Less managing. More teaching. Greater learning.

INSTRUCTORS...

Would you like your **students** to show up for class **more prepared**?

(Let's face it, class is much more fun if everyone is engaged and prepared…)

Want an **easy way to assign** homework online and track student **progress**?

(Less time grading means more time teaching…)

Want an **instant view** of student or class performance?

(No more wondering if students understand…)

Need to **collect data and generate reports** required for administration or accreditation?

(Say goodbye to manually tracking student learning outcomes…)

Want to **record and post your lectures** for students to view online?

(The more students can see, hear, and experience class resources, the better they learn…)

With **McGraw-Hill's Connect,**®

INSTRUCTORS GET:

- Simple **assignment management**, allowing you to spend more time teaching.
- **Auto-graded** assignments, quizzes, and tests.
- **Detailed visual reporting** where student and section results can be viewed and analyzed.
- Sophisticated **online testing** capability.
- A **filtering and reporting** function that allows you to easily assign and report on materials that are correlated to learning objectives and Bloom's taxonomy.
- An easy-to-use **lecture capture** tool.
- The option to **upload course documents** for student access.

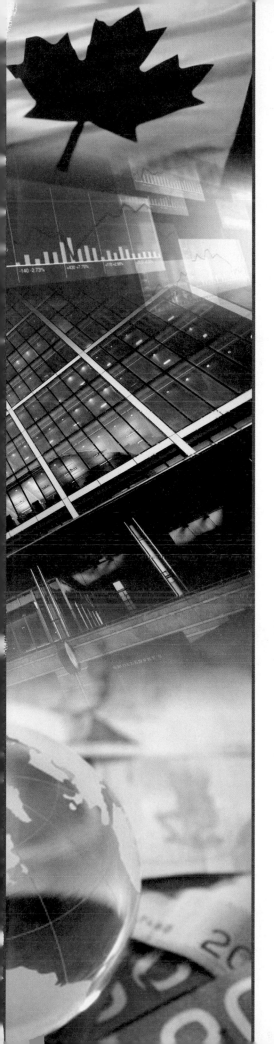

INTERMEDIATE ACCOUNTING

SIXTH EDITION

Thomas H. Beechy
Schulich School of Business
York University

Joan E.D. Conrod
Faculty of Management
Dalhousie University

Elizabeth J. Farrell
Schulich School of Business
York University

Ingrid McLeod-Dick
Schulich School of Business
York University

Mc
Graw
Hill
Education | McGraw-Hill
Ryerson

Intermediate Accounting
Volume 1
Sixth Edition

The Internet addresses listed in the text were accurate at the time of publication. The inclusion of a website does not indicate an endorsement by the authors or McGraw-Hill Ryerson, and McGraw-Hill Ryerson does not guarantee the accuracy of the information presented at these sites.

ISBN-13: 978-0-07-133947-6
ISBN-10: 0-07-133947-7

1 2 3 4 5 6 7 8 9 10   TCP   1 9 8 7 6 5 4

Printed and bound in Canada.

Care has been taken to trace ownership of copyright material contained in this text; however, the publisher will welcome any information that enables them to rectify any reference or credit for subsequent editions.

Director of Product Management: Rhondda McNabb
Product Manager: Keara Emmett
Executive Marketing Manager: Joy Armitage Taylor
Product Developers: Lindsay MacDonald and Chris Cullen
Senior Product Team Associate: Christine Lomas
Supervising Editor: Jessica Barnoski
Photo/Permissions Researcher: Steve Rouben, Photo Affairs, Inc.
Copy Editor: Karen Rolfe
Proofreader: Rohini Herbert
Plant Production Coordinator: Tammy Mavroudi
Manufacturing Production Coordinator: Lena Keating
Cover Design: Katherine Strain
Cover Images: Flag: Louis B. Wallach Inc./Getty Images RM; Graph: Saul Gravy/Getty Images (RM); Building: Shutterstock/Alex Saberi; Money: Vstock LLC/Getty RF.
Interior Design: Katherine Strain
Page Layout: Christopher Hudson
Printer: Transcontinental Printing Group

Library and Archives Canada Cataloguing in Publication

   Intermediate accounting / Thomas H. Beechy, Joan E.D. Conrod, Elizabeth J. Farrell,
Ingrid McLeod-Dick. — Sixth edition.

Includes index.
ISBN 978-0-07-133947-6 (v. 1).—ISBN 978-0-07-133882-0 (v. 2)

   1. Accounting—Textbooks.   I. Beechy, Thomas H., 1937–, author

HF5635.B466 2014   657'.044   C2013-905925-3

About the Authors

Thomas H. Beechy, York University

Thomas H. Beechy is a Professor Emeritus of Accounting at the Schulich School of Business, York University. He also is the Director of International Academic Development. Professor Beechy holds degrees from George Washington University (BA), Northwestern University (MBA), and Washington University (DBA). Before entering Canada in 1971, Professor Beechy taught for 10 years at Illinois Institute of Technology, after which he was employed at the Kellogg School of Business (Northwestern University) as a case writer. He has been active in research and publication for about 50 years, having published six books, including *Advanced Financial Accounting*, and numerous articles in accounting journals. Professor Beechy has been a leader in Canadian accounting education, emphasizing the importance of case analysis in developing students' professional judgement and accounting skills. He also has been an active researcher and advocate in both business and nonprofit financial reporting.

Joan E. D. Conrod, Dalhousie University

Joan E. D. Conrod is a Professor of Accounting in the Rowe School of Business at Dalhousie University. Her teaching excellence has been recognized through awards, such as the 2013 3M National Teaching Fellowship, the Dalhousie University Alumni Award for Teaching Excellence, and the AAU Distinguished Teacher award. She was awarded her FCA from the Nova Scotia Institute of Chartered Accountants in 1999. Joan is an active member of the University community and has served on the Dalhousie University Senate and the Board of Governors. She is a past president of the Canadian Academic Accounting Association. Joan has a lengthy history of involvement in professional accounting education. She has taught financial and managerial accounting courses to CA students across Canada, but particularly in Atlantic Canada, for 20 years. She has served on CA education committees at the local, regional, and national levels. Her publications include the text *Intermediate Accounting*, *Financial Accounting 3* for CGA-Canada, and a variety of case material and other publications.

Elizabeth J. Farrell, York University

Elizabeth J. Farrell is an adjunct professor and has taught at the Schulich School of Business for many years. She was awarded her FCPA, FCA from the Institute of Chartered Accountants of Ontario in 2013. In recognition of her excellence in teaching, she was awarded the Seymour Schulich Award for Teaching Excellence in 1999, 2003, and 2010 and was nominated for the award in 2004, 2005, 2006, 2007, 2008, and 2012. She was awarded the John Peace teaching faculty award in 2001 and 2012. She has taught financial accounting courses for over 20 years. Liz is assistant coordinator of the Institute of Chartered Accountants of Ontario's School of Accountancy, where she also has served as a seminar leader for many years. She has taught executive development courses for the Schulich Executive Education Centre (SEEC), as well as professional development courses for the ICAO and for CA firms. In addition to being a co-author of the *Intermediate Accounting*, she has also worked on an accounting case analysis software package; study guides; an IFRS Property, Plant, and Equipment, Intangible Assets and Impairment professional development course; *ASPE—A Comparison to IFRS*; *Guide to ASPE*; and a variety of case material and other publications.

Ingrid McLeod-Dick, York University

Ingrid McLeod-Dick is an adjunct professor and has taught at the Schulich School of Business for many years in its BBA, MBA, and EMBA programs. In recognition of her excellence in teaching, she received the John Peace part-time faculty teaching award in 2000 and was nominated for the Seymour Schulich Award for Teaching Excellence in 2000 to 2007 and 2012. She was awarded her FCA from the Ontario Institute of Chartered Accountants in 1994. Ingrid also served as a seminar leader for many years for the Institute of Chartered Accountants of Ontario's School of Accountancy. She currently teaches professional development courses for the ICAO. Her publications include the IFRS Financial Presentation and Disclosure course, and she is a contributing author to *Financial Reporting under IFRS* and *Guide to ASPE*, as well as a variety of case material.

Brief Table of Contents—Volume 1

Table of Contents—Volume 1

THE FRAMEWORK FOR FINANCIAL REPORTING — 1

CHAPTER 1

ACCOUNTING JUDGEMENTS — 35

CHAPTER 2

CHAPTER 6

REVENUE RECOGNITION   265

CHAPTER 6R

REVENUE RECOGNITION— REVISED IASB STANDARD   ONLINE

CHAPTER 7

FINANCIAL ASSETS: CASH AND RECEIVABLES   343

COST-BASED INVENTORIES AND COST OF SALES   405

CHAPTER 8

PROPERTY, PLANT, AND EQUIPMENT; INTANGIBLES; AND GOODWILL   463

CHAPTER 9

DEPRECIATION, AMORTIZATION, AND IMPAIRMENT   529

CHAPTER 10

FINANCIAL INSTRUMENTS: INVESTMENTS IN DEBT AND EQUITY SECURITIES   591

CHAPTER 11

APPENDIX

FUNDAMENTALS: THE ACCOUNTING INFORMATION PROCESSING SYSTEM   659

Preface

Welcome to the complex Canadian GAAP reporting environment! The vast majority of Canadian public companies prepare financial statements that comply with International Financial Reporting Standards (IFRS), as set by the International Accounting Standards Board (IASB) and contained in the *CPA Canada Handbook, Part I*. In contrast, Canadian private companies may choose to comply with either IFRS or Canadian Accounting Standards for Private Enterprise (ASPE), as contained in the *CPA Canada Handbook, Part II*. These two sets of GAAP are similar in many respects but quite different in other respects. This duality presents a huge challenge to accountants, managers, and financial statement users.

Clearly, accounting standards are ever expanding, and change is the norm; you might find the expanding universe of accounting knowledge to be intimidating. Intermediate accounting is the essential course for developing both the technical skills and the professional judgement that you need to succeed. We believe that neither technical knowledge nor professional judgement is sufficient on its own; it is the blend of the two that represents the value added by a professional accountant.

So that is what *Intermediate Accounting* will do for you: provide complete, appropriate technical knowledge while also developing your professional judgement. Both these elements are described in the broad range of topics in this text. We will clearly explain the standards, identify patterns, explore the impact of alternatives on users and uses of financial statements, and look forward to further changes that are on the horizon. Throughout this text, we stress the importance of ethical standards—an accountant must learn to recognize and respond appropriately in potentially challenging situations.

In selecting material to include in this book, we have assessed the realities of Canadian business practice and the choices that are currently available. We have a distinctly Canadian agenda, looking at the issues that matter in Canadian business. We are clear in our treatment of the body of knowledge. Our coverage does not get bogged down in the (sometimes twisted) past history of a given issue, nor does it speculate needlessly on what might or might not happen in the future. Our emphasis is on preparing you to apply the standards now in place, providing an overview of some expected changes, and moving to develop the necessary judgemental skills to apply those standards wisely and effectively. These same judgemental skills will serve you equally well even when standards change in the future, as they undoubtedly will.

After you master the contents of *Intermediate Accounting*, you will be able to account for the wide range of events and transactions found in this unique and challenging economic environment. We are proud that this text is now in its sixth edition. Many thousands of students have started their substantive study of the corporate reporting environment with this text. In addition, many people have supported the evolution of this book over the last 20 years, and we are very grateful for their encouragement and continued goodwill. In particular, Tom, Joan, and Liz are very pleased to welcome Ingrid McLeod-Dick to the author team for this edition; Ingrid is a great colleague who brings solid classroom experience and a history of expertise in professional accounting education.

IFRS AND ASPE

A Canadian agenda means that we all must master international standards. Every chapter is based first and foremost on IFRS. Differences between ASPE and IFRS are explained in a separate section, to provide clarity regarding one set of standards as compared with the other. Assignment material reflects both IFRS and ASPE so that applications reflect the dual GAAP environment.

TECHNICAL KNOWLEDGE

Accountants have to be able to account for things! There is a base level of expertise that must become part of every accountant's body of knowledge: how to record a receivable, capitalize a lease, account for a pension, or prepare a statement of cash flows. Some of the transactions that we must account for are very complex, and the specific rules must be mastered. An affinity for numbers is important.

PROFESSIONAL JUDGEMENT

Professional judgement, it is often said, is the hallmark of a profession. There are often different ways to account for the same transaction. Professional accountants must become expert at sizing up the circumstances and exercising judgement to determine the appropriate accounting policy for those circumstances.

Once an accounting policy has been established, management almost always must make accounting measurement estimates before the numbers can be recorded. Accounting estimates require the exercise of professional judgement.

Professional judgement is not acquired overnight. It is nurtured and slowly grows over a lifetime. In this book, we begin the development process by explicitly examining the variables that companies consider when evaluating their options, and the criteria that accountants use to make choices. Many opportunities to develop and improve judgement are provided in the case material.

ACCURACY

The text has been extensively reviewed and proofread prior to publication. Chapter material has been reviewed by professional accountants. All assignment materials have been solved independently by multiple individual "assignment checkers" in addition to the authors. Nevertheless, errors may remain, for which we accept full responsibility. If you find errors, please email the authors at **j.conrod@dal.ca, tbeechy@schulich.yorku.ca, efarrell@schulich. yorku.ca,** or **ing.mcleod@sympatico.ca**. Your help will be greatly appreciated.

TOPICAL REVIEW IDENTIFYING KEY CHANGES

Chapter 1

The book starts by exploring the multiple accounting frameworks in use in Canada for public companies and private companies—IFRS or U.S. standards for public companies, IFRS or ASPE or DBA for private companies. The chapter then explores the issue of international comparability and the difference between nations in their acceptance of IFRS—whether a nation adopts, adapts, or harmonizes with IFRS. While companies in different countries may use IFRS, the financial reports still imbed significant differences that arise from differences in nations' economic, business, and sometimes even religious practices.

After establishing the multiple GAAP frameworks, our attention turns to the basis of application of any framework. Before we can make judgements on choosing accounting policies and making accounting estimates, we must understand the many possible (and often conflicting) objectives underlying a company's financial reporting. Thus, the second major theme of the first chapter is how the many different factors and influences shape a company's financial reporting. This is fundamental material that supports professional judgement.

Chapter 1 has been extensively revised and rewritten for this edition, with new exhibits to further clarify the material.

Chapter 2

Chapter 2 has been completely rewritten in this edition. The primary focus is on the accounting choice process, emphasizing underlying assumptions, qualitative characteristics, and measurement methods. Having set the basic reporting framework in Chapter 1, Chapter 2 further develops the theme of professional judgement. This chapter explains the basic assumptions underlying financial reporting and then moves on to develop the qualitative characteristics that must be considered when developing professional approaches to accounting issues.

Ethical issues are strongly emphasized in this chapter, as they are throughout the book. After discussing the broad recognition issues for revenue and expense, the chapter then sets out the elements of financial reporting. The increased incidence of fair value measurement within IFRS requires that the traditional distinction between "revenue" and "gains" be modified, which is clarified both by discussion and by a revised exhibit.

By the end of Chapter 2, all of the factors and elements underlying the exercise of professional judgement have been laid out and clarified. These factors and elements underlie the professional judgements that students must make as they move through the text, particularly in the case material at the end of each chapter.

Chapter 3

Chapter 3 discusses the nature of income and the difference between the economic and accounting concepts of income. The statement of comprehensive income is explained, and a new section emphasizes the distinction between operating income and comprehensive income. The general presentation approach is explained, along with format variations that are accepted in practice.

In the previous edition, it was necessary to use non-Canadian examples in this chapter and the next. This was due to a lack of Canadian examples that illustrate the application of IFRS because Canadian companies had not yet switched to IFRS. In this edition, all financial statement examples in Chapters 3 and 4 (as well as the following chapters) are of Canadian companies.

Chapter 3 contains the book's primary discussion of asset disposals, discontinued operations, and restructuring. Discontinued operations is just one part of a broader issue of asset disposals. We have introduced asset disposals in this chapter to provide a clearer context for understanding discontinued operations. We discuss and provide examples of all forms of asset disposals, including abandonment, sales of individual assets, sale of asset groups, and discontinued operations. Because asset disposals are often connected with restructurings, we also present the criteria and reporting requirements for restructuring plans as well as the requirements for reporting constructive obligations that frequently accompany restructurings.

The chapter ends with a discussion of ASPE and the ways in which the reporting requirements for private enterprises using ASPE differ from enterprises reporting under IFRS.

Chapter 4

This chapter begins with a general discussion of the purpose and limitations of the statement of financial position. This discussion includes an explanation of the different ways in which the assets, liabilities, and shareholders' equity can be presented, depending on the individual regional practice.

Specific individual items on the statement are then discussed. IFRS requires certain items to be reported on the face of the statement but does not prescribe a specific format. In this edition, we have introduced rates-of-return analysis at this early stage in the book.

The next section discusses and illustrates the statement of changes in equity. We illustrate that the statement of changes in equity (SCE) includes not only the "normal" shareholder accounts (e.g., share equity and retained earnings) but also each of the various components of other comprehensive income.

In the fourth section, we have expanded the overview of accounting changes, including changes in estimate, changes in accounting policy, and error correction. Accounting changes are pervasive, and this section prepares students to understand accounting changes as they move through the specific topics that comprise the rest of the book. A full discussion of accounting changes is reserved for the end of the book, Chapter 21 (in Volume Two).

The final section is a discussion of disclosure notes. This section reflects the current disclosure requirements of IFRS, including related party transactions, segment reporting, contingencies, and guarantees. In this edition, we have expanded our discussion of segment reporting and provided a numerical illustration.

Chapter 5

The statement of cash flows (SCF) is dealt with in sequence, as a primary financial statement. The chapter deals with the mechanics of statement preparation, using both a format-free approach and the T-account method. The journal-entry-based worksheet approach is included in an appendix. Coverage is linked to the reporting example of International Forest Products, to emphasize IFRS presentation issues and judgemental presentation choices. Presentation of investment revenue cash flow, interest, and dividends paid is discussed and illustrated in a separate section later in the chapter. Statement of cash flows (SCF) issues are reviewed in every subsequent chapter of the text. And, new in this edition, there is a comprehensive SCF review at the end of Volume Two.

Chapter 6

Revenue is one of the most judgemental areas of accounting policy choice in the GAAP world. For the sixth edition of the book, we have more specifically outlined the five criteria required for revenue recognition. A consistent approach is used to apply these criteria to determine the appropriate revenue recognition for various types of transactions. Specifically, the chapter provides examples of revenue transactions, including sales with rights of return or warranty agreements, bill and hold arrangements, consignments, and licensing fees. Transactions involving multiple deliverables are explained, with examples of loyalty point programs and franchisee fees provided. Biological assets and agricultural produce are also discussed in the chapter.

In accounting for long-term contacts, we illustrate only the percentage-of-completion method, as this is the only method normally acceptable under IFRS. The completed-contract method is illustrated in the ASPE section at the end of the chapter. This separation helps students to better understand the difference between IFRS and ASPE as applied to long-term contracts. Barter transactions and exchanges of similar and dissimilar goods or services are important but challenging aspects of accounting. The chapter puts these transactions into a broader context and illustrates, based on IFRS, just how each of the various types of non-monetary exchanges should be measured and reported. Also new to this edition is the discussion of non-monetary transactions under ASPE.

New for the sixth edition is an Appendix that explains the details of the new standard on revenue recognition (effective for annual reporting periods beginning on or after 1 January 2017) and how it will be applied. There is also a supplemental chapter on Connect that goes into further detail, applying the new revenue recognition criteria to various types of revenue transactions. This supplement also includes some end-of-chapter questions related to this new standard.

Chapter 7

This chapter now deals with two important financial instruments: cash and receivables. Coverage of payables has been shifted to Volume Two. Classification and valuation decisions are central to the coverage of cash and receivables. Important topics, such as foreign currency translation (a must, in this age of globalization) and the IFRS rules governing the transfer of receivables, are incorporated. Material on bank reconciliations is in an appendix, and coverage of present- and future-value calculations is available online on Connect, as is a more extensive set of compound interest tables.

Chapter 8

This chapter conforms to the IFRS approach applying lower of cost or market valuation methods wherein the IFRS defines "market" as net realizable value. Also, we explain the process for writing inventory backup if NRV recovers before the inventory is sold. The allowance method of accounting for inventory writedowns is fully illustrated—the allowance method is the *only* feasible method when the LCNRV test is applied on a group basis.

Inventory valuation always raises the possibility of unethical behaviour. Therefore, the chapter includes discussion of the ethical issues surrounding inventory valuation and accounting.

Introductory accounting texts deal with inventory systems and the cost flow assumptions, and thus we present that more basic material in the Appendix, available for student review, if needed.

Chapters 9 and 10

Accounting for capital assets and intangible assets is challenging in the IFRS context. There are three possible models to consider depending on the type of asset: the fair value model, the revaluation model, and the cost model. Also, component accounting and depreciation add complexities to the accounting for capital assets. Impairment testing and reversals will create more volatility on the income statement using IFRS. These chapters systematically look at acquisition, amortization, impairment, and disposal considering both the IFRS standards and ASPE. The appendices cover the complexities related to investment property, government assistance, capital cost allowance, and the revaluation model.

Chapter 11

This chapter reflects coverage of IFRS 9, effective in 2015 but available for early adoption as a response from standard setters to the upheaval in financial markets. Accounting for amortized cost, fair value through profit and loss, fair value through other comprehensive income, cost, significant influence, and control investments is covered. Both policy and numeric issues are thoroughly explored. The chapter includes a number of helpful diagrams and figures to help clarify the roadmap through this complex territory. ASPE alternatives are very different in this area, and the choices are documented and described.

Volume One Appendix—Fundamentals: The Accounting Information Processing System

The Appendix reviews the accounting cycle from the original transaction to the journals, trial balance, and preparation of financial statements. Examples of adjusting journal entries are discussed as well as subsidiary ledgers and worksheet applications. Extensive examples are used to illustrate the accounting cycle.

Chapters 12 and 13

New in this edition, there are two chapters on liabilities to start Volume Two. Chapter 12 deals with operating payables, as well as notes payable and provisions. The chapter includes some examples of liability measurement that require discounting. We hope that this shorter chapter is a more appropriate way to start off a new term! This chapter fully reflects IFRS and ASPE standards in the area, and has complete case and problem material.

Chapter 13 delves into long-term debt, using bonds as an example. The chapter relies on discounted cash flow models for liability measurement, accompanied by the effective-interest method of amortization. Straight-line amortization is illustrated in the ASPE section. Various valuation and measurement complexities are covered, including the effect of upfront fees and derecognition scenarios. This chapter includes a section on the capitalization of borrowing costs.

Chapter 14

This chapter deals with straightforward shareholders' equity issues. Multicolumn presentation of the shareholders' equity statement, consistent with International Accounting Standard 1 (IAS 1), is completely incorporated. Classification and presentation of amounts in accumulated other comprehensive income, (e.g., from fair-value-through-other-comprehensive-income [FVTOCI] investments, and certain foreign currency gains/losses) is included, and is supported by assignment material. Summary charts have been incorporated, where appropriate.

Chapter 15

One major topic in this chapter is classification: debt versus equity, compound financial instruments, and the like. Classification is based on the substance of a financial instrument rather than its legal form. A major section covers the IFRS approach to share-based payments, emphasizing the estimates needed for measurement and forfeitures. Basic patterns for option accounting are established. Finally, the material on derivative instruments is included in this chapter. While many of the complexities of derivatives are appropriately left to advanced accounting courses, this introduction is vital. We think that the material is clear and understandable, at an appropriate level for Intermediate courses.

Chapters 16 and 17

Accounting for income tax remains two separate chapters, to acknowledge that many instructors prefer to spend two blocks of time on this most challenging area. The Chapter 16 material establishes a three-step process for typical situations. The focus of Chapter 17 remains accounting for the tax effect of losses—carrybacks and carryforwards. This is difficult material for students, but the Chapter 17 problems incorporate the prior-chapter material and allow solid reinforcement of the steps associated with tax accounting. The ASPE section explains the taxes payable or flow-through method that is available for private enterprises.

Chapter 18

The major change to this chapter is the introduction of IASB's new approach for lease accounting. The proposal requires all leases lasting longer than 12 months to be capitalized. At the time of writing this textbook, the proposed changes were still in Exposure Draft form and no effective implementation date had yet been specified. Although there is no doubt that a new standard will be issued, corporations will need at least three years to implement the change. A new standard cannot become effective before 2017. We present this new approach as an Appendix rather than in the main body of the text as the current standards will remain effective in the interim.

Chapter 19

Pensions and other post-retirement benefits are highly complex arrangements, with correspondingly complex accounting treatment. This chapter has been completely revamped to reflect up-to-date standards for defined benefit pension plans, both from IFRS and ASPE. We are pleased that the revised rules are easier to understand, but more importantly, the new standards result in better reflection of the economic position of such plans. The worksheet structure used is helpful to organize the material. This chapter also includes an example of accounting for other post-retirement benefits and appropriate coverage of defined contribution plans, since the latter are gaining in popularity.

Chapter 20

Earnings per share material includes an explanation of basic and diluted earnings per share (EPS). IFRS terminology is used throughout. The procedural steps associated with organizing a complex EPS question are emphasized to provide more comfort and support in this complicated area. There are a variety of useful summary figures and tables.

Chapter 21

Accounting policy changes and error corrections require restatement of one or more prior years' financial statements. Restatement is surely an important topic, given the number of fraud-based restatements reported in the public press in recent years. Also, the ongoing changes in accounting standards means that companies must often restate their accounts. This chapter deals with the theory and mechanics related to such restatement, reflecting current IFRS standards.

Chapter 22

The text concludes with a review of financial statement analysis and emphasizes the importance of accounting policy choice and disclosure in the analysis of published financial statements. New in the sixth edition is an in-depth discussion related to the type of information to gather specifically to assist with the analysis. Each of the ratios described in the chapter are calculated for the same sample company, and the results are analyzed, taking into consideration the entity's business and industry. There is an extensive case illustration, showing restatements, which demonstrates the importance of accounting policy choice.

Volume Two Appendix—Statement of Cash Flows

SCF topics have been explained in each chapter of the text, and students have had assignment material to reinforce each topic. However, some prefer to end the course with a comprehensive review of SCF topics, as review and reinforcement. This Appendix gathers material that will support this approach. The appendix is based on a T-account analysis, and has an appropriate range of assignment material.

ACKNOWLEDGEMENTS

Our initial draft of this text was reviewed by several colleagues with expertise in IFRS. Our manuscript benefitted significantly from the comments and suggestions from Judy Cumby, FCA, Ingrid McLeod-Dick, FCPA, FCA, and Marisa Morriello, CPA, CA. Many other reviewers had contributed valuable comments on the previous edition, which informed our decisions about coverage and approach for the sixth edition.

We are grateful to the team members who exhaustively checked the assignment material and the solutions, including Mike Lutes, CA; Andrew Bonner, CA; Borden Rhodes; James Rockwood; Chantelle Loucks; Alex Kogan, CPA, CA; Winnie Siu; Alex Fisher, CPA, CA; Marisa Morriello, CPA, CA; Marcella Augustina, CPA, CA; Susan Cohlmeyer, FCA; and Cara Chesney, CA. The residual errors are our responsibility, but these expert individuals have significantly improved our accuracy. A special thanks to Judy Cumby, FCA, Laura Cumming, CA, and Tammy Crowell, CA.

We appreciate the permissions granted by the following organizations to use their problem and case material:

- The Canadian Institute of Chartered Accountants
- The Certified General Accountants' Association of Canada
- The Ontario Institute of Chartered Accountants
- The Atlantic School of Chartered Accountancy
- The American Institute of Certified Public Accountants

We are grateful to the people at McGraw-Hill Ryerson who guided this manuscript through the development process. We appreciate the strong support of Keara Emmett, our Product Manager; Lindsay MacDonald and Chris Cullen, our Product Developers; and the production team, led by Margaret Henderson and including Jessica Barnoski and Tammy Mavroudi, who have all contributed in significant ways to this final product. And, of course, Karen Rolfe, copy editor, and Rohini Herbert, proofreader, have become welcome and active partners in this enterprise.

On a personal level, we would like to thank our friends and family members for their support and encouragement throughout the lengthy process of bringing this book to fruition, especially, in Toronto—Brian McBurney; in Halifax—Andrew, Yen, Meredith, and Daniel Conrod; in Richmond Hill—Ed Farrell, Catherine, Michael, and Megan Farrell; and in Collingwood—Michael Dick and Kenneth Dick.

Pedagogical Walkthrough

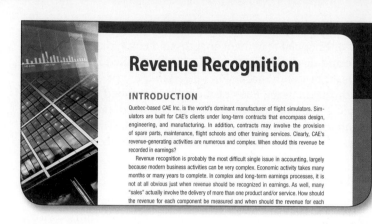

Revenue Recognition

INTRODUCTION

Quebec-based CAE Inc. is the world's dominant manufacturer of flight simulators. Simulators are built for CAE's clients under long-term contracts that encompass design, engineering, and manufacturing. In addition, contracts may involve the provision of spare parts, maintenance, flight schools and other training services. Clearly, CAE's revenue-generating activities are numerous and complex. When should this revenue be recorded in earnings?

Revenue recognition is probably the most difficult single issue in accounting, largely because modern business activities can be very complex. Economic activity takes many months or many years to complete. In complex and long-term earnings processes, it is not at all obvious just when revenue should be recognized in earnings. As well, many "sales" actually involve the delivery of more than one product and/or service. How should the revenue for each component be measured and when should the revenue for each

Introduction

Each chapter has an introduction that explains the objectives of the chapter in narrative form.

CONCEPT REVIEW

1. How is a *gain* different from a *revenue*?
2. List the five criteria that must be satisfied before revenue from the sale of goods can be recognized.
3. What measurement issues might arise in determining the amount of revenue to be recognized?

Concept Review

Throughout each chapter concept review questions are included. Students can stop and think through the answers to these basic questions, covering the previously explained material. This helps comprehension and focus! Answers to these questions can be found online on Connect.

EXHIBIT 3-6

DETERMINING IF A CONSTRUCTIVE OBLIGATION EXISTS

START

Is there a detailed plan identifying the necessary elements as set out in IAS 37(¶72)? — No

Yes

Will the plan start as soon as possible and be completed in a time frame that makes significant changes to the plan unlikely? — No

Yes

Yes — Has the entity started dismantling the plant prior to the year-end?

No

Yes — Has the entity started selling assets prior to the year-end?

Figures and Tables

Where appropriate, chapter material is summarized in figures and tables to establish the patterns and help reinforce material.

ETHICAL ISSUES

The reason for the conditions for reclassifying an asset as held-for-sale is to prevent managers from reclassifying assets as "current" for a short period and then reversing that decision later. For example, a company may have a lending covenant that requires a minimum current ratio. If these restrictions were not in place, an unethical manager could temporarily reclassify a *noncurrent* asset to *current*, claiming that it is held-for-sale, just to meet the current ratio requirement, and then reclassify it back to noncurrent after the reporting date had passed. Clearly, there is an ethical issue involved in the "held-for-sale" classification.

Ethical Issues

Many chapters discuss accounting issues that raise ethical concerns. These concerns are highlighted in the chapter. Where ethical issues are particularly problematic, we have included a separate "Ethical Issues" section to help students focus on the ethical aspects of policy choice.

Ethics assignment material has also been incorporated into the case material. Essentially, when an accountant makes a recommendation on a contentious choice of accounting policy, ethics are tested. Students exercise true-to-life ethical judgement when they have to make a tough judgement call and recommend an accounting policy that is "good" for one group but "bad" for another. These ethical overtones are highlighted in the case solutions to help instructors draw them out in discussion and evaluation.

ACCOUNTING STANDARDS FOR PRIVATE ENTERPRISES

Comprehensive Income

There is no SCI in Canadian ASPE; only an income statement should be provided. The concept of *other comprehensive income* does not exist in ASPE. Instead:

- Net income after taxes is transferred directly from the income statement to retained earnings (or via the statement of changes in retained earnings, if a separate statement is prepared);
- Unrealized foreign exchange translation gains or losses related to a foreign subsidiary (a component of OCI under IFRS) are reported as a separate component of shareholders' equity; and
- Any other nonearnings items that affect shareholders' equity are reported in shareholders' equity, as appropriate.

Under ASPE, *consolidated* financial statements are not required. The statements of a private enterprise are not issued to the public, and users are presumed to be knowledgeable. If a user wants consolidated statements, he or she can request them (or insist on them, in the case of a major provider of capital, such as an institutional investor).

Format

- ASPE does not specify a format other than the obvious fact that it should begin with "revenue" and end with "net income." There is no requirement for basing the expense disclosure on "functional" versus "nature of expense" approach as required by IFRS.

Accounting Standards for Private Enterprises

At the end of each chapter, there is a section that expands on essential items to understand for Accounting Standards for Private Enterprise (ASPE) in Canada. These sections include numeric examples, where appropriate. The ASPE sections provide students and instructors with a detailed, but easy-to-use guide to these important standards.

Looking Forward

In November 2012, the IASB began looking into a wide range of issues on presentation, disclosure and measurement. Among the issues on the IASB's Conceptual Framework agenda are a re-examination of the definitions of elements, definitions of liabilities, recognition principles, measurement principles, the distinction between equity and liability instruments, and measurements other than cost and fair value. In coming years, the Board is likely to issue new guidance on the format and presentation of items on the SFP.

This is a long-term project. We are not likely to see a resolution of these many issues for quite a while.

Looking Forward

Standards are constantly evolving and changing! To help keep abreast of forthcoming probable changes, at the end of each chapter we provide a discussion of key anticipated changes in IFRS and/or ASPE standards.

RELEVANT STANDARDS

CPA Canada Handbook, Part I (IFRS):
- IAS 1, Presentation of Financial Statements
- IAS 8, Accounting Policies, Changes in Accounting Estimates and Errors
- IAS 37, Provisions, Contingent Liabilities and Contingent Assets
- IFRS 5, Non-current Assets Held-for-sale and Discontinued Operations

CPA Canada Handbook, Part II (ASPE):
- Section 1520, Income Statement
- Section 3475, Disposal of Long-lived Assets and Discontinued Operations

Relevant Standards

At the end of each chapter, we provide a comprehensive list of the IASB and ASPE standards that are relevant to the material in that chapter. We have not quoted the standards directly in chapter material, and we have not provided paragraph references to either the IASB publications or *CPA Canada Handbook*. This omission is intentional—the two sources are harmonized but may use different words. Also, the IASB makes "annual improvements" that change the wording of some standards. Our focus is on the application of standards, not the technicalities of the wording.

SUMMARY OF KEY POINTS

1. Public companies must report *comprehensive income*, which has two components: (1) profit or loss (i.e., net income), and (2) *other comprehensive income*. OCI generally includes value changes that have been recognized in the SFP but are excluded from periodic earnings, either temporarily or permanently.

2. Comprehensive income can be presented either in one continuous statement, or in two consecutive statements with net income as the final line of the profit or loss statement (i.e., income statement) and also as the first line of the SCI, which must follow immediately on the same page.

3. Companies can report expenses in the profit and loss section either by *nature of expense* or by *function*. Under either presentation approach, two compulsory expense disclosures are (1) depreciation and amortization expense and (2) the cost of employee benefits.

4. Both IFRS and ASPE require a subtotal for net earnings from continuing operations (net of income tax). IFRS encourages companies to provide information, headings, and other subtotals that will help the financial statement reader understand the company's financial performance.

5. Income taxes must be allocated over two dimensions: *intraperiod*, which is within the financial statements of a reporting period, and *interperiod*, which allocates the income tax burden to the current and future years.

Summary of Key Points

A summary of key points concludes each chapter. This provides a list of the key ideas and reinforces the chapter material.

KEY TERMS

abandoned asset	idle asset
accounting income	income
basic EPS	interperiod tax allocation
cash-generating unit	intraperiod tax allocation
comprehensive income	multiple-step statement
constructive obligation	noncontrolling interest (NCI)
diluted EPS	provision
discontinued operation	recoverable amount
disposal group	restructuring plan
economic income	single-step statement
fair value less the cost to sell	statement of comprehensive income (SCI)
flipping	unusual items
held-for-sale	weighted average number of shares

Key Terms

Each chapter concludes with a list of key terms used and explained in the chapter.

REVIEW PROBLEM 3-1

The following information is taken from the adjusted trial balance of Killian Corporation at 31 December 20X5, the end of Killian's fiscal year:

Account	Amount
Sales revenue	$1,000,000
Service revenue	200,000
Interest revenue	30,000
Gain on sale of capital asset	100,000
Cost of goods sold[1]	630,000
Selling, general, and administrative expense[2]	170,000
Interest expense	20,000
Loss on sale of long-term investment	10,000
Loss from earthquake damage	200,000
Loss on sale of assets of discontinued business segment	60,000
Loss on operations of discontinued business segment	10,000

[1]Consists of depreciation of $30,000, employee wages and benefits of $40,000, and $580,000 of merchandise purchases less $20,000 increase in inventory.
[2]Includes depreciation of $35,000 and employee wages and benefits of $90,000.

Review Problem

From Chapter 3 onward, we provide at least one self-study review problem, with the solution. This provides an opportunity to practise the primary aspects of that chapter's content.

CASE 3-1

DELUCA SOLUTIONS INC.

Deluca Solutions Inc. is an Ontario-based manufacturer. The company is listed on the TSX, but the family of founder David Deluca retains control through multiple-voting shares.

Cases

More than 60 cases are included in *Intermediate Accounting*, and there is at least one new case in every chapter in the sixth edition. The cases portray realistic situations, usually with multiple financial reporting implications. Students must put themselves into the situation and grapple with the facts to arrive at the most appropriate accounting policies for the circumstances. A blend of professional judgement and technical skills is needed to respond to a case. Case coverage is not limited to "one chapter" bites but often integrates material learned to date. For those trying to build a base of professionalism, the use of cases consistently over the term is highly recommended. Cases can be assigned for class debriefing, class presentations, or written assignments.

TECHNICAL REVIEW

connect

TR4-1 Financial Statement Classification: The first list below shows the financial statements normally included in a company's annual financial statements. The second list shows some amounts that often appear in those financial statements.

A. SFP
B. Statement of comprehensive income—profit and loss section
C. Statement of comprehensive income—other comprehensive income section
D. Statement of cash flows
E. Statement of changes in shareholders' equity

B, D, E	1. Net income
_____	2. Retained earnings (opening)
_____	3. Translation gain/loss on foreign subsidiaries
_____	4. Provision for restructuring costs
_____	5. Cumulative translation gain or loss
_____	6. Dividends declared, unpaid at year-end
_____	7. Appropriation for factory reorganization
_____	8. Loss on discontinued operation
_____	9. Non-controlling interest in subsidiaries
_____	10. Investment property held-for-sale
_____	11. Cumulative effect of change in accounting policy
_____	12. Proceeds from issuance of common shares
_____	13. Unrealized gains/losses on hedge derivatives
_____	14. Deferred pension cost

Required:
Use the letters given in the first list to indicate the financial statement on which each item in the second list will appear. Some letters may be used more than once or not at all. The first item is completed for you as an example.

Technical Review

In this edition, we have added Technical Review exercises at the end of each chapter, preceding the somewhat more demanding assignment material. These technical exercises are directive, brief, and quantitative and encourage students to ensure they understand the chapter's basic quantitative aspects. We have provided five such exercises in each chapter (except in the introductory chapters; these are more conceptual than numerical in nature, and technical review is not the focus.)

Assignment Material

There is an extensive range of assignment material at the end of each chapter. The assignments provide the opportunity to "learn by doing."

 The technical review questions and many of the assignments are available online on Connect; the Connect logo identifies these questions. The Connect problems allow web-based iterations of the problem for assessment, immediate feedback, and extra practice.

★ Stars accompany each assignment to indicate length, with one star indicating a shorter assignment and three stars indicating a longer assignment.

 To help students practise on their own, we have selected a few assignments from each chapter and put their solutions online. These selected assignments are highlighted by the icon in the margin.

 Excel® templates for selected assignments provide an introduction to basic spreadsheet applications. These assignments are identified with the icon in the margin and are available online.

Integrative Problems

From time to time, we include integrative problems that formally deal with accounting topics covered in five or six chapters. These problems are a great pretest review!

SUPPLEMENTS

Connect

 McGraw-Hill Connect™ is a web-based assignment and assessment platform that gives students the means to better connect with their coursework, with their instructors, and with the important concepts that they will need to know for success now and in the future. With Connect, instructors can deliver assignments, quizzes, and tests easily online. Students can practise important skills at their own pace and on their own schedule. With Connect, students also get 24/7 online access to an eBook—an online edition of the text—to aid them in successfully completing their work, wherever and whenever they choose.

LearnSmart

No two students are alike. Why should their learning paths be? LearnSmart uses revolutionary adaptive technology to build a learning experience unique to each student's individual needs. It starts by identifying the topics a student knows and does not know. As the student progresses, LearnSmart adapts and adjusts the content based on his or her individual strengths, weaknesses, and confidence, ensuring that every minute spent studying with LearnSmart is the most efficient and productive study time possible.

SmartBook

As the first and only adaptive reading experience, SmartBook is changing the way students read and learn. SmartBook creates a personalized reading experience by highlighting the most important concepts a student needs to learn at that moment in time. As a student engages with SmartBook, the reading experience continuously adapts by highlighting content based on what each student knows and does not know. This ensures that he or she is focused on the content needed to close specific knowledge gaps, while it simultaneously promotes long-term learning.

INSTRUCTOR RESOURCES

Instructor Resources

- Instructor's Manual
- Instructor's Solutions Manual
- Computerized Test Bank
- Microsoft® PowerPoint® Lecture Slides

SUPERIOR LEARNING SOLUTIONS AND SUPPORT

The McGraw-Hill Ryerson team is ready to help you assess and integrate any of our products, technology, and services into your course for optimal teaching and learning performance. Whether it is helping your students improve their grades or putting your entire course online, the McGraw-Hill Ryerson team is here to help you do it. Contact your Learning Solutions Consultant today to learn how to maximize all of McGraw-Hill Ryerson's resources!

For more information on the latest technology and Learning Solutions offered by McGraw-Hill Ryerson and its partners, please visit us online: www.mcgrawhill.ca/he/solutions.

CHAPTER 1

The Framework for Financial Reporting

INTRODUCTION

Air Canada is a large international airline. The company has more than 300 aircraft and operates flights not only throughout Canada but also over an extensive international network. About 40% of its revenue is from Canada, while 60% is from flights from international flights, including those to the United States.

Air Canada (AC) is a public company with 277 million common shares outstanding. Its two classes of shares are traded on the Toronto Stock Exchange (TSX). Most of the shares are owned by Canadian investors, but many are owned by investors in the United States and other countries. AC has about 24,000 employees and innumerable creditors around the world. Many organizations and individuals have a significant interest in AC, whether as shareholders, employees, lessors, debt holders, government regulators, or customers. As a public company, AC must issue general-purpose financial statements for the use of its many current and potential stakeholders.

In contrast, Porter Airlines Inc. is a regional airline based in Toronto. Porter has dozens of planes instead of hundreds. Its shares are held by a small group of private investors. The company almost certainly has privately negotiated debt, although its sources and amount of financing are not public information. As a private company, Porter is under no requirement to disclose its financial details to the public. The company's shareholders and creditors can obtain the information they need directly from the company.

For accounting, the significant difference between AC and Porter is not in their relative sizes, it is in their status as public versus private companies. AC's financial statements must be prepared by using **International Financial Accounting Standards (IFRS)**, which constitute Part I of the *CPA Canada Handbook*. Porter, in contrast, may *choose* to be guided by **Canadian Accounting Standards for Private Enterprises (ASPE)** in Part II of the *CPA Canada Handbook*, rather than by IFRS.

Regardless of whether a company is public or private, financial reporting will be strongly affected by (1) entity-specific financial reporting objectives and (2) management's accounting judgements. A company's financial reporting objectives and judgements will have a major impact on the company's reported financial results.

This chapter begins with an overview of the Canadian approach to business enterprise financial reporting in Canada. Then we will discuss the objectives of financial reporting and how different objectives can affect financial reporting, even in public companies.

ACCOUNTING STANDARDS IN CANADA

As you already know from your introductory study of accounting, there are two related sets of financial reporting standards for Canadian business enterprises: International Financial Reporting Standards (IFRS) and Accounting Standards for Private Enterprises (ASPE). Both are contained in the *CPA Canada Handbook* as *Part 1* and *Part II*, respectively.

Nonpublicly accountable private enterprises can choose between IFRS and ASPE. The choice depends on management's reporting objectives and on the needs (and demands) of their financial statement users, primarily the providers of both debt and equity capital.

Authoritative Source of Canadian Standards

The accounting standard-setting body in Canada is the **Accounting Standards Board (AcSB)** of the Canadian Institute of Chartered Accountants (CICA). The authority of the CICA comes from the corporations acts of the federal and provincial governments. Each corporations act, including the federal *Canadian Business Corporations Act* (CBCA), requires auditors to report in accordance with generally accepted accounting principles (GAAP), and GAAP is defined in the regulations as compliance with the recommendations of the *CPA Canada Handbook*.

The GAAP requirement for public companies is enforceable by the provincial securities commissions. The commissions are responsible for enforcing the reporting standards for companies that are traded in their province. In the case of Air Canada, the primary regulatory agency is the Quebec Securities Commission (Autorité des marchés financiers) because Air Canada is based in Montreal. Since AC is traded on the TSX, the Ontario Securities Commission also has strong jurisdiction.

The AcSB had, for many decades, maintained Canadian standards by regular revisions and additions to the *CPA Canada Handbook*. With the rapid acceptance of IFRS around the world, the AcSB had to decide whether to maintain a separate standard-setting process or adopt IFRS. After extensive deliberation, the AcSB decided to follow a two-pronged approach for Canadian enterprises:

1. Public companies and other publicly accountable enterprises must use *International Financial Reporting Standards* (IFRS) for financial reporting for all reporting periods beginning on or after 1 January 2011. To meet legal requirements for corporate reporting, all of the IFRS standards are included in the *CPA Canada Handbook, Part I*. There is absolutely no difference between the *CPA Canada Handbook, Part I* and the authoritative English-language IFRS standards.

2. Private nonpublicly accountable enterprises have a choice between two options:

   a. Full IFRS, just as for public companies; or

   b. Canadian Accounting Standards for Private Enterprises (ASPE), as prescribed in the *CPA Canada Handbook, Part II*.

Although the sources for public versus private company standards differ, the content between the two sets of standards is substantially parallel. The private-company standards are somewhat less complex, place less reliance on fair-value measurements, and have far fewer disclosure requirements.

IFRS Overview

Organization International standards are developed and issued by the **International Accounting Standards Board (IASB)**, which is based in London, England. The IASB's oversight body is the not-for-profit IFRS Foundation, based in the U.S. state of Delaware. The IASB comprises 16 experts "with an appropriate mix of recent practical experience in setting accounting standards, in preparing, auditing, or using financial reports, and in accounting education." The board members are appointed by the IFRS Foundation.

In March 2013, the IASB website listed 16 board members, consisting of five from North America (five from the United States, one from Canada); five from Europe (United Kingdom, Netherlands, France, Sweden, Germany); two from the south Pacific (Australia, South Africa); three from Asia (two from China, one from Japan); and one from South America

(Brazil). Board members have international experience in accounting/auditing practice, accounting standard setting, and investment analysis; the IFRS Foundation emphasizes "broad geographic diversity" for Board membership.

The national representation of the IFRS Foundation is rather similar to that of the IASB, although its membership is somewhat broader in that six of its 22 trustees are from two each of Asia, Europe, and North America. Otherwise, the Anglo-Saxon and European complements are roughly the same as for the IASB members.

Adopt, Adapt, or Converge? The hope of the IFRS (and of many international corporations) is that all countries will use IFRS as their reporting standard for publicly accountable enterprises. In reality, it is not so simple. There actually are three different approaches in use, depending on the regulatory environment in each nation:[1]

1. **Adopt** When a country adopts IFRS, the country's pre-existing public company GAAP is ended, and IFRS is substituted in its place. Canada has "adopted" IFRS by including all standards directly into the *CPA Canada Handbook* without modification or any intermediate approval process.

2. **Adapt** Under this approach, a country uses IFRS, but not before reviewing each standard for suitability in that specific national environment. If the national regulatory body (often, the legislature) deems a particular IFRS to be unsuitable in some respect, then the standard is altered, such as by deleting one or more specific aspects of the standard before approving it for use in that country. Thus, the standards are *adapted* to the perceived national environment. This is the approach used in the European Union, where all standards must be approved by the EU Parliament before they go into effect.

3. **Converge** Under a convergence approach, a national standard setter revises its own national standards to reduce differences between an international standard and its own standard, such as "harmonizing" or converging standards on such topics as inventory accounting or revenue recognition. This is the approach used by such disparate countries as China and the United States. In the case of the United States, the FASB and IFRS work directly together to reduce differences between their standards. Indeed, it may be fair to suggest that the IFRS may modify some of its draft standards to be closer to the U.S. standards rather than the other way around.

Therefore, when looking at non-Canadian financial statements, the notes may contain a sentence, such as the following in an Australian mining company's 2012 annual report:

> The Group's financial statements have been prepared in accordance with IFRS as adopted by the European Union ('EU IFRS'), which differs in certain respects from the version of IFRS that is applicable in Australia.[2]

The nature of the differences then must be disclosed, although no alternative measurements are disclosed.

Translations and Authority The IASB prepares translations of IASs and IFRSs into many other languages, but these translations are not authoritative. Worldwide, only the English version of IFRS is authoritative. In case of dispute, it is the English version that must prevail. This is an issue because different languages have different linguistic practices and vocabularies. Other languages may not have exactly equivalent phraseology. However, since the companies in other countries will use the local-language version of IFRS, the outcome from applying IFRS may be rather different from that in English-speaking countries.

In Canada, however, there is an authoritative French version, since the standards must say the same thing in both English and French. The CICA prepares its own French translations

---

[1] Stephen A. Zeff and Christopher W. Nobes, "Has Australia (or Any Other Jurisdiction) 'Adopted" IFRS?" *Australian Accounting Review*, no. 53, vol. 20, Issue 2 (2010).

[2] *Rio Tinto 2012 Annual Report*, p. 145. Retrieved May 14, 2013, from http://www.riotinto.com/reportingcentre2012.

(as it always has done for Canadian standards). The IASB now uses the CICA translations as its own French-language standards.

Accounting Standards for Canadian Publicly Accountable Enterprises

A **publicly accountable enterprise** (**PAE**) is any company that either (1) has securities (either debt or equity, or both) issued to the public or that is in the process of issuing debt or equity to the public, or (2) is a for-profit private enterprise that holds assets in a fiduciary capacity for a broad group of outsiders as one of its primary businesses.

A **fiduciary enterprise** is any organization that acts in a trusteeship capacity for members of the general public. Examples are investment funds, mutual funds, pension funds, savings institutions, privately owned banks, credit unions, and other deposit-taking organizations; many such enterprises and organizations are private in the sense that they have no securities outstanding in public hands.

As well, governmental business enterprises must disclose their financial performance and thus are PAEs, regardless of whether or not they are intended to earn a profit. Examples include Canada Post, VIA Rail, Toronto Transit Commission, and the many port authorities across Canada. Government business enterprises are usually known as **crown corporations**.

In this book, we will use *public company* or *public enterprise* to indicate any type of publicly accountable enterprises, rather than encumber the text with excessive repetition.

Choice of GAAP Although IFRS is the normal reporting requirement for Canadian public corporations, the shares of some Canadian corporations are heavily traded in the United States. To enhance the acceptability of its shares in the U.S. financial markets, a Canadian company may choose to follow U.S. GAAP. The use of U.S. standards is accepted by the Ontario Securities Commission (OSC) and the TSX for trading in Canada, thanks to a mutual-recognition agreement between the Securities Exchange Commission (SEC) and the OSC. Conversely, if a Canadian corporation uses Canadian GAAP and its securities are traded in the U.S. financial markets, the SEC will accept IFRS-based reporting.

Although there is an SEC–OSC mutual recognition agreement, it is fairly rare for a Canadian company to use U.S. GAAP. Some Canadian U.S. GAAP users are listed on the New York Stock Exchange (NYSE). However, as of 2012, only 67 Canadian companies were listed on the New York Stock Exchange, and only a minority of those companies use U.S. GAAP. Thus, do not get distracted by this rarely used alternative. The basic reporting requirement for Canadian public companies is IFRS.

IFRS is the normal reporting requirement for lists on other securities exchanges around the world. Therefore, Canada's adoption of IFRS makes it relatively easy for Canadian public companies to list on foreign exchanges.

Legal and Regulatory Requirements In some special industries, such as investment funds, chartered banks, and regulated enterprises (e.g., telephone or cable companies), the normal provisions of IFRS may be supplemented by legal requirements. Canada's chartered banks, for example, are governed by Canada's *Bank Act*. IFRS still prevails, however, except for rare specific instances in which legal or regulatory requirements may take precedence.

Reporting Currency Canadian companies do not always prepare their financial statements in Canadian dollars. Under IFRS, a company should report in its **functional currency**, which is the currency in which most of a company's transactions are conducted. For example, if a Canadian company has most of its transactions in U.S. dollars, all non–U.S. currency flows and values are translated into U.S. dollars. Normally, such a company would also adopt the U.S. dollar as the company's **presentation currency**—the currency in which the financial statements are presented. IFRS requires an enterprise to disclose its presentation currency at the top of each financial statement.

For example, in the notes to its 2012 financial statements, Montreal-based Bombardier Inc., a manufacturer of airplanes (BA) and railroad equipment (BT), explains its use of U.S. dollars as follows:

Foreign currency translation

The consolidated financial statements are expressed in U.S. dollars, the functional currency of Bombardier Inc. The functional currency is the currency of the primary economic environment in which an entity operates. The functional currency of most foreign subsidiaries is their local currency, mainly the U.S. dollar in BA, and the euro, pound sterling, various other Western European currencies, and the U.S. dollar in BT.

Do not get confused between reporting in U.S. dollars and reporting using U.S. GAAP. There is no necessary relationship between the presentation currency and the reporting GAAP. This is illustrated by the reporting practices of three major Canadian companies:

- Barrick Gold Corporation reports in Canadian GAAP but U.S. dollars.
- Canadian National Railways reports in U.S. GAAP but Canadian dollars.
- IMAX Corporation (yes, the big-screen movie projection system) reports in U.S. GAAP and U.S. dollars.

Accounting Standards for Canadian Private Enterprises

A **private enterprise** is one that neither issues debt or equity securities *to the public* nor is in the process of doing so and also does not hold assets in a fiduciary capacity as one of its primary businesses. All of the company's shares are held privately and cannot be offered for sale on the open market. Usually, all of the shares are owned by the members of a single family and sometimes by senior executives as well. However, other investors can be involved. The fact that "outsiders" own part of the stock does not affect its status as a private enterprise.

The suppliers of capital to a private corporation are assumed to be either insiders or sophisticated investors who do not need the special protection given to members of the general public who may buy shares on the open market.

Private companies provide financial statements for a limited group of users, including managers, shareholders, taxation authorities, lenders, and other creditors. These users are presumed to have access to the information that they need, either as owners and/or managers or as bankers/creditors. Financial statements must also accompany each corporation's income tax form; tax authorities can demand additional information as well.

Canadian private companies have three financial statement reporting choices:

1. IFRS, the same as public companies;

2. Canadian ASPE, as prescribed in the *CPA Canada Handbook, Part II*; or

3. Tailored accounting policies, known as a disclosed basis of accounting.

A private company is often referred to as an **SME**, which refers to **small and medium-sized enterprises**. In some countries, accounting standards for SMEs are limited to companies below a certain size threshold of revenue, capital, or employees. However, some of Canada's largest corporations are private corporations (e.g., McCain Foods Ltd. and Bata Shoes—both companies have multi-billion-dollar annual revenues). Therefore, the SME appellation has never been used to refer to private-company accounting standards in Canada. There are no size thresholds. The choice between following IFRS versus Canadian ASPE is unaffected by a Canadian private corporation's size.

Using IFRS A private company may wish to use IFRS instead of following private-company Canadian standards because it competes with public companies for capital.

Despite the inability to sell shares to the public, private corporations can obtain substantial capital through **private placements**. A *private placement* is arranged by direct negotiation with the one or more suppliers of capital. Private capital suppliers include pension funds, investment funds, private equity investment companies, and major banks. In Canada, almost all major debt financing for both public and private corporations is by means of private placements.

Private placements also are a source of equity financing for private companies. Securities that are issued in a private placement cannot be publicly traded, and therefore a private company remains outside the jurisdiction of the securities acts and securities regulators.

Even though private companies' shares are not publicly traded, management nevertheless may choose to use IFRS so that the company's financial statements can be more easily compared with those of public companies. This is not simply a matter of competing for financing in Canada—for a large company, the competition for funds is international. A large private Canadian corporation is competing for debt and equity funds against companies from the United States, Europe, Asia, South America, and so on. To compete for capital effectively, an important financial reporting objective for a private company may be to issue financial statements that are comparable with those issued by public companies worldwide.

Other reasons that a private enterprise may choose to use IFRS include the following:

- The company is a subsidiary of a parent that reports on the basis of IFRS.
- The company may be considering issuing shares to the public in the foreseeable future and wishes to establish a pattern of IFRS compliance in the financial statements that it must submit as part of the company's prospectus.
- The company's controlling shareholders may intend to sell the company in the near future. Using IFRS may enhance the financial statements' credibility to prospective public-company acquirors.

Using ASPE   Most Canadian corporations are private, not public, companies. The AcSB has long recognized that private companies are unnecessarily burdened by the complex standards that were designed for public companies. Thus, upon adopting IFRS, the AcSB had to decide how to reduce the financial reporting burden for private companies. One alternative was to adopt the IASB's simplified version of IFRS for SMEs. An advantage of using IFRS-SME is that a nation does not need to maintain an accounting standard-setting structure of its own. Australia is an example of a country that has adopted IFRS-SME as its reporting requirement for private enterprises; Australia has gotten out of the business of accounting standard setting.

The other alternative was to continue home-grown standards as an option for Canadian private companies. After all, only a tiny proportion of Canadian corporations are public. By using Canada-specific standards instead of tying private companies to international standards, the AcSB would be better able to adapt private company reporting to the Canadian legal, regulatory, and capital environments.

After considering the alternatives, the AcSB opted to maintain national standards. The pre-existing standards in the *CPA Canada Handbook* were simplified by removing some of the reporting requirements that are less appropriate for private companies. Canadian accounting standards for private enterprises are based less on fair values and more on historical cost, and the disclosure requirements are less onerous.

As a result of continuing use of the *CPA Canada Handbook* instead of IFRS-SME, many private companies found that there was little change in their reports when they converted to ASPE, in contrast to the IFRS tsunami that hit Canadian public companies in 2011.

Using a Disclosed Basis of Accounting   In practice, private enterprises are not bound by GAAP unless an external user (such as a major lender) requires the company to use GAAP. While many private companies do abide by all accounting standards, many others deviate from the standards in one or more respects. The deviation is usually to make the statements more useful for specific users or to coincide with the income tax treatment of specific items. For example, a company may prepare statements to satisfy contractual requirements, such as compliance with the requirements of a major loan.

When non-GAAP accounting policies are used, the company is said to be reporting on a **disclosed basis of accounting (DBA)**. The description of DBA will normally be included in the accounting policy note to the financial statements, and the auditor's opinion (if any) will refer to the fact that the financial statements have been prepared in accordance with the accounting principles described in the accounting policy note.

Be cautious! We are not suggesting that a company can toss out all of GAAP. Deviations from GAAP usually are limited to just certain policies (e.g., using tax-based capital cost allowance [CCA] instead of accounting depreciation), except for very small companies that report on what is essentially a modified accrual basis.

Learning Multiple Sets of Standards Canada is using different accounting standards for public and private enterprises. Other countries are using yet other sets of standards (e.g., IFRS-SME). Does this mean that we all have to learn two or three different sets of standards? Well, not really.

IFRS is the biggie—the one that all professional accountants and investment managers around the world must understand. As your career takes you around the world, whether as a professional accountant, a financial expert, a private investor, or a company manager, you should be highly knowledgeable about IFRS.

On the other hand, most Canadian private companies will use ASPE, with fewer disclosure requirements and less reliance on fair values. Although these are two different sets of GAAP, they are very similar in many respects. The AcSB is unlikely to let Canadian ASPE deviate very far from the general principles and practices prescribed by IFRS.

Thus, there is a lot of convergence between ASPE and IFRS. Private-company GAAP can be regarded mainly as simplifying exceptions to IFRS rather than as a substantially different body of standards. Many of the principles and practices of international standards had already been incorporated into Canadian standards before the 2011 change-over to IFRS, although there were still many significant differences.

This book will discuss IFRS in the main text body of each chapter. At the end of each chapter, we will explain the ways in which Canadian ASPE differs from IFRS.

The Issue of Comparability

The point of establishing IFRS is not only to promote multiple exchange listings but also to greatly improve comparability between companies based in different countries. Previously, it was quite difficult to compare the financial statements of companies based in different countries. Even relatively minor differences between U.S. and Canadian reporting caused difficulties for analysts. To compare companies between more radically different standards (e.g., German versus United Kingdom) required detailed knowledge of both countries' accounting standards. But now that both Germany and the United Kingdom use IFRS for their consolidated statements, comparisons should be straightforward, right? Unfortunately, comparisons are not that simple.

The financial reporting of any company is strongly affected by its national environment. There are differences between countries regarding legal requirements, economic environment, political environment, regulation, and ways of doing business.

In the United States and Canada, the principal focus of general-purpose statements is on residual earnings for the shareholder. Other countries may place greater emphasis on other stakeholder groups or have different cultural practices. For example,

- Many countries base income tax on reported earnings; taxable income is equal to accounting income. Income tax minimization therefore becomes a dominant financial reporting objective.
- Corporations in Sweden are expected to provide information about social responsibility and environmental protection in their annual reports. Accounting information relating to these issues is highlighted in financial reporting.
- German financial reporting places a strong emphasis on creditor protection. The tendency is to understate earnings and to provide for income reserves that have no correspondence in IFRS or Canadian ASPE.
- Many countries emphasize employee protection. Information on employee compensation and benefits must be disclosed in considerable detail, in contrast to Canadian and U.S. practice, where only limited information about employee compensation and benefits is reported in the financial statements—only broad totals are provided.
- Companies that follow Muslim practice do not enter into lending relationships. Instead, banks and other sources of financing enter into equity-based arrangements. Therefore,

amounts that would be reported as interest expense in Canadian will be reported as dividends in companies based on Muslim principles.

- The "consolidated" statements of large Japanese conglomerates do not include the bulk of their related companies because there is no "parent" company. Each company within the large group holds just a small share (e.g., 1%–3%) of each other company. At least 60% of the shares are held within the group (called a *keiretsu*), and yet there is no company that "controls" any others. Thus, there is no comparison between the consolidated financial statements of General Motors (which includes all of its subsidiaries) and the consolidated statements of Mitsubishi or Toyota (which include only controlled foreign subsidiaries).

International comparisons of financial statements are fraught with hazards because of the many differences that arise. For example, a very high debt load is usually viewed in North America as a bad sign, while low debt is usually a sign of good management. In Germany and Japan, however, low debt indicates that the banks have no confidence in the company—banks will support only strong companies, and thus strong companies are able to access high levels of debt.

CONCEPT REVIEW

1. What is the difference between a public corporation and a private corporation? Which type is dominant in the Canadian economy?

2. How can private corporations obtain capital from outside investors without becoming public companies?

3. Why would a Canadian private enterprise choose to use IFRS instead of ASPE?

OBJECTIVES OF FINANCIAL REPORTING

Is XYZ Corporation making a profit or a loss this year? Well, that depends on how you measure it! To prepare the financial statements, managers and accountants must make many judgements. They must:

1. Choose appropriate measurement methods (i.e., accounting policies); and

2. Make suitable accounting estimates.

To help users understand the financial statements and the approximate nature of the information they contain, managers must also decide what additional information to disclose in both the statements and the notes.

As we will see throughout this book, management's choice of accounting policy and disclosure are constrained by the requirements of IFRS (for public companies) and Canadian ASPE (for private companies). Nevertheless, management must make policy choices in some areas and many estimates in applying the standards. A fairly small change in an estimate can have a very substantial impact on the company's reported results. Indeed, variations in a number of small estimates, such as from optimistic to pessimistic, can sometimes turn a profit into a loss, and vice versa. We will discuss this crucial issue of estimation more extensively later.

To exercise judgement, the accountant must have *criteria* against which to measure the suitability of alternatives. The most fundamental criteria for deciding on policies, estimates, and disclosures are the **objectives of financial reporting** for the specific reporting enterprise or organization.

To be useful to the users, the financial statements must convey information that is useful for their decision purposes. These decision purposes may vary widely, and the information that is suitable for one purpose may not be suitable for another purpose.

Financial statements often have direct economic impacts for either the enterprise or its stakeholders, or both. For example,

- Reported earnings may be used as the basis for employee profit sharing and/or management bonuses.
- Accounting methods may increase or decrease a corporation's income tax liability.
- The reported level of accounts receivable and inventories affects the level of financing provided by a bank through an operating line of credit.
- Reported earnings and reported net asset value affect the permitted return in regulated industries, such as cable companies and pipelines.
- Various reported numbers in the financial statements may trigger a default on loan requirements, known as **covenants**.
- In partnerships, cooperatives, and mutual insurance companies, the reported financial results affect the financial rewards of the partners, members, and policyholders.

In addition, many users' decisions are *evaluative* decisions that may not have immediate economic impacts, but do affect users' perceptions of the reporting enterprise and affect their relationship with (or stake in) the enterprise:

- Lenders evaluate the cash flow potential of a borrower to assess the ability of the borrower to service the loan (that is, to pay the interest and principal as they come due).
- Income tax authorities evaluate the financial statements to see whether the information that a corporation is reporting to its owners is compatible with (but not necessarily the same as) the information it is reporting to the Canada Revenue Agency (CRA).
- Employees evaluate an employer's ability to pay higher compensation (or the validity of employer requests for reductions in compensation).
- Shareholders assess management's ability to conduct the affairs of the enterprise.
- Security analysts evaluate public companies' performance and issue recommendations to buy, hold, or sell shares.
- Regulators evaluate a rate-regulated enterprise to see if the enterprise's earnings are reasonable.

To establish each enterprise's financial objectives, management must consider many aspects of the company and the users of its financial statements. Exhibit 1-1 illustrates the forces that shape a company's financial reporting objectives.

- The *facts* of the company's operations—for example, the sources of its capital; whether it is a public or private enterprise; the length of its operating cycle; the volatility (and predictability) of its revenues and costs.
- The financial reporting *constraints* facing the company—for example, whether an audit is required; whether the audit report must have an unqualified opinion; whether there are regulatory or statutory requirements to meet.
- The *power* of the users—for example, the ability of users such as securities regulators, major lenders, or shareholders to enforce their needs over those of other users or the managers.
- The needs of the financial statement *users*—for example, cash flow prediction; contract compliance; management performance.
- The motivations or objectives of the *preparers* (i.e., the managers)—for example, to minimize current taxes payable; to reveal as little about the company as possible; to show a smooth growth in earnings.

Before identifying the appropriate reporting objectives in a specific situation, the enterprise's facts and constraints must be taken into account. Once that is done, the needs of users and the motivations of preparers can be identified and ranked in order of priority. The cases at the end of each chapter will give you practice at identifying company-specific facts and constraints.

We will begin our discussion of financial reporting standards with a quick overview of *general purpose financial reporting*, after which we will move on to the more specific reporting objectives.

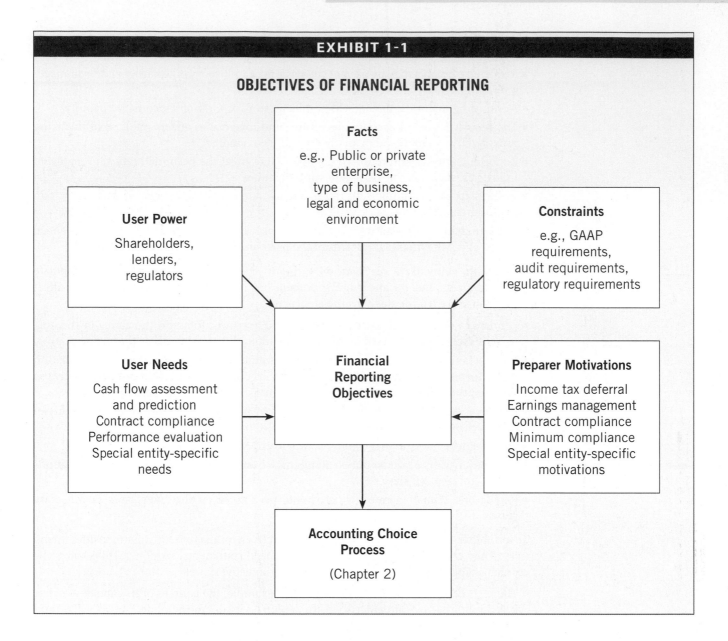

EXHIBIT 1-1

OBJECTIVES OF FINANCIAL REPORTING

Facts

e.g., Public or private enterprise, type of business, legal and economic environment

User Power

Shareholders, lenders, regulators

Constraints

e.g., GAAP requirements, audit requirements, regulatory requirements

User Needs

Cash flow assessment and prediction
Contract compliance
Performance evaluation
Special entity-specific needs

Financial Reporting Objectives

Preparer Motivations

Income tax deferral
Earnings management
Contract compliance
Minimum compliance
Special entity-specific motivations

Accounting Choice Process

(Chapter 2)

General Purpose Financial Reporting

Financial reporting for public companies is described as **general purpose financial reporting**. It is "general purpose" because the potential interest group is large and diverse. A public company's financial statements must serve the needs of current and prospective shareholders and other suppliers of capital, as well as other potential users. A public company's financial statements users can be anyone, anywhere. Public-company accounting standards have been developed to protect the interests of economic decision makers who are dependent solely on a company's financial statements.

The IASB focuses on the supplier of capital as the primary user group. The IFRS *Conceptual Framework for Financial Reporting* states that the objective is to provide useful information that can be used by "existing and potential investors, lenders and other creditors" in their decisions.

In practice, "general purpose" is too imprecise to be an effective guide for a specific enterprise. While the financial reporting objectives cited by the IASB are a guide to standard setting, companies have their own more specific reporting objectives. Accountants and managers must identify the appropriate reporting objectives for their own specific company.

For example, some companies, although publicly listed, really are controlled by a single individual, family, or institutional investor. The group of voting shares that gives control to a small group of shareholders is called a **control block**.

In the *Financial Post*'s annual listing of Canada's 500 largest corporations, known as the FP500, approximately half of the companies are public. Of the public companies, however, well over half have control blocks. Only about 20% of the companies in the FP500 list are "widely held" public companies.

Usually, a control block exists because a private, family-controlled corporation has issued shares to the public, while the original shareholders retain a majority of the outstanding *voting* shares. This is common in Canada for companies that find they need to "go public" to raise sufficient funds for expansion.

Another common Canadian practice is for a public corporation to issue two or more classes of shares, one class with multiple votes and another with few or no voting rights. Shares that have limited voting power are called **restricted shares**. Restricted shares enable a corporation to raise capital from the public without impairing the power of the controlling shareholders.

For example, Vancouver-based International Forest Products Limited ("Interfor," for short). has two classes of common shares outstanding. At the end of 2012, there were almost 55 million Class A shares and a little over one million Class B shares. Class A shares have one vote each, while Class B shares have 10 votes each and are entitled to elect 11 of the company's 12 directors. The holders of Class B shares are the company's founding family.

Interfor's Class B shareholders have a *control block*, in this case as the result of the number of directors they can elect rather than by the proportion of shares they own. When there is a control block, a company's financial reporting is unlikely to be dominated by a concern for the public shareholder. Instead, the reporting objectives of the controlling shareholder may well take precedence over those of the public investor.

When there is a control block, managers may focus primarily on satisfying the controlling shareholder—the needs and perceptions of other shareholders and lenders can become a secondary consideration. Alternatively, management may be especially concerned about meeting the requirements of a large major supplier of debt capital, such as a pension fund.

Users

"Users" can be grouped into two categories—(1) external users and (2) preparers:

- **External users** includes all nonmanagement users of the financial statements, such as investors, creditors, and employees.
- **Preparers** consists of the managers who make decisions in the three judgemental aspects of applying accounting standards—accounting policy, estimates, and disclosure—as well as the accountants who participate in and carry out those decisions by incorporating them into the accounts.

A manager is a *preparer* but may also be a *user* in a different role. A chief financial officer (CFO) of a large corporation is a preparer of the corporation's consolidated statements. On the other hand, that same CFO will use the financial statements of different business units and subsidiaries to evaluate their performance.

In Exhibit 1-1, each of the two boxes labelled "User Needs" and "Preparer Motivations" contains a summary listing of the primary financial reporting objectives. This list is by no means comprehensive because entity-specific objectives often arise.

Ethical Issues Accountants are part of the preparer group because accountants carry out the accounting and reporting decisions of management. Ethical issues can arise. Some accountants have gone to jail because they followed accounting instructions (or strong "hints") from senior executives that resulted in financial misrepresentation.

A professional accountant, whether internal or external (e.g., an auditor), must be prepared to resist management's pressure to misstate financial results, even if it leads to dismissal. It is bad to be temporarily unemployed, but it is far worse to be convicted of a crime.

EXTERNAL-USER OBJECTIVES

Assessing and Predicting Cash Flows

A financial reporting objective that has received much attention in both the professional and academic accounting literature is that of *cash flow assessment and prediction*—investors and creditors are interested in predicting the ability of the company to earn sufficient income and generate sufficient cash flows in the future to be able to pay the company's obligations and to provide a return to shareholders.

Bankers and creditors need to assess a business's ability to generate enough cash through its normal operations to be able to pay interest and to repay debt principal. The shareholders of public companies may also be interested in cash flow prediction because, in theory, share value is derived from the present value of the perpetual stream of future dividend payments. To the extent that earnings are retained instead of being paid out as dividends, the reinvested earnings increase the asset base and should generate increased cash flow (and increased dividends) in the future.

Assessment versus Prediction There is a subtle but important difference between the assessment of *current* cash flows and the prediction of *future* cash flows. To assess current cash flows, the nonmanagement financial statement user wants to understand the cash inflows and outflows of the enterprise in the current period. Normally, the user places particular emphasis on the *cash flow from operating activities* to assess the entity's ability to generate cash. The availability of other sources of financing is also important, as is the disposition of those funds: *How much cash is the company generating or raising externally, and what is the company doing with that money?*

Cash flow *prediction* requires extrapolating the current cash flow into future years. Users must make assumptions to do this, and accounting can help this process by measuring and/or disclosing the company's commitments to future cash flows (e.g., forthcoming lease and loan payments).

As all accountants are well aware, a company's operating cash flow for a year is very different from its earnings for that year. In the long run, however, earnings are the result of cash flows. Revenues and expenses arise from cash flows but differ from the actual cash flows to the extent that accountants engage in the processes of *accrual accounting* and *interperiod allocation* to estimate earnings. Financial analysts and bankers, too, are aware of the difference.

Earnings Quality Creditors and analysts who attempt to assess and predict future cash flows tend to prefer earnings measures that are supported by operating cash flows. For this reason, analysts often use the reported *cash flow from operating activities* to calculate *cash flow per share* for public companies. They compare the operating cash flow per share with the earnings per share.

If there is a high degree of correlation between the two measures, the company has **high-quality earnings**. If the two measures differ significantly, then the company is said to have **low-quality earnings**. The perceived quality of earnings is good when the relationship between operating cash flow and net income is fairly stable.

Sometimes a company will report positive earnings but negative cash flow from operations; this situation is not viewed kindly by analysts because it suggests that management may be manipulating earnings through accruals and interperiod allocations.

Effect on Financial Reporting Choices What impact does an objective of cash flow prediction have on financial reporting? The consequences of adopting cash flow prediction as a primary reporting objective include the following:

- Accounting policies are chosen that tend to reduce interperiod allocations. For example, costs that could be capitalized and amortized depending on management's estimates (e.g., development costs) or accounting policies (e.g., the numeric threshold for capitalization) may be expensed instead, so that the impact on earnings (as an expense) will coincide with the cash flow.

- Full disclosure of future cash flow commitments is given in the notes. There is a great deal of leeway permitted in disclosing future commitments of various kinds. Under a cash flow reporting objective, the choice is to provide fuller disclosure of future cash flows, and particularly to alert users to probable future changes in cash flows (positive or negative).

When cash flow assessment and prediction is the primary objective, financial reporting policies are chosen that provide the clearest indication of the cash flows underlying reported earnings. Accrual accounting and interperiod allocation are still used, but their use is restricted to those instances in which there is little or no choice, such as amortization of capital assets for profit-oriented enterprises.

Income Tax Deferral

A very common objective, particularly for private companies, is that of **income tax deferral** (also known as income tax *minimization*). Since there is a time value of money, why pay taxes this year if they can be delayed until next year? The cash saved by reducing this year's income tax bill can be invested to earn a return or can be used to service debt or pay dividends. A company has better things to do with its money than pay income taxes, if the payment can legitimately be delayed to a later year.

Financial Reporting versus Income Tax Reporting Canada Revenue Agency (CRA) is an agency of the federal government that interprets and enforces the nation's federal tax laws. The *Income Tax Act* and CRA have procedures and reporting requirements whose primary purpose is to collect taxes efficiently and effectively. At times, the government also uses tax law to attain specific social or economic objectives that Parliament considers important, such as encouraging investment in research and development.[3]

The general aim of the *Income Tax Act* is to collect tax revenue. In general, the act provides for taxation when cash is flowing so that revenues are usually taxed when they have been substantively realized and costs are deducted from taxable revenue when they are incurred. Taxation principles tend to emphasize cash flows because those flows normally can be measured quite clearly. There are exceptions to the cash flow emphasis in assessing taxable income, of course. For example, the taxation of revenue often is affected by the revenue recognition policy used by the business, which may differ significantly from the revenue cash flow. Nevertheless, tax law and tax regulations generally steer clear of interperiod allocations and subjective estimates.

The general principle of taxing on the basis of cash flows has an impact on the tax treatment of expenses. Expenses may be recognized for tax purposes in a way that is quite different from their accounting treatment. This is particularly true for costs that are viewed as assets for financial reporting purposes but that are viewed as expenses by CRA, such as development costs, pension costs, and long-term leases.

Similarly, the Canadian *Income Tax Act* has specific requirements for amortizing the cost of capital assets—the capital cost allowance (CCA). CCA is unrelated to depreciation or amortization expense for financial reporting purposes. Nevertheless, private companies may choose to amortize their capital assets on the same basis as CCA is calculated to simplify their financial reporting.

CRA does not require a corporation (or the owners of proprietorships and partnerships) to use the same reporting principles for tax as for accounting, or vice versa. However, corporations must attach their annual financial statements to the tax return. One of the basic parts of the corporate income tax form is a reconciliation of reported pre-tax accounting income to reported taxable income. The corporation must make it clear just what accounting differences caused any discrepancy between the net earnings reported to its shareholders and the

---

[3] For example, in 2007, the government provided incentive for investment by permitting highly accelerated CCA for new investments in equipment and machinery, an incentive that was renewed in 2011 and again 2013. Instead of amortizing over 14 years, companies were permitted to amortize over as little as 3 years.

taxable income reported to CRA. This is the principle of *exception reporting* as applied to the taxable income calculation.

Tax-Book Conformity   When corporations adopt the same accounting practices for financial reporting as for tax reporting, this is known as *tax-book conformity*. Many accountants believe that disclosure of variations between tax and book reporting on the tax return acts as a "red flag" for CRA and invites a tax audit.

Therefore, although there is no requirement in Canada (unlike some other countries, such as Germany and Japan) that tax reporting be identical to financial reporting, tax treatment of items may have an impact on financial reporting. The impact is most likely to be observed for revenue; CRA generally takes a dim view of a corporation's recognizing revenue in the income statement while deferring revenue recognition for tax purposes.

Tax Deferral versus Tax Evasion   When we discuss tax deferral, we are not talking about *cheating* on the income tax. There is some flexibility in the timing of reporting certain revenues and expenses on the corporate income tax return. To a limited extent, a company can affect the amount of tax that it pays through its selection of accounting policies. The use of legitimate options for reducing a company's current taxable income is known as *tax deferral* or *tax minimization*. In contrast, deliberate misstatement on the tax return is *tax evasion*, which is fraud.

Effect on Financial Reporting Choices   If a company wishes to minimize the amount of taxes that it pays, it will adopt accounting policies that tend to:

- Delay the recognition of revenue to the extent permitted by the *Income Tax Act*, particularly for long earnings cycles; and
- Speed the payment of expenses that can legitimately be deducted for tax purposes.

Why wouldn't every company attempt to reduce its income tax bill? The reason is that if the company adopts accounting policies that reduce taxable income, those policies may also reduce reported net income.

This might be a problem for managers whose compensation is tied to book income. A lower book income may also lead to a poorer performance evaluation and hence reduced promotion possibilities for managers. Furthermore, many executive compensation packages include significant amounts of stock options. Anything that lowers the firm's stock price will lower the value of those options.

As a result of the impact on reported earnings, income tax deferral is more likely to be an objective for private corporations and, to a lesser extent, for public corporations that have a strong family control block. The owner-managers of these types of corporations have independent sources of information about the company, and their bankers usually are kept closely informed about the activities of the corporation.

A tax-deferral objective is in the best interests of bankers and creditors, but they must recognize that reported earnings under a tax deferral objective will *look* poorer, but the cash flow will actually be better. In contrast, public corporations are likely to place less emphasis on tax deferral because their managers are more concerned about external stakeholder perceptions of the company's earnings ability.

Contract Compliance

External users often use financial statements as the basis for assessing whether an enterprise has complied with contract provisions. The most common type of financial statement contracting is for debt, particularly with bank loans and with issues of bonds (both publicly issued and privately placed). Debt contracts or agreements usually have provisions that require companies to maintain a certain level of performance, such as:

- Maximum debt-to-equity ratio;
- Maximum percentage of dividend payout;
- Minimum times-interest-earned ratio; and/or
- Minimum level of shareholders' equity.

These provisions are known as covenants or **maintenance tests**. If a company fails to meet the covenants, the lender (or trustee, in the case of publicly issued bonds) has the right to call the loan and force immediate repayment. Since the debtor seldom will be able to satisfy the call for repayment, the company is forced into reorganization or receivership.

Shareholders' agreements in private corporations also usually contain provisions that affect the valuation of shares if a shareholder decides to sell her or his shares. Since there is no public market for the shares of private corporations, there is no easily identifiable market price. In theory, the value of shares is a function of future earnings (and cash flow) and of the fair value of the corporation's net assets. In practice, most shareholders' agreements stipulate that the price is based on historical earnings and on net asset book values.

Effect on Financial Reporting Choices   Accounting policy choices and accounting estimates can have a significant effect on the ratios used in debt agreements and for share valuation in shareholders' agreements. For example, electing to use straight-line depreciation instead of accelerated depreciation for buildings and equipment will result in relatively higher earnings, higher shareholders' equity, lower debt-to-equity ratio, and higher times-interest-earned ratio (which is calculated as income before interest and taxes, divided by interest).

Therefore, some debt agreements (particularly in private placements) specify what accounting policies must be used for calculating the ratios. When specific policies are stipulated in the debt agreement, management's ability to select policies to enhance the ratios is restricted.

Similarly, the share valuation components of private company shareholders' agreements often contain specific provisions concerning the valuation of net assets. These provisions are not constrained by GAAP and therefore may be more suitable to the needs of the shareholders for a fair valuation of their shares than would a GAAP-based valuation.

Stewardship

A question commonly asked by lenders and investors is, "What did they do with my money?" A *steward* is a person who is responsible for managing an enterprise on behalf of someone else. The word originally applied to the person who managed large household estates on behalf of the owners. **Stewardship reporting**, therefore, focuses on showing the financial statement reader just how the resources entrusted to management's care were managed. Transparency is important—full disclosure should exist and the financial affairs should be transparent. Financial reporting should not be complicated by a large number of allocations that obscure the operating results for the year.

Effect on Financial Reporting Choices   The objective of stewardship is reflected in two ways: (1) minimization of interperiod allocations and (2) full disclosure.

Interperiod allocations make it difficult for financial statement readers to see how management is managing the funds entrusted to its care. For example, some types of expenditures either can be expensed immediately or can be capitalized (as an asset) and amortized. A stewardship objective would lead to expensing rather than capitalization.

In addition, the company may choose to provide more than the minimum mandatory disclosures concerning the company's financial position. The role of stewardship is especially clear in the case of mutual fund reporting, where the investment activity of the organization is fully reported each year to satisfy investors' natural inquisitiveness about the nature of the fund's investments and the level of investment activity during the year.

Performance Evaluation

Financial statement readers often use the statements to evaluate management performance. The common use of bonus schemes for managers that are based on reported earnings attests to the widespread use of financial statements for this purpose.

Performance evaluation is a reporting objective that benefits not only external users but also managers themselves. Managers are users of financial statements to (1) evaluate their own performance and (2) evaluate the performance of the managers of subsidiaries and other related companies in a corporate family of companies.

Effect on Financial Reporting Choices To be useful for performance evaluation, financial statements should reflect the basis on which management decisions are made to the extent possible. For example, suppose that a cruise line builds and introduces a new ship. There are substantial costs involved in set-up costs for a new ship. These costs are essential to successful operation of the ship. If performance evaluation is a reporting objective, these costs are carried as work-in-progress inventory to be matched against the revenue that they are intended to enhance. If, instead, cash flow prediction were the dominant objective, then it would be preferable for the costs to be expensed when incurred.

Managers are fully aware of the performance evaluation objective of financial statements, and managers of widely held public companies are apt to be quite sensitive to the earnings impacts of accounting policy choices. Therefore, managers have strong motivations to select accounting policies and make accounting estimates that will enhance their apparent performance. The issue of management motivations in financial accounting policy selection is important and is the subject of the next section.

CONCEPT REVIEW

1. What type of company is *required* to issue general purpose financial statements?

2. Explain the difference between *assessing* cash flows and *predicting* cash flows.

3. What is meant by *high-quality earnings*?

4. Since all companies would like to reduce the amount of income taxes they pay, why isn't *income tax minimization* always the primary objective of financial reporting?

5. What is a *control block*?

PREPARER MOTIVATIONS

The needs of external financial statement users are vital to developing appropriate financial reporting objectives for each specific enterprise. However, managers (i.e., preparers) have their own objectives or motivations that influence their selection of accounting policies and their accounting estimates. These motivations often conflict with external users' objectives and may dominate the accounting choice process if external users lack the power to enforce the dominance of their objectives. This section will briefly discuss the most common preparer motivations.

Earnings Management

Income Smoothing Managers often like to show a smooth record of earnings, free of annoying peaks and valleys. Widely fluctuating earnings are an indication of business risk, and managers often do not want investors or creditors to perceive the company as being risky. Thus, managers have strong motivation to show a smooth upward trend in earnings, year after year.

Income can be smoothed by taking advantage of the opportunities available for spreading both revenues and costs over several periods. The capitalize-and-amortize approach beloved by many managers is a reflection of wide acceptance of the income-smoothing motivation. In recent years, accounting standards have been revised to reduce the options for the capitalize-and-amortize approach, but the opportunity still exists in some contexts.

Accounting estimates provide the most fertile territory for income smoothing. By edging various accounting estimates up or down within a feasible range, management often can significantly affect net income. Remember that net income is a residual. Relatively small changes in estimates for revenues and expenses, such as the amount of accruals, the estimate of bad debts, or the writedown of inventory, can have a significant impact on this residual.

For example, suppose that a company's net income is 10% of total revenue. If total expenses are decreased by 1% through adjustments in estimates, the net income will increase by 10% (that is, from 10% to 11% of revenue), a significant change in most investors' eyes. Thus, shifting of earnings from one period to another is quite feasible.

The impact of accounting estimates is still largely invisible to the external user. IFRS has increased disclosure requirements for many estimates and even requires some sensitivity analysis, as we shall see in later chapters. Nevertheless, there are still many areas where management is not required to provide disclosure of estimates used; their impact is simply impounded in the numbers to which they relate.

Maximizing Earnings *Maximization of net income* is one of the most common management motivations, particularly in public companies. This motive stems from three powerful concerns:

1. To make it easier to comply with debt covenants and to provide a margin of safety between the covenant requirements and the reported numbers (i.e., to keep lenders from getting worried);

2. To positively influence users' judgements when they evaluate the performance of management (i.e., to help managers keep their jobs and to enhance their public standing); and

3. To enhance managers' compensation in the many corporations wherein management compensation is tied either to net income or to stock price performance (or both).

These concerns are particularly relevant for the managers of public companies because ownership is dispersed and there is a general concern on the part of the shareholders and the board of directors about the share price. Managers believe, with good reason, that share prices are affected by reported earnings.

There is a belief that investors in an efficient public market are able to "see through" accounting manipulations that are intended to maximize earnings. However, this ability may be effective only in the short run. In the long run, the information that is necessary to make adjustments for accounting policy differences usually disappears from view.

For example, the effects of a change in depreciation methods (such as asset life or depreciation method) are "transparent" for one year, but there is no way that an investor can adjust for the effect of the change in following years. There is no evidence that shareholders are able to "see through" complex earnings maximization objectives over the long run.

Minimizing Earnings Instead of *maximizing* reported earnings, management may wish to *minimize* reported earnings as an ongoing endeavour. In addition to the possible objective of minimizing income taxes, management may strive to reduce earnings for any of the following reasons:

- To avoid public criticism of earnings that may be viewed as "excessive";
- To avoid attracting competitors into a very profitable business;
- To discourage hostile takeover bids;
- To avoid the scrutiny of regulators or politicians; or
- To discourage large wage claims by employees or to justify management initiatives for wage reductions and cutbacks.

Accounting policies that *maximize* earnings include early revenue recognition and delayed expense recognition. Accounting policies for *minimizing* earnings are just the opposite: Delay revenue recognition, but expense every cost as soon as possible.

The "Big Bath" Sometimes, a corporation will elect to *maximize a loss* in one year as part of a longer-run strategy to *maximize earnings*. The philosophy is that if there will be an operating loss anyway, they might as well take advantage of the opportunity to load as many losses into that year as possible (known as "taking a **big bath**" or "taking a big hit").

It is not at all unusual to see a corporation (in a bad year) announcing changes to accounting estimates that increase the total loss, including substantial writedowns of investments and impairments of capital assets. If a company writes down its capital assets, less depreciation will be charged to expense in future years, thereby enhancing *future* earnings. This motivation has been diminished somewhat for public companies by Canada's move to IFRS because, in certain circumstances, IFRS requires assets to be written back up if fair value recovers in future years (as we will see in Chapter 10), but it still will be management's judgement as to whether asset values have "permanently" recovered or not.

Another ploy is to make a substantial provision (charged to expense) for the estimated amount of future liabilities, such as site restoration costs. If these liabilities turn out to have been overestimated, the company will be able to report a *gain* in future periods when the excess provision is "returned" to earnings.

Minimum Compliance

Minimum compliance refers to the motivation of managers to reveal the least amount of information that is possible while still complying with GAAP.

Minimum compliance may be a motivation for managers in a public company because management does not wish to give outsiders any more information about the company than is absolutely necessary. Managers may wish to maintain confidentiality about their business activities to keep competitors in the dark.

Minimum compliance is usually equated with *minimum cost* of providing accounting information. However, the buyers and sellers of public companies' shares may value a company's shares at a lower level if they feel that the company is giving less than full disclosure about its operations and financial position. Minimum compliance may save accounting and auditing costs but may bear a cost in reduced share prices and increased cost of capital.

Expanded Disclosure

The opposite to minimum compliance may be called **expanded disclosure**. Management may wish to disclose a great deal of information that is not required by GAAP. The motivation for expanded disclosure may simply be to indicate that the company and its management are "good citizens" that have nothing to hide and wish to provide the most informative financial statements possible. Sometimes expanded disclosure is motivated by the expected concerns of specific stakeholders.

For example, a company that might be accused of polluting the environment may choose to disclose its environmental record and its efforts to curb pollution and/or clean up an already-polluted environment. By providing additional disclosure, management may hope to forestall criticism of the company's pollution-control efforts.

In other situations, a company may provide expanded voluntary disclosures to reassure the capital markets that the company is a good investment. For example, management may include information on product demand in the financial statement notes or in management's discussion and analysis, such as (1) the value of current contracts for a service company, (2) the order backlog for a manufacturer, or (3) environmental protection initiatives for a company publicly perceived as a high polluter.

CONFLICTING OBJECTIVES

Virtually every enterprise, public or private, will have more than one financial reporting objective. For example, a company may want to maximize earnings, minimize income taxes, and maintain high-quality earnings. Each of these may be desirable on its own, but they conflict with each other. Minimizing income taxes conflicts with earnings maximization, while both may conflict with showing high-quality earnings (i.e., earnings that correspond closely with cash flow from operations).

Once a company's objectives have been identified, they then must be prioritized: which one is the most important, which one is second most important, and so forth. Only then can accounting choices of policy, estimates, and disclosures be made.

In the real world, accounting requires constant exercise of judgement. Despite the apparent "precision" of the numbers in financial statements, accounting reports are always approximations of the underlying economic phenomena.

ETHICAL ISSUES

External users' needs and managers' motivations often conflict. Managers are aware of users' objectives, and therefore managers may attempt to present the best picture of the corporation's operations and financial position. The resolution of this conflict depends on general concepts of fair presentation and often presents an ethical dilemma for management, the company's accountants, and auditors.

The investigation of the events underlying the collapse of a major U.S. Internet provider provides an example of an accountant who held her ground in the face of senior management pressure to make an unethical "estimate":

> In an … effort to reduce costs, Sullivan [the CFO] directed General Accounting to reduce the Wireless division's expense for line costs by $150 million. When General Accounting called Delores DiCicco, Vice President of Wireless Finance, requesting her to reduce her line costs, she was surprised because there was no support for the entry. Even after Yates [Director, General Accounting] made several follow-up calls, asking her to make the journal entry following Sullivan's instructions, DiCicco firmly refused. In response, Sullivan told DiCicco that she should make the entry because she would eventually find $150 million in savings from disputed billings … Still refusing, she argued that she would not book the entry until she found the savings. As a consequence, the requested journal entry was prepared in General Accounting.[4]

CONCEPT REVIEW

1. Why is it important to establish the financial reporting objectives for a company?
2. Give an example of how the reporting objectives of a public company may differ from those of a private corporation.
3. How might a shareholders' agreement influence a company's financial reporting objectives?
4. Why might the objectives of financial statement users conflict with the motivations of managers?

REQUIRED FINANCIAL STATEMENTS UNDER IFRS

Chapters 3 through 5 describe the various financial statements in detail. Under IFRS, a complete set of financial statements consists of the following:

1. Statement of financial position;
2. Statement of comprehensive income, consisting of:
   a. statement of profit or loss;
   b. statement of other comprehensive income;

---

[4] "Behind Closed Doors at WorldCom: 2001," *Issues in Accounting Education* (February 2004). Copyright © 2004 American Accounting Association. Full text of American Accounting Association articles available at http://aaahq.org/pubs.cfm. See also the *Report of Investigation by the Special Investigative Committee of the Board of Directors of WorldCom Inc.* by Beresford et al., March 31, 2003. Retrieved May 14, 2013, from http://fl1.findlaw.com/news.findlaw.com/hdocs/docs/worldcom/bdspcomm60903rpt.pdf.

3. Statement of changes in equity;

4. Statement of cash flows; and

5. A set of notes comprising a summary of significant accounting policies and other explanatory information.

Some general observations:

- All statements should be *comparative* statements, with both the current and the preceding year's amounts presented in comparative columnar format.
- *The statement titles shown above are not mandatory.* For example, the commonly used title of "balance sheet" can be used instead of "statement of financial position." Also, "statement of profit or loss" is primarily a European convention. Titles such as "income statement" and "statement of earnings" are quite acceptable.
- The statement of comprehensive income is a two-step statement that can instead be shown as two individual statements: (1) an income statement and (2) a statement of comprehensive income that begins with net income as its first line. If the two-statement format is used, the two statements must be presented in immediate succession.

Looking Forward—Whither the United States? A major exception in all this harmonization is the United States. The United States Financial Accounting Standards Board (FASB) and the IASB have been working to reduce and eventually eliminate differences between the two sets of standards, a process known as the *convergence project*. The ultimate goal is to have just one set of standards or (more likely) two sets of consistent standards.

In 2010, the U.S. SEC reconfirmed its support for the convergence project, stating that:

> The Commission continues to believe [in] a single set of high-quality globally accepted accounting standards and that this goal is consistent with our mission of protecting investors, maintaining fair, orderly, and efficient markets, and facilitating capital formation. As a step toward this goal, we continue to encourage the convergence of US GAAP and IFRS and expect that the differences will become fewer and narrower, over time, as a result of the convergence project.[5]

In this statement, the SEC is not saying that IFRS will be an acceptable reporting standard for U.S. companies, but only that U.S. GAAP and IFRS should be "converged" to eliminate or sharply reduce the differences.

In July 2012, the SEC issued a 137-page staff report on the practicalities of incorporating IFRS into the U.S. financial reporting system.[6] This was an extensive study of the practical aspects of moving to IFRS, including the burden of conversion, the lack of investor understanding, and the inconsistency of application in various countries, as we have mentioned above.

Although the report contains no conclusions or recommendations as to whether the United States should fully accept IFRS, there seem to be sufficient serious concerns about the wisdom of such a move. It seems highly unlikely that the United States will ever grant control of accounting standards to a "foreign" institution, no matter how closely involved the FASB may be in its deliberations.

As for those foreign companies (including Canadian) that are listed on U.S. stock exchanges, the SEC already accepts IFRS–based financial statements from non–U.S. companies. Therefore, the move to IFRS has greatly simplified reporting for Canadian companies

---

[5] Securities and Exchange Commission, Release no. 33-9109, pp. 1–2. http://www.sec.gov (go to "Regulatory Actions"; "Other Commission Orders, Notices, and Information"; "33-9109").

[6] Office of the Chief Accountant, United States Securities and Exchange Commission: "Work Plan for the Consideration of Incorporating International Financial Reporting Standards into the Financial Reporting System for U.S. Issuers." Retrieved May 14, 2013, from http://www.sec.gov/spotlight/globalaccounting standards/ifrs-work-plan-paper-052611.pdf

cross-listed on the NYSE or NASDAQ, even if the United States never fully accepts IFRS for reporting by domestically based public corporations.

ACCOUNTING STANDARDS FOR PRIVATE ENTERPRISES

Objectives of Financial Reporting

The AcSB defines the objective of financial statements in a very similar manner to the IASB. The emphasis clearly is on investors and creditors. Although the AcSB's definition refers to other users, the intended "other users" are advisors to investors and creditors, such as security analysts, financial advisors, and bond rating agencies. The AcSB specifically states that:

> It is not practicable to expect financial statements to satisfy the many and varied information needs of all external users of information about an entity. [ASPE 1000.09]

Required Financial Statements

Canadian accounting standards for private enterprises (ASPE) have a somewhat simpler set of financial statements:

1. Balance sheet (i.e., statement of financial position);

2. Income statement (*not* a statement of *comprehensive* income);

3. Statement of changes in retained earnings (*not* changes in all share equity balances);

4. Statement of cash flows; and

5. Disclosure notes.

Chapters 3, 4, and 5 explain the differences between IFRS and ASPE for each type of statement.

Presentation Currency

ASPE does not specify a presentation currency. The concept of *functional currency* does not appear in ASPE. Nevertheless, companies that have a functional currency other than the Canadian dollar will generally report on the basis of that currency. Thus, companies involved in products priced in U.S. dollars will normally report in U.S. dollars. This includes international transportation companies, computer game developers, software developers, gold producers, dealers in diamonds and other precious stones, and so forth.

Canadian subsidiaries of foreign parents may report in the parent's currency, although they may provide "convenience translations" into Canadian dollars for the benefit of their Canadian lenders and creditors.

RELEVANT STANDARDS

CPA Canada Handbook, Part I (IFRS):
- IASB, *Conceptual Framework for Financial Reporting, Chapter 1*
- IAS 1, *Presentation of Financial Statements*

CPA Canada Handbook, Part II (ASPE):
- Section 1000, *Financial Statement Concepts*
- Section 1400, *General Standards of Financial Statement Presentation*

SUMMARY OF KEY POINTS

1. General purpose financial statements are intended to serve the needs of economic decision makers who have no direct or special access to a corporation's financial information.

2. A publicly accountable enterprise is one that either (1) has issued securities (debt or equity) to the general public and therefore must abide by the regulations of the securities commissions in the jurisdiction(s) in which its securities are traded or (2) holds assets in a fiduciary capacity for a broad group of outsiders as one of its primary businesses.

3. In Canada, all publicly accountable enterprises must report in accordance with International Financial Reporting Standards (IFRS). International standards are set forth in the *CPA Canada Handbook, Part I.*

4. IFRS are developed by the International Accounting Standards Board (IASB). IFRS is the set of financial reporting standards that many nations have adopted or adapted for their public companies. All major securities exchanges around the world accept financial statements prepared on the basis of IFRS for nonresident companies, which increases the likelihood of a company being listed on multiple exchanges.

5. The vast majority of Canadian corporations are private corporations. Many are very small enterprises, while many others are subsidiaries of foreign parent corporations. Many large public Canadian corporations have a control block that is owned by an individual or a family. A private corporation's shareholders and lenders are presumed to have access to the information that they need.

6. Canadian private corporations have three choices for financial reporting: (1) IFRS, (2) Canadian accounting standards for private enterprises (ASPE), or (3) a disclosed basis of accounting. Large private companies that compete for capital internationally may choose to use IFRS to present financial statements that are directly comparable with those of public companies.

7. ASPE is maintained by the CICA's Accounting Standards Board (AcSB) and is set forth in the *CPA Canada Handbook, Part II.*

8. It is impossible to impose a single, dominant objective on financial reporting. The objectives of financial reporting must be determined with reference to each specific organization's environment and its stakeholders, and with regard to the users' decisions that the financial statements are intended to facilitate.

9. The reporting objective taken by the IASB for developing IFRS is to present information that will assist lenders, creditors, and shareholders in making their economic decisions.

10. Cash flow prediction is a financial reporting objective that is often appropriate for lenders, creditors, and shareholders. Financial stakeholders need to predict a corporation's ability to generate cash flow from operations and to service debt or to pay dividends. Under a cash flow objective, revenues and expenses are recognized in a way that corresponds (on an accrual basis) with cash flow.

11. Income tax minimization is another very common objective, especially for private corporations. Public corporations are less likely to have this as a primary objective because they may be more concerned about the perceptions of other users of the statements than about saving taxes in the short run. An income tax minimization objective leads to delayed revenue recognition and faster expense recognition.

12. Financial statement readers often use the statements to assess the corporation's adherence to contract requirements, such as those in loan agreements and shareholders' agreements.

13. A major reporting objective is that of performance evaluation. Statements that have been prepared to facilitate the evaluation of management's performance will use reporting policies that coincide as closely as possible to the basis for management's operating decisions.

14. Managers are the preparers of financial statements. Managers often have motivations that stem from their desire to influence the decisions of external users, particularly those of public companies. Managers may be tempted to adopt accounting policies and make accounting estimates that tend to maximize reported earnings, minimize earnings, smooth earnings, or show compliance with contract provisions such as loan covenants.

15. The motivations of preparers often conflict with the financial reporting objectives that are appropriate for external users in a particular situation. Accountants must use their professional judgement to try to reconcile such conflicts ethically and to avoid issuing financial statements that contain biased measurements.

KEY TERMS

accounting standards board (AcSB)
accounting standards for private
    enterprises (ASPE)
big bath
control block
covenants
crown corporation
disclosed basis of accounting (DBA)
expanded disclosure
fiduciary enterprise
functional currency
general purpose financial reporting
high-quality earnings
income tax defferal
International Accounting Standards
    Board (IASB)

International Financial Reporting
    Standards (IFRS)
low-quality earnings
maintenance tests
minimum compliance
objectives of financial reporting
presentation currency
private enterprise
private placements
publicly accountable enterprise (PAE)
restricted shares
shareholders' agreements
small and medium-sized enterprises
    (SME)
stewardship reporting

QUESTIONS

Q1-1   What is the difference between public and private companies? What are the accounting implications of this difference in Canada?

Q1-2   What is a control block? What are the accounting policy implications?

Q1-3   Who sets accounting standards for public and private companies in Canada?

Q1-4   What are the three different approaches that a Canadian private company must choose from for financial reporting?

Q1-5   Why would a Canadian private company choose to use IFRS instead of ASPE?

Q1-6   What is a disclosed basis of accounting? Explain.

Q1-7   What is the objective of general purpose financial reporting?

Q1-8   If a set of financial statements were meant to portray the cash flows of an organization, what kinds of accounting policies would likely be chosen?

Q1-9   What accounting policies would best serve the reporting objective of tax minimization?

Q1-10   What is income smoothing? Explain how managers can use accounting estimates to achieve this objective.

Q1-11 What is a "big bath"? Why might this practice help to achieve higher reported earnings?

Q1-12 What is a covenant? What kinds of accounting policies would be common among companies with severe restrictive covenants?

Q1-13 Describe how the motivations of managers are different than those of shareholders. What accounting policies might be commonly found if managers receive bonuses based on net income?

Q1-14 Explain why a comparison of the debt level of companies in different countries might be misinterpreted.

Q1-15 How do a country's economic and political environments impair comparability between its corporations and those of Canada?

CASE 1-1

RICHARD PLOUGHWRIGHT

Andriana Bessemer, a sole practitioner in a rural area, is working in her office when one of her most important clients, Richard Ploughwright, walks in. Mr. Ploughwright operates one of the largest dairy farms in the region.

"I'm sorry to barge in like this, but I've just been across the street to see my banker. He suggested that I ask you to explain some matters that affect my financial statements. You'll recall that I need to renew my loans each year. The new bank manager isn't very happy with the way my previous statements have been prepared. He has requested that I make some changes to my statements this year before he processes my loan renewal.

"The new banker wants me to switch from the cash basis of accounting to the accrual basis. I don't quite understand how that will help either him or me. The cash basis provides me with the information I need to evaluate my performance for the year—after all, what I make in a year is the cash left over and in the bank at the end of the year after tending my cattle, selling my milk, and maintaining my dairy barns and equipment. That ending amount of cash is what I use to pay my taxes and the bank. I know the income tax people will accept either the cash or accrual basis from farmers, so why the change for the banker?

"Also, he now wants me to value all of my cattle at market value. I can't see the benefit of valuing them at market value because I'll never sell cattle that are still productive. Anyway, some of the cattle are for breeding, not for milking.

"I know I must give the bank manager what he wants, but I'd really appreciate knowing why I must make these changes. After all, these changes are just going to increase your bill, which already seems rather high to me, so it'll be an extra cash drain for me."

Required:
Assume the role of Andriana Bessemer. Respond to Mr. Ploughwright.

CASE 1-2

MILTON KIDD

Sander Persaud is an audit manager for a national public accounting firm. Each summer, the firm recruits several university students as interns. One such intern is Milton Kidd, a high-performing student who has just finished his third year of university and who is majoring in accounting.

As a test of Milton's understanding of accounting, Sander has assigned him the task of reviewing three of the firm's recently acquired clients. Sander has asked Milton to give him a report in which he points out any significant differences between the three clients and the implications of those differences for the clients' financial reporting, with a ranking of importance for each client. He wants the report on his desk by the end of the day.

Brief descriptions of the new clients are as follows:

Breeze Inc.

Breeze Inc. is a new entrant into the mobile phone market. The company is incorporated in Ontario and is establishing a new network, initially covering only the "Quebec City to Windsor" corridor, which includes the cities of Montreal, Ottawa, and Toronto. This heavily populated corridor encompasses more than half the Canadian population and generates about 60% of the national GDP.

Since mobile phones use public airwaves, entrance to that market is strictly limited and is controlled by the national telecommunications regulator, the Canadian Radio-television and Telecommunications Commission (CRTC). The CRTC has regulatory power over many aspects of Breeze Inc.'s operations but does not control or limit the profits (or potential profits) of the company. Breeze Inc. entered the market as one of the winners of competitive bidding when the CRTC made new licences available.

Establishing a new network requires intensive infrastructure investment, both financial and intellectual. Breeze is being assisted by Telyu, a Japanese telecom company that operates a very advanced network in Japan. The cooperation agreement provides that Breeze will pay Telyu a fee of 2% of all revenue arising from Internet traffic on Breeze's network. That is, the fee does not apply to voice traffic, ordinary text messages, sales of handsets, revenue from advertising messages, or any other tangential revenue.

Breeze Inc. has a 12-member Board of Directors. Three of the seats are reserved for nominees from Fenzal Partners, an Egyptian venture capital firm that provided most of the financing for Breeze Inc., mostly in the form of a private placement of nonvoting preferred shares but also via some secured debt. The other nine board members are Canadian, including the Chair of the Board.

The company is a private company that has no intent to become a public company in the foreseeable future.

Saturn Software Systems Ltd. (SSS)

SSS designs large-scale custom software programs for health management and social agencies, both private and provincial. The company has been in existence for about eight years. The demands on the company's resources increased significantly in the most recent couple of years due to an increasing recognition among health care and social agencies that they need better computer-based client management systems. The company is owned equally by the two former university classmates, Rejean and Klaus, who founded the company.

SSS has been profitable from the beginning, but the increase in business has begun to strain the company's resources. SSS has tripled its staff over the past two years, thereby more than tripling the company's costs, both payroll costs and other related costs. The company has been perpetually short of cash because contracts-in-progress have grown much more quickly than finished projects.

This year, SSS's owners turned to the venture capital unit of a large Canadian public pension fund for financial support. SSS issued a new class of convertible nonvoting preferred shares to the fund. The dividends on the preferred shares must be paid before Rejean and Klaus can declare any dividends to themselves. Also, the fund has approval rights over any salary increases for the owners.

SSS has negotiated a substantial line of credit with the Sterling Bank of Canada. The credit line has restrictions on salary and dividend levels, as well as a requirement for prior approval of any additional debt financing.

Rejean and Klaus are not wealthy. They have put their heart and soul into SSS since its founding and are strongly committed to the success of the company and the welfare of their employees, all of whom enjoy a profit-sharing plan.

International Auto Parts Ltd. (IAP)

IAP is an Ontario-based manufacturer of auto parts originally known as Magnum Manufacturing Corporation. The company started more than 20 years ago and slowly built up business by supplying parts to the "Big 3" U.S. automobile companies. A major recession in the industry caused IAP to almost collapse, but it was saved by a substantial injection of capital by the founding family.

The additional capital not only saved the company but also enabled it to begin acquiring other small auto parts companies in the southern Ontario and Northern Michigan regions that had suffered near-collapse. As the auto industry recovered and sales rose, so did the fortunes of Magnum. The name was changed to International Auto Parts to reflect its dual-country nature and also because the company's senior managers envision expansion (and acquisitions) in Europe, as well as linkages with emerging auto companies in China. Over the past two years, IAP was able to obtain contracts to supply parts to the North American plants of two non–North American auto makers, one from Japan and one from South Korea.

IAP is a private, family-owned company that has a significant level of debt financing through investment funds and, to a lesser extent, through Canadian and U.S. banks. However, the owners recognize that to continue expansion through acquisitions, they will need to tap the public financial markets. An IPO (initial public offering) is definitely an expectation within another two or three years, depending on the state of the market. IAP plans to apply for a listing on the Toronto Stock Exchange in conjunction with an IPO.

Required:

Assume that you are Milton Kidd. Prepare the report for Sander Persaud.

CASE 1-3

INTERNATIONAL FASHIONS INC.

You are an accounting student who has obtained a summer internship with the national public accounting firm of Nash & Crosby. Your manager has been giving you various tasks to test your abilities and your perceptions.

The firm has recently acquired a new corporate audit client, International Fashions Inc. (IFI). Your manager has given you the previous year's financial statements (unaudited) and has asked you to conduct some research into the client's operations. You are to prepare a memo in which you describe the objectives that you believe should shape the financial reporting of the company.

After viewing the company's website and searching other information sources, you learn the following information:

- The company is an Ontario corporation founded in 1976. The corporate headquarters and executive offices are near Toronto.

- The shareholders are two brothers who immigrated to Canada from Hong Kong in 1972. The brothers are both active managers of the company and its affiliates. The directors are all members of the brothers' families.

- The company operates a chain of 126 women's fashion clothing stores. There is one store each in Toronto, Montreal, and New York City. All of the other stores are located in Hong Kong, Taiwan, Singapore, and mainland China (P.R.C.).

- Most of the company's clothing is produced by factories in Xiamen, China, by a separate company that is also owned by the two brothers. Two designers work full-time in the company's headquarters near Toronto to design the clothing that is manufactured in Xiamen.

- The stores in North America are owned and operated by IFI directly. Those three stores are the "flagship" stores, intended to give an upscale North American flavour to the company's products. To further enhance the Canadian "origin" of the company, all models used in IFI's advertising, in all markets, are Western rather than Asian. The company prefers to use high-profile international public figures and entertainers as its fashion models.

- The stores in Hong Kong, Taiwan, and Singapore are operated by three separate wholly owned IFI subsidiaries, one for each area. Some of the profits from these subsidiaries are returned to the parent company through management fees, while the rest remain in the subsidiary to finance expansion and store renewal.

- The stores in mainland China are operated through an IFI subsidiary that has a local partner. As a foreign corporation, the company is entitled to special tax advantages that are not available to Chinese companies. The China subsidiary must pay 35% of the subsidiary's net income to the partner.

- IFI, as a separate entity, currently has no long-term debt. IFI has relied almost exclusively on retained earnings to finance its growth for the past 20 years. In its early stages, the company narrowly averted bankruptcy caused by high debt and various supply problems. Since then, management has been reluctant to use debt financing. However, the company does stretch payment periods for its accounts payable and effectively forces the suppliers to bear the cost of the inventory until the product is sold. The accounts payable debt is on the books of whichever company (i.e., the IFI parent or each of the Asian subsidiaries) received the inventory. About two-thirds of the total company-wide accounts payable is owed to the brothers' Xiamen company.

- IFI is eager to rapidly expand the number of stores that it operates in cities in eastern China. Rapid expansion will require external sources of funds.

Required:
Prepare the memo for your manager.

TECHNICAL REVIEW

TR1-1 Chapter Overview: Indicate whether each of the following statements is true or false:

1. The IASB has authority for setting Canadian accounting standards.
2. All Canadian corporations must comply with international accounting standards.
3. Most Canadian corporations are listed on the Toronto Stock Exchange.
4. IFRS must be used for the financial statements of every Canadian public corporation.
5. The objective of general purpose financial reporting is to serve the information needs of a wide variety of users, including lenders, shareholders, employees, and regulators.
6. The primary objective of financial accounting is to reveal all information about an enterprise's financial performance.
7. If a corporation has a restrictive bond covenant that specifies a minimum times-interest-earned ratio, the corporation's management will be motivated to pick discretionary accounting policies that maximize income.
8. Income tax law has no impact on the accounting choices made by management.
9. The presence of a control block can have an impact on a public company's choice of accounting policies.
10. Any Canadian company that uses U.S. GAAP must prepare its statements in U.S. dollars.

TR1-2 Chapter Overview: Indicate whether each statement is true or false:

1. IFRS and the *CPA Canada Handbook, Part II*, have equal status in Canada for financial reporting.
2. In a private corporation, the needs of external users have no impact on the company's financial reporting objectives.
3. Canadian companies must always prepare their annual financial statements in Canadian dollars.
4. Canadian accounting standards are set by the *Canada Business Corporations Act*.
5. The debt and equity securities of a private company cannot be traded on public exchanges. Therefore, private companies have no external sources of financing.
6. A company may take a "big bath" in a loss year if management wishes to maximize future earnings.
7. A public company may not use a disclosed basis of accounting for external public financial reporting.
8. When an enterprise's primary reporting objective is cash flow assessment, the enterprise will use a cash basis of reporting rather than an accrual basis.
9. Any Canadian company may use IFRS.
10. The IASB cannot require transnational corporations to use IFRS.

TR1-3 GAAP and Reporting Currency: Indicate whether each statement is true or false. If the statement is false, provide a brief explanation of why it is false.

1. A private company based in Canada must follow the recommendations of the *CPA Canada Handbook*.
2. A company that reports in U.S. dollars must use U.S. accounting standards.
3. A company cannot report under Canadian accounting standards unless it uses Canadian dollars as the unit of presentation in its financial statements.
4. A Canadian company that is listed on the TSE may use U.S. accounting standards.
5. All companies listed on the NYSE must use U.S. accounting standards.
6. The U.S. SEC will accept financial statements from U.S.-listed foreign companies in their home-country accounting standards.
7. Each country that accepts IFRS commits to using the full set of standards.
8. A Canadian private enterprise does not have access to outside investors if it uses Canadian ASPE.
9. Under Canadian ASPE, a company must report in its functional currency.
10. A private Canadian company that is a subsidiary of a U.K. parent company may not report in British pound sterling unless the pound also is its functional currency.

TR1-4 Acronyms: The language of accounting is littered with acronyms, abbreviations for common organizations or phrases. Match the phrase or organization on the left with its abbreviation.

Phrase or Organization	Abbreviation
1. International Accounting Standards Board	A. AcSB
2. Accounting Standards for Private Enterprises	B. SEC
3. Accounting Standards Board	C. CICA
4. International Financial Reporting Standards	D. OSC
5. Toronto Stock Exchange	E. IFRS
6. Ontario Securities Commission	F. ASPE
7. Kentucky Fried Chicken	G. FASB
8. Canadian Institute of Chartered Accountants	H. DBA
9. Securities and Exchange Commission	I. TSX
10. Financial Accounting Standards Board	J. KFC
11. Disclosed Basis of Accounting	K. IASB

ASSIGNMENTS

 A1-1 IASB Standard Setting: The IASB is the standard-setting body for IFRS. Anyone who uses financial statements should understand the process by which standards are set.

Required:
Consult the IASB website (http://www.ifrs.org). Click "Standards development," and then "Standard setting process." Describe the process of standard setting in your own words, including some information about each step in the process.

 A1-2 International Comparisons: You have recently attended a conference on behalf of your manager. One speaker from a large bank, Mr. Stearns, stated:

> With the advent of international accounting standards, we now can easily compare the financial results of companies across borders when we are choosing high-quality companies to invest in. We no longer have to struggle with different accounting in different countries. Now, when we compare the "net income" line on an earnings statement from Japanese company with one from a British company, we can be confident that the net incomes are comparable because both companies are using IFRS.

Required:
Write a memo to your manager discussing the issues raised by this speaker.

 A1-3 Accounting Choices: For each of the situations listed below, state what judgements and/or estimates are necessary when preparing financial statements at each business's fiscal year-end of 31 January:

1. Due to slow sales volume during December, a toy store has an unexpectedly large inventory.
2. One of Sukkor Corporation's major clients has gone into creditor protection. The client accounts for 40% of Sukkor's outstanding accounts receivable. Sukkor has filed a court claim against the client (along with other unsecured creditors), but a loss of somewhere between 20% and 35% of the receivable is likely.
3. IMF Inc. has been sued by another company for trademark infringement. The other company has won a lower-court judgement against IMF for $1.5 million. IMF is appealing the decision to a higher court. IMF's lawyers are confident that IMF will win the appeal.
4. CanBuild Ltd. signed a fixed-price contract for construction of a 45-storey condominium apartment building in downtown Calgary. Construction has been underway for almost a full year, and about 60% of the estimated total costs have been incurred so far. Construction costs have been rising rapidly in Calgary. Now, however, condominium sales have stalled due to a recession.
5. Pacific Alliance has just finished producing a new children's computer-animated motion picture for DVD distribution. The total accumulated production cost is $3.4 million. Pacific Alliance has signed a distribution agreement with a major supplier of educational materials, including DVDs. Normally, Pacific Alliance's earlier movies of the same general type have a sales life of about three years—slow to start, then increasing acceptance, followed by market saturation and obsolescence.

 A1-4 Effect of Accounting Policies: A private company has two debt covenants in place:

a. *Maximum debt-to-equity ratio*: Current and long-term liabilities, excluding future income taxes, are divided by total shareholders' equity.
b. *Minimum times-interest-earned ratio*: Income before interest and taxes is divided by total interest expense.

Required:

For each of the accounting policy choices listed below, indicate which ratio(s), if any, would be affected, and whether the policy would increase or decrease the ratio.

1. Depreciation method is straight line, rather than declining balance.
2. Costs that could either be deferred and written off or expensed immediately are expensed immediately.
3. Interest expense could be measured using straight-line amortization for the debt discount; alternatively, the effective interest rate method could be used. The straight-line method results in lower interest expense in the early years and is the chosen policy.
4. An issue of preferred shares that has the characteristics of debt (guaranteed cash flows to the investor) is reclassified from equity to debt.
5. Warranty expense is accrued as sales are made, rather than expensing it as warranty claims are paid.
6. Revenue is recorded as goods are delivered, rather than when cash is later collected.

★ **A1-5 Reporting Alternatives:** For each of the situations below, explain whether the company can use its preferred basis of accounting:

1. A Great Lakes shipping company based in Thunder Bay, Ontario, wishes to use U.S. dollars as its presentation currency. Shipping on the Great Lakes is always priced in U.S. dollars. The company prefers to use IFRS rather than U.S. GAAP. The company is registered with the SEC and its common shares are listed on the NYSE.
2. The wholly owned Canadian subsidiary of a U.K. carpet manufacturer is primarily a sales arm, importing and selling carpets manufactured by its parent company. The parent wants the subsidiary to use U.K. GAAP (which is IFRS compliant) instead of the *CPA Canada Handbook* recommendations for private companies. The parent also wants the subsidiary's financial statements to be expressed in British pounds sterling.
3. A private Ontario-based auto parts manufacturer has rapidly expanding operations in Germany, India, and Russia. The company is negotiating with private investors to issue a new class of restricted-voting common shares. Because of the increasing globalization of the company, management wants to use IASB standards to facilitate possible future listings on the Frankfurt stock exchange.
4. An expanding publicly owned airline corporation is soliciting substantial new investment from private equity funds. One potential investor has requested that the corporation submit special private financial statements that do not follow certain recommendations of IFRS.

★ **A1-6 Non-IFRS Situations:** A manager of a medium-sized, private company recently complained to you as follows:

> I'm very confused! I thought that all companies had to comply with IFRS starting in 2011. Now, after all our work to convert our systems to be IFRS-compliant, I hear that there are many companies that don't use IFRS and that there may be are circumstances in which different versions of GAAP may be appropriate! Now what should we do?

Required:

Respond to the manager's concern, and be sure to distinguish between general purpose and special purpose financial statements.

★★ **A1-7 Reporting Situations:** Four different unrelated Canadian corporations are described below:

1. Privately owned Vancouver-based Moonburst Coffee Ltd. imports coffee beans from around the world, but mainly from South America. The company roasts and packages the coffee and distributes it to several B.C. retail grocery stores under its own Moonburst

label. The company owns and operates 47 retail coffee shops in British Columbia and has franchised 16 coffee shops in Seattle, Washington. Currently, the company is in negotiations with a large Canada-wide supermarket chain to supply coffee under the chain's private label brand, Chairman's Choice. To supply the chain, Moonburst will have to drastically increase its purchasing and processing capacity. To finance its expanded operations, Moonburst's owners are negotiating with four private investment firms for new equity. Three of the potential investment firms are based in the United States; the fourth firm is a large Canadian pension fund.

2. Pangal Inc. is a steel fabricating company based in Hamilton, Ontario. The company is listed on the TSX. The controlling shareholder, Nataraj Pangal, holds shares entitling him to 51% of the voting rights. Seventy percent of Pangal's output is sold to U.S. manufacturers and builders (in U.S. dollars), although contracts with non-American manufacturers are under negotiation and are expected to account for an increasing proportion of sales in future years. Pangal is considering the possibility of registering with the SEC and applying for a U.S. exchange listing.

3. Economics International (EI) is a Toronto-based consulting company. EI provides consulting services to European companies that have operations in Canada and in the United States. EI bills its clients in the currency of their home country, primarily in euros and pounds sterling. Some billings are in the Scandinavian currencies as well. About half of EI's consultants are based in Canada; the others are located in London and Brussels. EI's shares are owned by the consultants; to become a *senior* consultant, a consultant must make a substantial equity investment in EI.

4. Chorus Entertainment Corporation's (CEC) head office is in Montreal, while its executive offices are in Los Angeles. CEC's main operations are in Los Angeles, although CEC does maintain an animation studio in Vancouver and operates a sound stage in Toronto. CEC is privately owned, but it raises additional financing almost exclusively in the United States and through its industry contacts in Los Angeles.

Required:
For each of the four companies, discuss the most appropriate accounting standards to use: IFRS, U.S. GAAP, Canadian ASPE, or DBA. Also indicate the most appropriate presentation currency for each company.

★ **A1-8 Reporting Situations:** The reporting situations of two different companies are described below:

1. Stardust Explorations Inc. (SEI) is seeking significant new financing for a gold and diamond mining venture in northern Ontario. In their search for new financing, company directors have been visiting Australia, South Africa, China, and India. The directors have met some resistance because Stardust's financial statements are based on Canadian private-company standards and use the Canadian dollar as the unit of measure in the company's financial statements. Gold and diamonds are valued internationally in U.S. dollars.

2. A new-venture investment fund has invested significant amounts of money in the convertible debentures of privately owned Cerebral Conceptions Ltd. (CCL), a Nova Scotia company. CCL has been reporting in accordance with Canadian private-company accounting standards. Now, however, the investment fund would like for CCL to begin reporting on a near-cash basis, recognizing all except capital expenditures as expenses and delaying revenue recognition until the revenue has been realized as cash. CCL's management fears that such a change in accounting policy will prevent the company from receiving an unqualified audit report. Also, the company worries that the change will drastically increase the loss that CCL has been reporting, with possible repercussions from the company's retired founder, who currently is living on Vancouver Island.

Required:
For each of the two companies, recommend and justify an accounting approach that is appropriate under its particular circumstances.

★★ **A1-9 Objectives of Financial Reporting:** The IASB sets out the objectives of general purpose financial statements, but public companies and their managers have objectives that relate to their specific circumstances. Explain how managers' objectives impact the choice of accounting policies and the exercise of judgement.

★★ **A1-10 Impact of Differing Objectives:** Privately owned BlueScreen Corporation is primarily a retailer of computer equipment for individuals and small business. The effective cost of computer equipment and peripherals, at both the retail and manufacturing levels, has been declining rapidly for many years and shows every sign of continuing that decline.

The company also develops software intended for small business applications—that is, for companies with up to 500 employees. The software is sold in BlueScreen's own stores as well as through the company website. However, most sales come through general software distributors (e.g., download.com).

For sales through the distributors, purchasers can obtain a 30-day limited-feature trial by paying an initial fee equal to 10% of the retail price of the software. If the customer decides to buy after 30 days, the trial fee is credited to the total cost of the purchase. On average, about two-thirds of the trials result in final purchase. Software development is a continuous process, including updates of existing software.

Some of BlueScreen's accounting issues are as follows:

1. What inventory methods should be used for retail merchandise in its stores and warehouses.
2. How the software development cost should be accounted for.
3. How the company should account for tangible capital assets, such as the warehouse building (which it owns), stores (which are leased), and store fixtures.
4. All of the company's personnel—retail, managerial, and software development—are sent annually to professional development programs to keep their skills at the cutting edge of performance. The company spends many millions of dollars on these programs each year.
5. The company opens an average of 20 new stores each year. About five stores are closed each year.

Required:
Using the chart below, indicate the accounting policies that the company should choose for each of these issues under each of three *different* primary financial reporting objectives:

1. Earnings maximization
2. Cash flow prediction
3. Earnings minimization

Issue	Earnings Maximization	Cash Flow Prediction	Earnings Minimization
1			
2			
3			
4			
5			

★★ **A1-11 Accounting Policy Disagreement:** You have been hired as the assistant in the finance department of a medium-sized publicly traded firm. Realizing the importance of accounting to your new duties, you have recently completed an intensive introductory course in financial accounting. On this course, you learned that research costs are expensed during the period they are incurred but that development costs should be treated as an asset and amortized over their projected benefit period.

Over the prior two years, your company's R&D unit had achieved an important breakthrough in electronic copying. This year, the company spent a substantial amount of money to develop a revolutionary new type of copying equipment and bring it to a marketable stage.

Your superior, Matta Hari, wishes to treat the development costs as an expense in the current year rather than deferring and amortizing them. After all (she argues), the costs have already been incurred and the cash spent, and she would prefer that future earnings from the sale of the equipment not be burdened by amortization of the development cost. She also points out that the company's primary lender, one of the "Big 5" Canadian banks, is particularly interested in assessing the company's cash flow.

Ms. Hari has asked you to research the issue and submit a written report to her on this issue by tomorrow morning.

You have researched your firm's past practice in this area and reread the relevant accounting standard. Although your firm has not previously experienced the level of research and development expenses associated with the present project, past practice in your firm has been to expense these costs. Your reading of the accounting standard confirms what you recall from your course—that development expenditures should be capitalized and amortized if certain criteria have been met.

Required:
Explain the status of GAAP to this manager. Be sure to distinguish between general purpose and special purpose financial statements.

★★ **A1-12 Accounting Policies and Reporting Objectives:** Entities may have a variety of corporate reporting objectives specific to their circumstances, such as:

a. Assessing and predicting cash flows;
b. Minimizing current income taxes;
c. Complying with restrictive covenants (specifically, debt covenants that specify minimum levels of shareholders' equity); and
d. Evaluating management's performance.

Required:
For each of the accounting policies listed below, indicate which objectives of corporate reporting is best served. Each policy may serve more than one objective.

1. Capitalize and amortize start-up costs.
2. Disclose proposed environmental protection efforts.
3. Defer expenses to match them against revenue generated from the activity.
4. Delay recognizing revenue as long as possible.
5. Recognize each period's payments on long-term finance leases as expense when incurred (i.e., rather than capitalizing and amortizing the payments).

★★ **A1-13 Policy Choice:** Marcon Properties Ltd. is a diversified private company that owns approximately 60 retail properties that the company has operated as discount department stores. These stores are small, stand-alone properties that Marcon owns outright, although most properties are heavily mortgaged. In 20X1, the company decided, due to increasing losses from retail operations, that all discount department stores should be closed and properties converted to rental units. This process was successfully started in 20X1, with 22 of 60 properties signed to long-term rental agreements with tenants. It is now the end of 20X1, and all retail operations have ceased. There are 38 properties currently sitting vacant. Marcon believes that it can successfully lease the remaining properties over the next 9 to 23 months.

For the 20X1 fiscal year, an accounting policy issue has come up in relation to the vacant properties—whether the properties should be depreciated during the period they sit vacant prior to rental. Those in favour of recording depreciation point out that the properties continue to deteriorate during the period in which they are idle and that depreciation is meant to allow for obsolescence, not just wear and tear. Those who favour suspension of depreciation point out that amortization should be matched with the rental revenue that the properties will generate in the future.

Marcon is reporting a positive net income in 20X1, generated from a variety of other activities.

Required:

Explain which accounting policy you would expect to be adopted in the following independent circumstances. Note that in some circumstances, the company will be indifferent as to the policy chosen.

1. Marcon is a public company and wants to show a smooth upward earnings trend.

2. Marcon has a team of senior managers who are compensated with a cash bonus based on a percentage of annual net income. Senior managers will choose the accounting policy.

3. Marcon is a private company, financed 60% through debt and 40% through equity, and has debt covenants that specify minimum debt-to-equity and return on assets (net income divided by total assets.)

4. Marcon is managed by its major shareholders, who wish to minimize income tax payments.

5. Marcon's controlling shareholders are not directly involved in the business, and they wish to use the financial statements as a method to evaluate the stewardship and performance of managers.

6. Marcon has a team of senior managers who are compensated with a cash bonus based on a percentage of annual income. Assume *for this part only* that the company will report a loss in 20X1 from other sources and that managers will not receive any bonus this year.

CHAPTER 2

Accounting Judgements

INTRODUCTION

In 2011 and 2012, the former senior managers of a once-prominent Canadian electronics company, Nortel Networks Corp., were under attack in court for allegedly manipulating earnings through the use of "accounting reserves." The preliminary results for one quarter showed a potential profit. The senior managers then sent queries to the financial managers of their worldwide subsidiaries. The queries were about whether the subsidiaries had any accounting reserves in those subsidiaries that could be reversed or "unwound." After the subsidiaries reported back with suggested adjustments, head office made adjusting entries that turned the prospective profit into a loss. A similar process was used in subsequent quarters that then turned a preliminary loss into a profit, thereby triggering generous bonuses for the executives.

The issue in the court case was whether or not the executives intentionally manipulated earnings to trigger their bonuses. The defence was that in making the end-of-quarter adjustments, the company simply was following the accounting practice of adjusting estimates at the end of each accounting period.

Accounting estimates are, by definition, approximations. Theoretically, estimates are based on the facts of the situation and expectations about the future. But how well can we predict the future? Corporate loan loss predictions in 2007 certainly did not take into account the financial system meltdown that occurred in 2008 and could not possibly have done so.

Accounting choice is often a matter of professional judgement, but exercising that judgement can be difficult and contentious. The previous chapter pointed out that management's selection of reporting objectives can significantly affect both earnings and the statement of financial position. Within any accounting model and with any sets of reporting objectives, accounting estimates play a major role. Indeed, it has been suggested that net income should not be stated as a single number but, instead, should be a median number within a range—e.g., "Net income for the year is $4.2 million, plus or minus $1.8 million." The range is due to different feasible reporting practices and accounting estimates.

This chapter explains the underlying assumptions of our accounting model and discusses the qualitative criteria needed to provide useful information. These criteria are useful guides to standard setters when they develop accounting standards. The criteria are also guidelines for management when they adopt accounting policies and make accounting estimates. As we will continue to emphasize through this text, accounting is full of estimates—virtually every amount on a company's financial statements is the result of multiple estimates.

What we call "generally accepted accounting principles" (GAAP) is really a collection of assumptions, objectives, and measurement concepts leading to an accumulation of accounting practices and accounting standards. We lump these all together and call them GAAP. In this chapter, we will analyze the different components of GAAP to get a clearer picture of the structure of accounting principles and how they are applied.

CATEGORIES OF ACCOUNTING CONCEPTS

The general body of accounting concepts (or principles—the "P" in GAAP) consists of three different categories: *underlying assumptions, qualitative criteria,* and *measurement methods.* We can describe these as follows:

- **Underlying assumptions** form the basic foundation upon which all accounting measurement rests. For example, the accounting principle of *going concern* (also called *continuity*) is an underlying assumption.

- **Qualitative characteristics** are the criteria that, *in conjunction with the organization's reporting objectives, facts, and constraints,* are used to evaluate the possible measurement options and choose the most appropriate measurement methods *for a given situation.* The principles of comparability and understandability are examples of qualitative criteria.

- **Measurement methods** are the various ways in which financial position and the results of operations can be reported. The accounting principles of fair value and realizable value are examples of measurement methods, both of which are based on the underlying assumption of continuity.

Measurement methods are *how* transactions and events are measured and reported; qualitative criteria are *why* they are measured that way, provided that the underlying assumptions are valid in the particular situation.

For example, historical cost is a widely used measurement method in which assets are reported at their acquisition cost. Historical cost (a *measurement method*) is commonly used because it is perceived as being more verifiable (a *qualitative criterion*) than other alternative measurement methods. But the use of historical cost depends on the reporting enterprise's continuity as a functioning entity (an *underlying assumption*).

To set standards and to understand the accounting choice process, we must clearly differentiate between underlying assumptions, qualitative characteristics, and measurement methods. Otherwise one becomes hopelessly entangled in fuzzy conceptualization that fails to recognize implicit assumptions.

For example, *historical cost* is not a fundamental concept of financial accounting, but *verifiability* is. Without a high degree of verifiability provided by historical cost, accounting reports would have less credibility, and accounting would not serve its most basic societal mission of conveying useful information. But there are many situations in which historical cost is not the appropriate measurement method, situations in which fair value is both highly verifiable and more *relevant* (which is another qualitative criterion).

Limitations of the Concepts

The financial statement concepts established by standard setters pertain to general purpose financial statements. Statements prepared for a *specific* use may well have attributes different from those described in the International Financial Reporting Standards (IFRS) concepts. Since one of the primary purposes of defining the concepts is to help standard setters determine appropriate policies for wide application, their focus on generalities is appropriate. *But it also means that there are exceptions to the applicability of the concepts and conclusions!*

Structure of Accounting Policy Choice

To construct financial statements for a particular enterprise, we must:

- Determine the objectives of financial reporting;
- Make sure that the underlying assumptions are valid;
- Measure the elements of financial statements using situation-specific measurement methods that satisfy the qualitative criteria; and
- Prepare the financial statements.

The process is illustrated in Exhibit 2-1. Chapter 1 discussed the forces that shape an organization's financial reporting objectives. This chapter will focus on the concepts that interact when we make accounting choices for measurement and reporting:

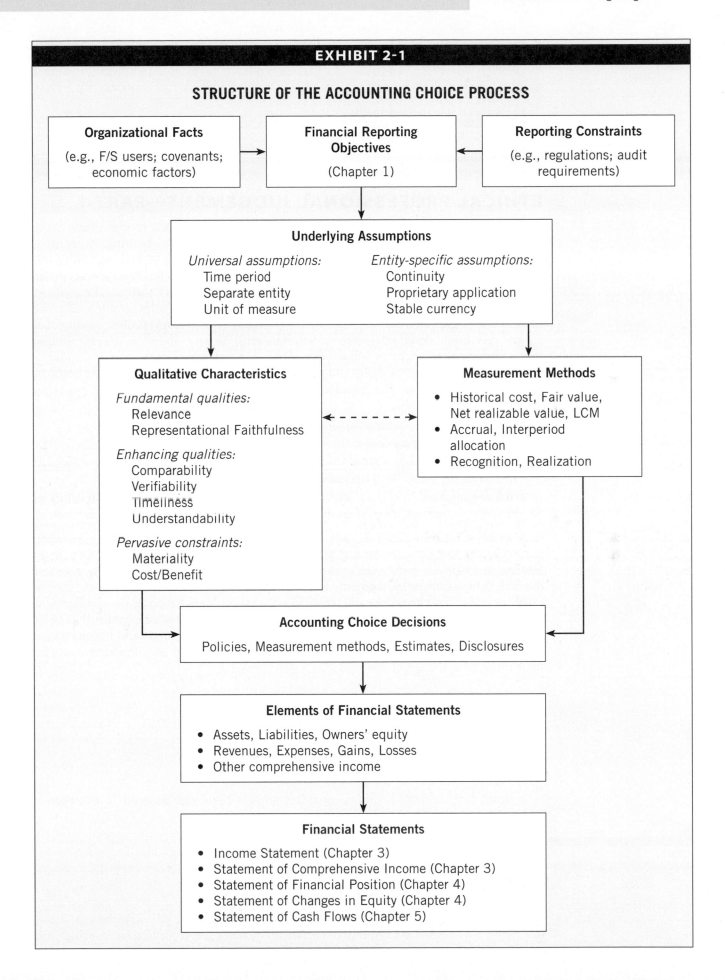

EXHIBIT 2-1

STRUCTURE OF THE ACCOUNTING CHOICE PROCESS

Organizational Facts

(e.g., F/S users; covenants; economic factors)

Financial Reporting Objectives

(Chapter 1)

Reporting Constraints

(e.g., regulations; audit requirements)

Underlying Assumptions

Universal assumptions:
Time period
Separate entity
Unit of measure

Entity-specific assumptions:
Continuity
Proprietary application
Stable currency

Qualitative Characteristics

Fundamental qualities:
Relevance
Representational Faithfulness

Enhancing qualities:
Comparability
Verifiability
Timeliness
Understandability

Pervasive constraints:
Materiality
Cost/Benefit

Measurement Methods

- Historical cost, Fair value, Net realizable value, LCM
- Accrual, Interperiod allocation
- Recognition, Realization

Accounting Choice Decisions

Policies, Measurement methods, Estimates, Disclosures

Elements of Financial Statements

- Assets, Liabilities, Owners' equity
- Revenues, Expenses, Gains, Losses
- Other comprehensive income

Financial Statements

- Income Statement (Chapter 3)
- Statement of Comprehensive Income (Chapter 3)
- Statement of Financial Position (Chapter 4)
- Statement of Changes in Equity (Chapter 4)
- Statement of Cash Flows (Chapter 5)

1. Underlying assumptions
2. Qualitative criteria
3. Accounting choices
   a. Financial statement elements
   b. Recognition and realization
   c. Measurement methods

ETHICAL PROFESSIONAL JUDGEMENT—PART 1

The process of making (or recommending) choices in accounting is the process of exercising **professional judgement**. Professional judgement is pervasive in accounting. Accounting standards frequently refer to the exercise of professional judgement. Indeed, one of the differentiating characteristics of IFRS and Accounting Standards for Private Enterprises (ASPE), in contrast to their Financial Accounting Standards Board (FASB) cousins south of the border, is that they place a great deal of reliance on professional judgement in preference to stipulating rigid rules. As well, judgement is pervasive in many aspects of accounting that are not specifically dealt with in accounting standards. As we examine various accounting topics throughout this text, we will emphasize their judgemental aspects.

Accountants must act ethically and exercise judgement to be fair to all stakeholders. In any specific situation, an accountant exercises **ethical professional judgement** by taking into account many factors:

- The users of the financial statements, and their *specific* information needs;
- The motivations of managers;
- The nature of the organization's operations (e.g., the type of ownership, the sources of financing, the nature of its operating or earnings cycle, etc.); and
- The organization's reporting constraints, if any (e.g., audit requirements, reporting to securities regulators, constraints imposed by foreign owners, etc).

Alternative measurement methods, both accounting *policies* and accounting *estimates*, are considered in light of the foregoing factors. Situation-appropriate measurement policies are chosen within the framework of the qualitative criteria, but only after making sure that the underlying assumptions are valid.

At the end of this chapter, we will return to a discussion of ethical professional judgement and the way that accounting policy choices are made. But first, we must examine the two of the three types of "accounting principles": (1) underlying assumptions and (2) qualitative criteria. The third type, measurement methods, will be discussed and illustrated topic by topic throughout the rest of this book.

CONCEPT REVIEW

1. Who uses financial statement concepts?
2. What are general purpose financial statements?
3. What factors must a professional accountant take into account to exercise ethical professional judgement?

UNDERLYING ASSUMPTIONS

Underlying assumptions provide the foundation of GAAP for for-profit enterprises, as shown in Exhibit 2-1. Six basic assumptions significantly affect the recording, measuring, and reporting of accounting information.[1] The assumptions can be grouped into two general categories: (1) **universal assumptions** that are essential to make financial reports feasible and meaningful, and (2) **entity-specific assumptions** that are very common but that actually depend on an individual entity's reporting circumstances:

Universal assumptions:

1. *Time period*—meaningful information can be assembled and reported for a time period that is less than the enterprise's life span.

2. *Separate entity*—the enterprise can be accounted for and reported independent of its owners and other stakeholders.

3. *Unit of measure*—the results of the enterprise's operations can be measured meaningfully in monetary terms.

Entity-specific assumptions:

1. *Proprietary approach*—the results of operations for a profit-oriented enterprise's operations should be reported from the viewpoint of its owners.

2. *Continuity*—the enterprise will continue in operation for a reasonable future period; also known as the *going-concern assumption*.

3. *Stable currency*—the value of the measurement currency (e.g., the Canadian dollar) does not change from year to year; the enterprise has generated a profit if its revenues are higher than the measurement basis (e.g., historical cost or fair value) of the resources used.

There are times when one or more of the entity-specific assumptions are not valid, in which case GAAP is not appropriate. GAAP might be useless or highly misleading if used when the assumptions are not valid.

Universal Assumptions

Time Period The operating results of any business enterprise cannot be known with certainty until the company has completed its life span and ceased doing business. In the meantime, decision makers need timely information. The **time-period assumption** states that it is feasible to provide useful information in shorter periods while the enterprise is still functioning instead of only at the end.

Although the reporting period varies, one year is the standard. Some companies use a calendar year, and others use a fiscal year-end that coincides with the low point in business activity over a 12-month period. Some businesses (such as retail stores and movie chains) report on a 52-week basis because their activity cycle is weekly (with an occasional 53-week year to catch up with the calendar). In addition, companies also report summarized financial information on an interim basis, usually quarterly for public reporting or monthly for internal purposes.

Separate Entity The **separate-entity assumption** means each specific, identifiable business entity is considered an accounting unit separate and apart from its owners and from other entities. The separate-entity assumption says that accounting, in essence, can draw a boundary around the business unit and account only for the business's activities, independent of the affairs of the owner(s).

This may be quite artificial. For example, an enterprise carried out as a corporation may be inseparable from its owner if it has a single shareholder who is the owner-manager and who co-mingles business and personal finances. The same is true for sole proprietorships

---

[1] An early, and still very relevant, study of the underlying assumptions of accounting was published by the American Institute of Certified Public Accountants as its *Research Study No. 1*: Maurice Moonitz, *The Basic Postulates of Accounting* (New York: AICPA, 1961).

and partnerships (for which each partner's share of the partnership income is included in each partner's individual tax return).

The accountant must be aware of the relationship between the business and its owner(s) and must take care to portray this relationship realistically. For example, loans by a controlling shareholder to the corporation are usually, in substance, equity infusions. These have the legal form of debt and are classified as such in the financial statements. However, lenders routinely insist that such loans be subordinated (i.e., made secondary) to their own loans and reclassify the shareholder loan as equity when performing any analysis of the company. The accountant must strive to disclose the nature of the shareholder loan so that any external user is able to understand that there is a special relationship between the creditor and the debtor.

This separate-entity accounting "boundary" does not necessarily correspond with the legal and tax status of an entity. Partnerships and sole proprietorships do not share the legal or tax status of separate entities; in law and in taxation, they are viewed as an extension of their owners. Partners and nonincorporated sole proprietors are fully liable for the debts of the business—the personal assets of the owners cannot legally be isolated from the business. There is no separate tax return for the partnership or sole proprietorship. Only one tax return is filed, by the individual proprietor or by each of the partners.[2]

Unit of Measure The **unit-of-measure assumption** means that the results of a business's economic activities can be reported in terms of a standard monetary unit throughout the financial statements. Simply stated, the assumption is that it is possible to prepare meaningful financial statements for an enterprise because everything of relevance can be measured using the dollar (or euro, or yen, or renminbi) as the unit of measure. Money amounts are thus the language of accounting: The common unit of measure enables dissimilar items, such as the cost of a tonne of coal and the amount of an account receivable, to be aggregated into a single total.

Unfortunately, the use of a standard monetary unit for measurement purposes poses a dilemma. If financial statements are to be meaningful, they must include complete relevant information to enable a user to make informed decisions. The unit-of-measure assumption implies that *if it cannot be measured, it cannot be reported.* And, by extension, that *if it cannot be reported, it cannot be used for decision making by external users.* Because of the unit-of-measure assumption, many important aspects of a modern business's operations are not included in the financial statements, such as:

- The value of in-house intellectual capital;
- The environmental impacts of the company's operations; and
- The value of customer goodwill and "human capital" (i.e., employees).

Many companies attempt to fill this information void with non-financial information, but its quality and consistency are often questionable. Another shortcoming is that supplementary information is not subject to audit.

Entity-Specific Assumptions

Proprietary Assumption The proprietary assumption is one of the fundamental assumptions of financial reporting for business accounting. There are two possible concepts for enterprise reporting:

- **Proprietary concept** An organization's financial condition and results of operations are reported from the point of view of the owners, or *proprietors.* All other claims on the assets are liabilities, and all payments other than those to the owners are expenses. Returns to owners are returns on capital and are not expenses. This is the dominant view of a business enterprise—all outsiders are paid off, and the owners keep the residual wealth.

---

[2] Limited liability partnerships (LLP) are an exception. These normally are professional service partnerships, particularly public accounting firms and legal firms that are not permitted to incorporate. Partners in LLPs, by definition, have limited personal liability for the firm's liabilities.

- **Entity concept** The owners are one of many participants, or stakeholders, in the enterprise. The **value added** by the enterprise (i.e., revenue minus purchases of goods and services from third parties) is distributed to the various *factors of production*, consisting of providers of capital (both interest on debt and dividends on equity), labour (wages, salaries, and benefits), and government (taxes and fees for services); any residual (i.e., retained earnings under the proprietary assumption) is reinvested in the enterprise. Under the entity view, the owners are just one of several groups that contribute to the enterprise—the corporation itself is the entity that benefits if there is residual wealth.

Another perspective is that if the enterprise is healthy, all contributors to the enterprise should benefit, not just the shareholders. This perspective coincides with the concept of **sustainable business enterprise**—that a business is sustainable in the long run only when value is created for all stakeholders, including employees, customers, owners, and creditors.

Value-added entity-basis reporting has some distinct advantages over proprietary reporting. Entity-basis reporting can enable a user (e.g., the government of a host country) to see whether a foreign-owned corporation is contributing to that nation's economy or is "milking" the economy for the benefit of nondomestic shareholders. Much of the information conveyed in a value-added report cannot be obtained from statements prepared by using the proprietary concept.

The proprietary concept is standard in the United States and Canada, where it is accepted without question. Note, however, that it is an *assumption*, not a fact of life. The proprietary concept is not so readily embraced in other parts of the world. In Germany, for example, employee representatives often occupy as many as 50% of the seats on a company's supervisory board, and the company's banks and major lenders are normally represented as well. While German consolidated financial statements are in conformity with IFRS (as required by the European Union [EU]), the general approach to corporate governance is to look after the welfare of the *corporation*, not just the welfare of the *shareholders*.[3]

Continuity The **continuity assumption** is also known as the **going-concern assumption**. Under the continuity assumption, the business entity is expected to continue operations into the future. This does not assume perpetual life but does assume that the business will continue to operate long enough to recover (or use up) the assets now in its possession and repay its outstanding liabilities. Financial statement preparers must assess the entity's ability to continue as a going concern, considering all available information.

Two occasions in which the continuity assumption is not valid are (1) when a business is a limited-life venture, and (2) when a business is in financial difficulty and is expected to be shut down or liquidated. In these circumstances, many commonly used measurement methods are not appropriate.

The continuity assumption provides a conceptual basis for many of the measurement methods used in accounting. For example, asset measurement assumes that the business's capital assets will be used up over their lifetime, which gives rise to the process of depreciation. If the entity is about to be ended, financial statements cannot be prepared on a going-concern basis—assets and liabilities will be valued at their net realizable value, not at their amortized carrying value.

The continuity assumption also justifies the classifications used in accounting. Assets and liabilities, for example, are classified as either current or long term on the basis of this assumption. If continuity is not a safe assumption, the distinction between current and long term loses its significance; all assets and liabilities become current.

Stable Currency Assumption The monetary unit of measure is often compared to a ruler, by which the dimensions of a business and its operations are measured. But unlike a ruler,

---

[3] German financial statements contain legally required special reserves that are taken from earnings and thus reflect the entity concept of protecting the enterprise rather than "unlocking maximum shareholder value"—the common mantra in North America.

which is always the same length, the value of a currency changes over time. The relative value of a currency can be measured in two ways:

1. In relation to the value of other currencies (its *exchange rate*); or

2. In relation to the amount of goods and services that it will buy (its *purchasing power*).

These two relative values are related. As the general purchasing power of a currency declines, its value in relation to currencies that have constant purchasing power also declines. A decline in the general level of purchasing power is a condition of *inflation*. Over time, the relative values of currencies of different nations will adjust to maintain their relative purchasing powers; this is known as maintaining **purchasing power parity**.

To keep operating successfully, any enterprise has to preserve its capital investment. This is the concept of **capital maintenance**. Annual profit can be measured only after keeping the same level of net assets from the beginning to the end of the year (excluding transactions with shareholders).

Usually, accounting is performed under the assumption that every dollar of revenue and expense has the same value, regardless of whether it was a 1950 dollar, a 1980 dollar, or a 2010 dollar. Dollars of different vintages are accounted for without regard to the fact that some have greater purchasing power than others. We call these **nominal dollars**, unadjusted for their purchasing power (inflation).

The assumption of an absolutely stable dollar is not correct, but it is used because inflation in most developed countries has been relatively modest. Unfortunately, over time, even modest annual rates of inflation can cause large cumulative changes in purchasing power. For example, Cdn\$100 spent in 1970 is equivalent in purchasing power to Cdn\$500 spent in 2010.

Alternative Capital Maintenance Approaches There are three approaches to capital maintenance:

- Financial capital maintenance measured in nominal monetary units;
- Financial capital maintenance measured in units of constant purchasing power; and
- Physical capital maintenance (also known as **productive capacity capital maintenance**).

We normally assume that the dollar is stable and does not change significantly from year to year. In contrast, **constant dollar capital maintenance** explicitly recognizes that not all dollars are created equal. If prices are rising (i.e., inflation), a dollar of capital at the end of the year is not worth as much as a dollar at the beginning of the year. Therefore, the enterprise must keep more nominal dollars invested in capital at the end of the year just to stay even, or to have *maintained* capital.

The **physical capital maintenance** concept recognizes that the prices of individual goods and services change at different rates and in different directions, some going up and some going down. A company's capital is invested in productive assets. The key to capital maintenance is that a company must be able to maintain the same level of service or *productivity*, not simply the equivalent dollars of investment.

Physical capital maintenance is a misnomer because the point is not to maintain the *physical* capacity but, rather, the *productive* capacity. No one would strive to maintain exactly the same computers, for example—they would maintain the computing *capacity*.

IFRS accepts both nominal dollar and physical/productive capacity capital maintenance concepts. The physical capacity concept may be used in regulatory situations. A good example is telecommunication companies. Telecom Italia, for example, uses physical capacity maintenance for its cellular phone network because its rates are regulated to maintain capacity plus a permitted maximum rate of return. Since the cost of electronic equipment keeps declining, the cost of maintaining capacity is not stable—it declines, which leads to lower rates for customers.

The apparently universal dominance of nominal dollar maintenance is somewhat misleading. Nominal dollar maintenance relies on historical cost as the basis of measurement. As accounting standards increasingly move toward fair values, the measurement of earnings incorporates more value changes. Changes in asset values reflect the expected productivity of those assets. Thus, the more we move to fair-value reporting (as in the investment and real property markets), the more we are unconsciously using productive/physical capital maintenance.

EXHIBIT 2-2

CAPITAL MAINTENANCE CONCEPTS

Capital Maintenance	Measure of Profit	Commentary
Nominal dollar financial capital maintenance	$1,500 − $1,000 = **$500**	Profits are reported after historical costs in nominal dollars are recovered.
Constant dollar financial capital maintenance	$1,500 − ($1,000 × 1.10) = $1,500 − $1,100 = **$400**	Profits are reported after inflation, ensuring that the purchasing power of the original investment is maintained.
Physical (productive capacity) capital maintenance	$1,500 − $1,350 = **$150**	Profits are reported only after the entity keeps enough capital to replace assets used.

Example To illustrate these possible assumptions, assume that an item of inventory is purchased for $1,000, held for one year and then sold for $1,500. Inflation during the period was 10%. It would cost $1,350 to replace the item in inventory at the end of the period because supplier price has increased. Under each of the three capital maintenance concepts, the profit under each method would be reported as shown in Exhibit 2-2.

CONCEPT REVIEW

1. Why may the separate-entity assumption be artificial for a small corporation with a single shareholder?
2. When might the continuity assumption not be valid?
3. What is the alternative to the proprietary concept?
4. Which underlying assumption is not appropriate in a country that suffers triple-digit annual inflation?

QUALITATIVE CRITERIA

Qualitative criteria are needed to establish accounting policies, as indicated in Exhibit 2-1. Many attempts to develop, clarify, and/or codify these criteria have been made, beginning way back in 1966.[4] The various conceptual frameworks have varied in detail, but they all reflect the same general ideas and qualitative hierarchy.

The discussion below will follow the IFRS *Conceptual Framework for Financial Reporting*, Chapter 3. Exhibit 2-3 presents a summary of the most recent IASB version of qualitative criteria.

---

[4] See *A Statement of Basic Accounting Theory* (American Accounting Association, 1966); *Statement of Financial Accounting Concepts No. 2: Qualitative Characteristics of Accounting Information* (Financial Accounting Standards Board, May 1980); and *Corporate Reporting: Its Future Evolution* (Canadian Institute of Chartered Accountants, 1980).

EXHIBIT 2-3

QUALITATIVE CHARACTERISTICS OF ACCOUNTING INFORMATION

Fundamental Characteristics
Relevance (the primary characteristic)
   Predictive value
   Confirmatory (*or* feedback) value
Faithful representation
   Completeness
   Neutrality
   Freedom from material error

Enhancing Characteristics
Comparability (*the goal*)
   Consistency (*the means*)
Verifiability, as:
   Representation of economic
      phenomena
   Application of a measurement
      method
Timeliness
Understandability

Pervasive Constraints
Materiality
Cost/benefit

Based on Chapter 3 of the IASB *Conceptual Framework for Financial Reporting*, "Qualitative Characteristics of Useful Financial Information."

Source: The International Accounting Standards Board, © 2012.

Fundamental Qualities

Relevance **Relevance** is the most important qualitative characteristic because it means that accounting information must be useful for decisions. Relevance refers to the capacity of accounting information to make a difference to the external decision makers who use financial reports. Relevance relates to the objectives of financial reporting. Chapter 1 pointed out that the accounting choices that are made when cash flow prediction is the primary reporting objective are not necessarily the same choices that are made when performance evaluation is the primary objective.

Two qualities that contribute to relevance are *predictive value* and *confirmatory value*:

1. **Predictive value**. Accounting information should be helpful to external decision makers by increasing their ability to make predictions about the outcome of future events. Decision makers working from accounting information that has little or no predictive value are merely speculating intuitively.

2. **Confirmatory value**. This also is known as **feedback value**. Accounting information should be helpful to external decision makers who are confirming past predictions or making updates, adjustments, or corrections to predictions.

Faithful Representation Information is reliable if users can depend on it as a sufficiently accurate measure of what it is intended to measure. Accounting information should represent what it purports to represent and should report the economic substance of transactions. This characteristic is known as **faithful representation**.

An important aspect of faithful representation is **substance over form**. As an example of accountants' efforts to portray substance over form, consider a company that leases a computer system. The legal form of the contract is a rental agreement, which would seem to suggest that payments made by the company should simply be reported as rent expense with no other financial statement impact.

However, suppose that the accountant discovers that this company decided to lease the computer instead of buying one outright with money borrowed from a bank. The lease term covers the entire expected useful life of the computer, cannot be cancelled by the company, and provides a full return of the cost of the computer plus a profit margin (in the form of interest) to the lessor. Now it appears as though, *in substance*, the company has acquired property rights over the computer, far more than a simple rental contract would imply. In substance, the company owns full rights to the use of the asset and is financing it with a lease agreement. Thus, to reflect *substance over form*, and to faithfully represent the substance of the transaction, the asset and the obligation should be shown on the balance sheet of the lessee; the subsequent statements of comprehensive income (SCIs) should reflect both depreciation of the computer and interest on the liability.

Faithful representation is closely related to the concept of reliability but has three additional subcomponents: *completeness*, *neutrality*, and *freedom from material error*:

- **Completeness:** To ensure that information faithfully represents the economic events or financial elements that it is purporting to measure, the information must not mislead or deceive. Information must give a faithful picture of the facts and circumstances involved, as a city map should accurately represent the layout of a city. If some important streets are omitted from the map, the map is far less useful than it could be because it lacks completeness.

- **Neutrality:** Financial reports are neutral if they do not influence a user's decisions or judgements to achieve a specific intended outcome. This characteristic is also known as *freedom from bias*. Accounting information is biased if the measurements result in consistent overstatements or understatements of the items being measured.

   The concept of neutrality is sometimes taken to mean that reported accounting information should not influence economic decisions. This view is weird—if information does not affect economic decisions, it is irrelevant and thus is useless. Lack of neutrality means the deliberate misstatement or exaggeration of information to influence decisions in a predetermined direction.

- **Freedom from material error:** Faithful representation does not imply "accuracy" in the sense that the measurement is completely free from error. Most accounting measurements are inherently uncertain, and that is why they are *estimates*. Estimates must be based on appropriate inputs and must reflect the best available information; biased estimates defeat faithful representation. If the extent of approximation is too great, measurements should be accompanied (in the notes) by an explanation of the degree of uncertainty. If statements are free from bias, overstatements and understatements must not exist, including any that may be introduced under the guise of "conservatism."

ETHICAL ISSUES

Preparers of financial reports should not attempt to induce a predetermined outcome or a particular mode of behaviour. For example, a set of financial statements should not be made to look "rosy" to influence potential investors to purchase a company's shares. Thus, there is a potential conflict between management's financial reporting objectives (or motivations) and the accountant's ethical professional responsibility.

Enhancing Qualities

Comparability Comparability is a factor when considering the relationship between two pieces of information. There are two aspects of comparability—*consistency*, which entails using the same accounting policies from year to year within a firm, and *uniformity*, which means that companies with similar transactions and similar circumstances use the same accounting treatments.

Consistency involves applying accounting concepts and principles from period to period in the same manner. There is a presumption that an accounting principle once used should not be changed. However, if consistency is carried too far, it adversely affects relevance. A change to a preferred accounting principle is permitted, even though this would impair consistency. This apparent conflict is usually resolved by retrospective restatement of financial statements to reflect the new policy, with appropriate note disclosure.

The principle of **uniformity** is a goal for which standard setters strive. The concept is that various companies should use the same accounting methods for the same economic events and phenomena. Companies' financial statements can be most readily compared with each other only when they use similar accounting policies and methods.

Verifiability If knowledgeable and independent observers can measure an economic event and arrive at generally the same result, the measurement is said to be verifiable. There are two aspects to **verifiability** in the IFRS framework:

- The accounting measure is a reasonable measure of the economic event, without material error or bias; and
- Independent observers, *using the same measurement methods*, would reach substantially the same conclusion.

The first aspect relates to faithful representation—that the measurement actually represents what it is supposed to. The second aspect is that the calculation or measurement can be replicated or reproduced by independent observers; this is the essence of the auditor's function.

Timeliness Accounting information should be reported soon enough for it to be useful for decision making. Like the daily news, stale financial information has less impact than fresh information. Lack of **timeliness** reduces relevance.

Understandability Information must be understandable to be useful to users in their decision-making process. **Understandability** does not mean that all information has to be reduced to the lowest common level or simplified so that the least sophisticated investor can understand it. Investors and creditors should have a reasonable understanding of business and economic activities, as well as some understanding of accounting. These users are expected to study the information with reasonable diligence. User groups include those who provide advice to investors and creditors; users who lack expertise are presumed to have obtained professional advice.

Pervasive Constraints

Materiality The term "**materiality**" is used to describe the significance of an item. Something is said to be material if its omission or misstatement would be likely to influence or change a user's decision. Essentially, it does not matter how an immaterial item is accounted for because errors or omissions relating to minor items would not lead to different decisions. Materiality may be caused by the relative size of an item or by its nature.

Regarding size, an essentially arbitrary limit of a small percentage (e.g., ranging from 2% to 5%) of income from continuing operations or of assets frequently is used to measure materiality. However, even a much smaller amount could affect investor or creditor perceptions.

For example, the auditors of Toronto-based Nortel Networks Limited insisted that the company disclose the reversal of "accounting reserves" of $80 million in its interim statements, even though the company had assets of $15.7 billion and quarterly revenue of $2.4 billion in the quarter. Such a small amount is only 0.3% of revenue and 0.005% of assets. The reason for the auditor's insistence was that the company's quarterly net earnings amounted to only $97 million. The reversal, which is a managerial judgement, amounted to 82% of the reported earnings.[5] Materiality might be determined by the nature of an item, not its size. For example, assume that a large company with a $500,000 materiality limit discovered a $100,000 payment that might have been a bribe. This item, which is immaterial dollar-wise, would have to be brought to the attention of the audit committee of the Board of Directors for further action because of its questionable legality.

The Cost/Benefit Tradeoff The concept of **cost/benefit effectiveness** holds that any accounting measurement or disclosure should result in greater benefits to the users than it costs to prepare and present. Benefits should exceed costs.

---

[5] "Nortel executives clashed with auditors, trial told." *The Globe and Mail*, 24 May 2012, p. B2.

In standard setting, this is a very difficult concept to implement, since the benefits of an individual accounting standard are very vague, while the costs of compliance are very real. Furthermore, the costs are borne by the companies, while the benefits are usually enjoyed by the external users. The cost/benefit perceptions of standard setters and of the preparers of financial statements do not always coincide, with the result that some standards enjoy less than full compliance, even by public companies.

For private companies that are not bound by a GAAP constraint, the cost/benefit trade-off is very pragmatic. In particular, if there are no external users of a private company's financial statements (other than the Canada Revenue Agency [CRA]), then there is no benefit to be derived from incurring higher accounting costs. Commonly, such companies will use accounting methods that coincide with their tax treatment, even though they may not be GAAP. Examples include (1) calculating depreciation/amortization expense on the same basis as capital cost allowance (tax depreciation), and (2) recognizing revenue on the same basis for accounting as for tax purposes.

Canadian accounting standards acknowledge this cost-benefit threshold by providing a somewhat simpler version of ASPE, as we described in the previous chapter. Canadian ASPE enables private companies to follow simpler accounting policies in some areas.

Trade-off Between Relevance and Faithful Representation

As discussed at the beginning of this section, there is often a trade-off between qualitative characteristics, but especially between relevance and faithful representation. For example, *timeliness* may have to be reduced to increase the degree of *verifiability*, or vice versa. If financial statements were delayed until all the future events that affect them were to come to pass, measurements would be far more verifiable. Uncollectible accounts, warranty reserves, and useful lives of depreciable assets would not have to be estimated and reliability would increase.

On the other hand, the timeliness of the financial statements would suffer, and thus the statements would lack relevance. Therefore, a degree of reliability is sacrificed to gain relevance. The relative importance of the characteristics changes from situation to situation and requires the exercise of professional judgement.

The extent of trade-offs is, in itself, subjective. This is particularly apparent in the standard-setting process, where there often is a vigorous debate about what is *relevant* and what is *measurable*. The concerns of the auditing profession often show up in the presence of standards that seem to emphasize verifiability. The historical cost measurement convention often seems to override what many observers perceive to be the relevance of other highly objective measurements.

CONCEPT REVIEW

1. How does relevance relate to financial reporting objectives?
2. Does the criterion of understandability mean that every person should be able to understand the financial statements?
3. What are the four *enhancing* qualities of accounting information?
4. Why must there often be trade-offs between different qualitative criteria?

ELEMENTS OF FINANCIAL STATEMENTS AND RECOGNITION

The building blocks of financial statements are called *elements*. **Elements** are the different *classes* of items in financial statements, as shown in the first column of Exhibit 2-4. The first three elements (assets, liabilities, and owners' equity/net assets) relate directly to the statement of financial position; the next three elements (revenues/gains, expenses/losses, and other comprehensive income [OCI]) relate directly to the SCI but are derived from the definitions of assets and liabilities. The definitions of these six elements are particularly important because they provide the basis for deciding whether or not to recognize the results of a transaction or event in the financial statements.

Elements of the Statement of Financial Position

Assets and Liabilities Assets and liabilities are central to the definitions, since all other definitions are *derived from* asset and liability definitions. That is, owners' equity equals assets minus liabilities. Revenues and gains are defined as increases in assets or decreases in liabilities; expenses and losses are decreases in assets or increases in liabilities. Obviously, the definitions emphasize the statement of financial position and the assets and liabilities that comprise it.

The definitions of assets and liabilities include three components and embody three time frames:

1. An asset must involve a *future benefit* (e.g., through a direct future cash flow or through its use in generating a future cash flow), and a liability must entail a future sacrifice (either a payment of cash or performance of service).

2. The reporting enterprise has a clear *present right* to the asset or obligation for the liability.

3. The asset or liability arose as the result of a *past transaction* or event.

Owners' Equity Owner's equity is a residual. It is not measured directly but is the difference between assets and liabilities. Thus it represents the enterprise's net assets. Primarily, owner's equity captures the results of transactions between the enterprise and its shareholders in their capacity as shareholders. This excludes non–share-related activities and transactions. There is nothing to stop a shareholder from having normal business transactions with the enterprise, but the results of those transactions must not be confused with the shareholder's role as an owner.

However, in addition to capturing the results of shareholders' ownership transaction, owners' equity also includes items of OCI. These items reflect changes in net assets that do not qualify for recognition as components of revenue or expense. Thus, owners' equity includes the net impact of all changes in assets and liabilities, regardless of whether they have been recognized in net income (profit or loss).

Elements of the Statement of Comprehensive Income

The IASB uses the term **income** to mean all increases in net assets that are flowing into the enterprise as the result of the operating activities of the company. The framework does not distinguish between "revenues" and "gains."

However, IAS18 does make a distinction between revenue and gains by defining **revenue** as "the *gross* flow of economic benefits during the period arising in the course of the ordinary activities of an entity." The distinction between *revenues* and *gains* is that gross revenues have directly related expenses, while gains do not and are reported net of any related expenses or losses.

In general, **gains** are increases in net assets that arise from two sources:

- Peripheral or incidental activities, such as sales of individual assets or income from investments; and

- Remeasurement of asset or liabilities, such as increases in the value of fair-valued assets (e.g., marketable investments or investment properties).

These distinctions are widely used in practice, but there really is no absolute rule about what we call *revenue* and what we call *gains*. Some companies will report all types of income as "revenue," whether from operating activities, peripheral items, or remeasurements.

The distinction between expenses and losses is similarly indefinite. **Expenses** normally relate to the ordinary activities of the company while **losses** relate to peripheral activities or downward remeasurements. But again, many companies will report all expenses and losses together in a single category.

For the ordinary operations of the company, revenues and expenses must be reported separately, not netted. However, gains and losses from peripheral activities may be reported "net"—gains net of related (or similar) expenses, and losses net of related income. For example, companies will usually report a net gain or loss from temporary investments. Income tax expenses can never be netted against gains or losses, however.

OCI includes only certain specific changes in net assets as prescribed by individual IFRS standards. Management does not have an option about whether to report such items in the net income (or "profit or loss") section of the statement or in the OCI section.

Recognition

Recognition is the process of measuring and including an item in the financial statements. A *recognized* item is given a title and numerical value. Recognition applies to all financial statement elements in all accounting entities.

Disclosure (i.e., information reported in the notes to the financial statements) is not the same as recognition. A *recognized* element is reported on the face of the financial statements and is directly incorporated into earnings and net asset measurements. In contrast, *disclosed* information is there for financial statement readers to use if they wish (and if they can figure out what to do with it). Disclosure is not a substitute for recognition.

In Exhibit 2-4, each element contains the same two basic criteria:

- The item's cost or value can be measured reliably; and
- The future benefit will flow to (or from) the reporting entity, either in the future or in the current reporting period.

Therefore, we can summarize the recognition process with three questions to be resolved:

- Does the item seem to be a financial statement element within the broad context of financial reporting?
- Does the item have a suitable basis of measurement, and can the amount be measured reliably?
- For assets and liabilities, is it probable that the economic benefits will be received or given up—that is, realized?

It seems obvious that financial statement elements are the things measured in financial statements—this is the first criterion. Next comes *measurability*. If an item cannot be measured, it cannot be recognized, even if it has a high probability of being realized. To be measurable, there must be both a basis of measurement (e.g., historical cost or fair value) and a reasonable estimate of the amount. *Probability* is the final criteria. It is entirely possible that an item that meets the first two recognition criteria will not be recognized because of failure of the last criterion—probability of realization (Exhibit 2-5).

Commitments Suppose that a company signs a three-year contract to hire a special consultant; the contract is noncancellable. Should the company recognize a liability? The company has committed to a cash outflow over the next three years, and the contract is noncancellable, but although a contract has been signed, there will not be a *transaction* until the consultant performs the contracted work. A liability does not arise until one of the parties to the contract has actually performed the contracted service or delivered the contracted product.

Therefore, the **commitment** would be viewed as an **executory contract**—a contract wherein neither party has yet fulfilled the requirements of the contract—and would not be recognized.

EXHIBIT 2-4

ELEMENTS OF FINANCIAL STATEMENTS*

Recognized	Elaboration
Statement of Financial Position (discussed in Chapter 4)	

1. An **Asset** is recognized in the statement of financial position (SFP) when:
  a. It is a resource controlled by the entity that arose as the result of past events;
  b. It is probable that the future economic benefits will flow to the entity; and
  c. The asset has a cost or value that can be measured reliably.
	If the entity has an expenditure that is *unlikely* to result in future economic benefits, it must be recognized as an *expense*, not as an asset.
	
	An entity will make some expenditures that are *likely* to result in future economic benefits, for example, research costs, but the future benefits cannot be measured with sufficient degree of reliability to satisfy the definition of an asset; therefore, they must be recognized as an expense.

2. A **Liability** is recognized in the SFP when:
  a. It is a present obligation arising from past events;
  b. It is probable that an outflow of resources embodying economic benefits will result from the settlement of the obligation; and
  c. The amount at which the settlement will take place can be measured reliably.
	Normally, a liability is not recognized for executory contracts in which neither side of the contract has performed the actions required by the contract.
	
	If circumstances require recognition of such a liability, recognition of a liability requires a balancing recognition of related asset(s) or expense(s).

3. **Owners' equity** (or **net assets**) is the residual of assets minus liabilities.	While total equity is a residual, it includes individual categories of items, such as various types of share capital, retained earnings, and individual components of other comprehensive income (OCI).
Statement of Comprehensive Income (discussed in Chapter 3)	

4. **Income** (including both revenues and gains) is an increase in future economic benefits that can be measured reliably with a sufficient degree of certainty, by way of:
  a. Inflows or enhancements of assets; and/or
  b. Reductions of liabilities.
	An essential characteristic of income is that it is an increase in the entity's net assets as the result of the company's operating activities, and *not* from **(a)** capital transactions, **(b)** the settlement of monetary liabilities, or **(c)** the sale of capital assets or investment assets.

5. **Expenses** (and **losses**) are decreases in future economic benefits that can be measured reliably and that result from the income-generating activities of an entity, by way of:
  1. Decrease in assets (by outflows or amortization); and/or
  2. Increase in liabilities.
	The essential characteristic of an expense or loss is that it must be incurred in conjunction with the company's income-generating process. Expenditures that do not qualify as expenses are treated either as assets, as OCI, or as distributions to owners.

6. **Other comprehensive income (OCI)** comprises increases and decreases in net assets that are:
  1. Specifically excluded from net income by IFRS; or
  2. Do not reflect transactions with owners in their capacity as owners.
	Components of OCI are the results of transactions with nonowners that are specifically excluded by IFRS from the measurement of profit or loss and must be included in OCI. Each type of item is a separate category of shareholders' equity, even though they do not reflect transactions with shareholders.

*Based on the IASB's *Conceptual Framework for Financial Reporting*, Chapter 4: "Recognition of the Elements of Financial Statements."

Source: The International Accounting Standards Board, © 2011.

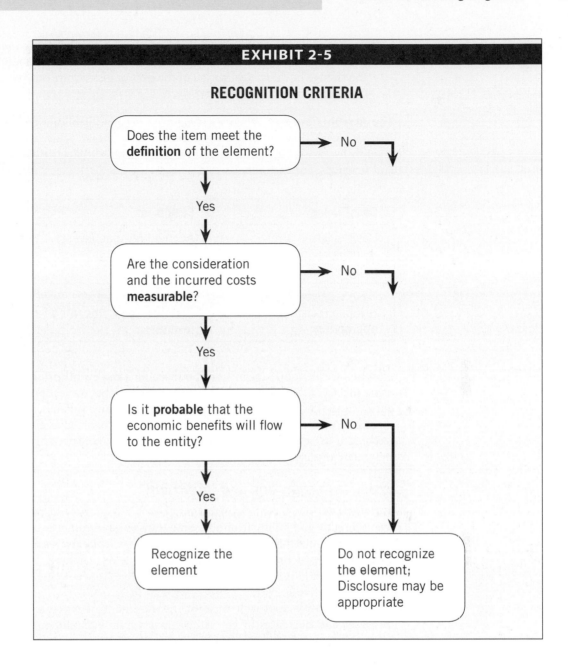

EXHIBIT 2-5

RECOGNITION CRITERIA

Recognition versus Realization

Recognition means that an item is recorded in the accounts. **Realization** is the process of converting an asset, liability, or commitment into a cash flow. Revenues are *recognized* when a credit sale is made but not *realized* until the receivable has been collected. Once realization has occurred, recognition *must* occur because there has been a cash flow impact that cannot be ignored in the accounts. For example,

- A customer pays in advance for goods yet to be produced and delivered; since the cash has been received (*realized*), it must be *recognized*. Revenue will not yet have been earned; the offsetting credit is to recognize unearned revenue.
- A company pays a retainer to a lawyer who will be acting on the company's behalf in the next fiscal year; the cash outflow triggers *realization*, which requires *recognition* of a prepaid expense.

However, recognition often occurs prior to realization. For example,

- A liability for a purchase of inventory is *recognized* when the goods are received—the offset is to recognize inventory as an asset. *Realization* occurs when the creditor is paid.

• A change in the value of cash held in a U.S.-dollar bank account is *recognized* at the balance sheet date—the offset is to a gain or loss account, depending on the direction of the change in value. *Realization* of the gain or loss occurs only when the U.S. dollars are converted to Canadian dollars.

The Accrual Concept   When we *recognize* assets and liabilities that have not yet been *realized* as a cash flow, we are using **accruals**. In contrast, when we have *realized* costs and receipts by a cash outflow or inflow, we use **deferrals** to delay their recognition as expenses and revenues. For example:

Cash Timing	Results in
Cash received after revenue recognition is appropriate	Accrued revenue (asset) (e.g., a receivable)
Cash received before revenue recognition is appropriate	Deferred revenue (liability) (e.g., unearned revenue)

When we recognize the effects of transactions and events prior to their realization, we are using the *accrual concept*. The accrual concept says that we recognize transactions when they occur. Cash flow may well happen in this period or in a different period.

In interperiod allocation, amounts originally recognized as assets are transferred to (i.e., *recognized* as) expense, and amounts recorded as liabilities are transferred to the income statement as revenue (or as reduction of expense).

Expense Recognition and "Matching"

Matching is "the simultaneous or combined recognition of revenues and expenses that result directly and jointly from the same transaction or other events."[6] Assets such as inventory are recognized in the same period as is the revenue from sale of a product. Interperiod allocation (e.g., depreciation) is a prime example of matching. The reason for depreciation and amortization is to match the costs of long-lived assets to the revenue generated by their use in productive activity.

An alternative approach to joint measurement of revenues and expenses is via the increases and decreases in net assets—assets minus liabilities, which we can call the **net asset principle of revenue/expense recognition**. When we generate revenue, we increase net assets by recording cash received or accounts receivable. The increase in net assets indicates that revenue has been earned. However, to fulfill our obligation to earn that revenue, we must use assets, such as inventory and cash, as well as long-lived assets, such as equipment, and we incur liabilities for labour and materials. These decreases in net assets (i.e., decreases in assets and increases in liabilities) are the expenses that we recognize in the same period as we recognize the revenue. Thus, matching is achieved, but the rationale is based on changes in assets and liabilities rather than on the concept of matching.

As a long-lived asset, such as equipment, is used up, its future usefulness decreases. For most assets, we do not try to measure the actual decrease in an asset's value; instead, we make an assumption that the remaining service potential has declined, thereby signalling that an expense should be recognized. Thus, we can justify interperiod allocation as an estimation of assets consumed rather than under the rubric of matching.

Be careful, though—some expenses related to long-term assets are recognized only when the measurable value of the asset has actually declined. An example is purchased goodwill, which is expensed only when its value has demonstrably been *impaired*.

---

[6] "Recognition of the elements of financial statements," ¶4.50. *Conceptual Framework for Financial Reporting*, Chapter 4. IASB 2011.

Illustration of Net Asset Principle To illustrate the net asset principle, assume that a home appliance is sold for cash with a 100% warranty on parts and labour in effect for 12 months from date of sale.

The cash from the sale is recognized as an asset immediately; the offset for this increase in net assets is revenue. Immediate costs (i.e., inventory) are recognized, but they are already consumed and have no future benefit. Therefore, those costs are recognized as expenses. These expenses include the costs of manufacturing and assembling the unit and the shipping and direct selling expenses incurred.

To fully measure the change in net assets, though, the estimated future liability implicit in honouring the warranty should also be recognized, even though the actual warranty cost may not be known until the next year. At the end of the year in which the sale occurs, the warranty expense should be estimated and recorded and thus recognized. In this way, the warranty expense is recognized in the same period as the revenue to which it is related, even though the cash may be expended at a later time.

You may notice that the net result of this example of the net asset principle is the same as would result under the matching concept—the estimated warranty cost is recognized in the same period as the sale that generated the probable estimated liability.

Professional Judgement The measurement of cost and the timing of expense recognition are matters that require a great deal of professional judgement. Almost all expense items in the income statement are the result of several interrelated judgements and estimates. Many of the following chapters in this book discuss issues of revenue and expense recognition at some length. Each chapter deals with recognition in the context of specific accounting issues, such as inventories, capital assets, leases, pensions, income tax, and so forth.

Cash Flow Is Central Before leaving the concepts of realization and recognition, we must stress that accounting recognition always relates to realized cash flows—past, present, and future. The recognition issue is always one of fitting the actual (or predicted) cash flows into time periods through a complex system of accruals and interperiod allocations. If actual cash flows deviate from those that we presumed in recognizing revenues and expenses, then we must adjust our accounts. *At no time can accounting recognize financial statement elements that are not based on actual or predicted cash flows.*[7]

CONCEPT REVIEW

1. What is the difference between accounting *realization* and *recognition*?

2. What is the difference between *accrual* and *interperiod allocation*?

3. What are the three criteria that must be met to justify recognition of an item in the financial statements?

MEASUREMENT

Measurement is the process of determining the amount at which an item is recognized in the financial statements. Measurement is integral to accounting choice, as indicated in Exhibit 2-1. In your introductory financial accounting course, you learned to use concepts of historical cost, net realizable value (NRV), lower-of-cost-and-NRV, and fair value. These concepts form the basis of the more specific measurement methods that you will learn in the following chapters of this book.

---

[7] There is one exception—the expense recorded for employee stock options is hypothetical and is never substantiated by actual cash flows. You will not have to bother with this until Volume Two, though.

Measurement methods encompass not only the process of attaching a number to a specific asset or a liability but also income measurement. The process of income measurement involves both (1) the initial measurement of a financial statement element and (2) the disposition or recognition of that measurement as it moves through the financial statements. IFRS recognizes that there are many potential measurement bases. The primary measurement methods used in IFRS are:

1. Historical cost

2. Current cost

3. Present value

4. Fair value

There are variations and alternatives within each approach.

Historical Cost

The **historical cost convention** specifies that acquisition cost be used for initial accounting recognition, especially for asset acquisitions. The cost principle assumes that assets are acquired in business transactions conducted at arm's length—that is, transactions between a buyer and a seller are at a fair market value prevailing at the time of the transaction.

The cost of the asset is based on the *value of the consideration given up*. If an asset is acquired via some means other than cash, **consideration** is whatever the buyer gives the seller as payment. For noncash transactions conducted at arm's length, the cost principle assumes that the fair value of the resources *given up* in a transaction provides reliable evidence for the valuation of the item acquired. This may be the amount of money paid, market value of common shares issued, or the present value of debt assumed in the transaction.

Sometimes, though, it is difficult to value the consideration given up, and then the fair market value of the assets *received* is referred to as a more reliable indicator. For example, if a company receives widely traded common shares valued at $50,000 in payment for land appraised at $60,000, the value of the shares should be used as the value of the consideration, since its value is less subjective than the appraised value of the land.

The historical cost convention provides guidance primarily at the initial acquisition date. Once acquired, the original cost basis of long-lived assets is then subject to amortization, depletion, depreciation, impairment, or write-up.

Current Cost

Current cost is what it would cost to replace an asset or, more precisely, to replace its productive capacity. Current cost is used primarily under the physical capital maintenance concept, as we discussed earlier in this chapter. It also is sometimes used for rate-setting purposes in regulated enterprises. There are several ways of measuring current cost, such as:

- Cost of acquiring a similar asset of similar remaining productivity (and age) on an established used-asset market. Motor vehicles are a good example of an asset type that can readily be measured this way.
- Cost of currently acquiring a similar asset, then deducting an estimated amount for depreciation. This measurement method is commonly called *depreciated replacement cost*.
- Applying a price index to a class of assets, when an appropriate index is available either through public sources or via a productivity index maintained by the entity itself. This approach is useful when the company has a very large number of similar or identical assets, either inventory items or common tools or equipment, such as computers and printers.

Current cost does not have much application in the normal run of business enterprise in North America, where financial capital maintenance is virtually ubiquitous.

Current cost and historical cost usually are identical at the time that an asset is acquired. However, this is not always the case if assets are acquired through an exchange of assets. We will discuss asset exchanges in Chapter 6.

Realizable Value

Historical cost and current cost are *entry values*—the cost of acquiring an asset. In contrast, **realizable value** is an *exit value*—what can be recovered when an asset is disposed of. For liabilities, it is the **settlement value**, or what it would cost to pay off the liability.

Realizable value has several variations, depending on the circumstances. You already are familiar with such concepts as lower-of-cost-or-NRV. You also know that a realizable value depends on whether an asset sale is forced (such as by bankruptcy) or is a sale in due course without pressure to sell.

The same is true of liabilities. The sacrifice required to settle a liability may be higher if it is settled prior to its maturity date. Or if settlement is delayed, the sacrifice may be either higher or lower than its face value or nominal amount. The true settlement price may be higher due to prepayment penalties or late-payment penalties; it could be lower due to changes in interest rates or due to a creditor's accepting less than full face value if the entity is in financial distress.

Present Value

Present value is the value of a future asset or liability with its interest component removed—its discounted value. Present value is the normal measurement method used for financial assets and liabilities with a maturity of more than one year after the SFP date. The present value may be fixed by contract, such as by the interest rate built into a mortgage. Alternatively, the present value could be an approximation based on expected future rates of return, such as in pension accounting.

A present value can be either an entry value or an exit value. When we initially record a long-term receivable, we discount it by using the current interest rate at the transaction date. The resulting present value is an entry value because it recognizes the interest rate at the time of the transaction.

However, suppose that a year later, we sell that receivable to another company. The buyer will be willing to pay only an amount based on the current rates of interest at the transaction date. If the current rate is higher than the historical rate, for example, the buyer will pay less to buy the receivable because its present value has gone down. That present value, based on the current interest rate, is an exit value (and also the realizable value).

Not all liabilities that appear to be financial liabilities are subject to present value reporting, however. A prime example is the balance of deferred income taxes, which is explicitly exempted from discounting by both IFRS and ASPE.

Fair Value

Fair value is a current measurement of the value of an asset or liability at the reporting date. It can be either an *entry value* or an *exit value,* which means that it could be measured as current cost, present value, or realizable (or settlement) value. Fair value is a slippery term—when using it, one must be very careful to understand what it means in any particular situation. Of course, fair value is always better than unfair value, which would be any value that violates the fundamental qualitative criteria of faithful representation and relevance.

Accounting standards have tended to define "fair value" in varying ways. To resolve confusion and to provide a comprehensive approach to fair valuation, the IASB issued IFRS 13 to be applied with any standard that permits or requires fair values.

Fair value is the price that would be received to sell an asset or paid to transfer a liability in an *orderly transaction* between market participants at the measurement date. An **orderly transaction** is one in which neither the buyer nor the seller is under undue pressure to enter the transaction. That means that the buyer does not have a special urgency to acquire the asset, and the seller does not have any strong pressure to sell, such as bankruptcy.

Although fair value has a relatively simple theoretical value, it can be very difficult to measure. Therefore, the IASB established a three-level *hierarchy* for measuring fair value:

• Level 1: quoted prices in active markets for identical assets;

- Level 2: prices for similar assets or that can be derived from observable market data; and
- Level 3: values derived by indirect valuation techniques, not verifiable by direct observation of market data.

These levels are stated in the order of priority. A reporting entity should not use an indirect method of measuring value if it is determinable directly. For example, quoted prices for an investment should be used, if available, and not an indirect valuation based on the prices of similar investments. It also should be a *current* price, not a forecasted price nor a historical average.

An asset should be valued in its *principal or most advantageous market*. For example, many corporations have art collections. Those collections can be of great value, but the value of each piece often will depend on what market it is being offered in. A painting by Vancouver artist Joe Average is likely to bring a better price in his home market of Vancouver rather than in a market where he is unknown. Vancouver would probably be the principal market for his work.

An asset also should be measured at its **highest and best use**. That is, if an asset has several possible uses, the valuation should be based on its most advantageous use. Sometimes the highest and best use is to use the asset by itself, on a stand-alone basis. Others might have a higher and better use when combined with other assets. For example, a conveyer system might not have much value on its own, but it probably would have a much higher value when used in the right type of production or distribution facility.

Fair value should not be adjusted for transaction costs. If an entity decides to sell an asset, the transaction costs are an expense in the period of the sale; estimated transaction costs should not be deducted from the fair value reported on the SFP prior to the sale.

Level 1—Direct Observation   This is the easiest measurement to understand. Level 1 uses quoted prices in active markets for identical items. For example, if Leslie Corporation holds common shares of Petro-Canada, the value of those shares at the end of Leslie's reporting year can easily be verified by looking at the Petro-Canada share price on the Toronto or New York stock exchanges. Brokerage fees (which are transaction costs) would not be deducted.

Level 2—Indirect Observation   If there are no quoted prices in active markets for identical items, the next-best alternative is to use a close approximation. The prices of similar assets can be used as the basis for estimation, or a price can be derived from observable market data.

For example, suppose that Leslie Corporation is a private equity firm that has invested in Ordeal Ltd. debt securities that were issued in a private placement. That is, the debt is all privately held and not traded publicly. There is no quoted market price, and thus level 1 valuation cannot be used.

However, Ordeal does have another debt issue that is publicly traded. Leslie can use the price for the publicly traded debt securities as the basis for estimating the fair value of the debt securities that it holds. Leslie may need to adjust the price to take into account any difference in the characteristics of the private versus public debt, but the resulting fair value will be a reasonable estimate.

Level 3—Unobservable Values   If the fair value of an asset (or liability) cannot be observed, either directly (level 1) or indirectly (level 2), what then? Level 3 identifies types of "unobservable inputs" that should be used to estimate the fair value. The term "unobservable" is rather unfortunate, because if it cannot be observed, how can it be measured? However, the real point is that other measures can be used that are based on the way that potential buyers would determine what price to pay if they were to buy it.

For example, suppose that Leslie Corporation owns some suburban land that is adjacent to its manufacturing plant. The company reports the land by the fair-value method as an investment property. Each piece of real estate is unique; the value of Leslie Corporation's land is estimated on the basis of several factors, such as:

- Property valuations in the broader region;
- Accessibility to highways and rail lines;

- Access to municipal services, such as water and sewage;
- Zoning restrictions;
- The probability of getting zoning changes to permit higher-value uses; and
- Interest rates.

Although the land could be valued on its basis as a stand-alone piece of real estate, that probably is not its highest and best use. The land most likely is more valuable to Leslie Corporation than it would be to most other users because it is adjacent to Leslie's current facilities. Even if Leslie Corporation went out of business, the combination of the vacant land and Leslie's currently used land could make the entire site especially valuable to another user or to a developer.

Obviously, fair values determined by level 3 methods will have less *faithful representation* than fair values determined on the basis of levels 1 or 2. But if levels 1 and 2 cannot be used, then level 3 estimates will be more *relevant* to the decision needs of users than historical cost; this is an application of qualitative criteria in accounting measurement.

The Crucial Importance of Estimates

Accounting practice requires seemingly endless estimates. Virtually every item on the SFP contains estimates, and those estimates flow through to the SCI, thereby affecting net income and comprehensive income. Estimates are required because, by definition, every asset or liability involves future benefit or future sacrifice—otherwise, they could not be reported on the SFP.

Perhaps the most tenuous of all estimates are those made for potential future liabilities. Pension costs are an outstanding example; those costs will not be realized until many years in the future but must be estimated in the current period. Some future liabilities have an even greater level of approximation, such as estimates for future cleanup or environmental remediation costs. Others include potential liabilities under patent or licence litigation.

The reason that we stress the importance of estimates is that fairly minor changes of estimates can trigger significant changes in earnings. Many academic research papers have established that companies that are about to go public tend to adjust their accruals in the immediately preceding period to "enhance" their apparent earnings potential. Indeed, other executives have been accused of intentionally manipulating earnings through adjustments in "reserves"—anticipated future costs—that shifted profits from one period to another.

CONCEPT REVIEW

1. What is the difference between an entry value and an exit value?

2. Determining fair values usually requires several estimates. What qualitative criteria underlie accounting standards' requirement for estimated fair values in certain situations rather than historical cost, which requires no estimation?

3. What are the three levels of fair value measurement?

4. What is meant by *highest and best use*?

ETHICAL PROFESSIONAL JUDGEMENT—PART 2

The Problem of Earnings Targets

The managers of public companies are under strong pressure to achieve *earnings expectations* or **earnings targets**. There are two sources of earnings targets: (1) the company's own projected earnings for the current fiscal period and (2) financial analysts' independent projections. When there are numerous financial analysts following a company, the average of analysts' predictions is often cited in the financial news as the target for management to achieve. Stock markets can react quite violently to "missed" targets, wherein the company's reported earnings fall below expectations. The reaction is particularly adverse when management is faced with the possibility of missing its own publicly announced earnings target.

When faced with this pressure to achieve targets, management is often tempted to use relatively small "adjustments." These adjustments can fall into two categories: (1) changes in measurement and (2) adjustments to reserves.

Measurement Variability

Measurement is a significant issue for those financial statement elements that are measured at fair value. Significant conflict can arise between the various qualitative criteria unless the basis of measurement is quite clear. Some fair values are reasonably obtainable, such as those at the first level of the fair value hierarchy. Others, however, are much more subjective.

For example, as we will discuss in Chapter 10, management may choose to use the revaluation method for qualifying capital assets, which requires periodic revaluations. There are various ways of estimating the fair value of capital assets. If appraisals are used for land and buildings, different appraisers will make different estimates of fair value. Management may be tempted to use the estimate that helps the company achieve its earnings target. Valuations should be undertaken to enhance users' decisions but not to influence them one way or the other. Unhappily, maintaining objectivity in such situations is easier said than done.

Management must be alert to the possibility of introducing bias into fair value measurements, either intentionally or subconsciously. When fair value measurements pertain to major assets or classes of assets, rather small variations in estimate can have a significant impact on net income when fair value changes are recognized in earnings, as they usually are.

Reserves

What are **reserves**? IFRS uses the term "reserves" only in reference to items in equity, such as "reserve for plant expansion."

In common practice, however, the term is often used for estimated liabilities that appear on the company's financial statements and that underlie reported expenses. At the simpler end, they include allowances such as the bad debt allowance, the estimated warranty liability, or an allowance for inventory obsolescence.[8]

At the more complex end of the range are such items as the estimated receivable asset for tax loss carryforwards and the estimated liability for asset restoration costs. Major companies have many such provisions in their balance sheets; a fairly modest adjustment can have a significant impact on reported earnings.

In the Introduction to this chapter, we cited the charges faced by former executives of Nortel Networks Corp. The allegation was that management used "reserves" to manipulate profits.[9] Estimates are always subject to debate and different interpretations. There is always more than one feasible or justifiable number for an estimate. The issue is which came first—the estimate or the profit goal? Even then, it is not so simple. In weak economic times, estimates are likely to reflect a pessimistic view, while the reverse is true in boom times. Thus, the influence of current events clearly affects estimates.

---

[8] Nortel Networks reversed an allowance for inventory obsolescence by $25.5 million thereby creating a gain, to offset another loss item. However, the company argued that $25.5 million was immaterial in the context of the $1 billion reserve for obsolete inventory. See "Accounting change not a material sum, Nortel trial hears," *The Globe and Mail*, 12 April 2012, p. B3.

[9] For example, see "Use of accounting reserves out in open, defence suggests," *The Globe and Mail*, 29 March 2012, p. B3.

> ### ETHICAL ISSUES
>
> #### Exercising Professional Judgement
>
> Accountants can find themselves in great difficulty if they carry out the demands of management to adjust earnings to match predictions. Indeed, prosecutors prosecute the accountants first, hoping they then will testify against their bosses. An ethical accountant will resist "orders" to manipulate estimates to achieve a desired result. Many chief accountants have, indeed, shown such strength and have emerged with their reputations intact (and not in jail).
>
> Professional judgement permeates the work of a professional accountant and requires the ability to build accounting measurements that take into account:
>
> - The objectives of financial reporting in each particular situation;
> - The facts of the business environment and operations; and
> - The organization's reporting constraints (if any).

The result of properly applied ethical professional judgement is fair financial information. Failure of ethical professional judgement may result in false or misleading information. Think about the steps required to apply professional judgement in an ethical fashion. The building blocks for accounting choice were illustrated in Exhibit 2-1.

1. The first judgement, upon which all else is built, is to determine the objectives of financial reporting for the specific reporting entity. There are usually multiple objectives, and the objectives must be ethically and appropriately prioritized to be able to resolve conflicts between them when decisions about specific accounting policies or estimates must be made. To develop the financial reporting objectives, we must consider important facts and constraints:

    a. The facts of the organization's operations and its economic environment must be determined to understand just what is to be measured. For example: Who are the users of the entity's financial statements? Is the entity bound by restrictive covenants or other contractual requirements? Is compensation based on accounting measures, such as net income? Fraud may interfere with fact finding, and an accountant must be very careful.

    b. The reporting constraints must be determined. Is the reporting enterprise a publicly accountable enterprise, bound by the reporting constraints of the securities commissions or regulators? Is it a private company that uses the financial statements only for its owner(s) and for income tax purposes? Is an audit required? If an audit is required (or desired by management), is a "clean" audit opinion necessarily needed? Can the enterprise report on the basis of disclosed (or tailored) accounting policies rather than IFRS or ASPE?

2. The underlying assumptions must be tested. In preparing the financial statements for the vast majority of Canadian business organizations, the normal underlying assumptions of continuity, nominal dollar financial capital maintenance, proprietary approach, and so forth are quite valid. But they cannot be taken for granted, and their appropriateness in the specific reporting situation must be evaluated.

3. Once the objectives have been discerned and prioritized, the facts and constraints determined, and the underlying assumptions evaluated, only then should the measurement choices or accounting policies be considered.

4. The measurement method must be consistent with the objectives, facts, and constraints. The measurement choices are further tempered by the qualitative criteria, especially in the realm of recognition. When should revenues be recognized? When should costs incurred or committed be recognized? When costs are recognized, should they be recognized as assets or as expenses? If they are recognized as assets, when should they be transferred to

expense? There are many ethical decisions to be made. Faithful representation may conflict with relevance, and both verifiability and understandability come into play.

5. The measurement and recognition criteria lead to the financial statement elements, which then are classified in a manner that is appropriate to the industry and consistent with the operational activities of the enterprise. The result is, finally, the financial statements themselves. To be appropriate for the specific reporting situation, the final financial statements must satisfy the specific reporting objectives that are at the foundation of the whole pyramid.

6. The ethical requirements are met if the financial statements are a fair representation of the underlying business activity.

Looking Forward

The basic principles outlined in this chapter do not change. However, the terminology does change from time to time as standards evolve. For example, in years past, "objectivity" was considered a fundamental accounting principle. Over time, accountants realized that objectivity really was a combination of more basic criteria, such as verifiability, neutrality, relevance, and faithful representation. Thus, accounting terminology has evolved as we have come to better understand the more basic components underlying measurement.

Similarly, the definitions of assets and liabilities have evolved over the years. As a continuation of this process, the IASB started a project in late 2012 to refine the definitions of assets and liabilities as well as attempt to define the concept of "financial performance."

We can expect changes in terminology and improvements in the definitions of financial statement elements in future years. Such evolution is characteristic of a profession that still, after all these years, is refining its theoretical underpinnings. Accounting is very much an applied art; it is not a science or a purely mathematical process.

CONCEPT REVIEW

1. List three different possible measurement bases for inventory.

2. How is the concept of matching usually applied to period costs?

3. Does full disclosure mean that all available information is provided in the disclosure notes?

ACCOUNTING STANDARDS FOR PRIVATE ENTERPRISES

Objectives and Qualitative Characteristics

The ASPE conceptual framework is very similar to that of IFRS. Some of the wording is different, and the positioning of the various qualitative characteristics differs, but overall there is no significant difference.

Financial statement objectives are "to communicate information that is useful to investors, creditors and other users" concerning the economic resources of an entity, and changes in those resources during the reporting period. A related objective also is to assess the entity's economic performance.

ASPE's qualitative characteristics are shown in Exhibit 2-6. You will observe that while the arrangement (and some of the wording) is different from that of IFRS, the substance is the same. The overall constraints of materiality and cost/benefit also apply within the ASPE framework.

The one difference between the frameworks of ASPE and IFRS is that ASPE includes the characteristic of conservatism as one component of reliability. The traditional understanding of conservatism is that when there is measurement uncertainty, amounts should be recorded that tend to lower earnings and/or net assets. However, ASPE discourages this traditional conservatism. Indeed, ASPE interprets conservatism as being an avoidance of optimistic amounts rather than favouring a downward bias:

> When uncertainty exists, estimates of a conservative nature attempt to ensure that assets, revenues and gains are not overstated and, conversely, that liabilities, expenses and losses are not understated. (¶1000.18d).

Financial Statement Elements

An explanation of the ASPE definitions of assets and liabilities is shown in Exhibit 2-7. The ASPE definitions are parallel to those of IFRS; although wording varies somewhat, there is no substantive difference. Similarly, the definition of equity is also the same—equity is the excess (deficiency) of assets over (under) liabilities.

Regarding liabilities, ASPE makes it clear that while an obligation must arise from past events, the obligation should be reported as a liability whether or not it is legally enforceable. A constructive or equitable obligation (e.g., environmental remediation not specifically legally required) is a liability, even if it may not be legally enforceable. "An equitable obligation is a duty based on ethical or moral considerations" (¶1000.30).

On the income statement (not SCI, since there is no "other comprehensive income" in ASPE) a definition difference is that ASPE draws a distinction between (1) revenues and expenses, which arise from the normal business activities of the entity, and (2) gains and losses, which are defined as arising from peripheral or incidental transactions and events. IFRS makes no such distinction—income is income, whether called revenue or a gain and whether from normal operations or from unusual transactions or activities.

EXHIBIT 2-6

ASPE QUALITATIVE CHARACTERISTICS

Principal Qualitative Characteristics	Pervasive Constraints
Understandability	Cost/benefit
Relevance	Materiality
Predictive value and feedback value	
Timeliness	
Reliability	
Representational faithfulness	
Verifiability	
Neutrality	
Conservatism	
Comparability	

Source: *CPA Canada Handbook, Part II*, Section 1000, © Chartered Professional Accountants of Canada, 2013.

EXHIBIT 2-7

ASPE DEFINITIONS OF ASSETS AND LIABILITIES

Assets	Liabilities
An asset is a resource acquired as the result of past events;	a. A liability is a present obligation or responsibility to others that arises from past events;
The entity can control access to the benefits; and	b. The duty or responsibility obligates the entity and leaves it little or no discretion to avoid it; and
The asset contributes directly or indirectly to future benefits that result in net cash flows.	c. In the future, the entity will be required to transfer or use assets, provide services or yield other economic benefits, at a specified or determinable date, on occurrence of a specified event, or on demand.

Measurement

Unlike IFRS, ASPE specifically cites historical cost as the primary basis of measurement. "Other bases" are listed as replacement cost (i.e., current cost in IFRS), realizable value, and present value. Curiously, fair value is not mentioned as a basis for measurement. However, the "financial instruments" section of ASPE is only partially harmonized with IFRS and requires some degree of fair value measurement. We will examine those specific differences later in the book.

Overall, the measurement methods in ASPE are basically the same as IFRS, although they are not necessarily applied in the same way. As we proceed through the following chapters of this book, we will point out specific differences between IFRS and ASPE concerning measurement requirements.

ASPE permits only nominal dollar capital maintenance. Neither constant dollar nor productive capacity are acceptable capital maintenance approaches for Canadian private enterprises using ASPE.

RELEVANT STANDARDS

CPA Canada Handbook, Part I (IFRS):
- IASB, *Conceptual Framework for Financial Reporting,* Chapters 3 and 4
- IFRS 13, *Fair Value Measurement*

CPA Canada Handbook, Part II (ASPE):
- Section 1000, *Financial Statement Concepts*

SUMMARY OF KEY POINTS

1. Accounting principles consist of three different sets of concepts: (1) underlying assumptions, (2) qualitative criteria, and (3) measurement methods.

2. *Underlying assumptions* include the basic postulates that make accounting measurements possible (such as *time period, separate entity,* and *unit of measure*), as well as underlying measurement assumptions that usually, but not always, are true in a given reporting situation. These measurement assumptions include *proprietary approach, continuity,* and *nominal dollar financial capital maintenance.*

3. There are two feasible alternatives to nominal dollar financial capital maintenance. One is constant dollar financial capital maintenance, in which the purchasing power of the capital investment is maintained rather than simply the nominal number of dollars invested. The other alternative is physical (or productive) capital maintenance, in which sufficient capital is maintained to achieve the same level of productivity.

4. *Qualitative criteria* are the criteria used in conjunction with an enterprise's financial reporting objectives to determine the most appropriate measurement methods to use in that particular reporting situation.

5. A fundamental qualitative criterion is that of *relevance*; relevance should be determined with reference to the users of the financial statements and the resulting financial reporting objectives. Relevance is enhanced if information is timely and has both predictive and confirmatory (i.e., feedback) value.

6. A second fundamental qualitative criterion is *faithful representation*, which means that an accounting measurement should be a sufficiently accurate measure of the reality of whatever it is measuring and should reflect economic substance. The attributes of faithful representation include *completeness, neutrality,* and *freedom from material error.*

7. *Neutrality* means that information is not biased in a way that would influence users' decisions in a particular direction. It does *not* mean that the information has no impact on users' decisions. For example, *conservatism* may not be used as a justification for overstating liabilities or understating assets. Accounting information should be unbiased.

8. Enhancing qualities are those that improve the quality of accounting information and/ or its usefulness. Enhancing qualities include *comparability, verifiability, timeliness,* and *understandability.*

9. Users are presumed to have a reasonable knowledge of financial reporting to interpret or understand accounting information. Financial statements are not prepared for naive or unsophisticated users.

10. *Materiality* and *cost* are *pervasive constraints* that underlie all accounting information. Information will be reported if it is *material,* meaning that the information has the capacity to influence users' decisions. The constraint of *cost* indicates that the cost of preparing accounting information should not outweigh its benefit to users.

11. There are trade-offs among qualitative characteristics. For example, the faithful representation and reliability of reported collectible accounts receivable may be improved by waiting to find out how many accounts seem uncollectible, but relevance would be diminished because the information would be less timely.

12. The *elements of financial statements* are the six types of accounts that appear on the statement of financial position and the statement of other comprehensive income: assets, liabilities, owners' equity, income, expenses (and losses), and other comprehensive income.

13. The IFRS asset and liability definitions require (1) a *future* benefit or sacrifice and (2) a reliably measurable cost, value, or settlement amount.

14. Initial accounting *recognition* occurs when the effects or results of a transaction or event are first measured and assigned to an account or *element*. To be recognized, or recorded, an item must meet the element definition, be measurable, and be probable.

15. *Recognition* is the process of measuring and including an item or event in the financial statements. *Realization* is the process of converting an asset, liability, or commitment into a cash flow.

16. *Realization* occurs when a cash flow occurs. Realization often occurs after recognition but can never occur prior to recognition because the cash flow forces recognition if it has not occurred previously.

17. The accrual concept relates to the recognition of receivables when the right to receive cash arises and to the recognition of liabilities when the obligation is created. Accrual does not refer to subsequent matching and interperiod allocations.

18. *Measurement* is the process by which numbers are attached to events and items that are reported in the financial statements.

19. *Measurement methods* are the various ways that the results of transactions and events can be reported in the financial statements. Measurement conventions include historical cost, the revenue recognition convention, expense recognition, and full disclosure. Measurement methods also encompass the process of earnings measurement.

20. Accounting is full of choices. Financial statements are constructed from the financial statement elements that have been recognized using measurement methods that optimize the qualitative characteristics and that are based on the appropriate underlying assumptions. The organization's reporting constraints as well as the facts of its business and environment all impact on the choice of accounting policy. The result is information that best satisfies the objectives of financial reporting in any given situation. This series of related decisions constitutes *ethical professional judgement in accounting*.

KEY TERMS

accruals
asset
capital maintenance
commitment
comparability
completeness
confirmatory value
consideration
consistency
constant dollar capital maintenance
continuity assumption
cost/benefit effectiveness
current cost
deferrals
earnings targets
elements
entity concept
entity-specific assumptions
ethical professional judgement
executory contract
expenses
fair value
faithful representation

feedback value
freedom from material error
gains
going-concern assumption
highest and best use
historical cost convention
income
losses
liability
matching
materiality
measurement
measurement methods
net asset principle of revenue/expense
    recognition
net assets
neutrality
nominal dollars
orderly transaction
other comprehensive income
owner's equity
physical capital maintenance
predictive value

present value	settlement value
productive capacity capital maintenance	substance over form
professional judgement	sustainable business enterprise
proprietary concept	timeliness
purchasing power parity	time-period assumption
qualitative characteristics (criteria)	underlying assumptions
realizable value	understandability
realization	uniformity
recognition	unit-of-measure assumption
relevance	universal assumptions
reserves	value added
revenue	verifiability
separate-entity assumption	

QUESTIONS

Q2-1 Identify the three different building blocks that comprise accounting principles.

Q2-2 Identify and describe the six underlying assumptions included in accounting principles.

Q2-3 Explain why the time-period assumption requires accruals and deferrals in accounting.

Q2-4 How does the continuity assumption relate to the use of historical cost in financial statement measurements of assets?

Q2-5 How are owners viewed under the entity assumption as compared with the proprietary assumption?

Q2-6 Which assumption or principle discussed in this chapter is most affected by the phenomenon of inflation? Give reasons for your choice.

Q2-7 Define both financial and physical capital maintenance, and explain the difference between them.

Q2-8 An item in inventory is sold for $1,500. It cost $1,000 and could be replaced from the supplier for $1,120. Inflation for the period is 4%. Give three different measures of income, and explain each.

Q2-9 What are the two fundamental qualitative characteristics of accounting information? Briefly explain each.

Q2-10 Explain the potential trade-off between the two fundamental qualitative characteristics.

Q2-11 "If the financial statements are to be understandable to users, they must be prepared in a very clear and simple manner for the benefit of those who are less sophisticated." Is this true? Explain.

Q2-12 Describe how consistency and uniformity promote comparability.

Q2-13 When a company evaluates an accounting policy with reference to its cost/benefit effectiveness, what benefits are under consideration? What are the costs?

Q2-14 The definitions of assets and liabilities involve a consideration of the three time dimensions of past, present, and future. Explain.

Q2-15 What is the difference between a *revenue* and a *gain* in ASPE, as contrasted with IFRS?

Q2-16 Contrast *recognition* and *realization*. Why can realization not precede recognition?

Q2-17 Explain what is meant by an *orderly transaction*.

Q2-18 What is the fair value hierarchy? What are the three levels?

Q2-19 Explain the meaning of *highest and best use*. What is the purpose of identifying highest and best use?

Q2-20 Describe the role of ethical professional judgement in the choice of accounting policies. What are the influencing factors?

CASE 2-1

AEROTRAVEL INC.

James Ehnes has recently completed his second year of accounting studies. He has just been hired as a summer intern at the auditing firm of Hetu & Fauré. James feels fortunate to have landed an internship in such a prestigious firm. His supervisor, Venus Yang, has handed him a lengthy description of the operations of AeroTravel Inc. (ATI) and has asked James to prepare a report in which he outlines the significant accounting policies that arise in this company. She also wants James's recommendations on how the company should account for the revenues and expenses relating to ATI's provision of services, as well as the balance sheet ramifications of his recommendations.

James knows that the purpose of this exercise is to test his understanding of the complex relationships underlying revenue and expense recognition. After reading through the description several times, he makes the following notes:

- ATI is a public company that operates loyalty reward plans for a wide range of clients involved in the travel business, including airlines, hotels, and package tour operators. ATI sells *loyalty units* to the clients, who, in turn, reward their customers or members with those loyalty units when they buy the clients' services or products. Clients' customers and members can then acquire products or services through ATI either for free or at a reduced price by using their loyalty points.

- ATI derives its cash inflows by selling loyalty units in bulk to each client. Each client then issues the points to the members of the client's loyalty plan. ATI receives payment directly from client companies for the loyalty units sold to the clients for their members.

- Loyalty plan members redeem loyalty units through ATI for rewards of travel, merchandise, or other services. ATI buys the airline seats, merchandise, or services from the vendor to provide the tangible rewards to members. For example, if a member of a client airline's loyalty plan books reward travel, ATI must buy the seat from the airline.

- The largest client is Trans-National Airways, which accounts for over 60% of ATI's business.

- Each year, Trans-National Airways is required by contract to buy a pre-established quantity of AeroTravel Miles from ATI.

- Conversely, each year ATI is required by the same contract to buy a minimum quantity of reward travel seats on Trans-National and its affiliates.

- The estimated redemption value of loyalty units outstanding (that is, those sold by ATI to its clients but not yet redeemed) are stated as deferred revenue on ATI's year-end SFP. Not all loyalty units are redeemed. ATI estimated that as of the end of 20X8, 18% of the outstanding loyalty units would not be redeemed, as compared with an estimate of 21% at the end of 20X7.

- When the company revises its estimated redemption rate at the end of a fiscal year, the company restates that year-end's balance of deferred revenue.

- In limited circumstances, ATI sells loyalty units directly to client plan members (rather than through the client company), such as to client plan members who wish to "top up" their point balance just enough to claim a desired reward.

- AIT also derives fees from client companies for direct marketing, for sales promotion, and for designing, developing, and administering loyalty programs for both existing and new client companies.

Required:
Ms. Yang wants the report on her desk first thing tomorrow morning. Assume that you are James Ehnes. Prepare the report for Ms. Yang.

CASE 2-2

DUBOIS LIMITED

Dubois Limited is a Vancouver-based private company established 30 years ago. Until very recently, all 16 of the shareholders have been relatives of the founder, Blanche Dubois. The company has been profitable in most years. In more recent years, however, it has become obvious that the company needed a capital infusion to remain competitive in the face of increased international competition; Dubois required substantial investment in more modern facilities and processes.

To obtain the needed funds, the Dubois Board of Directors sought private investment from nonfamily sources. After negotiating with several potential investors, the Board approved an investment by The Mangle Group, a private equity investment cooperative. After issuing the new shares to Mangle, the Dubois family members hold 65% of the outstanding common shares, with Mangle holding the remaining 35%.

The company holds a substantial line of credit with the Canadian subsidiary of a London-based international bank. The credit line is secured by a lien on all of the Dubois assets, based on 75% of accounts receivable, 60% of inventory, and 50% of buildings and equipment. The bank has been willing to maintain the credit line as long as the collateral is adequate and as long as Dubois is able to liquidate (i.e., fully pay off) the credit line at least once each calendar year.

In past years, the external auditor has given Dubois a qualified audit opinion because Dubois did not use a systematic depreciation method for its buildings. Instead, the company's policy was to obtain an independent assessment of its buildings. If the assessment was less than the buildings' book value, Dubois would record an "impairment" charge. The company's chief financial officer, Colleen Bissau, argues that the value of the building is much more relevant to the bank than an arbitrary "depreciated book value," and thus Dubois' method is more appropriate under the circumstances.

As a condition of its investment, The Mangle Group insists that Dubois obtain a "clean" (unqualified) audit opinion in the future so that Dubois' financial statements are more comparable with those of other companies in which Mangle has invested.

Following the Mangle investment, Dubois continues to be a private company. Dubois Limited reports on the basis of ASPE.

You have been approached by Ms. Bissau to advise the company's Board of Directors as to how Dubois Limited's financial reporting objectives and criteria for measurement methods may have changed from past years, following the new equity investment, and how they may change in the future if the company issues shares to the public.

Required:
Prepare the report for Ms. Bissau.

CASE 2-3

BLX SHIPPING LIMITED

BLX Shipping Ltd. is a Canadian company, one of over 500 international shipping lines operating worldwide. BLX had been a privately owned company until recently. However, in 20X2, the company issued 42% of its common shares to the public. The other 58% of BLX shares still are privately held, primarily by four family trusts.

In general, the company has been profitable (Exhibit 1), although results in 20X5, the most recent fiscal year, did not meet market expectations and share price declined from

$20 to $14. The company operates 32 container vessels with total capacity of 170,000 teu (a measurement of size used in the industry; the equivalent of a 20-foot shipping container).

The container shipping industry has experienced compound growth (in volume) of about 9% over the last 20 years, several times higher than the increase in global gross domestic product. However, the industry is highly price competitive as well as cyclical.

You have a friend who views the lower market price of BLX shares as a potential growth opportunity. Your friend knows that you are studying accounting and has asked you to consider two note disclosures in BLX's 20X5 financial statements that she finds curious:

Note 7

Revenue and costs directly attributable to loaded container movements are recognized when delivery of the container is completed. A substantial element of the cost of delivery of each container to its ultimate destination is estimated and accrued because there can be delays in determining the final charges from agents and suppliers throughout the world. Consequently, significant accruals are outstanding at each financial period-end. BLX has considerable experience in estimating costs of transporting containers.

However, your friend also notes that in the past year, BLX restated 20X4 and prior years' earnings by $41 million ($12 million related to prior years, and $29 million related to 20X4) primarily because costs were understated. According to the company's annual report:

The errors came to light during the implementation of a new financial accounting system and resulted from deficiencies in certain accounting and related business processes during a period of unprecedented increases in container shipping costs and adverse exchange rates.

After these systemic deficiencies were brought to light, the CFO left the company and was replaced.

Your friend wonders whether the company really has the experience to estimate the costs related to a shipment when the restatement implies otherwise. Accordingly, she has asked you to evaluate the two alternatives: recording revenue when the container is delivered versus revenue recognition at a later time when the costs are known with certainty. Shipping revenue is found in Exhibit 1.

EXHIBIT 1

BLX CONTAINER SHIPPING LTD.

(amounts in millions)

Year	20X5	20X4*	20X3*	20X2*	20X1**
Total revenue	$1,100	$ 939	$ 807	$ 795	$ 564
Revenue accrued at year-end	$ 316	$ 148	$ 244	$ 95	$ 152
Net income	$ 27.2	$30.6	$22.8	$41.7	$22.4
Costs associated with accrued revenue—as corrected in 20X4 restatement	$95	$60	$86	$36	$53
Dry-docking expenditures	$30	$10	$ 2	$24	$12
Amortization of dry-docking expenditures	$14	$18	$16	$17	$15

*As restated

**As restated; prior to public offering when company was private.

Note: Ignore income taxes.

Note 9

Dry-docking costs are capitalized and amortized over the dry-docking cycle, typically four years.

In dry-dock, a vessel is regularly subject to repairs and repainting, and sometimes refitting and upgrading (e.g., new engines). Your friend wonders why BLX does not use a different method of accounting for dry-docking costs, such as:

- Expensing the repairs as operating costs when incurred, as most businesses do; or

- Accruing one-fourth of the expense in each year between dry-dockings to create a reserve for dry-docking, since dry-docking is a necessary business expense to keep the vessels in good operating condition.

Your friend has asked you to evaluate the three alternative accounting policies as applied to BLX: (1) capitalization and amortization versus (2) immediate expensing versus (3) periodic accrual in advance. Your evaluation should include a review of the appropriate accounting concepts and the impact on financial statement users. Costs relating to dry-docking expenditures are found in Exhibit 1.

Required:
Prepare an appropriate analysis.

TECHNICAL REVIEW

connect

TR2-1 Underlying Assumptions: Indicate whether each of the following statements is true or false:

1. Nominal dollar capital maintenance assumes that earnings are distributable once the dollar level of investment has been maintained.
2. Nominal dollar financial capital maintenance is the only feasible basis for measuring earnings for a modern diversified business corporation.
3. The separate-entity assumption means that there must be no financial transactions between the business entity and its owners, except for the payment of dividends.
4. The continuity assumption means that it is feasible to prepare corporate financial statements at any point over the continuity of time.
5. The time-period assumption means that it is feasible to prepare meaningful annual financial statements, even though the entity still has many unfulfilled transactions outstanding.
6. The continuity assumption states that a business entity will last long enough for its assets to be used up and its liabilities settled.
7. The entity basis of reporting is the same as consolidated reporting, wherein all resources under the control of the shareholders of the parent company are combined into financial statements for the entire economic entity.
8. Under the proprietary assumption, financial statements are prepared from the point of view of the enterprise's owners.
9. The unit-of-measure assumption states that it is meaningful to express the affairs of an enterprise in currency units.
10. Because of the continuity assumption, it is impossible to prepare meaningful financial statements for a bankrupt company.

TR2-2 Qualitative Characteristics: Explain how the fundamental qualitative characteristics apply in each of the following situations:

1. A company acquires land in exchange for shares, but the shares are lightly traded and cannot be easily valued. The most recent trades have fluctuated widely. The company proposes to use its own internal expert's appraisal for the land.

2. A significant economic downturn occurs just as a company is preparing to issue its financial statements, three months after year-end. Because of the downturn, the collectability of its quite substantial accounts receivable is in doubt. The company's CFO proposes that the company delay the issuance of the financial statements for another two or three months, until the collectability of the accounts becomes clearer.

3. A private (not publicly accountable) construction company wishes to defer revenue recognition on each construction project until the project is finished, although most companies recognize revenue on a percentage of completion basis (which also is required under IFRS). The company's executives argue that since the completed-contract basis requires no estimates, it yields by far the most accurate (i.e., representationally faithful) measure of earnings.

4. The CEO of a major biotechnology company wishes to show the company's important internally generated assets on the balance sheet. She is concerned that financial statement users are deprived of relevant information when they assess the earnings potential of the firm. She proposes that the assets be measured and reported by computing the discounted future cash flows that will occur from their use.

5. A company uses many assets that were acquired through long-term rental contracts. The easiest way to measure the cost is by treating the monthly rent as an expense. However, the company's auditor insists that the leases be shown on the balance sheet as though the assets had been bought and a liability taken on, despite the significant number of estimates that are necessary to report it that way.

TR2-3 Concepts Identification: In the blanks provided to the left below, enter the letters of the underlying assumption, measurement method, qualitative criteria, or constraint most closely associated with the statements. Some letters may be used more than once and some may not be used at all.

A. Separate-entity assumption
B. Continuity assumption
C. Materiality
D. Time-period assumption
E. Cost/benefit
F. Revenue recognition

G. Matching
H. Historical cost
I. Unit-of-measure assumption
J. Faithful representation
K. Verifiability
L. Full disclosure

_____ 1. Any accounting method is acceptable for small items that will not change users' decisions.

_____ 2. Assumes that all financial statement elements can be meaningfully described in dollar terms.

_____ 3. Long-term assets that increase in value are not normally written up in the financial statements.

_____ 4. Assets and earnings should be neither understated nor overstated.

_____ 5. The estimated future cost of fulfilling warranties that may not arise until two years into the future are accrued in the period of the sale.

_____ 6. It is not necessary to use a complex accounting method for minor items that are highly unlikely to improve the decisions of financial statement users.

_____ 7. It must be possible to numerically confirm all amounts reported in the body of the financial statements.

_____ 8. The various costs associated with a revenue transaction may be deferred until the revenue is earned.

_____ 9. The personal transactions of owners should be kept separate from transactions of the business.

_____ 10. Significant recognized and many nonrecognized items should be fully described in the notes to the financial statements.

_____ 11. Enables historical cost, rather than liquidation values, to be used.

_____ 12. Enables measurement of the income and financial position of entities at regular intervals.

TR2-4 Capital Maintenance: Oundjian Corp. recently sold inventory for $140,000. The goods had originally cost $94,000. Inflation during the period was 5%. The goods could be replaced from their long-time supplier for $115,000. For simplicity, assume that there are no other costs of doing business.

Required:

1. Calculate a measure of accounting income, consistent with:
   a. Nominal dollar financial capital maintenance.
   b. Constant dollar financial capital maintenance.
   c. Physical capital maintenance, in nominal dollars.

2. Assume in each case in requirement 1 that the company collected revenue in cash and paid out 100% of net income in dividends to owners. Calculate the remaining cash balance. Explain the significance of the remaining cash flow in each case.

3. If the company were planning to replace the inventory, which capital maintenance concept allows it to keep enough money to accomplish this with no further investment or borrowing?

4. Which capital maintenance concept is dominant in Canada? Which one(s) is(are) acceptable under IFRS?

TR2-5 Capital Maintenance: At the beginning of 20X5, its first year of business, Marsalis Ltd. invested $64,000 in inventory and $300,000 in equipment. Total sales were $160,000. Of the initial inventory purchases, $25,000 remained in inventory at the end of the period. Leflore depreciated the equipment by 20% straight-line, taking a full year's depreciation in 20X5.

The replacement cost of the inventory, both that sold and that remaining in year-end inventory, had decreased by 10% by the end of the year. The replacement cost of the equipment, however, had increased by 3% over the year.

Required:

Determine the net income (using only the costs indicated above), under each of the following assumptions:

1. Nominal dollar capital maintenance.

2. Physical capital maintenance.

ASSIGNMENTS

★ **A2-1 Relevance versus Reliability:** Tannino Limited is a private investment company that manages investments for a group of about 30 wealthy individuals. The company is owned and managed by two experienced investment managers, each of whom owns 50% of the shares. The company merges all of its clients' money into a single investment fund. At the end of each period, the investors' investment accounts are increased or decreased by the percentage gain or loss for the entire investment fund.

A majority of the investments are in publicly traded companies, but a significant portion is invested in real estate and in private companies as (quite speculative) venture capital. The company is preparing its financial statements for its first fiscal year ended 31 December 20X4. GAAP is not a constraint. The two owner-managers are discussing the proper method of reporting the company's investment portfolio. On the one hand, they wish to present the most useful and relevant information to their investors, as well as to the bank that provides some debt financing. On the other hand, they are concerned about the reliability (i.e., faithful representation) of the reported asset values for various parts of the investment portfolio.

Required:

Discuss the trade-off between relevance and faithful representation for reporting the asset value of each of these various types of investments: (1) publicly traded securities, (2) real estate, and (3) venture capital in start-up businesses. Your discussion must be relevant to Tannino Limited's specific situation.

★ **A2-2 Relevance and Reliability:** Accounting measurements are enhanced by the presence of the qualities of predictive value, feedback value, comparability, verifiability, timeliness, freedom from bias, and representational faithfulness. For each of the following, indicate the quality demonstrated:

1. The value assigned to equipment is checked by referring to the original invoice.
2. Predictions concerning this year's income, issued 12 months ago, are compared with the actual results to assess the accuracy of the prediction.
3. Past trends are used to forecast this year's sales.
4. An outside expert is retained to assess the value of the recorded amounts for tangible and intangible capital assets.
5. Adjustments are made to financial statements that both increase and decrease net income despite the manager's preference to report lower net income.
6. Financial statements are issued four weeks after the year-end, even though this requires the use of estimates for some elements.
7. Preferred shares that have to be repaid on a given date are classified as a liability despite their legal status as equity.
8. The company releases estimates of operating results for the coming year, based on its budgets.
9. Cash received in advance of work done is recorded as a liability, unearned revenue.
10. Lawyers provide an estimate of the company's potential liability for product defects.

★ **A2-3 Questions on Principles:** For each of the following situations, indicate whether you agree or disagree with the practice described, list *one* accounting concept/assumption/ qualitative criteria/measurement method that is related to the situation (either followed or violated), and indicate how it is related:

1. Inventory that the company paid $450 for is carried on the balance sheet at $620 because it can be easily sold for $620.
2. The Book Printer Ltd. has an operating cycle of three years. It takes three years to have a book written, published, and marketed. The company, therefore, produces financial statements every three years.
3. WLZ Co. must estimate and record a warranty liability and has obtained three estimates— one for $75,000, one for $92,000, and one for $106,000. The company records $75,000.
4. Cambria Corporation has purchased a rare manuscript wanted by the major shareholder, whose passion is antiquities. The manuscript is kept at the shareholder's house for his sole use but is carried on the company's books as a long-term investment.
5. Elocom Ltd. has an account receivable *from* Maddox Ltd. for $40,000, and an account payable *to* Maddox Ltd. for $37,000. Elocom shows a net account receivable of $3,000, and no accounts payable, on its balance sheet.

6. Darlington Designs Ltd. has not fixed a $5,000 error in inventory accounting because it would have a trivial effect on cost of goods sold and net income.

 A2-4 Questions on Principles: If the following statements are true, write "True" after the statement. However, most are false. For a false statement, write "False," and *briefly* indicate why the statement is false.

1. Full disclosure involves telling financial statement users everything about the company's transactions.
2. Matching means that revenue is matched to the time period in which the enterprise does the work.
3. The continuity assumption means that a manufacturing company will stay in business long enough to use or sell its inventory.
4. The proprietary approach is the reason that dividends declared are classified on the retained earnings statement rather than on the income statement.
5. An asset is something owned by a company.
6. Relevance suffers when market values are included in the financial statements.
7. To preserve comparability, accounting policies may never be changed.
8. Many intangible assets are not recorded because of the nominal dollar capital assumption.
9. Materiality is based only on the relative size of the item.

 A2-5 Application of Principles: The following list of statements poses conceptual issues:

 a. The business entity is considered to be separate and apart from its owners for accounting purposes.
b. A transaction is always recorded in such a way as to reflect its legal form.
c. It is permissible for a company to use straight-line depreciation, even though the rest of the industry uses declining balance, because the company believes that straight-line better reflects the pattern of benefits received from these assets.
d. All details of transactions must be disclosed in the notes to the financial statements.
e. The lower-of-cost-or-market method must be used in valuing inventories.
f. The cost principle relates only to the income statement.
g. Revenue should be recognized only when cash is received.
h. Accruals and deferrals are necessary because of the separate-entity assumption.
i. Revenue should be recognized as late as possible and expenses as early as possible.

Required:

1. Indicate whether each statement is correct or incorrect.
2. Identify the principle(s) posited.
3. Provide a brief discussion of its (their) implications.

 A2-6 Realization versus Recognition: For each of the following transactions, indicate the point at which (1) the initial transaction is recognized and (2) the financial statement element is realized:

1. Inventory is purchased on credit on 1 August and is received on 14 August. It is paid for on 12 September.
2. A customer buys a product on credit on 13 November and takes immediate delivery, promising to pay on 1 February of the following year.
3. Expected warranty claims on products sold are accrued as the sales are made. Warranty claims are made at the end of the subsequent fiscal year. A cash payment is made to the customer at the beginning of the year following the claim.
4. A customer orders a custom-built machine and pays when the order is placed on 20 February. The machine is delivered on 10 March.

5. The company uses a substantial amount of electricity. The electric utility issues bimonthly bills (i.e., one every two months) three weeks following the two-month usage period.

6. A sale on credit is completed on January 20; the product is delivered on 1 February. Payment is received on 1 March.

★ **A2-7 Recognition of Elements:** In each of the following situations, identify the element or elements, if any, that would appear in financial statements. If no element is recognized, give the reason.

1. Unpaid electricity bill.
2. A patent on a new invention developed by a firm.
3. Professional development courses taken by employees at the company's expense.
4. Unissued common shares of a company that will likely be issued for cash next year.
5. A partially completed consulting project for a client.
6. The expenses of a lawsuit against the company.
7. Customer goodwill as indicated by a high percentage of satisfied return customers
8. A reputation for high-quality products.
9. Cash received from a customer for work to be done next year.
10. A Mercedes-Benz limousine leased for the company CEO.

★ **A2-8 Elements of Financial Statements:** Financial statement elements have specific definitions. To the right, some important aspects of the definitions are listed. Match the aspects with the elements by entering appropriate letters in the blanks. More than one letter can be placed in a blank.

Elements of Financial Statements	Important Aspect of the Definition of the Element
A. Assets	_____ 1. Using up of assets or incurrence of liabilities
B. Liabilities	_____ 2. Probable future economic benefits obtained by an entity
C. Owners' equity/net assets	_____ 3. Enhancement of assets or settlements of liabilities
D. Revenues	_____ 4. Residual interest in assets after deducting liabilities
E. Expenses	_____ 5. Increases in net assets from peripheral or incidental activities
F. Gains	_____ 6. Changes in net assets from peripheral or incidental transactions of the entity
G. Losses	_____ 7. Future sacrifices arising from past transactions
H. None of the above	_____ 8. Results from the entity's ongoing major or central operation

---

★ **A2-9 Questions on Principles:** For each of the following circumstances, give the letter item(s) indicating the accounting principle involved. Some letters may be used more than once, and some may not be used at all.

A. Continuity
B. Freedom from bias
C. Comparability
D. Cost/benefit effectiveness
E. Full disclosure
F. Historical cost
G. Relevance
H. Nominal dollar financial capital maintenance

I. Matching
J. Proprietary
K. Faithful representation
L. Revenue recognition
M. Separate entity
N. Time period
O. Unit of measure

1. Financial statements are prepared from the point of view of the owners.
2. A note describing the company's possible liability in a lawsuit is included with the financial statements, even though no formal liability exists at the balance sheet date.
3. Marketable securities are valued at market value.
4. The personal assets of partners are excluded from the partnership balance sheet, even though they are pledged as security for partnership loans.
5. A retail store uses estimates rather than a complete physical count of its inventory for purposes of preparing monthly financial statements.
6. Goodwill is recorded in the accounts only when it arises from the purchase of another entity.
7. An entity reports a $50 profit after buying a unit of inventory for $100 and selling it for $150, even though the cost to replace the unit has escalated to $112 due to inflation.
8. An advance deposit on a sale contract is reported as unearned revenue.
9. Accounting policies chosen for revenue recognition are the same as those of the entity's major competitors.
10. Capital assets are amortized over their useful lives.

★ **A2-10 Identification of Accounting Principles:** In each of the following cases, indicate the principle that appears to have been violated:

Solution

Case A   For its factory equipment, Unrequited Love Inc. used accelerated depreciation in 20X2; straight line in 20X3; and accelerated in 20X4.

Case B   Aaronist Ltd. sold a tract of land on credit by accepting a $55,000, two-year, non-interest-bearing note. The land account was credited (and notes receivable was debited) for $55,000. The going rate of interest was 10%.

Case C   JED Inc. always issues its annual financial report nine months after the end of the annual reporting period to ensure greater accuracy.

Case D   Idiomatic Inc. always recognizes its sales revenue when received in cash.

Case E   RBJ Corporation records interest income only on the payment dates.

Case F   Loran Company includes among its financial statement elements an apartment building owned and operated by the owner of the company.

Case G   The Adam Ltd. CEO refuses to permit the company to use notes or supplementary schedules in its financial reports because he believes that the financial statements are self explanatory.

★ **A2-11 Revenue Recognition:** Which of the following events would normally cause revenue recognition, assuming use of accrual accounting and transfer of title on delivery?

1. Collection of cash from a customer 30 days after the product is delivered.
2. Collection of cash from a customer 30 days before the product is delivered.
3. Delivery of a magazine as part of a prepaid 12-month subscription.
4. Inventory that cost $40,000 is known to have a replacement value of $67,000.
5. A financial institution loans $100,000 to a client; interest is due after 12 months; the financial institution is preparing financial statements two months after the loan was granted.
6. Goods are delivered to a customer with an invoice price of $26,000; the customer is notoriously slow in paying.

★ **A2-12 Recognition and Elements:** Indicate if each of the following items would be recognized in TelCan Ltd.'s financial statements for 20X3 and, if so, what elements would be recognized. For any items that would not be recognized, explain the reason for nonrecognition.

1. TelCan issued a purchase order to buy inventory early in the following year.

2. TelCan's share price has increased from $42 to $65 on the stock exchange.

3. The month of December has passed, and tenants occupying space in TelCan's building have not yet paid the rent. TelCan's rental agent believes that payment is reasonably assured.

4. TelCan sold the right to use its international industrial trademark to a Taiwanese computer manufacturer for the next five years.

5. TelCan experienced increases in the value of cash deposits held in U.S. dollars because of a stronger Canadian dollar.

6. TelCan invested in employee training costs to improve the company's future productivity.

7. TelCan's major competitor has liquidated and gone out of business. The company has purchased the competitor's customer list.

8. TelCan has a reasonably reliable estimate of the future cost of reaching a settlement on a pending patent infringement lawsuit.

★ **A2-13 Application of Principles:** The independent auditor of Fluidity Inc. found the following situations:

a. The company uses the straight-line method of measuring depreciation on manufacturing machinery, even though it knows that a method based on actual usage would provide better matching, more accurate income determination, and thus better information for financial statement users. However, the company uses the straight-line method because of the level of data needed to implement a usage method. The straight-line method is significantly cheaper to calculate.

b. For inventory valuation, Fluidity switched from FIFO to average cost and then back to FIFO for the same items during a five-year period.

c. Fluidity does not provide information about future contracts, called the "order backlog," in its financial statements. Such disclosure is quite common in the industry.

d. Fluidity follows a policy of depreciating plant and equipment on the straight-line basis over a period of time that is 50% longer than the historic use of similar equipment.

e. In its annual financial statements, the company reports interest expense as the *net* amount of interest expense less interest revenue. The amounts are very small, relative to the scale of Fluidity's business activities.

Required:

1. Identify and briefly explain the accounting principle that is directly involved in each situation.

2. Indicate what, if anything, the company should do in the future by way of any change in accounting policy.

★ **A2-14 Application of Principles:** An examiner's close inspection of the annual financial statements and the accounting records revealed that Mawani Inc. may have violated some accounting principles. The examiner questioned the following transactions:

a. Merchandise purchased for resale was recorded as a debit to inventory for the invoice price of $80,000 (accounts payable was credited for the same amount); terms were 2/10, n/30. Ten days later, Mawani Inc. paid the account at the net amount due, $78,400 ($80,000 less the 2% discount). The $1,600 discount was credited to revenue. The purchased goods were still shown in inventory at $80,000 at year-end.

b. Mawani Inc. recorded equipment depreciation expense of $227,000 as a debit to retained earnings and a credit to the equipment account.

c. Routine repairs on equipment were recorded as follows: debit equipment, $500; credit cash, $500.

d. The company sustained a $96,000 storm damage loss during the current year. The company had no insurance. Mawani Inc. reported the loss as follows:

Statement of retained earnings—storm loss	$24,000
Statement of financial position (assets): Deferred charge—storm loss	$72,000

e. Mawani's balance sheet showed accounts receivable of $95,000. This amount included a $42,000 three-year loan to the company president. The maturity date of the loan was not specified.

Required:

1. For each transaction, identify the inappropriate treatment and the principle(s) violated, if any.
2. Give the original entry that should have been made or the appropriate reporting.

★★ **A2-15 Implementation of Principles:** Carleton Builders Ltd. recorded the following summarized transactions during the current year:

a. The company originally sold and issued 100,000 common shares. During the current year, 94,000 of these shares were outstanding and 6,000 were repurchased from the shareholders and retired. Near the end of the current year, the Board of Directors declared and paid a cash dividend of $8 per share. The dividend was recorded as follows:

Retained earnings	800,000	
Cash ($8 × 94,000)		752,000
Dividend income ($8 × 6,000)		48,000

b. Carleton Builders Ltd. purchased a machine that had a list price of $90,000. The company paid for the machine in full by issuing 10,000 common shares (market price = $8.50). The purchase was recorded as follows:

Machine	90,000	
Share capital ($8.50 × 10,000)		85,000
Gain on purchase of equipment		5,000

c. Carleton needed a small structure for temporary storage. A contractor quoted a price of $769,000. The company decided to build the structure itself. The cost was $542,000, and construction required three months. The following entry was made:

Buildings—warehouse	769,000	
Cash		542,000
Revenue from self-construction		227,000

d. Carleton owns a plant located on a river that floods occasionally. A severe flood occurred during the current year, causing an uninsured loss of $97,000 (measured as the amount spent to repair the flood damage). The following entry was made:

Retained earnings, flood loss	97,000	
Cash		97,000

e. On 28 December, the company collected $76,000 cash in advance for merchandise to be shipped in January. The company's fiscal year-end is 31 December. This transaction was recorded on 28 December as follows:

Cash	76,000	
Sales revenue		76,000

Required:

1. For each transaction, determine which accounting principle (if any) was violated.
2. Explain the nature of the violation.
3. In each instance, indicate how the transaction should have been originally recorded.

★★ **A2-16 Implementation of Principles:** The bookkeeper for Branford Ltd. has drawn up a financial statement on 31 December 20X1. Some of the items on the draft balance sheet are as follows:

Cash	$400,000	Consists of 300,000 Canadian dollars in the bank, plus 100,000 Hong Kong dollars held in cash. The HK$ were received in full payment for a consulting assignment recorded as revenue in 20X1.
Marketable securities	$900,000	Represents the cost of a temporary investment in the common shares of another company.
Accounts receivable	$500,000	Recorded as revenue in December 20X1 for a customer order that had not been shipped by year-end.
Contract liability	$100,000	The amount of a contract with a construction firm for modifications to Branford Ltd.'s office space, expected to be undertaken in early 20X2.
Other liabilities	$ 1	Recorded as a result of a contractual (long-term) requirement to repair the roof of an office building that Branford rents for an advertising sign. The sign is to be removed and the roof repaired in January 20X7, at an estimated cost of $75,000.

Upon further inquiry, you discover that at 31 December 20X8, the Canadian dollar is worth HK$7.5. You also ascertain that the value of the marketable securities was $987,000 at 20X1 year-end.

Required:

1. Indicate what change, if any, you would make in reporting each of the preceding items.
2. In each case, discuss the accounting principle involved.

★★ **A2-17 Implementation of Principles:** One generally accepted accounting policy relates to contingent losses. If the loss is reasonably measurable and likely to be incurred, the amount is accrued in the financial statements. If the amount is not measurable or is not likely to be incurred, then the potential loss is disclosed but not recorded. Also, if the probability of payment cannot be determined (is not estimable) the possibility of a loss is disclosed but not recorded.

For example, this policy can be directly applied to lawsuits. If a company is being sued by a disgruntled ex-customer, and the matter is before the courts, there can be a long delay in dispute resolution. A company will record a loss from the lawsuit prior to the court decision only if an amount, if any, of the court-ordered award can be predicted, *and* it appears likely that the company will lose the lawsuit or agree to a settlement. If an amount is not recorded, the existence of the lawsuit is explained in the disclosure notes.

Required:

1. List the recognition criteria.
2. Explain the accounting policy for contingent losses with reference to the recognition criteria.

★★ **A2-18 Recognition Criteria:** Consider each of the following independent situations:

Case A The value of Coca-Cola's trademark has been estimated as worth billions of dollars. Yet, even though Coca-Cola reports over $12 billion of goodwill and other intangible assets, none of this reported value relates to the Coca-Cola trademark, which is unrecognized in the accounts despite its substantial commercial value.

Case B Air Canada purchases Aeroplan Miles® from Groupe Aeroplan Inc., a separate corporation. Air Canada is an Aeroplan partner providing certain Air Canada's customers with Aeroplan Miles®, which can be redeemed by customers for air travel or other rewards acquired by Aeroplan.

Under the CPSA, the companies' joint agreement, Aeroplan purchases passenger tickets from Air Canada to meet its obligation for the redemption of Aeroplan Miles® for air travel. The proceeds from the sale of passenger tickets to Aeroplan are included in Advance ticket sales. Revenue related to these passenger tickets is recorded in passenger revenues when transportation is provided.

For Aeroplan Miles® earned by Air Canada customers, Air Canada purchases Aeroplan Miles® from Aeroplan in accordance with the terms of the CPSA. The cost of purchasing Aeroplan Miles® from Aeroplan is accounted for as a sales incentive and charged against passenger revenues when the points are issued, which occurs upon the qualifying air travel being provided to the customer.

Case C Calgary-based Suncor Energy Inc. explores and develops sites within the Alberta oil sands. The company will be responsible for restoring the sites in the future. At 31 December 2011, the company reported an estimate of $3.43 billion in decommissioning and restoration costs. The following explanation appears in Suncor's disclosure notes (Note 4— Significant Accounting Estimates and Judgements):

> **Decommissioning and Restoration Costs**
>
> The company recognizes liabilities for the future decommissioning and restoration of exploration and evaluation assets and property, plant and equipment. These provisions are based on estimated costs, which take into account the anticipated method and extent of restoration, technological advances and the possible future use of the site. Actual costs are uncertain and estimates can vary as a result of changes to relevant laws and regulations, the emergence of new technology, operating experience, prices and closure plans. The expected timing of future decommissioning and restoration may change due to certain factors, including reserve life. Changes to assumptions related to future expected costs, discount rates and timing may have a material impact on the amounts presented.

Required:
For each of the preceding situations, discuss the issues relating to the recognition (or non-recognition) of relevant elements in each company's financial statements.

★★ **A2-19 Implementation of Principles:** Consider the following five reporting situations:

Case A The financial statements of Raychem Corporation included the following note:

> During the current year, plant assets were written down by $8,000,000. This writedown will reduce future expenses. Depreciation and other expenses in future years will be lower, and as a result this will benefit profits of future years.

Case B During an audit of the Silvona Company, the audit manager observed that certain liabilities, such as income taxes, seemed to be overstated. Also, some potentially obsolete inventory items seem to be undervalued, and the tendency is to expense rather than capitalize as many items as possible. Management states that "the company has always taken a very conservative view of the business and its future prospects." Management suggests that it does not wish to weaken the company by reporting any more earnings or paying any more dividends than are absolutely necessary because it does not expect business to continue to be good. Management points out that the lower valuations for assets do not cost the company anything but do create reserves for "hard times."

Case C   There was no comment or explanation of the fact that Simone Limited changed its inventory method from FIFO (first-in, first-out) to average cost at the beginning of the current reporting period. A large changeover difference was involved, and there was no retrospective restatement.

Case D   Current assets amounted to $314,000 and current liabilities, $205,000; the balance sheet of Nelta Corp. reported a single amount "Working capital, $109,000."

Case E   In 20X1, the Tryler Corporation switched its inventory method for financial reporting from LIFO (last-in, first-out) to FIFO due to a change in accounting standards that prohibits LIFO. Tryler publicly explained, "Our major competitors have consistently used the FIFO method. Therefore, the reported loss for 20X1 and the restated profit for 20X0 are on a comparable basis as to inventory valuation with competitors." The impact on opening balances is not material.

Required:
Analyze each of the preceding situations and indicate which accounting principles, as described in this chapter, are applicable in each situation.

connect   **LEARNSMART**   **SMARTBOOK**

For more information on the resources available from McGraw-Hill Ryerson, go to www.mcgrawhill.ca/he/solutions.

Statements of Income and Comprehensive Income

INTRODUCTION

Air Canada's 2012 consolidated statement of operations (which is the title Air Canada uses for its statement of comprehensive income) shows four earnings subtotals before arriving at the amount for net Income (loss): (1) operating Income, (2) Income/loss before income taxes and discontinued operations, (3) net income/loss from continuing operations, and (4) net income from continuing operations.

Similarly, Winnipeg-based New Flyer Industries (a manufacturer of heavy-duty transit buses) also shows four subtotals on its consolidated statement of profit or loss before arriving at the final amount for net earnings for the period—(1) gross profit; (2) earnings from operations; (3) earnings before finance costs and income taxes; and (4) earnings before income tax expense.

In contrast, Montreal-based BCE Inc. shows only one earnings subtotal on its consolidated income statement—earnings before income taxes—prior to the final amount for net earnings.

This chapter explains the various aspects of earnings and how they are displayed on the statement of comprehensive income (SCI). The chapter also explains what is not necessarily shown on the statement, such as major categories of expense.

This chapter focuses on the display of revenues, expenses, gains, and losses after they have been recorded. Accounting standards require that certain items of information be reported on the income statement or in the notes thereto. In general, however, the level of information provided in the profit or loss section of the SCI is left largely to the discretion of management, as is the style of presentation.

One item that requires special classification in the income statement is the reporting of discontinued operations. The main body of this chapter will conclude with a section on "discontinued operations" as well as other types of asset disposals.

Finally, as with all of the following chapters, we will end by explaining the income statement reporting requirements for private entities using ASPE.

NATURE OF INCOME

"Income" Terminology

The word "income" often is used to mean quite different things in accounting usage, as well as in everyday language. However, in IFRS, **income** means *all* amounts flowing into the entity through operations. IAS 1 (*Presentation of Financial Statements*) states:

> An entity shall recognise all items of income and expense in a period in profit or loss. (¶88)

"Income" in this sentence means *revenue* and *gains*, while "profit or loss" means *net income*. This can be a little confusing because we commonly use *income* for ancillary sources of revenue such as *interest income*.

Largely because of this confusion, most Canadian companies avoid the use of "income" and instead use *revenue* and "earnings." IFRS adopts the European tradition and refers to net income as "profit or loss." Although IFRS does not use the word "earnings" when defining revenue, it nevertheless is useful for avoiding confusion and is consistent with other common terminology, such as retained *earnings* and *earnings* per share.

The moral of this story is to be careful about what people mean when they say "income." Do they mean all sources of gain, or *revenue*, or *net income* (e.g., *earnings* or *profit or loss*)?

Accounting versus Economic Income

An economist defines income as a *change in wealth*, whether or not that change in wealth has been realized. Suppose that a company owns a parcel of land for which it paid $10,000 several years ago. A new highway has just been built next to the property, and several individuals have offered to pay $125,000 to $150,000 for the land. The firm has not yet agreed to sell. An economist would say that an increase in wealth has occurred because the land is worth more than historical cost. The wealth increase is called **economic income**, and it is based on an *events approach* rather than on a *transactions approach* to measuring profit or loss.

Using the transaction approach, an accountant would not recognize such an increase in wealth as income. Only if the land is sold to another party in an arm's-length transaction would the accountant recognize the increase in wealth as income. This is **accounting income**, based on the transactions approach.

Historically, accounting had been based strictly on the transactions approach and the historical cost measurement principle. Changes in value were recognized only when there was a transaction that *realized* the change in value. The only exceptions to the transaction approach occurred in the writedown or downward valuation of items, such as obsolete inventory and capital assets (both tangible and intangible).

Accounting standards under IFRS are moving more toward the concept of economic income. Accounting now recognizes not only value changes realized through transactions, but also certain types of value changes that have not been realized. A prime example is the reporting of financial assets and liabilities, many of which are reported on the statement of financial position (SFP) at fair values. Reporting based on fair values leads to accounting recognition of value changes as either realized or unrealized income.

But only some value changes are recognized and reported. Many other value changes, such as increases in the value of inventory, are not normally recognized in accounting. Therefore, accounting income is still quite different from economic income.

Comprehensive Income

Comprehensive income is defined as all changes to owners' equity that are *not* the result of transactions with the owners (i.e., the shareholders) in their capacity as owners. For example:

- The issuance of new shares, repurchase of outstanding shares, and the payment of dividends are examples of transactions with shareholders solely *in their capacity as owners* and will be reported as changes in equity, not as part of comprehensive income.
- In contrast, selling goods or services to a shareholder is a transaction with the shareholder that is *not* part of the relationship with the shareholder as an owner; it is a

transaction with the shareholder as a customer and will be reported as part of comprehensive income.

The concept of comprehensive income has two objectives:

- To eliminate all direct entries to shareholders' equity except those resulting from transactions with the shareholders; and
- To differentiate between (1) those value changes that are recognized both in net assets and in profit or loss and (2) those that are recognized in net assets (on the SFP) but are not recognized in the current year's earnings or net income.

There are two categories of comprehensive income:

1. Periodic profit or loss (also known as *net income* or *earnings*); and

2. Other comprehensive income (OCI).

The IASB permits two slightly different reporting formats:

- a continuous **statement of comprehensive income (SCI)** that starts with revenue, goes down to a total for net profit or loss (or "earnings") after tax and then continues to the items of *other comprehensive income*; or
- two separate statements consisting of (1) a statement of profit or loss; and (2) an SCI that begins with profit or loss as the first line.

When separate statements are prepared, the SCI must immediately follow the income statement in the company's financial statement presentation.

Classification Which items affecting net assets should be included in the computation of profit or loss and reported in the income statement? Or, to look at it another way, what items should be *excluded* from profit or loss and reported as a component of OCI?

The vast majority of items (other than transactions with owners) are included in profit or loss. In accounting terminology, this is the *all-inclusive* approach to earnings reporting— very few transactions or events are shown outside profit or loss.

Nevertheless, there are some items that are excluded from profit or loss. One type of item is reported in retained earnings, while the other three types are reported in OCI:

- Cumulative changes to retained earnings that are the result of (1) changes in accounting policies or (2) corrections of errors in prior periods. The retrospective effects of changes and corrections are reported as *changes to retained earnings*. Our detailed discussion of accounting changes occurs much later in this book, in Chapter 21.
- Certain specified changes in value are *recognized* in the SFP under IFRS but have not yet been *realized*. For the most part, these are value changes (1) that will be recognized in income only if and when realized or (2) that will be matched by an offsetting gain or loss in a future period. These items are reported in OCI.
- When companies have operations in foreign countries, the subsidiaries' financial statements must be converted to the parent's presentation currency so that they can be consolidated. The process is more complicated that it sounds because changes in exchange rates create an accounting gain or loss. This gain or loss has no economic significance; it is the mechanical result of the conversion process. Therefore, it is reported as an item of OCI.
- Currently, IFRS requires that net actuarial gains and losses relating to pension plans be reported as an item of OCI. Essentially, this is necessary to get the SFP to balance!

Other than these four types of value changes, the results of all transactions and all *recognized* value changes are reported in the profit or loss portion of the SCI.

We will explore the components of OCI as we go through the following chapters. For now, just accept that these nonowner changes in net assets are *excluded* from profit or loss but need to be reported somewhere—that "somewhere" is in the SCI as items of *other comprehensive income*. The rest of this chapter will focus on the "profit or loss," (or "net income" or "earnings") section of the SCI.

1. What are the different meanings often accorded to the term "income"?

2. Explain the difference between accounting income and economic income.

3. What general types of changes in assets and liabilities are *not* reported as part of net income? Where are such excluded items reported?

GENERAL PRESENTATION FORMAT

IFRS prescribes little detail for either the content or format of the SCI except for the clear division between *profit or loss* and *OCI*. Companies are quite free to use various presentation formats, as long as they do report those items that are specifically required by the various accounting standards.[1]

Line Items Required for Profit or Loss Section

In reporting a company's net earnings, IFRS requires a company to show the following minimum line items:

- Revenues, either (1) separated into categories, such as sales revenue, finance revenue, and investment income, or (2) shown in aggregate with note disclosure of the various income sources;
- Finance costs (which includes interest expense);
- The enterprise's share of earnings from associated companies and/or joint ventures;
- Income tax expense on continuing operations;
- Profit or loss on discontinued operations, net of tax;
- Net earnings; and
- Earnings per share.

This is a really short list! Note that it does not even mention any expense items except for finance cost and income tax expense.

There are three important additional disclosures that must appear either on the face of the SCI or in the notes:

- The amount of inventory charged to expense;
- Depreciation and amortization expense; and
- Employee benefits expense, which includes wages and salaries, payroll taxes, heath care costs, post-retirement benefits, and so forth.

Whether these items are shown on the face of the SCI or in a disclosure note depends on the presentation format, as we shall see in the next section.

Notwithstanding the list of required disclosures, materiality plays an important role. If particular items of income or expense are material, they must be disclosed either on the face of the SCI or in the notes.

Remember that this list of required disclosures is the IFRS requirement. For Canadian private enterprises that use ASPE, additional disclosures are required. The ASPE requirements are listed in the ASPE section at the end of this chapter.

IFRS requires that items of profit and loss be reported on a continuous basis. That is, the statement should start with revenues, and then other items should be subtracted (or added) to obtain net earnings. This may seem obvious, but in some countries (including Canada),

---

[1] This situation may or may not change. The IASB has been working on a revised framework for financial reporting for several years but with no end in sight.

it previously was possible to show gross revenue, then draw a line, and skip to "earnings except the undernoted," which then included the few specific items required by accounting standards. In some countries, it was even possible to avoid disclosing revenue, but not under IFRS.

Alternative Formats of the Income Statement

IFRS specifies two alternative formats that may be used for the "profit or loss" section of the SCI:

1. Classification by *nature of expense*; and

2. Classification by *function within the enterprise,*

Classification by *nature* of expense will classify expenses on the basis of input costs—what the money was spent on. Classification by *function* is an output-based presentation—what the expenditure was used for.

By Nature of Expense   Exhibit 3-1 shows the consolidated SCI for Air Canada. Air Canada classifies expenses by *nature*. It shows the expense incurred for each type input cost, such as fuel, maintenance, depreciation, and so forth. The "required" expense categories are all reported on the face of the statement, with details explained in the disclosure notes.

Note the column for note references—a company must cross-reference each line item (when relevant) to the disclosure notes wherein the reader can find more detailed information. For example, Note 20 will disclose the various sources of revenue within each major category of passenger and cargo.

By Function within the Enterprise   Bombardier presents its operating results classified by function. While Air Canada shows its total employee cost (classified by nature) on the face of its SCI, Bombardier's employee costs will be included in each of the major functional categories of cost of sales, SG&A, and R&D.

When a company reports on the basis of function, required information, such as employee benefit expense and amortization and depreciation expense, is shown in the notes to the financial statements. For example, in Note 10, Bombardier reports employee benefit costs totalling $6,035 million (for 2012); depreciation and amortization are reported in Note 19 (property, plant, and equipment) and Note 20 (intangible assets).

Bombardier's presentation is in two statements rather than in one continuous statement. Exhibit 3-2 shows the consolidated statement of income, while Exhibit 3-3 shows the consolidated SCI. As required by IFRS, the SCI immediately follows the statement of income in Bombardier's financial statements (and annual report).

Observe in the footnote to both statements that Bombardier's 2011 fiscal year was only 11 months long. This is because the company previously had reported on a fiscal year basis ending on 31 January each year. The company changed to a calendar year reporting basis for 2011, meaning that the 2011 fiscal year started on 1 February 2011, and ended on 31 December 2011.

Changes in fiscal year are not common, but they do happen occasionally. Companies may change their fiscal year-end to coincide with the reporting year of related companies or competing companies within an industry or for the benefit of major investors or lenders.

EXHIBIT 3-1

AIR CANADA
Consolidated Statement of Operations

		For the year ended 31 December	
(Canadian dollars in millions except per share figures)		**2012**	**2011**
Operating revenues			
Passenger	Note 20	$10,737	$10,208
Cargo	Note 20	488	481
Other		895	923
Total revenues		12,120	11,612
Operating expenses			
Aircraft fuel		3,561	3,375
Wages, salaries, and benefits		2,109	1,991
Benefit plan amendments	Note 9	(124)	—
Capacity purchase agreements	Note 21	1,072	1,003
Airport and navigation fees		992	1,007
Depreciation, amortization, and impairment		678	728
Aircraft maintenance		672	681
Sales and distribution costs		603	612
Aircraft rent		336	335
Food, beverages, and supplies		291	278
Communications and information technology		188	193
Other		1,305	1,230
Total operating expenses		11,683	11,433
Operating income		437	179
Non-operating income (expense)			
Foreign exchange gain (loss)		106	(54)
Interest income		37	36
Interest expense		(304)	(320)
Interest capitalized		18	4
Net financing expense relating to employee benefits	Note 9	(16)	(16)
Loss on financial instruments recorded at fair value	Note 17	(20)	(63)
Loss on investments in Aveos	Note 19	(65)	—
Other		(6)	(16)
Total non-operating expense		(250)	(429)
Income (loss) before income taxes and discontinued operations		187	(250)
Income taxes	Note 12	(1)	1
Net income (loss) from continuing operations		$ 186	$ (249)
Net loss from discontinued operations—Aveos	Note 19	(55)	—
Net income (loss)		$ 131	$ (249)
Net income (loss) attributable to:			
Shareholders of Air Canada		127	(255)
Non-controlling interests		4	6
		$ 131	$ (249)
Net income (loss) per share attributable to shareholders of Air Canada	Note 15		
Basic earnings (loss) per share from continuing operations		$ 0.66	$ (0.92)
Diluted earnings (loss) per share from continuing operations		$ 0.65	$ (0.92)
Basic and diluted loss per share from discontinued operations		$ (0.20)	$ —
Diluted earnings (loss) per share		$ 0.45	$ (0.92)

Source: Air Canada, 2012 Audited annual financial statements, page 4, www.sedar.com, posted 7 February 2013.

Bombardier uses common abbreviations for the various components of the income statement, including:

- SG&A—sales, general and administrative expense
- R&D—research and development
- EBIT—earnings before interest and income tax
- EBT—earnings before income tax

These abbreviations are known to any knowledgeable financial statement user and do not really need to be spelled out. Remember, accounting standards assume that financial statement readers are not naïve; users are expected to have a reasonable level of accounting sophistication.

The abbreviations in the SCI are as follows:

- OCI—other comprehensive income
- AFS—assets available for sale
- CCTD—cumulative currency translation difference
- NCI—non-controlling interest (an explanation follows below)

EXHIBIT 3-2

BOMBARDIER INC.

Consolidated Statements of Income

(In millions of U.S. dollars, except per share amounts)	Notes	For the fiscal years ended 31 December	
		2012	2011[1]
Revenues	5	$16,768	$18,347
Cost of sales	5, 16	14,269	15,444
Gross margin		2,499	2,903
SG&A	5	1,443	1,439
R&D	5, 6	299	271
Share of income of associates	5	(45)	
Other income	5, 7	(33)	
Special items	5, 8	140	—
EBIT		695	1,202
Financing expense	9	596	681
Financing income	9	(599)	(519)
EBT		698	1,040
Income taxes	11	100	203
Net income		$ 598	$ 837
Attributable to:			
Equity holders of Bombardier Inc.		$ 588	$ 837
NCI		10	—
		$ 598	$ 837
EPS (in dollars)	12		
Basic and diluted		$ 0.32	$ 0.47

[1] The fiscal year ended 31 December 2011, comprises 11 months of BA's results and 12 months of BT's results. See note 1—Basis of preparation for more details.

Source: Bombardier Inc., or its subsidiaries, 2012 Audited annual financial statements, page 130, www.sedar.com, posted 21 February 2013.

EXHIBIT 3-3

BOMBARDIER INC.

Consolidated Statements of Comprehensive Income

(In millions of U.S. dollars)	For the fiscal years ended 31 December	
	2012	**2011**[1]
Net income	$598	$ 837
OCI		
Items that may be reclassified to net income		
Net change in cash flow hedges		
Foreign exchange re-evaluation	(5)	16
Net gain (loss) on derivative financial instruments designated as cash flow hedges	163	(128)
Reclassification to income or to the related non-financial asset[2][3]	25	(40)
Income taxes	(64)	54
	119	(98)
AFS financial assets		
Net unrealized gain	6	26
Reclassification to income	(29)	(5)
Income taxes	6	(4)
	(17)	17
CCTD		
Net investments in foreign operations	75	(90)
Net gain (loss) on related hedging items	(18)	50
	57	(40)
Items that are never reclassified to net income		
Retirement benefits		
Net actuarial gains (losses)	172	(1,489)
Income taxes	(25)	234
	147	(1,255)
Total OCI	306	(1,376)
Total comprehensive income (loss)	$904	$ (539)
Attributable to:		
Equity holders of Bombardier Inc.	$891	$ (535)
NCI	13	(4)
	$904	$ (539)

[1] The fiscal year ended 31 December 2011, comprises 11 months of BA's results and 12 months of BT's results.

[2] Includes $22 million of gain reclassified to the related non-financial asset for fiscal year 2012 ($104 million of gain for fiscal year 2011).

[3] $2 million of net deferred loss is expected to be reclassified from OCI to the carrying amount of the related non-financial asset or to income during fiscal year 2013.

Source: Bombardier Inc., or its subsidiaries, 2012 Audited annual financial statements, page 131, www.sedar.com, posted 21 February 2013.

Non-controlling Interest

A consolidated income statement includes the revenues and expenses of both the parent company and of the subsidiaries that it controls. However, the parent may control a subsidiary without owning all of its shares. When the parent owns less than 100% of a subsidiary's shares, the shares that are held by others outside the consolidated entity are known as the **non-controlling interest (NCI)**.[2]

In a consolidated income statement, the net income amount includes *all* of the revenues and expenses of the parent and the subsidiary. However, the parent corporation's shareholders are not entitled to the benefit of that full amount (e.g., through dividends from the parent). Therefore, the final net income figure must be allocated proportionately to the controlling interest and the nonthat iscontrolling interest.

In Exhibit 3-3, Bombardier allocates its consolidated net income of $837 million completely to the equity shareholders of Bombardier, that is, its own shareholders, for the year ended 31 December 2011. However, for the year ended 31 December 2012, $10 million of the $598 million net income was allocated to NCI. This presentation format is required by IFRS.

Earnings per Share

A company must disclose its earnings per share (EPS), both basic and diluted, at the end of the income statement or, if the company is using a continuous statement of earnings and comprehensive income, then the EPS numbers must be shown at the end of the SCI. Both basic and diluted EPS must be shown. A company also must disclose the weighted average number of shares used in the EPS calculations, but this disclosure can be in the notes rather than on the face of the statement.

The **weighted average number of shares** is a simple calculation. For example, if a company had 10,000 shares outstanding at the beginning of the year and then issued another 6,000 at the beginning of the fourth quarter (and thus outstanding for just three months), the weighted average would be $10,000 + (6,000 \times 3/12) = 11,500$.

Basic EPS is the total net income divided by the weighted average of common shares outstanding during the year. Bombardier (see Exhibit 3-2) shows EPS of $0.32 for 2012, compared with $0.47 for 2011.

Diluted EPS is computed by using the weighted average of all shares that would have been outstanding if all conversion privileges had been exercised by the holders of convertible bonds, preferred shares, and so forth. While basic EPS is useful for historical comparisons, diluted EPS is forward looking—what will happen if conversion rights are exercised?

If the company reports any *discontinued operations* (which we shall discuss shortly), EPS must be reported in three steps:

- EPS (basic and diluted) for continuing operations
- EPS (basic and diluted) for discontinued operations
- Total EPS (basic and diluted)

Air Canada (see Exhibit 3-1) presents a full range of EPS amounts. The four EPS are for basic EPS and diluted EPS, and for both continuing operations and discontinued operations.

Note that EPS is based on *earnings attributable to shareholders of the parent corporation*. For Air Canada, EPS is based on the $127 million attributable to the shareholders of Air Canada, not on the $131 million total earnings.

EPS is *not* based on comprehensive income because, by definition, the items included in OCI are not a part of earnings in the reporting period, even though they may "recycle" into earnings in future periods. Items reported in OCI in this period will be recognized in earnings and EPS only when reported in earnings in a subsequent period.

[2] Some companies call this the *minority interest*, which is okay provided that the non-controlling interest is less than 50% of the outstanding shares.

Single-Step versus Multiple-Step Income Statements

Single-Step IFRS makes no prescription for the setup of the income statement. An income statement always starts with revenue, subtracts and adds things, and concludes with net income (or net earnings, or profit or loss). Theoretically, a company can display a single section for all "revenue and other income," followed by another single section for all "expenses and losses" (including income taxes), concluding with net income. This format is known as a **single-step statement**. There is just one step—*revenues* minus *expenses* equals *net income*.

In practice, a strict single-step income statement is extremely rare. All companies are required to segregate gains and losses of discontinued operations from net earnings (or loss) from continuing operations, as we will explain later in this chapter. As well, almost every company will segregate income tax expense from other expenses. Thus, a pure single-step statement is a rare sight, indeed.

Multiple-Step In contrast to a single-step income statement, most companies provide some sort of **multiple-step statement**, in which subtotals are presented after each section that presents certain types of income (or gain) and/or expense (or loss). IFRS encourages companies to provide additional line items, headings, and subtotals that are relevant to an understanding of the company's financial performance.

Both Air Canada and Bombardier Inc. use a multiple-step format. Air Canada (see Exhibit 3-1) has its first subtotal as "operating income," which includes the effect of all operating revenue and operating expenses (except income tax). In contrast, Bombardier (see Exhibit 3-2) draws its first subtotal for "gross margin." Gross margin is a common subtotal for manufacturing and mercantile entities, but it is optional.

Both companies present amounts for:

- Earnings before interest and taxes (EBIT); and
- Earnings before income taxes (EBT).

Many companies report these subtotals, but they certainly are not required. It is perfectly acceptable to simply include both interest expense and income tax expense as line items within the general expense category. Also, many companies will segregate **unusual items**, which usually are gains and losses that are not a part of normal earnings; such companies may highlight a subtotal labelled *earnings before unusual items*.

The IASB has shown some displeasure with multiple subtotals such as "earnings before unusual items" and EBIT. The Board is concerned that these "non-GAAP" measures of earnings suggest that there are several ways of measuring earnings, that is, by ignoring certain items of expense on the basis that they are nonrecurring or unusual.

The IASB's concern is that the qualitative criterion of *faithful representation* requires that all factors affecting profitability for a period should be taken into account in profitability analysis, both for feedback value and predictive value. Unusual items are a fact of life for all entities, especially for large companies.

One item that does require special attention is *discontinued operations*. The results of operations that have been discontinued (e.g., sold) during the reporting period are relevant for measuring profit or loss for the period but are irrelevant as a basis for predicting future earnings. Thus, if a company reports discontinued operations, additional subtotals *must* be provided both before and after discontinued operations—(1) earnings from continuing operations after tax and (2) earnings after discontinued operations net of tax.

Air Canada had a loss of $55 million from a discontinued operation. Later in this chapter, we will discuss the details underlying the reporting of discontinued operations.

Other Comprehensive Income

Exhibit 3-3 shows Bombardier's consolidated SCI. Bombardier presents a separate SCI following the statement of income. When separate statements are prepared, the first line of the SCI *must* be the net income shown on the last line of the income statement. The SCI format is straightforward:

- Net income/earnings/profit

- The items of OCI, segregated into two general categories:
  - Items that may be reclassified to earnings in a later period
  - Items that will never be reclassified to earnings
- The total comprehensive income allocated to the company's shareholders and NCI (if any).

As we noted earlier, there is no EPS calculation because "earnings" does not include items of OCI.

Bombardier's items in the first section (those that may be reclassified to net income) involve unrecognized (in earnings) foreign exchange changes and cash flow hedges for foreign exchange commitments. The first two lines are changes for 2011; the third line is the reclassification (known as *recycling*) of prior years' amounts to income (that is, moved from OCI to the income statement), while the fourth line represents the net income tax relating to the first three lines. Confusing? Well, do not worry about it now. You will have plenty of opportunity to fathom this mystery much later in your course.

The company also has an item labelled "CCTD." This means "cumulative currency translation difference." It arises because Bombardier has investments in foreign subsidiaries, but the Canadian dollar equivalent of those investments keep changing as currencies fluctuate. It is really just a mechanical outcome of the consolidation process, and it would get reclassified to net income only if and when the parent company sells or shuts down the one or more foreign subsidiaries. Again, you get to worry about this item much later in your accounting education.

Only one item appears in Bombardier's "never reclassified" section, and that is "net actuarial gains (losses)" relating to employees' pensions. Two other items that would be reported in this section are (1) revaluation surpluses and (2) fair value adjustments to certain types of financial instruments. Bombardier has neither of these items.

Net Income or Comprehensive Income?

If you are trying to understand a company's earnings, what is the "correct" measure of a company's earnings? IFRS seems to give us at least three options: (1) earnings after tax from continuing operations, (2) net income, or (3) comprehensive income.

The only EPS figures that IFRS requires are those based on net income, both before and after discontinued operations. There is no calculation of comprehensive income per share. Nevertheless, some financial analysts are beginning to emphasize comprehensive income rather than net income because they want to include all gains and losses in their calculations.

Including all of OCI in a periodic earnings analysis is unwise. As you go through the following chapters, you will come to understand the nature of the various items that flow through (or stay in) OCI. OCI is a mixed bag into which IFRS puts changes arising from valuations that we do not quite know what else to do with. One of those changes (translation of investment in foreign subsidiaries) is a purely mechanical result of the consolidation process; some others have more economic substance but relate to future periods, not the current period.

CONCEPT REVIEW

1. What are the two sections of the SCI? Explain the nature of the items that go into each section.

2. What components of net earnings are *required* by international accounting standards?

3. How might interest expense on long-term debt be presented differently in a single-step versus a multiple-step income statement?

INCOME TAX ALLOCATION

Intraperiod Tax Allocation

As the name implies, income tax allocation is the process of allocating a company's total income tax expense to various categories within the financial statements of any reporting period. If an item is shown *net of related tax*, it means that the tax consequences of the item have been determined and the reported amount is shown after these tax effects have been adjusted for.

Determining this amount is the process of **intraperiod tax allocation**. *Intra* means that the allocation is within the period and within the SCI and the components of shareholders' equity. The total amount of income tax expense (or benefit) must be reported along with the components to which they relate:

- Continuing operations;
- Discontinued operations;
- Items of other comprehensive income; and
- Other components of shareholders' equity.

For example, you can see in Exhibit 3-3 that Bombardier allocated income tax effects relating to each individual component of OCI. Intraperiod tax allocation also applies to the *cumulative effect of a retrospective change in accounting policy*, shown in the statement of changes in equity.

The crucial aspect is that net earnings from continuing operations should include only that portion of a company's total income tax expense that relates directly to continuing operations.

Interperiod Tax Allocation

A different aspect of reporting income taxes in the financial statements is known as *interperiod tax allocation*, although accounting standards consider it a form of liability recognition rather than tax allocation. **Interperiod tax allocation** is the allocation of a company's income tax liability to different reporting periods, which is covered in depth in Chapter 16.

Although we will not discuss interperiod allocation in depth here, you will see its results on most financial statements as amount for "deferred taxes" (or "future income taxes," which means the same thing). IFRS uses "deferred," which is what we will use in this book. You will often see a line for *deferred* (or *future*) *taxes* on either the face of the income statement or in the disclosure notes, as well as one or two lines on the SFP. The income statement usually shows only one line for income tax expense (or benefit) but that amount is almost always composed of two components:

- Current income tax (or benefit); and
- Deferred (or future) income tax (or benefit).

Usually, the components are shown in a note rather than on the face of the SCI.

"Current income tax" is the amount paid (or payable) to the government on taxable earnings in the current year. The amount of deferred income tax expense is not payable for current operations, nor is it a liability to the government. Instead, it reflects the possible impact of certain items of revenue and/or expense on future years' income taxes.

Some items of revenue and expense are taxed in one year but included in accounting earnings in a different year. When that happens, the current tax expense reflects only revenues and expenses actually reported (legally) on the company's income tax return. The calculation for deferred income taxes is intended to reflect the taxes that *would have been paid* if the company had reported exactly the same items of revenue and expense on the tax return as it reports on the income statement.

By far the most common source of deferred tax expense (and liability) arises from the difference between capital cost allowance (CCA) for tax purposes versus accounting depreciation and amortization expense. For a company following IFRS, it is almost impossible to avoid this difference.

If you see a deferred tax *gain* on the income statement (and an asset on the SFP), it almost always reflects the probable future benefits from tax loss carryforwards.

If this seems confusing, we are not surprised. Do not worry about it now. You will have plenty of time to worry about it next semester, when you get to chapters 16 and 17. The important point now is simply that the *deferred income tax expense does not represent a current cash flow*. Also, the deferred tax liability on the SFP does not mean that the company actually owes that amount to the government.

ASSET DISPOSALS, DISCONTINUED OPERATIONS, AND RESTRUCTURING

Sometimes a company decides to make significant changes in the way it operates. There are many reasons for making changes: for example, to cut costs and restore profitability, to make the company's production more efficient, or to meet competitive threats.

When a company decides that it can improve its operations, it can take several different approaches. The company can:

1. Shut down or abandon a part of its operations, laying off the employees, and selling some of the company's operating assets;

2. Significantly reorganize the company's operations, but still continue in the same businesses, which usually includes the disposal of at least one major asset or a group of assets; or

3. Sell a major business line as an operating unit (i.e., as a going concern) to the highest bidder, thereby transferring the operation to the buyer intact and as a functioning unit, which is known as a *discontinued operation*.

These are not really distinct scenarios but are points along a continuum, as shown in Exhibit 3-4. Many reorganizations and restructurings involve a combination of these approaches. The following sections will explain the accounting treatment of the different types of disposals.

Asset Disposals

Business enterprises frequently change their business operations by shutting down factories or distribution centres, dropping products, or eliminating product lines. Usually, a company is continuing in the same line of business but has decided that it can obtain greater efficiencies and improve earnings or eliminate losses by getting rid of excess assets (and, unfortunately, employees).

For accounting purposes, we can identify two different scenarios for asset disposals:

1. Disposing of individual noncurrent assets; or

2. Disposing of several assets as a group.

EXHIBIT 3-4

CONTINUUM OF ASSET DISPOSALS

Minor   Major

| Abandonment of a noncurrent asset | Sale of an individual noncurrent asset | Sale of an asset group | Discontinuance of a major line of business or geographic segment |

Under IFRS, assets put up for sale are reclassified from *noncurrent* to *current* on the SFP. They are classified as current assets because the intent is to sell them rather than hold them for productive use.[3]

Abandonment An **abandoned asset** is an asset that a company continues to own but has permanently stopped using. Old mine sites, for example, are often abandoned, even though they still contain resources; the mine is abandoned because the cost of extraction is greater than the value of the resource mined.

An abandoned asset should *not* be reclassified as a current asset because there is no plan to sell it. Depreciation stops, and the asset is written down to its **recoverable amount**, which is the higher of the *value in use* and **fair value less the cost to sell** the asset. If there is no fair value less costs to sell, the asset is written down to zero.

The asset is subject to impairment tests as long as the company owns it. If a periodic impairment test reveals that an abandoned asset's value has *increased*, the asset should be written up, but not to more than its original carrying value at the time of abandonment. The increase in value is recognized as a gain on the company's income statement.

An *abandoned* asset is not the same as an **idle asset**, which is an asset that the company temporarily is not using. In a recession, for example, many companies temporarily shut down factories, but they have not abandoned those assets. Idle assets continue to depreciate and are accounted for as productive assets, even though they currently are not producing.

Selling Individual Assets A company may decide to put an individual asset, or a series of individual assets, on the market for sale.

Current asset If the asset is a *current* asset, no special treatment is necessary as long as the carrying value of the asset does not exceed its recoverable amount. If the recoverable amount is less than the carrying value, a writedown is necessary; the loss will be reported in operating expenses.

An example of a current asset to be disposed of is inventory of a discontinued product line. The inventory's recoverable amount may have been higher than its carrying cost in the normal course of business, but the recoverable amount probably will be less once the inventory is declared as surplus inventory. The inventory will most likely be sold to an inventory clearance company at a price that is well below its carrying value. Thus, the inventory must be written down to its recoverable amount. The amount of any writedown is recognized in operating expenses.

Noncurrent asset Often, a company will put one or more individual *noncurrent* assets, such as a warehouse building, up for sale. The asset had been classified as a capital asset, but once it is removed from productive use and put on the market, it is subjected to an impairment test and written down to recoverable amount, if lower than carrying value. The asset may then be classified as an asset **held-for-sale** if it meets the necessary conditions. A held-for-sale asset is shown on the SFP as a current asset. When the asset is reclassified, depreciation or amortization ceases because it is no longer being held as a productive asset with future benefit beyond its recoverable amount.

Conditions for *held-for-sale* classification for a noncurrent asset Before an asset can be classified as "held-for-sale," two conditions must be satisfied:

1. The asset is available for immediate sale in its present condition; and

2. The asset's sale is *highly probable*, which means satisfying five requirements:
   - The price being asked for the asset must be reasonable, relative to the asset's current condition and fair value;
   - An active program to find a buyer must have been started;
   - Management must be committed to selling the asset;

---

[3] The treatment is a little different under ASPE, as we will explain at the end of the chapter.

- It is unlikely that the offer to sell will be withdrawn or that the terms of the offer will be changed significantly; and
- The sale is expected to take place within one year of the asset's being reclassified as "held-for-sale."

Events or circumstances may delay the sale beyond one year. If the delay is beyond the control of the company, the asset can continue to be shown as a current asset.

ETHICAL ISSUES

The reason for the conditions for reclassifying an asset as held-for-sale is to prevent managers from reclassifying assets as "current" for a short period and then reversing that decision later. For example, a company may have a lending covenant that requires a minimum current ratio. If these restrictions were not in place, an unethical manager could temporarily reclassify a *noncurrent* asset to *current*, claiming that it is held-for-sale, just to meet the current ratio requirement, and then reclassify it back to noncurrent after the reporting date had passed. Clearly, there is an ethical issue involved in the "held-for-sale" classification.

The "held-for-sale" two-step There are two steps to recording a noncurrent asset as held-for-sale:

1. A noncurrent asset that is intended for sale must first be "remeasured" to the lower of its carrying value and its fair value less costs to sell.

2. After remeasurement, the asset can be declared to be "held-for-sale" and classified as a current asset, provided that the five conditions listed above are satisfied.

In general, when any noncurrent asset is written down, the loss is reported as part of that period's net income. If the recoverable amount of the written-down asset increases later, the increase in value is reported in profit or loss as a gain. When a company writes up the asset, the write-up is limited to the extent of any prior writedowns, including any impairments recorded prior to the asset's classification as held-for-sale.

Example Suppose that in early September 20X4, near the end of the company's third fiscal quarter, Finagle Limited (a public company) completes installation of new package-handling equipment in its distribution centre in downtown Montreal. The old equipment is still serviceable but is not as efficient as Finagle's new equipment.

Finagle contacts a major industrial resale firm and requests that the firm put the old equipment on the market for sale. The resale firm believes that it can get a quick sale because there are many start-up companies in the Montreal area that can use serviceable low-cost package-handling equipment. Finagle therefore wishes to reclassify the equipment as held-for-sale.

The original cost of the equipment was $500,000; accumulated depreciation to the date of disuse (i.e., September 20X4) was $240,000, leaving a carrying value of the old equipment of $260,000. The resale firm estimates that the old equipment is worth about $250,000 on the resale market; the firm will charge 20% commission on the sales price. The commission is the "cost to sell." Therefore, the recoverable amount (fair value less cost to sell) is $200,000 (i.e., $250,000 × 80%). The process is as follows:

1. The accumulated depreciation to the date of abandonment will be offset against the original cost of $500,000, leaving a net book value of $260,000 in the equipment account:

Accumulated depreciation	240,000	
Equipment		240,000

2. Finagle will "remeasure" the old equipment by writing it down to $200,000, reporting the $60,000 loss in profit or loss:

Loss on equipment held-for-sale	60,000	
Equipment		60,000

3. Finagle then reclassifies the equipment from a noncurrent asset to current asset:

Equipment held-for-sale (current asset)	200,000	
Equipment (noncurrent asset)		200,000

This series of entries will (1) reclassify the equipment as a current asset at its net recoverable amount and (2) record the $60,000 writedown as a loss to be included in net income. Of course, these entries can be combined into a single compound entry:

Equipment held-for-sale (current asset)	200,000	
Accumulated depreciation	240,000	
Loss on equipment held-for-sale	60,000	
Equipment (noncurrent asset)		500,000

In December 20X4, a sudden economic crisis has the effect of freezing the capital market; few new companies are able to get going. The resale firm advises Finagle that the equipment now can probably be sold for no more than $180,000. Consequently, Finagle writes down the equipment to the new lower estimated recoverable amount: $180,000 × 80% = $144,000. The loss of $56,000 (that is, $200,000 − $144,000) is reported in Finagle's income statement with the following entry:

Loss on equipment held-for-sale	56,000	
Equipment held-for-sale		56,000

In March 20X5, the Canadian financial market begins to recover as the nation finds that the banking and financial system is still sound. The resale firm now begins aggressively marketing the equipment, asking a selling price of $260,000. For Finagle's first-quarter financial reports, under IFRS the company remeasures the equipment and writes it up to $208,000, disclosing the gain as a component of profit or loss:

Equipment held-for-sale	64,000	
Gain (recovery) on equipment held-for-sale		64,000

In July 20X5, the beginning of Finagle Limited's third quarter, the asset is sold for $270,000. The resale firm collects its 20% commission and remits the remaining $216,000 to Finagle. Since the carrying value at the end of the second quarter was $208,000, the company recognizes a gain of $8,000:

Cash	216,000	
Equipment held-for-sale		208,000
Gain on sale of equipment		8,000

In this example, Finagle met all five conditions for reclassifying the asset as held-for-sale:

- The asking price is realistic, according to expert opinion (i.e., the resale firm);

- An active program of sale was started;
- Management is committed to selling the asset;
- It is unlikely that management will withdraw or significantly change the terms of the offer to sell; and
- There is a reasonable expectation of selling it within a year.

Even though it took longer than a year to sell the equipment, the cause of the delay (a general economic financial crisis) was beyond the control of management.

Declassification as "held-for-sale" A noncurrent asset classified as held-for-sale may lose that classification because it no longer satisfies the criteria for held-for-sale classification. The company may have changed its mind about selling the asset, or market conditions have changed so that sale is no longer "highly probable." If that happens, the asset must be restored to its original classification at the lower of:

1. Its net recoverable amount at the date of the decision not to sell; or

2. What its carrying value would have been if the asset had not been reclassified in the first place, that is, if depreciation had continued as usual.

Effectively, this is the lower-of-cost-or-market rule.

Disposal Groups A **disposal group** is a group of assets that are being sold together in a single transaction. A disposal group can consist of both current and noncurrent assets, such as a combination of buildings, equipment, and inventory. As well, a disposal group can include liabilities that are specifically related to the assets in the group, such as a mortgage liability on a building.

Normally, a disposal group is an operating part of the business. For example, a company may decide to sell its warehousing operation to a third party that may be able to operate it more efficiently or at lower cost—this is a form of outsourcing, but with the basic working unit developed by the company and sold to an outside specialist. In this example, the disposal group of assets may include a building, equipment, land, inventory, supplies, and accounts payable.

When a company decides to sell a group of assets, the same general procedure is followed as we described above for a single noncurrent asset:

1. Initially, before classification as a held-for-sale asset, each individual asset and liability in the group is remeasured using the appropriate measurement rules for that item. In other words, the group is not remeasured as a whole, but by its individual components.

2. When the group is classified as held-for-sale, the assets of the group *as a whole* are reported separately as a current asset; the liabilities are reported separately from the company's other liabilities. The group's liabilities cannot be offset against the group assets in the SFP.

3. Future revaluations or remeasurements are based *on the group as a whole*. Individual asset values do not matter because the group will be sold as a whole for a single price.[4]

As with sales of single assets, decreases and subsequent recoveries in recoverable amount are reported in net income; recoveries are limited to the amount of any previous impairment losses. Also, depreciation (or amortization) stops at the date that the group is classified as held-for-sale.

There are two categories of disposal groups:

1. Asset groups that are stand-alone groups, such as the example of a warehousing operation cited above; and

2. Asset groups that are part of a *discontinued operation*.

The following sections will explain the special treatment given to discontinued operations.

---

[4] There are some exclusions from the statement that all of the items in the group are valued together as a group. The exclusions are "scoped out" items specified in IFRS 5, such as deferred taxes and some financial assets. We need not bother with these details at this point in the text.

Discontinued Operations

Although all of the types of asset sales that we have described above could theoretically be viewed as discontinued operations of some sort, the term "discontinued operations" has a quite specific meaning in accounting. The distinction is important because discontinued operations are given special recognition in both the SCI (profit or loss section) and the SFP.

One of the primary functions of the SCI is to provide a basis for investors and others to predict future earnings. If a company is selling a significant revenue-generating part of the company, that sale will have a material impact on predicting future earnings. Therefore, operating results of a discontinued operation are segregated so that financial statement users will not expect the revenues and earnings relating to this unit to continue into the future. The segregation happens not only in the year that the discontinuance decision is made but also for the prior year's comparative income statement (in retrospect).

Similarly, the assets and liabilities of a discontinued operation are segregated on the balance sheet. The assets of a discontinued operation are held-for-sale *current assets* under IFRS (but not under ASPE, as we will see later). Amortization is discontinued, and the *assets* are remeasured at their fair value less costs to sell. Liabilities are *not* remeasured except as may be required for financial instruments, which are discussed much later in the book.

Definition   When a company decides to exit from some part of its operations, the first financial reporting issue is whether termination of that part of the business fits the definition of a "discontinued operation."

To qualify as a discontinued operation, a disposal group must be a *cash generating unit* of the business that constitutes a major line of business or a significant geographic segment. IFRS 5 (see Appendix A) defines a **cash-generating unit** as a "group of assets that generates cash flows that are largely independent of the cash inflows from other assets or groups of assets." In other words, it has to be a unit that generates revenue from its own operations and that can be sold as an operating unit.

IFRS 5 defines a **discontinued operation** as *an operating segment* of a company that either (1) has been sold or (2) is held-for-sale. The "held-for-sale" requirement means that all of the conditions listed in the previous section for disposal of assets and asset groups must be satisfied—that is, an active program to find a buyer; a reasonable asking price based on fair value; expectation of sale within the next year; and so forth.

A crucial aspect of a discontinued operation is that the operation must be *separable* from the rest of the enterprise. That is, the operation must not be so well integrated with the other (continuing) operations that its cash flows cannot be separately identified.

Under IFRS, the special reporting requirements for discontinued operations should be applied only upon the discontinuance of major business segments. The special category of discontinued operations should not be cluttered with the disposal of relatively minor lines of business. Only the big ones matter because their discontinuance can have a significant impact on the decisions of financial statement users. As well, this limitation to major portions of a company's operations ties into the *segment reporting* that is required in the disclosure notes, as we shall discuss in the following chapter.[5]

There is one caveat, however. To qualify as a discontinued operation (or disposal group), the proceeds of the sale must be recovered mainly through a sale transaction, rather than through continuing use. Thus, a company cannot "sell" part of its operations to a third party and then continue to operate the unit and collect the sales price through revenue from the operation.

An operation is reported as discontinued when management has made the decision and has begun the process of selling it or shutting it down. It is quite likely that a plan of discontinuance will be begun in one fiscal year and finished in the next. Almost certainly, any discontinuance plan will extend over more than one public company's quarterly reporting

---

[5] ASPE does not require a discontinued operation to be a *major segment*. As long as the operation is a separable reporting unit, it can be reported as a discontinued operation, as we shall see in the ASPE section at the end of this chapter.

period. Therefore, an operation that is reported as discontinued may, in fact, still be in operation at the end of the fiscal period.

The past tense "discontinued" should not be taken too literally. Remember the one-year future time horizon. An operation that is *expected* to be sold or shut down within the next year is still reported as discontinued.

Example Suppose that an automobile manufacturer also manufactures buses. The bus business is a separate division of the larger company, with separate responsibility and reporting lines within the company and with separately measurable revenues and expenses. The manufacturer decides to sell its entire bus-manufacturing operation. In that case, the bus operation qualifies as a *discontinued operation* for accounting purposes.

To continue one step further, suppose that the automobile manufacturer decides to sell one of its brands, much as Ford Motor Company sold its Volvo line of cars to Chinese auto maker Geely. Even if Ford retained all of the factories that had made cars under the Volvo brand (and used those factories for other products), the sale of the brand is the discontinuance of a cash-generating unit because the cash flows relating to the Volvo brand will be transferred to the new owner.

Purpose-Bought Subsidiaries Occasionally a company will buy another company with the sole purpose of reselling it at a higher price. The practice of buying an asset only in order to resell it is known as **flipping** the asset. When the newly acquired company is purchased, it is reported as a discontinued operation from the date of its acquisition since the buyer's intent is to sell it.

Reporting Discontinued Operations

Statement of comprehensive income The results of discontinued operations should be reported in the SCI as a single line item *after* earnings from continuing operations. The results of discontinued operations should appear in the profit or loss section of the statement, *not* in OCI.

There are two broad components of the total amount reported as net earnings (or net loss) on discontinued operations:

- The net profit or loss, net of related income taxes, from operating the discontinued operation to the date of disposal or the end of the reporting period, if the disposal is not complete by year-end; and
- Writedowns of asset carrying values to *fair value less cost to sell*, and all realized gains or losses on disposal to the extent not previously recognized, net of related income taxes.

Thus, the single amount consists of (1) operating profits or losses plus (2a) completed sales, gains, and losses on assets or asset disposal groups sold, and (2b) uncompleted sales, writedowns to fair value less costs to sell for assets not yet sold. All amounts are *net of related income taxes*.

We will discuss the measurement of writedowns when we get to Chapter 10. The measurement criteria for disposing of a discontinued operation are the same as for disposing of an asset or an asset disposal group. For now, just bear in mind that the net profit or loss from discontinued operations is a combination of the current year's operating revenues and expenses plus the gains and losses on disposal, including any appropriate reduction of assets' book value to their fair value less costs to sell.

Statement of financial position On the SFP, the accounting basis of the assets (and related liabilities) is changed:

- The assets are reclassified as held-for-sale and are reported as a single current asset line item, labelled as *assets of discontinued operations held for sale*; and
- Liabilities are reclassified as a single current liability item as *liabilities related to discontinued operations*.

This is a significant change in status. When a long-lived asset is reclassified as "held-for-sale," its carrying value must be reduced to its fair value less costs to sell. Of course, if the cost-basis carrying value of the asset is below fair value less costs to sell, there will be no writedown. Also, once long-lived assets are reclassified as held-for-sale, amortization stops.

In summary, the effects on the SFP are:

- Depreciation and amortization ceases, effective on the date of the discontinuance decision.
- Current assets are carried at lower of cost or fair value less costs to sell except for those that are reported at fair value under IFRS, such as marketable equity securities.
- Capital assets (tangible and intangible) are carried at lower of amortized cost or fair value less costs to sell.
- All assets are grouped together and shown as a single "held-for-sale" current asset.
- Liabilities continue to accrue and are shown as a single current liability item.

Disclosure In the notes to the financial statements, the company should provide a description of the facts and circumstances leading to the disposal or expected disposal, along with the expected manner and timing of the disposal.

As well, the components of the single amount of net gain or loss from discontinued operations that is reported in the income statement should be disclosed. The components can be shown in the income statement, but companies almost always will put these details in the disclosure notes. The disclosed components should be:

- The revenue, expense, and pretax profit (or loss) of the discontinued operation;
- The income tax amount that is related to the pretax profit or loss;
- The gain or loss recognized on the remeasurement of assets and liabilities to fair value less costs to sell; and
- The income tax relating to the remeasurement gain or loss.

If the disposal is not finalized during the current fiscal year, there will be additional revenues, expenses, gains, and losses between the beginning of the following year and the date that the disposal is completed. Those amounts will be reported in that following period, when they are recognized, and must not be anticipated by any accruals in the year that the decision to discontinue was made. Subsequent-year adjustments must be reported separately as *discontinued operations* and not "hidden" in other revenues and expenses.

Adjusting Comparative Statements As we have seen, when a business segment is discontinued, the operating results for that segment are segregated from operations that will continue into the future. To improve comparability, the operating results of that segment should also be reclassified from continuing operations to discontinued operations in prior periods' income statements.

Reclassifying prior periods' results will enable financial statements readers to see more clearly the impact of this period's discontinued operations and thus to better analyze results of operations that are continuing beyond the current year-end.

Illustration The Board of Directors of Pacific Eastern Corporation (PEC), a large consumer products company, approved a plan to sell its Automatic Transmission Diagnostic Centres division at a Board meeting on 30 August 20X1. The division is a cash-generating unit of PEC. PEC engaged professional business valuators to appraise the fair value of the division's assets and solicited competitive bids from prospective buyers for the division. PEC then engaged the consultancy firm of KGMP to assist with the bidding and selling process. At 31 December 20X1, the following information is available:

- From 1 January 20X1 through 30 August 20X1, the division earned $7 million before tax.
- From 1 September through 31 December 20X1, the division earned an additional $2 million before tax.
- The evaluators estimate that the fair value less costs to sell of the division's net assets is $40 million; this is $5 million less than the $45 million carrying value on PEC's books.
- The bidding process closes on 31 January 20X2. Final negotiations and preparation for sale are expected to extend to at least the end of April, after which date PEC expects to have no continued interest in the division.

- PEC managers estimate that due to uncertainty surrounding the fate of the division, the division will probably lose $4 million between 1 January 20X2 and the closing date of the sale.
- PEC managers expect to receive a total purchase price of at least $50 million when the deal is finalized.
- PEC will have to pay a 5% commission to KGMP on any sale.
- PEC's marginal income tax rate is 30%.

The disposal of this division qualifies for reporting as a *discontinued operation* in 20X1 because the sale has been properly authorized, the division is a separate and separable division of the company, a plan is in place to actively sell the division, PEC will have no interest in the cash flows or operations after the sale, and the other criteria cited above appear to have been met.

The next issue is what amount should be reported in the discontinued operations section of PEC's 20X1 financial statements. The total reported amount on the income statement will be a net gain of $1,400,000, consisting of the following components (which should be reported in a disclosure note):

Earnings from operations for 20X1, before income tax ($7 m + $2 m)	$9,000,000
Reduction in carrying value of the assets to estimated fair value	(5,000,000)
5% commission to be paid on the estimated asset fair value less costs to sell of $40 million (that is, the estimated *cost to sell*)	(2,000,000)
Income tax expense related to all of the above [($9 m − $5 m − $2 m) × 30%]	(600,000)
Total gain (loss) on discontinued operations, net of tax, 20X1	$1,400,000

The gain of $1,400,000 is the division's profit, adjusted for the asset impairment and the cost to sell the division. The anticipated operating loss for 20X2 is not included, nor is the estimated gain or loss arising from the final sale.

Suppose that in 20X2, the division is sold to an Australian company for $53 million, minus the 5% commission and minus estimated additional income tax expense of $3 million. The net amount to be shown in PEC's 20X2 earnings is:

Sales price, gross	$53,000,000
Less carrying value of assets sold (net of cost to sell, recognized in 20X1)	(40,000,000)
Sales commission not previously recognized [($53 m − $40 m) × 5%]	(650,000)
Income tax expense not previously recognized	(3,000,000)
Profit on discontinued operation, 20X2	$ 9,350,000

Distinction between asset groups and discontinued operations The major difference in accounting for discontinued operations (as contrasted with other asset group disposals) is that both (1) gains and losses from disposals and (2) operating profit or loss are segregated and reported below earnings from continuing operations. In contrast, the gains and losses from other asset disposal groups continue to be reported as part of earnings from continuing operations, even though some companies may choose to segregate them as "unusual" items.

Disclosure Example Exhibit 3-5 shows the lower portion of the income statement for Armtec Infrastructure Inc., an Ontario-based manufacturer and marketer of construction

---

EXHIBIT 3-5

ARMTEC INFRASTRUCTURE INC.

Reporting Illustration—Discontinued Operations

Extract from the consolidated statements of earnings:

(in thousands of dollars, except share amounts)	Years ended 31 December	
	2011	2010
Net (loss) earnings from continuing operations attributable to owners of the company	$(269,793)	$ 4,896
Net earnings from discontinued operations (Note 21)	—	6,606
Net (loss) earnings attributable to owners of the company	$(269,793)	$11,502
Basic and diluted (loss) earnings per share or unit—continuing operations	$ (11.74)	$ 0.24
Basic and diluted earnings per share or unit—discontinued operations	—	$ 0.33
Basic and diluted (loss) earnings per share or unit	$ (11.74)	$ 0.57

Source: Aastra Technologies Limited, 2011 Audited annual financial statements, page 4, www.sedar.com, posted 22 March 2012.

Note 21. Discontinued operations

The assets and liabilities related to the cement packaging operation (the "Packaging Business"), which was not a core part of the Group's business, were presented as held for sale following Trustee approval on September 31, 2010. The transaction closed on 1 November 2010, and the Group recorded a gain on disposal of $5,230 including a deferred income tax recovery of $736. The results of operations of the Packaging Business have been segregated and presented separately as discontinued operations in the consolidated financial statements.

The results of the Packaging Business were as follows:

For the year ended 31 December	2010
Revenue	$7,155
Earnings before taxes from discontinued operations	1,329
Recovery of deferred income taxes	47
Net earnings from discontinued operations	1,376
Gain on disposal including deferred income taxes of $736	5,230
Net earnings from discontinued operations	$6,606

Source: Armtec Infrastructure Inc., 2011 Audited annual financial statements, page 44, www.sedar.com, posted 8 March 2012.

---

and infrastructure products, as well the disclosure note relating to discontinued operations. Armtec's statement of earnings presents EPS in the three-step format described earlier in this chapter—separately for continuing operations, discontinued operations, and total. Also, note that "Note 21" includes two components in deriving the net earnings from discontinued operations: (1) the net earnings for the period during which it operated plus (2) the gain on disposal. Both these components must be disclosed.

Restructuring

Restructurings are a fairly common phenomenon in most lines of business. If a company does not restructure its operations from time to time, it is apt to get out of date and begin to falter.

Companies often develop plans for major restructuring. Those plans may involve any or all of the disposal options that we have already discussed as well as significant additional costs. Restructuring usually requires relocation costs, retooling costs, training costs, and so forth. A particularly important aspect of most reorganizations involves the employees. Frequently, the employee group is reduced, sometimes quite drastically, thereby obligating the company to provide severance pay and other termination benefits, such as counselling services.

Definition of a Restructuring Plan   Restructurings show up rather often in financial statements. This is partially due to the rather restrictive guidelines for reporting discontinued operations, as we discussed above. If an operational change does not qualify under IFRS as a discontinued operation, it often ends up being reported as a restructuring. However, restructuring has its own definition and requirements under IFRS. IAS 37 defines a **restructuring plan** as a plan that has two characteristics:

1. The program must be planned and controlled by management; and

2. The program must significantly alter:

   a. The manner in which the business is conducted, and/or

   b. The scope of business in which the company is engaged.

Take special note of the words "*significantly alter.*" The IFRS does not want companies to clutter up its financial reporting by treating minor operational adjustments as restructurings. Only major alterations in an entity's operations may be reported as restructurings under IFRS. Major restructurings should be a flag to investors and creditors to expect a change in the nature of the entity's operations and therefore the earnings and cash flows in future periods.

The definition of a restructuring plan is one thing; it is quite another to decide (1) *what* costs can be recognized and (2) *when* they can be recognized. The costs to be recognized must only be direct expenditures arising from the restructuring plan, and they must not be related to the ongoing or continuing activities of the company.

For example, suppose a communications company has decided to restructure its mobile phone manufacturing facilities. Some employees will be let go, with severance pay and supplemental benefits. Those costs clearly are direct expenditures arising from the restructuring plan. However, other affected manufacturing employees will be retrained and relocated to other divisions of the company. Those costs cannot be included as costs of the restructuring because the employees will still be employed by the company.

The *future* costs of a formal restructuring plan can be recognized in the financial statements only if the future expenditures are a *constructive obligation*.

Definition of a Constructive Obligation   A **constructive obligation** is a liability of uncertain timing and amount that will arise in the future as a result of an entity's present or past practices and actions. Without the guidance of accounting standards, any company could set up a provision for future costs arising from current or past decisions. Indeed, in past years, many companies did set up "provisions" for poorly defined future costs of restructuring and other potential costs. It is easy for a company to "say" that it is going to take certain actions in the future, but it is something different to carry through with those actions. Without strong limitations on a company's ability to establish such provisions or "reserves," management can be strongly tempted to use these provisions as a way of manipulating profits by subsequent "adjustments" to the projected costs.

For example, it is not unusual for a company's management to announce that it will lay off thousands of employees, but then either not lay anyone off or lay off significantly fewer employees. While that outcome is good for the employees, it is not good enough to merit recognition of severance costs when the announcement is made.

Therefore, in order for a constructive obligation to exist, the company must not only have publicly communicated the restructuring plan in detail, it also must have taken specific actions to implement the plan. One example of a specific action is reaching agreement with the affected employee group for early retirements, layoffs, retraining, and termination of employees. Such an agreement would identify the employees affected, specify the timing of the various actions, and provide a reliable estimate of the costs.

Exhibit 3-6 shows a flow chart for deciding when a *provision for restructuring costs* can be recognized. If any step is not satisfied, the company cannot recognize the estimated future expense or the future liability as a provision in its financial statements—the restructuring plan should only be disclosed in the notes.

Provision for Restructuring Cost   A **provision** is *a reliably estimable liability for a probable cost that will arise due to a past action*. As you can see, the definition of a provision is derived from defining and recognizing the liability rather than the cost. This approach is in line with the definitions of financial statement elements that we discussed in Chapter 2. An expense arises from an increase in liabilities—thus, a restructuring cost is recognized in the income statement because the increase in liabilities (the constructive obligation) triggers recognition of an expense.

Since a provision must be based on reliable estimates, it follows that costs that cannot be reliably estimated must be excluded from the provision. Other costs can be added to the provision as they become reliably estimable. That means that not all of the costs for a restructuring plan will be recognized as a liability and as an expense in the first period. Both newly estimated costs and revisions of previously recognized costs will show up in the income statements throughout the years of restructuring, as well as in later years as payments are actually made (e.g., for separation payments).

One final important point—restructuring costs are reported as an expense under *continuing operations* in the profit or loss section of the SCI. The only exception arises when the restructuring plan will include the discontinuance of a major segment of the business or a geographic area of operations. Then, only the discontinued operation will be reported *below* the line for "earnings from continuing operations" while other restructuring costs will be reported as expenses *above* that line.

Disclosure Example   A good example of restructuring is provided by the annual financial statements of Wescast Industries Inc. of Guelph, Ontario. Wescast manufactures parts for automobiles and trucks. In the economic distress of 2008–2009, the Canadian auto parts manufacturing industry was hit hard by the near-bankruptcy of two of the Big-3 U.S. auto manufacturers. Many auto parts companies simply went out of business due to a complete loss of sales. Wescast survived but endured a significant loss.

To meet the crisis, the company undertook a major restructuring plan. In 2008, the company charged $72.7 million to expense as a "Restructuring charge." Most of the cost was for impairment of long-lived assets, but $13.5 million was the estimated cost for employee severance. During the year, the company wrote down its long-term assets by $58.3 million and paid out $2.4 million for severance, leaving a current liability for "Restructuring charge" of $12 million on the year-end 2008 balance sheet.

Exhibit 3-7 shows the Wescast disclosure note for restructuring that appeared in the company's 2011 financial statements. We can see in this note that the company:

- Paid out cash of $1,973,000 in 2010 and $356,000 in 2011 the debit for these expenditures would have been to the liability account, and thus they do not appear in the income statement.

- Reduced the estimated amount of the outstanding liability by $746,000 in 2010 and $146,000 in 2011 these amounts show up in the income statement as "Restructuring recovery."

- At the end of 2011, the company has a remaining current liability of $3,095,000, shown on the balance sheet as "Provisions."

EXHIBIT 3-6

RECOGNIZING A RESTRUCTURING PROVISION

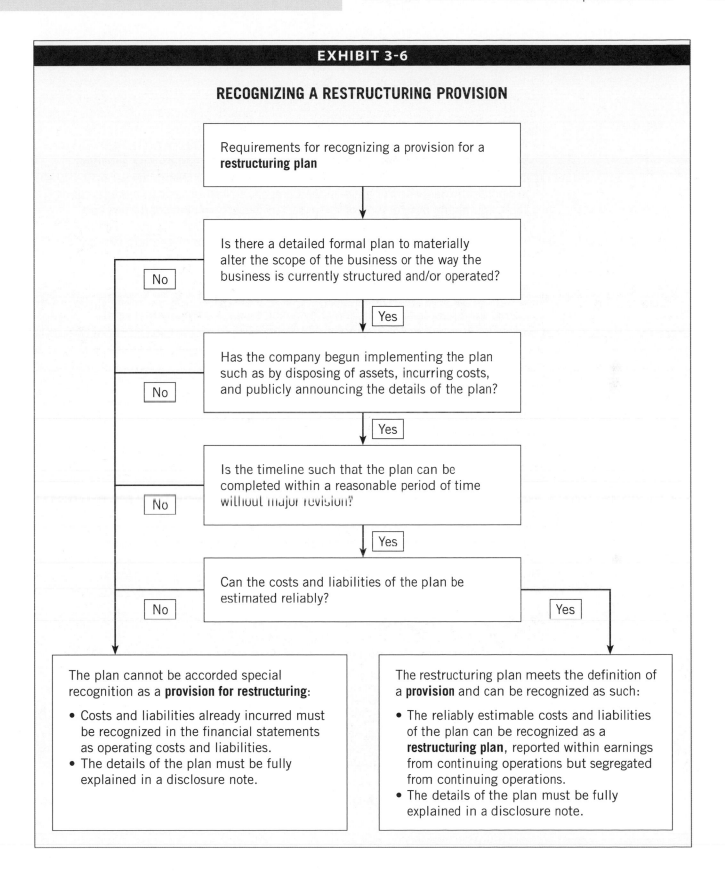

Requirements for recognizing a provision for a **restructuring plan**

Is there a detailed formal plan to materially alter the scope of the business or the way the business is currently structured and/or operated?

No

Yes

Has the company begun implementing the plan such as by disposing of assets, incurring costs, and publicly announcing the details of the plan?

No

Yes

Is the timeline such that the plan can be completed within a reasonable period of time without major revision?

No

Yes

Can the costs and liabilities of the plan be estimated reliably?

No

Yes

The plan cannot be accorded special recognition as a **provision for restructuring**:

- Costs and liabilities already incurred must be recognized in the financial statements as operating costs and liabilities.
- The details of the plan must be fully explained in a disclosure note.

The restructuring plan meets the definition of a **provision** and can be recognized as such:

- The reliably estimable costs and liabilities of the plan can be recognized as a **restructuring plan**, reported within earnings from continuing operations but segregated from continuing operations.
- The details of the plan must be fully explained in a disclosure note.

EXHIBIT 3-7

NOTE 5—PROVISIONS

Restructuring

The Company recorded a net recovery of expense of $146 (2010 – $746) related to its North American operations during 2011. Restructuring activities began in 2008 to adjust the Company's cost structure, to streamline various support activities, and to right-size the Company's North American manufacturing footprint, all in consideration of the expected industry market conditions and resulting lower demand for the Company's products in North America. The net recovery of expense of $146 in 2011 was due to fewer employee terminations than planned under the original restructuring plan as a result of improved North American automotive market conditions. The Company expects that the restructuring provision will be paid out by the end of 2014.

The following table highlights the activity and balance of the restructuring provision for the fiscal years ended 2010 and 2011:

(in thousands of Canadian dollars)	Employee Termination Benefits	Other	Total
December 28, 2009	$ 5,819	$ 497	$ 6,316
Cash payments	(1,960)	(13)	(1,973)
Recovery of expense	(743)	(3)	(746)
January 2, 2011	3,116	481	3,597
Cash payments	(209)	(147)	(356)
Recovery of expense	(146)	—	(146)
January 1, 2012	$ 2,761	$ 334	$ 3,095

Source: Wescast Industries Inc., 2011 Audited annual financial statements, page 19, www.sedar.com, posted 29 March 2012.

CONCEPT REVIEW

1. Explain the difference between an *idle* asset and an *abandoned* asset. What is the accounting treatment for an asset that a company is abandoning?

2. What are the two necessary conditions that must be satisfied for a noncurrent asset to be reclassified as *held-for-sale*?

3. What is a *disposal group*? How is a disposal group reported on the SFP?

4. Define a *cash generating unit*. Why must a *discontinued operation* be a cash-generating unit?

5. What is the reporting objective of the special treatment given to *discontinued operations*?

Looking Forward

In 2011, the IASB began the process of reconsidering the conceptual framework, including the role of comprehensive income. Respondents to a 2011 survey raised a number of issues concerning the SCI, such as the basic nature of comprehensive income and OCI, a lack of clarity between the roles of profit or loss and OCI in measuring an enterprise's performance, and a perception that OCI has become a "dumping ground" for controversial items.

In March 2013, the IASB released an early draft of a series of discussion papers on possible changes to the Conceptual Framework. One paper addresses issues that have been raised about the SCI. The paper attempts to set out a set of principles by which to improve the reporting framework. The goal is to improve the measurement of "financial performance," but it concedes that IFRS does not define what financial performance means.

One major suggestion is that only two general types of items should be reported in OCI: (1) bridging items and (2) mismatched remeasurements. The paper also raises the question of whether the term "comprehensive income" should be replaced by a more understandable term.

Interestingly (and perhaps a bit frighteningly), there are some who hold the view that there should be no differentiation between profit or loss and OCI. That is, the subtotal of profit and loss should be eliminated and only one final amount should be shown for comprehensive income.

Do not hold your breath to witness the outcome. Discussions on changes to the Conceptual Framework take a long time to work through. Nevertheless, there clearly has been a lot of discomfort expressed by both preparers and users with the present content of OCI, particularly those with items that are never recycled into profit or loss.

ACCOUNTING STANDARDS FOR PRIVATE ENTERPRISES

Comprehensive Income

There is no SCI in Canadian ASPE; only an income statement should be provided. The concept of *other comprehensive income* does not exist in ASPE. Instead:

- Net income after taxes is transferred directly from the income statement to retained earnings (or via the statement of changes in retained earnings, if a separate statement is prepared);
- Unrealized foreign exchange translation gains or losses related to a foreign subsidiary (a component of OCI under IFRS) are reported as a separate component of shareholders' equity; and
- Any other nonearnings items that affect shareholders' equity are reported in shareholders' equity, as appropriate.

Under ASPE, *consolidated* financial statements are not required. The statements of a private enterprise are not issued to the public, and users are presumed to be knowledgeable. If a user wants consolidated statements, he or she can request them (or insist on them, in the case of a major provider of capital, such as an institutional investor).

Format

- ASPE does not specify a format other than the obvious fact that it should begin with "revenue" and end with "net income." There is no requirement for basing the expense disclosure on "functional" versus "nature of expense" approach as required by IFRS.
- ASPE requires just one subtotal in the statement, and that is for "income or loss before discontinued operations." Other subtotals are permitted, but none is required.
- As with IFRS, discontinued operations are reported separately after earnings from continuing operations, net of income tax.

Thus, the default position for ASPE is a single-step statement to derive earnings from continuing operations, followed by a line for discontinued operations net of income tax. Otherwise, subject to the line item requirements below, items can be listed in whatever arrangement the company chooses.

Line Items

In general, all of the line items required by IFRS are also required under ASPE, *except* for information relating to total employee expenses, which is *not required*. Additional detail on some items is required:

- The amounts of major categories of revenue recognized
- The amount of inventories recognized as expense
- Income from investments should be disclosed not only in total but also broken down into earnings from:
    - Nonconsolidated subsidiaries;
    - Investments measured using the equity method;
    - All other investments measured at cost; and
    - All other investments carried at fair value.
- The amount of exchange gain or loss included in net income
- The amount of gain or loss recognized on long-lived assets (including disposal groups) disposed of or reclassified as held-for-sale
- Separately, the amounts charged for:
    - Amortization of property, plant, and equipment;
    - Impairment losses on property, plant, and equipment;
    - Amortization of intangible assets;
    - Impairment losses on goodwill; and
    - Impairment losses on intangible assets.
- Net gains and losses recognized on financial instruments
- Share-based compensation and other share-based payments
- Separately, interest expense related to:
    - Current liabilities;
    - Long-term liabilities; and
    - Capital lease obligations.
- Unusual revenues, expenses, gains and losses that are not normal business activities of the enterprise
- Government assistance credited directly to income
- Income taxes on continuing operations
- Net income (loss) after taxes relating to discontinued operations

While this may look like a long list, it really is not very significantly different from IFRS. Most of this detail is shown in the notes rather than on the face of the income statement.

Held-for-Sale Assets

IFRS classifies held-for-sale assets as current because the expectation is that they will be sold within one year. In contrast, ASPE continues to classify the assets as current or noncurrent, depending on their nature. The only exception is when a noncurrent asset is sold prior to the date of completion of the financial statements and the proceeds from the sale are expected within the next year. Note that this reclassification as "current" does *not* require the asset to be sold prior to the year-end but only prior to finalizing the year's financial statements.

When a company writes down an asset and classifies it as "held-for-sale," any subsequent increase in value is recognized in net income only to the extent that the asset had been written down *after* its classification as held-for-sale. The asset's initial remeasurement before its reclassification becomes the upper limit.

Restructuring

ASPE does not specifically deal with restructuring. However, the general concepts underlying the recognition of constructive obligations still would apply for private enterprises.

Earnings per Share

Earnings per share amounts are not required. Indeed, EPS is not even mentioned in ASPE. The reason is that private companies are very closely held, often by just one person or one family, and there is no widespread share ownership or fluctuating number of outstanding shares as in a public company. Dilution of earnings is not an issue.

RELEVANT STANDARDS

CPA Canada Handbook, Part I (IFRS):
- IAS 1, Presentation of Financial Statements
- IAS 8, Accounting Policies, Changes in Accounting Estimates and Errors
- IAS 37, Provisions, Contingent Liabilities and Contingent Assets
- IFRS 5, Non-current Assets Held-for-sale and Discontinued Operations

CPA Canada Handbook, Part II (ASPE):
- Section 1520, Income Statement
- Section 3475, Disposal of Long-lived Assets and Discontinued Operations

SUMMARY OF KEY POINTS

1. Public companies must report *comprehensive income*, which has two components: (1) profit or loss (i.e., net income), and (2) *other comprehensive income*. OCI generally includes value changes that have been recognized in the SFP but are excluded from periodic earnings, either temporarily or permanently.

2. Comprehensive income can be presented either in one continuous statement, or in two consecutive statements with net income as the final line of the profit or loss statement (i.e., income statement) and also as the first line of the SCI, which must follow immediately on the same page.

3. Companies can report expenses in the profit and loss section either by *nature of expense* or by *function*. Under either presentation approach, two compulsory expense disclosures are (1) depreciation and amortization expense and (2) the cost of employee benefits.

4. Both IFRS and ASPE require a subtotal for net earnings from continuing operations (net of income tax). IFRS encourages companies to provide information, headings, and other subtotals that will help the financial statement reader understand the company's financial performance.

5. Income taxes must be allocated over two dimensions: *intraperiod*, which is within the financial statements of a reporting period, and *interperiod*, which allocates the income tax burden to the current and future years.

6. Intraperiod tax allocation apportions income taxes to current operations, discontinued operations, items of OCI, and transactions involving share capital.

7. Interperiod tax allocation apportions income tax to current and future operations. Tax relating to future operations is *deferred* (or *future*) income tax and is the result of differences between asset and liability bases for tax and accounting purposes. Deferred tax does not represent a currently payable liability (or asset), and it cannot be reported on the SFP as a current liability (or asset) under IFRS.

8. When a company discontinues use of a noncurrent asset or a group of noncurrent and current assets, those assets may be abandoned or put up for sale. Amortization stops and the assets are remeasured to net recoverable amount. If sale is highly probable, the assets can be reclassified as "held-for-sale" current assets.

9. Held-for-sale assets are subject to impairment tests. If the recoverable amount declines, they must be written down. If the value subsequently increases, they should be written up, but not higher than the original "remeasured" value.

10. The gains or losses resulting from the sale or abandonment of an operating segment, whose activities represent a separate major line of business, must be reported, net of income tax effects, as a separate component of income, positioned after income from continuing operations.

11. Companies often restructure their operations to match their operations with the market and remain efficient and effective. When management establishes a formal restructuring plan and takes action to put it into effect, it may be appropriate for the company to establish a provision for restructuring cost. The provision is based on the obligations that the company undertakes in conjunction with the restructuring, such as for employee severance pay and related costs.

KEY TERMS

abandoned asset
accounting income
basic EPS
cash-generating unit
comprehensive income
constructive obligation
diluted EPS
discontinued operation
disposal group
economic income
fair value less the cost to sell
flipping
held-for-sale

idle asset
income
interperiod tax allocation
intraperiod tax allocation
multiple-step statement
noncontrolling interest (NCI)
provision
recoverable amount
restructuring plan
single-step statement
statement of comprehensive income (SCI)
unusual items
weighted average number of shares

REVIEW PROBLEM 3-1

The following information is taken from the adjusted trial balance of Killian Corporation at 31 December 20X5, the end of Killian's fiscal year:

Account	Amount
Sales revenue	$1,000,000
Service revenue	200,000
Interest revenue	30,000
Gain on sale of capital asset	100,000
Cost of goods sold[1]	630,000
Selling, general, and administrative expense[2]	170,000
Interest expense	20,000
Loss on sale of long-term investment	10,000
Loss from earthquake damage	200,000
Loss on sale of assets of discontinued business segment	60,000
Loss on operations of discontinued business segment	10,000

[1]Consists of depreciation of $30,000, employee wages and benefits of $40,000, and $580,000 of merchandise purchases less $20,000 increase in inventory.
[2]Includes depreciation of $35,000 and employee wages and benefits of $90,000.

Other information:

a. The income tax rate is 30% on all items.

b. There were 100,000 common shares outstanding throughout the year. No preferred shares are outstanding.

c. Assume that the capital cost allowance deductible for tax purposes is equal to the depreciation expense shown on the income statement.

Required:
Prepare in good form:

1. A single-step SCI by nature of expense.
2. A single-step SCI by function within the enterprise.
3. A multiple-step SCI by function within the enterprise.

REVIEW PROBLEM 3-1—SOLUTION

1. Single-step income statement, by nature of expense:

KILLIAN CORPORATION

Statement of Comprehensive Income

For the year ended 31 December 20X5, in Canadian dollars

Revenues and gains:	
Sales revenue	$1,000,000
Service revenue	200,000
Interest revenue	30,000
Gain on sale of capital asset	100,000
Total revenue and gains	1,330,000
Expenses and losses:	
Cost of merchandise purchased, less increase in inventory	560,000
Employee wages, salaries and benefits	130,000
Depreciation	65,000
Other operating expenses	45,000*
Interest expense	20,000
Loss on sale of long-term investment	10,000
Loss from earthquake damage	200,000
Income tax expense on continuing operations [see computations below]	90,000
Total expenses and losses	1,120,000
Income from continuing operations	210,000
Loss from discontinued operation (net of $21,000 income tax)	(49,000)
Net income and comprehensive income	$ 161,000
Earnings per share:	
Income from continuing operations	$ 2.10
Income (loss) from discontinued operation	(0.49)
Net income	$ 1.61

*($630,000 + $170,000) – ($560,000 + $130,000 + $65,000) = $45,000

Computation of income tax expense:

Total revenues		$1,330,000
Expenses from continuing operations, before income taxes:		
Merchandise cost	$560,000	
Employee cost	130,000	
Depreciation	65,000	
Other operating expenses	45,000	
Interest expense	20,000	
Loss on sale of long-term investment	10,000	
Earthquake damage	200,000	1,030,000
Taxable income		300,000
Tax rate		30%
Income tax expense on continuing operations		$ 90,000

2. Single-step income statement, by function:

KILLIAN CORPORATION
Statement of Comprehensive Income

For the year ended 31 December 20X5, in Canadian dollars

Revenues and gains:	
Sales revenue	$1,000,000
Service revenue	200,000
Interest revenue	30,000
Gain on sale of capital asset	100,000
Total revenue and gains	1,330,000
Expenses and losses:	
Cost of goods sold	630,000
Selling, general and administrative expense	170,000
Interest expense	20,000
Loss on sale of long-term investment	10,000
Loss from earthquake damage	200,000
Income tax expense on continuing operations [see computations below]	90,000
Total expenses and losses	1,120,000
Income from continuing operations	210,000
Loss from discontinued operation (net of $21,000 income tax)	(49,000)
Net income and comprehensive income	$ 161,000
Earnings per share:	
Income from continuing operations	$ 2.10
Income (loss) from discontinued operation	(0.49)
Net income	$ 1.61

Computation of income tax expense:

Total revenues		$1,330,000
Expenses from continuing operations, before income taxes:		
Cost of goods sold	$630,000	
Selling, general and administrative expenses	170,000	
Interest expense	20,000	
Loss on sale of long-term investment	10,000	
Earthquake damage	200,000	1,030,000
Taxable income		300,000
Tax rate		30%
Income tax expense on continuing operations		$ 90,000

3. Multiple-step income statement, by function:

KILLIAN CORPORATION

Income Statement

For the year ended 31 December 20X5

Sales revenue		$1,000,000
Cost of goods sold		630,000
Gross margin		370,000
Operating expenses:		
Selling, general, and administrative expenses		170,000
Income from continuing operations before the undernoted		200 000
Other revenues and gains:		
Service revenue	200,000	
Interest revenue	30,000	
Gain on sale of capital asset	100,000	330,000
Other expenses and losses:		
Interest expense	(20,000)	
Loss on sale of long-term investment	(10,000)	(30,000)
Income from continuing operations before unusual item		500,000
Unusual item: Loss from earthquake damage		(200,000)
Income from continuing operations before income tax		300,000
Income tax expense		90,000
Income from continuing operations		210,000
Loss from discontinued operation (net of $21,000 income tax)		(49,000)
Net income and comprehensive income		$ 161,000
Earnings per share:		
Income (loss) from continuing operations		$ 2.10
Income (loss) from discontinued operation		(0.49)
Net income		$ 1.61

Alternative arrangements of the information above the income from continuing operations line are allowed for all formats. In single-step statements, there commonly is a subtotal for *income from continuing operations before income tax*. In multiple-step statements, other revenues and other expenses are commonly combined into a single category of *other revenues and expenses* instead of being shown in two categories.

The amount of earnings from continuing operations should be identical in every presentation, as should all of the items below that subtotal.

REVIEW PROBLEM 3-2

In August 20X5, TLC Printing Ltd. installed a new six-colour printing press to enable the company to produce high-quality posters and handbills in high volume at low cost. The new printer replaced a four-colour printer that had been purchased in 20X0 for $550,000. Accumulated depreciation on the old printer amounted to $230,000 through the end of July 20X5.

TLC's management put the older printer up for sale through Like-New Inc., a used-equipment dealer. The asking price was $320,000, an amount that the dealer had evaluated the old printer to be worth on the open market. The dealer was confident of obtaining a fairly quick sale as there always were new start-ups in the commercial printing business. Upon sale, the dealer will retain a sales commission of 10%.

At the end of 20X5, the dealer informed TLC that due to new innovations in high-speed laser printers, the market for standard four-colour presses had declined. The dealer advised that a more likely resale price would be $290,000, although the public asking price would be retained at $320,000.

On 4 February 20X6, the dealer sold the printer to a corporation that wished to establish its own in-house printing capability. The sales price was $310,000.

Required:
Prepare the journal entries necessary to record for foregoing information in TLC's accounting records.

REVIEW PROBLEM 3-2—SOLUTION

a. 31 August 20X5—Offset the accumulated depreciation against the original historical cost:

Accumulated depreciation	230,000	
Equipment		230,000

The equipment now has net book value of $320,000.

b. 31 August 20X5—Remeasure the equipment to the lower of carrying value [$320,000] and its fair value less cost to sell [$320,000 − $32,000 = $288,000]: $320,000 − $288,000 = $32,000:

Loss on equipment held-for-sale	32,000	
Equipment held-for-sale		32,000

The old printer's book value now is $320,000 − $32,000 = $288,000, which is the estimated net sales value.

c. 31 August 20X5—Reclassify the printer from a noncurrent asset to current asset:

Equipment held-for-sale (current asset)	288,000	
Equipment (noncurrent asset)		288,000

31 December 20X5—Write down the equipment to the new lower estimated recoverable amount: $290,000 × 90% = $261,000. The loss of $27,000 (that is, $288,000 − $261,000) is reported in TLC's income statement with the following entry:

Loss on equipment held-for-sale	27,000	
Equipment held-for-sale		27,000

d. 4 February 20X6—Record the sale for a net amount (less $31,000 commission) of $279,000:

Cash	279,000	
Equipment held-for-sale		261,000
Gain on sale of equipment		18,000

QUESTIONS

Q3-1 What is the difference between *economic income* and *accounting income*?

Q3-2 How does *comprehensive income* differ from *net income*?

Q3-3 Why might the term "income" mean different things?

Q3-4 Under IFRS, what are the two alternative presentation formats for the profit or loss section of the SCI?

Q3-5 What is *noncontrolling interest* (*NCI*)? How does it arise?

Q3-6 What totals or subtotals does IFRS *require* in arriving at net income on the income statement?

Q3-7 What is the objective of providing subtotals within the income statement?

Q3-8 What are unusual items? How might they be reported on the income statement?

Q3-9 Define earnings per share (EPS). Why is it required as an integral part of the income statement?

Q3-10 What is the difference between *basic* EPS and *fully diluted* EPS?

Q3-11 What is the difference between *intraperiod* and *interperiod* income tax allocation? Explain how intraperiod tax allocation affects the statement of income and comprehensive income.

Q3-12 What is the difference between the accounting treatments of an *abandoned* noncurrent asset and an *idle* noncurrent asset?

Q3-13 What are the two primary conditions that must be satisfied for a noncurrent asset to be reclassified as a held-for-sale current asset?

Q3-14 What is a disposal group? What types of assets and liabilities may be included in a disposal group?

Q3-15 If an asset disposal group is reclassified as held-for-sale, what is its measurement basis?

Q3-16 When can a disposal group be reported as *discontinued operation* rather than simply as an asset held-for-sale?

Q3-17 A company has a segment that it decides to sell, effective 1 September, after incurring operating losses of $45,000 to date in the fiscal year. The segment, with net assets of $310,000, was sold for $240,000 on 1 November, after incurring further operating losses of $30,000. Assume a tax rate of 25%. What amounts would be disclosed in the income statement?

Q3-18 What is the definition of a *restructuring plan*?

Q3-19 Define a *constructive obligation*? When does such an obligation arise?

Q3-20 How can estimation errors arise when accounting for asset disposals such as disposal groups and discontinued operations?

CASE 3-1

DELUCA SOLUTIONS INC.

Deluca Solutions Inc. is an Ontario-based manufacturer. The company is listed on the TSX, but the family of founder David Deluca retains control through multiple-voting shares.

Deluca undertook modernization of its production facilities during fiscal year 20X4. As part of the modernization process, the following events occurred:

1. Production equipment has been replaced by newer systems. The old equipment will be sold if a buyer can be found. The company has not yet identified a method for finding a likely buyer for the equipment. At the time its use was discontinued, the equipment had a carrying value of $1,000,000. Deluca's production manager estimates that it could be sold for about half that price, at best.

2. The company discontinued using a small four-year-old building that has housed one part of a production process. Since the building is on Deluca's property, among the company's other buildings, it is not feasible to sell the building or to rent it to an outside organization However, it is quite possible that Deluca will find a use for it in some future year. The building originally cost $3,000,000 to construct and is being depreciated on a straight-line basis over 20 years.

3. A warehousing conveyor system is being replaced. A buyer for the old system, including supplies and spare parts, is actively being sought so that it can be dismantled to make room for the new system. The warehousing manager estimates that the cost of dismantling the system will be about $600,000. The buyer will be responsible for installation. It is expected that the buyer will cover the cost of shipping, although the relative cost of shipping (depending on the distance to the buyer's facilities) will have an impact on the equipment's realizable value. The equipment has a carrying value on Deluca's books of $4,600,000; Deluca is asking $4,000,000 for the equipment, which is less than the $5,000,000 value estimated by the company that is supplying Deluca's new conveyor system.

4. Deluca has decided that its production and sales for the Eastern Canada area would be more efficient and effective if the company transferred all of its assets in that region to Irving Corporation, an unrelated Halifax-based company. Deluca has negotiated to sell the assets to Irving Corporation for $1,250,000, effective 1 December 20X4. The equipment's current book value is $900,000. Effective 2 January 20X5, Irving Corporation will produce Deluca's products and also will maintain the inventory. Irving will manage the sales force for the eastern region, although all sales and accounts receivable will continue to be invoiced and collected by Deluca. Deluca will reimburse Irving Corporation for the cost of production and direct sales expense plus 50% of the gross margin.

5. The former employees in the Eastern Canada division were offered a choice of moving to the new Halifax owner or receiving six months of severance pay conditional on a promise not to seek employment from the new owner for at least one year. A survey of the affected employees indicated that 60% will elect to accept a transfer. The cost of severance pay for the other 40% is estimated to be $900,000, none of which will be paid out until after the end of the current fiscal year.

Deluca's general manager, Lindsey Adroit, is uncertain as to how the financial aspects of these changes will affect the company's financial statements. The company has a substantial line of credit with the bank, but the credit line is fully drawn, and the manager worries that the bank may reduce the credit line if the reorganization will have adverse effects on Deluca's financial statements.

You have recently been given a summer internship in Deluca's general accounting department. The manager is aware that you are enrolled in some higher-level accounting courses and would like you to prepare a report in which you summarize the reporting consequences of the company's reorganization activities.

Required:

Explain fully how each of these events should be accounted for by Deluca. What will be the impact on Deluca's financial statements for 20X4? To the extent possible, specify the numerical effect on both the income statement and the SFP.

CASE 3-2

HOSPITALITY INC.

Hospitality Inc. (HI) is a holding company that has wholly owned interests in the travel and entertainment industry. HI is listed on the Toronto Stock Exchange and is subject to the reporting requirements of the exchange and of the Ontario Securities Commission. The company has four operating divisions:

1. Travel Adventures Inc. (TAI) is a travel services company. The company sells vacation packages to vacation destinations, both at retail and at wholesale (i.e., to other travel agencies). TAI is incorporated in British Columbia and operates 12 retail travel offices in the province. The company also sells its package vacations throughout Canada through agencies in other provinces.

2. Sunsation Incorporated is a charter airline incorporated in Alberta that operates between Western Canada and various Caribbean and Central American vacation "sun destinations," and also to Hawaii. Sunsation's main customer is TAI. TAI buys bulk seat blocks on Sunsation's flights and resells the seats at retail (and at wholesale to other retail travel agencies). Sunsation also provides flights to sun destinations for an Alaska-based tour company. As a Canadian airline, Sunsation must operate the flights through Vancouver.

3. Elegance Limited is a hotel management company that manages hotels in the Caribbean, Costa Rica, and Mexico. Elegance is incorporated in the Cayman Islands—a "tax haven" that imposes no income taxes on corporations. Many (but not all) of TAI's tours are booked into Elegance's hotels.

4. Brookside Investments Corporation is a real estate company that owns and operates several commercial developments in Canada. Brookside also owns some of the hotels that are managed by Elegance, including all of the Mexican hotels that TAI uses for its tour groups.

The senior executives of each of the operating divisions report directly to the senior executives of HI.

In mid-20X1, the North American economy entered a severe recessionary period. The recession caused a significant decline in the vacation travel business in late 20X1 and throughout 20X2. TAI was forced to cancel about 30% of its planned 20X1 tours due to lack of client bookings. The decline in vacation travel caused many airlines to reduce flight frequency. Due to reduced bookings, Sunsation was no exception. To make matters worse, the general decline in the travel business enabled All-Alaska Airways (AAA) to lease long-range jet aircraft at reduced rates, thereby enabling AAA to take over the charter services that Sunsation had been operating from Alaska because AAA had no need to stop in Vancouver on the way from Alaska to warmer climes.

The multiple effects of the decline in vacation travel caused a sharp drop in revenue from all of HI's business segments, although TAI and Sunsation were affected more drastically than Elegance and Brookside. Elegance, operating through management contracts, and Brookside, with its nontravel-related commercial developments in Canada, have less direct exposure to the travel slump.

The recession has put HI's shares under extreme pressure, and two large HI shareholders demanded that the company "clean up its act" and put the company on sounder footing. Therefore, late in the third quarter of 20X2, HI's Board of Directors developed a restructuring plan. The major components of the plan are as follows:

Changes in Travel Adventures Inc.

Due to the slump in the travel business, HI's Board decided to revamp TAI's operations. TAI announced its intention to close all but two of its retail travel offices, leaving only a single office each in Vancouver and Victoria. The company intended to significantly reduce the volume of personal travel counselling. Instead, the company would focus on corporate business travel and will also develop a stronger Internet presence for selling its tour packages. In December,

HI publicly announced its intention to close 10 of its 12 offices in the first quarter of 20X3, offering transfers to some employees and generous severance packages to all full-time staff. Part-time employees would receive two week's pay after the offices close. TAI estimates the cost of severance packages at $1,340,000, although that amount had not been publicly announced.

TAI also contracted an Internet consultant to help the company develop a detailed request for proposals (RFP) for the planned website development. The RFP was expected to be issued in January 20X3, a development company retained in February, and a new online presence made public in March. HI budgeted $1.5 million for a full-featured website.

Sale of Hotel Properties

To generate some much-needed cash and to relieve HI of the burden of properties with negative cash flow, HI's Board of Directors decided to put the Mexican hotel group on the market. The Mexican hotels were owned by a wholly owned subsidiary of Brookside Investments Corporation.

On 23 November 20X2, after conclusion of a 60-day open bidding period, the HI Board accepted a purchase proposal from Lincoln Goodview Ltd. (LGL). LGL agreed to acquire all of Brookside's shares in the Mexican subsidiary for cash consideration of $250 million. LGL would acquire all of the division's assets and assume all debt related to the Mexican properties. The purchase price was $250 million, based on the fair value of the hotel assets less the present value of the related mortgage debt. The transaction was contingent upon the completion of LGL's due diligence review of the Mexican hotel group's books. LGL's due diligence was expected to be completed in February 20X3. In the meantime, Brookside would continue to operate the hotels and will receive all monies until the sale was finalized, which was expected to occur in February 20X3, pending approval by the Mexican authorities.

The net book value of the division's real estate asset portfolio was $930 million on 23 November 20X2. The appraised fair value on 23 November was $1,240 million. At 31 December 20X2, the fair value of the portfolio was $1,360 million. The fair value of the related debt was $790 million on 23 November and $780 million on 31 December.

In 20X1, the Mexican hotel subsidiary had total revenues of $160 million and net income of $10 million. Revenue for 20X2 was expected to be $110 million, with a net operating loss of approximately $18 million.

LGL agreed to keep Elegance's management contracts for the Mexican hotels in place for at least two years.

Sale of Retail Mall

In July 20X2, HI realized that the company needed to improve its consolidated working capital position to satisfy a debt covenant. Therefore, HI asked Brookside to find a buyer for one of its major retail malls. After reviewing its portfolio, Brookside managers decided to put a fairly new retail mall in suburban Toronto on the market. The mall seemed to be a good prospect for sale as it was located in a growing area populated mainly by fairly wealthy recent (incoming) immigrants from mainland China and was little affected by the recession. The mall had been constructed just three years ago and was carried on Brookside's books at $200 million, of which $15 million would have been charged to expense by the end of 20X2.

Because of the good future prospects for the region and the mall, Brookside decided to retain 51% interest in the mall and sell only 49%. Brookfield retained a facilitator for the sale, promising a 5% commission. Although there was no publicly announced asking price, the facilitator let it be known that Brookside would entertain only offers of $100 million or higher.

Several real property developers in the United States and Canada expressed interest. However, in December 20X2, Brookside accepted an offer from a large pension fund for $123 million, conditional on the buyer's due diligence investigation. The buyer gave Brookside a 10% deposit. The tentative closing date was 15 April 20X3.

Required:

What are the reporting implications of these three transactions? Explain how each would be shown on HI's consolidated statements for the year ending 31 December 20X2. Be specific.

CASE 3-3

KIDSaWARE

KIDSaWARE Incorporated (KWI) is a retailer of children's clothing that has been in operation for over 30 years. The stores are located in Ontario and Quebec.

Four years ago, KWI bought all of the shares of Prairie Kids Ltd. (PKL), an existing chain of retail children's clothing stores that operated throughout Alberta, Saskatchewan, and Manitoba. PKL was struggling against severe competition, particularly from Walmart. KWI had just had a successful initial public offering and believed that it could return PKL to profitability by injecting fresh capital to modernize the stores, coordinating PKL's marketing with KWI's and introducing KWI merchandise into PKL stores.

PKL was maintained as a separate corporate entity. The PKL store managers reported to the PKL district managers, as before, and the district managers reported to the sales manager of KWI. All corporate affairs were conducted through KWI's head office in Brampton, Ontario.

On 17 September 20X1, however, the KWI Board of Directors decided that the PKL venture was not successful, and the Board decided to put PKL up for sale. KWI paid a broker $100,000 to find a buyer for PKL. If an acquiror could not be found, PKL would be shut down.

In January 20X2, the broker did find a potential buyer. The buyer agreed to acquire PKL, effective 15 March, paying $0.15 per share for 100% of the PKL shares, plus assuming the outstanding debt and all future lease commitments (Exhibit 1). Because the potential buyer had no direct experience with children's wear, a condition of the sale was that KWI management would continue to be involved in managing PKL until the end of the next fiscal year—that is, through the Christmas 20X2 selling season.

Meanwhile, the audit committee was presented with a draft of the KWI income statement (Exhibit 2) that treated the PKL disposal as a discontinued operation. KWI's fiscal year ended on 31 January 20X2.

Required:

1. Assume that the disposal of PKL qualifies as a discontinued operation. Is the draft KWI presentation correct? If not, how should it be reported?
2. Assume instead that the disposal does not qualify as a discontinued operation but that PKL has become a held-for-sale asset as the result of the Board meeting on 17 September 20X1. How would the potential disposal of PKL be reported?
3. Does PKL qualify for reporting as a discontinued operation under IFRS? Explain.

Source: The Canadian Institute of Chartered Accountants, © 2010.

	EXHIBIT 1	

PRAIRIE KIDS INCORPORATED

Balance Sheet (Unaudited)

31 January 20X2

(thousands of Canadian dollars)	Book Values	Estimate Liquidation Values
Assets		
Accounts receivable	$ 584	$ 584
Inventory	10,846	3,841
Prepaid expenses	2,870	NIL
Capital assets	22,869	5,717
Total assets	$37,169	

(thousands of Canadian dollars)	Book Values	Estimate Liquidation Values
Liabilities		
Bank indebtedness	$ 8,051	$ 8,051
Accounts payable and accrued liabilities	18,389	18,389
Long-term debt	4,936	4,936
Deferred lease inducements	854	
	32,230	
Shareholders' equity		
Common shares (8,342,000 shares issued and outstanding)	17,573	
Deficit	(12,634)	
	4,939	
Total liabilities and shareholders' equity	$37,169	

Note 1. The rent expense for the year is $7,147. The minimum rental payments for the leases of the premises are as follows:

20X3	$ 7,253
20X4	$ 7,012
20X5	$ 6,889
20X6	$ 6,599
20X7	$ 6,156
20X8–20X12	$32,035

The rental payments for the store premises are guaranteed by KWI. The rent guarantee is limited to three years of minimum rental payments.

EXHIBIT 2

STATEMENTS OF COMPREHENSIVE INCOME (UNAUDITED)

Year ended 31 January 20X2

(thousands of Canadian dollars)	KWI Consolidated	PKL
Sales	$258,420	$48,421
Cost of sales and store, warehouse, and administrative expenses	(233,122)	(51,209)
Other expenses	(11,859)	(3,088)
Earnings before income taxes and discontinued operations	13,439	(5,876)
Income taxes (current and deferred)	(4,829)	—
Earnings (loss) from continuing operations	8,610	(5,876)
Loss from discontinued operations*	(9,664)	—
Net income (loss) and comprehensive income (loss)	$ (1,054)	$ (5,876)

*The loss from discontinued operations was calculated, in thousands of dollars, as:

Loss from PKLI's operations		$ (5,876)
Sale of 8,342,000 shares at $0.15 per share	$ 1,251	—
Broker's fee	(100)	—
Book value of PKLI's net assets	(4,939)	—
Loss on disposal at $0.15 per share	$ (3,788)	(3,788)
Loss from discontinued operations		$ (9,664)

TECHNICAL REVIEW

eXcel

connect

TR3-1 Accounting Income versus Economic Income: On 1 January 20X1, Tyler Trading Corporation was incorporated by Jim Tyler, who owned all the common shares. His original investment was $100,000. Transactions over the subsequent three years were as follows:

02 January 20X1	Purchased 20 units for resale at $5,000 each.
Throughout 20X1	Sold 12 units for an average of $8,000 each.
31 December 20X1	Remaining eight units have a selling market value of $6,000 each.
15 July 20X2	Bought six units for resale at $7,000 each.
Throughout 20X2	Sold nine units at an average of $12,000 each.
31 December 20X2	Remaining five units have a selling market value of $10,000 each.
Throughout 20X3	Sold all five remaining units at $9,000 each.

Required:

1. Calculate accounting income, based on transactions, for 20X1, 20X2, and 20X3. Assume FIFO.

2. Calculate economic income, based on events or changes in value, for 20X1, 20X2, and 20X3.

3. Compare total accounting income with total economic income, and explain your findings.

4. In what ways is accounting income superior to economic income? In what ways is economic income superior? Use the accounting principles from Chapter 2 to explain.

connect

TR3-2 Comprehensive Income: Acrimony Limited has the following balances in its general ledger on 31 December 20X8 (in thousands of Canadian dollars):

	Debit	Credit
Retained earnings, 31 December 20X7		$40,000
Sales revenue		18,000
Interest expense	$ 780	
Cost of sales	8,000	
Accumulated other comprehensive income, 31 December 20X7		1,350
Dividends paid	2,000	
Foreign currency gains and losses on 20X8 transactions		3,000
Income tax expense	1,120	
Selling and administrative expense	3,400	
Amortization on furniture and fixtures for 20X8	1,050	
Write-off of obsolete inventory	530	
Impairment of tangible capital assets	970	
Additional contributed capital		18,000
Loss on redemption of long-term debt	670	
Unrealized foreign currency translation loss on self-sustaining U.S. subsidiary for 20X8, net of $124 income tax	496	

Required:

Prepare, in good form, a statement of income and comprehensive income. Use a continuous format.

connect

TR3-3 Format of Statement of Comprehensive Income: The accounting records of Food Complex Limited, a publicly listed company, showed the amounts below for the year ended 31 January 20X7, in millions of Canadian dollars. The company had 40 million common shares outstanding throughout the fiscal year.

Dr./(Cr.)	Retail	Wholesale	Dairy	Bakery	U.S.	Total
Sales revenue	$(390)	$(251)	$(45)	$(65)	$(67)	$(818)
Cost of inventory expensed	160	134	12	18	—	324
Employee cost	43	28	17	15	22	125
Other operating expense	16	14	8	13	27	78
Restructuring cost	5					5
Gain on sale of marketable securities						(8)
Interest expense						12
Depreciation expense						96
General advertising expense						21
General corporation administrative expense						33
Loss on discontinued operation	(21)					(21)
Loss on translation of U.S. subsidiary (OCI)						6
Income tax expense (including $5 tax recovery on discontinued operation)						20

Required:
Prepare two different versions of the SCI as follows:

1. By nature of income and expense.
2. By function.

connect

TR3-4 Held-for-Sale Asset: On 13 September 20X1, Nitish Corporation's board of directors moved the company's operations into a newly constructed building and declared its old building available for sale. The original cost of the old building was $20 million; it was 40% depreciated. Other information is as follows:

a. On 15 September, a professional appraisal of the old building estimated its value as $10 million.
b. On 24 September, Nitish Corporation engaged a commercial property developer to place the building on the market for $10 million. Despite some softness in the market the developer expects to be able to sell the building within the next nine months. The developer charges a commission of 6% on final sale.
c. By 31 December, the commercial real estate market had "softened" considerably. Although the developer held the official asking price at $10 million, Nitish and the developer agreed they would consider offers as low as $8.5 million.
d. Despite receiving several "low-ball" offers from prospective buyers over the first two months of 20X2, Nitish's management did not accept any of the offers.
e. By 31 March 20X2, the end of Nitish's first reporting quarter, the market had improved considerably. The developer relisted the property at $11.5 million, its newly appraised value.
f. On 27 April 20X2, Nitish's board accepted an offer of $11.7 million.

Required:
Prepare the appropriate general journal entries to record the information above.

connect   **TR3-5 Disposal Group:** Drabinski Ltd. decided on 1 July 20X3 to dispose of an asset group consisting of land, a building, and equipment. An active plan of disposal is being carried out, and sale is highly probable within the following year. The assets' carrying values and estimated recoverable amounts at 1 July 20X3 are as follows:

	Cost	Carrying Value	Estimated Recoverable Amount
Land	$ 400,000	$ 400,000	$ 420,000
Building	2,700,000	1,500,000	900,000
Equipment	900,000	400,000	300,000
	$4,000,000	$2.300,000	$1,620,000

On 31 December 20X3, the net recoverable amount of the group is reliably estimated to be $1,640,000. On 1 April 20X4, the asset group is sold for $1,700,000, net of costs to sell.

Required:
Prepare journal entries that are appropriate to record the information above.

ASSIGNMENTS

★ **A3-1 Accounting Income versus Economic Income:** Hoskins & Sells is a partnership that was established in March 20X6. If a partner decides to leave the partnership, the value of her or his partnership share will be determined by the net book value of the partnership's net assets at the end of the last-preceding fiscal year.

The following transactions and events occurred during 20X6, in thousands of dollars:

- Acquired land for $200 and constructed a building at a cost of $800. Hoskins expects to use the building productively for about 20 years, after which the company will sell the building and move to new premises. Hoskins will amortize the building at a declining balance rate of 10% per year.
- Purchased furniture for $60. The useful life for the furniture is expected to be 10 years; it will be amortized on a straight-line basis, assuming no residual value.
- Had sales of $900 and operating and other expenses (excluding amortization) of $560.
- At the end of the year, fair value less costs to sell for the assets were as follows:
  - Land, $220
  - Building, $775
  - Furniture, $45

Required:
1. How much is Hoskins & Sells's accounting income?
2. Calculate the economic income.
3. If you were a partner in Hoskins & Sells, would you prefer for the partnership to report its earnings and value its net assets in accordance with accounting income or economic income? Explain.

A3-2 Interpreting the Components of Income: Excerpts from the statements of comprehensive income for Yaoming Adventures Limited for the years 20X2 through 20X4 are as follows:

(stated in millions of Canadian dollars)	20X4	20X3	20X2
Operating earnings from continuing operations, before unusual items and income tax	$30	$25	$20
Unusual items:			
Loss from earthquake damage	—	(40)	—
Gain on expropriation of property	—	—	35
Earnings (loss) from continuing operations, before tax	30	(15)	55
Income tax expense (recovery) on continuing operations	6	(3)	11
Earnings (loss) from continuing operations, after tax	24	(12)	44
Discontinued operations:			
Income from operations of discontinued segment, net of tax	—	10	15
Gain on disposal of discontinued segment, net of tax	50	—	—
Net earnings (loss)	$74	$ (2)	$59

Required:

1. Yaoming has experienced volatile earnings over the three-year period shown. Do you expect this to continue? Why, or why not?

2. Net earnings increased from a loss of $2 million in 20X3 to a profit of $74 million in 20X4, a very substantial increase. Suppose the company's common share price increased only approximately 20% during the same period. Why might this be the case? Relate the 20% increase in share price to the components of net income.

3. Would you expect net income in 20X5 to be more or less than the amount reported in 20X4? More specifically, assuming no new unusual, nonrecurring items, what amount would you estimate net income to be in 20X5?

 A3-3 Income Statement Format: The following items were taken from the adjusted trial balance of the Bremeur Corporation on 31 December 20X5. Assume an average 20% income tax on all items (including the divestiture loss). The accounting period ends 31 December. All amounts given are pretax and are subject to the same income tax rate. Bremeur had 30,000 shares outstanding at the beginning of the year. On 31 August 20X5, an additional 9,000 shares were issued; at the end of 20X5, 39,000 shares were outstanding.

Sales revenue from continuing operations	$695,200
Revenue in business segment being discontinued	75,000
Rent revenue	2,400
Interest revenue	900
Gain on sale of investments	2,000
Distribution expenses	136,000
General and administrative expenses	110,000
Operating expenses in business segment being discontinued	78,000
Interest expense	1,500
Depreciation and amortization	6,000
Settlement of legal claim agains the company	10,000
Asset impairments, discontinued operation	12,000
Cost of goods sold	330,000
Operating loss of discontinued operation to disposal date, before income tax	75,000

Required:

1. Prepare a single-step income statement.
2. Prepare a multiple-step income statement.

A3-4 Income Statement Formats: The information below pertains to the operations of Montreal Retail Corporation for the year ended 31 December 20X6:

Cost of merchandise sold	$102,000
Inventory warehousing cost	20,000
Accounts payable	120,000
Sales revenue	525,000
Accumulated depreciation	140,000
Sales returns	5,000
Unearned revenue	2,000
Depreciation expense	50,000
Rent revenue	4,000
Employee wages, salaries, and benefits	100,000
Interest expense	6,000
Investment revenue	3,000
Loss on disposal of geographic segment	30,000
Earnings from discontinued geographic segment	20,000
Distribution expenses	106,000
General and administrative expenses	46,000
Loss on sale of noncurrent assets	13,000
Income tax expense	?
Fire loss	20,000

Additional information:

- Functional costs do not include depreciation or employee costs.
- Depreciation expense pertains 50% to warehousing cost, 30% to administrative costs, and 20% to distribution expense.
- Employee wages, salaries, and benefits pertain 20% to warehousing and merchandising, 50% to administrative costs, and 30% to distribution expense.
- The company's income tax rate is 20%. Assume that the tax rate pertains to all elements of revenue, expense, gain, and loss.

Required:

1. Prepare an income statement on a functional basis, in a single-step format.
2. Prepare an income statement on the basis of nature of expense, using a multiple-step format.

A3-5 Comprehensive Income: Quebecor Inc. is a major provider of cable services and also the owner of many newspapers. The company reported the following items in its 20X11 financial statements (in millions of Canadian dollars, except per-share amounts):

a. Revenues	$4,206.6
b. Cost of sales and selling and administrative expenses	2,864.9
c. Noncontrolling interest in earnings	182.0
d. Financial expenses	322.9
e. Dividends	12.8
f. Income tax expense—continuing operations	141.9
g. Change in unrealized gain on translation of net investments in foreign operations	1.6
h. Restructuring of operations and impairment of assets	30.2
i. Gain on translation of investments	1.6
j. Reclassification to income of loss related to cash flow hedges (net of tax)	0.6
k. Premium over book value paid on repurchased shares	23.1
l. Diluted earnings per share from continuing operations	3.11

Required:

Identify whether each of the items above would be included in the SCI as (1) part of profit or loss or (2) OCI, or (3) in the statement of changes in shareholders' equity.

★ ★   **A3-6 Comprehensive Income, Intraperiod Tax Allocation:** Haliteck Corporation is based in Halifax. At the end of 20X4, the company's accounting records show the following items:

a. A $100,000 loss from hurricane damage.
b. Total sales revenue of $2,600,000, including $400,000 in the Decolite division, for which the company has a formal plan of sale.
c. Interest expense on long-term debt of $65,000.
d. Increase in fair value of marketable securities of $55,000.
e. Operating expenses of $2,100,000, including depreciation and amortization of $500,000. Of the total expenses, $390,000 (including $75,000 in depreciation and amortization) was incurred in the Decolite division.
f. Haliteck Corporation wrote down tangible capital assets by $35,000 during the year in order to reduce the Decolite division's assets to their estimated recoverable amount.
g. Haliteck has long-term debt that is denominated in U.S. dollars. Due to the weakening of the U.S. dollar during 20X4, the company has an unrealized gain of $20,000.
h. Haliteck has a subsidiary in France. The euro strengthened during the year, with the result that Norse had an unrealized gain of $15,000 on its net investment in the subsidiary.
i. Haliteck's income tax expense for 20X4 is $76,000. This amount is net of a tax recovery of $20,000 on the Decolite division and a $25,000 tax benefit from hurricane damage.
j. The company had 34,000 common shares outstanding at the beginning of the year; an additional 8,000 were issued on March 31.

Required:
Prepare a continuous SCI.

★ ★   **A3-7 Impairment; Bond Retirement:** In December 20X4, the Board of Directors of Mead Corporation approved a plan to dispose of the company's imaging products division. As a result, the company recognized an asset impairment loss before tax totalling $77,000,000. The imaging products division had incurred before-tax losses of $50,000,000 in 20X3 and $41,700,000 in 20X4.

In addition, during 20X4, the company retired an issue of bonds early. These bonds had a carrying value of $200,000,000 and were retired at a cost of $185,000,000, resulting in a pretax gain of $15,000,000. The company had never had such a transaction before.

The tax rate on all the above items is Mead Corporation's average income tax rate of 20%.

Assume that earnings from other sources, before income taxes, were $392,500,000 in 20X3 and $168,900,000 in 20X4. This does not include the bond retirement transaction. The average number of common shares outstanding was 62.2 million shares in 20X4 and 65.1 million shares in 20X3. Mead Corporation has no preferred shares outstanding.

Required:
Prepare the income statements for Mead Corporation for 20X3 and 20X4, beginning with income from continuing operations. Include earnings per share computations.

★ ★   **A3-8 Asset Disposals:** Panych Ltd. discontinued use of three assets during 20X2:

a. A brick kiln that originally cost $100,000 to construct was shut down and retired from service on 30 June. It is being depreciated over 25 years on a straight-line basis. The carrying value (i.e., the net book value) was $40,000 at the beginning of 20X2. Panych has no plans to use the kiln in the future, and it is not saleable since it cannot be moved and is on Panych's private property.
b. The company stopped using a movable concrete casting assembly on 1 April 20X2 due to lack of demand for the assembly to be moved to construction sites. Its use will be restored if and when construction demand picks up. The assembly's original cost was $120,000, and it was 50% depreciated on 1 January 20X2.
c. Panych ceased to use a company-owned cargo plane on 30 September. The plane cost $7,000,000 and now has a carrying value of $2,400,000. The company plans to find a buyer as quickly as possible and has engaged a dealer to look for a buyer. The agent expects to

find a buyer within the following six to eight months. The asking price is $2,000,000. The dealer will take a 3% commission on the sale.

Required:

How should each asset be reported on Panych's 20X2 year-end balance sheet? Be specific as to classification and amount. Prepare journal entries to properly record the change of status of each asset.

★★ **A3-9 Disposal Group:** Zhang Zinc Mines Ltd. decided on 1 April 20X8 to dispose of one of its mining properties in northern Ontario. The property consists of mineral rights (an intangible asset) and the on-site mining equipment. The mineral rights have a carrying value of $1,000,000 while the mining equipment has a net book value (after depreciation) of $400,000. Due to the currently depressed value of zinc on the world market, the value of the mineral rights is estimated to be $800,000. The recoverable amount of the mining equipment is very low, no more than $100,000 because most of the equipment is fixed to the property and cannot be moved at any reasonable cost. Zhang's Board of Directors has launched an active search for a resource company (or a speculator) to buy the mine; the board is confident of finding a buyer in no more than one year. As a public company traded on the TSX, Zhang must provide quarterly statements to the shareholders.

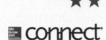

Required:

1. Prepare journal entries to recognize the mineral rights and equipment as a disposal group, including any reclassification entries, if necessary.
2. Assume that at 30 June (the end of the second quarter), the value of zinc has increased and the mineral rights are worth $1,150,000. Prepare any necessary journal entries to reflect the increase in value.
3. On 21 August (in the third quarter), Zhang signs a contract to convey all rights to the mine and the equipment to Rio Tonto Inc., an Australian-based mining company. The contract price is $1,350,000. Prepare the journal entry (or entries) to record the sale.

★★ **A3-10 Disposal Group:** Black Media Inc. owns and operates a large number of newspapers across Canada. On 1 October 20X5, the board of directors voted unanimously to dispose of one of those newspapers, *The Daily Con*. Black Media would continue to publish *The Daily Con* while a buyer was being sought. As Black Media was facing some financial problems, the Board hoped for a quick sale. The newspaper was Black Media's sole holding in that city, and thus the newspaper's assets and liabilities could easily be transferred to a new owner. The Board authorized an immediate search for possible buyers, and the company received several indications of interest by the end of 20X5. The net assets of *The Daily Con* can be summarized as follows:

Carrying Values, 30 September 20X5

	Cost	Accumulated Depreciation	Book Value	Estimated Recoverable Value
Cash			$ 20,000	$ 20,000
Accounts receivable			90,000	80,000
Inventory			110,000	90,000
Motor vehicles	1,400,000	800,000	600,000	300,000
Land	750,000	—	750,000	850,000
Building	2,500,000	2,000,000	500,000	600,000
Equipment and furnishings	450,000	350,000	100,000	80,000
Accounts payable	(120,000)		(120,000)	(120,000)
			$2,050,000	$2,010,000

Required:

1. Does the potential sale of *The Daily Con* qualify for treatment as a disposal group? Explain.
2. Give the appropriate entry or entries pertaining to *The Daily Con* on 1 October 20X5.
3. Assume that there is no change in recoverable amounts between 1 October and 31 December 20X5. Show how the year-end 20X5 SFP and SCI will be affected by the decision to sell *The Daily Con*.

★★ **A3-11 Discontinued Operations, Recording and Reporting:** On 1 August 20X5, Fischer Ltd. decided to discontinue the operations of its services division. The services division is not a separate corporation, but it is a major operating segment, financially and operationally. On 22 September 20X5, Fischer closed a deal to sell the division to Printemp Limited. Printemp will assume responsibility for the current liabilities (e.g., accounts payable and accrued liabilities) that pertain to the division. The facts pertaining to the sale are as follows:

Divisional assets, book values at 1 August 20X5 (cost of $950,000, less accumulated depreciation of $335,000)	$615,000
Division assets, estimated fair values at 1 August 20X5	550,000
Liabilities assumed by purchaser; fair value = book value	270,000
Purchase price paid by Printemp Limited	470,000
Division revenue to 22 September 20X5	690,000
Division profit (before taxes) to 22 September 20X5	55,000
Commission fee paid to the business brokerage that facilitated the sale	80,000
Fischer Corp. marginal income tax rate	30%

On 31 December 20X5, the after-tax net income, including the services division, was $400,000.

Required:

1. Give the entries to record the (a) reclassification and (b) sale of the services division.
2. Complete the 20X5 income statement, starting with income from continuing operations, after tax.
3. Explain what other disclosures and/or reclassifications are necessary in the 20X5 comparative financial statements and notes.

★★★ **A3-12 Discontinued Operations:** Salamander Inc. is a food processing company that operates divisions in three major lines of food products: cereals, frozen fish, and candy. On 13 September 20X1, the Board of Directors voted to put the candy division up for sale. The candy division's operating results had been declining for the past several years due to intense competition from large international players such as Nestlé and Cadbury.

The Board hired the consulting firm Atelier LLP to conduct a search for potential buyers. The consulting fee was to be 5% of the value of any sale transaction.

By 31 December 20X1, Atelier had found a highly interested buyer for the candy division, and serious negotiations were underway. The potential buyer was a food conglomerate based in Brazil; the company offered to buy the division for $4.5 million cash.

On 25 February 20X2, after further negotiations with the potential buyer, the Salamander Board accepted an enhanced Brazilian offer to buy the division for $4.7 million. The Salamander shareholders approved the sale on 5 March 20X2. The transfer of ownership took place on 31 March 20X2.

Salamander's income tax rate is 20%. Other information is as follows (before tax, in thousands of dollars):

	13 September 20X1		31 December 20X1
	Book Value	**Fair Value**	**Fair Value**
Candy division's net assets:			
Current assets	$ 910	$ 820	$ 740
Property, plant, and equipment (net)	4,400	3,200	3,400
Current liabilities	(900)	(900)	(900)
	$4,410	$3,120	$3,240
Net earnings (loss) of the candy division, net of tax:			
13 September to 31 December 20X1			450
1 January to 31 March 20X2			(560)

Required:

1. Prepare whatever journal entries are appropriate at 13 September 20X1, 31 December 20X1, 25 February 20X2, 5 March 20X2, and 31 March 20X2.

2. Assume that the after-tax earnings from continuing operations amounted to $5 million in 20X1. Prepare the lower section of the earnings section of the 20X1 SCI (in thousands of dollars).

★★★ **A3-13 Disposal of Business Segment:** NSC Ltd. has a 31 May fiscal year-end. NSC disposed of its Information Systems Group (ISG) on 31 January 20X3. ISG had a net loss (after taxes) of $37,700,000 in 20X3, to the date of disposal. The division was sold for $475,600,000 in cash plus future royalties through 31 May 20X4, which were guaranteed to be $30,000,000. The minimum guaranteed royalties were included in the computation of the 20X3 gain on the sale of the division. Actual royalties received in 20X4 were $35,500,000. Excerpts from comparative income statements found in the 31 May 20X4 financial statements are as follows:

	Year ended 31 May	
(in millions of Canadian dollars)	**20X4**	**20X3**
Earnings (loss) from continuing operations	$(29.3)	$(105.5)
Discontinued operations:		
Earnings (loss) on operations, net of income taxes of $6.0	—	(37.7)
Gain on sale of discontinued operation (net of income taxes of $1.2 in 20X4 and $34.0 in 20X3)	4.3	182.3
Net income (loss) from discontinued operations	4.3	144.6
Net income (loss)	$(25.0)	$ (39.1)

Required:

1. Determine the net book value of ISG at the date of disposal.

2. Why does NSC report a gain on the sale of the discontinued operation of $4.3 million in the year ending 31 May 20X4?

3. NSC reports an after-tax loss from discontinued operations of $37.7 million for the year ending 31 May 20X3. Over what period was the loss accrued?

★★ **A3-14 Restructuring:** Serena Limited is a Newfoundland-based manufacturer of building materials. In the fourth quarter of 20X1, the Serena Board of Directors agreed with senior management that the company needed to restructure its operations so as to be more competitive, as competition from abroad was beginning to become more intense. Therefore, the Board reviewed and accepted management's recommendations for the following series of actions:

a. Production of insulation products will cease. Instead, a Quebec company will be contracted to supply insulation products that will be sold under Serena's label. Serena's insulation production equipment will be sold, assuming a buyer can be found; if no buyer can be found, the facilities will be scrapped. The current carrying value of the facilities is $2,300,000. Serena's production manager estimates that the equipment could be sold for about $1 million, provided that Serena paid the dismantling (estimated at $100,000) and shipping costs (which would depend on the location of the buyer).

b. The 15 employees currently involved exclusively in insulation production will be given eight weeks' severance pay. The average wage is $800 per week. Eight other employees who are only partially involved in the insulation division will be reassigned to other duties within the organization.

c. The production processes in the adhesives division will be modernized and streamlined. Computer-controlling mixing will be introduced to maintain a more consistent product quality. The cost of the upgrade has been priced at $1,700,000. Employee retraining will be required, which will cost an additional $160,000. The old equipment will be dismantled and the salvage sent for recycling.

By the end of 20X1, the employees of the insulation division had been notified of the outsourcing of insulation products and the planned shut-down of production. Management set 20 April 20X2 as the changeover to outsourcing. Of course, the restructuring plan had become public knowledge by that time, a development that was causing some agitation in the provincial government.

By 20X1 year-end, Serena had entered into a contract for supplying the new computerized equipment for adhesives mixing; the value of the contract was $1,350,000 and Serena had paid a 10% advance to the supplier. Other equipment (estimated to cost $420,000) had not yet been ordered, although a nonbinding memorandum of agreement had been reached with a supplier.

Required:
Assume that Serena Limited is a public company. How would the events described above be reported in its financial statements at the end of 20X1? Be specific.

★★ **A3-15 Restructuring:** Leos Janacek is CEO and controlling shareholder of Mira Products, Inc., a Vancouver-based company listed on the TSX. Mira's principal business is the manufacture of furniture for small children. The company has two product lines: (1) home furniture and (2) institutional furniture for schools, hospitals, daycare centres, and so forth. Home furniture is produced under contract by a manufacturer in Quebec and accounts for about 20% of the company's revenue. The institutional division operates two production facilities on its own, one in British Columbia and another in the Czech Republic. Institutional furniture accounts for a little over 70% of the company's revenue and 90% of its net earnings.

Twelve years ago, Mira had purchased the net assets of a Quebec company that manufactures a well-known line of stuffed animals known as PitaPets, which is also the name of the company. PitaPets has contributed less than 10% of Mira's revenue and a miniscule portion of earnings. PitaPets' products are sold through different outlets than are Mira's furniture product lines.

Mr. Janacek, with the concurrence of the Mira Board of Directors, has decided to restructure the company. Mr. Janacek wants to modernize the Czech production facilities and sell PitaPets to obtain the necessary funds for modernization. Mira was never seriously involved with operating PitaPets, but had let the former owners continue to operate the firm with only broad overview by Mr. Janacek and his CFO.

Consequently, Mira Products Inc. took the following actions by the end of 20X4, the current fiscal year:

a. Operating through a broker, Mira reached agreement to sell the net assets of PitaPets to a U.S. company for $12 million cash, contingent on the buyer's due diligence inspection of PitaPets' books and operations. The closing date for the deal is set for 15 May 20X5. Mira will have to have responsibility for the employees of PitaPets, who will continue to work for that firm subject to any subsequent decisions made by PitaPets' new owners. The year-end 20X4 carrying value of PitaPets' net assets is $8.6 million.

b. Mira publicly announced to the business media (and to the employees) that the Czech operation would be upgraded. The announcement contained the following specifics:

i. Negotiations for equipment modernization were underway with a German manufacturer. Mira had made a deposit of €1 million as an indicator of good faith. The deposit is 90% refundable if Mira and the German manufacturer do not come to an agreement. The estimated equipment cost is €6.6 million. At the end of 20X4, the euro was worth C$1.40. The old equipment will be dismantled and taken away by the German manufacturer at no cost to Mira Products Inc. The carrying value of the old equipment is €1.2 million

ii. Mira will provide retraining to affected employees in the Czech plant. Mira signed a €80,000 contract with a Czech training firm to deliver training over a three-week period once the new equipment is installed. The targeted installation date is 17 June 20X5.

iii. Employees who are surplus to the Czech plant's needs after the modernization will be given six months' severance pay and assistance with finding a new position. The estimated cost of severance is €650,000. At the insistence of the Czech government, Mira deposited €150,000 toward the cost of the severance package in a special restricted account in a government bank.

Required:

Assume that Mira Products is a public company. How should this reorganization be reported in Mira Products Inc.'s financial statements for 20X4? Be specific.

★★   **A3-16 Analytical—Statement Classification:** The following transactions have been encountered in practice. Assume that all amounts are material.

a. A company decided to put the assets of one product line up for sale (intended to be sold within eight months) because management had decided to outsource production of that product to Vietnam. The company established a plan of sale and engaged an industrial broker. The assets consisted of inventory with a carrying value of $40,000 and equipment with a carrying value of $420,000. The estimated recoverable amount was $30,000 for the inventory and $280,000 for the equipment, before deducting a 5% broker's commission.

b. A company suffered a casualty loss (from a fire) amounting to $500,000. The company has had three fires in the last 10 years, but this was significantly more than any such loss experienced before by the company.

c. A company paid $175,000 damages assessed by the courts as a result of an injury to a customer on the company premises three years earlier.

d. A company sold a capital asset and recorded a gain of $70,000. The asset originally had a carrying value of $330,000 but had been written down to $300,000 in the prior year.

e. A major supplier of raw materials to a company experienced a prolonged strike. As a result, the company reported a loss of $150,000. This is the first such loss; however, the company has three major suppliers, and strikes are not unusual in the industry.

f. A Canadian company owns a majority of the shares of a publicly traded subsidiary in India. The shares have been held for a number of years and are viewed as long-term investments. During the past year, 10% of the shares were sold to meet an unusual cash demand. Additional disposals are not anticipated. In the process of translating the subsidiary's financial statements from rupees to the Canadian dollar, a translation adjustment arose from exchange rate changes that occurred over the year.

Required:

For each of the foregoing transactions, explain how financial statement elements will be affected and how the results of the transactions and events should be reported in each company's year-end financial statements.

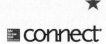

★ **A3-17 ASPE—Income and Retained Earnings Statements:** The 31 December 20X2 year-end trial balance for Dynamics Ltd., a private company, showed the following account balances:

	Dr./(Cr.)
Retained earnings, 31 December 20X1	$(7,800,000)
Sales revenue	(8,400,000)
Dividend income from investments	(60,000)
Cost of sales	4,500,000
Impairment on discontinued plant assets, held-for-sale (before tax)	700,000
General, selling, and administrative expenses	1,800,000
Interest expense	95,000
Reduction in prior years' earnings due to change in accounting policy, cumulative to 31 December 20X1 (before tax)	310,000
Dividends declared, to be paid 15 January 20X3	600,000
Loss due to bankruptcy of major client	135,000

The company pays income tax at a rate of 20%.

Required:

Prepare an income statement and a statement of retained earnings for the year ended 31 December 20X2

★★★ **A3-18 ASPE—Restructuring, Ethics:** Cayman Islands–based Harris Corporation is in the beauty industry. The company develops and produces a wide range of products for hair and skin care. The products are sold both at wholesale (through professional beauty supply stores) and retail (through various types of retail outlets and through hair and beauty salons and spas). Harris also owns a chain of hair styling salons that operate under the name "Hair First." The chain operates through three subsidiaries, each operating in a single province—Ontario, Alberta, and British Columbia.

In 20X3, Harris's Board of Directors approved a restructuring plan that had two principal components that are expected to be completed within the first six to eight months of 20X4:

a. To obtain additional working capital, Harris will sell the factory that produces the skin care products for $1.8 million to a new company that is being formed by the litigation attorney that Harris retains for the many patent infringement cases that beset the industry. Harris will then lease the factory back on a year-by-year basis for $180,000 per year. If the attorney wishes to sell the building, Harris has the "right of first refusal" (which means that Harris gets precedence over other potential buyers). Harris will continue to pay all costs associated with building maintenance and operation. The building originally cost $3 million to construct; its carrying value at the end of 20X3 is $1.3 million.

b. Due to intense competition in Ontario, Harris has decided to divest itself of the Ontario salons. Harris has reached a tentative deal to sell about 60% of the salons to a competitor for $2.4 million; the new owner will continue to operate those salons under the Harris brand, paying Harris a 2% royalty of all Harris products sold through the salons. The current carrying value of the salons (as a group) is $2.8 million. The remaining 40% of the salons will be closed and the staff laid off with four weeks' pay. Severance pay will amount to $600,000. Once all of the salons have been either sold or closed, the Ontario subsidiary will be liquidated and all funds will be transferred to Harris Corporation as the subsidiary's sole secured creditor.

Required:

1. How would these plans and events be reported in Harris's consolidated financial statements at the end of 20X1? Provide specific numbers, to the extent possible.

2. Comment on the ethical aspects of Harris Corporation's plans.

A3-19 ASPE—Restructuring: Return to A3-15 and assume instead that Mira Products is a private company reporting in accordance with ASPE. How would the reorganization affect Mira Products 20X4 financial reporting?

 A3-20 ASPE—Income Statement, Accounting Policies: You have been asked to prepare the financial statements for Ali Corporation, a private Canadian corporation, for the year ended 31 December 20X4. The company began operations in early 20X4. The following information is available about its business activities during the year:

a. On 2 January, Ali issued no par common shares for $600,000.
b. On 3 January, machinery was purchased for $510,000 cash. It was estimated to have a useful life of 10 years and a residual value of $80,000. Management is considering using either the straight-line amortization method or the declining-balance method at twice the straight-line rate.
c. On 4 January, Ali purchased 20% ownership in a long-term investment, ABC Company, for $90,000. During the year, ABC paid dividends of $7,000 and earned net income of $16,000. Ali can use either the cost method or the equity method of accounting for its investment in ABC.
d. Inventory purchases for the year were, in order of acquisition:

Units	Unit Cost	Total Cost
100,000	$4.20	$ 420,000
160,000	4.25	680,000
60,000	4.30	258,000
35,000	4.40	154,000
355,000		$1,512,000

Ali uses a periodic inventory system. There were 50,000 units in ending inventory on 31 December. Management is considering whether to use FIFO or weighted average as the inventory accounting method.
e. Sales during the year were $3,000,000, of which 90% were on account and 10% for cash.
f. Management has estimated that approximately 1% of sales on account will be uncollectible. During the year, $2,070,000 was collected on accounts receivable. When management scrutinizes the year-end outstanding accounts, it estimates that approximately 6% of the accounts will prove to be uncollectible.
g. Additional operating expenses for the year were $1,100,000.
h. On 31 December, the company paid a $10,000 cash dividend on common shares.
i. On 31 December, accounts payable pertaining to operating expenses and inventory purchases totalled $307,000.
j. The cash balance on 31 December was $205,000.

Required:

1. Choosing from the alternative accounting policies described above, prepare a single-step income statement for the year ended 31 December 20X4 that will produce the lowest net income.
2. What are the ethical implications to be considered when selecting from among alternative accounting policies?

(Source: [Adapted] © CGA-Canada. Reproduced with permission.)

≡connect **≡LEARNSMART** **≡SMARTBOOK™**

For more information on the resources available from McGraw-Hill Ryerson, go to www.mcgrawhill.ca/he/solutions.

CHAPTER 4

Statements of Financial Position and Changes in Equity; Disclosure Notes

INTRODUCTION

Quebec-based CAE Inc. is the world's leading supplier of flight simulators and integrated training facilities for the civil aviation industry. In 2012, the company employed 8,000 people around the globe and operated in more than 100 sites in 30 countries. CAE's 2012 statement of financial position (SFP) showed total assets of $3.2 billion. Assets include current assets; property, plant, and equipment; finite-life intangible assets; intangible assets (with indefinite life); goodwill; and deferred income taxes. All $3.2 billion is captured by only 12 lines on the SFP. Yet these assets are reported on a variety of different measurement bases and give only a general overview of the company's asset position.

On the equities side (i.e., liabilities and shareholders' equity), CAE reported a total of about $2.1 billion of liabilities, comprising a variety of short-term and long-term liabilities. The company had shareholders' equity of $1.0 billion, 54% of which was retained earnings.

When assets and liabilities are shown in such a summarized manner, how can a financial statement reader know what underlies a large summary number, such as the $1.3 billion that CAE reports for capital assets? That is where the disclosure notes come in. CAE provided 66 pages of notes to the 2012 consolidated financial statements. The notes contain much of the detail that a user may seek.

This chapter gives a general introduction to the SFP—its format and content as well as the nature and content of the disclosure notes. The various types of assets, liabilities, and shareholders' equity accounts will be discussed extensively in the chapters that follow.

STATEMENT OF FINANCIAL POSITION

The **statement of financial position** (SFP) is a summary statement of the assets and liabilities of an organization at a single point in time. It is like a financial photograph. But every photograph is *static*—it may yield a detailed and seemingly precise portrait, yet a photograph taken a little later may appear quite different.

The SFP is widely known as the **balance sheet**, especially in North America. Practice has swung back and forth over the decades. While "balance sheet" has been the long-time favourite, there have been occasional attempts to require or persuade reporting entities to use the SFP title. Although "balance sheet" continues to be a valid statement title, we will use "statement of financial position" or "SFP" in the context of discussing International Financial Reporting Standards (IFRS) because it is the term used throughout IFRS. Canadian accounting standards for private enterprises (ASPE), however, continues to use "balance sheet" in its standards.

The amounts shown on the SFP are a combination of historical costs, partially amortized historical costs, discounted present values, fair values, and residuals. Many of a company's most important assets (and liabilities, to a lesser extent) are not shown on the SFP at all. Some examples of "missing" assets are the values of trademarks, customer loyalty, and intellectual capital. Liabilities shown on the SFP do not include such items as loan guarantees and potential legal liabilities. We will discuss and illustrate all of these issues as we move through the following chapters. In this chapter, we are concerned with the general format and presentation of the SFP rather than with the measurement of individual items.

Items to Be Reported on the SFP

In Chapter 3, we saw that IFRS requires very little detail on the face of the income statement. In contrast, IFRS prescribes a minimum of 18 different line items to be shown on the face of the SFP, assuming they exist in the reporting company and are not immaterial. The full list is shown in Exhibit 4-1. This exhibit also indicates the chapters in this textbook in which each item is discussed in detail. Therefore, do not be alarmed if you do not know what some of these line items are. You will have ample opportunity to learn more about each of them later.

Classification and Presentation

IFRS permits two methods of classifying assets and liabilities on the SFP:

- On a current/noncurrent basis; or
- In order of liquidity, either decreasing or increasing.

Current–Noncurrent Presentation The most common presentation format is the current versus noncurrent classification. The definition of "current" depends on the operating cycle of the company. The **operating cycle** of a business is the average length of time from the expenditure of cash for inventory or raw materials, to the point of sale and the collection of accounts receivable. For most companies, the operating cycle is less than one year, but can be longer than a year in some industries—for example, construction or wine making. Since the normal audited accounting period is one year, one year is the lower limit on classifying assets and liabilities as current. Thus, we can define current items as follows:

- A **current asset** is one that is expected (or available) to be converted to cash or to be used in production within one year or the operating cycle, whichever is longer.
- A **current liability** is one that is due within one year or the operating cycle, whichever is longer.

If a company's operating cycle is longer than a year, the amount expected to be received or paid after 12 months should be disclosed. This post-12-month portion does not need to be shown as a separate line item on the SFP—note disclosure is adequate.

There is no requirement for any particular subclassification system within the current assets and current liabilities. Managers are trusted to use whatever headings and subtotals will help users to understand the company's operations.

EXHIBIT 4-1

LINE ITEMS TO BE SHOWN ON THE SFP

Assets	Liabilities and Shareholders' Equity
Cash and cash equivalents (Ch. 5)	Trade and other payables (Ch. 12)
Assets held-for-sale (Ch. 3)	Provisions—e.g., restructuring (Ch. 3 & 12)
Trade and other receivables (Ch. 7)	Financial liabilities (Ch. 12, 13 & 18)
Inventories (Ch. 8)	Current tax liabilities (Ch. 16)
Biological assets—e.g., farm products (Ch. 6 & 8)	Deferred tax liabilities (Ch. 16 & 17)
Investments reported on the equity basis (Ch. 11)	Liabilities included in disposal groups classified as held-for-sale (Ch. 3)
Financial assets (Ch. 7)	Non-controlling interests in subsidiaries (Ch. 11)
Intangible assets (Ch. 9 & 10)	Issued capital and reserves (Ch. 14 & 15)
Investment property—e.g., rental property (Ch. 9 & 10)	
Property, plant, and equipment (Ch. 9 & 10)	

Order of Presentation   IFRS does not prescribe the *order* of presentation within each of the current and noncurrent classifications, although an entity should be consistent from year to year in its form of presentation.

Current and noncurrent classification   When a current/noncurrent classification is used, the normal practice in North America is that within each current and noncurrent SFP segment, assets are presented in the descending order of liquidity and liabilities in the descending immediacy of their demand on cash. Current assets start with cash and go down to the least liquid form of asset. Current liabilities start with notes payable (such as short-term bank loans) and proceed to estimated liabilities.

In many other countries, the order of presentation is reversed from the North American practice. The least liquid and longest-term assets are listed first, with increasing levels of liquidity.

Presentation by liquidity   Some types of entities do not use a current/noncurrent classification at all because it does not suit the nature of the entity's operations. Instead, all of the assets and liabilities are presented in order of liquidity (either descending or ascending). This format generally is used by financial institutions such as banks, investment companies, and insurance companies.

Again, a descending order of liquidity (most liquid to least liquid) is normally used in North America, with the most liquid assets shown first, and the liabilities with the shortest maturity listed first. An ascending order is used in some other countries, however.

Other Regional Differences in Presentation   The two prescribed formats of (1) current/noncurrent and (2) order of liquidity apply to both the assets and liabilities, but that classification does not address other aspects of the SFP format. When using either of those two formats, there still can be differences in presentation.

In North America, the overall format of the SFP is to present assets first (current, and then long-term), followed by liabilities and capital. However, companies in many countries use a reverse format. For example, the separate-entity SFP of Daimler AG (the manufacturer of Mercedes-Benz vehicles) shows assets first, but in ascending order of liquidity. Long-term assets are shown first, followed by current assets in ascending order of liquidity. Thus, "cash" is at the bottom rather than the top of the list of assets. On the other side, the presentation is from share capital down to "other liabilities." This style of presentation is common in Europe. Yet another alternative is to show equity and liabilities first and then long-term assets, followed by current assets.

While IFRS defines the two alternative ways of sequencing items within each section, the standards do not prescribe any particular order of the sections themselves. This is due to long-standing practices; to achieve acceptance of the IFRS financial statement presentation standard, it was necessary to accommodate the existing practices around the globe.

Example

Exhibit 4-2 presents the consolidated SFP for Bombardier Inc. Note that it has three columns. The third column is headed 1 February 2011 because the company changed its fiscal year end from 31 January to 31 December, effective in 2011.

IFRS requires an SFP for the beginning and end of each fiscal period being used for comparing financial performance. Financial performance for a period is assessed on the basis of an SFP at each end of the period, plus the statement of comprehensive income (SCI) and statement of cash flows (SCF) for the period. That is, in order to adequately compare Bombardier's 2012 performance with that of 2011, we need a beginning and ending SFP for each of the two years.

Line Items   IFRS specifies that the SFP should contain 18 specific line items, to the extent that the entity has a material amount of those items. Bombardier shows 26 line items, a somewhat more detailed listing than required, especially since the company does not have six of the items listed in Exhibit 4-1, such as held-for-sale assets, investment property, and biological assets.

You will notice that there are no subdivisions within each of the current and noncurrent classifications. This linear presentation is increasingly popular among corporations, since there is limited space for detail. However, entities are free to present greater detail in the form of additional line items, headings, and subtotals that may help the reader understand the company's financial position. For example, PP&E (property, plant, and equipment) could be expanded by listing the major categories on the face of the statement with a subtotal for PP&E.

Note References   Bombardier shows a "Note" reference number for every asset and liability on its SFP except for the two lines for "Advances on aerospace programs." The basic financial statements contain very little detail, as we have also seen in Chapter 3 for the income statement. Companies tend not to provide such levels of detail on the face of the SFP because the detail is provided in disclosure notes. Since a detailed disclosure note must be provided for PP&E, Bombardier does not list the components of PP&E on the face of the SFP.

The final note reference is just below the bottom line of the SFP. This reference, "commitments and contingencies," alerts financial statement users that the company has commitments and contingent liabilities that cannot be measured with sufficient reliability to be shown on the statement but that the user should be aware of.

We will explore the contents of the disclosure notes more fully in a later section of this chapter.

PURPOSE AND LIMITATIONS

The Purpose of the SFP

The basic purpose of the SFP is to provide an overview of the asset and liability structure of the entity. It is *only an overview*. The assets are measured by a variety of methods, including the fair value of most monetary assets, the fair values of some nonmonetary assets, the historical cost of most nonmonetary current assets, and the remaining unamortized historical cost of the company's nonmonetary assets.

Similarly, liabilities have several different measure bases, including monetary commitments, fair values, discounted present values, estimated constructive obligations, and allocation of potential future taxes (undiscounted). Thus, the SFP is definitely not a precise portrait of an entity's financial position; the measurements are full of estimates and approximations, as well as choices of accounting policy. Instead, it is a framework from which to begin analysis and interpretation.

The SFP and the disclosure notes can also provide some insight into the *risk profile* of a business and its *financial flexibility*. Are the company's assets old and fully amortized or relatively new? Are there sufficient liquid assets to cover the short-term monetary liabilities? Is the organization in a position to finance new activities with relative ease without incurring excessive debt? These are important questions that the SFP and its accompanying disclosure notes help address.

EXHIBIT 4-2

BOMBARDIER INC.
Consolidated Statements of Financial Position

(in millions of U.S. dollars)	Notes	31 December 2012	31 December 2011	1 February 2011
		As at		
Assets				
Cash and cash equivalents	14	$ 2,896	$ 3,372	$ 4,195
Trade and other receivables	15	1,525	1,408	1,377
Inventories	16	7,729	7,398	7,307
Other financial assets	17	443	526	705
Other assets	18	683	559	648
Current assets		13,276	13,263	14,232
Invested collateral	30	—	—	676
PP&E	19	2,028	1,864	1,878
Aerospace program tooling	20	4,770	3,168	2,088
Goodwill	20	2,325	2,253	2,358
Deferred income taxes	11	1,452	1,506	1,294
Other financial assets	17	1,316	1,305	1,104
Other assets	18	623	505	462
Noncurrent assets		12,514	10,601	9,860
		$25,790	$23,864	$24,092
Liabilities				
Trade and other payables	22	$ 3,553	$ 3,210	$ 3,073
Provisions	23	1,062	1,078	1,198
Advances and progress billings in excess of long-term contract inventories	16	2,015	1,885	2,370
Advances on aerospace programs		3,053	2,788	2,989
Other financial liabilities	25	455	732	860
Other liabilities	26	2,236	2,262	2,214
Current liabilities		12,374	11,955	12,704
Provisions	23	524	594	614
Advances on aerospace programs		1,600	1,266	1,193
Noncurrent portion of long-term debt	24	5,360	4,748	4,645
Retirement benefits	21	2,997	3,226	1,975
Other financial liabilities	25	601	502	532
Other liabilities	26	957	902	908
Noncurrent liabilities		12,039	11,238	9,867
		24,413	23,193	22,571
Equity				
Attributable to equity holders of Bombardier Inc.		1,331	639	1,454
Attributable to NCI		46	32	67
		1,377	671	1,521
		$25,790	$23,864	$24,092
Commitments and contingencies	37			

Source: Bombardier Inc., or its subsidiaries, 2012 Audited annual financial statements, page 132, www.sedar.com, posted 21 February 2013.

For example, Bombardier's cash resources and trade receivables amount to about $4.4 billion (i.e., $2.9 billion + $1.5 billion), which is more than adequate to cover its short-term payables ("trade and other payables" plus "other financial liabilities") totalling $4.0 billion. Thus, the company's liquidity position appears to be fairly strong.

Liquidity   **Liquidity** is evidence of a company's ability to pay short-term debts from its current assets as well as to meet short-term and long-term obligations. Creditors are obviously interested in assessing liquidity. Beyond this, equity investors are interested in liquidity because it affects dividend payments. Unions examine liquidity to establish bargaining positions. Employees are concerned with the company's continuing ability to pay wages. Liquidity is a major concern to many financial statement users.

While the SFP provides some information about actions and strategy over the year, the SCF contains more information about the investing and financing activities of the company; we will take a look at SCFs in Chapter 5.

Rates of Return   The SFP and the disclosure notes also provide data needed to determine *rates of return*, as well as a variety of other ratios. One commonly used family of ratios is called **return on investment**. Return on investment (or ROI) can be measured in different ways. The most basic measure is the entity's **return on assets**—how much is the company earning on each dollar invested in assets?

Of course, the SCI has to provide the earnings information used to calculate these ratios. Bombardier's SFP shows total assets of $25,790 million at 31 December 2012, compared with $23,864 million on 31 December 2011, averaging $24,827 million over the year. The company's 2012 net income (from Exhibit 3-2) was $598 million for that period. Thus, the company earned a return of 2.4% on its average asset base over the eleven month period: $598 ÷ $24,827 = 2.4%.

Return ratios are very important to financial statement users, both lenders and equity investors, as they help determine the company's credit rating and share price. The figures used in ratio calculations will depend on the accounting policies chosen by the company, however, and therefore must be used with caution.

As well, return ratios work best for companies that have most of their assets on the SFP. Companies whose profitability is based mainly on unmeasured intangible assets may show a very high return on assets, but this is misleading, since the most important assets are not on the SFP. We will consider a different ROI ratio later in the chapter, following our discussion of the statement of changes in equity.

Limitations of the SFP

Amounts Shown on the SFP Are the Result of the Company's Reporting Policies   Even within the constraints of GAAP, alternative accounting policies are acceptable. Many amounts shown on the SFP are the result of a company's chosen accounting policies; different policies will result in different SFP amounts. For example, a company's choice of depreciation policy (e.g., *straight-line* or *declining balance*) will significantly affect the amounts shown for net capital assets, and thereby will affect the amounts shown for total assets and for net assets (i.e., owners' equity). Ratios such as ROI and debt-to-equity will be affected.

The Typical SFP Includes Many Estimated Amounts   The amounts reported on the SFP are affected not only by accounting *policies* but also by accounting *estimates*. For example, the amounts shown for capital assets will be affected not only by the application of a given depreciation policy (such as straight line) but also by the estimates used in applying the policy, such as each asset's useful life and estimated residual value. Other examples of estimates include the estimated loss from uncollectible receivables and the estimated liability arising from warranties.

The impacts of estimates are difficult, sometimes impossible, for an external financial statement user to figure out. As we will see, companies must disclose the nature of measurement uncertainty that could affect financial statement elements. Although the *nature* of measurement uncertainty is disclosed, the potential variation that could be caused by using different estimates (from within a range of feasible estimates) is disclosed in only a few instances, particularly for some financial instruments. However, a public company may disclose more information about sensitivity to estimation error in the **MD&A (Management's Discussion and Analysis)**.

Very Few Values on the SFP Are Current Values and Are Not Intended for Valuation Purposes Most major items on many companies' SFP are reported at historical cost, which is not always a relevant attribute. Investors and creditors may be far more interested in market values. Market value (or fair value) reporting is not a generally accepted practice except for certain types of financial instruments, some types of nonmonetary assets held-for-sale, and capital assets that the reporting enterprise chooses to remeasure at a fair value.

In a set of generally accepted accounting principles (GAAP) statements, market values may be disclosed for nonmonetary assets but generally are not. Companies may choose to prepare non-GAAP statements when market value is significantly different than cost and important decisions have to be based on market value, not cost.

The amounts reported for major asset categories such as plant and equipment may be significantly different from fair value or current replacement cost, given even a modest level of price changes. Individual companies are affected by this problem differently, depending on the date and rate of capital acquisitions, the rate of depreciation, and the level of specific price changes for the types of capital assets they use. Uncritical comparisons between companies can therefore be very misleading.

The historical cost–based SFP can have particularly little relationship to market values when a company's assets are primarily intangible. At least tangible capital assets are valued at their fair value on the date of acquisition; the often negligible cost of many *internally generated* intangible assets is not even close to their fair value. For example, a patent is often recorded only at the legal cost involved in registration. ROI and ratio comparisons are questionable in these circumstances.

Certain Assets and Liabilities Simply Do Not Appear on the SFP For a financial statement element to be recognized, an item must (1) meet the definition of an element, (2) be measurable, and (3) have probable future cash flows. If the recognition criteria are not met, elements are not recognized. Assets that do *not* appear on the SFP include intangible assets acquired at no reliably measurable cost, such as brand names, customer loyalty, and the expertise and skill of the workforce. These assets may have substantial future benefit—usually future revenue cash flows—but cannot be recognized because the future cash flows specifically relating to these "assets" are not measurable.

Significant tangible assets may not appear because they are rented or leased rather than owned. Only certain types of lease arrangements are recognized; most are not.[1] An airline, for example, may lease most or all of its aircraft under operating leases, with the result that the planes do not appear on its SFP. Clearly, however, the airline needs to have the aircraft to operate—they are necessary capital assets but are not recorded. Again, these financial statement elements are excluded from the financial statements because they do not meet the recognition criteria.

Examples of recorded liabilities include (1) some types of lease commitments, (2) hazardous waste cleanups whose cost cannot be reliably estimated, and (3) other unrecognized commitments, such as purchase commitments. Measurement is usually the problem—things that cannot be reliably quantified are not recorded.

Numbers Are Consolidated A company can be quite diversified. For example, Bombardier Inc. operates in four major sectors, each quite different from the others, with subsidiaries in Europe, Asia, and South America. It is not only diversified but also operates through a worldwide network of subsidiaries. Each of its many subsidiaries is a separate legal entity,

---

[1] This may change in coming years; the IASB is working on a revision of the accounting standard on leases, which probably will require all lease and rental agreements greater than one year to be capitalized at the present value of the net lease payments.

with title to its own assets and its own obligations to fulfill. Each subsidiary will prepare its own separate-entity financial statements that will be used by its own creditors and by the income tax authorities in its resident country.

The process of consolidation combines the assets and liabilities of the Bombardier parent corporation with the assets and liabilities of all of its subsidiaries around the world. The result, consolidated financial statements, is an *accounting fiction*. It is fiction because there is no legal entity that comprises all of those assets. Accounting is attempting to give shareholders a broad view of the resources under the *control* of the parent company. While consolidated statements do successfully portray the broad economic entity that goes under the name of Bombardier, most of those consolidated assets do not actually belong to the parent company, nor are most of those liabilities really obligations of the parent company.

Consolidated statements do not tell creditors what assets are available to satisfy their claims. A creditor, whether a trade supplier or a lender, has recourse only to the assets owned by the legal entity to which it has extended credit. Assets held by other corporations within the consolidated accounting group cannot be claimed. It is not unusual for one corporation in a consolidated group to go bankrupt while other corporations in the group remain healthy. The creditors of the bankrupt corporation would be out of luck if they based their lending decisions only on consolidated statements!

In North America, public companies may issue separate-entity statements (that is, non-consolidated) to specific users such as banks and creditors, but are not permitted to issue them publicly to shareholders or to the general public. Thus, as a Canadian company, Bombardier is permitted to issue the company's separate-entity statements only as *special purpose* statements when requested by individual users, such as the holders of the company's long-term debt. However, other countries, such as those in the European Union, either permit or require companies to issue separate-entity statements.

CONCEPT REVIEW

1. What is the definition of "current" for current assets and current liabilities?

2. Why may some of a company's major "assets" not appear on the SFP?

3. What interpretive problems arise from the fact that the financial statements of public companies are consolidated?

SPECIFIC SFP ITEMS

Most of this book is devoted to examining financial statement elements: their recognition, valuation, and required disclosures. This overview of SFP items cannot replace the detailed study that lies ahead of you. Instead, try to gain an appreciation for the overall nature of SFP accounts and their related disclosures.

Assets

Most companies classify assets into the required minimum of two categories: (1) current assets, and (2) noncurrent assets. Subcategories may be used if there are enough items to warrant a separate subcategory. The major categories and the items included therein are described below. Later chapters discuss each type of asset in more detail.

Current Assets

Cash and Cash Equivalents Cash available for operating activities is a current asset. Accounts held for designated purposes (e.g., bond sinking funds) are long term. Short-term, highly liquid investments are known as **cash equivalents** and usually are combined with the cash figure. Cash equivalents are defined as short-term (usually no longer than three months), interest-bearing investments, providing little risk of market value fluctuations.

Short-Term Investments Short-term investments must be readily marketable *and* intended to be held only for the short term. Examples include investments in both debt and equity securities. As noted, some short-term debt investments are cash equivalents that companies group with the cash account. Those that do not qualify as cash equivalents are shown separately as short-term investments. Cash equivalents and other short-term investments are reported at their current market value.

Trade and Other Receivables Trade receivables (i.e., *accounts receivable*) and other receivables should be reported net of estimated uncollectible amounts. Notes and loans receivable within the next year, including those to shareholders, will be reported as current assets. Any receivables pledged as security for an obligation of the firm should be disclosed.

Inventories Inventories usually are reported at the lower of cost or net realizable value. Fair value normally is defined as net realizable value for raw materials, work in process, and finished goods. In some sectors of the economy, inventories are valued at fair value (FV), whether FV is higher or lower than cost. An example is inventory of financial instruments held by investment companies (e.g., mutual funds or investment bankers) reported at market values. Also, biological assets (e.g., cattle, timber) are reported at fair value less costs to sell, even when FV is higher than cost. For long-term projects, inventories usually are reported at cost plus profits recognized when revenue is recognized throughout the earnings process.

Prepayments Prepayments, or prepaid expenses, are cash outlays made in advance of receipt of service. Rent paid in May for the month of June is an example. A short-term prepayment should be classified as a current asset. Prepaid expenses are current assets because by paying cash in advance, the company's cash outlays for the coming reporting period are reduced. A long-term prepayment should be classified as a noncurrent asset.

Assets Held-for-Sale The amount of any assets that are held-for-sale, that are part of a designated discontinued operation, or that comprise an asset disposal group should be reported separately. Discontinued operations and disposal groups were discussed in Chapter 3.

Noncurrent Assets

Assets are noncurrent if:

1. Assets will not be used in the next operating cycle or within 12 months, whichever is longer; or

2. Management plans to retain the assets beyond the next year or operating cycle, whichever is longer.

Financial Assets The principal types of financial assets are as follows:

- *Investments being held to maturity.* A company may invest in the long-term debt instruments of another company with the intent to hold the debt to maturity. This is common in Canada, as most corporate debt is privately placed and therefore is not available for trading. Investments held to maturity are reported at amortized cost. Amortization is calculated on the effective interest method, which will be discussed in Chapter 11. Any unamortized premium is added to the investment, and any unamortized discount is subtracted.

- *Long-term loans and receivables.* These are reported at amortized cost using the effective interest method, as with held-to-maturity investments.

- *Special funds.* Sometimes a company will set aside funds for long-term future use, either as required by contractual arrangements (e.g., compensating bank balances and non-registered pension funds) or as directed by the company's Board of Directors (e.g., expansion funds, share retirement funds, and long-term savings deposits). Special funds are segregated from funds available for current operations. Funds may include cash, but usually the cash is invested in interest-bearing securities. Special funds are shown at their accumulated amount in the fund—contributions plus interest earned to date.

Strategic Investments These are the reporting entity's investments in the shares of related companies, companies in which the reporting entity has significant influence over the related company's strategic operating policies. Such investments are carried at adjusted cost plus unremitted earnings, using the equity method (which we will discuss in Chapter 11).

Biological Assets These are investments in living plants or animals, such as timber stands or cattle, during their period of growth. Biological assets are measured at fair value less estimated cost to sell and becomes inventory for further processing.

Property, Plant, and Equipment This category includes all property, plant, and equipment (PPE) that are used in the company's production or service process, either directly or indirectly. The category is also known as **tangible capital assets**. Historically, tangible capital assets have often been called **fixed assets** because of their relative permanence—this term is generally discouraged because its meaning is not obvious. A wide variety of terminology is found in practice.

PPE includes both (1) items that are depreciated, such as buildings, machinery, and office furniture and fixtures; and (2) items that are not subject to depreciation, such as land. Tangible capital assets also include certain leased assets if the lease arrangement is capitalized (discussed in Chapter 18).

PPE is usually shown on the SFP at its net undepreciated amount—historical cost minus accumulated depreciation. However, if the recoverable amount of a capital asset has fallen below its net book value (or carrying value), the asset must be written down and a loss recognized in net income. If the recoverable amount increases in later years, the asset can then be written up again but only to the level that the carrying value would have been had no impairment loss been recognized (that is, to the prewritedown carrying value less additional depreciation that would have been taken).

A company can choose to use a *revaluation approach* for its PPE. Under this approach, the company can revalue individual assets to their fair value at the reporting date.

Investment Properties **Investment property** includes any land and/or buildings that are held for rental or for capital appreciation. Investment properties cannot be owner occupied. This category pertains mainly to real property development companies. Nevertheless, if any company holds property for rental or for capital appreciation, that property is accounted for as investment property. Investment properties can be reported either (1) on the cost basis (with depreciation, as appropriate for each type of property) or (2) at fair value.

Intangible Assets **Intangible assets** are long-lived assets that lack physical substance. Examples include brand names, copyrights, franchises, licences, patents, software, subscription lists, and trademarks. Intangible assets are usually shown net of accumulated amortization on the SFP, with the accumulated amortization disclosed in the notes.

Some intangible assets are not amortized because they do not have a finite life span. Goodwill acquired by buying another business is one example.

Whether amortizable or not, all intangible assets are subjected to regular *impairment tests* to ensure that they still have a value that is at least equal to their carrying value.

Liabilities

Most companies classify liabilities into two categories: (1) current liabilities and (2) noncurrent liabilities. Within noncurrent liabilities, the most common are (a) long-term financial liabilities, and (b) deferred liabilities, and (c) accrued retirement benefits. The major categories and the items included therein are described below. Later chapters discuss each type of liability in more detail.

Current Liabilities The current liabilities section of the SFP includes all obligations of the company that are due within one year or one operating cycle, whichever is longer. The following categories of current liabilities should normally be disclosed:

• Trade payables—amounts payable for goods and services that enter into the operating cycle of the business;

- Other current payables, such as accrued expenses for payroll and interest;
- Provisions for obligations that will be paid within the next year, either legally due or constructive obligations (such as a provision for restructuring costs, as discussed in Chapter 3);
- Income tax liabilities currently due;
- Financial liabilities other than those above, including short-term notes payable, short-term bank debt, and the current maturities of long-term debt; and
- Unearned revenue (such as rent collected in advance) that will be earned within the next year or operating cycle, whichever is longer.

Long-Term Liabilities A **long-term liability** is an obligation that is due beyond the next operating cycle or during the next reporting year, whichever is longer. Typical long-term liabilities are bonds payable, long-term notes payable, pension liabilities, deferred long-term revenues from customers (e.g., "Advances on aerospace programs" on Bombardier's SFP, Exhibit 4-2), and long-term finance lease obligations.

Long-term liabilities also will include any part of a financial instrument that is debt in substance, even though the instrument may be described by the company as share equity. This type of financial instrument is discussed in Chapter 15.

Offsetting Assets and Liabilities

Normally, assets and liabilities should not be offset against one another. *Offsetting* or *netting* is a procedure by which a liability is subtracted from an asset, or vice versa, and the resulting net amount is disclosed. Such practice defeats the objective of full disclosure and could permit a business to show more favourable ratios. Offsetting is permissible only when:

- A legal right to offset exists; and
- The entity plans to settle the items on a net basis or at least simultaneously.

For instance, it may be permissible to offset a $5,000 overdraft in one bank account against another account reflecting $8,000 on deposit in that *same* bank, provided the bank can legally offset the two deposit accounts.

CONCEPT REVIEW

1. What is the difference between tangible and intangible long-term assets?
2. In what order are assets normally presented on a Canadian company's SFP?
3. What are the two necessary conditions for a liability to be offset by an asset?

STATEMENT OF CHANGES IN EQUITY

A company must include a *statement of changes in equity* as part of its complete set of financial statements. The **statement of changes in equity** (**SCE**) discloses the components of equity and the changes in each component during the reporting period. The SCE reconciles the beginning and ending balances of each component of shareholders' equity. Although "statement of changes in equity" is the title used in IFRS, many companies use the fuller (and perhaps more descriptive) title, "statement of changes in shareholders' equity." Either title is completely acceptable.

Shareholders' equity accounts are derived from three sources:

- Accounts relating to transactions between the company and the shareholders such as (1) share issuance and redemption and (2) retained earnings;
- Components of *other comprehensive income (OCI)*; and
- Equity in the net assets that pertains to non-controlling shareholders of subsidiaries.

We will briefly explain each type of equity account in the following sections. Later chapters will explain each in more detail.

Contributed Capital

Share Capital   Share capital is the paid-in value or par value of the issued and outstanding preferred and common shares of the corporation. This amount is not available for dividend declarations.

Each share class should be reported at its paid-in amount, or, in the case of par value shares, at par value. Par value shares are found only in a very few provincial jurisdictions in Canada but may be found in other jurisdictions (e.g., in the United States, the United Kingdom, and Hong Kong).

Details of the terms and conditions of each class of share capital must be reported separately, including the number of shares authorized, issued, outstanding, and subscribed; also disclosed are conversion features, callability, preferences, dividend rates, and any other special features. Changes in share capital accounts during the period must be disclosed, along with outstanding options.

Share capital also will include any financial instrument (or the portion of a complex instrument) that might be described by the company as debt but that lacks the legal characteristics of debt. Financial instruments are discussed a little later in the chapter under "Specific Significant Disclosures."

Contributed Surplus   This is a subclassification of equity. **Contributed surplus** also is known as **additional paid-in capital**. The most common source of contributed surplus arises in conjunction with the issuance of *par value* or *stated value* shares. When par-value shares are used in a state, province, or country, it is normal for the actual share issue price to be well above the par or "stated" value of the shares.

For example, a share could have a par value of $1 but be issued at any price that the market is willing to pay. If a $1 par share is issued at $50, only $1 per share goes into the share capital account; the "excess" of $49 is credited to additional paid-in capital.

Once upon a time, par value was intended to be the original issue price of the shares. To stimulate sales of new issues, companies would sometimes discount the shares and sell them below par value. However, court judgements held shareholders liable for any "discount" if the company became insolvent, no matter who the current shareholder was. Thus, companies began setting par values far below expected issue prices, thereby avoiding any potential liability on the part of future shareholders as well as improving shares' marketability.

Other sources of contributed surplus are from transactions such as (1) the retirement of shares for less than the original amount paid in for the shares and (2) capital arising from recapitalizations or donations from shareholders.

The entity must maintain a separate account for each type of contributed surplus on the books but they all are combined into a single amount for the SFP. For each type, details and changes during the period must be disclosed.

Equity Components of Debt Instruments   Corporations sometimes issue debt securities that have some characteristics of debt and other characteristics of equity. For example, a company may issue debt securities that require the company to pay interest in cash each year but are convertible into common shares at maturity at the holder's option. The interest obligation is legally binding and must be treated as a debt obligation, while the holder's conversion option has some characteristics of share equity. As a result, the proceeds of the debt issue are shown partially as debt and partially as equity. Accounting for these "complex instruments" is explained in Chapter 15.

Retained Earnings   Retained earnings is essentially a corporation's accumulated net earnings since the company's inception minus dividends paid out. In many corporations, retained earnings is the largest amount in the owners' equity section. A negative balance in retained earnings is called a *deficit* and usually arises when a company experiences continuing operating losses.

Retained Earnings Reserves Retained earnings may be segregated into subclassifications called **reserves**. There are two types of reserves—*restrictions* and *appropriations*. Both types are created by debiting retained earnings and crediting the reserve account. The point of a reserve is to restrict dividends. Regardless of their origin, restrictions and appropriations (and any changes in their balances) must be shown on the SCE (or in the notes).

Restrictions A **restriction** is a reserve mandated by the provisions of a statute (i.e., by law), by contractual requirements, or by the bylaws of the corporation. Restrictions are rare in Canada, but they are common in some other countries (e.g., Germany) where "earnings reserves" are required by law. Restrictions may also be required by contract with lenders or bond holders so that a corporation's Board of Directors cannot freely declare dividends that may undermine the corporation's solvency.

Dividend restrictions usually exist to protect the interests of creditors, shareholders, or employees. They prevent management from paying out all earnings in good years and thereby leaving the company in bad financial state in poor years.

Appropriation In contrast, an **appropriation** is a voluntary reserve created by the Board of Directors. Since an appropriation is a voluntary action of the Board, the Board can also reverse, reduce, or eliminate the appropriation at any time.

Appropriations announce the Board's intention to designate a portion of assets for future use, such as for future plant expansion, or to provide for contingencies, such as a possible unfavourable outcome of a major lawsuit. However, an appropriation is not a substitute for a *provision* if the amount of a probable contingent liability is measurable.

When the need for a reserve has passed, the amount is returned to "unappropriated" retained earnings by reversing the entry that was made to create the reserve. *A reserve account is never debited directly for any reason.* For example, if an appropriation is created for plant expansion and the expansion occurs, the plant expansion is accounted for in the usual fashion, not by a direct charge to the retained earnings appropriation.

Items of Other Comprehensive Income

There are some changes in the reported value of net assets that standard setters do not want to appear in net income but that are reported instead as components of OCI. If value changes are not recognized in net income, their effect must be included elsewhere in shareholders' equity to make the SFP balance. A direct entry to retained earnings is not permitted because retained earnings should be directly affected by only two things: (1) net income and (2) other transactions with shareholders, such as dividends.

OCI consists of three types of items, each of which will be **recycled** into earnings in future periods:

- Changes in value that are recognized in the SFP but will be recognized later in earnings;
- Gains or losses in the current period that will have a matching offsetting loss or gain in a future period; and
- The translation gain/loss on foreign subsidiaries.

We will explain the components of OCI as they arise in later chapters. For now, just bear in mind that the items listed in the "other comprehensive income" section of the statement of comprehensive income have not yet been recognized in earnings.

Translation Gain or Loss on Foreign Subsidiaries When a company has a subsidiary in a foreign country, the subsidiary normally will keep its accounts and prepare its financial statements in its local currency. The parent company must translate those statements into its presentation currency before it is possible to combine the parent's and subsidiary's financial statements into consolidated statements.

Translating the subsidiary's assets and liabilities at the year-end exchange rate will inevitably result in a gain or loss compared with the investment account on the parent's books. The only way to get the consolidated statements to balance is to record a translation gain or loss. That gain or loss has no economic value; it simply is a mechanical result of the translation process. This is a topic covered in depth in "advanced accounting" courses—something to look forward to!

Each year's translation gain/loss is accumulated in an OCI account, usually labelled as "translation gain or loss" or as cumulative currency translation different (CCTD). Each year's change in the balance is recorded as an item of OCI. Such an account is normal for any company that has subsidiaries outside the parent's home country.

Non-controlling Interest in Subsidiaries

As we have emphasized, the financial statements of a public company are *consolidated*. Consolidated statements include 100% of the assets and liabilities of the parent plus 100% of those of its subsidiaries. However, sometimes the parent does not own 100% of the subsidiary. The amount *not* owned by the parent is called the **non-controlling interest** (also known as **minority interest**).

To make the parent's consolidated SFP balance, it is necessary to include an amount in equity to recognize the proportionate part of the subsidiary's net assets that are *not* owned by the parent. For example, suppose one company controls 80% of the shares of another company. The parent will combine 100% of the subsidiary's assets with the parent's assets, even though the parent holds only an 80% equity interest because the 80% ownership give the parent *control* over the subsidiary. The 20% equity of the outside shareholders must be reported on the right side of the statement to make it balance.

Non-controlling interest is shown as a component of consolidated equity but not as equity relating to the shareholders of the parent company. The NCI relates to the non-controlling shareholders' claim on the *subsidiaries'* net assets.

An example of non-controlling interest presentation can be seen in Exhibit 4-2. Bombardier's total shareholders' equity of $1,377 million is divided between $1,331 million relating to shareholders of the parent company, and $46 million relating to non-controlling shareholders' claim on the net assets of Bombardier's subsidiary companies.

Reporting Example 1

Exhibit 4-3 shows Softchoice Corporation's consolidated SCE. Softchoice is a business-to-business marketer of information technology hardware, software, and services. The company is based in Toronto and has a U.S. subsidiary.

The statement is in two sections, the top section for 2012 and the lower section for 2011. The statement has six numerical columns, the first of which is the number of shares. In 2012, the company repurchased 219,600 shares and issued 40,151 new shares for stock options that option holders exercised. Disclosure of share amounts is required, but the disclosure does not need to be in the SCE. The share information usually is disclosed in a note, especially for more complex capital structures.

The company has four types of shareholders' equity, each shown in individual columns: capital stock, contributed surplus, cumulative other comprehensive loss, and retained earnings. Note that Softchoice is reporting in U.S. dollars. On Softchoice's SFP, all four of these equity accounts are shown and totalled. It is not necessary to show each account on the face of the SFP, however; since these amounts are shown in the SCE, their disclosure in the SFP is not required. Just the total shareholders' equity is sufficient.

EXHIBIT 4-3

SOFTCHOICE CORPORATION

Consolidated Statements of Changes in Equity (in thousands of U.S. dollars)

Years ended 31 December 2012 and 2011

2012	Number of shares	Capital stock	Contributed surplus	Accumulated other comprehensive loss	Retained earnings	Total shareholders' equity
Balance, 1 January 2012	19,837,211	$26,548	$3,274	$(1,193)	$111,689	$140,318
Total comprehensive income (loss):						
Net income	—	—	—	—	27,656	27,656
Other comprehensive loss:						
Foreign currency translation adjustment	—	—	—	(106)	—	(106)
Total comprehensive income (loss)	—	—	—	(106)	27,656	27,550
Transactions with shareholders recorded directly in equity:						
Share options exercised	40,151	516	(194)	—	—	322
Share-based compensation	—	—	2,091	—	—	2,091
Repurchase of common shares	(219,600)	(336)	(2,264)	—	—	(2,600)
Dividends declared	—	—	—	—	(2,778)	(2,778)
	(179,449)	180	(367)	—	(2,778)	(2,965)
Balance, 31 December 2012	19,657,762	$26,728	$2,907	$(1,299)	$136,567	$164,903

2011	Number of shares	Capital stock	Contributed surplus	Accumulated other comprehensive loss	Retained earnings	Total shareholders' equity
Balance, 1 January 2011	19,780,039	$26,016	$2,054	$(1,142)	$89,569	$116,497
Total comprehensive income (loss):						
Net income	—	—	—	—	22,120	22,120
Other comprehensive loss:						
Foreign currency translation adjustment	—	—	—	(51)	—	(51)
Total comprehensive income (loss)	—	—	—	(51)	22,120	22,069
Transactions with shareholders recorded directly in equity:						
Share options exercised	8,599	108	(41)	—	—	67
Share-based compensation	—	—	1,722	—	—	1,722
Repurchase of common shares	(4,000)	(37)	—	—	—	(37)
Deferred share units exercised (note 18)	52,573	461	(461)	—	—	—
	57,172	532	1,220	—	—	1,752
Balance, 31 December 2011	19,837,211	$26,548	$3,274	$(1,193)	$111,689	$140,318

Source: SoftChoice Corporation, 2012 Audited annual financial statements, page 3, www.sedar.com, posted 19 February 2013.

Reporting Example 2

Exhibit 4-4 presents the SCE for Bombardier Corporation. Unlike the Softchoice Corporation, Bombardier presents the previous year's amounts first, followed by the most recent year (ending 31 December 2012). This style of presentation enables the company to show a continuous presentation, from 1 February 2011 through to 31 December 2011 and then through to 31 December 2012.

This is a somewhat more complex example. Bombardier has both preferred and common shares, contributed surplus, retained earnings, and four types of OCI: net actuarial losses, AFS (i.e., available for sale) financial assets, cash flow hedges, and CCTD, each of which is detailed in its own column. After the total column, the amounts relating to the non-controlling interest (NCI) is deducted, leaving the total equity attributable to the company's shareholders. Only the final total of the last two columns is reported on the face of the SFP (see Exhibit 4-2), which is all that IFRS requires.

Return on Investment   Now, let us return to the issue of *return on investment* (ROI) that we raised earlier in the chapter. We calculated that Bombardier had a return on total assets of 2.4% for the year ending 31 December 2011. But *assets* is just one measure of investment ROI. The shareholders are also likely to be interested in how much the company earned on the shareholders' investment.

Bombardier Corporation reported $671 million in shareholders' equity at the end of 2011 and $1,377 million at the end of 2012 (see Exhibit 4-2 or 4-3). Averaging these beginning and ending amounts gives us $1,024, If we use this amount to measure the company's rate of return on shareholders' equity, we would get an astounding ROI: $598 million net income divided by $1,024 million equity gives us a return of 57%.

However, it is not really that good. To find the shareholders' **invested capital**, we must add together the two classes of shares, the contributed surplus, and the retained earnings to find the invested equity. Adding these four amounts gives us $4,061 million at the end of 2011 and $4,450 million at the end of 2012. The average equity over 2012 amounted to $4,256.5 million. Dividing that average into $588 million net income gives us about 14% for 2012—still a good rate of return, but rather less than we would get without looking at the detail in the SCE:

$$\text{ROI} = \$588 \div \{[(\$347 + \$1,323 + \$2,273 + \$118) + (\$347 + \$1,342 + \$2,652 + \$109)] \div 2\} = 14\%$$

You will notice that we left out the NCI. That is because we are interested in the investment by Bombardier's shareholders, not by minority shareholders in the company's subsidiary.

In Chapter 22, we will take a much closer look at adjustments that may be required before any ratio analysis is done. Nevertheless, the crucial message is that the highly summarized amounts in the SFP should not be used for analysis without examining the other statements (including the SCE) and the notes. Conclusions based on partial information are useless at best and misleading at worst.

Precision   Incidentally, if you recalculate this ratio, you will get 13.8142%. This level of "precision" is meaningless. Accounting numbers incorporate many estimates. It is ridiculous to calculate any ratio to more than two significant digits. One should not try to be "precise" about ratios based on imprecise numbers.

EXHIBIT 4-4

BOMBARDIER INC.

Consolidated Statements of Changes in Equity

For the fiscal years ended (in millions of U.S. dollars)

Attributable to equity holders of Bombardier Inc.

	Share capital		Deficit		Contributed surplus	Accumulated OCI			Total	NCI	Total equity
	Preferred shares	Common shares	Other retained earnings	Net actuarial losses		AFS financial assets	Cash flow hedges	CCTD			
As at 1 February 2011	$347	$1,324	$1,702	$(1,978)	$131	$10	$(218)	$136	$1,454	$67	$1,521
Total comprehensive income											
Net income	—	—	837	—	—	—	—	—	837	—	837
OCI	—	—	—	(1,255)	—	17	(98)	(36)	(1,372)	(4)	(1,376)
	—	—	837	(1,255)	—	17	(98)	(36)	(535)	(4)	(539)
Options exercised	—	9	—	—	(1)	—	—	—	8	—	8
Repurchase of share capital	—	(2)	(12)	—	—	—	—	—	(14)	—	(14)
Dividends											
Common shares	—	—	(179)	—	—	—	—	—	(179)	—	(179)
Preferred shares	—	—	(25)	—	—	—	—	—	(25)	—	(25)
Shares distributed—PSU plans	—	50	—	—	(50)	—	—	—	—	—	—
Shares purchased—PSU plans	—	(58)	—	—	—	—	—	—	(58)	—	(58)
Share-based expense	—	—	—	—	38	—	—	—	38	—	38
Purchase of NCI	—	—	(50)	—	—	—	—	—	(50)	(31)	(81)
As at 31 December 2011	$347	$1,323	$2,273	$(3,233)	$118	$27	$(316)	$100	$ 639	$32	$ 671
Total comprehensive income											
Net income	—	—	588	—	—	—	—	—	588	10	598
OCI	—	—	—	147	—	(17)	119	54	303	3	306
	—	—	588	147	—	(17)	119	54	891	13	904
Options exercised	—	5	—	—	(2)	—	—	—	3	—	3
Dividends											
Common shares	—	—	(177)	—	—	—	—	—	(177)	—	(177)
Preferred shares	—	—	(29)	—	—	—	—	—	(29)	—	(29)
Capital distribution	—	—	—	—	—	—	—	—	—	(2)	(2)
Shares distributed—PSU plans	—	14	—	—	(14)	—	—	—	—	—	—
Share-based expense	—	—	—	—	7	—	—	—	7	—	7
Purchase of NCI	—	—	(3)	—	—	—	—	—	(3)	3	—
As at 31 December 2012	$347	$1,342	$2,652	$(3,086)	$109	$10	$(197)	$154	$1,331	$46	$1,377

Source: Bombardier Inc., or its subsidiaries, 2012 Audited annual financial statements, page 133, www.sedar.com, posted 21 February 2013.

ACCOUNTING CHANGES

We close the books at the end of each fiscal year. "Closing" means that we cannot reopen that year's accounts—the year is over. However, there are two circumstances in which, while we do not actually reopen the books, we do need to make changes to the financial statements of one or more prior years. This happens when:

1. Accounting standards have changed and we need to restate the financial results of one or more prior periods; or

2. We discover a material error in one or more prior periods, an error that must be corrected in those prior periods' financial statements.

In this section of the chapter, we will explain how these changes must be accounted for.

Changes in Accounting Policy

From time to time, a company changes an accounting policy that it has been using for a certain type of transaction or event. **Changes in accounting policy** can be either:

- *Voluntary* when accounting policy options are available because management decides that its previous policy inadequately reflects the nature of the company's operations; or
- *Compulsory* because new or changed accounting standards have come into effect that no longer permit the company's previous policy.

The International Accounting Standards Board (IASB) has regularly been introducing new standards or revisions to existing standards. The 2009 reporting year saw several very significant changes in standards. Substantial additional changes occurred in 2011, when Canada switched to IFRS. Significant changes took effect in 2013 when several new (or revised) IFRS came into effect. It seems that there also will be a number of changes in or around 2017. Between such major changes, the Board often makes small adjustments.

When a reporting entity changes an accounting policy, the historical comparability of the financial statements is reduced because the statements issued before the change in policy have been prepared on a different basis from those issued after the change. This lack of comparability can be overcome only if comparative amounts reported in prior years' statements are restated using the newly adopted principle. The resultant change in prior years' income also changes opening retained earnings in the current year.

For example, suppose that a company changes its inventory costing method in 20X2 to exclude storage costs that previously had been included in inventory cost. The change is due to the company's change to IFRS, which does not permit storage costs to be included as part of inventory cost. The company determines that the amount of storage costs included in the 20X1 ending inventory was $60,000. Since the 20X1 ending inventory had been subtracted in determining cost of goods sold for 20X1, an overstatement of inventory cost causes an understatement of cost of goods sold and an overstatement of net income. In 20X2, the 20X1 net income is in 20X2's opening retained earnings. To make the accounting policy change in 20X2, the company must reduce 20X2's opening inventory *and* opening retained earnings (net of income tax).

Assume an income tax rate of 30%. The cumulative effect of the change in accounting policy, net of applicable income taxes, is $60,000 × 70%, or $42,000. The entry in 20X2 to record the effect of the change in accounting policy is as follows:

Retained earnings—cumulative effect of change in accounting principle	42,000	
Deferred income tax liability	18,000	
Inventory—opening		60,000

The tax amount is deferred because the change is made for accounting purposes only—the tax return (and taxes payable) is not changed. We discuss this type of tax effect in Chapter 15.

The effect of a retrospective change in accounting policy usually is shown on the retained earnings statement as follows:

Opening retained earnings, as previously reported (assumed)	$400,000
Effect of change in accounting policy (net of tax)	(42,000)
Opening retained earnings, as restated	$358,000

The details of the nature and impact of the change would be provided in a disclosure note.

Occasionally, a new accounting standard permits *prospective treatment*. **Prospective treatment** means that the new policy is used for the current period and future periods, but past periods are left as is. This practice results in a loss of consistency, but it also avoids the necessity of digging into past records to determine exactly what the effect would be in prior years. Prospective treatment is also used as a practical matter when it is simply not feasible to reconstruct data for prior periods.

In other circumstances, the company can determine the impact of the change in accounting policy on opening balances in total but cannot reconstruct the detail needed to restate individual prior years. This will result in an adjustment to opening retained earnings, as illustrated, but no restatement of previous income statements. Again, practicalities force the use of less desirable disclosure of the effect of the new policy on prior years.

Changes in Accounting Estimates   A change in an accounting *estimate* is not the same as an accounting *error*. Errors are corrected retrospectively, while new estimates are always applied prospectively. A revised estimate is used for this year, and future years (or until revised again), but previous statements are *never* changed and retained earnings is not touched.

For example, we may discover in 20X6 that our estimate of the recoverable amount of year-end 20X4 inventory had been far too optimistic; the actual recoverable amount turned out to be significantly less than we had estimated. When we discover that fact, we are not finding an error; instead, we are finding that our 20X4 estimate had been incorrect. Therefore, the results of underestimating the year-end 20X4 inventory flow through to earnings in 20X3 and 20X4.

Prior-Period Error Corrections

Errors happen. They usually arise from classifying amounts and transactions incorrectly. When errors are discovered, they must be corrected. This sometimes involves restating the financial statements of prior years, and thus changing prior income, which is summarized in retained earnings.

In the year that we discover the error, we must make a correcting adjustment. The adjustment is to the beginning-of-year retained earnings for the *cumulative* impact of the change to prior earnings, net of income tax. Thus, the opening retained earnings is *restated*.

Then, the comparative financial statements are adjusted to give effect to the error correction. In effect, the transaction is backed out of the current income statement and into the appropriate prior year. A description of the error and its effect on the financial statements must be included in the disclosure notes.

Capital Transactions

The statement of changes in equity contains other increases and decreases in equity caused by capital transactions. Most capital transactions are share transactions. Since a corporation is dealing with itself (its owners) in share transactions, gains and losses caused by these transactions are not shown on the income statement because they are not arm's-length transactions.

For example, in 2011, BCE Inc. repurchased 3.5 million common shares for cancellation. The cost of the repurchase was $143 million. When shares are repurchased, the common stock account is debited for only $61 million and $4 million for the contributed surplus attributable to original issue price. The remainder of $78 million was charged to retained earnings. BCE would have recorded the transaction as follows (in millions):

Share capital—Common	61.0	
Contributed surplus	4.0	
Retained earnings	78.0	
Cash		143.0

ETHICAL ISSUES

Usually, errors are accidental. However, some "errors" can be perceived as intentional—management may have been trying to affect reported results by intentionally misclassifying some transactions. Prosecutors allege that major public companies (such as Nortel, WorldCom, Enron, Live Entertainment, Philip Services, and Tyco) deliberately misstated their financial results.

In accounting terms, the cause of errors is irrelevant. All errors are corrected in the same manner, whether they occurred innocently or not so innocently.

To illustrate the recording of a retrospective adjustment for an error correction, assume that a machine that cost the Bailey Retail Corporation $10,000 (with a 10-year estimated useful life and no residual value) was purchased on 1 January 20X2. Further, assume that the total cost was erroneously debited to an expense account in 20X2. The error was discovered on 29 December 20X5. A correcting entry would be required in 20X5. Assuming that any income tax effects are recorded separately, the entry is as follows:

29 December 20X5:		
Machinery	10,000	
Amortization expense, straight line (for 20X5)	1,000	
Accumulated amortization (20X2 through 20X5)		4,000
Retained earnings, error correction		7,000

The $7,000 retrospective adjustment corrects the 1 January 20X5 retained earnings balance on a pretax basis. The balance is understated by $7,000 before tax:

Understatement of 20X2 income ($10,000 − $1,000)	$9,000
Overstatement of 20X3 and 20X4 income ($1,000 × 2)	(2,000)
Net pretax understatement	$7,000

Assuming that the same error was also made on the income tax return, the entry to record the income tax effect of the error, assuming a 30% income tax rate, would be as follows:

Retained earnings, error correction ($7,000 × 30%)	2,100	
Deferred income tax liability		2,100

Appropriate reporting in the retained earnings column of the SCE is illustrated in Exhibit 4-5. Amounts other than the error correction are assumed.

EXHIBIT 4-5

BAILEY RETAIL CORPORATION
Statement of Changes in Equity (excerpt)

Year ended 31 December 20X5

(in thousands of Canadian dollars)

	Retained earnings
Balance, 1 January 20X5, as previously reported	$378,800
Correction of error (net of income tax of $2,100) (Note 6)	4,900
Balance, 1 January 20X5, as restated	383,700
Net income	81,200
Cash dividends declared and paid during 20X5	(30,000)
Balance, 31 December 20X5	$434,900

Note 6. Error correction—During the year, the company discovered that a capital expenditure made in 20X2 was incorrectly expensed. This error caused net income of that period to be understated and that of subsequent periods to be overstated. The adjustment of $4,900 (after income tax of $2,100) corrects the error.

Other charges to retained earnings arise from share issue expenses incurred on the issuance of new shares, taxes resulting from a change in control or triggered by dividend payments to shareholders, and adjustments to retained earnings caused by a reorganization.

CONCEPT REVIEW

1. What types of items will appear on the statement of changes in equity?

2. What is the normal approach to accounting for a change in accounting policy?

3. How are errors in prior years corrected? How does this differ from the way we correct the results of accounting estimates made in prior years?

DISCLOSURE NOTES

Disclosure notes are an integral part of the financial statements and must be presented if the statements are to be complete. If the financial statements are audited, so are the notes.

Disclosure notes can adhere to minimal disclosure requirements or be far more extensive; this is management's decision based on corporate reporting objectives and the needs of user groups. Unlike the purely quantitative financial statements, disclosure notes can provide qualitative as well as quantitative information. Readers can then make their own assessment of the potential ramifications of the information presented. Notes are sometimes complex and highly technical.

Notes are not a substitute for proper measurement and financial statement reporting.

General Classification of Disclosure Notes

The objective of disclosure notes is to provide information that will help users understand the financial position and operating results of the company. However, bear in mind that financial statements, including the notes, are intended for sophisticated financial statement readers—people who have a good basis of understanding of both financial reporting and of the operations of the company whose statements they are reading. Naïve readers peruse financial statements at their own risk.

The most important functions of the disclosure notes are to:

- Give a quick overview of the nature of the business;
- Explain the accounting policies that the company is using, both in general and for each specific financial statement element;
- Forewarn of new standards that have been issued but not have not yet come into effect—the disclosure of each new standard should indicate the potential impact on the enterprise's financial reporting;
- Provide additional detail for individual financial statement elements, both as required by IFRS and as necessary to enable readers to understand the amounts presented;
- Provide information about commitments and contingencies;
- Identify major underlying assumptions and estimates; and
- Provide information that is not presented elsewhere in the financial statements but is useful for understanding them.

The company should include cross-references to the notes from each financial statement item, as we have seen in the sample statements presented in Exhibits 4-2 and 4-3 and in Chapter 3. IFRS stipulates the general order in which the notes should appear.

Compliance Statement   The reporting enterprise should state that it is complying with IFRS. Sometimes, this takes a somewhat different appearance than simply a flat statement of compliance. For example, Australian mining company Rio Tinto states the following:

> The Group's financial statements have been prepared in accordance with IFRS as adopted by the European Union (EU IFRS), which differs in certain respects from the version of IFRS that is applicable in Australia referred to as Australian Accounting Standards (AAS).[2]

This type of statement shows up in companies that are based in countries where IFRS must be subject to legislative or regulatory approval. In the European Union (EU), for example, new IFRS become effective for EU companies only after they have been approved and adopted by the EU Parliament.

Accounting Policies   A summary of accounting policies, starting with the compliance statement, should be presented prior to any notes on specific items. The summary usually is presented as the first note to the financial statements, but it also can be presented in a separate summary of significant accounting policies immediately preceding the notes. The accounting policy notes should include:

- Specific accounting principles chosen for each financial statement element, with any choices between acceptable alternatives that management made, such as FIFO (first-in, first-out) versus average cost inventory valuation;
- Any changes in accounting policies or new accounting standards that have or are about to come into effect; and
- The methods of applying these principles, including methods specific to the industry in which the company operates, as well as important judgements that are required.

New Accounting Standards   New accounting standards do not come into effect immediately. Companies need time to adjust their accounting procedures and information collection before they can apply new standards. When a new standard is issued, a reporting entity should alert financial statement readers to the fact that the standard will be coming into

---

[2] *Rio Tinto 2011 Annual Report*, page 138. Retrieved 28 May 2013, from http://www.riotinto.com/documents/Investors/Rio_Tinto_2011_Annual_report.pdf.

effect, the date at which it will be effective, and the potential impact on the company's financial reporting. Often, a company will end its disclosure of a new standard with a statement such as "implementation of this standard is not expected to have a material impact on our financial statements." In other instances, the impact can be quite substantial. Regardless of the potential impact, each new standard must be explained to the reader.

Additional Detail As we have seen from the examples in this and the preceding chapter, financial statements are quite brief. Accounting standards require quite a bit of detailed information that does not appear on the face of the statements. Instead, the required detail is provided in individual notes relating to each item.

For example, on Bombardier Inc.'s 2012 SFP (see Exhibit 4-2), the company reports a single amount of $2,028 (million) for PPE. From disclosure note 19, we can learn that the total represents cost of $4,330 minus accumulated depreciation of $2,302. The major components were buildings ($2,166 less $1,175 depreciation) and equipment ($1,387 cost less $859 depreciation). We also learn that PPE includes assets under finance lease ($214 less $88 amortization). Further, the company tells us that total depreciation of $185 was charged against earnings in fiscal year 2012.

Bombardier leases some aircraft to other companies under operating leases. Those assets, amounting to $51 minus $12 amortization at year-end 2012, are included in Bombardier's PPE. Rental income during 2012 was $10.

Major Underlying Assumptions and Estimates Sophisticated financial statement readers are generally aware of the large number of estimates that underlie amounts in the financial statements. Nevertheless, it is appropriate to call attention to **measurement uncertainty**—the extent to which errors in significant estimates can affect the financial statements. Disclosing the nature and extent of measurement uncertainty requires a description of the estimated amount, the amount recorded, and an indication of possible dollar change that is possible. Disclosure might also include key assumptions, ranges, and the sensitivity of the range to changes in assumptions.

The notes should indicate those assumptions that have a potentially significant impact on the financial statements. A reporting entity should explain the nature of each source of estimation uncertainty that might have a significant impact on the carrying value of assets and liabilities.

Bombardier makes several sensitivity disclosures in the notes to its 31 December 2011 statements. For example:

- "A 1% increase in the estimated future costs to complete all ongoing production contract accounted for under the percentage-of-completion method would have decreased BT's gross margin for fiscal year 2012 by approximately $75 million ..."[3]

Bombardier's 2012 reported gross margin was $2,499 (see Exhibit 4-2), and thus a change in estimated costs would have reduced the margin by just 3.0%. However, as that cost increase flows through to earnings before taxes (EBT) of $698, EBT (and net earnings, assuming the tax impact would be been proportionate) would have gone down by almost 11%. Conversely, lowering the estimated future costs would have increased earnings. This example indicates how crucial it is to make "fair" estimates!

Information Useful for Understanding the Statements This can cover a wide range of information, such as:

- Contingencies;
- Guarantees;
- Segment reporting;
- Related party transactions;

---

[3] From Note 4, page 149 of the 2012 annual report. "BT" refers to the company's rail transportation division, which has numerous long-term contracts for rail systems in several parts of the world.

- Economic dependence;
- Unrecognized contractual commitments;
- Financial risk management objectives and policies; and
- Subsequent events.

We will briefly explain some of these disclosures in the following section. Others will be dealt with in the following chapters.

Specific Significant Disclosures

There are several disclosure requirements that are significant enough to warrant separate discussion because they are either new or relatively complex.

Contingencies A **contingency** is an event or transaction that will occur only if some other event happens. For example, a civil lawsuit poses a contingent gain for the plaintiff and a contingent loss for the defendant. However, the parties will not know whether they have a gain or a loss until the court reaches a decision.

Under IFRS, neither a contingent asset nor a contingent liability is recognized in the financial statements. Instead, the situation giving rise to the contingent event and its possible outcomes is described in the notes. When practicable, the note should also disclose a "best estimate" of its potential financial effect. It is then up to the users to assess the risks for themselves.

If and when a liability becomes *probable* rather than just *contingent*, the liability then should be recognized in the accounts as a *provision* (i.e., as a cost and a liability), as we discussed in the previous chapter.

Guarantees We are all familiar with a *guarantee* that relates to a product or service provided by the reporting enterprise. However, the concept of a guarantee goes beyond these simple (and usually estimable) warranty arrangements.

More broadly, a **guarantee** is an agreement by the reporting enterprise to pay compensation, to undertake to perform services, or to assume the obligation of another entity under certain conditions. Guarantees are really a type of *contingency*, but they are given special attention because they are so common in business affairs and because they can be the hidden elephant in a company's otherwise undisclosed contingent obligations.

For example, Bombardier Inc. sells small jets to regional airlines. The airlines often obtain debt or lease financing for the planes. To facilitate the sale, Bombardier will guarantee the debt by promising to pay the lender or lessor if the airline defaults on its obligations. In Bombardier's financial statements, the company describes the nature of these guarantees (along with other types of guarantees) in a disclosure note.

The company is able to quantify the extent of the risk—at 31 December 2012, the "maximum potential exposure" for credit risk from aircraft sales was $1,218 million. None of the amount appears as a liability in the company's SFP, however, because although the *exposure* is quantifiable, the actual amount of future liability is not predictable. Nevertheless, investors and creditors can see the maximum potential loss should the regional airline industry collapse. Bombardier also disclosed that "three regional airline customers accounted for 66% of the total maximum credit risk."

Other examples of guarantees that an entity should disclose include:

- A guarantee of debt of an affiliated corporation, such as a subsidiary;
- A promise to make good on nonperformance, such as when a subcontractor is unable to carry out the contracted services. This is known as a **performance guarantee**; or
- A promise to remedy any deficiency or shortfall of assets held by another entity. For example, a company may issue shares in payment for services received from another company, and guarantee that the value of the shares won't fall below a certain level. This is also known as **indemnification**.

When a company has given any guarantees, the nature and potential maximum amount of these guarantees should be disclosed in a separate disclosure note.

Segment Disclosures Consolidated financial information may mask important trends, risks, and opportunities for a diversified company. Therefore, public companies are required to disaggregate their reported results by operating segment.

An **operating segment** has three characteristics:

1. It engages in business activities that may generate revenues and incur expenses;

2. There is discrete financial information available for the segment; and

3. Its operating results are reviewed regularly by the entity's "chief operating decision maker" (e.g., the CEO or the chief operating officer), who evaluates the segment's performance and makes resource allocation decisions.

Although there may be many operating segments under this definition, a **reportable segment** is one that meets at least one of the following tests:

- Its revenue to external customers is at least 10% of the company's total revenue; or
- Its assets are 10% or more of the company's total assets; or
- The absolute value of its profit or loss is 10% or more of the greater of the absolute amounts of:
  - The combined earnings of all operating segments that did not report a loss, or
  - The combined reported loss of all operating segments that reported a loss.

To illustrate this last condition, consider a company that has six operating segments:

Segment	Profit or (Loss)
A	$150,000
B	70,000
C	(100,000)
D	25,000
E	(60,000)
F	(20,000)

The sum of segments A, B, and D is $245,000. The sum of segments C, E, and F is $180,000. The higher total is $245,000, and therefore the cut-off point for a reportable segment is $24,500. Since all segments except F have either a profit or a loss that is higher than $24,500, all but F are reportable segments.

Every public company must identify enough segments to explain 75% of its total revenue. If the total revenue of reportable segments does not add up to 75%, the company must report additional segments until the 75% threshold is met.

Once the reportable segments have been identified, the company must disclose selected information on each segment, including (1) revenue, (2) profit or loss, and (3) assets and liabilities. Other specific disclosures are required, too, such as interest revenue, interest expense, income tax expense, and depreciation and amortization.

The company must reconcile the disaggregated segment data to the numbers reported on the primary financial statements. As well, the company should disclose information about the geographic regions in which it operates. The data include (1) total revenue derived from each country in which the company operates and (2) the carrying value of noncurrent assets in each of those countries. Countries can be grouped into regions when individual countries do not account for a significant portion of business.

Segment disclosures can be quite long and complex if the company is involved in a large number of segments and geographic areas. Bombardier discloses two business segments—aerospace (BA) and rail transportation (BT). The 31 December 2012 segmented disclosures indicate, for example, that aerospace accounted for 51% of revenues and 46% of operating earnings (EBT).

The company reported geographic data for nine countries individually and for an "other" category within each of Asia-Pacific, Europe, and "Other." The nine individually identified countries accounted for 70% of Bombardier's revenue and 87% of its capital assets.

Canada accounted for only 7% of Bombardier's consolidated revenue but 38% of the company's total assets.[4] Canada does not qualify as a reportable segment under the revenue criterion (10%) but does qualify on the basis of the high proportion of assets held in Canada.

Related Party Transactions   When a firm engages in a transaction wherein one of the parties has the ability to influence the actions and policies of the other, the transaction is termed a **related party transaction**. Such transactions cannot be assumed to be at arm's length because the conditions necessary for a competitive, free market interaction are not likely to be present. Related parties include management, individuals, and/or corporations with significant shareholdings; other corporations with common major shareholders; family members of related parties; and so on. There can be a large number of related parties!

If a company has had related party transactions during the reporting period, the company should disclose the nature of the relationship as well as information about the nature of the transactions. The company should disclose the amount of the transactions and the amount of any outstanding balances, including commitments.

A broader disclosure recommended by IAS 24 is that related party transactions should be made separately for a long list of categories, including associated companies, joint ventures in which the reporting entity is a participant, and key management personnel of the company or its parent company (if any).

Furthermore, a public company that is a subsidiary of another company should disclose who its parent is, if the parent is also a public company. For example, Calgary-based Imperial Oil Ltd. is a publicly traded subsidiary of Exxon Mobile Corporation; Exxon owns 70% of Imperial's shares. IFRS requires Imperial to disclose that Exxon is its parent so that financial statement readers will know that transactions between those two companies are related party transactions for both of them.

The disclosure of related party transactions is intended to alert financial statement readers to the existence of these relationships, either individual or corporate. The disclosures do not include any measurement of the fair value of transactions (as opposed to the recorded value of the transactions), and therefore there is little opportunity for readers to judge the impact of the non-arm's-length transactions on the reporting enterprise's financial statements.

The thrust of IAS 24 is *disclosure*. In contrast, Canadian ASPE has some explicit *measurement* requirements pertaining to the measurement basis of goods and services traded between related parties, as we will see in the ASPE section at the end of this chapter.

Economic Dependence   Segmented reporting is intended to alert financial statement readers to the company's vulnerability to economic changes in its various business segments and in its geographic exposure. An additional vulnerability arises when a company depends on the business of one large customer or a small group of major customers. An auto parts manufacturer may sell all of its output to a single large automobile manufacturer, such as General Motors or Toyota. A medical research lab may perform all of its work under contract to a government health ministry. The company's continuance may depend on this customer's continued business. If the customer switches suppliers or goes bankrupt, the company may fail if it cannot quickly replace that business with new customers.

Financial statement readers need to know whether the company is highly dependent on one or a small group of customers. When a company is heavily dependent on certain few customers, this fact, and the volume of business involved, should be disclosed in the notes. The rule is that an entity must disclose each customer that represents 10% or more of the entity's revenue. It is not necessary to disclose who the customer is, although knowledgeable readers may well know from other sources or from their knowledge of the industry.

---

[4] In contrast, France accounted for a similar proportion of revenue (5.3%) but less than one percent of capital assets.

EXHIBIT 4-6

MAGNA INTERNATIONAL INC.

Disclosure of Economic Dependence

	2012	2011	2010
General Motors	$ 5,704	$ 6,202	$ 4,731
Fiat / Chrysler Group	4,637	3,864	3,102
BMW	4,100	4,191	3,090
Ford Motor Company	3,848	3,549	3,371
Volkswagen	3,835	3,187	2,567
Daimler AG	3,367	2,793	2,354
Other	5,346	4,962	4,250
	$30,837	$28,748	$23,465

Source: Magna International Inc. Audited annual financial statements, page 45, www.sedar.com, posted 8 March 2013.

For example, in its 2012 annual report, Canadian auto parts manufacturer Magna International Inc. reported its economic dependence on six large automobile companies for 83% of its revenues (in millions of U.S. dollars) as shown in Exhibit 4-6.

Subsequent Events What happens if the company unexpectedly sells a division soon after the end of the fiscal year? It is not an event of the past fiscal year, but shouldn't it be part of the report? Users have almost certainly learned about this significant event through the financial press or other sources, as news travels fast. The financial statements must retain their credibility and relevance by reflecting up-to-date information.

Therefore, disclosure is required for significant events that take place *after the end of the fiscal year*, but *before the date that the statements are completed*. The date that the entity's Board approves the statements is usually used as a cut-off date for reporting **subsequent events**.

There are two categories of subsequent events: (1) adjusting events and (2) nonadjusting events.

Adjusting events are those that occur after the year-end that require the company to make adjustments to the financial statements. Some events that take place *after* the year-end actually reflect economic conditions existing at the year-end; *these events must be recognized in the accounts*, and therefore are known as *adjusting events*. For example, if a major customer unexpectedly announces bankruptcy after the year-end, the accounts receivable relating to that customer at the year-end would be written down under the reasoning that the customer was actually insolvent at the end of the fiscal year, but this fact did not become known to the company until after the year-end.

This may appear to be the application of hindsight to financial reporting, but it really reflects a long-standing practice in financial reporting. The period between the year-end and the completion of the financial statements provides a reality check on the validity of many measurements, including uncollectible accounts, returns and allowances, and the net realizable value of inventory.

Other examples of adjusting events include (1) settlement of a court case related to events that took place before the reporting date, and (2) evidence uncovered of asset impairment existing at the reporting date. Such events can be taken into account *in retrospect*, as part of the accounting estimation process that occurs at every financial reporting date.

Nonadjusting events are those that do not require modification of the year-end results. Examples of nonadjusting events include:

• A decline in the market value of an investment after the reporting date;

• An event that results in a loss, such as fire or flood;

- Issuance of debt or equity instruments that changed the common shares, or potential common shares, outstanding; and
- Announcing or commencing a restructuring.

These events will affect the financial statements in the following year (that is, in the year that they actually occur). When nonadjusting events are known before the issuance of the most recent year's statements, they should be communicated to the financial statement readers as part of the reporting exercise.

CONCEPT REVIEW

1. In general, what functions are served by disclosure notes?
2. Why might financial statement users want to see *segmented information*? What companies are required to disclose segmented information?
3. Define a *related party transaction*.
4. What is measurement uncertainty?
5. Explain the difference between *adjusting* and *nonadjusting* subsequent events.

Looking Forward

In November 2012, the IASB began looking into a wide range of issues on presentation, disclosure and measurement. Among the issues on the IASB's Conceptual Framework agenda are a re-examination of the definitions of elements, definitions of liabilities, recognition principles, measurement principles, the distincion between equity and liability instruments, and measurements other than cost and fair value. In coming years, the Board is likely to issue new guidance on the format and presentation of items on the SFP.

This is a long-term project. We are not likely to see a resolution of these many issues for quite a while.

 ## ACCOUNTING STANDARDS FOR PRIVATE ENTERPRISES

Balance Sheet

Canadian ASPE continues to use the title "balance sheet," but use of that title is not required. "Statement of financial position" remains an acceptable alternative title. The general format of the balance sheet is the same as for IFRS. *CPA Canada Handbook, Part II,* section 1521, contains a list of items that should be "separately presented." Some of these items usually will appear on the face of the balance sheet, but some may be disclosed in the notes. The only items in the list that do not specifically appear in IFRS are:

- Prepaid expenses;
- Obligations under capital leases;
- Accrued benefit liability; and
- Asset retirement obligations.

However, disclosure of these items is implicitly contained in the specific standards that deal with those topics.

ASPE does not require separate disclosure of three asset categories that are specifically required in IFRS:

- *Investment property* is included in land and buildings, as appropriate;
- *Agricultural produce and biological assets* are reported as inventory and/or tangible capital assets, as appropriate; and
- *Provisions* are reported as liabilities, either current or noncurrent, as appropriate.

Of course, private enterprises may use these additional reporting captions if they so choose.

Equity

Section 3251 of the *CPA Canada Handbook, Part II* requires the "presentation of equity and changes in equity." The components of equity are:

- Share capital;
- Contributed surplus;
- Retained earnings;
- Reserves;
- Non-controlling interests; and
- Other components of equity.

Again, this list is essentially the same as under IFRS. "Other components of equity" is apt to be quite limited. One example of an "other component" is "foreign currency translation gain or loss" for a company that has one or more foreign operations (e.g., in the United States).

Bear in mind that ASPE contains no concept of "other comprehensive income," and therefore no specific equity accounts that derive therefrom.

Changes in Equity

ASPE requires a company to "present separately [the] changes in equity for the period." There is no prescription for format. In practice, the core equity statement for a private enterprise is likely to be the statement of retained earnings, presented either separately or as a continuation of the income statement—a "statement of income and retained earnings." Information on other changes in equity usually are presented in a disclosure note rather than in a formal statement format.

Disclosure Notes

Segments ASPE does not require segment disclosure.

Subsequent Events Section 3820 covers subsequent events, including those that require adjustment and those that require only disclosure. Although the *CPA Canada Handbook, Part II* does not use the terms "adjusted events" and "nonadjusted events," the substance of the recommendations is the same.

Contingent Liabilities Contingent liabilities are treated differently under ASPE. IFRS does not permit recognition of a contingent liability in the accounts until it becomes a *probable* liability, at which point it meets the IFRS definition as a provision. In contrast, ASPE is rather more specific by requiring that a contingent loss be recognized as an expense and a liability in the financial statements when:

- It becomes more likely than not that the company will become liable, and
- The amount of the future liability can be reasonably estimated.

Within the range of possible financial impacts, if one particular amount seems to be more likely than other estimates, that best estimate should be accrued. In many cases, there will be no clear best estimate, in which case the lowest amount in the feasible range should be used to measure the recognized liability and expense.

ASPE contains no specific requirement for *provisions*. Instead, ASPE accomplishes the same goal via the recognition requirements for the probable outcomes of contingent liabilities. A good example is the liability for losses from a lawsuit, which is a *provision* under IFRS but would be a *recognized contingency* under ASPE.

Related Party Transactions   ASPE makes a distinction between two types of transfers: (1) those in the normal course of business, such as a sale of merchandise, or (2) those that are not in the normal course of business, such as a transfer of property.

Related party transactions in the normal course of business must be recorded at the *exchange value* (usually fair market value). That is, a regular sale of inventory that happened to be to a related company would be recorded at the exchange value, not carrying value.

Related party transactions not in the normal course of business must be recorded at *carrying value*, which is the *book value of the transferor*. Cost would be carrying value for inventory, net book value for capital assets, and so on. Carrying value is considered appropriate because no transaction of substance has taken place—a different related party simply owns the asset in question. However, the exchange amount is also used to value the transaction if the transaction is (1) monetary (that is, if money changes hands), (2) the change of ownership interest is substantive, and (3) the exchange amount can be verified by independent evidence.

Financial statement users tend to assume that all transactions are recorded at fair market value, and the presence of related party transactions may make the financial statements difficult to interpret. ASPE recommends the following disclosures:

- The nature of the relationship(s) involved;
- A description of the nature of the transactions, including the dollar amounts, and the measurement basis used;
- Any amounts due to or from related parties as of the reporting date, and the terms and conditions thereof;
- Any contingencies or contractual obligations with related parties; and
- The amount of any doubtful accounts, whether expensed or provided for, that pertain to related party transactions or balances.

RELEVANT STANDARDS

CPA Canada Handbook, Part I (IFRS):
- IAS 1, Presentation of Financial Statements
- IAS 8, Accounting Policies, Changes in Accounting Estimates and Errors
- IAS 24, Related Party Disclosures
- IFRS 8, Operating Segments
- IAS 10, Events after the Reporting Period
- IAS 37, Provisions, Contingent Liabilities and Contingent Assets

CPA Canada Handbook, Part II (ASPE):
- Section 1521, Balance Sheet
- Section 3251, Equity
- Section 3260, Reserves
- Section 3290, Contingencies
- Section 3820, Subsequent Events
- Section 3840, Related Party Transactions

SUMMARY OF KEY POINTS

1. The SFP provides information about an entity's assets, liabilities, and equities. The SFP, taken together with other financial statements, provides information that is useful to financial statement users for assessing an entity's financial position, risk profile, financial flexibility, liquidity, and rates of return.

2. The amounts reported on the SFP are a mix of historical costs and fair values, which may reduce its relevance for certain decisions. The specific amounts reported are the result of the company's reporting policies. The SFP also contains many estimates, excludes assets and liabilities that GAAP deems unrecognizable, and often consolidates financial data from very different types of industry segments. Financial statement users must proceed with caution.

3. Classification of SFP items is governed by accounting standards and industry norms and characteristics, but leaves much room for management judgement. Most, but not all, SFPs classify current assets and current liabilities to facilitate evaluation of short-term liquidity. Other classifications follow the major asset, liability, and equity groups. Elements are often highly condensed and summarized on the SFP.

4. Various SFP categories have specific display and disclosure requirements to meet accounting standards and users' expectations.

5. Companies that are following IFRS must provide a statement of changes in equity (SCE), also known as a statement of shareholders' equity. The SCE provides a columnar reconciliation that includes a column for each individual item of shareholders' equity. The major categories are (1) share capital accounts, (2) individual categories of OCI, (3) equity of non-controlling shareholders in consolidated subsidiaries, and (4) retained earnings.

6. Retained earnings may be subdivided by two types of *reserves*—restrictions and appropriations. Restrictions are created either by law or contract. Appropriations are created voluntarily by the Board of Directors. Legal and contractual restrictions limit the amount that is available for dividends. In contrast, appropriations have no substantive effect; the Board of Directors can reverse them as easily as they are created.

7. Error corrections that affect the financial statements of prior periods are recorded (net of tax) as a change to opening retained earnings, and comparative statements are restated.

8. A change in accounting principle is normally applied retrospectively, with the cumulative effect of the change shown as an adjustment to opening retained earnings. Comparative financial statements should be restated. If this treatment is not feasible, only the cumulative effect is shown on the retained earnings statement. In certain circumstances, the change in principle is reflected prospectively. An accounting estimate is always changed prospectively.

9. Disclosure notes provide information regarding accounting policies, describe recognized and unrecognized items, and provide supplemental information regarding future cash flows and potential liabilities.

10. Important disclosures include segment disclosures, related party transaction data, economic dependence, subsequent events, contingencies and guarantees, and measurement uncertainty. Also, if a company's future is in doubt such that the continuity assumption might not apply, going-concern disclosures are needed.

KEY TERMS

additional paid-in capital
adjusting events
appropriation
balance sheet
cash equivalents
changes in accounting policy
contingency
contributed surplus
current asset
current liability
disclosure notes
fixed assets
guarantee
indemnification
intangible assets
invested capital
investment property
liquidity
long-term liability
management's discussion and analysis
   (MD&A)

measurement uncertainty
minority interest
nonadjusting events
non-controlling interest
operating cycle
operating segment
performance guarantee
prospective treatment
recycled
related party transactions
reportable segment
reserves
restriction
return on assets (ROA) ratio
return on investment (ROI) ratio
statement of changes in equity (SCE)
statement of financial position (SFP)
subsequent events
tangible capital assets

REVIEW PROBLEM 4-1

The post-closing SFP accounts of Ibsen Icons Inc. at 31 December 20X3 are as follows:

Account	Debit	Credit
Cash (overdraft)		$ 3,500
Accounts payable		15,000
Deferred income tax liability		20,000
Common shares		40,000
Preferred shares		24,000
Long-term investment in common shares of Grieg Graphics Inc.	$ 14,000	
Accounts receivable	19,000	
Income taxes payable		10,000
Loan from shareholder, due 1 July 20X9		40,000
Land	120,000	
Leasehold improvements (net of amortization)	30,000	
Furniture and equipment (at cost)	90,000	
Accumulated depreciation, furniture and equipment		30,000
Retained earnings—unappropriated		76,000
Deferred revenue		7,000
Notes receivable	7,500	
Goodwill	9,000	
Provision for restructuring costs (current)		9,000
Appropriation for plant expansion		11,000
Prepaid expenses	3,500	
Marketable securities available for sale	5,000	
Note payable to bank, due 15 October 20X4		25,000
Allowance for doubtful accounts		2,000
Supplies inventory	14,500	
	$312,500	$312,500

Required:
Prepare a classified SFP in good form.

REVIEW PROBLEM 4-1—SOLUTION

IBSEN ICONS INC.

Statement of Financial Position

31 December 20X3

Assets

Current assets:

Marketable securities		$ 5,000	
Notes receivable		7,500	
Accounts receivable	$19,000		
Less: allowance for doubtful accounts	2,000	17,000	
Supplies inventory		14,500	
Prepaid expenses		3,500	$ 47,500

Noncurrent assets:

Capital assets:

Land		120,000	
Furniture and equipment	90,000		
Less: accumulated depreciation	30,000	60,000	
Leasehold improvements (net)		30,000	
Goodwill		9,000	
		219,000	
Investment in Grieg Graphics Inc.		14,000	233,000
Total assets			$280,500

Liabilities and shareholders' equity

Liabilities:

Current liabilities:

Bank overdraft		$ 3,500	
Income taxes payable		10,000	
Bank note payable, due 15 October 20X4		25,000	
Accounts payable		15,000	
Provision for restructuring costs		9,000	
Deferred revenue		7,000	$ 69,500

Noncurrent liabilities:

Shareholder loan, due 1 July 20X9		40,000	
Deferred income tax liability		20,000	60,000
Total liabilities			129,500

Shareholders' equity:

Contributed capital:

Common shares		40,000	
Preferred shares		24,000	64,000

Retained earnings:

Appropriated for plant expansion		11,000	
Unappropriated		76,000	87,000
Total shareholders' equity			151,000
Total liabilities and shareholders' equity			$280,500

Capital assets could be separated into tangible and intangible categories. Deferred revenue and notes receivable are assumed to be within normal business practice for this company and therefore are classified as current.

REVIEW PROBLEM 4-2

On 1 January 20X5, the shareholders' equity for Svengali Controls Limited (SCL) included the following items (in thousands of dollars):

	Debit	Credit
Common shares		$12,000
Deficit	$250	
Preferred shares		2,500
Appropriation for plant expansion		1,000
Contributed surplus		250
Accumulated translation gain or loss on Mexican subsidiary		550

During the year ending 31 December 20X5, the following occurred:

a. Net income (after income tax) was $50,000.

b. Sixty thousand additional common shares were issued to existing shareholders for $50 each. The shares had no stated or par value.

c. The Board of Directors appropriated an additional $150,000 for plant expansion.

d. The company purchased and retired 1,000 of its preferred shares at their original issue price of $1,100 each. The shares had a stated value of $1,000 each, and had originally been issued to an institutional investor for $1,100 each.

e. SCL recorded a loss of $5,000 arising from a decline in the net asset value of the Mexican subsidiary due to a change in the exchange rate for the Mexican peso against the Canadian dollar.

Required:

a. Determine the amount of comprehensive income.

b. Prepare a statement of changes in equity for SIL for the year ended 31 December 20X5 in columnar format.

REVIEW PROBLEM 4-2—SOLUTION

a. Comprehensive income:

Net income	$50,000
Translation loss	5,000
Comprehensive income	$45,000

b. Statement of Changes in Equity, 31 December 20X5:

	Deficit	Appropriation for plant expansion	Translation gain/loss	Contributed surplus	Preferred shares	Common shares	TOTAL
Balances, 1 January 20X5	$(250)	$1,000	$550	$250	$2,500	$12,000	$16,050
Net income for 20X5	50						50
Change in translation gain/loss			(5)				(5)
Issuance of common shares						3,000	3,000
Redemption of preferred shares				(100)	(1,000)		(1,100)
Additional appropriation	(150)	150					—
Balances, 31 December 20X5	$(350)	$1,150	$545	$150	$1,500	$15,000	$17,995

Note: There is no prescribed sequence of columns or rows, except for the beginning and ending balances.

REVIEW PROBLEM 4-3

Kanga Corporation had the following transactions and changes during the fiscal year ended 31 December 20X7:

a. On 15 October 20X7, the Board of Directors declared $2.5 million in dividends, to be paid on 15 November 20X7. The dividends were to be paid to shareholders of record as of 30 October.

b. Two thousand new preferred shares were issued to a private equity fund on 17 May at $72 per share. The stated value of the shares was $65. These were a new class of shares, not previously issued.

c. Kanga Corporation has a wholly owned subsidiary in Mexico. The subsidiary's reporting currency (that is, for its own financial statements issued to creditors and regulators in Mexico) is the Mexican peso. When Kanga Corporation translated the year-end 20X7 financial statements to the Canadian dollar, Kanga's translated net investment had decreased from the beginning of the year, due to appreciation of the Canadian dollar, relative to the Mexican peso. The amount of the change was C$3.3 million.

d. On 15 March, Kanga redeemed $1.0 million outstanding debt securities for $0.9 million.

e. Near the end of 20X6 (the previous year), Kanga decided to discontinue its heavy maintenance division and began an active search for a buyer. Kanaga Corporation reported the division as a "discontinued operation" in its 31 December 20X6 financial statements. On 13 August 20X7, Kanaga's management signed a binding agreement to sell the company's heavy maintenance division to Industrial Innovations Inc. The net proceeds from the sale and transfer of the division to III were $1.2 million less than the carrying value of the division's net assets on Kanga's books at year-end 20X6.

f. On 31 December 20X7, Kanga's Board of Directors voted unanimously to reverse an appropriation of $15.2 million that had been established two years previously. The purpose of the appropriation was to reserve funds for plant expansion that the Board now decided to postpone indefinitely.

g. When preparing the 20X7 financial statements, management (with consultation with the auditors) decided that, in hindsight, the company had been using overly optimist estimates of the useful lives of certain categories plant and equipment for the past five years. Therefore, management agreed to reduce those estimates to a more realistic level.

h. When preparing the 20X7 financial statements, the company discovered that certain items in the year-end 20X6 inventory had been overstated by $200,000.

Required:
Explain briefly how each of these items would be reported in the 31 December 20X7 comparative financial statements, if at all. Ignore income tax effects.

REVIEW PROBLEM 4-3—SOLUTION

a. Retained earnings is reduced by $2.5 million.

b. The total issue price at $72 per shares was $144,000. Of that total, $130,000 would be reported in the preferred shares account and $14,000 as contributed surplus in the statement of changes in equity. The total $144,000 would be shown in the financing section of the SCF.

c. The change of $3.3 million (OCI) would be reported as a loss in the "other comprehensive income" segment of the SCI, and as a reduction (debit) in the "translation adjustment" column in the statement of changes in equity.

d. The gain of $0.1 million is reported as gain (other income) in the profit and loss section of the SCI.

e. This $1.2 million loss is reported in the profit and loss section of the SCI, in the "discontinued operations" section.

f. The reversal will appear in the retained earnings column of the SCE. The amount would not appear on the 20X7 year-end SFP.

g. The changes in estimates will affect depreciation in 20X7 and following years. Previous years' statements will not be restated; changes in estimates are always applied forward and never in retrospect.

h. The $200,000 inventory overstatement will be corrected by adjusting opening retained earnings downward by $200,000 to correct for the resultant overstatement of 20X6 earnings; 20X7 earnings will be increased as a result. The year-end 20X6 comparative SFP and SCI also will be restated to correct the error.

QUESTIONS

Q4-1   Describe the limitations of the SFP.

Q4-2   Describe the usual order of current asset accounts in North American SFPs and balance sheets.

Q4-3   Identify some of the differences between SFP presentations around the world.

Q4-4   What are capital assets? Distinguish between tangible and intangible assets.

Q4-5   Comment on the difficulties associated with evaluating the financial position of an entity whose primary assets are intangible.

Q4-6   What is an *impairment test*? What is its purpose?

Q4-7   Why is *deferred income tax* classified as a liability? Why might the amount be subject to question?

Q4-8   Explain the term "non-controlling interest."

Q4-9   Under what circumstances may a liability be offset against a related asset, such as offsetting a bank note payable against "cash in bank"?

Q4-10 What is shareholders' equity? What are its main components?

Q4-11 What is the usual format of the statement of changes in equity?

Q4-12 When may an item of OCI be recycled through net income?

Q4-13 List the primary types of disclosure notes. Give an example of each type.

Q4-14 Explain the difference between a *contingency* and a *provision* for future costs.

Q4-15 What is the purpose of segment disclosures?

Q4-16 Why might the presence of large volumes of related party transactions make it difficult to evaluate a company based on its financial statements?

Q4-17 What is *measurement uncertainty*? Why should it be disclosed?

Q4-18 A company has a machine that cost $21,000 when acquired at the beginning of Year 1. It had a 10-year useful life and a $1,000 estimated residual value. Toward the end of Year 5, the company discovered that, in error, the machine had been expensed when it was acquired. Straight-line depreciation is appropriate. What adjustment to opening retained earnings is appropriate in Year 5?

Q4-19 Describe how a change in accounting policy affects the financial statements.

Q4-20 What is meant by *appropriations* and *restrictions* on retained earnings? How are such items usually reported?

CASE 4-1

AUTOPART MANUFACTURING LIMITED

Autopart Manufacturing Ltd., incorporated 15 years ago, has grown to be a successful competitor in the cost- and quality-conscious auto parts manufacturing market. Autopart specializes in relatively standard replacement parts sold under store brand labels in hardware stores. Since people own cars longer than ever (now an average of 8.5 years), the auto repair business is a growth sector of the economy.

You have obtained the SFP for Autopart Manufacturing Ltd., and you have analyzed the basic financial structure of the company. You are thinking of investing in Autopart's common shares, but looking at the SFP, you are reminded of the definitions of financial statement elements. You have decided to see how well the balance sheet items conform to the definitions. In particular, it is important to explain to yourself exactly why each item is an asset, liability, or equity item. The SFP is shown in Exhibit 1, and the notes to the financial statements in Exhibit 2.

EXHIBIT 1

AUTOPART MANUFACTURING LTD.

Statement of Financial Position

(in thousands of Canadian dollars)

31 December	20X1	20X0
Asset		
Current assets		
Cash and short-term investments	$ 9,800	$ 4,390
Accounts receivable	12,464	12,570
Inventories (Note 1)	15,730	14,400
Total current assets	37,994	31,360
Capital assets		
Property, plant, and equipment (net) (Note 2)	21,529	19,200
Goodwill (Note 3)	5,100	4,750
Licences (Note 4)	1,640	1,490
Total capital assets	28,269	25,440
Other assets		
Future contract costs (Note 5)	1,950	2,300
	$68,213	$59,100
Liabilities and shareholders' equity		
Current liabilities:		
Accounts payable and accrued liabilities	$11,384	$15,875
Current portion of long-term debt	450	475
Other	615	655
Total current liabilities	12,449	17,005
Long-term liabilities (Note 6)	27,190	10,580
Commitments payable (Note 7)	—	1,900
Prepaid contract (Note 8)	1,650	2,900
Deferred income tax (Note 9)	950	890
Total liabilities	42,239	33,275
Shareholders' equity (Note 10)	25,974	25,825
	$68,213	$59,100

EXHIBIT 2

NOTES TO THE FINANCIAL STATEMENTS

As of 31 December

(in thousands of Canadian dollars)

Note 1. Inventories

	20X1	20X0
Raw materials	$ 6,700	$ 6,300
Finished goods	7,700	7,200
Supplies	400	380
Returnable containers	930	520
	$15,730	$14,400

Note 2. Property, Plant, and Equipment

	Cost	Accumulated depreciation	Net balance, 31 Dec. 20X1
Land	$ 990	$ —	$ 990
Buildings	5,910	696	5,214
Machinery and equipment			
Owned	11,480	2,600	8,880
Leased	3,720	200	3,520
Furniture and fixtures	2,600	310	2,290
Transportation equipment	1,120	485	635
	$25,820	$4,291	$21,529

Note 3. Goodwill

During the year ended 31 December 20X1, the company acquired 100% of the shares of Benn Mufflers Limited for $1,240 in cash. Benn Mufflers Limited had tangible assets, at fair value, of $890 on the acquisition date, and goodwill of $350 arose. The opening balance in the goodwill account is from a series of similar acquisitions over the past 12 years.

Note 4. Licences

The company manufactures certain auto parts under licence. Licences are acquired for cash at the beginning of the licence period, usually five years.

Note 5. Future Contract Costs

The company enters into three-year contracts with retailers, guaranteeing the company a market and specific shelf space for its goods. Payments are made to the retailers to secure these multiyear contracts. The payments are amortized against sales over the term of the related contracts.

Note 6. Long-Term Liabilities

	20X1
Term bank loans, 8%, maturing in 20X9	$17,830
Mortgages, 7%–10%, maturing in 20X3–20X6	6,910
Capital leases, 8.5%–14.3%, maturing in 20X3–20X9	2,900
	$27,640
Less: current portion	450
	$27,190

Note 7. Commitments Payable

In 20X0, the company set up a provision of $1,900 for potential losses relating to a guarantee provided for Carburetor King Limited, an associated company. Autoparts had guaranteed a bank loan of Carburetor King, and it appeared in 20X0 that financial difficulties within that company would trigger a payment by Autoparts under the guarantee. In 20X1, Carburetor King was sold and reorganized, and Autoparts was released from its guarantee after a payment of $400,000.

Note 8. Prepaid Contract

Certain customers in long-term contracts with the company prepay a portion of the estimated total contract value. This prepayment is taken into income over the life of the contract, in proportion to deliveries.

Note 9. Deferred Income Tax

Certain expenses, primarily depreciation, are reported in different periods for income tax and financial statement reporting purposes. The result is a future tax liability.

Note 10. Shareholders' Equity

	20X1
Common shares, unlimited shares authorized, 26,837 shares issued	$14,499
Contributed capital from share retirement	49
Retained earnings	11,426
	$25,974

CASE 4-2

WONDER AMUSEMENTS LIMITED

Wonder Amusements Limited (WAL) was incorporated over 40 years ago as an amusement park and golf course. Over time, a nearby city has grown to the point where it borders on WAL's properties. In recent years WAL's owners, who are all members of one family, have seen WAL's land values increase significantly. WAL's majority shareholder, Howard Smith, owns 55% of the outstanding shares and is no longer active in WAL's day-to-day activities.

Last year Howard hired a new chief executive officer, Leo Titan. Leo has a reputation for being an aggressive risk taker. Howard is committed to supporting Leo's plans and has the personal financial resources required to do so.

Eight months ago, WAL became the successful bidder for a new sports franchise, in conjunction with a minority partner. Under the terms of the franchise agreement, WAL is required to build a sports arena, which is currently being constructed. The arena is being built on a section of the amusement park. Another section of the amusement park is being relocated to ensure that the entrances to the arena are close to public transportation and parking. Consequently, some of the rides will be relocated. WAL is the sole owner of the arena at present.

The sports franchise is separately incorporated as Northern Sports Limited (NSL); WAL holds 75% of the shares in the company. Another bid is being prepared by NSL to obtain a second sports franchise so that the arena can be used more often. NSL will be required to lease space from WAL when the arena is completed, in about 22 months.

For the first two sports seasons, NSL will have to lease arena space from Aggressive Limited (AL). During this time, NSL does not expect to be profitable because:

- It may take time to build a competitive team;
- AL is charging a high rent and is not giving NSL a share of concession (e.g., hot dogs, drinks) revenue;

- AL cannot make the better dates (e.g., Saturday night) available to NSL to attract sports fans; and

- As a newcomer to the league, NSL is restricted with regard to the players who are available to it and the days of the week it can play in its home city.

Consequently, NSL has arranged to borrow funds from WAL and from others to finance costs and losses.

Your employer, Fabio & Fox, Chartered Accountants, has conducted the audit of WAL for several years. WAL has tended to be marginally profitable one year and then have losses the next year. The company has continued to operate because the directors knew that the real estate holdings were becoming increasingly valuable. For purposes of WAL's financial statements, Canadian ASPE is used by WAL.

Leo is expected to oversee the expanded accounting and finance functions in the company. Leo has met with you and the partner in charge of the WAL audit and has discussed various issues related to the year ending 30 September 20X7. His comments are provided in Exhibit 1.

You have been asked by the partner to prepare a report for him, which will be used for the next meeting with Leo. He would like you to discuss the accounting, audit, and tax implications related to your discussion with Leo. The partner wants a thorough analysis of all important issues as well as support for your position.

In your review of documents, and as a result of various conversations, you have learned the following:

1. The arena will be mortgaged, but only for about 50% of its expected cost. Lenders are concerned about the special-use nature of the arena and whether it will be successfully rented for other events, such as concerts.

2. The mortgage lenders to WAL and the minority shareholders in NSL are both expected to want to see appraisals and financial statements before deciding whether to invest. Covenants will be required by the lenders to ensure that excessive expenditures are not undertaken and that cash is preserved.

3. Leo does not intend to consolidate NSL until it is profitable. The investment in NSL will be reported on WAL's financial statements at cost. The WAL financial statements will be used for income tax purposes.

4. WAL's minority shareholders are not active in the business and want quarterly financial statements to monitor progress and assess Leo's performance. The minority shareholders have all expressed concern over Leo's growth strategy over the past year. Most are approaching their retirement years and are relying on WAL to supplement their retirement income.

Required:
Prepare the report.

EXHIBIT 1

Notes from discussion with Leo Titan

1. To build a road to the arena's parking lot, two holes of the 18-hole golf course will be relocated next spring. Costs of $140,000 are expected to be incurred this year in design, tree planting, ground preparation, and grass seeding to ready the area for next spring. These costs are to be capitalized as part of the golf course lands, along with related property taxes of $13,000 and interest of $15,000.

2. Approximately $600,000 will be required to relocate the rides that are currently on land that is needed for the arena. This amount is to be capitalized, net of scrap recovery on dismantled and redundant equipment of $60,000. Virtually all the rides were fully depreciated years ago.

3. In May 20X7, WAL acquired, for $4.25 million, all of the shares of an amusement park in a different city, when its land lease expired. The amusement park company was wound up and the equipment, rides, concessions, and other assets are being transported to WAL at a cost of $350,000. According to Leo, the estimated fair market value of WAL's net assets is $4.85 million, including liabilities of $1.20 million.

   WAL expects to spend approximately $400,000 in getting the assets in operating order and $500,000 on foundations and site preparations for the rides. Leo wants to "capitalize as much as possible."

4. To assist in financing the new ventures, WAL sold excess land to developers who intend to construct a shopping centre, office buildings, and expensive homes that will be adjacent to the golf course and away from the amusement park. The developers and WAL agreed to these terms:

Paid to WAL on 1 May 20X7	$ 6,000,000
To be paid to WAL on 1 March 20X8	10,000,000
To be paid to WAL on 1 March 20X9	8,000,000
	$24,000,000

   The land is to be turned over to the developers on or about 1 February 20X8, but the sale is to be reported in fiscal 20X7. The land was carried on WAL's books at $1.35 million; a pro-rata portion of the total land carrying value (at cost) will be allocated to the portion sold to the developers

5. An additional "contingent profit" will accrue to WAL if the developers earn a return on investment of more than 25% when they resell the newly constructed buildings. Leo wants a note to the 20X7 financial statements that describes the probability of a contingent gain.

6. The golf course has been unprofitable in recent years. However, green fees are to be raised and specific tee-off times will be allotted to a private club, which is currently being organized. Members of the private club will pay a nonrefundable entrance fee of $2,000 per member plus $100 per month for five years. The $2,000 is to be recorded as revenue on receipt. Approximately $350,000 is to be spent to upgrade the club facilities.

7. Leo wants to capitalize all costs of NSL on NSL's books until it has completed its first year of operations. In addition to the franchise fee, $20 million will have to be spent on the following:

Acquisition of player contracts	$12,000,000
Advertising and promotion	1,500,000
Equipment	3,200,000
Wages, benefits, and bonuses	6,800,000
Other operating costs	3,300,000
	26,800,000
Less revenue:	
Ticket sales	(6,000,000)
Other	(800,000)
	$20,000,000

   The value of players can change quickly, depending upon their performance, injuries, and other factors.

8. The new sports arena will have private boxes in which a company can entertain groups of clients. The boxes are leased on a five-year contract basis, and they must be occupied for a fixed number of nights at a minimum price per night. To date, 12 boxes have been leased for $15,000 per box for a five-year period, exclusive of nightly charges. A down payment of $3,000 was required; the payments have been recorded as revenue.

9. Three senior officers of WAL, including Leo, receive bonuses based on income before income taxes. The three have agreed to have their fiscal 20X7 bonuses accrued in fiscal 20X8 along with their fiscal 20X8 bonuses. Actual payments to them are scheduled for January 20X9.

Source: The Canadian Institute of Chartered Accountants, © 2010.

CASE 4-3

WPB LIMITED

The management of WPB Ltd. has spent the past year reorganizing the company's business activities. The company is a service provider to hospitals. Originally the company operated only in Canada, where hospital care is provided at government expense through public health care systems. After demonstrating successful operations, the company subsequently was invited by several African governments to extend its expertise to providing services on that continent, particularly as a result of the intense need for external support that arose from the ongoing AIDS crisis. The African operations were supported by the various nations' governments, with additional aid provided through the Stephan Louis Foundation. The Foundation requires WPB to provide audited financial statements each year as a condition for continuing its support.

WPB had been under pressure to decrease the cost of its services to hospitals as a result of severe budget pressure on the governments that bear the ultimate cost of hospital care. The company has consolidated some services, reduced its workforce, and sold some parts of its operations.

It now is 31 December 20X7, the end of the fiscal year. The vice president of Finance has requested your advice on the treatment of certain items in the company's financial statements. She has provided you with a description of the items about which she is uncertain (below), and she has requested that you prepare a report in which you recommend appropriate financial statement presentation and note disclosure for each item, in accordance with international accounting standards.

Items of Concern

1. In the last quarter of the year, we struck a deal with LaidLow Corporation to take over the ambulance service division that we had acquired in 20X4 from Asper Inc. for $12 million. The deal will not be finalized until 15 March 20X8, dependent on the results of Laidlow's due diligence inspection. We have operated the division as a separate unit, reporting directly to senior management. We struck the deal on 17 August 20X7. At that time, we estimated that the fair value of the division's assets was $24 million, of which $7 million is current assets, mainly billings receivable from the hospitals and other agencies for which we provided service. We estimated that the fair value of the $17 million noncurrent assets was $14 million at the end of the third quarter, 30 September 20X7, and we wrote the noncurrent assets down to that amount. Now, at 31 December, we have good reason to believe that the noncurrent assets are worth $16 million.

2. We also sold off some of our laboratory facilities to HealthCom Limited. HealthCom paid the purchase price of $5 million in its shares. The value of the HealthCom shares at the end of 20X7 was $5.5 million. We do not intend to hold these shares over the long term.

3. Our facilities in the nation of Albageria were confiscated by the government after a coup, and we had to terminate our operations in that country. The facilities cost us $3 million to establish and were carried on our books at $2.7 million at the time of the confiscation. We estimated that the value of the facilities at the date of the confiscation was $4.3 million. We received compensation of $4.0 million from the Canadian federal government's Export Development Corporation (EDC), which had provided us with "political risk" insurance.

4. We have billings receivable of US$13 million from African countries (not including Albageria). The billings are in U.S. dollars. We have arranged hedges for 90% of that amount. The Canadian dollar equivalent of the receivables at the time of billing was Cdn$14.4 million. At 31 December 20X7, the receivables were the equivalent of $15.3 million.

5. As the result of our restructuring activities during this past year, we estimate that we will have to make severance payments and give resettlement allowances of approximately $2.5 million during 20X8. The amount may vary up or down by $0.6 million, depending on whether our estimate of voluntary early retirements is correct.

6. We have guaranteed the operating lines of credit of several international agencies that co-operate with us in providing services abroad. The total amount of the guarantees varies, of course, because the draw on the credit lines fluctuates. At year-end 20X7, I would estimate that our total guarantees come to about $4.2 million. We do not expect any of these agencies to default on their credit obligations, however.

Required:

Prepare the report requested by the vice president. Be sure to consider the impacts on all of the year-end 20X7 financial statements.

TECHNICAL REVIEW

TR4-1 Financial Statement Classification: The first list below shows the financial statements normally included in a company's annual financial statements. The second list shows some amounts that often appear in those financial statements.

A. SFP
B. Statement of comprehensive income—profit and loss section
C. Statement of comprehensive income—other comprehensive income section
D. Statement of cash flows
E. Statement of changes in shareholders' equity

B, D, E	1. Net income
_____	2. Retained earnings (opening)
_____	3. Translation gain/loss on foreign subsidiaries
_____	4. Provision for restructuring costs
_____	5. Cumulative translation gain or loss
_____	6. Dividends declared, unpaid at year-end
_____	7. Appropriation for factory reorganization
_____	8. Loss on discontinued operation
_____	9. Non-controlling interest in subsidiaries
_____	10. Investment property held-for-sale
_____	11. Cumulative effect of change in accounting policy
_____	12. Proceeds from issuance of common shares
_____	13. Unrealized gains/losses on hedge derivatives
_____	14. Deferred pension cost

Required:

Use the letters given in the first list to indicate the financial statement on which each item in the second list will appear. Some letters may be used more than once or not at all. The first item is completed for you as an example.

TR4-2 Return ratios: Oleander Corporation had total assets of $1,200,000 on 31 December 20X3. At 31 December 20X4, total assets had increased to $1,400,000. Oleander's statement of changes in equity disclosed the following amounts at the beginning and end of 20X4:

	31 December 20X4	31 December 20X3
Class A shares	$345,000	$285,000
Class B shares	41,000	41,000
Contributed surplus	7,500	6,000
Translation reserve (OCI)	(15,000)	(17,000)
Hedge reserve (OCI)	(5,000)	(1,000)
Retained earnings	60,000	43,000
Total equity	$433,500	$357,000

The company's 20X4 statement of comprehensive income showed the following amounts:

Earnings from continuing operations, net of income tax	$53,000
Earnings (loss) from discontinued operations, net of income tax	(4,000)
Other comprehensive income	(2,000)
Comprehensive income	$47,000

Required:

Determine Oleander Corporation's (1) return on assets and (2) return on invested capital for the year 20X4 based on net income.

connect   **TR4-3 Change in Accounting Estimate:** Arboretum Limited has been depreciating its production equipment on a straight-line basis over 10 years, taking a full year's depreciation in the year of acquisition and assuming no residual value at the end of the equipment's life. The company had invested $1,200,000 in the equipment at the beginning of 20X1. At the beginning of 20X4, the company decided to adjust the equipment's total useful life from 10 years down to eight, but with an estimated residual value amounting to 5% of the equipment's original cost rather than zero.

Required:

How should this change be reported in Arboretum's comparative financial statements for 20X4? Determine the amount of depreciation expense to be shown for 20X4 and the comparative amount for 20X3.

connect   **TR4-4 Error Correction:** In preparing the year-end financial statements for 20X7, the controller of Risk 'n Save Inc. discovered that the opening inventory for 20X6 had been overstated by $20,000. The company has a 20% income tax rate.

Required:

1. How will discovery of this error change the amounts previously reported on the company's SFP and SCI for the years prior to 20X7?

2. What will be the impact on the company's 20X7 reporting? Prepare a journal entry to correct the error at the end of 20X7, if needed.

connect   **TR4-5 Segment Reporting:** Multi-Facet Corporation has eight operating segments. The revenue, profit and assets in each segment are as follows:

Segment	Revenue	Profit	Assets
A	$ 80,000	$ 7,000	$ 30,000
B	350,000	3,000	120,000
C	340,000	17,000	108,000
D	100,000	3,000	22,000
E	135,000	9,000	60,000
F	550,000	60,000	350,000
G	90,000	11,000	50,000
H	95,000	10,000	30,000
Total	$1,740,000	$120,000	$770,000

Required:

Determine which segments are reportable *segments*.

ASSIGNMENTS

★★ **A4-1 Current/Noncurrent Classification:** Consider each of the following separate situations that arose in 20X1:

a. Corporation G invested $65,000 in corporate bonds as a short-term investment. The year-end 20X1 market value of the bonds is $68,000.

b. Corporation A has the equivalent of C$200,000 cash in a bank in Elbonia. Elbonia's laws prohibit transferring the cash to the Canadian parent company. Corporation A has ongoing operations in Elbonia.

c. Corporation B received $72,000 from a customer as advance payment for special-order goods to be delivered in 20X3.

d. Corporation C has $400,000 in notes receivable from customers. The notes mature over a three-year period. The company normally sells its products on an instalment basis that requires payments over three years.

e. Corporation D made an advance payment of $330,000 into the employees' pension plan. The company will recognize the pension expense over five years beginning in 20X2.

f. Corporation H holds 10,000 shares in Theo Limited as a long-term investment; the shares cost $14 each. At year-end 20X1, the market value is $20 per share.

g. Corporation E has negotiated a two-year $600,000 loan from its bank to finance equipment. The bank will charge 6% interest per year, compounded. The loan will be repaid in a single lump sum in 20X3, including interest. The market rate of interest is 6%.

h. Corporation F has a major customer that recently went into receivership. As a result of an agreement among all creditors, Corporation F will receive payment on the customer's $240,000 outstanding account in equal instalments over a four-year period.

Required:
For each item indicate the amount(s) that will show as current and the amount(s) that will show as noncurrent in each company's 20X1 SFP.

★★ **A4-2 SFP/SCE Classification:** Dashall Ltd. has the following accounts in its year-end 20X7 trial balance:

a. Retained earnings.
b. Investment in equity securities of another company as a temporary use of cash.
c. Deferred income tax liability.
d. Note payable for equipment, payable in equal instalments over three years.
e. Income tax payable; the amount is being contested by Dashall Ltd.
f. Euro deposit account held in a New York bank.
g. Inventory held in a bonded warehouse (i.e., protected against improper entry). The product needs to be aged for five years before being finished and released for sale.
h. Foreign currency translation gain on Mexican subsidiary.
i. Investment in the marketable equity securities of another company in which Dashall Ltd. has significant influence.
j. Decline in fair value of assets in a division that is being discontinued; a buyer for the division is actively being sought.

Required:
Explain how each item would be reported on Imposing Ltd.'s 20X7 SFP and/or statement of changes in equity.

★ **A4-3 SFP/SCE Classification:** Abriel Limited, a public company, has the following accounts in its year-end 20X5 trial balance:

a. Dividends payable.
b. Compensating cash balance in Abriel's bank, being held by the bank as a partial "compensating balance" against a bank loan that will come due in early 20X7.

   c. Gain on repurchasing Abriel shares from a minority shareholder; the shares have been cancelled.

   d. Reserve for bond retirement.

   e. Translation loss on converting the pound sterling financial statements of a UK subsidiary to Canadian dollars.

   f. An empty warehouse not currently needed for storage.

   g. Security deposits by customers who order custom-designed products; if a customer cancels an order, Abriel keeps the deposit.

   h. Investment in marketable securities of an unrelated company; Abriel has held these securities for over two years.

   i. Provision for restructuring costs; these estimated costs are mainly for employee severance pay and retraining costs. The restructuring will take place over the next two or three years.

   j. A overdraft in one of Abriel's regional bank accounts; Abriel has more than sufficient funds in other accounts with the same bank.

Required:

Explain how each item would be reported on Imposing Ltd.'s 20X7 SFP and/or statement of changes in equity.

★★ **A4-4 Determining Values in the SFP:** The consolidated SFP of Mutron Lock Incorporated, is shown below.

MUTRON LOCK INCORPORATED

Consolidated Statement of Financial Position

As of 31 December 20X5

Assets

Current assets		
Cash and cash equivalents		$ 10,195
Marketable securities		a
Accounts receivable	$153,682	
Allowance for doubtful accounts	b	147,421
Inventories		201,753
Prepaid expenses		8,902
Total current assets		c
Noncurrent assets		
Land		12,482
Building (net)		d
Equipment and machinery	195,467	
Accumulated depreciation	(103,675)	91,792
Total capital assets		261,056
Investments		14,873
Other assets		7,926
Total assets		$661,774

Liabilities and shareholders' equity

Current liabilities	
Accounts payable	$ 85,476
Notes payable	e
Income taxes payable	6,421
Current portion of long-term debt	4,893
Accrued expenses	5,654
Total current liabilities	110,763
Long-term debt	122,004
Deferred income taxes	f
Total liabilities	g

Shareholders' equity
Preferred shares, no-par value (authorized
10,000 shares, issued 2,400 shares for $14,281)

Shareholders' equity	
Preferred shares, no-par value (authorized 10,000 shares, issued 2,400 shares for $14,281)	h
Common shares, no-par value (authorized 400,000 shares, issued 20,000 shares)	i
Total contributed capital	j
Retained earnings	206,471
Total Mutron Lock Inc. shareholders' equity	347,668
Non-controlling interest in subsidiaries	35,136
Consolidated shareholders' equity	382,804
Total liabilities and shareholders' equity	$ k

Required:

For each of the items (a) through (k) in the SFP above, calculate the amount that should appear for that item.

A4-5 Analyzing Data and Reporting on the SFP: Akerman Techonology Corporation is preparing its SFP at 31 December 20X5. The following items are under consideration:

a. Rent received in advance for the first quarter of 20X6, $16,000.
b. Note payable, long term, $80,000. This note was issued on 1 July 20X5 and will be paid in eight equal instalments. The first instalment, $10,000, will be paid 1 January 20X6. Interest will accrue at the rate of 6% per annum.
c. $200,000 bonds payable bearing interest of 8% per annum, maturing 31 December 20X9. Unamortized premium amounted to $5,000 at the end of 20X5.
d. Long-term note payable, $500,000, issued on 30 June 20X2 and maturing 30 June 20X6. Interest at 8% must be paid 30 June each year.
e. Restriction for bond sinking fund, $40,000; this restriction is required by provisions of the bond agreement.
f. On 28 January 20X6, prior to finalizing the 20X5 statements, the company issued new preferred shares to a private equity fund for $1,400,000. The new shares increased the equity base of the company by almost 40%. The fund will be used to retire existing long-term debt and for new production processes.

Required:

Show, with appropriate captions, how each of these items should be reported on the 31 December 20X5 SFP. If amounts are not quantifiable, describe the appropriate reporting that would be followed when numbers are available. Round amounts to the nearest $100.

A4-6 Financial Statement Classification: Listed below are some financial statement classifications coded with letters and, below them, selected transactions and/or account titles.

Code	Financial Statement Classification
	Statement of Comprehensive Income
A	Earnings/loss from continuing operations
B	Earnings/loss from discontinued operations
C	Other comprehensive income
D	Earnings per share
	Statement of Financial Position
E	Current assets
F	Noncurrent assets
G	Current liabilities
H	Noncurrent liabilities
I	Shareholders' equity

Statement of Changes in Shareholders' Equity

J   Beginning balance
K   An adjustment (addition to or deduction from) beginning balance
L   Change during the year—retained earnings
M   Change during the year—invested capital (not designated as a discontinued operation)
N   Change during the year—items of other comprehensive income

O   **Notes to the financial statements**

Response	Transaction or Account Title
A, E, I	0. Accrued interest on long-term receivables
_____	1. Provision for restructuring costs
_____	2. Accrued liability for employee post-retirement benefits
_____	3. Factory equipment designated for sale
_____	4. Translation gain on self-sustaining foreign subsidiary
_____	5. Appropriation for plant expansion
_____	6. Payment of $30,000 additional income tax assessment on prior year's income
_____	7. Cash dividends declared; not yet paid
_____	8. Estimated amount to be collected from a lawsuit against a competitor for patent infringement
_____	9. Earnings from a subsidiary that was purchased with the explicit intent to resell it at a higher price
_____	10. Exchange loss on accounts receivable balances in euros; the euro balances are hedged
_____	11. Amount paid when the company purchased and retired some of its own common shares; the amount paid was in excess of the shares' original issue proceeds
_____	12. Earnings after income tax from a division held for sale
_____	13. Loss due to expropriation of a plant in a foreign country
_____	14. Change in the translated net investment in a U.S. subsidiary
_____	15. Interest paid during the year plus interest accrued on liabilities
_____	16. Dividends received on shares held as an investment
_____	17. Damages paid as a result of a lawsuit by an individual injured while shopping in the company's store; the litigation lasted three years
_____	18. Cumulative effect of a change in accounting policy
_____	19. A $100,000 bad debt is to be written off—the receivable had been outstanding for five years. The company estimates bad debts each year and has an allowance for bad debts
_____	20. Adjustment due to correction of an error during current year; the error was made two years earlier

Required:

For each transaction or account title, enter in the space provided one or more code letters to indicate how that item will appear on the statements, either directly or implicitly. The first item, "0," is shown as an example. Comment on any doubtful items.

★★ **A4-7 Statement of Changes in Equity:** On 31 December 20X2, the balances of Argon Enterprises Inc.'s shareholders' equity accounts were as follows (all are credit balances):

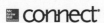

Capital stock	$303,000
Contributed surplus	6,000
Retained earnings	121,000
Currency translation differences	1,500
Mark-to-market adjustments on available for sale investments	28,600
Cash flow hedges	2,100
Actuarial gains and losses	1,600
	$463,800

Argon's statement of comprehensive income for the year ending 31 December 20X3 showed the following amounts, from "net profit for the year" through to "comprehensive income":

	31 December 20X3	31 December 20X2
Net profit for the year	$ 46,900	$62,100
Other comprehensive income (loss) net of applicable income tax:		
Currency translation differences	(4,500)	2,500
Mark-to-market adjustments on available for sale investments	(36,800)	7,200
Actuarial gains (losses)	2,100	(5,900)
Cash flow hedges	(500)	(150)
Total other comprehensive loss for the year	$(39,700)	$ 3,650
Comprehensive income for the year	$ 7,200	$65,750

Required:

Prepare a statement of changes in equity for Argon Enterprises Inc. for the year ended 31 December 20X3. The company declared no dividends during either 20X2 or 20X3.

★★ **A4-8 Statement of Changes in Equity:** The Atlantic Refinery Corporation (ARC) is a public company headquartered in St. John's, Newfoundland. On 31 December 20X5, the post-closing trial balance included the following accounts (in thousands of Canadian dollars):

	Debit	Credit
Investment in Mongolian subsidiary	$72,000	
Provision for future site restoration		$ 34,000
Common shares		170,000
Translation differential from Mongolian subsidiary		12,000
Convertible bonds		85,000
Equity portion of convertible bonds		5,000
Contributed surplus—premium on common shares issued		35,000
Goodwill (from purchase of Mongolian subsidiary)	18,000	
Investment in shares of upstream affiliate	36,000	
Retained earnings		533,000
Trademarks	6,800	

The following transactions and events occurred during 20X6:

a. Net income amounted to $47 million.
b. The value of trademarks was written off after ARC lost a patent protection lawsuit.
c. An additional $1.5 million of convertible bonds was transferred from the debt portion to the equity portion.
d. An accounting policy was changed due to a new IFRS taking effect in 20X6; the effect of retrospective restatement was to reduce prior years' earnings by an aggregate amount of $31 million.
e. The future liability for site restoration was increased by $5 million.
f. Common shares with a stated value of $15 million were repurchased on the open market for $20 million and cancelled. The original issue price of the shares amounted to $18, of which $3 million had been credited to contributed surplus.
g. A new class of preferred shares was issued to a major public sector pension plan for $85 million to finance future development.
h. Dividends totalling $24 million were issued during the year. Of that amount, $6 million were declared on 24 December 20X6, payable to shareholders of record on January 15, 20X7.
i. The translated amount of ARC's investment in Mongolian subsidiary declined by $2 million due to a rise in the value of the Canadian dollar.

Required:

Prepare a statement of changes in equity for Atlantic Refinery Corporation for the year ended 31 December 20X6. Explain assumptions you need to make, if any. [*Hint*: Not all of the accounts listed above are relevant to the CSE.]

★★ **A4-9 Rates of Return:** Refer to the data in **A4-7**. Assume that the assets of Argon Enterprises Inc. totalled $1,980,000 at the end of 20X1, $1,750,000 at year-end 20X2, and

 $2,120,000 at year-end 20X3.

Required:

1. Assume you are analyst for a private equity firm. Determine the following for each of 20X2 and 20X3:
   a. Return on assets
   b. Return on total shareholders' equity
   c. Return on invested capital
2. Explain the relevance and significance of these ratios for deciding whether or not your firm should invest in Argon Enterprises.

[*Hint:* You will need to calculate the year-end 20X1 shareholders' equity and invested capital balances by working backward from the amounts given in A4-7.]

★★ **A4-10 Rates of Return:** Po-Yen Devices Inc. and Kejia Computer Ltd. are competing businesses. Selected data from the financial statements for the two companies for the year

 ended 31 December 20X2 are shown below.

Year ended 31 December 20X2 (in thousands of Canadian dollars)	Po-Yen Devices	Kejia Computer
Sales revenue	$540,000	$270,000
Earnings from continuing operations, net of income tax	80,000	23,000
Net earnings, after income taxes	66,000	23,000
Comprehensive income	72,000	16,000
Current assets	$260,000	$110,000
Tangible capital assets, net	400,000	40,000
Total assets	$660,000	$150,000
Current liabilities	$120,000	$ 60,000
Long-term liabilities	360,000	—
Common shares	100,000	50,000
Retained earnings	80,000	40,000
Total liabilities and shareholders' equity	$660,000	$150,000
Number of common shares outstanding (thousands)	300,000	250,000

Required:

1. Compute the following ratios for both companies (for convenience, use 20X2 year-end balance sheet amounts instead of averages):
   a. Operating margin (i.e., earnings ÷ revenue)
   b. Return on assets
   c. Return on share equity
   d. Total debt-to-shareholder's equity
2. Evaluate the two companies, based on the ratios you have calculated. Which company do you think is more profitable?

★★ **A4-11 Error Correction:** On 23 November 20X7, when engaged in preparing for the 20X7 fiscal year-end, the chief accountant of Harper Limited discovered two accounting errors in the 20X5 statements:

a. A government ministry had paid $2.3 million in partial settlement of an amount due for a large contract. The contract revenue had already been recognized. However, the payment was accidentally credited to contract revenue instead of to accounts receivable and was included in taxable income.

b. Inventory purchases of $1.2 million had inadvertently been charged to equipment, a capital asset account, and had been amortized by 10% for each of 20X5 and 20X6. The accounting amortization rate is the same as the CCA rate for tax purposes. The ending and beginning inventories had been properly stated. Therefore, the mistake caused cost of sales to be understated by $1.2 million and pretax earnings to be overstated by the same amount.

Harper's income tax rate is 25%.

Required:

1. Calculate the earnings correction that Harper must show in the 20X7 financial statements. Where will these amounts be disclosed?
2. Prepare a general journal entry to record the correction of each error.

★★

A4-12 Error Correction: In May 20X5, the newly appointed controller of Butch Baking Corporation conducted a thorough review of past accounting, particularly of transactions that exceeded the company's normal level of materiality. As a result of his review, he instructed the company's chief accountant to correct two errors:

a. In 20X2, the company made extensive improvements to the baking process and installed a substantial amount of new equipment. The entire cost of the process improvements and equipment was accidentally charged to income as restructuring expense in 20X2. However, the equipment should have been capitalized and added to the factory equipment account. The cost of the equipment was $1,200,000. Butch depreciates its factory equipment on the straight-line basis over 10 years. A full year's depreciation is charged in the year that equipment is acquired.

b. A year-end cut-off error occurred in 20X3. A large shipment of nonperishable supplies arrived from China on the last day of 20X3 and had been left in the shipping containers outside the main plant. As a result, the supplies were recorded as received in 20X4 and had not been included in the year-end 20X3 inventory count. The account payable also had not been recorded in 20X3. The supplies cost $160,000.

Like most companies, Butch Baking presents a five-year financial summary in its annual report. The 20X4 summary contained the following information (in thousands of dollars, except EPS):

	20X0	20X1	20X2	20X3	20X4
Gross revenue	$ 15,000	$ 16,000	$ 17,500	$ 17,000	$ 18,000
Net income	1,980	2,100	850	2,300	2,100
Total assets	140,000	155,000	148,000	147,000	152,000
Total liabilities	50,000	65,000	70,000	69,000	73,000
Net assets	90,000	90,000	78,000	78,000	79,000
Earnings per share*	$19.80	$21.00	$8.50	$23.00	$21.00

*100,000 shares outstanding

Required:

1. Explain the impact of these two errors on the summary financial information.
2. Revise the financial summary.
3. Prepare the journal entry or entries that are necessary in 20X5 to correct the accounts as of 1 January 20X5.

★ **A4-13 Change in Accounting Policy:** The Hannam Company decided to change from the declining-balance method of depreciation to the straight-line method effective 1 January 20X7. The following information was provided:

Year	Net Income as Reported	Excess of Declining-balance Depreciation over Straight-Line Depreciation
20X3*	$(60,000)	$10,000
20X4	70,000	30,000
20X5	45,000	25,000
20X6	105,000	14,000

*First year of operations.

The company has a 31 December year-end. The tax rate is 22%. No dividends were declared until 20X7; $40,000 of dividends were declared and paid in December 20X7. Income for 20X7, calculated using the new accounting policy, was $210,000.

Required:

Assuming that the change in policy was implemented retrospectively, present the retained earnings reconciliation that would appear in Hannam's 20X7 statement of changes in equity.

★★ **A4-14 Change in Accounting Policy:** Moncton Developments Limited was established in early 20X2. During the first three years, the company followed the policy of expensing its development costs rather than capitalizing and amortizing them. The company followed this policy because in the early stages of the company's life, there was no reasonable assurance that the development costs would meet the criteria for capitalization. However, the company's development activities turned out to be very successful. Therefore, the company decided in 20X4 to change its method of accounting for product development expenses from expensing such items to capitalizing them and amortizing them over the period of expected benefit. To prepare for the change, the following data were gathered:

	20X4	20X3	20X2
Product development costs	$200,000	$150,000	$250,000
Depreciation and amortization, prior to change	70,000	70,000	60,000
Restated amortization, after policy change	120,000	110,000	90,000
Net income before income tax, old policy	840,000	770,000	300,000
Net income after income tax (at 30%), old policy	588,000	539,000	210,000
Earnings per share	$ 11.76	$ 10.78	$ 4.20

Moncton Developments has 50,000 common shares outstanding. The balance of retained earnings was $690,000 at 31 December 20X3. During 20X4, the company declared dividends of $50,000.

Required:

1. Determine the numerical impact of the policy change on net income and EPS for 20X2 and 20X3.
2. Prepare the retained earnings column (or section) of the 20X4 statement of changes in equity, giving appropriate treatment to the change in accounting policy.
3. Prepare an appropriate disclosure note.

★ **A4-15 Note Disclosures:** Note disclosures provide the following information:

A. Explain the accounting policies that the company is using.
B. Provide additional detail for financial statement components.

C. Identify major underlying assumptions and estimates.

D. Provide information not presented elsewhere in financial statements but that is useful for understanding them.

Typical notes include:

__B__   a. Description of income statement item, "discontinued operations"

_____   b. Amortization policy and amounts of accumulated amortization by asset class

_____   c. Revenue recognition policy

_____   d. Breakdown of the SFP amount shown for "other assets"

_____   e. Description of related party transactions

_____   f. Description of contingent loss that is not measurable

_____   g. Preferred share dividend rate

_____   h. Extent of reliance on major customers

_____   i. Sensitivity to variation in oil prices

_____   j. Description of subsequent event not relating to conditions before SFP date

_____   k. Information on key operating segments of the business

_____   l. Long-term debt note—interest rates, terms to maturity, five-year cash flow, market value

_____   m. Breakdown of inventory into component parts and description of valuation method

_____   n. Fair value of debt

Required:

For each note (a) to (n) above, indicate the type(s) of disclosure (letters A to D) provided. A note may provide more than one type of disclosure. The first one is done for you as an example.

 A4-16 Contingencies: Unlimited Possibilities Limited (UPL) is finalizing the financial statements for 20X5. The company's managers are uncertain how each of the following events and situations should be reported:

a. UPL is the guarantor on a $10 million bank loan that was obtained by another company controlled by the same shareholders who control UPL. The amount of the guaranteed loan is a material amount for UPL.

b. UPL has a subsidiary in Japan. UPL has reached agreement to sell the Japanese subsidiary to a Taiwanese company, subject to approval by regulators in Japan. When the sale closes, UPL will realize a profit of $20 million as the purchase price is $20 million higher than the subsidiary's net book value. Approval is expected, but it will be at least six months before the regulators issue their final ruling.

c. A minority shareholder alleges that UPL's controlling shareholders entered into transactions that had the effect of reducing the non-controlling shareholder's equity in the company. (In securities legislation this type of action is known as "shareholder oppression.") The non-controlling shareholder filed a complaint with the provincial securities commission, claiming damages of $50 million. The securities commission ruled in favour of the non-controlling shareholder. UPL is appealing the case and UPL's lawyers are confident that the court will overturn the ruling in approximately one year.

Required:

Discuss the appropriate reporting for each of these three items on UPL's 20X5 financial statements.

 A4-17 Contingencies, Subsequent Events: Zero Growth Limited has completed financial statements for the year ended 31 December 20X6. The financial statements have yet to be finalized or issued. The following events and transactions have occurred:

a. The office building housing administrative staff burned to the ground on 15 January 20X7.

b. On 15 November 20X6, a customer sued the company for $1,000,000 based on a claim of negligence leading to personal injury; Zero Growth is actively defending the suit and claims it is unfounded. Nothing has yet been recorded in the 20X6 financial statements in relation to this event.

c. On 1 February 20X7, Zero Growth received a $49,700 income tax reassessment for 20X5.

d. On 20 December 20X6, Zero Growth applied for a bank loan to replace an existing line of credit. The loan was granted on 2 January 20X7. This event was not recorded in 20X6 or reported in the draft 20X6 financial statements.

e. Zero Growth has reinterpreted a legal agreement entitling it to commission revenue for the sale of a client's products. Zero Growth's interpretation would entitle it to an extra $60,000 over and above amounts recognized in 20X6. The amount has not been recorded in the accounts. The client was billed for this amount in 20X6 but has disagreed with Zero Growth on the contract interpretation. Both parties have consulted their lawyers; resolution of the issue is not expected soon.

f. On 1 March 20X7, Zero Growth issued new common shares for cash. The new issue increased the total number of shares outstanding by 20%.

Required:
Discuss the appropriate accounting treatment for the contingencies and subsequent events described.

 A4-18 Subsequent Events: Northern Switching Ltd. (NSL) is a manufacturer of digital switching equipment and systems. The company has total assets of approximately $784 million. Each of the following events occurred after the end of NSL's 20X8 fiscal year, but before the statements had been finalized:

a. NSL finalized an agreement to sell a major production facility to Cascade Cable Corporation for approximately $84 million cash. The sale includes buildings of approximately one million square feet, fixtures, equipment, and 63 acres of land. The property has an amortized cost of $56 million on NSL's draft 20X8 SFP.

b. NSL reached agreement with an international banking corporation for credit support for up to $46 million of new sales to customers abroad.

c. The company has a U.S. subsidiary. NSL (i.e., the parent company) signed a repayment guarantee on a $100 million line of credit that Citibank issued to the subsidiary.

d. Marketable securities held by NSL at 20X8 year-end, reported on the year-end draft SFP at their market value of $27 million, were sold for $23 million.

e. The CEO of Crisco Corporation, NSL's major competitor, accused a senior NSL executive of improperly accessing confidential information via an employee-only portal on Crisco's website and using that information for competitive advantage. Crisco said that the company will file a lawsuit to recover $76 million in damages. NSL vehemently denies the allegation.

Required:
Discuss what disclosure, if any, NSL should give to each of these events in its 20X8 financial statements.

 A4-19 Subsequent Events: The auditor has completed her work on the financial statements of Leslie Kwok Incorporated (LKI) for the year ended 31 December 20X7. The auditor signed her audit opinion on 5 March 20X8; LKI's Board of Directors has not yet approved the statements. The following transactions and events occurred after 31 December 20X7:

a. On 27 January, LKI entered into a long-term lease for a private airplane for the company president and CEO. The lease requires payments of US$75,000 per month for 60 months.

b. On 28 January, LKI acquired all of the shares of Phan Limited by issuing LKI shares in exchange. The acquisition more than doubled the size of LKI, and the former shareholders of Phan now have a majority of the votes in LKI.

c. On 15 February, the Board of Directors of LKI decided to discontinue a major segment of the company's business due to continuing losses and a change of strategy.

d. The Royal Toronto Bank extended a $50 million line of credit to LKI on 5 March.
e. One of the company's major customers declared bankruptcy on 22 March. The customer accounted for 27% of LKI's revenue in 20X7.
f. On 31 March, LKI reached an agreement with a major institutional investor to issue $500 million in secured debentures through a private placement.
g. A new Board of Directors was elected on 7 April.
h. On 10 April, the new directors cancelled the lease on the private airplane. The contract calls for a cancellation penalty of US$1 million.

Required:
Discuss how each item should be reported in LKI's 20X7 financial statements as a *subsequent event*, if at all.

★ **A4-20 Segment Disclosure:** Union Carbolics Inc. has five operating segments. Segment operating data (in millions of Canadian dollars) for the year 20X6 are as follows:

Segment	Intersegment Sales	Sales to External Customers	Total Assets	Operating Profit (Loss)
Chemicals	$450	$1,500	$1,020	$ 90
Plastics	150	1,050	1,350	112
Adhesives	—	325	300	9
Solvents	—	275	255	(18)
Coatings	—	330	225	(21)
Totals	$600	$3,480	$3,150	$172

Required:
Identify which of these five segments are *reportable segments* under IFRS. Indicate the grounds on which you selected each identified segment.

★★ **A4-21 Segment Disclosure:** The following disclosure note is from the 31 December 20X4 financial statements of Riconda Limited:

The Company operates one operating segment, that being the design, manufacture, and sale of graphics and multimedia products for personal computers and consumer electronic devices.

	20X2	20X1	20X0
Sales			
Canada	$ 23,104	31,119	$ 41,175
U.S.	325,464	424,472	425,000
Europe	247,795	396,805	412,855
Asia-Pacific	441,446	430,669	307,320
Consolidated sales	$1,037,809	$1,283,065	$1,186,350
Product Sales			
Components	$ 481,083	$ 499,859	$ 390,238
Boards	548,053	778,015	796,112
Other	8,673	5,191	—
Consolidated sales	$1,037,809	$1,283,065	$1,186,350
Noncurrent Assets			
Canada	$ 54,162	$ 42,494	$ 36,590
U.S.	297,417	421,955	31,341
Europe	5,071	5,364	5,410
Asia-Pacific	706	919	1,051
Consolidated noncurrent assets	$ 357,356	$ 470,732	$ 74,392

Required:

1. What is the purpose of this disclosure note?
2. Evaluate the information presented. What does it tell you about the company's operations?
3. Review the requirements for segment disclosures. What information is lacking in the note above? Why?

 A4-22 Special Disclosures: Respond to the specific questions in each of the two cases, below.

Case A The following disclosure note is from the 31 October 20X2 financial statements of GreenWorld Limited, a mining company:

> The preparation of the financial statements, in conformity with generally accepted accounting principles, requires management to make estimates and assumptions that affect the reported amounts of assets and liabilities and disclosure of contingent assets and liabilities at the date of the financial statements and the reported amounts of revenues and expenses during the reporting period. The most significant estimates are related to the physical and economic lives and the recoverability of mining assets, mineral reserves, site restoration and related obligations, commodity contracts and financial instruments, and income taxes. Actual results could differ from those estimates.

Required:

1. What is the purpose of this disclosure note?
2. How could this note be made more meaningful to the financial statement user?
3. List four other financial statement elements (not listed above) that are affected by estimates.

Case B The following disclosure note is from the 31 December 20X2 financial statements of UMM Limited, a software company:

> UMM has entered into an agreement with Vitech Ltd., a shareholder, with respect to acquiring certain rights to Vitech's software, technology, services, and other benefits. In the current year, UMM acquired $200 (million) of specific software products from Vitech. These assets were recorded at the transaction price, which represents fair market value as determined by an independent appraisal. UMM has expensed $68 (million) in services received from Vitech in 20X2. Sales in 20X2 to Vitech amounted to $151 (million). These transactions were conducted in the normal course of business at prices established and agreed to by both parties.

Required:

1. What is the purpose of this disclosure note?
2. In general, what makes two parties related?
3. What measurement attribute has been used to record software assets, and revenues and expenses between these related parties? Comment.
4. What evidence has UMM gathered to support the value for software purchased?

 A4-23 Special Disclosures: Respond to the specific questions in each of the two cases, below.

Case A The following disclosure note appeared in the 31 December 20X5 financial statements of Dridell Corporation, a manufacturer of electronic equipment:

> Dridell is exposed to liabilities and compliance costs arising from its past and current generation, management, and disposal of hazardous substances and

wastes. As of 30 December 20X5, the accruals on the consolidated SFP for environmental matters were $27 million. Based on information available as of 31 December 20X5, management believes that the existing accruals are sufficient to satisfy probable and reasonably estimable environmental liabilities related to known environmental matters. Any additional liabilities that may result from these matters, and any additional liabilities that may result in connection with other locations currently under investigation, are not expected to have a material adverse effect on the business, results of operations, financial condition, and liquidity of Dridell.

Case B The following disclosure note is from the 31 December 20X2 financial statements of Zing Limited, a property developer:

> On 7 January 20X3, the Corporation contracted to acquire 60 residential housing units from a third party for a purchase price of $2.8 million, cash. On 24 January 20X3, the Company issued 240,000 stock options to senior officers of the company. These options have a three-year vesting period, with one-third vesting on each anniversary date.

Required:
For each of these two disclosure notes, explain:

1. What is the purpose of the note?
2. What types of management estimates are implied by this disclosure?
3. What implications might this note have for the financial reporting in future years, if any?

★★★ **A4-24 SFP Interpretation:** The SFP of Karmax Ltd. discloses the following assets:

KARMAX LIMITED

Statement of Financial Position (Extracts)

Year ended 31 December 20X6

(in thousands of Canadian dollars)

Assets	
Current assets	
Cash	$ 710
Short-term investments	416
Accounts receivable	1,011
Inventory	2,600
Prepaid expenses	410
Total current assets	$ 5,147
Tangible capital assets, net	14,755
Intangible capital assets, net	984
Long-term investments	1,077
Total assets	$21,963

The following information has been established in relation to market values (amounts in thousands of dollars):

	Market Value	Source
Short-term investments	$416	Quoted stock market price
Inventory	$4,190	Karmax price list
Tangible capital assets	$20,000–$25,000	Real estate appraisal
Long-term investment	$3,000	(Note 1)
Intangible capital assets	$10,000	(Note 2)

Note 1

The long-term investment is an investment in the common shares of a company owned and operated by the two sons of Karmax's major shareholder. The Karmax investment is 25% of the outstanding shares. The long-term investment is accounted for using the equity method. The sons' company has never sold shares to a nonfamily investor, and the Karmax shareholder provided this estimate of value.

Note 2

Karmax holds patents on a successful consumer product, licensed to various manufacturers. Significant annual royalties are earned; the recorded SFP value consists of legal fees paid during patent infringement cases. The $10 million estimate of market value is based on discounted future cash flow.

Required:

Prepare a brief report that contains:

1. An analysis of the reliability of the various market value estimates as a good predictor of future cash flows; and

2. An assessment of the usefulness of the (primarily historical cost) SFP to:
   a. A banker making a lending decision.
   b. An investor evaluating return on investment.

★★★   **A4-25 SFP Interpretation:** The SFP of a junior Canadian gold-mining company reports the following amounts (in $ thousands):

Assets
Current assets

Cash and cash equivalents	$ 8,260	
Accounts receivable, less allowance for doubtful accounts	20,338	
Taxes recoverable	200	
Inventories	20,800	
Prepaid expenses	500	
Investments (cost is equal to market value)	1,830	$ 51,928
Noncurrent assets		
Plant, equipment, and mine development costs, net		95,000
Goodwill		2,000
Total assets		$148,928

Liabilities and shareholders' equity
Current liabilities

Accounts payable and accrued liabilities	$ 6,550	
Royalties payable	560	$ 7,110
Noncurrent liabilities:		
Liability for site restoration costs	2,280	
Convertible bonds	12,000	
Deferred income taxes	1,830	16,110
Shareholders' equity		
Share capital	100,000	
Contributed surplus	1,128	
Cumulative exchange adjustment	500	
Retained earnings	23,000	
	124,628	
Non-controlling interest	1,080	
Consolidated shareholders' equity		125,708
Total liabilities and shareholders' equity		$148,928

Required:
1. Explain the meaning of the following accounts:
   a. Mine development costs
   b. Goodwill
   c. Liability for future site restoration costs
   d. Deferred income tax
   e. Non-controlling interest
   f. Cumulative exchange adjustment
   g. Contributed surplus
2. What items on the above SFP would most likely be estimated? Explain.
3. For what assets would you expect the market value and book value to be the most different? Explain.
4. As a potential shareholder, what additional information would be relevant to any decision to acquire shares in this company? Why is this information not presented with the audited financial statements?

★★ **A4-26 ASPE—Prepare an SFP:** The following trial balance was prepared by Vantage Electronics Corporation, a Canadian private enterprise, as of 31 December 20X5. The adjusting entries for 20X5 have been made, *except* for any related to the specific information noted below.

Vantage Electronics Trial Balance

31 December 20X5

Cash	$15,000	
Accounts receivable	15,000	
Inventories	17,000	
Equipment	22,400	
Land	6,400	
Building	7,600	
Prepaid expenses	1,100	
Accounts payable		$ 5,500
Note payable, 10%		8,000
Share capital, 2,500 shares outstanding		38,500
Retained earnings		32,500
Totals	$84,500	$84,500

Other information:
You find that certain errors and omissions are reflected in the trial balance below:

a. The $15,000 balance in accounts receivable represents the entire amount owed to the company; of this amount, $12,400 is from trade customers and 5% of that amount is estimated to be uncollectible. The remaining amount owed to the company represents a long-term advance to its president.
b. Inventories include $1,000 of goods incorrectly valued at double their cost (i.e., reported at $2,000). No correction has been recorded. Office supplies on hand of $500 are also included in the balance of inventories.
c. When the equipment and building were purchased new on 1 January 20X0 (i.e., six years earlier), they had estimated lives of 10 and 25 years, respectively. They have been amortized using the straight-line method on the assumption of zero residual value, and depreciation has been credited directly to the asset accounts. Amortization has been recorded for 20X5.
d. The balance in the land account includes a $1,000 payment made as a deposit on the purchase of an adjoining tract. The option to buy it has not yet been exercised and probably will not be exercised during the coming year.

e. The interest-bearing note dated 1 April 20X5 matures 31 March 20X6. Interest on it has not been recorded for 20X5.

Required:
Prepare a balance sheet with appropriate captions and subcaptions. Show the computation of the ending balance in retained earnings.

★★ **A4-27 ASPE—Redraft a Deficient SFP:** Rutgers e-Terminal Limited is a private corporation that is wholly owned by Mr. Adonis Rutgers. Mr. Rutgers also personally owns 40% of the common shares of a company named Princeton Corporation. A further 20% of the Princeton common shares are held by Rutgers e-Terminal Limited. The bookkeeper for Rutgers e-Terminal prepared the following SFP:

RUTGERS E-TERMINAL LIMITED
Financial Situation

For the year ending 31 December 20X3

Short-term assets		
Cash on hand	$ 600	
Cash in the Royal Dominion chequing account	15,200	
Overdraft in the ScotiaTrust chequing account	–3,800	
Accounts receivable (includes credit balances of $22,000)	52,600	
Automobile held for resale, fully depreciated (estimated market value, $10,000)	10,000	
Supplies on hand, at cost	1,800	
Inventory, at cost (estimated market value, $35,000)	37,900	
Final month's rent on office space (lease expires in 20X7)	3,000	
Investment in shares of subsidiary (market value, $150,000)	130,000	
		$247,300
Long-term assets		
Furniture	40,000	
Warehouse	500,000	
Prepaid expenses	4,500	
Note receivable from customer (issued 5 March 20X1, due on Mr. Rutger's demand)	30,000	
Loan receivable from shareholder	120,000	694,500
Total financial assets		$941,800
Liabilities		
Payable to suppliers	$175,300	
Amounts on purchase orders issued	50,000	
Reserve for depreciation on furniture	10,000	
Reserve for depreciation on warehouse	75,000	
Mortgage due to the Montreal National Bank	380,000	
Common shares of Rutgers e-Terminal held by Mr. Rutgers	150,000	
Accumulated surplus	101,500	
Total financial liabilities		$941,800

Required:
Prepare a corrected classified SFP, using appropriate terminology.

★★ **A4-28 ASPE—Redraft an SFP:** Prime Essentials Limited is a small private corporation. The owner plans to approach the bank for an additional loan or a line of credit to facilitate expansion. The company bookkeeper, after discussion with the owner of the company, has prepared the following draft SFP for the fiscal year ended 30 September 20X3, the company's first full year of operations:

PRIME ESSENTIALS LIMITED
Statement of Financial Position

Year ended 30 September 20X3

Assets	
Cash in the bank	$ 12,000
Patent	30,000
Goodwill	50,000
Equipment	120,000
Amounts owed by customers	32,000
Stocks and bonds owned by the company	10,000
Total	$254,000
Financing sources for assets	
Amounts owed to suppliers	28,000
Amount owed to owner for automobile expenses	6,000
Amount owed to owner's brother-in-law	20,000
Amount owed to bank	26,000
Earnings accumulated in the business	27,000
Shares paid for by owner	60,000
Cash flow from used-up portion of equipment	24,000
Increases in value	63,000
Total	$254,000

The bookkeeper has provided some notes on the amounts included in the draft SFP:

a. The owner invested $60,000 of his own money to start the business.
b. The patent was purchased from the owner's brother-in-law for $17,000. The owner believes that the patent could easily be sold for $30,000, and probably more.
c. The equipment is being depreciated at the same rate as allowed for income tax. Depreciation represents a source of financing for the company because it is added back to net income and increases the operating cash flow.
d. The owner uses his personal automobile for occasional business errands. He estimates that the company owes him $6,000 for his use of his personal car.
e. Because the business has been profitable from the very first, the owner estimates that he could sell the company at a $50,000 premium, thereby almost doubling his initial investment after only one year.
f. The bank gave a five-year loan to the company, with the provision that the company had to maintain a 25% "compensating balance" in its cash account until the loan is repaid.
g. The company holds some publicly traded shares in other companies. The value of these securities was $10,000 when the owner's brother-in-law gave them to the company as a loan on 1 April 20X3. On 30 September 20X3, their market value was $14,000. The company is free to sell the securities, but $10,000 plus one-half of any proceeds above $10,000 must be passed on to the brother-in-law. The brother-in-law also lent $10,000 cash to the company, repayable on demand.
h. One of the customers is a bit unsteady, financially. That customer owes $3,000.

Required:
Redraft the SFP. Provide an explanation for each change that you make. Explain any note disclosures that you think are needed.

★★★ **A4-29 ASPE—Criticize and Redraft a Deficient SFP:** The most recent SFP of Blackstone Tire Corporation, a private corporation, appears below:

Blackstone Tire Corporation SFP

For the year ended 31 December 20X5

Assets			
Current			
Cash			$ 23,000
Short-term investments			10,000
Accounts receivable			15,000
Merchandise			31,000
Supplies			5,000
Shares of Wilmont Co. (not a controlling interest)			17,000
			$101,000
Investments			
Loan to shareholder			82,500
Tangible:			
Building and land ($10,000)	$86,000		
Less: reserve for depreciation	40,000	46,000	
Equipment	$20,000		
Less: reserve for depreciation	15,000	5,000	51,000
Deferred			
Prepaid expenses			5,000
Total			$239,500
Debt and capital			
Current			
Accounts payable	$16,000		
Reserve for future, deferred income tax	17,000		
Customers' accounts receivable with credit balance	100	$ 33,100	
Fixed (interest paid at year-end):			
Bonds payable, 8.5%, due 20X9	45,000		
Mortgage, 11%	12,000	57,000	
Reserve for bad debts		900	
Capital			
Preferred shares, authorized and outstanding,			
6,000 shares	50,000		
Common shares, authorized 10,000 shares	67,000		
Earned surplus	22,500		
Donated capital	9,000	148,500	
Total			$239,500

Required:

1. List and explain in writing your criticisms of the above statement.

2. Prepare a complete SFP as far as possible, using appropriate format, captions, and terminology.

★★★ **A4-30 ASPE—Full Set of Statements; Comprehensive Income:** Amana Cement Corporation is a private corporation controlled by Amin Amana. The company's adjusted trial balance and other related data at 31 December 20X5 are given below. Although the company uses some obsolete terminology, the amounts are correct.

AMANA CEMENT CORPORATION

Adjusted Trial Balance

31 December 20X5

Debit balance accounts

Cash	$ 38,600
Land (used for building site)	129,000
Cost of goods sold	150,000
Short-term securities, at market (cost, $32,000)	42,000
Investment in U.S. subsidiary	100,000
Goodwill	120,000
Merchandise inventory	29,000
Office supplies inventory	2,000
Patent	7,000
Operating expenses	55,000
Income tax expense	17,500
Impairment of patent	7,500
Prepaid insurance	900
Building (at cost)	150,000
Land (held for speculation)	75,000
Translation loss on U.S. subsidiary, 31 December 20X4	12,000
Accrued interest receivable	300
Accounts receivable (trade)	22,700
Note receivable, 10% (long-term investment)	30,000
Subscriber lists (net)	22,000
Prepayments to pension fund in advance of expensing (long-term)	26,000
Dividends declared in 20X5, payable in 20X6	15,000
Correction of error from prior year—no income tax effect	15,000
	$1,066,500

Credit balance accounts

Reserve for bad debts	$ 1,100
Accounts payable (trade)	15,000
Revenues	275,000
20X5 translation gain on U.S. subsidiary	15,000
Deferred income tax	47,500
Note payable (short term)	12,000
Common shares, no par, 10,000 shares outstanding	170,000
Reserve for depreciation, building	90,000
Retained earnings, 1 January 20X5	202,500
Gain on new accounting policy	40,000
Accrued wages	2,100
Cash advance from customer	3,000
Accrued property taxes	800
Note payable (long term)	16,000
Rent revenue collected in advance	1,500
Bonds payable, 11% ($25,000 due 1 June 20X6)	175,000
	$1,066,500

Additional information (no accounting errors are involved):

a. Merchandise inventory is based on FIFO, lower of cost or net realizable value.

b. The patent is subjected to an annual impairment test. The impairment for 20X5 has already been recorded.

c. Operating expenses as given include depreciation and interest expense, and revenues include interest and investment revenues.

d. The "cash advance from customer" was for a special order that will not be completed and shipped until March 20X6; the sales price has not been definitely established because it is to be based on cost (no revenue should be recognized for 20X5).

Required:

Prepare the following:

1. Income statement (including EPS)
2. Statement of retained earnings
3. SFP

CHAPTER 5

The Statement of Cash Flows

INTRODUCTION

The statement of comprehensive income provides information about the results of operations. The statement of financial position includes information about the assets, liabilities, and equity of the company. What additional information can a statement of cash flows (SCF) provide?

Consider the 2011 financial statements of Cangene Corporation, a biopharmaceutical company in the business of developing, manufacturing, and marketing products to treat infectious diseases. The company had gross revenues of $150 million in 2011 and reported net earnings of $1.5 million. The statement of financial position shows cumulative retained earnings of $172 million and total assets of $266 million. Several asset and liability accounts show large changes in the year. What have been the company's major cash transactions during the year? An analyst could piece the changes together. Or the SCF could be consulted: the SCF shows the cash effect of significant operating, investing, and financing decisions.

The SCF for Cangene shows that the $1.5 million operating earnings actually represented significant cash inflows from operating activities of $15.7 million. Much of the difference is the result of non-cash expenses, such as depreciation and amortization, and a writedown of capital assets and goodwill because of impairment. These items decreased earnings but used no cash during the period. The SCF shows that the company spent $3.3 million in cash to redeem common shares and spent over $7.5 million on new plant and equipment. Thus, the cash implications of *strategic activity* during the year—positive cash outflow from operations, retiring some of the company's equity financing and major expenditure on new plant and equipment—is *most obvious* from the SCF. This statement provides important, easily identifiable insights into the actions of the company that have cash impact. It unravels the accruals and deferrals needed in the other statements.

This chapter discusses the preparation and interpretation of the SCF. As individual categories of assets, liabilities, and shareholders' equity are covered in following chapters, the cash flow impact of each topic will be reviewed at the same time.

Objectives of the SCF

Companies are required to include the **statement of cash flows** (SCF) as an integral part of their financial statements. Historical cash flows are often used as an indicator of the amount, timing, and uncertainty of future cash flows. Cash inflows must be measured against cash outflows, such as loan repayments, replacement of capital assets, and payments to owners. Therefore, the objective of the SCF is to disclose the historical cash flows of the enterprise during the reporting period for both feedback and predictive purposes.

Classification and Organization

The SCF is classified on the basis of the type of cash flow:

- **Operating activities** are the principal revenue-producing activities of the enterprise and the related expenditures. The cash inflow from operations is measured as the cash received from customers or clients. Cash outflows are those disbursements for operating activities, such as cash paid for inventories, wages and salaries, and overhead costs. Cash flow is not accrual accounting, and cash from customers is different from revenue recognized, just as cash paid for expenses is different from expenses recognized on the statement of comprehensive income.

  Operating activities relate to *net earnings*, not *comprehensive income*. Net earnings comprise revenues and expenses. If the company has recognized specific amounts that are part of other comprehensive income, these transactions or events are not included in operating activities. Therefore, *net earnings is the reference point for operating activities on the SCF*.

- **Investing activities** are those activities that relate to long-term assets and investments that are not cash equivalents—essentially capital assets and investments. The acquisition and disposal of property, plant, and equipment; intangible assets; other assets; and investments[1] are all included in this section. Changes in (current) operating assets, such as inventory and accounts receivable, are excluded from this section and included in operating activities.

- **Financing activities** relate to borrowings of the entity and contributed owners' equity. Changes in operating liabilities, such as accounts payable, are excluded from this section and included in operating activities.

Exhibit 5-1 lists some of the common transactions that fall into each category.

Definition of "Cash"

On the SCF, cash is defined as cash, plus cash equivalents, less any temporary bank overdrafts.

1. Cash Cash includes currency on hand, which is cash held for daily operating purposes in cash registers or petty cash funds. Cash also includes the amount that is held in the company's **current account**(s) with the bank, as long as these are due on demand, with no notice (delay before withdrawing funds) requirement.

2. Cash Equivalents Cash is a nonproductive asset, and therefore companies strive to keep their immediately accessible cash balance at a minimum. Companies place their cash in term deposits, guaranteed investment certificates, certificates of deposit, or other money market instruments to earn interest. These investments are **cash equivalents** and are part of cash on the SCF if they meet two conditions:

- They are held for the purpose of meeting short-term cash commitments and not for investing or other reasons; and
- They are readily convertible into a known amount of cash and are subject to an insignificant risk of change in value. Investments with a very short maturity, *at the time of purchase*, would qualify: Short maturity is suggested to be three months or less. There may be exceptional circumstances where a slightly longer term can be justified. Investments in common shares are excluded because they have no maturity date.

---

[1] Investments that are held for trading qualify as operating activity cash flows.

EXHIBIT 5-1

EXAMPLES OF CASH FLOWS BY CATEGORY

Operating Cash Flows

Inflows	**Outflows**
Receipts from customers	Payments to suppliers
Advance deposits from customers	Wages and salaries to employees
Income tax refunds	Rent and insurance payments
	Income tax payments, related to any year

Investing Cash Flows

Inflows	**Outflows**
Cash received from sale of property, plant, and equipment	Payments to buy property, plant, and equipment, including capitalized interest
Cash received from sale of investment property	Payments to buy investment property
Cash from sale of debt or equity investments	Cash flows capitalized as intangible assets, such as:
Collection of principal on loans to others	• legal fees
	• development costs
	Purchase of investments in the form of debt or equity securities of others
	Loans extended to others

Financing Cash Flows

Inflows	**Outflows**
Net proceeds of issuing debt or equity securities	Repayment of principal on bonds or bank loans
Cash proceeds received from bank loans	Repurchase of the entity's own shares

---

3. Overdrafts Companies might be authorized by their lenders to have an **overdraft**, which is a negative balance in the bank current account. For example, suppose that a company begins the year with a balance of $10,000 in its current account. By the end of the year, the cash balance is completely used up and more—there is a negative balance, or an overdraft, of $15,000 in the current account. The change in cash for the year is not simply the decline in cash from $10,000 to zero, but is the change from a $10,000 asset to a $15,000 liability—a decrease of $25,000.

Bank overdrafts are included as a component of cash and cash equivalents *when the bank balance fluctuates from positive to negative on a regular basis.* That is, if the current account is always overdrawn, it is in substance a bank loan and not a cash equivalent. The current account must be regularly positive and then swing to overdraft status (and then back) to qualify as "cash." Furthermore, the overdrafts have to be repayable at any time that the bank demands payment.

Many companies rely on a **line of credit**, which is a preapproved short-term bank loan. The borrowing limit has been negotiated with the lender in advance. Lines of credit often are used to cover seasonal fluctuations in cash flows. However, lines of credit and other types of short-term bank loans (and a permanently overdrawn cash account) normally are viewed as financing activities and are *not* part of the cash definition.

Reconciliation The components of cash and cash equivalents (including overdrafts) must be disclosed. The cash amount that is reported in the SCF must be reconciled to the equivalent items in the statement of financial position.

SCF Example

Exhibit 5-2 shows the SCF for International Forest Products Limited (INTERFOR), a Canadian company that produces wood products in British Columbia and in the U.S. Pacific Northwest for sale to markets around the world. Note that:

1. For all three categories, the cash flows can be either positive or negative. For example, investing activities include both cash outflows for purchase of property, plant, and equipment and cash inflows from disposal.

2. Positive and negative flows are *not* netted. For example, as shown, INTERFOR had a cash inflow of $100,000 in 2011 from new borrowing and also had a cash outflow of $146,000 to repay long-term debt.

3. The cash provided by operating activities is calculated *indirectly*, starting with *net loss* of the period and then adjusting to cash flow. This is the most common presentation approach—we will discuss an alternative later in the chapter.

Interpreting the Statement of Cash Flows

Interpretation involves examining the SCF for the major sources and uses of cash. The following questions must be considered, with professional judgement:

- Has operations provided cash or used cash?
- Why are earnings different than cash from operating activities? What are the major adjustments?
- What are the major investing activities that involved cash transactions?
- What are the major financing activities that involved cash transactions?
- How are these activities interrelated?
- Has cash, overall, increased or decreased for the period?
- How do the company's cash activities compare with prior years? With competitors?
- What accounting policy choice might affect classification of cash flows?

Since non-cash transactions are omitted from the SCF, it is important to review these transactions, included in the disclosure notes, to gather a complete picture of the company's strategic activities for the year. Only the cash transactions are included on the SCF.

Note that a company can report a loss and still have positive cash flows from operations. This commonly happens when net earnings include a large amount of depreciation of capitalized costs. Lenders may be quite willing to lend to such a company on the strength of the cash flow, despite the existence of losses, because they are convinced that there is adequate cash flow to pay the interest and principal.

Refer to the INTERFOR SCF in Exhibit 5-2. INTERFOR reported 2011 net loss of $13,453 (all amounts are in thousands), but cash flow from operating activities is positive, at $28,439. Depreciation and depletion expenses of $27,291 and $24,263, respectively, are added back—these expenses reduced earnings but did not require cash this period. Another major difference between cash generated by operating activities and earnings is the $25,613 outflow related to an increase in inventory.

In investing activities, there were outflows of $16,099 for the purchase of property, plant, and equipment, and $19,987 for additions to logging roads. A subsidiary was acquired, and this resulted in an inflow of the subsidiary's cash position to the consolidated entity. The acquisition itself was a non-cash transaction that is omitted from the SCF. In financing activities, INTERFOR raised $56,256 through share issuance. There was additional borrowing of $100,000, but higher debt repayment of $146,000. Overall, the cash balance increased by $1,134 this year, and the company ended the year with $10,435 in cash and cash equivalents.

EXHIBIT 5-2

INTERNATIONAL FOREST PRODUCTS LIMITED

Consolidated Statements of Cash Flows

(in thousands of Canadian dollars)

Years ended 31 December 2011 and 2010	2011	2010
Cash provided by (used in):		
Operating activities:		
Net loss	$ (13,453)	$ (5,193)
Items not involving cash:		
Depreciation of plant and equipment	27,291	27,475
Depletion and amortization of timber, roads, and other	24,263	18,521
Income tax expense	1,427	470
Finance costs	7,094	10,441
Other assets	238	(5)
Reforestation liability	(90)	(670)
Other liabilities and provisions	(2,761)	287
Equity in earnings of associate company	—	(11,431)
Writedown (reversals) of plant, equipment, and roads	(423)	809
Unrealized foreign exchange losses (gains)	191	(71)
Other expense (income)	(184)	25
	43,593	40,658
Cash generated from (used in) operating working capital:		
Trade accounts receivable and other	3,191	(13,461)
Inventories	(25,613)	(12,423)
Prepayments	(1,698)	(551)
Trade accounts payable and accrued liabilities	9,588	15,161
Income taxes refunded (paid)	(622)	396
	28,439	29,780
Investing activities:		
Additions to property, plant, and equipment	(16,099)	(10,745)
Additions to logging roads	(19,987)	(16,261)
Additions to timber and other intangible assets	(126)	(15,218)
Proceeds on disposal of property, plant, and equipment	273	1,325
Cash received on acquisition of subisidary	4,846	—
Investments and other assets	(921)	(4,383)
	(32,014)	(45,282)
Financing activities:		
Issuance of share capital, net of expenses	56,256	862
Interest payments	(5,629)	(8,881)
Funds from promissory note payable to associate	—	15,738
Additions to long-term debt	100,000	125,819
Repayments of long-term debt	(146,000)	(112,534)
	4,627	21,004
Foreign exchange gain (loss) on cash and cash equivalents held in a foreign currency	82	(3)
Increase in cash and cash equivalents	1,134	5,499
Cash and cash equivalents, beginning of year	9,301	3,802
Cash and cash equivalents, end of year	$ 10,435	$ 9,301

References to disclosure notes deleted.

Source: International Forest Products Limited, 2011 Annual Financial Statements, www.sedar.com, posted 17 February 2012.

CONCEPT REVIEW

1. What are the three categories of cash flows to be reported on the SCF?
2. What is the definition of cash on the SCF?
3. How does cash from operating activities differ from net earnings?

Basic Approach to Preparation

The statements of financial position and comprehensive income are prepared from the trial balance. Preparation of these statements involves classifying the general ledger accounts. The SCF, on the other hand, is a statement that is prepared by analyzing account balances and changes in balances. It is not enough, for example, to know by how much the equipment balance has changed over the course of an accounting period; one must analyze the sources of the accounting entries in the account. As a result, the SCF is usually a hand-prepared statement.

Analyzing Cash Flows If the statement explains cash flows, it seems logical to start by analyzing the cash in and out of the cash account(s). The entries to the general ledger cash account are usually summary entries from subsidiary records such as specialized journals or cumulative transaction records. For example, it should be possible to see how much cash was received from customers by summarizing the debits to the cash account from the collections on accounts receivable and/or from the summary posting of the daily cash receipts; cash paid to employees for wages and salaries can be obtained by looking at the payroll accounts, and so on.

Unfortunately, direct analysis of the cash account is difficult and time consuming. Therefore, the normal approach is to describe the cash activities by analyzing the changes in all of the *non-cash* accounts. Since one basic, indisputable characteristic of the statement of financial position (the balance sheet) is that it *balances*, cash flows can be determined by looking at the causes of the changes in all of the other accounts *except* cash (and cash equivalents.) For example, it is possible to quickly determine how much cash was received from customers by taking the total sales revenue figure and adjusting that accrual-basis amount by the change in trade accounts receivable for the period. If the balance in accounts receivable went up, then the company received less cash than was recognized in sales for the period; if the accounts receivable balance went down, then the company received more cash than was recognized in sales.

A Simple Example

The data for preparing the SCF for Simple Limited is shown in Exhibit 5-3.

The cash account shows a change from $20 at the beginning of the year to $35 at the end, for a net increase of $15. However, there is a short-term investment account. Investigation shows that it meets the required criteria and can be classified as a cash equivalent investment. It is therefore included with cash, and the net change in the balance of cash and cash equivalents is a *decrease* of $35:

	Ending	Beginning	Change	
Cash balance	$35	$20	$ 15	increase
Short-term investments	20	70	(50)	decrease
Total	$55	$90		
Net increase (decrease) in cash and cash equivalents			$(35)	decrease

---

EXHIBIT 5-3

SIMPLE LIMITED

Statement of Financial Position

(in thousands) 31 December	20X5	20X4
Current assets:		
Cash	$ 35	$ 20
Short-term investments	20	70
Accounts receivable	110	125
Inventory	100	135
	$ 265	$ 350
Capital assets:		
Plant and equipment	1,100	1,000
Accumulated depreciation	(250)	(300)
	850	700
Total assets	$1,115	$1,050
Current liabilities:		
Bank loan	$ 65	$ 50
Accounts payable	100	125
	165	175
Long-term note payable	300	330
Shareholders' equity:		
Common shares	100	100
Retained earnings	550	445
	650	545
Total liabilities and shareholders' equity	$1,115	$1,050

SIMPLE LIMITED

Statement of Comprehensive Income

Year ended 31 December 20X5

Revenue:	
Sales revenue	$2,000
Gain on sale of equipment	70
	2,070
Operating expenses:	
Cost of goods sold	1,100
Other expenses	640
	1,740
Net earnings and comprehensive income	$ 330

SIMPLE LIMITED

Statement of Changes in Equity

	Common shares	Retained earnings
Opening balance, 1 January 20X5	$100	$445
Net earnings and comprehensive income		330
Dividends declared		(225)
Closing balance, 31 December 20X5	$100	$550

Additional information:
 i. Other operating expenses include $200 of depreciation expense.
 ii. During the year, Simple sold equipment originally costing $310 for net proceeds of $130.

The SCF is shown in Exhibit 5-4. (The letters in the "key" column in Exhibit 5-4 refer to the explanations below.)

To explain the flows that resulted in the net decrease of $35, all of the changes in the *non-cash* accounts are analyzed, starting with information from the statement of comprehensive income, the statement of changes in equity, and the *additional information*, as follows:

a. Net earnings of $330 is the basis for determining cash flow from operating activities. For this company, there are no items reported on other comprehensive income that would make net earnings different from comprehensive income. *If net earnings were different from comprehensive income, the SCF would still start with net earnings.*

　　The amount of net earnings is placed first in the operating activities section of the SCF. Net earnings, of course, includes all revenues and expenses, so starting with this number places all revenues in operating activities as inflows, and all expenses in operating activities as outflows. Net earnings is then reconciled to the *real* cash inflow and outflow for revenue and expenses.

b. Dividends of $225 were declared (and paid) during the year. This amount is placed in the financing section. Note that net earnings of $330 less dividends of $225 completely explain the $105 increase in retained earnings during the year.

c. *Additional information* reveals that operating expenses includes $200 in depreciation. Since depreciation is an interperiod allocation of previous years' investment cash flows, its impact must be removed from net earnings. The $200 depreciation is *added back* to net earnings to eliminate the effect of this interperiod allocation.

d. *Additional information* reveals that equipment that originally cost $310 was sold for $130. The statement of comprehensive income also shows a gain from the sale of equipment

---

EXHIBIT 5-4

SIMPLE LIMITED

Statement of Cash Flows

Year ended 31 December 20X5	Key		
Operating activities:			
Net earnings	(a)	$330	
Add (deduct) to reconcile net earnings to net operating cash flows:			
Depreciation expense	(c)	200	
Gain on sale of equipment	(d)	(70)	
Decrease in accounts receivable	(e)	15	
Decrease in inventory	(f)	35	
Decrease in accounts payable	(g)	(25)	$485
Investing activities:			
Proceeds from sale of equipment	(d)	130	
Purchase of new equipment	(h)	(410)	(280)
Financing activities:			
Increase in current bank loan	(j)	15	
Dividends paid	(b)	(225)	
Reduction of long-term notes payable	(k)	(30)	(240)
Increase (decrease) in cash and cash equivalents			(35)
Cash and cash equivalents, 1 January			90
Cash and cash equivalents, 31 December			$ 55

amounting to $70. The following entry must have been made when the equipment was sold:

Cash	130	
Accumulated depreciation (to balance)	250	
Plant and equipment		310
Gain on sale of equipment		70

On the SCF, the $130 cash received is an investing activity; the $70 gain is eliminated (subtracted) from operating cash flow. The gain is eliminated for two reasons:

1. The sale of assets is not an operating activity but reflects a change in asset structure; the disposal of assets must be reported as an investing activity.

2. The gain does not measure the actual cash flow during the period, but instead it is the difference between the proceeds of the sale and the net book value of the asset. The net book value is the original expenditure for the asset, reduced by depreciation to date.

e. Accounts receivable decreased by $15 during the year. This means that customers paid more than the amount reported as sales. The $15 is added to net earnings in the operating section to restate the sales from an accrual to a cash basis.

f. Inventory decreased by $35. The change in inventory is a component of cost of goods sold (COGS). By definition, the beginning-of-year inventory was acquired in a previous period and not the current period. Therefore, a decrease in inventory indicates that less cash was paid for the goods than were sold during the year.

g. Accounts payable decreased by $25. The accounts payable adjustment is assumed to be primarily related to the inventory adjustment, since trade accounts payable relate largely to inventory purchases. This $25 decrease indicates that suppliers were paid more cash for goods and services than the company accrued during the period. The $25 decrease reduces the amount of cash from operating activities.

h. Plant and equipment increased by $100 during the year. However, this amount is the net result of both new investment and retirement of old equipment. From (d) (above), the disposal was $310. The amount of the 20X5 acquisition is determined as follows:

Beginning balance	$1,000
Original cost of equipment sold during the year	− 310
Equipment purchased during the year	+ ???
Ending balance	$1,100

The amount that makes the account balance is $410. This is an outflow for purchased equipment in the investing activities section.

i. Accumulated depreciation decreased by $50. Depreciation expense of $200 for 20X5 was added to this account, and accumulated depreciation on the equipment sold was $250. These two transactions combine to verify the $50 reduction and no additional entry to the SCF is needed.

j. The current bank loan increased by $15. This is a loan and not an overdraft; therefore, the loan is *not* included as a component of cash and cash equivalents. The increase in the loan is a source of financing and will go into the financing section of the SCF.

k. The long-term note payable decreased by $30. This represents a principal repayment and is an outflow in the financing activity section.

l. Common shares did not change during the period. There will be no item on the SCF relating to common shares.

The net result of entering all of these amounts in the SCF is that net decrease in cash of $35 is explained. In a disclosure note, the company will show the components of cash, that is, that both cash and cash equivalents are included.

CONCEPT REVIEW

1. When the operating activities section starts with net earnings, why is depreciation added to derive cash flow from operating activities? Is depreciation a source of cash?

2. Explain why a gain on the sale of equipment is subtracted in the reconciliation of earnings and operating cash flows.

3. Why is the change in the balance of accounts receivable included in the SCF?

4. If salaries payable increases during the year, why does this imply that salary expense exceeds salary payments?

Presentation of Operating Activities

There are two approaches for presenting the cash provided by (used in) operating activities:

- *Indirect presentation:* The operating activities section begins with net earnings, and all interperiod allocations and accruals are reversed out of net earnings.
- *Direct presentation:* The revenues and expenses are each adjusted to a cash basis of reporting and listed directly.

In Exhibit 5-4, the indirect method of presentation is used. Operating activities begins with net earnings of $330 and is then adjusted for depreciation, the accounting gain on sale of equipment, and changes in the balances of the other current assets and current liabilities related to operating items.

Exhibit 5-5 shows the operating activities section of Simple Limited's SCF, using the direct approach of presentation. The amounts are obtained as follows:

1. To convert from accrual-basis sales to cash received from customers, start with sales, and add the decrease in accounts receivable during the year ($15). This converts sales ($2,000) to cash received from customers ($2,015). This $15 adjustment is the same as adding the amount that customers owed at the beginning of the year ($125 opening balance) and subtracting the amount owing at the end of the year ($110 ending balance):

Sales, accrual basis	$2,000
Plus cash collected on opening accounts receivable	+ 125
Minus cash not collected at year-end	− 110
Cash received from sales during 20X5	$2,015

2. COGS requires two adjustments. The first adjustment is for the decrease in inventory of $35 during the year. Since inventory purchased in the previous year was used this year, the cash flow requirements for buying inventory were $35 less than the expense shown for COGS. Therefore, subtract the $35 decrease from the $1,100 expense to arrive at cash

---

EXHIBIT 5-5

SIMPLE LIMITED

Statement of Cash Flows
Sample of Direct Presentation of Operating Activities

Year ended 31 December 20X5

Operating activities:		
Cash received from customers ($2,000 + $15)	**(1)**	$2,015
Operating expenses:		
Cash paid to suppliers ($1,100 – $35 + $25)	**(2)**	(1,090)
Cash paid for other operating expenses ($640 – $200)	**(3)**	(440)
Cash provided by operating activities		$ 485

---

flow. Partially offsetting the decline in inventory is the decrease in accounts payable. The decrease in accounts payable of $25 indicates that more cash was expended to pay creditors (presumably, for inventory purchases and other expense components that comprise COGS). Therefore, it is necessary to increase the expense by $25 to arrive at cash flow. The $1,090 cash flow for COGS is lower than the expense by $10.

3. Other operating expenses are decreased by the $200 depreciation. Items such as depreciation and the gain on sale of equipment are not cash flows and are omitted in the SCF under the direct presentation approach.

Direct or Indirect? The standard permits either the direct or indirect method of reporting cash flows from operating, but enterprises are "encouraged" to report cash flows from operating activities using the direct method.

It is often argued that the direct approach is clearer to financial statement users because they do not have to untangle the adjustments that are made under the indirect approach. In particular, there is the concern that the indirect method encourages the idea that depreciation is a source of funds. The addback of depreciation is usually a large positive element in the operating section, and business people have often been heard to remark that they will be using their "depreciation funds" for certain projects. Of course, this is a mistaken impression, but the indirect presentation method certainly strengthens the myth.

Regardless of any possible advantages in clarity of using the direct approach, the indirect method of presentation has been, by far, the more dominant approach in practice. There is certainly no trend toward the direct method of presentation.

Two-Step Indirect Presentation

A common refinement of the indirect method of presentation is a two-step approach. First, net earnings is adjusted for interperiod allocations and nonoperating amounts, and then it is adjusted for changes in other working capital accounts. Changes in working capital are often included as a single, summary amount, with the detail included in a disclosure note. The operating section of Simple Limited's SCF is illustrated in Exhibit 5-6, using the two-step approach. (INTERFOR, in Exhibit 5-2, also uses a two-step presentation.)

Note the subtotal of $460 after "items not affecting cash" in Exhibit 5-6. This subtotal is just a matter of convenience and has no special meaning.

EXHIBIT 5-6

SIMPLE LIMITED

SCF Operating Activities Two-Step Indirect Presentation

Year ended 31 December 20X5

Operating activities:	
Net earnings	$330
Plus (less) items not affecting cash:	
Depreciation	200
Gain on sale of equipment	(70)
	460
Changes in other working capital items:	
Decrease in accounts receivable	15
Decrease in inventory	35
Decrease in accounts payable	(25)
Cash provided by operating activities	$485

Offsetting Transactions

Accounting standards emphasize that *offsetting should not occur in the SCF.* That is, gross cash receipts and gross cash payments must be reported separately for investing and financing activities.

Within the investing and financing activities of the enterprise, there often are transactions that, overall, have the effect of offsetting or partially offsetting each other. For example, if a company refinances its debt by retiring an outstanding bond issue and issuing new bonds, the *net* impact on the statement of financial position may be relatively minor. However, these activities demonstrate the company's ability to renew its capital structure. The cash flows associated with the refinancing should be disclosed separately and not offset, or netted.

Netting is permitted in limited circumstances. *If cash flows represent cash receipts and payments on behalf of a customer in relation to the activities of the customer, netting is appropriate.* For example, net cash flows would be reported if the company were a property management company that collected rent on behalf of a customer and turned that rent over to the customer, net of a management fee. Only the management fee is reported as a cash inflow.

Non-cash Transactions

Some transactions have a significant effect on the asset, liability, or equity structure of an entity without involving any direct cash flow at all. These non-cash transactions are economically similar to cash transactions *but are excluded from the SCF because no cash changes hands.* For example, settling a debt by issuing shares directly to the debt holder involves no cash but has the same effect as issuing the shares for cash and using the proceeds to settle the debt. Or an asset may be acquired without cash by entering into a mortgage or a long-term finance lease; the economic effect is the same as borrowing money to buy the asset.

Common types of non-cash transactions include:

- Retiring bonds through share issuance;
- Assuming finance lease obligations in exchange for leased assets;
- Converting preferred shares to common shares;

- Settling debt by transferring non-cash assets;
- Bond refinancing directly with existing bond holders;
- Converting bonds to common shares;
- Acquiring shares in another company in exchange for shares of the reporting enterprise; and
- Issuing a stock dividend, which increases common shares and decreases retained earnings.

At one point, non-cash transactions, such as those listed above, were required to be included in the SCF as both an inflow and an outflow. However, the current reporting standard specifically *excludes non-cash transactions* from the SCF on the grounds that such transactions are not cash flows. For example, the acquisition of a building (an investing activity) that is acquired through a finance lease (a financing activity) would not be shown on the face of the SCF because there was no cash involved. These transactions must be fully explained in the disclosure notes.

Note Disclosure When a non-cash transaction is excluded from the SCF, it is included in a disclosure note to make sure financial statement users are informed about the transaction. This information is often part of other disclosure notes: property plant, and equipment, common share disclosure, and so on. In our text assignments, a list of non-cash transactions should accompany a SCF to represent the note disclosure requirement.

Partial Cash Transactions Sometimes an acquisition will take place where part of the consideration is in cash and the remainder is a non-cash exchange. In this case, *the cash portion of the transaction* would be reported in the SCF while the non-cash portion would be omitted. For example, suppose that a building costing $4,000,000 is acquired by paying $1,000,000 cash and issuing a $3,000,000 long-term note to the vendor. The SCF would list only the $1,000,000 cash paid (as an investing activity), although the line item on the SCF should be referenced to the note that contains the details of the entire transaction.

Evaluation In one sense, the exclusion of non-cash transactions provides an appropriate focus on cash flows. On the other hand, the total exclusion of non-cash transactions from the SCF seems to give precedence to form over substance. For example, the purchase of another company (i.e., a business combination) through an issue of shares would not be reported in the SCF, while the issuance of shares for cash and the use of the proceeds to buy the company *would be* reported in the SCF.

Debt Transactions

Sometimes the interest rate stated on a debt security is different from the market interest rate on the date of issuance. The true amount of interest must be *classified consistently with interest payments (operating or financing)* and the true principal *classified as financing.*

Examples Consider the following examples:

1. A company borrows $100,000 and makes no annual payments of any kind but agrees to repay $125,000 in three years' time. The extra $25,000 is interest. In the SCF at maturity, $100,000 would be shown as a financing outflow and $25,000 is classified as an interest payment, in operating or financing.

2. A company issues a $1,000,000, 10% bond at a discount and receives $960,000 because market interest rates were higher than 10%. In the first year, interest paid is $100,000, but interest expense is $102,300 (amounts assumed), because interest expense includes discount amortization. On the SCF in the first year, financing activities show an inflow of $960,000 from the issuance of the bond, and the cash outflow for interest is $100,000. *Interest expense* has to be adjusted to *interest paid* by eliminating the $2,300 discount

amortization. In the final year, when $1,000,000 is repaid, $960,000 is repayment of principal and $40,000 is classified as interest paid, making $140,000 ($40,000 plus the annual $100,000) as the cash outflow for interest in the final year.

3. A company retires a bond with a face value of $400,000 for $410,000. The discrepancy of $10,000 is a call premium, not directly related to interest. A loss of $10,000 is reported in earnings because of the retirement. In the SCF, the $10,000 loss is added back in operating activities as an adjustment to earnings. The $410,000 repayment is shown as a financing activity, an outflow of cash.

CONCEPT REVIEW

1. If the SCF lists "cash received from customers," is the direct or the indirect method used in operating activities?

2. A company acquires a $75,000 asset by entering into a finance lease. No down payment is needed. Is this transaction listed on the SCF? Explain.

3. If a company borrows $300,000, and later repays $350,000, what is the correct explanation and cash flow classification of the $50,000 discrepancy?

INTERPRETATION ISSUES

Quality of Earnings

Investment analysts sometimes refer to the **quality of earnings** of a company that they are analyzing. This concept relates the amount of net earnings to the amount of cash flow from operating activities. A company is said to have high quality of earnings when there is a close correspondence between *net earnings* and *cash flow from operations*, a relationship that persists over several years. It does not necessarily mean positive cash flow from operating activities. Instead, quality of earnings is present if, when earnings increase, cash flows also increase. When earnings decline, cash flows also decline. *Correlation* of the two numbers is considered to indicate higher quality of earnings.

In contrast, a company that reports earnings that are not closely related to cash flows is said to have low quality of earnings. In some companies, cash flows and earnings have an erratic relationship. For example, a company can have high earnings but a negative cash flow from operations because of soaring receivables or expanding inventories; this situation often makes analysts a bit nervous. The next year, earnings may be stable but cash flow may soar if receivables and inventory are trimmed. While this is a positive cash flow trend, it does not indicate a stable relationship between cash flow from operating activities and net earnings.

Effect of Accounting Policy Choices on the Statement of Cash Flows

One of the reasons that users like to see the SCF is that "cash doesn't lie." Many financial statement users work on the premise that managers and accountants have little room to manipulate cash flows. However, companies may adopt accounting policies that have a significant and substantial effect on the measurement of net earnings and financial position.

Management influences policy decisions and makes significant estimates for most assets and liabilities, which affect the related revenue and expenses. These policies and estimates are influenced by external events and are not entirely under the control of management, but management has considerable influence. The underlying cash flow is not changed by accounting policies and estimates. It is reasonable to suggest, therefore, that the overall net cash flow for an accounting period is unaffected by accounting policy choices and estimates.

Policy and Cash Flow There is a certain type of accounting policy decision that affects the SCF by changing the classification of items on the SCF, and that is whether to expense or

capitalize one or more types of cost. If expenditures of a certain category (i.e., development costs) are charged to expense, they will be included as a deduction in net earnings and therefore be part of operating cash flow.

On the other hand, if those expenditures are capitalized, they will appear on the SCF as an *investing* activity. In subsequent years, amortization of capitalized costs is deducted in determining net earnings but is then added back to net earnings to derive cash flow from operating activities.

The result is that capitalized costs never enter into operating cash flow but will appear only as an investing activity. An organization that capitalizes and amortizes its development costs will show a consistently higher cash flow from operating activities than one that charges such costs to expense, all other things being equal.

ETHICAL ISSUES

Choice of accounting policy must be based on the facts, the user environment, and the competitive situation. Policies that are chosen to manipulate certain measurements, or foster erroneous conclusions by financial statement users, are not acceptable. However, accountants must be aware of the implications of choosing a certain policy. A decision to capitalize costs, and amortize them over the period of use instead of immediate expensing, will effectively transfer the cash outflow out of operating activities and show the outflow under investing activities.

CONCEPT REVIEW

1. If cash from operating activities increases as net earnings increase, and declines when net earnings declines, what does this imply about the quality of earnings?

2. If development costs are capitalized and amortized, how will they be reflected on the SCF? If they are expensed?

ANALYZING MORE COMPLEX SITUATIONS

T-Account Method

When preparing the SCF for Simple Limited, we used an informal, *ad hoc* approach. We went down the statement of financial position and filled in the appropriate amounts in the SCF. In the process, we explained all of the changes in the non-cash accounts and thus indirectly explained all of the changes in the cash accounts.

While the informal approach is completely acceptable, in complex situations it is easy to lose track. Therefore, it is common to use some form of T-account approach, or a spreadsheet (see the Appendix to this chapter), to force some discipline on the process and to help ensure that relevant transactions are not overlooked. The method used to organize information does not affect the final SCF. A more formal approach is useful because it:

- Provides an organized format for documenting the preparation process;
- Facilitates review and evaluation by others;
- Provides proofs of accuracy; and
- Formally keeps track of the changes in statement of financial position accounts and ensures that all accounts are explained.

The T-accounts used in this approach are not actual ledger accounts. Rather, they are work-spaces in account format used to accumulate the information necessary to prepare the SCF and

EXHIBIT 5-7

LING CORPORATION
Statement of Financial Position

As at 31 December	20X5	20X4
Assets		
Current assets:		
Cash	$ 50,000	$ 36,000
Short-term liquid investments,		
two-month original term	10,000	34,000
Accounts receivable	84,000	70,000
Inventories	42,000	30,000
Prepaid expenses	15,000	11,000
	201,000	181,000
Fixed assets:		
Land	50,000	50,000
Plant and equipment	740,000	615,000
Accumulated depreciation	(260,000)	(215,000)
	530,000	450,000
Capitalized development costs	82,000	76,000
Long-term investments	92,000	70,000
Total assets	$905,000	$777,000
Liabilities and shareholders' equity		
Current liabilities:		
Bank loan	$ 20,000	$ 5,000
Accounts payable	36,000	45,000
Dividends payable	10,000	5,000
	66,000	55,000
Long-term liabilities:		
Bonds payable	146,000	133,000
Deferred tax	27,000	24,000
Total liabilities	239,000	212,000
Shareholders' equity:		
Preferred shares	142,000	120,000
Common shares	230,000	180,000
Retained earnings	294,000	265,000
	666,000	565,000
Total liabilities and shareholders' equity	$905,000	$777,000

continued on next page

to explain all account balance changes. The cash T-account accumulates all changes in cash (and cash equivalents) and is divided into three sections, corresponding to the three SCF categories.

Example

The comparative statement of financial position and the statement of comprehensive income for Ling Corporation are shown in Exhibit 5-7, along with some important supplementary information.

EXHIBIT 5-7 *(cont'd)*

LING CORPORATION
Statement of Comprehensive Income

Year ended 31 December 20X5

Sales revenue	$960,000	
Gain on sale of equipment	4,000	
		$964,000
Operating expenses		
Cost of goods sold	597,000	
Interest expense	18,000	
Wages expense	131,000	
Other operating expenses	100,000	
Income tax expense	54,000	900,000
Net earnings and comprehensive income		$ 64,000

LING CORPORATION
Statement of Changes in Equity

	Preferred shares	Common shares	Retained earnings
Opening balance, 1 January 20X5	$120,000	$180,000	$265,000
Issued shares	22,000	50,000	
Net earnings and comprehensive income			64,000
Dividends declared			(35,000)
Closing balance, 31 December 20X5	$142,000	$230,000	$294,000

Additional information:
1. Cost of goods sold includes depreciation of $65,000.
2. Other operating expenses include amortization of capitalized development costs of $5,000.
3. During 20X5, the corporation issued preferred shares with a market value of $22,000 in exchange for 1,000 common shares of THB Corporation. The THB shares are being held as a long-term investment. Fair market value and cost are identical for long-term investments.
4. Old equipment was sold for $9,000; the original cost was $25,000.
5. Bonds with a face value of $20,000 were repurchased at par and retired.
6. Other operating expenses include a loss of $2,000 from liquidating the short-term investments. Net proceeds were $22,000.

From the statement of financial position, we can see that cash increased by $14,000 during the year. Short-term liquid investments, however, decreased by $24,000. Short-term liquid investments are *cash equivalents*, and thus the change in cash is really a decrease of $10,000.

	Ending	Beginning	Change	
Cash balance	$50,000	$36,000	$ 14,000	increase
Short-term investments	10,000	34,000	(24,000)	decrease
Total	$60,000	$70,000		
Net increase (decrease) in cash			$(10,000)	decrease

The task of the SCF is to explain the transactions that caused this decrease of $10,000 in cash and cash equivalents. As cash flows are identified by reconciling the individual asset, liability, and equity accounts, the offsetting cash effect is entered into the cash T-account.

T-Account Procedures

The starting point is to draw a simple T-account for each asset, liability, and equity account, including a single T-account for *cash and cash equivalents*. See Exhibit 5-8. The cash T-account has to be physically large; it is where all the information necessary for preparing the SCF will be accumulated. Within this cash T-account, three subsections are set up, one for each type of cash activity: operating, investing, and financing.

The second step is to insert in each T-account the beginning balance at the top, and the ending balance at the bottom. These are shown in green in Exhibit 5-8. Accuracy is critical. Alternatively, only the net change in the account may be used. This is a matter of personal preference.

The third step is to make reconciliation entries directly in the T-accounts that reconstruct the entries that were made during the year, including those made to cash. It is essential to cross-reference the entries so that it is straightforward to relate the different elements of a particular transaction. Generally, the place to start is with the reconciliation of retained earnings because it is where the net earnings for the year has been transferred. Net earnings is the top line in the operating activities section. Starting with net earnings also focuses attention on earnings and on the adjustments that are necessary to arrive at cash flow from operating activities.

Ling Corporation's statement of changes in equity reveals that the change in retained earnings consists of two items: (1) net earnings, and (2) dividends declared. The net $29,000 increase in the retained earnings balance came about as the result of $64,000 in net earnings and $35,000 in dividends declared. Therefore, the first reconciling entry is to enter net earnings:

a.

Cash: operating activities, net earnings	64,000	
Retained earnings		64,000

The second reconciling entry is to record the dividends declared:

b.

Retained earnings	35,000	
Cash: financing activities, dividends declared		35,000

These entries are posted in the T-accounts. Observe that these entries recreate the original entries to (a) close net earnings into the retained earnings account and (b) to record the declaration of dividends. Dividends are debited to the retained earnings account in the T-accounts and credited to cash. The actual cash paid for dividends will be later calculated after including the change in the dividends payable account.

The rest of the reconciliation entries are as follows, considering first the list of items of additional information in Exhibit 5-7:

c. Depreciation of $65,000 was expensed during the period. The entry is as follows:

Cash: operating activities, depreciation expense	65,000	
Accumulated depreciation		65,000

This entry is posted in the T-accounts, with the debit placed in cash, under *operating activities*.

EXHIBIT 5-8

LING CORPORATION
T-Account Analysis

Cash and cash equivalents

Opening	**70,000***		
Operating activities			
a) Net earnings	64,000	f) Gain on sale	4,000
c) Depreciation	65,000	i) Increase in accounts receivable	14,000
d) Amortization	5,000	j) Increase in inventory	12,000
q) Deferred tax	3,000	k) Increase in prepaid expenses	4,000
		o) Decrease in accounts payable	9,000
Investing activities			
f) Sale of equipment	9,000	l) Purchased plant and equipment	150,000
		m) Increased capitalized development costs	11,000
Financing activities			
h) Issued bond	33,000	b) Dividends declared	35,000
n) Increased short-term loan	15,000	g) Repaid bond	20,000
p) Increased dividends payable	5,000		
r) Issued common shares	50,000		
Closing	**60,000***		

*Cash plus cash equivalent investments

Accounts receivable

Op.	70,000		
i)	14,000		
Cl.	84,000		

Inventories

Op.	30,000		
j)	12,000		
Cl.	42,000		

Prepaid expenses

Op.	11,000		
k)	4,000		
Cl.	15,000		

Land

Op.	50,000		
Cl.	50,000		

Plant and equipment

Op.	615,000		
l)	150,000	f)	25,000
Cl.	740,000		

Accumulated depreciation

		Op.	215,000
f)	20,000	c)	65,000
		Cl.	260,000

Capitalized development costs

Op.	76,000		
m)	11,000	d)	5,000
Cl.	82,000		

Long-term investments

Op.	70,000		
e)	22,000		
Cl.	92,000		

Bank loan

		Op.	5,000
		n)	15,000
		Cl.	20,000

Accounts payable

		Op.	45,000
o)	9,000		
		Cl.	36,000

Dividends payable

		Op.	5,000
		p)	5,000
		Cl.	10,000

Bonds payable

		Op.	133,000
g)	20,000	h)	33,000
		Cl.	146,000

Deferred tax

		Op.	24,000
		q)	3,000
		Cl.	27,000

Preferred shares

		Op.	120,000
		e)	22,000
		Cl.	142,000

Common shares

		Op.	180,000
		r)	50,000
		Cl.	230,000

Retained earnings

		Op.	265,000
b)	35,000	a)	64,000
		Cl.	294,000

d. Amortization of capitalized development costs amounting to $5,000 was recorded during the year. The entry is entered in the T-accounts:

Cash: operating activities, amortization expense	5,000	
Capitalized development costs		5,000

e. The company acquired a $22,000 long-term investment in another company's shares in exchange for Ling's own preferred shares. No cash changed hands, so this is an example of a non-cash transaction. Even though the transaction resulted in a material change in the asset and equity structure of the company, it will not be reported on the SCF. Details of the transactions will be disclosed in a note to the financial statements. The effects of the increase of $22,000 on long-term investments and on preferred shares are recorded in the asset and equity T-accounts, with no corresponding entry to cash:

Long-term investments	22,000	
Preferred shares		22,000

f. Old equipment was sold for $9,000; the original cost was $25,000. A gain of $4,000 was reported, so the net book value at the time of sale must have been $5,000. That is, the gain is the difference between net book value and cash. In a gain situation, net book value is lower than cash received. If net book value is $5,000 and original cost is $25,000, then accumulated depreciation on the asset sold therefore must have been $20,000. That is,

Proceeds from sale		$9,000
Net book value of the asset sold:		
Historical cost	$25,000	
Accumulated depreciation	?	5,000
Gain on sale		$4,000

The "?" must be $20,000. The entry for the sale is as follows:

Cash: investing activities, sale of equipment	9,000	
Accumulated depreciation	20,000	
Plant and equipment		25,000
Cash: operating activities, gain on sale		4,000

g. Bonds with a face value of $20,000 were repurchased and retired at par, since there is no gain or loss reported in earnings.

Bonds payable	20,000	
Cash: financing activities, bonds retired		20,000

The only other piece of *additional information* in Exhibit 5-7 is that other operating expenses include a loss of $2,000 on liquidation of short-term investments. The initial reaction may be to eliminate this by adding it back to operating activities and to record $22,000 as an investing activity inflow. However, the catch here is that the loss relates to a component of cash. Since short-term liquid investments are a cash equivalent and included within the definition of cash, the loss really did cause cash and cash equivalents to decrease by $2,000. This amount is appropriately included in net earnings. Therefore, *there is no adjustment for gains and losses that are incurred within the cash and cash-equivalent accounts*, including foreign currency exchange gains and losses.

h. The reconciliation entries that have been described above are those that result from the information provided in Exhibit 5-7. However, there obviously have been other transactions during the year that caused as-yet unexplained changes in the asset, liability and equity accounts. An example is that of bonds payable. The bonds payable account grew from $133,000 to $146,000 during the year, a net increase of $13,000. However, to have a net increase of $13,000 after the $20,000 retirement, the company must have issued $33,000 in new bonds during the year:

Cash: financing activities, bonds issued	33,000	
Bonds payable		33,000

Reconciliations, such as this one, for the bond issuance sometimes are referred to as *hidden entries* because they become apparent only as the result of reconciling those changes that are known beforehand. That is, once the known elements are entered, as above, the remaining reconciliation entries are all balancing entries that simply record the change in each account that is required to explain the net change, *after* taking into consideration the reconciliation entries already made. Starting with the first non-cash account, accounts receivable, they are as follows:

i.

Accounts receivable	14,000	
Cash: operating activities		14,000

j.

Inventories	12,000	
Cash: operating activities		12,000

k.

Prepaid expenses	4,000	
Cash: operating activities		4,000

l.

Plant and equipment	150,000	
Cash: investing activities, purchase of equipment		150,000

The *net* increase of $125,000 in plant and equipment is due to acquisitions of $150,000 and the sale of equipment that originally cost $25,000.

m.

Capitalized development costs	11,000	
Cash: investing activities, investment in development costs		11,000

Since the net account increase was $6,000 *after* amortization, $11,000 must have been capitalized during the year.

n.

Cash: financing activities, increase in bank loan	15,000	
Bank loan		15,000

o.

Accounts payable	9,000	
Cash: operating activities		9,000

p.

Cash: financing, dividends	5,000	
Dividends payable		5,000

The change in dividends payable does not affect operating cash flows because dividends are a financing cash flow for this company. The change in dividends payable is posted to the financing portion of the cash T-account and reduces the cash outflow for dividends. This is logical—dividends payable increased, and therefore comparatively less of the dividends declared were actually paid. The dividend paid is shown as one number on the SCF, calculated as dividends declared combined with the change in the dividends payable account.

q.

Cash: operating activities	3,000	
Deferred tax		3,000

The $3,000 increase in the liability account for deferred tax represents the part of income tax expense that was not paid in cash.

r.

Cash: financing activities, common shares issued	50,000	
Common shares		50,000

Once all of the reconciliation entries are in the T-accounts, check for completeness by adding each T-account to make sure that the beginning balance plus the reconciliation entries equals the ending balance. Then total the inflows and outflows in the cash account to ensure that it adds correctly.

The cash account in Exhibit 5-8 now contains all of the information that is necessary for preparing the SCF. It is important to remember that Exhibit 5-8 is *not* the SCF in itself; it is only the data analysis that supports the SCF.

Statement of Cash Flows—Indirect Method

The SCF using the indirect approach for operating activities is shown in Exhibit 5-9. The indirect approach starts with net earnings, and makes all of the adjustments that are necessary to convert from the accrual basis to the cash basis. The two-step approach shown in Exhibit 5-9 is the most common format. The non-cash transaction is listed as a disclosure note.

EXHIBIT 5-9

LING CORPORATION

Statement of Cash Flows (Indirect Approach)

Year ended 31 December 20X5

Operating activities:		
Net earnings	$ 64,000	
Adjustments for items not affecting cash:		
Depreciation of plant and equipment	65,000	
Amortization of development costs	5,000	
Gain on sale of equipment	(4,000)	
Deferred tax	3,000	
	133,000	
Changes in working capital amounts:		
Increase in accounts receivable	(14,000)	
Increase in inventory	(12,000)	
Increase in prepaid expenses	(4,000)	
Decrease in accounts payable	(9,000)	
Cash provided (used) by operating activities		$ 94,000
Investing activities:		
Acquisition of plant and equipment	(150,000)	
Investment in development costs	(11,000)	
Proceeds from sale of equipment	9,000	
Cash provided (used) by investing activities		(152,000)
Financing activities:		
Increase in short-term bank loan	15,000	
Issuance of bonds	33,000	
Retirement of bonds	(20,000)	
Common shares issued	50,000	
Dividends paid ($35,000 – $5,000)	(30,000)	
Cash provided (used) by financing activities		48,000
Increase (decrease) in cash and cash equivalents		$ (10,000)
Opening cash and cash equivalents		$ 70,000
Closing cash and cash equivalents		$ 60,000
Supplemental disclosures:		
Cash payment for interest		$ 18,000
Cash payment for income tax ($54,000 – $3,000)		$ 51,000

Disclosure note:
Preferred shares were issued for 1,000 shares of THB Company, held as a long-term investment. The transaction was valued at $22,000.

Operating Activities—Direct Method

The operating activities section of the SCF can be presented using the direct method. The direct method may be prepared through the following steps:

1. Begin with the analysis of operating activities under the indirect method. Specifically, refer to the journal entry analysis (or the summary of adjustments to operating activities in the T-accounts in Exhibit 5-8).

2. Prepare a schedule to support the calculations for the direct method. This schedule should have three columns. In the first column, copy all profit and loss accounts, with all

expenses and losses in brackets. This column should total to net earnings. (See Exhibit 5-10, first column.)

3. Copy all the adjustments collected in Step 1 into the second column. Make sure the credit adjustments are in brackets. (See second column, Exhibit 5-10.) Sort the adjustments to the revenue or expense line to which they pertain. For example, accounts receivable is copied onto the revenue line, the adjustment for depreciation is on the COGS line, since the data state that depreciation is part of COGS, and so on.

4. Cross-add the schedule, entering cash flows in the third column. Note that non-cash items, such as depreciation and gains and losses, disappear as they are adjusted to zero.

5. Prepare the operating activities section of the SCF, using the numeric data from the third column, but changing the captions to appropriate cash flow descriptions, and then group cash flows, if that is considered desirable.

The final product is shown at the bottom of Exhibit 5-10. The $94,000 total cash from operating activities is the same as in Exhibit 5-9, but the presentation is different.

The investing and financing sections of the SCF are not dependent on the format chosen for the operating activities section and are not repeated here because they would be identical to those shown in Exhibit 5-9.

EXHIBIT 5-10

LING CORPORATION

Statement of Cash Flows Operating Activities Direct Method

Year ended 31 December 20X5	Profit and loss accounts	Adjustments (letter references refer to prior journal entries)		Cash flow
Sales revenue	$960,000	i.	(14,000)	$946,000
Gain on sale of equipment	4,000	f.	(4,000)	0
Cost of goods sold	(597,000)	c.	65,000	(553,000)
		j.	(12,000)	
		o.	(9,000)	
Interest expense	(18,000)			(18,000)
Wages expense	(131,000)			(131,000)
Other operating expenses	(100,000)	d.	5,000	(99,000)
		k.	(4,000)	
Income tax expense	(54,000)	q.	3,000	(51,000)
Net earnings and cash flow from operations	$ 64,000			$ 94,000

LING CORPORATION

Partial Statement of Cash Flows Operating Activities

Year ended 31 December 20X5

Operating activities	
Cash received from customers	$946,000
Cash paid to suppliers ($553,000 + $99,000)	(652,000)
Cash paid to employees	(131,000)
Cash paid for interest	(18,000)
Cash paid for income tax	(51,000)
Cash from operating activities	$ 94,000

CONCEPT REVIEW

1. What is the effect on the SCF of selling a short-term investment, classified as a cash equivalent, at a $3,000 loss?

2. A company acquires a substantial amount of capital assets by issuing its own common shares to the vendor. What is the impact of this transaction on the SCF?

3. What section(s) of the SCF will be identical regardless of whether the direct or the indirect method is chosen?

DISCLOSURE OF CASH FLOWS FOR INTEREST, DIVIDENDS, AND INCOME TAX

Classification

Reporting standards require decisions about the SCF classification of income tax, interest paid, interest received, dividends paid, and dividends received. Once a classification is chosen, it must be applied consistently from period to period.

Income Tax In general, income tax should be shown in the operating activities section. However, there are times when tax is specifically related to investing or financing activities. In these cases, tax may be classified as investing or financing. For example, there are times when capital transactions, such as dividend distributions, attract specific taxes. It seems logical that the related tax be shown with the cash flow. *This classification decision is based on the transaction that causes the income tax and is not based on the judgement of management.*

Dividends Paid Dividends paid have traditionally been classified in financing activities, as a voluntary payment to shareholders. Conceptually, classification in financing activities is appropriate if the company considers dividends paid to shareholders as an element related to obtaining financial resources. The reporting standard allows management to select an alternative classification of dividends as *operating activities*. This classification may be chosen to assist users in determining a company's ability to pay dividends out of operating cash flows.

Interest Paid Interest paid has traditionally been classified in operating activities because interest is an expense in earnings. The reporting standard recognizes, though, that interest, like dividends, may be viewed as a element related to obtaining financial resources. If dividends are classified in financing activities, then interest might be classified in a consistent manner. Accordingly, the reporting standard allows interest to be classified as either an operating or a financing outflow. In Exhibit 5-2, INTERFOR classified interest paid of $5,629 in *financing activities*.

Capitalized Interest Interest expense may be capitalized as part of the cost of various fixed assets and also investment properties. For example, if a company takes a year to construct a manufacturing facility, and interest of $600,000 is paid relating to money tied up in the project over this time, then the $600,000 is included in the cost of the asset and is not expensed. In this case, the $600,000 cash outflow is shown on the SCF in investing activities, with the acquisition of the manufacturing facility.

Dividends and Interest Received Interest and dividend cash flows received also offer a particular classification challenge. Traditional practice has been to include these cash inflows in operating activities. That is, interest income and dividend revenue are part of net earnings and stay there in the SCF, adjusted for changes in related accounts such as interest receivable or dividends receivable, if needed. However, the reporting standard allows management to select an alternative classification and place these cash inflows in investing activities, to reflect the philosophy that cash is a return on investment decisions.

Summary The management choice of classification of interest and dividends should rest on whether or not the payment is conceptually an operating item or if it should be traced to its root cause of *investing* or *financing*. One concern is that management might pick classifications to portray a particular impression of operating cash flows or other key reporting metrics. Another concern is that financial statements may not be comparable with those of competitors. Financial statement users will have to proceed with caution when benchmarking.

The judgemental choices, and their rationale, can be summarized as follows:

Cash Flow	Operating Classification	Alternative SCF Classification
Interest received	*Operating activities*—interest received is judged to be part of operating decisions	*Investing activities*—interest received should be viewed as part of the evaluation of an investment decision
Interest paid*	*Operating activities*—interest paid is judged to be part of operating decisions	*Financing activities*—interest paid should be evaluated with the financing strategy
Dividends received	*Operating activities*—dividends received are judged to be part of operating decisions	*Investing activities*—dividends received should be viewed as part of the evaluation of an investment decision
Dividends paid	*Operating activities*—indicates the company's ability to pay dividends from operating cash flow	*Financing activities*—dividends paid should be evaluated with the financing strategy

*Interest paid is an investing activity if capitalized on a qualifying asset such as fixed assets or investment properties.

Separate Disclosure Items

The reporting standard requires that cash flows associated with income tax, interest paid, interest received, dividends paid, and dividends received all be disclosed separately. This reporting requirement can be met by:

1. Using the direct method to show cash flows in the operating activities section of the SCF, which shows cash flows from each source; or

2. Using the indirect method of presenting cash flows in the operating activities section, *adding back the expense (deducting the revenue) and then listing the cash flows for the item separately.*

3. Reporting required cash flows as supplementary information (see Exhibit 5-8 for an example). This is not strictly in accordance with the reporting standard but is a common reporting practice.

Of course, the second approach makes the reconciliation in operating activities even more complex. In Exhibit 5-2, note that INTERFOR adds back income tax expense of $1,427 and financing costs of $7,094 in the operating activities section and then deducts $622 of income tax paid in the operating activities section and interest payments of $5,629 in the financing section. The expense and cash flow numbers are not identical because of changes in tax payable or other adjustments.

Reconciliation method To accomplish this disclosure though the indirect presentation approach (alternative 2, above), *basic account analysis does not change.* When *preparing* the SCF:

1. Add back the appropriate expenses and/or deduct revenues from net earnings.

2. Convert the revenue or expense to cash flow by applying the change in any related asset, liability, or equity account to the expense or revenue item. List the cash inflow or outflow in the SCF. *Do not relist on the SCF* any changes in payables, receivables, prepaids, and so on. that were needed to convert this item from accrual to cash amounts.

Example For RestCo, net earnings are $1,925, after income tax expense of $670, interest expense of $350, and interest revenue of $180. Assume that prior analysis had produced an operating activities section of the SCF as follows:

Year ended 31 December 20X2	
Operating activities:	
Net earnings	$1,925
Plus (less) items not affecting cash:	
Depreciation	390
Increase in deferred tax liability	65
	2,380
Changes in other working capital items:	
Increase in interest receivable	(50)
Decrease in tax payable	(35)
Decrease in interest payable	(110)
Decrease in accounts payable	(75)
Cash provided by operating activities	$2,110

If the company were to show the cash flows for interest and tax in the operating activities section, the result would be as follows; items that have changed are highlighted:

Year ended 31 December 20X2	
Operating activities:	
Net earnings	$1,925
Plus (less) items adjusting net earnings:	
Depreciation	390
Interest expense	350
Income tax expense	670
Interest revenue	(180)
	3,155
Changes in other working capital items:	
Decrease in accounts payable	(75)
	3,080
Cash paid for income tax ($670 + $35 − $65)	(640)
Cash paid for interest ($350 + $110)	(460)
Cash received for interest ($180 − $50)	130
Cash provided by operating activities	$2,110

Note that the $2,110 cash flow from operating activities has not changed, but the presentation is different. Expenses and revenues related to interest and income tax have been added and subtracted in the top section. Cash outflows and inflows for interest and income tax are now listed at the bottom.

The cash outflow for income tax begins with tax expense of $670. It then incorporates the two adjustments to the original SCF that relate to tax expense: the $35 change in tax payable and the $65 change in deferred tax. A decrease in payables requires cash, so the outflow is *higher* than the expense; add the $35. Some of the expense will not be paid until the future, so the $65 increase in deferred tax *reduces* the outflow. The same logic applies to interest paid. The calculation begins with the $350 expense and *adds* the $110 reduction to the interest payable because it uses cash. For interest revenue, the increase in interest receivable means that some of the revenue is not received this year, so the cash inflow is $50 less than the $180 revenue.

In all cases, if the reconciling item relates to an item where cash is shown directly, then the reconciling item is no longer listed separately on the SCF. Compared with the original SCF, the change in deferred tax, and the changes in interest receivable, tax payable, and interest payable have been left off because they are individually incorporated in cash flow amounts.

Ling Corp. Example The SCF for Ling Corporation in Exhibit 5-9 showed supplementary disclosure for the cash flow for interest and tax. If the company wished to continue to use the indirect presentation format in operating activities but show cash flows on the face of the SCF, the operating activities section would appear as follows (changed items are highlighted):

Year ended 31 December 20X5		
Operating activities:		
Net earnings	$ 64,000	
Adjustments:		
Depreciation of plant and equipment	65,000	
Amortization of development costs	5,000	
Gain on sale of equipment	(4,000)	
Interest expense	18,000	
Tax expense	54,000	
	202,000	
Changes in working capital amounts:		
Increase in accounts receivable	(14,000)	
Increase in inventory	(12,000)	
Increase in prepaid expenses	(4,000)	
Decrease in accounts payable	(9,000)	
	163,000	
Cash paid for interest	(18,000)	
Cash paid for income tax ($54,000 – $3,000)	(51,000)	
Cash provided (used) by operating activities		$ 94,000

As a final presentation alternative, remember that interest paid could be reclassified to the financing activities section.

Evaluation Adding back these expenses and revenues and replacing them with their cash flows change the operating activities from an indirect presentation to one that is partially indirect and partially direct. The direct method of presentation is far more logical, and it is clearer for financial statement readers. One might hope that companies would come to this realization and adopt the direct method of presentation.

CONCEPT REVIEW

1. What choices are available to classify dividends paid to shareholders on the SCF?

2. If a dividend payment of $50,000 to shareholders attracts $5,000 of tax for the company, what amount is shown as cash paid for dividends on the SCF?

3. If a company reported investment (interest) income of $320,000 and interest receivable increased by $18,000 during the year, how much cash was received from interest income?

SUMMARY OF ADJUSTMENTS IN OPERATING ACTIVITIES

To prepare the operating activities section of the SCF, it is necessary to convert accrual-basis earnings to the cash basis. There are certain types of adjustments that must be made to the accrual-basis earnings number:

Type of Adjustment	Reason for Adjustment	Examples
The effects of cost/revenue allocations must be reversed	• Revenue or expense item has no related cash flow this period • Intent is to arrive at earnings as if the item were not included	• Add back depreciation of all kinds • Add back increase in deferred tax, deduct decrease in deferred tax • Add back bond discount amortization • Add back writedown of assets • Add back non-cash compensation expense from stock options • Deduct investment revenue under the equity method
Certain transactions, the net effects of which are included in net earnings, must be reclassified as investing or financing activities	Gain or loss on sale of fixed assets or bond retirement (in earnings) does not equal cash flow	• Add back losses • Deduct gains
Accruals must be "backed out" of various asset and liability accounts to determine cash inflows and outflows in operations	• Revenue or expense item has caused an asset or liability account because cash flow is before or after revenue or expense recognition • Asset or liability accounts must be directly related to a revenue or expense account (e.g., sales is related to accounts receivable)	• Change in accounts receivable, accounts payable, prepaid expenses, inventory, etc. • See chart below for direction of change
Expenses or revenues must be "backed out" of earnings to allow classification elsewhere	• Tax expense is added back, and then cash paid for tax is reported on a separate line in operating activities • Interest expense and interest and dividend revenue are "backed out," and then cash paid or received is listed as a separate line in appropriate section of the SCF	• Add back expenses • Deduct revenues • List cash flows

When adjustments must be made for changes in working capital accounts related to operations, the protocol is:

Change in Account Balance during the Year

	Increase	Decrease
Asset (e.g., accounts receivable)	*Subtract* increase from net earnings	*Add* decrease to net earnings
Liability (e.g., accounts payable)	*Add* increase to net earnings	*Subtract* decrease from net earnings

Looking Forward

SCF issues are not now on the active agenda of either the IASB or the Canadian AcSB.

ACCOUNTING STANDARDS FOR PRIVATE ENTERPRISES

The SCF is required under accounting standards for private enterprises (ASPE) as part of a set of complete financial statements. The ASPE requirements for this statement are very similar to the IFRS presentation requirements, with the following differences:

1. Dividends paid *must* be classified as a financing activity.

2. Interest received and paid, and dividends received *must* be classified in operating activities. There is no choice of alternative classification.

3. Cash flow from investment revenue, cash paid for interest, and cash paid for income tax must be *disclosed*. This disclosure can be accomplished through a disclosure note and is not needed on the face of the SCF.

RELEVANT STANDARDS

CPA Canada Handbook, Part I (IASB):
  • IAS 7, Statement of Cash Flows

CPA Canada Handbook, Part II (ASPE):
  • Section 1540, Cash Flow Statement

SUMMARY OF KEY POINTS

1. Cash flow information discloses the historical pattern of cash flows in an enterprise for both feedback and predictive purposes. The information is used to predict future cash flows and to assess liquidity, the ability of a firm to pay dividends and obligations, the ability of a firm to adapt to changes in the business environment, the quality of earnings, and for other purposes.

2. The SCF classifies cash flows from operating activities, cash flows relating to investing activities, and cash flows relating to financing activities. In each category, *cash flow* includes both inflows and outflows.

3. Operating cash flows are related to the main revenue-producing activities of the business and are connected to the earnings process. Investing cash flows describe (long-term) capital asset and investment acquisitions and the proceeds from sale of these assets. Financing cash flows describe the sources of debt and equity financing and repayments of liabilities and equities, excluding liabilities directly relating to operations such as accounts payable.

4. The reporting basis for the SCF is the net cash position. The net cash position includes cash plus cash equivalent investments minus certain bank overdrafts. Cash equivalents include short-term liquid investments that are held for current needs and that bear little risk of change in value (maximum original three-month term).

5. Interpreting the SCF involves evaluating quality of earnings, major strategic sources and uses of cash, identifying trends, and benchmarking against industry norms.

6. There are two alternatives to present cash from operating activities—the direct and the indirect presentation methods. The indirect method reports operating activities by showing a reconciliation of net earnings with net cash flow from operating activities. Examples of adjustments are adding back depreciation, eliminating gains and losses, and adjusting for changes in operating working capital accounts. The direct method reports the cash inflows from the main classifications of revenues and cash outflows from the main classifications of expenses. Standard setters encourage companies to use the direct method but few Canadian companies use this formatting option.

7. In the investing and financing sections, gross cash flows are reported. Transactions are not offset, or netted, against other flows in the same category.

8. Non-cash transactions (e.g., acquiring plant assets with the vendor taking back a long-term note) are not shown as outflows and inflows on the SCF. These transactions must be described in the disclosure notes.

9. If debt is issued, only principal amounts are recorded in financing activities. Amounts that are in substance interest are classified consistently with interest expense.

10. Net cash flow is not affected by accounting policy choices or by management's accounting estimates. However, the reported cash flow from operations can be increased by capitalizing certain types of costs (e.g., development costs) because the costs are reclassified as investing activities and amortization has no effect on operating cash flows in future periods.

11. Cash paid for income tax, cash paid for interest, cash received for interest, and cash received for dividends must all be separately disclosed on the SCF. This can be accomplished through add-backs and deductions by using the indirect presentation method in operating activities, or through use of the direct presentation method.

12. Interest paid may be classified as an operating outflow or a financing outflow. The same two choices are available for dividends paid. Interest and dividends received may be classified as operating activities or investing activities. Once a classification alternative has been chosen, it must be applied consistently.

13. There are many approaches to preparing the SCF, including a format-free, *ad hoc* approach; T-accounts; and/or a worksheet. The same objectives apply to all—analyze transactions to identify all cash flows, reconciling items, and non-cash transactions.

KEY TERMS

capitalize
cash
cash equivalents
current account
financing activities
investing activities

line of credit
operating activities
overdraft
quality of earnings
statement of cash flows (SCF)

REVIEW PROBLEM 5-1

The Phillies Corporation assembled the following information to prepare its 20X7 SCF:

Statement of Financial Position, 31 December	20X7	20X6
Cash	$ 62,000	$ 50,000
Temporary investments	—	150,000
Accounts receivable, net	80,000	60,000
Inventory	30,000	18,000
Equipment, net of accumulated depreciation	650,000	300,000
Goodwill	70,000	90,000
Total assets	$892,000	$668,000
Accounts payable	$ 63,000	$ 48,000
Salaries payable	50,000	60,000
Interest payable	9,000	6,000
Income tax payable	22,000	12,000
Mortgage payable	110,000	120,000
Bonds payable	250,000	200,000
Common shares	170,000	150,000
Retained earnings	218,000	72,000
Total liabilities and shareholders' equity	$892,000	$668,000

Statement of Comprehensive Income, year ended 31 December 20X7	
Sales	$820,000
Gain on insurance settlement	10,000
Cost of goods sold	(380,000)
Depreciation expense	(100,000)
Impairment of goodwill	(20,000)
Other expenses	(49,000)
Interest expense	(22,000)
Income tax expense	(73,000)
Net earnings and comprehensive income	$186,000

Additional information:

1. Phillies declared $40,000 in dividends in 20X7.
2. Equipment (cost $100,000, accumulated depreciation, $60,000) was destroyed by fire.
3. The temporary investments had a three-month term when they were first bought.
4. Goodwill was written down by $20,000 because of impairment.

Required:

1. Prepare the 20X7 SCF for Phillies Corporation. Use the indirect method of presentation for the operating activities section. Phillies classifies dividends paid as a financing activity. Separate disclosure of cash paid for interest and income tax is not required.
2. Repeat the operating activities section of the SCF using the indirect method, showing cash flow for interest and income tax directly in the operating activities section of the SCF.

Use whichever method of preparation you feel most comfortable with (i.e., choose from among the format-free, T-account, or spreadsheet [see the Appendix to this chapter] methods). The suggested solution uses T-accounts.

REVIEW PROBLEM 5-1 —SOLUTION

The T-account analysis appears below. Other approaches are equally valid—it is the result that matters. The actual SCF is shown at the end of this solution. Explanations for T-account entries are as follows:

a. Net earnings are $186,000. The T-account entry records net earnings.

b. Increase in accounts receivable; less cash was received from customers than was recognized as revenue.

c. Increase in inventories; more cash was paid for inventories than was recognized as COGS.

d. Increase in accounts payable; less was paid to trade creditors than was recognized as expense.

e. Depreciation expense was removed from operating expenses—a non-cash expense.

f. Goodwill impairment (expense) removed from operating expenses—another non-cash expense.

g. Salaries payable decreased, requiring more cash.

h. Adjustment to write off destroyed equipment and to record the insurance proceeds; $10,000 gain removed from operating earnings, and proceeds of $50,000 ($40,000 net book value disposed at a gain of $10,000) recorded as an inflow in the investing activities section.

i. Increase in interest payable, indicating that less cash was paid for interest than the amount of interest expense accrued.

j. Increase in bond payable, implying issuance of bond, in the absence of other information.

k. Increase in common shares implies issuance of additional shares, in the absence of evidence to the contrary.

l. Increase in income taxes payable; less tax paid than accrued.

m. Dividends declared *and paid* (i.e., there is no dividends payable account, so all must have been paid).

n. "Plug" entry to account for the otherwise unexplained change in the balance of the equipment account; the increase must have been due to the purchase of new equipment.

o. Decrease in mortgage payable implies repayment of mortgage, in the absence of other information.

T-Account Analysis

Cash and cash equivalents

Opening	200,000		
Operating activities			
a) Net earnings	186,000	b) Accounts receivable	20,000
d) Accounts payable	15,000	c) Inventory	12,000
e) Depreciation expense	100,000	g) Salaries payable	10,000
f) Goodwill impairment	20,000	h) Gain on insurance settlement	10,000
i) Interest payable	3,000		
l) Income tax payable	10,000		
Investing activities			
h) Insurance proceeds	50,000	n) Equipment bought	490,000
Financing activities			
k) Issued common shares	20,000	m) Dividends paid	40,000
j) Bond issued	50,000	o) Mortgage repayment	10,000
Closing	62,000		

Accounts receivable, net		
Op.	60,000	
b)	20,000	
Cl.	80,000	

Inventory		
Op.	18,000	
c)	12,000	
Cl.	30,000	

Equipment, net				
Op.	300,000			
h)	60,000	e)	100,000	
n)	490,000	h)	100,000	
Cl.	650,000			

Goodwill			
Op.	90,000		
		f)	20,000
Cl.	70,000		

Accounts payable			
		Op.	48,000
		d)	15,000
		Cl.	63,000

Salaries payable			
		Op.	60,000
g)	10,000		
		Cl.	50,000

Interest payable			
		Op.	6,000
		i)	3,000
		Cl.	9,000

Income tax payable			
		Op.	12,000
		l)	10,000
		Cl.	22,000

Mortgage payable			
		Op.	120,000
o)	10,000		
		Cl.	110,000

Bonds payable			
		Op.	200,000
		j)	50,000
		Cl.	250,000

Common shares			
		Op.	150,000
		k)	20,000
		Cl.	170,000

Retained earnings			
		Op.	72,000
m)	40,000	a)	186,000
		Cl.	218,000

Requirement 1

PHILLIES CORPORATION

Statement of Cash Flows

Year ended 31 December 20X7

Operating activities:		
Net earnings		$ 186,000
Adjustments:		
Depreciation expense	100,000	
Impairment of goodwill	20,000	
Gain on insurance settlement	(10,000)	110,000
		296,000
Plus (less) changes in non-cash working capital:		
Increase in accounts receivable	(20,000)	
Increase in accounts payable	15,000	
Increase in inventories	(12,000)	
Decrease in salaries payable	(10,000)	
Increase in interest payable	3,000	
Increase in income tax payable	10,000	(14,000)
		282,000
Investing activities:		
Insurance proceeds from equipment destroyed by fire	50,000	
New equipment purchased	(490,000)	(440,000)
Financing activities:		
Issuance of bonds	50,000	
Dividends paid	(40,000)	
Reduction of mortgage principal	(10,000)	
Issuance of common shares	20,000	20,000
Net increase (decrease) in cash		(138,000)
Opening cash and cash equivalents		200,000
Closing cash and cash equivalents		$ 62,000

Requirement 2

PHILLIES CORPORATION
Partial Statement of Cash Flows
Operating Activities

Year ended 31 December 20X7

Operating activities:		
Net earnings		$186,000
Adjustments:		
Interest expense	22,000	
Income tax expense	73,000	
Depreciation expense	100,000	
Impairment of goodwill	20,000	
Gain on insurance settlement	(10,000)	205,000
		391,000
Plus (less) changes in non-cash working capital:		
Increase in accounts receivable	(20,000)	
Increase in accounts payable	15,000	
Increase in inventories	(12,000)	
Decrease in salaries payable	(10,000)	(27,000)
		364,000
Cash paid for interest ($22,000 − $3,000 increase in payable)		(19,000)
Cash paid for income tax ($73,000 − $10,000 increase in payable)		(63,000)
		$282,000

APPENDIX

SPREADSHEET METHOD

The main body of the chapter pointed out that the analytical method used to derive the SCF is not important; what matters is the result. This chapter has illustrated two approaches—the *ad hoc* approach and the T-account approach. Another method that is popular, especially when complete documentation is important, is the spreadsheet approach. In essence, the spreadsheet approach puts the T-account data into columnar form.

SPREADSHEET PROCEDURES

To set up the spreadsheet, transfer the accounts and account balances from the statement of financial position to a four-column spreadsheet. Exhibit 5-A1 demonstrates the set-up for Ling Corporation, based on the chapter example and data in Exhibit 5-7. The 20X4 asset, liability, and equity account balances are in the first column, and the 20X5 balances are in the last column. Reconciling entries are entered in the two middle columns.

EXHIBIT 5-A1

LING CORPORATION

Statement of Cash Flows Worksheet

Accounts	31 December 20X4	Key	Reconciliation Debit	Reconciliation Credit	Key	31 December 20X5
Assets:						
Cash	$ 36,000	(s)	$ 14,000			$ 50,000
Short-term investments	34,000			$ 24,000	(s)	10,000
Accounts receivable	70,000	(i)	14,000			84,000
Inventories	30,000	(j)	12,000			42,000
Prepaid expenses	11,000	(k)	4,000			15,000
Land	50,000					50,000
Plant and equipment	615,000	(l)	150,000	25,000	(f)	740,000
Accumulated depreciation	(215,000)	(f)	20,000	65,000	(c)	(260,000)
Capitalized development costs	76,000	(m)	11,000	5,000	(d)	82,000
Long-term investments	70,000	(e)	22,000			92,000
Total assets	$777,000					$905,000
Liabilities and shareholders' equity:						
Bank loan	$ 5,000			15,000	(n)	$ 20,000
Accounts payable	45,000	(o)	9,000			36,000
Dividends payable	5,000			5,000	(p)	10,000
Bonds payable	133,000	(g)	20,000	33,000	(h)	146,000
Deferred tax	24,000			3,000	(q)	27,000
Preferred shares	120,000			22,000	(e)	142,000
Common shares	180,000			50,000	(r)	230,000
Retained earnings	265,000	(b)	35,000	64,000	(a)	294,000
Total equities	$777,000		$311,000	$311,000		$905,000

continued on next page

EXHIBIT 5-A1 *(cont'd)*

LING CORPORATION

Statement of Cash Flows Worksheet

Accounts	31 December 20X4	Key	Debit	Credit	Key	31 December 20X5
			Reconciliation			
Components of the Statement of Cash Flows						
Operating activities:						
Net earnings		(a)	$ 64,000			
Non-cash items						
Depreciation expense		(c)	65,000			
Amortization of development costs		(d)	5,000			
Gain on sale of equipment				$ 4,000	(f)	
Working capital changes:						
Increase in accounts receivable				14,000	(i)	
Increase in inventory				12,000	(j)	
Increase in prepaid expenses				4,000	(k)	
Decrease in accounts payable				9,000	(o)	
Increase in deferred tax		(q)	3,000			$ 94,000
Investing activities:						
Proceeds from equipment sold		(f)	9,000			
Purchase of plant and equipment				150,000	(l)	
Development costs				11,000	(m)	(152,000)
Financing activities:						
Dividends paid				35,000	(b)	
Increase in dividends payable		(p)	5,000			
Bonds retired				20,000	(g)	
Increase in short-term bank loan		(n)	15,000			
Bonds issued		(h)	33,000			
Common shares issued		(r)	50,000			48,000
Subtotal			249,000	259,000		
Change in cash and cash equivalents:		(s)	10,000			$ (10,000)
			$259,000	$259,000		

The reconciling entries are exactly the same for the spreadsheet and the T-accounts. Refer to the chapter example for an explanation of the cross-referenced entries. One additional entry is needed on the spreadsheet to record the change in cash.

s. The final reconciling entry transfers the change in cash and cash equivalents to the lower spreadsheet section. The $14,000 increase in cash and the $24,000 decrease in short-term investments are reconciled as follows:

Cash	14,000	
Change in cash and cash equivalents	10,000	
Short-term liquid investments		24,000

Entering the net change into the lower part of the statement balances the inflows and outflows. Totalling the debit and credit columns in the upper part of the worksheet reveals that they are in balance (at $311,000). The total of the debit and credit columns is meaningless *except* for the important fact that they balance. Any imbalance would indicate a debit-credit imbalance in the reconciliation entries.

The lower section of Exhibit 5-A1 now contains all of the information that is necessary for preparing the SCF. This SCF is shown in Exhibit 5-9 in the chapter.

The disadvantage of spreadsheets is the time it takes to format and to do all the adding and balancing. Some of this challenge can be eliminated with the use of spreadsheet programs. Spreadsheets are commonly used in very complex situations or where work has to be carefully documented so that it can be reviewed.

SUMMARY OF KEY POINTS

1. The spreadsheet method is an alternative way to analyze information prior to preparing the SCF. The spreadsheet method is an analytical approach; it is *not* a method of presentation.

2. In setting up a spreadsheet, opening balances are entered in the first column of a four-column spreadsheet, and closing balances in the final column. Reconciling entries are entered in the middle two columns. Items that involve cash flow are collected at the bottom of the spreadsheet.

QUESTIONS

Q5-1   Compare the purposes of the statement of financial position, statement of comprehensive income, and SCF.

Q5-2   How is cash defined for SCF purposes? Why is disclosure of the definition important?

Q5-3   Explain the basic difference between the three classifications reported on the SCF: operating, investing, and financing.

Q5-4   List three major cash inflows and three major cash outflows properly classified on the SCF under (a) operating activities, (b) investing activities, and (c) financing activities.

Q5-5   During the year, a capital asset with an original cost of $750,000 and accumulated depreciation on the date of sale of $560,000 was sold for $216,000. What will appear on the SCF as a result of this transaction? Assume the indirect presentation approach.

Q5-6   During the year, a company records $100,000 in cash sales and $160,000 in credit sales, of which $40,000 was collected from customers. Also during the year, $80,000 was collected from last year's credit sales. How much cash was collected from customers? What is reflected on the SCF?

Q5-7   Explain why an adjustment must be made for depreciation to compute cash flows from operating activities if the indirect presentation approach is used.

Q5-8   Explain the difference between the direct and indirect presentation approaches to the operating activities section of the SCF. Use the following data to illustrate the difference: a company reports $116,000 of earnings, which includes sales of $750,000. During the year, accounts receivable increased by $47,000.

Q5-9   Why might the direct method of presenting cash flows from operating activities be preferable to the indirect method? Which presentation approach dominates current practice?

Q5-10 Describe the two-step method to disclose cash flows from operations using the indirect method.

Q5-11 A company repaid a loan for $75,000, but borrowed another $82,000. The balance in the loan account therefore increased by $7,000 during the year. How would these events be reflected on the SCF? Use this example to explain offsetting.

Q5-12 Give three examples of significant non-cash transactions. Are these items included in the SCF?

Q5-13 A company borrows $350,000 and repays $400,000 after several years. The difference relates to interest. What appears on the SCF and in what classification in the year the money is borrowed? Repaid?

Q5-14 Forward Co. reports a net loss of ($100,000) this year. In the prior year, net earnings was $30,000 and cash flow from operating activities was $60,000. Is its quality of earnings higher if cash flow from operating activities this year is $60,000 or ($75,000)?

Q5-15 Developing Ltd. spends $46,700 on development. Under what circumstances will this cash outflow be reported in operating activities in the year of the expenditure, and in what circumstances will it be shown as a cash outflow for investing activities?

Q5-16 A company has earnings of $150, after income tax of $40. Tax payable increased by $6 over the year. What would appear on the operating activities section if the company chooses to add back the expense and list cash flows for income tax separately in operating activities? What other revenue or expense accounts may be subject to this presentation alternative?

Q5-17 In what category(ies) of the SCF may income tax be presented? Interest paid? Interest received? Dividends paid? Dividends received? If judgement is involved, who makes the decision about where to classify these items?

Q5-18 Why would the gain on sale of temporary investments (classified as a cash equivalent) not be reflected on the SCF that is prepared using the indirect method to present operating activities?

Q5-19 Explain the types of reconciling items used to adjust from earnings to cash flows from operating activities using the indirect method.

Q5-20 What are the differences between ASPE and IFRS with respect to the SCF?

CASE 5-1

PURPLE LIMITED

"Frankly, if we continue to grow, we will be out of business soon."

This was the glum assessment of Kathy Lin, President and CEO of Purple Limited, a company that designs, manufactures, and retails women's fashion. Kathy has a 30-year history in the fashion business and has managed her own label for much of that time. In 20X0, she incorporated Purple, and the company grew rapidly. It was particularly known for its edgy fashion design, reasonable prices, and quick turnaround. Purple hires young designers and has established a highly efficient manufacturing and distribution system to place trendy clothes in stores ahead of her competition. Initially, designs had been sold only in Purple's own stores, but over the last two years, Purple began selling to larger chains. As a result, the scope of Purple has significantly increased as have revenues and profits. In fact, the company reported a loss of $1,345 in 20X0 but moved to earnings of $133 in 20X1, earnings of $2,580 in 20X2, and an impressive $6,245 in 20X3 (All figures in thousands.) Sales had more than tripled over the past three years. Capital assets purchased over this period were $16,000 in 20X0, $9,500 in 20X2, and $8,000 in 20X3.

"We are pretty much out of cash, and I have bills to suppliers that are due. My banker will provide some cash, but not enough to keep up with this—and all that borrowing is getting expensive. I'm not sure how we can post such high earnings and be so broke. Can you explain this to me and help me with a plan to get out of this mess? I need good advice, fast."

You are an accounting professional in public practice and have provided business advice to Kathy in the past. You agree to meet with her on this issue tomorrow and now are preparing a draft report for discussion. You decide that calculating cash flows from operating activities is a good place to start (Exhibit 1).

Required:
Prepare the draft report for discussion.

EXHIBIT 1

PURPLE LIMITED
Summarized Statement of Financial Position

At 31 December (in thousands)	20X3	20X2	20X1	20X0
Cash	$ 320	$ 1,680	$ 4,210	$ 5,870
Accounts receivable	29,240	18,450	3,060	2,940
Inventory	41,970	32,970	25,760	22,800
Prepaid assets	1,566	1,211	1,087	1,004
Plant and equipment (net)	22,720	17,650	11,290	14,600
Other assets	3,650	1,540	2,970	1,340
Total	$99,466	$73,501	$48,377	$48,554
Liabilities				
Accounts payable and accrued liabilities	32,119	26,404	18,813	16,824
Short-term debt	35,566	24,929	13,276	14,675
Long-term debt	20,150	15,800	12,500	13,400
Equity				
Common shares	5,000	5,000	5,000	5,000
Retained earnings (deficit)	6,631	1,368	(1,212)	(1,345)
Total	$99,466	$73,501	$48,377	$48,554

CASE 5-2

HUM PRODUCTS LIMITED

HUM Products Limited (HUM) is a consumer products company that designs, manufactures, markets, and distributes a diverse portfolio of consumer products, primarily in the recreational and leisure segments. The company's products enjoy strong positive brand recognition and include consumer goods such as bicycles, car seats, small boats, and strollers.

As a public Canadian company, HUM complies with IFRS. The company is currently evaluating alternative presentations for the SCF. You are an independent accounting professional, hired to provide some expertise in the area. Your charge from the CFO:

> We'd like to take a fresh look at our SCF, with your help. We'd like to see what our SCF would look like if we used the direct method to present operating activities, rather than the indirect method that we have always used in the past. It would probably be helpful if your analysis also included an analysis of our strategic operating,

investing, and financing decisions that are apparent from the SCF. I've provided you with the information you need (Exhibit 1). You can piece it together from this, I expect. Document your assumptions and we'll review it together next week. We'd also like you to evaluate the alternatives for presenting dividends and interest paid in the operating versus financing sections: a demonstration of the alternatives, and the impact on our key reporting numbers, would be helpful. We also struggle with the accounting policy for our development costs; they're pretty steady from year to year, and we expense them. But that's a judgement call; we're evaluating the capitalization and amortization decision as well. Perhaps you should analyze that issue, as well. We are meeting with the audit committee next week, and we need to present an analysis to them.

Required:
Prepare a report that responds to the requests of the CFO.

EXHIBIT 1

HUM PRODUCTS LIMITED
Statement of Financial Position

As of 31 December (in thousands)	20X4	20X3
Assets		
Current assets		
Cash and cash equivalents	$ 19,600	$ 22,500
Accounts receivable	316,300	286,900
Inventories	508,500	322,400
Prepaid expenses	16,300	10,600
	860,700	642,400
Property, plant, and equipment, net	159,800	140,400
Intangible assets, net	368,900	276,400
Goodwill	540,200	540,200
	$1,929,600	$1,599,400
Liabilities		
Current liabilities		
Bank indebtedness	$ 4,400	$ 5,800
Accounts payable and accrued liabilities	380,900	325,900
Income tax payable	30,600	25,500
Current portion of long-term debt	8,900	63,000
	424,800	420,200
Long-term debt	450,700	162,900
Pension obligations	20,100	20,900
Deferred tax	111,800	109,700
	1,007,400	713,700
Shareholders' equity		
Common shares	177,500	177,500
Retained earnings	744,700	708,200
	922,200	885,700
	$1,929,600	$1,599,400

continued on next page

EXHIBIT 1 *(cont'd)*

HUM PRODUCTS LIMITED

Statement of Comprehensive Income

For the year ended 31 December (in thousands)	20X4	20X3
Sales	$2,164,800	$1,792,500
Expenses		
Cost of sales	1,651,100	1,375,400
Selling, general, and administrative expenses	319,100	244,800
Depreciation	35,800	29,800
Amortization of intangibles	10,400	10,700
Development costs	10,900	9,000
Restructuring costs	700	14,600
Interest	21,200	23,800
	2,049,200	1,708,100
Earnings before income tax	115,600	84,400
Income tax		
Current	17,000	26,400
Deferred	2,100	(7,300)
	19,100	19,100
Net earnings and comprehensive income	$ 96,500	$ 65,300
Earnings per share		
Basic and diluted	$3.84	$2.60

CASE 5-3

WOMEN'S HOCKEY POWER

On 14 February 20X6, Dana Samuels e-mailed you, Chris Morgan, a public accountant. Samuels is a famous female Canadian hockey player. In anticipation of retirement from competitive ice hockey following the current season, Samuels incorporated Women's Hockey Power (WHP). WHP has established an excellent reputation for its coaching clinics aimed toward women's hockey and the quality of the Deek line of women's hockey equipment and accessories that it manufactures. In fact, the company has been so successful that Samuels hopes to go public when volumes are higher.

Another firm will audit WHP's financial statements, but Samuels would like you to analyze the attached information. She really does not have much time to discuss financial information at the moment, as hockey season is in full swing. She has, however, attached the partial 31 January unaudited financial statements (Exhibit 1) and some supporting explanations (Exhibit 2).

Samuels's request:

> Look at this financial information and correct anything that might be misstated. If there are things you can't correct or I'll need to deal with later, let me know what will have to be done. Please provide corrected GAAP-compliant financial statements and the necessary information. If you adjust any of the numbers in these financial

statements, I would like you to provide me with the supporting journal entries. I did take a little accounting once, and it will help me understand what you've done. And if there are any other issues I need to deal with before taking WHP public, please provide an explanation and your advice.

Required:
Prepare a report and revised financial statements for Samuels.

(Judy Cumby, adapted)

EXHIBIT 1

WOMEN'S HOCKEY POWER LTD.

Statement of Financial Position (draft)

31 January 20X6

Accounts receivable	$226,300
Inventory	150,020
Investment in Deek Inc.	100,000
Equipment	480,000
Accumulated depreciation	(106,700)
Total assets	$849,620
Bank overdraft	$ 7,000
Accounts payable	12,000
Wages and bonus payable	—
Interest payable	—
Income taxes payable	36,500
Unearned revenue	35,000
Note payable, 9%	100,000
Note payable, 7%, four payments of $120,000 due starting 31 May 20X6. Interest payable annually on 31 May	480,000
Loan payable, 8% to Regal Bank	75,000
Common shares	5,000
Retained earnings	99,120
Total liabilities and shareholders' equity	$849,620

WOMEN'S HOCKEY POWER LTD.

Selected Earnings Information (draft)

For the year ended 31 January 20X6

Selected accounts and balances include:	
Interest expense (all sources)	$ 12,700
Earnings before income tax	$141,600
Income tax expense (30%)	42,480
	$ 99,120

EXHIBIT 2

INFORMATION RELATED TO WOMEN'S HOCKEY POWER
For the year ended 31 January 20X6

1. WHP was incorporated on 1 February 20X5 and has a 31 January year-end. The company was formed by issuing common shares for cash. Samuels owns 60% of the common shares of WHP, and the remaining shares are owned by three teammates.

2. In anticipation of WHP becoming fully operational, WHP secured a loan of $75,000 from the Regal Bank on 1 May 20X5. The loan bears interest at 8% and is payable on demand. Principal payments of $5,000 are due each April 30. Interest is payable monthly. The loan covenants stipulate that the company's financial statements must comply with GAAP, and WHP's debt-to-equity ratio cannot exceed 6:1.

3. There is no SCF, and one must be prepared in proper format, so cash flows are more easily understood by lenders. All asset, liability, and equity numbers as of 31 January 20X5 were zero because WHP did not exist on that date.

4. On 1 September 20X5, WHP acquired all of the common shares of Deek Inc. (Deek), a women's sporting apparel company, by issuing a $100,000, 9% note payable to the former shareholder. This was felt to be a very clever strategic choice as Deek Inc. manufactures and distributes a line that enjoys popular brand recognition in the marketplace. In fact, Deek recorded net earnings of $40,000 in the period from 1 September 20X5 to 31 January 20X6.

5. On June 1, 20X5, WHP acquired equipment from Super Shot Inc., a company wholly owned by one of the WHP minority shareholders. As payment for the equipment, WHP signed a 7% note payable. The principal will be paid in four equal instalments of $120,000 with the first payment due on 31 May 20X6.

6. During the year, WHP conducted a number of successful hockey clinics. The amount in unearned revenue relates to clinics that were actually finished in December 20X5.

7. The WHP accountant is entitled to a bonus of 10% of before-tax earnings over $50,000 but no accrual has been made.

8. Point Shot, a hockey school company wholly owned by another minority shareholder, placed an order for $40,000 worth of hockey sticks in November 20X5. Point Shot, which has an excellent credit rating and history with WHP, e-mailed WHP and asked that it not ship the sticks until early March 20X6. Accordingly, WHP has not made any journal entries related to this transaction. The hockey sticks were fully manufactured by 31 January 20X6 at a cost of $15,000 and are in inventory. Point Shot will pay the full $40,000 during the first week of March.

TECHNICAL REVIEW

Note: In all assignment questions, unless directed otherwise, assume that dividends paid are financing activities, and assume that interest paid and received, and dividends received, are operating transactions.

TR5-1 SCF—Cash Definition: Selected accounts from the SFP of TMI Limited at 31 December 20X4 and 20X5, are presented below.

As at 31 December	20X5	20X4
Cash #1	$ 230,000	$ 20,000
Cash #2 (overdrawn at the end of 20X4)	15,000	(70,000)
Short-term investments (a cash equivalent)	300,000	—

Required:
Calculate the change in cash for the year.

TR5-2 SCF—Cash from Operating Activities: Selected accounts from the SFP of UVI Limited at 31 December 20X4 and 20X5, are presented below. UVI reported earnings of $407,000 in 20X5, and depreciation expense was $35,000.

As at 31 December	20X5	20X4
Accounts receivable	$160,000	$110,000
Inventory	200,000	240,000
Accounts payable	150,000	195,000
Short-term bank loan payable	75,000	102,000

Required:
Calculate cash from operating activities for the year.

TR5-3 SCF—Investing Activities: Selected accounts from the SFP of MNN Limited at 31 December 20X4 and 20X5 are presented below. Depreciation was $40,000 for equipment, $60,000 for buildings, and $75,000 for machinery. A new machine was purchased in 20X5, with 25% of the price paid in cash and the other 75% financed directly by the vendor through a long-term note. Other assets were purchased for cash.

As at 31 December	20X5	20X4
Equipment, net of accumulated depreciation	$530,000	$400,000
Buildings, net of accumulated depreciation	700,000	200,000
Machinery, net of accumulated depreciation	560,000	210,000

Required:
List the items that would be included in the SCF from these accounts for 20X5. Include the appropriate section (operating, investing, or financing). Also list the non-cash item disclosure.

TR5-4 SCF—Financing Activities: Selected accounts from the SFP of Norelco Limited at 31 December 20X4 and 20X5 are presented below. Norelco reported earnings of $280,000 in 20X5. There was a new $140,000 of notes payable this year that was direct financing (a note issued by the vendor) for a piece of machinery.

As at 31 December	20X5	20X4
Notes payable, long-term	$450,000	$700,000
Common shares	300,000	230,000
Retained earnings	610,000	540,000

Required:
List the items that would be included in the SCF from these accounts for 20X5. Include the appropriate section (operating, investing, or financing). List the non-cash item disclosure. Make logical assumptions about unexplained changes in accounts.

TR5-5 SCF—Cash Paid or Collected: Information related to various financial statement elements is provided for three cases:

Case A   Interest expense was $26,400. Interest payable had an opening balance of $11,200 and a closing balance of $7,300. The discount on bonds payable was amortized by $2,200 during the year.

Case B   Interest revenue was $125,700. Interest receivable increased by $72,100 during the year.

Case C   Sales revenue was $794,300. Accounts receivable increased from $104,100 to $119,700, and unearned revenue decreased by $12,000 during the year.

Required:
For each case, calculate the cash inflow or outflow related to the revenue or expense account.

ASSIGNMENTS

Note: In all assignment questions, unless directed otherwise, assume that dividends paid are financing activities, and assume that interest paid and received, and dividends received, are operating transactions.

★ **A5-1 Overview—SCF Classification:** The records of Mineola Limited provided the following data:

a. Purchased capital asset for $170,000; paid cash.
b. Purchased capital asset for $170,000; signed a long-term note with the vendor for $150,000 and paid $20,000 in cash.
c. Sold a capital asset for $34,000 cash; original cost, $90,000, accumulated depreciation, $70,000.
d. Sales revenue, $1,300,000; accounts receivable increased, $215,000.
e. Wages expense, $168,000; wages payable increased, $10,000.
f. Declared a cash dividend, $66,000; dividends payable decreased by $2,000.
g. Borrowed $107,000 cash from the bank.
h. Converted long-term bonds into common shares, $4,000,000.
i. Paid a note payable, $150,000 principal plus $6,000 interest.
j. Depreciation expense, $67,000.

Required:
For each of the above items, give:

1. The SCF category (operating, investing, financing), or indicate that the item is excluded from the SCF.
2. The item that would appear on the SCF (indirect presentation method for operating activities).

★ **A5-2 Overview—SCF Classification:** The main sections of the SCF are shown below with letter identification. Next, several transactions are given. Match the transactions with the SCF sections by entering a letter in each blank space. Assume loans and notes receivable are long-term investments not related to operating activities. State other assumptions or explanations, if needed.

STATEMENT OF CASH FLOWS:
A. Cash inflows (outflows) from operating activities (indirect method of presentation)
B. Cash inflows (outflows) from investing activities
C. Cash inflows (outflows) from financing activities
D. None of the above

TRANSACTIONS:

_____   1. Cash dividends declared but not paid
_____   2. Repurchase and retirement of common shares

_____ 3. Stock dividend declared and distributed to common shareholders

_____ 4. Proceeds from issuing bond payable

_____ 5. Sale of plant assets at a loss

_____ 6. Purchase of long-term investment

_____ 7. Purchase of a 30-day treasury bill with excess cash

_____ 8. Issuance of the company's own common shares, for cash

_____ 9. Acquisition of a building through a finance lease with no money changing hands at the inception of the lease

_____ 10. Acquisition of plant equipment assets; paid cash

_____ 11. Increase in prepaid expenses

_____ 12. Depreciation expense

_____ 13. Payment of debt, 90% cash and 10% common shares issued

_____ 14. Sale of land at a loss; proceeds will be received in the next fiscal year

_____ 15. Decrease in rent payable

★ **A5-3 Overview—SCF Classification:** The records of Corktown Corporation provide information about transactions and events of the year. The company is preparing a SCF using the indirect presentation approach for operating activities.

a. Issued common shares for cash, $625,000.

b. Bought land for $500,000; signed a long-term note with the vendor for $275,000 and paid $225,000 in cash.

c. Invested $50,000 of idle cash in a temporary investment with a 60-day term.

d. Sales revenue, $3,400,000; accounts receivable decreased, $145,000.

e. Invested $300,000 of idle cash in common shares of a public company. The shares will be sold in 30 days' time.

f. Sold equipment for $86,000 cash; original cost, $340,000, accumulated depreciation, $210,000.

g. Repaid a bank loan, paying out $100,000 for principal and $12,000 for interest.

h. Issued common shares for equipment with a fair value of $670,000.

i. Paid a cash dividend, $50,000.

j. Recorded goodwill impairment of $40,000.

Required:

For each of the above items list the item that would appear on the SCF, including its category (operating, investing, or financing), and amount. If the item is excluded from the SCF, list the required disclosure.

★★ **A5-4 Statement of Cash Flows:** The records of Rangler Paper Company provided the selected data given below for the reporting period ended 31 December 20X5.

Statement of financial position data	
Paid cash dividend Fin	$ 10,000
Established restricted construction cash fund (a long-term investment) to build a new building Inv	60,000
Increased inventory of merchandise Op	14,000
Borrowed on a long-term note Fin	25,000
Acquired five acres of land for a future site for the company; paid in full by issuing 3,000 shares of Rangler common shares, when the quoted market price per share was $15 N/A	45,000
Increase in prepaid expenses Op	3,000
Decrease in accounts receivable Op	7,000
Payment of bonds payable in full at book value Fin	97,000
Increase in accounts payable Op	5,000
Cash from disposal of old operational assets (sold at book value) Inv	12,000
Decrease in rent receivable Op	2,000

Statement of comprehensive income

Sales revenue	$400,000
Rent revenue	10,000
Cost of goods sold	(190,000)
Depreciation expense	(20,000)
Remaining expenses	(97,000)
Net earnings and comprehensive income	$103,000

Required:

Prepare the SCF. Use the indirect method for operations. Separate disclosure of cash paid for interest and income tax and investment income is not required. Group all changes in non-cash working capital in operations as one amount. Assume a beginning cash balance of $62,000.

★★ **A5-5 Statement of Cash Flows:** Denton Corporation's statement of financial position accounts as at 31 December 20X4 and 20X5 and information relating to 20X5 activities are presented below.

As at 31 December	20X5	20X4
Assets		
Cash	$ 230,000	$ 100,000
Short-term investments ꜰ∧	300,000	—
Accounts receivable ᴏᴘ	510,000	510,000
Inventory ᴏᴘ	680,000	600,000
Long-term investments ꜰ∧	200,000	300,000
Plant assets ɪɴᵥ	1,700,000	1,000,000
Accumulated depreciation ᴏᴘ	(450,000)	(450,000)
Patent ᴏᴘ	90,000	100,000
Total assets	$3,260,000	$2,160,000
Liabilities and shareholders' equity		
Accounts payable and accrued liabilities ᴏᴘ	$ 825,000	$ 720,000
Short-term bank debt ꜰ∧	325,000	—
Common shares ꜰ∩	1,170,000	950,000
Retained earnings	940,000	490,000
Total liabilities and shareholders' equity	$3,260,000	$2,160,000

Information relating to 20x5 activities:

- Net earnings for 20X5 were $690,000.
- Cash dividends were declared and paid in 20X5.
- Equipment costing $400,000 and having a net book value of $150,000 was sold for $150,000.
- A long-term investment was sold for $135,000. There were no other transactions affecting long-term investments in the year.
- Short-term investments consist of treasury bills with an original term of three months.

Required:

Determine the following amounts for Denton for the year 20X5:

1. Net cash from operating activities (indirect method)
2. Net cash from investing activities
3. Net cash from financing activities

★★ **A5-6 Statement of Cash Flows:** The financial statements for Fardy Limited are shown below:

Statement of Comprehensive Income

For the year ended 31 December 20X5

Sales revenue	$607,100
Investment revenue	12,500
Operating expenses, including cost of goods sold	264,400
Depreciation expense	35,000
Goodwill impairment	38,700
Administrative expenses	207,000
Interest expense	15,100
Gain on sale of investment	2,000
Income tax expense	24,600
Net earnings and comprehensive income	$ 36,800

Statement of Financial Position

As of 31 December	20X5	20X4
Assets		
Cash	$ 27,500	$ 30,000
Accounts receivable	102,500	70,000
Merchandise inventory	231,400	210,000
Prepaid insurance	2,600	6,400
Investments	25,000	40,000
Land	90,000	90,000
Capital assets, net of accumulated depreciation	478,000	310,000
Goodwill, net of impairment	57,900	96,600
	$1,014,900	$853,000
Liabilities and equity		
Accounts payable	$ 212,400	$189,000
Rent payable	7,500	5,000
Income tax payable	16,400	16,000
Bonds payable	370,000	300,000
Pension obligation	16,700	10,000
Common shares	324,000	270,000
Retained earnings	67,900	63,000
	$1,014,900	$853,000

During the year, the company purchased a capital asset valued at $10,000; payment was made by issuing common shares. Additional capital assets were acquired for cash. Changes in other accounts were typical transactions.

Required:

1. Prepare the SCF using the indirect method. Include required note disclosure of non-cash transactions. Omit the separate disclosure of cash flow for interest, investment income, and income tax.
2. Explain the company's cash transactions for the year, based on the SCF.

★★ **A5-7 Statement of Cash Flows:** Filbert Corp's 20X2 financial statements showed the following:

Sales		$842,100
Cost of goods sold	$320,000	
Depreciation	42,000	
Other operating expenses	125,900	
Income tax	72,400	
Loss on sale of equipment	5,100	
Gain on sale of investment	(3,200)	562,200
Net earnings and comprehensive income		$279,900

As at December 31	20X2	20X1
Cash	$ 113,800	$ 90,600
Accounts receivable	147,000	169,200
Inventory	308,000	289,000
Equipment	913,000	783,000
Less: accumulated depreciation	(379,000)	(377,000)
Investment	90,000	130,000
Total	$1,192,800	$1,084,800
Accounts payable	$ 101,800	$ 171,200
Income tax payable	16,300	11,600
Bonds payable	75,000	0
Common shares	504,000	504,000
Retained earnings	495,700	398,000
Total	$1,192,800	$1,084,800

Additional information:
During the year, equipment with an original cost of $164,000 was sold for cash.

Required:

1. Prepare the SCF, in good form. Include required note disclosure of non-cash transactions. Omit the separate disclosure of cash flow for interest, investment income, and income tax. Make logical assumptions regarding the nature of change in asset, liability, and equity accounts.

2. Explain the company's cash transactions for the year, based on the SCF.

★ **A5-8 Presentation—Direct Method, Operating Activities:** Refer to the data in A5-6.

Required:
Prepare the SCF, in good form, using the direct method in the operating activities section.

★★ **A5-9 Presentation—Direct and Indirect, Operating Activities:** The statement of financial position, statement of comprehensive income, and additional information are given below for Supreme Company.

Statement of Financial Position

As at 31 December	20X5	20X4
Debits		
Cash	$ 44,900	$ 40,000
Accounts receivable	52,500	60,000
Merchandise inventory	141,600	180,000
Prepaid interest	1,200	2,400
Investments, long term	—	30,000
Land	38,400	10,000
Capital assets	259,000	250,000
Patent (net)	1,400	1,600
	$539,000	$574,000
Credits		
Accumulated depreciation	$ 79,000	$ 65,000
Accounts payable	49,700	50,000
Wages payable	1,500	2,000
Income taxes payable	13,400	9,000
Bonds payable	50,000	100,000
Common shares	329,000	320,000
Retained earnings	16,400	28,000
	$539,000	$574,000

Statement of Comprehensive Income

For the year ended 31 December 20X5	20X5
Sales revenue	$399,100
Cost of goods sold	(224,400)
Depreciation expense	(14,000)
Patent amortization	(200)
Salary expense	(80,000)
Interest expense	(4,400)
Other expenses	(44,000)
Investment revenue	900
Gain on sale of investments	10,000
Income tax expense	(24,600)
Net earnings and comprehensive income	$ 18,400

Analysis of selected accounts and transactions:

a. Purchased capital asset, $9,000; payment by issuing 600 common shares.
b. Payment at maturity date to retire bonds payable, $50,000.
c. Sold the long-term investments for $40,000.
d. Reassessment for prior years' income taxes; paid during 20X5 and added to 20X5 tax expense, $6,600.
e. Purchased land, $28,400; paid cash.

Required:

1. Prepare the SCF, using the direct method in the operating activities section. Include a list of non-cash transactions that would be presented in the disclosure notes.
2. Prepare the operating activities section of the SCF using the indirect method in the operating activities section. Omit the separate disclosure of cash flow for interest, investment income, and income tax.

A5-10 Presentation—Direct and Indirect, Operating Activities: The following financial information is available for Buffalo Incorporated for the 20X3 fiscal year:

Statement of Financial Position

As at 31 December	20X3	20X2
Cash	$ 5,000	$ 20,000
Receivables	220,000	180,000
Marketable securities	190,000	230,000
Inventory	731,000	632,000
Land	330,000	410,000
Building	1,040,000	1,120,000
Accumulated depreciation, building	(470,000)	(380,000)
Machinery	1,080,000	875,000
Accumulated depreciation, machinery	(219,000)	(212,000)
Goodwill	110,000	110,000
	$3,017,000	$2,985,000
Current liabilities	$ 256,000	$ 331,000
Bonds payable	1,000,000	1,000,000
Preferred shares	1,048,000	843,000
Common shares	565,000	500,000
Retained earnings	148,000	311,000
	$3,017,000	$2,985,000

Statement of Comprehensive Income

For the year ended 31 December 20X3

Sales	$1,684,000
Cost of goods sold	1,103,000
Gross profit	581,000
Depreciation	
Building	110,000
Machinery	75,000
Interest	115,000
Operating expenses	361,000
Selling expenses	40,000
Gain on sale of land	(22,000)
Loss on sale of machine	27,000
	706,000
Net earnings (loss) before income tax	(125,000)
Income tax recovery	54,000
Net earnings (loss) and comprehensive income (loss)	$ (71,000)

Additional information:

1. Marketable securities were sold at their carrying value. The marketable securities are not cash equivalents.
2. A partially depreciated building was sold for an amount equal to its net book value.
3. Cash of $40,000 was received on the sale of a machine.
4. Preferred shares were issued for cash on 1 March 20X3. Dividends of $50,000 were paid on the noncumulative preferred shares.

5. On 1 September 20X3, 25,000 common shares were purchased and retired for $55,000, their original issuance price. On 1 November 20X3, 65,000 common shares were issued in exchange for machinery and valued at $120,000.

6. Because of its loss, the company received a refund of taxes paid in prior years of $54,000.

Required:

1. Prepare the SCF, in good form. Use the indirect method for cash flows from operations. Omit the separate disclosure of cash flows for interest, investment income, and income tax. Include a list of non-cash transactions that would be presented in the disclosure notes.

2. Repeat the operating activities section of the SCF, using the direct method for cash flows from operations.

★★ **A5-11 Presentation—Direct and Indirect, Operating Activities:** The accounting records of Laurent Company provided the following data:

Statement of Comprehensive Income

For year ended 31 December 20X8

Sales	$900,000
Cost of goods sold	(540,000)
Depreciation expense	(12,000)
Operating expenses	(192,000)
Net earnings and comprehensive income	$156,000

Statement of Financial Position

At 31 December	20X8	20X7
Debits		
Cash	$102,000	$ —
Accounts receivable - OP	54,000	57,000
Inventory + OP	75,000	60,000
Investment, long term Inv	—	9,000
Capital assets Inv	279,000	180,000
Total debits	$510,000	$306,000
Credits		
Bank overdraft starting cash	$ —	$ 15,000
Accumulated depreciation + OP	42,000	30,000
Accounts payable + OP	36,000	18,000
Short-term bank loan + Fin	12,000	9,000
Notes payable, long term	108,000	60,000
Common shares + Fin	240,000	150,000
Retained earnings	72,000	24,000
Total credits	$510,000	$306,000

Other information:

a. Paid a $24,000 long-term note payable by issuing common shares.

b. Purchased capital assets that cost $99,000; gave a $72,000 long-term note payable and paid $27,000 cash.

c. Sold the long-term investment at cost, for cash.

d. Assume that unexplained differences in asset, liability, and equity accounts flow from logical sources.

Required:

1. Prepare the SCF, using the two-step indirect method of presentation for the operating activities section. Omit separate disclosure of cash paid for interest and income tax. Include a list of non-cash transactions that would be presented in the disclosure notes.
2. Prepare the operating activities section of the SCF using the direct method.

★ **A5-12 Interpretation—Quality of Earnings:** Dromeda Limited has prepared the following comparison (in thousands):

31 December	20X5	20X4	20X3
Net earnings	$210	$670	$(145)
Cash flows from operating activities	535	560	510

The same information has been collected for Panel Corporation:

31 December	20X5	20X4	20X3
Net earnings	$210	$670	$(145)
Cash flows from operating activities	190	455	(50)

Required:

1. Which of the companies above illustrates higher quality of earnings? Explain.
2. Suggest four factors that would make cash flows from operating activities different from net earnings.

★ **A5-13 Interpretation—Quality of Earnings:** Oakland Limited owns a chain of golf courses. Members sign multiyear membership packages, with increasing payments in later years of the contract. Revenue is recognized evenly over the membership term, regardless of the cash flow pattern. The operating activities section of the SCF for the past two years is as follows:

OAKLAND LIMITED

Statement of Cash Flows

	20X3	20X2
Cash flows from operating activities		
Earnings for the period	$ 36,000	$ 31,500
Adjustment for:		
Depreciation and amortization	41,700	32,500
(Gains)/losses on sale of assets	(3,600)	(2,300)
Decrease/(increase) in accounts receivable	(4,200)	(3,300)
Increase/(decrease) in unearned revenue	7,400	61,100
Decrease/(increase) in other working capital accounts	(17,400)	(8,200)
Deferred income tax	9,300	6,900
Other	(1,000)	(700)
Net cash from operating activities	$ 68,200	$117,500

Required:

1. Does the above analysis suggest high quality of earnings? Explain.
2. Suggest two accounting policies that would contribute to lower quality of earnings, based on the adjustments above.

★ **A5-14 Interpretation—Quality of Earnings:** Minex Corporation owns a number of mine sites, and is involved in exploration, extraction, and refining. Output is sold under long-term contracts, where prices are set, but extraction and exploration decisions are influenced by commodity prices. The operating activities section of the SCF for the past two years:

MINEX CORPORATION
Statement of Cash Flows

	20X3	20X2
Cash flows from operating activities		
Income (loss) for the period	$ (7,300)	$ 43,200
Adjustment for:		
Depreciation and depletion	11,300	42,400
Deferred development cost amortization	20,700	32,400
Decrease/(increase) in accounts receivable	(2,600)	(6,300)
Increase/(decrease) in unearned revenue	4,200	(53,300)
Decrease/(increase) in other working capital accounts	7,400	6,100
Deferred income tax	9,300	17,100
Other	1,700	(300)
Net cash from operating activities	$44,700	$ 47,100

Required:

1. Does the above analysis suggest high quality of earnings? Explain.

2. Suggest two accounting policies that would contribute to lower quality of earnings, based on the adjustments above.

★★ **A5-15 Statement of Cash Flows—Indirect Method; Capital Assets:** Information related to capital assets is provided for three cases:

Case A	20X2	20X1
Capital assets	$180,000	$160,000
Accumulated depreciation	(60,000)	(70,000)
	120,000	90,000

The company sold an asset with an original cost of $40,000 and a net book value of $10,000 for a gain of $2,000. Other capital assets were acquired for cash.

Case B	20X2	20X1
Capital assets	$330,000	$320,000
Accumulated depreciation	(170,000)	(190,000)
	160,000	130,000

The company sold an asset with an original cost of $60,000 at a loss of $4,000. Depreciation expense was $25,000. Other capital assets were acquired for cash.

Case C	20X2	20X1
Capital assets	$600,000	$290,000
Accumulated depreciation	(160,000)	(110,000)
	440,000	180,000

The company sold an asset with an original cost of $80,000 and a net book value of $54,000 for a gain of $17,000. Capital assets of $200,000 were acquired by issuing a long-term note to the vendor for the full amount. Other capital assets were acquired for cash.

Required:

For each case, indicate the items that would appear on the SCF, along with their classification. Assume that the operating activities section reflects the indirect presentation format. Assume that unexplained account changes result from logical transactions.

★★★ **A5-16 Statement of Cash Flows—Direct and Indirect:** Financial statements for Wonder Company follow:

WONDER COMPANY

Statement of Financial Position

As of 31 December	20X4	20X3
Assets		
Current assets:		
Cash	$ 18,500	$ 16,000
Accounts receivable	515,000	490,000
Inventory	420,000	380,800
Total current assets	953,500	886,800
Land	350,000	150,000
Plant and equipment	1,760,000	1,209,000
Less: Accumulated depreciation	(890,800)	(878,000)
Patents	93,000	97,000
Total assets	$2,265,700	$1,464,800
Liabilities and shareholders' equity		
Liabilities:		
Current liabilities:		
Accounts payable	$ 290,000	$ 316,200
Salaries and wages payable	45,700	42,100
Income tax payable	106,900	99,300
Total current liabilities	442,600	457,600
Long-term debt	1,109,000	595,000
Total liabilities	1,551,600	1,052,600
Shareholders' equity:		
Common shares, no-par	183,000	180,000
Retained earnings	531,100	232,200
Total shareholders' equity	714,100	412,200
Total liabilities and shareholders' equity	$2,265,700	$1,464,800

WONDER COMPANY

Statement of Comprehensive Income

For the year ended 31 December 20X4

Sales revenue		$3,700,000
Less expenses:		
Cost of goods sold	$2,041,000	
Selling and administrative expenses	545,000	
Depreciation and amortization	185,000	
Rent expense	15,000	
Miscellaneous expenses	142,000	
Total expenses		2,928,000
Other revenues and expenses:		
Interest expense	34,600	
Gain on sale of equipment	(6,000)	
Loss on debt retirement	11,000	39,600
Earnings before income tax		732,400
Income tax expense		311,800
Net earnings and comprehensive income		$ 420,600

Additional information:

a. The company sold equipment that had an original cost of $292,000 and a net book value of $123,800. Other equipment was purchased for cash. Patent amortization was $4,000.

b. Long-term debt with a face value of $400,000 was repaid during the year and other long-term debt was issued at a lower interest rate.

c. The company issued shares for land during the period. Other common shares were retired (bought back and cancelled) at book value.

d. Assume unexplained changes in accounts stem from logical transactions.

Required:

1. Prepare the SCF, using the indirect method. Use the two-step method for operations. Omit the separate disclosure of cash flows for interest, investment income, and income tax.

2. Prepare the SCF, using the direct method to present cash flows in the operating activities section.

★★★ **A5-17 Statement of Cash Flows—Optional Spreadsheet:** Shown below are the statements of comprehensive income, the comparative statements of financial positions, and additional information useful in preparing the 20X5 SCF for Sells Company.

Statement of Comprehensive Income

For the year ended 31 December 20X5

Net sales	$300,000
Cost of goods sold	80,000
Gross margin	220,000
Depreciation expense	45,000
Amortization of intangibles	2,000
Other expenses	44,000
Interest expense	3,000
Income tax expense	65,000
Net earnings and comprehensive income	$ 61,000

Statement of Financial Position

As of 31 December	20X5	20X4
Cash	$ 32,000	$ 16,000
Accounts receivable	47,000	50,000
Other receivables	2,000	3,000
Inventory	32,000	30,000
Equipment	77,000	80,000
Accumulated depreciation	(5,000)	(6,000)
Intangibles, net	53,000	55,000
Total assets	$238,000	$228,000
Accounts payable	$ 60,000	$ 50,000
Income taxes payable	50,000	70,000
Interest payable	1,000	2,000
Bonds payable	—	32,000
Discount on bonds payable	—	(2,000)
Common shares	80,000	70,000
Retained earnings	47,000	6,000
Total liabilities and owners' equity	$238,000	$228,000

Additional information:

a. Equipment costing $66,000 with a book value of $20,000 was sold at book value. New equipment was also purchased; common shares were issued in partial payment.

b. The bonds were repaid at maturity; $2,000 of bond discount was amortized in 20X5 prior to the maturity date.

Required:

Prepare the 20X5 SCF, indirect method, for Sells Company. Omit separate disclosure of cash paid for income tax and interest in the operating activities section. The solution to this assignment features an optional spreadsheet.

 A5-18 Statement of Cash Flows, Partial: The following selected information is available for Smith & Co. Ltd., for the year ended 31 December 31 20X8:

Statement of Comprehensive Income

For year ended 31 December 20X8

Sales	$600,000	
Gain of sale of equipment	4,500	$604,500
Cost of goods sold		375,000
Operating expenses, including $45,000 of depreciation		66,000
Loss on sale of land		15,000
Net earnings and comprehensive income		$148,500

Selected Asset, Liability, and Equity Accounts

As of 31 December	20X8	20X7
Inventory	$ 56,000	$ 42,000
Equipment	550,000	460,000
Accumulated depreciation, equipment*	(322,000)	(316,000)
Land	200,000	250,000
Notes payable (long term)*	(60,000)	(80,000)
Common shares*	(490,000)	(415,000)
Retained earnings*	(352,000)	(306,000)

*Brackets denote a credit balance.

Other information:

1. Equipment with an original cost of $50,000 was sold for cash.
2. Other equipment was bought for cash.
3. There is no income tax expense.
4. Cash dividends were paid during the year as well as a $25,000 stock dividend that reduced retained earnings and increased common shares.

Required:

Present, in good form, the operating, investing, and financing section of the SCF for the year ended 31 December 20X8 as far as possible. Also list the non-cash transactions that would be separately disclosed. *Note:* You have not been provided with enough information (cash, other assets, and liabilities) to balance the SCF to the change in cash.

  A5-19 Statement of Cash Flows, Partial: Sternhill Limited reported the following selected balances:

Account Title	20X4	20X3
Machinery	$567,800	$344,900
Accumulated depreciation, machinery*	(214,800)	(123,600)
Bonds payable*	(300,000)	(200,000)
Common shares*	(780,000)	(500,000)
Preferred shares*	(50,000)	(300,000)
Retained earnings*	(467,500)	(356,900)

*Brackets denote a credit balance.

Other information:

1. There was a stock dividend of $50,000 on common shares and a cash dividend of $70,000.
2. Of the preferred shares, $100,000 were retired for cash, and $150,000 were converted into bonds payable.
3. Some common shares were issued for cash during the period.
4. Machinery with a net book value of $56,200 and an original cost of $97,300 was sold during the year at a loss of $2,100. Other machinery was purchased for cash.
5. Any unexplained change in the accounts should be assumed to be because of logical transactions.

Required:

List the items that would appear on the SCF for 20X4 as far as possible, considering the changes in the accounts above, and the other information. Organize your SCF appropriately (operating, investing, financing) and indicate whether each item is added or subtracted. Also list the non-cash transactions that would be separately disclosed. *Note:* You have not been provided with enough information (cash, other assets, and liabilities) to balance the SCF to the change in cash.

★★★ **A5-20 Statement of Cash Flows:** The following data were provided by the accounting records of NewFort Limited at year end, 31 December 20X9:

Statement of Financial Position

As of 31 December	20X9	20X8
Debits		
Cash	$ 21,000	$ 12,000
Accounts receivable	296,000	196,000
Inventory	362,000	393,000
Long-term investments	—	91,000
Property, plant, and equipment	1,196,000	960,000
Total debits	$1,875,000	$1,652,000
Credits		
Accumulated depreciation	$ 470,000	$ 576,000
Accounts payable	154,500	191,500
Interest payable	16,500	13,500
Deferred tax	71,000	47,000
Bonds payable	350,000	180,000
Common shares	480,000	250,000
Retained earnings	333,000	394,000
Total credits	$1,875,000	$1,652,000

Statement of Comprehensive Income

Year ended 31 December 20X9

Sales	$2,457,000
Cost of goods sold	(1,689,000)
Depreciation expense	(62,000)
Remaining expenses	(572,000)
Loss on sale of operating assets	(9,000)
Gain on sale of investments	36,000
Net earnings and comprehensive income	$ 161,000

Analysis of selected accounts and transactions:

a. Sold plant assets for cash; cost, $252,000; two-thirds depreciated.
b. Purchased plant assets for cash.

c. Purchased plant assets and exchanged unissued bonds payable of $190,000 in payment.
d. Sold the long-term investments for cash.
e. Retired bonds payable at maturity date by issuing common shares, $65,000.
f. Other changes in asset, liability, and equity accounts flow from logical sources.

Required:

1. Prepare the SCF, using the two-step indirect method to present the operations section. Omit separate disclosure of cash paid for interest and income tax in the operating activities section of the SCF. Include a list of non-cash transactions that would be presented in the disclosure notes.

2. Prepare the operating activities section of the SCF using the direct method.

★★ **A5-21 Statement of Cash Flow—Optional Spreadsheet:** Todd Corporation reported the following in its 20X4 financial statements:

TODD CORPORATION

Statement of Comprehensive Income

For the year ended 31 December 20X4

Sales	$624,000
Cost of goods sold	(330,000)
Depreciation expense	(48,000)
Patent amortization	(1,800)
Remaining expenses	(106,200)
Net earnings and comprehensive income	$138,000

TODD CORPORATION

Statement of Financial Position

As of 31 December	20X4	20X3
Cash	$129,000	$ 90,000
Investments, short term (common shares)	18,000	—
Accounts receivable	126,000	102,000
Inventory	90,000	60,000
Investments, long term	60,000	—
Property, plant, and equipment (net)	354,000	360,000
Patent (net)	16,200	18,000
Other assets	42,000	42,000
Total	$835,200	$672,000
Accounts payable	$132,000	$ 72,000
Accrued expenses payable	52,200	—
Bonds payable	120,000	240,000
Common shares	267,000	210,000
Retained earnings	264,000	150,000
Total	$835,200	$672,000

Required:

1. Prepare the SCF using the indirect method. Assume that unexplained changes in the accounts are caused by logical transactions. Omit separate disclosure of cash paid for interest and income tax. The solution to this assignment features an optional spreadsheet.

2. Prepare the operating activities section of the SCF using the direct method.

★ **A5-22 Calculate Cash Flows—Interest and Income Tax:** Information related to various financial statement elements is provided for three cases:

Case A   Interest revenue was $43,500. Interest receivable had an opening balance of $7,200 and a closing balance of $4,100.

Case B   Interest expense was $87,000. Discount amortization was $5,000 during the year. Interest payable had an opening balance of $5,500 and a closing balance of $6,700.

Case C   Tax expense was $170,700. The deferred tax liability had an opening balance of $46,000 and a closing balance of $51,500. Income tax payable declined by $11,200 during the year.

Required:
For each case, calculate the cash inflow or outflow related to the income statement element.

★★ **A5-23 Optional Presentation Alternatives, Direct Method:** The SCF for MacLaren Supplies Limited, using the direct method of presentation for operating activities, is shown below.

MACLAREN SUPPLIES LIMITED
Statement of Cash Flows

Year ended 31 December 20X5

Operating Activities		
Cash received from customers	$406,600	
Cash paid for operating expenses	(306,300)	
Cash paid for interest	(7,700)	
Cash paid for income tax	(20,200)	
Cash received from investment income	4,900	
Cash from operating		$77,300
Investing activities:		
Sold long-term investment	36,000	
Purchased fixed assets	(28,400)	
Cash from investing		7,600
Financing activities:		
Dividends paid	(20,000)	
Bonds payable retired	(60,000)	
Cash used for financing		(80,000)
Net increase in cash during the year		4,900
Cash balance, beginning of the year		16,000
Cash balance, end of the year		$20,900

Required:
1. Some of the items included in operating activities, above, may be presented in other sections of the SCF. Explain the alternatives open to the company. What alternative is open for dividends paid, now in financing activities?
2. Redraft the SCF, classifying all items identified in requirement 1 into sections *other than* operating activities.
3. Return to the SCF as presented in the question. Redraft the SCF, classifying interest and dividends paid in operating activities.
4. Explain why companies might choose the presentations provided in requirement 2 or 3.

★★ **A5-24 Optional Presentation Alternatives, Indirect Method:** The SCF for Wave Electronics Limited, using the indirect method of presentation for operating activities, is shown below.

WAVE ELECTRONICS LIMITED

Statement of Cash Flows

Year ended 31 December 20X2

Operating Activities		
Net earnings	$ 28,200	
Adjustments:		
Depreciation and amortization	14,200	
Income tax expense	16,000	
Interest expense	23,500	
Dividend revenue	(6,800)	
Gain on sale of investments	(10,000)	
	65,100	
Changes in working capital:		
Decrease in accounts receivable	7,500	
Decrease in inventory	18,400	
Cash paid for interest	(24,000)	
Cash paid for income tax	(11,100)	
Cash received from dividend revenue	5,600	
Cash from operating		$61,500
Investing activities:		
Sold long-term investment	45,000	
Purchased fixed assets	(138,400)	
Cash for investing		(93,400)
Financing activities:		
Dividends paid	(20,000)	
Bonds payable issued	60,000	
Cash for financing		40,000
Net increase in cash during the year		8,100
Cash balance, beginning of the year		(1,300)
Cash balance, end of the year		$ 6,800

Required:

1. Some of the items included in operating activities, above, may be presented in other sections of the SCF. Explain the alternatives open to the company. What alternative is open for dividends paid, now in financing activities?
2. Redraft the SCF, reclassifying all items identified in requirement 1 into sections *other than* operating activities.
3. Return to the SCF as presented in the question. Redraft the SCF, classifying interest and dividends paid in operating activities.
4. Explain why the presentation prepared in requirement 2 or 3 may be preferable.

★ **A5-25 Presentation of Interest and Tax, Indirect Method:** Return to the facts of A5-16.

Required:

1. Prepare the operating activities section of the SCF, using the indirect method of presentation but incorporating separate disclosure of income tax paid and interest paid within the operating activities section.
2. In what sections of the SCF could each of interest paid, investment revenue received, and dividends paid be classified?

★ **A5-26 Presentation of Interest and Tax, Indirect Method:** Return to the facts of A5-17.

Required:

1. Prepare the operating activities section of the SCF, using the indirect method of presentation, but incorporating separate disclosure of income tax paid and interest paid within the operating activities section.
2. In what sections of the SCF could each of interest paid, investment revenue received, and dividends paid be classified?

★ **A5-27 ASPE—Statement of Cash Flows:** Return to the facts of A5-24.

Required:

1. Prepare the operating activities section of the SCF incorporating ASPE classification and policy decisions. Include supplemental disclosure of interest paid, income tax paid, and dividend revenue received. Tax payable increased by $4,900, dividends receivable increased by $1,200, and prepaid interest increased by $500.
2. Explain the classification requirements that are different between ASPE and IFRS.

★★ **A5-28 ASPE—Statement of Cash Flows:** The records of HKL Company provided the following information for the year ended 31 December 20X8:

Statement of Comprehensive Income

For the year ended 31 December 20X8

Sales revenue	$180,000
Cost of goods sold	(131,000)
Depreciation expense	(10,000)
Insurance expense	(1,000)
Interest expense	(2,000)
Salaries and wages expense	(12,000)
Remaining expenses	(13,000)
Loss on sale of equipment	(2,000)
Income tax expense	(8,000)
Net earnings and comprehensive income	$ 1,000

Statement of Financial Position

As of 31 December	20X8	20X7
Cash	$ 61,000	$ 35,000
Accounts receivable	31,500	28,500
Inventory	15,000	10,000
Prepaid interest	1,400	2,400
Buildings and equipment	81,000	80,000
Accumulated depreciation	(21,000)	(20,000)
Land	81,100	40,100
Total	$250,000	$176,000
Accounts payable	$ 21,000	$ 18,000
Wages payable	1,000	4,000
Income tax payable	6,000	—
Notes payable, long-term	56,000	30,000
Common shares	143,000	100,000
Retained earnings	23,000	24,000
Total	$250,000	$176,000

Additional information:

a. Sold equipment for cash (cost, $15,000; accumulated depreciation, $9,000).
b. Purchased land, $20,000 cash.
c. Acquired land for $21,000 and issued common shares as payment in full.
d. Acquired equipment, cost $16,000; issued a $16,000, three-year, interest-bearing note payable.

Required:

Prepare the SCF, using the two-step indirect method. Analyze every account to ensure all changes are included. Assume unexplained changes are from logical sources. Include required note disclosure of non-cash transactions. Prepare separate disclosure of cash paid for interest and income tax, as is required by ASPE.

 A5-29 ASPE—Statement of Cash Flows: You are presented with the following data from Jake Doyle Inc. for the year ended 31 December 20X1.

JAKE DOYLE INC.

Statement of Financial Position

As at 31 December	20X1	20X0	Change
Debits			
Cash	$ 41,000	$ 32,000	$ 9,000
Accounts receivable	256,000	196,000	60,000
Inventory	342,000	393,000	(51,000)
Long-term investments	—	71,000	(71,000)
Property, plant, and equipment	1,105,000	960,000	145,000
Total debits	$1,744,000	$1,652,000	
Credits			
Accumulated depreciation	$ 484,000	$ 576,000	$ (92,000)
Accounts payable	124,500	201,500	(77,000)
Interest payable	3,250	3,500	(250)
Income tax payable	49,550	47,000	2,550
Bonds payable	300,000	180,000	120,000
Common shares	300,000	250,000	50,000
Retained earnings	482,700	394,000	88,700
Total credits	$1,744,000	$1,652,000	

JAKE DOYLE INC.

Statement of Comprehensive Income

For the year ended 31 December 20X1	
Sales	$1,523,000
Cost of goods sold	(689,000)
Depreciation expense	(68,000)
Interest expense	(16,800)
Income tax expense	(55,000)
Other expenses	(457,200)
Loss on sale of operational assets	(7,200)
Gain on sale of investments	6,540
Net earnings and comprehensive income	$ 236,340

Additional information:

a. Sold property, plant, and equipment for cash. Cost of the assets was $236,000; net book value was $76,000.

b. Purchased equipment and exchanged unissued bonds payable of $120,000 in payment.

c. Purchased other equipment for cash.

d. Sold the long-term investments for cash.

Required:

1. Calculate cash paid for each of interest and income taxes. This is required under ASPE as separate disclosure.

2. Prepare the investing section of SCF and any disclosure notes for non-cash investing activities.

(Judy Cumby, used with permission)

★★★ **A5-30 Integrative Problem, Chapters 1–5:** Account balances, taken from the ledger of Argot Flooring Limited as of 31 December 20X5, appear below.

Accounts payable	$280,000	Land	$ 398,000
Accounts receivable	632,000	General operating expenses	338,000
Accumulated depreciation,		Notes payable	232,000
building equipment	42,000	Notes receivable	120,000
Allowance for doubtful		Property tax expense	3,200
accounts	3,000	Cost of goods sold	1,042,000
Building and equipment	198,000	Cash	?
Common shares	204,100	Retained earnings,	
Dividends declared	80,000	1 January 20X5	806,400
Deferred tax liability	116,700	Revenue	2,632,000
Income tax expense*	334,600	Salaries expense	232,000
Interest revenue	5,000	Store supplies inventory	12,400
Inventory, 31 December		Unearned revenue	32,000
20X5	480,000		

*Assume this amount is properly stated after all subsequent adjustments are considered.

Additional information:

1. Store supplies were counted at 31 December and found to be valued at $5,600.

2. Depreciation of building and equipment is over eight years with an expected salvage value of $10,000.

3. Property taxes of $3,200 were paid on 1 October 20X5 and relate to the year 1 October 20X5 to 30 September 20X6.

4. The note payable was issued on 1 November 20X5 and has an annual interest rate of 12%. Interest must be paid each 30 October along with $30,000 of principal. Interest payable has not been recorded.

5. The note receivable has been outstanding all year. Interest at 10% is collected each 1 June. The note is due 1 June 20X11. Interest receivable has not been recorded.

6. The allowance for doubtful accounts now has a $3,000 credit balance. Aging of accounts receivable indicates that $76,000 of the accounts are doubtful.

7. Unearned revenue represents an advance payment from a customer; 75% was still unearned at year-end.

8. At year-end, $10,000 (at retail value) of goods were shipped to customers, but the sale was not yet recorded. Correctly, the goods were not included in closing inventory. The revenue must be recorded.

Required:
1. Explain the meaning of GAAP.
2. Identify common objectives of financial reporting.
3. Prepare adjusting journal entries to reflect the additional information provided above.
4. Explain the following (a) through (d), and give an example of an adjusting journal entry in requirement 3 caused by each:
   a. Time-period assumption
   b. Continuity assumption
   c. Accrual concept
   d. Revenue recognition convention
5. Prepare a multiple-step classified statement of comprehensive income, a statement of changes in equity, and a classified statement of financial position based on the adjusted accounts. There was no change in the common share account during the year.
6. Assume that accounts have changed (*after the entries made in requirement 3*) as follows over the period:

Accounts receivable (net)	$41,900	decrease
Interest receivable	no change	
Inventory	136,000	increase
Store supplies inventory	8,000	decrease
Prepaid property tax	no change	
Buildings and equipment	40,000	increase
Accounts payable	75,000	increase
Interest payable	4,640	increase
Notes payable	232,000	increase
Deferred tax liability	26,400	increase
Unearned revenue	24,000	increase

Prepare the operating activities section of the SCF using the indirect method of presentation.

Begin the SCF with net earnings. Include separate disclosure of cash flows on the face of the SCF for interest paid and received and income tax paid.

CHAPTER 6

Revenue Recognition

INTRODUCTION

Quebec-based CAE Inc. is the world's dominant manufacturer of flight simulators. Simulators are built for CAE's clients under long-term contracts that encompass design, engineering, and manufacturing. In addition, contracts may involve the provision of spare parts, maintenance, flight schools and other training services. Clearly, CAE's revenue-generating activities are numerous and complex. When should this revenue be recorded in earnings?

Revenue recognition is probably the most difficult single issue in accounting, largely because modern business activities can be very complex. Economic activity takes many months or many years to complete. In complex and long-term earnings processes, it is not at all obvious just when revenue should be recognized in earnings. As well, many "sales" actually involve the delivery of more than one product and/or service. How should the revenue for each component be measured and when should the revenue for each component be recognized?

This chapter will examine the nature of the earnings process and the various points at which revenue could be recognized, depending on the nature of the revenue-earning process. The chapter also deals with measuring the amount of revenue attached to separate activities within the same contract.

All of the issues in revenue recognition have a direct impact on profit or loss measurement—a relatively small change in revenue recognition can have a major impact on earnings. Therefore, there are many ethical implications associated with the choice of revenue recognition policies. This is an area where judgement plays a major role.

To enhance comparability and reliability across all types of revenue transactions, accounting standard setters have attempted to standardize and narrow revenue recognition choices by providing more explicit guidance. After many years of review and consultation, the IASB has revised the standard for revenue recognition, effective for annual reporting periods beginning on or after 1 January 2017. Due to the long implementation date, this chapter discusses revenue recognition under the standards that are currently in place and effective until the end of 2016. The new standard is explained in the Appendix to this chapter. There is a more detailed supplement based on the new standard, along with examples, on Connect.

DEFINITIONS

Revenue and Expense

What is revenue? It is not defined on its own as, for example "the value of goods and services delivered during the period." Instead, revenue and expense are defined by *changes in net assets* (i.e., assets less liabilities) that are not due to capital transactions with shareholders. As we explained in Chapter 2, IFRS defines revenue as follows:

- **Revenue** arises from (1) inflows of cash, increases in accounts receivable, or other increases in a business's assets, (2) settlements of its liabilities, or (3) a combination of the two. These inflows must be derived from delivering or producing goods, rendering services, or performing other activities that constitute a company's business operation over a specific period of time.

- Conversely, an **expense** arises from outflows of assets or increases in liabilities that result from delivering or producing goods, rendering services, or performing other activities that constitute a company's business operation over a specific period of time.

Thus, *revenue and expenses are defined by changes in assets and liabilities arising from earnings-generating activities.* This is the asset-liability definitional approach to measuring earnings. For example, suppose that a company sells merchandise on credit:

- Creating the account receivable increases assets. The increase is the result of an ongoing business operation, and therefore the increase in net assets constitutes *revenue.*

- Reducing inventory *decreases* assets. The reduction is the result of an ongoing business operation, and therefore the reduction in assets is an *expense.*

Exhibit 6-1 illustrates the interrelations and shows that changes to the SFP are connected to SCI amounts.

Gains and Losses versus Revenue and Expense

Revenue and expenses, by definition, arise in the course of a company's ordinary business activities. As you know from Chapter 2, **gains** and **losses** are also included in earnings but have a different nature. They may or may not arise from a company's ordinary course of business.

A gain or loss can arise from either:

1. Peripheral transactions or events (e.g., a gain on the sale of land or the sale of fixed assets) or

2. Transactions and events relating to the enterprise's principal lines of business (e.g., remeasurement of assets to recoverable amounts).

Presentation Gains and losses are often reported as a net amount; for example, the gain on sale of land is shown net of related costs. In contrast, revenue is reported at the gross amount with expenses listed separately. For example, assume that a company sold a piece of land for $100,000. The land has a cost of $75,000. The two presentation alternatives:

1. If the company was a developer whose normal business was land sales, revenue of $100,000 would be reported with cost of land sold reported at $75,000.

2. If the sale of land was peripheral, then a gain on sale of land for $25,000 would be reported.

The "method" of presentation alternatives is *based on the nature of the business.* In either alternative, the bottom line is not affected, but presentation is different, and as a result revenue trends and patterns are different.

Gross or Net Revenue?

To recognize and report revenue, a company must be entitled to the full benefits of the increase in net assets. For example, what should the on-line auction website eBay Inc. report as revenue—the total amount of sales that are transacted through its website, that is on

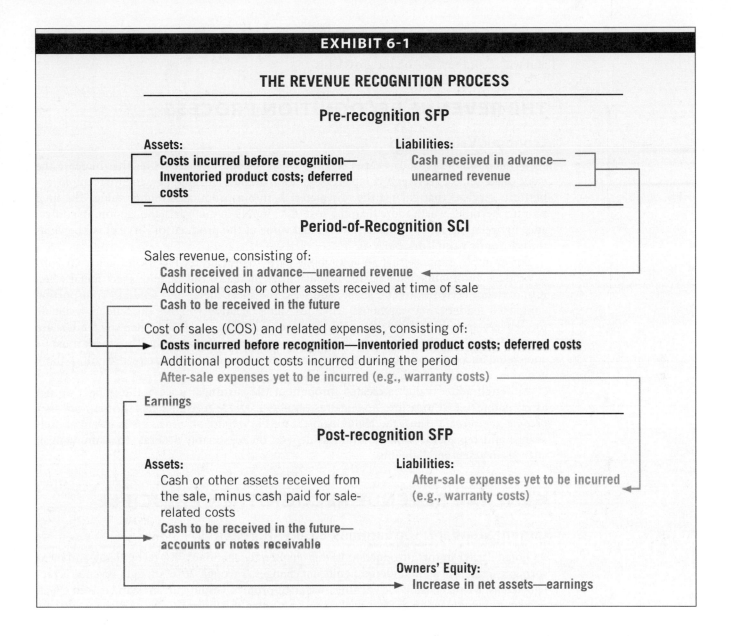

EXHIBIT 6-1

THE REVENUE RECOGNITION PROCESS

Pre-recognition SFP

Assets:
Costs incurred before recognition—Inventoried product costs; deferred costs

Liabilities:
Cash received in advance—unearned revenue

Period-of-Recognition SCI

Sales revenue, consisting of:
Cash received in advance—unearned revenue
Additional cash or other assets received at time of sale
Cash to be received in the future

Cost of sales (COS) and related expenses, consisting of:
Costs incurred before recognition—inventoried product costs; deferred costs
Additional product costs incurred during the period
After-sale expenses yet to be incurred (e.g., warranty costs)

Earnings

Post-recognition SFP

Assets:
Cash or other assets received from the sale, minus cash paid for sale-related costs
Cash to be received in the future—accounts or notes receivable

Liabilities:
After-sale expenses yet to be incurred (e.g., warranty costs)

Owners' Equity:
Increase in net assets—earnings

a **gross basis**? Or should it record only the eBay commission on those sales, that is, on a net basis?

If the full value of the sale was recorded, it would imply that the total sales value would increase eBay's net assets. But eBay has no control over the transaction prices. The company sets the commission and other fees that it charges, but the price of the item sold is set between the buyer and the seller. Therefore, eBay is not entitled to the full benefits of the negotiated price—only to the commission. This is true even though the company collects the purchase price from the buyer and then passes on the proceeds, net of commission, to the seller. In this example, eBay is an *agent* and will record revenue on a **net basis**.

Indicators that a company is actually *operating as an agent on behalf of another party* and it is the *other party's* responsibility to fulfill the contract are where the company:

• Bears no inventory risk at any time during the contract;

• Cannot change the price;

• Earns a commission; and

• Does not assume any credit risk.

In many cases, some of these indicators will be present and some absent. Professional judgment is required in the more complex cases to determine whether the company is acting as an agent or not. If the company has control of the goods or services for some period of time prior to the sale to the ultimate customer, the company is more likely acting as a *principal* and will record revenue on the gross basis.

THE REVENUE RECOGNITION PROCESS

Economic Value Added

At a *conceptual* level, a firm earns revenue when it engages in activities that increase the value of an item or service. A company buys raw materials and supplies, and then employees perform services that change the raw materials into a product of higher value. The final product becomes worth more than the cost of its inputs in materials and labour. The difference between the input cost and the eventual value of the product (or service) is known as the **economic value added** (EVA).

For example, suppose that an automobile parts manufacturer has a contract from Ford to produce automobile fenders. The manufacturer increases the value of sheet metal when it undertakes activities to cut, shape, and weld the sheet metal into fenders. Transporting completed fenders to a warehouse also adds value because it makes the fenders available for delivery and use by Ford. The earnings process is fully completed when the fenders are sold and delivered to Ford in return for cash or a promise to pay cash. Paperwork must be completed and cash collected. Any deficient fenders must be fixed or replaced. All of these activities, and many more, are part of the earnings process.

Although added value is created throughout the earnings process, the impact on net assets is difficult to measure. *Accountants cannot recognize revenue and expenses until they become measurable.* Thus, the ability to measure the *impact on net assets* is essential. Relevance and representational faithfulness depend on reasonably accurate measurement of changes in assets and liabilities.

GENERAL REVENUE RECOGNITION PRINCIPLE

Current Standard: The Earnings-Based Approach

As noted earlier in the introduction to this chapter, the standards for recognizing and measuring revenue will soon undergo significant changes. Through 2016, though, revenue is recognized as "earned" using the **earnings-based approach**. Under current standards in effect, revenue is recognized in the financial statements when the following conditions are met:

1. Performance is complete and has been accepted by the customer;

2. Consideration, as well as any future costs, can be measured with reasonable assurance; Consideration is the dollar value of the transaction. Usually, net assets increase, through an inflow of cash, a new accounts receivable, and so on. Less frequently, liabilities might be reduced as consideration, perhaps through forgiveness of debt; and

3. Collection is reasonably assured. Quantifiable bad debt can be accrued, and revenue still recognized. If the risk of noncollection is not quantifiable, revenue must be deferred until the uncertainty is resolved.

The application of these broad principles may appear to be simple and straightforward. Indeed, in many businesses, revenue recognition is not a major challenge. In other businesses, however, the challenge can be quite significant as we will see later in the chapter.

Revised Standard: The Contract-Based Approach

As these current standards have been found to be difficult to implement and apply consistently across industries, the IASB and FASB have completed a joint project to update revenue recognition standards for principles that could be used for any type of revenue transaction, regardless of industry. The new standard is effective for annual reporting periods beginning on or after 1 January 2017. This new standard requires companies to adopt a **contract-based approach**.

The "contract basis" of reporting revenue is based on *enforceable rights and obligations* as contained in a contract between buyer and seller. In such a contract, the seller makes a commitment to transfer the goods and/or services to the buyer—the **performance obligation**. In return, the buyer agrees to pay some amount of **consideration**.

The core principle of the contract-based approach is that the seller recognizes revenue at the time there is a transfer of promised goods or services to a buyer. The amount to be recognized is the expected amount of consideration for the transfer under the contract.

The discussion of the details of this new standard and how it will be applied to various revenue transactions is described in the Appendix to this chapter and also in supplemental material available on Connect.

The remainder of this chapter is based on the current standard that uses the earnings-based approach to revenue recognition.

Earnings-Based Revenue Recognition Requirements

There are two broad issues to consider for revenue recognition:

1. *When* to recognize revenue; and

2. *How much* to recognize as revenue in earnings.

When to Recognize Revenue for the Sale of Goods To determine when the sale of goods should be recognized, standard setters expanded on the general concepts of performance, measurability, and collection to come up with five specific criteria that must *all* be met to recognize revenue from the sale of goods. These criteria are:

1. The seller's performance is complete and the seller has transferred the significant risks and rewards of ownership to the buyer;

2. The seller retains no continuing managerial involvement or control over the goods sold;

3. The amount of revenue can be measured reliably;

4. It is probable that the benefit of the revenue will actually flow to the seller; and

5. The seller can reliably measure all costs relating to the transaction, past and future.

Revenue is recognized only when *all five* of the criteria have been satisfied. The trigger for revenue recognition is often called the **critical event**—the final event (whatever the last of the five criteria is, in fact, last) is the critical event for that transaction. "Critical event" is not an explicit phrase used in accounting standards but it is a useful idea to keep in mind.

In simple revenue transactions that involve the sale of a good, the recognition point (or critical event) is when the good is delivered and accepted by the customer, as long as all the other criteria have been met. In other cases, however, revenue may be recognized only when *cash is collected*. The critical event is cash collected because of uncertainties surrounding collection. We will look at these examples and others in this chapter.

Exhibit 6-2 summarizes a description of the revenue recognition criteria and issues to be addressed. We will see how the criteria are applied as we work through examples in this chapter.

When to Recognize Revenue for the Sale of Services The criteria for recognizing service revenue is similar to those for product sales. Revenue from services is earned when all of the following four criteria have been met:

1. Revenue can be measured reliably;

2. It is probable that the economic benefits of the transaction will flow to the service provider;

3. For long-term projects, the stage of completion can be measured reliably; and

4. All costs can be reliably measured.

At the point where all of the four criteria are met, the sale of services can be recognized. Note that one criterion listed is the ability to measure the stage of completion. This is important for projects that will span more than one reporting period. Later in this chapter, we will discuss the various methods for determining stage of completion.

EXHIBIT 6-2

THE FIVE CRITERIA TO BE MET FOR REVENUE RECOGNITION FOR THE SALE OF GOODS

Step	Description	Issues to Be Addressed
1. Seller's performance is complete and the seller has transferred the significant risks and rewards of ownership to the buyer.	Goods have been delivered. Seller has no more significant risks or responsibilities regarding the item sold. Seller will not benefit from the goods in the future. Buyer must accept the risks and rewards.	Indications of performance not being complete are when the seller agrees to provide after-sales support and warranties, the costs of which cannot be reliably estimated. Indications of future benefits would be if the seller continues to collect royalties or a portion of the product's revenue stream.
2. The seller retains no continuing managerial involvement or control over the goods sold.	The seller cannot retain the right to affect the buyer's use of the product and can retain no continuing interest or involvement in its future benefits.	Does the buyer have a right of return? If so, then the seller will continue to have involvement until the return period is over. If the revenue is contingent on the buyer's resale of the product, then the revenue is not recognized until this resale takes place.
3. The amount of revenue can be measured reliably.	There is no significant uncertainty of the amount of revenue; there should be no revenue that is contingent on future events or performance. Collection should be reasonably assured. The amount of revenue to be recognized is the present value of the discounted cash flows.	Examples of where revenue may not be reliably measurable are: • Total revenue from the sale depends on future performance of the asset sold; • The credit status of the customer is unstable and risk of default is high. • There is a possibility of a large proportion of products being returned and so the quantity sold cannot be reliably estimated. • If revenue is to be received over a long period of time, the present value of the cash flows must be determined as the revenue.
4. It is probable that the benefit of the revenue will actually flow to the seller.	There is a high probability that the seller will actually enjoy the economic benefits of the transaction.	The buyer needs to accept the goods and be satisfied. Revenue recognition may be delayed if: • Buyer must test the product to ensure that it works properly; e.g., software must be installed and tested before the buyer will accept the product and be willing to pay. • Buyer might have to ensure that the product properly meets the specifications outlined in the contract.
5. The seller can reliably measure all costs relating to the transaction, past and future.	There are no significant uncertainties about measuring the costs incurred in the past or any after-sale costs yet to be incurred in the future. Past costs and future costs must be measurable.	Past costs may be difficult to measure if the final contract price is unknown or under dispute. The seller must be able to estimate after-sales costs. This will depend on whether or not the seller has past experience with the product. If seller has no basis for reliable measurement, revenue recognition must be delayed until these costs are measurable or known.

How Much to Recognize as Revenue *How much* revenue to recognize can also be complex. There are two potential problems:

1. Assigning revenue to different parts of a complex contract, known as *multiple deliverables*; and

2. Measuring the amount of revenue when the contract amount may vary throughout the contract or payments are made over a long period of time.

The complexities of these issues will be illustrated in later examples.

CONCEPT REVIEW

1. How is a *gain* different from a *revenue*?

2. List the five criteria that must be satisfied before revenue from the sale of goods can be recognized.

3. What measurement issues might arise in determining the amount of revenue to be recognized?

TRANSFER OF GOODS AND SERVICES AT A SINGLE POINT IN TIME

Recognition at Delivery

In many cases, revenue recognition is straightforward. For example, consider a simple transaction that involves the sale of goods in a retail store on 30 November. The item has a price tag of $100. At the checkout counter, the customer receives a bill that lists the item, its price, and the terms of the sale. Applying the five criteria:

1. *Seller's performance is complete; the seller has transferred the significant risks and rewards of ownership to the buyer.* On 30 November, the item is delivered to the buyer and ownership is transferred.

2. *The seller retains no continuing managerial involvement or control over the goods sold.* In this case, there is no indication of after-sales service, warranties, or return policies.

3. *The amount of revenue can be measured reliably.* The amount of the sale is $100, as indicated by the price tag.

4. *It is probable that the benefit of the revenue will actually flow to the seller.* The customer pays for the item on 30 November, so all of the cash is collected by the seller.

5. *The seller can reliably measure all costs relating to the transaction, past and future.* As discussed earlier under (2), there are no future costs to be incurred.

Based on the five criteria, the critical event occurs when the item is delivered and paid for by the customer. On 30 November, cash is debited for $100 and revenue is credited for $100. That is, net assets increase. Cost of goods sold is also recorded and inventory is reduced.

We can make this a little more complicated and add a new fact that the customer prepaid a deposit of $75 to hold the item on 29 October. The $75 represents *unearned revenue* since the customer has paid some consideration, but the seller's performance is not yet complete and the seller still has control over the goods. The critical event has not yet occurred. On 29 October, the entry is as follows:

Dr. Cash	75	
Cr. Unearned revenue (liability account)		75

On 30 November, the customer now receives the item and pays the remaining $25. Performance is now complete, the seller no longer has control over the goods, and the critical event has occurred. The full amount of revenue is recognized. The entry on 30 November would be:

Dr. Cash	25	
Dr. Unearned revenue	75	
Cr. Sales revenue		100

Short-Term Service Revenue Revenue from *short-term* services rendered is recognized when the services have been completed and accepted by the client. Such services as hairdressing, carpet cleaning, and repairs to equipment might be examples of these types of services that are transferred at the date of delivery. There is no great challenge to accounting for these services. More of a challenge arises when service is provided over a long period of time and stage of completion must be assessed, which we will address later in this chapter.

Impact on Net Assets Recall that revenue has been defined as *a change in net assets.* Exhibit 6-3 illustrates a situation in which a company buys inventory, customizes it, and then holds it until sold. It is sold on account and 30 days later the customer pays the agreed consideration. Exhibit 6-3 traces the appropriate entries if delivery is considered to be the date of delivery. Costs for customization and predelivery are added to the inventory account, which is an asset. When the item is delivered, the sales price is accrued as an account receivable and inventory (including the customization and predelivery costs) is expensed. Note that:

- Net assets (i.e., assets minus liabilities) are increased only *at the date* of revenue recognition.
- Transactions *before* revenue recognition change an asset; the change is in the *composition* but not the *total* of net assets.
- Transactions *after* revenue recognition likewise change the *composition* but not the *total* of net assets.

This was a simple delivery of a good. The exact point of when revenue is earned can become more complicated when the customer has a right of return or the seller provides a warranty.

Sale with a Right of Return

In many industries, it is a customary business practice to allow customers to return unused products within a specified return period and receive a full refund or another type of product in exchange. In the textbook industry and manufacturing industries, for example, contract terms normally allow customers the right to return goods under certain conditions and over long periods of time, after control has been transferred. From an accounting perspective:

- *If the quantity of returns is reasonably predictable,* the company can recognize revenue at delivery for the estimated volume of goods that will not be returned. An *allowance for sales returns* representing the amount expected to be refunded on return must also be recorded at the time of the sale.
- *If returns are not predictable, revenue is deferred until the return situation is known.*

Example—Returns Predictable Under contract, Rigour Corporation delivers 200 units to Customer A on 1 March. The cost of each product is $90 and the sales price is $120. Rigour's documented policy is to allow a customer to return any unused product within 60 days and receive a full refund. Based on historical experience, Rigour estimates that 3% of the units will be returned. Rigour expects that the returned products can be resold.

Five Criteria Applying the five criteria:

1. *Seller's performance is complete; the seller has transferred the significant risks and rewards of ownership to the buyer.* As noted, Rigour delivers 200 units, but also "stands ready" to take back any unused product within 60 days of the sale. Rigour's performance is not complete until the return period is over or the amount of the returns can be reliably

---

EXHIBIT 6-3

REVENUE RECOGNITION: IMPACT ON NET ASSETS

Data

15 January	Inventory purchased, $14,500
17 January	Inventory repackaged and customized—labour and materials cost $2,250. Now ready for sale.
6 March	Inventory delivered to customer on account. Agreed-upon price, $28,000. Control is transferred to customer at the time of delivery.
30 April	Customer pays 100% of sales price.

	Revenue Recognized		
Date	**on Delivery**		
15 Jan.	Inventory	14,500	
	Cash, A/P, etc.		14,500
Effect on net assets	**None**		
17 Jan.	Inventory	2,250	
	Cash, A/P, etc.		2,250
Effect on net assets	**None**		
6 March	Accounts receivable	28,000	
	Sales revenue		28,000
	Cost of goods sold	16,750	
	Inventory		16,750
Effect on net assets	**Increase $11,250**		
30 April	Cash	28,000	
	Accounts receivable		28,000
Effect on net assets	**None**		

---

estimated. From past experience, Rigour estimates that 6 (200 × 3%) units with a total price of $720 ($120 × 6 units) may be returned.

2. *The seller retains no continuing managerial involvement or control over the goods sold.* In this case, the goods have been delivered to the customer, who now has control over the goods. However, due to the return policy, the seller still has involvement with the goods.

3. *The amount of revenue can be measured reliably.* The amount of the sale is $24,000 (200 × $120), as indicated by the contract. However, the final amount of revenue may be lower if returns are made.

4. *It is probable that the benefit of the revenue will actually flow to the seller.* There is no indication that the customer will not pay for the goods delivered, but this will be net of any returns.

5. *The seller can reliably measure all costs relating the transaction, past and future.* As discussed above, returns are possible. However, Rigour can *reliably measure* the returns as 3% of units sold.

Entries Delivery of the 200 units to the customer is the critical event since Rigour can reliably provide an estimate of the returns. Rigour records the sale of the 200 units for $24,000 and the offsetting account receivable. The estimate for the returns of $720 (6 units × $120) is recorded as *sales returns* with an offsetting amount to *allowance for sales returns*. For reporting purposes, the sales returns account will be netted against revenue and the allowance for sales returns will be netted against accounts receivable. Both sales returns and the allowance are *contra accounts*, and netting is required. The entries to record the sale on delivery to the customer:

1 March:		
Dr. Accounts receivable (200 × $120)	24,000	
Cr. Sales revenue		24,000
Dr. Sales returns	720	
Cr. Allowance for sales returns		720
Dr. Cost of goods sold (200 × $90)	18,000	
Cr. Inventory		18,000

Once the return period has passed, any remaining amount in the sales returns and the allowance for sales returns accounts is reversed. Assume that in the above example, there were only two units returned on 4 April and no additional products were returned by 29 April, the end of the return period. The entries:

4 April:		
Dr. Allowance for sales returns (2 × $120)	240	
Cr. Accounts receivable (or cash)		240
Dr. Inventory (2 × $90)	180	
Cr. Cost of goods sold		180
29 April:		
Dr. Allowance for sales returns ($720 – $240)	480	
Cr. Sales returns		480

Example—Returns Not Predictable If, on the other hand, there is little or no history about product returns, or if returns have been volatile over the recent past, it will not be possible to predict the level of returns. If no reasonably reliable estimates are possible, recognition of *all* of the sales revenue and the related cost of goods sold must be delayed until the return period is over. The critical event occurs after the end of the 60-day period on 29 April.

Assume the facts as in the prior example except that returns are not predictable at 3%. In fact, what happens is that 160 units are kept by the customer, and 40 units are returned on 29 April, the end of the return period. The $24,000 account receivable is recorded, as is the reduction in inventory on 1 March, but the gross margin on the sale is deferred and shown as a liability. On 29 April, returns must be recorded, but since the return period has expired and performance is complete, remaining revenue and cost of goods sold are recognized.

Entries

1 March:		
Dr. Accounts receivable (200 × $120)	24,000	
Cr. Deferred gross margin (liability account)		6,000
Cr. Inventory (200 × $90)		18,000
29 April:		
Dr. Deferred gross margin	6,000	
Dr. Cost of goods sold (160 × $90)	14,400	
Dr. Inventory (40 × $90)	3,600	
Cr. Accounts receivable (40 × $120)		4,800
Cr. Sales revenue (160 × $120)		19,200

Summary These points deserve special emphasis:

- If the future returns can be quantified reliably, the sale can be recorded on delivery and an estimate of the sales returns recorded.
- If risk cannot be quantified reliably, the sale can be recognized as revenue only after expiry of the return privilege. In this case, the entire consideration is deferred net of the related cost of goods sold.

ETHICAL ISSUES

In the past, some managers have used questionable revenue recognition policies. For example, a now-defunct producer of farm equipment forced its dealers to accept excess inventory at the end of the year so that the manufacturer could show high sales revenue. However, there was an implicit, unwritten, agreement that the manufacturer would take back the excess inventory in the following year and dispose of it elsewhere, such as in foreign markets, at a lower price if necessary. Similarly, some automobile manufacturers have been known to require dealers to accept the manufacturers' excess inventories at the end of the fiscal year.

Using the approach shown above, the right to return would require delayed revenue recognition. However, the "unwritten agreement" has to be clearly understood and reflected in the entries.

Sale with a Warranty or Service Agreement

Companies often provide a warranty with the sale of good or services. The warranty can be in the form of assurance that the product will operate as intended and meet specifications. Warranties can also require the seller to provide certain service or repairs for a period of time. Such warranties and service agreements may be provided at no extra cost to the customer. In other cases, there may be a separate warranty contract or a separate service agreement contract for which the customer must pay extra. Using a warranty as a generic example, there are two approaches to such an agreement:

Approach	Use If	Description
Cost deferral	The warranty is provided to give assurance that the product will meet agreed-upon specifications and the warranty is not sold separately.	Accrue the (reliably) *estimated costs* of the vendor's warranty obligation as a provision and an expense when revenue is recognized; future costs are charged to the warranty provision as they are incurred. The warranty provision must be adjusted at each reporting period to reflect actual/projected warranty cost.
Revenue deferral	The warranty provides the customer with future services in addition to product assurance, or the warranty can be purchased separately.	A proportionate part of the *sales revenue* is deferred as unearned revenue; the deferred revenue is recognized over time until the warranty or service agreement expires. Warranty or servicing costs are charged to expense as incurred. The proportion of revenue from *new* sales that is deferred may be adjusted periodically to reflect actual cost experience, but there is no adjustment of deferred revenue already on the books. The contract must be evaluated to see if it is an onerous contract (losing contract). If so, a provision must be recorded.

The *revenue deferral method* includes an element of profit (or loss) in the warranty contract, which is the difference between warranty revenue and expenses paid to meet warranty claims. There is no such profit using the *cost deferral method*. The *revenue deferral method* is easier to apply in practice because it does not require periodic adjustment of existing balances. In contrast, the deferred warranty cost provision requires review and adjustment at each reporting date.

Example On 6 March, Tudor Computers delivers manufacturing equipment to a buyer. The agreed-upon price is $28,000. Included in this price is a 12-month warranty that the equipment will be fixed or replaced if it does not perform to certain specifications. The company estimates that based on past experience, the warranty costs for defective product should be estimated at $3,900. Subsequently, warranty work results in expenditures of $3,700.

Five Criteria Applying the five criteria:

1. *Seller's performance is complete; the seller has transferred the significant risks and rewards of ownership to the buyer.* The seller's performance is not complete with respect to the potential costs of warranty work that might have to be completed. As long as this risk can be estimated reliably, the revenue for the sale can be recorded at the point of delivery, along with an estimate of these costs.

2. *The seller retains no continuing managerial involvement or control over the goods sold.* The goods have been delivered to the customer, who now has control over the goods. However, there is future involvement if warranty work is subsequently required.

3. *The amount of revenue can be measured reliably.* The amount of the sale is $28,000, as indicated by the contract.

4. *It is probable that the benefit of the revenue will actually flow to the seller.* There is no indication that the customer will not pay for the goods delivered.

5. *The seller can reliably measure all costs relating the transaction, past and future.* As discussed earlier under (1) and (2), there are potential additional costs for warranty work. However, Tudor can reliably measure this at $3,900 and these costs can be recognized at the time of the sale. Cost deferral is used for the warranty as it is not sold separately.

Entries—Cost Deferral The journal entries required are shown in the first column of Exhibit 6-4. The warranty results in a separate expense and provision that is recorded when the sale is recognized. When $3,700 of expenditures is required under the warranty, this is *not* expensed, but rather reduces the provision. The $200 unneeded provision is reversed at the end of the warranty period, resulting in an expense recovery.

Remember, it is *very* important that the warranty provision be measured correctly. The SFP must reliably reflect the obligations of the company. *Detailed engineering studies and review of warranty experience are required to ensure that the provision is correctly valued.* It can be increased (decreased) with additional expense (expense recovery) recognized, if needed.

Entries—Revenue Deferral Assume now that the warranty was sold separately and is valued at $5,000.[1] This means less revenue is allocated to the manufacturing equipment itself. The value allocated to the manufacturing equipment is the residual of $23,000 after the warranty of $5,000 is factored out of the $28,000 contract. This time, the warranty is initially recognized as deferred revenue and is reported as warranty revenue as time passes. The warranty costs are expensed as incurred.

In this case, if warranty expenses are projected to exceed deferred revenue, the contract is considered to be an *onerous contract* and a loss is recorded. This is a topic considered in Chapter 12.

---

[1] This is now an example of a contract with multiple deliverables. These contracts will be separately addressed later in the chapter.

EXHIBIT 6-4

WARRANTY: COST DEFERRAL VERSUS REVENUE DEFERRAL

Date	(a) Cost Deferral for Warranty		(b) Revenue Deferral for Warranty	
6 March	Accounts receivable 28,000		Accounts receivable 28,000	
	Revenue—sale of		Revenue—sale of	
	equipment	28,000	equipment	23,000
			Deferred revenue—	
			warranty	5,000
	Warranty expense 3,900			
	Provision for warranty	3,900		
Subsequently			Deferred revenue—	
			warranty 5,000	
			Revenue—warranty	5,000
	Provision for warranty 3,700		Warranty expense 3,700	
	Cash	3,700	Cash	3,700
End of warranty period	Provision for warranty 200			
	Recovery of			
	warranty expense	200		

Delayed Revenue Recognition Often, after-sale costs can be measured reliably for the company's sales as a whole, based on historical experience, even if the follow-up costs of individual sales might turn out to be quite substantial. For example, automobile manufacturers recognize revenue and accrue warranty expense using the cost deferral method when they sell cars, even though they might have to issue a *product recall* to fix design problems detected later.

But if potentially significant costs *cannot* be reliably estimated for the class of buyers as a whole, performance has not been completed, since there is still significant risk with the seller. In these circumstances, *no revenue can be recognized until the uncertainty is resolved.* (That is, criteria (1) and (5) above in the revenue analysis would dictate no revenue being recognized.) This is highly undesirable for the seller, and thus considerable effort will be invested in estimating the warranty obligation!

Bill-and-Hold Arrangements

A **bill-and-hold arrangement** is a contract between a buyer and seller wherein the buyer is billed for a product, but the product is not delivered until some specific future point in time. Delivery is often at the buyer's request. This type of arrangement might be used if the buyer does not yet have the space or need for the product but wishes to have guaranteed access to the product and thus the buyer is willing to sign a firm contract.

Example An electronics dealer may agree to accept (and pay for) 10,000 units of a new cell phone, to be delivered at the dealer's choice in stages at various points in time over the next six months. The dealer then has a guaranteed source of supply, although no price flexibility. The dealer benefits from the transaction if demand for the new phone exceeds the manufacturer's production capacity because later orders might not be filled in a timely fashion. When should the manufacturer recognize revenue?

Revenue recognition is often triggered when the goods are delivered. However, in a bill-and-hold situation, revenue may be recognized before delivery if the buyer has accepted the risks and rewards of ownership. Transfer of risks and rewards (control) of the units shifts to the buyer when the buyer takes title and all of the following conditions are met:

- The buyer has acknowledged the deferred delivery instructions;
- Delivery is probable;
- The buyer's inventory is separately identified as belonging to the buyer (i.e., held apart from the seller's other inventory);
- The inventory is ready to be delivered; and
- The customary payment terms apply to the invoice.

Only in these special situations can the seller recognize the revenue prior to the delivery of the product.

ETHICAL ISSUES

If revenue recognition prior to delivery was generally applicable, sellers could ask "friendly" buyers to enter into bill-and-hold agreements so that the seller could recognize revenue on existing inventory. The agreements could provide various escape clauses for the buyer so that the buyer could avoid the purchase requirements. Examples of such clauses might give the buyer cancellation clauses, generous return rights, and the right to renegotiate the price. To avoid such abuses for revenue recognition, stringent specific conditions have been established for revenue recognition prior to delivery to be acceptable.

Consignment Arrangements

No revenue should be recognized if the buyer's obligation to pay the seller is **contingent** on the resale of the product. If payment is contingent on resale, this is a **consignment arrangement**. This is a marketing arrangement in which the owner of the product (the *consignor*) ships the product to another party (the *consignee*), who acts as a sales agent. The consignee does not purchase the goods but assumes responsibility only for their care and resale. Upon sale, the consignee remits the proceeds (less specified expenses and commission) to the consignor. *Goods on consignment are part of the inventory of the consignor until sold by the consignee.* They are not a sale of the consignor when *shipped* to the consignee, but only when they are *sold* by the consignee.

Example Company A delivers goods to Company B, which is to sell the goods to the final customer C. How and when revenue is recognized will depend on which party has risks and rewards of ownership of the goods. If A retains control until sale to C, then this is a consignment arrangement. B likely has the ability to return the goods if not sold and has no obligation to pay for the goods. When B ultimately sells the goods to C, B *as an agent* can report as revenue only the fee or commission that it has earned. A will report the full sales price of the goods as revenue because it was the party that transferred risks and rewards of ownership to the final customer. The commission earned by B will be a cost to A. (In general, recall that a seller reports gross revenues only if the seller has control over the goods being sold.)

On the other hand, if B holds the goods and can make product, pricing, location and promotion decisions, B may, in fact, have the risks and rewards of ownership related to the goods. B might have ownership, even if B has the ability to return the goods. This would be a very different situation and be accounted for as *a sale with the right of return,* as we have seen. Accordingly, the nature of the relationship between A and B has to be carefully analyzed.

ETHICAL ISSUES

When inventory is counted, consignment goods are a potential problem for both the consignor and the consignee.

Inventory is sitting in the consignee's warehouse or showroom and looks exactly like inventory from other arrangements that the consignee, in fact, owns. Owned inventory is the consignee's asset and consigned inventory is the consignor's inventory. Both company staff and auditors need to clearly and accurately identify which is which. On the other side of the coin, the consignor has inventory that may be in geographically disbursed locations, with a broad range of consignees. Managing inventory record and verifying the accuracy of widely spread inventory are significant challenges. A business model that relies on consignment arrangements involves this additional risk.

There are numerous unfortunate examples of unethical consignees reporting consignment goods as their own, resulting in inflated inventories on the financial statements.

Product financing arrangements include agreements in which a sponsoring company (Company S) sells a product to another company (Company T). Then, in a related transaction, S agrees to repurchase the product at some future point in time if T has been unable to resell the product. This is consignment selling in a different legal form, and it is clear that the control of the goods has not passed from S to T.

In these kinds of product-financing agreements, the sponsoring company must record a liability (deferred revenue) at the time the proceeds are received. The sponsoring company can neither record a sale nor remove the product from its inventory account. Only when the product is sold to an outside party without a related repurchase agreement can the sponsoring company record sales revenue.

Licensing Fees

Licensing arrangements allow a customer to use intellectual property, such as software, music, franchises, and trademarks. Licence agreements can be designed to either transfer a right to use the licence or a promise to provide access to the seller's intellectual property for a period of time. Revenue is recognized in one of two patterns, depending on the contract terms:

1. *Recognize revenue at a point in time.* If the license has a perpetual life, making it impossible to determine over what period of time the customer would receive the related benefits, then this type of license is treated as a sale of a good. That is, once all criteria have been met for recognition (in particular, that there are neither additional costs nor performance still to be completed by the seller), revenue is recognized at the point of delivery. For example, the licensing fee for software would be recognized as revenue once the customer has installed and begins to use the software.

2. *Recognize revenue over time.* In other cases, the licence grants the buyer limited access to the seller's intellectual property for only a fixed period of time. In this case, the revenue would be recognized over the period of time covered by the licence.

Recognition at Cash Collection

What happens if a sale is complete and the seller has no future involvement but the credit default risk is high for the customer? In this case, the following two criteria have not been met:

1. *The amount of revenue can be measured reliably.* The amount of realizable revenue cannot be estimated reliably due to substantial credit risk; and

2. *It is probable that the benefit of the revenue will actually flow to the seller.* Since the customer's default risk is high, it is not probable that the seller will actually receive the cash and benefits from this transaction.

When this is the case, cash collection becomes the critical event, and revenue is not earned until cash has been collected.

This situation is not uncommon in certain types of retail operations, where a dealer sells to people who have shaky credit history or no credit history at all (e.g., first-time users of credit). The buyer may be given a deferred payment plan (e.g., "no payments for 18 months!" as the ads scream), or the buyer may be allowed to pay by instalments. The dealer knows that a significant proportion of buyers will not be able to finish their payments, but the outcome depends on future economic conditions that cannot be reliably predicted.

Accounting practice has developed two approaches to dealing with this problem: the *instalment* method and the *cost recovery* method. These methods have arisen through practice rather than through authoritative pronouncements.

Instalment Sales Method   If future customer defaults cannot be predicted reliably, a company that sells its products on an instalment plan may choose to use the *instalment sales method* of accounting. Revenue under the **instalment sales method** is recognized when cash is collected rather than at the time of sale. Under this method, revenue (and the related COS) is recognized only when realized. For example, the instalment method may be used to account for sales of real estate when the down payment is relatively small and ultimate collection of the sales price is not reasonably assured.

Suppose that Truro Limited makes $80,000 of instalment sales in 20X2. The inventory cost $60,000, and thus the gross margin is $20,000, or 25% of sales. The sale is recorded with a *deferred* gross margin. The deferred gross margin is reported as unearned revenue in the liabilities section of the SFP because it represents net profit that has not yet been recognized is earnings. The entry at the date of sale is as follows:

Instalment accounts receivable	80,000	
Inventory		60,000
Deferred gross margin (liability account)		20,000

Recording the sale does not result in an increase in the company's net assets because the increase of $20,000 in assets (that is, the increase from $60,000 inventory to $80,000 accounts receivable) is completely offset by the $20,000 increase in the unearned revenue account—deferred gross margin.

If $10,000 is subsequently collected, this represents $10,000/$80,000, or 12.5% of the transaction. The entries to record the collection and to recognize a proportionate part of the deferred gross margin are as follows:

Cash	10,000	
Instalment accounts receivable		10,000
Deferred gross margin ($20,000 × 12.5%)	2,500	
Cost of goods sold	7,500	
Sales revenue		10,000

It is the second entry that records the increase to net assets that is the sign of revenue recognition. The increase in net assets is accomplished by reducing the amount of the deferred gross margin.

Cost Recovery Method   On occasion, the collectability of the customer's payment is so questionable that a company will use the **cost recovery method**. This method generally is used when a customer represents an extreme credit risk.

Why sell to such a customer? The cost recovery method is most frequently applied when substantial costs have been invested in a contract or product, the customer develops a financial problem, and the seller is trying to make the best of a bad situation. Since the eventual recovery of the full contract price is in doubt, the seller recognizes no *profit* until all costs are covered.

Return to the prior example, now modified. Suppose that Truro Limited sells $80,000 of product to a customer whose financial stability is suddenly uncertain. Truro decides to use the cost recovery method because the likelihood of receiving full payment is unpredictable. The cost of goods sold is $60,000. Suppose that the customer makes one payment of $45,000, followed by another payment of $35,000. If Truro uses the cost recovery method, the entry at the time of sale will be exactly the same as under the instalment sales method:

Accounts receivable	80,000	
Inventory		60,000
Deferred gross margin		20,000

When the first cash payment is received, the receivable is reduced and the entire amount is recognized as revenue, but an equal amount of cost of goods sold is also recognized. No profit is reported in earnings:

Cash	45,000	
Accounts receivable		45,000
Cost of goods sold	45,000	
Sales revenue		45,000

When the second payment is received, the remaining revenue of $35,000 is recognized, as is the remaining $15,000 of cost of goods sold. The residual $20,000 reflects recognition of the deferred gross margin:

Cash	35,000	
Accounts receivable		35,000
Cost of goods sold	15,000	
Deferred gross margin	20,000	
Sales revenue		35,000

The cost recovery approach is highly skewed toward later profit recognition and does a poor job of reflecting performance and cash flows. Its use is justified *only* in the face of extreme uncertainty regarding cash collection.

CONCEPT REVIEW

1. Explain how revenue is recognized for a sales contract that has a right of return.

2. Explain the difference between cost deferral and revenue deferral for contracts that involve a warranty arrangement.

3. What criteria must be met before a bill-and-hold contract may result in revenue recognition before delivery?

4. How is a consignment arrangement different from a sale with the right of return?

5. When would licence revenue be recognized for a contract that allows the customer, under license, to use a manufacturing process for five years?

6. Explain the difference between the instalment sales method and cost recovery.

TRANSFER OF GOODS AND SERVICES OVER TIME

Long-term service contracts and construction contracts are types of revenue transactions where performance is completed over time rather than at a specific point in time. Revenue is also measured *over time*. The problems (and potential estimation errors) that are inherent in multiperiod recognition are offset by the relevance and timeliness of the information that is provided to financial statement readers. Thus, there is a trade-off between the qualitative characteristics of *relevance* on the one hand, and *verifiability* on the other.

Service revenue is earned when all of the following four criteria have been met:

1. Revenue can be measured reliably;

2. It is probable that the economic benefits of the transaction will flow to the service provider;

3. For long-term projects, the stage of completion can be measured; and

4. All costs can be reliably measured.

We now look at the challenges of *measuring stage of completion*. Remember that recognizing revenue based on its stage of completion is often referred to as the **percentage-of-completion method**. The mechanics of this method will be reviewed in a later section.

Measuring Progress Over Time

For contracts that are recognized over time, the key is to recognize revenue based on a measure of progress of the performance. Various methods can be used to measure this progress:

1. **Output methods** recognize revenue based on the *value of the work performed to date.* Examples of this would be units produced or milestones achieved. Basically, the question is, "What has been finished?" Results to date are compared with expected total results when the contract is completed. Output measures also include the basic passage of time—the customer has the service provided for the time promised. Examples are (1) the number of kilometres of highway completed compared with total kilometres to be completed and (2) progress milestones established in a software development contract. The difficulty with this method is that in many contracts, mid-project outputs are not easily observed.

2. **Input methods** recognize the revenue based on *value of the effort performed to date.* The effort devoted to a project to date is compared with the total effort expected to be required to complete the project. Examples are (1) costs incurred to date compared with total estimated costs for the project and (2) labour hours worked compared with total estimated labour hours required to complete the project. Often input methods can be easier to apply than output methods because measuring inputs is straightforward. In fact, if costs are incurred evenly over the contract, revenue can be recognized on a straight-line basis. The difficulty with this method is that costs incurred might not be linear with real progress; for example, if there was a learning curve, wastage, or failed initiatives.

Over Time Some long-term services are really a series of short-term performances. Service contracts that provide the same type of service throughout the contract would be recorded evenly over the life of the contract. For example, assume that an entity provides monthly payroll services to a customer. The contract is for six months, and the customer pays a consideration of $24,000. As each payroll run is provided, it is being consumed immediately by the customer and therefore meets the criteria to be recognized as time passes. The contract is really a series of monthly payroll runs and falls neatly under an output measure of progress, as described above. The revenue will be recognized evenly over the six months, at $4,000 each month.

Similarly, consider the sale of a service contract on heating and air conditioning systems. The contract states that the service company will perform routine servicing of the system on a monthly basis as needed, providing whatever labour and materials are necessary without additional charge. Again, this contract would be recorded with the passage of time *as an output measure,* since the benefits are conferred and used at the same time and a proportionate part of the consideration is recorded as revenue month by month.

Nonrefundable Payments

Nonrefundable upfront fees might be charged at the beginning of a contract. For example, initiation fees are often paid when a person joins a golf club. However, just because these fees are nonrefundable does not mean they can be immediately recognized as revenue by the golf club. The contract must be assessed to determine when the *performance* with respect to these fees is completed. *This is an output measure.* In the case of a golf club, a new member paying an initiation fee has the ability to use the golf course generally over the rest of the member's life, as long as annual dues are paid. If the company determines that the member will be able to use the golf course for 35 years, the initiation fee is recognized evenly over this period.

Suppose that a client pays a nonrefundable $100,000 lump sum to a law firm on 1 January. This payment guarantees that for one year the law firm will provide service as needed, *for extra compensation* over and above the $100,000. The law firm is committing to provide the client with *access* for $100,000, nothing more. This type of payment is commonly referred to as a *retainer.* The amount would be recorded as unearned revenue when received and then transferred to revenue month by month because the revenue is earned evenly throughout the contract term. It does not matter whether the client actually required no service in a particular month or if the law firm was billing an extra $2 million in legal services rendered. The law firm *stood ready* to supply the service on demand as the contract requires, and thus the passage of time dictates revenue recognition.

In other cases, revenue recognition for an upfront fee is at *one point in time.* For example, think about an upfront fee that relates to the transfer of goods and services to a customer. The question is, when is this revenue earned? If the revenue is earned at the point of delivery, then that is the point when the entire upfront fee is recognized as revenue.

Each *contract must be reviewed to see when the underlying performance is complete* and all recognition criteria have been met to earn the revenue. At this point, the nonrefundable deposit can be transferred from unearned revenue to revenue.

MEASUREMENT OF CONSIDERATION

One of the criteria for revenue recognition for goods and services refers to a reliable measure of the *amount* of revenue. This is the amount that the company expects to be paid. In most cases, this amount will be quite obvious. In other cases, depending on the complexity of the customer contract, the consideration may vary. For example, if the customer is entitled to discounts or rebates depending on volume of product purchased, this could impact the final cash received. *Companies must estimate the amount of cash they expect to receive.* Alternatively, a delayed payment stream may decrease the value of the cash paid.

Delayed Payment Contracts

Some contracts spread the cash payments to be made by the buyer over future periods. For example, a $5 million contract may be payable at $1 million a year for five years. If interest is charged over and above the $5 million (or on the outstanding balance), then this separate interest revenue is recognized as time passes. However, if the contract *appears to be interest free,* the accounting treatment must recognize *substance over form* and acknowledge that there is no real economic truth to an interest-free contract. Interest is included in the $5 million price and must be accounted for separately. This means that the amount of revenue is the *present value* of the *future cash flows.* The difference between the discounted amount and the gross amount is *imputed interest,* which is *recognized as time passes.* This is independent of the timing of the revenue recognition for the sale contract itself. (In practice, if the consideration is paid within a year, then there is no need to present value the cash flows because the amount of any difference would not be material.)

We will return to an examination of present value techniques in our discussion of notes receivable in Chapter 7. However, since discounting affects revenue recognition, we will provide a brief example.

Example Assume that a company delivers new manufacturing equipment to a customer on 1 January 20X1. The contract specifies that $4 million be paid on delivery and another $3 million is due on 1 January 20X3. Applying the five criteria:

1. *Seller's performance is complete; the seller has transferred the significant risks and rewards of ownership to the buyer.* The seller's performance is complete, since the manufacturing equipment has been delivered and there are no future costs to be incurred. All risks and rewards have been transferred at the date of delivery.

2. *The seller retains no continuing managerial involvement or control over the goods sold.* The goods have been delivered to the customer, who now has control over the goods.

3. *The amount of revenue can be measured reliably.* The amount of the sale is $7 million, as indicated by the contract. However, although $4 million is paid on delivery, the remaining $3 million will not be received for two years. The $3 million must be discounted. Assuming that the appropriate discount rate is 6%, this has a present value of $2,670,000.[2] This results in the total consideration being $6,670,000, including the $4 million initial payment. There is also $330,000 ($3,000,000 − $2,670,000) of imputed interest involved in this contract, which will be recognized as time passes.

4. *It is probable that the benefit of the revenue will actually flow to the seller.* The customer has paid $4 million, and there is no indication that the remaining $3 million will not be paid in 20X3 when it comes due.

5. *The seller can reliably measure all costs relating the transaction, past and future.* There appear to be no future costs to be incurred.

The critical event is the delivery date, and revenue of $6,670,000 is recognized on 1 January 20X1. Imputed interest of $330,000 is recognized as time passes.

Entries On 1 January 20X1, revenue of $6,670,000 is recognized along with cash of $4 million and a long-term receivable of $2,670,000 as follows:

Dr. Cash	4,000,000	
Dr. Long-term receivable	2,670,000	
Cr. Sales revenue		6,670,000

In subsequent periods, the company will recognize interest revenue as time passes. The accounting treatment of discounted long-term receivables is illustrated in Chapter 7.

Non-cash Consideration

What happens when part or all of the consideration is not cash, but some other form of asset, good or service? In these cases, the transaction price is determined to be the fair value of the non-cash consideration. When it is impossible to determine the fair value of the consideration that is received, then the company can use the estimated selling price of the goods or services being transferred. We will discuss nonmonetary transactions later in this chapter.

MULTIPLE GOODS AND SERVICE CONTRACTS

A contract has **multiple deliverables** if it includes a *bundle of goods and/or services* in a single contract. Examples of different goods and/or services, which constitute *multiple deliverables*, are:

- Delivery of goods;
- Provision of a service;

---

[2] More detail is provided in Chapter 7. Calculation of present value is explained in a unit available on Connect.

- Granting licences for the use of intangible property; and
- Granting options to the customer to receive additional goods or services at discounted prices.

Multiple deliverables make the timing and amount of recognition of revenue for the contract challenging. Ideally, each separately identifiable component of such an agreement should be accounted for individually as a separate revenue-generating activity provided that there is **objective and reliable evidence** of the fair value of the separate components. The overall revenue stream should be allocated to the stand-alone components on the basis of the relative fair values of the components. Each deliverable is then treated as a separate revenue transaction and assessed against the five criteria to determine the point that the related revenue is earned.

Multiple Deliverables Consider a software company that sells an advanced processing system to a client. The sales contract also includes three years of technical service as well as periodic software updates at a reduced rate. There appear to be three separate deliverables under this contract. The company has agreed to deliver (1) the processing system, (2) the updates, and (3) the technical services. Ideally, each promised good or service in such an agreement should be accounted for individually as a separate revenue-generating activity provided that each component can be measured at its fair value using objective and reliable evidence.

Separately identifiable The term "each separately identifiable component" should not be taken too literally. If a contract seems to have four different components but there is no objective and reliable estimate of the fair value of one component, then that component should be combined with another component to form a single unit for accounting purposes.

Allocation of Consideration Once each stand-alone component has been identified, it is necessary to *allocate the total contract consideration to the individual items*. This allocation is calculated based on the relative **stand-alone value** of each good and service being delivered. The *stand-alone value* is, as its name implies, the fair value of that component when sold on its own. Two approaches to allocation are possible:

1. The **relative fair value method**, where the allocation of revenue is based on the relative stand-alone values of each component in the contract; and

2. The **residual value method,** where the fair value of the initial component is reliably measurable while the values of subsequent components are not. In such a case, the residual method can be used. Under this approach, the fair value of the initial component is recognized, and the remaining (i.e., "residual") revenue is allocated to the remaining component or components and treated as a single component.

The relative fair value method To illustrate the *relative fair value method*, suppose that on 20 December 20X4 Crease Computers Ltd. enters into a $900,000 contract with a customer to supply a sophisticated mainframe computer plus three years of regular service. The computer has a selling price of $800,000 and the service is sold separately for $200,000. There are two deliverables in the contract. Since stand-alone values can be determined for each of these components, they can be treated as separate deliverables. The contract price of $900,000 is allocated as follows (in thousands):

Revenue from sale of computer	$900 × [$800 ÷ ($800 + $200)]	= $720
Revenue from service contract	$900 × [$200 ÷ ($800 + $200)]	= 180
Total revenue		$900

For each separate component, we assess the recognition criteria to determine when revenue is earned and recognized. The sale of the mainframe is earned on delivery, once the customer accepts. The service maintenance is earned over three years.

If the customer is paying for the entire contract at the outset and the computer is delivered to the customer on 20 December 20X4, the journal entry to record the sale will appear as follows:

20 December 20X4:		
Cash	900,000	
Revenue—sale of equipment		720,000
Unearned revenue		180,000

Since the performance of the service will likely happen evenly over time, the revenue from the service contract normally will be recognized evenly over each of the following three years:

31 December 20X5, 20X6, and 20X7:		
Unearned revenue	60,000	
Revenue—service contracts		60,000

If the company does not sell each component separately, a stand-alone price could still be estimated by estimating the price that competitors would normally charge for similar items or using a cost-plus-margin approach.

The residual value method In limited circumstances, the stand-alone price of the initial component to be delivered may be determinable, but the remaining item(s) may not be reliably measurable. Examples of this would occur when the item is not sold separately. In these circumstances, the residual value method may be used.

In the preceding example, assume that the stand-alone value of the service contract cannot be determined using objective and reliable information. Crease would then allocate the $900,000 total consideration as $800,000 to the computer and the residual of $100,000 to the services.

Fair values unavailable If there is no objective and reliable evidence of the fair value of any of the components separately, they must be accounted for as a single contract. In that situation, the *critical point* comes into play—revenue can be recognized only at the point at which it is possible to objectively and reliably measure the remaining costs to be incurred. Then, the seller should recognize the revenue *except for an amount of revenue that is equal to the estimated remaining costs plus a reasonable profit.* The *unrecognized* portion of revenue is deferred for recognition in future periods when the remaining service is performed.

Examples of Multiple Deliverable Contracts

Two common examples of contracts that have several performance obligations are customer loyalty programs and franchise fees.

Customer Loyalty Programs Many companies have loyalty point programs to cement customer relationships, provide promotional opportunities, and track buyer behaviour. At the time of a sale, the customer not only receives the goods or service but also receives points that can be used toward future purchases. From the company's perspective then, there are two separate deliverables that are entered into at the time of sale—the sale of the good or service and the right to the customer to use the points toward a future sale.

For example, Drug Store Inc. (DSI) has a program that awards one customer loyalty point for every $10 of goods purchased. During the month, the company sold $250,000 of goods in the store and awarded 25,000 points, which can be redeemed and used toward future purchases. The stand-alone selling price for the goods sold is $250,000. Based on past experience, DSI expects that only 90% of the points will actually be redeemed. The stand-alone selling price of the points is determined to be $0.90 per point, making a total of $22,500 for the value of the points.

Based on the relative stand-alone prices of the two deliverables, the sales for the month would be reported as follows:

			Allocation of consideration
Goods sold	$250,000	[$250,000 ÷ $272,500] × 250,000	$229,360
Points sold	22,500	[$22,500 ÷ $272,500] × 250,000	20,640
Total	$272,500		$250,000

Dr. Cash	250,000	
Cr. Sales revenue		229,360
Cr. Provision for loyalty program awards		20,640

Each year, the remaining points outstanding need to be assessed for redemption rates (known as "breakage") and adjusted accordingly. This provision will be covered again in Chapter 12.

Franchise Fees Franchise fee arrangements are often complex, making revenue recognition decisions challenging.

Suppose that a doughnut chain (franchisor) "sells" one of its stores to an entrepreneur for an upfront franchise fee of $500,000 plus 2% of the store's gross revenues on a monthly basis. For this fee, the doughnut chain agrees to allow the entrepreneur to use the chain's trade name and sell its product for 20 years. The franchisor also will provide market know-how as needed for a term of five years, employee training, and all necessary equipment.

Clearly, a franchise fee contract has multiple deliverables. The franchisor is delivering many services over a (potentially) extended period of time. Stand-alone items must be identified through research and investigation. The problem is to determine which of those components has a reliably measurable value, since many are unique. It is determined that the rights to the trade name, product sale, and market experience cannot be individually separated but, in combination, a stand-alone value can be determined. This constitutes one deliverable. Training and equipment are also each sold separately and each has a stand-alone value. These are two more deliverables, making three in total.

The next step is to allocate the $500,000 to each of the three separate identifiable components and assess each separately using the criteria to determine when revenue is earned. In this case, the training and equipment would be recognized on delivery when performance is complete and risks and rewards have been transferred. The right to use the trade name and market know-how would be recognized with the passage of time (over the five years) commencing when the entrepreneur opens his business and starts to use them.

CONCEPT REVIEW

1. Under what circumstances must revenue be recognized over the term of the contract?
2. Explain the two methods used to determine progress over time.
3. If a contract requires cash of $10 million to be paid in five years' time, will $10 million of sale revenue be recognized? Explain.
4. What does it mean if a contract has multiple deliverables?
5. Explain the residual value method.

LONG-TERM CONTRACTS

In some instances, a company enters into a long-term contract, one that requires economic activity that spans several fiscal years. Examples include construction contracts and development of large-scale custom software. If the seller waits until the project or contract is completed to recognize revenue, the information on revenue and expense included in the financial statements will be *verifiable*, but it may not be *relevant* for decision making because the information is not timely. Therefore, use of the percentage-of-completion method is required to reflect the results of the enterprise's economic activity during the period. This method is more relevant, but relies on estimates and so is less verifiable.

Percentage-of-Completion Method

For a long-term contract, revenue is recognized using the percentage-of-completion method. The objective is to measure the economic activity (i.e., work accomplished on the construction project) during the year. To apply the percentage-of-completion method, the contractor (e.g., the seller) must meet the revenue recognition criteria, as described earlier in this chapter. That is, criteria for recognizing service revenue are:

- Revenue can be measured reliably;
- It is probable that the economic benefits of the transaction will flow to the service provider;
- For long-term projects, the stage of completion can be measured reliably; and
- All costs can be reliably measured.

Note particularly the third criteria; that is, the contractor must be able to measure the stage of completion.

If these criteria are met, the percentage-of-completion method very clearly *relates the revenue to the work performed*. Revenue is recognized in an amount equal to the percentage of the contract value that is achieved during the year. Of course, judgement plays an important role in determining whether the criteria are met.

Criteria not met If the criteria are not met, *a cost recovery approach should be used*, similar to that previously illustrated for sales when collection is uncertain. Revenue is equal to collections, and an offsetting expense is recognized; there is no profit. Instead, all profit is recognized with final collections. Finally, in cases where the company lacks information to determine stage of completion *and is not expected to be contractually able to recover the costs incurred to date,* revenue would not be recognized until the contract is completed (completed-contract method). The completed-contract approach is allowed under ASPE in certain circumstances; see the final section of this chapter for an example.

Example

Ace Construction Corporation has entered into a $1.5 million contract to construct a building, starting construction on 1 February 20X1. The planned completion date is 1 August 20X3, and thus the contract spans three fiscal years for Ace. Initially, total costs to complete the contract are estimated at $1.35 million, so the contract is initially expected to generate gross profit of $150,000. For this example, Ace uses the costs incurred to date, an *input measure*, to assess the stage of completion for the contract.

The data shown in Exhibit 6-5 show the progress of the three-year construction period. The actual data for each of the three years becomes known as each year goes by. That is, in 20X1, Ace does not know the 20X2 or 20X3 information.

The total construction costs were originally estimated at $1,350,000, of which $350,000 was incurred in 20X1. In 20X2, another $550,000 in costs was incurred, bringing the total spent to $900,000 ($350,000 + $550,000). Estimated total project costs, including past and current costs but also all anticipated costs to complete the project, rose by $10,000 in 20X2, to $1,360,000. In 20X3, Ace finished the project and spent $465,000, bringing total costs to $1,365,000, another $5,000 higher than expected. Contract gross profit over the three years therefore drops from the original estimate of $150,000 to an actual gross profit of $135,000.

EXHIBIT 6-5

ACE CONSTRUCTION CORPORATION

Construction Project Fact Sheet, Three-Year Summary Schedule

Contract Price: $1,500,000	20X1	20X2	20X3
1. Estimated total costs for project	$1,350,000	$1,360,000	$1,365,000
2. Costs incurred during current year	350,000	550,000	465,000
3. Cumulative costs incurred to date	350,000	900,000	1,365,000
4. Estimated costs to complete at year-end	1,000,000	460,000	—
5. Progress billings during year	300,000	575,000	625,000
6. Cumulative billings to date	300,000	875,000	1,500,000
7. Collections on billings during year	270,000	555,000	675,000
8. Cumulative collections to date	270,000	825,000	1,500,000

Construction companies do not wait until the end of the project to collect their money. Instead, **progress billings** are made throughout the duration of the project. The amount of progress billings is based on contract and negotiated based on the contractor's need for cash to pay for materials and wages as the work is performed and as verified by an independent facilitator. Ace's contract allows progress billings of $300,000 in 20X1 and $575,000 in 20X2, with the balance to be billed when the project is complete.

Estimating Revenue To establish the revenue and gross profit to be recognized in a given year:

First, use the relative proportion of the total costs that have been incurred to date to determine the cumulative percentage completed as of the end of the year. Multiply this percentage by the contract price to determine cumulative revenue to date.

Second, subtract revenue recognized in prior years, if any; the result is revenue for the current year.

Recognize this amount of revenue, along with the costs incurred in the year, to determine gross profit for the year.

For Ace, year by year, the cumulative estimated percentage-of-completion and cumulative revenue to date would be:

	20X1	20X2	20X3
Cumulative costs incurred to date	$ 350,000	$ 900,000	$1,365,000
Estimated total costs	1,350,000	1,360,000	1,365,000
Cumulative percent completed	26%	66%	100%
Cumulative Revenue:			
20X1: $1.5 million × 26%; 66%; 100%	$390,000	$990,000	$1,500,000

The percentage completed is computed by dividing the estimate of *costs incurred to date* by the *estimated total costs*. For example, estimated total costs at the end of 20X1 ($1,350,000) equals costs incurred to date ($350,000) plus estimated costs to complete at the end of 20X1 ($1,000,000). This percentage is multiplied by the $1.5 million contract value to determine cumulative revenue to date.

The percentages shown above have been rounded to the nearest full percentage point. The "exact" percentage for 20X2, to be precise, is 66.17647 … %. But there is no point in calculating the percentage-of-completion to more than two digits. We are working with estimates here, and it is silly to be "precise" in calculating percentages that are based on approximations.

The second step is to subtract revenue previously recognized, and the result is revenue that is recognized in each specific year.

	20X1	20X2	20X3
Cumulative revenue (above)	$390,000	$990,000	$1,500,000
Less: revenue previously recognized	—	(390,000)	(990,000)
Recognized revenue for the year	$390,000	$600,000	$ 510,000

Costs incurred are expensed. Gross profit is the difference between revenue and costs incurred in the period:

	20X1	20X2	20X3	Total
Recognized revenue for the year (above)	$390,000	$600,000	$510,000	$1,500,000
Costs incurred in the current year	350,000	550,000	465,000	1,365,000
Gross profit for the year	$ 40,000	$ 50,000	$ 45,000	$ 135,000

Recording The entries to record the costs incurred on construction, the progress billings, and the collections are shown in Exhibit 6-6. In sequence:

- Project costs are charged to inventory ("construction-in-progress") as incurred.
- Billings on contracts increase accounts receivable and are credited to a contra-inventory account ("billings on contracts").
- Cash received reduces accounts receivable.
- At year-end, in 20X1 and 20X2, or when the contract is completed in 20X3,
  - The contractor estimates the percentage of the contract that has been completed to date; and
  - The estimated percentage of completion is used to measure the amount of contract gross profit to be recognized. Revenue recognized and related costs of construction are recorded through an entry that increases the *construction-in-progress account by the gross margin earned in the year.*
- When the contract is completed in 20X3, the *billings on contracts* and the **construction-in-progress inventory** accounts are closed out. (These accounts should be the same amount once the contract is completed.)

By adding the "earned" gross profit to the inventory, the inventory is increased to its net realizable value. The gross profit is debited to the construction-in-progress inventory thereby raising the inventory carrying value to estimated *net realizable value*—total revenue less the estimated cost to complete plus unearned gross profit.

Note that the balance of the construction-in-progress inventory account is *not* reduced each year as the revenue and related costs are recognized in the SCI. Recognized gross profit is disaggregated into revenue less costs of construction. The offset to the inventory account is the billings on contracts account.

Total actual gross profit on the contract will not be known until the project is completed; what is recognized each period is based on many estimates, as we discuss shortly.

EXHIBIT 6-6

JOURNAL ENTRIES—PERCENTAGE-OF-COMPLETION ACCOUNTING FOR LONG-TERM CONSTRUCTION CONTRACTS

	20X1		20X2		20X3	
To record costs of construction:						
Construction-in-progress inventory	350,000		550,000		465,000	
Cash, payables, etc.		350,000		550,000		465,000
To record progress billings:						
Accounts receivable	300,000		575,000		625,000	
Billings on contracts		300,000		575,000		625,000
To record cash received:						
Cash	270,000		555,000		675,000	
Accounts receivable		270,000		555,000		675,000
To recognize gross profit:						
Construction-in-progress inventory	40,000		50,000		45,000	
Costs of construction	350,000		550,000		465,000	
Revenue—long-term contracts		390,000		600,000		510,000

Reporting Results As a result of these entries:

- Accounts receivable will reflect the balance owing.
- The construction-in-progress inventory account will be higher than the costs incurred to date, since it includes the gross profit that has also been earned to date.
- When the project is completed, the billings on contracts will completely offset the construction-in-progress inventory. A final journal entry is needed to remove both accounts:

Billings on contracts	1,500,000	
Construction-in-progress inventory		1,500,000

Exhibit 6-7 gives a summary of the balances and recognized amounts for each of the three years.

Measurement Issues

It is important to understand the estimates and approximations that underlie the percentage-of-completion method. Virtually every cost, revenue, and percentage-of-completion figure reflects not just one but multiple estimates.

Input versus Output Measures The goal is to have a realistic *measure of progress made toward completion of the contract.*

Measuring progress toward completion of a long-term project can be accomplished by using input measures, output measures, or simply the passage of time. This measurement issue was described earlier in the chapter. Remember, though, that these measurements are very subjective.

Output measures seem to directly address the issue of the *degree of completion* and seem preferable. Output is subjective and the company may have to rely on an expert to say that a building is, say, 65% versus 72% complete. However, input measures are also subjective, and

---

EXHIBIT 6-7

FINANCIAL STATEMENT PRESENTATION—PERCENTAGE-OF-COMPLETION ACCOUNTING FOR LONG-TERM CONSTRUCTION CONTRACTS

Year-End Amounts on SFP and SCI

	Years ending 31 December		
	20X1	20X2	20X3
SFP:			
Current assets:			
Accounts receivable	$ 30,000	$ 50,000	
Inventory:			
Construction in progress	390,000	990,000	
Less: Billings on contracts	300,000	875,000	
Construction in progress in excess of billings	$ 90,000	$115,000	
SCI:			
Revenue from long-term contracts	$390,000	$600,000	$510,000
Costs of construction	350,000	550,000	465,000
Gross Profit	$ 40,000	$ 50,000	$ 45,000

---

may be misleading when a constant relationship between the input measure and progress of the final product is tenuous.

Despite their shortcomings, input measures are most frequently used because they are the most readily available.

Estimating Input   Input measures rest on *cost to date* versus *cost to complete*. Obviously, the cost to complete is an estimate. It may be somewhat off the mark because large-scale projects are often begun before the final design is even completed. Complications often arise during construction, and costs mount up.

Cost to date can also be problematic. Only direct costs should be included in cost estimates; general administrative overhead or selling costs cannot be included in estimated contract costs. *Direct costs* include:

- Direct labour and materials costs and all other costs that relate directly to the project, including design costs, costs of outsourcing, and fees charged by subcontractors;
- Costs that relate to contract activity in general and can be allocated to individual projects or contracts, such as equipment depreciation, insurance, and other construction overheads; and
- Any other costs that the client must pay for as part of the contractual agreement.

Care must be taken with costs included. For example:

- Cost overruns on projects might cause erroneous levels of completion to be estimated. These costs, which would include cost of wasted materials and labour, should ideally be immediately expensed and excluded from the input measures. Tracking inefficiencies is not simple, though.
- One-time, upfront expenditures for quantities of materials and supplies to be used during the construction period may skew input measures. If all the raw materials for the project are delivered up front, for instance, a large percentage of input cost is recorded with no real construction progress made. These types of costs should ideally

be separated and included in input measures based on usage rather than being included at the time of incurrence.

Estimating Revenue The contract price itself may also be an estimate. True, any long-term construction contract starts out with a contract price, but that initial contract price rarely ends up being the final revenue figure. Modifications, or change orders, may be made to the contract as it progresses. Careful analysis will have to be done to determine how these modifications impact the performance obligation and the amount of the consideration related to the contract.

Extent of Estimates To summarize, in relation to a construction project:

- Output measures, if used, may provide a subjective measure of completion;
- Input measures rely on estimated cost to complete, which will change each period;
- Input measures also rely on the costs incurred to date, which also involve judgement; and
- The estimated total contract price will change from period to period.

It is safe to say that the percentage-of-completion method is a complete approximation! It represents a trade-off between conflicting qualitative characteristics—*verifiability* is sacrificed for *timeliness* and *relevance*.

Measurement Not Possible If the company cannot measure progress with *reasonable assurance* but expects to be able to recover the costs incurred to date, then the cost recovery method would be used.

Accounting for Losses on Long-Term Contracts

When the costs exceed revenues, losses result. Two situations are possible:

1. There is a loss in the current year, but the overall contract remains profitable.

2. The contract becomes unprofitable overall and is thus an *onerous contract*.

Loss in the Current Year Return to the Ace example in Exhibit 6-5, using the percentage-of-completion method. Suppose Ace's costs incurred to the end of 20X2 are as shown, but the estimate to complete the contract has increased to $550,000. Total costs of $900,000 have already been incurred in 20X1 and 20X2. Therefore, the total estimated cost of completing the contract is now $1,450,000. The contract will still generate a gross margin of $50,000, so it is still a profitable contract overall.

Using the revised cost estimates at the end of 20X2, the completion percentage becomes 62%; $900,000 ÷ $1,450,000. The cumulative amount of revenue that will be reported at the end of 20X2 is $1,500,000 × 62% = $930,000.

Exhibit 6-8 shows the revised calculation. A loss is recorded for 20X2. In effect, the loss is caused by estimation errors in 20X1—the future costs to complete were estimated at too low a level, which caused too much gross profit to be recognized in 20X1. The impact of this corrects itself in 20X2.

Overall Contract Loss—Onerous Contracts A test must be done to see if the unfinished portion of a long-term contract is *onerous*, or *not profitable*. A contracted performance obligation is an **onerous contract** when the *consideration yet to be received* is less than the *lowest cost of settling the obligation*. This *lowest cost* is determined to be the lower of:

1. The costs required to satisfy and complete the obligation; and

2. The amount the company would have to pay to cancel and exit the contract, if this is allowed.

When a contract represents an onerous contract, expected losses are recognized in the current year, before they are realized.

EXHIBIT 6-8

PERCENTAGE-OF-COMPLETION METHOD: LOSSES ON LONG-TERM CONTRACTS DUE TO CHANGES IN COST ESTIMATES

Overall Profit; Loss in an Individual Year

	20X1	20X2	20X3
Costs incurred to date	$ 350,000	$ 900,000	$1,450,000
Estimated total costs	1,350,000	1,450,000	1,450,000
Percent completed	26%	62%	100%
Cumulative revenue recognized:			
$1.5 million × 26%; 62%; 100%	$ 390,000	$ 930,000	$1,500,000
Less: revenue previously recognized	—	(390,000)	(930,000)
Recognized revenue for the year	$ 390,000	$ 540,000	$ 570,000
Costs incurred during the year	350,000	550,000	550,000
Gross margin (loss)	$ 40,000	$ (10,000)	$ 20,000

For example, assume that at the end of 20X4, there was $250,000 of remaining revenue in a contract, and expected costs to complete were $450,000. The contract will end in 20X5. The contractor investigates and discovers that it would cost $625,000 to cancel the contract or have another contractor complete the work. Thus, $450,000 is the lowest cost alternative. This is an onerous contract because a loss of $200,000 is expected *in 20X5*. The $200,000 expected loss would be recorded *in 20X4*, with a credit recorded to a special provision (an estimated liability) for onerous contracts. This is recorded in 20X4 as follows:

Loss on contract	200,000	
Provision for onerous contract		200,000

At each reporting date, this *onerous test* would be updated and changes in the liability reported in profit or loss for the period. At the end of the contract, the onerous liability would be derecognized, or eliminated in the books. Onerous contracts are also addressed in Chapter 12.

CONCEPT REVIEW

1. Why might the use of input measures to measure progress in a contract lead to misleading information?

2. What estimates are required to use the percentage-of-completion method?

3. When is a long-term contract an onerous contract?

Agricultural Produce and Biological Assets

IAS 41 gives special attention to **agricultural produce** and **biological assets**. Biological assets are unique in that they are living and growing assets owned by a company. Examples of biological assets include livestock (cattle, milk cows, and pigs), plants, trees, and vineyards. The accounting standards measure biological assets using a *fair value approach* because changes in fair values of these assets is seen to have a direct relationship with expected future economic cash flows.

Definitions The basic definitions are as follows:

- *Biological assets* are living animals or plants (including trees, such as orchards and timberlands).
- *Agricultural produce* is the harvested product of a company's biological assets (e.g., wheat, fruit, milk, timber).
- *Harvest* involves separating the agricultural produce from the biological asset (e.g., picking apples in an orchard) or ending its life (e.g., cutting trees).
- *Products that are the result of processing after harvest* are products that have taken the agriculture produce and *done something else with it*, such as turning milk into butter or cheese, or grapes into wine.

Measurement Biological assets and agricultural produce are *recognized* only when:

- The company controls the asset as the result of past events (e.g., planting crops or trees, or buying animals to raise to maturity);
- It is probable that the future economic benefits of the asset will flow to the reporting entity; and
- The asset's fair value can be reliably measured.

At each reporting date, the biological assets are *measured at their fair value less costs to sell*. In cases where the fair value cannot be measured reliably at the time of initial recognition, the biological asset will be measured at cost less accumulated depreciation and accumulated impairment losses. The *change in value during the reporting period is recognized in earnings for the year*. Costs incurred during the period are recognized as expenses.

At the time of harvest, agricultural produce is valued at its fair value less costs to sell. This will become the cost of the item used for inventory valuation purposes. *Agricultural produce is not subsequently remeasured to a new fair value as the inventory valuation rules of lower of cost and net realizable value will apply.*

Reporting Example As an example of biological assets, consider the following disclosures by Andrew Peller, a large Canadian winery:

Note 2 (F) Inventories

Inventories are valued at the lower of cost and net realizable value. Cost is determined on an average cost basis. The Company utilizes a weighted average cost calculation to determine the value of ending inventory (bulk wine and finished goods). Average cost is determined separately for import wine and domestic wine and is calculated by varietal and vintage year.

Grapes produced from vineyards controlled by the Company that are part of inventories are measured at their fair value less costs to sell at the point of harvest.

Note 2 (H) Biological Assets

The Company measures biological assets, consisting of grape vines, at fair value less costs to sell. Agricultural produce, consisting of grapes grown on vineyards controlled by the Company, is measured at fair value less cost to sell at the point of harvest and becomes the basis for the cost of inventories after harvest.

Gains or losses arising from a change in fair value less costs to sell are included in the consolidated statement of earnings in the period in which they arise.

Excerpt from Note 3

Fair Value of Biological Assets

Determining the fair value of grape vines involves making assumptions about how market participants assign the value of a vineyard between vines, land and other assets. The fair value of vineyards at 1 April 2010 was determined by an accredited appraiser and a portion of this fair value was in respect of vines. Changes in the fair value of vines may occur as a result of changes in numerous factors, including vine health and expected future yields.

To estimate the fair value of controlled vines planted on leased land, discounted cash flows over the estimated remaining life of vines or the remaining lease term, whichever is shorter, were used. The fair value of vines on leased land reduces to $nil as the lease nears its expiration date. Assumptions used include the discount rate, expected yields, grape price trends and annual growing cost trends.

To estimate the fair value of vines in the middle and later stages of development, the estimated fair value of mature vines was reduced by the net discounted cash outflows necessary to bring the vines to a fully developed state.

Fair Value of Grapes at the Point of Harvest

Where possible, the fair value of grapes at the point of harvest is determined by reference to local market prices for grapes of a similar quality and the same varietal. For grapes for which local market prices are not readily available, the average price of similar grapes is used.

Source: Andrew Peller Limited *2012 Annual Report,* Excerpts from p. 33, 34 and 39, Note 2(F), Note 2(H) and Note 3. Retrieved 5 June 2013 from http://www.andrewpeller.com

---

Peller reports its vineyards and grapes not yet harvested as biological assets. These assets are reported at fair value less costs to sell at each reporting period. Once the grapes are harvested, they are agricultural produce and are recognized at fair value less costs to sell as their deemed cost for inventory valuation.

Application To illustrate accounting for biological assets, suppose that a farmer buys hogs for $150,000 at the end of 20X0. The purchase is recorded as a biological asset of $150,000, offset by the decline in cash.

During 20X1, the hogs are sheltered, fed, and otherwise cared for at a cost of $35,000. At the end of 20X1, the fair value less cost to sell hogs of that age, type, and weight is $200,000. On the farmer's SFP, the "hogs" biological asset is written up by $50,000; the $50,000 gain is recognized in earnings as a "gain on biological asset—hogs." The $35,000 cost of caring for the hogs is charged as an expense. The net profit from raising hogs in 20X1 is $15,000.

Note that the increase in value is recorded as a gain, not as revenue. We usually reserve the term "revenue" for products that have been sold during the period rather than products held over the period. Regardless of what we call it, the increase in asset value is recognized in earnings because we have increased net assets. The resources expended to care for the hogs have decreased net assets, and therefore an expense has been recognized.

Further costs for raising the hogs of $55,000 are incurred in 20X2. That expenditure of resources will be recorded as an expense of the period. Near the end of 20X2, the hogs are slaughtered, an act that converts the hogs (as biological assets) to agricultural produce (as carcasses); the fair value less costs to sell at the time of slaughter for the carcasses is $300,000. On the 20X2 SFP, the classification of the asset has changed from biological assets (hogs) to inventory (carcasses). During the year, the value of hogs increased from $200,000 (at the beginning of 20X2) to $300,000 at the time of harvest. The net increase of $100,000 is reported in earnings as a gain on biological assets. The $55,000 cost of raising the hogs in 20X2 is charged to expense.

In 20X3, the hog carcasses are now part of inventory and valued at the *lower* of cost ($300,000 at the time of harvest) and net realizable value. As part of the processing, the carcasses are cut up into pork chops and processed into other pork products. Additional costs to process the inventory were $25,000. Finally, the pork products are sold in the commercial market for $400,000. The total cost of goods sold is $325,000 ($300,000 + $25,000). Earnings of 20X3 will show the following:

- Revenue from sale of pork products of $400,000; and
- Cost of goods sold of $325,000.

Exhibit 6-9 shows the financial statement effects of this series of events.

Biological Assets Not Immediately Salable In the previous illustration, the biological asset (hogs) have a market price at various stages of maturity, which we used for valuation (i.e., the value changed from $150,000 to $300,000 as the hogs matured). These prices would be obtainable, and verifiable, in commodity markets with reference to the age and weight of livestock. Other biological assets do not have such reference prices.

For example, consider standing timber—that is, trees destined for harvest but still standing and growing. There is no market for immature trees that are not yet of a size to become lumber. However, there is a market for mature felled trees, or logs. The value of mature logs must be used to measure the net realizable value of the immature growing trees, but many adjustments are required.

Brookfield Asset Management Inc. states that

> … The fair value of standing timber is calculated as the present value of anticipated future cash flows for standing timber before tax and an annual terminal

---

EXHIBIT 6-9

ILLUSTRATION OF BIOLOGICAL ASSET ACCOUNTING

(in thousands)

Year/Events	Gain or Revenue	Expense	Net Earnings	Y/E Balance, Biological Assets	Y/E Balance, Inventory
20X0: Buy hogs	Nil	Nil	Nil	150	Nil
20X1: Raise hogs	**Gain** $50	Costs to tend hogs $35	$15	+ 50 ⎯⎯ 200	Nil
20X2: (1) Raise hogs;	**Gain** $100	Costs to tend hogs $55	$45	+100	
(2) Convert to carcasses				−300 (transfer to inventory) ⎯⎯ 0	+300 ⎯⎯ 300
20X3: (1) Process into pork products in inventory				Nil	+ 25 ⎯⎯ 325
(2) Sale of pork products	**Revenue** from sale of products $400	Cost of goods sold $325	$75		−325 ⎯⎯ 0

date of approximately 75 years. Fair value is determined based on existing, sustainable felling plans and assessments regarding growth, timber prices and felling and silviculture costs. ... (2011 Annual report, page 102; retrieved 6 June 2013, from http://www.brookfield.com)

To determine the fair value of its biological assets, Brookfield must look ahead to the salability of that type of mature wood logs, adjust for the current age of the trees, deduct felling and forestry costs, and then use discounting to bring expected net cash flows to the current year-end.

CONCEPT REVIEW

1. What is the difference between a biological asset, agricultural produce, and an inventory item?

2. How are biological assets valued?

3. If agricultural produce has a fair value increase during the time it is held, when is this increase included in earnings?

NON-MONETARY TRANSACTIONS

Most transactions are based on a transfer of money. However, two entities can exchange assets, goods, or services without any money changing hands. Logically enough, these are called **non-monetary transactions**. Measurement issues can be quite significant for a non-monetary transaction if there is no obvious way to measure the value of the exchange.

Remember that **non-monetary assets**, such as inventory and fixed assets, *do not have a value that is fixed in terms of dollars*, and their fair value can be subjective. **Monetary assets,** on the other hand, are assets whose value is fixed in terms of dollars. In addition to cash, monetary assets include receivables and investments in bonds.

Monetary transactions are those where an exchange has one "side" primarily based on any *monetary asset*; non-monetary transactions lack this anchor. However, a transaction can be "non-monetary" and still have some small cash component. Relatively small amounts of cash might be used to equalize an exchange, to make up for agreed-upon differences in value of the non-monetary assets exchanged.

Valuation Alternatives There are two general approaches to valuation of a non-monetary transaction:

- The **fair value method**, in which the asset or service acquired is valued on the basis of fair value, or
- The **book value method**, in which the asset or service acquired is valued at the carrying (book) value of the asset or service given up.

These alternatives are explored in the situations that follow.

Barter Transactions

Sometimes, two entities exchange (or **barter**) goods or services. Some exchanges involve similar goods while others involve dissimilar goods; similarity/dissimilarity should be based on common sense and be fairly obvious. The two categories are treated differently because the intent of the exchange is quite different.

Exchange of Similar Goods or Services An exchange of goods of *similar nature* is treated as a straight exchange, valued at book value with *no revenue or expense* recognized.

Suppose that an oil company has ample supply in storage in Ontario but is short of supply in Newfoundland. Another company has a reasonable supply in Newfoundland but is running low in Ontario. The two companies can agree to an exchange of a fixed and equal quantity of inventory, which is in the best interests of both. The ultimate sales are to customers in the two provinces. *The goods acquired are valued at the carrying value of the goods given up.* Assume that the Ontario inventory for the first company has a cost of $189,000 and a fair value of $265,000. No revenue or change in value is recorded, and the entry is:

Inventory—Newfoundland	189,000	
Inventory—Ontario		189,000

Exchange of Dissimilar Goods or Services When the goods or services exchanged are dissimilar, the amount of revenue is measured at fair value, using the fair value of the consideration *received*. If the fair value of the consideration received cannot be determined, then the fair value of the goods or services given up may be used to value the transaction. Establishing fair value often involves professional judgement.

For example, suppose that an accountant regularly prepares the tax return for a resort owner. Depending on the year and the amount of work involved, this has cost the resort owner between $1,000 and $2,000. For the past year, the resort business has been depressed, and the resort company has very little cash. The accountant agrees to accept her payment in the form of an all-inclusive one-week vacation at the resort. Since the transfer is of dissimilar goods and services, the accountant should record revenue as the value of the vacation that she is receiving.

That raises a problem for her, however. Just what is the value of the vacation? There is the official list price, known in the hotel trade as the "rack rate," but rack rates are frequently discounted. Hoteliers discount heavily to attract business, based on the season and demand. The accountant searches on-line and can find much cheaper rates, which seem more reasonable than the rack rate. But on-line prices vary significantly based on timing—school vacation and holiday weeks are more expensive weeks than shoulder-season prices.

The hotelier has a similar problem. Effectively, he has sold a week's vacation and received a tax return as consideration. He must decide what value to assign to the accountant's services. After all, it might be a slow period for the accountant too, which is why she was willing to accept hotel accommodation instead of finding another client who will pay cash. It is a valuation challenge for both parties! There is no requirement for the two parties to the transaction to record a common value; each reaches her or his own decision about the value each has received.

Assume that the accountant has made her reservation for a week in March and has a firm reference point through an on-line quote for a $1,500 value. This is close to the amount she billed in cash last year for the tax return, something she knew when she agreed to the terms of the exchange. As a result, the amount seems reasonable to her. The entry is:

Prepaid vacation asset	1,500	
Revenue—tax return preparation		1,500

Exchanges of Fixed Assets

Fixed assets are often exchanged for other fixed assets. For example, old equipment is traded in on the purchase of new equipment. These transactions do not give rise to *revenue,* but rather may generate *gains and losses.* Gains and losses are the appropriate classification because the exchange is peripheral and not part of customer-related revenue-generating activities. Again, the two alternative valuation approaches for the transaction are *fair value* versus *book value.*

Illustration of Valuation Alternatives Assume that Company 1 and Company 2 decide to exchange assets. Since Company 1's asset is worth $40,000 versus the $45,000 for Company 2's asset, Company 1 will pay $5,000 to make the exchange even. This monetary amount is low in relation to the value of the transaction, so the transaction is still classified as non-monetary. The facts are:

	Co. 1	Co. 2
Asset original cost	$76,400	$91,600
Accumulated depreciation	58,000	61,900
Net book value	$18,400	$29,700
Fair value of asset	$40,000	$45,000
Cash to change hands: $5,000, paid by Co. 1 to Co. 2		

Here are the two alternative ways to record the transaction on Company 1's books:

At Fair Value			At Book Value		
New asset	45,000		New asset**	23,400	
Accumulated			Accumulated		
depreciation, old	58,000		depreciation, old	58,000	
Gain on exchange*		21,600	Cash		5,000
Cash		5,000	Old asset		76,400
Old asset		76,400			

*$40,000 – $18,400
**$5,000 + $18,400

Both entries record the disposal of the old asset, removing its original cost and accumulated depreciation from the books. Both record the $5,000 cash paid. But they differ significantly in the valuation of the new asset and recognition of a gain or loss.

Under fair value treatment, the new asset is recorded at its $45,000 fair value, and a gain is recorded as the difference between the $18,400 book value of the old asset and its fair value, or trade-in value—$40,000. Under the book value alternative, the new asset is recorded at a deflated value—the book value of the old asset, $18,400, plus $5,000 cash paid. No gain is recorded. There is quite a difference between $45,000 and $23,400, a valuation difference that affects earnings, assets on the SFP, and the level of depreciation expense in years to come.

Now we can consider the circumstances in which each method is acceptable.

Commercial Substance As we saw above, accounting treatment of *barter transactions for goods and services* relied on a judgement of whether the exchanged items were similar or dissimilar. In contrast, accounting treatment of non-monetary exchanges of fixed assets relies on a judgement of whether the transaction has *commercial substance*. That is:

Use the Fair Value Method If:	Use the Book Value Method If:
• the transaction has *commercial substance*—the net present value or the configuration of cash flows is significantly altered by the exchange.	• The transaction has no *commercial substance*; the configuration of cash flows has not changed; or
	• The exchange has been in the ordinary course of business to facilitate a sale to a third party; or
	• Fair values cannot be determined; or
	• The exchange is a distribution to shareholders (part of a restructuring, spin-off, or liquidation).

Commercial substance exists if there is a significant change in the company's cash flows after the exchange. A transaction has commercial substance when:

- The configuration (i.e., the risk, timing, or amount) of the cash flows of the asset received differs significantly from the configuration of the cash flows of the asset given up; or
- The present value of the after-tax cash flow from use of the new asset is significantly different from that of the old asset. (The present value of the cash flows is called the "entity-specific value" of the asset.)

Significance is measured relative to the fair value of the assets exchanged, not to the overall operations of the company, and is a matter for professional judgement.

As stated above, certain circumstances dictate use of the book value method:

- If the transaction lacks commercial substance.
- The transaction is in the normal course of business and is part of a chain of transactions that will culminate in the transfer to a third party. For example, a parcel of assets might be assembled to meet contract requirements. Profit (or loss) will be recognized only when the sale to the eventual third party takes place.
- Fair values are not reliably determinable for either asset in the exchange. Undeterminable fair values exist when alternative measures of fair value are very different, or probabilities cannot be reliably assigned to different estimates in a range of fair values.
- The gain and loss is derived from transactions with shareholders in their role as shareholders. When the non-monetary transaction is a distribution to shareholders, the company receives nothing in return. These distributions should not trigger a gain or a loss and are recorded at book value.

Use of the book value approach in the absence of commercial substance is logical. If commercial substance is absent, there is no real difference in cash flows to the company "before" versus "after" the transaction. Companies should not be able to trade similar assets and record a gain or loss that has little economic substance.

Sources of Fair Values Where do fair value numbers come from? *Fair value* is ideally determined in an orderly market transaction and is the price agreed to between market participants on the measurement date. Unfortunately, used equipment can be pretty thinly traded, and fair value can be hard to establish. Here are some of the alternatives:

- Base fair value on prices actually observed in market transactions of identical assets; this is the ideal!
- Obtain quoted cash prices from suppliers of new and used assets. Remember, though, that the cash price is lower than the list price for many assets, and list price must be adjusted downward to cash price if this is the case.
- When a quoted cash price is unavailable, a company can invite bids for the asset to be exchanged. The highest reasonable bid for the asset in question is used as the fair value. However, this approach is not always appreciated by the companies that invest time and energy submitting quotes, only to discover that the asset was not really to be sold!
- Appraisal is another commonly used approach, although appraisals are notoriously subjective.
- Fair value can also be determined based on prices for *similar* but not identical assets, adjusted for obvious differences, such as age, operating efficiency, and capacity.
- A less reliable but commonly used alternative is published information on the average price of specific used assets, such as the *Kelley Blue Book Auto Market Report* for automobiles.

As stated above, if fair value cannot be reliably determined for either of the assets in a swap, the book value method must be used.

Fair Value of Which Asset? The general rule in the fair value method for fixed assets is that the fair value of *the asset being given up* should be used to record the asset acquired. If, however, the fair value of the asset received is more clearly evident, this fair value should be used.

(This is different from the valuation rule for barter transactions, explained above, where the fair value of the good or service received is the primary reference point; instead, *fixed assets start with the asset given up*.)

Sometimes, both fair values are known but are not consistent with each other. Remember, two arm's-length companies would not trade assets unless the fair value of each was similar. Practical common sense should dictate measurement. For example, if an asset with a reported fair value of $25,000 was exchanged for an asset with a reported fair value of $32,000, and no cash changed hands, one of the fair values is clearly incorrect. *A determination must be made as to which fair value is more reliable, and the valuation flows from there.*

Sometimes, one fair value is known but not the other. In this case, the exchange is valued at the known fair value, adjusted for cash paid. Consider the following cases:

	Case 1	Case 2	Case 3
Fair value of (old) asset given up	$44,000	$100,000	$73,000
Fair value of (new) asset received	50,000	?	?
Cash paid	10,000	4,000	—
Cash received	—	—	50,000

In Case 1, the values indicate some measurement uncertainty. The cash paid of $10,000 plus the fair value of the old asset of $44,000 equals $54,000, but the new asset is reportedly worth $50,000. In this situation, the two fair values must be assessed to see which is more reliable, and then, *either:*

- the $50,000 is used as the reliable value, and is used to record the new asset, and therefore the "real" fair value of the old asset would be treated as $40,000; *or*
- the new asset is valued at $54,000, relying on the $44,000 fair value of the old asset.

In Case 2, the fair value of the new asset is unknown, and its fair value must be implied by the value of the old asset, $100,000. However, the company also had to pay $4,000 to get the new asset, so the new one must have been worth $104,000.

In Case 3, the fair value of the new asset is again unknown. The old asset was worth $73,000, but the company received $50,000 in the exchange. Therefore, the new asset must have been worth $23,000.

Fair Market Value Cap

When non-monetary assets are exchanged and the book value method is used, the new asset is recorded at the book value of the old asset. However, *the highest value that can be recorded is the fair value of the acquired asset, regardless of other valuation rules.* This is known as the **fair market value cap**. For example, consider the following exchange (facts assumed), recorded at book value because the transaction lacked commercial substance.

New asset	97,000	
Accumulated amortization, old asset	56,000	
Old asset		153,000

The new asset is valued at the $97,000 book value of the old asset. Now, assume that there was reliable information available that indicated that the fair value of the new asset was $80,000. This is the *maximum value* that can be used for the new asset, and the entry becomes:

New asset	80,000	
Accumulated amortization, old asset	56,000	
Loss on asset exchange ($97,000 – $80,000)	17,000	
Old asset		153,000

Of course, what is really implied in this situation is that the old asset was overvalued at the time of exchange and was worth only $80,000 to the new owner, not its $97,000 book value. Overvaluation of assets is a failure in financial reporting and should be caught prior to the exchange. Each year, a thorough review of depreciation methods and rates, coupled with an impairment review, should minimize this risk.

Examples of Non-monetary Asset Exchanges

The following information for Regina Corporation is used in the examples that follow:

Asset Transferred—Crane	
Original cost	$90,000
Accumulated depreciation, updated to date of exchange	$60,000

1. Transaction has commercial substance

   a. *Fair values are determinable; no cash payment.* Assume that the crane has a fair value of $47,000 and is exchanged for a truck whose value cannot be reliably measured; no cash is paid or received. The book value of the crane is $30,000; therefore, a $17,000 gain is recognized. The entry is:

Equipment—truck	47,000	
Accumulated depreciation—crane	60,000	
Equipment—crane		90,000
Gain on disposal of the crane		17,000

   b. *Fair values are determinable; with cash payment.* Assume that the crane's fair value is not easily determinable but that the truck has a fair value of $33,000. In addition, Regina receives $12,000 cash. The acquired truck is recorded at its fair value. The entry is:

Equipment—truck	33,000	
Cash	12,000	
Accumulated depreciation—crane	60,000	
Equipment—crane		90,000
Gain on disposal of the crane		15,000

   c. *Fair values are not determinable; no cash payment.* Assume that neither fair value is reliably measurable. The acquired truck is recorded at the book or carrying value of the crane, the carrying value of the asset given up. There can be no gain or loss recognized on the transaction:

Equipment—truck	30,000	
Accumulated depreciation—crane	60,000	
Equipment—crane		90,000

2. Transaction does not have commercial substance

   a. *Fair values are determinable; no cash payment.* Assume that the crane has a fair value of $47,000 and is exchanged for another crane whose fair value is not more reliably measurable. There is no cash payment. Because the transaction does not significantly affect Regina's cash flows, the acquired crane is recorded at the book value of the crane being given up. There can be no gain or loss recognized on the transaction:

Equipment—crane 2	30,000	
Accumulated depreciation—crane 1	60,000	
Equipment—crane 1		90,000

b. *Fair values are determinable; with cash payment.* Assume that the old crane's fair value is not easily determinable but that the new crane has a fair value of $33,000. In addition, Regina receives $12,000 cash. Since there is no commercial substance to the transaction, the acquired crane is recorded at the old crane's book value minus the cash received. The entry is:

Equipment—crane 2	18,000	
Cash	12,000	
Accumulated depreciation—crane 1	60,000	
Equipment—crane 1		90,000

Whenever cash is involved in a transaction without commercial substance, the new asset is always recorded at the book value of the old asset, *minus any cash received or plus any cash paid.* Fair values are irrelevant. No gain or loss may be recognized.

c. *Fair values are determinable; with cash payment and fair value cap.* Assume that the old crane's fair value is not easily determinable but that the new crane has a fair value of $14,000. In addition, Regina receives $12,000 cash. Since there is no commercial substance to the transaction, the acquired crane is recorded at the old crane's book value minus the cash received ($18,000 = $30,000 book value less $12,000) to a maximum of $14,000. A loss of $4,000 is recorded. The entry is:

Equipment—crane 2	14,000	
Cash	12,000	
Accumulated depreciation—crane 1	60,000	
Loss on exchange of assets	4,000	
Equipment—crane 1		90,000

CONCEPT REVIEW

1. What is *commercial substance*? What is its significance?
2. When should the book value approach be used for recording capital asset exchanges?

INTEREST AND DIVIDEND REVENUE

Sales revenue by definition arises from a *contract with a customer* for goods and services that are part of the entity's normal operating activities. In some cases, the entity will receive other forms of *revenue* that are not part of its normal business activities but still arise from a contract. Examples are rental revenue and interest revenue. These types of revenue are recognized as stipulated by the contract. *The most common pattern is to recognize these amounts as time passes.*

Other types of revenue do not arise from contract. For example, consider dividend revenue, which is the result of an intercorporate investment. Dividend revenue is subject to complex revenue recognition rules, depending on the classification of the investment that gave rise to the dividend. For a passive investment, IFRS 9 dictates that dividend revenue is recognized when all three of the following criteria are met:

- The entity has a right to receive the dividend;
- It is probable that economic benefits will flow to the entity; and
- The amount can be measured.

These are all topics for later chapters, including Chapters 7, 11 and 18.

CHOOSING A REVENUE RECOGNITION POLICY

This chapter has illustrated many different ways in which revenue can be recognized. Depending on the nature of a company's operations, the determination of appropriate revenue recognition policies may be the single most pervasive and most difficult accounting policy choice. After all, revenue is the top line in the SCI and earnings is carefully watched by financial statement users!

Although there may seem to be many alternatives, *revenue recognition policy is not a free choice*. The policy is, first and foremost, a function of the contracts and terms that govern the revenue activity of the enterprise. When there is more than one revenue-generating activity, then there *may* be a different policy for each. For example, a retail company that engages in straightforward sales activity for cash or credit will probably recognize sales revenue at the point of delivery, while interest revenue on outstanding credit card balances will be recognized as time passes.

A chosen revenue recognition policy must satisfy the general recognition criteria of *performance*, *measurability*, and *probability of collection*. The products or services must be delivered to and accepted by the customer. Revenue and any future costs must be measurable with reasonable assurance. The eventual collection (in cash) must be highly probable. Revenue may be earned over time or at a specific point in time, depending on the nature of the transaction. It is important to bear in mind that the act of revenue (and expense) recognition *increases the net assets of the company*. The initial increase may be through an increase in cash, accounts receivable, or the value of inventories, but ultimately the amount must be realizable in cash.

ETHICAL ISSUES

Companies bring a variety of motives to the revenue recognition policy decision. Firms that are anxious to show increasing sales and profits sometimes have followed questionable and possibly even improper accounting procedures. A relatively innocent-looking example occurs when a firm records revenue for goods that have been ordered for a later delivery. For example, suppose a firm receives an order in December for goods that the customer desires to receive in mid-January and agrees to pay for the goods by the end of December. Should the sale be recorded in December or January? We saw earlier in this chapter, that these types of bill-and-hold transactions can be recorded prior to delivery *only if certain criteria are met*.

Even more problematic is a "sale" recorded for goods shipped to a customer that regularly purchases such goods in approximately the amounts shipped but which has not yet ordered the goods! There have also been cases where the invoices for goods shipped after the fiscal year-end are *backdated* to the current fiscal year to record them as sales in the earlier period. Yes, this really happens, but it is not acceptable, either ethically or under IFRS. Such actions are deliberate attempts to mislead users and are tantamount to fraud.

One last example is misrepresenting the types of revenue and the related costs. In 2011, Hewlett-Packard (HP) acquired the software company Autonomy for US$11.1 billion. In November 2012, HP accused Autonomy of deliberately misrepresenting revenue on its financial statements that HP had used to determine the acquisition price. Specifically, HP reported that Autonomy had reported hardware sales as software sales as seen from the quote below:

> … The mischaracterization of revenue from negative-margin, low-end hardware sales with little or no associated software content as "IDOL product," and the improper inclusion of such revenue as "license revenue" for purposes of the organic and IDOL growth calculations. … The use of licensing transactions with value-added resellers to inappropriately accelerate revenue recognition, or worse, create revenue where no end-user customer existed at the time of sale. This negative-margin, low-end hardware is estimated to have comprised 10-15% of Autonomy's revenue.[3]

Accounting standard setters have developed criteria in an attempt to discourage the most egregious revenue recognition and disclosure practices. However, bear in mind that revenue recognition often involves a lot of estimates—expected consideration, allocation to the separate performance obligations, future costs, management intent, and customer acceptance (and returns). There still is a lot of flexibility for unscrupulous managers to manipulate revenue recognition. All accountants must be on guard!

Accounting Policy Presentation and Disclosure

The disclosure related to revenue is very extensive, reflecting not only its importance in determining earnings but also the fact that policy in this area is judgemental in many cases. Historically, revenue disclosures have been criticized by financial statement users, including regulators. They noticed that disclosure was commonly "boilerplate," generic disclosures copied from examples in accounting standards. Companies must provide *specific, helpful information* in the disclosure notes.

From Earnings Companies must disclose the amount of revenue actually recognized in earnings. Revenue must also be segregated into different categories depending on its nature, timing, amount, and uncertainty. Construction contract revenue must be disclosed, including the methods used to determine stage of completion and contract revenue earned in the period.

From the SFP SFP accounts related to revenue recognition include inventories, prepaid costs, receivables, unearned revenues, and any onerous performance obligations. Disclosure must provide the user with information on these specific accounts. For construction contracts, the gross amount due from/to customers must be disclosed.

Policy and Estimates Disclosure notes must not only deal with revenue recognition policy but also describe the nature of revenue from construction contracts. For construction contracts in progress, aggregate costs and profits, total advances received and the amount of retentions must be disclosed.

Critical estimates and decisions must be disclosed. For example, companies must indicate how performance is measured in cases where the contract revenue is recognized over time and how the consideration is allocated when there is more than one deliverable in the same contract. For onerous performance obligations, disclosure is required about the amount,

---

[3] Eric Savitz, "HP alleges fraud in autonomy deal; takes $8.8 B charge." *Forbes*, 20 November 2012. http://www.forbes.com/sites/ericsavitz/2012/11/20/hp-alleges-fraud-in-autonomy-deal-takes-8-8b-charge/ retrieved November 21, 2012.

nature, why it was concluded these were onerous, and when the company expects to complete the related obligations.

The spirit of good disclosure is not captured in long lists of required items. The key is to provide information designed to give the user insights into the nature, timing, and risk of the revenues and its related cash flows.

REVENUE ON THE STATEMENT OF CASH FLOWS

Accounting tends to recognize revenue at a particular point or with the passage of time in a more continuous earning cycle. On occasion, revenue recognition also coincides with the cash inflow, but that circumstance is quite rare. Usually, a company recognizes revenue prior to receiving the cash.

To report cash flow from operations, the accruals relating to revenue recognition must be removed. This was demonstrated in Chapter 5.

If the *indirect* method is used for reporting cash from operations, the adjustments are made to reported earnings, the starting point for cash flow from operations. The primary adjustments are as follows:

- Any increase in accounts receivable or notes receivable must be deducted from earnings; a decrease in receivables would be added.
- Expenses that have been accrued (but not yet paid in cash) must be added back to earnings; examples include warranty provisions.
- Expenses that have been prepaid or set up as construction-in-progress inventory (i.e., paid in cash but not yet expensed) must similarly be deducted from earnings; examples include direct materials not yet used in the performance of a contract.
- Unearned revenue must be added to earnings; the cash has been received but revenue has not yet been recognized.

If the company uses the *direct* method of reporting cash from operations, the starting point is the amount of revenue as reported on the SCI (i.e., the profit or loss section of the SCI) must be adjusted as follows:

- Deduct increases in accounts receivable (and notes receivable); decreases in those assets would be added to reported revenues, since more cash was received than had been reported as revenue.
- Add (deduct) any increase (decrease) in deposits or other amounts prepaid by customers or unearned revenue.
- Expenses would be adjusted by the amounts of changes in accrued expenses and prepaid expenses.

CONCEPT REVIEW

1. When is interest revenue recognized?
2. On the statement of indirect cash flows what adjustments are required for unearned revenue?

Looking Forward

As previously mentioned, the IASB has a new standard on revenue, *Revenue from Contracts with Customers*. The new standard will be effective for years beginning on or after 1 January 2017, and requires companies to adopt a *contract-based approach*. Using this approach, revenue transactions are analyzed by looking at the commitment, or *performance obligation*, that the seller makes, in exchange for the *consideration* paid by the buyer.

The new standard is explained in the Appendix to this chapter. There is a more detailed supplement based on the new standard, along with examples, on Connect.

ACCOUNTING STANDARDS FOR PRIVATE ENTERPRISES

Revenue

Most of the principles concerning revenue recognition are essentially the same as those of IFRS, although the rationale is often different. IFRS adheres more stringently to the "definitional" approach of assets and liabilities than does the *CPA Canada Handbook, Part II*.

One major difference in the revenue recognition between ASPE and IFRS is that for long-term contracts, ASPE permits use of *either the percentage-of-completion method or the completed-contract method*. However, the completed-contract method should be used only when "the enterprise cannot reasonably estimate the extent of progress toward completion."[4]

Completed-Contract Method

Under the **completed-contract method**, there is no recognition of the project in the income statement until the project is completed and has been legally accepted by the customer.

Return to the example used to illustrate percentage-of-completion earlier in this chapter. The facts and estimates relating to the Ace Construction Corporation are repeated in Exhibit 6-10 for convenience, along with the journal entries to record construction costs, billings, and cash collection.

EXHIBIT 6-10

ACE CONSTRUCTION CORPORATION

Completed Contract Accounting

Construction Project Fact Sheet, Three-Year Summary Schedule

Contract Price: $1,500,000	20X1	20X2	20X3
1. Estimated total costs for project	$1,350,000	$1,360,000	$1,365,000
2. Costs incurred during current year	350,000	550,000	465,000
3. Cumulative costs incurred to date	350,000	900,000	1,365,000
4. Estimated costs to complete at year-end	1,000,000	460,000	—
5. Progress billings during year	300,000	575,000	625,000
6. Cumulative billings to date	300,000	875,000	1,500,000
7. Collections on billings during year	270,000	555,000	675,000
8. Cumulative collections to date	270,000	825,000	1,500,000

Journal Entries to Record Construction in Progress

	20X1		20X2		20X3	
Construction-in-progress inventory	350,000		550,000		465,000	
Cash, payables, etc.		350,000		550,000		465,000
Accounts receivable	300,000		575,000		625,000	
Billings on contracts		300,000		575,000		625,000
Cash	270,000		555,000		675,000	
Accounts receivable		270,000		555,000		675,000

---

[4] *Revenue, CPA Canada Handbook, Part II*, Section 3400.18.

These are the same entries as for percentage-of-completion in Exhibit 6-6 except that there is no entry at the end of each year to recognize construction revenue and construction expense on the SCI. On the SFPs during the construction period, the construction-in-progress inventory is reported as total accumulated costs to date less the total billings to date.

The accumulated balances at the end of the project (20X3) are as follows:

Billings on contracts	$1,500,000
Construction-in-progress inventory	$1,365,000

Only when the contract is complete and the buyer has accepted the project are revenue and expense recognized. The accumulated amount of billings on contracts is recognized as sales revenue, and the accumulated amount of construction-in-progress inventory on completion of the contract is recognized as cost of construction. These two entries increase net assets and thereby recognize profit:

Billings on contracts	1,500,000	
Revenue from long-term contracts		1,500,000
Costs of construction	1,365,000	
Construction-in-progress inventory		1,365,000

Advantages of Completed-Contract Method The completed-contract method has the advantage of delaying profit measurement until substantially all of the costs and revenues are known. There may be some remaining costs that are roughly similar to warranty costs; these can be estimated and accrued.

The completed-contract method ranks high on the qualitative characteristic of *verifiability* because there is so little estimation involved. On the other hand, the method is perceived as lacking in the qualitative attributes of *relevance* and *timeliness* because the benefit of the contractor's economic activity during the year is not reflected on the SCI as long as the project is underway. Therefore, the completed-contract method is not very helpful if the dominant reporting objective is performance evaluation.

The completed-contract method may appear to be quite useful for income tax deferral, since there is no taxation until the project is complete. This advantage is severely limited in Canada, however, because Canada Revenue Agency (CRA) permits use of the completed-contract method for tax purposes only for contracts lasting two years or less. Percentage-of-completion *must* be used for tax purposes for all longer contracts. Since CRA requires percentage-of-completion for longer contracts, there is little or no benefit to using completed contract for financial reporting purposes in a private enterprise.

Non-monetary Transactions

Under ASPE, if the non-monetary transaction has commercial substance, the transaction is reported at the fair value of either the asset given up or the asset received, depending on which value is more reliably measurable. In comparison, IFRS would use the fair value of the asset given up to determine the value of the transaction. (Only in cases where the asset received had a more reliable measure would it be used under IFRS.) The transaction is measured at the carrying value of the asset given up if there is no commercial substance, neither of the items has a reliably measurable fair value, or the transaction is a nonreciprocal transfer to the owners. This is similar to IFRS.

Under ASPE, for barter transactions where non-cash consideration is received in return for goods and services, if the exchange has commercial substance, the fair value of the asset given up is used as discussed above. If the exchange has been in the ordinary course of business to facilitate a sale to a third party, then the exchange is measured at the carrying value of the good or service given up. Under IFRS, only in cases where there is an exchange of dissimilar goods and services is the fair value of the asset received used to record the revenue.

Biological Assets ASPE does not require biological assets to be carried at fair value less costs to sell. Under ASPE, biological assets are reported at cost. A lower of cost or NRV valuation would be applied, consistent with other types of inventories.

Disclosure

Disclosure under ASPE is far less extensive than under IFRS. Under ASPE, the revenue recognition policy for each type of revenue transaction must be disclosed including how multiple elements within a single contract and nonmonetary sales are determined and valued. On the face of the SCI or in the notes, the major categories of revenue must be separately disclosed.

RELEVANT STANDARDS

CPA Canada Handbook, Part I (IFRS):
- IAS 11, Construction Contracts
- IAS 18, Revenue
- IAS 41, Agriculture

CPA Canada Handbook, Part II (ASPE):
- Section 3400, Revenue
- Section 3831 Non-monetary Transactions

SUMMARY OF KEY POINTS

1. Revenue arises from increases in net assets resulting from performance of the company's normal business activities. Expenses arise from decreases in net assets from the company's normal business activities. Gains and losses can arise from normal business activities or peripheral transactions.

2. Sales revenue is reported at a net amount—commission only—when the entity is acting as an agent. Indications of an agency relationship include the following: The entity does not have primary responsibility to fulfill the order, bears no inventory or credit risk, and has no influence on the price.

3. Revenue is recognized using the earnings-based approach. Revenue from the sale of goods is recognized when all of the following five criteria have been met: (1) Performance is complete, risks and rewards have been transferred and accepted by the customer; (2) the seller has no continuing managerial involvement or control over the goods sold; (3) the amount of revenue can be measured reliably; (4) benefits of the revenue will flow to the seller; and (5) the past and future costs can all be measured reliably.

4. The critical event that triggers revenue recognition is the last transaction or event that satisfies all of the revenue recognition criteria. The primary critical events are delivery (the most common critical event), after delivery (if there are significant uncertainties

about measurement, or remaining costs), or at cash collection (after delivery; caused by uncertainty about collection).

5. When cash collection is uncertain, the instalment method or the cost recovery methods of revenue recognition may be used. The instalment sales method of revenue recognition delays recognition of gross profit until cash is collected. The cost recovery method is a conservative method in which no profit is recognized until all costs associated with the sale item have been recovered in cash. All subsequent cash collections are profit.

6. Special accounting treatment is required for sales transactions with a right of return or warranties. In both cases, the amount of returns or warranty claims must be estimable to record the sale at the time of delivery, with the estimate of returns and warranties recorded. Warranties may also involve revenue deferral in certain circumstances. Bill-and-hold arrangements may be recognized as revenue prior to delivery only if specific criteria have been met.

7. Service revenue may be recognized at a single point of time or over a period of time. Service revenue is earned and recognized when all of the following criteria are met: (1) Revenue can be measured reliably; (2) it is probable that the economic benefits of the transaction will flow to the service provider; (3) for long-term projects, the stage of completion can be measured reliably; and (4) all costs can be reliably measured.

8. *Output methods* and *input methods* can be used to measure the stage of completion over time. Output measures recognize revenue based on the value of the work performed to date. Output measure include the passage of time. Input measures recognize revenue based on the value of the effort expended to date.

9. If consideration is received over a period longer than one year, the present value of the cash received must be used to determine the total value of the consideration. Interest revenue will be earned on this contract throughout the period of payment.

10. When a contract has *multiple deliverables*, the contract must be separated into separate identifiable components if the goods and services to be delivered have independent stand-alone values. Each separately identifiable component is accounted for individually as a distinct revenue-generating activity provided that there is objective and reliable evidence of the fair value for each component. The *relative fair value method* is used to allocate a contract's consideration into its separate deliverables. The *residual value method* may be used only when the fair value of the first deliverable is reliably measurable but the subsequent deliverables are not.

11. Long-term contracts are accounted for by using the *percentage-of-completion method*. Revenues and expenses are recognized each accounting period based on the effort expended, which is determined as an estimate of the percentage-of-completion. Losses are recognized when probable, and contracts are reviewed to see if they are onerous contracts.

12. Biological assets are living plants and animals and are measured at the fair value less costs to sell at each reporting period. Agricultural produce is measured at fair value less costs to sell at the time of harvest, which becomes the deemed cost for inventory.

13. The valuation of barter transactions depends on the types of goods or services being exchanged. Exchanges of *similar* goods and services are valued at the carrying value of the goods or services being given up. For *dissimilar* goods or services, the exchange is valued at the fair value of the items received, as is the nature of a sales transaction.

14. When non-monetary assets are exchanged and the transaction has commercial substance, the transaction is valued at fair market value and a gain or loss on the exchange is recorded. The transaction is valued at book value with no gain or loss if there is no commercial substance, the exchange is to facilitate a sale to a third party, when fair values are not available, or if the exchange is a distribution to owners. Regardless, an asset cannot be recorded at a value higher than fair value.

15. Revenue recognition policies must be chosen carefully and satisfy the core principle that revenue is recognized when control of the goods and services is transferred to the

customer and the performance obligation is complete. There is extensive disclosure related to revenue recognition policies and critical estimates required in measuring revenues.

16. For long-term contracts, ASPE requires use of the completed-contract method in certain circumstances. Percentage-of-completion is used in other circumstances. Under completed-contract, revenues and expenses are recognized only when the contract obligations are completed. Costs incurred in completing the contract are accrued in an inventory account, and progress billings are accrued in a contra-inventory account.

KEY TERMS

agricultural produce	gross basis
backdated	input methods
barter	instalment sales method
bill-and-hold arrangement,	licensing arrangements
biological asset	losses
book value method	monetary assets
commercial substance	multiple-deliverables
completed-contract method	net basis
contingent	non-monetary assets
control	non-monetary transaction
consideration	nonrefundable upfront fees
consignment	objective and reliable evidence
construction-in-progress inventory	onerous contract
contract asset	output methods
contract-based approach	percentage-of-completion method
contract liability	performance obligation
cost recovery method	product financing arrangements
critical event	progress billings
distinct	refund liability
earnings-based approach	relative fair value method
economic value added	residual value method
expense	revenue
fair market value cap	right to recovery asset
fair value method	separate and distinct
gains	stand-alone values

REVIEW PROBLEM 6-1

Cromax Corporation is a Canadian public company whose shares are listed on the TSX. The company has a December fiscal year-end. The following transactions and events occurred in 20X5. For each item, review the five criteria for revenue recognition, determine the critical event, and prepare the appropriate journal entries required to record the transactions. Assume all amounts are material.

1. Cromax has entered into a contract with Lukin Company to deliver 1,000 switch boxes for a total amount of $150,000. Each switch box sells for $150 each and has a cost of $95. Cromax has stipulated in the contract that Lukin may return any of the items within 45 days and receive a full refund. Based on historical experience, Cromax estimates that 4% of the items will be returned. Cromax also expects any returns can be resold. Cromax delivered all of the goods on 1 March, and Lukin accepted them at this time. On 1 April, Lukin returned 30 items. On 18 April, Lukin paid the final balance owing.

2. Cromax entered into a contract with Almate Limited to deliver 250 photocopiers and provide two years of on-site service. The total contract consideration was $300,000. Cromax

often sells individual photocopiers at a price of $1,100 each. The maintenance agreements are also sold separately, with a one-year maintenance cost being approximately $115 per photocopier. On 1 August, Cromax delivered the 250 photocopiers. At various times throughout August to December, Cromax sent its technicians to do regular maintenance on all the machines.

REVIEW PROBLEM 6-1—SOLUTION

1. Reviewing the five criteria for revenue recognition:
   a. *Seller's performance is complete; the seller has transferred the significant risks and rewards of ownership to the buyer.* The seller's performance is not complete with respect to the potential costs of items that might be returned even though delivery has been made and the buyer has accepted the items. As long as this risk can be estimated reliably, the revenue for the sale can be recorded at the time of delivery, along with an estimate of these costs.
   b. *The seller retains no continuing managerial involvement or control over the goods sold.* The seller has no control over the goods, which are in the hands of the buyer at the time of delivery. However, there may be continuing involvement when the items are returned.
   c. *The amount of revenue can be measured reliably.* The amount of the sale is $150,000, as indicated by the contract. However, there is a possibility that items may be returned. Since Cromax can reliably measure the estimate of the returns, the revenue can be recognized at the point of delivery, rather than after the return period.
   d. *It is probable that the benefit of the revenue will actually flow to the seller.* There is no indication that the customer will not pay for the goods delivered except that any items returned will not be paid for.
   e. *The seller can reliably measure all costs relating the transaction, past and future.* As discussed earlier, Cromax has the information to reliably measure all past and future costs.

On 1 March all of the items were delivered and assumed accepted by Lukin. This is the critical event and when revenue is earned and recognized. However, there is still uncertainty about how many items will be returned before the 45 day period ends. Cromax estimates the amount of returns to be 4% which is 40 (1,000 × 4%) items. Each item has a selling price of $150 and a related cost of $95.

The following journal entries are required:

1 March
Dr. Accounts receivable (1,000 × $150)	150,000	
Cr. Revenue (1,000 × $150)		150,000

Dr. Sales returns (40 × $150)	6,000	
Cr. Allowance for sales returns		6,000

Dr. Cost of goods sold (1,000 × 95)	95,000	
Cr. Inventory		95,000

1 April
Dr. Allowance for sales returns	4,500	
Cr. Accounts Receivable (30 × $150)		4,500
Dr. Inventory (30 × $95)	2,850	
Cr. Cost of goods sold (30 × $95)		2,850

14 April (end of 45-day period from point of delivery)
Dr. Allowance for sales returns (10 × $150)	1,500	
Cr. Sales returns (10 × $150)		1,500

18 April
Dr. Cash (150,000 − 4,500)	145,500	
Cr. Accounts receivable		145,500

2. Reviewing the five steps for revenue recognition:

a. *Seller's performance is complete; the seller has transferred the significant risks and rewards of ownership to the buyer.* At the time of delivery of the photocopiers, the seller's performance is not complete with respect to the maintenance agreement. However, this contract is a multiple deliverable contract and can be spilt into two deliverables: the delivery of the photocopiers and the delivery of the maintenance services.

b. *The seller retains no continuing managerial involvement or control over the goods sold.* The seller has no control over the goods, which are in the hands of the buyer at the time of delivery. There will be continuing involvement until the maintenance contract is finished.

c. *The amount of revenue can be measured reliably.* The amount of the sale is $300,000, as indicated by the contract. However, the $300,000 must be split into the two deliverables, since there appears to be stand-alone values that can be reliably measured for each one.

d. *It is probable that the benefit of the revenue will actually flow to the seller.* There is no indication that the customer will not pay for the goods delivered.

e. *The seller can reliably measure all costs relating the transaction, past and future.* The only ongoing costs are the maintenance costs, which will be recognized as incurred.

As given in the problem, Cromax has an agreement with the customer obligating it to deliver 250 items to Almate and provide two years maintenance service. There are two deliverables, and we need to determine if they can be separately identified and reported. We are told that Cromax sells individual photocopiers for a price of $1,100 each. This would indicate a stand-alone price for the photocopiers. Cromax also provides separate maintenance agreements priced at $115 per photocopier per year, which would be the stand-alone price for this service. These are separate components with observable and reliable stand-alone values, and therefore there are two deliverables. We can use the relative method to allocate the total consideration of $300,000 as seen below.

	Stand Alone Values	Relative Calculation	Allocation of Consideration $
Revenue from sale of 250 photocopiers	250 × $1,100 = 275,000	275,000/332,500 × $300,000	248,120
Revenue from sale of two-year maintenance agreement	250 × $115 × 2 years = $57,500	57,500/332,500 × $300,000	51,880
Total	$332,500		$300,000

The performance related to the photocopiers is complete on delivery. The performance for the maintenance service will be over the passage of time.

On 1 August all of the items were delivered and assumed accepted by Lukin. This is the critical event for the performance related to the photocopiers and the point in time when revenue for the sale of the copiers is recognized. The maintenance contract is a two-year service contract. The services will be provided and consumed over the term of the contract, likely with the passage of time. Consequently, the maintenance contract is recognized as unearned and will be recognized over the next 24 months commencing 1 August at $2,162 per month ($51,880/24).

The following journal entries are required:

```
1 August
Dr. Accounts receivable                              300,000
    Cr. Revenue for sale of copiers                             248,120
    Cr. Unearned revenue—maintenance contract                    51,880
```

Each month, Cromax would recognize the maintenance service revenue as follows:

31 August, 30 September, 31 October,
   30 November, and 31 December
Dr. Unearned revenue—maintenance contract   2,162
   Cr. Revenue—maintenance services   2,162

(Source: Atlantic School of Chartered Accountancy, © 2010.)

REVIEW PROBLEM 6-2

Precision Punctual Construction Company (PPCC) has agreed to build a 10-storey office building for Mountain Bank Limited on land owned by Mountain Bank. The contract calls for a contract price of $15,000,000 for the building, with progress payments being made by Mountain as the construction proceeds. The period of construction is estimated to be 30 months. The contract is signed on 1 February 20X5, and construction begins immediately. The building is completed and turned over to Mountain Bank on 1 December 20X7.

Data on costs incurred, estimated costs to complete, progress billings, and progress payments over the period of construction are as follows:

($ thousands)	20X5	20X6	20X7
Costs incurred this period	$ 1,500	$ 7,875	$ 3,825
Costs incurred to date	1,500	9,375	13,200
Estimated costs to complete at year-end	10,500	3,125	0
Estimated total costs of project	12,000	12,500	13,200
Progress billings this period	1,200	6,000	7,800
Progress payments received this period	825	6,300	7,875

Required:

Part I
As outlined in the contract, Mountain will own the building as it is being constructed. Show the relevant SFP and SCI items for 20X5, 20X6, and 20X7 for PPCC.

Part II
Assume that PPCC controls the building during construction and title transfers only at the end of the project. Show the relevant SFP and SCI items for 20X5, 20X6, and 20X7 for PPCC.

REVIEW PROBLEM 6-2—SOLUTION

Part I
Financial statement items: (in thousands of dollars)

	31 Dec. 20X5	31 Dec. 20X6	31 Dec. 20X7
Statement of Financial Position:			
Accounts receivable	$ 375	$ 75	0
Inventory:			
Construction in progress	$1,875	$11,250	0
Less: Billings on contract	(1,200)	(7,200)	0
Construction in progress			
In excess of billings	$ 675	$ 4,050	0
SCI:			
Revenue from long-term contracts	$1,875	$ 9,375	$3,750
Cost of construction	(1,500)	(7,875)	(3,825)
Gross profit	$ 375	$ 1,500	$ (75)*

*This is an example of a current-year loss on a contract that is profitable overall.

Part II

Financial statement items: (in thousands of dollars)

	31 Dec. 20X5	31 Dec. 20X6	31 Dec. 20X7
Statement of Financial Position:			
Current assets			
Accounts receivable	$ 375	$ 75	0
Construction in progress—inventory	$1,500	$9,375	0
Current liabilities			
Billings on contracts	$1,200	$7,200	0
Statement of Comprehensive Income:			
Revenue from long-term contracts	$ 0	$ 0	$15,000
Cost of construction	0	0	(13,200)
Gross profit	$ 0	$ 0	$ 1,800

APPENDIX

2017 REVENUE RECOGNITION STANDARD

In 2013, the IASB released a new standard titled "Revenue from Contracts with Customers." This new standard replaces IAS 11 (Construction Contracts) and IAS 18 (Revenue). The revenue recognition principles were revised to ensure that revenue recognition standards were applied consistently across all types of revenue transactions, regardless of industry. The new standard requires the application of the *contract-based approach*. In this appendix, a description of this approach is provided, along with a discussion of the core principles and the five steps to revenue recognition. Also briefly discussed is how long term-contracts are to be recognized; as well as contracts with multiple deliverables. Chapter 6R, Revenue Recognition—2017 Standard is available on Connect and goes into more detail (and provides examples of how these five steps are to be applied.)

The Contract-Based Approach

The "contract basis" of reporting revenue is based on enforceable rights and obligations as contained in a contract between buyer and seller. In such a contract, the seller makes a commitment to transfer the goods and/or services to the buyer—the *performance obligation*. In return, the buyer agrees to pay some amount of *consideration*. Consideration is the dollar value where usually net assets increase, through an inflow of cash, a new accounts receivable, and so on. Less frequently, liabilities might be reduced as consideration, perhaps through forgiveness of debt.

The core principle of the contract based approach is that the seller recognizes revenue at the time there is a transfer of promised goods or services to a buyer. The amount to be recognized is the expected amount of consideration for the transfer under the contract.

This core principle sounds simple. Indeed, in many businesses, revenue recognition is not a major challenge. In other businesses, however, the challenge can be quite significant. There are two general issues:

1. *How is the SFP affected?* That is, accounting policy must dictate *when and how much* to recognize for any *contract assets or contract liabilities* on the statement of financial position; and

2. *How is the SCI affected?* Accounting policy must dictate *when and how much* to recognize as *revenue* in earnings.

Recognition on the Statement of Financial Position From the perspective of the statement of financial position, as performance progresses during a contract, a *contract asset* or *contract liability* may arise depending on how much the customer has paid (if any) in comparison to how much work has been completed by the seller.

A **contract asset** results when the seller has transferred the good or service to the customer but has only a conditional right to the consideration dependent on some further future performance. (As we will see, a contract asset differs from an account receivable; an account receivable is recorded once the transfer is complete and the entity has an unconditional right to be paid.)

A **contract liability** arises when the customer has paid consideration, but the seller still has the obligation to transfer the goods and services.

Recognition in the Statement of Comprehensive Income As stated above, the seller recognizes revenue at the time there is a transfer of promised goods or services to a buyer.

When to recognize revenue can be very straightforward; for example, when a customer takes delivery of all the goods on one date. In other cases, it can be complex.

How much revenue to recognize can also present problems. There are two potential problems:

- Assigning revenue to different parts of a complex contract, known as *separate performance obligations*; and
- Measuring the amount of revenue when the contract amount may vary throughout the contract or payments are made over a long period of time.

The complexities of these issues will be illustrated in later examples.

Contract-Based Revenue Recognition Requirements

To determine when revenue should be recognized, five steps must be addressed for each customer contract:

1. Identify the contract with the customer;

2. Identify separate performance obligations, if they exist.

3. Determine the overall contract price;

4. Allocate the contract price to the separate performance obligations; and

5. Determine when the performance obligation is satisfied and revenue can be recognized.

Refer to Exhibit 6A-1, where the specific criteria for assessing each of these steps are listed. These criteria will be described in the sections which follow.

EXHIBIT 6A-1

THE FIVE STEPS FOR REVENUE RECOGNITION

Step	Description	Criteria to Be Met
1. Identify the contract with the customer.	Contract: Is written, oral or implied by common business practice; and Must be enforceable.	Commercial substance exists; Buyer and seller are committed to perform; Rights regarding transfer of goods and services can be identified; and Payment terms are specified.
2. Identify separate performance obligations, if they exist	Does the contract involve **separate and distinct** goods and services to be provided?	Separate and distinct when: Company regularly sells these separately; or Customer can use on its own.
3. Determine the overall contract price.	Consider discounts, rebates, incentives, penalties and present value of future payments.	Two methods can be used: Expected value method (using weighted probability of various outcomes); or The most likely amount.
4. Allocate the price to the separate performance obligations identified in Step 2.	Pro-rate the price based on the *stand alone value* of each separate performance obligation.	*Stand alone value* can be determined: As the price the item is separately sold for; or Estimated based on competitor's selling price; or Estimated based on the cost plus margin approach. In cases where a stand-alone value cannot be determined for each obligation, the residual approach is acceptable.
5. Determine when the performance obligation is complete and revenue can be recognized.	Completion occurs when **control** of the good or service is transferred to the customer. Note that completion can be at a single point in time, or over the period of the contract.	Indications of transfer of control: Seller has right to payment; Legal title, physical possession and/or significant risks and rewards have been transferred; and Customer has accepted the item.

Collectability Collectability refers to the customer's ability to pay the consideration agreed to in the contract. *The company must assess whether or not the contract asset or the receivable is fully collectible.* Any amounts estimated to be uncollectible are shown as a separate expense in the SCI. Changes in these estimates are included in the expense section of the statement of profit or loss.

Specific Examples

Sales with Right of Return A sale with a right of return has a single performance obligation, but the seller "stands ready" to accept any returns from the buyer until the return period expires. In recording this sales transaction, the accounting treatment depends on whether returns are predictable:

- *If the quantity of returns is reasonably predictable,* the company can recognize revenue at delivery for the estimated volume of goods that will not be returned. A **refund liability** representing the amount expected to be refunded on return must also be recorded at the time of the sale. At the same time, there is a quantity of items that the company will recognize as a **right to recovery asset** representing the cost of the items to be returned.

- *If returns are not predictable, revenue is deferred until the return situation is resolved.*

Sales with Warranty or Service Agreement The accounting for a sale transaction with a warranty depends on the nature of the warranty. If the warranty is provided to give assurance that the product will meet agreed-upon specifications and is not sold separately, the cost deferral method is used. Revenue is recorded at the gross amount, and an estimate for the warranty costs is recognized as a provision. If the warranty provides the customer with future services in addition to product assurance or the warranty can be purchased separately, then the contract has multiple deliverables and the revenue deferral method is used. The contract is split into separate performance obligations (sale of goods, sale of warranty) and each is recognized individually when performance is completed. As a result, a portion of the contract revenue will be deferred and recognized over the warranty period.

Performance Completed Over Time The 2017 IASB standard allows the completed-contract method to be used in certain cases for long-term contracts. The standard provides the following guidance to determine if contract revenue is recognized at a point in time or over a period of time using the percentage-of-completion method. Revenue is recognized using the percentage of completion method if *at least one* of the following criteria is met:

1. The *customer controls the asset throughout the contract period* and the *company is creating or improving that asset over time.*

2. The performance under the contract *yields an asset with no alternative use to the seller* and at least one of the following criteria applies:

   - For a pure service contract, the *customer receives and consumes the benefits of the contract as it progresses.* If another company took over the existing contract, there would be no need to reperform the services provided prior to the date of transferring the contract. In these cases, the seller has earned the right to payment for performance completed to date.

   - The work completed to date on a partially completed asset *cannot be sold* to another customer (either due to contractual limitations or without substantial rework). Additionally, the *entity has a right to payment for work completed to date and it expects to fulfill the requirements of the entire contract.*

If one of these criteria is met, the percentage-of-completion method is used. If none of the criteria is met, then the completed contract method is used, as illustrated in the ASPE section of the chapter.

Multiple Goods and Service Contracts A contract has *multiple deliverables* if it includes a *bundle of goods and/or services* in a single contract. Examples of different goods and/or services, which constitute *separate performance obligations*, are:

- Delivery of goods;
- Provision of a service;
- Standing ready to deliver or take back goods and services, if required (similar to the warranty obligation discussed earlier);
- Granting licenses for the use of intangible property; and
- Granting options to the customer to receive additional goods or services at discounted prices.

Multiple deliverables make the timing and amount of recognition of revenue for the contract challenging. Refer again to Exhibit 6A-1, which outlines the five-step process used for contract-based revenue recognition decisions:

- *Step two* in the assessment of a contract requires an entity to determine if the contract is made up of more than one performance obligation. *Revenue is recognized for each separate performance obligation as the performance obligation is satisfied.*
- *Step four* then requires the consideration to be allocated to each of these separate obligations.

Distinct performance obligations First, let us examine Step 2. When is there more than one performance obligation in a contract? Consider a software company that sells an advanced processing system to a client. The sales contract also includes three years of technical service as well as periodic software updates at a reduced rate. There appear to be three distinct goods and services under this contract. The company has obligations to deliver (1) the processing system, (2) the updates, and (3) the technical services. Ideally, each promised good or service in such an agreement should be accounted for individually as a separate revenue-generating activity, provided that each is distinct. A good or service is **distinct** if one of these criteria is met:

1. The company regularly sells the good or service separately,

2. The customer can use the good or service on its own or with other resources that it can readily obtain.

Not distinct The term "distinct" should not be taken too literally. In cases where the products in the contract are *not distinct*, they will be treated as a single performance obligation. In this case, revenue would be recognized in one pattern only. Goods and services that are highly interrelated and integrated, or where significant customization of the bundle of goods and services is required, are not distinct.

If a contract seems to have four different components but there is no separate sales market (stand-alone value) for some of them, then those components should be combined with another component to form a single unit for accounting purposes.

Allocation of Consideration Next, we move on to Step 4. It is necessary to *allocate the consideration to the individual items.* This allocation is calculated based on the relative *stand-alone value* of each good and service being delivered. The *stand-alone value* is, as its name implies, the fair value of that performance obligation when sold on its own. Two approaches to allocation are possible:

1. The *relative value method*, where the allocation of revenue is based on the relative stand-alone values of each component in the contract, and less commonly,

2. The *residual value method*, where allocation of revenue is complicated because one (or more) components has a highly variable or uncertain stand-alone value, and this component is allocated the residual contract value after other, known components are valued.

Long-Term Contracts Under the new standard, there are two ways to approach accounting for long-term contracts:

1. The *percentage-of-completion method*, used for contracts where the customer controls the asset throughout the contract period, and the contractor's performance obligation is met gradually over the length of the contract; or

2. *The completed contract method*, used for contracts where control over the asset is not transferred to the customer until the end of the contract, and the contractor's performance obligation is met at the single point in time at the end of the contract.

The key factor in determining the revenue recognition point is whether the customer controls the asset during the construction period. In every case, a contract must be reviewed to see if performance of the contract enhances or creates an asset that the customer controls. Control is indicated by:

- Title transfer,
- Physical delivery, or
- Transfer of risks and rewards of ownership.

Refer to Connect for further in-depth discussion of the 2017 standard for revenue recognition and examples of how the new standard is to be applied.

SUMMARY OF KEY POINTS

1. Revenue is recognized using the contract-based approach. The contract outlines the seller's performance obligation to deliver goods and services and the consideration that the buyer agrees to pay. The seller recognizes revenue at the time the performance obligation is complete; that is, when the promised goods and services have been transferred to the customer. The amount of revenue is the consideration that the buyer has agreed to pay.

2. There is a five-step process used to determine how and when revenue from a customer's contract will be recognized. The five steps include (1) identifying the contract; (2) identifying separate performance obligations; (3) determining the contract price; (4) allocating the price to the separate performance obligations; and (5) determining when performance is complete and revenue is recognized.

3. On the SFP, *contract assets, contract costs, and contract liabilities* will be reported as the contract progresses. Once revenue is recognized, accounts receivable or cash will be reported.

4. Special accounting treatment is required for sales contracts with a right of return, sales contracts that involve warranties, and contracts that involve multiple deliverables.

5. Long-term contracts may be accounted for using either the *percentage-of-completion method* or the *completed-contract method*. A key factor is control over the asset under construction. The *percentage-of-completion* method is used for contracts where the company will recognize revenue over the term of the contract. The *completed-contract* method is used where the company recognizes revenue at a single point in time. For the percentage of completion method, revenue can be recognized using input measures or output measures.

QUESTIONS

Q6-1   Explain the relationship between the definition of revenue and the definitions of assets and liabilities.

Q6-2   When is revenue earned in economic terms? How does this relate to typical accounting revenue recognition?

Q6-3   What are the five criteria required to be met to recognize revenue?

Q6-4   Under the "earnings approach," when is performance complete?

Q6-5   Under what conditions is revenue reported on a net basis?

Q6-6   Why is revenue typically recognized on delivery?

Q6-7   Under what circumstances is revenue recognized prior to delivery?

Q6-8   What conditions must be met for revenue to be recognized when a customer has the right to return purchased products? What accounting entries are used until all conditions are met?

Q6-9   Explain the two different methods for recognizing warranties and when each method is appropriate.

Q6-10   Describe the difference between (1) the instalment sales method and (2) the cost recovery method of recognizing revenue. When is each method appropriate?

Q6-11   Using the percentage of completion method, why is the ending inventory of construction-in-progress not equal to the accumulated costs incurred to date? Explain the amount of the difference.

Q6-12   What is an onerous loss on a contract? When is the provision for the loss recognized?

Q6-13   How are gains or losses from biological assets recognized?

Q6-14   How is revenue measured in a barter transaction of dissimilar items?

Q6-15   Company A gives up a noncurrent asset with a carrying value of $12,000 and a fair value of $20,000 in exchange for another noncurrent asset owned by Company B. Company B's asset has a carrying value of $17,000 and a fair value of $26,000. No cash is exchanged. There is no commercial substance to the transaction. What value should Company A assign to the new asset?

Q6-16   Return to the facts of Question 6-15. Assume that Company A pays $5,000 cash in addition to exchanging its noncurrent asset. Also, assume this time that there is commercial substance to the transaction. What value should Company A assign to the acquired asset?

Q6-17   Under ASPE, the completed contract method is allowed in limited circumstances. Explain what these circumstances are and how contracts are reported under this method.

CASE 6-1

SOLAR POWER INC.

Solar Power Inc., (SPI) is a public company manufacturing and distributing solar panels. SPI has been in existence for 10 years; the last three have been as a public company. To date, the company has experienced growth rates slightly higher than industry averages. Historically, the company had only been a distributor of solar panels and solar power consulting. However, due to the high demand for solar panels and a potentially growing market in Canada, management decided to open its own manufacturing facility in Canada. To finance this growth, the company obtained a bank loan. The maximum amount of the loan outstanding at any time cannot exceed three times the company's last 12 months' EBITDA (earnings before interest, taxes, depreciation, and amortization). The company is required to file interim statements with the banker so that EBITDA amount can be monitored.

SPI primarily sells two types of products: RHP-1 and CSP-2. RHP-1 products are solar panels that the company manufactures for residual use only. These products are sold primarily to individual home owners and home builders. The panels come in five different sizes that are suitable for installation on residential house roofs.

CSP-2 products are solar panels that are imported from a German supplier and are sold to the commercial market to be used on large commercial buildings. For these products, SPI acts as a distributor. These panels come in eight different sizes. Both types of products can be installed either when the building is being constructed or any time after the completion of the building. The company sells all of the accessories required to install these panels.

SPI also provides services for installation and consulting. In most cases, installation is for the products that SPI sells, although the company has started to provide installation services to other solar panel sellers in the industry. Consulting contracts are generally performed for companies looking for energy cost reduction solutions.

During 20X9, SPI entered into the following contracts:

1. On 16 March, SPI signed a contract with Sharone Company for a total $4 million. Sharone was building a new addition to its manufacturing facility and has decided to install solar panels to reduce its annual operating electricity costs. The contract price includes the CSP-2 solar panels, installation, a two-year warranty and a five-year maintenance agreement that starts as soon as installation is completed. Separate selling prices for the panels and installation and a one-year maintenance contract are $3,200,000 for the panels and installation and $300,000 each year for the maintenance contract. Generally, the panels can be installed within four months of the date the contract is signed. A nonrefundable deposit of 10% of the contract is due on the signing of the contract. Another 75% is due on delivery and installation. The remaining 15% is due six months or later after the installation date when all deficiencies have been resolved. Delivery and installation was completed on 31 August 20X9. The warranty is for assurance that the product will work within its specifications. SPI estimates that based on past experience, warranty costs will be approximately $150,000 on this size of contract. The company has recognized $3.3 million in revenue for 20X9.

2. On 5 May, SPI entered into a contract with Bakers Builders Inc. to supply RHP-1 panels. Bakers is a home builder that is currently building 3,000 homes that are energy efficient. However, Baker does not want to take delivery until the panels are needed. Baker has agreed to be invoiced for all of the panels but will ask for delivery at different points in time for the next six months. The total contract amount of $6,000,000 was invoiced to Baker on 15 May and Baker paid the full amount on 18 June. The panels are ready for delivery and have been set aside in a separate part of the warehouse. It is expected that there will be still 15% of the panels left to be delivered by the end of SPI's fiscal year-end. The company reported revenue of $5.1 million related to this contract in 20X9.

3. On 8 September, SPI entered into a unique agreement for the sale and installation of CSP-2 panels on the building of a local restaurant. The restaurant's owner, Fred Mason, is planning to sell most of the electricity generated back to the grid. As he currently does not have the cash flow to finance the upfront cost of the panels and installation, he has proposed that SPI receive payment for these panels based on 50% of the amount of credit that Mason receives when he sells the power back to the grid. The amount would be determined monthly and immediately remitted to SPI for a period of two years from the date of installation. The normal selling price of this installation would have been $20,000, and management believes that this contract may yield $25,000 or more over the two-year period. The installation was completed on 10 October and the two year period commenced on this date. SPI recorded a sale and related receivable of $25,000 in

October. To date, SPI has received $2,700 from Mason, which was recorded against the account receivable.

4. During 20X9, SPI entered into an arrangement with Solutions Co. to distribute its RHP-1 product in all of Solution's retail stores. The contract specifies the following: (a) Solution Co. will have some product on hand for demonstration purposes, which will be given at no cost. (b) Once the customer decides he or she wants to make a purchase, Solutions will call the order into SPI. Solutions will invoice the customer and be responsible for collection. Solutions will be required to remit to SPI on the date of invoice 85% of the sale proceeds; Solution may retain 15%. SPI will ship the product directly to the customer's home and install the product, if requested by the customer.

It is now one month before the fiscal 31 December 20X9 year-end. You have just been hired as an accounting manager responsible for the revenue reporting for the company. The CFO has asked you to prepare a memo outlining how SPI should recognize the revenue from these four contracts during 20X9. Particularly, the CFO wants you to identify the impact on the SFP and SCI and state how this will impact the amount of financing available.

Required:

Prepare the memo, as requested.

CASE 6-2

BELLA BEAUTY INC.

Bella Beauty Inc. (BBI) has been in operations for just over five years and is a private company following ASPE. The company designs and manufactures high-end maternity clothing under the brand name of BBI Chic™. BBI experienced initial success; however, the company has struggled somewhat over the past 12 months due to the general economic downturn. BBI management has recently concluded that their target market is too narrow as many women are not willing to pay a premium for clothing they will wear only for a few months. Management has therefore decided to launch a more affordable clothing line that will be labelled BBI Trend™. They expect that by offering two different lines, they will be better poised to compete in the maternity clothing market.

The main obstacle BBI faces is that it does not have sufficient capital to design, manufacture, and market the BBI Trend™ line. The company has applied for a $150,000 extension of its operating facility from the bank. The bank is willing to discuss an extension as soon as BBI's audited financial statements for the year ending 31 December 20X8 are finalized. BBI has been forewarned that its debt-to-equity ratio as of fiscal year-end will be a determining factor in whether it will be granted the extension. The bank prefers a ratio below 2.5. The bank is also interested in reported *income from continuing operations*. Reporting income from continuing operations that is fairly consistent with the prior year would demonstrate that BBI is able to survive during trying economic conditions.

The following information is available concerning BBI and its 31 December 20X8 draft financial statements:

BBI's customers are maternity boutiques across Canada. Sales in December were strong for two main reasons:

- As a one-time offer, BBI offered special sales terms to many of its customers. Customers that placed their order in time for December delivery and paid in cash were granted the right to return their unsold merchandise at any time up until 15 April 20X9. Customers liked this option because it mitigated the risk of losses due to slow 20X9 sales. BBI was pleased to offer this deal as it increased customer satisfaction and resulted in December sales of $50,000. BBI's products have an average margin of 40%.

- During fiscal 20X8, BBI entered into a deal with a well-known chain of maternity boutiques, Piper Inc. In November 20X8, Piper Inc. placed a custom order for silk T-shirts that would bear its store logo. Piper Inc. had very specific design specifications and contracted with BBI the right to refuse the delivered product and demand free rework should the T-shirts not meet its specs. The T-shirts were delivered on 15 December 20X8. Unfortunately, Piper Inc. rejected the T-shirts on the basis that they had tags sewn into the necks rather than silk-screened directly onto the fabric as was requested. BBI quickly admitted its mistake and had the T-shirts returned to be reworked. The reworked product was redelivered to Piper Inc. on 5 January 20X9. Piper Inc. accepted the delivery and paid in full shortly afterward. Due to the uniqueness of the order, Piper Inc did not qualify for the special sales terms. Since performance was "substantially complete" in 20X8, BBI recorded these sales totalling $8,000 in its 20X8 financial statements.

The sales manager for BBI performed a detailed analysis of margin by product in November. He determined that BBI's evening dresses were generally selling at negative margins. Based on this analysis, it was decided that BBI would no longer design and manufacture evening dresses. BBI would try to sell the remaining inventory on hand by discounting its prices. Since this portion of the clothing line would no longer continue, it was determined that losses on sales of evening dresses would be reported as part of discontinued operations for the year ending 31 December 20X8. Total losses from evening dress sales amounted to $600,000 ($408,000 after tax) in 20X8. Luckily, the equipment used to design and manufacture evening dresses is also used for other products and therefore is still in use.

BBI is currently taking legal action against a retail company with a chain of maternity stores that is based in the United States. BBI filed a lawsuit on 31 October 20X8 when it was discovered that the recently opened U.S. retail chain was operating under the same name. BBI is demanding that its name no longer be used and the defendant pay $15,000 in damages. BBI's lawyers are very confident that they will be successful with this claim. For this reason, BBI has recorded a gain of $15,000 in its 20X8 financial statements. The lawsuit is expected to be settled in late 20X9.

BBI reports the following on the 20X8 draft financial statements:

Income from continuing operations—$78,000 (2007—$85,000)
Total assets—$450,000
Total liabilities—$300,000

You are the auditor for BBI. It is now February 20X9 and you are preparing for a meeting with BBI's manager of financial reporting. At the meeting, you plan to discuss contentious accounting issues identified and any concerns you have regarding the 20X8 financial statements. BBI follows Canadian ASPE.

Required:
Prepare detailed notes to use in your meeting with BBI's manager of financial reporting. You must evaluate valid financial reporting alternatives and establish adequate support for your conclusions.

CASE 6-3

TIME-LICE BOOKS LTD.

Time-Lice Books Ltd. (TLBL) is a well-established public company that publishes a wide variety of general interest nonfiction books. The company is incorporated under the *Canada Business Corporations Act*, and the heirs of Harold Lice, the firm's founder, hold 30% of the shares. The heirs do not take any active interest in the affairs of the company but rely on the advice of their professional financial advisor, Mr. Jin-Shan Dai, in voting their shares. The remaining 70% of the shares are widely distributed and are traded on the TSX.

TLBL distributes about 25% of its books through retail booksellers (including on-line), but the bulk of the sales (75%) are made directly to end consumers by direct mail and Internet advertising. About half of the direct mail and Internet sales are for *book series*, and the company has decided to review its accounting policy for this segment of the business. TLBL is also exploring the possibility of selling its books electronically for use on e-readers.

A *book series* is a set of books on a particular topic. Rather than publishing all of the books at once, the approach is to issue one book at a time, at two- to four-month intervals. Topics of some series that have recently begun are *Saving the Planet*, *Great Impressionist Artists*, *Time-Lice Guides to Home Maintenance*, and *Lives of Great Accountants* (a particularly popular series).

When TLBL decides to start a new series, the first step is to design an elaborate and expensive full-colour advertising brochure for the series. This brochure is then mailed to about two million homes in Canada, using TLBL's own mailing list plus purchased mailing lists. An electronic version of the brochure is also disseminated via the Internet. The first book of the series is offered free of charge to anyone who returns a postage-paid card or requests a copy via Internet.

While the sales campaign is going on, TLBL contracts writers to prepare the text of the first book in the series and begins design of the book. However, actual production of the book does not occur until the direct sales campaign has ended and the number of copies needed has been determined from the returned postal cards and Internet requests.

The second book is produced about two months after the first has been mailed out, and it is sent to all those customers who received the first (free) volume. However, customers are then asked either to subscribe to the entire series at a fixed price or to return the second volume without charge. Company experience has been that, on average, 80% of the customers elect to subscribe and about 15% return the second book. The other 5% neither subscribe nor return the book, and TLBL takes no action against these subscribers except to send them a letter and to delete their names from its mailing lists. While 80% is the average subscription rate, the rate for specific series may vary anywhere from 70% to 85%.

Customers who do subscribe have a choice of paying for the entire series all at once, or paying for each book (at a higher per-unit price) as it is sent. Roughly half of the customers elect each alternative, although there has been a trend toward advance payment via credit card or PayPal.

The advertising brochure and sales campaign is the largest single cost incurred. The writers of the books are under a fixed-fee contract with TLBL and do not receive royalties. The layout and design work on each volume is performed by TLBL's salaried designers. Although printing costs have been escalating sharply, the cost to print and bind each book has lately been about $5. The books are sold to customers at about $30 per copy. All customers may cancel their subscriptions at any time. The advance-payment subscribers must send a letter of cancellation, but few do so. The instalment subscribers may cancel simply by returning one of the volumes within 15 days of receipt whereupon they are sent no more volumes in the series. At some point before the conclusion of the series, 20% to 30% of instalment subscribers cancel.

Required:
Evaluate the revenue and expense recognition alternatives for TLBL for the book series.

CASE 6-4

THOMAS TECHNOLOGIES CORPORATION

Thomas Technologies Corporation (TTC) is an engineering services company based in Calgary. The company's Class B common shares are listed on the Toronto Stock Exchange. The Class A common shares are all owned by Theodore Thomas, the company founder, and his immediate family. The Class A shares are multiple voting shares that assure that the Thomas family retains voting control over the company.

The company's shares have risen sharply in price over the past two years, driven mainly by the strength of the Alberta economy and the need for engineering services by the many resource and exploration companies based in Calgary. Stock analysts have been very enthusiastic about TTC shares and analysts have issued very favourable earnings forecasts for TTC's 20X4 year-end results.

In 20X4, TTC entered into special long-term contracts with two of its largest clients. The company's accounting staff recorded the transactions as directed by the TTC chief financial officer. The two transactions were as follows:

1. TTC entered into a three-year contract with Howard Limited to provide engineering services. The services would be rendered on an as-needed basis over the three years. The contract stated that Howard would pay $3 million to TTC at the start of the contract and the remaining amount would be paid over the next two years: $2 million one year later in 20X5, and $1.6 million in 20X6. Howard made the first payment as required in 20X4. TTC recorded the payment as revenue for 20X4. The cost of services rendered by TTC to Howard is not separately tracked but is part of the regular service provided by TTC to many clients.

2. TTC and Parker Inc. signed an agreement on 14 October 20X4. As one part of the agreement, TTC designed and built a special purpose piece of equipment for Parker. Parker did not solicit bids from other manufacturers due to the close working relationship that has been established between Parker and TTC over the years. It is possible, however, that similar equipment could have been obtained for about 20% less from a heavy equipment manufacturer in Japan. The agreement provided that Parker would pay $5.6 million for the equipment. The equipment was delivered to Parker on 22 December 20X4. Parker paid 40% of the purchase price on 30 December, with a promise to pay the remaining 60% within the first 90 days of 20X5. The equipment cost TTC $3.4 million to construct. The agreement provided that Parker could not sell or otherwise convey the equipment to any other user.

   In addition to the equipment sale, the agreement stipulated that Parker would pay $1.5 million per year for the next four years as a service contract. The price is about 25% less than TTC would normally charge a client for that type of service.

   TTC recorded revenue of $5.6 million for the equipment, and included $3.4 million in cost of services. The company also recorded the first years' service revenue by crediting $1.5 million to revenue and debiting accounts receivable—long term. This revenue was matched by charging $1.0 million to cost of services (for the estimated cost of providing the service) and crediting an equal amount to estimated service liability.

It now is January 20X5. You are working for the audit firm of Andrew, Athens, and Argoyle on the annual audit of TTC. The audit manager is preparing to meet with the TTC CFO tomorrow morning. She has asked you to prepare a memorandum in which you set out your views on the accounting used by TTC for these two contracts, with a recommendation on whether or not to accept TTC accounting, and any alternatives that you propose.

Required:
Prepare the memorandum for your audit manager.

TECHNICAL REVIEW

TR6-1 Net versus Gross: Crane Inc. is an agent for Phillips Co. and negotiates sales contracts between Phillips and the final customer for heating and air conditioning units. By agreement, Crane is to receive a commission of 15% on each sale. During the last quarter, Crane negotiated sales of 100 furnaces for total sales of $60,000. The cost of each furnace is $37,000.

Required:
Calculate the amounts that would be recognized and reported by Phillips and Crane for the last quarter.

TR6-2 Prepaid Deposits and Revenue Recognition: Clothes Are You is an upscale dress shop. On 15 August, Sally, a regular customer, came in and put a deposit down on two dresses—$50 on one dress and $100 on a suit. The deposit was a total of $150, which represented 20% of the total retail value of the clothes. On 21 August, Sally came in again to the store and decided to take the dress. She paid the remaining amount of $200 and took the dress home. On 2 September, Sally came in and paid the full amount remaining for the suit.

Required:
Prepare the journal entries that Clothes Are You would use to record these transactions.

TR6-3 Licensing Fees: Spreadsheets Made Easy (SME) is a company that designs and sells spreadsheet software. Corporate customers purchase licences for the number of users in their company that can access the software from their network at any point in time. The licences are granted for two years at which time the licence expires and can no longer be used by the customer. On 1 November 20X1, SME sold 50 licences to a customer for a total consideration of $60,000. SME has a February year-end.

Required:
Prepare the journal entries that would be recorded by SME related to this transaction for its February 20X2 year-end.

TR6-4 Output Measure: CCS is a construction company that builds roads in the NWT. CCS uses the percentage-of-completion method and measures completion based on the number of kilometres completed. In November 20X9, CCS signed an agreement with the NWT government to build 50 kilometres of new road for a total consideration of $40 million. The contract would likely take three years to complete and start in the spring of 20X10. Over the next three years, 15 kilometres were completed in 20X10, 22 kilometres in 20X11, and 13 in 20X12.

Required:
Calculate the amount of revenue that would be recognized in 20X10, 20X11, and 20X12.

TR6-5 Customer Loyalty Program Revenue Recognition: Rock Gasoline decided to implement a customer loyalty points program. For each litre of fuel sold, the customer would earn 1 point. The points could be accumulated and redeemed later for gas, products in the store, or a car wash. In May, Rock has sales of $60,000, which represented 48,000 litres. The fair value of all of the loyalty points awarded on these sales was $1,500.

Required:
Prepare the journal entry required to record the sales for May for Rock.

ASSIGNMENTS

★ **A6-1 Revenue Recognition—Gross or Net:** Each of the following situations is independent:

a. A company sells books through the Internet. The company obtains the books from the publishers and carries them in inventory for immediate shipment. Customer payment is by credit card.

b. An interior design company operates a showroom. Furniture manufacturers send samples of their products to the showroom for display. When a customer orders furniture, the company transmits the order to the manufacturer, and the manufacturer ships the products directly to the customer. Customers pay a deposit by cash or credit card, with the balance due (cash or credit card) when the product is delivered.

c. CanLight Ltd. is a company that sells electrical lighting fixtures. The fixtures are produced in China and shipped to CanLight by container ship. The producer pays shipping costs and retains title to the fixtures both while in transit and while they are in CanLight's inventory. CanLight markets and sells the fixtures to builders for inclusion in new construction. When a sale is made, CanLight delivers the fixtures to the building site and invoices the builder. When the builder pays the invoice, CanLight sends 70% of the cash to the producer by international bank transfer.

Required:

For each of the preceding situations, explain:

1. Whether the seller should report the gross amount of the sales transactions as revenue; and

2. Your basis for deciding whether to recognize gross or net revenue.

★ **A6-2 IFRS—Revenue Recognition:** For each of the following independent items, indicate when revenue should be recognized.

a. Interest on loans made by a financial institution, receivable in annual payments.

b. Interest on loans made by a financial institution, receivable in three years when the customer, who has an excellent credit rating, will make payment.

c. Recognition of revenue from the cash sale of airline tickets, where the travel purchased will occur in the next fiscal period.

d. Transportation of freight by a trucking company for a customer; the customer is expected to make payment in accordance with the terms of the invoice in 60 days.

e. Growing, harvesting, and marketing of Christmas trees; the production cycle is 10 years.

f. Building houses in a subdivision, where the project will take two years to complete and each house must be individually sold by the contractor. The contractor owns each house until title is transferred to the new owner.

g. Building houses in a subdivision, where the project will take two years to complete and the contractor is building the houses under a contract with the local government. The local government owns the land and the homes as they are constructed.

h. Selling undeveloped lots for future retirement homes in a western province, with very low down payment and long-term payment contracts.

i. Sale of a two-year parking permit by a parking garage, with one-half the sale price received at the time of the sale, and the remainder to be received in equal monthly payments over the period of the permit.

j. A fixed-price contract with the government to design and build a prototype of a space arm; the costs to complete the project cannot be reliably estimated. The government owns the space arm throughout the contract.

★★   **A6-3 IFRS—Revenue Recognition, Four Cases:** The cases given below for 20X5 are independent of each other. In each instance, assume that the accounting period ends 31 December.

Case A   On 31 December 20X5, Zulu Sales Company sold a machine for $100,000 and collected $30,000 cash. The remainder plus 10% interest is payable 31 December 20X6. Zulu will deliver the machine on 5 January 20X6. The buyer has an excellent credit rating.

Case B   On 17 April 20X5, the law firm of Pearlstein and Wolf received $30,000 from a client. The payment was a retainer for legal services to be provided, as needed, from 1 May 20X5 though 30 April 20X6. During 20X5, additional work was provided to the client and billed accordingly.

Case C   On 15 November 20X5, Victor Cement Company sold a tonne of its product for $500. The cement was delivered on that date. Victor agreed that the buyer could pay for the product with three units of its own merchandise commonly sold for $200 each. The buyer promised to deliver the merchandise around 31 January 20X6.

Case D   On 2 August 20X5, Remer Publishing Company collected $720 cash for a three-year subscription to a monthly magazine, *Investor's Stock and Bond Advisory*. The first issue will be mailed to subscribers in December 20X5.

Required:

Write a brief report covering the following for each of the four situations:

1. When revenue should be recognized.
2. Any entry that should be made on the transaction date.
3. An explanation of the reasoning for your responses to requirements (1) and (2).

★★   **A6-4 IFRS—Revenue Recognition, Critical Event:** Each of the following situations is independent of the others:

a. Carnegie Corporation commissions, produces, and sells books through faith-based non-profit organizations. The books are sold on the basis that a maximum of 50% of the quantity purchased can be returned within six months. Payment is due within 30 days of the end of the return period. Carnegie has a good historical record of the proportion of books returned, on average.

b. Maxwell Limited is a gatherer and distributor of coffee beans. The beans are purchased from harvesters in Brazil and Columbia, roasted, and packaged in large burlap bags. Maxwell then resells the bagged beans to food processors, coffee houses, and grocery chains in North America. Coffee beans have an open trading market and are traded on several major commodity exchanges in the United States. Raw beans can be purchased and/or sold in the open market at any time.

c. Heckinger Inc. manufactures customized private-label bottled water for a large retail chain. The product is sold under the chain's "Director's Choice" in-house label. Just prior to shipping the customized product, the chain voluntarily entered creditor protection. Under creditor protection, creditors cannot force payment of their claims until a judge approves a comprehensive plan for settling the claims of all creditors, a process that can take several years. Since the product had already been customized, Heckinger did deliver the product, believing that it would be better off in the long run to receive some payment instead of scrapping the product.

d. Nevo Corporation develops large-scale custom software. Nevo's main area of expertise is in designing complex systems for managing health care. It takes the company an average of three years to complete a project, from concept and specifications through programming, debugging, and testing. The client makes interim payments as Nevo accomplishes "milestones" that are specified in the contract. Nevo offers "turn-key" service, in which Nevo is responsible for installation in the client's facilities (including additional hardware, if necessary), on-site testing, and training for the client's staff. Nevo has never failed to deliver a contract on time and on budget, provided that the client does not change the system specifications while the system is being designed.

Required:
For each situation, explain when revenue is recognized and how costs and payments should be accounted for both before and after revenue is recognized under IFRS.

★★ **A6-5 ASPE—Revenue Recognition, Critical Event:** Luke Windows Limited manufactures custom-made windows for homes. The company deals directly with some individual customers, but mainly does business with contractors that are building tract housing under contract with a developer—that is, a real property development company that is constructing a large number of houses in a single new development.

For tract housing, Luke bids on the contract according to specifications given by the developer. The costs of preparing the bid are not substantial, but they are not insignificant either. If Luke wins the contract, the company then sets up a production line in the factory to manufacture the windows according to specification. As the windows are finished, they are stored in Luke's factory temporarily, until the contractor is ready to receive them. When they are delivered to the building site (usually in batches, not all together), the contractor is responsible for any damage or breakage that occurs. Also, the contractor is responsible for proper installation. Luke also provides a warranty to replace any defective windows if there is found to be a failure in the design or construction of the window after testing and inspection period by the developer (discussed in the following paragraph).

The houses are built (and sold) in batches. The sales from one batch help the developer to finance the next batch. After each batch of houses is finished and has been standing empty through a few rain or snow storms, the developer inspects for any failure in design, construction, or installation. If all is satisfactory, the developer authorizes payment for that part of the development. Payment is made to the contractor, who then is responsible for paying Luke. In the unlikely event that the contractor does not pay Luke, Luke can establish a "lien" on the houses that requires the developer (or the new owners who have purchased the houses) to satisfy Luke's claim.

Depending on the size of the housing development, the entire project, from bid preparation to final collection can take anywhere from two to five years. Each batch of houses usually is completed within about 18 months. However, Luke's construction and delivery of the windows for a batch seldom takes more than two months.

Required:
1. From the information given, identify the point at which Luke should recognize revenue from windows for tract housing. Explain your reasoning.
2. Using the revenue recognition point identified in requirement (1), explain how Luke should account for costs and revenues related to this project over time.

★★★ **A6-6 IFRS—Revenue Recognition:** Shawinegan Development Company (SDC) conducts research and development on specific projects under contract for clients; SDC also conducts basic research and attempts to market any new products or technologies it develops.

In January 20X4, scientists at SDC began research to develop a new industrial cleaner. During 20X4, $3,160,000 of costs were incurred in this effort. Late in July 20X5, potentially promising results emerged in the form of a substance the company called Scourge. Costs incurred through the end of July 20X5 were $1,540,000. At this point, SDC attempted to sell the formula and rights to Scourge to Pride and Glory Industries Limited (P&G), for $16,000,000. P&G, however, was reluctant to sign before further testing was done. It did wish, though, to have the first option to acquire the rights and formulas to Scourge if future testing showed the product to be profitable. SDC was very confident that Scourge would pass further testing with flying colours. Accordingly, the two companies signed an option agreement that allowed P&G to acquire the formulas and rights to Scourge any time before 31 December 20X6. Testing costs on the product incurred by SDC for the remainder of 20X5 amounted to $1,800,000.

On 5 January 20X6, P&G exercised its option and agreed to purchase the formulas and rights to Scourge for $16,000,000. P&G paid $4,000,000 immediately with the balance payable on 31 December 20X7. The formula was to be completed and delivered within 18 months. The credit risk rate associated with P&G was determined to be 6%.

In April 20X7, SDC delivered the formulas and samples of Scourge to P&G Industries. Additional testing costs incurred by SDC during 20X6 amounted to $540,000; in 20X7, $260,000.

Required:

1. When should revenue be recognized by SDC from its work on Scourge? Why?

2. Assume that the total costs of $7,300,000 actually incurred by SDC over the years 20X4 to 20X7 had been accurately estimated in 20X4. Determine the amount of revenue and expense that should be recognized each year from 20X4 to 20X7, assuming revenue is to be recognized:
   a. At the time the option is signed.
   b. At the time the option is exercised.
   c. At the time the formulas are delivered.

   Note that the $3,160,000 *research* costs must be expensed in all alternatives to comply with accounting standards for research costs. *Development* costs may be deferred if appropriate. Do not attempt journal entries—your solution should focus on SCI presentation.

★★★ **A6-7 Entries for Critical Events:** Maypole Industries imports goods from Taiwan and resells them to domestic Canadian markets. Maypole uses a perpetual inventory system. A typical transaction stream follows:

18	July	Purchased goods for resale for $456,000
24	August	Goods repackaged and ready for sale. Cost incurred, $60,000
10	September	Goods delivered to customer. Agreed-on price, $712,000
22	November	Customer paid

Required:

1. Prepare journal entries assuming the following critical events:
   a. Delivery to customer.
   b. Cash receipt.
   c. Customer agrees to be invoiced in August once the goods have been repackaged and are ready for sale and accepts title to the goods. However, the customer requests that the goods not be shipped until Maypole is given directions as to where and when to ship.

2. Explain the circumstances under which each of these methods would be appropriate.

★★ **A6-8 ASPE—Entries for Critical Events:** Dominum Corporation is a mining company that mines, produces, and markets teledine, a common mineral substance. The mineral is mined and produced in one large batch per year, as the mine is accessible only for a brief period in the summer due to severe weather conditions at the mine site. Dominum has an advance purchase contract with one customer that takes all of Dominum's output each year. The agreement allows the customer to return product that is defective for up to 60 days from the date of delivery. Transactions in 20X6 were:

30	August	186,000 tonnes of teledine ore removed from mine, at a cost of $4,300,000.
30	September	All of the ore refined to 115,000 tonnes of teledine, at a cost of $640,000. A deposit is receive from the customer for $1,350,000 (10% of the contract amount).
15	October	All of the teledine delivered to the customer, total contract price, $13,500,000. At this point, 50% of the contract amount is received. Dominum estimates, based on historical experience, that 7% of the goods might be returned.

25	November	Five percent of the teledine is returned for full credit; ore had been improperly refined and the teledine was unusable; customer given full credit for $675,000 and the unusable teledine scrapped. No other returns are anticipated.
30	November	Customer fully paid the final amount owing.

Required:

1. Assess the five steps for revenue recognition and determine when the performance obligation is complete.

2. Prepare all the journal entries to record these events assuming the critical event is at the point of delivery.

★★

A6-9 Unconditional Right of Return: In 20X5, Balla Shoe Corporation developed a new product, an electric shoe tree. To increase acceptance by retailers, Balla sold the product to retailers with an unconditional right of return, which expires on 1 February 20X6. Balla has estimated returns on the new product will be 10%. The following information is available regarding the product:

Sales—20X5	$360,000	
Cost of goods sold—20X5	240,000	
Returns 20X5	18,000	(cost, $12,000)
Returns—January 20X6	12,000	(cost, $8,000)

All sales are on credit. Cash collections related to the sales were $80,000 in 20X5. The remaining cash owing from the 20X5 sales was collected in February 20X6. Balla uses a perpetual inventory system. Assume all returned goods were in working condition and placed into inventory.

Required:

1. Assess the criteria to determine the point of the critical event.

2. Give journal entries for sales, returns, and collections related to the new product in 20X5 and 20X6. How much sales revenue should Balla recognize in 20X5?

★★★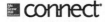

A6-10 Unconditional Right of Return: McLaughlin Novelty Corporation developed an unusual product, electric clip-on eyeglass wipers. McLaughlin felt the product would appeal to hikers, joggers, and cyclists who engaged in their sports in rainy climates. Because retail establishments were skeptical about the market appeal of the product, McLaughlin sold the product with a declining unconditional right of return for up to 10 months, with 10% of the right-of-return amount of the purchase expiring each month for 10 months. Thus, after the retailer had the product for one month, only 90% could be returned. After two months, only 80% could be returned, and after 10 months, the right of return was fully expired.

McLaughlin had no basis for estimating the amount of returns. Consistent with the terms McLaughlin offered its customers, all retailers paid cash when purchasing the clip-on eyeglass wipers but received cash refunds if goods were returned. McLaughlin had its first sales of the product in September 20X5. Sales for the remainder of the year and returns prior to 31 December 20X5, were as follows:

Month of Sale	Units Sold	Sales Price	Monthly Sales	Units Returned
September	10,000	$10	$100,000	2,500
October	12,000	10	120,000	1,000
November	15,000	12	180,000	1,000
December	11,000	12	132,000	0
Totals	48,000		$532,000	4,500

Each unit of product costs McLaughlin $6 to produce.

Required:

1. Show the journal entries to record the four months of sales transactions, including the deferral of gross margin. Prepare one summary entry.
2. Show a summary entry to record the returns in 20X5.
3. Compute the amount that McLaughlin can record as (realized) sales for 20X5. How much is the gross margin? Record the revenue recognition entry.
4. For the above transactions, total returns in all of 20X6 were as follows:

Month of Sale	Units Returned
September	1,000
October	2,000
November	2,500
December	4,000

Show the entries to record the returns in 20X6 and to record sales revenue and cost of sales from the 20X5 shipments of this product.

 A6-11 Licensing Fees: GoRight Inc. (GRI) is a franchisor who sells the rights to its trademark to franchisees. The franchisee pays an upfront, nonrefundable deposit of $1,000. GRI will then check the background and credentials of the franchisee prior to signing a licensing agreement. This takes only about four days to complete. If the franchisee passes this screening, then a contract is signed with GRI. The contract states that for consideration of $150,000, the franchisee will have the right to use the trademark for a period of three years. The three year period commences at the beginning of the month the contract is signed. At the end of the three-year period, the contract can be extended for another two years on payment of an agreed upon amount at that time. The franchisee may pay the $150,000 in three instalments starting on the date that the contract is signed. (The upfront fee is part of the $150,000 total.) In other words, on signing of the contract, $50,000 is due, and then another $50,000 is paid in the next 30 days and the final $50,000 payment is due in 60 days (from the date of signing the contract). Failure to pay the amounts on time will forfeit the franchisee's right to use the trademark and a refund of only 95% will be repaid. The 5% is kept to cover administrative costs incurred. In 20X4, GRI signed 20 contracts with various franchisees as detailed below. GRI has a December year-end.

	Number of Licence Agreements Signed	Amount Paid to Date $	Payments Not Yet Received
April 20X4	3	450,000	0
July 20X4	8	1,200,000	50,000 (note 1)
October 20X4	5	700,000	
November 20X4	4	400,000	200,000
Total	20	2,750,000	250,000

Note 1: All franchisees made their payments on time, except for one who owed his last payment of $50,000. The rights to this franchise were revoked in November 20X4.

Required:

1. Give the required entries for 20X4 summarized for the year.
2. Give the related balances that would be reported on the 20X4 SCIs and SFP.

 A6-12 ASPE Cost Recovery Method: The Trusett Merchandising Company has an inventory of obsolete products that it formerly stocked for sale. Efforts to dispose of this inventory by selling the products at low prices have not been successful. At the end of the prior year (20X4), the company reduced the value to a conservative estimate of net realizable value of $15,000. On 1 March 20X6, Trusett sold this entire inventory to Watson Trading Company for $21,000 cash. However, prior to sale, Trusett is concerned about collectability of the account and has decided to use the cost recovery method to record this transaction. Subsequent cash collections have been as follows: 20X6—$4,000; 20X7—$5,000; and the final payment in 20X8 was $8,000.

Required:
Give the 20X6, 20X7, and 20X8 entries for Trusett Merchandising Company to record revenues and cost of sales.

A6-13 IFRS—Customer Loyalty Program: Beaver Limited is a retail company that sells sporting goods. The company has a customer loyalty program that allows customers to earn points based on sales made. These points can be accumulated and used for future purchases. One customer loyalty point is awarded for every $1 of purchases. During March 20X4, the company recorded sales of $1,725,000 to customers who were accumulating points. The stand alone value of these goods sold was $1,725,000. Beaver has also determined that each point has a fair value of $0.017. The customer loyalty account had a balance of $870,000 at the beginning of March. During the month of March, customers used 1,200,000 points to purchase goods in the store.

Required:
Prepare the entries for the above transactions for the month of March 20X4.

A6-14 Warranty—Two Accounting Methods: On 30 April 20X2, Neuman Limited sells a product to a customer for $600,000. The product carries a one-year assurance warranty. Neuman management estimates that the probable cost of fulfilling the warranty will be $50,000. Between 1 May and 31 December 20X2, the actual warranty cost was $20,000. On 31 December 20X2, management decides that the remaining warranty provision (i.e., the additional warranty costs still to be incurred) will be no more than $13,000. Between 1 January and 30 April 20X3, the additional cost was $11,000.

Required:
1. Prepare the entries concerning the sale and the warranty for 30 April 20X2 through 30 April 20X3.
2. Assume instead that the warranty can be sold separately and is valued at 10% of the total contract value. Prepare the relevant journal entries for 30 April 20X2 through 30 April 20X3.

A6-15 Warranty—Two Accounting Methods: Chapnik Equipment Corporation (CEC) produced custom-designed machinery for a long-time customer. The direct cost to produce the machinery was $1.4 million. CEC sold the equipment to the customer for $2.0 million. The machinery was delivered, installed, and tested during September 20X1. At the end of September, the customer declared satisfaction with the machinery and signed a formal declaration of acceptance. CEC guaranteed the equipment for a full two years after acceptance, agreeing to correct any defects or operational problems that might occur before 30 September 20X3.

At the time of the sale, CEC management estimated that the eventual warranty cost would be no more than $100,000, since CEC had considerable experience with this general type of machinery. Subsequent experience was as follows:

a. Repair costs during the remainder of 20X1 amounted to $25,000.
b. At the end of 20X1, CEC managers decided that the total warranty cost might be as much as $130,000 by the end of the warranty period.
c. During 20X2, total warranty costs amounted to $40,000.
d. At the end of 20X2, management revised their estimate of remaining warranty cost to just $20,000.
e. Additional warranty costs during 20X3 (i.e., up to the end of the warranty period) were $15,000.

Required:

Prepare the entries concerning the sale and the warranty that the company would make from 30 September 20X1 through 30 September 20X3 under each of the following two assumptions:

1. Assume that warranty cost is in the form of an assurance.
2. Assume instead that CEC also sells the warranty as a separate service. CEC management estimates that of the $2 million total revenue, 6% should be allocated as revenue relating to the warranty. The warranty-related revenue will be recognized in earnings straight-line through the warranty period.

 A6-16 Multiple Deliverables: BigBoy Equipment Inc. sells heavy-duty forklift trucks. Model 217A has a stand-alone price of $140,000. BigBoy offers to sell the 217A inclusive of a three-year service contract for $180,000.

Required:

Prepare a journal entry to record the sale of one Model 217A forklift truck plus service contract for $180,000 assuming:

1. A comparable service contract is sold separately for $60,000. BigBoy uses the relative fair value method for multiple deliverables.
2. The service contract has a variable stand-alone value ranging from $30,000 to $70,000 and BigBoy uses the residual method.

 A6-17 Multiple Deliverables: Dominion Mobile Incorporated provides cell phone services. The company conducts a special sales campaign in which new subscribers will get a high-end cell phone for only $100 if they sign a 36-month contract that has a service fee of $100 per month. Thus, the total price of the cell phone plus 36 months of service is $3,700.

The company normally sells the phone for $1,000. Current subscribers pay $60 per month for comparable service but are not permitted to take advantage of the $100 cell phone offer.

Required:

Determine how a customer contract for $3,700 should be recognized.

★★ **A6-18 Multiple Deliverables:** Milbank Appliance Corporation (MAC) sells major appliances (such as refrigerators, stoves, etc.) at retail. MAC sells its top-line home refrigerator, the Zero-Line, for $7,500. The refrigerator comes with a one-year unconditional assurance warranty on all parts and labour except for the electronic control panel, which is limited to a 90-day warranty. This warranty has an expected cost of $250.

For an additional $500 at the time of the refrigerator purchase, the warranty on the control panel can be extended to one year. This warranty can be purchased only when the refrigerator is purchased new from a MAC-licensed dealer. It is not offered as a separate item by any other company. This is an assurance warranty.

As well, MAC offers a three-year extension to the basic one-year warranty, which includes annual servicing of the refrigerator. The cost is $1,250 if it is purchased along with the refrigerator. The extended warranty can also be purchased later (but prior to expiry of the basic warranty) for $1,500. The extended warranty can be purchased by owners of Zero-Line refrigerators from other dealers, provided that the customer can show dated proof of purchase (i.e., the original sales contract).

Required:

Explain how revenue should be recognized in each of the following situations. Use the relative fair value method. Be specific, with calculations.

a. MAC sells a refrigerator with a three-year extended warranty for $8,000.
b. For a total price of $9,000, MAC sells a refrigerator together with the control panel one-year extended warranty and a three-year extended warranty.

★★ **A6-19 IFRS—Biological Assets and Agricultural Produce:** Timber Resource Inc. is a forestry company. The company owns timber resources in northern Quebec. The company produces lumber from these resources. During 20X3, the company cut trees into logs with a fair market value of $600,000. The selling costs at the time of harvest were 5% of fair market value. At the end of the year, about 20% of these logs have not yet entered production. The 80% that have entered production required $175,000 of production costs to produce lumber into fixed cut lengths that are now available for sale to various customers. By the end of the year, 40% of the lumber was still on hand and ready for sale. There was no work-in-progress at the year-end. Fair value information for assets owned at the year-end is provided below:

	Timber	Logs	Lumber
Fair value at end of 20X2 (before selling costs)	$8,900,000	$110,000	$295,000
Fair value at end of 20X3 (before selling costs)	$9,350,000	$125,000	$310,000

Costs to sell are estimated to be 5% for timber, 5% for logs and 7% for lumber.

Required:

1. Prepare the journal entries to record the transactions during 20X3 as well as any entries needed to adjust year-end balances.
2. Show relevant balances in the SCI and SFP related to the transactions above.

★ **A6-20 IFRS—Biological Assets and Agricultural Produce:** The following list contains various products:

a. Yarn
b. Lumber
c. Sheep
d. Eggs
e. Trees
f. Frozen omelets
g. Wool
h. Chickens
i. Logs (felled trees)

Required:

1. In this list, identify those items that may qualify as biological asset, agricultural produce, and inventory. In addition match up the biological asset with its agricultural produce and its processed inventory. Prepare your answer using the following table:

Biological Asset	Agricultural Produce	Inventory

2. Explain how each of the three types of assets—biological assets, agricultural produce, and inventory—is measured at each reporting period.

★★ **A6-21 IFRS—Percentage-of-Completion Method:** Star Construction Corporation has a contract to construct a building for $10,950,000. The building is controlled by the customer throughout the term of the contract. Total costs to complete the building were originally estimated at $8,850,000. Construction commenced on 4 February 20X5. Actual costs were in line with estimated costs for 20X5 and 20X6. In 20X7, actual costs exceeded estimated costs by $150,000.

Total construction costs incurred in each year were as follows:

20X5	$2,700,000
20X6	$4,500,000
20X7	$1,800,000

Progress billings based on the amount of work completed were collected each year. Star Construction uses the percentage-of-completion method. The percentage-of-completion is based on costs incurred compared with estimated total costs of the project.

Required:

1. Calculate the revenues and gross profit for the construction project for each of the three years.

2. Prepare all of the journal entries for revenue recognition for each year until completion in 20X7.

(Source: [Adapted] © CGA-Canada. Reproduced with permission.)

★★   **A6-22 ASPE—Construction Contract:** Thrasher Construction Company was contracted to construct a building for $975,000. The building is owned by the customer throughout the contract period. The contract provides for progress payments. Thrasher's accounting year ends 31 December. Work began under the contract on 1 July 20X5, and was completed on 30 September 20X7. Construction activities are summarized below by year:

20X5   Construction costs incurred during the year, $180,000; estimated costs to complete, $630,000; progress billings during the year, $153,000; and collections, $140,000.

20X6   Construction costs incurred during the year, $450,000; estimated costs to complete, $190,000; progress billing during the year, $382,500; and collections, $380,000.

20X7   Construction costs incurred during the year, $195,000. Because the contract was completed, the remaining balance was billed and later collected in full per the contract.

Required:

1. Give Thrasher's journal entries to record these events. Assume that percentage-of-completion is measured by the ratio of costs incurred to date divided by total estimated construction costs.

2. Provide the balances that would be shown on the SCI and SFP for this contract for each year.

3. Now assume that the company uses the completed-contract basis for this construction contract. Prepare the journal entries required to record the events from 20X5 to 20X7. Also calculate the balances that would be shown on the SCI and SFP for this contract for each year.

★★   **A6-23 Construction Contract:** Buildit Corp. was contracted to construct a building for $1,600,000. The contract provided for progress payments. Buildit's accounting year ends 31 December. Work began under the contract on 1 March 20X3 and was completed on 30 November 20X5. Construction activities are summarized below by year:

20X3   Construction costs incurred during the year, $470,000; estimated costs to complete, $830,000; progress billings during the year, $380,000; and collections, $290,000.

20X4   Construction costs incurred during the year, $700,000; estimated costs to complete, $210,000; progress billing during the year, $990,000; and collections, $870,000.

20X5   Construction costs incurred during the year, $195,000. Because the contract was completed, the remaining balance was billed and later collected in full per the contract.

Required:

1. Give Buildit's journal entries to record these events. Assume that percentage-of-completion is measured by the ratio of costs incurred to date divided by total estimated construction costs.

2. Provide the balances that would appear on the SCI and SFP for this contract for each year.

★★ **A6-24 IFRS—Construction Contract, Revenue Change:** Catalina Construction Corporation signed a contract to build an apartment building for $5,600,000. The customer controls the building throughout the contract period. Construction began in October 20X4 and was scheduled to be completed in May 20X6. Catalina has a 31 December year-end. Data for the first two years of the contract were as follows:

(in thousands of dollars)	20X4	20X5
Costs incurred during year	$ 850	$2,900
Estimated additional costs to complete	4,200	900
Billings during year	700	2,900
Cash collections during year	650	2,600

Late in 20X5, the client made some design changes to the apartment layouts in the upper floors. After negotiations, Catalina agreed to a contract amendment that increased the total price to $6,400,000 and delayed the completion date until 31 October 20X6. Catalina estimated that the contract change would increase total costs by $600,000 (not included in the $900,000 "costs to complete" for 20X5 above).

Actual costs incurred during 20X6 were $1,650,000. The full remaining contract price was billed during 20X6. By the end of 20X6, the client had paid the full contract price except for the 10% holdback permitted by law for 90 days.

Required:

Prepare the journal entries for Catalina. Use costs incurred to date divided by total estimated construction costs to measure percentage complete. Round your estimate of revenue to the nearest thousand.

★★★ **A6-25 Construction Contract—Loss, Revenue Change:** Banks Construction Company was contracted to build an office block on a fixed-fee basis for $3,200,000. Construction began in September 20X4 and was scheduled to be completed in May 20X6. Banks has a 31 December year-end. Data related to the contract are summarized below:

(in thousands of dollars)	20X4	20X5	20X6
Initial estimated cost	$3,000		
Estimated additional costs to complete	2,500	$ 950	$ —
Costs incurred during year	600	1,850	850
Billings during year	450	1,400	1,350
Cash collections during year	400	1,200	1,600

Required:

1. Prepare the journal entries to record work on this contract. Use costs (in thousands) incurred to date divided by total estimated construction costs to measure percentage-of-completion. Round all percentages to the nearest whole number.
2. Prepare presentation of this contract on the statement of financial position and SCI for each of the three years.
3. Assume instead that in 20X5, Banks and the client agree to change orders that increase the total revenue from $3,200 to $3,600. For each of the three years, how would this change affect (a) the amounts shown on Banks' SCI and (b) the carrying value of inventory?

★★ **A6-26 Asset Exchanges—Five Situations:** Consider each of the following independent situations:

a. GYT Company exchanges a machine that cost $4,000 and has accumulated depreciation of $2,560 for a similar machine. GYT also receives $25 in the exchange. The fair market value of the old asset is $750. The fair market value of the new asset is $725. There is no commercial substance to the transaction.

b. FST Company exchanges a machine that cost $4,000 and has accumulated depreciation of $3,560 for a similar machine. FST also receives $25 in the exchange. The fair market value of the old asset is $750. The fair market value of the new asset is $725. There is no commercial substance to the transaction.

c. LKC Company pays $250 and exchanges a machine that cost $3,000 and has accumulated depreciation of $1,900 for a similar machine. The fair market value of the old asset is undeterminable. The fair market value of the new asset is $690. The transaction has commercial substance.

d. HRT Company pays $250 and exchanges a machine that cost $2,000 and has accumulated amortization of $1,400 for a similar machine. The fair market value of the old asset is $435. The fair market value of the new asset is $680. The transaction has commercial substance.

e. AML Company pays $500 and exchanges a machine that cost $9,000 and has accumulated depreciation of $8,400 for a similar machine. The fair market value of the new asset is $1,580. The transaction has commercial substance.

Required:
For each situation, determine:

1. The value at which the acquired asset will appear on the company's statement of financial position.
2. The amount of gain or loss that will be recorded on the company's statement of comprehensive income.

(Judy Cumby, adapted)

★★ **A6-27 Asset Exchanges—Four Situations:** Ricardo Heavy Hauling has some earth-moving equipment that cost $432,000; accumulated amortization is $288,000. Ricardo traded equipment with another construction company. The fair value of Ricardo's old equipment is estimated to be $225,000, and the fair value of the equipment being acquired is estimated to be $285,000. Four different possible scenarios are presented below:

a. The new equipment will perform essentially the same tasks as the old equipment. The estimate of the fair value of the new equipment is the more reliable of the two estimates. The exchange is a straight swap and no cash changes hands.

b. The new equipment has very different functions than the old equipment. The new equipment will permit Ricardo to attract new business that it had previously been unable to obtain. The fair value estimate of the new equipment is the more reliable of the two estimates. The exchange is a straight swap and no cash changes hands.

c. In addition to exchanging its old equipment, Ricardo pays $24,000 cash. The characteristics of Ricardo's operating cash flows will change as a result of the exchange. The fair value of the old equipment is the more reliable estimate.

d. Assume the same facts as in (c) above, except that the exchange will not significantly alter Ricardo's cash flows.

Required:
For each scenario, prepare the journal entry to record the exchange.

★★ **A6-28 ASPE—Asset Exchanges, Two Transactions:**

a. A large truck, which cost Company A $100,000 ($60,000 accumulated depreciation), has a market resale value of $70,000. The truck is traded to a dealer, plus a cash payment of $20,000, for a new truck that will perform essentially the same services as the old truck but will look a lot nicer to the customers. The new truck has a list price of $95,000, although discounts of 3% to 4% may be negotiable.

b. Rochester Shipping Company received a new ferry that has a normal purchase price of $1.30 million. In exchange, the company gave the vendor a parcel of land and a building located on the waterfront. The market value of the land and building is $1.15 million.

The land cost $300,000; the building cost $700,000 and is 30% depreciated. The vendor will use the land and building to operate a maintenance facility. The new ferry will enable Rochester Shipping to launch a new ferry service across Lake Ontario. The ferry was available because the buyer for whom it had been built went bankrupt and was unable to take delivery. The boat remained unsold for two years before Rochester was able to negotiate the exchange. Because the boat had been dormant for so long, it needed some upgrading and maintenance. Rochester agreed to pay for the necessary work, which was estimated to cost $350,000.

Required:
Prepare the journal entry to record each of these two independent transactions.

★★ **A6-29 SCF Impact:** XYZ Company had a variety of revenue transactions during the year. Below are the balances on the SFP related to its revenue transactions.

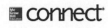

	Closing Balance 20X8 $	Closing Balance 20X9 $
Accounts receivable	675,000	890,000
Unearned revenue	128,000	172,000
Provision for warranties	24,000	35,000

Required:
Using the information in the table, indicate the line items that would appear on the SCF with respect to the related items and the amounts. The company uses the indirect method.

★★ **A6-30 Revenue and Expense Recognition:** Pewter Publishing Company (PPC) prepares and publishes a monthly newsletter for an industry in which potential circulation is limited. Because information provided by the newsletter is available only piecemeal from other sources and because no advertising is carried, the subscription price for the newsletter is relatively high. To increase circulation, PPC recently purchased a contact list from the industry's trade association for $110,000. PPC then engaged in a campaign to increase circulation. The campaign involved extensive use of long-distance telephone calls to industry members on the list who were not current subscribers. The telephone cost of the campaign was $38,000 plus salary payments to individuals who made the calls amounting to $51,000.

As a direct result of the campaign, new one-year subscriptions at $175 each generated revenue of $294,350. New three-year subscriptions at $450 each generated revenue of $225,450, and new five-year subscriptions at $625 each generated $187,500. Cancellations are rare, but when they occur, refunds are made on a half-rate basis (e.g., if a subscriber has yet to receive $100 worth of newsletters, $50 is refunded).

The subscription campaign was conducted during August 20X0. New subscriptions began with the October 20X0 issue of the monthly newsletter. The company's accounting year ends 31 December.

Required:
Identify the specific accounting issues involved in recognizing revenue and costs for PPC. Calculate the related assets, liabilities, revenue, and expenses that would be reported by the company for 20X0 on its SFP and SCI.

Adapted from: Copyright 1994–2000 by the American Institute of Certified Public Accountants, Inc. All rights reserved.

For more information on the resources available from McGraw-Hill Ryerson, go to www.mcgrawhill.ca/he/solutions.

CHAPTER 7

Financial Assets: Cash and Receivables

INTRODUCTION

One objective of financial reporting is to provide information to allow financial statement users to assess the financial position of an entity. Levels of current financial assets are critical when assessing the *liquidity* and viability of an operation. For example, consider Aastra Technologies Limited, a Canadian public company involved in developing and marketing products and systems for accessing communication networks, including the Internet. At the end of the 2011 fiscal year, the statement of financial position (SFP) reports $129,933 (thousand) in cash and $167,142 (thousand) in accounts receivable out of total assets of $567,525. That is, these two assets alone represent 52% of total assets. Correct measurement and presentation of these assets is important to the company's overall financial picture.

This chapter explores accounting principles for the recognition, measurement, and reporting of several critical financial assets: cash, accounts receivable, and notes receivable. This material is based on IFRS 9, effective in 2015, with early adoption permitted. Financial instruments that are investments are discussed in Chapter 11.

This chapter deals with both presentation issues and valuation. The financial instruments discussed in this chapter are initially recorded at fair value, which is the exchange amount. This is *book value,* or *cost.* The recorded value is maintained, subject to allowances that reduce various receivables for such factors as bad debts, cash discounts, and sales allowances. Receivables must reflect the present value of future cash flows. Accordingly, *amortized cost* is the valuation approach when the time value of money is a factor in valuation. In some circumstances, these financial assets might be remeasured to a (new) fair value at a later year-end date.

This chapter also examines the issue of when to *derecognize* accounts receivable as the result of a transaction called a *transfer*, which can be accounted for as a sale of the receivables or as a loan, depending on the terms of the transfer.

Most students will already be familiar with present value calculations. If practice is needed, a review is included on Connect.

FINANCIAL ASSETS

Financial assets comprise a wide range of financial statement elements, including cash, accounts/notes receivable, many investments, and derivatives. In this chapter, the discussion of financial assets is limited to cash and accounts/notes receivables. These elements are financial assets because they are either:

1. Cash; or

2. A contractual right to receive cash from another entity.

Cash obviously qualifies as a financial asset. Accounts/notes receivable represent the contractual right to receive cash. This cash claim has been fixed through a transaction, such as the sale of goods or services, or borrowing. In contrast, balances, such as inventories and fixed assets, are not financial assets, even though they eventually will be converted into cash because their cash value is not known with certainty in advance. The amount of cash to be obtained from nonfinancial assets will depend on future market conditions.

Financial assets include balances that represent assets to be received in a *determinable* amount of cash. An example of a *determinable* amount is a cash deposit held in foreign currency. The foreign currency cash deposit (or a foreign account receivable) represents a claim to cash, whose value in Canadian dollars is *determinable* from the current exchange rate.

Monetary Items Financial assets are, by their nature, **monetary items**. Cash is a monetary item and so are receivables because they represent a claim to cash *where the amount is fixed by contract or agreement.* Like financial assets, monetary items have two key aspects: cash must be involved, and the amount of cash must be fixed (or determinable) by contract or agreement.

Classification

Accounting standards require that companies classify each financial asset. All financial assets are initially recognized at the *transaction value,* which is *fair value* on that date. This is then the *cost* of the financial instrument. *Classification then determines the subsequent measurement of the financial asset.* The asset may be carried at cost, amortized cost, or the asset may have to be remeasured to fair value at each reporting date:[1]

Classification	Summarized Classification Criteria	Initial Valuation	Subsequent Valuation
1. Amortized cost	Two conditions must be met: 1. Objective is to hold financial asset to collect contractual cash flows; and 2. Contractual cash flows are solely principal and interest	Fair value, which is the transaction value and establishes the cost of the financial instrument; ADD Transaction costs, if any	Cost or Amortized cost
2. Fair value through profit or loss (FVTPL)	All other financial assets Assets that meet the amortized cost criteria can nonetheless be classified as FVTPL if: a. Loans and receivables will be sold in the short term; and b. Management wishes to avoid an accounting mismatch (related/ hedged financial instruments are FVTPL)	Fair value, which is the transaction value and establishes the cost of the financial instrument	Fair value; gains and losses from change in fair value in earnings

---

[1] Reflects content of IFRS 9, effective 2015, with early adoption allowed.

CASH AND CASH EQUIVALENTS

Classification of Cash Cash is measured at fair value in the FVTPL category, and if fair value changes, any gain or loss is included in earnings. Cash balances are not ordinarily subject to such fair value fluctuations, so this classification decision presents few challenges. If fair value were to change, however, because of foreign currency fluctuations and so on, any change in fair value is recorded as a gain or loss in earnings.

Cash Equivalents Cash equivalents are items that can readily be converted to cash. On the SFP, cash and cash equivalents are often lumped together, appropriately described.

Cash equivalents are limited to investments that are highly liquid and have little risk of price fluctuation—**money market instruments**—but not investments in common shares. Cash equivalents are usually classified as FVTPL.

The most common examples of cash equivalents are **treasury bills** (**T-bills**), **guaranteed investment certificates** (**GICs**), **commercial paper** (short-term notes receivable from other companies), and money market funds. To be classified as a *cash equivalent*, the term of these investments must be *short*—90 days maximum at the acquisition date—to minimize possible price fluctuations caused by interest rate changes or market conditions.

Asset-backed commercial paper Of course, the unexpected can happen. In the liquidity crunch that spiked in 2007, some short-term **asset-backed commercial paper (ABCP)** turned out to be highly risky because the issuers lacked liquid resources to repay. ABCP is a short-term investment instrument secured by assets, such as trade receivables or mortgage receivables. In this case, cash equivalents that should have been subject to very little price fluctuation turned out to be the cause of large losses.

Under a court-supervised restructuring program, pools of ABCP held as cash equivalents by many companies were replaced with notes receivable of varying maturities. The investor companies would then have to reclassify these investments as FVTPL financial instruments, now long-term investments, valued at their (lower) fair value. With hindsight, the risk of these investments was such that they should not have been classified as cash equivalents.

Overdrafts An **overdraft** is a negative bank account balance. Overdrafts occur when the dollar amount of cheques honoured by the bank exceeds the account balance. An overdraft is reported as a separate current liability on the SFP despite the fact that it may be classified with cash on the statement of cash flows (SCF). Netting with other cash accounts is not allowed on the SFP.

However, if a depositor overdraws an account but has positive balances in other accounts *with that same bank*, it is appropriate to net the negative and positive balances on the SFP as long as:

- The bank has the legal right to offset, which is usual; and
- The company *plans to settle the overdraft in this way*—by a transfer from one of the other accounts.

Accounts with different financial institutions may never be netted against each other, since they fail the first condition above.

Compensating Balances A **compensating balance,** or a *restricted balance*, is a minimum balance that must be maintained in a depositor's account as support for a separate loan borrowed by the depositor. Companies might consider such compensating balances as long-term assets and therefore not include them in the current cash account because they are not currently available for use. However, the practice is often to include these balances in cash and disclose the restrictions in notes to the financial statements. The same approach is used for any cash held offshore that has usage restrictions imposed by a foreign country; the amounts are typically included in cash and restrictions are disclosed.

Foreign Currency The Canadian dollar value of cash holdings in foreign currency fluctuates with changes in the relevant exchange rate. To arrive at the Canadian dollar equivalent, it is necessary to multiply the amount of foreign currency by the *current exchange rate.* Gains and losses are included in earnings.

For example, assume that DGF Group Limited has a U.S. bank account, with US$4,500 on deposit at year-end. The money was received as a result of a cash sale that took place when the exchange rate was US$1.00 = Cdn$1.07, and was recorded at a Canadian dollar amount of 4,815:

Cash, U.S. dollars [$4,500 × $1.07]	4,815	
Sales		4,815

At the end of the year, the exchange rate is US$1.00 = Cdn$0.95. The current Canadian dollar equivalency must be established:

Exchange loss	540	
Cash, U.S. dollars [$4,500 × ($0.95 − $1.07)]		540

Of course, foreign cash holdings could be converted to the current exchange rate every time the rate changes, but this is a lot of extra work, and valuation is usually important only at reporting dates. The cash is included on the SFP at the 31 December exchange rate, $0.95, or $4,275.

Internal Control Over Cash

The need to safeguard cash is crucial. Cash can be stolen in a lot of creative ways in addition to simply being physically picked up; for example, cheques can be issued to fictitious suppliers. The risk of theft is directly related to the ability of individuals to access the accounting system and obtain custody of cash. Firms address this problem through an **internal control system**, which is a planned organizational design meant to protect all assets and the integrity of the information system. A sound internal control system for cash increases the likelihood that the reported values for cash and cash equivalents are accurate and may be relied on by financial statement users.

A fundamental principle of internal control is *division of duties*—the person who handles cash must not also be responsible for the books. This is called "segregation of duties." The functions of cash handling and record keeping must be separated, so it will be difficult to embezzle cash unless two people agree together (or *collude*) to take the money. Internal control is built largely on the principle that dishonest collusion is significantly less likely than individual action.

ETHICAL ISSUES

If the bookkeeper handles cash, it is both possible and occasionally tempting for him or her to set cash aside for personal use and cover up the cash shortage by making a fictitious entry in the books. In a large enterprise, quite a large amount of cash (in personal terms) can go missing before anyone starts to notice it. Modest embezzlement may unfortunately go undetected for years. A robust internal control system will reduce any such opportunities.

Bank Reconciliation as Internal Control By comparing the bank account to the cash general ledger account, the company can ensure that the books are being kept accurately. The **bank reconciliation** provides the correct cash balance for the SFP and information for adjusting entries. A bank reconciliation analyzes the firm's cash account versus the bank's reported cash amount to ensure that transaction recording is complete and accurate. Since cash forms a part of so many transactions, *the accuracy of the cash account is often a good surrogate for the accuracy of other accounts.* Thus, the bank reconciliation is an important internal control. Of course, it is crucial that the individual who is in charge of cheques and/or deposits is not also in charge of the bank reconciliation—it would be too easy to cover up something. It is not appropriate for individuals to check their own work; there is no segregation of duties.

Bank Reconciliation Adjustments A bank reconciliation begins with the two cash balances (bank and book), lists the specific items that are different between those balances, and ends with the true cash balance, as follows:

Adjustments to the Bank Balance	Adjustments to the Book Balance (Adjustments to be Journalized)
Starting point: Cash balance per the bank statement	*Starting point:* Balance per the books
Add: Outstanding deposits	*Add:* Deposits recorded by the bank but not yet recorded by the company (e.g., customers that paid by direct deposit)
Deduct: Outstanding cheques	*Deduct:* Charges recorded by the bank but not yet recorded by the company (e.g., expenses paid by direct transfer and not yet recorded on the books, service charges, customers' cheques returned NSF [not sufficient funds])
Add or deduct: Bank errors in recording transactions	*Add or deduct:* Company errors in recording transactions
Ending point: Adjusted cash balance	*Ending point:* Adjusted cash balance

The adjustments to the book balance usually represent transactions processed by the bank that the company has not yet recorded or transactions that the company has improperly recorded. These items are journalized to establish the accuracy of the accounting records. Bank reconciliations are illustrated in the Appendix to this chapter.

Reporting Cash and cash equivalents are reported as the first asset on the SFP. Companies are required to show the components of cash, which they often do in conjunction with the statement of cash flows. Others provide a breakdown in the disclosure notes. For instance, Aastra Technologies Limited, in its 31 December 2011 financial statements, provides disclosure of the components of its cash account (in thousands):

Note 4 Cash and Cash Equivalents

	2011	2010	2010 (1 Jan.)
Cash	$ 70,667	$59,905	$ 39,426
Cash equivalents	59,266	30,799	74,170
	$129,933	$90,704	$113,596

Investments held, which mature in less than 90 days from the original purchase date, are classified as cash equivalents....Generally, cash equivalents are comprised of bankers' acceptances, term deposits, and treasury bills. There is no asset-backed commercial paper classified as cash and cash equivalents at 31 December 2011, 31 December 2010, or 1 January 2010. At 31 December 2011, 31 December 2010, and 1 January 2010, none of the company's cash was restricted.

Source: Aastra Technologies Limited, 2011 Annual Financial Statements, page 23, www.sedar.com, posted 8 March 2012.

CONCEPT REVIEW

1. What is the definition of a financial asset?

2. What are the two categories of financial assets that relate to cash and receivables, and how is each category valued?

3. What is the valuation problem for cash that is denominated in a foreign currency?

4. What is the basic principle of internal control?

5. Why is it necessary to perform a regular bank reconciliation?

ACCOUNTS RECEIVABLE

Classification of Accounts Receivable As financial assets, accounts and notes receivable are usually in the *amortized cost* category. They are initially recognized at the transaction value, which is fair value on the transaction date. They are subsequently measured at amortized cost (AC), subject to valuation allowances. They are classified as FVTPL if they were to be sold or were part of a hedging arrangement.

Accounts receivable are called *trade accounts receivable*, if they are amounts owed by customers for goods and services sold in the firm's normal course of business. These receivables are supported by sales invoices or other documents rather than by formal written promises to pay. *Notes receivable* are also amounts receivable but are usually supported by formal promissory notes. *Nontrade receivables* arise from many other sources, such as tax refunds, contracts, investments, finance receivables, sale of assets, and advances to employees. Receivables may be current or noncurrent assets, depending on the expected collection date.

Individual accounts receivable for customers with credit balances (from prepayments or overpayments) are reclassified and reported as liabilities on the SFP if they are material. Credit balances should not be netted against other accounts receivable, but netting is a common practice if the amounts are small (i.e., immaterial).

Valuation Allowances

The receivable balance is meant to be an approximation of the cash that will be collected. Say, a company has $2,000,000 in accounts receivable at the end of 20X8. This may not be the amount of money it will actually collect. Usually, adjustments have to be made at year-end to reduce receivables to *net realizable value*, for such things as:

- Cash discounts;
- Sales returns and allowances[2]; and
- Allowance for doubtful accounts.

Cash Discounts Companies frequently offer a cash discount, or sales discount, for payment received within a designated period. Cash discounts are used to increase sales, encourage early payment by the customer, and increase the likelihood of collection. Sales terms might be 2/10, n/30, which means that the customer is given a 2% cash discount if payment is made within 10 days from sale; otherwise, the full amount net of any returns or allowances is due in 30 days. Theoretically, the sale and the receivable should be recorded at the lowest cash price, or the net amount after deducting the discount. This would be $980 for a $1,000 sale, if the discount for prompt payment is 2%. In practice, though, sales are usually recorded gross

---

[2] Accounting for transactions with the right of return will be significantly different when revised IASB standards governing revenue recognition are adopted, likely in 2017. See the Appendix to Chapter 6.

because it is easier to relate the account receivable to the (gross) invoice if they are the same amount. The entry on sale, for the gross method is:

| Accounts receivable | 1,000 | |
| Sales revenue | | 1,000 |

The entry on collection is:

Cash	980	
Sales discounts (a contra account to sales)	20	
Accounts receivable		1,000

Under the gross method, if material cash discounts are expected to be taken on outstanding accounts receivable at year-end, an adjusting entry is required to *decrease net sales* and to *reduce net accounts receivable* to the estimated amount collectible. To illustrate, assume that the $2 million of accounts receivable mentioned above all have terms of 2/10, n/30, and are recorded gross. Management expects 60% of these accounts to be collected within the discount period. There is no balance in an allowance account. The adjusting entry on 31 December 20X8 is:

| Sales discounts [$2,000,000 × 2% × 60%] | 24,000 | |
| Allowance for sales discounts | | 24,000 |

The sales discounts account is a contra account to sales, and reduces sales to the net amount. The allowance for sales discounts account is a contra account to accounts receivable and reduces accounts receivable to the net cash value. If there had been a $3,000 credit balance in the allowance account prior to this entry, the entry would have been made for $21,000 ($24,000 − $3,000).

During 20X9, the allowance can then be used to absorb the discounts taken when payment is made. The following entry would be recorded, assuming that the estimates were correct:

Allowance for sales discounts	24,000	
Cash	1,176,000	
Accounts receivable [$2,000,000 × 60%]		1,200,000

Alternatively, and more commonly, the sales discounts account can be directly debited each time customers use discounts during the year, and the allowance can be adjusted up or down at the end of each reporting period.

Sales Returns and Allowances Return privileges are frequently part of a comprehensive marketing program required to maintain competitiveness. Sales returns and allowances are significant amounts in some industries, including retailing and book publishing. Of course, if returns are material and unestimable, sales revenue cannot be recorded until after the uncertainty is resolved. This issue was discussed in Chapter 6. This chapter deals with the more likely case, *estimable returns.*[3]

Sales returns occur when merchandise is returned by the customer; *sales allowances* occur when a company gives a price reduction to a customer who is not completely satisfied with

---

[3] This chapter is based on existing 2014 standards. Refer to the Appendix to Chapter 6 for a discussion of the accounting approach to sales contracts with the right of return that will prevail when revised revenue standards are implemented, likely in 2017.

purchased merchandise but does not actually return it. For example, if a sale of $10,000 (2/10, n/30) is recorded, then an allowance of $2,000 is granted, and finally the customer pays within the discount period, the sequence of entries would be as follows:

| Accounts receivable | 10,000 | |
| Sales revenue | | 10,000 |

| Sales returns and allowances (a contra account to sales) | 2,000 | |
| Accounts receivable | | 2,000 |

Cash [$8,000 × 98%]	7,840	
Sales discounts [$8,000 × 2%]	160	
Accounts receivable		8,000

At the end of the year, the problem again is to reduce recorded receivables to their probable cash flow or net realizable value, which is net of returns. The company must estimate and recognize the returns and allowances expected for the accounts receivable outstanding at the end of 20X8. Assume that total estimated sales returns and allowances relating to the closing receivables balance is $9,000, and there is no balance in the allowance for sales returns account. The company records an adjusting entry on 31 December 20X8:

| Sales returns and allowances | 9,000 | |
| Allowance for sales returns and allowances | | 9,000 |

If there had been a $5,000 credit balance in the allowance account prior to this entry, the entry would have been made for $4,000 ($9,000 – $5,000). Remember that the sales returns and allowances account is a contra account to sales and the allowance is a contra account to accounts receivable.

When accounts receivable that arose in 20X8 are reduced in 20X9 because of returns, the reduction in accounts receivable can be charged to the allowance account. It is usually easier, though, to charge the reduction directly to the sales returns and allowances account and adjust the balance in the allowance account at the end of each reporting period.

Allowance for Doubtful Accounts When sales are on account, some amount of uncollectible receivables is generally inevitable. Firms attempt to develop a credit policy that is neither too conservative (leading to excessive lost sales) nor too liberal (leading to excessive uncollectible accounts). Past records of payment and the financial position of customers are key factors to consider.

If uncollectible receivables are both likely and estimable, an amount of uncollectible accounts must be recognized so that accounts receivable and earnings are not overstated. This is a form of asset valuation that is a common theme in financial reporting: Assets may not be overvalued. Because accounting recognition criteria require companies to anticipate a writedown before actually giving up on a particular account, the writedown is made to an allowance account, called the **allowance for doubtful accounts**, or the *allowance for uncollectible accounts*. This allowance is a contra account to accounts receivable that represents the portion of outstanding receivables whose collection is doubtful. Estimated uncollectibles are recorded in bad debt expense, an operating expense usually classified as a selling expense.

For example, if this company estimates that $120,000 of the $2,000,000 in receivables will not be collected, and the existing credit balance in the allowance account is $12,000, the adjusting entry is as follows:

Bad debt expense	108,000	
Allowance for doubtful accounts		
[$120,000 − $12,000]		108,000

Available information This estimate of uncollectible amounts is made at the end of the reporting period but takes into consideration *all facts known at the date of the review.* For example, if the company became aware in January that a customer who owed money was in financial distress, the allowance established for the 31 December accounts receivable would include the customer's likely uncollectible balance. The allowance is estimated in January, when available information sheds light on the 31 December status of the customer. This is an example of a *subsequent event* that must be recorded in the current year.

Write-off and Recovery Two other events must be considered:

1. The write-off of a specific receivable; and

2. The collection of an account previously written off.

The adjusting entry for bad debt expense creates the allowance for doubtful accounts for future uncollectible accounts. When specific accounts are determined to be uncollectible, they are removed from the accounts receivable and that part of the allowance is no longer needed. The bad debt estimation entry had previously recognized the estimated economic effect of future uncollectible accounts. Thus, write-offs of specific accounts do not further reduce net assets unless they exceed the estimate.

For example, the following entry is recorded by a company deciding not to pursue collection of R. Knox's $1,000 account:

| Allowance for doubtful accounts | 1,000 | |
| Accounts receivable, R. Knox | | 1,000 |

This write-off entry affects neither earnings nor the net amount of accounts receivable outstanding. The write-off entry changes only the components of net accounts receivable, not the net amount itself (amounts assumed):

	Before Knox Write-Off	After Knox Write-Off
Accounts receivable	2,000,000	$1,999,000
Allowance for doubtful accounts	(120,000)	(119,000)
Net accounts receivable	$1,880,000	$1,880,000

When amounts are received on account after a write-off, the write-off entry is reversed to reinstate the receivable and cash collection is recorded. Assume that R. Knox is able to pay $600 on account some time after the above write-off entry was recorded, but no additional payment is expected. These entries are required:

Accounts receivable, R. Knox	600	
Allowance for doubtful accounts		600
Cash	600	
Accounts receivable, R. Knox		600

The net effect of these two entries is to increase cash and *reinstate* the allowance for doubtful accounts to the extent of the cash recovery. The reason for reinstating the allowance is that since $600 cash was collected, the writedown of $1,000 was excessive; the writedown should have been for only $400. The adjustment of $600 to the allowance will have a direct (or indirect) effect on the amount of bad debt expense recorded in the next year.

Reporting The SFP presentation of net accounts receivable provides focus on the realizable cash amount. In our example, the net balance is $2,000,000 less the $24,000 allowance for cash discounts, less the $9,000 allowance for sales returns, and less the $120,000 allowance for doubtful accounts. This is reported as follows:

Accounts receivable, net	$1,847,000

While allowances do not have to be shown separately on the SFP, the allowance for doubtful accounts, in particular, must be included in the disclosure notes. The itemized changes in the allowance from the beginning to the end of the year are also disclosed.

Aastra Technologies Limited reports the following information in its 2011 annual report (in thousands):

Note 6 Trade and Other Receivables

	2011	2010	2010 (1 Jan.)
Trade receivables	$158,348	$176,560	$174,875
Allowance for doubtful accounts	(7,139)	(9,515)	(11,623)
Net trade receivables	151,209	167,045	163,252
Other receivables	15,933	16,932	11,830
	$167,142	$183,977	$175,082

Source: Aastra Technologies Limited, 2011 Annual Financial Statements, page 25, posted 8 March 2012.

Note that the 2011 allowance is 4.5% of 2011 trade receivables, which are shown net in the SFP but gross in the disclosure notes. The allowance was 5.3% of trade receivables in 2010 and 6.6% the prior year. Additional disclosure shows the change in the allowance for doubtful accounts, showing that bad debt expense was $1,043 (thousand) in 2011, write-offs were $918 (thousand), and there were recoveries and reversals.

The movement in the allowance for impairment in respect of trade receivables during the year was as follows:

	2011	2010
Balance, 1 January	$9,515	$11,623
Impairment loss recognized	1,043	1,437
Receivables written off during the year as uncollectible	(918)	(1,478)
Reversal of impairment	(1,016)	(597)
Recovered amount	(1,443)	(411)
Foreign exchange translation differences	(42)	(1,059)
Balance, 31 December	$7,139	$ 9,515

Source: Aastra Technologies Limited, 2011 Annual Financial Statements, page 35, posted 8 March 2012.

Valuation of the Allowance for Doubtful Accounts

The previous section illustrated that when an allowance for doubtful accounts is established, the entry increases bad debt expense and increases the allowance. There are two approaches to determining the amount of the entry: the *aging method* and the *credit sales method*.

Aging method This approach begins with the reported value of accounts receivable. Accounts receivable are examined item by item, *or* aged, *or* analyzed statistically. This will determine net realizable value and the value of an appropriate allowance. The allowance is then increased *to* this amount, *which involves adjusting for the opening balance*. This is called the **aging method,** because accounts receivable are usually aged to provide a basis for the allowance.

Credit sales method This approach begins with the recorded credit sales amount. Bad debt experience over time is correlated to credit sales to establish a percentage of sales that is normally uncollectible. The allowance is then increased *by* this amount, *irrespective of the opening balance*. This is called the **credit sales method** because bad debts are linked to credit sales.

Exhibit 7-1 presents background information for several examples. The pre-adjustment $500 *debit* balance in Rally's allowance account does not necessarily indicate that past estimates of bad debt losses were too low, although this is one explanation. Alternatively, it is possible that some receivables originating in 20X2 were written off and the debit balance does not yet reflect the estimate for bad debts based on 20X2 sales.

Aging Method This method emphasizes the net realizable value of accounts receivable and uses historical data to estimate the percentage of accounts receivable expected to become

---

EXHIBIT 7-1

RALLY COMPANY

Information for Bad Debt Estimation Examples

1 January 20X2 balances:	
Accounts receivable (debit)	$101,300
Allowance for doubtful accounts (credit)	3,300
Transactions during 20X2:	
Credit sales	500,000
Cash sales	700,000
Collections on accounts receivable	420,000
Accounts written off as uncollectible during 20X2	3,800

After posting entries for sales, collections, and write-offs, accounts receivable and the allowance for doubtful accounts appear as follows:

Accounts Receivable

1 Jan. 20X2 balance	101,300	Collections	420,000
Credit sales	500,000	Write-offs	3,800
31 Dec. 20X2 balance	177,500		

Allowance for Doubtful Accounts

Write-offs	3,800	1 Jan. 20X2 balance	3,300
31 Dec. 20X2 balance *before* adjustments	500		

uncollectible. Exhibit 7-2 illustrates Rally's aging schedule and the application of the collection loss percentages. The $177,500 receivable balance is divided into four age classifications with a collection loss percentage applied to each age category. This percentage is usually based on past experience. Rally's collection loss *percentages* (logically) increase with the age of the accounts because when accounts are collected, good accounts are removed from each category, and what is left is more likely to be uncollectible.

The computation in Exhibit 7-2 indicates that the allowance account should be increased to $5,690 (credit). Because the allowance balance is $500 (debit) before adjustment, the entry is for $6,190, yielding an ending $5,690 balance.

Bad debt expense [$5,690 + $500]	6,190	
Allowance for doubtful accounts		6,190

Had the allowance balance been a $500 credit before adjustment, bad debt expense would have been $5,190 ($5,690 – $500). Since the allowance is $5,690, net accounts receivable will be shown on the SFP at $171,810 ($177,500 – $5,690).

Total accounts receivable Aging may be more cumbersome than is warranted, and a composite rate, *based on the accounts receivable total,* may be used. Assume that experience leads Rally Company (see Exhibit 7-1) to use a single 3% composite rate. Therefore, the required ending allowance credit balance is $5,325 (3% × $177,500). The allowance account currently has a $500 debit balance, so the adjusting entry increases the allowance account to $5,325 through an entry for $5,825 ($5,325 + $500).

Bad debt expense [$5,325 + $500]	5,825	
Allowance for doubtful accounts		5,825

EXHIBIT 7-2

RALLY COMPANY

Accounts Receivable Aging Schedule

31 December 20X2

Customer Account	Balance 31 Dec. 20X2	Current	31–60 days	61–90 days	Over 90 days
Denk	$ 500	$ 400	$ 100		
Evans	900	900			
Field	1,650		1,350	$ 300	
Harris	90			30	$ 60
King	800	700	60	40	
Zabot	250	250			
Total	$177,500	$110,000	$31,000	$29,500	$7,000
Percent estimated uncollectible		0.2%	1.0%	8.0%	40.0%
Amount estimated uncollectible		$ 220	$ 310	$ 2,360	$2,800

Total amount to include in allowance: $220 + $310 + $2,360 + $2,800 = $5,690

The estimated net realizable value of accounts receivable is $172,175 ($177,500 − $5,325) in this case, a reasonable approximation.

Credit Sales Method This method emphasizes relationships between credit sales and bad debt expense. The average percentage relationship between actual bad debt losses and net credit sales is established on the basis of experience. The percentage must be updated periodically to approximate the rate of actual write-offs. Once established, the percentage is applied to a period's net credit sales to determine bad debt expense.

Assume that in the past, 1.2% of Rally's credit sales had not been collected. Barring changes in Rally's credit policies or major changes in the economy, Rally expects this rate to continue. Under this method, the following is the required 20X2 adjusting entry, which increases the allowance by a percentage of credit sales.

Bad debt expense [$500,000 × 1.2%]	6,000	
Allowance for doubtful accounts		6,000

After this entry is posted, the balance in the allowance account is $5,500 ($6,000 from the adjusting entry less the prior $500 debit balance). *The credit sales method directly computes bad debt expense without regard to the prior balance in the allowance account.* Rally would report $172,000 ($177,500 − $5,500) of net accounts receivable in the 20X2 SFP.

Evaluation of Methods Either method of estimation is acceptable for financial reporting as long as the resulting allowance is reasonable. Statistical support for the rates used to establish the allowance under either method helps establish this reasonableness.

The credit sales and aging methods may be used together. Each is used to validate the other, although only one may be used in the accounts. For interim financial statements, many companies base monthly or quarterly adjusting entries on the credit sales method because of its simplicity. At the end of the year, they may age their accounts receivable to check the reasonableness of the allowance balance. It is also fairly standard to evaluate the allowance with reference to major accounts receivable in various categories, in conjunction with the year-end audit or review. This evaluation uses all known facts at the date of the review including subsequent payments and defaults.

The general condition of the economy, the economic health of specific customers, and the seller's credit policy and collection effort affect the rate of account write-offs. Over time, this rate changes, necessitating adjustment to the percentages applied to credit sales or aged receivables. If the unused balance in allowance for doubtful accounts is found to increase each year, the estimate of uncollectibles can be decreased to reflect actual experience. Alternatively, if the allowance is inadequate, future estimates will increase.

Direct Write-off of Uncollectible Accounts

In some limited circumstances, receivables are written off directly, with no allowance used. No adjusting entry is made at the end of an accounting period under the direct write-off method. Instead, bad debt expense is recognized only when an account is acknowledged to be finally uncollectible. The entry for the direct write-off of a $2,000 account receivable from M. Lynx is as follows:

Bad debt expense	2,000	
Accounts receivable, M. Lynx		2,000

Normally, bad debts are estimated, and an allowance is set up. Use of the direct write-off method creates several unavoidable problems:

- Prior to this entry, accounts receivable are reported on the SFP at a value higher than their net realizable value because it is virtually certain that not all receivables are collectible.

- The write-off is often recorded in a different year from the year of the original sale that created the account receivable, overstating net earnings. At the extreme, if bad debts are material and inestimable, revenue cannot be recognized until the uncertainty is cleared up—usually on collection.
- Direct write-off opens the potential for profit manipulation by arbitrary selection of the year in which to record the write-off.

For these reasons, the direct write-off method is not normally appropriate. Only *new operations with no basis to estimate bad debts*, or those with *immaterial bad debts*, may use the direct write-off method.

FVTPL Classification

Various receivables may sometimes be classified as FVTPL financial instruments. If this is the case, they are valued at fair value at reporting dates after initial recognition. Specifically, if the receivables are to be sold to a third party (see the section on transfers of receivables later in the chapter), then they *must* be classified as FVTPL. In other circumstances, management may designate certain loans and receivables as FVTPL. This might be appropriate, for example, if various hedging strategies were in place, and management wished to have both the hedged asset and the hedged liability in the same category for valuation purposes. When an asset is carried at fair value, fair value is remeasured at reporting dates, and gains and losses are recorded in earnings.

Speeding Cash Flow from Sales

Credit Card Transactions At one point in time, many retail stores offered credit to customers—in fact, some built a business primarily on offering credit (e.g., consider People's Credit Jewellers, now usually just called People's). Now, most retailers prefer to accept third-party credit cards and receive their money upfront, letting the customers owe the credit card company. Retailers are charged a fee by the credit card company, which is a percentage of the total sale but prefer this arrangement because they avoid bad debts, there is no delay in receiving cash, and they hope that customers will spend more when they can charge their purchases. There are not many cash-only businesses these days. Retail customers expect to be able to use credit cards.

Other retailers have expanded their credit-granting operations into separate credit card companies. These operations earn profits by charging interest on overdue accounts. Their largest expenses are the cost of funds (interest) and bad debts.

Assume that a merchant has $2,000 in credit card sales. The credit card company deducts a commission for its services and the money is electronically transferred. Assuming that the fee is 2%, the appropriate entry is as follows:

Cash	1,960	
Credit card fees expense [$2,000 × 2%]	40	
Sales		2,000

The merchant does not always receive the cash immediately. Sometimes, for low-volume credit card sales, the merchant must accumulate credit card sales in batches. These documents are deposited with a bank acting as agent for the credit card company. The company receives its money by direct deposit after the request is reviewed and processed.

Debit Card Transactions Most merchants accept debit cards. The primary difference between a debit card and a credit card is from the point of view of the customer: A debit card will remove the transaction amount immediately from the customer's bank account, while a credit card is paid when due. The merchant has to go through the same motions for debit cards as with credit cards: An agreement must be negotiated with the sponsoring financial institution for a fee (again a percentage of the transaction amount) and payment terms. All transactions are authorized through automated point-of-sale systems, and the merchant receives the cash immediately through direct deposit.

Loans Secured by Accounts Receivables If a company has a $100,000 account receivable from a creditworthy customer that will not pay for 45 days, how can the company get cash sooner? One alternative is to encourage the customer to pay sooner, and a variety of policies are usually explored to speed collection. Then what? One common course of action is to go to a financial institution and borrow money using the account receivable as collateral.

This is not very complicated on the books: A loan is recorded, and interest expense is accrued as time passes. When the account is collected, the financial institution is repaid. Assets pledged as collateral are disclosed in the financial statements. Of course, it is less common to make credit arrangements for one receivable at a time: The overall balance of accounts receivable, and usually inventory, too, are used to secure working capital loans. These current loans payable are a relatively permanent part of the capital structure for most companies.

CONCEPT REVIEW

1. Why is it necessary to establish an allowance for doubtful accounts?
2. What other allowances, in addition to doubtful accounts, might be necessary to value accounts receivable correctly?
3. What is the purpose of an aging schedule?
4. Name two ways to speed collection of sales revenue.

TRANSFER OF RECEIVABLES

Derecognition of accounts receivable simply means that the accounts are taken off the SFP. This automatically happens when cash is collected because the company has no further right to cash flow from the contract. However, derecognition can be far more complex.

Accounts receivable can be *transferred* to another party to speed cash flow. One example of a transfer is *factoring,* where individual accounts receivable are passed over to a financial institution, which then collects from the customer. This is a common business arrangement in certain industries. A transfer might be a far more complex transaction, where accounts receivable are bundled together and sold as a portfolio to a financial institution subject to certain guarantees and administrative functions. This is also called a **securitization**.

Agreements to transfer receivables are made either:

- on a **notification basis**—customers are directed to remit to the new party holding the receivables, the finance company, or
- on a **non-notification basis**—customers continue to remit to the original seller, which then, in turn, remits to the finance company.

Receivables can be transferred with recourse or without recourse. **Recourse** means that the finance company can come back to the company that sold the account receivable for payment if the account turns out to be uncollectible. Recourse arrangements often allow the company to replace defaulted receivables with "good ones" in the event of default.

Alternative Accounting Treatments A transfer of accounts receivable may be recorded as a sale or a borrowing, depending on the terms of the transfer, as we will see below. The two accounting alternatives are described as follows:

1. *A sale/derecognition.* The accounts receivable come off the books of the selling company and a financing fee is recognized. This represents *derecognition* of the accounts receivable.

2. *A borrowing.* The accounts receivable are left on the books of the selling company, and the amount received from the finance company is recorded as a loan until the customer actually pays. Payment by the customer triggers derecognition of the account receivable and repayment of the loan.

To illustrate a transfer recorded as a sale, consider the following case. Largo Incorporated (the **transferor**), now has a large volume of accounts receivable on its books. Largo sells $200,000 of its accounts receivable on 15 August 20X2. The buyer is a finance company (the **transferee**). The finance company charges a 12% financing fee. The entry to record the transfer as a *sale,* which *derecognizes* the accounts receivable, is:

Largo Incorporated			Finance Company		
Cash	176,000*		Accounts receivable	200,000	
Finance expense	24,000**		Deferred financing		
Accounts receivable		200,000	revenue***		24,000
			Cash		176,000

*$200,000 − (12% × $200,000)
**12% × $200,000; expensed immediately
***Deferred and recognized in earnings over the collection period.

This looks relatively straightforward. Accounts receivable can be sold, like any other asset! Now, what if an identical transaction was recorded as a *borrowing*?

Largo Incorporated			Finance Company		
Cash	176,000		Note receivable	200,000	
Discount on note payable	24,000		Discount on note		
Note payable		200,000	receivable*		24,000
			Cash		176,000

*Recognized in earnings as time passes.

Note that the accounts receivable stay on Largo's books and are joined by a loan. The discount on the loan is amortized to finance/interest expense and revenue over the life of the note. This transfer was on a non-notification basis. When the receivables are collected by Largo, the money is remitted to the finance company, and the note is repaid:

Largo Incorporated			Finance Company		
Cash	200,000				
Accounts receivable		200,000			
Notes payable	200,000		Cash	200,000	
Cash		200,000	Notes receivable		200,000
Finance expense*	24,000		Discount on notes		
Discount on notes			receivable	24,000	
payable		24,000	Finance revenue*		24,000

*Recognized in earnings as time passes.

Evaluation The sale/derecognition alternative effectively uses a journal entry to *net off* the loan against the assets being financed, with the difference recorded as an expense. That is, the receivables come off the books, the loan never goes on the books, and as a result, both assets and liabilities are lower. The SFP may suggest a different business model—fewer receivables and less debt—than really exists. Certain key financial ratios, such as debt/equity, the current ratio, and return on assets, would also be affected. Furthermore, an analyst attempting to determine the period of time between when inventory is purchased and cash collected from customers (sometimes called the *cash-to-cash cycle*) might be misled. As a result, many analysts use note disclosure information on recorded transfers to reinstate transferred accounts receivable and recognize related notes payable before performing ratio analysis, although this is difficult to do accurately. Chapter 22 will give you a taste of these kinds of adjustments.

ETHICAL ISSUES

The sale/derecognition alternative may reflect genuine business realities. Risk (of delayed collection or noncollection) may be appropriately transferred or shared, and the core business activities are all that remains. On the other hand, derecognition may be an attempt to portray the business cycle in a more favourable light for investors or creditors. Derecognition is appropriate only when it reflects economic reality.

Derecognition has been subject to significant scrutiny in financial markets because many financial institutions, especially in the United States, transferred and derecognized large portfolios of mortgage receivables. When residential real estate markets in the United States crumbled during the period between 2006 and 2008, these mortgage receivables had high default rates. Various legislative initiatives made *the transferor* assume responsibility for losses in some cases despite contractual terms to the contrary. Thus, the risks of receivables that had been derecognized came back to the transferor. In other cases, the transferee was significantly destabilized because of the transfers.

Criteria for Classification The criteria for establishing whether a transfer qualifies for derecognition have changed several times over the last decade and are still under review. The most recent set of standards makes it more difficult for a transfer to qualify for derecognition, and thus derecognition will become less commonly recorded. Borrowing treatment will prevail. The challenge for standard setters is that the terms of transfer contracts are both ingenious and aggressive and are often structured to allow sale/derecognition treatment.

Classification is assessed at the level of the consolidated entity. That is, before making any accounting policy decisions, all subsidiaries and special purpose entities (SPEs) (see section below) must be added in, and then only transfers that go *outside the complete economic entity* are considered. Furthermore, a decision has to be made as to whether the criteria are applied to all or part of a financial asset. Then, derecognition would be allowed if and only if *BOTH the following tests are met*:

Test 1: The account receivable is transferred
The account receivable is considered to be transferred if:

1. *The rights to the cash flows from the asset have been completely transferred.* This is the simplest case—a clean sale, and the transferee (the finance company) has the right to all cash flows and accepts all the risks. The transferor (the company, or vendor) is no longer involved in any way. Since the finance company would expect to be compensated for accepting such risk, a transfer that met this condition would be expensive for the company.

2. *The transferor (the company, or vendor) retains the contractual rights to the cash flows but assumes a contractual obligation to pay the cash flows to the transferee (the finance company).* In this contractual obligation, the terms must represent a 'real" transfer of the original account receivable. The terms must require that:

   a. There is no obligation to pay the finance company unless cash is actually received from the accounts receivable,

   and

   b. The company is not permitted to use the original accounts receivable for collateral in another transaction or sell the accounts receivable to another party, *and*

c. The cash flows from the original account receivable must be passed on to the finance company without material delay.

Test 2: The risks and rewards of ownership are passed to another party

The risks and rewards of ownership are considered to be passed to another party if:

1. The company's exposure to variability in the amounts and timing of cash flow are different before versus after the transfer; and

2. If transfer of risks and rewards is not clear-cut, then the company must assess control over the receivables; if control has not been retained, then this is an indication that risks and rewards have passed. For example, if the receivables can be resold by the transferee without the consent of the transferor, then derecognition is appropriate because the transferor has no effective control over the receivables and the risks and rewards of ownership have been passed to the transferee.

Clearly, these two tests are highly detailed and quite restrictive. This will limit the cases for which a transfer can be recorded as a sale.

Examples The complexity of these arrangements, with their extensive call and put options, makes accounting in this area very specialized. This discussion only scratches the surface. Two examples follow.

Case 1 *Transfer recorded as a sale/derecognition.* Assume that Largo sells $200,000 of accounts receivable to a finance company with no recourse on 15 August 20X2. The parties agree that uncollectible accounts will amount to $3,000; that is, the transferee is expecting to be able to collect only $197,000 of accounts receivable. If loan losses are higher or lower, the fact that there is no recourse to Largo means that the transferee will have losses or gains. The negotiated $3,000 amount is already in the allowance for doubtful accounts of Largo. The financing fee is 15%.

Assume that conditions are met to record this transfer as a sale/derecognition, and the accounts receivable will be derecognized. That is, there has been a transfer (Test 1) and the risk and rewards of ownership have passed (Test 2). The difference between the book value of receivables transferred and cash received from the finance company is recognized immediately as an expense.

Cash {$200,000 − $3,000 − [15% ×		
($200,000 − $3,000)]}	167,450	
Allowance for doubtful accounts*	3,000	
Finance expense [15% × ($200,000 − $3,000)]	29,550	
Accounts receivable		200,000

*Debit to bad debt expense if not already part of allowance estimate.

Largo receives $197,000, the net "good" receivables balance, less the (hefty) $29,550 financing fee on $197,000. The allowance for doubtful accounts is reduced.

Case 2 *Transfer recorded as a borrowing.* In a transfer recorded as a borrowing, the receivables stay on the books, and a loan is recorded. The transferor recognizes the difference between the assets received from the finance company and the book value of the receivables as interest *over the term of the loan*. This is in contrast to the sale/derecognition example, in which the financing fee was immediately recognized as an expense. Assume the same facts as Case 1, except that Largo accepts recourse and also retains the option to repurchase the receivables. This means that Largo has not transferred the risks and rewards of ownership, and fails Test 2. The transaction is recorded as a borrowing as follows:

Cash {$200,000 − $3,000 − [15% × ($200,000 − $3,000)]}	167,450	
Discount on payable to finance company [15% × ($200,000 − $3,000)]	29,550	
Payable to finance company		197,000

The discount account is a contra account to the payable to finance company account and represents the total interest expense to Largo. The discount account is amortized as interest expense over the loan term using the effective interest method. Largo records sales adjustments, such as sales discounts and returns, as they occur and reduces the receivable from the customer and payable to the finance company as customers remit cash. No adjustment is made for bad debts because the allowance is already appropriate. Write-offs would be recorded when the facts dictate. At the end of the arrangement, Largo must pay any outstanding balance on the payable, whether or not customers have remitted on time.

It is worth noting that the payable to the finance company must be shown as a current liability on the SFP and may *not* be netted with the related accounts receivable. Netting is appropriate only when there is a legal right to net, *and* intent to net. While intent is present in this case, there is no legal right to net, and the balances must be shown as the separate elements they really are.

Allowance for Bad Debts Review the entry for Case 1 again, and note that the allowance for bad debts was debited because of the $3,000 of problematic accounts transferred. *If the allowance was inadequate, or did not include any provision for these accounts, bad debt expense might be debited.* Similarly, when the transaction is recorded as a loan, there might be an additional allowance of $3,000 set up, with a corresponding debit to bad debt expense, if the allowance were deemed inadequate at this time. However, this decision to acknowledge additional bad debt expense need not be part of the transfer transaction. The adequacy of the allowance is reviewed regularly in the reporting cycle, based on aging or credit sales, and transfer of accounts receivable does not have to disturb this routine. Alternatively, some companies may choose to record some bad debt expense as needed when accounts are transferred.

Disclosure Companies are required to disclose information to allow financial statement users to understand the relationship between transferred financial assets that are still on the SFP and the related liabilities. In addition, information must be provided to assess the nature and risks associated with derecognized financial assets. An example of disclosure of transfer of accounts might appear as follows:

In the 2012 fiscal year, the Company completed a new trade accounts receivable securitization agreement with a financial institution that requires the sale of trade accounts receivable be recorded as a sale from an accounting perspective and accordingly trade accounts receivable sold under these agreements are derecognized on the consolidated statement of financial position at 31 December 2013 and 2012. Under these agreements, The Company retains a very limited recourse obligation for delinquent accounts receivable. The agreements expire in 2015.

At 31 December 2013, trade accounts receivable under these agreements amounted to $508.6 million (2012, 530.4 million). In return for the sale of these receivables, the Company received cash of $502.3 million (2012, $525.1) on the settlement date.

Transfer of Accounts Receivable to a Special Purpose Entity

Another structure that may be used for the transfer of accounts receivable involves a **special purpose entity** (SPE). This is a separate entity that carries out a specific part of a company's business but is not legally controlled by the company; the SPE has a separate shareholder group. Often, the "parent" company owns no shares of the SPE at all. The SPE holds the accounts receivable as assets, using them as security for loans from outside investors. However, the transactions typically involve the parent company continuing to hold the *financial risk* of the receivables and loans, through contractual arrangements. The parent company would also gain benefits if the collection operations are profitable.

The use of SPEs may be a legitimate and low-cost way to segregate a particular kind of asset, and raise money using these assets as collateral. SPEs might also be used to manipulate financial reporting and keep accounts receivable and liabilities off the company's SFP. To avoid manipulation, there are accounting standards that require SPEs to be consolidated, despite the fact that the parent company owns no shares in the SPE. **Consolidation** involves combining the financial statements of the two companies. If the SPE is consolidated, the receivables and loan balances would come back onto the parent's SFP. After that, any transfer arrangement *with third parties* can be evaluated to see if derecognition is the correct accounting treatment.

Consolidation is considered appropriate when the parent company has power over the SPE, from whatever source, plus the parent has the right (or exposure to) to *variable returns* from the activities of the SPE, *and* the ability to use power over the SPE to affect returns. If the operations of the SPE are conducted for the primary benefit of the parent company, it seems obvious that irrespective of share ownership, the SPE is part of the parent's economic entity and should be consolidated. Consolidation of SPEs is covered in depth in advanced accounting courses.

CONCEPT REVIEW

1. What does *derecognition* mean?
2. What financial statement ratios will be especially affected by a derecognition entry?
3. Why is the allowance for doubtful accounts part of a derecognition entry?
4. What is an SPE, and how can it be used to transfer accounts receivable?

NOTES RECEIVABLE

Notes receivable may arise from loans and also from normal sales, extension of the payment period of accounts receivable, exchanges of long-term assets, and advances to employees. Notes are a written promise to pay a specified amount at a specified future date (or a series of amounts over a series of payment dates). Some notes formalize **collateral security** for the lender. Collateral security represents assets of the borrower that the secured lender can seize if the note goes into default. The examples in this chapter illustrate the accounting treatment for both the note receivable and the note payable, since they are mirror images.

Compared with accounts receivable/payable, notes receivable/payable usually provide:

- Extended payment terms;
- More security and a solid legal footing for the payments;
- A formal basis for charging interest; and
- Negotiability.

Valuation Notes receivable and payable are initially valued at fair value, which is the exchange value of the date of initial recognition. Fair value is established *using the effective interest method. If the note carries a stated interest rate equal to market interest rates, or has a very short term, then valuation issues are immaterial and stated values are used.* When the stated and market interest rates are different, and term is more than a year (i.e., not short), then present values must be used to establish initial fair value.

Terminology The borrower is the *maker* of the note and the lender is the *payee*. The **face value**, or **maturity value**, is the dollar amount stated on the note. The face value is the amount, excluding interest, payable at the end of the note term, unless the note requires that principal repayments be made according to an instalment schedule. The total interest over the life of the note equals the difference between total cash inflows and cash outflows.

Notes may be categorized as **interest-bearing** or **non-interest-bearing** notes. Interest-bearing notes specify the interest rate to be applied to the face amount in computing interest payments. Non-interest-bearing notes do not state an interest rate but command interest through the difference between cash lent and (higher) cash repaid. Notes receivable with stated interest rates below market rates may be used by companies as a sales incentive.

Interest-bearing notes, in turn, can be divided into two categories according to the type of cash payment required: (1) notes whose cash payments are interest only, except for the final maturity payment and (2) notes whose cash payments are *blended*, and include both interest and principal. Actually, there are an unlimited number of principal and repayment options. Payment schedules are not limited to those used in the examples below.

The **stated interest rate** in a note may not equal the market rate prevailing on obligations involving similar credit rating or risk. The **market interest rate** is the rate accepted by two parties for loans of equal profile. The loans must have identical amounts, with identical credit risk, terms, and conditions for the rate to be appropriate.

If the rate is not given, but the value of the transaction is known, the rate can be determined by equating the present value of the cash flows called for in the note to the market value of the transaction. The rate can be determined with a computer program or calculator that determines the correct rate iteratively—that is, by trial and error.

Effective Interest Method

The effective interest method requires that the *market rate is used to value the note and the transaction. The market rate is also used to measure interest revenue or expense. The stated rate is used to determine the cash interest payments.* If an interest rate differential between the market and stated rates is not material, it can be ignored. This might be true when the term is less than one year.

Example 1: Interest-bearing note On 1 April 20X2, Lionel Company sold merchandise for $12,000 to Baylor Company and received a two-year, 4% note. Interest is payable each 31 March, and the principal is payable at the end of the second year. *The stated and market interest rates are equal.* The entry to record the sale is as follows:

Lionel			Baylor		
1 April 20X2			1 April 20X2		
Note receivable	12,000		Inventory (1)	12,000	
Sales (1)		12,000	Note payable		12,000

(1) If this were a loan transaction instead of a sale, Lionel and Baylor would pay or receive cash

Accounting for this note is very simple because the 4% interest rate charged is also the market rate. Cash interest received equals interest revenue recognized over the terms of the note, as indicated in the remaining entries. The computation for interest assumes months of equal length; in practice, interest is accrued by day if it is material.

31 December 20X2 and 20X3—Adjusting entries

Lionel			Baylor		
Interest receivable	360*		Interest expense	360	
Interest revenue		360	Interest payable		360

*$12,000 × 4% × 9/12

31 March 20X3 and 20X4—Interest payments

Lionel			Baylor		
Cash	480		Interest payable	360	
Interest receivable		360	Interest expense	120	
Interest revenue		120*	Cash		480

*$12,000 × 4% × 3/12

31 March 20X4—Payment at maturity

Lionel			Baylor		
Cash	12,000		Note payable	12,000	
Note receivable		12,000	Cash		12,000

Example 2: Different market and stated rates Assume the same facts for the Lionel and Baylor $12,000 sale as illustrated in Example 1. This time, though, while the stated rate on the note is 4%, the market interest rate is assumed to be 10%. Assume also that the inventory sold does not have a readily determinable market value. To value the transaction, it is necessary to calculate the present value of the note, including both principal and interest:

Present value of maturity amount:	
$12,000(P/F, 10%, 2) =	$ 9,917
Present value of the nominal interest payments:	
$480(P/A, 10%, 2) =	833
Present value of the note at 10%	$10,750

Notes are recorded at gross (face) value plus a premium or minus a discount amount (the gross method), or at the net present value (the net method). The two methods are illustrated below.

1 April 20X2:

	Gross			Net	
For Lionel Company					
Note receivable	12,000			10,750	
Discount on note receivable		1,250			—
Sales (1)		10,750			10,750
For Baylor Company					
Inventory (1)	10,750			10,750	
Discount on note payable	1,250			—	
Note payable		12,000			10,750

(1) If this were a loan transaction instead of a sale, Lionel and Baylor would pay or receive cash

Under either method, the net book value of the note is $10,750, the present value. The discount account is a contra account to notes receivable or payable. Since the note is disclosed net of its discount on the SFP, the two methods are identical in presentation. In the remaining parts of the example, only the gross method will be illustrated, as it is more comparable with accounting for bonds payable, which you will see in Chapter 13. However, both recording conventions are common in practice.

In each year of the note, the market rate of interest is applied to the beginning balance of the net note receivable to compute interest. This approach, called the **effective-interest method**, results in a constant rate of interest throughout the life of the note. The calculations may be organized in a table:

(1) Opening Net Liability/ Receivable	(2) Interest Expense/ Revenue 10% Market Rate (1) × 10%	(3) Interest Paid/ Received 4% Stated Rate $12,000 × 4%	(4) Discount Amortization (2) – (3)	(5) Closing Net Liability/ Receivable (1) + (4)
$10,750	$1,075	$480	$595	$11,345
$11,345	1,135	480	655	12,000

The net notes receivable and payable balance is always the present value of remaining payments. For example, the $11,345 balance is the present value on 31 March 20X3, of the remaining payment (principal plus interest), a payment that is due on 31 March 20X4.

$12,480(P/F, 10%, 1) = $11,345

If the fiscal year corresponded with the dates of the note, the interest and payment information from this table would correspond directly to the interest entry, that is:

Hypothetical full year entry—31 March 20X3:

Lionel			Baylor		
Cash	480		Interest expense	1,075	
Discount on note receivable	595		Discount on note payable		595
Interest revenue		1,075	Cash		480

Since the fiscal year is different from the dates of the note, accruals must be made that also include discount amortization. In this case, the year-end is 31 December, or 9/12 of the year. The entries at the end of the fiscal year are as follows:

31 December 20X2:

Lionel			Baylor		
Interest receivable ($12,000 × 4% × 9/12)	360		Interest expense	806	
Discount on note receivable	446		Discount on note payable		446
Interest revenue ($10,750 × 10% × 9/12)		806	Interest payable		360

Entries on cash payment:

31 March 20X3:

Lionel			Baylor		
Cash ($12,000 × 4%)	480		Interest expense	269	
Discount on note receivable	149		Interest payable	360	
Interest receivable		360	Discount on note payable		149
Interest revenue			Cash		480
($10,750 × 10%					
× 3/12)		269			

In the second year of the note:

31 December 20X3:

Lionel			Baylor		
Interest receivable	360		Interest expense	851	
Discount on note receivable	491		Discount on note payable		491
Interest revenue			Interest payable		360
($11,345 × 10%					
× 9/12)		851			

Entries on cash payment:

31 March 20X4:

Lionel			Baylor		
Cash ($12,000 × 4%)	480		Interest expense	284	
Discount on note receivable	164		Interest payable	360	
Interest receivable		360	Discount on note payable		164
Interest revenue			Cash		480
($11,345 × 10%					
× 3/12)		284			

After the 31 March 20X5 entry, the net notes receivable and payable balance is $12,000, the face value. The discount account balance is zero, and the note is paid.

31 March 20X4:

Lionel			Baylor		
Cash	12,000		Note payable	12,000	
Note receivable		12,000	Cash		12,000

Straight-Line Measurement of Interest Expense/Revenue

Another approach to measuring interest, the straight-line method, amortizes an equal amount of discount each period. The straight-line method produces the same interest amount each period but shows a varying rate of interest period by period (i.e., "interest ÷ note" will vary). It is less accurate for this reason and is not permitted under IFRS standards. However, it is much simpler and may yield results that are not materially different from the effective interest method. In this example, the straight-line method results in discount amortization of $625 ($1,250 ÷ 2 years) and interest revenue or expense of $1,105 ($625 + $480) in both years. The straight-line approach is permitted under ASPE.

Example 3: Blended payments Consider a 10%, $4,000, two-year note receivable of Vancouver Sea Lines that requires interest to be paid on its face value. This is an interest-bearing note, and the annual interest of $400 ($4,000 × 10%) is due at the end of each year of the note term. The $4,000 face amount is due at the end of the second year. In total, $800 of interest is required over the term of the note. In notes of this type, the original principal is not decreased by the yearly payment.

Now assume instead that Vancouver's note requires blended payments, involving *two equal* annual amounts due at the end of each year. These payments *each* contain some interest and some principal in the amount necessary to extinguish the receivable. The payment is computed as follows:

$4,000 = Present value of an annuity = Payment × (P/A, 10%, 2)
$4,000 ÷ (P/A, 10%, 2) = Payment
$2,305 = Payment (rounded)

Payment	Interest Component	Principal Component
1	$400 ($4,000 × 10%)	$1,905 ($2,305 − $400)
2	210 ($4,000 − $1,905) × 10%	2,095 ($2,305 − $210)
	$610	$4,000

Total interest for the second type of note ($610) is less than for the first note ($800) because part of the first payment of $2,305 is a principal payment, which reduces the principal on which interest is paid in the second period. Vancouver would record the note and its payments as follows:

Initial entry:		
Note receivable	4,000	
Cash (etc.)		4,000
First payment:		
Cash	2,305	
Interest revenue		400
Note receivable		1,905
Second payment:		
Cash	2,305	
Interest revenue		210
Note receivable		2,095

Sometimes, blended payment notes may not include an explicit disclosure of the interest rate. The implicit interest rate must be calculated before the transaction can be recorded. For example, assume that on 30 June 20X5, a firm sells equipment with a cash price of $10,000 and receives in exchange a note receivable that requires a payment of $6,000 on 30 June 20X6, and another $6,000 on 30 June 20X7. The note does not explicitly mention interest, but $2,000 of interest is implicit in the note ($6,000 × 2) − $10,000. The interest rate is computed using the present value of an annuity as follows:

$10,000 = $6,000 × (P/A, i, 2)
$10,000 ÷ $6,000 = 1.66667 = (P/A, i, 2)

A calculator equipped for present value tells us that $i = 13.066\%$. This rate should be comparable with the rate incurred by the debtor on similar financing.

Impairment

Notes receivable will be an asset only if the maker of the note pays—both principal and interest are to be considered in this regard. Revenue cannot be recognized; that is, interest cannot be accrued unless it is collected or collectible. Impairment is an issue if there is objective evidence that there is a "loss event"—logically, some objective indication that there is a decrease in the estimated future cash receipts that will flow from the note receivable. An allowance for doubtful notes receivable must be established if the collection is uncertain.

In calculating the extent of such an allowance, the following information may be considered and compared with the book value of the loan receivable:

1. *The total present value of the cash flows expected from the maker of the note over its remaining life.* While some customers will pay nothing, it is quite common to get partial payment, or even complete payment, several months or years late. To assess the fair value of this cash flow, the present value is calculated using the interest rate set for the original loan.

2. If there are a range of possible amounts, the *best estimate within the range of outcomes is used.*

3. *The fair value of any collateral security (assets)* that the lender can legally repossess. This collateral is valued at its fair value, and costs to obtain and sell the collateral must be deducted.

For example, assume that a note receivable was on the books for $4,800, including both principal and accrued interest to date, and the customer has encountered financial difficulties. As a result, the cash flows associated with the note are expected to have a present value of $1,200. Some of this will come from a cash payment from the customer and some from the net proceeds of selling repossessed collateral assets. A $3,600 loan loss or impairment expense is recognized, and an allowance for doubtful accounts is established.

Impairment is hard to estimate. It is extremely challenging to make accurate predictions of cash flows to be received from a party in financial difficulty and to assess appropriate interest revenue recognition on remaining balances as time passes. This presents special challenges because impairment losses can be reversed. There is some room to be pessimistic, take large loan losses, and then watch income bounce back with loan loss recoveries.

Transfer of Notes Receivable

Rather than hold a note receivable to maturity, a company may transfer notes receivable, a transaction that may be recorded as a borrowing or as a sale/derecognition. For a discussion of the related issues on transfers, refer to "Transfer of Receivables."

CONCEPT REVIEW

1. What is the effective interest method?
2. What is a low-interest loan? How is it valued?
3. What happens to the discount on a note receivable over time?
4. What is a blended payment?

FOREIGN CURRENCY RECEIVABLES

If a company has accounts or notes that are receivable or payable in foreign currencies, they must be *restated to Canadian dollars* at the current exchange rate at the year-end date. When the receivable is first recorded, the then-current exchange rate is used. For example, suppose that Talud Limited has a sale to a customer in Europe for €10,000 when the exchange rate was €1 = $1.25. The sale would be recorded as follows:

Accounts receivable (€10,000)	12,500	
Sales (€10,000 × $1.25)		12,500

The receivable is stated (or *denominated*) in euros, not in dollars. The sale is recorded at the Canadian dollar–equivalent of the European sales price. However, when the European company pays the account, it will pay €10,000, not $12,500. The cash receipt must be recorded at the current exchange rate. Suppose that the customer pays the €10,000 when the exchange rate is €1 = $1.19. Talud will receive only $11,900 in Canadian currency when it converts the cash. The exchange loss is recognized in current period earnings.

Cash (€10,000 × $1.19)	11,900	
Foreign exchange gains and losses	600	
Accounts receivable		12,500

Exchange Gain or Loss The difference between the Canadian equivalent of the receivable and of the cash receipt is charged to an *exchange gain or loss* account. Exchange gains and losses are netted in this account, and the net balance is reported in earnings. It is important to understand that changes in the exchange rate following the initial transaction *do not affect the amount initially charged or credited to sales*. In the Talud Limited example above, the sales account is not affected by the subsequent exchange rate change.

Similarly, if inventory or fixed assets (such as equipment) are purchased in a foreign currency, changes in the exchange rate between the date of purchase and the date of payment will not affect the originally recorded value of the asset. *Historical cost is determined by the exchange rate at the date of the purchase transaction*. Subsequent gains and losses on the outstanding monetary balance are recognized directly and immediately in earnings.

Year-End Assume instead that at Talud's year-end date, the receivable (recorded at $12,500) is still outstanding. The receivable must be translated to the then-current exchange rate. If the exchange rate at the year-end date is €1 = $1.30, the value of the account receivable will be $13,000 (€10,000 × $1.30). The increase of $500 in the Canadian equivalent of the €10,000 balance would be recorded as follows:

Accounts receivable ($13,000 – $12,500)	500	
Foreign exchange gains and losses		500

STATEMENT OF CASH FLOWS AND DISCLOSURE

SCF The statement of cash flows is designed to explain the change in cash and cash equivalents over the period and as a result is the major element of disclosure related to cash. Components of cash as defined on the SCF (i.e., cash equivalents, if any) must be reconciled to the SFP. The change in accounts and notes receivable is an adjustment in operating activities to reconcile earnings to cash flow from operating activities. If notes receivable arise from investing activities rather than operating activities, then the change in this account would be classified in investing activities on the SCF.

Disclosure Accounting standards require disclosure of information that will allow users to evaluate the significance of financial instruments in an evaluation of financial position and performance. Financial instrument disclosure is extensive; this recap provides the highlights only. Companies must disclose the following:

1. The *carrying amounts* for financial instruments in each category. For some categories, this is amortized cost or cost. For others, carrying value is fair value.

2. Regardless of what is used for carrying value, disclosure must be made of fair value, and a description provided of the methods used to estimate fair value. For many of the financial instruments in this chapter, cost and fair value are identical.

3. When a financial instrument has been valued at fair value, details about the change in fair value are required, in addition to the maturity value and methods used to assess fair value and its components.

4. The important components of each financial statement category. For example, receivables from outside customers are shown separately of receivables from related parties, receivables for tax refunds, and so on.

5. Collateral for accounts/notes receivable, along with the terms and condition of use.

6. A reconciliation of the changes in any allowance for credit losses (bad debts), and an analysis of past due accounts that have not been written down or for which no bad debt allowance has been provided.

7. Extensive disclosure that allows the financial statement users to evaluate the effect of netting arrangements (i.e., transfer of receivables that has resulted in derecognition). This essentially involves disclosing the major terms of the transaction(s).

8. Various revenue and expense amounts must be disclosed separately, including interest income.

9. Information on *credit risk, liquidity risk,* and *market risk,* as appropriate. As part of this, objectives, policies and processes for managing risk must be disclosed. Such disclosure is extensive and includes both qualitative and quantitative elements. Disclosure of interest rates and terms of receivables would be included as a matter of course.

Example As an example of disclosure of carrying and fair value, consider the following extract from the 2011 Aastra Technologies Limited annual financial statements. Note that the methods to determine fair value are described, and refer to price quotes and discounted cash flow. Fair value is equal to carrying value for trade and other receivables but not for finance lease receivables, for which fair value is determined through present value. The decline in fair value would be caused by changes in interest rates.

---

15. FINANCIAL INSTRUMENTS

(a) Fair values and classification of financial instruments

The fair values of financial assets and liabilities, together with the carrying amounts shown in the consolidated statement of financial position, are as follows:

	2011		2010	
	Carrying amount	Fair value	Carrying amount	Fair value
Cash and cash equivalents, measured at fair value	$129,933	$129,933	$ 90,704	$ 90,704
. . .				
Loans and receivables, measured at amortized cost:				
Trade and other receivables	167,142	167,142	183,977	183,977
Finance lease receivables	44,805	42,283	41,750	39,601
. . .				

The following summarizes the significant methods and assumptions used in estimating the fair values of financial instruments reflected in the table above:

(i) The fair values of cash equivalents and short-term investments are determined by the quoted market values for each of the investments in an active market at the reporting date.

. . .

(iii) The carrying amounts of cash, trade and other receivables and trade and other payables approximate their fair values due to the short-term nature of these financial instruments.

(iv) The fair values of finance lease receivables, acquired lease receivables, and loans payable are estimated using the discounted cash flow method. The interest rates used to discount estimated cash flows are based on the government yield curve at the reporting date plus an adequate credit spread.

. . .

Source: Aastra Technologies Limited, 2011 Annual Financial Statements, page 33, posted 8 March 2012.

Looking Ahead

The financial instrument standards have been under constant review and revision since they were first issued and remain a work in progress. For example, the measurement of impairment of financial assets is currently being reconsidered. Changes in disclosure requirements have been continuous. In addition, the requirements that must be met for a transfer of financial assets to qualify for sale/derecognition have also changed regularly; the most recent version in the chapter might well change again.

ACCOUNTING STANDARDS FOR PRIVATE ENTERPRISES

The ASPE requirements for cash, accounts receivable, and notes receivable are largely similar to IASB standards. The following differences are noted:

- In terms of classification, *CPA Canada Handbook, Part II* requirements specify that any cash held in a foreign country that is subject to restrictions, and cannot be used for general purposes, is not classified as cash. Under IASB standards, this restriction is simply disclosed in the notes and does not affect cash classification.
- With respect to the classification of a transfer of accounts receivable (as a sale/derecognition or a borrowing), the ASPE approach focuses on surrender of control. That is, if the *transferee* has control over the receivables, the transferor will derecognize the accounts receivable. This is a different set of criteria than that established by the IASB, and thus a transaction that might result in derecognition for a private enterprise might be recorded as a borrowing by a company that complies with IASB standards.
- Required note disclosure under ASPE is far less onerous. For example, there is no requirement to show a continuity schedule for the allowance for doubtful accounts and significantly less disclosure for financial instruments in general.
- Amortization of a premium or discount on a note receivable or payable may be accomplished through the straight-line method. The effective interest method is not required.

Straight-Line Method

The straight-line method will amortize the discount on a note receivable to interest income over the life of the receivable, with the same dollar amount recognized each period. Interest revenue will therefore be measured as cash received plus discount amortization. While this is not consistent with the measurement model established through discounting, it is expedient. The following example will illustrate straight-line amortization.

Example: Straight-line amortization On 1 April 20X2, Lee Company sold merchandise for $7,000 to Vish Company and received a two-year, 3% note. Interest is payable each 31 March, and the principal is payable at the end of the second year. *The market interest rate is 9%*. To value the transaction, it is (still) necessary to calculate the present value of the note, including both principal and interest:

Present value of maturity amount:	
$7,000(P/F, 9%, 2) =	$5,892
Present value of the nominal interest payments:	
$210(P/A, 9%, 2) =	370
Present value of the note at 9%	$6,262

The entry to record the sale is as follows:

1 April 20X2:

Note receivable	7,000	
Discount on note receivable		738
Sales		6,262

Interest expense for each year can be organized in a table, with discount amortization of $369 ($738 ÷ 2) each year:

(1) Opening Net Liability/ Receivable	(2) Interest Expense/ Revenue Cash Paid + Discount Amortization (3) + (4)	(3) Interest Paid/ Received 3% Stated Rate $7,000 × 3%	(4) Discount Amortization Discount ÷ # of periods	(5) Closing Net Liability/ Receivable (1) + (4)
$6,262	$579	$210	$369	$6,631
$6,631	579	210	369	7,000

Entries are identical in approach to those of the effective interest method.

Note, however, that the effective interest rate implied by interest revenue is 9.2% in the first year ($579 ÷ $6,262) and then 8.7% in the second year ($579 ÷ $6,631). This rate would be exactly 9%, and true to the substance of the transaction, if the effective interest method were used to measure interest revenue.

CONCEPT REVIEW

1. If a sale for €50,000 is finalized by a Canadian company when the exchange rate is €1 = $1.22, and paid by the customer when the exchange rate is €1 = $1.19, what Canadian dollar amount is recorded as a sale? What amount of cash is collected?

2. What is included in a continuity schedule for the allowance for doubtful accounts?

3. If the discount for three-year note is $1,200, and the (annual) cash received is $600, how much is recorded as interest revenue if the straight-line method is used?

RELEVANT STANDARDS

CPA Canada Handbook, Part I (IFRS):
- IAS 1, Presentation of Financial Statements
- IAS 21, The Effects of Changes in Foreign Exchange Rates
- IAS 32, Financial Instruments: Presentation
- IAS 39, Financial Instruments: Recognition and Measurement
- IFRS 7, Financial Instruments: Disclosure
- IFRS 9, Financial Instruments
- IFRS 10, Consolidated Financial Statements

CPA Canada Handbook, Part II (ASPE):
- Section 1510, Current Assets and Current Liabilities
- Section 1650, Foreign Currency Translation
- Section 3000, Cash
- Section 3020, Accounts and Notes Receivable
- Section 3025, Impaired Loans
- Section 3855, Financial Instruments—Recognition and Measurement
- Section 3861, Financial Instruments—Disclosure and Presentation
- Section 3862, Financial Instruments—Disclosures
- Section 3863, Financial Instruments— Presentation

SUMMARY OF KEY POINTS

1. Financial assets are those that are cash, or the contractual right to receive cash. Monetary items are those that will be paid or received in fixed or determinable amounts of money.

2. Cash is a financial asset. Cash equivalents, also financial assets, are certain kinds of short-term investments.

3. A bank reconciliation is an internal control mechanism. Reconciliation of the book balance to the correct cash balance provides the data for end-of-month adjusting entries for cash and provides insights as to the accuracy of recording.

4. In a bank reconciliation, adjustments to the bank are made for outstanding cheques and deposits, and bank errors. The book balance is adjusted for unrecorded items and errors.

5. Accounts receivable are financial instruments that are classified as amortized cost but may, in some circumstances, be classified as FVTPL and carried at fair value. Doubtful accounts, cash discounts, and sales returns and allowances represent adjustments to the recorded value of receivables, which are necessary to provide an estimate of net realizable value.

6. The allowance for doubtful accounts can be estimated through aging or a percentage-of-sales method.

7. Debit and credit card transactions may replace sales on account to speed the cash cycle. Accounts receivable can also be used as collateral for a loan to speed the cash cycle.

8. Accounts receivable can be transferred to a finance company to obtain immediate cash. The key accounting issue is whether the transfer of accounts receivable is treated as a sale/derecognition or borrowing. Derecognition is allowed if the accounts

receivable are transferred, and if risks and rewards of ownership have genuinely passed to another party.

9. Notes receivable (and payable) that have low interest or no interest, and are longer than one year in duration, are recorded using the effective interest method. This method uses the present value of all cash payments to be received using an appropriate market rate of interest. Interest is based on the market interest rate and the outstanding principal balance at the beginning of the period. Impaired notes are reduced to the present value of future cash flows.

10. Transactions that are denominated in a foreign currency are recorded at the exchange rate that exists at the transaction date. Monetary balances (i.e., cash and receivables) are restated to the exchange rate that exists on the year-end date. Foreign exchange gains and losses are recognized in earnings.

11. Extensive disclosure is required for financial instruments, including carrying value, fair value, details of contractual requirements, and continuity schedules for allowances, in addition to information on credit risk, liquidity risk, and market risk.

KEY TERMS

aging method
asset-backed commercial paper (ABCP)
allowance for doubtful accounts
bank reconciliation
cash equivalents
collateral security
commercial paper
compensating balance
consolidation
credit memo
credit sales method
debit memo
derecognition
effective-interest method
face value
financial assets
guaranteed investment certificate (GIC)

interest-bearing
internal control system
market interest rate
maturity value
monetary items
money market instruments
non-interest-bearing
non-notification basis
notification basis
overdraft
recourse
securitization
special purpose entity
stated interest rate
Treasury bill (T-bill)
transferee
transferor

REVIEW PROBLEM 7-1

At the end of 20X5, three companies ask you to record journal entries in three different areas associated with receivables. The fiscal year of each company ends on 31 December.

1. *Mandalay Company—uncollectible accounts receivable.* Mandalay Company requests that you record journal entries for its bad debt expense and uncollectible accounts receivable in 20X5. Mandalay's 1 January 20X5 balances relevant to accounts receivable are as follows:

Accounts receivable	$400,000 (dr.)
Allowance for doubtful accounts	20,000 (cr.)

During 20X5, $45,000 of accounts receivable are judged to be uncollectible, and no more effort to collect these accounts will be made. Total sales for 20X5 are $1,200,000, of which $200,000 are cash sales; $900,000 was collected on account during 20X5.

a. Assuming that Mandalay uses the credit sales method to estimate bad debt expense and uses 4% of credit sales as its estimate of bad debts, provide the journal entries to record write-offs and bad debt expense for 20X5. Also, provide the 31 December 20X5 amount for net accounts receivable.

b. Assuming that Mandalay uses the aging method to estimate net accounts receivable and uses 9% of total accounts receivable as its estimate of uncollectibles, provide the journal entries to record write-offs and bad debt expense for 20X5. Also, provide the 31 December 20X5 amount for net accounts receivable.

2. *Berkshire Company—transfer of accounts receivable.* Berkshire Company requests that you record journal entries for accounts receivable transferred in 20X5:

> On 1 January 20X5, Berkshire transferred $45,000 of accounts receivable with no recourse to a finance company, on a notification basis. Bad debts are estimated to be $2,500, an amount that is already part of the allowance for doubtful accounts. The financing fee is 10%. Criteria for derecognition are met.

3. *White Mountain Company—accounting for long-term notes*: White Mountain Company requests that you record journal entries for a note it received in 20X5. On 1 January 20X5, White Mountain Company sold merchandise for $12,000 and received a $12,000, three-year, 6% note; 12% was the current market rate of interest at that time. Interest is paid annually at the end of each year, and the principal is due at the end of the third year. Provide journal entries from inception to final payment. Use the gross method to record the note.

REVIEW PROBLEM 7-1—SOLUTION

1. Mandalay Company

a. *Summary entry for write-offs during 20X5:*

Allowance for doubtful accounts	45,000	
Accounts receivable		45,000

Adjustment on 31 December 20X5:

Bad debt expense ($1,000,000 × 4%)	40,000	
Allowance for doubtful accounts		40,000

Statement of financial position amounts at 31 December 20X5:

Accounts receivable	$455,000*
Allowance for doubtful accounts	(15,000)**
Net accounts receivable	$440,000

*$400,000 + $1,000,000 − $900,000 − $45,000
**$20,000 − $45,000 + $40,000

b. *Summary entry for write-offs during 20X5:*

Allowance for doubtful accounts	45,000	
Accounts receivable		45,000

Adjustment on 31 December 20X5:

Bad debt expense	65,950*	
Allowance for doubtful accounts		65,950

Calculation of adjustment:

Ending gross accounts receivable		$455,000
Required allowance balance ($455,000 × 9%)		$ 40,950
Allowance balance before adjustment for 20X5:		
Beginning balance, 1 January 20X5	$ (20,000)	
Write-offs during 20X5	45,000	25,000
Increase necessary to adjust balance		$ 65,950

Statement of financial position amounts at 31 December 20X5:

Accounts receivable	$455,000
Allowance for doubtful accounts	(40,950)
Net accounts receivable	$414,050

2. Berkshire Company

Cash ($45,000 − $2,500 − (10% × $42,500))	38,250	
Allowance for doubtful accounts	2,500	
Financing fee (10% × $42,500)	4,250	
Accounts receivable		45,000

3. White Mountain Company

Present value of note

$12,000 (P/F, 12%, 3)		$ 8,541
$720 (P/A, 12%, 3)		1,729
		$ 10,270

a. *1 January 20X5:*

Note receivable	12,000	
Sales revenue		10,270
Discount on note receivable		1,730

b. *31 December 20X5:*

Cash	720	
Discount on note receivable ($1,232 − $720)	512	
Interest revenue ($10,270 × 0.12)		1,232

c. *31 December 20X6:*

Cash	720	
Discount on note receivable ($1,294 − $720)	574	
Interest revenue ($10,270 + $512) × 0.12		1,294

d. *31 December 20X7:*

Cash	720	
Discount on note receivable	644	
Interest revenue ($10,270 + $512 + $574) × 0.12		1,364

e. *31 December 20X7:*

Cash	12,000	
Note receivable		12,000

APPENDIX

BANK RECONCILIATION

The purpose of a bank reconciliation is to ensure that transactions in both the company's cash account and the bank's cash account have been recorded accurately. This involves comparing every deposit and cheque/charge in both accounts. Items that are different are reconciling amounts, which may lead to adjusting entries.

Review the information in Exhibit 7A-1 for North Company.

The bank statement reported an ending $23,760 balance, and the cash account reflects an ending $23,230 cash balance. These figures are reconciled to $23,160, as shown in Exhibit 7A-2. Here are the steps to follow:

Step 1 Compare all deposits made in the bank account with those in the books. If there are differences, determine why. If the bank has processed something that should be on the books, adjust the book balance. If the bank has made errors or if deposits are in transit, adjust the bank balance. If the company has made errors adjust the balance per the books. A careful bank reconciliation includes a comparison of the dates of deposits—there should be no delays in getting money to the bank. Deposits in transit from the prior month should clear in the first few days of the next month, and this month's deposits in transit should relate only to the last day or two.

Step 2 Compare all cheques and charges that went through the bank account to the cash disbursements journal. All cheques and direct payments that the bank processed should be in the cash disbursements journal this month or have been outstanding last month. Bank fees must be recorded on the books. If the bank has made errors or cheques are still outstanding, adjust the bank balance. If the bank has processed something that should be on the books, adjust the book balance. If the company has made errors, adjust the balance per the books. Again, watch for irregularities; cheques are usually cashed after only a short delay.

Step 3 Make journal entries for all adjustments *to the book balance*. The company must also inform the bank of any errors made by the bank so that they can be corrected before the end of next month.

Adjustments Review the bank reconciliation in Exhibit 7A-2 in detail. Examine the deposits and then the cheques/charges. When they are not identical, either the bank balance or the book balance has to be adjusted.

a. *Deposits.* For North Company, compare (cross off) the list of deposits in the bank versus those on the books (or last month's reconciliation.) Each item should be in both places. Circle the items that are in one place *or* the other, but not both, *or* if the items are for different amounts. These are the reconciling items.

The first deposit in the bank was the outstanding deposit from last month (see last month's bank reconciliation at the bottom of Exhibit 7A-1.) It was recorded in the books last month and now has cleared; so it needs no adjustment. There is a $1,000 deposit made by a customer directly to the bank account. This should be recorded by the company and is added to the balance per the books.

All other deposits are identical until the end of the month, when there is a deposit of $2,700 in the books that is not in the bank. This is an outstanding deposit, made too late to be reflected in the bank statement. It is added to the bank balance in Exhibit 7A-2.

b. *Cheques and charges.* Compare cheques cleared through the bank account with cheques recorded in the books and the cheques that were outstanding last month. For North Company, compare (cross off) the two lists. Circle the items that are in one place or the other or are for different amounts. These are the reconciling items.

Outstanding cheques at the end of June are, first, *the outstanding cheques from last month that have not yet been cashed* and, second, any cheques written this month that

EXHIBIT 7A-1

NORTH COMPANY
Information for Bank Reconciliation

30 June 20X8

Bank Statement Summary:

Opening balance, 1 June	$23,000
Deposits (see below)	12,600
Cheques and charges (see below)	(11,740)
Service fees	(100)
Ending balance, 30 June	$23,760

Deposits		Cheques and Charges			
1 June	$ 2,000	2 June #61	$1,000	17 June #65	$ 150
8 June	3,000	7 June #63	2,000	23 June #60	1,100
17 June	4,500	9 June #66	3,000	27 June #67	2,300
18 June	1,000*	14 June #64	1,420	29 June	250**
22 June	2,100	15 June NSF***	520		
Total	$12,600				$11,740

*Customer Franklin paid his outstanding account receivable through a direct deposit to North's bank account.

**Direct payment for utilities processed by bank.

***NSF: Customer Treetoe's $500 cheque, deposited on 1 June, was returned NSF; there was a $20 bank fee.

Balance per Books: *transactions recorded in the cash account in the general ledger:*

Opening balance, 1 June	$23,900
Deposits (see below)	12,300
Cheques (see below)	(12,970)
Closing balance, 30 June	$23,230

Deposits and cheques:

Deposits		Cheques			
June 8	$ 3,000	#60	$1,100	#65	$ 150
June 17	4,500	#61	1,000	#66	3,000
June 22	2,100	#62	900	#67	2,100*
June 30	2,700	#63	2,000	#68	1,300
	$12,300	#64	1,420		
					$12,970

*This cheque was actually for $2,300 and was to a supplier, on account.

The bank reconciliation at 31 May:

Bank balance	$23,000
Add: deposit outstanding	$2,000
Deduct: cheque outstanding (#59)	($1,100)
Book balance	$23,900

EXHIBIT 7A-2

NORTH COMPANY BANK RECONCILIATION

30 June 20X8

Bank statement		
Ending bank balance, 30 June		$23,760
Additions:		
Deposits in transit, 30 June	2,700	
Deductions:		
Cheques outstanding 30 June		
(#59, $1,100; #62, $900; #68, $1,300)	(3,300)	(600)
Adjusted balance		$23,160
Book balance		
Ending book balance, 30 June		$23,230
Additions:		
Accounts receivable collected by bank		1,000
Deductions:		
NSF cheque, Treetoe, $500, plus $20 NSF fee	(520)	
Bank service charges	(100)	
Utility payment	(250)	
Error in recording cheque	(200)	(1,070)
Adjusted balance		$23,160

---

have not been cashed. There are three such cheques, and they are subtracted from the bank balance in the reconciliation.

There was an NSF cheque returned from a deposit; this amount has reduced North's bank balance but is not recorded on the books. There was a $100 bank service charge that reduced North's bank balance. There was a $250 utilities payment put through the bank account; this is a direct payment, presumably preauthorized by the company. All these items must be recorded on the books and are recorded as reconciliation deductions *on the book side*.

Finally, one cheque was recorded correctly by the bank and incorrectly by North. Since this was the company's error, it affects the book balance. There must be an additional $200 reduction on the book side.

There were no bank errors in this example, but if there were, the adjustment would be made to the *bank side* of the reconciliation. For example, if the bank charged a cheque of a different company to this account, or charged too much in service fees, the bank balance would be adjusted and the bank notified to correct its error.

Book and bank balances are now reconciled to the same value, $23,160.

Balancing But what if the two amounts are *not* equal? What if it did not work? Then, the reconciler gets to do it again ... and again ... until it does work! The nightmare is that a $10 difference is really a $10,000 error in one direction and a $10,010 error in the other direction! So the bank reconciliation really is expected to "work." Here are a couple of techniques to help find common errors:

1. If a reconciling item is deducted when it should have been added (or vice versa), the unreconciled amount will be *double* the item. Therefore, try dividing the unreconciled amount by 2, then look for an item of that amount. That is, if $170 is the unreconciled amount, look for an $85 item that is added when it should be subtracted, or vice versa.

2. Transposition errors are *always* divisible by 9. For example, if $5,012 was written as $5,102, the unreconciled amount will be $90. If $5,012 was written as $5,210, the error will be $198, which also is divisible by 9.

Of course, if there are multiple errors, these suggestions will not help much. In practice, after things have been very carefully reviewed a few times to make sure there is no possibility of large counterbalancing errors, small differences are written off to miscellaneous expense.

Adjusting Entries Each of the reconciliation items on the book side requires an adjusting journal entry to correct the cash balance. *There are no entries in North's books for items that are reconciling items to the bank balance.*

A. *Account receivable collected by bank.* An account receivable for $1,000 was collected by the bank but was not recorded by North. Usually, the bank informs the company immediately, but if the item has not been recorded by month-end, it shows up as a reconciling item and is recorded at that time.

Cash	1,000	
Accounts receivable		1,000

B. *Not sufficient funds (NSF) cheque.* The $500 cheque from customer Treetoe, which was not supported by sufficient funds in Treetoe's chequing account, was returned to North by the bank. North had deposited the cheque, increased cash, and decreased accounts receivable, but the bank was unable to get any money from Treetoe's account. Again, the company is usually informed immediately so that it can pursue its delinquent customer. However, if there are delays, or the NSF cheque occurs late in the month, it is a reconciling item and will be recorded at that time. Note that the company will try to recover the bank fee charged as well as the original receivable.

Accounts receivable, Treetoe	520	
Cash		520

Is this really a bad debt? Treetoe might be delinquent, but no company will give up after only one try—it will create a receivable when an NSF cheque is received. The receivable may end up as part of the amount included in the allowance for doubtful accounts.

C. *Bank service charges and direct payments.* The bank debited North's account for $100 of bank charges in June. There was also a payment for $250 of utilities, a direct charge to the bank account. North deducts these amounts from the cash account as reconciling items and records an entry:

Miscellaneous expense (or Bank service charge expense)	100	
Utilities expense	250	
Cash		350

D. *Error in recording.* North recorded a $2,300 cheque in the cash disbursements journal as $2,100, debiting accounts payable and crediting cash for *too little*. The book balance of cash and accounts payable is now overstated by $200 ($2,300 − $2,100). North corrects the recording error as a reconciling item and makes an entry.

Accounts payable	200	
Cash		200

This entry corrects the cash disbursement amount and reduces the payable. Correction entries of this kind always either debit or credit the cash account, and the other side of the entry is made to whatever the first cheque was charged to: in this case, accounts payable. It helps to reconstruct the original (incorrect) entry.

Bank Debit and Credit Memos Deposits and withdrawals may take place that are initiated by the bank or others rather than by the company. These show up on the bank statement as debit and credit memos and include such items as interest earned, cash collected by the bank from customers, and service charges. For a bank, a depositor's cash balance is a liability, the amount the bank owes to the company. A bank **debit memo** describes a transaction from the bank's point of view—a decrease in liability to the account holder. Therefore, a debit memo reports the amount and nature of a *decrease* in the company's cash account. A **credit memo** indicates an *increase* in the cash account. Since this debit-credit memo terminology is derived from the bank's point of view, it seems backward to the debit and credit convention in the company's cash account. This tends to create a little confusion.

SUMMARY OF KEY POINTS

1. To prepare a bank reconciliation, deposits and cheques/charges are compared between the bank account and the cash account in the general ledger. Where there are differences, there are reconciliation items.

2. Common adjustments to the bank balance in a bank reconciliation are outstanding cheques, outstanding deposits, and bank errors.

3. Common adjustments to the books in a bank reconciliation are deposits recorded by the bank but not yet in the books, charges recorded by the bank but not yet in the books, and recording errors made in the books.

4. Adjusting journal entries are prepared for the adjustments in a bank reconciliation that affect the books.

QUESTIONS

Q7-1 Indicate the likely financial instrument classification of (a) cash, (b) cash equivalents, and (c) accounts receivable. How is each type of financial instrument valued initially? At subsequent reporting dates?

Q7-2 ABC Company has US$160,000 in a U.S. bank account. It received this money from a customer, for a cash sale, when the exchange rate was US$1 = Cdn$1.02. At year-end, the exchange rate is US$1 = Cdn$0.97. At what amount is the sale recorded? What amount of cash is reported on the end-of-year statement of financial position?

Q7-3 Why is internal control over cash so important? What is a major component of internal control?

Q7-4 Briefly explain the basic purposes of a bank reconciliation. Who should perform the reconciliation?

Q7-5 A company allows 10% of gross sales to be returned within a month of sale, and estimates that potential returns amount to $25,000 at year-end based on December sales. The allowance for sales returns is now $10,000 (credit). What entry should be made?

Q7-6 At the end of an accounting period, a company has $4,000,000 recorded in accounts receivable, all from sales. It is not likely that the company will collect all of the

$4,000,000, even though all the sales really took place. Give three reasons that collections might not equal $4,000,000.

Q7-7   It sometimes happens that a receivable that has been written off as uncollectible is subsequently collected. Describe the accounting entries in such an event.

Q7-8   Under what circumstances should the direct write-off method for bad debts be used?

Q7-9   A company has a credit balance of $700 in its allowance for doubtful accounts. The amount of credit sales for the period is $80,000, and the balance in accounts receivable is $15,000. Assume that the bad debt estimates are as follows: (a) related to accounts receivable, 8% composite rate, or (b) related to credit sales, 0.4%. What would be the balance of the allowance for doubtful accounts and the bad debt expense, if (a) the aging method were used (composite rate) and (b) the credit sales method were used?

Q7-10   Describe several different ways a company could speed cash flow associated with accounts receivable.

Q7-11   A company with $200,000 in receivables could sell them for $169,000 without recourse or for $195,000 with recourse. What do the terms "with recourse" and "without recourse" mean? Why is the "without recourse" alternative more expensive? How could the transfer be recorded?

Q7-12   Under what conditions will a transfer of receivables be recognized as a sale/derecognition? As a borrowing? What financial statement ratios are particularly affected by these alternatives?

Q7-13   A company transferred accounts receivable of $10,000 for $8,500. Uncollectible accounts are estimated at $700, and this amount is already in the allowance for doubtful accounts. Give the required entry, assuming that the transaction is recorded as (a) a borrowing and (b) a sale/derecognition. What tests must be assessed to determine the correct accounting treatment?

Q7-14   Why is a note receivable sometimes preferred to an account receivable?

Q7-15   How is a note receivable valued if it is (a) a no-interest note and (b) a low-interest note? Assume in all cases that the note had a term of two years. How would your answer change if the note had a term of two months?

Q7-16   Compute the present value of a $20,000, one-year note payable that specifies no interest, although 10% would be a realistic rate. What is the true amount of the principal and interest?

Q7-17   Assume that $6,000 cash is borrowed on a $6,000, 10%, one-year note payable that is interest bearing and that another $6,000 cash is borrowed on a $6,600 one-year note that is non–interest bearing. For each note, give the following: (a) face amount of the note, (b) principal amount, (c) maturity amount, and (d) total interest paid. The market interest rate is 10%.

Q7-18   A company has an account receivable from a U.S. customer, for US$100,000. The receivable arose when the exchange rate was US$1 = Cdn$1.08. At year-end, the rate is US$1 = $1.01. What amount of total exchange gain or loss will the company report for the year?

Q7-19   Under what conditions will a transfer of receivables be recognized as a sale/derecognition under ASPE?

Q7-20   If the discount for two-year note is $700, and the cash received for interest is $900, how much is recorded as interest revenue if the straight-line method is used?

CASE 7-1

MELVILLE CREDIT UNION

The Melville Credit Union has operated in small-town, rural Nova Scotia for the last 27 years. In the summer of 20X4, after decades of operation as a prosperous paper mill, the Lancaster Mersey Mill was abruptly shut down. Lancaster had been a major employer of many clients of Melville Credit Union. In fact, of the 1,000 residents of the town in which Melville operates, over 320 were employed by Lancaster.

The following information relates to loans receivable of Melville as of 30 June 20X4:

	30 June 20X4	30 June 20X3
Loans receivable	$4,306,190	$3,164,000
Less: allowance for doubtful accounts	427,312	412,375
	$3,878,878	$2,751,625

Aging:
As of 30 June 20X3:

	Current	Over 30 days	Over 60 days	Over 120 days	Total
Loans receivable	$1,020,000	$872,000	$762,000	$510,000	$3,164,000

As of 30 June 20X4:

	Current	Over 30 days	Over 60 days	Over 120 days	Total
Loans receivable	$1,105,612	$632,000	$1,432,578	$1,136,000	$4,306,190

You, Karilyn Zinck, are in charge of the field work for the Melville audit. Melville has been a client of your firm for many years and has always received an unmodified audit report. Your audit senior reported the following discussion that took place between her and Colin Rodenizer, the chief accountant at Melville:

Audit Senior: Colin, I noticed a lot of "for sale" signs on the houses as I drove here on my way to the Credit Union.

Colin: Yes, sadly that is true. Now that the mill has shut down many of our residents have decided to move. Well, many have lost their jobs and pretty much have to move.

Audit Senior: How have house sales been going?

Colin: Not really well, and the situation is getting worse by the day. We are now stuck with a number of homes ourselves, because we've had to foreclose on a number of mortgages that are not collectible. This is the first time this has happened in many years. I'm not sure how to account for these homes that we now own.

Audit Senior: You would think that low interest rates and low property values would entice more sales.

Colin: We hope that will help! Oh right, I'm also not sure what to do about the interest on these loans. Our system has been accruing interest on all of the loans receivable.

Required:

You are now working to identify the accounting issues that flow from the above information. You have scheduled a meeting with the audit partner tomorrow and decide, in advance of the meeting, to document the issues/areas of concern in a memo. The memo will include the quantitative impact of issues, to the extent possible.

(Tammy Crowell, used with permission)

CASE 7-2

MITRIUM CORP.

Mitrium Corp. is a large privately held company that manufactures frozen ice cream products, which are sold to large and small retailers across North America. The shares of this company are held by 12 individuals, some of them related and some of them not. Four of these shareholders are actively involved in the management of the company and are compensated with bonuses based on earnings. There are annual dividend payouts to provide some return to the remaining shareholders. The company has been prosperous in the past but the current retail grocery market, slowly being taken over by private-label goods, is proving a challenge for Mitrium. However, the company is actively engaged in manufacturing private-label goods and enjoys healthy sales and profit margins in several of its flagship products, which have strong brand recognition with the end consumer.

The VP Finance has come to you has come to you, a staff member, for commentary on two key financial ratios (Exhibit 1) based on the draft statement of financial position (Exhibit 2) for the most recent fiscal year. She has isolated these ratios because they are the subject of loan covenants. Specifically, one chartered bank provides the $6 million financing that appears as long-term debt on the statement of financial position. As part of this lending agreement, the current ratio on audited financial statements must not go below 2:1, and the debt-to-equity ratio must not go above 12:1. If either of these ratio requirements is violated, or if interest is not paid annually, the debt becomes payable on demand. The current ratio condition is not met in the financial statements, although it is very close. The VP Finance suspects that the draft financial statements will change based on the additional information she has provided to you (see Exhibit 2). Your task is to analyze this additional information and restate the ratios, providing any commentary or advice you feel is appropriate.

Required:
Prepare a report to the VP Finance that responds to her concerns. The tax rate is 40%.

EXHIBIT 1

MITRIUM CORP.

Debt Covenant Ratios

Ratio	Definition	Calculation (Based on Draft Statements)
Current ratio	$\dfrac{\text{Current assets}}{\text{Current liabilities}}$	$\dfrac{\$2,360}{\$1,211} = 1.95$
Debt/equity	$\dfrac{\text{Total debt}}{\text{Total owners' equity}}$	$\dfrac{\$8,808}{\$867} = 10.2$

EXHIBIT 2

MITRIUM CORP.

Draft Statement of Financial Position 31 December 20X8

(in thousands)

Assets
Current assets:

Cash		$ 300	
Accounts receivable	$1,443		
Allowance for doubtful accounts	(12)	1,431	
Inventory		533	
Prepaid expenses		96	$2,360

Capital assets:

Property, plant, and equipment	7,293
Other assets	22
Total assets	$9,675

Liabilities
Current liabilities:

Bank indebtedness	$ 405	
Accounts payable and accrued liabilities	576	
Current portion of long-term debt	230	
Total current liabilities		$1,211

Long-term liabilities:

Secured bank debt, 6%	1,442
Secured bank debt, floating interest rate	6,000
Deferred tax	155
Total liabilities	8,808

Owners' Equity

Common share capital	583	
Retained earnings	284	
Total owners' equity		867
Total liabilities and owners' equity		$9,675

Additional information (all amounts in thousands):

At year-end, there was a balance of $22 in the cash account in the general ledger, a $300 bank balance less $278 in outstanding cheques. Cash is shown as the balance before outstanding cheques, which have been reclassified as accounts payable.

In 20X8, certain accounts receivable were transferred to a financial institution on a nonrecourse basis. The transfer was accounted for as a sale/derecognition of accounts receivable. An undivided percentage interest in the designated pool of receivables was transferred, with Mitrium retaining the right to repurchase the receivables and use them as collateral against the 6% bank loan. Servicing of the accounts receivable is done by Mitrium on a fee-for-service basis. At the end of the year, $210 of accounts receivable had been transferred. This transaction took place on 20 December and is expected to be of a 45-day duration. Mitrium recognized finance expense of $1.9 and reduced (debited) the allowance for doubtful accounts by $4 when the transfer was recorded. This was felt to be an accurate representation of the doubtful accounts in this account receivable population.

Of the remaining accounts receivable, $412 is receivable from one grocery chain, which is wholly owned by a shareholder of Mitrium. This account has been outstanding for some time, but Mitrium has had the shareholder personally pledge his share investment in Mitrium as security in the event of nonpayment. Activity in the account this fiscal year is:

Opening balance	$256
Sales	455
Payments on account	(341)
Interest accrued	42
Closing balance	$412

Of this amount, the $42 interest and $106 of sales are current and the remainder is over 90 days past due.

Mitrium instituted a sales discount program for all customers this year with the intent of speeding collections of accounts receivable. The discount program allows 1% of the invoice to be deducted if payment for the invoice is received by Mitrium within 10 business days of the invoice date. This program has been quite successful and Mitrium feels that its accounts receivable balances are lower this year as a result. However, since many of the company's highest credit rating customers use these discounts, Mitrium feels that the traditional noncollection percentage for current accounts receivable should likely triple this year. Other categories (30 days past due, etc.) are expected to be stable.

Sales data for the latter portion of December 20X8 are as follows:

Date: December 20X8	Business Day	Sales on Account (thousands)	Percentage Using Sales Discount as of 31 December
11	Yes	$53.4	54%*
12	Yes	71.2	53%*
13	Yes	68.9	61%*
14	Yes	56.7	45%*
15	Yes	48.1	24%
16–17	No	—	—
18	Yes	81.6	12%
19	Yes	41.3	14%
20	Yes	24.4	9%
21	Yes	22.2	12%
22	Yes	51.4	5%
23–26	No	—	—
27	Yes	10.4	4%
28	Yes	78.4	2%
29	Yes	46.4	0%
30–31	No	—	—

*Discount period now expired.

The allowance for doubtful accounts has not yet been addressed in the year-end financial statements. An aging of accounts receivable shows the following:

Status	Amount	Percentage Uncollectible*
Current	$ 424	3%
30 days past due	208	8%
60 days past due	231	10%
90+ days past due	580	40%
	$1,443	

*Based on prior experience. These percentages exclude the receivable from the grocery chain described above, which has not been included in the allowance in any prior year.

CASE 7-3

STEVE'S GROCERY INC.

Steve's Grocery Inc. (SGI) owns and operates a chain of six grocery stores located throughout Nova Scotia. The stores are located in rural communities and SGI's head office is located in Halifax. Because SGI stores provide jobs within small, rural communities and SGI's head office has a policy of employing individuals coping with mental and physical disabilities, SGI receives some grant funding from the Nova Scotia Department of Community Services (DCS). DCS requires that SGI's financial statements be audited each year. Details of the grant funding agreement between SGI and DCS are included in Exhibit 1.

You have been the auditor of SGI for many years and have a good working relationship with SGI's sole shareholder, Steve Marcus. You admire Steve's integrity and commitment to improving his community and are impressed with how SGI's corporate culture reflects Steve's core values. You recently met with Steve to discuss the upcoming audit for the year ending 28 February 20X9. Notes from your meeting, which took place on 25 March are as follows:

- Steve hired a new manager of accounting in November 20X8. Marci Lucas is a professional accountant and is now in charge of accounting and finance for SGI. Marci has already made some year-end adjustments to the financial statements so that everything is in good shape for the visit from the auditors. (These journal entries, which include Marci's supporting notes, are in Exhibit 2.)

- Steve, who knows little about accounting, has recently been taking an on-line accounting class to help him develop a basic understanding of GAAP and financial reporting requirements. He is currently learning about accounting for bad debts and thinks that SGI should switch to the allowance method. He knows that the direct write-off method has been used in the past and is surprised that you (as his auditor) have signed off on it, since this method is not recommended per GAAP. He would like you to explain your position on this issue.

- Steve is in the process of designing a bonus plan for SGI employees. The bonuses paid will be based on earnings of SGI. The tentative bonus calculation will call for all earnings before taxes and bonuses in excess of $100,000 to be paid out as bonuses. The first bonus will be based on *next year's* reported earnings before taxes and bonuses (i.e., earnings for the year ending 28 February 2010.) Steve believes this calculation will result in a generous bonus pool, since SGI's earnings before taxes historically averages $200,000 – $250,000.

Required:

Prepare a memo to your client analyzing any financial reporting and other issues you identify. Identify any additional information you will need from your client to resolve these issues.

EXHIBIT 1

(Excerpts from)
GRANT FUNDING AGREEMENT BETWEEN:
STEVE'S GROCERY INC (SGI)
AND NOVA SCOTIA DEPARTMENT OF COMMUNITY SERVICES (DCS)

Clause 2: On an annual basis, DCS will reimburse SGI for 10% of the total salary and wage expenses incurred by the six grocery stores. The following condition must be met in order to receive the above reimbursement:

> "At least 30 individuals in total must be employed on a full-time basis by the six SGI grocery stores."

Clause 3: On an annual basis, DCS will reimburse 50% of salary and wage expenses paid to employees who are coping with physical or mental disabilities. Any physical and mental disabilities must be documented by a medical doctor.

Clause 5: Salary and wage expenses per the audited annual financial statements will form the basis for the reimbursement calculations. Detailed records must be kept for salaries and wages such that a DCS auditor can easily track what was reported as salaries and wages for the different categories of employees (i.e., employees with mental or physical disabilities must be tracked separately). SGI is responsible for calculating the reimbursement owing and submitting the claim to DCS within 60 days of each fiscal year-end.

Clause 6: A DCS auditor may be assigned to audit SGI's reported salary and wage expenses without notice. Any abuse discovered in the preparation of a reimbursement claim will result in a cancellation of this agreement.

EXHIBIT 2

MARCI'S ADJUSTING JOURNAL ENTRIES FOR THE YEAR ENDING
28 FEBRUARY 20X9

AJE#1:

Sales returns and allowances	5,000	
Allowance for sales returns		5,000

Supporting notes: SGI grocery stores sold a bulk order to McMichael Distributors, a company that has been supplying grocery items to communities in the far north for the past three years. McMichael sends a container load of nonperishable groceries to a community, for re-sale to residents. McMichael can often sell for less than the conventional—and expensive—grocery store in the community but takes the risk that they send items in the container that no one wishes to purchase. SGI agreed that McMichael had six months to pay, but the SGI bookkeeper feels that some products might be returned if sales are low.

AJE#2:

Salaries and wage expense	14,000	
Repairs and maintenance expense	15,000	
Building		29,000

Supporting notes: During the year, a lot of work was done to the head office building. This was capitalized in asset accounts by the SGI bookkeeper. However, it is better classified as expense for the period. Details as to the costs incurred are as follows:

The building roof was reshingled at a cost of $12,000. The shingles are made of tin, and cost more than standard shingles but the roofer assured me the extra cost would be worth it as tin shingles do not need to be replaced as often as regular shingles. It was good that we completed this repair as the roof was leaking prior to fixing it. Additional insulation was added to the building at a cost of $7,000. We also had the exterior of the building repainted at a cost of $10,000. Of the total cost incurred of $29,000, I recorded the portion relating to the labour charges as salaries and wage expense and the portion relating to materials used as repairs and maintenance expense. I believe this will better reflect how much we spent on actual materials versus the labour for the trades people hired to perform the work.

AJE#3:

To be determined …

Supporting notes: The reimbursement for eligible salary and wages expenses for fiscal 20X9 has yet to be prepared. I have been too busy with my other responsibilities to prepare this calculation. I plan to record this in late April, in the 20X10 fiscal year, after I have the audit behind me and the financial statements are issued.

(Laura Cumming, adapted)

TECHNICAL REVIEW

TR7-1 Cash—Bank Reconciliation: Vish Limited reported a cash balance of $36,000 in the general ledger, but the bank statement reported a balance of $27,900 at the end of September 20X9. You have ascertained that the bank cashed a cheque on this account, in the amount of $5,500, which was actually issued by Mish Limited; this was an error made by the bank. There was also an outstanding deposit of $4,900, an amount that was deposited by Vish at the end of September after the bank cut-off. Outstanding cheques were $2,500, and there was an error made by Vish's bookkeeper, who recorded a cheque to a supplier at $1,200 when it was really $2,100. Bank fees of $400 have not yet been recorded by Vish, and neither was a direct deposit of $1,100 by a customer, who paid Vish directly to Vish's bank account.

Required:
Prepare a bank reconciliation as of the end of September, 20X9.

TR7-2 Accounts Receivable—Allowances: The accounts of Quickly Company provided the following 20X4 information at 31 December:

Accounts receivable balance	$600,000 (dr.)
Allowance for sales discounts	5,500 (cr.)
Allowance for sales returns	2,000 (cr.)
Allowance for doubtful accounts	40,000 (cr.)

In fact, the allowance for sales discounts is not needed at the end of 20X5, the allowance for sales returns should be $14,000, and aging shows that the allowance for doubtful accounts should be $65,000.

Required:
1. Prepare journal entries to adjust all allowances.
2. By how much have these entries changed earnings?
3. What is the net balance of accounts receivable that will be included on the SFP?

TR7-3 Accounts Receivable—Bad Debts: The unadjusted net accounts receivable on the books of Elantra Limited as of 31 December 20X4 are as follows:

Accounts receivable	$100,000
Less: Allowance for doubtful accounts	10,000
	$ 90,000

Two alternatives are being considered for estimating the allowance at the end of 20X4:

Alternative 1: Percentage of credit sales; Sales revenue was $3,000,000, of which 40% was on credit and 1% might be uncollectible

Alternative 2: Aging; 40% of the accounts are current and 5% might not be collected, and the remainder is past due and 30% might not be collected.

Required:
For each alternative, calculate the bad debt expense, the balance in the allowance for doubtful accounts, and the net accounts receivable on the SFP at the end of 20X4.

TR7-4 Transfer of Receivables: Hum Corp. has accounts receivable of $460,000. The company transfers these accounts receivable to a financial institution. There are no bad debts associated with these accounts receivable. Proceeds of $444,500 are received from the transfer. The transfer is on a non-notification basis, which means that the customers pay Hum, and Hum remits the cash to the financial institution. The customers pay $460,000 to Hum on schedule, and the cash remittance is forwarded to the financial institution.

Required:
Record all journal entries for the sequence of events assuming:

1. the transfer is recorded as a sale/derecognition, and
2. the transfer is recorded as a borrowing.

TR7-5 Notes Receivable: Dharma sold a piece of equipment at the beginning of Year 1, receiving a $10,000, two-year 1% note. Interest is paid at the end of each year. Market interest rates are in the range of 10%.

Required:
1. Calculate the present value of the note receivable.
2. Prepare entries for the sale, and cash collection each year for two years.

ASSIGNMENTS

★ **A7-1 Financial Assets:** The disclosure note of HOSA Products Limited showed the following (in millions):

	FVTPL	Amortized Cost	Total Carrying Value	Total Fair Value
Cash	$116	$ —	$116	$116
Cash equivalents	542	—	542	542
Accounts receivable	165	699	864	864

Required:

1. Define financial instrument and financial asset.
2. With respect to cash, explain why the asset is classified as FVTPL. Under what circumstances would the fair value of cash change from the originally recognized value?
3. What is the definition of a cash equivalent?
4. With respect to accounts receivable, explain the difference between the accounting treatment of financial instruments classified as FVTPL and those classified as amortized cost. Why are some elements likely placed in one category versus the other?
5. What is the most likely reason that fair value and amortized cost are equivalent?

★ **A7-2 Accounts Receivable—Allowances:** The accounts of Polaris Company provided the following 20X5 information at 31 December 20X5:

Accounts receivable	$ 1,899,000 (dr.)
Allowance for sales discounts	23,500 (cr.)
Allowance for sales returns	5,700 (cr.)
Allowance for doubtful accounts	134,900 (cr.)
Total credit sales revenue during 20X5	23,589,000

Investigation showed the following:

a. Examination of an aging of accounts receivable showed that accounts of $106,200 should be written off. Of the remaining balance, $216,000 was doubtful at year-end.
b. Estimated sales discounts inherent in the closing accounts receivable balance were $17,200. Terms of 1/10, n/45 were granted to customers. Accounts receivable were recorded gross, and the discounts taken were recorded when taken by the customers in a discounts account, reported contra to the sales account.
c. Customers are allocated sales allowances when goods have flaws. Based on past experience, $9,500 of price reductions might be given. When price reductions are granted during the year, the sales returns account, a contra account to sales, is increased.

Required:

1. Prepare year-end adjusting entries with respect to accounts receivable and the related allowances.
2. Show how the net accounts receivable appear on the statement of financial position on 31 December 20X5.

★ **A7-3 Accounts Receivable—Allowances and Entries:** The net accounts receivable on the books of GJY Corporation as of 1 January 20X3 are as follows:

Accounts receivable	$562,000
Less: Allowance for sales discounts	12,000
Allowance for doubtful accounts	41,300
	$508,700

During the year, the sales discount allowance is left unchanged, with discounts recorded directly in the sales discounts account. Allowances are adjusted at year-end. Summarized transactions during 20X3 are as follows:

a. Sales revenue was $1,240,000, of which 70% was on credit.
b. Customers paid off $985,000 of the outstanding accounts receivable. Of this reduction to the accounts receivable, $600,000 was paid in time to earn a 2% discount.
c. Accounts of $15,300 were written off at year-end.
d. There were recoveries of previously written-off accounts in the amount of $2,800.
e. At year-end, analysis of accounts receivable indicates that an allowance of $7,900 is needed for sales discounts.
f. At year-end, the allowance for doubtful accounts is increased by 1% of gross credit sales.

Required:

1. Prepare journal entries for the above transactions.
2. Show how the net accounts receivable appear on the statement of financial position on 31 December 20X3.
3. Do you have any concerns about the level of the allowance for doubtful accounts? Explain.

A7-4 Accounts Receivable—Allowances: At 31 December 20X8, Security Controls Limited reported gross accounts receivable of $1,240,900. Investigation showed the following:

a. Customers are permitted to return 2% of annual sales for full credit, as long as goods are returned in good condition within 30 days of delivery. Based on past years' experience, $25,100 of goods might be returned. As returns are received during the year, the sales returns account, a contra account to sales, is increased. An allowance for sales returns exists, at $19,600, unchanged from the previous year-end.
b. The credit balance in the allowance for doubtful accounts was $91,200 after write-offs for the year but before any bad debt adjustment. Bad debt expense is based on a percentage of receivables. Based on the latest available facts, $140,000 will not be collected due to collection issues.
c. Terms of 1/10, n/30 were granted to all customers. Accounts receivable were recorded gross, and the discounts taken were recorded when taken by the customers in a discounts account, reported contra to the sales account. Estimated discounts inherent in the closing accounts receivable balance were $15,300. The allowance for sales discounts account was established at $14,900 last year and has not been adjusted since.

Required:

1. Prepare year-end adjusting entries with respect to accounts receivable.
2. Show how the net accounts receivable would appear on the statement of financial position on 31 December 20X8.

★★ **A7-5 Accounts Receivable—Estimation of Allowances:** Information related to accounts receivable is given for two cases:

Case 1 Technology Solutions uses the credit sales method to estimate bad debt expense. Sales this year were $5,600,000, of which 70% were on credit. History has shown that 1.2% of credit sales will be uncollectible over time. The company reported a balance of $677,200 of accounts receivable at the end of the year before any adjustment. The allowance for doubtful accounts was $14,900, and the allowance for sales discounts was $6,000 before adjustment. Analysis shows that receivables of $24,500 must be written off, and approximately $3,900 of cash discounts will be taken when existing accounts receivable are collected.

Case 2 At the beginning of the year, Health Products Corp. has a balance of $2,450,000 in accounts receivable and $220,000 in the allowance for doubtful accounts. Sales for the year were $19,300,000, of which 70% were on credit. Cash payments on account were $12,905,000. Sales returns were $340,000. Accounts of $107,600 were written off, but $32,900 was subsequently recovered and collected. This $32,900 cash payment was in addition to the collections previously mentioned. At year-end, a review indicated that 8% of outstanding accounts receivable were uncollectible, but that there was no risk of further sales returns.

Required:

For each case above, show how net accounts receivable would be reported on the statement of financial position, and calculate bad debt expense for the year.

★★ **A7-6 Accounts Receivable—Estimation of Allowances:** Information related to accounts receivable is given for two cases:

Case 1 Zhang Corporation used the credit sales method to estimate bad debt expense. In 20X3, the opening balance of accounts receivable was $320,500. Credit sales were $2,545,000 Collections during the year were $2,596,500. The opening balance of the allowance for doubtful accounts was $41,800. Accounts receivable of $34,200 were written off, and $2,100 of previously written of accounts were subsequently paid by the customer. This $2,100 is in addition to the $2,596,500 collections previously mentioned. Over time, 0.8% of credit sales have been uncollectible.

Case 2 Mobile Technology Limited reported an unadjusted balance of accounts receivable of $1,285,000 at 31 December 20X3, along with a credit balance in the allowance for doubtful accounts of $83,100 and an allowance for sales discounts of $6,000. At year-end, the company determined that an allowance of $12,500 for sales discounts was needed. They also decided that $53,400 of accounts receivable were uncollectable and should be written off. Of the remaining receivables, it was determined that 40% were current, and of the remaining *net* current balance, an allowance for doubtful accounts of 3% of the net balance was needed. The remaining 60% of outstanding accounts receivable were past due and an allowance for doubtful accounts of 10% of the outstanding balance was needed.

Required:

For each case above, show how net accounts receivable would be reported on the statement of financial position, and calculate bad debt expense for the year.

★★ **A7-7 Accounts Receivable—Estimation of Bad Debt Expense:** The accounts of Long Company provided the following 20X5 information at 31 December 20X5 (end of the annual period):

Accounts receivable balance, 1 January 20X5	$ 51,000
Allowance for doubtful accounts balance, 1 January 20X5	3,000
Total sales revenue during 20X5 (on credit)	160,000
Uncollectible account to be written off during 20X5 (ex-customer Slo)	1,000
Cash collected on accounts receivable during 20X5	170,000

Estimates for bad debt losses:

a. Based on credit sales, 1%.
b. Based on ending balance of accounts receivable, 8%.
c. Based on aging schedule (excludes Slo's account):

Age	Accounts Receivable	Probability of Noncollection
Less than 30 days	$28,000	2%
31–90 days	7,000	10
91–120 days	3,000	30
More than 120 days	2,000	60

Required:

1. Give the entry to write off customer Slo's long-overdue account.

2. Give all entries related to accounts receivable and the allowance account for the following three cases:

   Case A—Bad debt expense is based on credit sales
   Case B—Bad debt expense is based on the ending balance of accounts receivable
   Case C—Bad debt expense is based on aging

3. Show how the results of applying each case above should be reported in 20X5 earnings and on the 20X5 statement of financial position.

4. Briefly explain and evaluate each of the three methods used in Cases A, B, and C.

5. On 1 August 20X6, customer Slo paid his long-overdue account in full. Give the required entries.

★★ **A7-8 Accounts Receivable—Allowance for Doubtful Accounts:** The accounting records of Sine.Com Limited provided the following for 20X9:

Balance in accounts receivable, 1 January 20X9	$ 90,000
Balance in accounts receivable, 31 December 20X9	120,000
Balance in allowance for doubtful accounts, 1 January 20X9	3,000 (cr.)
Accounts already written off as uncollectible during 20X9	5,500

Cash sales were $900,000, while credit sales were $650,000. Recently, Sine.Com's management has become concerned about various estimates used in its accounting system, including those relating to receivables and uncollectible accounts. The company is considering various alternatives with a view to selecting the most appropriate approach and related estimates.

For analytical purposes, the following 20X9 alternative estimates have been developed for consideration:

a. Bad debts approximate 0.75% of credit sales.
b. Bad debts approximate 0.4% of total sales.
c. Six percent of the uncollected accounts receivable at year-end will be uncollectible.
d. Aging of the accounts receivable at the end of the period indicated that 80% would incur a 2% loss, while the remaining 20% would incur a 10% loss.

Required:

1. For each of the four alternatives listed above, give the following:
   a. 20X9 adjusting entry
   b. Ending 20X9 balance in the allowance account
   c. An evaluation of the alternative

2. Explain which of the four alternatives you would recommend.

(Atlantic School of Chartered Accountancy, used with permission)

★★ **A7-9 Accounts Receivable—Allowance for Doubtful Accounts:** Accounts receivable for Pressure Oil Ltd. were reported on the statement of financial position prepared at the end of 20X8, as follows:

Accounts receivable		$122,900	
Less: Allowance for doubtful accounts	$3,530		
Allowance for sales returns	670	4,200	$118,700

In 20X9, the following transactions took place:

Sales on account	$841,610
Cash collected on account	799,430
Sales returns and allowances given to customers	3,210
Accounts written off	2,150
Accounts previously written off but recovered	650

Additional information:

The company sells goods on account. At the end of the year, accounts receivable are aged and the following percentages are applied in arriving at an estimate of the charge for doubtful accounts.

	Estimated loss
Current accounts	0%
Accounts 1–2 months overdue	7%
Accounts 3–6 months overdue	20%
Accounts 7–12 months overdue	50%
Accounts more than 1 year overdue	95%

At the end of the year, most of the accounts receivable are current. However, the aging schedule (after write-offs and recoveries) shows the following:

Accounts 1–2 months overdue	$7,500
Accounts 3–6 months overdue	6,100
Accounts 7–12 months overdue	2,500
Accounts more than 1 year overdue	880

An analysis shows that the allowance for sales returns should have a balance of $2,200 at the end of the year.

Required:

1. Give the entries required to record the transactions listed above and also to adjust the accounts. Sales returns and allowances should be entered directly in the sales returns and allowances income statement account. The allowance for sales returns is adjusted at year-end only.

2. Calculate the balance for accounts receivable and the related allowances as at 31 December 20X9, and show these accounts as they will appear on the statement of financial position.

A7-10 Accounts Receivable—Alternatives for Allowance for Doubtful Accounts: At 31 December 20X9, the end of the annual reporting period, the accounts of Huron Company showed the following:

a. Sales revenue for 20X9, $2,950,000, of which one-quarter was on credit.

b. Allowance for doubtful accounts, balance 1 January 20X9, $22,700 credit.

c. Accounts receivable, balance 31 December 20X9 (prior to any write-offs of uncollectible accounts during 20X9), $383,400.

d. Uncollectible accounts to be written off, 31 December 20X9, $19,800. These accounts are all in the "past due over 90 days" category.

e. Aging schedule at 31 December 20X9, showing the following breakdown of accounts receivable (prior to any write-offs of uncollectible accounts during 20X9):

Status	Amount
Not past due	$210,800
Past due 1–60 days	60,000
Past due over 60 days	89,100
Past due over 90 days	23,500

Required:

1. Give the 20X9 entry to write off the uncollectible accounts.

2. Give the 20X9 adjusting entry to record bad debt expense for each of the following independent assumptions concerning bad debt loss rates:
   a. On credit sales, 1.8%.
   b. On total receivables at year-end (after write-off), 4.2%.
   c. On aging schedule: not past due, 0.8%; past due 1–60 days, 1.8%; past due over 60 days, 11%, and past due over 90 days, 80%.

3. Show the amount that would be reported on the 20X9 statement of financial position relating to net accounts receivable for each assumption.

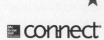

★ **A7-11 Transfer of Accounts Receivable:** Belanger Ld. reports a current ratio of 2-to-1 in its 20X2 financial statements. The statement of financial position shows current assets of $2,540,500 and current liabilities of $1,284,000. Accounts receivable are $745,900 of the current assets. Foote is considering transferring $440,000 of the accounts receivable with a 90-day term to a financial institution. There are no bad debts associated with these accounts receivable. Proceeds of $421,200 are expected from the transaction.

Required:

1. What criteria must be met for the transfer of accounts receivable to qualify for derecognition?
2. Prepare journal entry to record the transfer as (a) a sale/derecognition and (b) a borrowing.
3. Recalculate the current ratio reflecting first (a) and then (b) in requirement 2.
4. Why might a financial statement analyst restore transferred accounts receivable to the statement of financial position before performing a ratio analysis? What ratios other than the current ratio would be especially affected?

★ **A7-12 Transfer of Accounts Receivable:** The following two cases are independent:

Case A   Appa Apparel manufactures fine sportswear for many national retailers and frequently sells its receivables to financing companies as a means of accelerating cash collections. Appa transferred $600,000 of receivables from retailers to a financing company and has no control over, or continuing interest in, the accounts receivable. The receivables were transferred without recourse on a notification basis. The financing company charged 12% of the receivables total. There were no bad debts.

Required:

1. Should Appa record the transfer of receivables as a sale/derecognition or as a borrowing? Why?
2. Record all entries related to the transfer for Appa.

Case B   Bappa Apparel manufactures fine sportswear for many national retailers and frequently sells its receivables to financing companies as a means of accelerating cash collections. Bappa transferred $600,000 of receivables from retailers to a financing company. The receivables were transferred with recourse on a notification basis. The financing company charged 8%. Bappa has no obligation to the financing company other than to pay the account of a retailer in the event of a default. However, Bappa retains legal control over the receivables, and the financing company may not sell the accounts receivable to a third party. There were no bad debts.

Required:

1. Should Bappa record the transfer of receivables as a sale/derecognitionor as a borrowing? Why?
2. Record Bappa's entries related to the transfer.

★★ **A7-13 Transfer of Accounts Receivable:** On 1 April 20X5, XCourt Company transferred $75,000 of accounts receivable to Prima Finance Company to obtain immediate cash. Consider the two following independent circumstances.

Required:

1. The transfer agreement specified a price of $64,200 on a no-recourse, notification basis that effectively transferred legal control to Prima. Prima is permitted to resell the accounts receivables without permission from XCourt. Give the entry/entries that XCourt Company should make. The $10,800 reduction from face value represents a $6,800 financing fee and $4,000 of expected bad debts that are already in the allowance for doubtful accounts. Explain the basis for your response.
2. The transfer agreement specified a price of $70,000 on a with-recourse, notification basis. The $5,000 reduction from face value is related to expected bad debts, $2,000, and

a $3,000 financing fee. The bad debt amount is already in the allowance for doubtful accounts. XCourt retained the right to repurchase the receivables; Prima is not permitted to resell the accounts receivable unless XCourt is given first refusal on the transaction. Give the entry/entries that XCourt should make.

3. Explain the difference to the statement of financial position between requirements 1 and 2.

★ **A7-14 Transfer of Accounts Receivable:** Lincraft Corp. reports a current ratio of 3-to-1 in its 20X2 financial statements. The statement of financial position shows current assets of $3,116,500 and current liabilities of $1,040,100. Lincraft has accounts receivable of $1,267,300. The company transfers $970,000 of these accounts receivable to a financial institution. There are $33,600 of bad debts associated with these accounts receivable, an amount that is already in the allowance for doubtful accounts. Proceeds of $889,450 are received from the transfer. The transfer is on a non-notification basis, which means that the customers pay Lincraft and Lincraft then remits the cash to the financial institution. The customers pay $936,400 to Lincraft on schedule, $33,600 is written off to the allowance at the appropriate time, and the cash remittance is forwarded to the financial institution.

Required:

1. Record all journal entries for the sequence of events assuming:
   a. The transfer is recorded as a sale/derecognition, and
   b. The transfer is recorded as a borrowing.
2. Calculate the current ratio, after the initial entry in requirements 1a and 1b, and comment on the result.

★★ **A7-15 Notes Receivable:** MacDonald Company sells large construction equipment. On 1 January 20X5, the company sold Chowdury Company a machine at a quoted price of $60,000. MacDonald collected $20,000 cash and received a two-year note payable for the balance.

Required:

1. Give MacDonald's required entries for the two years, assuming an interest-bearing note, face value $40,000. (8% interest, simple interest, payable every 31 December.)
2. Assume that the market interest rate is still 8%. Give MacDonald's required entries for the two years, assuming a 2% interest-bearing note, face value $40,000. Prepare the entries based on the gross basis.
3. Compare the interest revenue and sales revenue under requirements 1 and 2.

★★ **A7-16 Notes Receivable:** The following cases are independent:

Case A   On 1 May 20X8, Jain Company sold merchandise to a customer and received a $110,000 (face amount), one-year, non-interest-bearing note. The going (i.e., market) rate of interest is 6%. Discounting must be used to value the transaction. The annual reporting period for Jain Company ends on 31 December. The customer paid the note in full on its maturity date.

Case B   On 15 April 20X8, Hall Company sold merchandise to a customer for $175,000, terms 2/10, n/30. The sale is recorded gross, at $175,000. Because of nonpayment by the customer, Hall agreed to accept a $175,000, 5%, 12-month note on 1 May 20X8 to replace the account receivable. This is a market interest rate. The annual reporting period ends 30 September. The customer paid the note in full on its maturity date.

Required:
For each case:

1. Give all entries related to the notes receivable through to maturity. Use the gross method to account for accounts and notes receivable.
2. List the items and amounts that will be reported on the 20X8 statement of comprehensive income and statement of financial position.

★★   **A7-17 Notes Receivable:** MacWilliams Limited sold a $45,000 piece of machinery to a customer on 1 January 20X6, and took back a two-year, 1% note receivable. The customer has to pay interest every 31 December, but the $45,000 principal is due only after two years. Market interest rates are in the range of 5%.

Required:

1. What is the present value of the note receivable?
2. Record the sale/loan on 1 January 20X6, the interest each 31 December (two times) and the loan repayment on 31 December 20X7. Use the gross method to record the note.
3. If present value was disregarded, and the transaction recorded at its face value, would accounts be misstated in the financial statements? Explain.
4. Record the transaction, interest and repayment on the books of the customer.
5. Repeat requirement 2, assuming that MacWilliams has a fiscal year-end of 31 October.

★   **A7-18 Notes Receivable:** Bento Corporation took a $500,000 four-year note receivable from a customer in connection with a major sale transaction. The note required annual blended payments, to be paid at the end of each year. The market interest rate is 4%.

Required:

1. Calculate the required blended payment. Round to the nearest dollar.
2. Prepare a schedule that shows the annual interest and principal portion of the four payments.
3. Prepare journal entries to record the initial sale transaction and each payment.

★★   **A7-19 Notes Receivable:** Cambria Limited took a $250,000 two-year note receivable from a customer in connection with a major inventory sale transaction on 1 January 20X5. The note required annual end-of-year interest payments of 4%, and the principal was due at the end of 20X6.

Required:

1. Prepare journal entries to record the initial sale transaction and each payment on the books of Cambria, assuming that the market interest rate is 4%.
2. Assume now that the market interest rate is 8%. Calculate the present value of the note, and prepare a schedule that shows the annual interest.
3. Prepare journal entries to record the initial sale transaction and each payment on the books of Cambria, consistent with requirement 2. Use the gross method to record the note.
4. What accounts are different between requirements 1 and 3? Explain.
5. Prepare journal entries to record the initial sale transaction and each payment on the books of the customer who bought inventory and owes the note, consistent with requirement 2.

★   **A7-20 Notes Receivable:** Omega Chemicals Limited took a $420,000 two-year note receivable from a customer in connection with a major sale transaction on 1 May 20X7. The note required annual 31 April interest payments of 3%, and the principal was due on 31 April 20X9. Omega has a 31 December year-end.

Required:

1. Prepare journal entries to record the initial sale transaction and each payment on the books of Omega, assuming that the market interest rate is 3%.
2. Assume now that the market interest rate is 5%. Calculate the present value of the note, and prepare a schedule that shows the interest for each year of the note receivable.
3. Prepare journal entries to record the initial sale transaction and each payment on the books of Omega, consistent with requirement 2. Use the gross method to record the note.

4. What accounts are different between requirements 1 and 3? Explain.

★★ **A7-21 Notes Receivable—Impairment:** On 1 January 20X5, Spencer Inc. sold merchandise (cost, $8,000; sales value, $14,000) to Bryden, Inc. and received a non-interest-bearing note in return. The note requires $15,730 to be paid in a lump sum on 31 December 20X6.

In February 20X6, Bryden requested that the terms of the note be modified so that the $15,730 payment be paid at the end of 20X11. Spencer refused Bryden's request.

During 20X6, however, news of Bryden's deteriorating financial condition prompted Spencer to reevaluate the collectibility of the note. Consequently, the modified terms requested by Bryden were accepted as of 31 December 20X6.

Required:

1. Prepare the entry to record the sale by Spencer, assuming a perpetual inventory system. Also prepare the 31 December 20X5 adjusting entry. Use the net method. You will need to establish the interest rate implicit in the original note.

2. Prepare the entry to record the impairment on 31 December 20X6. (Compare the book value of the note at 31 December 20X6 with the present value of the newly acknowledged cash flow stream using the same interest rate as in requirement 1. No interest revenue is accrued in 20X6.)

★ **A7-22 Foreign Currency Receivables:** Gerung Limited is a Canadian company that had the following transactions in 20X7:

a. Sold goods to a customer in France on 25 November for 110,000 euros.
b. Sold goods to a U.S. customer on 25 November for US$40,000.
c. Sold goods on 1 December, to a British customer for 70,000 euros.
d. On 15 December, the customer in transaction (a) paid.

At year-end, the other two accounts receivable were still outstanding.

EXCHANGE RATES

Canadian Equivalencies	Euro	US$
25 November	1.55	1.02
1 December	1.61	0.98
15 December	1.42	1.01
31 December	1.47	1.03

Required:

Calculate the exchange gain or loss to be reported in 20X7, the accounts receivable on the 31 December 20X7 statement of financial position, and the sales revenue to be recorded from the transactions listed above.

★★ **A7-23 Foreign Currency Receivables:** Golden Limited had the following transactions in 20X5:

a. Sold goods on 1 June to a British customer for 70,000 euros with payment to be in four months.
b. Sold goods to a U.S. customer on 15 June for US$150,000; payment was due in one month.
c. Sold goods to a British customer on 15 July for 20,000 euros; settlement was to be in two months.
d. Received payment from the U.S. customer in (b) on 15 July.
e. Received payment from the British customer in (c) on 15 September.
f. Received payment from the British customer in (a) on 1 October.

EXCHANGE RATES:

Canadian Equivalencies	Euro	US$
1 June	1.45	1.07
15 June	1.40	1.11
15 July	1.42	1.09
15 September	1.36	1.03
1 October	1.32	1.06

Required:
Prepare journal entries for the above transactions.

 A7-24 Comprehensive: April Ltd. reported various selected balances in its 31 December 20X7 unadjusted trial balance:

Accounts receivable	$1,800,000 dr.
Special accounts receivable	225,000 dr.
Accounts receivable—U.S.	116,000 dr.
Allowance for doubtful accounts	158,050 cr.
Allowance for sales discounts	45,000 cr.

The following transactions and events are noted:

1. An analysis of accounts receivable indicates that $800,000 are still in the discount period. An allowance of $80,000 is needed for sales discounts.

2. An analysis of accounts receivable indicated that $198,000 of accounts receivable should be written off. Of the remaining balance, 80% was current, and, after the allowance for sales discounts, approximately 5% was deemed doubtful. Of the 20% noncurrent, 75% was doubtful.

3. The U.S. account receivable was recorded when the exchange rate was $1.16. The exchange rate at year-end was $1.12.

4. The special account receivable was a single account receivable from a customer with an excellent credit rating that was transferred to a financial institution at a discount rate of 4% during the period. The cash collected from the financial institution was credited to an account called "Miscellaneous credits." Management has determined that this transaction was to be recorded as a sale/derecognition but has not yet made the necessary entry.

5. The company has a note receivable that has not yet been recorded. The note is a $70,000, three-year note that bears an interest rate of 4%. Interest is paid annually. The note was issued on 1 November 20X7 because of a sale. The market interest rate for accounts of this risk is 8%.

Required:
Provide journal entries to reflect the above items.

 A7-25 ASPE—Notes Receivable: Epsilon Limited accepted a $300,000 two-year note receivable from a customer in connection with a major inventory sale transaction on 1 January 20X5. The note required annual end-of-year interest payments of 2%, and the principal was due at the end of 20X6.

Required:

1. Assume that the market interest rate is 7%. Calculate the present value of the note, and prepare a schedule that shows the annual interest using the straight-line method of amortization.

2. Prepare journal entries to record the initial sale transaction and each payment on the books of Epsilon, consistent with requirement 1. Use the gross method to record the note.

3. Prepare a schedule that shows the annual interest using the effective interest method of amortization.

4. Compare interest revenue as calculated in requirements 1 and 3. Which is more accurate? Explain. What method(s) are permitted under ASPE? IFRS?

★★ **A7-26 ASPE—Notes Receivable:** Sumarah Corporation accepted a $225,000 two-year note receivable from a customer in connection with a major inventory sale transaction on 1 October 20X5. The note was interest-free, although market interest rates were in the range of 8%.

Required:

1. Can the company record a sale for $225,000? Explain.

2. Calculate the present value of the note, and prepare a schedule that shows the annual interest using the effective interest method. Prepare a second schedule using the straight-line method.

3. Compare the two alternate measures of interest revenue as calculated in requirement 2. Which is more accurate? Explain. What method(s) are permitted under ASPE? IFRS?

4. Prepare journal entries to record the initial sale transaction and each payment on the books of Sumarah, using the straight-line method. Use the gross method to record the note.

★★★ **A7-27 Bank Reconciliation (Appendix):** The August bank reconciliation for C&C Limited:

Balance per bank	$151,570
Plus: outstanding deposits	17,900
Less: Outstanding cheques ($11,245, $650, $1,570, $890, $120)	(14,475)
Cash, per general ledger	$154,995

September information, per books:

Opening balance: $154,995

Cash Receipts Journal Deposits:		Cash Disbursements Journal Cheques:	
7 Sept.	$ 4,600	1030	$ 11,000
11 Sept.	42,500	1031	24,650
14 Sept.	17,800	1032	24,780
22 Sept.	13,400	1033	75
25 Sept.	21,600	1034	8,165
30 Sept.	13,210	1035	7,900
30 Sept.	1,750	1036	40,420
	$114,860		$116,990

September information, per bank:

Opening balance: $151,570

Deposits:		Cheques:	
$ 17,900		$ 1,570	
4,600		890	
42,500		175 (cheque of C&S Co.)*	
17,800		90 (service charges)	
5,750 (direct deposit by customer		11,000	
on account)		24,780	
13,400		120	
21,600		9,700**	
$123,550		24,650	
		$72,975	

*Charged to this account in error

**For automobile; incorrectly recorded as $7,900 by company.

Required:

1. Prepare a bank reconciliation, in good form, at the end of September.
2. Prepare any adjusting journal entries required as a result of the reconciliation.

A7-28 Bank Reconciliation (Appendix): Ample Company carries its chequing account with Commerce Bank. The company is ready to prepare its 31 December bank reconciliation. The following information is available:

a. The 30 November bank reconciliation showed the following:
   i. Cash on hand (held back each day by Ample Company for change), $400 (included in Ample's Cash account).
   ii. Deposit in transit, #51, $2,000.
   iii. Cheques outstanding, #121, $1,000; #130, $2,000; and #142, $3,000.

b. Ample Company cash account for December:

Balance, 1 December	$ 64,000
Deposits: #52—#55, $186,500; #56, $3,500	190,000
Cheques: #143—#176, $191,000; #177, $2,500; #178, $3,000; and #179, $1,500	(198,000)
Balance, 31 December (includes $400 cash held for change)	$ 56,000

c. Bank statement, 31 December:

Balance, 1 December	$ 67,600
Deposits: #51—#55	188,500
Cheques: #130, $2,000; #142, $3,000; #143—#176, $191,000	(196,000)
Account receivable collected for Ample Co.	6,720
Cash received from foreign customer: prepayment on order; not yet recorded by Ample Co.	10,000
NSF cheque, Customer Belinda	(200)
United Fund (automatic charitable donation per transfer authorization signed by Ample Co.)	(50)
Bank service charges	(20)
Balance, 31 December	$ 76,550

Required:

1. Identify by number and dollars the 31 December deposits in transit and cheques outstanding.
2. Prepare the 31 December bank reconciliation.
3. Prepare all journal entries.

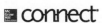

A7-29 Bank Reconciliation (Appendix): The general ledger of Michelle Co. Ltd. showed a cash balance of $25,160 on 31 December 20X2, while the bank showed a balance of $59,400. The following facts were available:

a. The bank collected $11,560 as a direct deposit for one of Michelle's customer as a payment on account. A $15 fee was charged by the bank for administration. Michelle has yet to record either of these amounts.
b. Michelle paid a utilities bill of $390 through direct transfer from its bank account but has not yet recorded the payment.
c. There was an outstanding deposit of $16,800 at the end of December.
d. The bank had charged a cheque of $2,600, written by Mitchell Corp., to Michelle's bank account. The bank has been contacted about the error, and will reverse the cheque in January.
e. A deposit of $1,300 from a customer on account was recorded by Michelle for $3,100. The bank noticed the error and deposited the correct amount of money, but the deposit is incorrectly recorded on Michelle's books.
f. Michelle's bank account shows a deposit of $22,000 in December, which is an increase in Michelle's bank loan. The amount has not been recorded by Michelle.

g. At the end of November, outstanding cheques were $8,185. This month, cheques were issued for $199,000, and cheques of $184,900 cleared the bank account.

Required:

1. Prepare a bank reconciliation, in good form, at the end of December 20X2.
2. Prepare any adjusting journal entries required as a result of the reconciliation.

★★★ **A7-30 Bank Reconciliation (Appendix):** Various information for Helix Company in relation to the cash account:

General Ledger:

Balance, 1 April	$16,420
Plus: cash receipts journal	45,700
Less: cash disbursements journal	(42,980)
Balance, 30 April	$19,140

Information from the journals:

Cash Receipts Journal Deposits:		Cash Disbursements Journal Cheques:	
4 April	$ 2,100	670	$ 440
5 April	13,550	671	16,100
19 April	650	672	1,180
26 April	23,800	673	450
30 April	5,600	674	12,600
		675	7,900
		Service charges	265
		676	4,045
	$45,700		$42,980

The March bank reconciliation:

Balance per bank	$19,730
Plus: Outstanding deposits	500
Less: Outstanding cheques ($450, $1,670, $1,355, $335)	(3,810)
Cash, per general ledger	$16,420

April information, per bank:

Opening bank balance	$19,730
Deposits: $500, $2,100, $13,550, $10,000 (loan from bank), $5,500 (direct deposit from customer for cash sale) $650, $23,800	56,100
Cheques: ($1,180, $12,600, $265 (service charges), $1,355, $4,900 (direct payment to supplier on account), $1,200 (interest), $450 (March cheque), $1,560 (direct payment for insurance), $4,450 (recorded in error as $4,045 in books; to supplier on account)	(27,960)
Closing bank balance	$47,870

Required:

1. Prepare a bank reconciliation in good form at the end of April.
2. Prepare any adjusting journal entries required as a result of the reconciliation that should be made at 31 December, based on your bank reconciliation.

■ connect ■ LEARNSMART ■ SMARTBOOK™

For more information on the resources available from McGraw-Hill Ryerson, go to www.mcgrawhill.ca/he/solutions.

CHAPTER 8

Cost-Based Inventories and Cost of Sales

INTRODUCTION

A few years ago, the Italian-based international dairy company Parmalat SpA—well known in Canada for its Lactantia, Beatrice, and Astro brands—was found to have overstated assets and net income by as much as $20 billion over several years, the largest fraud in European history. A large part of the misstatement was in the inventory accounts. Parmalat executives allegedly recorded fictitious purchases of inventory, followed by fictitious sales to customers.[1] Parmalat was hardly the first and certainly will not be the last company in which inventory fraud has occurred. Similar high-profile frauds involving fictitious inventories have occurred in many industries including retail, gold mining, and pharmacy distribution.

Inventories typically represent the largest single current asset of manufacturing, wholesale and retail companies. In today's competitive economic climate, inventory accounting methods and management practices are profit-enhancing tools. Better inventory systems can increase profitability; poorly conceived systems can drain profits and put businesses at a competitive disadvantage. The success of Walmart is largely the result of finely tuned inventory and supply chain systems.

Good inventory and profit control depends on up-to-date, efficient, and reliable inventory accounting systems. No matter how sophisticated a company's electronic inventory systems may be, physical inventory still must be counted. Between counts, inventory amounts often are *estimated* for special reporting purposes, such as monthly or quarterly statements, or to test for possible "missing" inventory. Toward the end of this chapter, we will explain the two estimation methods: gross profit method and retail method.

This chapter covers the accounting methods used to value and report inventories on the statement of financial position. Inventory valuation simultaneously affects measurement of cost of sales (COS) and net income. The main body of this chapter will not dwell on the basic concepts of cost flow and of perpetual inventory—those concepts are discussed in introductory accounting textbooks. However, we have included these basic concepts in the Appendix to this chapter, just in case you need to refresh your memory.

---

[1] You may wonder why auditors did not detect the fraud earlier. One of the basic postulates of auditing is that top management is not lying to the auditors. If top management is deliberately misleading auditors or hiding parts of the business, it is not easy for an auditor to uncover these systemic frauds.

Bases of Inventory Valuation

Exhibit 8-1 shows the various classifications of inventory. For accounting purposes, there are two important bases for inventory valuation:

- Historical cost, subject to lower-of-cost-or-NRV (net realizable value) valuation; and
- Market value, either NRV or fair market value, depending on the type of inventory.

There is one very important point to remember: *inventory valuation is based on historical cost unless accounting standards specifically state otherwise.* Historical cost, modified by NRV, is the "default" valuation method for inventory.

EXHIBIT 8-1

TYPES OF INVENTORY

Inventories Based on Historical Cost

Classification	Measurement Basis
Retail & wholesale	
Goods available for sale	Laid-down cost, net of rebates*
Manufacturing	
Raw materials	Laid-down cost, net of rebates[†]
Work in progress	Accumulated direct labour and materials costs + allocated manufacturing overhead to date[†]
Finished goods	Total accumulated direct labour and materials costs + allocated manufacturing overhead[†]
Supplies	Cost of items used in production or service delivery but too inexpensive to allocate to individual products or product classes*
Long-term service contracts	
Work in progress	Direct labour and other direct costs + allocated service overhead[§]
Long-term construction contracts —completed contract method	
Construction in progress	Total material, labour, and overhead cost to date[§] (see Chapter 6)

Inventories Based on Market Value

Classification	Measurement Basis
Biological assets, agricultural produce at point of harvest, and minerals	NRV when widely used in the industry; otherwise, the lower of cost or NRV (see Chapter 6)
Financial instruments held for trading (e.g., by securities dealers or financial institutions)	Fair market value minus cost to sell (see Chapter 7)

*Subject to lower-of-cost-or-NRV valuation by item or by group.
[†]Subject to NRV valuation based on the selling price of finished goods.
[§]Subject to NRV valuation based on the finished contract price.

COST-BASED INVENTORIES

General Nature of Inventory

We typically think of inventories as tangible goods and materials, such as raw materials, work in process, finished goods, or merchandise held by retailers. But, depending on the nature of the company's business, inventory may include a wider range of costs incurred and held in an inventory account.

A very common type of inventory for many businesses is *work in progress*, which also is known by other names, such as *work in process* or *contracts in progress*. The only types of business that do not have work in process inventories are (1) mercantile businesses (retail and wholesale) and (2) entities providing short-term services. Most inventories consist of accumulated costs that have been incurred in an as-yet incomplete earnings process. Once the earnings process is complete, the inventory is moved from asset to expense and is recognized in the income statement in the same period as the revenue is recognized.

For example, a professional services firm, such as a software development company or a law firm, may accumulate the costs of fulfilling a particular contract as "inventory" until the contract has been substantially completed and the criteria for revenue recognition have been met.

Even in companies that deal with physical goods, tangible raw materials and purchased parts are likely to be a relatively small part of the total cost. Most of the inventory cost is likely to consist of such costs as labour and overhead.

Items that may be capital assets for one company may be inventory for another. Machinery and equipment, for example, is inventory for the company that manufactures it. It becomes a capital asset for the company that buys and uses the assets. Even a building, during its construction period, is an inventory item for the builder.

Cost-Based Inventory Policy Issues

Since COS is often the largest single expense in measuring profit or loss and since inventory is an integral part of current and total assets, accounting policies in this area can cause net income and net assets to change significantly. There are four basic policy issues:

1. Items and costs to include in inventory

2. Application of lower-of-cost-or-NRV valuations

3. Cost flow assumptions for measuring COS

4. Choice of accounting procedure: periodic versus perpetual systems

Strictly speaking, the choice of periodic or perpetual systems is a *procedural* choice rather than a *policy* choice, but the choice can affect financial reporting and thus should be viewed as an accounting policy choice.

This chapter focuses on the first two issues. Introductory accounting textbooks discuss (1) cost flow assumptions and (2) periodic versus **perpetual inventory systems** quite extensively. Therefore, we have relegated these two topics to the Appendix of this chapter. If you need to refresh your knowledge, read the Appendix.

Items to Include in Inventory

Inventory should include all goods that are *both* (1) owned by the company and (2) intended for resale or use within the company, regardless of their physical location. These are not trivial requirements—at any time, a business may hold goods that it does not own, or it may own goods that it does not hold. Therefore, care must be taken to identify the goods that should be included in inventory.

Goods *purchased and in transit* should be included in the purchaser's inventory if ownership has passed to the purchaser. Passage of title for goods in transit depends on the terms of the shipping contract. In some cases, title automatically transfers to the buyer when the goods are given to the carrier (e.g., a trucking or railroad company). This is sometimes described as FOB (free on board) *shipping point*. In other cases, the seller has title until the carrier delivers the goods to the final customer. This is sometimes described as FOB *destination*. There are at least a dozen common shipping arrangements, so contracts must be carefully scrutinized to establish the point at which ownership of goods in transit is legally transferred from the seller to the customer.[2] This is called **title transfer** (or *transfer of title*), and it is an important element in inventory accounting.

Goods that are owned by a company but are out on **consignment** (i.e., held by agents) should be included in inventory. Goods should be *excluded* from inventory if they (1) are held for sale on commission or on consignment but owned by someone else or (2) have been received from a supplier but rejected and are awaiting return to the supplier for credit.

Repurchase Agreements Some suppliers enter into **repurchase agreements** to sell and buy back inventory items at prearranged prices if they are not resold by a certain date. This practice has several advantages. Inventory is, in effect, "parked" outside the company, so the supplier may be able to avoid finance and storage expenses that would be incurred if the inventory stayed in-house.

The buyer usually pays all or most of the retail value of the inventory covered in the repurchase agreement until the goods are reacquired by the seller, again at a prearranged price. However, when a repurchase agreement exists, the inventory must remain on the seller's books. In effect, repurchase agreements may be loans from customers rather than sales because the vendor has an obligation to pay back the customer if the goods are not resold.

Special sales agreements exist in some industries, including those selling items to retailers; sporting goods manufacturers and book publishers are good examples. These agreements permit goods to be returned if not sold. Should such goods be considered sold when delivered to the retailer? Revenue recognition rules suggest that these goods should be considered as sales only if returns can be reasonably estimated or if the return privilege has expired. Otherwise, the items remain in the seller's inventory account.

Although legal ownership is a useful starting point to identify items that should be included in inventory, a strict legal determination of ownership does not automatically mean that those items should be included. The sales agreement, industry practices, and other evidence of intent should be considered.

Elements of Inventory Cost

The basic principle for measuring inventory cost is that the cost of inventories should include *all costs incurred to bring the inventories to their present location and condition*. The cost should be net of any discounts, rebates, or other concessions that effectively reduce the cost.

Raw Materials and Goods Purchased for Resale In general, inventory cost is measured by the total cash equivalent outlay made to acquire the materials or goods. For goods intended for resale, the cost to prepare them for sale is also included. These costs include materials purchase cost and incidental costs incurred until the goods are ready for sale to the customer. Cost includes "freight-in" and other shipping costs incurred by the buyer, as well as customs charges and excise duties. The total of these costs is known as the **laid-down cost**. Sales taxes may or may not be included—we will explain this in the following section.

When freight charges and other incidental costs incurred in connection with the purchase of tangible inventory are part of the laid-down cost, they should be attributed to the specific goods to which they pertain. However, specific identification often is impractical. For example, an individual supplier may ship many different types of inventory in a single shipment. Therefore, freight costs are commonly recorded in a special account, such as freight-in, which is allocated and added to inventory and to cost of goods sold for reporting purposes.

Certain other incidental costs often are not included in inventory valuation but are reported as separate expenses, even though they theoretically are a cost of goods purchased. Examples include insurance costs on goods in transit, material handling expenses, and

---

[2] For international transactions, additional shipping arrangements include CIF (shipper bears responsibility for "Customs, Insurance and Freight") and DPD (shipper is responsible for "Duty Paid and Delivered").

import brokerage fees. These expenditures are usually not included in determining inventory costs because the cost of allocating them to specific purchased goods is not worth the benefit.

Storage, warehousing, and distribution costs are *not* normally included as an element of inventory cost. Although those costs are a necessary cost of inventory handling, IFRS requires that they be treated as period costs and charged to expense when incurred. An exception arises when storage is a necessary part of the production process before further production or processing. Examples would be the storage costs for (1) aging wine prior to its bottling or (2) holding cheese for maturation prior to packaging.

Companies in some industries regularly offer **cash discounts** on purchases to encourage timely payment from buyers. The intent is to speed cash inflow. Terms of 2/10, n/30, for example, means that if the invoice is paid within 10 days, a discount of 2% can be taken. Alternatively, the full balance, *n*, is due in 30 days. Most buyers make timely payments and take advantage of cash discounts because the savings are normally quite substantial.[3] In fact, some companies borrow money to take advantage of cash discounts. Inventory should be recorded at the lowest available cash price, which is 98% of the invoice price in this example. *Lost discounts are a cost of financing and should not be included in inventory amounts.*

General, selling, and administrative (GS&A) expenses are never included as an element of inventory cost. GS&A costs are not directly related to the acquisition of inventory.

"Sales" Taxes Two types of taxes that often are assessed on purchases are *sales tax* and *value added tax*. Retail customers do not usually make any distinction between these two types of tax, since the buyer must pay them regardless of what they are called. However, there is an important difference that has an effect on how we record inventory cost:

- A merchant adds the amount of a **sales tax** to the price of goods thereby creating a liability for the seller because the tax must be remitted to the government. The buyer must absorb the full cost of the tax.
- A merchant adds the amount of a **value added tax** (VAT) to the price of all goods sold regardless of the nature of the purchaser. The VAT collected creates a liability to the government. However, the merchant also *pays* VAT on materials, supplies, and goods that the merchant buys. The amount paid is called an *input tax credit*, and the merchant deducts the amount paid for inputs from the amount owed to the government on sales. In other words, everyone along the entire supply chain is liable only for the net difference between the amount collected on sales and the amount paid on purchases. Only the final consumer gets stuck with bearing the full amount of the tax.

In Canada, we have both types. There is a **provincial sales tax** (PST) in some provinces and a federal **goods and services tax** (GST) in all provinces and territories. For example, a $100 pair of shoes will cost you $112 in Manitoba, including 7% PST and 5% GST.[4]

Consumers normally refer to both PST and GST as "sales tax," but they really are two quite different types of tax. To make things more confusing, five provinces have combined their PST with the federal GST to end up with a **harmonized sales tax** (HST). Although HST is viewed as a sales tax by consumers, it really is a value added tax—the effect of "harmonizing" the two taxes was that the previous PST was converted into a VAT, thereby extending it to all goods and services (with some legislated exemptions, such as food).

---

[3] Discounts for prompt payment actually are very expensive for the vendor. If a 2% discount speeds customers' payments by 20 days, on average, then the annual interest rate is equivalent to 37%. The vendor is far better off to *not* give a discount and to borrow from the bank to finance the receivables (or sell the receivables to a factor or finance company). To make matters worse, some large customers will blithely deduct the discount from their payment even if they pay quite late; the customer views the discount as a price reduction rather than a reward for quick payment.

[4] GST and HST are completely visible in Canada. In most other countries, VAT is "hidden" in the price of goods and services. It is there, though, and at far higher rates—e.g., 15% to 27% in Europe, although most are around 20%.

What this distinction means for accounting is that our treatment of taxes paid on purchases depends on the type of tax:

- Sales taxes are not refundable and therefore are considered part of the laid-down cost for inventory.
- VAT (GST or HST) is not included in the cost of inventory because it is refundable. Instead it is debited to a "taxes payable" account to offset the VAT collected on sales revenue. If more is paid on purchases than collected from sales, the company will receive a refund from the government.

There is one exception to the principle that organizations recover GST/HST on purchases. Not-for-profit (NFP) organizations get a rebate from the government for just two-thirds of the HST/GST paid. The nonrefundable one-third theoretically should be added to inventory cost. In practice, the amounts may be immaterial and may instead be reported as a period cost (i.e., an expense) rather than as a part of inventory cost.

We will not pursue this issue any further at this point. You will be delighted to know that it is covered in more detail in Chapter 12.

Service Contracts A service company such as a law firm or a consulting company does not have physical inventory available for sale. Aside from some inventory of *supplies*, service inventory consists exclusively of **work in progress**, which is the accumulated costs of contract work performed to date for which the company has not yet recognized the revenue. There are two elements of cost:

- *Direct costs.* These are mainly the costs of personnel who are directly engaged in providing the service. Direct costs also include any material or equipment (e.g., special computer equipment or software) that is necessary to complete a particular service contract.
- *Overhead costs.* Overhead consists of costs that are necessary to complete service contracts but that cannot be attributed specifically to individual contracts, such as supervision and service-related equipment (e.g., company-owned laptop computers). Overhead includes supplies and other small costs that are theoretically assignable to specific contracts but are not worth the effort to assign.

Inventory for a service provided does not include general administrative or selling costs. GS&A costs are recognized as expenses when incurred.

As a practical matter, when service contracts are short-term contracts, normally only the direct costs are inventoried; overhead costs usually are treated as period costs. When the contract is complete and the revenue is recognized, the inventoried costs are transferred from *work in progress* on the SFP to *cost of services* provided (or some similar title) on the income statement.

The approaches for recognizing revenue from long-term contracts were explained in Chapter 6.

Manufactured Goods In a retail or wholesale business, there is just one type of inventory—the laid-down cost of goods available for sale. In a service company, we also will see just one inventory type—work in progress. In contrast, a manufacturing or producing company will normally have three types of inventory:

- *Raw materials*—the laid-down cost of raw materials and purchased small parts that will be used in production
- *Work in progress*—the costs incurred on goods that are in production, but not yet finished; work in progress includes raw materials, direct labour, and an allocation of production overhead
- *Finished goods*—the cost of goods manufactured and ready for sale, including raw materials, direct labour, and allocated production overhead

The overall cost of turning raw materials into a finished item is called its **conversion cost**. Raw materials are *converted* into finished goods by applying labour and incurring overhead costs. The movement of costs through the accounting system is as follows:

- The cost of purchased raw materials and parts starts out in raw materials inventory.

- When raw materials enter production, their cost is transferred to work in progress, with direct labour and overhead costs added to work in progress.
- When production is complete, the accumulated costs are transferred to finished goods.
- When the goods are sold, the cost is transferred from finished-goods inventory to COS.

Overhead should be allocated on the basis of *normal capacity*. **Normal capacity** is the operating level at which the factory is expected to operate most of the time, not full capacity or maximum capacity. You will study cost allocation systems in management accounting courses, but the significant point for financial accounting is that the cost of inventory should *not* absorb all of the manufacturing costs if the manufacturing plant is operating below normal capacity. The costs of idle capacity are expensed as a period cost.

Standard costs may be used for inventory costing purposes, provided that the standards are based on normal capacity and are regularly reviewed and revised.

Supplies Inventory   In addition to the inventory types described above, most companies also have an inventory of supplies. *Supplies* are items that are used in the productive activities of the company but that are either (1) used during production (e.g., lubricant for machinery) or (2) too small to try to keep track of individually, even though they may enter the product directly (e.g., adhesives, bolts, rivets, and small spare parts). Supplies inventories often are very small, and thus they often are included in raw materials inventory as being immaterial and are not separately reported in the statement of financial position (SFP) or in the disclosure notes.

Periodic or Perpetual Recording Method

Inventory cost may be measured by either a periodic inventory system or a perpetual inventory system. The essential difference between these two systems from an accounting point of view is the *frequency with which the cost flows are calculated*.

In a *periodic* system, the inventory is physically counted at least once each year and then the total inventory cost is calculated from cost records using the chosen cost flow policy (e.g., FIFO or average cost).

In a full accounting *perpetual* system, the inventory cost is continuously updated for each purchase and sale. After each change in inventory quantities, the total cost of inventory is recalculated, using the chosen cost flow policy.

Note that for accounting purposes, a perpetual system exists only when the total inventory cost is continually updated. In contrast, some companies use a perpetual system for *quantities only*, which often are linked to an automated purchasing system. The dollar cost is calculated only at the end of each accounting period. These quantity-only systems are not perpetual systems as far as accounting and financial reporting is concerned.

The Appendix to this chapter contains a more extensive discussion of this topic.

Cost Flow Assumptions

There are only three cost flow assumptions acceptable under IFRS:[5]

1. Specific identification

2. First-in, first-out (FIFO)

3. Average cost

The specific identification and FIFO methods are not affected by the decision to use periodic or perpetual inventory systems—the cost allocated to inventory and COS will be the same under each method. In contrast, average cost *is* affected by the inventory system. The Appendix to this chapter illustrates the details.

Specific identification is used only when inventory items are not ordinarily interchangeable. Specific identification is applied to special-order inventory items that are significantly unlike other items. Most often these are very large items, such as ships or custom-designed

---

[5] LIFO (last-in, first-out) is not acceptable under IFRS. It remains acceptable in the United States and Japan, but its use is rare when prices are fairly stable.

yachts. However, the sheer size of the item is not really a factor. Large airplanes cost hundreds of millions of dollars, but they come off a production line and can be costed by FIFO (first-in, first-out) or average cost despite the fact that there is some relatively minor adaptation of specific models for specific airline customers. Essentially, every Canada Regional Jet, Boeing 777, or Airbus A380 is the same and is not accounted for by specific identification.

The "workhorses" of inventory cost flow assumptions are (1) FIFO and (2) average cost. In hand-kept bookkeeping systems, FIFO was more popular, especially for perpetual systems because there was no need to continuously recalculate the cost as under the average cost method. With the almost universal adoption of computer-based accounting systems, however, the average cost method has increased dramatically in popularity, especially as it works well with point-of-sale bar code scanners.[6]

CONCEPT REVIEW

1. Identify the accounting policy issues to be decided when accounting for inventory.

2. What classifications of inventory does a manufacturer have?

3. What are the three elements of cost that should be included in a manufacturer's finished-goods inventory cost?

APPLYING LOWER-OF-COST-OR-NRV VALUATION

Estimating Net Realizable Value

GAAP requires that most inventories be valued either at *laid-down cost* or at **net realizable value** (**NRV**), whichever is lower. The NRV is the estimated selling price in the normal course of business, minus (1) estimated costs of completion (if any) and (2) the estimated amount of any costs that are necessary in order to make the sale. For finished goods, there will be no costs of completion but there may be sales commissions or brokerage fees, and there may be special concessions (such as free shipping) that are necessary to close the sale. These costs must be subtracted from the year-end selling price to find NRV.

For example, suppose a retailer has an inventory consisting of a single line of office electronics products, all purchased during 20X2 at a cost of $150 per unit. The retail price was $200 at the time of acquisition. Late in the year, stiff competition in the electronics and office products market causes retail prices to drop significantly. At year-end, the retailer's remaining inventory can be sold in the normal course of business for no more than $160 per unit.

The year-end retail price of $160 is above the original unit cost of $150, but what is the NRV of the unit? To determine the NRV, the retailer must subtract any direct costs of making the sale. If the retailer pays a 15% commission to the salesperson, the $24 sales commission must be subtracted from the $160 sales price. The NRV is $160 − $24 = $136. The carrying value of the inventory must be written down from its historical cost of $150 to its NRV of $136, a loss of $14 per unit. This $14-per-unit loss must be reported in the retailer's 20X2 financial statements, the period during which the market price decline took place.

For work in process, the costs of completing the product or project must be estimated and then subtracted, as well as any further costs to sell (e.g., commissions), to find NRV.

Raw materials and work in process inventories seldom are written down. That is because these inventories will be used in the production of finished goods. The recoverable cost of these items depends on the sales price of the finished good, not of the inventory item itself. If the final selling price is stable, the inventory item's cost may be fully recoverable and thus should

---

[6] The use of bar code scanners does not necessarily mean that a company is accounting for *costs* on a perpetual basis. Often, the bar code system is used only to keep track of inventory *quantities*, not costs.

not be written down. However, a writedown is required if any items of raw materials become obsolete and therefore will not be used or will not be used in the manner originally intended.

The determination of NRV is fairly straightforward in concept, but its application requires estimating (1) sales value (which can be difficult in a rapidly changing market) (2) costs of completion and sale, and (3) current or potential obsolescence.

Exceptions to Writedowns

There are two situations in which a writedown to lower of cost or NRV may not occur:

1. The amount of writedown does not necessarily depend on an inventory item's NRV at the reporting date. A writedown is always determined *after* the reporting date, when the financial statements are being prepared. A company takes a broader look at the cost/price situation around the reporting date. If it appears that the low NRV was a year-end anomaly and prices recovered thereafter, management may decide that it is not appropriate to write the inventory down.

2. The NRV is *not* the amount that could be obtained by selling the inventory to another party to dispose of (e.g., to a clearance house) unless such a sell-off is foreseen at the date on which the financial statements are finalized. The sales price of any item is the estimated selling price in the normal course of business. This principle is known as the *best and highest use* of the asset.

Aggregation

Normally, the lower-of-cost-or-NRV test is applied by class of inventory item—that is, by each type of inventoried product treated as a group of individual items. However, in some circumstances, it is acceptable to group related asset types and apply the NRV test for the group as a whole.

Aggregation is appropriate if the inventory classes within a product group have a strong relationship with each other and cannot realistically be evaluated independently of each other. An example would be digital cameras in a camera store, all of which have the same general characteristics and end uses. Another example would arise when a camera store deliberately offers popular high-end cameras for sale at below cost to generate sales of ancillary products, such as expensive batteries or additional lenses. In such cases, the NRV test can be applied to the group as a whole.

Exhibit 8-2 shows the application of each approach. Inventory is valued at $67,500, a loss of $3,500, if the individual approach is used. If valued in groups, inventory is reported at $69,000, a loss of $2,000. The amount of any writedown must be disclosed.

Consistency in application over time is essential. The item-by-item basis produces the most conservative inventory value because units whose NRV exceeds cost are not allowed to offset items whose NRV is less than cost. This offsetting occurs to some extent when inventory is valued in groups. The more you aggregate, the less you write down.

How should inventory be grouped? There is no easy answer to this question. In general, there should be a relationship between the items that are grouped together. The groupings should not be arbitrary, and they should reflect the sales reality of the organization. Inventories should be not evaluated by general classification of such raw materials or finished products or by geographic region.

However, the products in a single product line can be grouped together because they represent a "product" in the broad sense of a range of related products. For competitive reasons, some products may be sold at a loss to support the sales of products that are highly profitable.

Therefore, some degree of offsetting within categories seems appropriate given the nature of sales efforts in general and the fact that NRV requires a lot of estimation.

Reversing Writedowns

What happens if the NRV goes back up after inventory has been written down? Prices may rise due to the failure of a major competitor, a shortage of supply, a change in the economic outlook, or many other reasons.

EXHIBIT 8-2

APPLICATION OF LOWER-OF-COST-OR-NRV VALUATION TO INVENTORY GROUPS

Inventory Types	Cost	NRV	Lower of Cost or NRV Applied to: Individual Items	Groups
Group A:				
Item 1	$10,000	$ 9,500	$ 9,500	
Item 2	8,000	9,000	8,000	
	18,000	18,500		$18,000
Group B:				
Item 3	21,000	22,000	21,000	
Item 4	32,000	29,000	29,000	
	53,000	51,000		51,000
Total	$71,000	$69,500		
Inventory valuation under different approaches			$67,500	$69,000

Suppose that an item of inventory is written down from $150 historical cost to $136 NRV in 20X2. In 20X3 the estimated $160 sales price goes up to $180. Sales commission remains at 15%, which is $27 on a sales price of $180. NRV has increased to $153: $180 − $27. The increase in NRV is $17 per unit (i.e., $153 − $136), but the reversal is limited to the amount of the original writedown, which was $14 per item. Cost-based inventory cannot be written up above its historical cost.

The writedown should be reversed by $14 for those items still in inventory thereby restoring the unit inventory carrying value to $150. On the income statement, the increase in NRV is recognized as a *reduction in the COS*, not as a separately recognized gain. The amount of the reversal must be disclosed in the notes.

In practice, reversals seldom occur. The normal expectation is that inventory will turn over within a year, and usually several times during a year. It is unlikely that written-down inventory will still be on the books a year later. If the inventory still is in stock, it probably will merit an additional writedown rather than a reversal due to obsolescence or due to inability to sell in the marketplace. Reversals are more likely to occur for shorter reporting periods, such as monthly or quarterly reporting.

Recording Writedowns—Using a Valuation Allowance

There are two methods of recording writedowns:

1. *Direct inventory reduction method.* The carrying value of individual inventory items is adjusted in the inventory accounts by the amount of any writedown. After adjustment, the inventory carrying values will show the NRV as the new carrying value. This method is possible only when NRV is applied to individual items.

2. *Inventory allowance method.* The writedown is not entered into the inventory accounts but is recorded separately in a contra inventory account, *allowance to reduce inventory to NRV*. The inventory remains at historical cost on the books but is reported on the net of the valuation account. Assume that the company illustrated in Exhibit 8-2 had an existing allowance of $2,500 and decided to apply NRV by individual items. The entry would be as follows:

Holding loss on inventory	1,000	
Allowance to reduce inventory to NRV		
($2,500 − $3,500)		1,000

In both methods, the amount of the writedown (and any reversal) is reported in the income statement or disclosed in the notes; it must not be hidden in *COS* or *cost of goods sold* as once was common.

The direct reduction method is practical only if NRV has been applied item by item. Only then can individual inventory items be written down in the subsidiary records. If NRV has been applied to inventory groups, it is impossible to record the writedown to specific inventory items.

Bear in mind that the SFP inventory account is a *control account*—it must be possible to reconcile the detailed subsidiary inventory records by classes and items to the balance in the control account. Companies generally prefer to keep the original cost amounts in the detailed inventory records so that those records can be easily reconciled to the control account. This is true regardless of whether writedowns are applied item by item or in groups.

The valuation allowance method *must* be used when NRV is applied to groupings so that the detailed subsidiary records will correspond with the balance in the inventory control account. However, the valuation allowance method is not limited to group writedowns; it may also be used when item-by-item lower of cost or NRV is applied.

A significant advantage to using a valuation allowance is that reversals can be handled very easily. If NRV rises after an initial writedown, only the allowance is adjusted; the inventory accounts themselves are not touched.

In practice, the valuation method is the most common approach, especially in large enterprises that have innumerable asset classes in many divisions operating in widespread locations.

ETHICAL ISSUES

NRV valuations require estimations. Both the current selling price and the costs to complete and sell must be determined. In a stable market, these estimates may be not too difficult. In a volatile market, both estimates may require quite a lot of judgement.

The difficulty of estimating NRV allows room for income manipulation, especially if inventories are substantial. Inventory can be written down in one year and sold at a substantial profit in a later year. Sometimes this happens with no intent to mislead if weak market conditions and poor selling prices dictate writedowns. A subsequent price recovery may be unexpected.

In other cases, unethical decisions may drive high write-offs in a "big bath" scenario. Managers who receive bonuses based on net income may be particularly motivated if tentative net income in the first year, or writedown year, is below the level needed to trigger a bonus. In businesses with a thin profit margin, relatively small estimation errors can have a significant impact on reported net income.

CONCEPT REVIEW

1. What is the definition of NRV?

2. In what situations can different items of inventory be aggregated and evaluated on the basis of lower of cost or NRV for the group as a whole?

3. What are the reasons for using a valuation allowance for inventory writedowns rather than using the direct inventory reduction method?

OTHER ISSUES FOR COST-BASED INVENTORIES

Damaged and Obsolete Inventory

Special inventory categories are created for items that are damaged, shopworn, obsolete, defective, trade-ins, or repossessions. These inventory items are valued at NRV.

To illustrate accounting for damaged inventory, assume that Allied Corp. suffers fire damage to 100 units of its regular inventory. The items, which originally cost $10 per unit (as reflected in the perpetual inventory records), were marked to sell before the fire for $18 per unit. No established used market exists. The company should value the item for inventory purposes at its NRV. Allied estimates that after cleaning and making repairs, the items would sell for $7 per unit; the estimated cost of the repairs for all the units is $150, and the estimated selling cost is 20% of the new selling price. Given these data, the total inventory valuation for the items is as follows:

Estimated sale price (100 × $7)		$700
Less: Estimated cost to repair	$150	
Estimated selling costs ($700 × 20%)	140	(290)
NRV for inventory		$410

Damaged inventory is segregated in a separate account as part of the writedown entry:

Inventory, damaged goods	410	
Loss from fire damage	590	
Inventory (100 × $10)		1,000

Losses on Purchase Commitments

To lock in prices and ensure sufficient quantities, companies often contract with suppliers to purchase a specified quantity of materials during a future period at an agreed unit cost. Some purchase commitments (contracts) are subject to revision or cancellation before the end of the contract period; others are not. Each case requires different accounting and reporting procedures. A loss must be accrued on a purchase contract when:

- The purchase contract is not subject to revision or cancellation, *and*
- A loss is both likely and material, *and*
- The loss can be reasonably estimated.

Assume that the Bayshore Limited enters into a noncancellable purchase contract during October 20X2 that states, "During 20X3, 50,000 tanks of compressed chlorine will be purchased at $5 each," a total commitment of $250,000. At the end of 20X2 the current replacement cost of the chlorine is $240,000. Thus, a $10,000 loss is likely.[7]

When a purchase contract binds a company to a price that will result in losses for the company, the contract is known under IFRS as an **onerous contract**. At the end of 20X2, the loss on the purchase commitment would be recorded as follows:

Estimated loss on onerous purchase commitment ($250,000 − $240,000)	10,000	
Estimated liability on onerous purchase commitment		10,000

The estimated loss is reported in the profit and loss section of the 20X2 statement of comprehensive income, and the liability is reported on the SFP. When the goods are acquired in 20X3, merchandise inventory (or purchases) is debited at the current replacement cost, and

---

[7] This is known as an *opportunity cost* because the company missed the opportunity to buy the chlorine at a lower price.

the estimated liability account is debited. If, at the date of delivery, the replacement cost goes down further, to $235,000, the purchase entry would be as follows:

Materials inventory (or purchases)	235,000	
Estimated liability on onerous purchase commitment	10,000	
Loss on onerous purchase commitment	5,000	
Cash		250,000

This treatment records the loss in the period when it became *likely*—$10,000 in 20X2 and an additional $5,000 in 20X3. Note that inventory is never recorded for more than its replacement cost at the date of acquisition, $235,000 in this example.

If there were a full or partial recovery of the purchase price, the recovery would be recognized in the period during which the recovery took place. Thus, if in 20X3 the materials had a replacement cost at date of delivery of $255,000, the purchase entry would be as follows:

Materials inventory (or purchases)	250,000	
Estimated liability on onerous purchase commitment	10,000	
Recovery of loss on onerous purchase commitment		10,000
Cash		250,000

Review the three criteria for accounting loss recognition listed above.

- What if the contract were cancellable? Then the loss is no longer likely, and the amount would not be accrued.
- What if the loss were not estimable? Recognition criteria are not met, and again no entry can be made.
- What if commodity prices are going up, not down? Then a loss is not likely, and no entry is appropriate.

Gains never are recognized. Disclosure of the contracts and terms is appropriate when the contracts are significant, or out of the ordinary, or when a loss is present that cannot be reasonably estimated.

Inventory Errors

In our discussion so far, we have focused mainly on the relationship between inventory and COS. Obviously, we will not get the correct COS if we have problems with our inventory calculations.

But inventory interacts with more than just COS. Incoming inventory relates directly to accounts payable and purchases, while outgoing inventory relates directly to accounts receivable and revenue. Because of the sheer volume of transactions involving inventory, it takes special vigilance to avoid errors.

There may be some estimation errors in inventory, especially in lower-of-cost-or-market estimates, in work-in-process inventories relating to long-term contracts, or in estimation techniques, such as the retail inventory method (which we will discuss shortly). However, estimates are a fact of life in accounting. They may turn out to be wrong, but they are not errors—we just do the best we can with the information that we have at the time we exercise our professional judgement.

Cut-Off Errors A primary type of error is **cut-off errors**. "Cut-off" refers to the year-end closing of the books. When we reach the end of a fiscal period, we must draw a line between transactions at (1) the period just ending and (2) the start of the next period. In theory, this is a simple exercise. In practice, accurate cut-offs are both crucial and difficult.

Assuring proper cut-off is a major accounting (and auditing) control issue due to the sheer volume of activity and the need to coordinate all of the accounting activities that involve inventory. Think about a factory. New inventory is delivered almost continuously during every day, and finished goods are shipped to customers all day long. If the factory operates 24 hours a day, when do we stop counting for last year and start counting for next year? Consistency is crucial. If we say that the year-end inventory is the amount in our factories, warehouses, and offices at midnight on 31 December, we must use that same cut-off time each year. The physical count of inventory must be taken as of that specific time, even though inventory is flowing in and out of our factory while the physical count is taking place over the following days.

Counting inventory is only part of the problem. We must be sure that goods shipped on the closing days of the year have also been invoiced to the customers—revenue and accounts receivable must include last-minute shipments. Goods and raw materials flowing into the factory in the final days must be included in purchases and accounts payable. Similarly, we must ensure that revenue has not been recorded for shipments that will not be made until the early days of the next year.

We also must make sure that no invoices were invoiced to customers prior to shipment of the goods. Unethical managers may be tempted to delay or accelerate shipments around year-end to manipulate income.

An example of cut-off weakness is the disclosure of "material weaknesses" and "significant deficiencies" in internal control by American Dairy Inc. (a Chinese company, despite the "American" name) in the company's 2009 10-K filing with the Securities and Exchange Commission (SEC):

- We did not effectively and timely assess the accounting treatment for transactions, including sales, purchases, inventory, taxation, acquisition of assets, asset valuations and capital assets.

- We did not have formal period-end closing procedures in place, which did not allow effective identification, approval and detection, of routine and nonroutine accounting journal entries.

As a result of this (and other) deficiencies, the company was unable to receive an auditor's attestation report regarding internal control over financial reporting.[8]

Counting Errors Sometimes, inventory is simply miscounted. Parts of an inventory tally may go missing, or a storage area or facility (e.g., a small warehouse in a foreign country) may be overlooked when the physical inventory count is taken. Correcting this type of error is fairly straightforward.

Suppose that a company discovers in 20X7 that its 20X6 year-end inventory was overstated by $750,000. The error is discovered after its 20X6 financial statements were issued. An overstatement of ending inventory leads to an (1) understatement of COS, (2) overstatement of income, and (3) overstatement of retained earnings. Therefore, the correction in 20X7 will be recorded as follows:

Retained earnings	750,000	
Inventory (1 January 20X7)		750,000

When the 20X7 financial statements are prepared, the comparative 20X6 financial statements must be restated to show the correct inventory and income amounts. Errors are always corrected by restatement and never by showing special charges or credits in the income statement.

Self-Correcting Errors Some errors self-correct over time. Suppose that the 20X6 inventory overstatement is not discovered until 20X8. If the year-end 20X7 inventory was correct, then there will be no misstatement of earnings in 20X8 because both the beginning and ending inventories for 20X8 are correct. However, the reported earnings for both 20X6 and 20X7 will be misstated by the amount of the inventory error—$750,000 too high for 20X6

---

[8] American Dairy Inc. Form 10-K/A, retrieved 24 June 2013, from http://www.sec.gov/Archives/edgar/data/789868/000114420409038758/v155283_10ka.htm.

and $750,000 too low for 20X7. No accounting entry is necessary in 20X8, but the prior years' statements will need to be restated.

We already touched on accounting changes in Chapter 4, and later in the book, we have devoted a full chapter (Chapter 21) to accounting changes, including error correction. Therefore, we will not elaborate further at this point in the text.

INVENTORY ESTIMATION METHODS

Many companies, large and small, rely on the periodic inventory method. Does this mean that they cannot prepare monthly or quarterly statements without also taking a physical inventory? It is quite expensive to conduct inventory counts and therefore physical counts may be done only at the end of each fiscal year. So what can be done when interim statements must be prepared?

The answer is quite simple: Inventory can be *estimated*. In a small business, the owner or inventory manager might be able to provide a reasonably accurate estimate. For larger businesses, a more formal calculation is made by using such methods as the *gross margin method* or the *retail inventory method*. It is important to understand that these are estimation methods. They necessarily introduce some level of unreliability to the financial results, a difficulty that is offset by providing more timely information.

Estimation methods are also useful for providing a cross-check on the results of accounting inventory systems. It should be possible to reconcile the estimated inventory (or, more importantly, COS) to a physical inventory count or to the accounting records of perpetual inventory. Obviously, the reconciliation will not be exact, but there should be a rough similarity between the results of the accounting inventory system (periodic or perpetual) and the estimated inventory. Large discrepancies raise questions of the accuracy of the accounting system, the effectiveness of the system of internal control, or the possibility of theft.

For example, a local manufacturer of fruit juices and soft drinks also distributed Coca-Cola syrup to restaurants and bars. The Coca-Cola syrup was, in fact, the company's biggest single seller and was also the most profitable product. Despite high sales, the company was only marginally profitable. A gross profit analysis revealed that the recorded COS was much too high, given the level of sales. A closer examination revealed that the inventory of syrup was too low for the amount that was actually recorded as being sold. It finally was discovered that due to supervisors' lack of vigilance in reconciling each driver's sales with the inventory loaded onto the truck, it was possible for unethical truck drivers to sell jugs of syrup "on their own account," pocketing the money.

Estimation methods are used primarily in mercantile firms: retailing and wholesaling. They are less useful in manufacturing but still are used for finished-goods inventories.

Estimates of inventory cannot be used for audited annual financial statements—a physical count is required.

Gross Margin Method

The **gross margin method** (also known as the *gross profit method*) uses a constant gross margin to estimate inventory values based on current sales levels. The **gross margin rate** (i.e., gross margin ÷ sales) is estimated on the basis of recent past performance and is assumed to be reasonably constant in the short run. The gross margin method has two basic characteristics:

1. It requires the development of an *estimated gross margin rate* for different lines or products.

2. It applies the rate to *relevant groups of items*.

Estimating by Gross Margin Method   Estimating the ending inventory by the gross margin method requires five steps, as illustrated in Exhibit 8-3:

Step 1   Estimate the gross margin rate on the basis of prior years' sales: gross margin rate = (sales − cost of sales) ÷ sales.

EXHIBIT 8-3

GROSS MARGIN METHOD

	Known Data	Estimated Results*
Net sales revenue (base amount)	$10,000	$10,000
Cost of goods sold:		
Beginning inventory	$ 5,000	$ 5,000
Add: Purchases	8,000	8,000
Goods available for sale	13,000 (1)	13,000
Less: Ending inventory		7,000 (4)
Cost of sales		6,000 (3)
Gross margin		$ 4,000 (2)

*Computational steps:
Gross margin rate (estimated as percent of sales based on last year's results) = 40%
(1) Goods available for sale, above: $13,000
(2) Gross margin: $4,000 (i.e., $10,000 × 40%)
(3) Cost of sales: $6,000 ($10,000 − $4,000)
(4) Ending inventory $7,000 ($13,000 − $6,000)

Step 2 Compute total cost of goods available for sale in the usual manner (beginning inventory plus purchases) based on actual data provided by the accounts.

Step 3 Compute the estimated gross margin amount by multiplying sales by the estimated gross margin rate.

Step 4 Compute COS by subtracting the computed gross margin amount from sales.

Step 5 Compute ending inventory by subtracting the computed COS from the cost of goods available for sale.

Uses of the Gross Margin Method The gross margin method is used to:

- Test the reasonableness of an inventory valuation determined by some other means, such as a physical inventory count, or from perpetual inventory records. For example, assume the company in Exhibit 8-3 counted inventory, and got a figure of $10,000. The gross margin method provides an approximation of $7,000, which suggests that the physical count may be overvalued and should be examined.

- Estimate the ending inventory for interim financial reports prepared during the year when it is impractical to count the inventory physically and a perpetual inventory system is not used.

- Estimate the cost of inventory destroyed by an accident such as fire or storm. Valuation of inventory lost is necessary to account for the accident and to establish a basis for insurance claims and income taxes. This is an example of a case where it would be helpful to know the markup on cost (i.e., gross profit ÷ COS) since cost is used for the insurance claim and to establish the loss.

- Develop budget estimates of COS, gross margin, and inventory for budgets.

Limits on Accuracy Is the gross margin method accurate? Well, it depends on whether or not gross margins really are fairly constant in the short run. If retail prices are slashed this year to spur consumer demand, or if theft has increased, the gross margin method will overstate earnings and inventory, perhaps significantly. Similarly, the results will not be accurate if the product mix changes a lot in the current period.

For example, if a company has traditionally sold about half its volume in a high-profit category, and half in a low-profit category, the historical gross profit margin will reflect this mix. In the current year, if volumes fall off in the high-profit side, the estimation method will produce inaccurate results. It is better to do separate estimates for each different product line. Mis-estimates will be uncovered at the end of the year, when inventory is actually counted—which may result in an unpleasant surprise for those who relied on the interim statements.

Retail Inventory Method

The **retail inventory method** is often used by retail stores, especially stores that sell a wide variety of items. In such situations, perpetual inventory procedures may be impractical, and a complete physical inventory count is usually taken only once annually. The retail inventory method is appropriate when items sold within a department have essentially the same markup rate and articles purchased for resale are priced immediately. Two major advantages of the retail inventory method are (1) its ease of use and (2) reduced record-keeping requirements, compared with perpetual inventory systems.

The retail inventory method uses both *retail value* and *actual cost* data to:

1. Compute a ratio of cost to retail (referred to as the *cost ratio*);

2. Calculate the ending inventory at *retail value*; and

3. Convert that retail value to an estimated lower of cost or NRV by applying the computed cost ratio to the ending retail value.

Application of the retail inventory method requires that internal records be kept to provide data on:

- Sales revenue;
- Beginning inventory valued at both cost and retail;
- Purchases during the period valued at both cost and retail;
- Adjustments to the original retail price, such as additional markups, markup cancellations, markdowns, markdown cancellations, and employee discounts; and
- Other adjustments, such as interdepartmental transfers, returns, breakage, and damaged goods.

The retail inventory method differs from the gross margin method in that it uses a computed cost ratio, based on the *actual* relationship between cost and retail for the current period, rather than on historical ratio. The computed cost ratio is often an average across several different kinds of goods sold.

Estimating by Retail Inventory Method The retail inventory method is illustrated in Exhibit 8-4. The steps are as follows:

Step 1 *Determine cost of goods available for sale at cost and retail.*
The total cost of goods available for sale during January 20X2 is determined to be $210,000 at cost and $300,000 at retail, as shown in Exhibit 8-4.

Step 2 *Compute the cost ratio (i.e., the ratio of cost to sales).*
The **cost ratio** is calculated by dividing the total goods available for sale at *cost* ($210,000) by the same items at *retail* ($300,000). In this example, the cost ratio is ($210,000 ÷ $300,000) = 0.70, or 70%, as shown in Exhibit 8-4. This is an *average cost* application of the retail method, because both beginning inventory and purchases are included in determining the cost ratio.

Step 3 *Compute closing inventory at retail (goods available for sale at retail, less sales).*
This is done by taking the total cost of goods available for sale at retail ($300,000) minus the goods that were sold in January ($260,000), resulting in the value of the ending inventory at retail ($40,000), as shown in Exhibit 8-4.

Step 4 *Compute ending inventory at cost.*
This is done by applying the cost ratio (70%), derived in (2), to the ending inventory at retail ($40,000), derived in (3). The result is an ending inventory of $28,000 at cost (i.e., $40,000 × 70%).

EXHIBIT 8-4

RETAIL INVENTORY METHOD, AVERAGE COST

	At Cost	At Retail
Goods available for sale:		
Beginning inventory	$ 15,000	$ 25,000
Purchases	195,000	275,000
Total goods available for sale (1)	$210,000	300,000
Cost ratio:		
$210,000 ÷ $300,000 = 70%; average,		
January 20X2 (2)		
Deduct January sales at retail		260,000 (3)
Ending inventory:		
At retail		$ 40,000
At cost ($40,000 × 70%)	$ 28,000 (4)	

Markups and Markdowns The data used for Exhibit 8-4 assumed no changes in the sales price of the merchandise as originally set. Frequently, however, the original sales price on merchandise is changed, particularly at the end of the selling season or when replacement costs are changing. The retail inventory method requires that a careful record be kept of all changes to the original sales price because these changes affect the inventory cost computation. To apply the retail inventory method, it is important to distinguish among the following terms:

- **Original sales price.** Sale price first marked on the merchandise.
- **Markup.** The original or initial amount that the merchandise is marked up above cost. It is the difference between the purchase cost and the original sales price, and it may be expressed either as a dollar amount or a percentage of either cost or sales price. Sometimes this markup is called "initial markup" or "markon."
- **Additional markup.** Any increase in the sales price above the original sales price. The original sales price is the base from which additional markup is measured.
- **Additional markup cancellation.** Cancellation of all, or some, of an additional markup. Additional markup less additional markup cancellations is usually called *net additional markup.*
- **Markdown.** A reduction in the original sales price.
- **Markdown cancellation.** An increase in the sales price (that does not exceed the original sales price) after a reduction in the original sales price markdown.

The definitions are illustrated in Exhibit 8-5. An item that cost $8 is originally marked to sell at $10. This item is subsequently marked up $1 to sell at $11, then marked down to a sales price of $7.

Using the retail method, all additional markups, markup cancellations, markdowns, and markdown cancellations are included in the early calculations that determine goods available for sale, both at cost and at retail. However, to provide a conservative cost ratio that approximates lower of cost or NRV, the denominator of the cost ratio *excludes net markdowns.*

See the example in Exhibit 8-6. If all of the markups and markdowns had been included in the cost ratio, the cost ratio would have been 72% (i.e., $6,840 ÷ $9,500). Applying that ratio to the estimated inventory at retail would have given an estimated ending inventory of $720 at cost. However, when the $500 net markdowns (i.e., $600 markdowns minus $100 markdown cancellations) are *excluded* from the cost ratio, the cost ratio becomes 68.4% (i.e., $6,840 ÷ $10,000), thereby yielding a lower estimated ending inventory of $684. *This lower value approximates the lower of cost or NRV.*

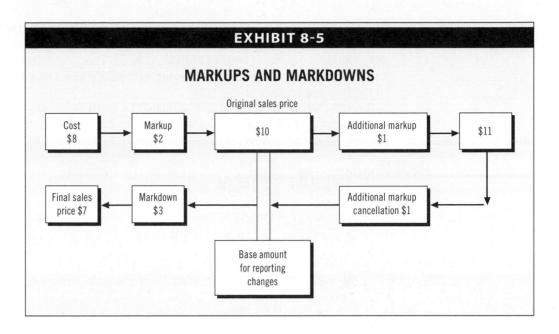

EXHIBIT 8-5

MARKUPS AND MARKDOWNS

Uses of the Retail Inventory Method Like the gross margin method, the retail inventory method is used to estimate the amount of the ending inventory at NRV and cost of goods sold.

A physical inventory count must be taken at least annually as a check on the accuracy of the estimated inventory amounts. The retail inventory method provides a test of the overall reasonableness of a physical inventory but has greater accuracy than the gross margin method in a retail environment.

The retail inventory method also can be quite useful if the entity regularly takes physical counts of inventory (e.g., monthly) and then converts the physical counts to a dollar value

EXHIBIT 8-6

RETAIL INVENTORY METHOD, LOWER OF COST OR NRV

	At Cost	At Retail
Goods available for sale:		
Beginning inventory	$ 550	$ 900
Purchases during period	6,290	8,900
Plus: additional markups during period		225
Less: additional markup cancellations		(25)
		$10,000
Less: markdowns		(600)
Plus: markdown cancellations		100
Total goods available for sale	$6,840	$ 9,500
Cost ratio (excluding net markdowns):		
$6,840 ÷ $10,000 = 68.4%		
Deduct:		
Sales		(8,500)
Ending inventory:		
At retail		$ 1,000
At cost, approximating lower of cost or NRV ($1,000 × 68.4%)	$ 684	

at retail. Remember, retail prices are much easier to determine on the selling floor than cost! The retail value can then be converted to cost by applying the retail inventory method without needing to know the costs of individual items. This derived inventory value may be used for interim external reporting if sufficient evidence is accumulated to support the accuracy of the cost percentages.

Like the gross margin method, though, the retail inventory method is subject to estimation errors. A lot of its accuracy depends on how carefully the company keeps track of markups and markdowns and other data needed to develop accurate cost ratios.

CONCEPT REVIEW

1. Why would a company use an inventory estimation method?

2. What is the basic difference between the gross profit method and the retail inventory method?

3. Why are markdowns excluded from the cost ratio when the retail inventory method is used?

REPORTING ISSUES

Statement of Cash Flows

Inventory costs represent expenditures. However, the expenditures do not make their way to the income statement until the inventory is sold. Therefore, the amount of inventory expenditures that are included in cost of goods sold in any accounting period will be different from the amount that was spent to acquire inventory. The statement of cash flows (SCF) must show the cost of inventory *paid for*, not the cost of inventory *sold*.

If cash flow from operations is calculated by the indirect method, net income must be adjusted by the change in inventory during the period:

- An *increase* in inventory means that the cash flow to purchase inventory was higher than the amount of expense reported as cost of goods sold—the increase must be subtracted from net income to reflect higher cash outflow.

- A *decrease* in inventory means that the cash flow to acquire inventory was less than the amount of expense reported as cost of goods sold—the decrease must be added to net income.

A further adjustment must be made for a manufacturing, resource, or service company. The COS (or cost of services provided) of such companies almost always includes amortization (e.g., depreciation on facilities or depletion on resources). Any depreciation or amortization that has been charged to inventory, whether to work in process or finished goods, must be added back to net income when determining the cash flow from operations.

Inventory Disclosures

The following disclosures are required in the financial statements:

- The dollar amount of inventory that is recognized as expense for the period; normally, this is included as part of COS, cost of goods sold, or cost of services provided. The amount of inventory consumed must be disclosed; it cannot be buried in COS without disclosure, as had often been done in the past.

- The major categories of inventory (e.g., raw materials, finished goods, contracts in progress, etc.).

- The basis for valuation for each inventory category (e.g., FIFO, average cost, lower-of-cost-or-NRV, NRV).

- Amount of any writedown recognized as expense in the period.
- The amount of any reversal of writedowns, and the reasons for the reversal.
- The amount of inventories carried at fair value less the cost to sell (e.g., commodity inventories carried by dealers or brokers).
- The carrying value of any inventories that have been pledged as collateral for liabilities.

Exhibit 8-7 shows New Flyer Industries Inc.'s inventory note disclosure for 2012. The company not only shows the year-end amounts of each category of inventory but also discloses the cost of inventories recognized as expense during the period, as required by IFRS. New Flyer recorded inventory writedowns in both fiscal years and reversed a previous writedown in 2012.

EXHIBIT 8-7

NEW FLYER INDUSTRIES INC.
Disclosure Note for Inventory

4 INVENTORIES

	December 30, 2012	January 1, 2012
Raw materials	$ 59,338	$45,454
Work in process	62,753	46,340
Finished goods	2,621	1,697
	$124,712	$93,491

	Fiscal 2012	Fiscal 2011
Cost of inventories recognized as expense and included in cost of sales	$732,312	$751,120
Write-down of inventory to net realizable value in cost of sales	1,124	1,828
Reversals of a previous write-down in inventory	192	—

Source: *Consolidated Financial Statements of New Flyer Industries Inc.*, page 18, www.sedar.com, posted 20 March 2013.

ETHICAL ISSUES

As we stated in the Introduction to this chapter, inventory accounting has often been abused. By its nature, inventory accounting requires many judgements and estimates. These issues are particularly challenging in manufacturing, where more decisions must be made about whether a cost should be a part of inventory or an expense of the period.

Ethical issues also surround the year-end cut-off. Internal controls must be strong enough to resist unethical managers' attempts to manipulate income by accelerating or delaying the recording of shipments and sales invoices.

Assigning Costs to Inventory Applying costs to the physical count, whether periodic or perpetual, requires careful tie-in. This is especially important when input costs change significantly during the period, such as for natural resources like oil, copper, and gold. Management may be tempted to be less than completely accurate in allocating overall purchase cost to inventory versus COS.

Accurate Cut-Off It is essential to maintain a consistent and effective cut-off at the end of each reporting period. Cut-off errors, whether accidental or deliberate, can have a significant impact on net income. Inventory shipments, sales recording, and accounts payable accounting must be carefully coordinated. Estimates such as damaged goods, missing inventory, probable returns, and cash discounts, offer additional opportunities for misstatement.

Major financial reporting software, such as SAS, has internal control safeguards that can guarantee that sales, accounts receivable, inventory, and accounts payable records are in harmony. Cut-off is more easily controlled through the use of these systems. Accounting software for smaller companies (or for those that have designed their own systems) is less likely to have effective built-in cut-off safeguards.

False Transactions As past frauds have repeatedly illustrated, inventories can be used by senior managers to generate apparent earnings by creating complex fake transactions through nonexistent purchases and sales. It is very difficult for external audit procedures to detect fraud by senior executives; an underlying assumption of external auditing is that senior managers are not lying to the auditors.

However, internal auditors and accountants often become aware of suspicious transactions. Most wrongdoing by senior management has been uncovered by internal accountants, not by external auditors. It is the company accountant's responsibility to watch for suspicious account activity and to alert the Board of Directors' Audit Committee that something improper might be going on.

Writedowns One very difficult ethical area is the use of inventory writedowns. The need for a writedown is a matter of judgement. Management may refuse to write down inventory, even in the face of slow-moving inventory and strong competitive pressures. Conversely, management may write down inventory prematurely. Management's decisions can be the result of an unintentionally inaccurate assessment of NRV or of a temporarily prevailing business mood. In either case, the writedown is legitimately motivated.

In other cases, however, management has used inventory writedowns as a way of manipulating profit. This is a problem not only with inventory but also with capital assets, as we shall discuss in Chapter 10. There have been many instances of management opposing demands by auditors to write down obviously obsolete inventory so as not to reduce net income. There have been many other instances of management writing down inventories excessively in order to shift profits from the current year to a future year.

We have seen that lower-of-cost-or-NRV valuation requires many judgements. A primary issue is just how to measure NRV. How should the potential selling price be estimated—as a year-end spot rate or as a prediction for the expected inventory turnover period? How can *costs to complete and sell* be estimated? What level of aggregation should be used? All of these questions are subject to significant estimation errors. The task of the accountant is to ensure that these questions are answered reasonably.

When the allowance method is used to reduce cost to NRV, an additional concern arises because the methodology and the reasonableness of the estimates are subject to audit review only at year-end. Interim results are not audited; management may be tempted to use inventory valuation allowances to "adjust" quarterly earnings to meet analysts' quarterly earnings projects or management's own earnings targets. The allowance method permits earnings to be shifted from one quarter to another within a fiscal year.

Conclusion Inventory accounting raises many opportunities for improper accounting. Company accountants can get drawn into significant ethical dilemmas if they are not careful.

Looking Ahead

Inventory accounting is a stable issue. The IASB has no projects on its work plan that relate to inventories.

ACCOUNTING STANDARDS FOR PRIVATE ENTERPRISES

Accounting for inventories under ASPE is substantially identical to IFRS. As in IFRS, LIFO is not permitted—inventory cost valuation methodology is the same. The few differences are as follows:

- **Onerous contracts**—The term "onerous contract" is not contained in ASPE. However, the effects of such contracts still should be recognized, as indicated in the chapter, but the term "onerous" is not used.

- **Writedowns**
  - ASPE does *not* require disclosure of the amounts of inventory writedowns.

- **Special inventories**—ASPE contains no special disclosure requirements for biological assets, agricultural produce, minerals, or mineral products.
  - For *biological assets*, "existing practice" prevails, which essentially means the lower of cost or NRV both for products in growth and for products at the point of harvest.
  - IFRS does not yet have a standard on the extractive industries. ASPE contains an Accounting Guideline on recognition and measurement of *oil and gas exploration* using the "full cost" method. However, the guideline neither encourages nor rejects the use of full cost accounting. Both full cost and successful efforts alternatives are permitted.

- **Presentation**—ASPE specifies only the following disclosures:
  - Inventory accounting policies, including the cost method used.
  - The total carrying value of inventories, classified as is appropriate for the enterprise (i.e., as supplies, raw materials, work in progress, and finished goods).
  - The amount of inventories recognized as expense during the period (which is similar to the IFRS requirement)

RELEVANT STANDARDS

CPA Canada Handbook, Part I (IFRS):
- IAS 2, Inventories
- IAS 41, Agriculture

CPA Canada Handbook, Part II (ASPE):
- Section 3031, Inventories

SUMMARY OF KEY POINTS

1. Inventories are assets that consist of material owned by the business and held either for future sale or for consumption in manufacturing or service provision. Inventories include raw materials, supplies, work in process (or progress), and finished goods or merchandise available for sale.

2. The cost of inventories includes all costs that were required to bring the inventories to their present location and condition but does not include inventory holding costs, such as insurance, storage, and distribution.

3. Work in process and finished-goods inventories of manufacturers should include raw materials, direct labour, and an allocation of manufacturing overhead determined on the basis of normal capacity.

4. All goods owned at the inventory date, including those out on consignment, should be counted and valued.

5. Either a periodic or a perpetual inventory system may be used to track inventory. Computer technology now makes it easier and less costly to use a perpetual system.

6. For accounting purposes, inventory systems are "perpetual" only when they track costs as well as quantities. Quantity-only systems provide inventory quantities, which is helpful, but does not provide the inventory costs.

7. The only cost flow assumptions that are acceptable under both IFRS and ASPE for cost-based inventories are (1) specific identification, (2) average cost, and (3) FIFO. Neither IFRS nor ASPE permits LIFO.

8. Net realizable value of inventory is measured as the current final sales price less costs to complete and to sell. If sales prices decline, NRV may be less than cost, in which case NRV, instead of historical cost, is used as the carrying value of inventory.

9. Raw materials and work-in-process inventories should be written down to NRV only if the cost cannot be recovered by the final selling price of the finished goods.

10. If the NRV of inventories goes up after it has been written down, the writedown should be reversed to the extent of the NRV recovery but never in excess of the historical cost.

11. Lower-of-cost-or-NRV valuation can be performed either item-by-item or by groups of related or similar items.

12. When lower-of-cost-or-NRV valuation is conducted on an item-by-item basis, inventory writedowns can be recorded either directly in the inventory accounts or by using a valuation account; when lower-of-cost-or-NRV valuation is conducted by groups, the allowance method *must* be used for writedowns.

13. Inventory estimation methods may be used either when inventory valuations are needed for interim reporting or as a double-check on the reasonableness of physical inventory counts. They also can be used to test for the possible existence of fraud or theft.

14. Occasionally, a company will enter into a purchase commitment that requires the buyer to purchase a minimum amount of goods at a fixed price. This usually is done to avoid the apparent likelihood of increasing future prices. Sometimes, however, prices decline, and the buyer must therefore pay higher than market prices. When this occurs, the buyer must record inventory at the current market price rather than at the higher contract price; the difference is reported as a loss. Such situations are called "onerous contracts" under IFRS; that term is not used in ASPE.

15. Adequate inventory cut-off procedures at the end of each fiscal period are crucial because inventory affects not only the income statement (via COS) but also the balances of inventory, accounts receivable, and accounts payable.

16. The gross margin method is used to estimate inventory values when it is difficult or impractical to take a physical count of the goods. The method is most accurate when profit margins are stable.

17. The retail inventory method applies the ratio of actual cost to sales value with the ending inventory at sales value to estimate the inventory value. When net markdowns are excluded when calculating the cost ratio, the resulting valuation is an estimate of lower of cost or NRV.

18. When inventory is valued at NRV, changes in value are reported in income in the period in which they occur. Under IFRS, the amount of any writedowns or reversals must be disclosed; ASPE has no similar disclosure requirement.

19. Companies must report the dollar amount of inventories that have been recognized as expense in the reporting period; inventory costs may not be "buried" in more general categories of expense.

20. The cash flow from operations is affected by (1) changes in inventory levels and (2) amortization and other interperiod allocations that have been included in the inventory. Cash flow must be adjusted to reflect the amount of inventory *purchased* rather than sold and must be adjusted by adding back any amortization.

KEY TERMS

additional markup	moving average
additional markup cancellation	net realizable value (NRV)
cash discounts	normal capacity
consignment	onerous contract
conversion cost	original sales price
cost ratio	periodic inventory system
cut-off errors	perpetual inventory system
first-in, first-out (FIFO)	provincial sales tax (PST)
goods and services tax (GST)	repurchase agreements
gross margin method	retail inventory method
gross margin rate	sales tax
harmonized sales tax (HST)	shrinkage
laid-down cost	specific identification
last-in, first out (LIFO)	title transfer
markdown	value added tax
markdown cancellation	weighted average system
markup	work in progress

REVIEW PROBLEM 8-1

Dominion Vacuums Ltd. sells three general types of vacuum cleaners at retail. Each one is sold in both a basic model and a deluxe model. Information relating to the inventory at the end of 20X3 was as follows:

Inventory Type	No. of Units	Laid-Down Cost	Net Realizable Value
Upright models:			
Basic	20	$ 60	$ 70
Deluxe	10	75	90
Canister models:			
Basic	34	50	40
Deluxe	14	80	85
Shop-Vac models			
Basic	16	40	35
Heavy duty	22	120	150

Required:

1. Determine the total amount of ending inventory under each of the following two bases:
   a. For each individual model, and
   b. By type of model—floor, canister, and Shop-Vac.
2. Prepare the adjusting entry that will be necessary to reduce inventory to NRV under each of the two bases.

REVIEW PROBLEM 8-1—SOLUTION

1. The amount of inventory under each method is as follows:

Inventory Type	Units	Inventory Value at: Cost	NRV	Lower of Cost or NRV Applied by: a. Individual Item	b. General Type
Upright models:					
Basic	20	$1,200	$1,400	$1,200	
Deluxe	10	750	900	750	
		1,950	2,300		$1.950
Canister models:					
Basic	34	1,700	1,360	1,360	
Deluxe	14	1,120	1,190	1,120	
		2,820	2,550		2,550
Shop-Vac models:					
Basic	16	640	560	560	
Deluxe	22	2,640	3,300	2,640	
		3,280	3,860		3,280
Total		$8,050			
Inventory valuation				$7,630	$7,780

2. The adjusting entry under each method is as follows:

   a. Using the individual item approach:

Holding loss on inventory	420	
Inventory		420
($8,050 − $7,630) = $420		

   b. Grouping by model type:

Holding loss on inventory	270	
Allowance to reduce inventory to LC/NRV		270
($8,050 − $7,780) = $420		

REVIEW PROBLEM 8-2

Super-Sell Inc. operates a discount store in downtown Edmonton. The store prepares financial statements monthly as required by Super-Sell's bank. A physical inventory is taken only on 31 January, the end of the fiscal year. Estimated inventory amounts are used for the monthly statements.

The 31 January inventory was $100,000. During February, Super-Sell purchased goods for sale amounting to $130,000. The average markup was 100% on cost. February sales revenue was $300,000.

Required:
Determine the estimated amount of inventory at 28 February using the gross margin method.

REVIEW PROBLEM 8-2—SOLUTION

Note that the 100% is the amount of *markup on cost, not the gross margin.* Goods costing $1 are marked for sale at $2.00. The gross margin percentage therefore must be computed as follows:

$1 ÷ $2 = 50%

- Cost of goods available for sale:

Opening inventory	$100,000
Purchases	130,000
Total	$230,000

- Sales amounted to $300,000. At a 50% gross margin, cost of goods sold was $150,000.

- Ending inventory = goods available for sale – cost of goods sold:

Ending inventory = $230,000 – $150,000 = $80,000

APPENDIX

PERIODIC VERSUS PERPETUAL SYSTEMS

Periodic Inventory System

In a **periodic inventory system**, unit costs are applied to the ending inventory quantities to derive the ending inventory valuation. The costs are applied by using the specific cost flow assumption (e.g., FIFO or average cost). Cost of goods sold (or cost used in production or in a service contract) is determined by subtracting the ending inventory value from the cost of goods available for sale.

In a periodic system, purchases are debited to a purchases account, and end-of-period adjusting entries are made to close the purchases account, to close out beginning inventory and to record the ending inventory as an asset (i.e., the ending inventory replaces the beginning inventory in the accounts). Additional accounts, for costs tracked separately (e.g., freight-in or customs duties) are also closed at this time. Finally, any contra accounts to purchases, such as accounts for purchase returns and allowances or purchase discounts, must also be closed.

Under a periodic system, COS is computed as a residual amount (beginning inventory plus net purchases less ending inventory) and, for all practical purposes, cannot be verified independently from an inventory count except by use of an estimation method, as we discussed in the main body of the chapter. The lack of verifiability is one reason that estimation methods may be used as a check.

Perpetual Inventory System

In a *perpetual inventory system* for accounting, both the quantities and costs of each receipt and each issue of an inventory item are recorded in the detailed inventory records to maintain an up-to-date perpetual inventory balance at all times. The result of the perpetual system is verified at least once a year by physically counting the inventory and matching the count to the accounting records. Thus, the perpetual inventory system provides the units and costs of inventory and cost of goods sold at any time. The unit costs applied to each issue or sale are determined by the cost flow assumption used.

It is important to make a distinction between tracking the *physical flow* of goods and the *costing* of goods. Many companies maintain an ongoing record of physical flows as quantity information only. A continuous tracking of physical flows does not constitute a perpetual inventory system (from an accounting standpoint) unless the costs associated with those flows are simultaneously tracked. A good example is provided by supermarkets that use automated scanners at checkout stations to keep track of physical inventory levels but assign accounting values to the physical flows only periodically.

Periodic versus Perpetual Systems—Illustration

To illustrate the periodic versus the perpetual systems, consider the following data for Lea Limited:

	Units	Unit Cost	Total
Beginning inventory	500	$4.00	$2,000
Purchases	1,000	4.00	4,000
Goods available for sale	1,500		$6,000
Less: Sales	900		
Ending inventory, as calculated	600		
Ending inventory, based on physical count	580		

Note that there should have been 600 units on hand, not 580; 20 must have been either damaged and discarded or stolen. The amount by which the physical count falls short of the expected level of inventory is generally (and euphemistically) referred to as **shrinkage**. However, it also is possible that the sales records are not completely accurate.

Based on the prior data, the computation of the COS yields the following amounts:

Beginning inventory (carried forward from the prior period): 500 × $4	$2,000
Merchandise purchases (accumulated in the purchases account):	
1,000 × $4	4,000
Total goods available for sale during the period	6,000
Less: Ending inventory (quantity determined by a physical count):	
580 × $4	2,320
Equals: Cost of sales (a residual amount)	$3,680

Periodic Recording At the beginning of the year, the balance of the inventory account will be the $2,000 cost of the 500 units that were on hand. The entries to record the purchases and COS under a periodic inventory system are as follows:

To record the purchases		
Purchases	4,000	
Accounts payable		4,000
To reallocate the cost of opening inventory and		
purchases		
Cost of sales	3,680	
Inventory (closing, per count)	2,320	
Inventory (opening)		2,000
Purchases		4,000

A variation on the second entry above is to explicitly recognize the shrinkage of 20 units as an expense, instead of hiding it in cost of goods sold:

Cost of sales (900 × $4)	3,600	
Inventory shrinkage expense (20 × $4)	80	
Inventory (closing, per count: 580 × $4)	2,320	
Inventory (opening)		2,000
Purchases		4,000

The inventory shrinkage expense will appear as an expense on the income statement.[9]

Under a periodic inventory system, the inventory is counted at least once a year. For interim financial statements, however, the amount of inventory may be estimated. If a perpetual record of only the physical units of inventory is maintained, then only the cost of that inventory needs to be estimated. If the company maintains no perpetual inventory count, then both the quantity and unit cost must be estimated.

Perpetual Recording When a perpetual inventory system is used, detailed perpetual inventory records, in addition to the usual ledger accounts, are maintained for each

---

[9] It may be shown as a separate expense line on an income statement prepared for management use. However, it will not be found on published income statements. In public financial statements, the amount is included in COS.

inventory item, and an inventory control account is maintained in the general ledger. The perpetual inventory record for each item must provide information for recording receipts, issues, and balances on hand, both in units and in dollar amounts. With this information, the physical quantity and the valuation of goods on hand at any time are available from the accounting records. A physical inventory count is still necessary but only to verify the accuracy of the perpetual inventory records. A physical count is made annually to compare the inventory on hand with the perpetual record and to provide data for any adjusting entries needed (errors and losses, for example).

When a difference is found between the perpetual inventory records and the physical count, the perpetual inventory records are adjusted to the physical count. In such cases, the inventory account is debited or credited as necessary for the correction, and COS is increased or decreased. The loss may be accumulated in a separate account, such as inventory shortages, to keep track of inventory shrinkage for internal purposes.

In the Lea Limited example above, the company began the year with 500 units in inventory, at a cost of $4 per unit. The purchase of 1,000 additional units is recorded as a debit to the inventory account (*not* to a purchases account):

Inventory (1,000 × $4)	4,000	
Accounts payable		4,000

When goods are sold, two entries are made; one to record the sale and the other to transfer their cost to COS. Assuming that Lea sells 900 units at a price of $10:

Accounts receivable (900 × $10)	9,000	
Sales revenue		9,000
Cost of sales (900 × $4)	3,600	
Inventory		3,600

The company will end the accounting period with an inventory balance of $2,400 (600 × $4). At the end of the year, a physical count would reveal only 580 units, and the additional expense would be recorded (it may also be recorded in a separate expense account):

Cost of sales	80	
Inventory ($2,320 – $2,400)		80

Thus at the end of the period, both the perpetual and periodic systems report identical inventory ($2,320) and COS ($3,680) amounts.

Choosing a Method

The choice of a periodic or a perpetual system is one of practicality—which method gives the best cost/benefit relationship?

A perpetual inventory system is especially useful when inventory consists of items with high unit values or when it is important to have adequate, but not excessive, inventory levels. Computer technology has made perpetual inventory systems far easier and much less expensive to maintain than was the case in manual systems. Thus, computerized perpetual inventory systems are now very widespread.

Thanks to robotics and computer technology, automated inventory systems can not only account for the inventory but also manage the stocking and handling of inventory goods and materials. For example, a store may have a point-of-sale perpetual inventory system (using bar codes) to keep track of its merchandise and to facilitate prompt reordering of popular items. This is information that a periodic system could not possibly provide on a timely basis.

The choice of method depends on whether the company really needs to have *both* quantity information and cost information at its fingertips for control purposes:

- Does the company need to know exactly how many units it has at any point in time? If so, then it needs a perpetual system *for quantities* but not necessarily for costs. Point-of-sale computer terminals that read bar codes are very useful for maintaining quantity flow information but are not necessarily tied to the accounting records.
- Does the company need to know exactly how many units it has on hand, how old they are, *and how much they cost* on a regular basis (e.g., weekly or monthly)? The need for frequent interim financial statements will make perpetual tracking of costs more useful.

Bank operating lines of credit are often tied to the carrying value of receivables and inventory. If, for example, a company's bank is willing to lend up to 60% of the carrying value of the inventory, it is necessary to know at least monthly (and to report to the bank) the value of the inventory. In this case, a perpetual system makes sense. Also, full information on quantities and costs may be needed for insurance purposes. If a company has a fire in its warehouse or on the plant floor, how much inventory has been lost? Only a computerized perpetual inventory can provide the information necessary to file a convincing insurance claim.[10]

Even with the most sophisticated perpetual system, it still is necessary to take a physical inventory at the end of each fiscal year. A physical inventory is necessary not only to satisfy the auditors but also to verify the integrity of the perpetual system. If there is a significant difference between the count revealed by the physical inventory and the quantity of inventory that the perpetual system says should be there, there can be only two reasons: (1) there is a problem with the perpetual system, or (2) someone is stealing the inventory. Prompt investigation and remedial action is required in either case.

COST FLOW METHODS

At date of acquisition, inventory items are recorded at their cash equivalent laid-down cost. Subsequently, when an item is sold, net assets decline and expenses increase as a result of the transfer of the item's cost from inventory to cost of sales. The cost value assigned to the end-of-period inventory of merchandise and finished goods is an allocation of the total cost of goods available for sale between that portion sold (cost of sales) and that portion held as an asset for subsequent sale (ending inventory).

Each cost flow assumption gives a different result on the income statement and the SFP, since both cost of sales and inventory are affected by the chosen assumption. There is no difference in reporting the cash flow from operating activities, however.

The major cost flow methods are:

- Specific cost identification;
- Average cost; and
- FIFO.

A numeric example of these three methods is shown below, applied to both perpetual and periodic systems.

Specific Identification

This method is, in theory, the most straightforward of all the methods. At the end of the year (periodic method) or on each sale (perpetual method) the specific units sold, and their specific cost, are identified to determine inventory and cost of sales. In the example in Exhibit 8A-1, there are 300 units left in closing inventory. **Specific identification** under

---

[10] This emphasizes the importance of maintaining backup computer records at remote locations (or in the "cloud"); perpetual inventory records will be of no use if they are destroyed in the same catastrophe that destroyed the inventory itself.

EXHIBIT 8A-1

CHASE CONTAINER CORPORATION INVENTORY DATA

Transaction Date	Purchased	Units Sold	On Hand
1 January—Inventory @ $1.00			200
9 January—Purchase @ $1.10	300		500
10 January—Sales		400	100
15 January—Purchase @ $1.16	400		500
18 January—Sale		300	200
24 January—Purchase @ $1.26	100		**300**

The costs to be allocated; goods available for sale:

Beginning inventory	200 × $1.00 =		$ 200
Purchases	300 × $1.10 =	$330	
	400 × $1.16 =	464	
	100 × $1.26 =	126	920
Cost of goods available for sale			$1,120

The $1,120 is allocated between ending inventory and cost of sales, using one of the cost flow assumptions described.

---

a periodic system reveals that at the end of January, there are 100 units from the 9 January purchase, 100 units from the 15 January purchase, and 100 units from the 24 January purchase. The calculations are:

Ending inventory = (100 × $1.10) + (100 × $1.16) + (100 × $1.26) = $110 + $116 + $126 = **$352**

Cost of sales = ($1,120 − $352) = **$768**

In practice, specific identification may not be so simple for most businesses because it is inconvenient and difficult to establish just which items were sold and what their specific initial cost was. However, it is the method used when each product or service is unique (and substantial), such as for shipbuilding, special-order heavy equipment, custom software, construction contracts, consulting operations, and so forth.

Average Cost

When the average cost method is used in a periodic system, it is called a **weighted average system**. A weighted average unit cost is computed by dividing the sum of the beginning inventory cost plus total current-period purchase costs by the number of units in the beginning inventory plus units purchased during the period. That is,

$$\text{Average cost} = \frac{\text{Opening inventory} + \text{Purchases}}{\text{Units in opening inventory} + \text{Units purchased}}$$

Exhibit 8A-2 illustrates application of the weighted average method under a periodic system for the Chase Container Corporation using the data given in Exhibit 8A-1.

When the average cost method is used in a perpetual inventory system, a **moving average** unit cost is used. *The moving average provides a new unit cost after each purchase.* When goods are sold or issued, the moving average unit cost at the time is used. Application of the moving average concept in a perpetual inventory system is shown in Exhibit 8A-3, based on Exhibit 8A-2.

For example, on 9 January, the $1.06 moving average cost is derived by dividing the total cost ($530) by the total units (500). The January ending inventory of 300 units is costed at

---

EXHIBIT 8A-2

CHASE CONTAINER CORPORATION

Weighted Average Inventory Cost Method, Periodic Inventory System

Goods Available	Units	Unit Price	Total Cost
1 January—Beginning inventory	200	$1.00	$ 200
9 January—Purchase	300	1.10	330
15 January—Purchase	400	1.16	464
24 January—Purchase	100	1.26	126
January—Total available	1,000		$1,120
Weighted average unit cost ($1,120 ÷ 1,000)		1.12	
Ending inventory:			
31 January (300 × $1.12 = $336)	300	1.12	$ 336
Cost of sales*	700	1.12	784*
Total cost allocated			$1,120

*(400 × $1.10 from 10 January) + (300 × $1.16 from 18 January) = $440 + $348 = $784

EXHIBIT 8A-3

CHASE CONTAINER CORPORATION

Moving Average Inventory Cost, Perpetual Inventory System

	Purchases			Sales			Inventory Balance		
Dates	Units	Unit Cost	Total Cost	Units	Unit Cost	Total Cost	Units	Unit Cost	Total Cost
1 January							200	$1.00	$ 200
9 January	300	$1.10	$330				500	1.06(a)	530
10 January				400	$1.06	$424	100	1.06	106
15 January	400	1.16	464				500	1.14(b)	570
18 January				300	1.14	342	200	1.14	228
24 January	100	1.26	126				300	1.18(c)	354
Ending inventory									$ 354
Cost of sales						$766			766
Total cost allocated									$1,120

(a) $530 ÷ 500 = $1.06
(b) $570 ÷ 500 = $1.14
(c) $354 ÷ 300 = $1.18

---

the latest moving average unit cost of $1.18 ($354 ÷ 300). The COS for the period is the sum of the sales in the total cost column, $766.

Moving average requires a lot of calculating if it is done by hand, but the inventory system being computerized does not make a significant difference. Indeed, on a computerized system, moving average cost is the easiest method to use.

First-in, First-out

The **first-in, first-out (FIFO)** method treats the first goods purchased or manufactured as the first units costed out on sale or issuance. *Goods sold (or issued) are valued at the oldest unit costs, and goods remaining in inventory are valued at the most recent unit cost amounts.* Exhibit 8A-4 demonstrates FIFO for the periodic system.

Exhibit 8A-5 demonstrates the perpetual system. Using the perpetual system, a sale is costed out either currently throughout the period or each time there is a withdrawal. In Exhibit 8A-5, issues from inventory on 10 January and 18 January (FIFO basis) are costed out as they occur. FIFO always produces the same numeric results whether a periodic or perpetual system is used.

Last-in, First-out—The Banished Option

The **last-in, first-out (LIFO)** method of inventory costing matches inventory valued at the most recent unit acquisition cost with current sales revenue. When the cost of inventory is rising, LIFO attempts to give an approximation of *economic income* by recognizing that replacement inventory must be purchased at a cost closer to the most recent purchases rather than the oldest purchases, as under FIFO.

LIFO was most popular during periods of high inflation, even though the inventory account on the SFP was reported at the oldest stock (and prices). The lower, out-of-date inventory value on the SFP was tolerated to measure accounting income in a manner that is closer to economic income.

The IFRS prohibited LIFO effective in 2005. The IASB argued that LIFO "is not a truly systematic method," but that argument seems somewhat bogus since it is quite systematic in practice. More revealingly, the IASB argues (correctly) that LIFO is "inconsistent with the measurement of inventories for balance sheet purposes."

The latter argument is the crux of the matter—the IASB believes that income should be measured only by changes in asset and liability accounts. LIFO gives the poorest approximation of inventory asset value compared with the other approaches, and thus IFRS rejects it. Nevertheless, most inventory valuation remains at historical cost rather than NRV and in any period of rapidly changing prices (up or down), any historical cost basis will unavoidably

---

EXHIBIT 8A-4

CHASE CONTAINER CORPORATION

FIFO Inventory Costing, Periodic Inventory System

Beginning inventory (200 units at $1)	$ 200	
Add purchases during period (computed as in Exhibit 8A-1)	920	
Cost of goods available for sale		$1,120
Deduct ending inventory (300 units per physical inventory count):		
100 units at $1.26 (most recent purchase—24 January)	$ 126	
200 units at $1.16 (next most recent purchase—15 January)	232	
Ending inventory		**358**
Cost of sales		**$762***

*Can also be calculated as 200 units on hand 1 January at $1 plus 300 units purchased 9 January at $1.10, plus 200 units purchased 15 January at $1.16.

EXHIBIT 8A-5

CHASE CONTAINER CORPORATION
FIFO Inventory Costing, Perpetual Inventory System

Dates	Units	Purchases Unit Cost	Purchases Total Cost	Units	Sales Unit Cost	Sales Total Cost	Units	Inventory Unit Cost	Inventory Total Cost
1 January	200	$1.00	$200						
9 January	300	1.10	330				200	1.00	200
							300	1.10	330
10 January				200	$1.00	$200			
				200	1.10	220	100	1.10	110
15 January	400	1.16	464				100	1.10	110
							400	1.16	464
18 January				100	1.10	110			
				200	1.16	232	200	1.16	232
24 January	100	1.26	126				200	1.16	232
							100	1.26	126

Ending inventory ($232 + $126) $ 358
Cost of sales $762   762
Total cost allocated $1,120

---

distort earnings. Paradoxically, the IASB states that the banishment of LIFO "does not rule out specific cost methods that reflect inventory flows that are similar to LIFO."[11]

Some countries (e.g., the United States and Japan) permit LIFO valuation for income tax purposes if it is also used on the company's financial statements. This poses a problem for companies that operate in such countries. The attitude of the IASB, however, is that it is a problem for the tax authorities to consider, rather than for the accounting standard-setting board, which seems a rather curious attitude for a standard setter when legislation runs counter to the standard setter's preferences. Thus, the IFRS's prohibition of LIFO is a barrier to the United States adopting IFRS in the foreseeable future.

CONCEPT REVIEW

1. Explain the essential differences in accounting for inventories under the periodic and perpetual inventory systems.

2. Does the choice of periodic or perpetual systems have any impact on the COS for a year? Explain.

3. Grocery stores usually use bar code scanners for ringing up prices at checkout. Does the use of bar code scanners necessarily mean that the store has a perpetual inventory system for measuring cost of sales?

---

[11] These quotations are from "Basis for Conclusions on *IAS2 Inventories*," paragraphs BC13, BC14, and BC 19.

REVIEW PROBLEM 8-3

The inventory data for the Black Eagle Lounge Inc. for the beginning of June is shown below. Compute the inventory value at 30 June, using both perpetual inventory and periodic inventory approaches, under each of the following methods:

1. Specific cost identification
2. Average cost
3. FIFO

     1 June—no inventory on hand
     2 June—bought one case of Red Hook Ale @ $10
     13 June—bought one case of Red Hook Ale @ $16
     24 June—sold one case of Red Hook Ale @ $20*
     28 June—bought one case of Red Hook Ale @ $18
     *This case of Red Hook Ale was purchased on 13 June.

REVIEW PROBLEM 8-3—SOLUTION

At 30 June, there are two cases of ale on hand. The carrying value of the 30 June inventory is shown below under each method:

1. Specific cost identification:
    Periodic $(1 \times \$10) + (1 \times \$18) = \$28$
    Perpetual $(1 \times \$10) + (1 \times \$18) = \$28$

2. Average cost:
    Periodic $[[(1 \times \$10) + (1 \times \$16) + (1 \times \$18)] \div 3] \times 2$ remaining
           $= \$14.67 \times 2 = \$29.34$

    Perpetual (moving average):

	Units		Total Inventory	
Average Bought (Sold)	Cost per unit	Total Cost	Units	Cost
1	$10	$10	1	$10.00
1	16	26	2	13.00
(1)	(13)	13	1	13.00
1	18	31	2	15.50

3. FIFO:
    Periodic $(1 \times \$16) + (1 \times \$18) = \$34$
    Perpetual $(1 \times \$16) + (1 \times \$18) = \$34$

Comments:

• Under specific identification, *periodic* and *perpetual* always give the same result because the cost of each specific item sold is identified. Therefore, the same inventory amount is shown for both.

• Average cost yields different results under the periodic and perpetual methods because the numbers of items and their costs are averaged together differently under a moving average (perpetual) than under a historical tabulation of purchases (periodic).

• FIFO always yields the same result under both periodic and perpetual methods.

QUESTIONS

Q8-1   In general, why should financial statement users and preparers be especially concerned about inventories?

Q8-2   List and briefly explain the usual inventory classifications for a trading entity and a manufacturing entity.

Q8-3   Which of the following items should be included in inventory?

    a. Goods held by our agents for us
    b. Goods out on consignment
    c. Goods held by us but awaiting return to vendor because the goods do not meet our criteria
    d. Goods returned to us from buyer without explanation
    e. Goods held by us for sale on commission
    f. Goods sold under conditional resale agreements, where we have agreed to repurchase the items that our customer does not resell, and reimburse the customer for carrying costs incurred
    g. Merchandise at a convention for display purposes
    h. Merchandise at our branch for sale

Q8-4   State whether or not each of the following should be included in or excluded from cost of inventory of a for-profit enterprise:

    a. Shipping costs, FOB
    b. Canadian sales tax paid on purchases
    c. Cost of storing inventory in a warehouse
    d. Insurance on inventory on hand
    e. Costs of distributing goods to regional distribution centres
    f. Customs duty when importing from abroad

Q8-5   Why is the lower-of-cost-or-NRV rule applied to inventory valuation?

Q8-6   When should a company continue to carry an item of raw material inventory at historical cost even when its NRV is less than cost?

Q8-7   Estimate the value of ending inventory, assuming the following data:

Cost of goods available for sale	$180,000
Sales	160,000
Gross margin (on sales)	30%

Q8-8   Explain why it is important to decide whether to apply the lower-of-cost-or-NRV test by individual inventory items versus by categories.

Q8-9   What is an *onerous contract*? List the three conditions that are necessary for a purchase commitment to be considered as an onerous contract under IFRS.

Q8-10 Explain how a purchase made under an onerous contract must be recorded and reported.

Q8-11 List the required financial statement disclosures for inventory. Indicate any differences between IFRS and ASPE.

Q8-12 Explain three reasons that an enterprise would use the valuation method of recording writedowns rather than directly writing down its inventory to net realizable value.

Q8-13 Explain the gross margin method. What basic assumption is implicit in the gross margin method?

Q8-14 Explain the approach of the retail method for estimating inventories. What data must be accumulated to apply the retail method?

Q8-15 Why is the year-end inventory cut-off so important? What are the complexities inherent in ensuring that the year-end inventory cut-off is correct?

Q8-16   Explain three different cost flow assumptions that can be used to measure cost of sales. Which alternative will always result in the highest net income when prices are rising?

Q8-17   Distinguish between a *weighted average* and a *moving average* in determining inventory unit cost. When is each generally used? Explain.

Q8-18   Briefly explain the differences between periodic and perpetual inventory systems. Under what general circumstances is each used?

Q8-19   Zena Ltd. purchases goods from a supplier for $200,000, plus 12% harmonized sales tax. How should Zena record this purchase?

Q8-20   When a company uses a perpetual inventory system, why is it still necessary to take a physical count or measurement of inventories?

CASE 8-1

ALLIANCE APPLIANCE LTD.

Alliance Appliance Ltd. (AAL) is an assembler and distributor of household appliances: primary kitchen equipment as well as washing machines and driers. AAL assembles the appliances from components received mainly from Germany and some also provided by Japanese parts manufacturers.

AAL does not sell directly to end-users. The company's direct customers are retail appliance sales dealerships across Canada and, to a lesser extent, in the northern United States. Although the dealers sell primarily to homeowners, they also do contract work for institutional purchasers. Such institutional purchasers primarily are real estate developers who are building new or re-equipping existing apartment and condominium buildings. AAL works closely with such developers to meet their needs at a reasonable cost.

Alliance Appliance is based in Windsor, Ontario, where it operates its assembly plant and also has its principal warehousing facilities. The company has a second distribution centre in Vancouver for western Canada.

AAL also has a distribution centre near Detroit, Michigan, to serve its customer base in the northern United States. The Michigan distribution centre is deemed essential for quick delivery to customers in the United States—rapid delivery is important, but shipments across the United States–Canada border can be delayed by security and customs procedures, which leads to a backup of shipments waiting to cross the border.

Each distribution centre stocks AAL's most popular models. High-end models, all customized models, and all orders from institutional purchasers are assembled (and customized, if necessary) to order in the company's assembly plant. Each distribution centre also stocks spare parts that can be shipped to firms that are licensed to repair AAL appliances either under warranty or post-warranty.

All of AAL's common shares are owned by the company's CEO, Douglas Beck, an engineer who migrated from Hungary to Canada 34 years ago and built up the business over three decades. Substantial external financing comes from two sources:

- International banking company HSBI provides ongoing banking services via operating loans secured by AAL's accounts receivable, inventory and capital assets. HSBI also facilitates AAL's international transactions with the United States, Germany, and Japan.

- Toronto-based private equity firm Oxwell Inc. holds convertible preferred shares in AAL, shares that had been issued to provide financing for a plant upgrade in 20X3 and the 20X5 investment in the Michigan warehousing facility. These are voting shares that Oxwell can be converted into common shares at any time.

As a Canadian private enterprise, AAL reports on the basis of ASPE. The company's annual financial statements are submitted to the AAL Board, to HSBI, and to Oxwell Inc.

The Board and Oxwell also receive AAL's unaudited quarterly statements. HSBI does not receive the quarterly statements, but the bank requires a monthly update on the balance of accounts receivable and inventories because the bank's operating loans cannot exceed the sum of 75% of accounts receivable plus 50% of inventory.

It now is April 20X8. At some time over the next four or five years, Oxwell expects to convert its shares to common and then sell them to one or more investors. One potential option is that if the stock market is strong, Oxwell might choose to sell the shares through an initial public offering (IPO). If such an option were to be chosen, AAL would need to restate its accounts on the basis of IFRS. Even if other private investors acquire the Oxwell shares (i.e., instead of through an IPO), the potential pool of buyers would be increased if AAL used IFRS.

Therefore, in early 20X8, the AAL Board commissioned a review of how a change to IFRS would impact AAL's 20X7 financial reporting. AAL's CFO contacted Henry & Higgins, the company's auditors, and asked them to provide a well-qualified person to assess the impact of any change. In response to the request, H&H assigned a senior staff auditor, Maxwell Davies, to prepare a report that provides the information requested by AAL.

After extensive review of AAL's accounting records, Maxwell has assembled the following information that may be relevant to the assignment:

a. AAL uses the titles "Balance Sheet," "Statement of Income," "Statement of Cash Flows" and "Statement of Retained Earnings" for its primary financial statements.

b. The company's income statement has no subclassifications of expense items; all expenses (including income tax expense) are listed in summary fashion with no subtotals—just a final amount for "net income." The company does not report earnings-per-share amounts.

c. Preferred dividends paid to Oxwell Inc. are reported only in the retained earnings statement.

d. AAL provides a one-year full guarantee on its products when sold to the final user. The company estimates the approximate future cost of making good on the guarantees, an estimate that is adjusted at every year-end. AAL also guarantees the bank loans of the Michigan facility.

e. AAL has a high volume of foreign-currency transactions for purchases (in euros and in yen) and a somewhat lesser volume relating to sales and related costs in U.S. dollars. The foreign currency gains and losses (due to currency fluctuations between the transaction date and the payment or settlement date) are included as part of "finance expense" on the income statement.

f. The company has a three-year parts contract with the Canadian subsidiary of a Japanese company. The contract commits AAL to acquire 2,400 units per year of a certain type of washing machine motor at a cost of Cdn$150 each. The motors are manufactured in Japan. When the contract was entered into at the end of October 20X5, the value of the Japanese yen was increasing, and AAL management wished to protect the company from further price increases. During 20X6, however, the yen unexpectedly began to drop in value. As a result, identical motors are now available directly from Japan at a price equivalent to Cdn$130. AAL has attempted to reopen negotiations with the supplier but to no avail.

g. In 20X5, the company wrote down the carrying value of its entire inventory of 25-inch and 27-inch wall ovens due to increased consumer interest in 30- and 36-inch ovens. In late 20X6, however, company line managers reported that the builders of new high-rise centre-city condominium buildings were installing the narrower (i.e., "European design") ovens due to the small kitchen spaces in new buildings as well as to many downtown tenants' lack of interest in cooking.

h. During 20X6, AAL exchanged a disused building in the outskirts of Ottawa (previously a local distribution terminal, no longer in use) for an empty lot near its assembly plant.

The acquired land will be used for parking for its delivery vans. AAL recorded the transaction at the value of the lot received because the value of the land was more reliably measureable than was the value of the building given up. The transaction had commercial value.

i. The Michigan distribution centre is legally owned by a wholly owned subsidiary of AAL. The subsidiary conducts its operations in U.S. dollars. The cumulative annual gains/losses on translating the net assets of the subsidiary from US$ to Cdn$ are reported as a separate component of shareholders' equity, as required by ASPE.

j. AAL ships its finished products from Windsor to Vancouver by train. In late 20X6, AAL's Board of Directors approved moving the Vancouver distribution centre to a location with better rail access. The move will occur in mid- to late-20X7. Therefore, in its 20X6 balance sheet, the company wrote down the soon-to-be-vacated building to its estimated recoverable value and reclassified it as a held-for-sale asset (long term).

Required:

Assume the role of Maxwell Davies, and prepare the report requested by AAL.

CASE 8-2

TERRIFIC TITLES INC.

Terrific Titles Inc. (TTI) is a major publisher of books for postsecondary education. TTI is a Canadian public corporation. One of TTI's major shareholders is Global Holdings PLC (GHC), a London-based media company.

In early 20X4, TTI's executives were preparing a bid to buy 80% of Ashwin Book Corporation of Canada (TLC). At present, all of TLC's common shares are owned by the company's CEO, Ashwin Joshee. If the sale goes through, Mr. Joshee will retain 20% and will continue as CEO and president of TLC for at least the following five years.

TLC is a niche publisher that evolved from Mr. Joshee's early endeavours in "vanity press," wherein authors self-publish their own books. Now, however, TLC has a strong line of business books for the college and university market. A particularly strong aspect of the business is the accounting line, including such widely used titles as *Indeterminate Accounting* (by the eminent authors Conchee and Beerod) and *Accounting Theory for Fun and Profit* (by Elizabeth Farroff). TTI is eager to acquire this line under the TLC imprint, provided that a reasonable price can be negotiated with Mr. Joshee. TTI's strategy is to acquire prominent high-quality publishing lines and expand them into international brands with the help of GHC, utilizing GHC's financial and market strengths.

Ian Fanwick is an accountant employed as an analyst by TTI's strategic development department. The department's executive director, Helen O'Malley, has asked Ian to prepare a report on certain accounting issues pertaining to TLC. She is concerned that TLC does not have adequate accounting controls in place, and she needs assurance that TLC's reported earnings and net assets are properly reported. She needs to know if any of the company's reported 20X3 numbers need to be adjusted before she finalizes TTI's bid for 80% of TLC's shares

After receiving Ms. O'Malley's request, Ian visits TLC's head office in downtown Windsor, Ontario. The notes from his visit are as follows:

- TLC occupies 100% of a small building in a light-industrial area. TLC leases the building on a series of five-year leases, renegotiated at each renewal. The rental is $100,000 per month, and the current lease has 10 months to run. Rental rates in the area have been rising at about 6% per year.

- TLC has a small permanent staff. Acquisition is retained in-house, but developmental editing and production are outsourced to freelancers, as is common in the industry. TLC's production level is erratic because several of the books need revision at the same time. In contrast, TTI has a substantial in-house staff for editing and production because TTI's large and more varied book list ensures a more constant level of activity.

- TLC, like other publishers, ships to book retailers (including college and university bookstores) on terms of 2%/90 days, net/6 months. TLC pays normal shipping costs, usually via truck from TLC's Winnipeg warehouse. Air express for urgent orders is at the customer's cost unless the urgency is TLC's fault (e.g., out-of-stock, or delayed publication). The company also gives a free copy (known as a "comp," for *complimentary*) of a textbook to any faculty member who requests it, whether or not the book is adopted for his her or his course.

- Revenue is recorded when the books are shipped, FOB destination. The buyer is normally invoiced within 30 days of shipment. When a buyer pays within the 2% discount period, the discount is charged to interest expense.

- TLC accepts unlimited returns of unsold books within six months from the invoice date. In practice, as a small publisher, TLC accepts later returns, but only from colleges and universities to maintain good relationships with textbook selection committees. TLC does not accept returns of used or damaged books. Returned books are placed back in inventory at their original cost.

- Standard practice in the textbook business is that textbooks are never discounted by the publisher. Retailers usually add a 25% markup, although some "discount" booksellers apply a smaller markup. The usual author royalty is 15% of the wholesale price, split among the authors as designated by the publishing contract. Sales representatives receive a commission of 15% on all institutional sales; on average, for all titles, 90% of sales are to colleges and universities.

- Each successful textbook is revised once every three years. The time span between the start of revision and the release of the book is 12 to 20 months.

- TLC provides supplementary material to instructors free of charge. Supplemental material usually consists of instructors' manuals, solution manuals, and PowerPoint™ presentations. These materials are essential for selling the books; no instructor would adopt a book that did not have the usual range of supporting resources. The cost of developing these materials is recorded as a deferred charge and amortized over the time span until the next revision—usually three years. Printing cost also is treated as a deferred charge.

- Increasingly, these supporting resources are being provided online rather than by print, which saves the publisher quite a lot of cost. TLC is not yet providing online resources for either the instructor or the students but plans to do so within the next two years. In 20X3, TLC spent $135,000 on developing an improved website to provide supplementary resources for both students and instructors for the company's various books. The improved website is not expected not go "live" until early 20X6, after a sufficient quantity of electronic resources has been developed. The development cost was recorded as an intangible asset.

- Due to an impending major change in accounting standards effective in 20X6, the only accounting textbook to go through the revision cycle in 20X3 was *Accounting Theory for Fun and Profit*, as it would not be significantly affected by the changes—the sixth edition of this book was released in January 20X4.

- About 75% of TLC's list will need to be issued in new editions by the end of 20X5 or the beginning of 20X6. TLC's acquisition editors are currently negotiating with authors for new editions, while the production department is lining up copy editors, technical checkers, typesetters, and so on, as well as blocking time at the printing presses and binderies—on average, it takes four to eight weeks to print and bind a book's print run, depending on the size of the run. Press runs are for 1,500 to 6,000 copies, depending on the book's popularity.

- After release of a new edition, a small inventory of that book's previous edition is kept in stock for one or two years to satisfy residual demand by instructors who do not wish to switch to the new edition. All other copies are sent for recycling after release of a new edition.

- TLC carries its inventory of books and supplementary instructor resources at cost. Inventory cost for each title includes all editorial and publishing costs for that edition plus an allocation of general overhead. The total inventory cost is then divided by the number of copies in the initial print run to determine the cost per unit.

Required:
Assume the role of Ian Fanwick. Prepare the report for Ms. O'Malley.

CASE 8-3

SIEGFRIED AIR CONTROL LTD.

Siegfried Air Control Ltd. (SAC) manufactures and installs air conditioning and ventilation systems, mainly for businesses but also for home use. The company was founded 18 years ago by a group of five professional engineers, who had previously worked for a multinational air conditioning company based in Germany. The five engineers are the only shareholders. Additional financing is provided through bank loans and a bank line of credit. The line of credit is limited to 70% of SAC's accounts and notes receivable plus 50% of the book value of inventory.

Over the years, SAC developed a sophisticated air conditioning system that could be installed in older buildings without the need for extensive reconstruction. The AirRing System, as it was called, was very popular for old residences and commercial buildings.

AirRing evolved through several designs over the years. In 20X4, due to severe energy shortages, SAC developed a new energy-efficient model (Sigmund) that reduced energy consumption by 40% and also substituted a new type of refrigerant that was safe for the environment, unlike refrigerants in prior years that caused damage to the ozone layer if they leaked into the atmosphere.

The only difficulty with Sigmund was that both the condenser and the air-handler (the fan unit that circulates the air) were appreciably larger than the older, less efficient, models. The larger size meant that customers that had to replace their old air conditioning units would need to provide larger spaces for both units—not always an easy task in older buildings.

SAC began manufacturing, selling, and installing Sigmund in 20X5. Most of the components were subcontracted to other manufacturers in the region and in Europe. Subcontractors were intentionally scattered so that the exact design of the new system would not be immediately obvious to competitors. Of course, SAC knew that other companies would successfully copy its design through reverse engineering. Therefore, SAC set a high price on the new systems at the beginning to recover the development costs before similar systems became available from other manufacturers.

The total cost to manufacture Sigmund was $10,000 for a medium-sized unit suitable for homes. Commercial systems were custom-designed to specifications and could run up to a million dollars to manufacture and install.

It is now the end of 20X5. The VP, Finance, who is one of the founding engineers and shareholders, is pondering the proper presentation of some transactions and events. Because it is a private company, SAC has never been audited. Nevertheless, SAC's shareholders want the company's financial statements prepared on the basis of GAAP so that the bank does not ask any awkward questions and perhaps force an expensive audit in future years.

You, Theresa Tie, have been hired as an accounting expert to advise the company on the proper treatment of the following matters:

1. The company has been charging all direct manufacturing costs to inventory—raw materials, direct labour, and the full cost (including taxes, foreign exchange gains and losses, and shipping costs) of subcontracted components. All other costs are charged to expense in the year incurred.

2. Accounts payable includes several million dollars worth of unpaid subcomponent costs that were invoiced to SAC in euros. On advice from the bank, SAC hedged the euro commitment when the company signed the subcontracting agreement and established the euro price of the subcontracted components. Due to the strength of the Canadian dollar (compared with the euro), the Canadian dollar value of the accounts payable has decreased by $156,000.

3. Historically, SAC has incurred very little cost in honouring its warranties on its equipment and installations. These costs have been charged to expense when incurred. Callbacks for service on newly installed Sigmunds have been largely the result of their having been installed in small spaces with inadequate ventilation, which has caused the overall cost of honouring warranties on Sigmund to be higher than usual in the short run.

4. SAC has an inventory of older units (the Erda model) that are about to become obsolete in Ontario due to pending new regulations on energy and refrigerant. Some customers are hurrying to purchase the Erdas in advance of the effective date of the new regulations. Unsold units can be shipped into the United States and sold through another company but would have to be discounted by at least 50% below Erda's usual selling price, which is about 10% below the recorded inventory cost. SAC would have to pay shipping costs to get the units to the United States.

5. In October 20X6, SAC signed a contract to retrofit an old factory building that is being converted into condominiums. The contract price is $1,200,000; SAC's estimated cost is $1,000,000. By the end of the year, SAC had spent $600,000 on the project, including the $250,000 cost of the compression and air-handling equipment that had not yet been installed. Just before the end of the year, the SAC project supervisor advised SAC that due to more difficult conversion problems than expected, an additional $150,000 would probably have to be spent. The project supervisor estimated that about 40% of the physical work had been finished.

Required:

Prepare a memorandum to the VP, Finance, in which you identify and analyze alternative accounting treatments for these five issues. Recommend which treatments SAC should adopt.

TECHNICAL REVIEW

TR8-1 Inventory Holding Gains/Losses: Arganon Limited had the following ending inventory balances for each of the past six years:

	Cost	Net Realizable Value
20X3	$ 0	$ 0
20X4	12,000	14,000
20X5	15,000	13,000
20X6	18,000	17,000
20X7	20,000	16,000
20X8	22,000	23,000

Required:
For each year, 20X4 through 20X8, determine the holding loss (gain) under lower-of-cost-or-NRV valuation and the adjusting entry (if any) necessary at the end of each year.

TR8-2 Lower of Cost or NRV: Halicon Ltd. applies LCNRV valuation. The company's inventory at the end of the year is as follows:

		Per Unit	
Inventory Classification	Quantity	Cost	Net Realizable Value
Class 1:			
Halicon basic models	50	$100	$120
Halican super models	30	150	140
Class 2:			
Private brand—regular	120	90	100
Private brand—deluxe	60	130	140
Private brand—super deluxe	40	200	150

Required:
Determine the amount of any adjustment that is required to inventory, assuming inventory is valued under lower-of-cost-or-NRV valuation under each of the following valuation methods:

1. By individual type of item
2. By class of inventory

TR8-3 Onerous Contract: In February 20X3, La Fondue Limited signed a two-year contract with a Quebec cheese supplier to provide a minimum of 1,500 kilograms of fine cheese for fondue at a fixed price of $20 per kilogram. By the end of October, La Fondue had purchased 650 kg at the agreed-upon price. In early November, however, the open market price of the cheese dropped to $17 per kg due to excess capacity in the dairy industry. On 18 November, La Fondue placed an order for 110 kg at the contract price of $20. The cheese is received on 27 November and full payment of $3,000 is made on 10 December.

Required:
Prepare any journal entries that are necessary on La Fondue's books to record the events in November and December.

TR8-4 Gross Margin Method: Tate Tasers Inc. is preparing interim financial statements for the quarter ending 31 March 20X1 and needs to estimate the value of inventory on hand at the end of the quarter. Physical inventory counts are taken only at the end of the fiscal year. The following information is available:

Beginning inventory	$ 400,000
Purchases	900,000
Sales	1,500,000
Sales returns (to stock)	40,000
In-bound shipping on purchases	26,000
Out-bound shipping to customers	42,000
HST on purchases	117,000
HST on net sales	190,000
Import duties	40,000
Inventory storage costs	6,000

The average gross margin ratio is 30%.

Required:
Using the gross margin method, determine the cost of ending inventory and the cost of sales for the quarter.

∎connect

TR8-5 Retail Inventory Method: Redux Ltd. estimates its quarterly inventory by the retail inventory method. The following data are available for the quarter ended 30 September 20X6:

	Cost	Selling Price
Inventory, 1 July 20X6	$362,000	$ 537,000
Markups		195,000
Markup cancellations		38,000
Markdowns		60,000
Markdown cancellations		23,000
Purchases	830,000	1,500,000
Purchase returns and allowances	16,000	25,000
Sales		1,680,000
Sales returns and allowances		80,000

Required:
Prepare a schedule to compute the estimated inventory at 30 September 20X6.

ASSIGNMENTS

★ **A8-1 Inventory Cost—Items to Include in Inventory:** The bookkeeper for Interior Advances Ltd. (IAL) is uncertain which of the following items he should include when he calculates the inventory balance for the year-end financial statements:

a. Goods counted in the physical inventory, including $4,100 in HST and $1,500 in import brokerage fees	$36,000
b. Gross invoice cost of goods received and included in inventory count but not yet paid for; IAL can deduct a 2% discount if the invoice is paid within 30 days of year-end	6,000
c. Warehousing cost for inventory	2,000
d. Goods shipped to a wholesale distributor; the distributor has the right to return up to 33% of the goods if they are not sold within three months; not included in inventory count	9,000
e. Items included in inventory count that have been returned by customers for repair (counted at original sales price, which was 50% above cost)	3,000
f. Cost of goods on consignment to Big Box Inc. (including 20% commission that will be due to IAL if and when it sells the goods)	10,000
g. Total expected cost of goods in inventory that are being modified by the company for private-branding for Canada Designs Limited; 40% of the cost has been incurred by year-end	14,000

Required:
Determine the amount of ending inventory that should be reported on Interior Advances' SFP.

★ **A8-2 Inventory Cost—Items to Include in Inventory:** Grundig Enterprises Ltd. (in thousands of dollars)

a. Physical count, 31 December 20X3	Cdn$120,000
b. Advance payment for inventory due before year-end but not yet received	10,000
c. HST (refundable) on inventory, not included in the above amounts	9,000

d. California sales not refundable tax paid on part of the inventory
included in physical count   3,000

e. Cost of items received from a supplier for testing, included in
physical count; items are returnable after testing if they do not
meet specifications   5,000

f. Import excise tax paid on inventory acquired from a supplier in China   4,000

g. High-value inventory purchased and held in a bonded warehouse in
California, not included in above count (Cdn$1.05 = US$1.00)   US$22,000

Required:

Determine the amount of ending inventory that should be reported on Interior Advances' SFP.

 A8-3 Inventory Cost—Items to Include in Inventory: Gerard Limited reported inventory of $689,600 and accounts payable to suppliers of $456,300 for the year ended 31 December 20X6. The company has a periodic inventory system, and the inventory value given is the result of the physical count.

a. The inventory count took place on 31 December. Late in the day on 31 December, goods with a cost of $54,300 and a retail price of $98,500 were delivered to a customer. These goods had been counted earlier in the day and were included in the inventory count. The company did not record the sale until 3 January due to the New Year's break.

b. Goods from a supplier, in transit on 31 December, were neither counted nor recorded as a purchase and account payable as of 31 December. The goods, with a cost of $37,500, legally belonged to Gerard while they were in transit over the year-end.

c. Goods received from a supplier on 30 December were counted and included in inventory, but the invoice had not been recorded as a purchase or accounts payable by the end of December. The invoice was for $51,100.

d. On 4 January 20X7, a $5,000 bill for freight for the month of December was received. The freight was for goods bought from a supplier and delivered to the Gerard warehouse. None of these goods has been resold.

e. The inventory count was subsequently determined to include $21,900 of goods on consignment from a supplier; the goods have to be paid for only if they are sold to Gerard's customers.

f. Gerard had goods with a recorded cost of $12,700 that were properly recorded as a purchase and account payable, and counted in inventory. However, the goods were damaged and Gerard entered into negotiations with the supplier that resulted in a discount of $4,000 off the price. The negotiations were completed in early January 20X7.

g. Market value of remaining inventory *after* any adjustments appropriate for items (a)–(f), at NRV, was determined to be $605,000. The allowance to reduce inventory to NRV, unchanged for the end of the last fiscal period, was $32,200.

Required:

1. Calculate the correct balances for inventory (net) and accounts payable, as of 31 December 20X6.

2. Calculate the holding loss on inventory that will appear on the income statement for the year ended 31 December 20X6.

3. Assume that cost of goods sold had been calculated to be $2,211,400 based on the original physical count. What is the new cost of goods sold? Assume that the holding loss on inventory is reported as part of cost of goods sold.

 A8-4 Inventory Discounts and Rebates: Majestic Stores Incorporated, a large Canadian publicly traded electronics dealer, buys large quantities of a flat-screen LCD television model that costs $500 and sells for $990. The supplier provides a rebate of $25 per set if Majestic buys 200 or more sets during the calendar year. Between 1 February and 1 December 20X1, Majestic purchased 150 sets, which were recorded in inventory at $75,000 (150 × $500). By December 15, 130 of these units had been sold. On 15 December, Majestic ordered

50 more sets, FOB destination, for $500 each. Majestic received the sets on 22 December and promptly made a request for the rebate. Majestic sold an additional 40 sets by 31 January 20X2, the end of Majestic's fiscal year. The rebate cheque arrived on 20 February, after Majestic's accountants had closed the books.

The supplier provides terms of 2/10, n/30. The supplier paid a total of $1,760 in freight charges, including $375 paid in January for the last order of 50 sets.

Required:

1. Calculate the ending inventory value at 31 January 20X2. Majestic uses FIFO.
2. What entry should be made relative to the rebate on 31 January 20X2? Why?
3. What entry would be made on 20 February 20X2?

★★ **A8-5 Inventory Policy Issues:** Consider each of the following independent situations:

Case A Inventory was received and was recorded at the invoice price of $56,000. The goods had neither been sold nor paid for at year-end. Consequently, a 2% discount was not taken.

Case B In the lower-of-cost-or-market valuation at year-end, replacement cost was used as the definition of "market." The evaluation resulted in a writedown of $135,500. The company reports that although its supplier's prices were lower for certain products at year-end, thus causing the writedown, both its prices to its own customers and its direct selling costs had remained at constant levels.

Case C Inventories costing $65,000, with a sales price of $97,000, were with a customer on consignment. These goods were excluded from the physical inventory count, and the $97,000 sale was recorded in the current fiscal year because final sale was reasonably assured—in the past, this customer has always been able to sell all the goods sent on consignment.

Case D At the end of 20X4, Sino-India Inc. entered into a binding commitment to buy 150 units of a certain type of inventory at a cost of $16,000 per unit by the end of 20X7. In 20X5, the company bought 70 units, all of which were used in production. In 20X6 the company purchased 45 units and recorded them in inventory at $720,000 (i.e., 45 × $16,000). The market value per unit had been $17,000 during 20X4, dropped to $14,000 in 20X5, and rose again to $15,500 by the date of the 20X6 acquisition.

Required:
For each situation, describe the accounting policy decision. Describe the impact that the chosen policy has had on the income statement and SFP. If the company's policy is not correct or if there is an alternate policy that should be considered, explain the alternative.

★ **A8-6 Lower of Cost or NRV:** Harpo Marks Corporation produces and sells forklift trucks. Model 17A (the "Chico") has a list price of $70,000. The production cost for the 20 finished Chicos in inventory at the end of 20X4 was $60,000 per unit. Due to recent improvements in manufacturing flow, the cost of new production is expected to be $54,000 in the next year. The list price for Chico will be reduced by $5,000 at the beginning of 20X5. The price reduction will reflect the reduced manufacturing cost and undercut the prices of generally comparable competing models made by other manufacturers. The Chico model often is sold below the list price; the actual discount varies by customer but is usually 10% less than list price for the regular industrial clients that comprise 40% of HMC's sales. Individual nonrepeat buyers receive smaller discounts, averaging about 3%. HMC's sales agents receive a 6% commission on the actual sales price. The buyer bears the cost of shipping.

Required:

1. What value should be used for the lower-of-cost-or-NRV test? What amount of writedown is required?
2. Assume that early in 20X5 the company sells five Chicos for $63,000 each. How much gross profit will be recorded, assuming that the company uses FIFO?

★   **A8-7 Lower of Cost or NRV—Income Effects:** Hessian Limited has been suffering the effects of strong price competition on a particular inventory item from an overseas company that has moved into Hessian's Canadian market. At the end of 20X6, Hessian management decided that the carrying cost (at historical value) of its year-end inventory was not recoverable and that Hussein would have to reduce its prices drastically to meet the competitor's prices. Management estimated that inventory currently carried at $20,000 (at historical cost) will have a NRV of $16,000. Hessian normally priced its products at 50% above historical cost.

Early in 20X7, Hessian's competitor unexpectedly withdrew from the Canadian market because of financial difficulties in its home country. Consequently, Hessian restored the prices of its goods to full premarkdown selling price. By the end of 20X7, 60% of the inventory had been sold.

Required:

1. Prepare the journal entry for 31 December 20X6 to write down the inventory to NRV. Use the direct writedown method.

2. Prepare a summary journal entry to record the sale of the goods (and the cost of sales) in 20X7 and the writeup of remaining inventory.

3. Suppose that Hussain Limited's net income (after the writedown) was $50,000 in 20X6 and $60,000 in 20X7. What would each year's net income have been if Hussain Limited had not written down the inventory?

★★   **A8-8 Lower of Cost or NRV—Direct Writedown versus Allowance Method:** At the end of 20X2, Rontu Inc. has four inventory items, two of which management believes should be written down. The cost and estimated NRVs of the items are as follows:

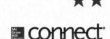

		Per Unit	
	Quantity	Cost	NRV
Item A	100	$85	$80
Item B	260	40	45
Item C	150	70	50
Item D	200	50	60

Required:

1. Determine the amount by which the inventory should be written down if lower-of-cost-or-NRV valuation is applied item-by-item. Prepare the journal entry to record the writedown.

2. Items A and B are related, while Items C and D are related. Determine the inventory writedown if lower-of-cost-or-NRV valuation is applied by category. Prepare the journal entry to establish an inventory allowance.

3. Suppose that in 20X3, the NRV of Item A rises to $90 by the end of the year. Prepare journal entries to record the recovery in value, if feasible, under each of the two methods.

4. Explain the advantages and disadvantages of using an allowance instead of direct writedown.

★★   **A8-9 Lower of Cost or NRV—Allowance Method:** At the end of 20X6, OverBright Lighting Limited has a large stock of incandescent lighting fixtures that are becoming obsolete due to a new trend to low-energy fluorescent and LED lighting fixtures. The current inventory of incandescent fixtures has a laid-down cost of $340,000. The sales manager of OverBright estimates that the inventory can be sold through the normal course of business over the next several reporting quarters for approximately $300,000. Sales personnel are given a 10% commission on sales. In addition, OverBright will grant an additional 5% sales bonus for sales of these almost-obsolete fixtures, intended to make up for the reduced sales prices as well as an additional incentive to sell them.

In early 20X7, OverBright's production manager decided that the fixtures can be adapted to not only accept the new LED lighting but also compete quite effectively with new products coming on the market. During 2007, the fixtures are converted at a cost of $50,000. The sales manager estimates that after the conversion, the newly adapted inventory can be repriced to fetch $370,000 (before 10% sales commission) in the market.

Required:
Using the valuation allowance method, prepare the appropriate journal entries to record inventory adjustments at the end of each of 20X6 and 20X7.

★★ **A8-10 Lower of Cost or NRV—Allowance Method:** The records of Loren Movers Ltd. contained the following inventory data:

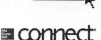

		20X1		20X2	
		Cost	NRV	Cost	NRV
Category 1					
	Item A	$10,000	$ 9,000	$ 5,000	$ 3,000
	Item B	40,000	35,000	10,000	9,000
	Item C	25,000	33,000	45,000	52,000
		$75,000	$77,000	$60,000	$64,000
Category 2					
	Item D	$18,000	$16,500	$12,000	$10,500
	Item E	20,000	4,000	4,000	1,000
	Item F	42,000	42,000	56,000	54,000
		$80,000	$62,500	$72 000	$65,500

Required:
1. Calculate two different amounts that could justifiably be recorded as the allowance to reduce inventory to lower-of-cost-or-NRV at the end of 20X1.
2. Record the 20X1 lower-of-cost-or-NRV adjustments (if any) for each of the two amounts from requirement (1), using the valuation allowance method.
3. Record the 20X2 lower-of-cost-or-NRV adjustments (if any) under each of the two lower of cost or NRV methods, using the valuation allowance.

★★ **A8-11 Lower of Cost or NRV—Two Ways to Apply:** The information shown below relating to the ending inventory was taken at lower of cost or NRV from the records of Components Corporation:

Inventory Classification	Quantity	Per Unit Cost	Per Unit NRV
Keyboards			
Stock A	12	$47	$40
Stock B	20	38	35
Stock C	18	50	55
Hard drives			
Stock X	30	90	85
Stock Y	60	80	90
CD burners			
Stock D	60	38	33
Stock E	200	50	58

Required:
1. Determine the valuation of the above inventory at cost and at lower of cost or NRV, assuming application of lower-of-cost-or-NRV valuation by (a) individual items, and (b) classifications.

2. Give the entry to record the writedown, if any, to reduce ending inventory to lower of cost or NRV. Assume periodic inventory and the allowance method.

3. Of the two applications described in (2) above, which one appears preferable in this situation? Explain.

★★ **A8-12 Lower of Cost or NRV and Foreign Currency:** StarCross Ltd. is a public company incorporated in Alberta and traded on the Toronto Stock Exchange. In December 20X7, StarCross management decided that cost exceeded NRV for a significant portion of the inventory. Consequently, the company wrote the Class A inventory down from $700,000 to $300,000 and the Class B inventory down from $850,000 to $650,000.

In June 20X8, the value of Class B inventory rose to $730,000. Half of the Class B was sold for $380,000 in November of that year.

In March 20X9, the Class A inventory was sold in bulk for a price of €200,000. At the time of the sale, €1 = Cdn$1.70.

Required:

1. Prepare all entries, assuming that the direct writedown method is used for lower of cost or NRV.

2. Prepare all entries, assuming instead that the allowance method is used for lower of cost or NRV.

★ **A8-13 Obsolete Inventory:** Olson Metrics Ltd. has been the dominant firm in its field. The company's most popular product has been the Model T, which carries a retail price of $350. The Model T costs $250 per unit to produce.

Recently, the company introduced a new version, Model A, priced at $380. When the model A was released, Olson reduced the retail price of the remaining 1,000 units of Model T to $300. Despite the sharp price reduction, the demand for the Model T dropped sharply. Therefore, Olson decided to sell 600 of the remaining units on consignment through FloorMart Inc. as a private label product at $220 per unit. FloorMart will collect a commission of 20% per unit. Olsen will lower the price of the remaining 400 units in inventory to $280.

Required:
Prepare any journal entry(ies) that are necessary to record the effects of the above information.

★ **A8-14 Purchase Commitment:** Cabernet Incorporated is a BC-based wine producer. In anticipation of a particularly bounteous grape harvest and a potential problem in obtaining a sufficient volume of shipping crates, Cabernet entered into a noncancellable agreement with Lumber Products Ltd. to supply 200,000 wooden crates at a price of $12 per crate plus 7% PST and 5% GST. During the current fiscal year, Cabernet purchased 50,000 crates.

Near the end of the year, however, a restrictive tariff on the import of crates from the United States was lifted. Crates then became readily available from other suppliers for only $9.

Required:

1. Prepare the journal entry to record the purchase of crates during the current fiscal year.

2. Prepare the journal entry to record the impact of the price drop. What two conditions are necessary for Cabernet to recognize a loss on the contract?

★★ **A8-15 Loss on Purchase Commitment:** During 20X5, Brokeback Corporation signed a contract with Alpha Inc. to purchase 20,000 subassemblies at $45 each during 20X6.

Required:

1. On 31 December 20X5, the end of the annual accounting period, the financial statements are to be prepared. Assume that the cost of the subassemblies is dropping and the total

estimated current replacement cost is $850,000. Under what additional contractual and economic conditions would note disclosure only be required? Prepare an appropriate note.

2. What contractual and economic conditions would require accrual of a loss? Give the accrual entry.

3. Assume that the subassemblies are received in 20X5 when their replacement cost was $830,000. The contract was paid in full. Give the required entry, assuming the entry in (2) was made, and a periodic inventory system is used.

★ **A8-16 Inventory—Error Correction:** On 31 December 20X5, Office Systems Ltd.'s books showed an ending inventory valuation of $490,000 based on a periodic inventory system. The accounts for 20X5 have been adjusted and closed. Subsequently, the bookkeeper prepared a schedule that showed that the inventory should be $569,800, not $490,000.

a. Merchandise in store (at 40% above cost)	$490,000
b. Merchandise purchased, in transit (shipped FOB destination, estimated freight, not included, $800), invoice price	9,000
c. Merchandise held for later shipment to Davis Electronics at sales price, 40% above cost (already billed to Davis Electronics)	16,800
d. Merchandise out on consignment at sales price (including markup of 50% on selling price)	24,000
e. Merchandise (office equipment) removed from the warehouse and now used in the company's marketing office (at cost)	20,000
f. Merchandise out on approval, sales price = $10,000, cost = $4,000	10,000
Total inventory as corrected	$569,800

Income tax rate = 30%

Required:

1. Review the items making up the list of inventory. Compute the correct ending inventory amount.

2. The income statement and SFP now reflect a closing inventory of $490,000. List the items on the income statement and SFP for 20X5 that should be corrected for the above errors; give the amount of the error for each item affected.

★★ **A8-17 Inventory-Related Errors:** McGoo-Hillock Publishers Inc. prepared its draft 20X4 financial statements in February 20X5. The draft income statement showed a tentative net income of $550,000. After the draft statements were prepared, but prior to their approval and release, the external auditors discovered several errors:

a. Inventory of $25,000 that was received from an offshore publisher on 29 December 20X4 (and included in the 31 December 20X4 physical inventory count) had not been recorded as an account payable until well into January 20X5.

b. The company had shipped books worth $120,000 to a distant customer on 28 December 20X4. The revenue (and account receivable) was recorded by Nicodemus on 4 January 20X5.

c. Although the company's internal auditors had discovered a calculation error in the worksheets for the 31 December 20X4 physical inventory, the error had never been corrected. Year-end 20X4 inventory actually should have been $50,000 greater than recorded and reported.

d. Books costing $80,000 were shipped to a large chain of bookstores in the final week of the fiscal year; a sale (and receivable) of $125,000 had correspondingly been recorded. However, the bookstore chain actually had accepted the books only on consignment.

Required:

1. What effect will correction of these errors have on the net income for the year ended 31 December 20X4? What will be the revised 20X4 net income?

2. Suppose that these errors were not discovered until *after* the 20X4 statements were released. What adjustment(s), if any, should the company make on its books in 20X5?

★★ **A8-18 Inventory Errors:**

Case A When the accounting staff of Nicodemus Limited was preparing the first-quarter 20X5 interim financial statements, they discovered an error in the 31 December 20X4 financial statements. Inventory costing $265,000 had been in transit and was not received until 4 January 20X5. The accounts payable department had recorded the purchase as an account payable on 28 December 20X4. Title to the inventory had passed to Nicodemus on 27 December, the date that the supplier had loaded the shipment onto the shipping company's trucks. Nicodemus uses a periodic inventory method.

Case B Internal auditors for Basu Corporation discovered during 20X4 that finished goods inventory of $400,000 had been shipped to a customer on 30 December 20X3, the last working day of the year. The ending inventory for 31 December 20X3 had been properly stated on the basis of the year-end physical count. However, the shipment was not recorded until 4 January 20X4, when sales revenue of $640,000 was recorded. Basu uses a perpetual inventory system.

Required:

1. What impact did the errors have on each company's financial statements?
2. What correcting entry should each company make when the error is discovered?

★ **A8-19 Gross Margin Method:** You are auditing the records of Xiao Yu Corporation. The company took a physical inventory under your observation. However, the valuations have not
 been completed. The records of the company provide the following data: sales, $800,000 (gross); returned sales, $35,000 (returned to stock); purchases (gross), $500,000; beginning inventory, $320,000; freight-in, $16,000; and purchase returns and allowances, $14,000. The gross margin last period was 25% of net sales; you anticipate that it will average 30% for the year under audit.

Required:
Estimate the cost of the ending inventory and the cost of sales using the gross margin method. Show all calculations.

★★ **A8-20 Gross Margin Method:** The manager of Seaton Books Limited, a book retailer, requires an estimate of the inventory cost for a quarterly financial report to the owner on
 31 March 20X5. In the past, the gross margin method was used because of the difficulty and expense of taking a physical inventory at interim dates. The company sells both fiction and nonfiction books. Due to their lower turnover rate, nonfiction books are typically marked up to produce a gross profit of 37.5%. Fiction, on the other hand, generates a 28.6% gross profit. The manager has used the average gross profit of 33.333% to estimate interim inventories.

   You have been asked by the manager to estimate the book inventory cost as of 31 March 20X5. The following data are available from Seaton's accounting records:

	Fiction	Nonfiction	Total
Inventory, 1 January 20X5	$100,000	$ 40,000	$140,000
Purchases	600,000	200,000	800,000
Freight-in	5,000	2,000	7,000
Sales	590,000	160,000	750,000

Required:
(Round gross margin percentages to one decimal place.)

1. Using the average gross profit margin of 33.3%, compute the estimate of inventory as of 31 March 20X5, based on the method applied to combined fiction and nonfiction books.
2. Compute the estimate of ending inventory as of 31 March 20X5, based on the gross margin method applied separately to fiction and nonfiction books.
3. Which method is preferable in this situation? Explain.

★★ **A8-21 Retail Inventory Method:** Hi-Valu Ltd. estimates its quarterly inventory by the retail inventory method. The following data are available for the quarter ended 30 June 20X9:

	Cost	Selling Price
Inventory, 1 June	$226,000	$ 336,000
Markups		122,000
Markup cancellations		38,000
Markdowns		88,000
Markdown cancellations		43,000
Purchases	519,600	940,000
Purchase returns and allowances	9,000	16,000
Sales		1,050,000
Sales returns and allowances		50,000

Required:

1. Prepare a schedule to compute the estimated inventory at 30 June 20X9.
2. Explain why the retail inventory method approximates lower-of-cost-or-market valuation.

★★ **A8-22 Retail Inventory Method:** Auditors are examining the accounts of Acton Retail Corporation. They were present when Acton's personnel physically counted the Acton inventory; however, the auditors made their own tests. Acton's records provided the following data for the current year:

	At Retail	At Cost
Inventory, 1 January	$ 300,000	$180,500
Net purchases	1,453,000	955,000
Freight-in		15,000
Additional markups	31,000	
Additional markup cancellations	14,000	
Markdowns	8,000	
Employee discounts	2,000	
Sales	1,300,000	

Inventory at 31 December (per physical count valued at retail) = $475,000

Required:

1. Compute the ending inventory at lower of cost or NRV as an audit test of the overall reasonableness of the physical inventory count.
2. Note any discrepancies indicated. What factors should the auditors consider in reconciling any difference in results from the analysis?
3. What accounting treatment (if any) should be accorded the discrepancy?

★★★ **A8-23 Gross Margin and Retail Inventory Methods:** The records of Diskount Department Stores Inc. provided the following data for 20X5:

Sales (gross)	$800,000
Sales returns	2,000
Additional markups	9,000
Additional markup cancellations	5,000
Markdowns	7,000
Purchases:	
At retail	850,000
At cost	459,500
Purchase returns:	
At retail	4,000
At cost	2,200
Freight on purchases	7,000

Beginning inventory:	
At retail	80,000
At cost	45,000
Markdown cancellations	3,000

1. Estimate the valuation of the ending inventory and cost of goods sold using the gross margin method. Last year's gross margin percentage was 51%.

2. Estimate the valuation of the ending inventory and cost of goods sold using the retail sales method, which approximates lower-of-cost-or-NRV valuation.

3. Which method is likely to be more accurate? Comment.

★★★ **A8-24 Inventory Concepts—Recording, Adjusting, Closing, Reporting:** Gamit Ltd. completed the following selected (and summarized) transactions during 20X5:

a. Merchandise inventory on hand 1 January 20X5, $105,000 (at cost, which was the same as lower of cost or NRV).

b. During the year, purchased merchandise for resale at cost of $200,000 on credit, terms 2/10, n/30. Immediately paid 85% of the cash cost.

c. Paid freight on merchandise purchased, $10,000 cash.

d. Paid 40% of the accounts payable within the discount period. The remaining payables were unpaid at the end of 20X5 and were still within the discount period.

e. Merchandise that had a quoted price of $3,000 (terms 2/10, n/30) was returned to a supplier. A cash refund of $2,940 was received because the items were unsatisfactory.

f. During the year, sold merchandise for $370,000, of which 10% was on credit.

g. A television set caught fire and was damaged internally; it was returned by the customer. The set was originally sold for $600, of which $400 cash was refunded. The set originally cost the company $420. Estimates are that the set, when repaired, can be sold for $240. Estimated repair costs are $50, and selling costs are estimated to be $10.

h. Operating expenses (administrative and distribution) paid in cash, $120,000; includes the $10 (in thousands).

i. Excluded from the purchase given in (b) and from the ending inventory was a shipment for $7,000 (net of discount). This shipment was in transit, FOB shipping point at 31 December 20X5. The invoice had arrived.

j. Paid $50 cash to repair the damaged television set; see (g) above.

k. Sold the damaged television set for $245; selling costs allocated, $10.

l. The ending inventory (as counted) was $110,000 at cost, and $107,000 at NRV. Assume an average income tax rate of 40%.

Accounting policies followed by the company are as follows:

(1) The annual accounting period ends 31 December.

(2) A periodic inventory system is used.

(3) Purchases and accounts payable are recorded net of cash discounts.

(4) Freight charges are allocated to merchandise when purchased.

(5) All cash discounts are taken.

(6) Used and damaged merchandise is carried in a separate inventory account.

(7) Inventories are reported at lower of cost or NRV, and the allowance method is used.

Required:

1. Give the entries for transactions (b) through (k).

2. Give the end-of-period adjusting entries.

3. Prepare a multiple-step income statement for 20X5. Assume that 20,000 common shares are outstanding.

4. Show how the ending inventory should be reported on the SFP at 31 December 20X5.

★★★ **A8-25 Statement of Cash Flows:** Thistle Corporation reported the following items in its 20X5 financial statements:

	20X5	20X4
From the SFP:		
Inventory, at lower of cost or market	$ 951,000	$ 841,000
Accounts payable	616,000	596,000
Estimated liability on noncancellable purchase commitments	8,000	—
From the income statement:		
Cost of goods sold*	$4,900,000	$4,100,600
Loss on purchase commitment	8,000	—

*Includes loss due to decline in market value

From the notes:
Inventories are carried at FIFO cost, net of an allowance to reduce finished goods inventory to the lower of cost or NRV of $65,000 (20X4, $46,000).

At year-end, the company has outstanding purchase commitments in the amount of $13,400 (20X4, $6,600). The market value of these goods is equal to, or exceeds, the purchase commitment cost except as accrued in the financial statements.

Required:

1. What items would appear on the cash flow statement as a result of the inventory transactions of the year? Assume the use of the indirect method of presentation in the operating activities section.

2. Assume instead that the company uses the direct method of presentation in the operating activities section. How much did the company pay for inventory during the period?

★★★ **A8-26 ASPE—Accounting Policies:** The president of Aggressive Limited has come to you for advice. Aggressive is a newly established company with prospects for high growth. Decisions must soon be made concerning accounting policies for external financial reporting. The following information pertains to the company's first year of operations (in thousands of dollars):

Revenue	$48,000
Purchases	18,000
Closing inventory—FIFO	6,000
Closing inventory—average cost	4,800
Depreciation—straight line	2,400
Depreciation—declining balance	4,800
Advertising and promotion expense	2,400
Amortization of advertising and promotion over five years	480
Other expenses	5,000
Income tax rate	20%
Common shares outstanding	1,200

Note: The choice of depreciation method will have no effect on income taxes; maximum CCA on capital assets will be claimed for tax purposes. Advertising and promotion expenses are tax deductible as incurred, again, regardless of accounting policy.

Required:

1. Prepare a columnar income statement. In column 1, show net income assuming the use of FIFO, declining-balance depreciation, and expensing of advertising and promotion. In successive columns, show the individual impact of each of the following policy changes on net income:
   a. In column 2, average cost;

b. In column 3, straight-line depreciation;

c. In column 4, amortization of advertising and promotion; and

d. In column 5, the combined effects of the alternatives presented separately in columns 2 through 4.

2. As president, which accounting policies would you choose? Explain.

★★ **A8-27 Inventory Cost Methods (Appendix):** The inventory records of Acme Appliances Limited showed the following data relative to a food processor in inventory (the transactions occurred in the order given):

Transaction	Units	Unit Cost
1. Inventory	30	$19.00
2. Purchase	45	20.00
3. Sale	50	
4. Purchase	50	20.80
5. Sale	50	
6. Purchase	50	21.60

Required:

Compute the cost of goods sold for the period and the ending inventory, assuming the following (round unit costs to nearest cent):

1. Weighted average (periodic inventory system)
2. Moving average (perpetual inventory system)
3. FIFO

★★★ **A8-28 Inventory Cost Methods (Appendix):** The College Store Inc. inventory records showed the following data relative to a particular item sold regularly (transactions occurred in the order given):

Transaction	Units	Unit Cost
1. Beginning inventory	3,000	$5.00
2. Purchase	27,000	5.20
3. Sales (at $13 per unit)	−10,500	
4. Purchase	9,000	5.50
5. Sales (at $13.50 per unit)	−24,000	
6. Purchase	4,500	6.00
7. Ending inventory	9,000	

Required:

1. Complete the following schedule (round unit costs to nearest cent and total costs of inventory to the nearest $10):

	Ending Inventory	Cost of Goods Sold	Gross Margin
a. FIFO			
b. Weighted average			
c. Moving average			

2. Prepare journal entries, including year-end adjusting entries to establish ending inventory, if needed, for the two average calculations (b) and (c) above. Assume that the weighted average method is used with a periodic system and the moving average method with a perpetual system.

3. Explain how your entries in (2) would be different if a standard cost system were used, with the standard cost established at $5.50 at normal capacity.

★★★
eXcel

A8-29 Inventory Cost Methods (Appendix): The records of Cordova Corporation showed the following transactions, in the order given, relating to the major inventory item:

	Units	Unit Cost
1. Inventory	3,000	$6.90
2. Purchase	6,000	7.20
3. Sale (at $15)	4,000	
4. Purchase	5,000	7.50
5. Sale (at $15)	9,000	
6. Purchase	11,000	7.66
7. Sale (at $18)	9,000	
8. Purchase	6,000	7.80

Required:
Complete the following schedule for each independent assumption (round unit costs to the nearest cent; show computations):

	Units and Amounts		
Independent Assumptions	**Ending Inventory**	**Cost of Sales**	**Gross Margin**
a. FIFO			
b. Weighted average, periodic inventory system			
c. Moving average, perpetual inventory system			

★★★   **A8-30 Inventory Policy Comparison:** Carlton Inc. and Dennis Ltd. are two North American manufacturers of auto parts. The two firms use different inventory cost flow accounting policies. This question asks you to determine some of the differences due to the reporting. The two firms report the following selected information for 20X1:

	($ thousands)	
	Carlton Inc.	**Dennis Ltd.**
Earnings from continuing operations	$ (538)	$ (3,432)
Cost of sales	24,803	71,826
Net earnings per share (continuing operations)	(2.22)	(7.21)
Assets (total)	43,076	174,429
Inventories	3,571	6,215
Total shareholders' equity	6,109	22,690
Comparative units sold: United States and Canada (millions)	1.661 units	3.114 units
Comparative units sold: Worldwide (millions)	1.866 units	5.346 units

CARLTON INC.
Note 1: Summary of Significant Accounting Policies
Inventories are valued at the lower of cost or NRV. The cost of approximately 41% and 49% of inventories at 31 December 20X1 and 20X0, respectively, is determined on an average cost basis. The balance of inventory cost is determined on a first-in, first-out (FIFO) basis.

Note 2: Inventories and Cost of Sales
Inventories are summarized by major classification as follows (in thousands of dollars):

	31 December	
	20X1	20X0
Finished products, including service parts	$1,192	$1,114
Raw materials, finished, production parts, and supplies	873	1,100
Work-in-process	1,476	911
Other	30	25
Total	$3,571	$3,150

If inventories valued by FIFO had instead been valued on an average cost basis, inventory would have been $239 million and $208 million lower at 31 December 20X1 and 20X0, respectively (see Note 1). Total manufacturing cost of sales aggregated $24.81 million, and $24.13 million for 20X1 and 20X0, respectively.

DENNIS LTD.

Note 1: Accounting Policies (Inventory Valuation)
Inventories are stated at the lower of cost or market. The cost of substantially all North American inventories is determined by the average cost method. The cost of the remaining inventories is determined substantially by the first-in, first-out (FIFO) method.

If FIFO were the only method of inventory accounting used by the company, inventories would have been $1,323 and $1,331 higher than reported at 31 December 20X1 and 20X0, respectively. The major classes of inventory at 31 December were as follows (in thousands of dollars):

	20X1	20X0
Finished products	$2,979.2	$3,628.2
Raw materials and work-in-process	2,800.9	3,025.7
Supplies	435.2	461.5
Total	$6,215.3	$7,115.4

Required:

1. Are prices rising or falling in the 20X1 supplier markets in which Dennis (and Carlton) buys? How do you know?
2. Compare Dennis's and Carlton's inventory levels and comment on the comparison.
3. Is it desirable to have similar companies using different inventory cost flow policies? If not, why do accounting standard setters not require uniformity?

CHAPTER 9

Property, Plant, and Equipment; Intangibles; and Goodwill

INTRODUCTION

The main focus of this chapter is on the very broad category of long-lived assets—both tangible and intangible. Long-lived assets of many descriptions have future benefit to companies because they contribute to the revenue stream. For example, Maple Leaf Foods Incorporated, operating in the food service business, reports hog and poultry stock (biological assets), in addition to the more classic tangible assets, such as land, buildings, machinery, equipment, and assets under construction. Intangible assets include computer software, trademarks, customer relationships, poultry production quotas, delivery routes, and goodwill. These are quite a diversified collection of assets, but all necessary to operate in this industry!

In addition to having many different types of long-lived assets, companies can report using three different models. For example, Brookfield Asset Management Incorporated, which is a global asset management company, uses all three models for its long-lived assets. The company uses the cost model for intangibles and some items of property, plant, and equipment; the revaluation model for renewable power generating, utilities, transport, and energy assets; and the fair value model for biological assets and investment properties. Each of these models will have a very different impact on the financial statements.

This chapter will examine the issues surrounding the measurement and recording of long-lived assets, both tangible and intangible, and goodwill. Major topics in this chapter are acquisition cost and measurement models. The determination of acquisition cost may be complex because decisions must be made about what expenditures to include and exclude from capital cost. In addition, assets must be divided into significant parts or components. Companies must decide which measurement model they want to use for their long-lived assets. The appendices to this chapter discuss the accounting for investment properties and government assistance. Chapter 10 continues on this topic and deals with accounting for long-lived assets following acquisition, including amortization, impairment, revaluation, and fair value model.

CATEGORIES OF LONG-LIVED ASSETS

Long-lived assets may be separated into five types:

1. Property, plant, and equipment;
2. Investment property;
3. Biological assets;
4. Intangible assets; and
5. Goodwill.

Property, Plant, and Equipment   An item of **property, plant, and equipment** can be defined as a *tangible item, acquired for use in the revenue-producing activities of the enterprise and expected to be used for more than one period.*

Items of property, plant, and equipment are tangible assets. These assets have a physical presence; the word "tangible" means, literally, that the asset can be touched. Tangible assets include land, buildings, equipment, furniture, leasehold improvements, and other such physical assets. Tangible assets also include long-lived property held to generate revenue through rental, such as office buildings, apartments, cars and trucks, industrial property, furniture, computers, airplanes, and so on.

These tangible assets are held for use in the production or supply of goods and services or for rental to others. These tangible assets may also be used for administrative purposes or for maintenance of other capital assets. They must be separately identifiable and are acquired to be used on a continued basis for more than one period. These assets are not intended for sale in the ordinary course of business.

It is important to distinguish between items of property, plant, and equipment, and inventory. A computer is an item of *property, plant, and equipment* to the company that buys and uses it, but it was *inventory* to the manufacturer that made it and to the dealer that sold it. It is not the asset itself that governs classification as property, plant, and equipment; it is the intended *use* of the asset that matters. If an asset is held-for-sale, it is not property, plant, and equipment. Long-lived assets that were originally acquired for use in generating revenue but are no longer intended for that purpose cease to be classified as property, plant, and equipment. Instead, they become investment properties or assets held-for-sale and are given a different classification on the balance sheet as discussed earlier in Chapter 3.

Investment Property   **Investment property** is a unique classification of land and/or buildings that are held for rent (e.g., apartment buildings) or capital appreciation (e.g., vacant land held for future sale). Appendix 1 discusses the accounting for investment property.

Biological Assets   **Biological assets** are a unique classification for living plants and animals. The accounting for these types of assets, when classified as inventory, was discussed in Chapter 6. Biological assets can also be long-lived assets (e.g., vines in a winery).

Intangible Assets   **Intangible assets** are long-lived assets that do *not* have a physical substance. They are separately identifiable and often arise from legal or contractual rights. These assets are held to generate revenue, and are not intended for sale in the ordinary course of business. They can be purchased or internally generated. Examples include customer lists, copyrights, patents, subscription lists, mineral rights, franchises, computer software, quotas, licences, and trademarks.

Goodwill   *Goodwill* is not a *separately identifiable* asset. Goodwill arises as a residual in the purchase of other assets acquired in a business combination. The superior earning potential of the purchased entity is assumed to be the reason that goodwill exists.

VALUATION OF LONG-LIVED ASSETS

There are three possible models used in the valuation of long-lived assets. The most common model used in practice for valuation of long-lived assets is the cost model. All items in a class must use the same model. The discussions in this chapter focus on the cost model.

Cost Model

Long-lived assets are normally recorded using the **cost model.** The cost model records the assets at cost less accumulated depreciation and accumulated impairment losses since acquisition. This cost is acquisition price and includes all costs directly attributable to the acquisition, construction, development, or betterment of the asset including installing it in the location and in the condition necessary for its intended use.

Cost is usually the *fair value* at the date of purchase. That is, the asset is bought for its fair value as of the date of acquisition. As time passes, the fair value of the asset will change as the price for a comparable asset changes in the market, due to changes in technology and supply and demand forces. Since long-lived assets are held for lengthy periods of time, (depreciated) historical cost and fair value may be quite different. The cost model does not attempt to reflect the current value of capital assets, just the sacrifice made to acquire them.

Revaluation Model

Entities with property, plant, and equipment; intangible assets with an active market; and exploration and evaluation costs for mineral resources can choose to use the cost model or the **revaluation model.** This model uses fair value as its measurement base. The argument is that when these assets are pledged as collateral for loans, or in a number of other circumstances, the fair value of long-lived assets may be highly relevant to financial statement readers. The revaluation model revalues the assets to fair value. A key aspect of this model is that revaluation does not always occur every year. The asset is recorded at the revalued amount less accumulated depreciation and accumulated impairment losses in between valuations. This is often referred to as the *revalued amount.*

Fair Value Model

Investment property can choose to use the cost model or the **fair value model.** The key difference between this model and the revaluation model is that fair value is determined every year. Depreciation is not recorded with the fair value model. The fair value model is discussed further in Appendix 1 in this chapter and the revaluation model is discussed later in Appendix 2 to Chapter 10.

CONCEPT REVIEW

1. What are the five types of long-lived assets?
2. What is the difference between tangible and intangible capital assets?
3. What are the three valuation models used for measuring long-lived assets?

RECOGNITION OF PROPERTY, PLANT, AND EQUIPMENT

General Recognition Criteria

Costs for property, plant, and equipment can be recognized as an asset if there is a probable future economic benefit that will flow to the company and the cost of the asset can be measured reliably. Initial recognition is straightforward as we will see later in the chapter. However, subsequent costs can be added to the initial cost only if they will increase future economic benefits. Costs incurred to maintain the asset have to be expensed.

Component Accounting

A unique consideration for recognition of property, plant, and equipment is **component accounting.** The definition of a component is driven by depreciation, which is discussed in

Chapter 10. On initial recognition, if an asset has significant components that depreciate at different rates, the asset is separated into these components. A critical word here is "significant"! Not every part will be significant. Similar items would be grouped. For example, in its significant accounting policy note, Air Canada identifies the following components for its aircraft: airframe, engine, cabin interior equipment and modifications, spare engine and related parts "rotables," and major maintenance. Costs related to routine maintenance are expensed.

Spare Parts

Spare parts are included in either inventory or as a cost of property, plant, and equipment. As indicated above, Air Canada includes aircraft, engine, and rotable spares as a separate component. These spare parts are used for more than one period and can be used only with the plane. Minor spare parts that will be used in the current period are usually considered inventory unless they can be used only with an item of property, plant, and equipment. Major spare parts that are expected to be used in more than one period will be included in property, plant, and equipment.

A unique type of spare part is standby equipment, which is often viewed as a backup in case of failure of a part. For example, in the utility industry a reliable source of power is critical so its facilities would include backups for key components (e.g., transformers in case the original component fails).

Most spare parts are minor and included in inventory. Minor spare parts are expensed when used.

Costs (Safety or Environmental)

Involuntary costs incurred by the company for safety or environmental reasons must be capitalized. On the surface, these costs would appear to not meet the definition of an asset since there often is no future benefit from the cost on its own. For example, if a building needed to install a new sprinkler system to meet the fire code, these costs on their own would not provide an increased benefit to the company. The logic is that the future benefit is derived from the use of the asset as a whole. If the costs were not incurred to meet the fire code, the building would be shut down, and there would be no future benefits.

Voluntary costs for environmental or safety reasons would be capitalized only if they had a future benefit on their own. Otherwise, they would be expensed.

Basket Purchase of Several Assets

Occasionally, several assets are acquired for a single lump-sum price that may be lower than the sum of the individual asset prices, to encourage the sale. In other cases, the assets are attached (e.g., land and building, vines and land in a winery). This type of acquisition is called a **basket purchase**, group purchase, or lump-sum purchase. A portion of the single lump-sum price must be allocated to each asset acquired.

Any portions of the lump-sum price directly attributable to particular assets in the group are assigned in full to those assets. For example, land survey costs and back property taxes applicable to land are assigned only to the land account. Allocation of the remaining lump-sum price to each asset is necessary. Under the cost principle, the sum of the individual asset account balances at acquisition is limited to the lump-sum price.

Allocation is based on the relative fair values of the several assets involved. The company would determine the appropriate method of valuing the asset from the fair value hierarchy in the standard for fair value measurement discussed in Chapter 2. This value may be market prices for similar assets, current appraised values, or a present value of future net cash flows. The seller's book values are not relevant because they do not reflect the current value of the assets.

Each asset is valued according to the ratio of its value to the total value of the group; this valuation is called the *proportional method*.

To illustrate the proportional method, assume that $90,000 is the negotiated acquisition price paid for land, a building, and machinery. These assets are appraised individually. The best available indications of fair value are determined to be the following: land, $30,000;

building, $50,000; and machinery, $20,000. The cost apportionment of the single lump-sum price and the entry to record the transaction are as follows:

	Appraised Asset Value	Apportionment of Cost	Apportioned Cost
Land	$ 30,000	30%* × $90,000	$27,000
Building	50,000	50% × $90,000	45,000
Machinery	20,000	20% × $90,000	18,000
Total	$100,000		$90,000

*30% = $30,000 ÷ $100,000

To record the basket purchase:

Land	27,000	
Building	45,000	
Machinery	18,000	
Cash		90,000

Subsequent Costs

After acquisition, many costs related to capital assets are incurred. Examples include repairs, maintenance, betterments, replacement of major parts, and major inspections or overhauls. Expenditures that are incurred to replace a major part or a major inspection are capitalized.

The service potential of assets and their estimated useful life at acquisition assume a certain minimum level of maintenance and repair. Costs for maintenance are expensed in the period incurred. Some companies expense all post-acquisition expenditures less than a certain dollar amount (e.g., $1,000). This policy is acceptable because the amounts are not material.

Expenditures that result from accident, neglect, intentional abuse, or theft are recognized as losses. For example, if a computer workstation is damaged during installation, the repair cost is recognized as a loss. After repair, the asset is no more valuable than it was before the mishap. Outlays made to restore uninsured assets damaged through *casualty*, or accident, are also recorded as losses. They do not enhance the utility of the asset beyond the value before the casualty.

Significant post-acquisition expenditures fall into four major categories:

1. Maintenance and ordinary repairs;

2. Additions;

3. Replacement major part or betterment; and

4. Major inspection.

Maintenance and Ordinary Repairs

Maintenance expenditures include lubrication, cleaning, adjustment, and painting incurred on a continuous basis to keep assets in usable condition. Ordinary repair costs include outlays for parts, labour, and related supplies that are necessary to keep assets in operating condition but do not add materially to the use of assets nor prolong their useful life significantly. Ordinary repairs usually involve relatively small expenditures. *Many expenditures made to capital assets are repairs and expensing is the norm.* Keep this in mind as a rule of thumb—capitalization may look too tempting at times!

Many firms accrue repairs each month, and charge actual repairs to the accrued repair liability account to report smooth monthly expenses. This makes some sense, especially in a business where regular repairs and maintenance are all done in a regular slack season. For external reporting purposes, interim or year-end reports, any remaining balance in the liability account is reversed so that repair expense represents the amount actually spent during the year.

Additions

Additions are extensions, enlargements, or expansions of an existing asset. An extra wing or room added to a building is an example. Additions represent capital expenditures and are recorded in the capital asset accounts at cost. Related work on the existing structure, such as shoring up the foundation for the addition or cutting an entranceway through an existing wall, is part of the cost of the addition and is capitalized. Consideration would need to be made if the addition should be classified as a separate component.

Replacement of Major Part or Betterment

The replacement of a major component of an item of property, plant, and equipment is often referred to as a **betterment**.

Betterments may be replacements or renewals. A *replacement* is the substitution of a major component of an item of property, plant, and equipment with one of comparable quality. For example, a betterment could be the replacement of the seats in an airplane or the replacement of the lining in the oven of a bakery. *Renewals* involve large expenditures, are not recurring in nature, and often increase the utility or the service life of the asset beyond the original estimate. Examples include the replacement of an old roof with a new roof or replacing the interior walls of a building.

The cost of the betterment is capitalized and any carrying amount of the part that is being replaced is recognized as a loss on the income statement.

To illustrate, assume that a shingle roof with an original cost of $20,000 and now 80% depreciated is replaced by a new fireproof tile roof costing $60,000. The two entries to record the betterment are as follows:

To remove old component accounts		
Accumulated depreciation (old roof, $20,000 × 80%)	16,000	
Loss on asset improvement	4,000	
Building (old roof)		20,000
To record cost of new component		
Building (new roof)	60,000	
Cash		60,000

Major Inspection

Costs of **major inspections** are capitalized (e.g., the costs related to an overhaul of an airplane engine). Similar to the replacement of major parts, any remaining carrying amount from the previous inspection is derecognized.

CONCEPT REVIEW

1. What is component accounting?

2. How are spare parts and major inspections accounted for in property, plant, and equipment for initial recognition, and when they are replaced?

3. What is the difference in accounting for involuntary or voluntary costs related to safety or environmental costs?

4. Why is it necessary to allocate the overall cost of a basket purchase of assets to the individual assets in the basket?

5. What is the difference between accounting for repairs and for betterments?

MEASUREMENT OF PROPERTY, PLANT, AND EQUIPMENT

Elements of Cost

The cost of an item of property, plant, and equipment can include the purchase price, directly attributable costs, and dismantling or site restoration costs. Certain costs are not allowed to be included (e.g., start-up costs, relocation costs, initial operating losses).

Carefully analyze Exhibit 9-1 for common practices for tangible assets, such as buildings, machinery and equipment, land, and land improvements. Note in particular the conventions surrounding land. Since land does not depreciate, but other capital assets do, a decision to capitalize an amount in the land account means that there is no impact on net income until the land is sold. The exception to this relates to site restoration costs. As discussed later, the amount added to the land for the site restoration costs is depreciated. In particular, note that land cost includes costs specifically related to obtaining clear title to the land, such as legal fees and back property taxes. Any costs associated with preparing the land for its intended use, such as clearing existing structures and excavation, are also capitalized to the land account. Other expenditures, for things that will wear out over time, are put in a separate land improvements account, which is depreciated. These expenditures include nonpermanent landscaping as well as fences and paving.

Capitalization Norms

Accounting practice has developed steadily in this area, and there is normal practice surrounding the typical kinds of costs that should be capitalized versus expensed in each category. Common practices for capital expenditures are summarized in Exhibit 9-1. Careful analysis will show that each capitalized item creates some sort of future enhancement of cash flows. Often this results from the fact that the expenditure is required to get the capital asset into operation.

Self-Constructed Assets Many capital assets are not purchased but are constructed by the enterprise. The cost of a constructed asset is the sum of the expenditures relating to its construction. These costs may not reflect the fair value of the asset, even at the time of its creation. A tangible item may be constructed at a lower cost than its purchase price. For example, a utility employs its personnel to extend transmission lines and construct pipelines. All costs directly associated with the construction are capitalized to the constructed asset. These costs include incremental material, labour, and overhead costs.

Overhead Cost Overhead incurred during construction, *if it is directly attributable to the construction or development activity*, is included in the cost of self-constructed or self-developed assets. Overhead costs could include some portion of utility costs, maintenance on equipment used, supervision, and so on. General overhead costs are not allowed to be capitalized (e.g. administrative costs).

Many accountants contend that failure to allocate some portion of the overhead to self-construction projects causes an undervaluation of self-constructed assets. On the other hand, others argue that assets are often self-constructed during slack periods when the production facility and workers would otherwise be idle. Using this line of reasoning, no overhead should be capitalized because of the income-manipulation potential associated with this "make-work" project. Companies that want to show high asset values will tend to interpret "overhead" quite broadly and will allocate significant amounts of overhead cost to the project.

Interest Cost The period required for construction of long-lived assets can be lengthy. There is general agreement that time-related costs, including interest, property taxes, and insurance during construction, should be capitalized to the asset under construction. Interest must be capitalized if you have a "qualifying asset." This is an *asset* where a substantial time period is needed to get the item ready for use or sale. After all, if the asset were purchased rather than self-constructed, the purchase price would normally include a cost

---

EXHIBIT 9-1

COMMON CAPITALIZATION PRACTICES: PROPERTY, PLANT, AND EQUIPMENT

Capital Asset	Capitalize
Buildings, purchased	• Purchase price • Cost of modifications
Buildings, constructed	• Architectural fees • Payments to contractors • Cost of permits • Excavation costs • Legal fees, closing costs
Buildings, self-constructed	• Direct construction costs • Excavation costs • Reasonable apportionment of overhead • Legal costs, permits, etc. • Interest on *specific* construction loans and general interest
Machinery and equipment	• Invoice cost, net of discounts • Taxes, freight, and duty • Special platforms, foundations, other required installation costs • Costs of building modifications necessary for installation
Land	• Cost of preparing asset for use, including testing • Purchase price • Back taxes on acquisition, paid to release title • Legal fees, closing costs • General land preparation costs, including grading, filling, draining, and surveying • Cost of removing structures and other obstructions, if land is acquired for development (proceeds from salvaged materials reduce the cost capitalized) • Special assessments for local government-maintained improvements, including streets, sidewalks, sewers, and streetlights • Property taxes, insurance, and other holding costs incurred on land not in current productive use (may be expensed on grounds of expedience and conservatism) • Landscaping and other property enhancements, if permanent
Land improvements	• Site restoration costs • Driveways, parking lots, fencing • Streets and sidewalks that the company must maintain • Landscaping, if not permanent

component to cover the seller's financing expenses during construction. Also, many firms would be unable to construct assets without debt financing.

Interest is usually a period cost, not eligible for capitalization. For qualifying assets where a substantial amount of time is required to get the asset ready for use, interest costs must be capitalized. The amount of interest capitalized includes loans specific for the construction as well as a portion of general borrowings. The amount of general borrowings is determined using a capitalization rate considering the weighted average cost of borrowings.

Capitalization of interest starts when three conditions are met: Expenditures are incurred for construction; the entity incurs interest costs; and construction activities have started. Capitalization stops temporarily if there is an extended period of time where there is no active construction, for example, a strike shutting down the construction site for an indefinite period of time. Once the strike is over, interest would again be capitalized. Capitalization ends when the construction of the asset is complete. This issue will be discussed further in Chapter 13.

Incidental Revenues or Expenses Any profits or losses from incidental operations that occur before or during construction are not capitalized. These are treated as a separate event in the income statement. For example, a company might have demolished a building and decided to operate a parking lot on the land prior to beginning construction of a new facility. Any revenues and expenses from operating the parking lot are included in net income.

Fair Market Value Cap The actual cost of a self-constructed asset does not necessarily equal fair market value at the point of acquisition. Using the higher market value would result in recording a gain on construction. A company cannot record a gain as the result of expenditures! The lower construction cost is ultimately reflected in higher net income through lower depreciation expense in future years.

Consistent with the valuation of other assets, the maximum valuation allowed for self-constructed assets is fair market value. If total capitalized cost exceeds the market value of a similar asset of equal capacity and quality, the excess is recognized as a loss. Failure to do so carries forward cost elements that have no future benefit and causes overstated depreciation in future years.

Example To illustrate the accounting for a self-constructed asset, assume that Kelvin Corporation completes a project with total construction costs as follows:

Material	$200,000
Labour	500,000
Incremental overhead	60,000
Applied overhead	40,000
Capitalized interest	100,000
Total	$900,000

Kelvin has recorded costs in an account called equipment under construction. If the asset's market value at completion equals or exceeds $900,000, the summary entry to record the completion of the project is:

Equipment	900,000	
Equipment under construction		900,000

If the asset's market value is only $880,000, the entry is:

Equipment	880,000	
Loss on construction of equipment	20,000	
Equipment under construction		900,000

It is important to watch capitalization practices very carefully—many firms, with a desire to maximize earnings or assets by deferring costs, seize on self-construction as an opportunity to try to defer lots of interesting things. Others wish to capitalize as little as possible. Remember, though, that the higher asset value generated is a base for future depreciation and potential impairment.

Impact of Policy Choice Expenditures might be capitalized and depreciated or immediately expensed. If you do not expense now, you will expense later. That is, capitalized costs, in almost all cases, are carried to net income through depreciation. The two approaches will provide different income and asset values throughout the life of the asset.

ETHICAL ISSUES

Is there any room for choice or manipulation? Some firms are quick to disclaim any future benefit associated with a variety of expenditures related to capital assets. They expense these amounts immediately. For whatever reason, these companies seem to be attempting to minimize current net income and net assets and enjoy lower future depreciation expenses. A company may also prefer to expense rather than capitalize if it has cash flow prediction as a primary reporting objective. By including the expenditures in current expenses, a company achieves a net income figure that is closer to the actual cash flow.

At the other end of the spectrum, some companies are very aggressive in their capitalization policies, seeking higher current income and capital assets, and accepting higher future depreciation. For example, a regulated public utility will generally capitalize as many costs as possible because the enterprise's permitted (i.e., regulated) profit is based on its regulated rate of return multiplied by the asset base. The higher the asset base, the larger is the profit it is entitled to earn.

Materiality plays a role in this area, as well. Small capital expenditures are often expensed on the basis that the more correct capitalization and depreciation would not produce results different enough to cause investors to make different decisions.

Capital Assets Financed with Low-Interest Debt

Sometimes, payment terms for an asset stretch out over a long period. This presents no special accounting problems, unless the debt bears a reduced interest rate, perhaps offered by the vendor to encourage purchase. In such a case, the asset is recorded at the most objective amount, considering:

1. The cash equivalent price, or fair value of the capital asset, versus
2. The present value of the future cash payments required by the debt agreement discounted at the prevailing (market) interest rate for that type of debt.

When a low-interest debt instrument is issued it is recorded at its face value as a liability net of any discount. The difference between the face value and the (lower) fair value of the asset is the *discount on note payable*. The discount is amortized over the term of the debt, thereby increasing interest expense each period. The fair value of the asset may be calculated as the present value of the loan plus any cash paid.

Example To illustrate the purchase of a capital asset on credit, assume that Cobb Corporation purchases equipment on 1 January 20X2, with a $600 cash down payment and a $1,000, one-year 12% note payable due on 31 December 20X2. The stated interest rate is equal to the current market rate, so the present value of the note equals its face value. That is,

$$P = (\$1,000 + \$120) \times (P/F, 12\%, 1)$$
$$= \$1,120 \times .89286$$
$$= \$1,000$$

The asset is recorded at the sum of the cash down payment plus the present value of the note because the cash equivalent price of the asset is not available. The recorded amount is:

Equipment value = Cash down payment + Present value of note
= $600 + $1,000 = $1,600

Cobb's entries to record the asset and the note are as follows:

1 January 20X2

Equipment	1,600	
Cash		600
Note payable		1,000

Assume instead that Feller Company acquires a machine on 1 January 20X2, with a non-interest-bearing note that requires $8,615 to be paid on 31 December 20X2, 20X3, and 20X4. The note has no explicit interest, but the prevailing interest rate is 14% on liabilities of similar risk and duration. The face amount of the note is $25,845 ($8,615 × 3). The cash equivalent cost of the machine is unknown, so the asset is recorded at the present value of the three payments discounted at 14%.

Recorded cost = $8,615 × (P/A, 14%, 3)
= $8,615 × 2.32163
= $20,000 (rounded)

Feller's entries to record the asset and the note are as follows:

1 January 20X2

Net Method		
Equipment	20,000	
Note payable		20,000

The discount of $5,845 ($25,845 − 20,000) on the note payable reduces the net note payable balance to the present value of the future cash flows ($20,000). The discount is amortized to interest expense over the life of the liability using the effective interest method.

Capital Assets Acquired in Exchange for Equity Securities

When equity securities (e.g., common shares) are issued to acquire capital assets, this is a non-monetary transaction. Non-monetary transactions were discussed earlier in Chapter 6. When they relate to shares, special guidance exists that records the value of the capital assets received at the fair value of capital asset received unless that measurement is not reliably measurable and only then the fair value of the shares is used.

Donated Assets

Shareholders and other parties occasionally donate assets and services to corporations. For example, shareholders may donate valuable paintings to adorn the corporate boardroom.

The assets cost the company nothing; that is, they are obtained in a *non-reciprocal transfer*, meaning that the company gives nothing in return. Does that mean that the assets need not be recognized? If the SFP is to provide a record of assets controlled by the entity, and the income statement is to record the costs of doing business, then it seems logical to include these assets at fair value. But the entity sacrificed no resources to obtain the assets. If the assets are depreciable, recorded assets will create an expense in future years, as they are used. Should future years' income be reduced because of a charge created in such a way? Is the return on shareholders' investment understated in such circumstances? It is a thorny issue.

Current practice in Canada is often to record the asset at its fair value and increase a shareholders' equity contributed capital account. Depreciation based on the market value of the donated asset is matched against future revenue presumably generated by the assets. There is no specific IFRS guidance for non-reciprocal transfers.

Example   To illustrate accounting for a donated asset, assume that a building (fair market value $400,000) and the land on which it is located (fair market value $100,000) are donated to Sui Limited. A $5,000 legal and deed transfer cost for the land is borne by Sui, which records the donation as follows:

Building	400,000	
Land	105,000	
Cash		5,000
Contributed capital—donated assets		500,000

Government Assistance

To help fund the purchase or construction of property, plant, or equipment, government funding is often available. In some cases, this funding may come with a catch or strings attached requiring specific criteria to be met before the loan can be forgiven. However, other funding has no criteria. The alternatives for government assistance are discussed further in Appendix 2 to this chapter.

Site Restoration Costs or Decommissioning Liabilities

Some companies may have a legal requirement, either through legal statute or contract, to incur costs when an asset (or group of assets) is retired. Or they could have a **constructive obligation**, which is a management practice of incurring costs at the end of an asset's life. With a constructive obligation, the expectation by outsiders is that the company will incur this cost. For example,

- Companies often are required by law to restore mine sites to their original condition.
- Landfills must be covered, capped (e.g., with concrete), and perhaps landscaped when they are full.
- Companies that use rooftops for billboard advertising or for relay antennas usually are required by contract to physically remove billboards or antennas at the end of the contract and to repair the roofs as well.

These **site restoration costs** or **decommissioning obligations** are recognized when there is a legal or contractual commitment or a constructive obligation.

Initial Recognition   When a legal or constructive obligation exists, the cost of fulfilling that obligation must be recognized when the asset is acquired. Or it would be recognized at the time an obligation is known, for example, legislation changes creating an obligation that did not exist previously. The process is as follows:

- Estimate the amount required and the timing of the future cash flows;
- Discount the cash flow at a pretax rate that reflects the risks related to that liability;
- Credit a provision for the present value of the estimated liability; and
- Capitalize the amount, that is, increase the acquisition cost of the asset by the amount of the estimated liability.

For example, suppose that on 2 January 20X0, Firkin Limited purchased equipment for $500,000 to install in a leased building. The company is legally required by the building lease to remove the equipment at the end of 10 years. The estimated cost of removal is $70,000.

To recognize the liability, the $70,000 must be discounted at an appropriate interest rate. Suppose that the pretax rate that reflects the risks is 5%. The future obligation must be discounted at 5% for 10 years:

$$P = \$70,000 \times (P/F, 5\%, 10) = \$70,000 \times 0.61391 = \$42,974$$

The asset purchase and the retirement obligation are recorded as follows:

To record the purchase of equipment Equipment	500,000	
Account payable (to equipment vendor)		500,000
To record the legal obligation to remove the *equipment in the future* Equipment	42,974	
Provision—decommissioning		42,974

The asset's beginning book value will be $542,974.

Subsequent Depreciation and Accrual Once the asset and the retirement obligation have been recorded, the combined book value must be depreciated. Assuming that Firkin uses straight-line depreciation with zero residual value, the initial book value will be depreciated at $54,297 per year. The depreciation is recorded exactly the same way as any other depreciation expense. For 20X0, the entry will be:

Depreciation expense—equipment	54,297	
Accumulated depreciation—equipment		54,297

If the obligation related to land instead of equipment, only the portion added to the land for the site restoration costs would be depreciated, not the value of the land itself.

Interest In addition to depreciation expense, an expense must also be recorded to reflect the increase to the liability because of the passage of time. The retirement obligation was recorded at its present value. By the end of 10 years, the obligation must be $70,000 on Firkin's books, not $42,974. Therefore, Firkin must accrue an expense each year to build up the total obligation to $70,000. The increase is calculated using the same interest rate as was used in the initial measurement, which was 5%. The expense is recognized as interest expense.

For 20X0, the accrual will be:

Interest expense [$42,974 × 5%]	2,149	
Provision-decommissioning		2,149

At the end of 20X0, the book value of the obligation will be $42,974 + $2,149 = $45,123. For 20X1, the interest accrual will be $45,123 × 5% = $2,256. Each year's accrual is based on the accumulated obligation at the end of the preceding year and considers any changes to the discount rate.

Remeasurement In addition to amortizing the cost and accruing interest on the obligation, Firkin must also adjust the amount of the obligation if there is a change in the amount or timing of the expected retirement obligation cash flows or a change in the discount rate to reflect current market rates. In Firkin's case, the timing could change if the lease term is extended, or if the estimated amount changes. The current cost is quite likely to change from year to year as legislation changes, technology changes, and cost components change due to increasing or decreasing prices.

CONCEPT REVIEW

1. In initial measurement of property, plant, and equipment, what costs are eligible for capitalization, and what kind of costs are not eligible?

2. Under what circumstances can a company capitalize interest or borrowing costs?

3. When must a company record the present value of the costs of future asset retirement? How is the present value calculated?

INTANGIBLE ASSETS

Elements of Cost

Intangible assets are similar to property, plant, and equipment in that their cost is capitalized. As we will discuss in the next chapter, intangible assets with a definite life are amortized and those with an indefinite life are tested only for impairment. Note that if the intangible asset is internally generated, certain criteria will have to be met to qualify for capitalization; these will be reviewed in a later section. If the intangible asset is purchased, then the purchase price is capitalized. Legal costs are a major part of the recorded cost of intangible assets. This includes the legal costs to register these assets, and also legal costs for successful defence of the restricted use of these assets. Refer to Exhibit 9-2 for the common capitalizable costs for specific intangibles such as copyrights, trademarks, franchise fees. Costs related to introducing a new product or service (e.g., advertising) and conducting business in a new location (e.g., training) are not allowed to be capitalized.

Specific intangibles can be quite significant. For example, the 2011 financial statements for Telus Corporation show an intangible asset of $4.867 billion for "spectrum licences." This one intangible asset is 25% of Telus's total assets of $19.9 billion. Telus does not amortize the spectrum licences because they are assumed to have an indefinite life.

Many intangible assets are internally generated or developed by the enterprise. The cost of an internally generated intangible asset is the sum of the expenditures relating to its construction or development. Similar to our previous discussion for constructed buildings, interest costs for intangible assets developed over a long period of time are capitalized. These costs may not reflect the fair value of the asset, even at the time of its creation. An intangible asset may be developed for far less than it would cost to buy it fully developed from someone else.

Indeed, internally generated or developed assets may not be available for purchase at any price; they often are unique, which is what gives them their revenue-generating value. Examples include computer software and natural resource deposits. The capitalized value for these assets is not, was not, and was never intended to be, fair value at acquisition. It is undeniably difficult to interpret the earnings potential of companies with significant assets of this nature, without detailed knowledge of the assets beyond that provided in the financial statements.

Internally generated or developed assets may not be recorded at costs that *exceed* fair value. Fair value may be determined with reference to future benefits: future cash flow. This can be hard to establish. It may be impossible to determine whether an intangible asset is worth what was spent to develop it, until its development is complete. For example, the costs of developing a mining site are capitalized until it is known whether the value of the mineral resources is worth continued development of the mine site.

EXHIBIT 9-2

COMMON CAPITALIZATION PRACTICES: INTANGIBLE ASSETS

Patents	• Purchase price, transfer and legal fees if bought from another entity • If internally generated, criteria must be met to justify capitalization • Development costs to internally develop a patented item; research costs are expensed • Legal and other necessary documentation costs to register the patent, if self-developed • Costs of a successful court defence (unsuccessful defences are expensed, along with the now-worthless patent)
Industrial design registrations (e.g., a five-year renewable registration of the shape, pattern, or ornamentation of a manufactured item)	• Acquisition and registration cost, as per patents • If internally generated, criteria must be met to justify capitalization • Successful defence costs, as per patents
Copyrights	• Acquisition and registration cost, as per patents • If internally generated, criteria must be met to justify capitalization • Successful defence costs, as per patents
Trademarks and trade names	• Acquisition cost, as per patents • If internally generated, criteria must be met to justify capitalization • Legal and other necessary documentation costs to register the trademark, if self-developed • Successful defence costs, as per patents
Brands	• Acquisition cost • If internally generated cannot recognize
Customer Lists	• Acquisition cost • If internally generated cannot recognize
Publishing titles	• Acquisition cost • If internally generated cannot recognize
Franchise rights	• Initial franchise fees, not related to annual volumes • Legal fees, closing costs
Internally developed intangibles	• Specific criteria must be met to justify capitalization
Leasehold improvements (alterations, improvements, or refurbishing of leased space)	• Invoice cost, installation costs
Resource exploration and evaluation costs	• Resource exploration and development costs incurred • Present value of site restoration costs
Computer software costs	• If internally generated, criteria must be met to justify capitalization
Website development costs	• If internally generated, criteria must be met to justify capitalization • Application and infrastructure costs capitalized • Graphics costs capitalized • Some content development capitalized, depending on longevity and nature

SPECIFIC INTANGIBLE ASSETS

Internally Generated Intangibles

The criteria that must be met for any internally generated or developed intangible asset are:

1. First, the asset must be an *identifiable* intangible, which means that the intangible asset must be separable or able to be divided from an entity, or the asset must derive from contractual or legal rights; and

2. Second, the recognition criteria must be met:
    a. The intangible asset must be controlled by the entity as a result of past transactions or events;
    b. Future economic benefits must flow from the intangible asset; for example, markets for the related product or the internal usefulness of the intangible asset must be clearly established; and
    c. The cost must be reliably measurable.

These criteria are an attempt to provide some rigour over the cost-deferral practices of some companies.

Prohibited Internally Developed Intangibles Certain items are prohibited from being recognized as intangible assets, since it is difficult to separate these items from developing the business as a whole or internally generated goodwill. Internally generated brands, mastheads, publishing titles, and customer lists are not eligible for capitalization. These same items if purchased would be recognized as an intangible asset, since the purchase price indicates fair value.

Costs in Research and Development Phase

To determine if an internally generated asset meets the criteria for recognition, it is considered if activities are in the research or development phase. Broadly defined, research and development (R&D) includes the activities undertaken by firms to create new products and processes or to improve old ones and to discover new knowledge that may be of value in the future. For many firms, R&D is a very important part of ongoing activities and can be a significant expenditure. These expenditures are undertaken because the R&D effort is expected to more than pay for itself in the future by providing the firm with competitive, profitable products and processes.

R&D programs are undertaken by entities with a clear expectation of future profitable results. Their future benefits establish them as assets. Why do accounting standards recommend that all research and many development costs be expensed? Typically, research costs fail the recognition criteria of "probability." That is, one cannot be certain that future cash flows will accrue. Unfortunately, for some firms, expensing research costs means that the firm's most valuable asset is not shown at all on its balance sheet and that current period expenses are overstated.

Research versus Development Phase *Research* is defined as original and planned investigation undertaken with the hope of gaining new scientific or technical knowledge and understanding. Such investigation may or may not be directed toward a specific practical aim or application. *Development*, on the other hand, is the application of research findings or other knowledge into a plan or design for the production of new or substantially improved products and such before commercial production begins. The distinction matters because the accounting treatment is different for research costs and development costs.

Accounting Requirements for Capitalization Essentially, the accounting standards require that all research costs be expensed. Development costs for any internally generated intangible assets may be capitalized *after* certain specific criteria are met but otherwise must be expensed as well. The following criteria must *all* be met for a development asset to be capitalized:

1. The asset must be proven to be technologically feasible so it will be available for sale or use;

2. Management must have the intent to complete and then produce and market, or use, the asset;

3. The entity must be *able to* use or sell the asset;

4. The probable future economic benefits for (or external market or internal usefulness) of the product or process is clearly established;

5. Adequate resources exist, or are expected to be available, to complete the project; and

6. Costs can be reliably measured.

These criteria are subject to some potential for manipulation. Management plays a large role in assessing technological feasibility, future markets, and available resources. If management wishes to capitalize identifiable development costs for products or processes that the company is undertaking, it will be a brave auditor who tries to challenge this. Note that expenditures initially recognized as an expense may not subsequently be restated and capitalized if the criteria are met at a later date.

Ineligible Costs Certain costs are not eligible for capitalization. Costs that would *not* meet the capitalization criteria and therefore would be expensed as incurred are:

1. The costs of starting up a business (start-up costs);

2. Training;

3. Advertising and promotion; and

4. Costs of relocating or reorganizing all or part of an entity.

Computer Software Costs

Computer software is often a tricky area to determine if it is an item of property, plant, and equipment or an intangible asset. Computer software is often internally generated for either internal use or developed to be sold as a product.

Classification of Computer Software Where does computer software belong? Some software may be part of a tangible asset. For example, a piece of machinery may require software to be operated. In this situation professional judgement will be used to determine which part is more significant. If integrated into an item of property, plant, and equipment, it is a separate component and accounted for as a tangible asset. If not an integral part of a tangible asset, then it is classified as an intangible asset.

Internally Generated Computer Software Companies may develop software for use in the business or to be sold as a product. The criteria previously discussed for capitalization of an internally generated intangible asset would apply.

Companies that develop software for their own use are typically involved in expensive, large-scale systems and program development. The capitalization criteria as outlined for internally developed intangibles would apply. Companies that develop large-scale systems will usually meet the deferral criteria and will accordingly capitalize their software development costs. A common amortization period is three to five years.

However, many different measures of cost can be used, and there is significant variation in practice. For example:

1. Should all costs be capitalized, from the very beginning of the project, or should early feasibility and systems development studies be expensed?

2. Should only direct costs be capitalized, or should indirect and overhead costs also be capitalized?

Companies that develop software as a product may have a somewhat different approach. Software product development, like most other types of product development activities, has an initial period of feasibility testing to determine whether a proposed product is technically and financially feasible. Costs incurred during this period are viewed as research costs rather than as development costs and are written off. Technological feasibility (and a defined product) is usually considered to be present only when a *working model* exists. Of course, other criteria must also be met (a market must exist, and there must be management intent and adequate resources to take the product to market) before development costs can be deferred.

EXHIBIT 9-3

GENERIC EXAMPLE OF ACCOUNTING POLICY DISCLOSURE FOR COMPUTER SOFTWARE

ABC Company for the year ended 31 December 20X3

(i) Computer Software

ABC Company acquires computer software through purchases from vendors and internal development. Computer software that is an integral part of computer equipment is presented in property and equipment. All other computer software is treated as an intangible asset. ABC Company includes computer software under development in intangible assets. The assessment of whether computer software is an integral part of computer hardware is made when the software development project is complete and placed into use. Costs for internally developed computer software include directly attributable costs, including direct labour and overheads associated with the software development project. Expenditures on research activities as part of internally developed computer software are recognized in earnings when incurred.

Reporting Practice Review Exhibit 9-3 (see above) for an example of a generic disclosure note.

Remember that there is a lot of judgement involved in deciding whether the capitalization criteria have been met. Financial reporting objectives play a big role in the selection *and application* of accounting policies. The financial analyst community has tended to look unfavourably on software companies that capitalize a lot of their development costs. Therefore, to please the investment community, software companies tend to be conservative when applying capitalization policies.

Website Development Costs

Another type of software development cost is the sometimes material amount that companies spend to create websites. The companies may be traditional enterprises with more traditional marketing channels, or they may base their business model on electronic transactions or a blend of both strategies. That is, websites may be used to promote or advertise products or services, replace traditional products or services, and/or sell things.

How should the costs of website development be accounted for? Again, the listed criteria for internally developed intangible assets must be satisfied in order to support capitalization. Standard Interpretation Committee, SIC 32, breaks down website development costs into five areas:

Type of Website Expenditure	Accounting Policy Suggested; Deferral Criteria Must Also Be Reviewed
Costs incurred in the planning stage	Expense as incurred
Costs incurred for website application and infrastructure	Capitalize and amortize
Costs incurred to develop graphics	Capitalize and amortize
Costs incurred to develop content	Either expense or capitalize/amortize, depending on nature of costs
Operating costs	Expense as incurred

So, what is the overall theme? If costs are very early in the process (planning), then there is nothing tangible to pin the asset flag on, and the costs must be expensed. After that, the question is always whether there is a long-term benefit from the expenditure. Future benefits support asset treatment, otherwise, the expense category wins. One other small wrinkle is that if the website is used only for advertising, all costs must be expensed.

Exploration and Evaluation Assets

Exploration and evaluation (E&E) assets relate to costs that oil and gas companies and mining companies incur in exploring and evaluating their resource properties. *Exploration and evaluation of mineral resources* is the process of seeking mineral deposits, oil, natural gas, and so on after the entity has obtained legal rights to explore. It also involves deciding technical feasibility and commercial viability of these resources.

Much exploration is fruitless; that is the nature of the business. Most costs after the exploration and evaluation stage are necessary, since development of the site is not undertaken unless there is reasonable assurance of generating enough revenue from the site to recover the development costs. However, it can take years to develop a mine site or an oil field. How should the costs of exploration and development be accounted for? Costs are divided into three phases: pre-exploration and evaluation phase; exploration and evaluation phase; and post-exploration and evaluation phase.

Pre-exploration and Evaluation Phase Costs incurred prior to obtaining the legal right to explore are in the pre-exploration and evaluation phase. Costs in this stage are expensed, since before an entity obtains the legal right, it does not have the access to any future benefits from that site. How can you have control over a future benefit if you do not even have the legal right to explore?

Exploration and Evaluation Phase Once the legal right to mine or explore the property for resources has been obtained, the entity can capitalize costs until technical feasibility and commercial viability of the resource is reached. Examples of these activities could include acquisition costs for rights to explore the area, geological surveys and mapping, exploration, and test drilling of potential sites. Any removal or restoration costs for activities related to these mineral resources would need to be recognized. Of course, capitalization of costs would stop if it was established that there was no technical feasibility or commercial viability.

Post-exploration and Evaluation Phase After technical feasibility and commercial viability have been established, the same principles as property, plant, and equipment or intangibles apply to these costs. This phase is often referred to as *development and production*. Costs that are considered for property, plant, and equipment and intangible assets—materials and services, employee benefits, fees to register legal rights, interest costs, and other directly attributable costs—would be eligible for capitalization.

Successful Efforts Method The accounting for post-exploration and evaluation costs uses the successful efforts method. The **successful efforts method** accumulates costs by site. If a site has been determined to be unproductive, costs are expensed. The costs of successful sites are segregated as a deferred charge and amortized.

Under the *successful efforts method*, unsuccessful efforts are written off *once they are determined to be unsuccessful*. The costs are initially capitalized, since the effort may last more than one reporting period and the results are not known, but the accumulated costs relating to that site are charged to the income statement when management gives up the effort. Note that this is a management decision; timing of that decision will determine which accounting period's earnings bear the cost.

This method requires management to segregate costs by geographic area. There is a great deal of flexibility in this regard. One company may decide to segregate its successful sites on the basis of geological formation, while another may choose to use national boundaries as the definition of area. Some may view the United States and Canada as a single area, while others may view Oklahoma as one area, Alberta as another, and the Atlantic Provinces' offshore fields as yet another. Management choice is at the core of the successful efforts method.

CONCEPT REVIEW

1. What is the difference between the R&D phase for internally generated intangibles?
2. In general, when is it appropriate to capitalize costs in the development phase?
3. Is computer software always classified as an intangible asset?
4. Explain the successful efforts method of accounting for exploration and evaluation costs.

DERECOGNITION OF LONG-LIVED ASSETS

Derecognition of long-lived assets occurs on disposal or when the asset no longer will provide future benefits to the company. The disposal of long-lived assets may be *voluntary* as a result of a sale, exchange, or abandonment; be *involuntary* as a result of a *casualty*, such as a fire, or storm; or be government action, such as expropriation. Component accounting requires derecognition when major parts are replaced.

Cost Model

If the asset to be disposed of is subject to depreciation, it is depreciated up to the date of disposal to update the recorded book value. Applicable property taxes, insurance premium costs, and similar costs are also accrued up to the date of disposal. At the date of disposal, the original cost of the asset and its related accumulated depreciation are removed from the accounts.

The difference between the book value of a long-lived asset and the amount received on disposal is recorded as a *gain* or *loss*. Ideally, the gain or loss is segregated from ordinary income and reported in the income statement separately as part of income from continuing operations.

Disposals that are not the choice of the company are called **involuntary conversions**. This may happen in a natural disaster or as the result of a government expropriation. Involuntary conversions are unusual items.

To illustrate the disposal of a capital asset, assume that on 1 February 20X1, Brown Company paid $32,000 for office equipment with an estimated service life of five years and an estimated residual value of $2,000. Brown uses straight-line depreciation and sells the asset on 1 July 20X5, for $8,000. The entries for Brown, a calendar-year company, at date of disposal are as follows:

Depreciation expense	3,000*	
Accumulated depreciation—equipment		3,000
*($32,000 − $2,000) × (1/5) × (6/12)		
Cash	8,000	
Accumulated depreciation—equipment	26,500**	
Equipment		32,000
Gain from disposal of equipment		2,500
**($32,000 − $2,000) × (53 months used) ÷		
(60 months total useful life)		

However, the economic value of Brown Company is unaffected by the disposal. Brown received an asset worth $8,000 (cash) for an asset worth $8,000. Why is a gain recognized? Brown depreciated the equipment faster than it declined in value. The book value ($5,500) is less than market value ($8,000) at the date of disposal. If depreciation exactly reflected all changes in value, there would be no gain or loss from disposal. *The accounting gain in this example is a correction for excessive depreciation charges recognized before disposal.* In effect, the gain records a change in estimate.

If the asset is destroyed in an accident and was insured, then the entry will mirror the one recorded above. That is, the insurance proceeds will be received in cash, and the difference between cash and net book value will determine the gain or loss.

This approach is also used when an asset is abandoned or destroyed and was not insured, when there are no proceeds. The loss recognized equals the book value of the asset at disposal. For the Brown Company example, the loss recognized would be $5,500.

The costs of dismantling, removing, and disposing of plant assets are treated as reductions of any proceeds obtained from disposal. Therefore, the resulting gain is reduced, or the resulting loss is increased by these costs. If Brown Company incurs $500 in disposal costs, the net cash debit is $8,000 − $500, or $7,500, reducing the gain to $2,000 in the original example.

When the decision to sell or abandon plant assets is made near the end of a fiscal year, an estimated loss from disposal is recognized in that year if the loss is estimable. Gains are not recognized before disposal, however.

Derecognition using the revaluation model is discussed in Appendix 2 in Chapter 10.

Replacement of Major Parts

Component accounting requires an asset to be segregated into its major components. If a major part (component) is replaced, any remaining carrying amount of that part is derecognized at the time of replacement and recorded as a loss in the income statement. The new part would then be recorded as an asset and depreciated.

CONCEPT REVIEW

1. What is an involuntary conversion?

2. Why would a company dispose of a capital asset at a loss? Is the company necessarily in a worse position economically after doing so?

3. How would you interpret the gain on the disposal of a capital asset?

4. What happens when a major part that has been recognized as a separate component is replaced in an asset?

EXCHANGES OF NON-MONETARY ASSETS

Long-lived assets are often exchanged for other non-monetary assets. Remember that monetary assets are those whose value is fixed in terms of dollars, such as cash and receivables. Non-monetary assets, such as inventory and capital assets, *do not have a value fixed in terms of dollars.*

Non-monetary transactions are any exchange of non-monetary assets, liabilities, or services for other non-monetary assets, liabilities, or services, or any exchange that has little or no monetary consideration involved. Valuation of the acquired asset is the substantive issue in non-monetary asset exchanges. This valuation determines whether a gain or loss is recognized.

The valuation alternatives and accounting for non-monetary transaction are explained in Chapter 6.

GOODWILL

Goodwill is a common intangible asset. It represents the value associated with favourable characteristics of a firm that result in earnings in excess of those expected from identifiable assets of the firm. Goodwill is *internally generated* but is recorded only when *purchased*, along with identifiable tangible and intangible assets that constitute an operating unit. Goodwill typically cannot be separated from those identifiable assets. In the absence of an arm's-length transaction, it is difficult to measure the value of goodwill that a firm creates as it engages in business activities.

A few examples of factors that cause enhanced financial performance are:

- A superior management team;
- An outstanding sales organization;
- Especially effective advertising;
- Exceptionally good labour relations;
- An unusually good reputation for total quality; and
- A highly advantageous strategic location.

For accounting purposes, **goodwill** is the difference between the actual purchase price of an acquired firm or operation and the estimated fair market value of the identifiable net assets acquired (assets less liabilities, valued at fair value).

Measuring Goodwill The value of goodwill is calculated indirectly in an acquisition of a business unit. The steps are as follows:

1. *Establish the cost of the acquisition.* This is the value of whatever the purchaser gives up to acquire the business unit. The cost is measured as the cash payment plus the fair value of shares or assets given to the seller.

2. *Establish the fair value of all identifiable assets and liabilities assumed.* The fair value of the *net* assets acquired is the total fair value of the assets minus the total fair values of the liabilities:

Fair value of tangible and identifiable intangible assets − Fair value of liabilities
= Fair value of net assets acquired

---

3. *The cost less fair value of net identifiable assets is goodwill.* Goodwill is the excess purchase cost that cannot otherwise be assigned to specific assets or liabilities:

Cost of acquisition (#1) − Fair value of net assets acquired (#2) = Goodwill

---

In completing Step 2, the purchaser would consider if there were any items acquired in the purchase that would meet the definition of an intangible asset and should be assigned a value instead of just allocating that amount to goodwill. Examples of the type of assets are provided in five categories:

- Marketing-related intangibles (e.g., Internet domain name);
- Customer-related intangibles (e.g., customer list);
- Artistic-related intangibles (e.g., book);
- Contract-based intangibles (e.g., employment contract); and
- Technology-based intangibles (e.g., computer software).

As discussed earlier, some intangibles can be recognized only when they are purchased and not when they are internally developed. For example, a customer list can be capitalized on purchase but would be expensed if internally developed. This allocation of the purchase consideration between other identifiable intangibles and goodwill becomes critical when we get to the discussion of amortization and impairment in Chapter 10. We will see then that goodwill is not amortized but is tested for impairment, whereas the other intangibles, such as customer lists, would be amortized over their limited lifespan. As a result, this allocation of the purchase price has implications on amortization costs and earnings in subsequent years.

Example Assume that Hotel Company is considering the acquisition of the net assets of Cafe Corporation. Hotel Company obtains financial statements and other financial data on Cafe and estimates the fair value of Cafe's identifiable assets at $530,000 and the fair value of the liabilities at $400,000. See Exhibit 9-4.

The fair value column in Exhibit 9-4 shows that several assets have an estimated fair value different from their book value as reported in the published historical cost financial statements. Fair values include specific identifiable intangibles, such as customer lists.

The total fair value of Cafe's identifiable net assets is determined to be $130,000 ($530,000 total assets less liabilities of $400,000). Assume that Hotel negotiates a purchase price with the owners to acquire Cafe as of 31 December 20X4, for $202,000. Goodwill inherent in this price is $72,000, that is, the purchase price of $202,000 less current market value of the identifiable net assets of $130,000. The entry Hotel Company makes to reflect the acquisition of Cafe's operations, at their *fair values*, is as follows:

Cash	30,000	
Receivables	85,000	
Inventory	60,000	
Other current assets	30,000	
Plant and equipment	235,000	
Other assets	90,000	
Goodwill	72,000	
Short-term notes payable		85,000
Accounts payable		45,000
Other current liabilities		30,000
Long-term debt		240,000
Cash		202,000

EXHIBIT 9-4

CAFE CORPORATION BALANCE SHEET BOOK VALUE AND FAIR VALUE

As of 31 December 20X4	Book Value	Fair Value
Assets		
Cash	$ 30,000	$ 30,000
Receivables	90,000	85,000
Inventory	60,000	60,000
Other current assets	33,000	30,000
Plant and equipment (net)	220,000	235,000
Other assets	85,000	90,000
Total assets	$518,000	$530,000
Liabilities		
Short-term notes payable	$ 85,000	$ 85,000
Accounts payable	45,000	45,000
Other current liabilities	30,000	30,000
Long-term debt	250,000	240,000
Total liabilities	410,000	400,000
Shareholders' equity	108,000	
Total liabilities and equities	$518,000	
Net assets at fair market value		$130,000

Recording this $72,000 goodwill asset implicitly means that Hotel was willing to pay for anticipated superior earnings/cash flow from Cafe's operations. These superior results could be caused by a superior location, reputation for service or quality, and so on.

Do you *know* that goodwill is present, just because Hotel paid more than the fair value of the net assets? After all, Hotel may have been outbargained by the old owners of Cafe. The $72,000 could be the result of an inflated price. Just because the price is arm's length does not mean that it is meaningful. Accountants always make the comfortable assumption that goodwill explains excess purchase price. But beware—the assets acquired are supposed to provide a return consistent with the existence of goodwill, or the goodwill does not, in substance, exist.

In the 1990s, many companies purchased Internet-based developing enterprises (the so-called "dot-com" companies) at prices that turned out to be exorbitant. There were very few identifiable assets in the acquired businesses, and therefore almost all of the purchase price was accounted for as goodwill. When the stock market for the dot-coms collapsed, any prospect of future earnings collapsed as well.

If it becomes apparent that superior earnings ability does not really exist, the goodwill does not meet the definition of an asset, and its carrying value must be written down as an impairment loss. The moral of this story is that goodwill must be regularly reviewed with reference to profit performance to ensure continued recognition of goodwill is appropriate. This issue will be reviewed in Chapter 10.

Negative Goodwill

When the fair market value of the identifiable net assets acquired is *higher* than the purchase price, the acquiring firm has made what is sometimes called a *bargain purchase*. Goodwill is negative, that is, **negative goodwill** has been created. Even though it would seem that the seller could benefit from selling the assets individually rather than selling the firm as a whole, such situations do occasionally occur. For example, the seller may be in financial difficulty and have an immediate cash need. Alternatively, the seller may not have the time or resources to take on the risks of selling the assets separately.

If there is negative goodwill, the fair value of the assets acquired are reassessed. Assets with subjective or uncertain fair values would be written down. For example, one of the items acquired in the purchase may be an intangible asset, for example, customer lists, where an estimate was made of fair value that could have a variance. This type of "soft asset" would be reassessed to see if a writedown is appropriate. Any remaining excess after the reassessment is recognized immediately as a gain in the income statement.

Form of Acquisition

In the previous example, one company bought the net assets of another company, and goodwill was directly recorded on the purchaser's books. In many acquisition transactions, the acquiring company buys the shares of the target company, which is then left to operate as before, only with new shareholders.

At *reporting dates*, the two sets of financial statements are combined, or *consolidated*, to produce a report of the economic activity of the combined entity. In consolidation, the assets of the target company are recorded at fair value at the date of acquisition, and the goodwill inherent in the purchase price is recorded. The nature of goodwill is identical, but the form of the transaction is different. We will take a brief look at consolidation in Chapter 11.

LONG-LIVED ASSETS ON THE STATEMENT OF CASH FLOWS

Investments in long-lived assets are shown as *investing activities* on the statement of cash flows (SCF), provided that the acquisition is for cash. If a long-lived asset is acquired in a non-cash transaction, the transaction will be described in the notes to the financial statements, but it would not be reported as part of the SCF because no cash was involved. If cash was only part of the consideration to acquire a long-lived asset, then only the cash portion will be shown.

Gains and Losses

Gains and losses on the sale of long-lived assets are non-cash items, from the viewpoint of operating activities. These are excluded from cash flow operations either through adjustment (indirect presentation) or omission (direct presentation). When an asset is sold for cash, what appears on the SCF is the amount of the proceeds (i.e., the cash actually received) for the asset. The proceeds are shown in the investing activities section as a cash *inflow*.

If a long-lived asset is disposed of through a non-cash transaction or exchange, the transaction will not appear on the SCF, but will be disclosed in the notes.

Cash Flow Reporting of Capitalized Costs

An interesting wrinkle to the issue of capitalizing instead of expensing certain costs is the impact that the capitalization policy has on the reporting of cash flows.

It is obvious that the accounting policy decision to capitalize or expense a cost will not affect actual cash flows. The cost has been incurred and either has been or will be paid in cash. The accounting policy choice is only of whether to put the cost on the balance sheet (as an asset) or on the income statement (as an expense). Consider these differences in *cash flow reporting*, however:

- Costs that are accounted for as expenses are included in the cash flow from *operations*.
- Costs that are capitalized as assets are included in the *investing activities* section of the SCF.
- Depreciation on capitalized assets is deducted in determining net income but is removed from cash flow from operations either by adding it back in the indirect approach, or leaving it out in the direct approach.

For example, assume that Lorimer Limited spends $100,000 on development costs during 20X2, and that net income before deducting the development costs is $300,000. If the development costs are capitalized, they will be depreciated straight-line over the five years *following* their incurrence (i.e., from 20X3 through 20X7).

If Lorimer's management decides to expense the development costs (i.e., it decides that not all of the deferral criteria have been met), the net income for 20X2 is $200,000, and that amount is shown in the SCF as the cash flow from operations (ignoring the many other adjustments that may be made to net income to convert it to cash flow).

If the 20X2 costs are capitalized and depreciated, however, an interesting thing occurs. Because the costs are not charged as an expense, that $100,000 is shown as an investing activity outflow rather than being included in operations. Cash flow from operations therefore is reported as $300,000. In 20X3, $20,000 of the development costs (i.e., one-fifth) are depreciated and charged against net income. In the operations section, however, depreciation is added back to net income, and therefore the effect of the depreciation is removed. The result is that *if costs are capitalized, they will never affect reported cash flow from operations.*

ETHICAL ISSUES

A company that follows a policy of capitalizing as many expenditures as possible will, over time, show a consistently higher cash flow from operations than one that expenses those costs. While this may not fool a sophisticated user of the financial statements, management may choose to follow the capitalize-and-amortize approach consistently in an attempt to increase the company's apparent operating cash flow used to evaluate some debt covenants.

PRESENTATION AND DISCLOSURE

Property, plant, and equipment; goodwill; biological assets; and investment property must be presented as separate line items on the statement of financial position (SFP). Other intangible assets may be aggregated and then presented as a separate line item.

Companies are required to disclose the cost of each major category of property, plant, and equipment and each class of intangibles either on the SFP or in the notes. Segregation by major asset category is important, as the various categories of capital assets are associated with different levels of business risk and may have dissimilar useful lives and amortization policies. Typically, tangible capital assets are shown as one net amount on the balance sheet, with the required detailed breakdown shown in the disclosure notes.

Extensive note disclosure is required by class, including measurement base, depreciation methods, useful lives or depreciation rates (intangibles if indefinite or finite lives), gross carrying amount and accumulated depreciation, restrictions, expenditures related to construction, contractual commitments, and third-party compensation for impaired assets. In addition, a reconciliation of beginning balance of the carrying amount to the ending balance for the period is required, showing additions, assets held-for-sale, acquisitions in business combination, impairment losses, reversals of impairment losses, depreciation, net exchange differences due to foreign currency, and any other changes.

For example, Exhibit 9-5 contains the asset portion of the 2011 consolidated balance sheet for High Liner Foods Incorporated. This excerpt demonstrates the separate reporting for long-lived assets (e.g., property, plant, and equipment, intangible assets, and goodwill). Exhibit 9-5 shows the extracts from the significant accounting policy note as well as the specific note disclosure for property, plant, and equipment, intangible assets, and goodwill. Note 6 for property, plant, and equipment and note 5 for intangible assets and goodwill illustrate the required reconciliations of the beginning and ending balances. Notes 5 and 6 show additions from acquisitions.

EXHIBIT 9-5

HIGH LINER FOODS INCORPORATED

Extract from Consolidated Balance Sheet

High Liner Foods Incorporated Consolidated Balance Sheet

(In thousands of Canadian dollars)	Notes	December 31, 2011	January 1, 2011	January 2010
ASSETS				
Current:				
Cash and cash equivalents		$ 3,260	$ 598	$ 1,953
Accounts receivable	9	84,920	50,452	57,963
Income tax receivable		3,557	701	1,288
Other financial assets	22	1,346	890	1,590
Inventories	8	261,330	131,980	119,308
Prepaid expenses		3,019	1,889	2,024
Total current assets		357,432	186,510	184,126
Noncurrent:				
Property, plant, and equipment	6	99,933	67,269	69,061
Deferred income taxes	20	1,695	2,403	3,628
Other receivables and miscellaneous assets		1,210	814	406
Investment in equity accounted investee	7	275	157	—
Employee future benefits	14	94	91	118
Intangible assets	4,5	103,109	31,239	19,965
Goodwill	4,5	126,787	39,819	35,983
		333,103	141,792	129,161
		$690,535	$328,302	$313,287

continued on next page

EXHIBIT 9-5 *(cont'd)*				
(In thousands of Canadian dollars)	Notes	December 31, 2011	January 1, 2011	January 3, 2010
LIABILITIES AND SHAREHOLDERS' EQUITY				
Current:				
Bank loans	12	**$120,980**	$ 42,725	$ 23,051
Accounts payable and accrued liabilities	10	**108,553**	60,065	49,905
Provisions	11	**675**	550	1,423
Other current financial liabilities	22	**793**	2,334	3,989
Income taxes payable		**1,990**	3,230	29
Current portion of long-term debt	13	**2,543**	4,426	4,582
Current portion of finance lease obligations	13	**1,064**	972	864
Total current liabilities		**236,598**	114,302	83,843
Noncurrent:				
Long-term debt	13	**237,438**	43,912	49,920
Other long-term financial liabilities	22	**—**	207	928
Long-term finance lease obligations	22	**2,599**	3,045	2,700
Deferred income taxes	20	**41,099**	9,895	5,705
Employee future benefits	14	**11,274**	9,630	6,991
Total liabilities		**529,008**	180,991	150,087
Shareholders' equity				
Common shares	16	**78,067**	78,326	106,098
Contributed surplus		**8,406**	8,917	—
Retained earnings		**76,770**	65,557	59,240
Accumulated other comprehensive loss		**(1,716)**	(5,489)	(2,138)
Total equity		**161,527**	147,311	163,200
		$690,535	$328,302	$313,287

Commitments (note 15)
See accompanying notes

HIGH LINER FOODS INCORPORATED SELECTED NOTE DISCLOSURES FOR LONG-LIVED ASSETS (ALL AMOUNTS FOR 31 DECEMBER 2011)

Extracts from Significant Accounting Policy Note

PROPERTY, PLANT, AND EQUIPMENT

(i) Recognition and measurement

Items of property, plant, and equipment are measured at cost less accumulated depreciation and accumulated impairment losses. Cost includes expenditures that are directly attributable to the acquisition of the asset, including the present value of the expected cost for the decommissioning of the asset after its use, if the recognition criteria for a provision are met. The cost of self-constructed assets includes the cost of materials and direct labour, any other costs directly attributable to bringing the assets to a working condition for their intended use, the costs of dismantling and removing the items and restoring the site on which they are located, and capitalized borrowing costs. Cost also may include capitalized borrowing costs and transfers from other comprehensive income of any gain or loss on qualifying cash flow hedges of foreign currency purchases of property, plant and equipment.

continued on next page

EXHIBIT 9-5 (cont'd)

When parts of an item of property, plant and equipment have different useful lives, they are accounted for as separate items (major components) of property, plant, and equipment. An item of property, plant, and equipment is derecognized upon disposal or when no future economic benefits are expected from its use or disposal. Any gain or loss on the derecognition of the asset is determined by comparing the proceeds from disposal with the carrying amount of property, plant, and equipment and is recognized net within other income in profit or loss.

(ii) Subsequent costs

The cost of replacing a part of an item of property, plant, and equipment is recognized in the carrying amount of the item if it is probable that the future economic benefits embodied within the part will flow to the Company, and its cost can be measured reliably. The carrying amount of the replaced part is derecognized. The costs of the day-to-day servicing of property, plant, and equipment are recognized in income as incurred.

(iii) Depreciation

Depreciation is calculated over the depreciable amount, which is the cost of an asset, or other amount substituted for cost, less its residual value. Depreciation is recognized in income on a straight-line basis over the estimated useful lives of each component part of an item of property, plant, and equipment, since this most closely reflects the expected pattern of consumption of the future economic benefits embodied in the asset. Leased assets are depreciated over the shorter of the lease term and their useful lives unless it is reasonably certain that the Company will obtain ownership by the end of the lease term. Land is not depreciated.

The estimated useful lives for the current and comparative periods are as follows:

Building structure	60 years
Major building components	15–30 years
Production equipment	10–25 years
Furniture and fixtures	10–25 years
Computer hardware and peripherals	4–5 years
Software components	4–11 years

Depreciation methods, useful lives and residual values are reviewed at least at each financial year end and adjusted if appropriate.

GOODWILL

Goodwill acquired in business combinations is initially measured at cost being the excess of the cost of the business combination over the fair value of the acquired interest in the identifiable assets, liabilities, and contingent liabilities. Following initial recognition, goodwill is measured at cost less any accumulated impairment losses. Goodwill will be reviewed for impairment annually, or more frequently if events or changes in circumstances indicate that the carrying value may be impaired. For the purpose of impairment testing, goodwill acquired in a business combination is, from the acquisition date, allocated to each of the Company's cash-generating units that are expected to benefit from the synergies of the combination, irrespective of whether other assets or liabilities of the Company are assigned to those units or groups of units.

Impairment is determined by assessing the recoverable amount of the cash-generating unit to which the goodwill relates. Where the recoverable amount of the cash-generating unit is less than the carrying amount, an impairment loss is recognized. Impairment losses relating to goodwill cannot be reversed in subsequent periods. Where goodwill forms part of a cash-generating unit and part of the operation within that unit is disposed of, the goodwill associated with the operation disposed of is included in the carrying amount of the operation when determining the gain or loss on disposal of the operation. Goodwill disposed of in this circumstance is measured based on the relative values of the operation disposed of and the portion of the cash-generating unit retained.

continued on next page

EXHIBIT 9-5 (cont'd)

INTANGIBLE ASSETS

Intangible assets acquired separately are measured on initial recognition at cost. The cost of intangible assets acquired in a business combination is fair value as at the date of acquisition. Following initial recognition, intangible assets are carried at cost less any accumulated amortization and any accumulated impairment losses.

The useful lives of intangible assets are assessed to be either finite or indefinite. Intangible assets with finite lives are amortized over the useful economic life and assessed for impairment whenever there is an indication that the intangible asset may be impaired.

The amortization period and the amortization method for an intangible asset with a finite useful life are reviewed at least at each financial year end. Changes in the expected useful life or the expected pattern of consumption of future economic benefits embodied in the asset are accounted for by changing the amortization period or method, as appropriate, and treated as changes in accounting estimates. The amortization expense on intangible assets with finite lives is recognized in the income statement in the expense category consistent with the function of the intangible asset.

Intangible assets with indefinite useful lives are tested for impairment annually at the cash-generating unit level. Such intangibles are not amortized. The useful life of an intangible asset with an indefinite life is reviewed annually to determine whether indefinite life assessment continues to be supportable. If not, the change in the useful life assessment from indefinite to finite is made on a prospective basis.

The Company's intangible assets consist of brands that have been acquired through a business combination and have indefinite useful lives requiring impairment testing annually or more frequently when an indication of impairment exists.

Gains or losses from derecognition of an intangible asset are measured as the difference between the net disposal proceeds and the carrying amount of the asset and are recognized in the income statement when the asset is derecognized.

The estimated useful lives for the current and comparative periods are as follows:

Brands	2–8 years
Customer relationships	10–20 years
Indefinite lived brands	Indefinite, subject to impairment testing annually

RESEARCH AND DEVELOPMENT COSTS

Research and development costs include all costs relating to the activities that support the development and manufacturing of new or improved products or processes. Research activity costs are expensed as incurred. Development expenditures on an individual project are recognized as an intangible asset when the Company is able to demonstrate the following:

- The technical feasibility of completing the intangible asset so that it will be available for use or sale;
- Its intention to complete and its ability to use or sell the asset;
- How the asset will generate future economic benefits;
- Its ability to use or sell the intangible asset arising from the project;
- The availability of resources to complete the asset; and
- The ability to clearly identify the related costs on an individualized basis for a specific project during the development phase.

Following initial recognition of the development expenditure as an asset, the cost model is applied requiring the asset to be carried at cost less any accumulated amortization and accumulated impairment losses.

Amortization of the asset begins when development is complete and the asset is available for use or sale. It is amortized over the period of expected future benefit. Amortization is recorded in cost of sales.

continued on next page

EXHIBIT 9-5 (cont'd)

High Liner monitors the level of product development costs and process development costs against all the criteria set out above. These include the requirement to establish that a flow of economic benefits and the ability to use or sell the product or process developed is probable, before costs are capitalized. For High Liner this is evident only shortly before a product is launched into the market or a process is integrated into production. The level of costs incurred after these criteria have been met is currently not material.

BORROWING COSTS

Borrowing costs that are directly attributable to the acquisition, construction, or production of an asset, which necessarily takes a substantial period of time to get ready for its intended use or sale, form part of the cost of that asset. All other borrowing costs are expensed in the period they occur. Borrowing costs consist of interest and other costs that an entity incurs in connection with the borrowing of funds.

The Company capitalizes borrowing costs for all eligible assets where construction was started or proceeded on or after the IFRS transition date January 3, 2010.

Extracts from Notes

5. GOODWILL AND INTANGIBLE ASSETS

Goodwill is tested for impairment annually (as at the first day of the Company's fourth quarter) and when circumstances indicate the carrying value may be impaired. The Company's impairment test for goodwill and intangible assets with indefinite useful lives was based on fair value less costs to sell as of the IFRS transition date and as of the fiscal year end 2011. The method used to determine the Company's fair value less costs to sell uses a discounted cash flow model. The key assumptions used to determine the recoverable amount for the different cash-generating units for the most recently completed impairment calculations for fiscal 2011, fiscal 2010, and the IFRS transition date as at January 3, 2010 are discussed below. The Company has not identified any indicators of impairment at any other date and, as such, has not completed an additional impairment calculation.

The following table outlines the carrying amount and classification of the Company's intangible assets for the periods ending December 31, 2011, January 1, 2011, and January 3, 2010:

(Amounts in thousands as restated (note 26 (c)(i)))	Brands 2–8 Yrs	Customer relationships 10–20 Yrs	Indefinite lived brands	Total intangible assets	Goodwill	Total goodwill and intangible assets
Cost						
At January 3, 2010	$ 729	$11,498	$10,322	$ 22,549	$ 35,983	$ 58,532
Additions from acquisitions (note 4)	—	11,312	2,188	13,500	5,079	18,579
Translation adjustment of U.S.-based assets	(7)	(671)	(488)	(1,166)	(1,243)	(2,409)
At January 1, 2011	$ 722	$22,139	$12,022	$ 34,883	$ 39,819	$ 74,702
Additions from acquisitions (note 4)	2,499	33,969	37,721	74,189	87,666	161,855
Translation adjustment of U.S.-based assets	(35)	(37)	(326)	(398)	(698)	(1,096)
At December 31, 2011	**$3,186**	**$56,071**	**$49,417**	**$108,674**	**$126,787**	**$235,461**
Accumulated amortization						
At January 3, 2010	$ 281	$ 2,303	$ —	$ 2,584	$ —	$ 2,584
Amortization	72	1,132	—	1,204	—	1,204
Translation adjustment of U.S.-based assets	(7)	(137)	—	(144)	—	(144)
At January 1, 2011	$ 346	$ 3,298	$ —	$ 3,644	$ —	$ 3,644
Amortization	79	1,744	—	1,823	—	1,823
Translation adjustment of U.S.-based assets	3	95	—	98	—	98
At December 31, 2011	**$ 428**	**$ 5,137**	**$ —**	**$ 5,565**	**$ —**	**$ 5,565**
Carrying value January 3, 2010	$ 448	$ 9,195	$10,322	$ 19,965	$ 35,983	$ 55,948
Carrying value January 1, 2011	$ 376	$18,841	$12,022	$ 31,239	$ 39,819	$ 71,058
Carrying value December 31, 2011	**$2,758**	**$50,934**	**$49,417**	**$103,109**	**$126,787**	**$229,896**

continued on next page

EXHIBIT 9-5 (cont'd)

Goodwill acquired through business combinations and brands with indefinite lives have been allocated to two cash-generating units for impairment testing purposes.

The cash-generating units have been based on geography, Canada and the U.S., which is consistent with the Company's identified operating and reportable segments. Canada and the U.S. operating units are determined to be the smallest identifiable group of assets that generate cash inflows and are largely independent of the cash inflows from other assets.

Carrying amount of goodwill and brands allocated to each of the cash-generating units are as follows:

(Amounts in thousands) as restated (note 26 (c)(i))	Carrying amount of goodwill	Carrying amount of brands and customer relationships with indefinite useful lives
Canada		
January 3, 2010	12,474	1,040
January 1, 2011	12,474	1,040
December 31, 2011	**12,474**	**1,040**
U.S.		
January 3, 2010	23,509	9,282
January 1, 2011	27,345	10,982
December 31, 2011	**114,313**	**48,377**
Total Company		
January 3, 2010	35,983	10,322
January 1, 2011	39,819	12,022
December 31, 2011	**126,787**	**49,417**

The recoverable amount of the cash-generating units has been determined based on the fair value less costs to sell ("FVLCS"). In determining the FVLCS of each of the Canadian and U.S. cash-generating units ("CGUs"), we utilized a discounted cash flow methodology. The discounted cash flow technique provides the best assessment of what each CGU could be exchanged for in an arm's-length transaction as fair value is represented by the present value of expected future cash flows of the business together with the residual value of the business at the end of the forecast period. The discounted cash flow was applied on an enterprise value basis, where the after-tax cash flows prior to interest expense are discounted using a weighted average cost of capital ("WACC"). The cash flow projections, covering a five-year period, were based on financial projections approved by senior management using assumptions that reflect the Company's most likely planned courses of action, given Management's judgment of the most probable set of economic conditions, adjusted to reflect the perspective of the expectations of a market participant.

The WACC (discount rate applied) terminal capitalization rate and growth rate applied to each CGU's cash flow projection are outlined in the following table:

	Discount rate (WACC)	Terminal capitalization rate	Growth rate
Canada			
October 2, 2011 valuation date	10.1%	2%	2–3%
October 3, 2010 valuation date	11.8%	2%	2–3%
January 3, 2010 valuation date	12.7%	2%	1–4%
U.S.			
October 2, 2011 valuation date	12.0%	2%	2–3%
October 3, 2010 valuation date	11.4%	2%	2–4%
January 3, 2010 valuation date	11.9%	2%	2–4%

continued on next page

EXHIBIT 9-5 (*cont'd*)

Summary of key assumptions used in determining the fair value less costs to sell

The discounted cash flow calculation used for the two cash-generating units is most sensitive to the following assumptions:

- Discount rate applied (WACC);
- Gross margins and raw materials price costs;
- Inflation;
- Market share during the projection period;
- Growth rate used to extrapolate cash flows beyond the projection period; and
- Costs to sell.

DISCOUNT RATE

The discount rate reflects the current market assessment of the risk specific to comparable companies of High Liner. The discount rate was based on the average weighted average cost of equity and cost of debt for comparable companies to High Liner within the industry. The cost of equity was calculated using the capital asset pricing model. The debt component of the WACC was determined by using an after-tax cost of debt.

GROSS MARGINS, INCLUDING RAW MATERIAL PRICES AND CURRENCY FLUCTUATIONS

Gross margins are based on average values achieved in the three years preceding the start of the projection period. These are increased over the projection period for anticipated efficiency improvements. The projected gross margins are then updated to reflect anticipated future changes in the price of inputs (primarily raw materials and commodity products used in processing, such as cooking oil, wheat, fuel and boxboard), which are obtained from published indices for the countries from which raw materials are sourced, as well as forward-looking data relating to specific commodities. Forecast figures are used where data is publicly available, otherwise past actual raw material price movements have been used as an indicator of future price movements combined with Management's industry experience and analysis of the seafood and commodity markets.

INFLATION

Estimates are obtained from published indices for the countries in which they operate.

MARKET SHARE DURING THE PROJECTION PERIOD

These assumptions are important because, as well as using industry data for growth rates, management assesses how the unit's position, relative to its competitors, might change over the projection period. Management expects the Company's share of the Canadian frozen seafood market to be stable over the projection period, whereas Management expects the U.S. position, relative to its competitors, to continue to strengthen.

GROWTH RATE USED TO EXTRAPOLATE CASH FLOWS BEYOND THE PROJECTION PERIOD

Growth rates used to extrapolate the Company's projection were determined using published industry growth rates in combination with inflation assumptions and the input of each management group based on historical trend analysis and future expectations of growth. The growth rates used in the five-year projection declined by 0.5% each year until the terminal period where the growth rate was assumed to be equal to inflation.

COSTS TO SELL

Each CGU's costs to sell have been estimated to approximate 3% of the CGU's enterprise value. The costs to sell reflect the incremental costs, excluding finance costs and income taxes, that would be directly attributable to the disposal of a CGU, including legal costs, marketing costs, costs of removing assets and direct incremental costs incurred in preparing the CGU for sale.

SENSITIVITY TO CHANGES IN ASSUMPTIONS

With regards to the assessment of the fair value less costs to sell for each of the CGUs, management believes that no reasonably possible change in any of the above key assumptions would cause the carrying value of the CGU to materially exceed its recoverable amount.

continued on next page

EXHIBIT 9-5 (cont'd)

6. PROPERTY, PLANT AND EQUIPMENT

(Amounts in thousands)	Land	Production equipment	Building structures	Major building components	Computer hardware and peripherals	Software components	Furniture and fixtures	Equipment under finance lease	ITCs	Total
Cost										
At January 3, 2010*	$2,304	$ 41,884	$10,376	$ 29,752	$ 6,565	$ 2,687	$1,319	$ 4,293	$ (852)	$ 98,328
Additions	—	2,004	—	1,216	303	198	4	1,526	(37)	5,214
Acquisition of a subsidiary (note 4)	—	2,591	—	—	—	—	—	—	—	2,591
Disposals	—	(3,242)	—	(562)	(3,260)	(174)	(203)	(542)	—	(8,083)
Impairment	—	(79)	—	—	—	—	—	—	—	(79)
Effect of exchange rates	(103)	(1,839)	(302)	(274)	255	(26)	59	(244)	—	(2,674)
At January 1, 2011	$2,201	$ 41,319	$10,074	$ 29,832	$ 3,863	$ 2,685	$1,179	$ 5,033	$ (889)	$ 95,297
Additions	—	3,471	65	1,514	625	1,417	19	620	(259)	7,572
Acquisition of a subsidiary (note 4)	932	22,518	14,557	6,301	1,384	2,146	—	—	—	48,438
Disposals	—	(387)	—	(327)	(648)	(9)	(7)	(520)	—	(1,898)
Effect of exchange rates	30	818	(88)	47	(196)	(24)	(26)	71	—	538
At December 31, 2011	**$3,163**	**$ 67,739**	**$24,708**	**$ 37,873**	**$ 5,028**	**$ 6,215**	**$1,165**	**$ 5,204**	**$(1,148)**	**$149,947**
Accumulated depreciation										
At January 3, 2010*	$ —	$ (5,999)	$ (2,566)	$(13,263)	$(4,887)	$(1,378)	$ (822)	$ (727)	$ 375	$ (29,267)
Depreciation for the year	—	(4,159)	(212)	(1,316)	(603)	(341)	(45)	(644)	38	(7,282)
Acquisition of a subsidiary (note 4)	—	(19)	—	—	—	—	—	—	—	(19)
Disposals	—	3,229	—	662	3,260	174	203	386	—	7,914
Effect of exchange rates	—	(44)	72	314	42	10	10	222	—	626
At January 1, 2011	$ —	$ (6,992)	$ (2,706)	$(13,603)	$(2,188)	$(1,535)	$ (654)	$ (763)	$ 413	$ (28,028)
Depreciation for the year	—	(4,817)	(207)	(1,360)	(608)	(383)	(61)	(508)	43	(7,901)
Acquisition of a subsidiary (note 4)	—	(7,722)	(2,341)	(2,059)	(939)	(1,825)	—	—	—	(15,386)
Disposals	—	110	—	252	646	6	7	387	—	1,408
Effect of exchange rates	—	201	11	(118)	(32)	23	(5)	(187)	—	(107)
At December 31, 2011	**$ —**	**$(19,220)**	**$ (5,743)**	**$(16,888)**	**$(3,121)**	**$(3,714)**	**$ (713)**	**$(1,071)**	**$ 456**	**$ (50,014)**
Carrying amounts										
At January 3, 2010	$2,304	$ 35,885	$ 7,810	$ 16,489	$1,678	$1,309	497	$3,566	$ (477)	$ 69,061
At January 1, 2011	$2,201	$ 34,327	$ 7,368	$ 16,229	$1,675	$1,150	525	$4,270	$ (476)	$ 67,269
At December 31, 2011	**$3,163**	**$ 48,519**	**$18,965**	**$ 20,985**	**$1,907**	**$2,501**	**452**	**$4,133**	**$ (692)**	**$ 99,933**

*(note 26 (c) (ix)) Please refer to note 19 for additional information related to depreciation expense.

Source: High Liner Foods Incorporated 2011 Annual Financial Statements, www.sedar.com, posted 26 May 2012.

CONCEPT REVIEW

1. Do all companies with goodwill have the asset listed on the SFP? Why is it often not recorded?

2. How is goodwill calculated when net assets are bought?

3. What is negative goodwill, and how is it recorded on the SFP?

4. When there is a non-monetary exchange of assets, what will be recorded on the CSF?

5. Suppose that a company is very aggressive at capitalizing expenditures related to intangible assets. How will the capitalization of large amounts of expenditures affect the CSF, compared with a company that expenses many of the same types of expenditures?

6. What long-lived assets have to be shown separately on the SFP?

Looking Ahead

Long-lived assets are not now on the agenda of either the IASB or the Canadian AcSB.

ACCOUNTING STANDARDS FOR PRIVATE ENTERPRISES

There are many aspects to accounting for capital assets, and many different standards that govern accounting policy in this area. Overall, standards for publicly accountable enterprises are similar to accounting standards for private enterprises, but there are also many specific differences. Exhibit 9-6 summarizes some of the obvious areas where standards for publicly accountable enterprises and private enterprises are different.

EXHIBIT 9-6

COMPARISON OF INTERNATIONAL STANDARDS VERSUS ACCOUNTING STANDARDS FOR PRIVATE ENTERPRISES FOR LONG-LIVED ASSETS

Accounting Policy	Accounting Standards for Private Enterprises Standard	Accounting Standards for Publicly Accountable Enterprises
Valuation rule for capital assets	Historical cost is normally used.	Historical cost is permitted, but companies may also revalue many long-lived assets, by class, to fair value. This applies to property, plant, and equipment, and certain intangibles.
Involuntary safety and environmental costs	Capitalize only if future benefit.	Costs must be capitalized to the asset.
Interest capitalization	Interest may be capitalized. Only interest on specific loans may be capitalized. If capitalized, note disclosure required.	Interest on qualifying assets must be capitalized. Specific guidance provided on the calculation. Includes specific and general borrowings.
Self-constructed assets	Incidental revenues and expenses are included in the costs of the constructed asset.	Incidental revenues and expenses are recognized in net income.
Decommissioning obligations (asset retirement obligations)	Recognition of legal obligations on asset acquisition.	Recognition of legal and constructive obligations. Annual assessment for all estimates and discount rate.
Internally generated intangible assets	If meet criteria to capitalize development costs, management accounting policy choice to capitalize or expense.	If they meet criteria to capitalize, development costs must capitalize.

RELEVANT STANDARDS

CPA Canada Handbook, Part I (IFRS):
- IAS 16, Property, Plant, and Equipment
- IAS 23, Borrowing Costs
- IAS 37, Provisions, Contingent Liabilities and Contingent Assets
- IAS 38, Intangible Assets
- IFRS 6, Exploration for and Evaluation of Mineral Resources
- IFRIC 1, Changes in Existing Decommissioning, Restoration and Similar Liabilities
- SIC-32, Intangible Assets—Web Site Costs

CPA Canada Handbook, Part II (ASPE):
- Section 1582, Business Combinations
- Section 3061, Property, Plant, and Equipment
- Section 3064, Goodwill and Other Intangible Assets
- Section 3110, Asset Retirement Obligations
- Section 3831, Non-monetary Transactions
- Section 3850, Interest Capitalized—Disclosure Considerations
- AcG–16, Oil and Gas Accounting—Full Cost

SUMMARY OF KEY POINTS

1. Long-lived assets include property, plant, and equipment; investment property; biological assets; intangible assets; and goodwill.

2. The three models used in valuation of long-lived assets are the cost model, the revaluation model, and the fair value model. The most common model in practice is the cost model.

3. Costs for property, plant, and equipment are recognized if there is a probable future benefit and the cost can be measured reliably. These costs may include spare parts and involuntary safety or environmental costs.

4. Component accounting is the separation of an asset into significant components.

5. Assets acquired in a basket purchase must be individually valued using the proportional method.

6. Subsequent expenditures are typically repairs, which are expensed. If the expenditure is the replacement of a major part, betterment, or major inspection, the costs are capitalized.

7. Capital assets are recorded at cost, including cost to install assets and prepare them for use. Specific guidelines exist to aid in classification of expenditure for various asset categories, including buildings, self-constructed assets, machinery and equipment, land, and land improvements.

8. Self-constructed assets are recorded at cost, which includes reasonable amounts of overhead and includes interest. Incidental revenues or expenses during construction period are recognized in net income. Self-constructed assets may not be valued at an amount higher than fair value.

9. Capital assets purchased with low-interest debt are valued at the cash equivalent price or at the present value of the cash payments required.

10. Donated assets are valued at fair value and give rise to contributed capital.

11. If there is a legal requirement or constructive obligation to incur costs when an asset is retired, the present value of this is recorded as an asset and liability when the asset is acquired. As time passes, estimates are adjusted, the asset is depreciated, and the liability is increased through interest expense.

12. Specific intangible assets are recorded at cost, if purchased externally, or the cost to develop the asset, if internally generated. Legal costs are a major component of the cost of most intangible assets.

13. All costs in the research phase and many in the development phase must be expensed as incurred. Costs in the development phase or internally developed intangible assets

may be capitalized if specific criteria, including marketability or economic value, are met. Since the criteria are based on management estimates, substantial variation in practice can arise.

14. The practice of capitalizing some operating costs, such as training, promotion, and other start-up costs is prohibited.

15. Website development costs are subject to either capitalization or expensing, depending on the nature of the cost. Planning, some content costs, and all operating costs are expensed. Website application, infrastructure costs, and some content costs are capitalized. If the website is used solely for advertising, then all costs must be expensed.

16. Resource companies may incur costs related to exploration and evaluation of their resource properties. Costs incurred prior to obtaining the legal right to explore must be expensed. Costs incurred after the legal right has been obtained up until technical feasibility and commercial viability can be capitalized.

17. When assets are sold or otherwise retired or disposed, the difference between proceeds, if any, and book value is the gain or loss on disposal. The gain or loss is, in substance, a correction of the recorded depreciation over the period that the asset was used. If a major part is replaced, the carrying amount of the original part is removed and recognized as a loss.

18. Goodwill is recognized on the purchase of another business unit. It is measured as the excess of acquisition cost over the fair value of identifiable net assets acquired.

19. On the SCF, cash expenditures to acquire long-lived assets and cash received on sale are reported as investing activities. Long-lived assets acquired in a non-cash exchange are not included on the SCF. Some expenditures will be operating outflows if the item is expensed and investing outflows if the item is capitalized.

20. Different types of long-lived assets must be presented as separate line items on the SFP. Extensive note disclosure is required for long-lived assets, including assets, by major category and the accumulated amortization for each category. In addition, reconciliations of beginning and ending balances are required for each class.

KEY TERMS

basket purchase	investment property
betterment	involuntary conversions
biological assets	major inspection
constructive obligation	negative goodwill
component accounting	non-monetary transactions
cost model	property, plant, and equipment
decommissioning obligation	revaluation model
fair value model	site restoration costs
forgivable loan (see Appendix)	spare parts
goodwill	successful efforts method
intangible assets	

REVIEW PROBLEM 9-1

The following four questions are independent.

1. *Plant asset cost classification.* Maldive Company completed the construction of a building. The following independent items are the costs and other aspects relevant to the purchase of the lot and construction:

Cash payments to contractor	$100,000
Total provincial nonrefundable sales tax on materials used in construction in addition to payments made to contractor	3,000
Cost of land (building site)	50,000
Gross cost to demolish old building on land	20,000
Proceeds from salvage of old building	5,000
Power bill for electricity used in construction	2,000
Interest on loans to finance construction	3,000
Net incidental profit from operating parking lot until construction started	5,000

What is the final recorded cost (i.e., carrying value) for *each* of the land and building?

2. *Accounting for debt incurred on acquisition.* The Round Wheel Barn Company purchases a tractor by making a down payment of $10,000. In addition, Round Wheel Barn signs a note requiring monthly payments of $2,000, starting one month after purchase and continuing for a total of 20 months. The contract calls for no interest, yet the prevailing interest rate is 24% per annum on similar debts. What is the cost (and initial carrying value) of the asset? What is the interest expense that should be recognized for the month following purchase?

3. *Post-acquisition costs.* After one-quarter of the useful life had expired on equipment with an original cost of $100,000 and no residual value, a major component of the equipment is unexpectedly replaced. The old component was expected to last as long as the equipment itself. Company records indicate that the component originally cost $20,000 and had no expected residual value. The replacement component cost $30,000 and has no usefulness beyond that of the equipment. What is the entry to record the replacement? Assume straight-line depreciation.

4. *Acquisition of intangibles.* Growth Company acquired Technology Company during the year and paid $2 million for the company. Growth obtained the following for its purchase price:

	Net Book Value	Fair Market Value
Inventory	$1,250,000	$1,300,000
Property, plant, and equipment	1,500,000	1,750,000
Liabilities	1,200,000	1,200,000

In addition, Growth obtained technology from projects in progress with an estimated value of $200,000. What is the journal entry to record the acquisition?

REVIEW PROBLEM 9-1—SOLUTION

1. Cost components of the land and building:

Land		Building	
Land cost	$50,000	Cash payments to contractor	$100,000
Demolition	20,000	Sales tax on materials	3,000
Salvage proceeds	(5,000)	Power bill	2,000
		Capitalized loan interest	3,000
Total land cost	$65,000	Total building cost	$108,000

The incidental net revenues from operating the parking lot would be recognized in net income.

2. The cost of the tractor is the present value of the monthly payment annuity:

$$P = \$10,000 + \$2,000(P/A, 2\%, 20) = \$42,703$$

Interest cost for the first month is the present value times the monthly interest rate:

$$\$32,703 \times 2\% = \$654$$

3. The new component is a replacement of an old component and, as such, is a *substitution*. It is not a betterment because it does not improve or extend the functioning of the asset. The entries to remove the old component and substitute the new are as follows:

Loss on asset replacement	15,000	
Accumulated depreciation ($20,000 ÷ 4)	5,000	
Equipment		20,000
Equipment	30,000	
Cash		30,000

4. The acquisition of Technology Company would create negative goodwill of $50,000. The technology acquired would have a soft value and would likely be written down to $150,000. If it was established that the technology was worth $200,000, there would be a gain.

Inventory	1,300,000	
Property, plant, and equipment	1,750,000	
Technology in progress	150,000	
Cash		2,000,000
Liabilities		1,200,000

APPENDIX 1

INVESTMENT PROPERTY

Assets that are classified as investment property have the option of using the cost model or the fair value model. Assets considered investment property can include land and or buildings that are rented out or held for capital appreciation. For example, a company can be holding vacant land to sell or an apartment building earning rental income. Property held for use in the business or held for administrative purposes cannot be classified as investment property. For example, administrative offices or land used for a golf course would not be investment property. Of course, everything is not always clear-cut. A company could have a portion of the property being used or providing a service. For example, an apartment building may provide security and maintenance, and one of the apartments in the building may be occupied by the apartment manager. In this case, this operating component would be considered insignificant, and the apartment building could still be classified as investment property.

Initial recognition is similar to other items of property, plant, and equipment. The option of using the fair value model is unique; a company elects to use the cost model or the fair value model for all investment property. However, the fair value model is the preferred model and measures the assets at fair value at every reporting date. Fair value is for the asset as a whole and the concept of component accounting is not used. Both increases and decreases in the value are recognized in the income statement in that period. The asset is not depreciated.

Example To illustrate the accounting for investment property, assume that an apartment building met the classification as investment property. The building had a fair value in year one of $1,000,000. Assume that at the next reporting date, fair value had increased to $1,250,000. The following entry would be recorded for the building:

Building ($1,250,000 − $1,000,000)	250,000	
Unrealized gain: income statement		250,000

Transfers can occur between investment property and inventory or property, plant, and equipment if the use of the property changes. For example, if a rental building is now going to be used for the head office of the company, the building would change from investment property (fair value model) to property, plant, and equipment (cost model or revaluation model).

Exhibit 9A-1 provides an illustration from the 2011 annual report for Brookfield Asset Management Incorporated where the fair value model is used.

EXHIBIT 9A-1

BROOKFIELD ASSET MANAGEMENT INCORPORATED

Extract from Significant Accounting Policy Note and Note 15

8. INVESTMENT PROPERTIES

(in millions)	2011	2010
Fair value at beginning of year	**$22,163**	$19,219
Additions	**1,442**	689
Acquisitions through business combinations	**5,846**	1,416
Disposals	**(2,050)**	(802)
Fair value adjustments	**1,377**	778
Foreign currency translation	**(412)**	863
Fair value at end of year	**$28,366**	$22,163

continued on next page

EXHIBIT 9A-1 (*cont'd*)

The fair value of investment properties is generally determined by discounting the expected cash flows of the properties based upon internal or external valuations. All properties are externally valued on a three-year rotation plan.

(in millions)	Dec. 31, 2011	Dec. 31, 2010
Properties where valuations are performed by:		
External valuators	$10,095	$ 5,160
Internal appraisals	18,271	17,003
Fair value recorded in financial statements	$28,366	$22,163

The key valuation metrics of our commercial office properties are presented in the following table:

	United States		Canada		Australia	
	Dec. 31, 2011	Dec. 31, 2010	Dec. 31, 2011	Dec. 31, 2010	Dec. 31, 2011	Dec. 31, 2010
Discount rate	7.5%	8.1%	6.7%	6.9%	9.1%	9.1%
Terminal capitalization rate	6.3%	6.7%	6.2%	6.3%	7.5%	7.4%
Investment horizon (years)	12	10	11	11	10	10

The key valuation assumptions of our Brazilian retail properties include a discount rate of 9.6% (2010 – 10.0%), a terminal capitalization rate of 7.3% (2010 – 7.3%) and an investment horizon of 10 years (2010 – 10 years).

INVESTMENT PROPERTY

	2011			2010		
	Land	Building	Total	Land	Building	Total
Cost						
Balance, beginning of financial year	$ 8,084	$5,995	$14,079	$3,729	$3,044	$ 6,773
Transfers	4,325	327	4,652	4,386	2,951	7,337
Disposals	(723)	(2)	(725)	(31)	—	(31)
Balance, end of financial year	$11,686	$6,320	$18,006	$8,084	$5,995	$14,079
Amortization						
Balance, beginning of financial year	$ —	$1,309	$ 1,309	$ —	$ 889	$ 889
Amortization for the financial year	—	325	325	—	420	420
Transfers	—	—	—	—	—	—
Balance, end of financial year	$ —	$1,634	$ 1,634	$ —	$1,309	$ 1,309
Net book value			$16,372			$12,770
Net book value at January 3, 2010						$ 5,884

The fair value of investment property approximates its carrying value.

Source: Brookfield Asset Management Incorporated 2011 Annual Financial Statements, www.sedar.com, posted 28 November 2011.

Looking Ahead

Investment property is not now on the agenda of either the IASB or the Canadian AcSB.

ACCOUNTING STANDARDS FOR PRIVATE ENTERPRISES

ASPE does not have a separate standard for investment property. The option of classifying assets as investment property and using the fair value model is not an alternative. It is treated the same as all other property, plant, and equipment

RELEVANT STANDARDS

CPA Canada Handbook, Part I (IFRS):
- IAS 40, Investment Property

CPA Canada Handbook, Part II (ASPE):
- No standard

SUMMARY OF KEY POINTS

1. Land and/or buildings can be classified as investment property and use the cost or fair value model.

2. The fair value model records investment property at fair value every reporting date. Any changes in fair value are recognized in the income statement for that period. The asset is not depreciated.

APPENDIX 2

GOVERNMENT ASSISTANCE

Assets sometimes are acquired with monetary assistance from various levels of governments. This may be in the form of a cash grant. The terms of the grant may require the firm to maintain certain employment levels or pollution-control levels. If the conditions are not met, the firm may be required to refund the amounts received. This form of assistance is referred to as a **forgivable loan**. The forgivable loan is treated similarly to a government grant and recognized when there is reasonable assurance that the conditions will be met. Another common program is in the form of an investment tax credit, which reduces the amount of *income tax payable* based on a set percentage of eligible capital expenditures for the period.

Basically, accounting standards require that government assistance toward the acquisition of property, plant, and equipment in any form should be either:

1. Deducted from the related assets with any depreciation calculated on the net amount; or

2. Recorded as deferred income that is recognized over the life of the asset. The deferred income would be amortized to income on the same basis as the related depreciable assets are depreciated.

The choice allowed is really just a presentation issue; there is an identical impact on net income. The major decision is that the government assistance is deferred with property, plant, and equipment, and recognized on the income statement with depreciation.

Example To illustrate accounting for a government grant, assume that machinery costing $100,000 was eligible for assistance of 30%. The machinery has a 10-year life with no salvage value. Because both the *net method* and *deferral method* of accounting are acceptable, both sets of journal entries are provided.

	Net Method		Deferral Method	
Record purchase:				
Machinery	100,000		100,000	
Cash		100,000		100,000
Record receipt of government assistance:				
Cash*	30,000		30,000	
Machinery		30,000		—
Deferred government grant		—		30,000

*Cash is debited if government assistance is in the form of money. If assistance was investment tax credit, taxes payable would be debited.

	Net Method		Deferral Method	
Record straight-line depreciation expense at the end of years 1 to 10:				
Depreciation expense	7,000		10,000	
Accumulated depreciation		7,000		10,000
Deferred government grant	—		3,000	
Depreciation expense		—		3,000

The effect on income is the same under either method. The difference is on the balance sheet where, using the deferral method, the gross amount of the property, plant, and equipment would appear. The deferred government grant may be presented either netted against the asset (as a contra account), or shown under liabilities on the balance sheet. Which method would you choose if you were trying to maximize assets to reassure creditors? Companies often prefer higher asset values.

Government assistance can have a major impact on cash flows. As a result, under either the net method or the deferral method, the cash flows reported on the SCF (as investment activities) will show separately the gross amount paid for the asset and the gross amount received for the government assistance.

Other Government Assistance Before we leave government assistance, it is worth mentioning that government assistance can be obtained for a wide variety of purposes, not just the acquisition of property, plant, and equipment. The purpose of the government assistance governs its accounting. For example, if the assistance is to offset current expenses, then accounting for government assistance must reflect that fact and recognize government assistance on the income statement when the related expenses appear. Companies would have a choice of netting the government assistance against the related expenses or recognizing as income in the current period. If assistance is for future expenses, then assistance should be deferred and recognized when the expenses are recognized.

Government assistance is sometimes in the form of forgivable loans. The loans are forgiven when certain conditions are met, such as maintenance of a stated level of employment or volume sales for specific periods of time. In these circumstances, management must assess the conditions that are attached to the "loan." If the conditions are deemed likely to be met, the "loan" is recorded as a grant and the conditions and unforgiven balance are disclosed in the notes. Should management's expectations prove wrong and the loan becomes repayable in the future, this event should be accounted for in the period that conditions change. Note disclosure is required of the criteria to be met to inform users.

Finally, government assistance may be the transfer of an asset (e.g., land for the use of the company at no cost). These non-monetary government grants may be recorded at fair value or the entity may record at a nominal amount.

Looking Ahead

Government assistance is not currently on the agenda of either the IASB or the Canadian AcSB.

ACCOUNTING STANDARDS FOR PRIVATE ENTERPRISES

Accounting standards for private enterprises requires non-monetary grants to be recorded at fair value. Recording at a nominal amount is not allowed.

RELEVANT STANDARDS

CPA Canada Handbook, Part I (IFRS):
- IAS 20, Accounting for Government Grants and Disclosure of Government Assistance
- IAS 41, Agriculture
- SIC-10, Government Assistance—No Specific Relation to Operating Activities

CPA Canada Handbook, Part II (ASPE):
- Section 3800, Government Assistance
- Section 3805, Investment Tax Credits

SUMMARY OF KEY POINTS

1. Government assistance for property, plant, and equipment, in the form of grants, forgivable loans, or tax credits, is amortized to net income over the life of the related asset. On the balance sheet, the grant amount is shown in a separate deferred liability account.

2. Other government assistance is recognized on the income statement when the related expenses, meant to be supported by the assistance, are also recognized.

QUESTIONS

Q9-1   To what category of long-lived assets would the following assets belong: (a) vines in a winery (b) an apartment building for rent, (c) a manufacturing facility, (d) dairy cows on a farm, or (e) a patent?

Q9-2   Why might a company prefer to value capital assets at fair value rather than historical cost? Is this allowable under all accounting standards?

Q9-3   Your company is in the airline industry. What are some possible components of your airplanes?

Q9-4   The fire code has changed and your buildings are now required to install a new sprinkler system. These systems do not add any value to the operations. How would the costs be treated, and what is the logic?

Q9-5   When several capital assets are purchased for a single lump-sum consideration, cost apportionment is usually employed. Explain how you would determine the allocation to different categories. Why is apportionment necessary?

Q9-6   When are subsequent costs capitalized rather than expensed?

Q9-7   Explain the impact on income, net assets, and cash flow over an asset's life of a decision to capitalize or write off certain expenditures made at the time of the purchase of a capital asset.

Q9-8   Some businesses construct capital assets for their own use. What costs should be capitalized for these assets? Explain what policy to follow for (a) general company overhead, (b) costs of construction in excess of the purchase price of an equivalent asset from an outsider, and (c) interest on construction loans (d) incidental revenues and expenses.

Q9-9   A shareholder decides to donate a truck to be used in the business. What is the appropriate accounting for this donation?

Q9-10 Under what circumstances must a company record a liability for future costs of retiring an asset? What judgements are necessary to record a retirement obligation? What is the offsetting debit?

Q9-11 Suppose that an asset retirement liability is recorded and that the original estimates are not changed in subsequent years. Is any accounting treatment required for the liability in the intervening years until retirement? Explain.

Q9-12 What is the difference between the research and development phases of an internally generated intangible asset? How must a company account for costs in the research phase? For costs in the development phase?

Q9-13 What criteria have been suggested to determine whether an internally generated intangible asset can be capitalized?

Q9-14 Why would advertising and promotional expense, which might have a long-term positive effect on a company's reputation, not qualify for capitalization?

Q9-15 What is the most appropriate treatment for costs incurred in planning features of a company's website?

Q9-16 An asset is purchased for $10,000 and has a net book value of $2,000 after three years, at which time it is sold for $4,500. Explain the meaning of the $2,500 gain.

Q9-17 A major spare part is replaced in a machine at a cost of $100,000. There is a remaining carrying amount of the old part of $2,000. How is the $2,000 treated?

Q9-18 What items commonly are reported on the SCF in relation to capital assets?

Q9-19 Define goodwill, and describe how it is calculated.

Q9-20 What is negative goodwill? How does it arise? How is it treated for accounting purposes?

CASE 9-1

C2C

C2C is a small Canadian public company that services thousands of travellers on an annual basis. The company is a small personal transportation business that has the mission of getting people where they want to go in the cheapest, fastest way possible. C2C offers its customers many modes of transportation, such as taxi (for short trips), bus, and short-haul air trips. C2C only offers trips to certain destinations within Canada and the United States. C2C was founded in 20X2 and became a public company during 20X3. You have recently been hired as a student to assist the controller. It is now 20X4 and you have been asked by your boss to review some information pertaining to an upcoming acquisition of a small company, Blades, that runs out of Vancouver, British Columbia. Blades is currently a private company and follows accounting standards for private enterprises but has never had an audit. The controller obtained a listing of some of the significant accounting policies at Blades. She has asked you to review the policies and provide comments where the policy does not meet the IFRS requirements and what can be done to correct the policy. She has also asked you to ignore any transitional issues in your analysis and does not want you to provide any advice regarding whether the acquisition should move forward.

Background Information: Blades

Blades is a small private company located in Vancouver, British Columbia. Blades was founded in 20X2 by two men, Clarke Walker and Lee Parnes. During 20X3, Clarke passed away, and Lee put the business up for sale. Blades is a transportation company, which earns a similar level of revenue and profit as C2C.

Significant Accounting Polices at Blades

Revenue Recognition

At Blades there are several revenue streams. The revenue recognition treatment for each stream is described below:

Short-Haul Customer Transportation
Revenue is recognized at the point in time that the customer pays for the flight.

Short-Haul Cargo Transportation
In general, the customer is required to pay for the delivery once the item is delivered to its final destination. Under most circumstances, Blades is required to air transport the goods to the destination country and then provide ground transportation from the airport to the final destination (by truck). Once delivered, the customer is invoiced, and payment is collected within two weeks of delivery. Revenue is recognized once upon collection of the payment.

Incidental Revenue

Blades provides onboard food, beverage, and entertainment to its guests for a small fee. Revenue is recognized when the good or service is purchased.

Frequent-Customer Program

Blades provides a points program for its customers. This program allows its customers to accumulate points (that expire after 10 years if not used). The customer can redeem the points for travel rewards at a future point in time. Blades recognizes a liability when the point is awarded to the customer and also a promotional expense.

Property, Plant, and Equipment

Blades' most significant long-term asset is its aircraft. Blades owns and operates 4 airplanes and leases 10. Blades includes the purchase price and any other costs incurred to get the aircraft ready for flight in the cost of the asset with the exception of testing fees, and costs incurred to alter the aircraft to meet environmental regulations (which are both expensed). Every five years, each aircraft requires a major overhaul. These costs are expensed as incurred. Each aircraft is depreciated on a straight-line basis over 20 years, which is reflective of the asset's useful life.

At all times, Blades ensures that it has two extra engines on hand (as they tend to have a shorter useful life than the aircraft and will need to be replaced during the asset's useful life.) These engines are classified as spare parts inventory, which is included in total inventory.

From time to time, Blades contacts a company to construct assets. For example, in 20X4 Blades hired a contractor to construct a new hanger to house the aircraft. At that time, all costs relevant to the construction of the asset were capitalized, with the exception of any interest costs incurred during the construction period. These costs were expensed.

Blades owns a small piece of land adjacent to the airport, where it stores chemicals that are required to operate the aircraft. Due to the nature of the storage, the government requires that Blades restore the land at the end of its use. Blades has estimated it will likely incur about a million dollars of expenses to restore the land. This amount is disclosed in the notes to the financial statements.

Required:

Prepare the requested report.

(Sara Stonehouse)

CASE 9-2

WINERY INCORPORATED

Winery Incorporated (WI) is a private corporation formed in 20X8. Prior to 20X8, WI had been operating as a partnership by the Verity family. Due to their success and desire to expand, they have made the decision to incorporate so that they will have additional sources of financing. They are just establishing their accounting policies for their first year-end as a corporation. Their previous financial statements as a partnership were used for filing their tax returns and management purposes. They were not audited or reviewed.

WI grows grapes and produces wines in Ontario. The company also produces beer, spirits, and juices. It has a small store on the property where staff operate winery tours and sell wine. WI incorporated to raise additional capital to expand the operations by planting additional vines and expanding operations to produce organic wines.

In 20X8, to finance the expansion of the winery WI obtained a bank loan with Big Bank. Previously, when WI operated as a partnership, the bank had provided a line of credit, and the owners had provided personal guarantees. The loan now has the personal guarantees removed, and instead the bank requires annual audited financial statements and has a financial covenant that stipulates a minimum current ratio. WI is considering adopting GAAP for public companies to be comparable with its competitors.

You have recently been hired to develop new accounting policies for WI's 31 December year-end. Previously, the partnership used the cash basis of accounting. The owners know this will no longer be suitable for their corporation. You have been asked by the owners to discuss alternatives and provide recommendations on the appropriate accounting policies for events below that have occurred during 20X8.

1. WI spent $500,000 expanding its operations by planting new vines that were purchased in France. These vines are certified as being organic and will produce a red wine. The vines will produce grapes indefinitely as long as they are properly taken care of during the year.

2. WI obtained a winery licence during 20X8 from the Ministry. This licence allows WI to distribute wine in western Canada. The license does not have an expiry date.

3. Wine can take over two years to mature. The premium wine is stored in oak caskets to age.

4. A customer can purchase WI's wine in the store at the winery, at the LCBO, or starting in 20X8 through WI's new website. WI invested $70,000 in acquiring software for its computer system. WI spent an additional $10,000 on the following costs to develop the website—consulting fees to a website consultant, graphics design, and costs for training employees on the use of a website and for the company's web domain.

5. A customer can become a member of WI's new wine club. To join the club, a $200 annual fee is paid. In return, the member is shipped one bottle of red wine and one bottle of white wine a month. As part of the annual fee members receive a free subscription to *Wine Digest*, which could be purchased on its own. If a member likes the wine, he can then order a case through the website at a 10% discount.

6. Early in 20X8, WI's wine maker in error added too much yeast to the wine in the vats (large containers that the juice ferments in to make the wine). Initial tasting of samples from those vats indicates that the wine is spoiled. WI fired the winemaker, since the wine had a market value of $1 million. The winemaker has sued WI for wrongful dismissal.

7. Until the new vines are producing crops in 20X9, WI entered into an agreement to purchase some grapes from Chile for production. To protect itself from foreign exchange fluctuations, WI entered into a hedge. If hedge accounting was elected this would be a cash flow hedge.

8. WI received a forgivable loan of $1 million. This loan is forgiven if WI hires five additional employees for the next two years and produces a specified amount of organic fruit each season for use in its organic wines.

Required:
Prepare the requested report.

Part A: Assume that WI will adopt accounting standards for public companies.
Part B: Assume that WI will adopt accounting standards for private companies.

CASE 9-3

THOR LIMITED

Thor Ltd. (TL) is a Canadian company that produces, sources, and supplies agriculture products, including farm equipment, fertilizer, and seed. These products are sold to large and small distributors across Canada. TL deals with some large farm accounts directly.

Sales volumes are healthy and stable, but profit margins are thin and have been squeezed by rising fuel prices. Transportation is a major cost item.

James Watkins manages a project for TL. He is paid a salary of $60,000 and has been promised a bonus of 100,000 performance units if this project breaks even in the current period. Performance units are the bonus system used by TL. Units must be held for three years and are then assigned a value based on a formula that considers the overall profit performance of the company, along with key customer and employee satisfaction data. In the last valuation round, one unit was worth $3.15.

The project is a no-tillage agricultural precision planting system called Land-Plant. It is a patented process over which TL owns the world patent rights. This system minimizes moisture loss, makes rich topsoil less likely to be blown or washed away after planting, and reduces the release of carbon dioxide (a greenhouse gas) into the environment. Since the latter is a major goal of the Kyoto accord, the federal government has announced that Canadian farmers could get funding of up to $1 billion for adopting such zero-plowing systems and adopting other energy-saving practices. For farmers, the system also allows lower operating costs, precision planting, decreased soil compaction, and more precise application of needed fertilizers. While there are several no-till or low-till technologies on the market, TL's product line is of high quality and is being very well received at agricultural shows. Land-Plant is capable of placing seed and fertilizer in optimal relative positions while leaving 90% of the surface undisturbed.

Costs of the project to date (in thousands):

| | | Current Year | | | |
Description	Prior Year	1st Quarter	2nd Quarter	3rd Quarter	4th Quarter
Development costs	$1,698				
Legal costs re: patent	134	$60	$ 10		
Independent product testing		82			
Production planning			156	$ 18	
Market research	20	47	12		
Sales and marketing support				56	$ 76
Production set up				41	
Production training				29	
Production equipment (1), (2)				3,423	
Production cost over-runs (3)				225	
Administrative costs (4)	35	35	35	35	35
Production costs (5)				366	1,914

1. The production equipment is expected to have a service life of eight years, or approximately 18,000 manufacturing hours. It was used in the third and fourth quarter of the current year, for 570 hours.
2. The expenditure on manufacturing equipment will entitle TL to an investment tax credit (income tax relief) equal to 20% of the cost of the equipment.
3. Quality concerns with the initial units produced led them to be scrapped.
4. Watkins' salary is $15 per quarter, plus an administrative fee of $20 for overall supervision and accounting/systems support.
5. In the third and fourth quarter, a total of 48 good units of the 3300T Land-Plant system were produced. These costs exclude amortization on related assets.

Financing of this project was uncertain until the third quarter of the current year. While TL's Board of Directors has been very enthusiastic about the project, and has funded the development work, TL had no deep well of financing as would be needed to finance the project. Then, late in the second quarter, TL was approved as an Eligible Business Corporation under the provincial *Small Business Venture Capital Act*. This allowed the company to issue 50,000 preferred shares in a private placement at $100 per share. The individual shareholders are entitled to a 30% investment tax credit on their investment. These shares were successfully issued in the third quarter. This funding plus a lending arrangement secured the project and production was geared up.

Production was limited to the latter part of the third quarter and all the fourth quarter. Manufacturing operations were increased to full capacity to meet demand. Fortunately for Watkins, he had a backlog of orders from marketing efforts, especially trade shows. He sold 42 units of model 3300T before the end of the fourth quarter at an average price of $67,400. In all other divisions, TL ships essentially the same day as the order is received and thus recognizes revenue when orders are received. Because of the size and complexity of the Land-Plant equipment, it can take up to a week to have the unit shipped. Investigation showed that four units of model 3300T were not yet shipped at the end of the fourth quarter, although they were completed and ready for shipment.

In addition, invoices show that 12 units of model 3300T were to dealers who were told that if the units did not sell in six months, they could be returned to TL with no penalty or charge. Watkins views this as a clever marketing strategy because he is confident that if the units are shown to agriculture producers, they will be very impressed with the operation and ingenuity of the system. He plans more volume under this plan in the coming year.

Overall market demand for the system is hard to predict because much depends on continued federal government support for the system, and the development of rival systems by competitors. Watkins feels that he likely has three to five years before competition is much of a factor, but he acknowledges that this is largely a guess.

Watkins has requested a preliminary income statement, along with a discussion of the accounting issues. He knows that any income statement used for performance evaluation will have to be in accordance with GAAP, as it will be based on the information that is used for external reporting and TL's lenders require GAAP financial statements. The tax rate is 40%.

Required:
Prepare the information requested by Watkins.

Part A: Assume that TL will adopt accounting standards for public companies.
Part B: Assume that TL will adopt accounting standards for private companies.

CASE 9-4

PENGUINS IN PARADISE

"The thing you have to understand is how these stage plays work. You start out with just an idea, but generally no cash. That's where promoters like me come in. We find ways of raising the money necessary to get the play written and the actors trained. If the play is a success, we hope to recover all those costs and a whole lot more, but cash flow is the problem. Since less than half of all plays make money, you cannot get very much money from banks.

"Take my current project, *Penguins in Paradise (PIP)*. You only have to look at the cash inflows to see how many sources I had to approach to get the cash. As you can see, most of the initial funding comes from the investors in the limited partnership. They put up their money to buy a percentage of the future profits of the play.

"The money that the investors put up is not enough to fund all the start-up costs, so you have to be creative. Take reservation fees, for example. You know how tough it is to get good seats for a really hot play. Well, *PIP* sold the right to buy great seats to some dedicated theatregoers this year for next year's performance. These amounts are nonrefundable, and the great thing is that the buyers still have to pay full price for the tickets when they buy them.

"Consider the sale of movie rights. Lots of good plays get turned into movies. Once the stage play is a success, the movie rights are incredibly expensive. My idea was to sell the movie rights in advance. *PIP* got a lot less money, but at least we got it upfront when we needed it.

"The other sources are much the same. We received the government grant by agreeing to have at least 50% Canadian content. We also negotiated a bank loan with an interest rate of 5% a year plus 1% of the gross revenue of the play, instead of the usual 16% annual interest a year. Even my fee for putting the deal together was taken as a percentage of the profit, so just about everybody has a strong interest in the play's performance."

Required:

Prepare a memo addressing the major financial accounting issues to be established by *PIP*. Include your recommendations. Do not prepare financial statements.

(Reprinted (or adapted) from Case: 9-4 Penguins in Paradise, with permission Chartered Professional Accountants of Canada, Toronto, Canada. Any changes to the original material are the sole responsibility of the author (and/or publisher) and have not been reviewed or endorsed by the Chartered Professional Accountants of Canada.)

Summary of Cash Flows for the Period Ended 31 December 20X4
(in thousands of dollars)

Cash inflows:	
Investor contributions to limited partnership	$6,000
Bank loan	2,000
Sale of movie rights	500
Government grant	50
Reservation fees	20
	8,570
Cash outflows:	
Salaries and fees for rehearsal period	3,500
Costumes and sets	1,000
Miscellaneous costs	1,260
	5,760
Net cash inflows	$2,810

TECHNICAL REVIEW

TR9-1 Lump-Sum Purchase: Bell Incorporated (BI) purchased a group of assets together from one of their competitors whose owner had recently decided to retire and stop operations. BI paid $500,000 for land, building, equipment, and a patent. Independent appraisals had been completed on all assets prior to the sale. These appraisals indicated the following fair values for the assets: land $250,000; building $225,000; equipment $75,000; and patent $50,000.

Required:
Give the entry to record the purchase; show computations.

TR9-2 Self-Constructed Asset: Mappleback Incorporated had recently completed construction of a new manufacturing facility. Prior to the approval of the building permits the company operated a parking lot on the land. This parking lot had revenues net of costs of $50,000. Total construction costs were as follows:

Material	$300,000
Labour	600,000
Incremental overhead	120,000
General overhead	50,000
Interest costs	100,000
Cost permits	20,000

Required:

Provide the total amount of construction costs that would be capitalized to the cost of the building.

TR9-3 Decommissioning Cost Obligation: Manufacturing Incorporated (MI) purchased land on 1 January 20X2, which it started to operate as a gravel pit. The gravel pit will be operating for the next 20 years. At the end of the 20 years MI will be required to incur an estimated cost of $5 million to restore the land. This is required by government legislation. The interest rate that reflects the risks to MI is 8%.

Required:

1. Provide the journal entry for the restoration costs on 1 January 20X2.
2. Provide all required adjusting journal entries on 31 December 20X2.

TR9-4 Goodwill: Hendrie Incorporated acquired all of the assets and liabilities of Smith Corporation for $1,250,000 cash on 1 January. The book values and fair values of the assets of XYZ as of the date of acquisition were:

	Book Value	Fair Value
Accounts receivable	$150,000	$150,000
Inventory	225,000	350,000
Property, plant, and equipment	300,000	550,000
Land	200,000	400,000

In addition, XYZ had liabilities totalling $320,000 at the date of acquisition and a customer list estimated to have a fair value based on discounted future cash flows of $75,000.

Required:

1. Prepare the journal entry necessary for Hendrie Incorporated to record the acquisition.
2. Prepare the journal entry necessary for Hendrie Incorporated to record the acquisition assuming the purchase price was $1,200,000. It was determined that the value of all of the assets was reasonable.

TR9-5 Disposal of Capital Assets: O'Callaghan Incorporated (OI) is in the highway construction business. OI's property, plant, and equipment account includes heavy construction equipment. The following transactions relate to the disposal of two of their pieces of equipment.

- Equipment One—OI decided to dispose of one of its pieces of heavy machinery and replace it with a newer, more efficient model. OI received $125,000 cash on the sale of the machine. At the date of the sale, the machine had a net book value of $60,000. The original cost of the equipment was $500,000.
- Equipment Two—OI recognizes the scoop separate from the rest of the equipment, since it is a significant part that needs replacing. The scoop was replaced this year at a cost of $200,000. The scoop was depreciated separately. The net book value of the scoop at the date of replacement was $25,000.

Required:

Provide the journal entry for the two pieces of equipment.

ASSIGNMENTS

★ **A9-1 Valuation Model:** For each of the following assets, explain the available choices in valuation models:

a. Rental apartment buildings
b. Manufacturing facility
c. Vacant land held for eventual sale
d. Vines in a winery
e. Agriculture quotas
f. Timber
g. Customer lists

★ **A9-2 Component Accounting:** For each of the following assets, identify the possible components:

a. Airplane
b. Wind farm
c. Manufacturing facility
d. Cruise ship
e. Hydro lines

★ **A9-3 Lump-Sum Purchase:** Scarlett Incorporated purchased a tract of land with an office building and equipment included. The cash purchase price was $900,000 plus $50,000 in fees connected with the purchase. The following data were collected concerning the property:

	Appraisal Value	Vendor's Book Value	Original Cost
Land	$220,000	$ 80,000	$ 80,000
Equipment	360,000	170,000	550,000
Office building	440,000	260,000	720,000

Required:
Give the entry to record the purchase; show computations.

★★ **A9-4 Repairs and Other Expenditures:** Rundle Incorporated has various transactions in 20X6:

a. Plant maintenance was done at a cost of $35,200.
b. The entire manufacturing facility was repainted at a cost of $44,000.
c. The roof on the manufacturing facility was replaced at a cost of $66,200. At the same time, various upgrades were done to the electrical systems at a cost of $43,800. These upgrades to the electrical system were required to be in compliance with the current safety codes. Neither of these transactions increased the life of the manufacturing facility, although the safety of the facility was enhanced. The carrying amount of the original roof was $2,000 and the carrying amount of the replaced wiring is zero.
d. The company bought a piece of machinery at an auction at a price of $80,500. The machinery had an appraised value of $95,000, so Rundle was pleased to get this bargain. The company knew that the machine had to be painted and tuned up. Sales tax of 14% was paid on the purchase price.
e. The machine was delivered to Rundles' manufacturing facility. The freight bill was $1,600.
f. The machine was painted and tuned up, at a cost of $5,200. In the process of the tune-up, it was discovered that the machine needed additional unexpected repairs, which were done at a cost of $12,000.

Required:

Provide journal entries to record the transactions listed above. Justify your decisions. All items were acquired for cash.

★ **A9-5 Acquisition Cost:** The following cases are independent.

Case A   Timmis Limited bought a building for $2,120,000. Before using the building, the following expenditures were made:

Repair and renovation of building	$210,000
Construction of new paved driveway	55,000
Upgraded landscaping	8,400
Installation of high-speed cable	32,000
Deposits with utilities for connections	5,000
Sign for front and back of building, attached to roof	26,000
Installation of fence around property	28,000

Case B   Ling Company purchased a $65,000 tract of land for a new manufacturing facility. Ling demolished an old building on the property and sold the materials it salvaged from the demolition. Ling incurred additional costs and realized salvage proceeds as follows:

Demolition of old building	$62,000
Routine maintenance (mowing) done on purchase	5,000
Proceeds from sale of salvaged materials	22,400
Legal fees	18,000
Title guarantee insurance	11,200

Required:

1. What balance would Timmis report in the building account?
2. What balance should Ling report in the land account?
3. If any items in the list above are excluded from the building and land accounts, indicate the appropriate classification.

★★ **A9-6 Acquisition Cost:** An examination of the property, plant, and equipment accounts of James Company, disclosed the following transactions:

a. On 1 January 20X4, a new machine was purchased at a list price of $45,000. The company did not take advantage of a 2% cash discount available upon full payment of the invoice within 30 days. Shipping cost paid by the vendor was $200. Installation cost was $600, including $200 that represented 10% of the monthly salary of the factory superintendent (installation period, two days). A wall was moved two feet at a cost of $1,100 to make room for the machine.

b. On 1 January 20X4, the company purchased an automatic counter to be attached to a machine in use; the cost was $700. The estimated useful life of the counter was 7 years, and the estimated life of the machine was 10 years.

c. On 1 January 20X4, the company bought plant fixtures with a list price of $4,500, paying $1,500 cash and giving a one-year, non-interest-bearing note payable for the balance. The current interest rate for this type of note was 15%.

d. During January 20X4, the first month of operations, the newly purchased machine became inoperative due to a defect in manufacture. The vendor repaired the machine at no cost to James; however, the specially trained operator was idle during the two weeks the machine was inoperative. The operator was paid regular wages ($850) during the period, although the only work performed was to observe the repair by the factory representative.

e. During January 20X5, the company exchanged the electric motor on the machine in part (a) for a heavier motor and gave up the old motor and $600 cash. The market value of the new motor was $1,250. The parts list showed a $900 cost for the original motor, and it had been depreciated in 20X4 (estimated life, 10 years).

Required:

1. Prepare the journal entries to record each of the above transactions as of the date of occurrence. Explain and justify your decisions on questionable items. James Company uses straight-line depreciation.

2. Record depreciation at the end of 20X4. None of the assets is expected to have a residual value except the fixtures (residual value is $500). Estimated useful lives: fixtures, 5 years; and machinery, 10 years. Give a separate entry for each asset.

★ **A9-7 Expenditure Classification:** Consider each of the following items:

a. Cost of an oil change on the company's truck.
b. Cost of major brake replacement in a large piece of construction equipment that is expected to be completed every two years.
c. Lawyers' fees associated with a successful patent application.
d. Lawyers' fees associated with an unsuccessful patent application.
e. Cost development website used exclusively to advertise new products.
f. Cost permits for building construction.
g. Cost to demolish an old building that is on a piece of land where a new building will be constructed.
h. Future costs to restore land used for mine at end of its useful life.
i. Costs required to remove asbestos in building to bring it up to new safety code.
j. Cost to excavate land to make it flat for a building site.
k. Cost of replacing tires in construction equipment expected to last two years.
l. Cost of installing a new roof on the company's building.
m. Cost to add new functions to a software package unique to the company.
n. Routine maintenance of website.

Required:

For each of the above items, give the name of the account to which the expenditure should be charged; that is, what account should be debited? Be specific.

★★★ **A9-8 Asset Acquisition:** At 31 December 20X4, certain accounts included in the property, plant, and equipment section of Hint Corporation's balance sheet had the following balances:

Land	$1,200,000
Buildings	2,600,000
Leasehold improvements	1,600,000
Machinery and equipment	3,200,000

During 20X5, the following transactions occurred:

a. Land site number 101 was acquired for $6,000,000. Additionally, to acquire the land, Hint paid a $360,000 commission to a real estate agent. Costs of $60,000 were incurred to clear the land. During the course of clearing the land, timber and gravel were recovered and sold for $32,000.

b. A second tract of land (site number 102) with a building was acquired for $1,200,000. The closing statement indicated that the land value was $800,000 and the building value was $400,000. Shortly after acquisition, the building was demolished at a cost of $80,000. A new building was constructed for $600,000 plus the following costs:

Excavation fees	$24,000
Architectural design fees	32,000
Building permit fee	8,000

The building was completed and occupied on 30 September 20X5.

c. A third tract of land (site number 103) was acquired for $3,000,000 and was put on the market for resale.

d. Extensive work was done to a building occupied by Hint under a lease agreement that expires on 31 December 20X14. The total cost of the work was $500,000, as follows:

	Cost	Useful life Item (years)
Painting of ceilings	$ 20,000	1
Electrical work	180,000	10
Construction of extension to current working area	300,000	25
	$500,000	

The lessor paid half the costs incurred for the extension to the current working area.

e. During December 20X5, $240,000 was spent to improve leased office space.

f. A group of new machines was purchased subject to a royalty agreement, which requires payment of royalties based on units of production for the machines. The invoice price of the machines was $540,000, freight costs were $4,000, unloading costs were $6,000, and royalty payments for 20X5 were $88,000.

Required:
Disregard the related accumulated depreciation accounts.

1. Prepare a detailed analysis of the changes in each of the following balance sheet accounts for 20X5:
   a. Land
   b. Buildings
   c. Leasehold improvements
   d. Machinery and equipment
2. What items would appear on the SCF in relation to the accounts in part (1)?

★★ **A9-9 Self-Constructed Asset:** Snowsports Company operates a snowsports resort for skiers and snowboarders. The company has recently decided to replace an existing old chair lift with a new high speed quad chair and expand the hill to allow for increased capacity. The work was completed from April to November. Snow Sports incurred the following costs for the expansion:

Invoice price high-speed quad chair lift	$3,000,000
Costs to dismantle old chair lift	55,000
Cash received for sale used chair lift	300,000
Shipping costs for delivery	35,000
Landscape architect fees, grading expansion hill	12,000
Permit costs	8,000
Clearing trees/grading land for expansion	85,000
Installation concrete bases for chair lift	180,000
Helicopter rental to install towers for chair lift	160,000
Labour installation ski lift	500,000
Training employees on maintenance and operation	15,000
Testing of chair lift	50,000
Interest costs loan for construction	120,000
General overhead costs	60,000
Annual routine maintenance	90,000
Purchase tools required for annual maintenance	150,000

Required:

1. Identify which of the costs listed above would be included in the cost of an item of property, plant, and equipment.
2. Identify if the costs would be included in land, ski lift, or tools.
3. Calculate the total costs for land, ski lift, and tools.

★★ **A9-10 Self-constructed Asset:** Brazilia Corporation needed a warehouse and maintenance facility on its company site, which already housed three manufacturing/storage facilities and the company head office. The lowest outside bid for the facility was $6,400,000. Brazilia believed that it could successfully construct the facility and have more control over the construction process. Accordingly, it began construction on company-owned land in 20X5. The facility was completed in 20X6. Costs related to the project have been accumulated in one account, "manufacturing facility":

Materials	$2,132,400
Subcontracted work (primarily electrical and plumbing)	691,800
Direct labour; plant workers assigned to construction tasks	911,600
Direct labour; construction workers hired specifically for this project	247,200
Plant foreman used for construction supervision; salary and benefits	69,800
Direct labour; plant maintenance workers assigned to construction tasks	106,400
Engineering and architectural services	433,400

Additional information:

a. Overhead is assigned in the plant to cover supplies used, electricity, occupation costs, maintenance, and so on in the production environment at a rate of $0.57 for every dollar of direct plant labour. This is reasonable for the warehouse project.

b. A loan was negotiated to cover the cash flow needed for construction. Interest of $151,800 was paid on this loan.

c. Of the $911,600 of plant workers' time assigned to construction tasks, 70%, or $638,120, relates to time that would otherwise have been idle.

d. The administrative office handled the planning and paperwork related to the construction. The staff worked full-time on this for approximately six months, representing salary and benefit costs of $114,000.

e. The executive team (chief executive officer and chief financial officer of the company, primarily) devoted approximately 10% of their time to this project during construction. The compensation package for these two individuals was $640,000 for this period.

Required:

1. Prepare a schedule showing the costs that can be capitalized for the building. If any items are not capitalized, explain why not.

2. What, if anything, would change in your answer if the outside bid on this project had been $4,800,000? Explain.

3. Under what circumstances can loan interest be capitalized as part of the cost of self-constructed assets? Explain.

★ **A9-11 Donated Assets:** Markus Company received two donations during the year. A long-term client donated a piece of artwork from their personal art collection to display in their entrance way as a thank-you for all of the years the company had completed work for him immediately. The artwork was appraised at $80,000. Markus also received during the year a vacant building as a donation. The building has a 20-year estimated remaining useful life ($50,000 residual value), which was recognized in the donation agreement at the time the company was guaranteed occupancy. Transfer costs of $35,000 were paid by the company. The building originally cost $1,200,000, 10 years earlier. The building was recently appraised at $650,000 market value by the city's tax assessor. Anticipating occupancy within the next 10 days, the company spent $250,000 for repairs and internal rearrangements, expected to have value for 8 years. There are no unresolved contingencies about the building and Markus Company's permanent occupancy.

Required:

1. Give all entries for Markus Company related to (a) the donations, (b) the renovation, and (c) any amortization at the end of the first year of occupancy, assuming that Markus uses straight-line amortization.

2. What would appear on the SCF in relation to the transactions recorded in requirement (1)?

3. What objections are raised concerning the accounting policy of capitalizing and depreciating a donated asset? Explain.

★★ **A9-12 Capital Asset Accounting:** McNally Corporation reported various transactions in 20X2:

a. Equipment with an original cost of $65,000 and accumulated depreciation of $52,000 was deemed unusable and was sold for $500 scrap value.

b. A new machine was acquired for $75,700. The invoice was marked 2/10, n/30, but McNally did not pay in time to take advantage of the 2% discount for early payment and thus paid the gross amount of $75,700. Wiring was improved to accommodate the needs of the new machinery at a cost of $500. Related software to install in the machine required for operation was purchased for $3,000. Installation and testing of the new machinery cost $2,500.

c. Regular machine maintenance was carried out for $22,000.

d. A major overhaul was done on heavy machinery for a cost of $75,000. This overhaul is expected to be completed every five years.

e. The building roof was replaced during the period at a cost of $44,800 to improve the insulation in the building and save on heating costs. The old roof had an original cost of $20,400 and was three-quarters depreciated.

f. Two machines were acquired for a lump-sum amount of $53,800. One machine had an appraised value of $40,000 and the other, $20,000.

g. Land and building were acquired from a member of the Board of Directors in exchange for 325,000 of the company's own common shares. The land was appraised at $75,000 and the building, $400,000. The facility will be used for long-term storage. The market value of common shares has been around $1.25 per share this year, with weekly highs and lows ranging from $1.80 to $0.95, respectively.

h. The company spent $630,000 in a research lab program this year. It was successful in developing three new commercial projects, which represented $244,000 of the expenditures budget. Legal fees associated with the three successful projects amount to $55,000.

i. McNally paved its factory parking lot, previously a dirt lot, at a cost of $160,100.

Required:
Prepare journal entries to record the transactions listed above. State any assumptions made.

★ **A9-13 Decommissioning Cost Obligation:** Charlie Networks Ltd. (CNL) has a 10-year renewable lease contract with Mercator Limited (ML), the owner of a tall building in a

major city. CNL is permitted to erect a transmission tower on the top of the building. CNL's contract with ML requires CNL to dismantle the tower if and when CNL discontinues its use. CNL expects to use the tower for only 10 years due to the rapid advance in transmission technology that is likely to render the tower obsolete in 10 years. The lease payments to ML are $180,000 per year.

CNL constructed the tower at the beginning of 20X6 at a cost of $2,100,000. CNL estimates that dismantling and removal of the tower will cost $180,000, at 20X6 current prices. The pre-tax interest rate that reflects risks is 6%. CNL plans to use straight-line amortization; the company's policy is to take a full year's amortization in the year of acquisition but none in the year of disposal.

Required:

1. Prepare the journal entry to record construction of the tower and the decommissioning cost obligation.

2. Prepare the necessary adjusting entries pertaining to the tower and the decommissioning cost obligation for each of the years ending 31 December 20X6 and 20X7. Assume that there is no change in the estimated cost of the tower's removal.

★ **A9-14 Costs in Research and Development Phases:** Airfield Answers Corporation had several expenditures in 20X5:

a. Testing new plastic prior to use in commercial production
b. Redesign of prototype to improve performance
c. Testing electronic instrument components during their production
d. Study of the possible uses of a newly developed fuel
e. Start-up activities for the production of a newly developed jet
f. Construction of a prototype for a new jet model
g. Design of a new, more efficient wing for an existing airplane
h. Portion of vice-president's salary, related to the time spent managing the research lab
i. Experimentation to establish the properties of a new plastic just discovered
j. Current period amortization taken on the company's laboratory research facilities
k. Salary of lab technician working on clinical trials of new drug

Required:

1. Explain the accounting policies required for costs in the research and development phases.
2. Which of the above expenditures are considered research? Development? Neither?

★ **A9-15 Costs in Research and Development Phases:** Processes Limited is involved in the R&D of new processes to make manufacturing more efficient and environmentally friendly. The company has been working on a number of new projects for the past three years. On 31 October 20X5 the company was able to demonstrate the feasibility and potential markets for its latest project. In fact, it has a company that has already indicated it will purchase the technology for use in its manufacturing process when work is completed. Processes Limited has a 31 December year-end. It has incurred the following expenditures for this project:

Research costs expensed in 20X2 to 20X5	$2,200,000
Development costs incurred prior 31 Oct. 20X5	1,800,000
Development costs incurred 31 Oct. to 31 Dec. 20X5	1,200,000
Advertising costs to launch new product	800,000

Required:

1. Indicate how each expenditure should be accounted for and why.
2. How would your answer be different if there was no potential interest in the product at this time.

★★ **A9-16 Costs in Research and Development Phases:** Victor Medical Solutions Limited has a major scientific program underway, financed through an issuance of common shares. The program has an expected budget in excess of $55 million, and $17.9 million has been spent to date.

The program targets technology to reduce the chronic inflammation associated with cardiovascular disease. To successfully market an end-product from this project, the company has to meet rigorous testing standards established by government agencies. In Phase I testing, the product must be shown to be safe in animals. In Phase II testing, the product must be shown to be safe in humans. In rigorous Phase III testing, the product must be shown to be effective in treating the condition better than available treatments on the market, or show other advantages over available treatments (e.g., fewer side effects).

As a result of the scientific program, Victor has twelve compounds in Phase I testing, three in Phase II testing, and one compound in a 2,000 individual Phase III test. All costs to date for all projects have been expensed.

Required:

1. Explain the required accounting treatment of costs in the R&D phases.

2. Why are assets not established for research and many development initiatives?

3. Do you agree with Victor Medical Solutions's accounting policies for its scientific programs? What will be the impact on its financial statements, and how would you expect investors to react to the company's financial information?

★★ **A9-17 Costs Software Development** Innovative Incorporated has recently designed and developed its own payroll system for use in its own business. If there is a market the company may also decide to sell it to outside companies. Work on this project was completed over an 18-month period. The following costs were incurred in development of the software:

Conceptual design work	$ 3,200
Evaluation and decision on alternative options	4,100
Evaluation and consideration software requirements for options	9,500
Final selection of option	2,300
Software design work	50,000
Software coding	28,000
Testing of software	12,000
Data conversion costs information from old system	8,300
Staff training on new software	2,100
Allocation variable overhead costs	5,500
Allocation general and administrative costs	8,800
Ongoing software maintenance	4,500

Required:

1. Indicate how much would be accounted for as an intangible asset for software. Explain why a cost is included or not included.

2. Are software costs always classified as an intangible asset? Explain why or why not.

★★ **A9-18 Intangible Assets:** Cameras Limited is a new company whose only operation is the development of a new kind of video camera that will link to home computers and easily allow image transfer. The camera will come with a program to allow editing, so customers can edit their home movies and, for example, airbrush pictures and alter backgrounds. The camera and software are protected by several patents and copyrights, but technology in the area is moving quickly, and competition is fierce from competing products with different technology.

By the end of 20X6, a prototype existed and was being used to solicit orders. The product itself is due out in the second quarter of 20X7, in time for the Christmas season, which represents the vast majority of the annual camera-buying volume.

In 20X6, various costs were incurred: design costs ($675,800), engineering costs ($244,600), software development costs ($397,500), and market research costs ($68,900). Administration costs amounted to $670,000. Interest on bank loans was $62,500. Legal costs to register patents and copyrights amounted to $82,200. In addition, manufacturing equipment costing $450,000 was purchased and installed. It was used briefly to manufacture the prototype in the second quarter of 20X6, but is primarily idle and will continue to be idle until the first quarter of 20X7. At that time, production will begin in earnest.

Required:

Discuss classification of the various costs listed above. As part of your response, include a list of any additional information you would like to have.

★★ **A9-19 Website Development:** Worldwide Tours Corporation (WTC) established a new division in 20X8. The mandate of this new division is to establish a presence in the growing luxury eco-tourism travel business. This division will offer, through a sophisticated website, on-line quotes for travel packages to a variety of ecologically interesting locations. The website will include ratings of the various packages, including video clips of locations and interviews with local experts. WTC will underwrite various packages and place clients with other operators, earning a commission. Initial market research indicates that there is a demand for objective information about travel opportunities and increased purchasing over the Internet.

In 20X8, WTC incurred the following costs in relation to the operation:

Manager salaries (half planning)	$246,000
Rented space	52,000
Software purchased	90,200
Consultant's fees—graphics design	71,800
Computer equipment purchased; four-year life	64,800
Operating costs—heat, power, etc.	42,100
Travel and research costs re: travel packages	55,800
Preparation of content	63,100
Promotion of website to customers	81,300

The website is just recently up and running at the end of 20X8. The winter months of 20X9 will be the first real test of the viability of the service.

Required:

1. Provide recommendations as to how to account for the expenditures listed above. Be specific.

2. How would your answer above be different if the website was used only for advertising and promotion of the company?

★★

A9-20 Intangible Assets: Transactions during 20X5, the first year of the newly organized Nancy's Discount Foods Corporation, included the following:

2 Jan.   Paid $12,000 lawyer's fees and other related costs to register the name and trademark of the company in various jurisdictions.

31 Jan.   Paid $5,500 for television commercials advertising the grand opening. This advertising increased customers' awareness of the company name and location.

1 Feb.   Paid $7,300 to an image consultant to create a logo and distinctive packaging.

1 May   Acquired a patent from an existing patent holder for $20,200. The patent will not be used in the operations of the corporation but rather will be held as a long-term investment to produce royalty revenue.

1 Oct.   Obtained a licence from the city to conduct operations in a specific location. The licence, which cost $12,000, runs for one year and is renewable.

1 Nov.   Acquired another business and paid, after analysis, $35,000 cash for its goodwill. Recorded only the goodwill.

31 Dec.   Paid $10,000 in legal fees in an unsuccessful patent defence related to the patent acquired on 1 May, which, as a result of the lawsuit, now appears to be questionable in its revenue-generating capacity.

Required:
Give the journal entry that Nancy should make for each of the above transactions.

★

A9-21 Disposal of Capital Assets: Machinery that cost $96,000 on 1 January 20X1 was sold for $36,000 on 30 June 20X6. It was being depreciated over a 10-year life by the straight-line method, assuming its residual value would be $6,000.

A building that cost $850,000, residual value $50,000, was being depreciated over 20 years by the straight-line method. At the beginning of 20X6, when the structure was 15 years old, an additional wing was constructed at a cost of $250,000. The estimated life of the wing considered separately was 15 years, and its residual value was expected to be $10,000.

The accounting period ends 31 December.

Required:

1. Give all required entries to record:
   a. Sale of the equipment, including depreciation to the date of sale.

    b. The addition to the building: cash was paid.

    c. Depreciation on the building and its addition after the latter has been in use for one year.

2. Show how the building and attached wing would be reported on a balance sheet prepared immediately after entry 1(c) was recorded.

★★ **A9-22 Disposals:** Parry Incorporated recorded the following asset disposals during the year:

a. A computer system with an original cost of $23,800, 80% depreciated, was judged obsolete during the period and scrapped.

b. Automotive equipment, a large truck with an original cost of $50,800, 50% depreciated, was exchanged for a smaller truck. The smaller truck had a fair value of $25,000. The smaller truck will be used for the same general functions, but it is hoped that it will be more efficient and cost less money in gas. The larger used truck had a fair value of $23,000, and Parry paid $2,000 in the exchange.

c. Parry sold machinery with an original cost of $60,000 for $45,000 cash at the end of the year. It had held the machinery for three years. Originally, Parry had planned to hold the machinery for eight years, and charged straight-line depreciation, with an estimate of a $10,000 salvage value. At the beginning of the second year, Parry had spent $3,000 on routine maintenance of this machine, and another $5,000 to build a special base for it in the plant that improved its efficiency. The base is now worthless.

d. A trademark, with an amortized cost of $12,000, representing primarily unamortized legal fees, was sold for $75,500 cash.

e. Parry sold a piece of land with an original cost of $180,000 during the period. It accepted 20,000 common shares of the purchasing company, $30,000 in cash, and a five-year non-interest-bearing note that requires end-of-year payments of $50,000 per year for five years. The market interest rate is 7%. The purchaser's shares are widely traded in the stock market, and they have had a market value of about $2 per share in the last 12 months but have ranged from $1.10 to $5 in a volatile market. The land has been appraised a number of times over the years, with values ranging from $220,000 to $310,000.

Required:

1. Provide journal entries to record the disposal transactions listed above. Record the note receivable in (e) using the net method.

2. What would appear in the investing activities section of the SCF as a result of each of these transactions?

★ **A9-23 Goodwill:** Parent Corporation purchased all of the assets and liabilities of Sub Corporation for $800,000. The following assets and liabilities were purchased:

	Book Value	Fair Market Value
Accounts Receivables	$ 70,000	$ 70,000
Inventories	84,000	128,000
Capital assets (net)	410,000	520,000
Patents	0	138,000
Liabilities	(85,000)	(85,000)

Required:
What is the appropriate amount that would be recorded for goodwill, and what is the initial journal entry on acqusition?

★★ **A9-24 Goodwill Calculation:** During 20X4, the Evergreen Corporation entered into negotiations to buy Pine Company. During December 20X4, a final cash purchase price of $267,000 was agreed on. Evergreen will acquire all assets and liabilities of Pine Company, except for the existing cash balances of Pine.

The 31 December 20X4 balance sheet prepared by Pine Company is shown below in column (a), and the revised market values added later by Evergreen Corporation are shown in column (b).

PINE COMPANY BALANCE SHEET

At 31 December 20X4	(a) Book Values of Pine Co.	(b) Market Values of Evergreen Corp.
Assets		
Cash	$ 20,000	—
Accounts receivable (net)	58,000	$ 54,000
Inventory	160,000	90,000
Property, plant, and equipment (net)	309,000	285,000
Land	11,000	40,000
Franchise (unamortized balance)	19,000	21,000
Total	$577,000	
Liabilities and shareholders' equity		
Current liabilities	$ 37,000	37,000
Bonds payable	200,000	200,000
Shareholders' equity	340,000	—
Total	$577,000	

Required:

1. Compute the amount of goodwill purchased by Evergreen Corporation.
2. Give the entry for Evergreen Corporation to record the purchase of Pine Company.

★ **A9-25 Investment Property (Appendix)** Real Estate Company (REC) has a large number of apartment buildings that it holds for rent. In addition, it is holding land for capital appreciation. REC will either sell the land if the price is right or use it to build additional rental property. This land has a fair value of $10,000 at the beginning of 20X8. During the year, further acquisitions were made of land totalling $110,000. REC disposed of an old apartment building with a carrying amount of $80,000, for $120,000. At the 20X8 year-end date, the land had increased by $220,000, and the apartment buildings had decreased by $40,000 due to a downturn in the real estate market.

Required:

1. What are the options available for recording the land and apartment buildings?
2. How would the changes be accounted for during the year?

★★ **A9-26 Investment Property (Appendix)** On 1 January 20X2, Rental Incorporated purchased an apartment building. Apartments in this area are high in demand, and a wait list exists for potential tenants. The following costs were incurred for the purchase: cash $8,000,000; legal fees $1,200,000; upgrades to landscaping $80,000, and fresh painting of the lobby $55,000. The fire code also required the installation of a new sprinkler system for $120,000. On 31 December 20X3, the fair value of the apartment building was estimated to be $10 million and in 20X4 $11.5 million. In 20X5, a decision was made to add a new wing on excess land that allowed additional apartment units. The cost of this expansion was $5,000,000. On December 31, 20X5 the fair value of the apartment building was estimated to be $18 million. The building has a security system, and an apartment manager provides routine maintenance.

Required:

1. What are the options available for recording the land and apartment buildings?
2. Assuming the fair value model is selected, provide the journal entries for 20X2, 20X3, 20X4, and 20X5.

★★   **A9-27 Government Assistance (Appendix):** On 1 July 20X4, Theriout Corporation

acquired a manufacturing plant in Cape Breton for $1,750,000. The plant, employing 50 workers, began operation immediately and is expected to be in operation for 16 years with no residual value. In connection with the purchase, the following government assistance was received:

a. Theriout received a loan from the provincial government to help buy the capital assets, in the amount of $1,200,000. The loan need not be repaid as long as the plant operates for at least 10 years and employs an average of 25 people each year. Theriout is optimistic about the prospects for the plant but is mindful of the high rate of business failure in Cape Breton.

b. Theriout received a subsidy for salary costs of $1,000,000 for the next two years as long as it meets the criteria in requirement (a) of hiring an average of 25 people per year.

Required:

1. Provide the entry to record the loan to purchase capital assets and the salary subsidy. Explain your choice of entry.

2. How much net depreciation expense on the manufacturing plant would be recorded in the year ended 31 December 20X4? Provide calculations.

★★   **A9-28 Government Assistance (Appendix):** The Gysbers Company Limited has

embarked on a two-year pollution-control program that will require the purchase of two smokestack scrubbers costing a total of $600,000. One scrubber will be bought in 20X5 and one in 20X6. These scrubbers qualify for an investment tax credit of 20%. In addition, the federal government will lend Gysbers $100,000 for each scrubber installed. Provided that emissions are reduced 95% by the end of 20X8, the loans will be forgiven. The federal funds are received as the expenditures are made. If the emission standards are not met, the loan will have to be repaid. In 20X5, it was impossible to predict the success that the company would have with the scrubbers.

Gysbers will depreciate the devices over 20 years, straight-line (no residual value), and will take a full year's depreciation in the year installed. The purchase and installation schedule is as follows:

		Cost
January 20X5	Scrubber 1	$300,000
January 20X6	Scrubber 2	300,000
Total		$600,000

Required:

1. Prepare journal entries to record the purchase of Scrubber 1 and Scrubber 2, and the receipt of the federal loans.

2. Prepare journal entries to record depreciation and amortization for the year ending 31 December 20X6.

3. Assume that after testing in early 20X9, it is found that the emissions have been reduced only 85%. After negotiations, it was agreed that 45% of the loans will be repaid to the government in February 20X9. The balance of the loan will be forgiven. Prepare the journal entries to record the repayment and reclassification in 20X9.

★   **A9-29 Self-Constructed Asset (ASPE):** Lucas Incorporated had recently completed construction of a new manufacturing facility. Prior to the approval of the building permits the company operated a parking lot on the land. This parking lot had revenues net of costs of $65,000. Construction will take place over an 18-month period. Total construction costs were as follows:

Material	$320,000
Labour	550,000
Incremental overhead	120,000
General overhead	50,000
Interest costs on general loan	100,000
Cost permits	20,000

Required:
Provide the total amount of construction costs that would be capitalized to the cost of the building using ASPE.

★ **A9-30 Expenditure Classification (ASPE):** Refer to the facts in A9-7.

Required:
For each of the above items, using ASPE, give the name of the account to which the expenditure should be charged; that is, what account should be debited? Be specific.

CHAPTER 10

Depreciation, Amortization, and Impairment

INTRODUCTION

Armtec Infrastructure Inc. is a company in the construction and infrastructure business operating in Canada. During 2011, it recognized an impairment loss on goodwill of $139.8 million, bringing the balance for its goodwill account to zero. In addition, impairment losses were recognized on property, plant, and equipment and intangibles, bringing the total impairment loss to $268.5 million. The goodwill was written off to reflect a significant decline in the price of the common shares.

Management chooses depreciation and amortization methods. As well, management assesses the future economic benefit of long-lived assets and goodwill and decides whether the assets should be written down as *impaired*. The primary emphasis in this chapter is on the *judgement* issues in post-acquisition capital asset accounting. Management's many estimates and choices must be viewed in the context of financial reporting objectives as well as the more theoretical factors that influence choice.

There also are occasions when assets of a company may be written *up*. Previously written down property, plant, and equipment; certain intangibles assets; and held-for-sale assets can be restored to their pre-writedown value in subsequent periods. The flexibility to write assets down and up, as long as reasonably justifiable at the time, gives managers flexibility in their quest to "manage earnings."

Finally, there are times when the assets of a company can be completely revalued, thereby establishing a new basis of accounting for those assets. The revaluation model is discussed in Appendix 2 to this chapter rather than in the main body of the chapter, since the cost model is the predominant model in practice.

REVIEW OF DEFINITIONS—DEPRECIATION AND AMORTIZATION

A review of terminology is probably the best place to start. *Long-lived assets*, both tangible and intangible, produce revenue through use rather than through resale. They can be viewed as quantities of *economic service potential* to be consumed over time in the earning of revenues.

Accounting principles call for recognizing an expense when the future economic benefit of an asset declines. As most assets are used, their future benefit declines. Depreciation and amortization are an attempt to recognize the declining future benefit on a systematic and rational basis. Depreciation and amortization are not intended to mimic the decline in market value of an asset—only its declining future benefit. Alternatively, depreciation and amortization can be viewed as *matching* the costs of long-lived assets against revenue over their useful lives. The basic definitions are as follows:

- **Depreciation** is the periodic allocation of the cost of a tangible asset over its useful life.
- **Amortization** is the periodic allocation of the cost of an intangible asset over its useful life.
- **Depletion** may be used to describe depreciation of the costs of acquiring and developing natural resources.
- **Residual value** is the estimated net recoverable amount from disposal or trade-in of the asset at the end of its estimated *useful* life. It is the portion of an asset's acquisition cost that is not consumed through use.
- **Depreciable amount** is total capitalized asset cost *minus* estimated residual value—the total amount of depreciation or amortization to be recognized over the useful life of the asset.
- **Net book value** (carrying value) is an asset's original cost *plus* any capitalized post-acquisition costs *minus* accumulated depreciation or amortization to date and *net* any accumulated impairment losses or reversals.
- **Impairment** arises when the fair value of an asset is less than its carrying value.

NATURE OF DEPRECIATION AND AMORTIZATION

Depreciation is the term that applies to the interperiod allocation of the cost of a tangible asset. *Amortization* is the term that applies to intangible assets. What do these terms *not* represent? There are many misconceptions:

- Accumulated depreciation or amortization does not represent cash set aside for replacement of assets.
- Depreciation or amortization does not imply the creation of a separate cash fund for asset replacement.
- Depreciation or amortization does not measure the decline in market value during the period.

In everyday conversation, people often use "depreciation" to describe a decline in market value—for example, "A new car will depreciate by 25% as soon as you drive it off the dealer's lot." The accounting meaning of the term "depreciate" is quite different. Financial statements generally present the cost of tangible or intangible assets, not market value. However, as we have discussed in Chapter 9, the option of fair value does exist with the revaluation and fair value model. The focus of this chapter will be the cost model.

The Conceptual Basis of Depreciation or Amortization

The amount of depreciation or amortization recognized is not linked to the decline in an asset's utility or market value in a given period. However, the *inevitable eventual* decline in value justifies periodic recognition of depreciation or amortization. The decline in utility of long-lived assets is caused by:

- Physical factors, mainly usage (wear and tear from operations, action of time and the elements, and deterioration and decay); and

- Obsolescence (the result of new technology).

Assets rendered obsolete are often in good condition and still capable of supplying the service originally expected of them. However, technological advances may have rendered their operating costs uneconomic. Obsolescence also occurs when facility expansion renders certain assets unusable under new operating conditions or when demand for the product or service supplied by the asset declines.

Technological change does not automatically mean that older equipment is obsolete, however. If the older equipment meets the *present needs* of the company, obsolescence is not a factor. For example, in the computer industry, new computer chips substantially increase computer speeds and capabilities. For many companies, continual upgrades to state-of-the art hardware are not cost effective. Older computers will still run required software, and they are not obsolete. Of course, software upgrades sometimes require hardware upgrades as well, and this is the point at which obsolescence becomes a factor.

The Requirement to Recognize Depreciation or Amortization Expense

Generally, long-lived assets must be depreciated or amortized. Why?

- Depreciation or amortization is an allocation of capital cost. Operations must bear this cost as a cost of assets used during the period. The general requirement for depreciation or amortization is based on the declining future benefit of a long-lived asset. Recognizing this decline in the asset's future usefulness will match the costs of providing services to the revenue generated.
- Depreciation or amortization is justifiable based on an *eventual* decline in market value, often caused by obsolescence.

Long-lived Assets Not Depreciated or Amortized

There are six asset categories that do not have to be depreciated or amortized:

1. Land Land is not at risk due to obsolescence, nor does it suffer from wear and tear. Therefore, land is not depreciated. We hope you find this intuitively appealing! Of course, if the land is a mining site, then the situation is far different, and depletion would be recorded. Or if the land value has been increased due to decommissioning or site restoration costs, then only the additional value added to the land is depreciated, not the initial land value.

2. Investment Property When the fair value method is chosen to measure investment property, the property is adjusted to fair value every reporting date and not depreciated. Any changes in value are automatically accounted for, since they are reported in the income statement each period. The fair value method discussed in the appendix to Chapter 9 is very common in the real estate industry, since these businesses would normally have rental properties.

3. Held-for-Sale Capital Assets If an asset meets the criteria to be classified as a held-for-sale capital asset as discussed in Chapter 3, it is not being used in the business and therefore does not suffer from wear and tear. Therefore, these assets are not depreciated but are tested for impairment at each reporting date.

4. Biological Assets If an asset meets the definition of a biological asset, as discussed in Chapter 6, it has unique accounting in the standard for agriculture. Many biological assets mature over time rather than decline in value.

5. Intangible Capital Assets with an Indefinite Life If an asset will continue to provide service over the foreseeable future without its future benefit being reduced, it has **indefinite life**. Intangible assets with an indefinite useful life should not be amortized.

For example, a trademark can legally and effectively be protected forever. If the product associated with the trademark has indefinite sales potential, the trademark would not be amortized. At some point, the situation might change, and the asset may decline in value, but the value of the trademark does not decline with use. Indeed, in an economic sense, a trademark can increase in value the more it is used, as it becomes better known and trusted by customers.

"Indefinite" does not mean "infinite," however. Trademarks sometimes become outdated and must be updated or replaced. CBC and Air Canada have both updated or replaced their trademark designs in recent years. The old designs may have no more useful economic life, at which point they must be written down. Some companies amortize the costs of acquiring or designing a trademark, even though the trademark has an endless legal life because the company recognizes that the trademark may lose its effectiveness over time.

Useful lives have to be reviewed annually, and if the useful life becomes limited, amortization of these assets must commence. Intangible assets that are not amortized must be reviewed for impairment on an annual basis.

6. Goodwill   The useful life of goodwill is assumed to be indefinite. Goodwill is not amortized but is subject to an annual review for impairment. We will discuss the goodwill impairment test later in this chapter.

CONCEPT REVIEW

1. What are the main causes of the decline in value or usefulness of property, plant, and equipment over time?

2. Why is depreciation or amortization expense not necessarily an accurate measure of the decline in value of long-lived assets?

3. Which assets are not amortized? Why?

COMPONENT DEPRECIATION ACCOUNTING

In Chapter 9, we introduced the concept of component accounting. This is the separation of an asset into separate parts that are significant. Now we will discuss **component depreciation accounting**. Each significant part is depreciated. Remember, the critical word here is "significant"! In our Air Canada example in Chapter 9, in its significant accounting policy, note that the company identifies the following components for its aircraft: airframe, engine, cabin interior equipment and modifications, spare engine and related parts "rotables," and major maintenance. Note that some of these components are physical (e.g., spare parts) and others are nonphysical (e.g., overhaul of engine). Each of those components would be depreciated separately. In practice, this will create a lot of work to identify major components and then on an ongoing basis to keep track of depreciation, revisions in estimates, cost of replacements, and on and on.

Separation into components requires significant professional judgement. Parts that would have a similar useful life and depreciation method can be grouped together. The remainder of insignificant parts would be grouped together and depreciated. An entity would have the choice of depreciating any part separately if it chose to, even if it was not significant.

Separation into components should be accomplished when the asset is first acquired, even though not all events are known at purchase. If a major part is replaced or an unanticipated overhaul is required, the cost of the major part or overhaul can be used to estimate what the original amount would be in the asset. This amount would then be derecognized when the major part was replaced or overhaul completed.

Why is all this extra work necessary? When an asset is viewed as a whole, it does not reflect the pattern of consumption since some parts or components will be used up faster than others. The effect of this is lower depreciation than if the asset was viewed as components.

Exhibit 10-1 illustrates component depreciation of an asset assuming an asset would have four major significant components.

EXHIBIT 10-1

DATA FOR COMPONENT DEPRECIATION OF ASSET

Component	Quantity	Original Unit Cost	Residual Value	Useful Life	Annual SL Depreciation
A	10	$50,000	$5,000	15 years	$3,000
B	4	20,000	4,000	10 years	1,600
C	6	7,000	600	8 years	800
D	20	3,000	0	3 years	1,000

Total annual depreciation: 10($3,000) + 4($1,600) + 6($800) + 20($1,000) = $61,200

Total asset acquisition cost: 10($50,000) + 4($20,000) + 6($7,000) + 20($3,000) = $682,000

Total depreciable cost: $682,000 − 10($5,000) − 4($4,000) − 6($600) = $612,400

CONCEPT REVIEW

1. Why is an item of property, plant, and equipment segregated into components for depreciation?

2. How are the components determined?

3. What is done with the insignificant parts that are not treated as a separate component?

ACCOUNTING POLICY CHOICE

The only general requirement for a depreciation or amortization method is that it should be *rational and systematic*; most importantly, it needs to reflect the pattern of consumption of future economic benefits. The choices are:

1. *Based on equal allocation to each time period*—the straight-line (SL) method. This is used when the loss of service potential is largely a function of time, or when the utilization of the asset is expected to be fairly constant over its useful life. Straight line also is generally used as a "default" method; if the company is not sure about what the usage pattern or future benefit decline will be, SL is the simplest method to use. For limited-life intangible assets, when the pattern of economic benefits cannot be reliably determined, an SL amortization method normally is used. This is the most common method in practice.

2. *Based on inputs and outputs* (variable charge)—

   a. Service-hours (SH) method; or

   b. Productive-output (PO), or units-of-production, method.

   These methods are used when there is a physical capacity constraint; the more intensely the asset is used, the faster its future benefit declines. It also is used when the asset's utilization is apt to vary significantly from period to period and its utilization can be measured reliably, such as for equipment used in mining operations.

3. *Accelerated methods* (decreasing charge)—the diminishing-balance (DB) method or often referred to as declining balance method. This is used particularly for assets that are

subject to rapid obsolescence, such as computer equipment and software, or for assets that will see heavy use in the earlier years and declining use as they get older.

Conceptual Analysis

In theory, at least, the depreciation or amortization method should describe the pattern of consumption of future economic benefits—nature and use of the asset. For example, assume that a delivery truck has an estimated useful life of five years or 300,000 kilometres. Depreciation based on distance driven might yield a more accurate matching of expense and revenue than depreciation based on useful life in years. Based on this reasoning, the methods based on usage appear to be the most logical unless obsolescence is a major factor, in which case straight line is appealing.

However, GAAP allows choice with few guidelines: All methods are rational and systematic, and an evaluation of the nature of use of an asset can be subjective. Why aren't depreciation methods narrowed down? The reason is that there is a lack of one "correct method," really. The amount of revenue or cash produced by the use of one specific capital asset is usually impossible to determine clearly. Revenues are not generated by assets used in isolation. Rather, they are produced by a number of assets and people working together. It is impossible to associate specific revenues (benefits) to specific assets and, thus, impossible to allocate the cost of most operational assets on the basis of benefits or revenues.

As an allocation, depreciation is *incorrigible*—it cannot be supported or refuted without question. If you cannot establish one right way, then all rational and systematic methods are equally acceptable. Companies tend to let corporate reporting objectives, rather than pattern of use, dictate policy choice. This makes comparisons difficult.

Factors Influencing Choice

How do companies pick an accounting depreciation or amortization policy? Here is a summary of factors considered:

- *Nature and use of asset.* To promote matching, the pattern of consumption of future benefits is evaluated to establish the most logical depreciation or amortization pattern. The pattern of usage is often a good indicator of the pattern of consumption of future benefits or pattern of revenue generated.

- *Corporate reporting objectives.* On a situation-by-situation basis, it is important to analyze the various elements that drive reporting objectives. Is there a bonus based on net income? Is the entity regulated? Is it held under restrictive loan covenants governing debt-to-equity ratios, profitability, and so on? These factors have a powerful impact on the accounting policies chosen.

- *Industry norms.* Comparability is an important qualitative characteristic of financial reporting. Companies' financial statements are used by investors, creditors, and others to assess their performance relative to their competition. Using the same depreciation method helps. Depreciation methods, such as units of production for natural resources, become generally accepted within an industry.

- *Parent company preferences.* Is the company a subsidiary of another company (the parent)? If so, its financial statements will be combined, or *consolidated*, at the end of the fiscal year. These consolidated financial statements are more meaningful if all constituents follow the same accounting policies, and thus the parent company often dictates key policies to its subsidiaries. A lot of Canadian companies are wholly owned subsidiaries of foreign parents (usually American). Those subsidiaries usually do what their parents tell them, which may include accounting methods not widely used by Canadian-owned enterprises. (Of course, like all children, the subsidiaries sometimes disobey their parents.)

- *Simplified reporting.* Many smaller firms do not really care what amount of depreciation is booked but are interested in keeping their financial statements simple. Therefore, it seems logical to use an accounting policy that results in depreciation that coincides with the required tax treatment (which generally is a form of diminishing-balance method, as we will see in Appendix 1 to this chapter).

- *Accounting information system costs.* The company must keep detailed information about acquisition costs, post-acquisition costs, useful life, residual value, and accumulated depreciation. Which system is the least complex?

The latitude in selection of depreciation methods and the variety of estimates of useful life and residual value are at odds with the uniformity and consistency objectives of financial reporting. The large dollar amount of depreciation expense reported, combined with the inherently arbitrary nature of depreciation, results in a potentially difficult comparison problem for financial statement users.

Estimates Required

Depreciation or amortization methods require that the preparer make the following estimates:

1. Acquisition cost;

2. Useful life; and

3. Residual value.

Component accounting for property, plant, and equipment will require these estimates for each major component or part—not for the asset as a whole.

Acquisition Cost At first glance, acquisition cost may appear to be a solid amount, not an estimate. In some cases, the cost of an asset is readily determinable. However, acquisition cost often is a bit of an approximation even for tangible assets because ancillary acquisition costs, such as excise taxes, shipping costs, and installation costs, either are estimated or ignored. Thus, the measurement of "historical cost" is governed by various policies concerning capitalization (versus expensing), as we discussed in the previous chapter.

Useful Life An estimate of useful life for items of property, plant, and equipment requires assumptions about potential obsolescence, intensity of use, and adequate maintenance. The useful life of the asset is often shorter than its economic life due to a management practice of replacing assets after a specified time frame. What is important is the consumption of future benefits, which considers many factors. For example, an asset may not be used during a strike, so it is idle but may still have a consumption of future benefits through normal wear and tear. It is especially difficult to estimate the useful life of an intangible asset. Often, the real question is how long the intangible asset will be used or can generate revenue.

It is important to take a hard look at many factors for long-lived assets:

1. The expected use of the asset;

2. The legal life of an intangible asset (Exhibit 10-2) plus any renewal provisions;

3. The effects of economic factors, along with demand and competition;

4. Potential obsolescence;

5. The level of maintenance expenditures required (high maintenance implies an end to useful life);

6. The expected use of another asset or process that is related to the intangible asset (e.g., a patent for a process versus the machinery that runs the process); and

7. The asset management policy of the company. For example, it may have a corporate policy of disposing of an asset after a specific period of time.

The estimate of useful life must be reviewed at every reporting date. Estimates of useful life do change with new information and experience from the use of that asset. For example, a new technology could be introduced that changed the expected use of the asset. Because expectations have now changed, it would be treated as a change in an estimate and adjusted prospectively.

EXHIBIT 10-2

LEGAL LIFE OF CERTAIN INTANGIBLE ASSETS

Patent	20 years from date granted; but registration period is also covered
Industrial design	Five years; renewable for a further five years' registration
Trademark	15 years; renewable for infinite successive periods
Franchise	Unlimited unless specified in contract with franchisor
Copyright	Life of the author plus 50 years

Residual Value To estimate residual value, consideration is given to the costs of dismantling, restoring, and disposing of the retired asset. Future removal and site restoration costs also reduce residual value and can be material. These include all costs to dismantle and restore a property. These costs are particularly important for natural resources. For example, if the estimated realizable value upon retirement of an asset is $2,500 and estimated dismantling and selling costs are $500, the net residual value is $2,000.

This estimate is reviewed every reporting date based on current prices. In practice, the residual value for a tangible asset is often assumed to be zero. This is logical when an asset will be held almost until the end of its physical life and removal cost is low. An *intangible* asset usually has a residual value of zero. There would have to be an established market for similar intangible assets, or a specific sale agreement, to justify a residual value higher than zero. Over time, the residual value may increase (e.g., with inflation) so that eventually it may exceed the carrying amount. If the residual value is above the carrying amount, depreciation would then be zero.

Depreciation or Amortization Period

Depreciation or amortization does not start, is not recognized (i.e., useful life does not begin) until the asset is in its intended condition and location and is available for use. This is the same point at which you would stop capitalizing initial costs to the asset. When facilities are temporarily idle, straight line and accelerated methods continue because these methods are based on the passage of time, not use. Items of property, plant, and equipment may become temporarily idle or retired from use for a period of time (e.g., strike) when manufacturing facility and equipment are not being used. In that case, depreciation does not stop unless the asset has already been fully depreciated. Continued recognition of depreciation reflects increasing obsolescence and reduced future economic usefulness of the asset. As discussed below, some methods are based on the number of units produced. These methods would have no depreciation in a period of inactivity. Of course, the asset could still be impaired.

Depreciation or amortization stops in one of two situations. Either the long-lived asset is derecognized (e.g., sold) or classified as held-for-sale assets. When a company permanently stops using a capital asset, the asset is reclassified as **held-for-sale** and depreciation stops. If the asset's fair value is less than its carrying value, the asset is written down to its fair value and the loss is recognized in income. The accounting for held-for-sale capital assets is discussed in Chapter 3.

Assets should not be depreciated or amortized below residual value under any method or system. Although declining-balance methods do not use residual value in calculating periodic depreciation expense, a determination should be made at the end of each accounting period to ensure that book value is higher than residual value. Where the residual value of individual assets is relatively small, however, this test often is not performed and the assets are depreciated to zero.

Spare Parts Major spare parts are a separate component and depreciated separately. Often, spare parts are bought in advance of when they are used in an asset so that they are available when a machine or other asset breaks down. Depreciation of these parts would not begin until they are replaced in the asset and being used.

Standby Equipment A unique type of equipment is standby equipment that is ready for use as a backup and is rarely used in many cases. These items would start to be depreciated when they are ready for use. The expected pattern of consumption may be difficult to determine because it may be linked to the piece of equipment it is acting as standby or backup for, which has a definite life.

CONCEPT REVIEW

1. What is the most popular method of depreciation or amortization in Canada?
2. Name three factors that influence management's choice of depreciation or amortization policy.
3. What estimates must be made before a capital asset can be depreciated or amortized?

DEPRECIATION AND AMORTIZATION METHODS

Exhibit 10-3 summarizes the depreciation or amortization formulas for four depreciation or amortization methods. Each of the four depreciation or amortization methods will be illustrated in the following sections, using the data shown in Exhibit 10-4. Exhibit 10-5 shows depreciation or amortization schedules for the four methods.

Remember, terminology differs in practice between items of property, plant, and equipment, which are depreciated, and intangible assets, which are amortized. The SL method is the common method used for intangible assets, while all methods are used for tangible assets.

Straight-Line Method

The **straight-line (SL) method** is based on the assumption that an asset provides equivalent service, or value in use, each year of its life. The SL method relates depreciation or amortization directly to the passage of time rather than to the asset's use, resulting in a constant amount of depreciation or amortization recognized per time period. The formula for computing periodic SL amortization, with its application to the asset in Exhibit 10-4, is:

Yearly SL depreciation or amortization

= (Acquisition cost − Residual value) ÷ Estimated useful life in years

= ($6,600 − $600) ÷ 5

= $1,200 per year

The SL method is logically appealing. It is especially appropriate for a tangible asset when the use of the asset is essentially the same each period, and repairs and maintenance expenditures are constant over the useful life. The method is less appropriate for assets whose decline in service potential or benefits produced relates not to the passage of time but rather to other variables, such as units produced or hours in service. The SL method is common for buildings.

EXHIBIT 10-3

DEPRECIATION OR AMORTIZATION FORMULAS

Straight-line (SL) method:
Annual SL depreciation or amortization = (Acquisition cost − Residual value)
÷ Estimated useful life in years

Service-hours (SH) method:
Depreciation rate per service hour = (Acquisition cost − Residual value)
÷ Estimated service life in hours

Annual service-hour depreciation = Depreciation rate per service hour
× Hours of usage

Productive-output (PO) method:
Depreciation rate per unit of output = (Acquisition cost − Residual value)
÷ Estimated productive output in units

Annual productive-output depreciation = Depreciation rate per unit of output
× Units produced

Declining-balance (DB) method:
Annual DB depreciation = (Acquisition cost − Accumulated depreciation)
× DB rate

EXHIBIT 10-4

DATA USED TO ILLUSTRATE DEPRECIATION OR AMORTIZATION METHODS

Acquisition cost, 1 January 20X1 $ 6,600
Residual value   600
Estimated useful life:
  Years   5
  Service hours   20,000
  Productive output in units   10,000

Activity	Service Hours	Units Produced
20X1	3,800	1,800
20X2	4,000	2,000
20X3	4,500	2,400
20X4	4,200	1,800
20X5	3,500	2,000
	20,000	10,000

The SL method is the most popular method, by far. Ease of use partially explains the method's popularity. It is also popular because it provides a stable, smooth depreciation or amortization pattern. A relatively low amount is expensed in the asset's first year, which is popular with firms that want to maximize earnings and net assets in the short run.

For intangible assets, SL amortization must be used if the pattern of economic benefits cannot be determined.

EXHIBIT 10-5

DEPRECIATION OR AMORTIZATION SCHEDULES—FOUR METHODS

Straight-Line Method

Year	Amortization/ Depreciation Expense	Accumulated Depreciation/ Amortization	Cost	Net Book Value
1 January 20X1			$6,600	$6,600
31 December 20X1	$1,200	$1,200	6,600	5,400
31 December 20X2	1,200	2,400	6,600	4,200
31 December 20X3	1,200	3,600	6,600	3,000
31 December 20X4	1,200	4,800	6,600	1,800
31 December 20X5	1,200	6,000	6,600	600 (residual)
Total	$6,000			

Service-Hours Method

Year	Service Hours	Depreciation Expense	Accumulated Depreciation	Cost	Net Book Value
1 January 20X1				$6,600	$6,600
31 December 20X1	3,800	(3,800 × $.30) = $1,140	$1,140	6,600	5,460
31 December 20X2	4,000	(4,000 × $.30) = 1,200	2,340	6,600	4,260
31 December 20X3	4,500	(4,500 × $.30) = 1,350	3,690	6,600	2,910
31 December 20X4	4,200	(4,200 × $.30) = 1,260	4,950	6,600	1,650
31 December 20X5	3,500	(3,500 × $.30) = 1,050	6,000	6,600	600 (residual)
Total	20,000	$6,000			

Productive-Output Method

Year	Units Produced	Depreciation Expense	Accumulated Depreciation	Cost	Net Book Value
1 January 20X1				$6,600	$6,600
31 December 20X1	1,800	(1,800 × $.60) = $1,080	$1,080	6,600	5,520
31 December 20X2	2,000	(2,000 × $.60) = 1,200	2,280	6,600	4,320
31 December 20X3	2,400	(2,400 × $.60) = 1,440	3,720	6,600	2,880
31 December 20X4	1,800	(1,800 × $.60) = 1,080	4,800	6,600	1,800
31 December 20X5	2,000	(2,000 × $.60) = 1,200	6,000	6,600	600 (residual)
Total	10,000	$6,000			

Declining-Balance Method

Year	Depreciation Expense	Accumulated Depreciation	Cost	Net Book Value
1 January 20X1			$6,600	$6,600
31 December 20X1	(40% × $6,600) = $2,640	$2,640	6,600	3,960
31 December 20X2	(40% × $3,960) = 1,584	4,224	6,600	2,376
31 December 20X3	(40% × $2,376) = 950	5,174	6,600	1,426
31 December 20X4	(40% × $1,426) = 570	5,744	6,600	856
31 December 20X5	256*	6,000	6,600	600 (residual)
Total	$6,000			

*Should be 40% of $856, or $342, but limited to $256 so that net book value does not go below residual value.

Methods Based on Units of Service

Depreciation methods that associate periodic amortization with measurable use of long-lived assets include the SH method and PO method (also called the *units-of-production method*). These methods are rational and systematic and logically match expense and revenue if the asset's utility is measurable in terms of service time or units of output to reflect the pattern of consumption of the asset. These methods would be used for tangible assets.

These methods do not relate depreciation to the passage of time, as the other methods do. Depreciation expense under these methods is not recorded when assets are idle, and thus they are appropriate when production volumes vary greatly from period to period, provided that obsolescence is not as much of a factor in determining useful life as wear and tear. If obsolescence is an important factor, an asset's utility decreases whether used or not, and these methods will not portray this reality.

Service-Hours Method The **service-hours (SH) method** is based on the assumption that the appropriate depreciation is directly related to the amount of time the asset is in use.

Depreciation rate per service hour = (Acquisition cost − Residual value)
÷ Estimated service life in hours
= ($6,600 − $600) ÷ 20,000 = $0.30

Yearly SH depreciation, 20X1 = Depreciation rate per service hour
× Hours used
= $0.30 × 3,800 = $1,140

Exhibit 10-5 illustrates the service-hours method for the life of the asset.

Productive-Output method The **productive-output (PO) method** is similar except that the number of units of output is used to measure asset use. A constant amount of depreciable cost is allocated to each unit of output as a cost of production, so annual depreciation amounts fluctuate with changes in the volume of output:

Depreciation rate per unit of output = (Acquisition cost − Residual value)
÷ Estimated productive output in units
= ($6,600 − $600) ÷ 10,000 = $0.60

Yearly PO depreciation, 20X1 = Depreciation rate per unit of output
× Units produced
= $0.60 × 1,800 = $1,080

Exhibit 10-5 illustrates the PO method over the life of this asset.

The SH and PO methods can produce different results, depending on the ratio of machine-hours to units produced. For the asset under study, 2.11 machine-hours were required to produce one unit in 20X1 (3,800 ÷ 1,800), while in 20X2 that figure was reduced to 2.00 (4,000 ÷ 2,000), indicating a greater efficiency. The SH method, therefore, yielded slightly higher depreciation per unit of output in 20X1 than in 20X2. If the yield ratio is constant, the two methods would produce identical results and the firm would choose the one that is easier to implement.

The PO method is commonly used to measure depletion of natural resources. For example, assume that a company incurs costs of $4,000,000 to lease, explore, and develop a mine site that is expected to produce two million tonnes of coal. The land can be sold for $500,000 after mining is finished. The depletion per tonne is $1.75: ($4,000,000 − $500,000) ÷ 2,000,000. Annual depletion is based on the actual production level. For these companies, mining equipment and even buildings are often also depreciated on a units-of-production basis.

Estimates A significant difficulty in usage methods is an accurate estimate of total projected activity. Annual usage data are also needed to apply the method. Often, the extra cost of this data is not worth the effort. Remember, too, that if usage is relatively constant, the result will not be materially different from the SL method. Another problem arises when the running time of an asset varies without a corresponding effect in the output of service. For example, the increasingly heavy traffic in urban areas causes vehicles to run many more hours per week with no increase in their productive service.

Diminishing-Balance Method

A **diminishing-balance (DB) method** recognizes greater amounts of depreciation early in the useful life of tangible assets and lesser amounts later. A DB method is based on the assumption that newer assets produce more benefits per period because they are more productive and require less maintenance and repair. This method matches more of the acquisition cost against the revenue of these earlier periods when greater benefits are obtained. A smoother pattern of total annual operating expense is often the result because the sum of annual depreciation and maintenance expense is more constant than is likely with SL amortization. Remember, this method must still reflect the pattern of consumption of the future benefits of the asset. The one DB method that is in use in Canada is the declining-balance method.

Declining-Balance Method The declining-balance method is significantly different from other methods in two ways:

1. Residual value is not subtracted from cost when computing depreciation. It is still considered, but in a different way. Declining-balance depreciation stops when the net book value of the asset is equal to residual value.

2. The depreciation rate is applied to a declining (*net*) balance rather than to a constant cost.

How do companies arrive at a depreciation rate? A formula exists that can be used to find the rate that will reduce the book value of the asset to its estimated salvage value at the end of its estimated useful life, but the formula is never used in practice. Instead, firms may pick a fairly arbitrary rate, based on their assessment of useful life, on industry norms, or perhaps on corporate reporting objectives.

Another approach is to use the rates established by income tax regulations for capital cost allowance (CCA). CCA is mostly a declining-balance method but uses straight line for some types of assets. CCA does not work in exactly the same way as declining-balance amortization, but if the same rates are used (and a half-year's depreciation is charged in the year of acquisition), the tax and book depreciation are often identical, and deferred (future) income tax balances are minimized as a result. The CCA system is briefly described in Appendix 1 to this chapter. Tax-based rates often are used by private companies for simplicity. This practice would be acceptable only if those rates reflected the pattern of consumption of the asset's life.

Another approach to determining the rate is called **double-declining balance (DDB)** depreciation, which uses a rate equal to twice the SL rate. For example, the asset in Exhibit 10-3 has a 20% straight-line rate (the reciprocal of the years of life; 1/5 = 20%), and so the DDB rate would be 40%. This is a fairly aggressive depreciation rate—40% of the capital cost would be written off in the first year. If this capital asset is a piece of machinery, its CCA rate is set (in Class 8) at 20%. Depreciation rates, which must be disclosed, should be reviewed by financial statement users to see if they are aggressive or not and if they reflect the pattern of consumption of an asset's life.

For our example, assume that the firm has chosen a 40% DB rate.

Annual DB depreciation = (Acquisition cost − Accumulated depreciation) × DB rate

20X1 DB depreciation = $6,600 × 40% = $2,640

20X2 DB depreciation = ($6,600 − $2,640) × 40% = $1,584

See Exhibit 10-5 for the complete set of calculations. Note, in particular, the last line, where depreciation expense *stops* when accumulated depreciation equals the $6,000 depreciable cost, leaving the $600 residual value intact. Thus, the maximum depreciation for 20X5 is $256 ($6,000 − $5,744) rather than $342 (40% of $856).

CONCEPT REVIEW

1. When is a company most likely to use a usage-based depreciation method?
2. What is *double* about DDB depreciation?
3. Why might a company want to use a depreciation method that coincides with tax-basis CCA?

ADDITIONAL DEPRECIATION OR AMORTIZATION ISSUES

Additional depreciation or amortization issues include information required for component accounting, fractional-year depreciation or amortization, depreciation related to decommissioning costs (asset retirement obligations), and group depreciation.

Information Required for Component Depreciation Accounting

The requirement for component depreciation accounting requires that a company obtain specific information and track this information in its information system. When a new asset is required, its company will need to determine the following information:

- Identification of significant major parts or components
- For each significant major part or component
  - Acquisition cost
  - Residual value
  - Useful life
  - Depreciation method and period

Components are grouped together to determine depreciation when they have a similar useful life method of depreciation. The remaining parts that are not considered significant would be depreciated together. Since these remaining items may have very different useful lives or patterns of consumption, this may not be straightforward. The company may need to estimate using approximation techniques, a method that would provide faithful representation of the consumption pattern.

Fractional-Year Depreciation or Amortization

The calculations illustrated in Exhibit 10-5 assume that the company takes a full year of depreciation or amortization in the year that the asset was acquired. This seems logical in the specific example because the asset was assumed to have been purchased on 1 January. However, most long-lived assets are not placed in service at the beginning of a reporting period, nor do disposals occur neatly at the end of a year. Firms adjust for fractional periods in two different ways. Some compute the exact amount of depreciation or amortization for each fractional period, and others apply an accounting policy **convention**. A *convention* is a standardized shortcut.

Exact Calculation Approach This approach computes the "precise" amount of depreciation or amortization for each fractional period. For example, assume that an asset costing $20,000 with a residual value of $2,000 and useful life of four years is placed into service on 11 April 20X1. The firm has a calendar-year reporting cycle. The asset in question is used only 265/365 of a year in 20X1. Under SL depreciation or amortization, the asset's fractional service period is applied to the annual depreciation or amortization amount, as illustrated:

Depreciation or amortization expense for 20X1 = ($20,000 – $2,000) × (1/4)
$$\times (265/365)$$
$$= \$3,267$$

Depreciation or amortization expense for 20X2 through 20X4
$$= (\$20,000 - \$2,000) \times (1/4)$$
$$= \$4,500 \text{ per year}$$

Depreciation or amortization expense for 20X5 = ($20,000 – $2,000) × (1/4)
$$\times (100/365)$$
$$= \$1,233$$

The SH and PO methods automatically adjust for fractions of a year. The number of hours used or units produced in the partial-year period is applied to the depreciation rate in the normal manner.

Recognized depreciation expense.
  20X1 depreciation = $ 20,000 × 40% × 265/365 = $ 5,808
  20X2 depreciation = ($ 20,000 – $5,808) × .40 = $ 5,677, etc.

Using declining balance, the rate for the first year is simply the assumed annual rate times the fraction of the year during which the asset was owned. For an annual depreciation rate of 40%, the first year's depreciation will be 40% × 265/365 = 29%. For the following years, the rate will be the normal 40% applied to the asset's net book value at the beginning of each year.

The word "exact" should not be interpreted too literally. The "exact" approach usually means that amortization or depreciation is calculated only to the nearest month. Seldom will a company try to figure out amortization or depreciation to the exact day—what would be the benefit? Amortization or depreciation involves selecting one from among many possible policies and applying it to amounts that are estimates. There is nothing less "precise" in accounting than depreciation or amortization, and therefore it makes no sense at all to try to be highly precise about a highly arbitrary number!

Accounting Policy Convention Approach To avoid tedious fractional-year depreciation or amortization, many firms adopt a policy convention. Conceptually, these conventions may not be ideal but consider the cost benefit tradeoff. And at the end of the day, the difference between an exact calculation and one of the conventions below must be immaterial.

Examples of conventions in current use are:

1. *Half-year convention.* Under this approach, a half-year's depreciation or amortization is charged on all assets acquired or disposed of during the year. The implicit assumption is that assets are acquired throughout the year and as a result are, on average, acquired in the middle of the year.

   Annual amortization or depreciation expense is the amortization or depreciation rate multiplied by the simple average of the beginning and ending balances of the asset accounts. Given that depreciation or amortization is an approximation at best, this assumption is as good as any. This method also has the added convenience that it coincides with the convention used for income tax purposes in the year of acquisition.

2. *Full-first-year convention.* A full year's depreciation or amortization is charged to all assets that exist at the end of the year, including those acquired throughout the year. No depreciation or amortization is taken on assets disposed of during the year. This is particularly

popular in group depreciation or amortization methods, which generally are based on the asset account balance at the end of the year. Due to the need to split assets into major components, group depreciation as discussed below will not be common in practice.

This method bases depreciation or amortization expense on the ending balances. It is easily calculated without reference to transactions during the period. Since there is no amortization or depreciation in the year of an asset's disposal, last-year fractional amortization or depreciation can be completely ignored.

3. *Final-year convention.* Annual depreciation or amortization is determined solely on the basis of the balance in the capital asset accounts at the *beginning* of the period. Assets disposed of during a period are depreciated or amortized for a full period, and assets purchased during a period are not depreciated or amortized that period. The underlying assumption is that assets are seldom fully productive when they are first put into service.

In this method, depreciation or amortization expense is based solely on the *opening* balances in the asset accounts. This permits rapid calculation of adjusting entries at the end of the period. When pro-forma budgeted financial statements are prepared, the amount of depreciation or amortization is known with assurance, thereby avoiding unexpected (and uncontrollable) increases in overhead costs charged to operating divisions or departments.

When a company has high capital expenditures and increasing asset bases, this method tends to lower the amount of depreciation or amortization taken each period, thereby enhancing net income.

When a company reports on an interim basis, such as quarterly, these conventions may be applied to the *quarter* instead of to the *year*. For example, the half-year convention becomes the *half-quarter* convention—one half-quarter's depreciation or amortization is taken on all assets acquired or disposed of during the quarter.

Regardless of the convention chosen, the same policy should be used consistently.

Depreciation Related to Decommissioning Costs (Asset Retirement Obligations)

Land is not at risk due to obsolescence nor does it suffer from wear and tear. Therefore, land is not depreciated. With decommissioning costs related to land, the amount of the obligation is added to the value of the land. This is often referred to as a bump-up to the related asset. The initial land value is not depreciated, but the additional value added to the land for the obligation is depreciated. Depreciation would occur over the period of benefit from the costs of the obligation.

Group Depreciation

Unique features of certain tangible assets, as well as practical considerations, may cause firms to modify the application of standard amortization methods. We call these adaptations "amortization systems" because amortization is calculated on a *group* of assets rather than on individual assets, thereby dramatically reducing accounting costs. Physical control of individual assets still must be maintained, but detailed accounting records are maintained only for each group as a whole. This group method is appropriate only when the assets are small, have no significant components, and have a short useful life. A good example of this type of asset would be tools, dyes, and patterns that would have very short useful lives. The approach used for these homogeneous assets is called **group depreciation**.

Group accounts work on the principle of averaging. When assets are accounted for individually, the estimated useful life for each asset is almost certain to be incorrect. For a group of assets as a whole, however, the law of averages can be applied. As long as the estimates are correct *on average*, the depreciation will be correct.

An advantage of a group system is that no gains or losses are recorded on the routine disposals of assets. Gains and losses on the disposal of individual assets really are the result of estimation errors in determining depreciation. Group methods, in contrast, offset the gains and losses within the asset group account, thereby eliminating any possibility of earnings manipulation through management's adroit timing of asset disposals.

Group systems are not only theoretically sound but also much easier for accounting purposes. When a company is accounting for many similar assets (which can easily involve thousands of units for such assets as tools and dyes), the record keeping for individual-asset accounting is an enormous burden, even in computerized systems. Group accounts do away with the need to maintain that level of detail and reflect an apt application of the cost/benefit constraint. Of course, the company must still maintain adequate *physical* control over the assets.

Although the original cost for each asset acquired is maintained, only one control account for each group of assets and accumulated depreciation is used. Gains and losses are not recognized on disposal. Instead, the asset control account is credited for the original cost of the item, and the accumulated depreciation account is debited for the difference between cash received and the original cost of the item.

For example, assume that in 20X8 a company sells a tool that it had acquired in 20X7 for $1,000. The company received $200 from the sale of the asset. The asset is part of a group account that is depreciated at the rate of 50% per year, by the SL method. When the asset is disposed of, only two pieces of information are needed for recording the sale: (1) the original cost of the asset, and (2) the net proceeds from the sale. The sale is recorded as follows:

Accumulated depreciation—tools	500	
Property, plant, and equipment—tools		500
Cash	200	
Accumulated depreciation—tools		200

The full cost of the asset is removed from both the asset account and the accumulated depreciation account, and the disposal proceeds are credited to the accumulated depreciation account. There is no attempt to calculate the book value for the asset or any gain or loss.

If we collapse these two entries into a single compound entry, the entry becomes:

Cash	200	
Accumulated depreciation—tools	300	
Property, plant, and equipment—tools		500

Effectively, the entry is telling us that if the estimates of residual value and useful life were estimated correctly for this asset, its net book value would have been $200 at disposal. Of course, we cannot make such precise estimates on individual assets, but we can make very good estimates *on average* for any particular type of asset. The control account for each class of asset can be monitored over time, and the group depreciation rate can be adjusted to reflect actual experience, much as we regularly adjust bad debt expense estimates on the basis of experience.

Some companies simplify this system even further by not attempting to identify the actual cost of the asset retired. Instead, a FIFO (first-in, first-out) approach is often used (oldest unit is sold first, just as with inventory).

CONCEPT REVIEW

1 What information is required for implementing component depreciation when a new asset has been acquired by a company?

2. Why is land depreciated if there is a decommissioning cost?

3. Why are group systems of depreciation useful for small-value assets that do not have significant components?

REVIEW OF DEFINITIONS—IMPAIRMENT

A review of terminology is a good place to start for understanding impairment testing. Long-lived assets are subject to impairment testing, even if they are depreciated or amortized. In understanding impairment testing, the basic definitions are the following:

- **Impairment loss** is the amount by which the carrying amount of an asset or cash-generating unit exceeds its recoverable amount.
- **Cash-generating unit (CGU)** is the smallest group of assets that will generate cash inflows. These independent cash inflows are largely independent of the cash flows of other assets or groups of assets.
- **Recoverable amount** is the *higher* of fair value less costs of disposal and value in use.
- **Fair value less costs of disposal** is the amount that could be received from the sale of the asset between two unrelated parties less the cost incurred in the sale.
- **Value in use** is the *discounted cash flows* (cash inflows and cash outflows) from the use of the asset and disposal.

IMPAIRMENT OF LONG-LIVED ASSETS

Long-lived assets may or may not have a determinate, finite life span. The carrying value will stay on the balance sheet for many years. However, an asset's real economic value to the enterprise may decline significantly over the years. Possible overvaluation of assets can be a major issue for long-lived assets. Therefore, one has to critically examine long-lived assets and goodwill periodically and ask, "Do these assets still have the ability to generate cash inflows commensurate with their net book value?"

It is important to understand that the question is not, "What is market value?" Market value is the value at which an asset can be sold, which implies that it is, in fact, available for sale. In contrast, assets that are listed as long-lived assets or goodwill are not for sale. These assets provide value to the operation through their ability to increase net assets through profitable operation.

An **impairment test** is the process of comparing the carrying value of an asset with its *recoverable amount*. If the asset's recoverable amount is less than its carrying value on the company's books, the asset has suffered impairment. Since we cannot report an asset at a carrying value that is higher than its recoverable amount, the asset's carrying value must be reduced by the amount of the impairment. The writedown is charged to expense on the income statement, never directly to retained earnings.

Impairment tests already are quite familiar to us, in the form of lower-of-cost-or-net realizable value valuations for inventory and for other short-term assets. However, accounting standards tend to use the term "impairment" only for assets that have a long life: **long-lived assets**.

A basic assumption underlying impairment tests is that the asset is intended to be used in the company's operations and that its cost is recoverable. If the cost is completely unrecoverable through operations or sale, the asset does not meet our definition of an asset and therefore must be written off in full immediately.

Impairment tests are applied to all long-lived assets, both (1) assets with limited lives and (2) assets without limited lives, including land and some intangibles. However, the process of testing for impairment is somewhat different between goodwill and other types of long-lived assets. Therefore, we will look at impairment tests separately for each type.

An annual impairment test must be completed even if there are no factors that indicate impairment for intangible assets with indefinite lives, intangible assets not yet available for use, and goodwill.

Reversal of impairment losses is allowed for all long-lived assets except for goodwill. Impairment losses and any reversals are shown separately on the income statement. They may well be part of a restructuring charge or discontinued operations, if circumstances warrant. This means increased volatility in the income statement.

Impairment testing below refers to the cost model being used. The revaluation model and the treatment of impairment is discussed in Appendix 2 to this chapter.

Basic Steps in Impairment Testing of Long-lived Assets

In completing the impairment testing, the following steps are taken:

1. Identification of an asset or CGU;

2. Review of external and internal impairment indicators;

3. If required, annual impairment testing, or if, indication of impairment, then measurement of the recoverable amount; and

4. If impairment, write down to recoverable amount and allocate the impairment loss.

Cash-Generating Units The impairment test seldom is applied to individual assets. Assets function together in a company to generate cash flows and earnings. Therefore, impairment tests normally are applied to CGUs—defined earlier as a group of assets for which identifiable cash flows are largely independent of the cash flows of other assets or groups of assets. A store may have many different assets (e.g., building, equipment, and software) and all may function together as a CGU. For impairment tests, a CGU is the lowest level in a company at which it is possible to determine or identify the cash flows from a particular group of assets. Impairment may be one single asset that has identifiable cash inflows or a number of assets at an operating division level.

For example, a company may have patents on several products and processes, all of which use the same facilities for production and administrative support. If sales of one product are killed by a new product from a competitor, there has not necessarily been an impairment—the impairment test is applied to the cash flows from the assets used in production. The cash flow from the CGU is generated by all of the assets working together to produce several products.

Liabilities will be included in the group only when the recoverable amount could not be determined without including this liability. For example, a CGU could not be sold unless the buyer assumed the liability. Examples could include a mortgage debt and asset retirement obligations.

Held-for-sale assets may be subject to individual impairment tests, but even that may be rare. Most held-for-sale assets are the net assets of discontinued operations that are awaiting disposal. It is the discontinued operation as a whole that is tested for impairment, not individual assets.

Review of Impairment Indicators Sometimes asset impairment is as plain as day, such as when a building is destroyed in a fire. In such a case, the asset is written off and the insurance proceeds (if any) reduce the loss (and can even create a reported gain if the insurance proceeds are greater than the asset's net book value).

Intangible assets with indefinite lives and intangible assets not yet available for use must be tested for impairment annually. For all other long-lived assets, both the internal and external impairment indicators must be assessed each reporting date. Examples of such circumstances include:

- A significant change in the business environment, such as a new product from a competitor that makes the company's product or processes obsolete;
- Physical damage to the asset;
- A history of operating and/or cash flow losses that indicate that the company is not able to recover the cost of the asset;
- A probability of greater than 50% that the company will retire or dispose of the asset significantly earlier than planned; or
- Loss of a patent infringement lawsuit that has a significant effect on overall operations.

If annual impairment testing is required or an external or internal factor indicates possible impairment, then the CGU is tested for impairment.

How to Measure The impairment loss is the amount by which the carrying value of the CGU exceeds its recoverable amount. The recoverable amount is the higher of fair value less costs of disposal and value in use. An asset can recover its value from use in the business or from selling the asset. Fair value is interpreted to mean the amount that the asset group could be sold for in a fair and open transaction between willing parties, neither party being under any particular obligation to sell or buy. The difficult part is to measure fair value. One could try to piece together a fair value for the group by assembling market values for individual assets, but that would deny the synergy and productivity that is achieved when assets function together in an operating environment.

Although it makes little sense to add together the values of individual assets within a CGU, the CGU as a whole may have a measurable fair value. A group of assets can be sold to another company as an operating unit, similar to a discontinued operation. The price that a buyer would pay will be based on the *discounted* present value of the CGU's estimated future cash flows.

Estimating future cash flows (and the probabilities attached to those cash flows) is not the job of the accountant. That is the task of management with the assistance of professional business valuators. But once management estimates the fair value, the accountant must ensure that the impairment is properly recorded.

Allocating the Impairment Loss—Individual Asset The impairment loss may relate to an individual asset. The carrying amount of the individual asset is then written down to the recoverable amount, and an impairment loss is recognized on the income statement. The maximum amount of the impairment loss is the carrying amount of the asset unless a liability is required to be recognized in another standard (e.g., decommissioning costs related to an asset). After an impairment loss has been recognized, estimates related to that asset should be reviewed (e.g., useful life, residual value and depreciation method).

Allocating the Impairment Loss—Group of Assets in CGU As we have just seen, impairment losses are often applied to a group of assets in a CGU. But the assets usually are recorded individually on the books, not in groups. So, how should the overall impairment loss be allocated to the assets?

The first rule is that the amount of an impairment loss should be allocated on the basis of the carrying amount of the individual long-lived assets. This is done on a pro-rata basis. Suppose that Justus Limited has the following assets in its recreational products group:

	Carrying Value (thousands)
Land	$ 400
Building	640
Equipment	560
	$1,600

A change in the competitive environment suggests that the recoverable amount of this division may be less than its carrying value. Management conducts an impairment test and concludes that the recoverable amount based on the estimated discounted present value of the future cash flows of the asset group is $1,000. Fair value less costs of disposal could not be determined for these assets. The impairment loss is $600—the excess of $1,600 carrying value over $1,000 recoverable amount.

The impairment loss must be allocated to the long-lived assets. The $600 impairment loss will be allocated to the assets in proportion to their carrying value:

Asset	Carrying Value	Proportion	Allocation of Impairment Loss	Adjusted Carrying Value
Land	$ 400	25%	$150	250
Building	640	40%	240	400
Equipment	560	35%	210	350
	$1,600	100%	$600	$1,000

The allocation of the impairment loss should not reduce the carrying amount of an asset below: the higher of (1) its fair value less costs of disposal or value-in-use if they can be readily determined, or (2) zero. For example, suppose that an Internet service provider (ISP) shows as an asset the historical cost for a subscriber base that it purchased from another company. An ISP subscriber list has a fairly readily determinable value. If the ISP is consistently losing money, it is probable that the company's assets are impaired. Nevertheless, that does not indicate that the subscriber list has no value of its own—another company may use it quite profitably. If an impairment loss is recognized, the carrying value of the subscription base should not be reduced below the higher of its fair value less costs of disposal or value-in-use. Instead, a greater portion of the impairment loss should be allocated to the other long-lived assets, such as equipment and limited-life intangibles.

In the example above, assume the recoverable amount of the land is $320. Assets should not be written down below their fair value. In that case, the allocation must be (1) to reduce the land's carrying value by $80 (from $400 to $320), and then (2) to allocate the remaining $520 impairment loss to the remaining assets:

Asset	Carrying Value	Proportion	Allocation of Impairment Loss	Adjusted Carrying Value
Land	400	—	$ 80	320
Building	640	53%	276	364
Equipment	560	47%	244	316
	$1,600	100%	$600	$1,000

Reversal of Impairment Losses What goes down may go back up. Reversal is allowed for all long-lived assets with the exception of goodwill. Impairment losses may be reinstated if the fair value of the asset has recovered and should be recognized in income immediately.

The problem with reversing an impairment loss is that this provides yet another method by which management may be tempted to "manage" or smooth earnings—take an impairment loss in a high-income year and restore it in a low-income year. To guard against such manipulation, the international standard provides guidelines on how to ascertain that an impairment loss has occurred and when the value has recovered.

At each reporting date, an entity considers if there are factors that would indicate an impairment loss should be reversed partially or completely. These are often the opposite of factors that would indicate impairment. Examples of such circumstances include:

- A significant change in the business environment, such as a competitor leaving the market and increasing the market share for the company;
- Increased cash flows from the use of an asset that indicate the company will recover the cost of the asset;
- A probability of greater than 50% that the company will keep the asset significantly longer than planned; or
- Winning a patent infringement lawsuit that has a significant effect on overall operations.

Reversal of an impairment loss must indicate that there will be an increase in the value in use of the asset or fair value through sale of the asset.

Allocating the Reversal of an Impairment Loss—Individual Asset The reversal of an impairment loss may relate to an individual asset. The carrying amount of the individual asset is then written up to the carrying value the asset would have been without the impairment. This would be the carrying amount (net of depreciation or amortization) if no impairment loss had been previously recognized. An impairment reversal is then recognized on the income statement. After the reversal of an impairment loss has been recognized, estimates related to that asset should be reviewed (e.g., useful life, residual value, and depreciation method).

Allocating the Impairment Loss Reversal—Group of Assets in CGU The reversal of an impairment loss will be allocated to the assets in proportion to their carrying values. This reversal is allocated only to assets in the CGU that were decreased in recognizing previous impairment losses. If a reversal of an impairment loss is recognized, the carrying value of the assets should not be increased higher than their recoverable amount. Instead, a greater portion of the reversal of the impairment loss should be allocated to the other long-lived assets on a proportionate basis.

Let us return to our previous example, where we had an impairment loss of $600. A change in the competitive environment has improved our sales and our recoverable amount of this division may be more than its carrying value. Management determines that the recoverable amount based on the estimated discounted present value of the future cash flows of the asset group is $1,400. Fair value less costs of disposal could not be determined for these assets. The reversal of the impairment loss is $400—the excess of $1,400 recoverable amount over $1,000 carrying amount.

The reversal of the impairment loss must be allocated to the long-lived assets. The $400 impairment loss will be allocated to the assets in proportion to their carrying value:

Asset	Carrying Value	Proportion	Allocation of Reversal of Impairment Loss	Adjusted Carrying Value
Land	$ 250	25%	$100	350
Building	400	40%	160	560
Equipment	350	35%	140	490
	$1,000	100%	$400	$1,400

Disclosure Disclosure requirements for impairment losses are straightforward. The basic requirements are:

- A description of the impaired asset or CGU and the facts and circumstances leading to the impairment;
- The amount of the impairment loss, and an indication of where it appears in the income statement if it is not presented separately on the face of the income statement;
- The amount of any reversals of impairment loss and an indication of where it appears in the income statement if it is not presented separately on the face of the income statement; and
- The method used for determining recoverable amount.

Reversals of impairment arise from subsequent reviews of the impaired assets where the conditions that gave rise to the original impairments are deemed no longer to apply.

Goodwill Impairment

The testing of impairment for goodwill must be done on an annual basis. Similar to a group of assets above, goodwill is tested as part of a CGU. As we saw in Chapter 9, goodwill is measured as a residual, as the excess of the purchase price paid for a unit over the fair value of its net assets on the acquisition date.

The key measuring unit for goodwill impairment is the *cash-generating unit*. Goodwill is allocated to the CGUs to which it relates, which may be more than one. The impairment test is similar to that described above for other assets.

The carrying amount of the CGU including goodwill is compared with the recoverable amount of the CGU, including goodwill. If the recoverable amount is above the carrying amount of the CGU, there is no impairment. If the recoverable amount is below the carrying amount, an impairment loss is recognized.

Individual assets within a CGU will be tested before testing a CGU, including goodwill. This is to ensure that individual impairment losses are recognized before considering impairment of goodwill.

If there is an impairment loss in a CGU, it should be first allocated to the goodwill and then on a proportionate basis to the other assets based on their carrying amount. Let us return to our previous example but now assume that the assets of the CGU include goodwill.

A change in the competitive environment suggests that the recoverable amount of this division may be less than its carrying value. Management conducts an impairment test, determining that the recoverable amount based on the estimated discounted present value of the future cash flows of the asset group is $1,000. Fair value less costs of disposal could not be determined for these assets. The impairment loss is $800—the excess of $1,800 carrying value over the $1,000 recoverable amount.

The impairment loss must be allocated to the long-lived assets. The $800 impairment loss will be allocated first to goodwill and then to the assets in proportion to their carrying value:

Asset	Carrying Value	Proportion	Allocation of Impairment Loss	Adjusted Carrying Value
Goodwill	$ 200		$200	$ 0
Land	400	25%	150	250
Building	640	40%	240	400
Equipment	560	35%	210	350
	$1,800	100%	$800	$1,000

Reversal of Goodwill Impairment Goodwill is not allowed to be reversed if there is reversal of impairment in a CGU. All assets within the CGU would be increased on a proportionate basis of their carrying amount except for goodwill.

In our previous example, we had an impairment loss of $800. A change in the competitive environment has improved our sales, and our recoverable amount of this division may be more than its carrying value. Management determines that the recoverable amount based on the estimated discounted present value of the future cash flows of the asset group is $1,400. Fair value less costs of disposal could not be determined for these assets. The reversal of the impairment loss is $400—the excess of $1,400 recoverable amount over $1,000 carrying amount.

The reversal of the impairment loss must be allocated to the long-lived assets. The $400 impairment loss will be allocated to the assets in proportion to their carrying value:

Asset	Carrying Value	Proportion	Allocation of Reversal of Impairment Loss	Adjusted Carrying Value
Goodwill	$ 0		$ 0	$ 0
Land	250	25%	100	350
Building	400	40%	160	560
Equipment	350	35%	140	490
	$1,000	100%	$400	$1,000

The Role of Judgement It would be impossible to overemphasize the role of judgement when evaluating the need for an impairment writedown. Since fair values are estimates, often based on future cash flow projections, the optimism and pessimism of management will have a profound effect on the end result. There is significant temptation to take a bath in poor years and record large writedowns.

DISCLOSURE REQUIREMENTS

Not surprisingly, the requirement to disclose depreciation or amortization policy is front and centre in the disclosure requirements. If you are going to let companies pick a policy, it is crucial that financial statement readers be told about the choice. Thus, companies should disclose for each major category of depreciable long-lived assets:

- The depreciation or amortization method used, including the depreciation or amortization period or rate;
- The accumulated depreciation or amortization of each major category;
- The amount of depreciation or amortization charged to income for the period;
- The amount of any impairment loss or writedown during the period; and
- The amount of any reversal of an impairment loss or writedown during the period.

Exhibit 10-6 shows an example of depreciation of property, plant, and equipment, amortization of intangible assets, and an impairment loss from Armtec Infrastructure Inc. Note on the Consolidated Statement of Earnings the separate line disclosure of the impairment loss of $268.5 million. Note 9 and Note 10 show the allocation of the impairment loss to property, plant, and equipment as well as to intangible assets. Note that in the CGU an impairment loss of $139.8 is first allocated to goodwill, which has been reduced to zero, and then to the other assets within the CGU.

EXHIBIT 10-6

ARMTEC INFRASTRUCTURE INC.

Consolidated Statement of Earnings Years Ended Dec. 31, 2011

(in thousands of Canadian dollars unless otherwise noted)

For the years ended December 31	Note	2011	2010
Revenue	29	$ 453,605	$ 462,205
Cost of sales	18	398,934	377,896
Gross margin		54,671	84,309
Selling, general and administrative	18	72,191	68,250
Impairment of assets	9, 10, 14	268,571	—
Other (gains) losses—net	19	958	(1,846)
(Loss) earnings from operations		(287,049)	17,905
Finance (income) expense—net	20	33,788	23,745
Loss before taxes		(320,837)	(5,840)
Income tax recovery	11	51,044	10,736
Net (loss) earnings from continuing operations attributable to owners of the Company		(269,793)	4,896
Net earnings from discontinued operations	21	—	6,606
Net (loss) earnings attributable to owners of the Company		$(269,793)	$ 11,502
Basic and diluted (loss) earnings per share or unit—continuing operations	22	$ (11.74)	$ 0.24
Basic and diluted earnings per share or unit—discontinued operations	22	$ —	$ 0.33
Basic and diluted (loss) earnings per share or unit	22	$ (11.74)	$ 0.57

continued on next page

EXHIBIT 10-6 (*cont'd*)

ARMTEC INFRASTRUCTURE INC. SELECTED NOTE DISCLOSURES FOR IMPAIRMENT (ALL AMOUNTS FOR DECEMBER 31, 2011)

Extracts from Significant Accounting Policy Note

(k) Impairment

(ii) Non-financial assets

The carrying amounts of the Group's non-financial assets, other than inventories and deferred tax assets, are periodically reviewed to determine whether there is any indication of impairment. Non-financial assets that have an indefinite useful life or are not ready for use are not subject to amortization and are tested annually for impairment. Non-financial assets that are subject to amortization are reviewed for impairment whenever events or changes in circumstances indicate impairment. An impairment loss is recognized for the amount by which the asset's carrying amount exceeds its recoverable amount.

The recoverable amount of an asset or cash-generating unit is the greater of its value in use and its fair value less costs to sell. In assessing value in use, the estimated future cash flows are discounted to their present value using a pre-tax discount rate that reflects current market assessments of the time value of money and the risks specific to the asset. For the purpose of impairment testing, assets are grouped together into the smallest group of assets, known as the cash-generating unit, that generate cash inflows from continuing use that are largely independent of the cash inflows of other assets or group of assets. The goodwill acquired in a business combination, for the purpose of impairment testing, is allocated to groups of cash-generating units that are expected to benefit from the synergies of the combination.

Impairment losses are recognized in the Group's statement of earnings. Impairment losses recognized in respect of cash-generating units are allocated first to reduce the carrying amount of any goodwill allocated to the units and then to reduce the carrying amounts of the other assets in the unit, or group of units, on a pro rata basis. An impairment loss in respect of goodwill is not reversed. In respect of other assets, impairment losses recognized in prior periods are assessed at each reporting date for any indications that the loss has decreased or no longer exists. An impairment loss is reversed if there has been a change in the estimates used to determine the recoverable amount. An impairment loss is reversed only to the extent that the asset's carrying amount does not exceed the carrying amount that would have been determined, net of depreciation or amortization, if no impairment loss had been recognized.

Extracts from Notes

Note 9. Property, plant and equipment

Net book value	Note	Land, building and leaseholds	Machinery and equipment	Machinery and equipment under finance lease	Furniture and fixtures	Construction-in-progress	Total
Balance—January 1, 2011		$90,629	$84,273	$3,887	$2,860	$3,938	$185,587
Additions		314	2,439	2,006	104	2,182	7,045
Reclassification		2,385	2,126	250	114	(4,875)	—
Disposals		(13)	(97)	(292)	—	—	(402)
Impairment of assets	10	(11,828)	(43,600)	—	(1,501)	—	(56,929)
Depreciation		(2,226)	(10,548)	(2,036)	(772)	—	(15,582)
Balance—December 31, 2011		79,261	34,593	3,815	805	1,245	119,719
Net book value comprised of:							
Cost		99,537	124,600	8,705	6,031	1,245	240,118
Accumulated depreciation and impairment		(20,276)	(90,007)	(4,890)	(5,226)	—	(120,399)
Balance—December 31, 2011		$79,261	$34,593	$3,815	$ 805	$1,245	$119,719

continued on next page

EXHIBIT 10-6 (cont'd)

Net book value	Note	Land, building and leaseholds	Machinery and equipment	Machinery and equipment under finance lease	Furniture and fixtures	Construction-in-progress	Total
Balance—January 1, 2010		**$91,080**	**$92,145**	**$5,196**	**$3,178**	**$ 493**	**$192,092**
Additions		803	5,048	1,053	529	5,106	12,539
Reclassification		938	723	—	—	(1,661)	—
Disposals		(43)	(2,514)	(189)	(1)	—	(2,747)
Depreciation		(2,149)	(11,129)	(2,173)	(846)	—	(16,297)
Balance—December 31, 2010		90,629	84,273	3,887	2,860	3,938	185,587
Net book value comprised of:							
Cost		96,855	120,153	7,272	5,813	3,938	234,031
Accumulated depreciation		(6,226)	(35,880)	(3,385)	(2,953)	—	(48,444)
Balance—December 31, 2010		**$90,629**	**$84,273**	**$3,887**	**$2,860**	**$3,938**	**$185,587**

Net book value at January 2010 comprised of:	Land, building and leaseholds	Machinery and equipment	Machinery and equipment under finance lease	Furniture and fixtures	Construction-in-progress	Total
Cost	$95,160	$117,436	$6,577	$5,288	$493	$224,954
Accumulated depreciation	(4,080)	(25,291)	(1,381)	(2,110)	—	(32,862)
Balance—January 1, 2010	**$91,080**	**$ 92,145**	**$5,196**	**$3,178**	**$493**	**$192,092**

Depreciation of property, plant and equipment has been allocated to the Group's statement of earnings as follows:

For the years ended December 31	2011	2010
Cost of sales	$12,628	$13,174
Selling, general and administrative	2,954	2,920
Net earnings from discontinued operations	—	203
	$15,582	**$16,297**

The Group leases various vehicles under cancellable finance lease agreements and machinery primarily under noncancellable finance lease agreements. Specific machinery is pledged as security for finance leases. The leased equipment secures lease obligations (see Note 14(e)). The leases mature over various dates from 2012 to 2017.

continued on next page

EXHIBIT 10-6 (cont'd)

Note 10. Goodwill and other intangible assets

Net book value	Note	Goodwill	Trademarks and tradenames	Customer lists and contracts	Licenses and non-compete agreements	ERP systems	Intangibles-in-progress	Sub-total other intangible assets	Total goodwill and other intangible assets
Balance—January 1, 2011		**$139,822**	**$41,703**	**$63,128**	**$23,900**	**$4,745**	**$ —**	**$133,476**	**$273,298**
Additions—externally developed		—	—	200	800	—	—	1,000	1,000
Additions—internally developed		—	—	—	—	417	—	417	417
Impairment of assets		(139,822)	(23,472)	(29,841)	(15,722)	(2,785)	—	(71,820)	(211,642)
Amortization		—	(2,322)	(5,024)	(3,386)	(1,010)	—	(11,742)	(11,742)
Balance—December 31, 2011		—	15,909	28,463	5,592	1,367	—	51,331	51,331
Net book value comprised of:									
Cost		139,822	50,940	85,209	37,527	8,425	—	182,101	321,923
Accumulated amortization and impairment		(139,822)	(35,031)	(56,746)	(31,935)	(7,058)	—	(130,770)	(270,592)
Balance—December 31, 2011		**$ —**	**$15,909**	**$28,463**	**$ 5,592**	**$1,367**	**$ —**	**$ 51,331**	**$ 51,331**
Balance—January 1, 2010		**$142,900**	**$44,195**	**$70,520**	**$24,831**	**$2,362**	**$1,814**	**$143,722**	**$286,622**
Additions—externally purchased		—	—	—	2,868	—	—	2,868	2,868
Additions—internally developed		—	—	—	—	1,873	304	2,177	2,177
Reclassification		—	—	—	—	2,118	(2,118)	—	—
Disposals	21	(3,078)	—	(1,868)	(239)	—	—	(2,107)	(5,185)
Amortization		—	(2,492)	(5,524)	(3,560)	(1,608)	—	(13,184)	(13,184)
Balance—December 31, 2010		139,822	41,703	63,128	23,500	4,745	—	133,476	273,298
Net book value comprised of:									
Cost		139,822	50,940	85,009	36,727	8,008	—	180,684	320,506
Accumulated amortization		—	(9,237)	(21,881)	(12,827)	(3,263)	—	(47,208)	(47,208)
Balance—December 31, 2010		**$139,822**	**$41,703**	**$63,128**	**$23,500**	**$4,745**	**$ —**	**$133,476**	**$273,298**
Net book value at January 1, 2010 comprised of:		**Goodwill**	**Trademarks and tradenames**	**Customer lists and contracts**	**Licenses and non-compete agreements**	**ERP systems**	**Intangibles-in-progress**	**Sub-total other intangible assets**	**Total goodwill and other intangible assets**
Cost		$142,900	$50,940	$87,147	$34,171	$4,017	$1,814	$178,089	$320,989
Accumulated amortization		—	(6,745)	(16,627)	(9,340)	(1,655)	—	(34,367)	(34,367)
Balance—January 1, 2010		**$142,900**	**$44,195**	**$70,520**	**$24,831**	**$2,362**	**$1,814**	**$143,722**	**$286,622**

continued on next page

EXHIBIT 10-6 (cont'd)

Amortization of intangibles has been allocated to the Group's statement of earnings as follows:

For the years ended December 31	2011	2010
Cost of sales	$ 1,228	$ 1,900
Selling, general and administrative	10,514	11,069
Net earnings from discontinued operations	—	215
	$11,742	$13,184

(a) Significant carrying amounts

As at December 31, 2011, the following intangible assets have individually significant carrying amounts for the Group:

Description	Remaining amortization period	Carrying amount
Customer relationship recognized upon acquisition within the Prairie region	129 months	$9,866
Tradename recognized upon acquisition within the Prairie region	156 months	9,021
Customer relationship recognized upon acquisition within the Eastern region	148 months	4,918
Customer relationship recognized upon acquisition within the Pacific region	138 months	4,594
License recognized upon acquisition within the Central region	151 months	3,243

(b) Allocation of goodwill

The aggregate remaining carrying amounts of goodwill allocated to each of the Group's cash-generating unit groups, for the periods indicated, are as follows:

As at	December 31, 2011	December 31, 2010	January 1, 2010
Eastern region	$ —	$ 21,313	$ 21,313
Central region	—	52,307	52,307
Prairie region	—	45,590	48,668
Pacific region	—	20,612	20,612
	$ —	$139,822	$142,900

(c) Impairment testing for cash-generating units containing goodwill

The Group carries out its impairment test annually or more frequently if there is an indicator of impairment. Previous to June 30, 2011, September 30, 2011 and December 31, 2011 the next most recent tests were performed for both the Transition Date of January 1, 2010 and December 31, 2010. The Group has aggregated its cash-generating units into regions ("CGU groups") for the purposes of the goodwill impairment test. The carrying value of the goodwill has been allocated for impairment testing purposes to these CGU groups.

During 2011, the Group determined that an indicator of impairment existed due to a significant decline in the price of the Company's common shares listed on the TSX during the second through fourth quarters of 2011. As a result, the Group determined that $139.8 million of goodwill has been impaired (Eastern region—$21.3 million, Central region—$52.3 million, Prairie region—$45.6 million and Pacific region—$20.6 million), and this impairment was recorded within 'impairment of assets' on the Group's statement of earnings. With the full amount of the Group's goodwill being written off an additional impairment of $125.7 million reduced on a pro rata basis the other long-lived assets of the cash-generating unit groups (Eastern region—$19.1 million, Central region—$75.6 million, Prairie region—$27.5 million and Pacific region—$3.5 million). The pro rata calculation resulted in $56.9 million of property, plant and equipment and $68.8 million of other intangibles to be impaired in the four CGU groups. Transaction costs comprising of $3.0 million related to the Revolving Credit Facility were written off during 2011 (Note 14).

continued on next page

EXHIBIT 10-6 *(cont'd)*

The recoverable amounts of the CGU groups as at January 1, 2010 and December 31, 2010 were determined using a value in use methodology. No impairment was indicated as a result of these tests. The impairment tests at December 31, 2011 were calculated under both a value in use and fair value less cost to sell methodology. The impairments recorded were measured as the difference between the carrying value and fair value less costs to sell of the CGU groups as fair value less costs to sell was the higher of the values obtained in the Group's determination of recoverable amounts.

The key assumptions to which the recoverable amounts of each of the CGU groups are most sensitive include growth rates for revenue, future margins on products and discount rates applied to cash flow projections. The recoverable amounts of the CGU groups were determined similarly for the periods under review by discounting the future cash flows generated from the continuing use of the units. Cash flows and future margins were projected based on past experience and actual operating results using approved cash forecasts covering a five-year period that were extrapolated using growth and margin rates that did not exceed the long-term average for the CGU groups under review and the market in which the Group operates. The discount rates were based on the Group's weighted average cost of capital using a standard capital structure and reflect specific risks relating to the CGU groups for those periods under review.

The calculation of the recoverable amounts was based on the following key assumptions as at December 31, 2011:

	Growth rate for the terminal period	Post-tax discount rate
Eastern region	2.5%	14.5%
Central region	2.5%	14.5%
Prairie region	2.5%	14.5%
Pacific region	2.5%	14.5%

As at December 31, 2010:

	Growth rate for the terminal period	Post-tax discount rate
Eastern region	2.0%	14.0%
Central region	2.0%	14.1%
Prairie region	2.0%	14.1%
Pacific region	2.0%	14.3%

As at January 1, 2010:

	Growth rate for the terminal period	Post-tax discount rate
Eastern region	2.0%	14.9%
Central region	2.0%	15.0%
Prairie region	2.0%	14.9%
Pacific region	2.0%	14.7%

Source: Armtec Infrastructure Inc., 2011, Consolidated Statement of Earnings, www.sedar.com, posted 5 April 2012.

STATEMENT OF CASH FLOWS

Depreciation or amortization expense is an add-back to the operations section of the statement of cash flows (SCF), if the common indirect form of presentation is used. It is important to remember that depreciation or amortization is a little different from other expenses, because depreciation or amortization is a non-cash expense. Clearly, the company has to pay out cash or other resources to obtain the capital asset, but the timing of the cash paid is likely to be a lot different from the timing of the expense recognition.

Any writedowns of long-lived assets or reversals of writedowns, including impairment of goodwill, are a non-cash charge to income. Like depreciation or amortization, they are added back to net income.

CONCEPT REVIEW

1. In general, when is it necessary to write down property, plant, and equipment? How can we determine the value to which it should be written down?

2. Describe the steps followed to determine whether there has been an impairment of a long-lived asset.

3. What happens if there is a reversal of an impairment loss?

ETHICAL ISSUES

The importance of accounting estimates has been emphasized throughout this book. Depreciation or amortization requires not only a choice of method but also estimates of useful life and residual value. A choice of method, once made, normally is not changed. The requirement that similar assets be depreciated or amortized by similar methods helps to maintain consistency in measurement.

However, over the life of a long-lived asset, it is quite possible for a company to change any or all of the asset's (1) depreciation or amortization method, (2) useful life, or (3) residual value. If a company lengthens an asset's useful life, for example, is it really because the asset will be useful longer than expected, or is it because management seeks to improve the company's apparent profitability? Auditors can scrutinize the rationale behind changes in management's estimates, but their scrutiny will have little effect unless the new estimates are quite obviously outside the feasible range.

There are two aspects that help limit the ability of management to act unethically in setting estimates relating to depreciation or amortization. One is that if the company's policies and estimates get out of line with industry practice, the nonconformity will be apparent to investors and bankers, especially those who deal often with a specific industry. Nonconformity will cause statement users to suspect management's motivations and will discount the stock price or be hesitant to extend loans.

The second is that investors take changes in accounting estimates into account—efficient markets are not fooled by accounting changes in the short run. But even subtle changes can have important long-term effects on net income. Do investors really remember all of the past changes in management estimates when evaluating a company's performance?

While depreciation or amortization estimates and revisions offer some scope for unethical behaviour, impairments offer a far more fertile area for bias, either intentional or unintentional. Impairment tests are based on estimates of fair values. In turn, fair value is based on estimates of *future* cash flows. By their nature, estimates of future cash flows cannot be verified. Managers may be pessimistic when they estimate future cash flows from an asset group, for example, because the company has not been successful at making its products profitable. Even when it is clear that the future cash flows of a CGU are in decline, management must estimate how quickly and how severe the decline will be.

Managers can hire professional appraisers to help estimate future cash flows and thus the fair value of assets and CGUs. Ideally, more than one appraiser is used. Professional appraisers are assumed to be essentially in agreement if their estimates of fair value are within 10% of each other. A variation of 10% in the fair value of an asset or CGU may not seem very significant. However, a relatively small variation in estimated fair value can have a major impact on the net income in the year of the writedown. The variation also affects the future earnings and EPS of the company by lowering depreciation or amortization after the writedown. Furthermore, management can write the asset back up again, partially or completely if the future cash flows turn out to be better than expected.

Writedowns can be a very effective tool for enabling managers to "manage" the company's reported earnings.

An additional facet relating to *goodwill* impairment tests is that the test is performed at the level of the CGU. By rearranging the organization's CGUs, the need to perform impairment tests on specific operating units can be eliminated.

In summary, the practices for depreciation or amortization and for impairment tests are not as objective and verifiable as they may seem at first glance. Auditors and financial statement users must be vigilant against manipulation of reported results, as must the senior accountants working within the company itself.

Looking Ahead

An Exposure Draft titled "Clarification of Acceptable Methods of Depreciation and Amortization" was issued on 5 December 2012. The content of this Exposure Draft clarifies that the "consumption of future" benefits is the key principle behind depreciation or amortization. For this reason a revenue-based method should not be used to calculate depreciation or amortization. Long-lived assets are not now on the agenda for the Canadian AcSB.

ACCOUNTING STANDARDS FOR PRIVATE ENTERPRISES

The standards are similar for depreciation and impairment; however, there are some important differences.

Component Depreciation

Standards for publicly accountable enterprises require component depreciation. ASPE states that component depreciation should be done "if practicable," which has translated to many Canadian companies not using component depreciation.

Minimum Depreciation

Standards for publicly accountable enterprises have no provision for minimum depreciation. Scrap value is irrelevant—only residual value and estimated useful life are relevant for determining the amount of depreciation. In standards for private enterprises depreciation is the higher of cost less salvage value over the life of the asset, and cost less residual value over the life of the asset. The standard states quite explicitly that depreciation is zero if an asset's residual value is equal to or greater than its carrying value. Depreciation will commence only if and when the residual value drops below the asset's carrying value.

It is worth noting that while ASPE uses the word "amortization" to include all forms, including depreciation and depletion, standards for publicly accountable enterprises explicitly use the word "depreciation" when referring to amortization of tangible capital assets.

Determination of Impairment Losses

Standards for publicly accountable enterprises review impairment indicators every reporting date. If a factor indicates impairment, then a one-step test is used to determine impairment. The carrying amount is compared with the recoverable amount, which is the higher of value in use and fair value less costs to sell. If impairment exists then the asset is written down to its recoverable amount.

Standards for publicly accountable enterprises have one impairment test for property, plant, and equipment; intangible assets; and goodwill. Standards for private enterprises have a different test for long-lived assets, which includes property, plant, and equipment and intangible assets that are amortized. There is a separate test for intangible assets that are not amortized and goodwill.

For long-lived assets, ASPE performs the impairment test only if an event or circumstance indicates impairment, which is often referred to as a "trigger." A two-step test is used to determine impairment. The carrying amount is compared with the undiscounted cash flows from use and disposal (recoverable amount). If this indicates impairment, the carrying amount is compared with fair value. If impairment exists, then the asset is written down to its fair value.

For intangible assets with indefinite lives, they are again tested for impairment when there is an indication of impairment. When the carrying amount is higher than fair value an impairment loss is recognized.

For goodwill, it is tested as part of a reporting unit. Goodwill impairment is recognized when the carrying amount of the reporting unit as a whole including goodwill is higher than the fair value of the reporting unit.

Reversal of Impairment Losses

Standards for publicly accountable enterprises do permit the reversal of impairment losses if the circumstances change and the fair value of an asset or CGU goes up after an impairment loss has been recorded. The carrying value of the asset or of the assets in an asset group should be increased by the amount of any subsequent increase in the fair value of an impaired asset or CGU. The increase should be recorded as a gain on the income statement. The reversal is really a correction of accounting estimates that were made in the period of the original writedown. Goodwill impairments should never be reversed. A subsequent increase in goodwill is viewed as internally generated goodwill, which is never recorded.

ASPE does not allow for the reversal of any impairment losses related to long-lived assets.

Revaluation Accounting

Another major difference in the standards for publicly accountable enterprises is they permit routine revaluation (to fair value) of property, plant, and equipment. ASPE, in contrast, does not permit revaluation. The use of the cost model is an *option* under standards for publicly accountable enterprises, not a *requirement*. When revaluation accounting is used, all of the items in an asset class should be revalued to avoid selective revaluation of only certain assets. The asset values should be kept up to date.

If assets are revalued (upward), the increase in value is credited directly to shareholders' equity as *revaluation surplus*. Subsequent depreciation is based on the revalued amount, not on historical cost. The revaluation surplus is transferred directly to retained earnings without going through the income statement. The transfer can be either:

1. When the asset is retired; or

2. Year by year, calculated as the difference between (a) depreciation based on the revalued carrying value and (b) depreciation based on historical cost.

Appendix 2 to this chapter contains an illustration of revaluation accounting.

If the revaluation is downward, the reduction in carrying value first reduces any revaluation surplus relating to that asset. If the asset's carrying value is reduced to below its historical cost, the difference between the historical cost and the new lower valuation is treated as an impairment loss.

RELEVANT STANDARDS

CPA Canada Handbook, Part I (IFRS):
- IAS 16, Property, Plant, and Equipment
- IAS 36, Impairment of Assets
- IAS 38, Intangible Assets
- IAS 40, Investment Property
- IFRS 5, Non-current Assets Held for Sale and Discontinued Operations

CPA Canada Handbook, Part II (ASPE):
- Section 3061, Property, Plant, and Equipment
- Section 3064, Goodwill and Other Intangible Assets
- Section 3063, Impairment of Long-lived Assets
- Section 3475, Disposal of Long-lived Assets and Discontinued Operations

SUMMARY OF KEY POINTS

1. Depreciation or amortization is a rational and systematic process of allocating depreciable or amortizable cost (acquisition cost less residual value) to the periods in which long-lived assets are used. Depreciation refers to items of property, plant, and equipment while amortization refers to intangible assets. Depreciation or amortization expense for a period does not represent the change in market value of assets, nor does it necessarily equal the portion of the asset's utility consumed in the period. Depreciation or amortization is justified on the basis of eventual decline in value, through physical wear and tear and obsolescence.

2. Goodwill, land, investment property, held-for-sale capital assets, biological assets, and intangible assets with an unlimited life are not depreciated or amortized.

3. Component depreciation accounting is the depreciation by significant component.

4. Several methods of depreciation or amortization are rational and systematic and acceptable under GAAP: the straight-line (SL), service-hours (SH), productive-output (PO), and diminishing-balance (DB) methods. Factors affecting choice include individual corporate reporting objectives, information processing costs, a desire to minimize income tax temporary differences, industry norms, and parent company preferences.

5. Three factors contribute to the determination of periodic amortization expense: original acquisition cost and any capitalized post-acquisition costs, estimated residual value, and estimated useful life or productivity measured either in service hours or units of output. The key factor is that depreciation or amortization must reflect the pattern of consumption of future benefits.

6. For all methods, the estimated residual value is the minimum book value. Except for the declining-balance methods, depreciable or amortizable cost (cost minus residual value) is multiplied by a rate or fraction to determine periodic depreciation or amortization. Declining-balance depreciation is based on cost less accumulated depreciation and ceases when net book value equals residual value.

7. For assets acquired during an accounting period, an accounting convention, such as the half-year convention, is usually used in practice.

8. The group depreciation system is an alternative to depreciation methods applied individually to assets. These systems save accounting costs and are justified under cost-benefit and materiality constraints.

9. Long-lived assets subject to depreciation or amortization must be reviewed for potential writedown on a regular basis. A loss is recognized when the recoverable amount is less than carrying value. The loss equals the difference between the asset's carrying value and the asset's recoverable amount. Recoverable amount is based on the higher of fair value less costs of disposal and value in use (estimated future *discounted* cash flows).

10. Intangible assets not subject to amortization are written down to recoverable amount if the carrying value exceeds the recoverable amount.

11. Goodwill must be evaluated annually and written down if the value is impaired. This is done by comparing the recoverable amount of a cash-generating unit (CGU) (including goodwill) to its carrying value. If the recoverable amount is lower than the carrying value, then the impairment loss is allocated first to goodwill and then to other assets in the CGU.

12. Reversal of an impairment loss is permitted for all long-lived assets except for goodwill.

13. Depreciation or amortization is not a cash flow; the cash flow occurred when the capital asset was acquired. Depreciation and amortization and impairment writedowns are added back to net income when cash flow from operations is determined on the statement of cash flows (SCF).

14. Companies should disclose the depreciation or amortization method chosen for major categories of long-lived assets, the depreciation or amortization period or rate, and the amount of depreciation or amortization charged to income for the period.

15. Standards for publicly accountable enterprises differ from standards for private enterprise in some significant ways: (1) component depreciation is required; (2) they require no minimum amortization test; (2) impairment losses on assets and asset groups can be reversed; and (3) historical cost accounting is not required—long-lived assets can be reported at appraised values instead.

KEY TERMS

amortization
cash-generating unit (CGU)
component depreciation accounting
convention
diminishing-balance (DB) method
depletion

depreciable amount
depreciation
double-declining balance (DDB) method
fair value less costs of disposal
group depreciation

held-for-sale
impairment
impairment loss
impairment test
indefinite life
long-lived assets
net book value

productive-output (PO) method
recoverable amount
residual value
service-hours (SH) method
straight-line (SL) method
value in use

REVIEW PROBLEM 10-1

The following cases are independent.

1. *Partial-year depreciation.* Whitney Corporation purchased equipment on 1 April 20X4 for $34,000. The equipment has a useful life of five years and a residual value of $4,000. The year-end is December 31. What is depreciation for 20X4 and 20X5, using declining-balance depreciation at a 40% rate?

2. *Asset impairment.* Rancho Company purchases equipment on 1 April 20X3 for $34,000. The equipment has a useful life of five years, with a residual value of $4,000, and is depreciated using the straight-line method and the half-year convention. At the end of 20X5, Rancho suspects that the original investment in the asset will not be realized; the total remaining future cash inflows expected to be generated by the equipment, including the original residual value, amounts to $10,000 (undiscounted) and $8,000 (discounted). The equipment's fair value less costs of disposal at 31 December 20X5 is $7,000. Determine whether the asset is impaired and, if so, the impairment loss at 31 December 20X5.

3. *Component depreciation.* Baja Company has a large asset that it just purchased that has a number of significant components. The company has determined that the straight-line method reflects the pattern of consumption of future benefits. Component A is a major spare part that had an original cost of $100,000 and a residual value of zero and an estimated life of five years. Component B is a major overhaul that had an original cost of $20,000 and a residual value of zero and an estimated life of two years. Component C is the frame of the asset that has an original cost of $185,000 and a residual value of $5,000 and an estimated life of 20 years. The remaining components grouped together that are insignificant have an original cost of $16,000 and a residual value of $1,000 and an estimated life of three years. What is the depreciation expense?

REVIEW PROBLEM 10-1—SOLUTION

1. Depreciation for 20X4: $34,000 × 40% × 9/12 = $10,200
   Depreciation for 20X5: ($34,000 − $10,200) × 40% = $9,520

2. Book value of equipment at 31 December 20X5:

Cost	$34,000
Accumulated depreciation, 31 December 20X5:	
($34,000 − $4,000) ÷ 5 × 2.5 years	15,000
Net book value	$19,000

The asset is impaired because the higher of the discounted future cash flow of $8,000 and fair value less costs of disposal $7,000 is $8,000. This is less than the $19,000 book value. Since the remaining cost cannot be recovered through operations, the asset must be written down to its fair value of $8,000. This is a loss of $11,000.

3. Depreciation for 20X5 = A ($100,000 − 0)/5 = $20,000
   = B ($20,000 − 0)/2 = $10,000
   = C ($185,000 − 5,000)/20 = $9,000
   = D ($16,000 − 1,000)/3 = $5,000

The total depreciation for all components is $ 44,000.

APPENDIX 1

CAPITAL COST ALLOWANCE

The *Income Tax Act* does not allow the deduction of accounting depreciation or amortization expense in the determination of taxable income. Instead of depreciation or amortization, the taxpayer must either (1) deduct the expenditure from taxable income in the year that it is incurred or (2) use the form of depreciation or amortization mandated by the *Income Tax Act*. There is no choice between these two treatments; the tax treatment depends on the type of expenditure (i.e., on the type of capital asset for accounting purposes).

Just because an expenditure (or group of expenditures) is classified as a capital asset for accounting purposes does not mean that Canada Revenue Agency (CRA) will view it as a capital asset. Many of the costs that are capitalized for accounting purposes are viewed as expenses for tax purposes. This is particularly true of a large number of expenditures that accountants tend to capitalize as intangible assets, particularly when they are self-developed assets, such as development costs.

Expenditures that are considered by the *Income Tax Act* to be capital assets are subject to depreciation or amortization for tax purposes, but the depreciation or amortization is completely independent of accounting depreciation or amortization. Under GAAP, depreciation or amortization is intended to allocate an asset's historical cost to the accounting periods in which the asset is used. In contrast, tax depreciation or amortization is geared to the economic goals of the federal government, which change in response to economic conditions and the fiscal policies of Parliament. For example, the 2005 federal budget increased the CCA rate for manufacturing and processing equipment from 30% to 50% for the following seven years to encourage investment.

The Capital Cost Allowance System

Tax depreciation or amortization is known as *capital cost allowance,* or *CCA*. Basically, the CCA system is a group depreciation method. CCA requires the grouping of assets into various CCA classes established by CRA regulations. An exception to the group requirement is that buildings that are held for rental (i.e., "income properties") are treated individually; each one is a separate "class."

Most classes provide a maximum rate of depreciation or amortization that approximates double-declining balance (DDB) depreciation or amortization, although some classes use the equivalent of straight-line (SL) depreciation or amortization. Classes and rates for some of the more common assets are shown in Exhibit 10A-1, with the prescribed maximum rate shown in parentheses for the declining-balance classes.

An important point is that the rates are *maximums*. A tax-paying company does not have to use the maximum rate and, in fact, does not need to deduct any CCA at all if the company chooses not to do so. CCA is an optional deduction.

Why would a company not want to deduct CCA? Because it is not making any taxable income! If a company's taxable income is insufficient to absorb all of the CCA, the CCA can be "saved" to offset against future earnings. Regardless of whether or not a company takes CCA in a year, however, the CCA cannot be doubled up in future years. The maximum remains the same, but the base on which CCA is calculated is higher because the company did not take CCA in past years.

The basic rules for the capital cost allowance system can be explained (for most classes) as follows:

1. When assets are purchased, their purchase price (capital cost) is added to the balance (unamortized capital cost, or UCC) of the appropriate asset class. UCC is similar to the accounting concept of net book value—the initial capital cost minus accumulated CCA.

2. When assets are sold, either (1) the proceeds or (2) the capital cost, whichever is lower, is deducted from the balance in that asset's class.

3. Assets are considered to be purchased in the middle of the taxation year (i.e., the half-year convention).

EXHIBIT 10A-1

SAMPLE CCA RATES

Asset Classes Using Declining-Balance CCA

Class 1 (4%)	Buildings or other structures, including component parts acquired after 1987
Class 8 (20%)	Tangible capital property and machinery or equipment not included in another class
Class 9 (25%)	Aircraft, including furniture, fittings or equipment attached, and their spare parts
Class 10 (30%)	Automobiles, vans, trucks, electronic data processing equipment and systems software, and timber-cutting equipment
Class 12 (100%)	Jigs, patterns, tools, utensils costing less than $200, linens, computer software (except systems software)
Class 39 (25%)	Manufacturing and processing equipment acquired after 1987

Asset Classes Using Straight-Line CCA

Class 13	Leasehold improvements (life of lease plus one renewal period; minimum five years, maximum 40 years)
Class 14	Patent, franchise, concession, or licence (life of asset) with a limited life

4. The maximum CCA deductible for a particular class is the balance of unamortized capital cost (UCC), *after adjusting for the half-year rule in the year of purchase*, multiplied by the CCA rate for that class.

Exhibit 10A-2 provides an example of a calculation for CCA. Iles Machine Shop begins business in January 20X1 and purchases four lathes (class 8) for $5,000 each. A fifth lathe is purchased in 20X2 for $5,700. In 20X3, one of the original lathes is sold for $1,200 and is replaced with another lathe costing $6,500. In 20X4 one of the lathes is sold for $1,100.

EXHIBIT 10A-2

EXAMPLE OF CALCULATING CAPITAL COST ALLOWANCE

20X1 UCC opening balance		0
Additions (4 × $5,000)		$20,000
CCA for 20X1; ($20,000 × 20% × 1/2 year)		(2,000)
20X2 UCC opening balance		$18,000
Additions		5,700
CCA for 20X2; ($18,000 × 20%) + ($5,700 × 20% × 1/2)		(4,170)
20X3 UCC opening balance		$19,530
Additions	$6,500	
Proceeds on disposal	(1,200)	
Net additions		5,300
CCA for 20X3; ($19,530 × 20%) + ($5,300 × 20% × 1/2)		(4,436)
20X4 UCC opening balance		$20,394
Proceeds on disposal		(1,100)
CCA for 20X4; [($20,394 − $1,100) × 20%]		(3,859)
20X4 UCC closing balance		$15,435

When net asset additions take place, *the net addition is subject to the half-year convention* (see 20X2 and 20X3 in Exhibit 10A-2). However, when there is a net asset disposal, the entire amount is deducted prior to determining the CCA for the year (see 20X4 in Exhibit 10A-2).

The amount deducted on an asset disposal is the lower of (1) the proceeds and (2) the asset's capital cost. Proceeds up to the original capital cost are credited to the asset pool. If the proceeds on sale are higher than the original capital cost, the excess is treated as a capital gain for tax purposes. It is possible (but unlikely) that high proceeds will drive the pool into a negative balance. The negative unamortized capital cost (UCC) is reported as taxable income. More likely, though, proceeds up to capital cost just reduce the positive balance of UCC and reduce the future CCA claimable in that class.

When *all* of the assets in a class are disposed of, any remaining balance is treated as follows:

- A positive UCC balance is deducted as a terminal loss in determining taxable income.
- A negative UCC balance is added to taxable income as *recaptured* CCA.

In effect, this treatment is similar to the gain or loss on disposal of plant assets on the assumption that either too little or too much amortization (i.e., CCA) was taken over the lives of the assets. Any proceeds received in excess of the assets' capital (original) cost are treated as a capital gain for tax purposes.

SUMMARY OF KEY POINTS

1. Accounting depreciation or amortization has no tax impact; depreciation or amortization of capital assets for tax purposes is governed by the *Income Tax Act* and regulations and is completely independent of accounting depreciation or amortization.

2. Income tax depreciation or amortization is called the *capital cost allowance (CCA)* system.

3. The CCA system groups capital assets into *classes* of assets of similar types. Except for certain buildings, assets are not depreciated or amortized individually.

4. The regulations specify a depreciation or amortization *rate* to be used for each class of asset; the rate is a maximum—a company can claim less CCA in any year if management so chooses, without losing the maximum deduction in future years.

5. The half-year rule is applied to assets acquired during a taxation year.

6. Gains and losses are not recognized on the disposal of capital assets in a class, unless all of the assets in the class are disposed of. Proceeds on disposal of individual assets are credited to the asset class.

APPENDIX 2

REVALUATION MODEL

Historical cost or the cost model has long been the generally accepted basis for reporting long-lived assets in Canada. On rare occasions, however, a company may restate one or more of its capital assets upward, generally by using appraisal values. The general use of appraised values has not been a common practice in Canada prior to the adoption of international accounting standards.

The revaluation model is an allowed alternative to the cost model for property, plant, and equipment; intangible assets with an active market; and mineral reserves. The cost model is the predominant model, since, as we will see, the revaluation model involves a lot of bookkeeping and costs. This model is also less popular than the fair value model that is an allowed alternative for investment property (as discussed in the Appendix to Chapter 9). The differences between these two models will be explained in this appendix.

The revaluation model uses fair value as the basis of measurement every time a revaluation is completed. In between revaluations, the asset is carried at its revalued amount less subsequent accumulated depreciation and subsequent accumulated impairment losses. The revaluation model is selected by class of assets. For example, the revaluation model could be selected for the classes that include land and buildings, and the cost model could be selected for all other classes of assets. It is important to explain a key difference between the fair value model and the revaluation model. Using the fair value model provides fair value every reporting date, while the revaluation model has fair value only when a revaluation is done, which does not need to be every year. In the periods between revaluations, the assets are carried at their revalued amounts less subsequent accumulated depreciation and accumulated impairment losses.

How Is Fair Value Determined? Fair value is the base for the revaluation model. Therefore, to use this model, a company must be able to determine fair value. The fair value hierarchy discussed in Chapter 2 would provide guidance on fair value measurement. Fair value does not need to be an appraised value. Appraisals would be appropriate where available (e.g., for land and buildings). Fair value could also be an estimate based on the present value of future cash flows or an estimate based on depreciated replacement cost. For example, a specialized piece of machinery that is rarely sold could use the replacement cost of a similar machine to estimate fair value. If the existing machinery was 50% depreciated and the replacement cost of a similar machine was $100,000, fair value based on depreciated replacement cost would be $50,000. Management has a range of valuation methods or choices in estimating fair value.

Frequency of Revaluations The frequency of revaluations depends on the volatility of the fair value of the asset. If the asset value changes frequently, revaluation may be completed every year. If the asset value is not very volatile, the revaluation could be up to every five years. Like any other accounting policy choice, the revaluation period selected must be consistent unless the volatility of the fair value of the asset has changed. This is another difference between the revaluation and fair value model. The fair value model requires a fair value every year.

Depreciation and Impact of Accumulated Depreciation Depreciation is taken every year and prior to the revaluation. A revaluation is completed after taking depreciation expense and after the accumulated depreciation is eliminated. There are two methods of eliminating accumulated depreciation. Method one is the simplest method and common in practice:

- Method One (Elimination Method): The cost of the asset is restated to its revalued amount and the accumulated depreciation is eliminated.
- Method Two (Proportionate Method): The original cost of the asset and the accumulated depreciation is restated proportionately so the net carrying amount after revaluation equals its revalued amount.

Impact of Revaluation and Revaluation Surplus Changes due to revaluation may impact either other comprehensive income (OCI) or net income. Whether or not net income is affected will depend on the direction of the change and the accumulated revaluation changes to date. The flowchart in Exhibit 10A-3 helps illustrate the impact of changes.

Case A: Carrying amount increased—illustrated on left side of the flowchart

- First revaluation—the increase is recognized in OCI and then accumulated in the revaluation surplus in equity.
- Subsequent revaluation—the first question is, has there been a previous downward revaluation? If yes, then the increase is recognized in the statement of profit and loss (net income) up to the amount of the previous downward revaluation, and any excess is recognized in OCI and then accumulated in the revaluation surplus in equity. If no, then the entire increase is recognized in OCI and then accumulated in the revaluation surplus in equity.

Case B: Carrying amount decreased—illustrated on right side of the flowchart

- First revaluation—the decrease is recognized in net income.
- Subsequent revaluation—the first question is, has there been a previous upward revaluation? If yes, then the decrease is recognized first by a decrease in OCI, which will then decrease the amount accumulated in the revaluation surplus up to the amount of the previous upward revaluation and recognize any excess in net income. If no, then the entire decrease is recognized in the statement of profit and loss (net income).

This is a difference between the fair value and revaluation model. With the fair value model, all increases and decreases are recognized in net income.

Now let us use an example to illustrate how this works. A company decides to use the revaluation model for a machine. On 1 January, it purchased a new machine for $100,000 and determined that the machine has a five-year useful life with zero residual value. The straight-line depreciation method is being used and the machine has no significant components. The company has decided that the machine has a volatile fair value and will revalue every year.

The carrying amount for the machinery at the end of the first year is $100,000 − 20,000 = $80,000. We will assume on revaluation the machine has a fair value of $95,000.

The fair value is $95,000 and the carrying amount is $80,000. There are two methods of accounting for the accumulated depreciation.

- Elimination method—the accumulated depreciation of $20,000 is eliminated and the increase in the value of the machine of $15,000 is recognized in OCI.

Accumulated depreciation	20,000	
Machinery		5,000
OCI—revaluation surplus		15,000

- Proportionate method—revalue the original cost by grossing it up to $118,750 (95,000 ÷ 4 = 23,750 × 5 years = $118,750). Annual depreciation on the grossed-up amount would be $118,750 ÷ 5 = $23,750 compared to $20,000; therefore, accumulated depreciation is adjusted by $3,750.

Machinery	18,750	
Accumulated depreciation		3,750
OCI—revaluation surplus		15,000

Accumulated Revaluation Surplus The accumulated revaluation surplus is transferred to retained earnings on derecognition or as the asset is used.

Note Disclosure Additional note disclosure is required when the revaluation method has been selected by a company. Note disclosure is required for the following:

a. The date of the revaluation;
b. Whether or not an appraiser was used and, if so, the name and qualifications;
c. The methods used to determine fair value;
d. The amount of the revaluation surplus; and
e. For each class, the carrying amount of the asset if the cost model had been used.

To sum up, a lot of extra work is involved in the use of the revaluation model.

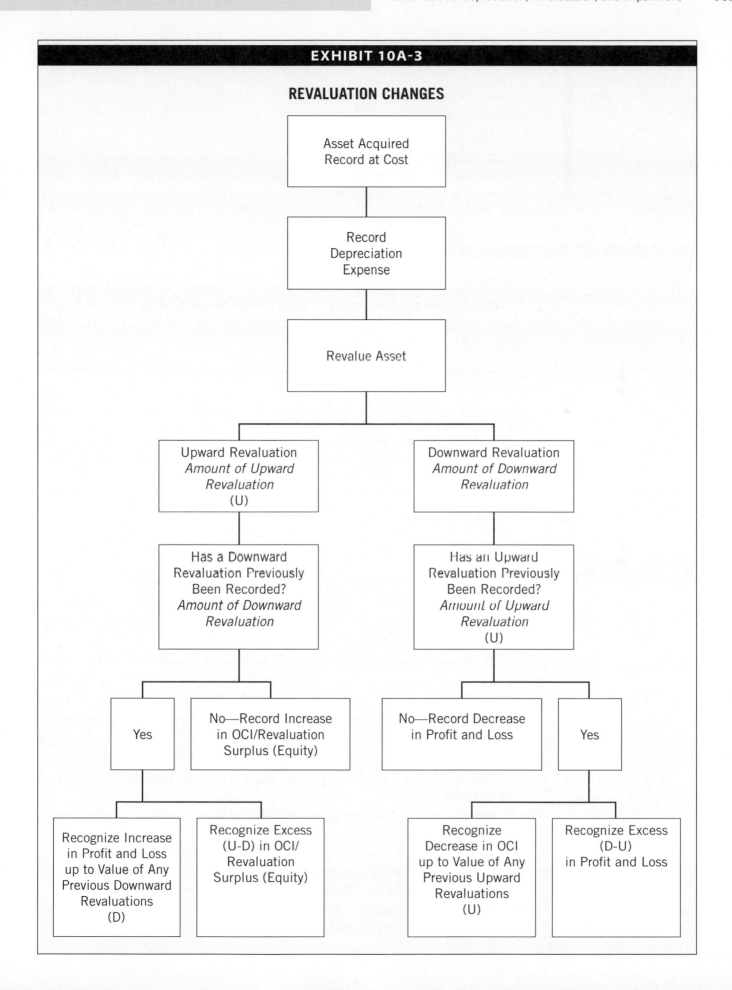

EXHIBIT 10A-3

REVALUATION CHANGES

Asset Acquired Record at Cost

Record Depreciation Expense

Revalue Asset

Upward Revaluation
Amount of Upward Revaluation
(U)

Downward Revaluation
Amount of Downward Revaluation

Has a Downward Revaluation Previously Been Recorded?
Amount of Downward Revaluation

Has an Upward Revaluation Previously Been Recorded?
Amount of Upward Revaluation
(U)

Yes

No—Record Increase in OCI/Revaluation Surplus (Equity)

No—Record Decrease in Profit and Loss

Yes

Recognize Increase in Profit and Loss up to Value of Any Previous Downward Revaluations (D)

Recognize Excess (U-D) in OCI/ Revaluation Surplus (Equity)

Recognize Decrease in OCI up to Value of Any Previous Upward Revaluations (U)

Recognize Excess (D-U) in Profit and Loss

RELEVANT STANDARDS

CPA Canada Handbook, Part I (IFRS):
- IAS 16, Property, Plant, and Equipment
- IAS 38, Intangible Assets

CPA Canada Handbook, Part II (ASPE):
- Section 3061, Property, Plant, and Equipment

SUMMARY OF KEY POINTS

1. The revaluation model is an alternative to the cost model for property, plant, and equipment, intangible assets with an active market; and mineral reserves.

2. Fair value is the base for the revaluation model and could be an appraisal or estimated fair value.

3. Revaluations are done with sufficient regularity depending on the volatility of the fair value of the asset.

4. Depreciation is taken every year. The revaluation adjustment can be made using either the elimination or the proportionate method. The changes in the revaluation can impact either the net income or OCI, depending on the direction of the change, and previous recorded changes in value. The OCI adjustments accumulate in an equity account called the *revaluation surplus*.

QUESTIONS

Q10-1 Compare and explain the terms "amortization," "depletion," and "depreciation."

Q10-2 What effect do changes in the current market value of the asset being depreciated or amortized have on depreciation or amortization estimates?

Q10-3 What type of long-lived assets are not depreciated, and why?

Q10-4 For what purpose are assets separated into components and depreciated by component?

Q10-5 Why is disclosure of depreciation or amortization methods and rates so important?

Q10-6 List the several factors a firm would consider in choosing a depreciation or amortization method.

Q10-7 Why might an asset with a 30-year physical life correctly be depreciated over only 14 years?

Q10-8 What is unique about the depreciation period for major spare parts or standby equipment?

Q10-9 Why is straight-line depreciation or amortization so popular in practice?

Q10-10 What is a diminishing-balance method of depreciation? Under what circumstances would this method generally be appropriate?

Q10-11 Explain the accounting policy alternatives that a company may use for assets acquired during the reporting year.

Q10-12 Explain what is meant by *group depreciation*. Under what circumstances is such a method appropriate?

Q10-13 What is an *impairment* in the value of property, plant, and equipment? How is it measured and reported?

Q10-14 Assume that the fair value of a cash-generating business unit is estimated at $17,000,000, while carrying value of the net assets is $22,000,000. What is the problem? What is the next step?

Q10-15 What estimates have to be made when recording an impairment of a long-lived asset?

Q10-16 Can an impairment loss be reversed?

Q10-17 What are the differences in impairment testing for property, plant, and equipment in standards for publicly accounting enterprises compared with standards for private enterprises?

Q10-18 When is the revaluation model allowed as an alternative to the cost model?

Q10-19 What are some key differences between the fair value and the revaluation models?

Q10-20 If revaluation accounting is used, how are revaluation decreases and increases treated?

CASE 10-1

ROCK GROUP LIMITED

You were recently approached by one of your clients, Wendy Wonders, the Chief Financial Officer of Rock Group Limited (RGL), a Canadian public company with a 31 December year-end. RGL manufactures and sells power precision hand-tools and accessories, such as hammers and drills.

To complement RGL's existing products, RGL is interested in purchasing 100% of the common shares of Scrulox Screws Inc. (SSI), a private company reporting under Accounting Standards for Private Enterprises (ASPE).

SSI was identified as an acquisition target because of its complementary product offerings, extensive internally generated customer database, and overall strong financial results, including a consistent gross margin on all sales of 60%. As of 31 December 20X2, the carrying value of SSI's net assets, excluding the customer database, was $29 million (fair market value of $50 million), which includes two manufacturing plants with a carrying value of $11 million each (fair market value of $19 million each). SSI's customer database is estimated to have a fair market value of $0.8 million.

SSI's financial statements have never been audited. The purchase price for SSI is based on two times net income for its year ended 31 December 20X2, which currently is estimated at $52 million (2 × $26 million SSI preliminary net income).

It is now 1 April 20X3. You have met with Wally, SSI's bookkeeper and primary shareholder, to obtain additional information on SSI. Notes from this meeting are included in Exhibit 1.

Wendy would like you to review SSI's accounting under ASPE for the year ended 31 December 20X2 and provide your comments. For each significant transaction, she would also like to understand what alternatives and possible adjustment (if any) needs to be recorded to reflect the transaction under IFRS.

As this is the first acquisition of a company for RGL, Wendy is unsure of the initial and subsequent accounting for SSI.

Required:

Prepare a report that responds to Wendy Wonders' requests and concerns. Be specific and quantify, wherever possible.

EXHIBIT 1

NOTES FROM MEETING WITH SSI BOOKKEEPER

- In anticipation of being purchased by a public company, on 29 December 20X2, SSI signed a contract with a new controller, proficient in International Financial Reporting Standards (IFRS), and agreed to pay her $165,000 per year starting 1 February 20X3, her first day of work. Wally is excited to have a controller who will be able to teach him the fundamentals of IFRS!

- SSI's manufacturing plant in Barrie, Ontario, produces electric drills, with annual net cash flows of $10 million and manufacturing assets of $25 million. SSI management is committed to opening a new plant in Hamilton, Ontario, which will produce solar drills that power on solar energy and therefore do not require electricity. As a result, production at the Barrie plant will be adjusted to reflect the change, resulting in annual projected cash-flows of $5 million expected for the next five years, after which, the plant will be shut down.

- As the new plant is set to open in the future, no accounting entries have been recorded.

- To support the building of the new Hamilton plant, the Government of Ontario has provided SSI with $10 million to help with the cost of purchasing new manufacturing equipment and to support payroll costs of the various individuals directly involved in the construction project, including architects, construction workers, project managers, and those individuals indirectly involved in the project, such as marketing personnel who are promoting the new solar hammer.

- Wally recorded the receipt of the government funds as revenue. Wally notes that if the government grant was not received, SSI would be forced to obtain a bank loan to fund the construction at a costly interest rate of 8%.

- On 30 July 20X2, SSI made an $80,000 upfront payment to Print Inc. to print the new 20X3 SSI product catalogues, featuring the upcoming solar drill. The catalogues were delivered to SSI on 5 October 20X2 and will be distributed to the public in the spring of 20X3, at which point SSI will record an expense of $80,000.

- On 24 March 20X2 SSI's Estevan, Saskatchewan, plant was the victim of theft. As of the last inventory count on 31 December 20X1, the plant had $1.8 million worth of products. SSI's records indicate that sales from 1 January to 24 March were $1.48 million and during that same time, purchases were $1.3 million. SSI's insurance will cover the cost of the lost inventory once Wally has filed the claim. Wally is not sure how much inventory was lost and therefore has yet to record an entry.

- Adjacent to the Estevan plant, SSI owns a parcel of land that is currently vacant and held for undetermined future use. Due to the increasing population of Estevan, the land has been gradually increasing in worth. To better reflect the true value of the land, Wally recorded the land at fair value on the balance sheet, increasing the carrying value from $1 million to $6 million.

(Alex Fisher)

CASE 10-2

ROAD SAFETY INCORPORATED

You have just been hired as an accounting advisor by Road Safety Incorporated (RSI), a company that manufactures road safety equipment (e.g., crash barriers, traffic lights, and electronic information signs). RSI was founded in 20X4 and has grown rapidly over the last five years. In 20X7, the company had its first profit with annual sales of over

$8 million, which is the highest level of sales in the company's history, and taxable income of $3 million.

RSI has needed to raise financing to develop a new product, "traffic sensors," which will identify traffic jams and warn motorists through the company's electronic information signs of problems and alternative routes. Part of the funding for product development has come from a bank loan. The bank requires an annual audit and specifies a maximum debt-to-equity ratio. At the end of 20X6, RSI was close to the maximum debt-to-equity ratio. This year will be the first year that RSI will have an audit completed.

You have just completed a meeting with the President of RSI, Nancy O'Callaghan. Nancy and other family members own all of the Class A common shares in RSI. They have 10 votes per share. During that meeting, she made the comments below. Nancy has requested that you draft a memo to her identifying alternative accounting policies as well as your overall recommendations for each issue.

"Our turnaround is for a large part due to the hiring of Tom, our new CEO. We were thrilled when he left our major competitor in January to join our team. He is such a valuable asset that we offered him a bonus of 10% of net income each year. Look at what he has accomplished! We are out of the red thanks to him. Besides increasing efficiency, he even had time to develop these new accounting policies.

"In the past all of our assets were recorded at cost and depreciated. Tom has just told us that we can recognize increases in some of these assets. For example, we have some vacant land that is just sitting there until we decide what to do with it. Also, we know our building used for administration and manufacturing has skyrocketed in value. Both can be shown at fair value, which is more relevant! And as an extra bonus, we will not need to record any depreciation on these assets. The bank will be very happy if we show higher values on our statement of financial position. And just think of how much stronger our earnings will be, which will make our shareholders happy.

"We offer a minimum 10-year guarantee with our products. If something does not work, we will fix it within a minimum of 24 hours at no cost. Speed is critical, since our equipment saves lives. Our products are of such high quality we anticipate few if any warranty costs. For that reason, Tom decided to keep the accounting simple—when and if we do any work we will record an expense.

"Another account Tom said not to worry about is that thing called *deferred taxes*. Whoever thought up that accounting rule? To keep life simple, income tax expense will equal the amount that we pay to the government for our taxes. On the other hand, when we can look good Tom said we should take advantage of those options. We have past taxable losses of $2 million that Tom said we can record as an asset.

"We have never amortized or tested goodwill for impairment, since goodwill is being built up in our business, not used. In fact, Tom reassured me that it will never go down in value, since our business is continuing to grow. This year for the first time, on Tom's advice, we acquired another private company that provides additional products to add to our line. That increased our goodwill even more.

"To preserve our cash reserves, Tom obtained some needed computer technology for our traffic sensors by having RSI issue some Class B common shares. The value of these shares for the financial statements has yet to be determined. This computer technology is leading edge with nothing comparable in the marketplace.

"Some of our manufacturing machinery, especially the robotics equipment, has major parts that need to be replaced every few years and requires major inspections and overhauls. Tom said we do not need to worry about that from an accounting point of view. That is just a business issue. Straight-line depreciation will be the simplest, and to minimize our information system costs, the machinery will just be depreciated based on the total carrying amount of the machinery."

Required:
Part A: Prepare the report for Nancy, assuming RSI is a public company.
Part B: Prepare the report for Nancy, assuming RSI is a private company and will use ASPE.

CASE 10-3

OMEGA PROPERTIES LIMITED

Omega Properties Limited (OPL) is a public corporation that manages 63 hotels under 3 brand names in 5 countries. The main shareholder is Isadora Duncan, who owns 10% of the total outstanding shares in the form of multiple voting shares that carry 15 votes per share. All other shares carry one vote per share. Isadora Duncan is OPL's founder and chief executive officer.

Omega Properties Limited has three operating divisions, each of which is a wholly owned subsidiary of OPL:

- Omega Hotels, Ltd., which operates midrange hotels;

- Xanadu Hotels and Resorts Corporation, a group of luxury hotels; and

- Alpha Express Inc., a small chain of low-cost hotel properties.

The divisions operate largely autonomously, each setting its own operating policies that best suit conditions for its market segment. The senior executives of each division report directly to their counterparts in OPL's head office. The subsidiaries' financial results are fully consolidated with those of OPL.

It is now early December 20X7. OPL Chief Financial Officer Gary Drabinsky is considering how to reflect certain events and transactions that have occurred during the fiscal year ending 31 December 20X7. He has requested your advice as an external professional accountant, and has provided you with the information shown in Exhibit 1.

EXHIBIT 1

1. Alpha Express Inc. was purchased by OPL in late 20X3 for $227 million cash. The fair value of OPL's net assets at that time was $192 million. For the first two years that OPL owned Alpha, Alpha achieved the expected profit and cash flow returns. In 20X6, however, the low-cost hotel segment suffered a downturn due to a mild recession. As well, 20X6 saw increased competition from big chains in that market, such as Holiday Inn Express. Now OPL and Alpha executives believe that Alpha will be underperforming for the foreseeable future. Indeed, it is quite possible that the OPL Board of Directors will decide to sell or dismantle Alpha during 20X8. As an alternative, OPL is thinking of combining Alpha with the main Omega Hotel chain, which continues to be quite profitable.

2. In early 20X7, Xanadu entered into a 10-year contract to manage a luxury hotel in Mumbai. OPL agreed to provide $63 million in loans to the hotel's owners to obtain the contract. The loans are to be used by the hotel's owners for remodelling and upgrading of facilities to meet Xanadu's standards. By the end of 20X7, OPL had paid $54 million, of which $23 million related to obtaining the management contract and $31 million was part of the loan.

3. During the year, OPL sold a hotel in Hawaii for net proceeds of $140 million. The property had a net book value of $93 million. OPL recorded a gain of $47 million before taxes. The sales contract stipulates that if the hotel's net operating cash flow over the

next three years falls below certain benchmarks, as specified in the sales contract, OPL will be required to refund up to 20% of the sales proceeds. OPL senior management believes that it is highly unlikely that any repayment will be necessary.

4. Omega owns and manages a hotel in New Orleans. The hotel was badly damaged by a severe hurricane in late October 20X6. Just prior to the hurricane, the hotel was enjoying high occupancy and was very profitable. Its net book value was $144 million but its estimated fair value was well over $200 million. The hotel was closed immediately after the hurricane and remained closed through the remainder of 20X6 pending an opportunity for engineers and others to assess the extent of the damage. In 20X7, it became apparent that although the damage could be repaired at a tolerable cost, the future business prospects were not good due to the almost complete absence of either business or leisure travellers. Therefore, in April 20X7, the OPL Board of Directors decided to sell the property and engaged a commercial real estate broker for that purpose. The broker estimated that OPL should expect the property to sell for no more than $37 million in its present condition.

5. The Xanadu division owns no hotels. The division operates exclusively through management contracts. In many cases, the hotels are owned by an investor who also owns 22% of OPL's limited voting shares.

6. In addition to managing hotels under its own brand, OPL also earns fee revenue in both its Omega Hotels and Xanadu divisions by designing and supervising the construction and fitting out of hotels that OPL will neither own nor operate. OPL also earns commissions as a percentage of the cost of goods and materials purchased by these clients through OPL's centralized purchasing system. These fees are treated as a reduction in the cost of operating the central purchasing system.

7. Xanadu entered into a five-year contract for $20 million that permits an unrelated party to use the Xanadu brand name for a new hotel in Japan. Xanadu can cancel the contract if the hotel does not hold to Xanadu's high standards of maintenance and service; no money need be refunded if Xanadu cancels the contract. The contract is renewable by mutual consent. Xanadu has received half of the money, with the rest due in annual instalments of $2 million. The agreement also permits the hotel to use the Xanadu central reservation system at a fee that is half of the fee normally charged to non-OPL properties.

Required:

Prepare a report for Mr. Drabinsky in which you point out any reporting problems and recommend appropriate reporting and disclosure, based on the information that you received from him.

TECHNICAL REVIEW

TR10-1 Depreciation: Manufacturing Incorporated purchased a machine on 1 January 20X2 for $500,000. The estimated physical life of the machine is 15 years, but the estimated useful life to Hawkrigg is 10 years. The equipment has an estimated residual value of $20,000. The equipment was ready for use on 1 January 20X2.

Required:

1. Calculate depreciation expense for 20X2 and 20X3 using the straight-line method.
2. Assume the machine is anticipated to produce 800,000 units. In 20X2 the machine produced 150,000 units and in 20X3 120,000 units. Calculate depreciation expense for 20X2 and 20X3 using the productive-output method.
3. Calculate depreciation expense for 20X2 and 20X3 using the declining-balance method using 40%.

TR10-2 Component Depreciation: XYZ Incorporated, a public company, has a building it purchased for $400,000. It is estimated the building has a useful life of 25 years and zero residual value. The building has three major components. XYZ uses the straight-line method of depreciation.

Component	Unit Cost	Useful Life
A	$ 80,000	5 years
B	$120,000	10 years
C	$200,000	25 years

Required:

1. What is the amount of depreciation in year one? Provide the journal entry.
2. What would be the impact if component A was a major spare part that was replaced at the end of the fourth year instead of year five? The new major spare part had a cost of $100,000. Provide the journal entry.

TR10-3 Component Depreciation: The company has a major asset that has just been purchased and has been segregated into the following significant components made up of spare parts and major inspections. Component D is all of the insignificant components grouped together with an average cost and useful life.

Component	Quantity	Original Unit Cost	Residual Value	Useful Life
A	2	$120,000	$5,000	12 years
B	1	40,000	0	3 years
C	5	8,000	500	6 years
D	10	2,000	0	2 years

Required:

1. Assuming straight-line is the appropriate method of depreciation, what is the amount of depreciation in year one?
2. What would be the impact if component B was a major spare part that was replaced at the end of the second year instead of the third year as originally predicted? The new major spare part has a value of $50,000. Identify the specific journal entry that would be required when the major spare part was replaced.

TR10-4 Recoverable Amount: Innovative Incorporated has a piece of equipment with a carrying amount of $175,000. Technology has changed, indicating that the machine may be impaired. A new machine with updated technology could be purchased for $350,000. A used machine of similar vintage is listed on Kijiji for $160,000. The estimated discounted cash flows from continuing to use the asset are $148,000. The undiscounted cash flows from the use of the asset are $180,000. The estimated value if the company sold the asset less commission costs is $155,000.

Required:

1. What value would be used to compare with the carrying amount to determine if there is impairment?
2. What is the amount of impairment?

TR10-5 Impairment: Food Incorporated, a public company, has a machine that processes and packages tuna in oil. This machine cannot be used for any other purpose. The machine originally cost $100,000 and is being amortized on a straight-line basis over 20 years. The carrying amount of the machine on 31 December 20X2 is $20,000. Recent health studies have shown that due to contamination, eating tuna is bad for your health. Undiscounted cash flows for the machine are $22,000. Discounted cash flows for the machine are $17,000. The machine is unique; therefore, there is no fair value.

Required:

1. Is the machine impaired? Provide the journal entry if there is impairment.
2. At the beginning of the following year new evidence comes out rebutting the evidence that tuna is bad for your health. In fact, studies have shown it is very healthy to eat fish. The company has also been able to package the tuna in water instead of oil. Can any previous impairment be reversed? If yes, provide the journal entry.

ASSIGNMENTS

★ **A10-1 Depreciation Policy:** Nancy O'Callaghan, the president of Clean Enterprises, is proposing the following amortization policy for property, plant, and equipment:

> I want to keep things simple and minimize any deferred tax liabilities. I propose we use the CCA rates for declining-balance depreciation for all of our assets. These are the tax rules! I know that the equipment will last a longer period of time, but I prefer the fast write-off to be conservative.

Required:

Is this depreciation policy acceptable? Write a brief memo to the president explaining your position.

★ **A10-2 Depreciation:** Manufacturing Incorporated had the following disclosure in its significant accounting policy note:

The amortization of PP&E is calculated on a straight-line basis over the following useful lives:

Buildings	5 to 75 years
Equipment	2 to 15 years
Other	3 to 20 years

Required:

1. Why is there a range for useful lives?
2. How could a building have a useful life of only five years and equipment for two years?

★ **A10-3 Valuation Models:** The following are the three valuation models demonstrated in Chapters 9 and 10:

a. Cost model
b. Revaluation model
c. Fair value model

Required:

Explain how depreciation and impairment is accounted for in each of these models. Discuss the differences among the models.

★ **A10-4 Depreciation or Amortization Policy:** The methods of depreciation or amortization demonstrated in the chapter include the following:

a. Straight-line.
b. Units-of-production.
c. Declining-balance.

Required:
Indicate the likely choice of depreciation or amortization method expected under each of the following circumstances:

a. The company has land that has site restoration costs (asset retirement obligations) that will be completed in 10 years.
b. The company is a mining company and assets to be depreciated are mine exploration and evaluation costs.
c. The company has a number of intangible assets with a limited life span.
d. The company wishes to portray stable income and expense patterns over time.
e. The company has a backup transformer that is installed and ready to use, even though it may never be brought into operation.
f. The company wants to minimize bookkeeping costs by keeping allocation methods simple.
g. The company expects to use the asset heavily in initial years and less as it grows older.
h. The company expects to use the asset sporadically, but the asset will not wear out unless used.
i. Technological obsolescence is a significant factor in estimating the useful life of the asset.
j. The company wants to minimize its deferred tax liability balances.
k. The company is a subsidiary of a parent that uses straight-line depreciation.

★ **A10-5 Amortization or Impairment:** Technology Incorporated (TI) has the following intangible assets:

Case A   TI acquired a patent from another company that expires in 10 years. The purpose of the purchase was to eliminate competition for one of its top selling products. Based on market surveys their product will continue to have sales for at least the next eight years. TI intends to hold the patent but not manufacture the product.

Case B   TI acquired a second patent from another company that expires in 15 years. The company intends to manufacture the product. Based on market surveys, this product will have strong sales for at least the next 10 years or until another competitor enters the market with a similar product.

Case C   TI acquired a quota that can be renewed indefinitely at a minimal cost. TI's intention is to continue to renew the quota. These quotas are high in demand and very difficult to obtain.

Case D   TI has a registered trademark that it has used for 10 years for one of its top-selling products. TI intends to renew the trademark indefinitely.

Required:
Should the intangible assets be amortized or just tested for impairment? If amortized, what is the appropriate period? Support your response.

★ **A10-6 Component Depreciation:** You have been asked to consider the following situations.

Case A   The company purchased a machine for $50,000 cash. It is estimated the machine will have a useful life for 10 years but it has a part that will need to be replaced every two and a half years. The cost to replace this part is $500.

Case B   The company purchased a second machine for $40,000 cash. It is estimated the machine will have a useful life for 10 years but it has a part that will need to be replaced every two years. The cost to replace this part is $8,000.

Case C   The company purchased a third machine for $100,000 cash. This machine requires a major overhaul every three years that costs $25,000.

Required:
For which machines is it likely there would be component depreciation, and why?

★ **A10-7 Component Depreciation:** You have been asked to explain the appropriate policy for depreciation for the following two cases for a major utility:

Case A The utility has a number of transformers in its transformer stations that transform power from a high voltage to a lower voltage that is the required voltage for customers. To ensure that major customers that require a reliable source of power at all times (e.g., hospitals) have it, the utility installs two transformers. The first transformer is on-line continuously and has a useful life of 50 years. The second transformer is installed as a backup in case the first transformer fails. This is referred to as standby equipment. This means the hospitals will not lose their power supply. The second transformer is rarely used but is considered essential to customers that cannot afford to lose their power.

Case B The utility has other customers for which it is not critical that they have a reliable source of power at all times. They can afford to have a short period of time without power while the transformer is replaced. Spare transformers are kept in the storage facility until they are needed for installation. On installation, the utility replaces the existing transformer, which then has a useful life of 50 years. Transformers are not subject to obsolescence.

Required:
What is the appropriate accounting policy in these two unrelated cases?

★★ **A10-8 Depreciation Computation:** Mace Company acquired equipment with components that are not significant and cost $36,000, which will be depreciated on the assumption that they will last six years and have a $2,400 residual value. Several possible methods of amortization are under consideration.

Required:
1. Prepare a schedule that shows annual amortization expense for the first two years, assuming the following (show computations and round to the nearest dollar):
   a. Declining-balance method, using a rate of 30%.
   b. Productive-output method. Estimated output is a total of 210,000 units, of which 24,000 will be produced the first year; 36,000 in each of the next two years; 30,000 the fourth year; and 42,000 the fifth and sixth years.
   c. Straight-line method.
2. Repeat your calculations for requirement (1), assuming a useful life of 10 years, and a DB rate of 20% that reflects the longer life, but the same number of units of production. The residual value is unchanged. What conclusion can you reach by comparing the results of (1) and (2)?
3. What criteria would you consider important in selecting a depreciation method?

★★★ **A10-9 Depreciation Schedule:** Quick Producers acquired factory equipment on 1 January 20X5, costing $78,000. In view of pending technological developments, it is estimated that the machine will have a resale value upon disposal in four years of $16,000 and that disposal costs will be $1,000. Quick has a fiscal year-end that ends on 31 December. Data relating to the equipment follow:

Estimated service life:

Years	4
Service-hours	20,000

Actual operations:

Calendar Year	Service Hours
20X5	5,700
20X6	5,000
20X7	4,800
20X8	4,400

Required:
Round to the nearest dollar, and show computations.

1. Prepare a depreciation schedule for the asset, using
   a. Straight-line depreciation.
   b. Declining-balance depreciation, using a 40% rate.
   c. Service-hours depreciation.
2. Express straight-line depreciation as a percentage of original cost.
3. Explain whether:
   a. The rate of 40% was a good choice for declining-balance depreciation.
   b. The 20,000 estimate of total service hours was accurate.

★★   **A10-10 Interpreting Depreciation Disclosures:** Portions of the 20X2 financial statements
of William's Company, a paint manufacturer, are reproduced below (in thousands of dollars):

Partial Income Statement for the year ended 31 December 20X2

Net sales	$2,266,732
Total expenses	2,079,455
Income before income tax	187,277
Income tax	64,611
Net income	$ 122,666

Note 1: Significant Accounting Policies

Property, Plant, and Equipment. Property, plant, and equipment are stated on the basis of
cost. Depreciation is provided principally by the straight-line method. The major classes of
assets and ranges of depreciation rates are as follows:

Buildings	2%–6%
Machinery	4%–20%
Furniture and fixtures	5%–20%
Automobiles and trucks	10%–33%

Note 16: Property, Plant, and Equipment Schedules

Cost	Beginning	Additions	Retirements	Other	Ending
Buildings	$191,540	$11,574	$ (960)	($7,185)	$194,969
Machinery	404,156	43,968	(16,319)	466	432,271

Total Accumulated Depreciation

	Beginning	Additions	Retirements	Other	Ending
Buildings	$ 62,843	$ 7,422	$ (769)	($4,951)	$ 64,545
Machinery	211,662	37,085	(12,302)	(845)	235,600

Required:
1. What method of depreciation is used by Williams?
2. What are the average estimated useful lives of buildings owned by Williams?
3. What percentage of the useful life of buildings remains, on average, at the end of the year?
4. What is the book value of machinery retired in the year?
5. Depreciation on buildings and machinery was what percentage of (a) total expenses and
   (b) pretax earnings?

★★   **A10-11 Analysis of Three Depreciation Methods—Maximize Income:** On 1 January
20X5, Lee Company, a tool manufacturer, acquired new industrial equipment for $2 million.
The new equipment had a useful life of four years, and the residual value was estimated to be
$220,000. Vello estimates that the new equipment can produce 20,000 tools in its first year.

Production is then estimated to decline by 2,000 units per year over the remaining useful life of the equipment.

The following depreciation methods are under consideration:

a. Declining-balance (50% rate)
b. Straight-line
c. Units-of-output

Required:

Which depreciation method would result in maximum income for financial statement reporting for the three-year period ending 31 December 20X7? Prepare a schedule showing the amount of accumulated depreciation at 31 December 20X7, under each method selected. Show supporting computations in good form.

 A10-12 Identify, Recalculate Depreciation: Beans Company purchased a special machine at a cost of $81,000 plus provincial sales tax of $6,480 (non-recoverable). The machine is expected to have a residual value of $6,000 at the end of its service life.

To assist in preparing the journal entries for depreciation of this machine, your assistant prepared the following spreadsheet:

BEANS COMPANY

Cost of asset			$87,480
Asset's residual value			6,000
Years of service life			4
Output in units	Year 1	1,400	
	Year 2	1,300	
	Year 3	1,000	
	Year 4	1,100	
Total expected output			4,800

	Method 1		Method 2		Method 3	
Year	Depreciation Expense	Accumulated Depreciation	Depreciation Expense	Accumulated Depreciation	Depreciation Expense	Accumulated Depreciation
1	$21,870	$21,870	$27,265	$27,265	$21,870	$21,870
2	16,403	38,273	25,318	52,583	21,870	43,740
3	12,302	50,575	19,475	72,058	21,870	65,610
4	36,905	87,480	21,422	93,480	21,870	87,480
Total	$87,480		$93,480		$87,480	

The spreadsheet includes statistics relating to the machine and calculates depreciation using three different methods—productive output, straight-line, and declining balance at a 50% rate. However, due to some carelessness, your assistant made at least one error in the calculations for each method.

Required:

1. Identify which method is the:
   a. Productive method.
   b. Straight-line method.
   c. Declining-balance method (50% rate).
2. Describe the error(s) made in the calculations for each method.
3. Recalculate depreciation expense for Year 2 under each method.

★★★   **A10-13 Depreciation and Depletion—Schedule, Entries:** Gaspe Mining Corporation
bought mineral-bearing land for $600,000 that engineers estimate will yield 400,000 kilo-
grams of economically removable ore. The land will have a value of $80,000 after the ore is
removed.

To work the property, Gaspe built structures and sheds on the site that cost $160,000;
these will last 10 years, and because their use is confined to mining and it would be expensive
to dismantle and move them, they will have no residual value. Machinery that cost $144,000
was installed at the mine, and the added cost for installation was $3,000. This machinery
should last 15 years; like that of the structures, the usefulness of the machinery is confined
to these mining operations. Dismantling and removal costs when the property has been fully
worked will approximately equal the value of the machinery at that time; therefore, Gaspe
does not plan to use the structures or the machinery after the minerals have been removed.

In the first year, Gaspe removed only 12,000 kilograms of ore; however, production was
doubled in the second year. It is expected that all of the removable ore will be extracted
within eight years from the start of operations.

Required:
Prepare a schedule showing (1) unit and total depletion and depreciation and (2) net book
value of the assets for the first and second years of operation. Use the units-of-production
method of depreciation for all assets.

★   **A10-14 Component Depreciation:** Highway Construction Incorporated (HCI) bought
a large piece of construction equipment at the beginning of 20X5.

- The construction equipment was a large piece of heavy equipment with an original cost
  of $600,000. This equipment was broken out into four components. The shell of the
  equipment is $200,000 and anticipated to last 10 years. The motor costs $180,000 and
  needs to have a major overhaul and inspection every three years. The tires cost $20,000
  and need to be replaced every two years. The shovel at the front of the equipment costs
  $170,000 and needs to be replaced every five years. The remainder of the cost, $30,000,
  is made up of insignificant parts. These are grouped together and are replaced on average every two years.
- Expected residual value at the end of 10 years for the shell is $8,000. The residual value
  for the remaining components is zero.
- HCI uses straight-line amortization for all construction equipment.

Required:
1. What is the depreciation expense for 20X5 assuming a full year's worth of depreciation?
2. How would the amount of depreciation differ with component depreciation compared with
   taking depreciation on the construction equipment without breaking it into components?
3. What is the logic behind component accounting?

★★   **A10-15 Depreciation:** The following information relates to Hawkrigg Corporation's
purchase of equipment on 15 June 20X7:

Invoice price	$210,000
Discount for early payment (if paid by 30 June)	$1,050
Shipping costs	$ 2,000
Installation	$ 1,500
Testing	$ 3,000

The equipment was installed and tested during the week of 22 June 20X7. Hawkrigg paid
the invoice price on 1 July 20X7. The equipment was ready for use on 30 June and put into
production on 3 July 20X7. Hawkrigg management uses straight-line depreciation for the
company's equipment and expects to use the asset for six years. The estimated residual value
is zero. Their fiscal year end is 31 December.

Required:

1. What is the book value of the equipment after installation?
2. Compute depreciation expense for 20X7, using the straight-line method, under each of the following assumptions:
   a. Exact, to the closest month
   b. Full first-year convention
   c. Half-year convention
3. Calculate depreciation expense for both 20X7 and 20X8 under each of the methods in requirement (2), using double-declining balance (DDB) depreciation.

A10-16 Fractional-Year Depreciation: Jackson Company's records show the following machinery acquisitions and retirements during the first two years of operations:

| | Acquisition | | Retirement | |
Date	Cost of Machinery	Estimated Useful Life (years)	Acquisition Date	Original Cost
1 January 20X5	$200,000	10		
1 April 20X5	80,000	5		
1 December 20X6	10,000	10		
31 December 20X6			20X5*	$28,000

*Part of machinery acquired on 1 January 20X5.

Required:

1. Compute depreciation expense for 20X5 and for 20X6 and the balances of the machinery and related accumulated depreciation accounts at the end of each year, using straight-line amortization. Machinery is depreciated according to the number of months of ownership in the year of acquisition or retirement. Assume no residual values. There are no sale proceeds upon retirement. Show computations and round to the nearest dollar. Set up separate columns in a schedule for machinery and for accumulated depreciation.

2. Compute depreciation expense for 20X5 and for 20X6 and the balances of the machinery and related accumulated depreciation accounts at the end of each year using straight-line depreciation. Machinery is depreciated for one-half year in the year of acquisition. Machinery retired is depreciated for one-half year in its year of retirement. Assume no residual values. There are no sale proceeds upon retirement. Show computations and round to the nearest dollar. Set up separate columns in a schedule for machinery and for accumulated depreciation.

3. Comment on the differences between requirements (1) and (2).

> Source: Copyright 1994–2000 by the American Institute of Certified Public Accountants, Inc. All rights reserved. Reprinted with permission.

A10-17 Comprehensive Intangibles—Accounting and Amortization: Bright Designs Limited began operations in 20X5 and, at the end of its first year of operations, reported a balance of $1,203,000 in an account called "intangibles." Upon further investigation, it is discovered that the account had been debited throughout the year as follows:

5 Jan.	Organization costs; legal fees. Economic life is indefinite.	$ 20,000
1 Feb.	Patent registration; legal fees re: patent with 20-year life to be used in research activities.	10,000
1 July	Operating expenses, first six months.	440,000
1 Aug.	Goodwill; excess of purchase price of an advertising company paid over tangible assets acquired.	320,000
10 Nov.	Copyright acquired; remaining legal life is 29 years but economic life is 10 years.	42,000

30 Nov.	Trademark registration; legal fees. The trademark is expected to have an indefinite economic life.	16,000
5 Dec.	Staff training costs; staff is expected to stay with the company for an average of three years; however, there are no employment contracts.	55,000
31 Dec.	Research costs incurred over the year; 40% of all research costs are properly classified as internally generated intangibles. The product developed will begin commercial production next year.	300,000
		$1,203,000

Required:

1. Prepare a correcting entry that reallocates all amounts charged to intangibles to the appropriate accounts. State any assumptions made.

2. Calculate amortization expense on intangible assets for 20X5. Straight-line amortization, to the exact month of purchase, is used. All residual values are expected to be zero.

★★   **A10-18 Component Depreciation:** A large piece of equipment acquired on 1 January 20X5 by Kapadia Company has four major components for depreciation. Details regarding each component are given in the schedule below:

eXcel

Component	Cost	Estimated Residual Value	Estimated Life (Years)
A	$100,000	$10,000	10
B	45,000	0	5
C	76,000	16,000	15
D	12,400	400	8

Required:

1. Calculate the depreciation for 20X5. Give the entry to record depreciation after one full year of use.

2. At the end of 20X6, it was necessary to replace component B, which was sold for $12,000. The replacement component cost $50,000 and will have an estimated residual value of $5,000 at the end of its estimated five-year useful life. Record the disposal and substitution, which was a cash acquisition.

3. Assume that the machine was depreciated as a whole on a straight-line basis over 15 years; and not broken into components. Provide the requested information in requirement (1).

★★   **A10-19 Asset Impairment—Five Situations:** Each of the following five cases is independent:

a. Marlene Incorporated produces several lines of office furniture. All of the furniture is sold through sales agents who sell the full array of lines. Each line is developed by the company internally, and the development costs are capitalized and amortized over 12 years. After several years of high revenue, one of Marlene's lines has recently suffered a significant decline. Marlene is considering shutting down production and discontinuing the line. About 40% of the development cost has not yet been amortized.

b. Antigonish Actuators Limited (AAL) has a production and sales division in northern Ontario. The divisional vice-president reports directly to the AAL CEO. AAL is decentralized, and the Northern Ontario division is one of several such divisions. The Northern Ontario division has operated at a loss for the past two years, and future prospects seem dim. The division has substantial property, plant, and equipment.

c. Canadian Wheels Corporation operates hardware and automotive stores throughout Canada. A few years ago, the company opened a series of stores in the northwestern United States. The new stores have not been doing well, and the company is thinking of selling them or shutting them down.

d. Capital Helicopter Services Corporation (CHSC) provides helicopter services for other corporations, mainly those in the resource industry that need extensive helicopter services for offshore oil and gas platforms, forestry operations, and otherwise inaccessible field operations. In addition, the company operates a separate division within Canada that manufactures airframe parts for manufacturers. This division is completely separate from the company's other operations and has a separate reporting line directly to the company's senior management. The division generates more than 10% of the company's overall revenues. However, the division has become only marginally profitable, and CHSC management has decided to sell the division and has put a plan for disposition in place.

e. Several years ago, Robertson Connectors Corporation (RCC) purchased the patents for a new type of connector. The new connector has enjoyed great success until recently. A competitor introduced a new product that is almost the same as RCC's product and that can be used interchangeably. RCC launched a patent infringement suit against the competitor, and RCC management was confident of success. In 20X4, however, the court ruled against RCC, thereby leaving the competitor free to continue its product. RCC management is considering whether to appeal the decision.

Required:

For each situation, explain whether an impairment test is necessary. If you need more information, explain what information you need and why you need it.

★ **A10-20 Asset Impairment:** Softsweat Incorporated is a software development company. It has several products on the market, including the widely used PlayMark animation software. The cash flows from PlayMark are clearly distinguishable within Softsweat. The company has recorded development costs of $2.8 million relating to PlayMark, which is being amortized on a straight-line basis over seven years. At the end of 20X5, the carrying value was $1,960,000. Softsweat maintains a separate account for accumulated amortization on PlayMark.

In 20X5, a large U.S. company, Macrosoftie, released a competing product that has been hailed as a substantial improvement over PlayMark. However, the competing product requires installation of a great deal of additional Macrosoftie software to make the new product run efficiently. In addition, the high price may delay its acceptance by some users.

Because of the new competition, Softsweat management decided that an impairment test should be made. In January 20X6, as the 20X5 financial statements were being prepared, the company hired a professional business valuator. The valuator's appraisal was that the fair value of PlayMark at the end of 20X5 was $1,000,000.

Required:

1. Prepare the necessary adjusting journal entry to record the results of the impairment test.
2. Suppose that in 20X6, the Macrosoftie product was found to be unreliable and that the sales of PlayMark returned to almost their 20X4 level. The fair value of PlayMark therefore was $1,600,000 at the end of 20X6. How (if at all) would this change be recorded in Softsweat's financial statements for 20X6?

★ **A10-21 Asset Impairment:** Zoe Incorporated has a large piece of machinery where management has assessed and determined there is potential impairment. This piece of machinery has independent cash inflows. The following information relates to the machine:

- Carrying amount $4 million.
- The machine could be sold for $ 3 million less a 10% commission.
- If the company was forced to sell immediately, the proceeds would likely be $2.5 million.
- If the machine continues to be used in production, it is anticipated to generate $1.5 million of cash flows for the next five years. It would require annual maintenance costs of $100,000 a year. The equipment could be sold for $50,000 at the end of the five years.
- Assume Zoe has a discount rate of 6%.

Required:

Is the machine impaired? If so, what is the amount of the impairment loss?

★   **A10-22 Asset Group Impairment:** The abrasives group of Chemical Products Incorporated (CPI) has been suffering a decline in its business, due to new product introductions
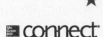
by competitors. At 31 December 20X5, the assets of the abrasives cash-generating unit are shown as follows (in millions) on the company's balance sheet:

	Cost	Accumulated Depreciation	Net Book Value
Equipment	800	$360	440
Fixtures	250	110	140
Patent rights	160	140	20
	$1,210	$610	$600

An impairment test indicates that the fair value of the abrasives cash-generating unit's assets is $500 million. The assets are not separable—they must be operated or sold together as a group.

Required:

Prepare an adjusting journal entry to record the impairment.

★★   **A10-23 Goodwill Impairment:** Information has been collected regarding Black Company's cash-generating unit that includes goodwill. At 31 December 20X5, the assets of the

Black Company's cash-generating unit are shown as follows (in millions) on the company's balance sheet:

	Cost	Accumulated Depreciation	Net Book Value
Goodwill	$ 400	$ 0	$ 400
Equipment	1,400	800	600
Building	2,100	600	1,500
Patent rights	200	80	120
	$4,100	$1,480	$2,620

An impairment test indicates that the fair value of Black Company's cash-generating unit's assets is $1,800 million. The assets are not separable—they must be operated or sold together as a group.

Required:

Prepare an adjusting journal entry to record the impairment. If the impairment was reversed, how would the reversal be accounted for among the assets in the cash-generating unit?

★   **A10-24 Goodwill Impairment:** Information has been collected regarding Casey Incorporated cash-generating unit that includes goodwill. At 31 December 20X5, the assets of the

Casey's cash-generating unit are shown as follows (in millions) on the company's balance sheet:

	Cost	Accumulated Depreciation	Net Book Value
Goodwill	$ 2,000	$ 0	$ 2,000
Equipment	15,000	4,000	11,000
Land	8,000	0	8,000
Property	33,000	8,000	25,000
	$58,000	$12,000	$46,000

An impairment test indicates that the fair value of Casey's cash-generating unit's assets is $41,000 million. The assets are not separable—they must be operated or sold together as a group.

Required:
Prepare an adjusting journal entry to record the impairment.

★ **A10-25 Statement of Cash Flows:** Idea Limited reflected the following items in the 20X5 financial statements:

Income statement

Depreciation expense, machinery	$600,000
Amortization expense, patent	120,000
Loss on sale of machinery	50,000
Gain on sale of land	60,000

Balance sheet

Decrease in land account	$800,000
Increase in net patent account	130,000
Decrease in net machinery account	912,000

The only entry through the land account was a sale of land. The other accounts may reflect more than one transaction.

Required:
List the items that would appear on the statement of cash flows as a result of the above items. Indicate in which section each item would appear. Assume that the indirect method is used for the operating activities section. State any assumptions that you make.

★★★ **A10-26 Comprehensive Long-lived Asset Transactions and Depreciation:** MH Plumbing Incorporated (MH) is the largest plumbing contractor in Moncton, Alberta. Information on selected transactions/events is given below:

a. On 15 January 20X2, MII purchased land and a warehouse building for $455,000. The land was appraised at $175,000, while the building was appraised at $375,000.

b. During January and February 20X2, MH spent $53,200 on the warehouse building, renovating it for its expected use as a storage and shipping facility.

c. MH used the warehouse building from February 20X2 until August 20X7. The building was expected to have a 20-year life and a residual value of $11,000.

d. In late August 20X7, MH traded the warehouse and land for another facility on the other side of town. The second facility was slightly larger. MH paid $33,750 to the vendor, and $19,800 in legal fees as a result of the transaction. The new warehouse was appraised at $425,000, and the new land at $180,000. This warehouse facility was expected to have a useful life of 18 years and a residual value of $7,800.

e. MH used the new warehouse facility from August 20X7 until February 20X9. At that time, a fire destroyed the warehouse. MH received $356,800 from the insurance company.

f. MH called for tenders for construction of a new warehouse building in March 20X9, but the lowest bid was $788,000. The company decided to self-construct and began in May 20X9. Monies spent were as follows:

Architect fees	$ 80,000
Removing debris from building site	13,400
Material cost for construction	245,800
Labour cost for construction	199,600
Parking lot	45,200
Specific overhead assigned to construction	24,800
Interest on loans related to construction	34,100

g. MH received a $100,000 investment tax credit in 20X9 as a result of the building activities, which reduced 20X9 taxes payable.

h. MH occupied its new warehouse in September 20X9. It was appraised at $650,000. It was expected to last for 25 years, and have a residual value of $20,000.

Required:

Prepare journal entries to record all transactions listed above, including annual depreciation to the end of 20X9. Record annual depreciation using a declining-balance method of 10% for buildings, and 5% for parking lots. MH records a full year of depreciation in the year of acquisition and no amortization in the year of disposal. Justify any decisions made with respect to accounting policy or application.

(Source: (Adapted) © CGA-Canada. Reproduced with permission.)

★★★ **A10-27 CCA Calculations (Appendix 1):** Dixon Company purchased several small pieces of equipment in May 20X5 for $600,000, which qualifies as a Class 8 asset for tax purposes.

30 September 20X6	Sold equipment bought in 20X5 for $40,000; proceeds, $22,400
1 February 20X7	Sold equipment bought in 20X5 for $80,000; proceeds, $39,600
31 August 20X7	Bought Class 8 equipment for $50,000
16 November 20X8	Bought Class 8 equipment for $72,000

Required:

Calculate CCA and the closing UCC balance for 20X5 to 20X8.

★★ **A10-28 Revaluation Model (Appendix 2):** Real Estate Incorporated (REI) has made the decision to use the revaluation model for its land. This is the only tract of land in this class. REI has a 31 December year-end. The following are independent situations.

Case A   REI purchased a tract of land in 20X1 for $100 million. At 31 December 20X1, the land was valued at $130 million.

Case B   REI purchased a tract of land in 20X1 for $140 million. At 31 December 20X1, the land was valued at $110 million. At 31 December 20X2, the land was valued at $160 million.

Case C   REI purchased a tract of land in 20X1 for $120 million. At 31 December 20X1, the land was valued at $170 million. At 31 December 20X2, the land was valued at $110 million.

Required:

1. For each case explain the impact on other comprehensive income, revaluation surplus, and statement of profit or loss (income statement).
2. What would be the difference if the fair value model was selected by REI?

★★ **A10-29 Asset Impairment (ASPE):** Refer to the facts in A10-21 and assume the company is following the accounting standards for private enterprises.

Required:

Is the machine impaired? If so, what is the amount of the impairment loss?

★★ **A10-30 Asset Impairment (ASPE):** Gardner Incorporated manufacturers products in two plants. One of the plants is an area where there has been a downturn in the market, and indications are that there has been potential impairment. Gardner has determined that the asset group includes land, building, equipment, and a mortgage. Management anticipates using the plant for the next 10 years. The net book value of the assets in the asset group are as follows:

Land	$ 60,000
Building	550,000
Equipment	210,000
Mortgage	(225,000)

Annual cash flows from continuing to operate the plant over the next 10 years are $50,000 a year. The plant would be demolished at the end of 10 years. The estimated residual value of the land and equipment is $80,000. The appropriate discount rate for Gardner is 5%.

Gardner has considered selling the assets and using the cash to help open a new facility. The market value of the assets was estimated by appraisers to be $700,000 less a commission of 10%. The buyer would assume the mortgage.

Required:
Is the asset group impaired? If so, what is the amount of the impairment loss?

CHAPTER 11

Financial Instruments: Investments in Debt and Equity Securities

INTRODUCTION

The cash flow associated with an investment in the securities of another company can be straightforward. Such an investment is usually purchased for cash, produces an annual cash flow of interest or dividends that can be recorded as investment revenue, and is sold for cash. What can be so complicated?

The challenge is that investments are acquired for different purposes, and this distinction affects accounting policies. Notably, there are different approaches to valuation of the investment account and investment revenue.

The cost and fair value of an investment may be very different. Fair value information might be far more relevant to a financial statement user and informative as long as fair value is objectively determinable with respect to securities markets. As a result, many investments that are financial instruments must be valued at fair value on the statement of financial position.

However, some investments are not held for resale, and fair value is less relevant. Long-term investments in voting shares may be used to establish a strategic intercompany relationship through which the investor corporation can control or significantly influence the operating and financing strategies of the investee. The carrying value of these investments will not reflect fair value. For example, Brookfield Asset Management Inc. shows an investment on its 2011 statement of financial position, carried at $4.1 billion, but discloses that the fair value of this investment is $2.9 billion.

What earnings should be reported for a strategic investment? Since the investor can control or influence the dividend policy of the investee, dividends are not the result of an arm's-length transaction, and the amount could be manipulated. The investor's share of the investee's earnings is more informative but is not cash flow. For example, in 2011, Brookfield reported $2.2 billion of investment revenue from all its strategic investments but then reported in the disclosure notes that cash distributions were quite different, at $0.2 billion.

This chapter explores the alternatives and provides an overview of this complex area. Keep in mind, though, that many accounting programs devote an entire course to investment accounting, so this is only the proverbial tip of the iceberg! Standards are in transition in this area. This chapter reflects IFRS 9, effective in 2015, with early adoption permitted. Companion material based on IAS 39 is available on Connect.

CATEGORIES AND CLASSIFICATION OF INTERCORPORATE INVESTMENTS

Investment Objectives

Companies invest in the securities of other enterprises for a variety of reasons. The investment can be a **passive investment**, meant primarily to increase investment revenue, or a **strategic investment**, meant to enhance operations in some way. Reasons for investments include:

- *Investment of idle cash.* Companies often have cash on hand that is not needed at present but will be needed in the future. Rather than allow idle cash to remain in a low-interest bank account, companies find money market investments with short terms that provide a higher return. These **cash equivalent** investments typically have low risk and are easily converted to cash.

  Some investments will generate return through interest or dividends but also may be sold at a gain if the market price has increased. These investments will likely be of higher risk and/or longer term, but the intent is still to sell the investment when money is needed for other activities and/or when the price is attractive.

- *Active investment portfolio.* Companies may own securities in a portfolio that is actively traded as part of the normal course of business, generally yielding a return because of price fluctuations or a dealer's margin. Such a portfolio might be used to offset, or hedge, gains or losses from other financial statement elements but might also be based on planned appreciation in various business sectors.

- *Long-term investments to generate earnings.* Some companies are active lenders, and have portfolios of loan assets. In other cases, resources are invested for the long term in securities to increase investment revenue. These investments are usually money market instruments (e.g., bonds), and the intent is to keep the investment for interest and principal cash flows.

- *Strategic alliances.* An investment, especially in voting shares, may establish or cement a beneficial intercompany relationship that will increase the profitability of the investing company, both directly and indirectly. Strategic decisions may be made to invest in suppliers, customers, and even competitors.

- *Legal frameworks.* Companies may choose to establish operations in one large company with numerous branches or organize activities in a set of smaller companies, all or partially controlled by a central holding company. This may be done for tax reasons, to allow outside shareholders a small stake in particular operations, to satisfy legal requirements in particular jurisdictions, and/or to limit potential liability claims to particular portions of the enterprise. The resulting corporate structure may be quite complex.

Categories and Classification Criteria

Securities are **financial instruments.** *A financial instrument is any contract that gives rise to both a financial asset of one party and a financial liability or equity instrument of another party.* In the context of intercorporate investments, financial assets are defined as any contractual right to receive cash or another financial asset from another company or a contractual right that is the equity instrument of another entity. Investment in debt securities (loans, bonds) and share investments meet this definition. Accounting alternatives for investments are summarized in Exhibit 11-1.

Overview of Alternatives   As shown in Exhibit 11-1:

- An *investment in* a *debt instrument* of another entity can be classified as an amortized cost (AC) investment, or as a fair-value-through-profit-and-loss (FVTPL) investment.

- An *investment in common shares* of another company may be an FVTPL investment, a fair-value-through-other-comprehensive-income (FVTOCI) investment, or, in limited

EXHIBIT 11-1

CLASSIFICATION OF INVESTMENTS

circumstances, a cost investment. If the investment in common shares is a strategic investment, it may be a subsidiary, an associate, or a joint arrangement.

Classification depends on many factors, as we will see. The classifications and decisions factors are defined in the sections that follow.

Initial Recognition *All investments are initially measured at fair value.* This is the *acquisition cost* of the investment, appropriately measured, and is the *transaction value.* If there are transaction costs, these costs are also included in the investment cost, unless the investment is classified as an FVTPL investment, or a subsidiary, in which case transaction costs are expensed. The classification alternatives determine *subsequent* measurement of asset carrying value and investment revenue.

Amortized Cost Investments Amortized cost (AC) investments must meet two tests:

1. The asset must be held and managed within a business model whose objective is to hold assets to collect contractual cash flows, *and*

2. The financial asset must have contractual terms that give rise, on specified dates, to cash flows that are solely payments of principal and interest on the principal amount. *Interest* is defined as compensation for the time value of money and credit risk.

Classification of an investment with contractually determined cash flows is based on the entity's *business model for managing the asset.* For example, if a company buys a bond with a 10-year maturity date and manages the bond as part of a portfolio while interest and then principal are repaid, it is classified as an AC investment. On the other hand, if the business model governing the portfolio includes the directive to sell the investment if the price is appealing, or to manage the portfolio for trading gains, then the bond is not AC. The AC category will include bonds and other money market instruments *but excludes common shares because shares lack contractually determined cash flows.*

Objective of the AC Portfolio The primary objective of an AC portfolio must be to *hold the investments* to collect contractual cash flows. *However, the investment does not have to be held until it matures.* For example, a bond investment might be sold if the credit rating of the issuer were to decline and no longer meets the investment policies set by the investor. The investor might sell the investment if the business model indicated a need to change the duration of the investment portfolio. The AC portfolio might be partially liquidated if the investor needed cash for capital expenditures. Such transactions should be infrequent, or the necessary overall objective for the portfolio—to hold the investments to collect interest and principal—might be called into question.

ETHICAL ISSUES

Many financial statement measurements and classifications rest on the judgements and the representations of management. Auditors need to rely on management integrity and thus must evaluate this integrity. Auditors must be prudent and skeptical when reviewing management representations, which would include the objectives of an investment strategy. Management must demonstrate, through action, that the stated intent is real.

Fair-Value-through-Profit-and-Loss Investments The **fair-value-through-profit-and-loss (FVTPL) investment** category covers investments that do not qualify as AC investments, and investments that are not designated by management or circumstances to be in another category. Accordingly, *this category is a catch-all* except that:

- Some investments must be accounted for using the cost method, when fair value cannot be established; and
- Management can designate investments as FVTOCI if the OCI treatment is preferable.

Logically, an FVTPL investment is:

- An investment in shares or bonds that is managed on a fair value basis internally. This would be done in accordance with a documented risk management or investment strategy. Performance would be evaluated on a fair value basis. In this category, the investment is *held for the purpose of resale*, or the investment is part of a portfolio of investments managed together for trading profit.
- An investment in shares or bonds that should be subject to the FVTPL accounting rules (change in fair value in earnings) because doing so eliminates or significantly reduces a measurement or recognition inconsistency (called an "accounting mismatch.") This might occur if a related (hedged) financial instrument were required to be in the FVTPL category. Logically, related items should be treated equivalently so gains and losses offset.
- An investment that does not qualify as an AC investment because either:
  – The investment lacks the contractual cash flows necessary to allow it to be classified as an AC investment; or
  – It is a bond investment that is not managed to collect the contractual cash flows but, rather, held for resale.

Investments in this category are revalued to fair value each reporting date, with the change in fair value included in earnings. Clearly, fair value must be determinable for this accounting method to be feasible. Techniques for estimating fair value (valuation models) are reviewed in a subsequent section.

Fair value-through-Other-Comprehensive-Income Investments This category is determined by management designation; *any equity investment* that is designated by management as a **fair-value-through-other-comprehensive-income (FVTOCI) investment** is included. The process is as follows:

- Only equity investments can be FVTOCI; investments in bonds or loans do not qualify.
- The election to classify an investment as FVTOCI must be made when the investment is initially recognized.
- The election to classify an investment as FVTOCI is irrevocable.
- The investment cannot be *held for trading*, which means that it cannot have been acquired primarily for resale.

Investments in this category are revalued to fair value each reporting date, with the change in fair value included in **other comprehensive income (OCI)**. The cumulative amount is collected in a separate equity reserve account (accumulated other comprehensive income, or AOCI).

When the investment is sold, the AOCI amounts may remain in the separate equity reserve account or be transferred directly to another equity account, most logically to retained earnings. In either case, *any gain or loss on sale is permanently excluded from earnings.*

Investments would be included in this category because the accounting treatment is considered desirable: Unrealized gains and losses caused by an increase or decrease in fair value are isolated in equity and bypass earnings. The category might be desirable to manage earnings, but adds considerable complexity to the financial statements because unrealized amounts are part of comprehensive income and the equity reserve account.

Cost Investments Investments in shares in this category are valued at cost until they are sold, at which time gains and losses are realized and included in earnings. This category description applies only to *equity investments. If an investment in a bond is to be carried at cost, it is an AC investment.* The cost category applies primarily to:

1. Investments in shares during the year on separate-entity financial statements; consolidation is the external reporting approach at reporting dates; and

2. Investments in shares for which fair value cannot be established.

Subsidiaries A **subsidiary company** exists when the investor (**parent company**) has **control** over the investee. Control exists when the investor has:

1. Power over the investee; *and*

2. Exposure, or rights, to variable returns; *and*

3. The ability to use its power to affect the amount of the returns.

Percentage share ownership is a primary input to this decision, and control *should* exist if an investor owns a simple majority of voting shares, or 50% plus one vote, since this should establish the right to elect the majority of the Board of Directors. Control might exist with less than 50% of the shares if the investor has the practical ability to unilaterally direct the activities that affect investment return. Other indications of a subsidiary might be the power to elect or remove a majority of the Board of Directors or the ability to appoint or approve the investee's key management personnel.

Many corporations are "run" by a major shareholder who owns the largest single block of shares, perhaps because other shareholders are not active. If the block of shares owned by the major shareholder is less than 50% of the voting shares, then *accounting control* must be assessed, based on the facts of the situation. Could the other shareholders realistically gather enough power (through the support of enough voting shareholders) to control the company? If that scenario is far-fetched (all other shares are widely held by diverse and unorganized investors), then control may exist for the major shareholder. In other cases (shares are held by a small group of related investors who could easily cooperate to outvote the major shareholder), there is no control by that major shareholder. Control does not have to be exercised to exist, though: If a shareholder has voting control but has never exercised it, the shareholder still has control. The real test is if the investor could exercise control if desired, and a majority of voting shares confers this right.

Investment in Associates An **associate** company exists when the investor company has the ability to exercise significant influence over the company. **Significant influence** is defined as the power to participate in financial and operating policy decisions of the investee, even though the investor does not control the investee. Significant influence can be obtained through several means and not just by equity investment. Possible evidence of significant influence includes:

- Representation on the Board of Directors;
- Participation in policy-making processes;

- Material intercompany transactions;
- Interchange of managerial personnel; or
- Provision of technical information.

Normally, ownership of 20% or more of an investee corporation's shares is deemed to suggest that significant influence exists. The burden of proof shifts at this line: If an investor *has* significant influence and owns less than 20%, the investor must prove *why* it has significant influence. If the investor has more than 20% and does *not* have significant influence, the investor must prove that significant influence *is not* present.

It is important to not put *too* much weight on the percentage of share ownership, though; a great deal depends on who owns the other shares as well as on the other (nonownership) financial and operating relationships between the investor and the investee corporations. For example, ownership of 30% of an investee corporation may not give the investee significant influence (or any influence) if the other 70% is held by a single shareholder who will not tolerate any influence. Conversely, an ownership interest of 15% may give the investor virtually unchallenged influence if ownership of the other 85% is widely dispersed. It is the substance that matters, not the percentage ownership.

Note, however, that *control* is present only when the investor meets all three of the criteria listed in the prior section.

Joint Arrangement   Another type of strategic equity investment is a **joint arrangement**, where an economic activity is undertaken by two or more investors and *control is shared*.

Joint arrangements are distinct because of joint control, or *joint decision making*, regardless of ownership percentage. *There must be a contractual arrangement in these circumstances that gives joint control over the operation.* Joint control means that the investors must together agree on key decisions before they are implemented. This feature of joint control means that majority ownership, or even the right to appoint the majority of the Board of Directors, does not confer control.

Joint arrangements are quite common in mining operations and in oil and gas ventures. The investors all contribute something to exploration activities, and all share in any wealth generated. For example, a small mining company may have exploration rights over a property and agree to work the property with a larger joint arrangement partner. This large investor provides management, working capital, and capital assets in exchange for a certain percentage of the profits. However, key decisions over when and where to explore, when to put the property into commercial production, and so on are subject to *shared control established through a contract*.

Joint arrangements can be joint ventures or joint operations. The legal terms of the arrangement will dictate whether the joint arrangement is a joint venture or a joint operation. A **joint venture** (JV) exists when the investors have rights to *net assets* of the operation—that is, a residual equity (net assets) interest. The equity method is used for joint ventures. A **joint operation** (JO) exists when the investors have *direct rights* to the assets and liability of the arrangement. An investor in a joint operation includes, in the investor's financial statements, the financial statements elements in which it holds a direct interest.

CONCEPT REVIEW

1. Under what circumstances is an investment in bonds classified as an AC investment? As a FVTPL investment?
2. Can an investment in common shares be classified as an AC investment? Explain.
3. Why might management choose to classify an investment as FVTOCI instead of FVTPL?
4. An investor owns 40% of the shares of another company. Is this evidence enough to conclude that significant influence exists?

ACCOUNTING FOR INVESTMENTS—OVERVIEW

There are six approaches to account for investments. For a summary of the application of accounting methods, refer to Exhibit 11-2. The highlights of the accounting methods themselves are summarized in Exhibit 11-3. This section is an overview; there are examples and further clarification in later sections of this chapter.

Amortized Cost Method

The amortized cost method is used to account for bonds classified as AC investments. In the amortized cost method:

- The original investment is recorded at its investment cost. This is initial book value or carrying value, but it also represents fair value on the purchase date. Cost excludes any accrued interest.
- Transaction costs, such as brokerage fees, are included in acquisition cost and capitalized.
- Interest is recorded as investment revenue, using the effective-interest method. That is, interest revenue will reflect the yield rate, rather than the stated rate. Any premium or discount is amortized to earnings over the life of the investment. This will change book

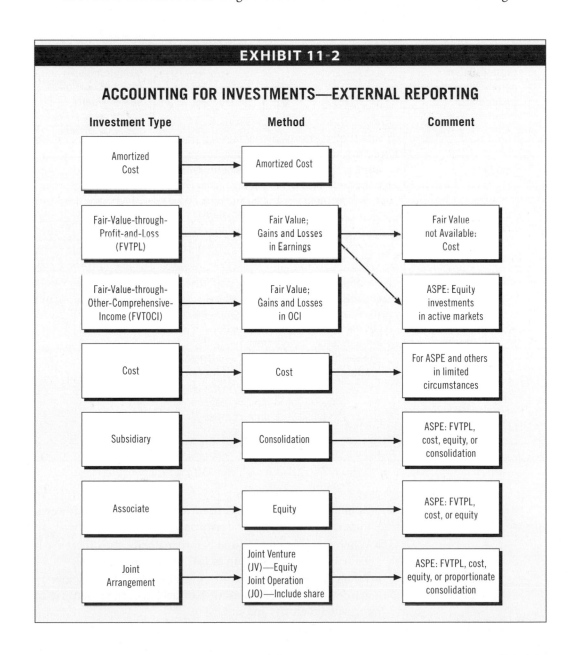

EXHIBIT 11-2

ACCOUNTING FOR INVESTMENTS—EXTERNAL REPORTING

Investment Type	Method	Comment
Amortized Cost	Amortized Cost	
Fair-Value-through-Profit-and-Loss (FVTPL)	Fair Value; Gains and Losses in Earnings	Fair Value not Available; Cost
Fair-Value-through-Other-Comprehensive-Income (FVTOCI)	Fair Value; Gains and Losses in OCI	ASPE: Equity investments in active markets
Cost	Cost	For ASPE and others in limited circumstances
Subsidiary	Consolidation	ASPE: FVTPL, cost, equity, or consolidation
Associate	Equity	ASPE: FVTPL, cost, or equity
Joint Arrangement	Joint Venture (JV)—Equity Joint Operation (JO)—Include share	ASPE: FVTPL, cost, equity, or proportionate consolidation

EXHIBIT 11-3

ACCOUNTING FOR INVESTMENTS
Summary of Accounting Methods

Method	Carrying Value	Investment Revenue	Unrealized Holding Gains and Losses	Realized Gains and Losses
Amortized cost (Bonds)	Amortized cost	Interest—effective-interest method	—	Included in earnings; should be rare
Cost (Shares)	Cost	Dividends	—	Included in earnings
Fair-value-through-profit-and-loss	Fair value	Interest or dividends	Included in earnings	Included in earnings; only the *annual change in value* in the year of sale
Fair-value-through-other-comprehensive-income	Fair value	Dividends	Included in other comprehensive income; part of shareholders' equity as a separate reserve	May be transferred to another equity account (retained earnings) when realized or may remain in separate reserve
Equity	Cost plus unremitted earnings to date	Share of investee earnings adjusted for fair value depreciation and unrealized intercompany profits	—	Included in earnings; should be rare
Consolidation	Investment account replaced with financial statements elements of investee for reporting	Investment revenue represented through inclusion of investee revenue and expense elements; adjusted for fair value depreciation and unrealized intercompany profits	—	Included in earnings; should be rare

value. Book value is *amortized cost* and will move toward maturity value, becoming maturity value on the maturity date.

- When an investment is sold before maturity, the difference between proceeds and book value is recorded as a gain or loss on sale in earnings.
- When an investment matures, cash increases and the investment decreases. There is no gain or loss on the maturation of debt securities because cash received is equal to the recorded maturity amount.

Cost Method

The **cost method** is used to account for investments in shares in some limited circumstances. In the cost method:

- The original investment is recorded at its investment cost. This is book value or carrying value, but it also represents fair value on the purchase date.
- Transaction costs, such as brokerage fees, are included in acquisition cost and capitalized.
- Dividends declared are recorded as investment revenue.
- When an investment is sold, cash increases and the investment decreases. There will be a gain or loss on the sale of shares that is included in earnings.

Fair-Value-through-Profit-and-Loss Method

For FVTPL investments, the **fair value method** is applied:

- The investment is originally recorded at cost. This is fair value on the purchase date.
- Transaction costs, such as brokerage fees, are *immediately expensed*.
- Interest on bond investments is recorded as investment revenue using the effective-interest method. Dividends on share investments are recorded as investment revenue when declared.
- At the end of each reporting period, the investments are revalued to fair value, whether this is higher or lower than the existing balance in the investment account.
- The investment is reported at fair value on the statement of financial position.
- **Holding gains and losses,** defined as the difference between the existing balance in the investment account (the new fair value) and the prior investment account balance (the old fair value), are recorded in earnings. That is, earnings includes the change in value of the investment each year, whether **realized holding gains or losses** (realized through sale) or **unrealized holding gains or losses** (unrealized because the investment is still held).

Fair-Value-Through-Other-Comprehensive-Income Method

For FVTOCI investments:

- The investment is originally recorded at cost. This is fair value on the purchase date.
- Transaction costs are *part of the cost of the investment*.
- Interest or dividends declared are recorded as investment revenue.
- At the end of each reporting period, the investments are revalued to fair value, whether this is higher or lower than the existing balance in the investment account.
- The investment is reported at fair value on the statement of financial position.
- *Holding gains or losses* are reported annually in *other comprehensive income*. The change is included on the statement of comprehensive income. The cumulative amount of such gains and losses are segregated in a separate equity reserve account (AOCI). The gains and losses *may be recycled* out of this separate equity account *to another equity account* (most logically, retained earnings) when the investment is sold and the holding gains are realized. Holding gains may also be left permanently in the separate reserve account. This choice is up to the company.

Earnings Volatility The difference between the two versions of the fair value method obviously relates to where the change in fair value is recorded in the financial statements. For FVTPL investments, these changes in value are included in earnings and then retained earnings. For FVTOCI investments, realized and unrealized changes in value are collected in a reserve account in equity. Amounts may be transferred to retained earnings when realized but will never be part of reported earnings. Realization is a traditional test for revenue recognition, which is not applied to investments in either of these categories.

Remember, though, that if investment fair values are volatile, inclusion of holding gains in earnings introduces volatility to earnings. Companies with FVTPL portfolios have registered concern about this volatility, and standard setters continue to grapple with these issues.

Equity Method

The **equity method** is used for associate companies and for joint ventures. Under the equity method:

- The original investment is recorded at its acquisition cost; this is initial book value and represents fair value on the purchase date.
- The investor's proportionate share of the investee's earnings (subject to certain adjustments) is recognized as investment revenue and as an increase to the investment account.
- Dividends are recorded as a decrease in the investment account and *not as investment revenue*. This reduces book value.
- When the investment is sold, the difference between proceeds and book value is recorded as a gain or loss on sale in earnings.

At any point in time, the equity method investment account consists of:

1. The cost of the investment, plus

2. The investor's cumulative share of the investee's adjusted earnings since the investment was made, minus

3. The investor's cumulative share of dividends from the investee since the shares were purchased.

The difference between the investor's share of the investee's earnings and the dividends received (item 2 less 3, above) is called **unremitted earnings** and increases book value above cost.

Consolidation Method

When an investor controls an investee, **consolidation** is required. The parent investor must prepare consolidated statements so that the financial statements reflect the assets, liabilities, revenues, and expenses of the entire economic entity, consisting of the parent and all of its subsidiaries.

When consolidated statements are prepared, the investment account relating to a subsidiary disappears entirely from the statement of financial position. Instead, the subsidiary's assets and liabilities are added to those of the parent and are reported together as a single economic entity. If the parent owns less than 100% of the subsidiary's shares, the equity interest of the minority shareholders is shown as a separate equity account on the parent's consolidated statement of financial position. This is called the **non-controlling interest (NCI)**. In consolidated financial statements, the fair value of the subsidiary's assets is recorded as of the acquisition date and intercompany transactions are eliminated.

Recording versus Reporting

It is very important to make a distinction between the way an investor records investments in its books and the way that the investment is reported in the investor's published financial statements. *Reporting* may involve cost, fair value, equity, or consolidation. *Recording may well be different during the year.*

For example, an investor may account for a strategic investment by using the cost method during the year simply because it is the easiest method; this is the investor's *recording method*. When financial statements are prepared, a different *reporting method* (e.g., consolidation) may be required. In that case, the accounts relating to the investment are adjusted by means of a worksheet and/or adjusting entries.

Public companies may prepare nonconsolidated (or separate-entity) statements for specific users, such as their lenders, *as well as* consolidated general purpose statements. Indeed, knowledgeable lenders will insist on seeing a corporation's nonconsolidated statements if they have immediate recourse only to the assets and cash flows of the specific legal entity to which they are making the loan. As well, nonconsolidated statements are essential for income tax purposes because each corporation is taxed separately (with some exceptions), and the corporation's separate-entity financial statements must be attached to the tax return.

CONCEPT REVIEW

1. Where are unrealized holding gains and losses recognized in the financial statements when using the fair value method for FVTOCI investments?

2. Under the equity method, investment revenue is present even if there are no dividends declared. Why is this the case?

3. How are transaction costs, such as brokerage fees, accounted for if an investment is classified as FVTPL? FVTOCI?

4. Will an investment in a subsidiary (asset) account appear on a set of consolidated financial statements? Explain.

ESTIMATING FAIR VALUE

Since financial statements will reflect **fair value** for some investments, it stands to reason that fair value must be carefully estimated. After all, estimated fair value is not substantiated by the objective evidence of a transaction of the reporting entity. Fair value is defined as the *price that would be received to sell an asset in an orderly transaction between market participants.*

When there is an *active market for an identical investment*, quoted prices provide objective evidence of fair value. A fair value referenced to active markets has a high degree of validity, and is referred to as a "Level 1" measure of fair value. Price quotes, whether from a stock exchange, dealer, broker, industry group, or pricing service, are an indication of actual transactions that have taken place at arm's length. The *bid price* is the appropriate measure, since it establishes the presence of a buyer (versus the *ask price*, which is offered by a vendor.)

If there is *no active market*, then *fair value must be estimated using a valuation technique* that incorporates all factors that market participants consider when establishing prices. For example, when trading is light, markets are not active. Recent bid prices may be acceptable if economic or firm-specific conditions have not changed. In particular, a recent price might not be relevant if significant events have taken place after the bid date.

Valuation models attempt to set a value that would have been valid in an arms length transaction motivated by normal business considerations. Fair value can be inferred by referencing another "similar but not identical" transaction and then adjusting the market price for differences in term and risk. Discounted cash flow and option pricing models can also be used. The result is an *inferred fair value*. Such an estimate is referred to as a "Level 2" measure of fair value. The reasonableness of any result must be carefully considered before the value can be used in the financial statements.

An estimate of fair value becomes less reliable when more estimates or adjustments have to be made. In the presence of extensive extrapolations, and unobservable data, a fair value is referred to as a "Level 3" estimate. For example, if a discounted present value model is used that incorporates many internal estimates, the use of estimated *unobservable data* makes the resulting fair value a Level 3 estimate.

The following extracts from the 31 December 2011 financial statements of Brookfield Asset Management Inc. define the three fair value levels and show the portion of financial instruments valued at each level.

Fair Value Hierarchical Levels

Fair value hierarchical levels are directly determined by the amount of subjectivity associated with the valuation inputs of these assets and liabilities and are as follows:

Level 1 – Inputs are unadjusted, quoted prices in active markets for identical assets or liabilities at the measurement date.

continued on next page

Level 2 – Inputs (other than quoted prices included in Level 1) are either directly or indirectly observable for the asset or liability through correlation with market data at the measurement date and for the duration of the instrument's anticipated life. Fair valued assets and liabilities that are included in this category are primarily certain derivative contracts, other financial assets carried at fair value in an inactive market and redeemable fund units.

Level 3 – Inputs reflect management's best estimate of what market participants would use in pricing the asset or liability at the measurement date. Consideration is given to the risk inherent in the valuation technique and the risk inherent in the inputs in determining the estimate. Fair valued assets and liabilities that are included in this category are power purchase contracts, subordinated mortgage-backed securities, interest rate swap contracts, derivative contracts, certain equity securities carried at fair value which are not traded in an active market and the non-controlling interests share of net assets of limited life funds.

Assets and liabilities measured at fair value on a recurring basis include $1,820 million (2010—$2,087 million) of financial assets and $618 million (2010—$580 million) of financial liabilities which are measured at fair value using valuation inputs based on management's best estimates. The following table categorizes financial assets and liabilities, which are carried at fair value, based upon the level of input to the valuations as described above:

(millions)	Dec. 31, 2011		
	Level 1	Level 2	Level 3
Financial assets			
Cash and cash equivalents	$2,027	$ —	$ —
Other financial assets			
Government bonds	225	299	—
Corporate bonds	8	194	—
Fixed income securities	108	—	114
Common shares	329	—	1,037
Accounts receivable and other	720	113	669
	$3,417	$606	$1,820

Source: Brookfield Asset Management Inc., 2011, Annual Financial Statements, page 116, www.sedar.com, posted 20 March 2012.

Fair Value Not Determinable Fair value may not be determinable when there is no active market for the financial instrument *and valuation models are not considered to be accurate.* This might happen if there were a broad range of values, suggested by different techniques, or no reasonable reference transactions. This should not be a common situation. In these circumstances, the standard suggests that *cost must be treated as though it were fair value.* Essentially, this means that the cost method is used—the investment is not revalued at reporting dates but is carried at cost.

The danger with this valuation approach is that fair value might be lower than cost, with the result that the asset is overvalued. Guidance is accordingly provided to help identify the conditions under which cost would not be a reasonable approximation of fair value. Usually, these are circumstances under which fair value is lower than cost. The investor is expected to consider a broad range of information that is available about the investee. Such information might include the performance of the investee in comparison with budget, technological risks, the health of the economy in general, the performance of competitors, any evidence of financial distress apparent in transactions with third parties, and any evidence of internal fraud or external litigation.

Fair Value in Distressed Markets

Through turbulent financial markets in 2007 and 2008, large financial institutions, particularly in the United States, recognized significant losses when they wrote down investments consisting of mortgage-backed securities. One issue was how to measure *fair value* for these investments. Some institutions might have been forced to "dump" comparable securities at short notice and at artificially low prices because of their internal financial constraints. These *actual transactions* then created reference prices for portfolios of investments in all financial markets and all companies.

Some claimed that these fair values were not realistic and that the reference prices forced writedowns that further exacerbated financial constraints.

As a result of these concerns, standard setters were put under considerable pressure to suspend the requirements for fair value accounting for these assets. The U.S. Financial Accounting Standards Board (FASB) not only made some concessions for U.S. financial institutions but also provided further guidance on measurement of fair value where markets were "not orderly." The changes were greeted with relief by some but triggered loudly expressed dismay from others, who consider fair values highly informative.

THE AMORTIZED COST METHOD

Using the amortized cost method, interest-bearing debt securities are recorded at cost, which is fair value on the date of acquisition. Fair value is the present value of the cash flow streams, discounted at the market interest rate. Any transaction costs, such as brokerage fees, are included in cost.

Accrued Interest If the debt security is purchased between interest dates, accrued interest since the last interest payment date is paid by the new investor. Accrued interest is not part of investment cost but is recorded as interest receivable.

Accrued interest must be paid on acquisition because at each interest date, the *full periodic interest* is paid to whoever holds the securities regardless of how long they have been held. When debt securities are sold between interest dates, the seller collects accrued interest, which is recorded as interest revenue. For the new investor, the accrued interest is recorded separately from the cost of the security itself.

Note that interest calculations will be done by month in this text, but financial markets will make these adjustments counting by day.

Example

To illustrate the cost basis for a bond investment, assume that on 1 November 20X1, Able Company purchases face amount of $30,000 of Charlie Corporation 8% coupon bonds at 100 plus accrued interest. The bonds mature on 31 December 20X7. Interest is paid semiannually on 30 June and 31 December. Able classifies this investment as an AC investment. Transaction costs are capitalized on acquisition. Commissions on sale are netted with proceeds received.

Bond prices are quoted as percentages of the face value of the bond. A quote of 98 implies that a $30,000 face amount bond has a market price of $29,400. Able paid par, or 100, and so paid $30,000. The bond price is based on the present value of the cash flows, discounted at the market interest rate. The quoted price does not include accrued interest, which also must be paid to the seller of the bond.

Because the bond is purchased between interest dates, accrued interest must be paid by Able for the period 1 July to 31 October. The Able bond purchase occurred on 1 November four months after the last interest payment on 30 June, and two months before the next payment at the end of December. Therefore, Able has to pay four month's interest *up front*. When Able receives six months' interest in December, cash will net out to two months' interest earned.

Acquisition The entry to record the acquisition is as follows:

Investment in Charlie Corporation bonds	30,000	
Accrued interest receivable ($30,000 × 8% × 4/12)	800	
Cash		30,800

Revenue When interest is received on 31 December, a portion of it represents the accrued interest recorded at the acquisition date:

Cash ($30,000 × 8% × 6/12)	1,200	
Investment revenue: Interest		400
Accrued interest receivable		800

Maturity When an AC investment comes due, the investor receives the face value plus interest for a full six months, since maturity occurs on an interest date:

Cash	31,200	
Investment revenue: Interest		1,200
Investment in Charlie Corporation bonds		30,000

Sale If the AC security is sold before maturity, the difference between book value and the selling price (net of accrued interest), less commissions and other expenses, is recorded as a gain or loss.

Suppose that on 31 March 20X2 Able Company sells its Charlie Corporation bonds at 105 plus accrued interest and incurs commissions and other expenses of $550. The cash generated includes three months of accrued interest, or $600 ($30,000 × 8% × 3/12) plus the net proceeds from the bond itself, $30,950 (($30,000 × 105%), less $550 commissions.) The gain on the sale is $950 because the proceeds of $30,950 are greater than the cost of $30,000.

The entry to record the sale is as follows:

Cash ($30,950 + $600)	31,550	
Investment revenue: Interest		600
Investment in Charlie Corporation bonds		30,000
Gain on sale of investment		950

Gains and losses on sale are recognized in earnings.

Amortization of Premium or Discount

What happens if debt securities are bought for an amount other than par value, for example, at 98 or 104? This is fair value and can be greater or less than the face amount of the debt because of interest rate differentials. The difference between fair value and par value is called a **premium** or **discount**. When fair value is higher than par value, the excess is called a *premium*. If fair value is less than par value, the difference is called a *discount*. The premium or discount must be amortized to interest revenue to properly measure the yield on the investment and also to bring the carrying value up (or down) to par value at maturity. Otherwise, interest revenue over the life of the investment is misstated, and a substantial gain or loss will be recognized at maturity.

Issuance Price To ascertain fair value, the present value of the cash flows associated with the debt is calculated using the market interest rate as the discount rate. For example, assume that Marcus Corp. purchased Baker Company bonds when the market interest rate was 6%. The Baker bonds had a $500,000 maturity value, paid 5.5% interest semi-annually, and had a five-year life. The fair value is calculated as follows:

Principal $500,000 × (P/F, 3%, 10)	$372,045
Interest $13,750 × (P/A, 3%, 10)	117,290
Fair value (Present value)	$489,335

Both the principal of $500,000 and the semi-annual interest payments of $13,750 ($500,000 × 5.5% × 6/12) must be included in the present value calculation. Note that the discount rate used is 3%. This is the 6% market rate multiplied by 6/12 because payments and compounding are semi-annual. The number of periods is 10, which is the five-year life multiplied by two payments per year. Principal is a lump sum, and the interest amount is an ordinary annuity.

The fair value on this investment is $489,335, which is 0.97867 of face value ($489,335/ $500,000). This investment would therefore be quoted at a fair value of 97.867; *fair value quotes in the bond market are based on a percentage of par value.* Acquisition would be recorded as follows:

Investment in debt securities: Baker bonds	489,335	
Cash		489,335

Since the bond will mature at $500,000, the $10,665 ($500,000 − $489,335) *discount* must be amortized to interest revenue over the life of the investment.

Amortization Methods There are two methods of amortization, the **straight-line method** and the **effective-interest method**. The straight-line method is simpler, but the effective-interest method is preferable because it provides a constant yield on the recorded value of the investment. *IFRS standards require use of the effective-interest method.* However, the difference between the two is not material if the original difference between cost and fair value is small, which is often the case. Both methods will be illustrated in this chapter.

Example: Effective-Interest Method Using the effective-interest amortization method, interest revenue is measured using the market interest rate in effect when the bonds were issued. Investment carrying value is multiplied by the market interest rate to obtain interest revenue. The difference between cash received and interest revenue is the premium or discount amortization. The investment value changes by the amortization amount, and the investment book value changes to face value at maturity.

Effective-interest method calculations are illustrated in Exhibit 11-4. Note the following:

- The cash payment amount is constant each period, consistent with the terms of the bond. This is the stated interest rate of 2.75% each six months, or 5.5% × 6/12.
- Interest revenue is a constant percentage of the bond carrying amount. To obtain interest revenue, multiply the bond carrying value by the market interest rate. For example, the first amount is $14,680, or 3% of $489,335.
- Amortization is the difference between the cash payment and interest revenue. On the first line, this is $930, or $14,680 less $13,750.
- The bond carrying value grows each period by the amortization amount. On the first line, this is $489,335 plus $930, to equal $490,265.
- The bond carrying value is increased to par value by the end of the 10-period amortization process.

EXHIBIT 11-4

EFFECTIVE-INTEREST AMORTIZATION

Period	Cash Payment	3% Interest Revenue	Amortization	Bond Carrying Value
0				$489,335
1	$13,750	$14,680	$ 930	490,265
2	13,750	14,708	958	491,223
3	13,750	14,737	987	492,210
4	13,750	14,766	1,016	493,226
5	13,750	14,797	1,047	494,273
6	13,750	14,828	1,078	495,351
7	13,750	14,861	1,111	496,462
8	13,750	14,894	1,144	497,606
9	13,750	14,928	1,178	498,784
10	13,750	14,966*	1,216	500,000

*$14,964 + $2 rounding error

Interest revenue is recorded for the first period as follows:

Cash	13,750	
Investment in debt securities: Baker bonds	930	
Investment revenue: Interest		14,680

Example: Straight-Line Method Using the straight-line method, interest revenue is measured as a constant amount each period. That is, interest revenue is cash received plus the discount amortization, or cash received minus the premium amortization. The investment value changes by the amortization amount, and the investment book value approaches face value at maturity. The straight-line amortization method calculations are illustrated in Exhibit 11-5. Note the following:

- The cash payment, interest revenue, and amortization are constant each period.
- Amortization is obtained by dividing the discount of $10,665 ($500,000 − $489,335) by 10, which is the number of interest payments.
- Interest revenue is the sum of cash payment plus amortization, or $13,750 plus $1,067 or $1,066.
- The bond carrying value is increased to par value by the end of the 10-period amortization process.

Purchase at Premium Suppose Marcus paid *more* than the face of the bonds because the market interest rate was 4% when the bonds were purchased. In this case, the fair value would be:

Principal $500,000 × (P/F, 2%, 10)	$410,175
Interest $13,750 × (P/A, 2%, 10)	123,511
Fair value (Present value)	$533,686

The excess paid over the face amount is a *premium*. At acquisition, the bonds would be recorded at $533,686, but over the period to maturity, the $33,686 premium would be

EXHIBIT 11-5

STRAIGHT-LINE AMORTIZATION

Period	Cash Payment	Interest Revenue	Amortization	Bond Carrying Value
0				$489,335
1	$13,750	$14,817	$1,067*	490,402
2	13,750	14,817	1,067	491,469
3	13,750	14,817	1,067	492,536
4	13,750	14,817	1,067	493,603
5	13,750	14,817	1,067	494,670
6	13,750	14,816	1,066	495,736
7	13,750	14,816	1,066	496,802
8	13,750	14,816	1,066	497,868
9	13,750	14,816	1,066	498,934
10	13,750	14,816	1,066	500,000

*($500,000 − $489,335) = $10,665; $10,665/10; rounded

amortized, reducing the carrying amount (and reducing investment revenue below cash received) each year. Using the effective-interest method, the amortization table would appear as in Exhibit 11-6. Only the first three interest periods have been included here. The table is constructed as for a discount situation except that the carrying value begins at a value *higher* than face value, the interest revenue is cash received *less* premium amortization, and the investment carrying value is *reduced* to face value over the life of the investment.

EXHIBIT 11-6

EFFECTIVE-INTEREST AMORTIZATION

Period	Cash Payment	2% Interest Revenue	Amortization	Bond Carrying Value
0				$533,686
1	$13,750	$10,674	$3,076	530,610
2	13,750	10,612	3,138	527,472
3	13,750	10,550	3,200	524,272
etc.				

The first interest payment would be recorded as follows:

Cash	13,750	
Investment in debt securities: Baker bonds		3,076
Investment revenue: Interest		10,674

Impairment

The fair value of an AC debt security will fluctuate whenever market interest rates change. The fair value of the investment will also fluctuate if the credit rating of the borrower changes because the risk attached to future cash flow is changed. An increase in credit risk increases the risk premium appropriately included in the discount rate.

When the value of an investment falls below its acquisition cost, assets may be overstated. Prudence might dictate loss recognition. However, since the security is not held for sale, and its maturity value is assured, fair value is not a relevant measurement attribute. Therefore, the loss is not necessarily recorded.

Impairment reflects a decline in fair value that must be recorded in the year. Investments must be reviewed to see if there has been a "loss event," or circumstances that have triggered a decline in fair value that must be recorded. A loss event will trigger an impairment if the event changes the expected cash flows from the investment and may be the combination of circumstances rather than one event. Examples are:

1. Significant financial difficulty of the investee;

2. A breach of contract, such as failure to pay required interest or principal on outstanding debt;

3. Concessions granted by the investor because of financial difficulties;

4. Probable bankruptcy or financial reorganization;

5. Disappearance of an active market for the investment because of financial difficulties; and

6. Observable data that indicate cash flows of the investee have decreased.

These situations must be evaluated to see if there is real impairment. For instance, if an active market for an investment disappears because a once-public company has gone private but the company is still in good financial position, there is no impairment. Similarly, a downgrade in credit rating does not mean impairment unless it is accompanied by one of the above conditions.

When an impairment loss must be recorded, it is measured as the difference between the investment's carrying value and fair value. Fair value is estimated as the present value of revised expected cash flows, taking into account the new economic circumstances of the investee.

Example Review the facts of the Baker bond given above, originally purchased for $489,335. After three years, if the effective-interest amortization method is used, the carrying value of the bond is $495,351. Assume that this investment has become impaired. Baker is in financial reorganization, and the fair value of the bond is $213,500 because interest and principal payments have been reduced significantly as part of the financial reorganization.

The impairment is recognized:

Impairment loss ($495,351 – $213,500)	281,851	
Investment in debt securities: Baker bonds		281,851

Alternatively, the impairment can be recorded in a valuation allowance:

Impairment loss	281,851	
Allowance for impairment loss: Baker bonds		281,851

The allowance is shown as a *contra account* to the investment on the statement of financial position. The loss would be reported in earnings. The investment account now has a net balance of $213,500. (Note that for tax purposes, such losses are deductible only when realized, so the impairment loss is tax deductible only when the [reduced] payments are actually accepted.)

Reversals Impairment losses are reversed as long as the improvement in fair value (i.e., the recovery of impairment loss) can be related objectively *to an event* occurring after the impairment was recognized. Reversals cannot be used to record the asset at an amount that is higher than the *otherwise valid amortized cost*. For example, assume that an AC bond had an amortized cost of $194,000. The borrower encounters cash flow problems, the present value of the bond is recalculated to be $165,000, and an impairment loss of $29,000 is recorded.

A year goes by. Assume that if the amortized cost approach had been used uninterrupted, the carrying value of the investment would have been $196,000. If new revenue streams come into play, improving cash flow, and fair value is now $175,000, a recovery of $10,000 ($175,000 − $165,000) is recorded. If fair value were to have been estimated at $209,000, the highest value that could be recorded is the amortized cost *reference value*, or $196,000.

THE COST METHOD

The cost method is used for investments in shares, particularly when fair value is not available.

Example: Share Investment

To illustrate the cost method for an investment in shares, assume that on 1 November 20X1, Able Company purchases 50,000 shares of Phillips Company common shares for $20 per share. Commissions and legal fees with respect to the purchase are $50,000; these are capitalized. This investment gives Able control of Phillips, and Able will consolidate at year-end. *During the year, however, Able will record the investment using the cost method.*

Acquisition The entry to record the purchase is as follows:

Investment in Phillips Company common shares	1,050,000	
Cash [(50,000 shares × $20) + $50,000 fees]		1,050,000

Investment Revenue On 31 December, Phillips declares a dividend of $0.50 per share. The dividend is recorded when declared:

Dividends receivable (50,000 × $0.50)	25,000	
Investment revenue: Dividends		25,000

The dividend is paid on 13 January, and the cash receipt is recorded.

Cash	25,000	
Dividend receivable		25,000

Sale If the investment is sold, the difference between book value and the selling price, less commissions and other expenses, is recorded as a gain or loss. Assume that the shares of Phillips Company common shares were sold for $2,300,000, less $61,000 of fees and commissions.

Cash ($2,300,000 − $61,000)	2,239,000	
Investment in Phillips Company common shares		1,050,000
Gain on sale of investment		1,189,000

Impairment

Shares accounted for using the cost method must be regularly evaluated for impairment. The same factors that indicate impairment of an AC bond investment apply to a share investment. Impairment evidence also includes any significant changes that suggest that the cost of the investment in the equity instrument may not be recovered. This might involve adverse developments in the technological, market, economic, or legal environment. A significant or prolonged decline in the fair value of an investment in an equity instrument below its cost is also objective evidence of impairment.

CONCEPT REVIEW

1. A debt security is bought for $14,700, including $700 of accrued interest, and sold for $14,900, including $900 of accrued interest. Why is there no gain or loss on sale?

2. How is the fair value of a bond determined?

3. Is interest revenue on an AC investment necessarily equal to the cash entitlement? Explain.

4. Under what conditions would an impairment loss on an AC investment be reversed?

THE FAIR-VALUE-THROUGH-PROFIT-AND-LOSS METHOD

The fair value method recognizes that financial statement users find fair value more relevant than the historical cost of the investment. Therefore, at reporting dates, the carrying value of an investment is adjusted to fair value. In the FVTPL method, gains and losses are included in earnings when the change in value is recognized, whether the gains and losses are *unrealized* or *realized through sale*. Dividend and interest revenue are recorded during the year, as appropriate.

Example Assume that on 1 December 20X5, YZone bought 5,000 shares of Gerome Limited, a public company, for $26.75 per share plus $1,200 in broker's fees. The investment is classified as FVTPL. *The commission is expensed for FVTPL investments on a purchase transaction.*

Investment in Gerome Ltd. shares (5,000 × $26.75)	133,750	
Commission expense	1,200	
Cash		134,950

YZone also purchased on 1 December 20X5 a $100,000, 6%, eight-year Provincial Hydro bond that pays interest each 1 December and 1 June, at a price of $106,528, to yield 5%. Because the bond was purchased on an interest date, there was no accrued interest. There was also no commission paid. This investment is classified as FVTPL.

Investment in Provincial Hydro bonds	106,528	
Cash		106,528

Investment Revenue Dividends would be recorded when declared. None is declared in 20X5. Bond interest is accrued on 31 December using the effective-interest method.

Accrued interest receivable ($100,000 × 6% × 1/12)	500	
Investment revenue: Interest ($106,528 × 5% × 1/12)		444
Investment in Provincial Hydro bonds		56

Fair Value Adjustment At year-end, fair value is determined through reference to active stock market quotations. The Gerome shares are trading for $24.75 and the bonds are trading at 107. This means that the shares must be reflected in the financial statements at

$123,750 (5,000 shares at $24.75) and the bonds at $107,000. An entry is made to record changes in fair value:

Investment in Provincial Hydro bonds		
($107,000 – ($106,528 – $56))	528	
Investment revenue: Holding gain:		
Provincial Hydro Bond		528
Investment loss: Holding loss: Gerome Ltd. shares		
($133,750 – $123,750)	10,000	
Investment in Gerome Ltd. shares		10,000

The 107 bond price is quoted exclusive of accrued interest, and *fair value is NOT adjusted for brokerage fees* that would have to be paid if the securities were actually sold.

Reporting At the end of 20X5 the financial statements will reflect the following:
Investments on the statement of financial position:

Assets:	
Investment, Gerome Ltd. shares	$123,750
Investment, Provincial Hydro bonds	107,000

In earnings:

Investment revenue: Interest revenue	$444 (cr.)
Investment loss: Holding loss	(10,000) (dr.)
Investment revenue: Holding gain	528 (cr.)
Commissions expense	(1,200) (dr.)

Second Year In 20X6, YZone has further transactions with respect to its FVTPL investments. Interest on the Provincial Hydro bonds is paid on 1 June and 1 December. YZone originally paid $106,528 for a yield to maturity of 5%. Although the carrying value was "topped up" to fair value at the end of Year 1, *the original measurements are used through the bond's life for interest revenue measurement.*
To record receipt of interest on 1 June:

Cash ($100,000 × 6% × 6/12)	3,000	
Investment revenue: Interest ($106,528 × 5%		
× 5/12)		2,219
Investment in Provincial Hydro bonds (to balance)		281
Accrued interest receivable (previously recorded)		500

To record receipt of interest on 1 December:

Cash ($100,000 × 6% × 6/12)	3,000	
Investment revenue: Interest		
(($106,528 – $281 – $56) × 5% × 6/12)		2,655
Investment in Provincial Hydro bonds		345

The carrying value of the bond is now $106,374, which is the fair value of $107,000 at the end of year 1, less premium amortization of $626 ($281 + $345) in Year 2. The bond is sold on 1 December for 109, less a broker's fee of $300:

Cash (($100,000 × 109%) – $300)	108,700	
Investment in Provincial Hydro bonds		
(carrying value, $107,000 – $281 – $345)		106,374
Investment revenue: Gain on sale of investment		2,326

Note that the commission is netted with the proceeds, and effectively netted with the reported gain. *The commission is not separately expensed in a sale transaction.* Gerome Ltd. paid a $0.43 per share dividend in 20X6:

Cash (5,000 × $0.43)	2,150	
Investment revenue: Dividend revenue		2,150

The Gerome Ltd. shares are still unsold at year-end. Their quoted share price is now $31.50, or a total of $157,500. Since the shares are now recorded at $123,750, a holding gain is recorded:

Investment in Gerome Ltd. shares		
($157,500 – $123,750)	33,750	
Investment revenue: Holding gain:		
Gerome Ltd. shares		33,750

Reporting At the end of 20X6 the financial statements will reflect the following: Investments on the statement of financial position:

Assets:	
Investment, Gerome Ltd. shares	$157,500

In earnings:

Investment revenue: Interest revenue	$ 4,874
Investment revenue: Dividend revenue	2,150
Investment revenue: Gain on sale of investment	2,326
Investment revenue: Holding gain	33,750

Third Year In 20X7, the Gerome Ltd. shares are sold for $30.50 per share, or a total of $152,500 (5,000 × $30.50), less $1,700 in broker's fees:

Cash ((5,000 × $30.50) – $1,700)	150,800	
Investment revenue: Loss on sale on investment		
($150,800 – $157,500)	6,700	
Investment in Gerome Ltd. shares		157,500

Again, the commission paid is netted with the proceeds. Overall, there has been a $17,050 gain on the shares: selling price of $150,800 versus original cost of $133,750. This has been recognized as a $10,000 loss in 20X5, a $33,750 gain in 20X6 and a loss of $6,700 in 20X7.

Impairment

The above example reflected an unrealized holding loss for the Gerome Ltd. shares at the end of 20X5. The fair value method automatically tracks any decrease in fair value through the financial statements and any subsequent recovery of fair value, so *no separate impairment test is needed*.

Other Issues

Investments Made in a Foreign Currency   Often, an investor will purchase equity or debt instruments that are priced in a foreign currency. The purchase price must be converted into Canadian dollars for recording on the Canadian investor's books and reporting in the investor's financial statements. To record the purchase, the exchange rate on the date of purchase is used.

Shares   For example, assume that LeBlanc Limited purchases an FVTPL investment, 20,000 shares of AllAm Incorporated, a U.S. corporation. The purchase price is US$65 per share, for a total of US$1,300,000. At the time of the purchase, the U.S. dollar is worth Cdn$1.07. The purchase would be recorded in Canadian dollars as follows:

Investment in AllAm Inc.	1,391,000	
Cash (US$1,300,000 × Cdn$1.07)		1,391,000

This entry establishes the cost of the investment to LeBlanc and will be the carrying value of the investment. Next year, if the fair value is US$68 per share and the exchange rate is $1.10, the fair value is a total of $1,496,000 (20,000 shares × $68 × $1.10). *No attempt is made to segregate the foreign exchange impact.* The entry to revalue the investment:

Investment in AllAm Inc. ($1,496,000 − $1,391,000)	105,000	
Investment revenue: Unrealized holding gain:		
AllAm shares		105,000

If this investment were FVTOCI (see the next section), the entire $105,000 revaluation amount would be recorded in OCI and the equity account, AOCI. Again, there is no separate treatment for the exchange gain or loss.

Bonds   An investment in foreign currency–denominated *bonds* must be restated at each reporting date to the equivalent amount in Canadian dollars, using the exchange rate at the reporting date (known as the spot rate). For debt instruments, *the exchange gain or loss is included in earnings as a separate element*.

For example, assume that LeBlanc Limited purchases an FVTPL investment, a U.S. $1,000,000 bond at par, when the U.S. dollar is worth Cdn$1.07. The purchase would be recorded:

Investment in bonds	1,070,000	
Cash (US$1,000,000 × Cdn$1.07)		1,070,000

At the end of Year 2, if the fair value is 102 and the exchange rate is $1.10, *both factors must be separately acknowledged in the entry*. Overall, the bond must be revalued to

Cdn$1,122,000 (US$1,000,000 × Cdn$1.10 × 102). However, the exchange gain on the carrying value is $30,000. This is the newly translated par value, or $1,100,000 (US$1,000,000 × Cdn$1.10) versus the existing book value of $1,070,000. Then, there is a *holding gain* measured as the difference between the $1,100,000 versus fair value of $1,122,000:

Investment in bonds (Cdn$1,122,000 – Cdn$1,070,000)	52,000	
Foreign exchange gain (US$1,000,000 × (Cdn$1.10 – Cdn$1.07))		30,000
Investment revenue: Unrealized holding gain: bonds (Cdn$1,122,000 – Cdn$1,100,000)		22,000

That is, the bond is first adjusted to the current exchange rate, which creates an exchange gain or loss *in earnings*. Second, the bond is adjusted to fair value, which creates an unrealized holding gain, also included in earnings. *This is different than the investment in shares scenario*, where both the change in the exchange rate *and* the change in fair value create investment revenue. The distinction is important for classification but does not change reported earnings, since both gains are included in income for FVTPL investments.

THE FAIR-VALUE-THROUGH-OTHER-COMPREHENSIVE-INCOME METHOD

The fair value method, with gains and losses recognized through other comprehensive income (FVTOCI), is similar in structure to our previous example. The difference between the two fair value methods lies in the entries to record changes in value and the entries on sale. Under FVTOCI, changes in fair value are recorded in other comprehensive income and are permanently excluded from earnings. The cumulative gain or loss is recorded in an equity reserve. This method may be applied only to *equity investments* that are irrevocably designated FVTOCI on initial recognition.

Example Assume that on 1 December 20X5, when YZone bought 5,000 shares of Gerome Ltd. for $26.75 per share plus $1,200 in broker's fees, that the investment was classified as FVTOCI.

Investment in Gerome Ltd. shares ([5,000 × $26.75] + $1,200)	134,950	
Cash		134,950

Note that transaction costs are capitalized and are not expensed.

Fair Value Adjustment At year-end, fair value is determined to be $24.75 per share, or a total of $123,750:

OCI: Holding loss: Gerome Ltd. shares ($134,950 – $123,750)	11,200	
Investment in Gerome Ltd. shares		11,200

The holding loss on the Gerome Ltd. shares includes the write-off of the broker's fees that were capitalized on acquisition.

Reporting Gains and losses caused by changes in fair value are not recorded as earnings but rather as an element of other comprehensive income and part of a separate equity account. The financial statements appear as follows:

On the statement of comprehensive income:

Net earnings (assumed)	$157,800
Other comprehensive income:	
Holding losses on FVTOCI investments	(11,200)
Comprehensive income	$146,600

On the statement of changes in equity:

	AOCI: Equity Reserve: Holding (Loss) or Gain	Retained Earnings
Opening balance (assumed)	$ 0	$651,000
Comprehensive income	$(11,200) dr.	157,800
Closing balance	$(11,200) dr.	$808,800

On the statement of financial position:

Assets:	
Investment, Gerome Ltd. shares	$123,750
Equity:	
Retained earnings	808,800
Reserve: holding loss	(11,200)

Second Year In 20X6, Gerome Ltd. paid a $0.43 per share dividend:

Cash (5,000 × $0.43)	2,150	
Investment revenue: Dividend revenue		2,150

Note that the FVTOCI category dictates treatment of changes in fair value but *dividends are still investment revenue*. The Gerome Ltd. shares have a fair value of $157,500 at year-end.

Investment in Gerome Ltd. shares		
($157,500 − $123,750)	33,750	
OCI: Holding gain: Gerome Ltd. shares		33,750

Reporting At the end of 20X6, the equity reserve includes the *cumulative amount* of holding gains and losses to date. The financial statements will reflect:
On the statement of comprehensive income:

Net earnings (assumed)	$177,100
Other comprehensive income:	
Holding gain on FVTOCI investments	33,750
Comprehensive income	$210,850

On the statement of changes in equity:

	AOCI: Equity Reserve: Holding (Loss) or Gain	Retained Earnings
Opening balance	$(11,200)	$808,800
Comprehensive income	33,750	177,100
Closing balance	$ 22,550	$985,900

On the statement of financial position:

Assets:	
Investment, Gerome Ltd. shares	$157,500
Equity:	
Retained earnings	985,900
Reserve: holding gain	22,550

To prove the $22,550 amount in equity, compare the original cost of the Gerome Ltd. shares, $134,950, and their current fair value of $157,500. The result is $22,550.

Third Year In 20X7, the Gerome Ltd. shares are sold for $30.50 per share, less $1,700 in broker's fees:

Cash ((5,000 × $30.50) − $1,700)	150,800	
OCI: Holding loss: Gerome Ltd. shares	6,700	
Investment in Gerome Ltd. shares		157,500

The holding gains may remain permanently in the equity reserve. Alternatively, if the company wishes, the cumulative holding gains, which are now entirely realized, may be transferred to retained earnings:

OCI: Holding gains ($11,200 − $33,750 + $6,700)	15,850	
Retained earnings		15,850

Reporting The financial statements will reflect the following:
On the statement of comprehensive income:

Net earnings (assumed)	$42,600
Other comprehensive income:	
Holding loss on FVTOCI investments	(6,700)
Comprehensive income	$35,900

On the statement of changes in equity:

	AOCI: Equity Reserve: Holding (Loss) or Gain	Retained Earnings
Opening balance	$22,550	$ 985,900
Comprehensive income	(6,700)	42,600
Transfer to retained earnings on realization	(15,850)	15,850
Closing balance	$ 0	$1,044,350

On the statement of financial position:

Equity:	
Retained earnings	$1,044,350

Impairment

As for FVTPL investments, there is no separate impairment test needed because fair value is the measurement attribute, whether high or low.

Comparison

Both fair value methods report the share investment asset account on the statement of financial position at fair value. Both methods report dividends declared as investment revenue. Neither method requires an impairment test. The difference between the methods lies in the treatment of changes in fair value in earnings: These amounts are in earnings (and retained earnings) under FVTPL and excluded from earnings under FVTOCI. Under FVTOCI, realized amounts may be transferred from the equity reserve to retained earnings, which means that the final destination can be the same.

Total earnings, however, will remain different between the two methods. Under FVTPL, increases and decreases in fair value will cause earnings to increase and decrease. Commissions and brokerage fees are immediately expensed, decreasing earnings. Under FVTOCI, changes in fair value and commission/brokerage fees bypass earnings. Since both retained earnings and the equity reserve are in equity, total equity is not affected. *However, the level, pattern, and potential variability of earnings are different.* Accordingly, the classification decision must be made carefully and thoughtfully by management.

CONCEPT REVIEW

1. A FVTPL investment is bought for $10,000 and has a fair value of $14,000 at the end of the first year, $16,000 at the end of the second year, and then is sold for $21,000 in the third year. What amount of gain is recorded in earnings in the third year?

2. Assume that the same investment is classified as a FVTOCI investment. What gain is included in earnings in the third year?

THE EQUITY METHOD

The equity method presents a radically different approach to measurement of investment revenue and investment valuation.

Illustration In its simplest form, the equity method requires that the investment account represent the investor's proportionate share of the acquired value of the associate and that the investment revenue represent the investor's proportionate share of the associate's income. Assume, for initial simplicity, that Teck Computer Company (TCC) makes an investment of $100,000 for 40% of the voting shares of RPP Software (RPP) on 1 January 20X1. In 20X1, RPP has earnings of $30,000 and pays dividends totalling $10,000. If the investment is accounted for by the equity method, TCC will make the following two entries at the end of 20X1:

To record TCC's share of RPP's earnings:

Investment in RPP Software	12,000	
Investment revenue: Share of earnings of associate ($30,000 × 40%)		12,000

To record receipt of dividends from RPP:

Cash ($10,000 × 40%)	4,000	
Investment in RPP Software		4,000

Note that dividends from the associate *are not recorded as investment revenue.* Under the equity method, the investor company records its proportionate share of the associate's earnings as investment revenue and increases its investment account by this amount. When the associate pays dividends, its net worth is reduced, and thus the investment account of the investor is reduced. Dividends are viewed as a *disinvestment,* that is, a return of the investment to the investor, rather than a return *on* the investment.

Following the two entries for 20X1, the investment account for RPP will reflect the following:

Investment in RPP Software, at Equity

Original investment	$100,000
Proportionate share of earnings of associate ($30,000 × 40%)	12,000
Dividends received from associate ($10,000 × 40%)	(4,000)
Ending balance	$108,000

Included in earnings:

Investment revenue: Share of earnings of associate	$12,000

The difference between investment revenue and dividends is the amount of earnings accruing to the investor that the associate retained, or the *unremitted earnings* of the associate. This is $8,000 in this example. Thus, the equity-based investment account is equal to the original investment plus the investor's proportionate share of the associate's unremitted earnings. This is also the *cumulative increase in the associate's retained earnings since the investment was made.* However, the $108,000 asset value no longer reflects the cost of the investment. This $108,000 number is not fair value, either, and is hard to interpret.

Discontinued Operations If the associate reports earnings from discontinued operations, the investor company must report its proportionate share of these items in earnings separately, in the same way as if they were incurred by the investor company. However, separate disclosure is needed only if they remain material items in earnings of the investor, which is rare.

Other Comprehensive Income If the associate reports items in other comprehensive income, the investor company must report its proportionate share of these items in OCI separately, as for discontinued operations.

Equity Method Adjustments The equity method is typically more complex than this simple example. It is usually necessary to make certain adjustments to the amount of investment revenue that is recorded on the investor's books. Two factors must be considered:

1. When an investor company acquires the equity securities of an associate company, it will usually pay more for the securities than their book value because tangible assets are undervalued or intangible assets are present but not recorded. In this situation, the investor's subsequent proportionate share of the investee's earnings must be adjusted to reflect *depreciation of the underlying fair value of the net assets acquired and impairment of goodwill, if any.* Therefore, it is necessary to:
   a. Measure the book value versus the fair value of net identifiable assets acquired;
   b. Compare the proportionate fair value to the price paid; and
   c. Determine the amount of goodwill, if any.

   The fair values of identifiable assets and goodwill are not explicitly recorded under the equity method, but the investor's share of income must be decreased by appropriate depreciation on the fair values of depreciable assets and any writedown caused by an impairment of goodwill.

2. If the investor and the associate have transactions with each other during the year, there may be *unrealized unconfirmed* profits from these transactions recorded in earnings. For example, assume that the investor sold inventory to the associate at a profit of $25,000. If the associate subsequently sold these goods to a third party, then the intercompany sales price is validated, or realized, in this subsequent transaction, and no particular accounting concerns arise. However, if the inventory is still held by the associate, then the profit is *unrealized* and *unconfirmed* through sale to an independent third party. It is not acceptable to recognize an increase in earnings if all that has happened is a sale to a "customer" that the vendor can significantly influence. Therefore, the investment revenue recognized must be adjusted for *unrealized, unconfirmed intercompany profits of both companies.*

Example: Equity Method

On 2 January 20X1, Giant Company purchased 3,600 shares of the 18,000 outstanding common shares of Small Corporation for $300,000 cash. Two Giant Company senior executives were elected to the Small Corporation Board of Directors. Giant is deemed to be able to exercise significant influence over Small's operating and financial policies, so the equity method of accounting for the investment is appropriate.

Acquisition Giant records its investment as follows:

Investment in Small, at equity	300,000	
Cash		300,000

Fair Values and Goodwill The net assets (assets less liabilities, or equity) of Small at 2 January 20X1, and estimated fair values, are as follows:

	Book Value	Fair Value	Difference
Cash and receivables	$ 500,000	$ 500,000	$ 0
Plant and equipment, net (10-year remaining life)	500,000	700,000	200,000
Land	150,000	170,000	20,000
Total assets	$1,150,000	$1,370,000	
Less: liabilities	(150,000)	(150,000)	0
Net assets; also equal to equity	$1,000,000	$1,220,000	$220,000

Giant bought 20% of Small's shareholders' equity, which has a book value of $200,000 ($1,000,000 × 20%); therefore, $200,000 is the proportion of Small book value purchased by Giant. However, Giant paid $300,000 for its 20% interest in Small. The accounting problem is to determine why Giant paid that much and then to account for the acquisition price accordingly. The $100,000 excess paid over net book value is related to fair value adjustments, and goodwill.

First, each asset and liability is examined to see if book value properly states fair value. To the extent that some assets were undervalued, the $100,000 excess is explained. If there is a remaining unexplained residual, it is attributed to goodwill. This is based on the assumption any excess paid is because there is an unrecorded intangible asset, which promises future cash flow.

The "difference" column above shows the specific assets whose fair value exceeds book value. Giant acquired a portion (20%) of each of these items, including the amount by which fair value exceeds book value.

	Book Value	Fair Value	Difference	20% of Difference
Plant and equipment (10-year remaining life)	$500,000	$700,000	$200,000	$40,000
Land	150,000	170,000	20,000	4,000
Totals			$220,000	$44,000

Giant, then, has acquired a 20% interest in Small at a cost of $300,000, and the items acquired can be represented as follows:

Purchase price (of 20% interest)		$300,000
20% of the net book value of Small ($1,000,000 × .20)		200,000
Excess relating to fair values and goodwill		100,000
20% of difference between fair value and book value:		
Plant and equipment (20% × $200,000)	$40,000	
Land (20% × $20,000)	4,000	44,000
Goodwill		$ 56,000

Thus, $44,000 of the $100,000 excess purchase price that Giant paid can be identified with specific assets. The remaining difference, $56,000, cannot be specifically identified with any asset and therefore represents goodwill. Goodwill is just the "leftover" but should represent positive cash flows expected from the investment. Goodwill can also be computed as follows:

Computation of Goodwill Purchased by Giant Company		
Purchase price (of 20% interest)		$300,000
Fair value of identifiable assets	$1,370,000	
Less: Fair value of liabilities	(150,000)	
Total	$1,220,000	
Fair value of 20% of identifiable net assets acquired: ($1,220,000 × 20%)		(244,000)
Goodwill		$ 56,000

Subsequent Depreciation The equity method requires that Giant record its initial $300,000 investment in Small in one investment account, despite the fact that it has many components. No formal recognition is given to the various component parts of the investment. However, the amount of investment revenue recognized annually will be changed as a result of these components.

When Small uses or disposes of any of the fair value elements, either in the normal course of business or by asset sale, Giant must record appropriate adjustments to its investment account through the annual entry that recognizes investment revenue. For example, depreciation is too low with reference to fair value. If the plant and equipment has a remaining useful life of 10 years and Small uses straight-line depreciation, Giant needs to increase the depreciation expense for Small by $40,000 divided by 10 years, or $4,000 each year for the next 10 years.

Next, goodwill must be considered. Goodwill is not amortized, but must be evaluated for possible impairment. If there is an impairment, investment revenue must be decreased accordingly. In this example, goodwill has been evaluated for potential impairment, but no writedown is required in 20X1.

No annual adjustment need be made for the excess of fair value over book value for the land. When Small sells the land, an adjustment is then made, showing that the cost of 20% of the land from the Giant perspective is understated by $4,000 on Small's books. Giant's proportionate share of any gain on disposal of the land would be decreased by $4,000.

Unconfirmed Unrealized Profits In 20X1, Small sold goods to Giant for $46,000, but none has been resold by Giant at year-end. The goods originally cost Small $38,000, and thus Small has recorded an $8,000 profit that has not been confirmed by a transaction with an outside party. Since Giant owns 20% of Small and records only 20% of Small's income, it must eliminate 20% of the gain, or $1,600 of the $8,000 unrealized profit.

Investment Revenue Giant's revenue from its investment in Small must be calculated with reference to the fair value items described above. Suppose that for the fiscal year ending 31 December 20X1, Small reports the following:

Net earnings before discontinued operations	$ 73,000
Net earnings from discontinued operations	30,000
Net earnings	$103,000
Cash dividends, paid on 31 December	$ 50,000

Investment revenue is a combination of Giant's share of a variety of items.

Small's net earnings before discontinued operations ($73,000 × 20%)	$14,600
Additional depreciation on plant and equipment fair value ($40,000 ÷ 10)	(4,000)
Elimination of unrealized intercompany profit in inventory ($8,000 × 20%)	(1,600)
Net investment revenue, based on net earnings before discontinued operations	$ 9,000
Giant's share of net earnings from discontinued operations ($30,000 × 20%)	$ 6,000

The investment revenue for 20X1, after all the adjustments, is $9,000 based on net earnings before the discontinued operation and $6,000 of net earnings from discontinued operations. These two items would be shown separately on Giant's statement of comprehensive income.

Investment revenue is a total of $15,000 ($9,000 + $6,000). If no adjustments had been made, Giant would have recorded a total of $20,600 of investment revenue ((($73,000 + $30,000) × 20%). This result of the equity method is quite common; less than you might expect is recorded as investment revenue. This happens because the investor very often pays more than book value for its interest in the associate, and the resulting depreciation of fair values reduces earnings. Then, too, intercompany transactions are quite common, and elimination of unrealized profits will also reduce earnings.

Entries   At 31 December, Giant would make the following entries to reflect its interest in the earnings of Small:

Investment in Small, at equity	15,000	
Investment revenue: Share of earnings of associate		9,000
Investment revenue: Share of earnings of associate from discontinued operations		6,000

To record the receipt of cash dividends paid by Small:

Cash ($50,000 × 20%)	10,000	
Investment in Small, at equity		10,000

Balance in Investment Account   After these entries are posted, the balance in the investment in account is $305,000.

Beginning balance (acquisition price)	$300,000
Proportionate share of Small's earnings	15,000
Dividends received	(10,000)
Investment account balance, 31 December 20X1	$305,000

The total investment revenue Giant reports from its investment in Small is $15,000. Since Giant received $10,000 of this in the form of cash dividends, the net increase in its investment is the *unremitted earnings* of $5,000.

Unrealized Profit Elimination

The example shown above involved an intercompany unrealized profit that had been recorded by the associate. This is called an **upstream** profit because the transaction went from the bottom of the investment river (the associate) to the top (the investor). Since the investor picks up only its share of the associate's income, it also picks up only a partial, or 20%, elimination of the profit.

Assume instead that the transaction in the Giant example is **downstream**, a sale from the investor to the associate. Again, none of the inventory is sold at year-end. In this case, Giant has recorded, as part of gross profit, an $8,000 amount that has not been confirmed by a sale to an outside party. *No adjustment is made to the investor's sales or gross profit.* Again, investment revenue is reduced by the investor's share of the $8,000 unrealized profit, or $1,600. The rule is that both upstream and downstream profits are *fractionally eliminated* (the investor's share only).

Goodwill Impairment

The procedures for evaluating goodwill for potential impairment were explained in Chapter 10. If goodwill had to be written down, investment revenue is reduced by the amount of the writedown. This may well create an investment loss for the year, and the *investment account* would be reduced as a result. This is the obvious result of a writedown: Assets go down!

CONCEPT REVIEW

1. What adjustments must be made to the investor's share of associate earnings to arrive at equity method investment revenue?

2. Explain what is meant by unrealized profits. Why should they be eliminated when the investor's share of earnings is calculated?

3. Does the balance of the investment account represent fair value if the equity method is used? Explain.

CONSOLIDATION

A parent company is required to consolidate its financial statements with those of its subsidiaries when general purpose financial statements are issued. The parent company uses the cost or equity method to account for the investment during the year, but, at the end of the reporting period, must prepare consolidated financial statements for reporting to its shareholders and other financial statement users. Consolidated statements are prepared by combining the separate sets of financial statements into one, which are intended to portray the activities of the whole enterprise. This is an application of *substance over form* because consolidated statements portray the economic entity that exists *in substance* rather than relying on the *legal form* that has been used to organize the activities of an enterprise.

Consolidation is accomplished using the *acquisition method*. The parent and the subsidiary are combined as of the acquisition date. Fair values of the subsidiary's assets are recognized based on this acquisition transaction, including goodwill. Prior results are not combined.

It is important to understand that consolidation *does not happen on any one company's books*. Financial statements from the parent and the subsidiary are imported to a spreadsheet and adjusted, and then the consolidated financial statements are produced.

Consolidation Process Consolidation is mostly an additive process; the financial statements are added together, line by line. Common adjustments include the following:

1. The investment account must be eliminated from the parent company's financial statements, and the corresponding equity accounts must be eliminated from the subsidiary's financial statements. Dividends reported are only those dividends paid by the parent.

2. The net assets of the subsidiary are valued at fair value, not book value, on the date of acquisition. This not only includes all recorded asset and liabilities but also involves valuing elements such as intangible assets that might not be on the subsidiary's books. Most significantly, any goodwill inherent in the purchase price will be recorded. This reflects the fact that the parent has acquired assets, including intangible assets, at fair value.

3. Since fair values are recognized, these values must be depreciated in subsequent years.

4. Goodwill is not amortized. Goodwill is written down if impaired. The impairment test must be done on an annual basis.

5. Any portion of the subsidiary that is consolidated but is owned by a minority, or non-controlling, subsidiary shareholder must be recognized as a separate equity account. The non-controlling interest is assigned a portion of net assets, at fair value, and a portion of earnings. Several approaches are acceptable to value the non-controlling interest, with the choice focused around goodwill valuation.

6. Intercompany receivables and payables, gains and losses, and revenues and expenses must be eliminated so that the financial statements will reflect only transactions with outsiders.

7. If there are any intercompany unrealized profits at year-end, these must be eliminated so that earnings are not misstated.

Connection to the Equity Method The calculations and adjustments that are required for the equity method are also required for consolidation. That is, data must be gathered to establish the fair value of net assets acquired and amount of goodwill. These amounts are recognized and then depreciated or evaluated for impairment. Intercompany unconfirmed profits are eliminated. In consolidation, however, all the different financial statement elements are recognized separately. In the equity method, the net assets are *subsumed in the investment account and the investment revenue line in earnings.*

RECLASSIFICATION

It happens that circumstances change, and investment classification has to be revisited. *Reclassification should not be common.* Points to note are as follows:

- Reclassification of AC investments is appropriate only when the objective of the entity's business model for managing the assets has changed.
- Classification of a FVTOCI investment may be made only on initial recognition and is irrevocable; transfers to and from this class are not permitted.
- Investments may move from FVTPL to being strategic investments if control or significant influence is established. Strategic investments may move into FVTPL if control or significant influence is lost.

Reclassifications are primarily driven by the facts of the situation. Sometimes, reclassifications are caused by the actions of others; for example, significant influence may be lost if another shareholder becomes dominant. Other times, it is an internal change of business model or intent that changes.

Reclassification of AC Investments Reclassification into or out of an AC investment portfolio is permitted *only when the objective of the entity's business model for managing those assets has changed.* This type of change would be infrequent. The change would be dictated by senior management in reaction to significant internal or external factors that can be demonstrated to external parties.

One example might be to reclassify an existing portfolio of bonds or loans receivable from FVTPL to AC. Perhaps the portfolio had been held for resale but now is being held to collect the contractual cash flows. The change in business model was dictated because the company acquired the expertise to manage the portfolio internally and changed its strategy accordingly. Alternatively, if an AC bond portfolio is put up for sale because the company changes its business model and no longer wishes to invest or loan, then the portfolio is no longer AC.

Transfer Value If investments are reclassified, they are transferred to the alternative portfolio at an appropriate value, which is often fair value. For example, if a FVTPL investment is transferred to the associate category, the transfer takes place at the investment's existing carrying value, fair value, and the investment is then accounted for using the equity method with fair value as the starting point. A transfer into FVTPL begins with the fair value on the transfer date. Refer to Exhibit 11-7 for examples of reclassification rules.

DISCLOSURE AND SCF REQUIREMENTS

Current versus Long-Term Investments

Should investments be classified as current or long-term assets in the SFP? The answer will have a significant effect on the current liquidity picture portrayed. An investment is current if it is:

- Classified as a *cash equivalent* (money market financial instruments with an initial term of 90 days or less; see Chapter 5); or
- Expected to be realized during the company's normal operating cycle or within 12 months, or investments held for trading.

FVTPL investments, FVTOCI investments, and AC investments about to mature may all be current. Investments in associates are long-term investments.

Disclosure of Financial Instruments

All AC, FVTOCI, and FVTPL investments are financial instruments. Financial instrument disclosure is extensive but should be limited to material areas to avoid overwhelming the financial statement users. The objectives of disclosure are to ensure that information is available to assess the significance of financial instruments for the company's financial position,

---

EXHIBIT 11-7

EXAMPLES OF RECLASSIFICATION RULES

Transfer from	Transfer to	Transfer Value	Prior Gains and Losses
Fair value through other comprehensive income (1)	Transfers not permitted	Transfers not permitted	—
Any appropriate category	Fair value through profit and loss	Fair value at reclassification date	Include cumulative gain or loss to date (fair value less carrying value on date of transfer) in earnings
Any appropriate category	Associate; significant influence established	Existing carrying value (often fair value)	No additional gain or loss recorded; equity method applied to carrying value of investment account as the starting point

(1) Note: Category open only on initial acquisition of an investment and designation is irrevocable.

the nature and extent of risks associated with financial instruments, and how those risks are managed. Some of the disclosures include the following:

1. The important components of each financial statement category (i.e., various types of investments).

2. Information related to value, by category. Methods used to assess fair value and its components must be explained. When a financial instrument has been valued at fair value, detail about the change in fair value is required.

3. Information related to the legal terms of the investments, including maturity dates, interest rates, collateral, and so on.

4. Various revenue and expense amounts and AOCI reserve amounts that must be disclosed separately, including interest revenue and expense, holding gains, and so on.

5. Information on exposure to *credit risk, liquidity risk,* and *market risk,* as appropriate. Objectives, policies, and processes for managing risk must be disclosed. Such disclosure is extensive, and includes both qualitative and quantitative elements.

6. Accounting policy information that is required as a matter of course for all financial statement elements.

Disclosure Example

IFRS 9 was published in 2009, and must be adopted in 2015. It is available for early adoption in the meantime. Refer to Exhibit 11-8, which contains extracts from the 31 December 2011 financial statements of Aston Hill Financial Inc., an early adopter of IFRS 9. Some of its investments are classified as FVTPL and some as FVTOCI. The FVTOCI investments have fair value estimated through Level 3 approaches.

EXHIBIT 11-8

FINANCIAL STATEMENT EXTRACTS ASTON HILL FINANCIAL INC.

Extracts from December 31, 2011 Financial Statements

From the SFP:

	December 31, 2011
Assets	
Current assets	
Cash and cash equivalents	$ 7,415
Investments at fair value through profit or loss	1,773
Trade and other receivables	3,745
Prepaid expenses	156
Notes receivable	342
	13,431
Prepaid deposits	149
Investments at fair value through other comprehensive income	5,880
Intangible assets	45,310
Property and equipment	727
Deferred sales commissions	308
Deferred income tax asset	—
Total assets	$65,805

continued on next page

EXHIBIT 11-8 (cont'd)

From the SCI:

...

	December 31, 2011
Net income for the period	$ 1,326
Other comprehensive (loss) income ("OCI"):	
Net change in fair value of investments through other comprehensive income	(2,404)
Deferred tax on net change in fair value of investments through other comprehensive income	464
Other comprehensive (loss) income for the period, net of tax	(1,940)
Total comprehensive (loss) income for the period	$ (614)

4. DETERMINATION OF FAIR VALUES

...

a) Financial assets and liabilities at fair value through profit or loss:

Non-derivative financial assets and liabilities at fair value through profit or loss are classified as held for trading and are reported at fair value through profit and loss. The fair value of a financial instrument is the amount of consideration that would be agreed upon in an arm's length transaction between knowledgeable, willing parties who are under no compulsion to act. Level 1 fair values are determined by reference to quoted bid or ask prices, as appropriate, in the most advantageous active market for that instrument to which the Company has immediate access. Level 2 fair values are determined using the net asset value per unit of each investment.

b) Financial assets at fair value through other comprehensive income:

The Company's investment in Sword Energy Inc. is a financial asset reported at fair value through other comprehensive income. The fair value of a financial instrument is the amount of consideration that would be agreed upon in an arm's length transaction between knowledgeable, willing parties who are under no compulsion to act. Estimated fair value is determined on the basis of the expected realizable value of the investments if they were disposed of in an orderly fashion over a reasonable period of time. The Company uses estimation techniques to determine fair value which include using recent arm's length market transactions between knowledgeable, willing parties, if available, reference to the current fair value of another instrument that is substantially the same, discounted cash flow analysis, multiple earnings analysis, and reserve based valuations.

Comparative figures and references to disclosure notes have been deleted.

Source: Aston Hill Financial Inc., 2011 Annual Financial Statements, pages 4, 6 and 38, www.sedar.com, posted 26 March 2012.

Disclosure of Strategic Investments

There are extensive disclosures relating to strategic investments, that is, associates, subsidiaries, and joint arrangements. The overall objectives of disclosure with respect to strategic investments are to allow financial statements users to evaluate:

- The impact of the investments on financial position, operating results and cash flows; and
- The risks associated with the investments.

There is an extensive array of information required to meet these objectives.

Statement of Cash Flows

Financial instruments that are considered to be *cash equivalents* are included in the definition of cash when the statement of cash flows (SCF) is prepared. Consequently, investments in cash equivalents do not appear on the SCF but instead are included in the cash balance.

For other investments in debt and equity securities, the cash flow impacts occur in three ways:

1. There is a cash outflow when an investment is purchased. The initial cash outflow is reported as an investing activity on the SCF.

2. Cash payments are received by the investor (dividends or interest). This cash flow may be classified in operating activities or investing activities, as we saw in Chapter 5. This is a management choice that must be applied consistently.

3. Cash is received when the investment is sold or is redeemed at maturity. This is an investing cash flow.

When the recorded values of FVTOCI investments or FVTPL investments change because of changes in fair value, this is a non-cash event; it does not appear on the statement of cash flows. For FVTPL investments, gains and losses in earnings are adjusted in operating activities as non-cash amounts. For FVTOCI investments, other comprehensive income is affected, but no adjustments are needed to earnings on the SCF.

On sale, the net cash proceeds that the company receives when it sells or redeems an investment security are reported as a positive (inflow) amount in the investing activities section of the SCF. Any gain or loss on disposal must be removed from earnings when computing the operating cash flow, since a gain or loss is not cash flow but is merely the difference between the cash proceeds and the investment's carrying value at the time of the sale. Note also that premium or discount amortization in investment revenue on AC investments is a non-cash item and must be included as a reconciliation item in operating activities.

Reporting the periodic cash flows for dividends received on strategic investments presents a somewhat greater challenge. If the investment is being reported on the equity basis, then:

- Cash received as dividends must be reported on the SCF, as cash flow from investment revenue. This is included in either operating activities or investing activities; and

- The investor's share of the investee's earnings must be removed from earnings when calculating cash flow from operating activities.

If the strategic investment gives the investor control over the investee and the parent prepares consolidated statements, the cash flows between the parent and subsidiary are eliminated on consolidation and do not appear on the statement of cash flows at all. A consolidated SCF is prepared.

Looking Ahead

IFRS 9 was issued in 2009 to be effective in 2013, later changed to 2015. Early adoption is allowed, but in the meantime, the classification rules of IAS 39 apply. The following major differences between IAS 39 and IFRS 9 can be highlighted:

1. Certain financial instrument categories have *different names* under the two standards:

	Investment Categories	
	in IFRS 9	**in IAS 39**
1	Amortized cost	Held-to-maturity
2	Fair-value-through-other-comprehensive income (FVTOCI)	Available-for-sale
3	Fair-value-through-profit-and-loss (FVTPL)	Fair-value-through-other-comprehensive income (FVTPL) (same name)
4	Loans and receivables	Loans and receivables (same name)

2. Investment categories have *different classification criteria* under the two standards; IFRS 9 relies on a *business model* classification for amortized cost investments, while IAS 39 relies on *positive intent* to hold to maturity. In the fair value categories, the catch-all is FVTPL under IFRS 9 and is available-for-sale (FVTOCI) for IAS 39. Management designation is required for FVTOCI under IFRS 9, but management designation is the criterion for FVTPL for IAS 39. Remember, though, that an investment in bonds may not be designated as FVTOCI under IFRS 9.

A comparison of the investment classification criteria:

	Investment Classification Criteria	
	IFRS 9	**IAS 39**
1. Amortized cost/Held-to-maturity	AC investments must meet two tests: • The asset must be held and managed within a business model whose objective is to hold assets to collect contractual cash flows. • The financial asset must have contractual terms that give rise on specified dates to cash flows that are solely payments of principal and interest on the principal amount.	An investment that has a defined maturity date, fixed or determinable payments, and for which there is *positive intent* to hold to maturity.
2. Fair-value-through-other-comprehensive-income/Available-for-sale	An investment *designated by management* as fair-value-through-other-comprehensive-income. Note that: • Only equity investments can be FVTOCI; investments in bonds or loans do not qualify; • The election to classify an investment as FVTOCI must be made when the investment is initially recognized and is irrevocable; and • The investment cannot have been acquired primarily for resale.	Any investment that is a financial instrument and is not in the other two categories; this is the *catch-all category* of investments.
3. Fair-value-through-profit-and-loss	Any investment that is a financial instrument and is not in the other two categories; this is the *catch-all category* of investments.	An investment *designated by management* as held for trading; part of a portfolio managed for short-term profit or acquired principally for resale; also certain qualifying financial instruments designated by management as FVTPL

3. Under IAS 39, the held-to-maturity category is *tainted* if an investment is reclassified out of the category and/or sold prior to maturity. The category is closed as a result of the tainting rule; any other investments in the category are reclassified, and no investments may be classified as held-to-maturity for the two fiscal years after the tainting takes place. *There is no such tainting rule under IFRS 9 in the amortized cost method.*

4. Under IAS 39, when an investment is accounted for as an available-for-sale investment, using FVTOCI, *OCI amounts are reclassified to earnings when the investment is sold or matures.* Under IFRS 9 and its version of the FVTOCI category, OCI amounts are *permanently excluded from earnings.* The amounts may be reclassified to another equity account when the investment is sold, but can never be reclassified to earnings.

ACCOUNTING STANDARDS FOR PRIVATE ENTERPRISES

Passive Investments ASPE allows *significantly* different accounting policies for investments compared with IFRS. Passive investments (i.e., other than strategic investments) are accounted for as follows:

Investment Classification	ASPE	IFRS
Equity securities for which prices are quoted in an active market	Fair value through profit and loss (FVTPL)	Classification as FVTPL or FVTOCI
Any other investment, as designated by management	Fair value through profit and loss (FVTPL)	Classification as AC, FVTPL, or FVTOCI
All others	Cost or amortized cost	As above

Essentially, the cost method is permitted, *unless the investment has a fair value established in an active market.* In this case, fair value is both relevant to users and reliably determinable, and therefore it must be reflected in the financial statements. *There is no use of comprehensive income* for private companies, though, so unrealized gains and losses are included in earnings and FVTOCI is not an option.

Strategic Investments For *strategic investments,* the following policies apply:

Investment Classification	ASPE	IFRS
Associate	Cost* or Equity	Equity
Subsidiary	Consolidation or Cost* or Equity	Consolidation
Joint venture	Cost* or Equity or Proportionate consolidation	Equity

*If share prices are quoted in active markets, cost is not permitted, but FVTPL is the alternative.

Note the significant breadth of alternatives allowed for private companies. While private companies can choose the alternative that conforms to IASB standards, ASPE allows major alternatives. This reflects the fact that there are different financial statements users for private companies, and the cost of compliance is high for more complex accounting policies, especially when fair values must be estimated. It is up to each private company to assess its reporting information needs and proceed accordingly.

Joint arrangements are not a classification contemplated by ASPE.[1] *Joint ventures* are the classification for investments with shared control. Under ASPE, joint ventures can be accounted for through the cost method or the equity method, but a third alternative

---

[1] This topic is under consideration by Canadian standard setters.

is proportionate consolidation. Under **proportionate consolidation,** the parent and investee financial statements are added together. However, *only the investor's percentage share* (e.g., 40%) of the investee's assets, liabilities, revenues, and expenses is added to the investor's own financial elements under proportionate consolidation. This differs from a regular consolidation, where *all* the subsidiary's assets and so on are included regardless of the ownership interest, partially offset by the non-controlling interest accounts.

Another difference between ASPE and IFRS is found in the application of the amortized cost method. *ASPE allows use of straight-line amortization,* while IFRS requires use of the effective-interest method, unless the difference between the two is immaterial.

Under ASPE, there is no choice for the classification of cash flow from investment revenue. This cash flow must be included in operating activities.

There are a myriad of small differences between ASPE and IFRS, in addition to the major policy differences listed above. For example, under ASPE in the equity method, downstream profits are eliminated *in their entirety,* while under IFRS, such elimination is fractional. Impairment tests proceed differently under the two models. And, of course, there are significant differences in the extent and nature of required disclosure.

Comparison of Equity and Cost Method

Under ASPE, a significant-influence investment may be accounted for using the cost method instead of the equity method. Refer to the Small Company example earlier in the chapter. If Small were accounted for using the cost method, the following entries would be made. The entries are compared to the equity method, side-by-side, for clarity.

Entries	Alternative 1: Cost Method Is Appropriate		Alternative 2: Equity Method Is Appropriate	

a. Entry to date of acquisition:
  Investment in Small
    Cash
	300,000	300,000	300,000	300,000

b. Entry at year-end to record earnings reported
    by Small:
  Investment in Small
    Investment revenue, earnings
    Investment revenue, discount operations
	No entry		15,000	9,000
				6,000

c. Entry for a cash dividend:
  Cash
    Investment revenue
  Cash
    Investment in Small
	10,000	10,000	10,000	10,000

d. Entry to reflect change in fair value	None, unless impairment		None, unless impairment	

The two methods are significantly different in how they define investment revenue, whether they recognize underlying net asset fair value and goodwill, treatment of dividends of the associate, and the value reported for the investment.

RELEVANT STANDARDS

CPA Canada Handbook, Part I (IFRS):
- IAS 1, Presentation of Financial Statements
- IAS 18, Revenue
- IAS 21, The Effects of Changes in Foreign Exchange Rates
- IAS 27, Consolidated and Separate Financial Statements
- IAS 28, Investments in Associates
- IAS 32, Financial Instruments: Presentation
- IAS 36, Impairment of Assets
- IAS 39, Financial Instruments: Recognition and Measurement
- IFRS 3, Business Combinations
- IFRS 7, Financial Instruments: Disclosure
- IFRS 9, Financial Instruments
- IFRS 10, Consolidated Financial Statements
- IFRS 12, Disclosure of Interests in Other Entities
- IFRS 13, Fair Value Measurement

CPA Canada Handbook, Part II (ASPE):
- Section 1582, Business Combinations
- Section 1590, Subsidiaries
- Section 1600, Consolidated Financial Statements
- Section 1651, Foreign Currency Translation
- Section 3051, Long-Term Investments
- Section 3055, Interests in Joint Ventures
- Section 3856, Financial Instruments

SUMMARY OF KEY POINTS

1. Companies invest in the securities of other entities for a variety of reasons, including increasing return on idle funds, managing an active investment portfolio, managing a long-term investment portfolio of loans or equity instruments, creating strategic alliances, and creating appropriate legal vehicles for business activities.

2. Investments must be classified as amortized cost, fair-value-through-profit-and-loss, fair-value-through-other-comprehensive-income, or cost. If the investments are strategic, they are classified as subsidiaries, associates, or joint arrangements.

3. Investments are classified as AC only if they are managed within a business model whose objective is to hold assets to collect contractual cash flows, and whose cash flows are for principal and interest only. FVTPL encompasses most other investments, and those investments management designates as FVTPL. FVTOCI investments are equity securities designated by management as FVTOCI on initial recognition. Cost investments are those with no ascertainable fair value, and those using the cost method during the year in unconsolidated financial statements.

4. Amortized cost investments are recorded at cost and interest revenue is accrued as time passes. Any premium or discount is amortized to income over the life of the investment, using the effective-interest method. The straight-line method can be used if it is not materially different than the effective-interest method.

5. FVTPL investments are accounted for using the fair value method, where the investment is remeasured to fair value at each reporting date. Gains or losses are recognized in earnings. Interest revenue is recognized as time passes and dividends are reported as investment revenue when declared.

6. FVTOCI investments are accounted for using the fair value method, where the investment is remeasured to fair value at each reporting date. Gains or losses are recognized in other comprehensive income and accumulated in an equity reserve account (AOCI). These gains and losses may be transferred to another equity account (retained earnings) when realized through sale or may remain in the equity reserve account. Dividends are reported as investment revenue when declared.

7. Cost method investments in common shares are valued at cost, with gains and losses on sale recorded only when the investment is sold. Dividends are reported as investment revenue when declared.

8. AC investments are subject to impairment tests, where a decline in value caused by a "loss event" is recorded as a loss, which may be reversed if an event causes fair value to improve in a later fiscal period. Cost method investments must also be evaluated for impairment.

9. Certain equity instruments are classified according to the power of the investor within the corporate governance structure of the investee. If the investor controls the investee, the investment is a subsidiary and is consolidated. Consolidation requires combining the financial statements of the parent and the subsidiary at reporting dates. If the investor has some influence but does not have control, the investee is an associate that must be accounted for using the equity method. A joint arrangement is present when power is shared; a joint venture is one that conveys an investment in net assets and is accounted for using the equity method.

10. In the equity method, the investment is first recorded at cost (initial fair value), but the balance of the investment account changes to reflect the investor's proportionate share of the investee's adjusted earnings less dividends. Investment revenue includes the investor's share of profits (or losses) less depreciation of fair values present at acquisition, goodwill impairment, and elimination of unrealized intercompany profits.

11. Certain investments may be reclassified from one category to another. The reclassification generally takes place at fair value, and any gains and losses are subject to specific rules depending on the reclassification category.

12. Investments are classified as current assets if they are a cash equivalent or will be realized in the next year. Otherwise, the investment is long term.

13. Extensive disclosure is needed for investments. Exact disclosures vary, depending on how the investment is classified. The objectives are to provide information on the risks associated with the investments and information regarding the impact/significance of the investments on financial position, operating results, and cash flows.

14. The statement of cash flows reflects cash paid for investments, cash received on sale, and cash received as investment revenue. Investment revenue is either operating or investing, at management's choice. Non-cash items are adjusted in operations when the indirect method of presentation is used.

15. ASPE allows choices for investment accounting. Many investments can be accounted for using the cost method. If investments are equity investments where there are prices quoted in an active market, they must be FVTPL. Strategic investments may be accounted for using the cost, FVTPL, equity, or consolidation alternatives, depending on the classification and management assessment of reporting objectives.

KEY TERMS

amortized cost (AC)	impairment
associate	joint arrangement (JA)
cash equivalent	joint operation (JO)
consolidation	joint venture (JV)
control	non-controlling interest (NCI)
cost method	other comprehensive income (OCI)
discount	parent company
downstream	passive investment
effective-interest method	premium
equity method	proportionate consolidation
fair value	realized holding gains or losses
fair value method	significant influence
fair-value-through-profit-and-loss investment (FVTPL)	straight-line method
	strategic investment
fair-value-through-other-comprehensive-income investment (FVTOCI)	subsidiary company
	unrealized holding gains or losses
financial instruments	unremitted earnings
holding gains or losses	upstream

REVIEW PROBLEM 11-1

On 1 January 20X5, Acme Fruit Company has the following investments:

	Net Carrying Value at 1 January 20X5
FVTPL investments:	
Apple (2,000 common shares)	$19,000
Quince (10,000 common shares)	50,000
Cherry (5,000 common shares)	40,000

To date, the company has recognized in earnings a $5,000 holding loss with respect to the Apple shares, a $5,000 holding gain with respect to the Quince shares, and a $2,000 holding gain with respect to the Cherry shares.

The following transactions occur during 20X5:

a. On 1 February 20X5, Acme purchases $30,000 of face amount bonds issued by Plum Incorporated for $29,500 plus accrued interest. The bonds have a coupon rate of 8%, pay interest semi-annually on 30 June and 31 December, and mature on 31 December 20X9. The investment is classified as an AC investment.

b. Dividends of $0.75 per share are received on the Apple common shares on 30 May.

c. Interest on the Plum bonds is received on 30 June and 31 December. Total amortization of the discount has been calculated to be $109 in 20X5.

d. On 1 July, the Quince shares are sold for $58,000. The proceeds are used to buy 1,000 Banana Company shares for $40 per share. These shares are classified as FVTOCI.

e. On 30 November, Apple shares are sold for $21,000.

f. At 31 December, the fair values of the various investments are determined to be as follows:

i. Cherry common	$57,500
ii. Banana common	33,000
iii. Plum bonds (excluding accrued interest)	31,000

g. The Cherry and Banana shares are short-term investments at year-end, while the Plum bonds are long term.

Required:

1. What amount of investment revenue or loss, from all sources, is reported in earnings for 20X5?

2. Show the change in other comprehensive income for the year to be included on the SCI, and the cumulative equity reserve account that would be reported on the SFP at the end of 20X5.

3. Show the accounts and amounts related to the investments that are reported as assets at the end of 20X5.

REVIEW PROBLEM 11-1—SOLUTION

1. Investment revenue:

Plum bonds:		
Interest: $30,000 × 8% × 11/12	$2,200	
Discount amortization: (given)	109	$ 2,309
Apple dividends: 2,000 shares × $0.75		1,500
Holding gain: sale of Quince shares		8,000
Holding gain: sale of Apple shares		2,000
Holding gain: Cherry shares ($57,500 – $40,000)		17,500
Total investment revenue		$31,309

2. Change in other comprehensive income, 20X5:

Holding loss: Banana shares ($40,000 – $33,000)	$ 7,000 (dr.)
AOCI: Equity reserve, 31 December, 20X5	$ 7,000 (dr.)

3. Investment assets at 31 December 20X5:

Temporary investments ($57,500 + $33,000)	$90,500
Long-term investments ($29,500 + $109)	$29,609

QUESTIONS

Q11-1 Why do companies invest in the securities of other enterprises?

Q11-2 How can a debt investment be classified? An equity investment? How should each category be accounted for?

Q11-3 What are the differences between the FVTPL and FVTOCI categories?

Q11-4 What factors indicate that significant influence may be present between an investor and an associate? How would such an investment be reported?

Q11-5 What factors indicate that control exists between an investor and an investee? How would such an investment be reported?

Q11-6 What is the distinguishing feature of a joint arrangement? A joint venture? How are joint ventures accounted for?

Q11-7 How is fair value estimated?

Q11-8 On 1 August 20X4, Baker Company purchased $50,000 face amount of Sugar Company 6% coupon value bonds for $43,200. The market interest rate was 8% on this date. The bond pays interest semi-annually on 31 July and 31 January. At the fiscal year-end for Baker, the bonds have a fair value of $45,000. Show the journal entries (a) to record the investment and (b) to record investment revenue and any other needed adjustments at 31 December. The investment is classified as an amortized cost investment and the effective-interest amortization method is used.

Q11-9 What conditions may indicate that the value of an investment recorded at cost or amortized cost has been impaired? How is an impairment recorded for an AC investment? Why is impairment not an issue for FVTPL or FVTOCI investments?

Q11-10 An investor purchased 100 shares of Zenics at $20 per share on 15 March 20X4. At the end of the 20X4 accounting period, 31 December 20X4, the stock was quoted at $19 per share. On 5 June 20X5, the investor sold the stock for $22 per share. Assuming this is a FVTOCI investment, give the journal entry to be made at each of the following dates:

- 15 March 20X4
- 31 December 20X4
- 5 June 20X5

Q11-11 On 31 December 20X1, ABC Company owned 10,000 shares of A Company. This investment had been purchased in 20X1 at a cost of $23 per share. At the end of 20X1, the fair value was $24 per share. At the end of 20X2, the fair value was $28 per share. The investment was sold in 20X3 at $30 per share. No dividends were declared in any year. This is a FVTOCI investment. What would be included in other comprehensive income on the SCI, the equity reserve for holding gains on the SFP (cumulative), and earnings, in each of 20X1, 20X2, and 20X3? Realized holding gains are transferred to retained earnings.

Q11-12 On 31 December 20X1, XYZ Company owned 10,000 shares of B Company. This investment had been purchased in 20X1 at a cost of $21 per share. At the end of 20X1, the fair value was $26 per share. At the end of 20X2, the fair value was $29 per share. The investment was sold in 20X3 at $33 per share. There were no dividends in any year. The investment is classified as a FVTPL investment. What would be included in other comprehensive income on the SCI, the holding gain reserve on the SFP (cumulative), and earnings in each of 20X1, 20X2, and 20X3?

Q11-13 The 31 December 20X3 statement of financial position shows FVTOCI investments at $456,800, and accumulated other comprehensive income at $169,000. The investments were purchased in 20X3. Interpret these two values. At what amount were the investments originally purchased?

Q11-14 A FVTPL investment is carried at $550,000, and unrealized gains of $35,000 have been recorded in earnings to date. The investment is sold for $520,000. What gain or loss is included in earnings in the year of the sale?

Q11-15 On 1 July 20X2, a company bought an investment in IBM bonds at par for US$50,000 when the exchange rate was US$1 = Cdn$1.12. The investment is classified as FVTPL. The company paid cash on the acquisition date. At 31 December, the exchange rate was US$1 = Cdn$1.09. The fair value was US$52,000. Prepare journal entries to record the purchase of bonds and any adjusting entries at year-end. Disregard any interest accrual.

Q11-16 Assume that Company R acquired, as a long-term investment, 30% of the outstanding voting common shares of Company S at a cash cost of $100,000. At the date of acquisition, Company S reported net assets and total shareholders' equity of $250,000. The fair value of the depreciable assets of Company S was $20,000 greater than their net book value at the date of R's acquisition. Compute goodwill purchased, if any.

Q11-17 Assume the same facts as in Q11-16. Net assets that were undervalued at acquisition have a remaining estimated life of 10 years (assume no residual value and straight-line depreciation). There is no goodwill impairment. How much investment revenue would Company R report using the equity method if Company S reported $80,000 of earnings after one year of ownership?

Q11-18 Investor Limited owns 35% of Machines Limited and has significant influence. The investment was made five years ago, when Machine's fair values equalled book values; $40,000 of goodwill was inherent in the purchase price. Goodwill is not impaired. In the current fiscal year, Machines reported $225,000 in income. This includes a $50,000 profit on inventory sold to Investor Limited, which Investor has not yet resold. How much investment revenue will Investor report using the equity method?

Q11-19 Equity income, and consolidated income, is usually lower than one would predict by simply adding the investor's income and the pro-rata share of the investee's income. Why does this happen?

Q11-20 Under what circumstances is an investment reclassified from the AC classification to the FVTPL classification? Can an AC investment be classified as FVTOCI? Explain.

Q11-21 What accounting policy(ies) will a private enterprise use to account for investments? Why are these different alternatives than those available to those companies that comply with IFRS?

CASE 11-1

SPACEINFO CORP.

"Will, I think these deals will provide an answer to our third-quarter profit shortfall." Florence Decoste, the CFO of SpaceInfo Corp. (SI), was all smiles as she placed several thick files on Will Blackburn's desk. "We've got revenue of $5 million here, along with an increase in the fair value of an investment that will easily push us over our third-quarter earnings targets. We're convinced that fourth-quarter economic recovery will solidify our core markets, so we will have healthy trends by the end of the fiscal year."

Will, one of the company's financial analysts, was pleased with the news that financial results would improve. The accounting and finance area group of SI had been tense all week, ever since projected third-quarter data for the company had surfaced, which indicated the potential for a significant shortfall. SI is a public company, offering on-line green pages (product and contact information) coupled with software that enables companies to gather information concerning potential customers' hits on web pages. This information could then be used to target particular users and geographic areas.

SI felt its business model was strong, but in a soft economy, the company was struggling. Senior management was concerned that analysts' expectations be met for third quarter revenue and profit projections. The company's share price had already dropped from a high of $12 to $2.06, and further declines were feared.

Florence continued, "Will, I want you to review these contracts and draft journal entries to book these transactions for us. If you have any questions and concerns, get them documented in a brief report I can take to the Executive Committee. We meet tomorrow at noon. They seem to have an interest in these transactions. I'm sure you won't find anything to alarm them. We all want to stay employed, don't we?"

As Will reviewed the documentation in the files, he began to outline the nature of the transactions.

First, SI was planning to invest $8 million cash in Harp Limited, a cell phone apps company. SI was prepared to purchase 2 million shares at $4 per share, for a 6% ownership position in the company. SI was not taking on any managerial or Board of Directors role with the company. Will noticed, though, that one of the major shareholders of Harp was George Francesca, the brother-in-law of John Yu, SI's President and CEO. Will knew that

SI had over $12 million in cash, the residual from the public offering that had taken place last year. The investment in Harp was to be accounted for at fair value, with changes in fair value through earnings.

A second, unrelated contract was for services SI was to provide to Harp, all in the third quarter of this year. The contract, for $5 million, would be a major advertising and information campaign for Harp. Cash would be paid to SI at the end of the third quarter. The services to be provided were standard activities of SI, but the size of the contract was unusual for a company the size and scope of Harp; in particular, a company the size of Harp might spend $3 million per year on marketing efforts, and this contract related to one medium and one-quarter of the fiscal year.

A third contract arranged a $10 million technology product acquisition by Harp Limited from GTT Limited, a third party. Harp was buying technology from GTT, in line with its product mix. In this contract, $10 million was to be paid in the third quarter, with $3 million directly from Harp and the additional $7 million raised through a loan that SI was to guarantee.

Finally, the fourth contract arranged for GTT to invest $8 million in Harp, in exchange for 1,600,000 shares; this represented a fair value of $5 per share.

Required:

As Will, prepare the requested report for the Executive Committee.

CASE 11-2

WILD ONES LIMITED

In May 20X1, a group of outdoor enthusiasts formed Wild Ones Limited (Wild Ones). Wild Ones operates in central Newfoundland and is involved in a variety of outdoor adventure activities. Start-up capital was provided from an inheritance that one of the owners had received and modest savings of the other owners. For the first eight months of operations, co-op students looked after basic financial record keeping. An unaudited balance sheet as of 31 December 20X1 is presented in Exhibit 1.

It is now 24 January 20X2, and you, a Professional Accountant, have just been hired by Wild Ones on a part-time basis to take on financial accounting responsibilities for the company's first fiscal year-end of 30 April 20X2. During its first year of operations, Wild Ones secured financing from the Regal Bank and the Atlantic Canada Opportunities Agency (ACOA), details of which are contained Exhibit 2. The terms of these lending agreements require Wild Ones to prepare its financial statements in accordance with Accounting Standards for Private Enterprises (ASPE) and to have audited financial statements. The firm of Jake and Malachy, public accountants, will be completing the audit of Wild One's financial statements.

Wild One's owners explain that they want you to analyze the information presented and then:

- Explain the changes you believe are required;
- Prepare any necessary 31 December 20X1 adjusting journal entries; and
- Prepare a revised balance sheet.

Required:

Prepare a report that addresses the requests of the owners.

EXHIBIT 1

WILD ONES LIMITED
Balance Sheet, 31 December 20X1
(unaudited)

Assets:

Cash	$ 4,500
Accounts receivable	42,000
Inventory	84,000
Investment in River Rafters	38,000
Promotional costs	12,000
Total Assets	$180,500

Liabilities:

Accounts payable	$ 3,200
Loan payable to Regal Bank	9,500
Loan payable to ACOA	150,000
Total Liabilities	$162,700

Shareholders' Equity:

Common shares	$ 2,500
Retained earnings	15,300
Total Equity	$ 17,800
Total Liabilities and Equity	$180,500

EXHIBIT 2

WILD ONES LIMITED
Events Occurring in the Eight Months Ended 31 December 20X1

1. Shortly after Wild Ones was formed, its owners decided to invest in River Rafters, another privately owned outdoor adventure company operating in central Newfoundland. Wild Ones paid $44,000 in return for 22% of the common shares of River Rafters, a company which has operated in the area for 15 years. The owners of Wild Ones were also given two of the six seats on River Rafter's Board of Directors.

   Poor weather during 20X1 meant that River Rafters had a particularly unusual and unprofitable year. River Rafter's total net loss for the period of time that Wild Ones has owned shares was $33,000. However, because River Rafters has had such a record of success and has significant cash on hand, it paid its usual dividend to owners this fall. Wild One has recorded their receipt of $6,000 in dividends as a debit to cash and a credit to the asset account, Investment in River Rafters, leaving a balance of $38,000 in the investment account: $44,000 purchase price less $6,000 of dividends received.

2. To gear up for winter operations, in September Wild Ones secured a loan with the Regal Bank. The loan bears interest at 9% and requires end-of-month payments of interest and also a specified principal amount. Wild Ones has made all payments as scheduled. The terms of the loan require Wild Ones to supply the bank with audited financial statements prepared in accordance with ASPE and to not exceed a specified debt-to-equity ratio. If the debt covenant is violated, the loan will become immediately due.

continued on next page

3. On 1 October 20X1, Wild Ones secured $150,000 of financing from the ACOA. The loan requires interest payments of 1% of the loan each 1 October, beginning in 20X2 and going through to 20X5. The principal payment is due in full as one payment of $150,000 at the end of four years (1 October 20X5). Wild One must provide ACOA with audited financial statements prepared in accordance with ASPE within 90 days of its fiscal year-end. No interest has been recorded because none is due at 31 December.

4. The owners tell you that you do not need to make any income tax entries or adjustments at this time.

5. Through the fall, Wild Ones worked on developing a prototype of a new snowshoe design. The company field-tested the prototype with a variety of independent adventure guides in northern Canada. Reviews were favourable, so Wild Ones immediately began manufacturing snowshoes in a rented facility. Sales during December were brisk and profitable. The company has outstanding sales orders for inventory to be delivered in January and is forecasting steady sales through North and South America for at least three years. The co-op student explained that the accounting for this venture was pretty easy. The snowshoe development costs of $81,000 were charged to repairs expense. $12,000 spent on a promotional event in South America in November was capitalized and will be written off over three years of expected sales.

(Judy Cumby, used with permission)

CASE 11-3

QUINN INC.

Quinn Inc. (QI) was formed in March 20X8 when Devon Goodman, Scott Adams, and Chase Beson pooled their resources and talents to take advantage of a booming economy in western Canada. The company selected 28 February as the date of its year-end. Beson had been making basic accounting entries for the first 10 months of operation and prepared a draft unaudited statement of financial position as of 31 December 20X8 (Exhibit 1). There is some information provided about the events of the year (Exhibit 2). Beson is entitled to sell his shares in QI to Goodman, based on a multiple of QI's net income for the year ended 28 February 20X9. Goodman now owns 21 shares of QI.

It is now 27 January 20X9. Two weeks ago, Goodman hired you, Chen Ngu, Public Accountant, to be QI's Chief Financial Officer. Goodman has requested a revised statement of financial position as of 31 December 20X8 and revised net earnings for the 10 months ended 31 December 20X8. She also asks that you provide her with journal entries to support adjustments you make to the draft 31 December statement of financial position and earnings figures provided by Beson. She is interested in accounting choices that present QI as a strong company, but she has specified that generally accepted accounting principles must be adopted. QI is not subject to income tax.

Required:
Respond to the requests of Devon Goodman.

(Judy Cumby, used with permission)

EXHIBIT 1

QUINN INC.

Balance Sheet

31 December

ASSETS	Unaudited 20X8
Cash	$ 7,200
Accounts receivable, net	254,000
Inventory	50,800
Investments	80,000
Investment in Procurement Inc.	375,000
Capital assets, net of depreciation	50,000
TOTAL ASSETS	**$817,000**

LIABILITIES	
Accounts payable	$ 62,900
Loan payable	600,000
	$662,900

SHAREHOLDERS' EQUITY	
Common shares, 41 shares issued	$ 4,100
Reserve: Holding loss	(50,000)
Retained earnings (earnings to date)	200,000
	$154,100
TOTAL ASSETS AND SHAREHOLDERS' EQUITY	**$817,000**

EXHIBIT 2

QUINN INC.

Events Occurring in the 10 Months Ended 31 December 20X8

1. QI develops and manufactures electronic devices used for personal identification. Operation of the electronic devices depends on two components: the identification cards held by authorized users and a card reader/programming device. If the card reader recognizes the card as legitimate, the cardholder will be granted access (to a building, specific room, etc.). On average, each programming device can process 80 identification cards. QI tells its customers that it will throw in the programming device "for free," but the reality is that the identification cards will not work with any device other than the proprietary technology in QI's programming device.

   QI has sold several sets of electronic cards and programming devices to a number of customers who are quite pleased with the technology's accuracy and speed. However, in mid-December, QI delivered four programming devices and 320 electronic cards to a property management company, SpaceCo Inc. SpaceCo is not satisfied with the programming devices, as there have been a number of access errors. QI loaned SpaceCo some of its demo units until it can get replacement ones manufactured for SpaceCo in March. SpaceCo's personnel are not pleased with the situation and are threatening to not pay the balance of its account when it comes due in early February.

continued on next page

Beson has recorded journal entries that reflected the sale to SpaceCo:

Unit	Unit Price	Quantity	Total Price
Programming device	$ 0.00	4	$ 0
Electronic cards	$ 543.75	320	$174,000
Total revenue			$174,000

Unit	Unit Cost	Quantity	Total Cost
Programming device	$2,800	4	$ 11,200
Electronic cards	$ 280	320	$ 89,600
Total cost			$100,800

SpaceCo paid 20% (or $34,800) in cash upfront. QI recorded a receivable for the remaining $139,200.

2. On 1 July, QI paid $300,000 for 40% of the common shares of Procurement Inc., a private company that provides equipment and services to oil exploration companies operating in Alberta. Procurement's business was booming through the summer. In response to falling oil prices and a global credit crunch, many companies started to scale back their oil exploration activities in the fall. However, Procurement's operations were not affected by these factors and the company reported a profit of $75,000 for the six months ended 31 December 20X8. Beson has increased the investment to $375,000 and booked $75,000 investment earnings.

3. QI Inc. decided to take some of its cash and invest it in publicly traded companies to earn short-term profits. On 15 July, QI purchased 5,000 shares of PZQ Ld, a public company, at $26 per share. Unfortunately, PZQ was hit hard by economic issues and by 31 December 20X8, its shares were trading at $16 per share. Beson recorded the unrealized loss of $50,000 in equity as a reserve.

4. QI did not declare or pay dividends during the year.

CASE 11-4

NORTHERN ENERGY LIMITED

Northern Energy Limited (NEL) is a large Canadian private company organized in three operating segments: propane operations, trucking, and mineral explorations. Financial statements have not been audited, and NEL has simply used the cost method for its investments. NEL is now considering issuing debt in a public offering, which would mean adoption of IFRS. You, a public accountant consulted on reporting issues, have been asked to prepare a report for circulation to the Board of Directors and shareholders, to help them understand the implications of this potential shift. They specifically wish to understand what financial statement elements might change with revised investment reporting.

Investments reported on the 20X6 statement of financial position:

Investment	Accounting Method	Net Book Value (in thousands)
Nico Investments Ltd., common shares	Cost	$416.3
Canner Ltd., 5% nonvoting preference shares	Cost	174.0
Later Corp., common shares	Cost	675.3
Placement Resources Corp., common shares	Cost	455.2
Trufeld Trucking Ltd., 8% bonds	Cost*	266.8
Lu Trucking, common shares	Cost	45.8

*Amortized cost

Additional information is contained in Exhibit 5.

Required

Prepare the report.

EXHIBIT 1

NEL INVESTMENTS

Later Corp., Common Shares

Later Corp. (LC) is a nationwide courier company, whose shares were acquired by NEL in 20X2. NEL purchased 57.4% of the outstanding shares from the founder of LC on his retirement; the remaining shares are owned by management and two family members of the founder. LC had real estate assets that were significantly undervalued in its financial statements, prompting NEL to pay a significant premium over book value for the company.

The LC Board of Directors consists of 14 members. NEL has the right to appoint eight directors, but to date has nominated only four individuals. The other four slots of NEL are filled by continuing members whom NEL found acceptable.

Nico Investments Ltd.

NEL owns 80% of the common shares of Nico Investments Ltd. (Nico), which manufactures and distributes aluminum wheels. The remaining shares are owned by Frank Nico, the founder. Nico has had persistent challenges with its product and markets and has achieved breakeven results at best since NEL acquired the shares in 20X0, although prospects are positive. Nico reports a deficit on its financial statements but is solvent. Nico has never declared dividends. NEL has guaranteed loans of Nico. Nico has a nine-member Board of Directors, of which NEL appoints seven members, including the chair, who is Frank Nico. According to the terms of signed shareholder agreements, Mr. Nico can veto certain decisions of the Board dealing with operating and financing issues.

Trufeld Trucking Ltd., 8% Bonds

These 8% bonds pay interest semi-annually and mature in 20X14. The par value is $275,000. NEL provided this debt financing to Trufeld, a long-time "friendly" competitor in NEL's trucking business. The two companies often enter joint bids for long-term hauling contracts, and take on freight for the other if overbooked. The bonds are secured against assets in Trufeld's trucking fleet. NEL has one member on the Trufeld Board of Directors as a result of the bond investment. NEL expects to collect interest and principal on the bond, and will not resell it.

continued on next page

Canner Ltd., 5% Nonvoting Preference Shares

NEL purchased these preferred shares in 20X4, when Canner came to NEL looking for equity financing. NEL purchases product from Canner for its propane operations. Canner is a closely held private company. Money was needed for an expansion, but Canner was unwilling to agree to the terms presented by lenders. Canner is located in a small town, and many of its workers are shareholders and are related through family ties. Canner has a six-member Board of Directors, and NEL places one member on the Board. To date, this has been a positive experience for all concerned, as the Canner Board of Directors has been receptive to the suggestions of the NEL representative; many improvements and modernization of governance and operations are being considered. Canner pays regular dividends.

Placement Resources Corp., Common Shares

Placement Resources is a mineral exploration company with active exploration going on in Northern Manitoba. NEL owns 10.2% of the common shares. NEL became involved in this company in 20X5, at the suggestion of a major shareholder of NEL. This shareholder owns 14% of NEL and 44% of Placement. After appropriate investigation, NEL purchased a common share interest and has been very pleased with the results. NEL estimates that the shares owned have a current fair value of at least $900 (thousand), although this is an estimate because Placement is traded only over the counter. Placement has had an erratic operating history, with high net income in some years when exploration is successful and losses in other years. In good years, dividend payouts are material. NEL has two members on the 11-member Board of Directors; the NEL shareholder has four members on the Board and is highly influential.

Lu Trucking, Common Shares

The common shares of Lu Trucking represent 24.3% of the voting shares and were purchased in 20X4, when NEL was considering acquiring this rival trucking company. Lu Trucking is a private company. The remaining shareholders of Lu were not enthused about a transfer of ownership. NEL originally had one member on the nine-member Board of Directors but has ceased to appoint a representative because relations were poor. NEL has attempted to sell these shares several times to other shareholders of Lu, with little success, as they are unable to agree on a price. Lu pays regular, although modest, dividends.

TECHNICAL REVIEW

TR11-1 Amortized Cost; Bond: On 1 January 20X2, Investor Company purchased $1,000,000 of Operating Corporation 5% bonds, classified as an AC investment. The bonds pay semi-annual interest each 30 June and 31 December. The market interest rate was 6% on the date of purchase. The bonds mature on 30 December 20X11.

Required:

1. Calculate the price paid by Investor Company.
2. Construct a table that shows interest revenue reported by Investor, and the carrying value of the investment, for the first two interest periods. Use the effective-interest method.
3. Give entries for the first interest payment based on your calculations in requirement 2.

TR11-2 Fair Value Method; Bond: On 1 January 20X2, Lucky Company purchased $5,000,000 of Fire Corporation 3% bonds, classified as an AC investment. The bonds pay semi-annual interest each 30 June and 31 December. The market interest rate was 4% on the date of purchase. The bonds mature on 30 December 20X11. At the end of 20X2, the bonds had a fair value of $4,800,000.

Required:

1. Calculate the price paid by Lucky Company.
2. Construct a table that shows interest revenue reported by Lucky for the first two interest periods. Use the effective-interest method.
3. Give entries for the first year assuming that the investment is classified as FVTPL.

TR11-3 FVTPL: On 30 June 20X2, King Limited purchased 10,000 shares of Prince Inc. for $12,000 plus $1,000 in commission. In 20X2, the company received a $500 of dividends, and the shares had a fair value of $16,000 at the end of the year. In 20X3, there were no dividends and the shares were sold for $22,000 less a $500 commission.

Required:

1. Prepare journal entries for 20X2 and 20X3, if the company uses the:
   a. Cost method.
   b. Fair-value-through-profit-and-loss method.

TR11-4 FVTOCI: In 20X1, FYY Limited purchased 500 shares of Humor Inc. for $6,000 plus $500 in commission. The shares had a fair value of $19,000 at the end of 20X1, $25,000 at the end of 20X2, and $40,000 at the end of 20X3. In 20X4, the shares were sold for $31,000 less $500 in commission. In each of 20X1, 20X2 and 20X3, dividends of $1,200 were received.

Required:

1. Prepare journal entries for 20X1 to 20X4, if the company uses the:
   a. Cost method.
   b. Fair value through other comprehensive income method; realized amounts are transferred to retained earnings.

TR11-5 Equity Method: On 3 January 20X4, Windsor Company purchased 30% of the shares of Brampton for $565,000 cash. Windsor will use the equity method. On this date, Brampton has $2,000,000 of assets, $1,600,000 of liabilities, and $400,000 of equity. Book values reflect for values except for $800,000 of equipment, which has a five-year life and a fair value of $1,000,000. In 20X4, Brampton pays $30,000 of total dividends and reports earnings of $100,000.

Required:

1. Calculate goodwill on acquisition, and the annual extra depreciation on investee equipment at fair value.
2. Prepare 20X4 journal entries for Windsor Company.
3. At the end of 20X4, what is the balance in the investment account?

ASSIGNMENTS

 A11-1 Classification: The following investments are held by investors that are public companies:

a. A $5,000,000 5% publicly traded 10-year bond of Tree Limited. The bonds are held for short-term capital appreciation, as the investor is expecting interest rates to change.
b. A $4,000,000, 5% publicly traded bond that matures in 10 years. The bond is in a portfolio that is managed with the objective of collecting interest and principal.
c. Common shares of Shrub Limited, amounting to 30% of the outstanding shares. The remaining shares are equally divided among four other investors. Each investor has two

representatives on the 10-member Board of Directors. All strategic decisions must be unanimously agreed to by the Board members.

    d. Common shares of Plant Limited, amounting to 30% of the outstanding shares. The remaining shares are equally divided among eighteen other investors. The investor has two seats on the 10-member Board of Directors.

    e. Common shares of Maple Inc., amounting to 3% of the outstanding common shares. Maple Inc. is a company whose shares are thinly traded on the over-the-counter (OTC) market.

    f. Common shares of Elm Inc., amounting to 5% of the outstanding common shares. Elm is publicly traded. Management wishes gains and losses caused by changes in fair value to bypass earnings.

    g. Common shares of Beech Limited, amounting to 16% of the voting shares. The investor has four members on the 10-member Board of Directors, and has extensive intercompany transactions with Beech.

    h. Common shares of Spruce Corp., amounting to 60% of the common shares of Spruce. The seven-member Board of Directors consists of four members appointed by the investor.

Required:

How should the investor classify each of the above investments? What accounting method should be used for each?

★ **A11-2 Classification:** For each situation below, indicate how the investment would be classified, and how it would be accounted for. The investor is a public company.

    a. Common shares are bought in a public company whose shares are broadly held and widely traded. The company is a supplier of the investor. The investor owns 30% of the voting shares, and puts three people on a 16-member Board of Directors. The intent is to hold the investment for a considerable period of time because of strategic ties.

    b. Twenty-year, fixed rate bonds. Management expects interest rates to fall and the price of the bonds to increase significantly over the coming year. The investment will be sold when this happens. The investor wishes gains and losses to be excluded from earnings because of volatility.

    c. A mining company has been incorporated to develop a mineral reserve. The investor has agreed to contribute equipment and expertise to physically mine the site, in exchange for 55% of the shares and six members on the 10-member Board of Directors. The remaining shares are held by the company who owned the mineral rights to the property.

    d. To invest idle cash, common shares are bought in a large, public company, a tiny fraction of the outstanding common shares. The shares are pledged as collateral against demand bank loans. The fair value of the shares, and market conditions, are regularly evaluated to see if the shares should be held or sold. The investor wishes gains and losses to be excluded from earnings because of volatility.

    e. Investment in $8,000,000 of 20-year bonds, part of a portfolio that is held to generate principal and interest cash flows.

    f. Common shares are bought in a large public company, whose shares are broadly held and widely traded. The investor owns 5% of the voting shares, sits on the Board, and is the largest single shareholder. The fair value of the shares and market conditions are regularly evaluated to see if the shares should be held or sold.

    g. Common shares are bought in a small, family-owned business. The investor is the only nonfamily shareholder. The shares constitute 30% of the voting shares, and the investor has one member on an eight-member Board of Directors, all of the rest of whom are appointed by members of the family investor group. Fair values for the shares are not available as they are rarely sold.

★ **A11-3 Classification:** Consider the following investment categories:

    A. AC investment
    B. FVTPL investment
    C. FVTOCI investment

D. Associate
E. Subsidiary
F. Joint venture
G. Cost

An investor company that is a public company has the following items:

a. SRY Ltd. preferred shares, paying a dividend of $1.25 per share. The shares are not intended to be sold in the near future but are publicly traded.
b. Investment of $10,000,000 in five-year Smith Corporation publicly traded bonds, 8% interest payable semi-annually. The securities will be held as part of a portfolio that is managed for principal and interest cash flows.
c. Investment in Ng common shares bought with idle cash in expectation that the price per share will rise in the short term. The investor wishes gains and losses to be excluded from earnings to reduce volatility.
d. Investment of $2,000,000 in Howard Corporation publicly traded bonds. The securities will be held until the investor needs short-term cash, or until interest rates swing and increase the price of the bonds, whichever comes first. The investor wishes gains and losses to be excluded from earnings because of volatility.
e. Shares in Farmo Company, a supplier. The shares owned amount to 40% of the shares outstanding and allow the investor two seats on the 11-member Board of Directors and the right to net assets. The other 60% of the shares are owned by the two brothers who started the company. All major decisions must be agreed to unanimously by the three major shareholders.
f. Investment in Goldkam Company, a customer in financial difficulty. The shares owned amount to 15% of the shares outstanding and allow the investor two seats on the 11-member Board of Directors. The other 85% of the shares are owned by the close-knit family that started the company. Because the investor is a customer, and has provided financing, there is evidence the investor has been influential in Board decisions.
g. Shares in Chen Company, a supplier. The shares owned amount to 60% of the shares outstanding and allow the investor six seats on the 11-member Board of Directors. The investor has never appointed any member of the Board because the investor is pleased with the way to company is now run and has been content to be a silent investor.
h. Shares in Kondor Ltd, a customer. The shares owned amount to 5% of the publicly traded shares outstanding. The company has no immediate intention of selling the shares but will do so if the price increases or if the investor needs money for other strategic purposes.
i. Shares in Lin Ltd, a customer. The shares owned amount to 8% of the shares outstanding. Lin is a private company and shares are rarely traded. The company has no immediate intention of selling the shares but will do so if the investment become liquid and the shares can be sold at a reasonable price.

Required:
Classify the items above into one of the investment categories, as appropriate. State any assumptions made.

★ **A11-4 Estimating Fair Value:** Timmins Ltd owns a number of investments in the common shares of other companies that qualify as FVTPL investments. Accordingly, fair value must be established for each. Consider the following cases that relate to fair value:

Case A Lakehead Corp. is a publicly traded company, with active trading. On the five days around the year-end date of Timmins, the fair value per share of Lakehead was $4, $16, $12, $12, and $6. At the time, Lakehead was renegotiating a major contract with an overseas customer. Two weeks later, the contract was finalized, and common share price steadied in the $12 range.

Case B Guelph Ltd. is a company whose shares are traded OTC. Trading is sporadic. No share transactions of any size took place around the year-end date of Timmins. Review of trading records show several offerings with an ask price of $6 to $8 per share, but bid prices were in the $4 per share range, and no transactions were completed.

Case C Ajax Corp. is a company whose shares are traded OTC. Trading is sporadic. Two major share transactions have taken place over the last two months, one at $4 per share and one at $6.50 per share.

Case D Whitby Corp. is a company whose shares are traded OTC. Trading is sporadic. No major transactions have taken place in the last six months. Two valuation models have been used to suggest a market value for the shares; one indicates a price of $22 per share and the other $16 per share.

Required:

In each case, explain the problematic element in determining fair value. Suggest additional required information, if appropriate.

★★

A11-5 Amortized Cost Method—Debt Investment: On 1 July 20X8, Sun Company purchased $4,000,000 of Moon Corporation 6.2% bonds, classified as an AC investment. The bonds pay semi-annual interest each 30 June and 31 December. The market interest rate was 6% on the date of purchase. The bonds mature on 30 June 20X13.

Required:

1. Calculate the price paid by Sun Company.
2. Construct a table that shows interest revenue reported by Sun, and the carrying value of the investment, for each interest period for four interest periods. Use the effective-interest method.
3. Give entries for the first two interest periods based on your calculations in requirement 2.
4. How much interest income would be reported for the year ended 31 December 20X9? What would the balance of the investment account be at this time?

★★

A11-6 Amortized Cost Method—Debt Investment: On 1 June 20X8, Ghana Company purchased $7,000,000 of Monaco Corporation 5.8% bonds, classified as an AC investment. The bonds pay semi-annual interest each 30 May and 30 November. The market interest rate was 6% on the date of purchase. The bonds mature on 30 May 20X13.

Required:

1. Calculate the price paid by Ghana Company.
2. Construct a table that shows interest revenue reported by Ghana, and the carrying value of the investment, for each interest period for four interest periods. Use the effective-interest method.
3. Give entries for 20X8, including the year-end accrual, based on your calculations in requirement 2.
4. How much interest income would be reported for the year ended 31 December 20X9? What would the balance of the investment account be at this time?

★★

A11-7 Amortized Cost Method—Debt Investment: On 1 July 20X2, New Company purchased $600,000 of Old Corporation 5.5% bonds, classified as an AC investment. The bonds pay semi-annual interest each 30 June and 31 December. The market interest rate was 5% on the date of purchase. The bonds mature on 30 June 20X5.

Required:

1. Calculate the price paid by New Company.
2. Construct a table that shows interest revenue reported by New Company, and the carrying value of the investment, for each interest period to maturity. Use the effective-interest method.
3. Give entries for the first three interest periods based on your calculations in requirement 2.

★★★

A11-8 Amortized Cost versus Fair Value Method—Debt Investment: On 1 January 20X5, Franco Ltd. purchased $400,000 of Gentron Company 5% bonds. The bonds pay semi-annual interest each 30 June and 31 December. The market interest rate was 6% on the date of purchase. The bonds mature on 31 December 20X10.

Required:

1. Calculate the price paid by Franco Ltd.

2. Assume that the bond is classified as an AC investment. Construct a table that shows interest revenue reported by Franco, and the carrying value of the investment, for four interest periods. Use the effective-interest method.

3. Give entries for the first four interest periods based on your calculations in requirement 2.

4. Assume instead that the bond is classified as a FVTPL investment, and the fair value at the end of 20X5 was $385,000, and was $391,500 at the end of 20X6. Give entries for each interest period in 20X5 and 20X6, and adjust the bond to fair value *at the end of each fiscal year*. (That is, the bond is not adjusted to fair value at each interest payment date, just at the reporting date.)

5. Show how the bond would be presented on the statement of financial position at the end of 20X5 and 20X6, if it were (a) AC and (b) FVTPL.

★★★

A11-9 Amortized Cost versus Fair Value—Debt Investment: On 1 May 20X7, Bertrum Limited purchased $1,000,000 of Fox Corp. 6.2% bonds, classified as an AC investment. The bonds pay semi-annual interest each 1 May and 1 November. The market interest rate was 6% on the date of purchase. The bonds mature on 1 November 20X11.

Required:

1. Calculate the price paid by Bertrum Limited.

2. Construct a table that shows interest revenue reported by Bertrum, and the carrying value of the investment, for each interest period to maturity. Use the effective-interest method.

3. Give entries for 20X7 and 20X8 for Bertrum Limited, including adjusting entries at the year-end, which is 31 December.

4. Assume that Bertrum sold the bonds on 1 February 20X9, for 99 plus accrued interest. Give the entry to record interest revenue to 1 February, and the entry for the sale.

5. Assume instead that the investment is classified as FVTPL. Repeat entries for 20X7, assuming that the fair value of the bond was $1,050,000 on 31 December. Contrast the asset valuation using this method to that produced under the amortized cost method.

★

A11-10 Fair Value Method—Comprehension: At the end of 20X9, Canfrax Corp. Limited reported an unrealized loss on Comet Co shares of $24,600 in earnings. Investments were reported on the statement of financial position as follows:

Long-term assets: investments:	
Star Co. common shares	$1,370,100
Comet Co. common shares	434,700
Shareholders' equity; OCI reserve account:	
Star Co. shares, unrealized gain	$ 150,300

Required:

1. Why are the investments classified as long term? Under what circumstances would they be classified as current?

2. What do the values reported as long-term investments represent? How is this value measured?

3. How have the Star Co. shares been classified? Explain. What criteria must be met for them to be classified in this way? Could the investment have been classified as AC? Explain.

4. Shares were purchased in 20X9. What price would originally have been paid for the Star Co. shares? Comet Co. shares?

5. If the Star Co. shares are sold for $1,500,000, and the Comet Co. shares are sold for $435,000, what gain or loss is included in earnings?

★★   **A11-11 Fair Value Method:** On 1 November 20X8, Porter Company acquired the following FVTPL investments:

- Minto Corporation—2,000 common shares at $15 cash per share
- Pugwash Corporation—700 preferred shares at $25 cash per share

The annual reporting period ends 31 December. Quoted fair values on 31 December 20X8 were as follows:

- Minto Corporation common, $12
- Pugwash Corporation preferred, $27

The following information relates to 20X9:

2 March	Received cash dividends per share as follows: Minto Corporation, $2.10; and Pugwash Corporation, $1.25.
1 October	Sold 200 shares of Pugwash Corporation preferred at $29 per share.
31 December	Fair values were as follows: Minto common, $23, and Pugwash preferred, $26.

Required:

1. Give the entry for Porter Company to record the purchase of the securities.
2. Give the adjusting entries needed at the end of 20X8.
3. List the amount that would be reported in 20X8 earnings and the asset amounts on the statement of financial position.
4. Give all entries required in 20X9.
5. List the amount that would be reported in 20X9 earnings and the asset amounts on the statement of financial position.
6. Repeat requirement (5), assuming that both the investments were originally designated FVTOCI investments. Include the balance of the AOCI equity reserve for holding gains for the SFP amounts. The holding gain amounts are not reclassified after realization.

★★   **A11-12 Fair Value Method:** London Ltd. reported the following transactions and information regarding the shares of Dolma Corp:

- 15 October 20X2, purchased 3,000 shares at $42 per share plus $1,200 commission.
- 1 December 20X2, received $0.50 per share cash dividend.
- 31 December 20X2, fair value is $38 per share.
- 1 December 20X3, received $0.50 per share cash dividend.
- 31 December 20X3, fair value is $45 per share.
- 15 November 20X4, sold 1,000 shares at $41 per share less $450 commission.
- 1 December 20X4, received $0.50 per share cash dividend.
- 31 December 20X4, fair value is $40 per share.

Required:

1. Show the amounts and accounts that would be reported in earnings and the statement of financial position for 20X2, 20X3, and 20X4 if the company uses the:
   a. Cost method.
   b. FVTPL method.
   c. FVTOCI method; realized amounts are transferred to retained earnings.
2. Explain when each of the above methods would be appropriate for this investment.

★★ **A11-13 Fair Value Method:** On 30 April 20X2, Marc Company purchased 4,000 shares of Spencer Limited for $17 per share plus $400 in commission. In 20X2, the company received a $0.65 per share dividend, and the shares had a fair value of $16 per share at the end of the year. In 20X3, the dividend was $1.05 per share, and the fair value was $20 per share at the end of the year. In 20X4, the shares were sold for $18 per share less a $550 commission.

Required:

1. Show the amounts and accounts that would be reported in earnings and the statement of financial position for 20X2, 20X3, and 20X4 if the company uses the:
   a. Cost method.
   b. FVTPL method.
   c. FVTOCI method; realized amounts are transferred to retained earnings.
2. Explain when each of the above methods would be appropriate for this investment.

★★ **A11-14 Fair Value Method:** During 20X2, Morran Company purchased shares in two corporations and debt securities of a third. The share investments are classified as FVTOCI and the bond investment is FVTPL. Transactions in 20X2 include:

a. Purchased 3,000 of the 100,000 common shares outstanding of Front Corporation at $31 per share plus a 4% brokerage fee.
b. Purchased 10,000 of 10,000 outstanding preferred shares (nonvoting) of Ledrow Corporation at $78 per share plus a 3% brokerage fee.
c. Purchased an additional 2,000 common shares of Front Corporation at $35 per share plus a 4% brokerage fee.
d. Purchased $400,000 par value of Container Corporation, 9% bonds at 100 (par) plus accrued interest. The purchase is made on 1 November; interest is paid semi-annually on 31 January and 31 July. The bond matures on 31 July 20X7.
e. Received $4 per share cash dividend on the Ledrow Corporation shares.
f. Interest is accrued at the end of 20X2.
g. Fair values at 31 December 20X2: Front shares, $34 per share; Ledrow, $82 per share; Container Corporation bonds, 98.

Required:

1. Give the entries in the accounts of Morran Company for each transaction.
2. Give the items and amounts that would be reported in 20X2 earnings, and all amounts on the statement of financial position.
3. Repeat requirements 1 and 2, assuming that all the investments are FVTPL investments. Note that for FVTPL investments, all acquisition fees are expensed immediately.

★★ **A11-15 Fair Value Method:** Cudmore Ltd. had two FVTPL investments at the end of 20X4, disclosed on the SFP as follows:

Kelowna Ltd.	1,000 shares	$ 67,500
Burnaby Corp.	6,000 shares	52,800
		$120,300

By the end of 20X4, unrealized losses of $4,500 related to the Kelowna Ltd. shares and unrealized gains of $9,600 related to the Burnaby Corp. shares had been included in earnings.

During 20X5, Cudmore sold the Kelowna Ltd. shares after receiving a dividend of $2 per share. Cudmore received $54,000 for the shares, less an $800 commission. Cudmore also received a dividend of $1 per share on the Burnaby Corp. shares, and then sold 2,000 shares for $9.60 per share, less a $500 commission. Cudmore bought 500 Wilton Ltd. shares for $18,000 plus a $500 commission. This is an FVTPL investment.

At the end of the year, the fair value of the Kelowna Ltd. shares was $51,000, Burnaby Corp. shares were $11.20 per share, and Wilton Ltd. shares had a total fair value of $16,000.

Required:

1. List the items that would be included in 20X5 earnings with respect to the investments.
2. List the items that would appear on the 20X5 statement of financial position with respect to the investments.
3. What criteria would have to be met to show these investments as current assets? Long-term assets?

 A11-16 Fair Value Method; Foreign Currency: On 14 June 20X9, Friedland Limited purchased 20,000 shares of Gerstan Limited for US$6.20 per share, plus US$1,700 in commissions and fees. The shares were purchased from a broker on account, with later cash payment. On 14 June 20X9, the exchange rate was US$1 = Cdn$1.09. The shares were held as a FVTPL investment. The account was settled with the broker on 1 August 20X9, when US$1 = Cdn$1.11.

On 1 July 20X9, Friedland bought a US$1,000,000 five-year bond at par value, when the exchange rate was US$1 = Cdn$1.08. Friedland paid cash on the acquisition date. There was no accrued interest. Management classified this bond as a FVTPL investment.

At 31 December 20X9, Gerstan shares had a quoted fair value of US$7 per share, the bonds were trading at 104, and the exchange rate was US$1 = Cdn$1.07.

Required:

1. Provide the journal entry to record purchase of the bond on 1 July.
2. Provide journal entries to record the acquisition of the Gerstan shares on 14 June, and payment to the broker in August.
3. Provide the 31 December 20X9 adjustment that must be made to reflect fair values and/or exchange rate changes. No interest accrual need be made. Explain the components of the Gerstan adjustment.

 A11-17 Fair Value Method; Impairment: Micah Corporation purchased an $850,500 investment in the common shares of Fortune Corporation on 15 July 20X5. The investment is a FVTPL investment. Fortune is a private company and few shares are bought and sold. Micah was speculating that the value of the Fortune common shares might increase dramatically when a major contract bid was accepted. Unfortunately, the bid was rejected in 20X6, and Micah management suggested that Fortune shares might be worth only half the price paid. Micah continued to hold the investment throughout 20X7, waiting for positive developments that would increase share value. There was no re-estimate of fair value in 20X7. The shares were finally sold in 20X8 for $477,100.

Required:

1. Assume that the Fortune Company FVTPL shares are carried at cost at the end of 20X5. Why might cost be appropriate? What criteria must be met for a subsequent value lower than cost to be recorded?
2. When the fair value of an investment written down subsequently increases, is the increase in value recorded? Is net income affected? Explain.
3. List the accounts and amounts that would appear in earnings and the statement of financial position for 20X5 to 20X8, inclusive. Assume that the management estimate of fair value was accepted as valid in 20X6. What evidence would be used to establish validity?
4. Repeat requirement 3 assuming that the investment was designated FVTOCI when it was initially acquired.

 A11-18 Equity Method: Premium Investments Ltd. bought 40% of the outstanding common shares of Trans-BC Operations Ltd. in early 20X5 for $598,000. Premium Investments has significant influence. On this date, Trans-BC Operations had assets and liabilities as follows:

	Book Value	Fair Value
Assets	$1,560,000	$1,820,000
Liabilities	$ 657,000	$ 657,000

Most of the difference between fair value and book value for assets was related to a depreciable fixed asset with a $65,000 book value and a $305,000 fair value. This asset has a five-year remaining life. The remainder of the difference between book value and fair value related to land.

In 20X5, Trans-BC Operations earned $245,000 and declared and paid common dividends of $90,000. Goodwill was not impaired in 20X5.

Required:

1. How much goodwill is inherent in the purchase price? How (and when) will goodwill affect investment revenue?

2. How much investment revenue will Premium Investments report in 20X5?

3. What is the balance in the investment account on Premium Investments' books at the end of 20X5?

★★   **A11-19 Equity Method:** On 1 January 20X5, Zan Company purchased 5,000 of the 20,000 outstanding common shares of Woo Computer Corporation (WC) for $120,000 cash.

 Zan had significant influence as a result of the investment and will use the equity method to account for the investment.

On 1 January 20X5, the statement of financial position of WC showed the following book values (summarized):

Assets not subject to depreciation	$150,000*
Assets subject to depreciation (net)	120,000**
Liabilities	40,000
Common shares	180,000
Retained earnings	50,000

*Fair value, $170,000; difference relates to land.
**Fair value, $140,000, estimated remaining life, 5 years.

Assume there is no impairment of goodwill. Additional subsequent data on WC are as follows:

	20X5	20X6
Earnings	$40,000	$65,000
Cash dividends declared and paid	15,000	20,000
Fair value per share	$17	$31

Required:

1. Provide the investor's entries or give the required information for:
   a. Entry at date of acquisition.
   b. Amount of goodwill purchased.
   c. Entries at 31 December 20X5 to recognize investment revenue and dividends.
   d. Entries at 31 December 20X6 to recognize investment revenue and dividends.

2. Are any entries needed to recognize a writedown to fair value at the end of 20X5 or 20X6? Explain.

3. Reconstruct the investment account, showing the opening and closing balances and all changes in the account.

4. How much investment revenue would be reported each year if the cost method was used? What would be the balance in the investment account?

★★   **A11-20 Equity Method:** On January 1, 20X6, Loffer Limited purchased 35% of Ming's common shares for a price of $575,000. The remainder of the shares in Ming are closely held by family members of the founder of the company. Loffer considers this a strategic investment, acquired to get a toehold in a critical consumer goods market. Loffer is a supplier of components to Ming.

On this date, the assets of Ming had a book value of $500,000, liabilities were $100,000, and equity was $400,000. Loffer paid significantly more than book value for its interest because of important patents held by Ming; the fair value of these patents is not recorded on the books. The patents give Ming a distinct competitive advantage, expected to last for at least 10 years before new technologies would develop to provide alternatives for customers. In the meantime, Ming is able to charge premium prices.

Loffer was entitled to place two members on the 10-person Board of Directors as a result of its investment. Loffer's Board members have felt that they were influential throughout 20X6 in strategic decisions. In 20X6, Ming reported earnings of $200,000 and paid dividends of $40,000.

Required:

1. Discuss whether significant influence is present.
2. Assuming that this is an investment in an associate, why is the dividend cash flow not considered the appropriate measure of investment earnings?
3. Will Loffer's share of earnings be calculated as a simple percentage of earnings? Why not?
4. What value for the patents is implied by Loffer's purchase price? Why does this impact future earnings?
5. If the investment is accounted for using the equity method, what will be the balance in the investment account at the end of the year? Assume all the excess paid over book value relates to patents and there are no intercompany unconfirmed profits at year-end. Does this balance represent fair value?

★★★   **A11-21 Comprehensive Investments:** Ruiz Imports is a public company. It reported the following at the end of 20X5:

FVTOCI investment, Barker Co. 10,000 shares		
($271,000 cost)		$ 316,000
FVTPL investments		
Chowdury Co., 14,000 shares	$908,000	
Sawicki Co., $70,000 par value, 10% bond, due		
31 December 20X7; originally purchased at par	74,000	$ 982,000
AC investment		
Duval Co. bonds, $200,000 par value, 9% bond,		
semi-annual interest; due 30 June 20X8		
(the market interest rate was 10% on acquisition)		195,672
Investment in associate, Binod Ltd., 15,000 shares,		
equity method		1,239,000
Shareholders' equity		
Reserve—unrealized holding gains (re: Barker Co.)		45,000

The following transactions and events took place in 20X6:

a. Dividends received, Barker Co, $0.50 per share, Chowdury Co., $1 per share, Binod Ltd., $2.50 per share.
b. Semi-annual interest was received on both bonds on 30 June.
c. Early in July, the Barker Co. shares were sold for $406,000, and the Chowdury Co. shares were sold for $62 per share. Holding gains and losses in reserves are not reclassified on realization.

d. One thousand Wong Ltd. shares were acquired for a total of $134,000. This is an FVTPL investment.

e. Ruiz owns 30% of the voting shares of Binod Ltd. Binod Ltd. reported earnings of $200,000 for 20X6. There was $108,000 of goodwill inherent in the original purchase price, and a fair value allocations on equipment, on which annual depreciation of $3,400 must be recorded.

f. The Sawicki Co. bond was sold for $71,400 plus accrued interest on 1 October 20X6.

g. Lucky Co. shares were acquired as a FVTPL investment, 300,000 shares for a total cost of $89,000.

h. Semi-annual interest was received on the Duval Co bond at the end of December.

i. Wong Co. paid a dividend of $0.40 per share.

j. Fair values on 31 December 20X6: Wong Ltd., $125 per share; Lucky Co., $0.65 per share; Barker Ltd., $62 per share; Chowdury Co., $95.

Required:

1. List the accounts and amounts that would appear in earnings. Also calculate the change in accumulated other comprehensive income for the year ended 31 December 20X6.

2. List the accounts and amounts that would appear on the statement of financial position for the year ended 31 December 20X6.

★ **A11-22 Consolidation—Explanation:** In 20X1, Pepper Company bought 75% of S Company's common shares, establishing control over the Board of Directors. Pepper 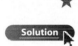 Company used the cost method to account for its investment in S Co. during the year, but prepared consolidated financial statements at the end of the fiscal year, which are shown in summary form:

	Pepper Co.	S Co.	Consolidated
Statement of Financial Position			
Cash	$ 11,000	$ 12,000	$ 23,000
Accounts receivable	22,000	19,000	37,000
Inventory	14,200	9,200	22,400
Capital assets	83,000	64,300	154,000
Investment in S Co.	74,000	—	—
Intangible assets	—	—	4,967
	$204,200	$104,500	$241,367
Current liabilities	$ 30,000	$ 9,000	$ 35,000
Long-term liabilities	4,000	2,500	6,500
Non-controlling interest	—	—	25,942
Common shares	100,000	60,000	100,000
Retained earnings	70,200	33,000	73,925
	$204,200	$104,500	$241,367
Statement of Earnings and Comprehensive Income			
Sales and other revenue	$ 96,000	$ 63,000	$146,750
Cost of sales	80,500	49,000	120,500
Operating expenses	2,500	4,900	7,533
Net earnings	$ 13,000	$ 9,100	$ 18,717
Non-controlling interest in earnings			1,992
Comprehensive income	$ 13,000	$ 9,100	$ 16,725

Required:

1. Why does the parent company use the cost method during the year?

2. Identify the accounts on the consolidated statements that do not appear on either of the unconsolidated statements. Explain the meaning of each new account.

3. Identify the accounts or amounts that appear on the unconsolidated financial statements that do not carry over to the consolidated amounts. Explain why they have been eliminated.

4. What is the most likely reason that the unconsolidated accounts receivables and current liabilities do not add to the balance shown in the consolidated financial statements?

★ **A11-23 Reclassification:** On 31 December 20X6, Kirwan Company's investments in equity securities were as follows:

	Carrying Value	AOCI: Equity Reserve: Holding Gains and Losses (Cumulative)
FVTOCI investment		
Goldhar Corp., common shares	$ 920,000	$34,700 loss
FVTPL investment		
McKinley Corp., common shares	669,700	
AC investment		
Walsh Ltd. 7% bonds, $300,000 par value	297,000	
Significant-influence investment Orr Ltd.	1,456,000	

Required:

1. Explain what the carrying value for each investment represents.
2. What was the original cost of the FVTOCI investment?
3. Kirwan reclassified the AC investment to a FVTPL investment on this date, when its fair value was $316,000. Explain how the reclassification will be reflected in the financial statements. How is fair value established?
4. Kirwan reclassifies the Orr common shares as a FVTPL investment when the fair value is $1,568,500. What accounting is required for this reclassification?
5. What is the rule for classifications in and out of the FVTOCI category?

★ **A11-24 Statement of Cash Flows:** For each of the following transactions, identify the item(s) that would appear on the statement of cash flows. Assume that the indirect method of presentation is used in the operating activities section and cash flow from investing revenue is classified in operating activities. Identify the appropriate section (i.e., operating, investing, financing) and whether the item is an inflow or an outflow, or an add-back or deduction in operating activities.

a. Purchased common shares of XTech Ltd. for $130,000, a FVTOCI investment.
b. The common shares in item (a) were revalued to $190,000 fair value at year-end, and $60,000 of unrealized holding gain was recognized in an equity reserve.
c. Guaranteed Investment Certificates (GICs) with a short term were purchased for $250,000, a FVTPL investment that is considered a cash equivalent.
d. The company owns an AC investment of $276,000, a $300,000, eight-year bond bought at a discount in previous years. The bond pays annual interest of 3%, and $6,200 of discount amortization had been recorded in the current year.
e. The company owns 47,000 shares of Apps Co., over which it has significant influence. In the current year, investment revenue of $99,000 was recorded, and cash dividends of $46,000 were received.
f. Common shares of Android Ltd. were purchased for $210,000, a FVTPL investment.
g. The common shares in item (f) were revalued to $175,000 fair value at year-end.
h. The XTech common shares in (a) and (b) were sold for $200,000. A gain of $10,000 was recognized in OCI.
i. The GICs in (c) were sold for $251,000. A gain of $1,000 was recorded.

A11-25 Statement of Cash Flows: The following comparative data are available from the 20X4 statement of financial position of Abraham Holdings Ltd:

	20X4	20X3
Current investments:		
FVTPL investments	$ 675,000	$550,000
Long-term investments:		
FVTOCI investments	1,050,000	887,000
Agrium bonds, at amortized cost	515,000	509,300
Investment in Falcon Ltd., at equity	1,101,100	950,000
Shareholders' equity:		
Reserves		
Unrealized holding gains	35,900	32,100

In 20X4, the following transactions took place and are properly reflected in the accounts, above.

a. There were no purchases or sales of FVTPL investments during the year.
b. Dividends of $60,000 were received from Falcon Ltd. No shares of Falcon were bought or sold during the year.
c. FVTOCI investments, with a carrying value of $36,200 and cumulative holding gains of $11,000 to date, were sold for $57,100. Holding gains and losses in reserves are not reclassified on sale.
d. FVTOCI investments were purchased during the year.
e. FVTPL and FVTOCI investments were adjusted to fair value at year-end.

Required:
What items would appear on the 20X4 statement of cash flows? Assume the operating section uses the indirect method of presentation. Cash inflow from investment revenue is classified in operating activities.

 A11-26 ASPE—Classification: Return to the facts of A11-1. Assume now that the investor is a private company that complies with ASPE.

Required:
How should the investor classify each of the investments? What accounting method should be used for each?

 A11-27 ASPE—Classification: Return to the facts of A11-2. Assume now that the investor is a private company that complies with ASPE.

Required:
How should the investor classify each of the investments? What accounting method should be used for each?

 A11-28 ASPE—Amortized Cost Investment: Return to the facts of A11-7. Assume now that New Company is a private company that complies with ASPE. Straight-line amortization will be used rather than the effective-interest method.

Required:
1. Calculate the price paid by New Company.
2. Construct a table that shows interest revenue reported by New Company, and the carrying value of the investment, for each interest period to maturity. Use the straight-line method.

3. Give entries for the first three interest periods based on your calculations in requirement 2.

★★   **A11-29 ASPE—Amortized Cost Investment:** On 1 January 20X8, Khalil Ltd. purchased $2,000,000 of six-year, Harvest Ltd. 5.4% bonds. The bonds pay semi-annual interest each 30 June and 31 December. The market interest rate was 6% on the date of purchase. Khalil is a private company that complies with ASPE and uses straight-line amortization.

Required:

1. Calculate the price paid by Khalil Ltd.
2. Construct a table that shows interest revenue reported by Khalil and the carrying value of the investment for four interest periods. Use the straight-line method.
3. Give entries for the first four interest periods based on your calculations in requirement 2.

★★   **A11-30 ASPE—Cost versus Equity Method:** On 3 January 20X4, TA Company purchased 2,000 shares of the 10,000 outstanding shares of common stock of UK Corporation for $14,600 cash. TA has significant influence as a result of this acquisition. At that date, the statement of financial position of UK Corporation reflected the following:

- Nondepreciable assets, $50,000 (book value is the same as fair value)
- Depreciable assets (net), $30,000 (fair value, $33,000)
- Total liabilities, $20,000 (book value equals fair value)
- Shareholders' equity, $60,000

Assume a 10-year remaining life (straight-line method) for the depreciable assets. Goodwill is not impaired over the time period in question.

Required:

1. Give any required entries for TA's books for each item (a) through (d) below, if applicable, assuming that the cost method is used.
   a. Entry at date of acquisition
   b. Goodwill purchased—computation only
   c. Entry on 31 December 20X4 to record $15,000 earnings reported by UK
   d. Entry on 31 March 20X5 for a cash dividend of $1 per share declared and paid by UK
2. Repeat requirement 1 above, assuming that the equity method is appropriate.
3. Why might TA use the cost method if it has significant influence?

■ connect·   ■ LEARNSMART·   ■ SMARTBOOK™

For more information on the resources available from McGraw-Hill Ryerson, go to www.mcgrawhill.ca/he/solutions.

Fundamentals: The Accounting Information Processing System

ACCOUNTS, TRANSACTION RECORDING, AND FINANCIAL STATEMENTS

This appendix is a review of the mechanics of the accounting information processing system. Transactions and events are recorded in accounts, which describe specific financial statement elements. These elements are reported to investors, creditors, and other interested readers in periodic financial statements.

Accounts

There are eight major types of accounts, grouped under two headings: **permanent accounts** (assets, liabilities, and owners' equity accounts) and **temporary accounts** (revenues, expenses, gains, losses, and dividends). Permanent accounts are also called "**real accounts**," and temporary accounts are also called "**nominal accounts**." The permanent accounts appear on the statement of financial position. *Temporary* accounts, which are revenues, expenses, gains, and losses, appear on the statement of comprehensive income and are closed out at the end of each fiscal year. Dividends are closed directly to retained earnings and reported on the statement of changes in equity.

The **accounting identity** states the relationship between the balances of the permanent accounts:

$$\text{Assets} = \text{Liabilities} + \text{Owners' Equity}$$

Recording Transactions

To maintain the accounting identity, every transaction recorded must affect at least two accounts. This protocol, called the **double-entry system**, records the change in a resource or obligation and the reason for, or source of, the change.

Complementing the double-entry system, the **debit–credit convention** is used as a recording and balancing procedure. This convention divides accounts into two sides. The debit (dr.) side is always the left side, and the credit (cr.) side is always the right side. These terms carry no further meaning and cannot be interpreted as "increases" or "decreases," since, depending on the account type, a debit or a credit can record an increase or decrease to the account balance. This is illustrated in the T-accounts summarized in Exhibit A-1. The **T-account** is a form of account used for demonstrating transactions; its skeletal form takes the shape of the letter T. The T-account reflects the general format of ledger accounts, as we will discuss later.

EXHIBIT A-1

DEBIT/CREDIT IMPACT ON T-ACCOUNTS

Permanent Accounts

Assets		=	Liabilities		+	Owners' Equity	
Debit entries *increase* assets	Credit entries *decrease* assets		Debit entries *decrease* liabilities	Credit entries *increase* liabilities		Debit entries *decrease* owners' equity	Credit entries *increase* owners' equity

Temporary Accounts

Expenses		Revenues		Dividends	
Debit entries *increase* expenses	Credit entries *decrease* expenses	Debit entries *decrease* revenues	Credit entries *increase* revenues	Debit entries *increase* dividends	Credit entries *decrease* dividends

Losses		Gains	
Debit entries *increase* losses	Credit entries *decrease* losses	Debit entries *decrease* gains	Credit entries *increase* gains

---

The debit–credit convention is a convenient way to check for recording errors. When the sums of debits and credits are not equal, an error is evident.

Financial Statements

At the end of a reporting period, after all transactions and events are recorded in accounts, **financial statements** are prepared. The financial statements report account balances, changes in account balances, and aggregations of account balances, such as earnings and total assets. The financial statements include the *statement of comprehensive income, statement of changes in equity, statement of financial position,* and *statement of cash flows.*

- The statement of comprehensive income (SCI) reports revenues, expenses, gains, and losses and thus shows profit or loss for the year. Items that are specified to be included in other comprehensive income (OCI) are summarized and added to the profit or loss to arrive at comprehensive income.
- Both earnings and other comprehensive income items change equity. The statement of changes in equity shows the opening and closing balances of every equity account for the company, with each change listed separately.
- The statement of financial position (SFP) reports assets, liabilities, and owners' equity. This statement is commonly called a *balance sheet*; the terms will be used interchangeably in this text.
- The statement of cash flows (SCF) lists sources and uses of cash.

The steps leading to these financial statements are discussed in the rest of this appendix.

The AIS and the Accounting Cycle

An **accounting information system** (AIS) is designed to record accurate financial data in a timely and chronological manner, facilitate retrieval of financial data in a form useful to management, and simplify periodic preparation of financial statements for external use. The design of the AIS, to meet the company's information requirements, depends on the firm's size, the nature of its operations, the volume of data, its organizational structure, and government regulation.

The accounting cycle, illustrated in Exhibit A-2, is a series of sequential steps leading to the financial statements. This cycle is repeated each reporting period, normally a year. Companies may combine some of these steps or change their order to suit their specific needs. Depending on the information-processing technology used, certain accounting cycle steps can be combined or in some cases omitted. Most accounting systems are computerized, in whole or in part. The fundamental nature of the process, however, is the same regardless of the technology used.

The first three steps in the accounting cycle require the most time and effort. The frequency of posting, step 3, depends on the volume and nature of transactions and the technology used. For example, on-line systems may update inventory accounts immediately when there is a sale or purchase. Steps 4 through 9 generally occur at the end of the fiscal year. The tenth step, the posting of reversing entries, is optional and occurs at the beginning of the new accounting period.

THE IMPACT OF TECHNOLOGY

Computerized systems have many advantages, including speed and accuracy. The norm is to use a customized or off-the-shelf computer program that will facilitate the following steps in the accounting cycle (refer to Exhibit A-2):

- Journalizing transactions, adjustments, closing, and reversing entries;
- Posting entries;
- Preparing trial balances; and
- Preparing financial statements.

What is left for the accountant to do? First, identification and control of transactions and adjustments is crucial. The accountant manages the entire process, ensuring that information entered is accurate and complete. Second, many elements in financial reporting require the exercise of professional judgement—choice of accounting policy, impairment testing, composition of the notes to the financial statements, and so on. These tasks require qualified decision makers.

Regardless of how the steps in the accounting cycle are performed, they accomplish the same task—posting is posting, manual or computerized. The accountant has to understand this process to manage it.

THE ACCOUNTING CYCLE

The annual accounting cycle includes 10 steps, explained in the following section.

Step 1: Identify Transactions or Events to Be Recorded

The first step is the requirement to identify transactions and events that cause a change in the firm's resources or obligations and to collect relevant economic data about those transactions. Events that change a firm's resources or obligations are categorized into three types:

1. *Exchanges of resources and obligations between the reporting firm and outside parties.* These exchanges are either **reciprocal transfers** or **nonreciprocal transfers**. In a reciprocal transfer, the firm both transfers and receives resources (e.g., sale of goods for cash). In a nonreciprocal transfer, the firm either transfers *or* receives current or future resources (e.g., payment of cash dividends or receipt of a donation). All exchanges require a journal entry.

EXHIBIT A-2

THE ACCOUNTING CYCLE

1. Identify Transactions or Events to Be Recorded
Gather information, generally in the form of source documents, about transactions or events.

↓

2. Journalize Transactions and Events
Identify, assess, and record the economic impact of transactions on the firm in a chronological record (a journal), using journal entries that facilitate transfer to the accounts.

↓

3. Post from Journal to Ledger
Transfer information from the journal to the ledger.

↓

4. Prepare Unadjusted Trial Balance
Provide a convenient listing of ledger accounts to prove debit–credit equality and provide a starting point for adjusting journal entries.

↓

5. Journalize and Post Adjusting Journal Entries
Record accruals, expiration of deferrals, estimations, and other events to ensure the accuracy and completeness of the accounts.

↓

6. Prepare Adjusted Trial Balance
Establish debit–credit equality and simplify preparation of the financial statements.

↓

7. Prepare Financial Statements
Summarize financial information in a form that will be useful to decision makers.

↓

8. Journalize and Post Closing Entries
Close temporary accounts and update retained earnings.

↓

9. Prepare Post-closing Trial Balance
Establish debit–credit equality after the closing entries.

↓

10. Journalize and Post Reversing Journal Entries
Optional step; simplifies certain subsequent journal entries and reduces accounting costs.

2. *Internal events within the firm that affect resources or obligations but do not involve outside parties.* Examples are recognition of depreciation of property, plant, and equipment and the use of inventory for production. These events also generally require a journal entry. However, other events, such as increases in the value of the company's brand resulting from superior management and good customer service, are not recorded.

3. *External economic and environmental events beyond the control of the company.* Examples include casualty losses and changes in the fair market value of financial assets and investment properties.

Transactions are events requiring a journal entry. Transactions are often accompanied by a source document, generally a paper record that describes the exchange, the parties involved, the date, and the dollar amount. Examples are sales invoices, freight bills, and cash register receipts. Certain events, such as the accrual of interest, are not signalled by a separate source document. Recording these transactions requires reference to the underlying contract supporting the original exchange of resources. Source documents are essential for the initial recording of transactions in a journal and are also used for subsequent tracing and verification, for evidence in legal proceedings, and for audits of financial statements.

Step 2: Journalize Transactions and Events

Journals Transactions are recorded chronologically in a **journal**—an organized medium for recording transactions in debit–credit format. A **journal entry** is a debit–credit description of a transaction that includes the date, the accounts and amounts involved, and a brief description. A journal entry is a temporary recording, although journals are retained as part of the audit trail; account balances are not changed until the information is transferred to the ledger accounts in Step 3.

Accounting systems usually have two types of journals: the **general journal** and **special journals**. The general journal has a flexible format and can be used to record any entry. Non-repetitive entries and entries involving infrequently used accounts are recorded in this journal. To save time and increase accuracy, repetitive entries are recorded in special journals, which have a predetermined, rigid format. If special journals are not used, all transactions are recorded in the general journal. Special journals are discussed later in this appendix. The general journal is used to illustrate most entries in this text.

The journal entry step is not absolutely essential; transaction data can be recorded directly into the accounts. However, the journal entry step has significant advantages, and it is standard practice to record all transactions first in a journal. Transaction processing is more efficient, and less costly, if transactions are grouped in a journal and processed together. By using journals, review and analysis of transactions is much simpler and the accounts consume less storage space. Also, a chronological list of transactions is provided. Transactions can be difficult to reconstruct without a journal because the debits and credits are located in different accounts. Journals are typically part of the paper trail relied on by auditors. The journal entry also ensures that the debits and credits are balanced prior to posting in the general ledger.

Some companies use computerized systems to bypass the traditional journal entry step. Retailers, for example, record relevant information about a transaction by using bar codes printed on product packages. Optical scanning equipment reads the bar code and the transaction is recorded directly in the relevant ledger accounts.

Exhibit A-3 illustrates an entry in a general journal. This entry records the purchase of equipment financed with cash and debt. Equipment is *debited* and recorded at the value of the resources used to acquire it. The names of the accounts *credited* are listed below and are indented.

Step 3: Post from Journal to Ledger

Transferring transaction data from the journal to the ledger is called **posting**. Posting reclassifies the data from the journal's chronological format to an account classification format in the ledger, which is a collection of the formal accounts.

EXHIBIT A-3

PAGE J-16   **GENERAL JOURNAL**

Date 20X5	Accounts and Explanation	Posting Ref.	Debit	Credit
2 Jan.	Equipment	150	15,000	
	Cash	101		5,000
	Notes payable	215		10,000
	Purchased equipment for use in the business. Paid $5,000 cash and gave a $10,000, one-year note with 5% interest payable at maturity.			

Posting Exhibit A-4 illustrates a section of a general ledger in T-account form. This ledger depicts three general ledger accounts after posting the journal entry shown in Exhibit A-3. Posting references and page numbers are used in both the journal and the ledger to ensure that an audit trail exists—that is, to indicate where an item in the account ledger came from and to which account the item was posted. Posting references also serve to confirm that an entry was posted.

When the $5,000 cash credit from the general journal entry of Exhibit A-3 is posted to the cash ledger account, "101" is listed in the journal to indicate the account number *to which* the credit is posted. Similarly, in the cash ledger account, "J-16" indicates the journal page number *from which* this amount is posted. Cross-referencing is especially important when posting large numbers of transactions, detecting and correcting errors, and maintaining an audit trail.

Ledgers Accounting systems usually have two types of ledgers: the general ledger and subsidiary ledgers. The **general ledger** holds all the accounts, grouped according to the basic elements of financial statements. Subsidiary ledgers support general ledger accounts that comprise many separate individual accounts. For example, a firm with a substantial number of customer accounts receivable will maintain one ledger account per customer, stored in an accounts receivable subsidiary ledger. The individual customer account is called

EXHIBIT A-4

GENERAL LEDGER (EXCERPTS)

		Cash				Acct. 101
20X5 1 Jan.	Balance	18,700	20X5 2 Jan.	J-16		5,000

		Equipment				Acct. 150
20X5 1 Jan.	Balance	62,000				
2	J-16	15,000				

		Notes Payable				Acct. 215
			20X5 2 Jan.	J-16		10,000

the "subsidiary account." The general ledger holds only the "control account," the balance of which reflects the sum of all the individual customer account balances. Only the control accounts are used in compiling financial statements.

For example, assume that a firm's accounts receivable consists of two individual accounts with a combined balance of $6,000. The firm's general and subsidiary ledgers might show these balances:

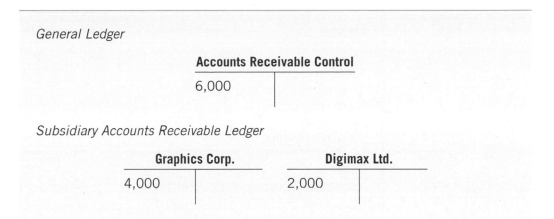

General Ledger

Accounts Receivable Control

6,000

Subsidiary Accounts Receivable Ledger

Graphics Corp.   **Digimax Ltd.**

4,000   2,000

Step 4: Prepare Unadjusted Trial Balance

An unadjusted trial balance is prepared at the end of the reporting period, after all transaction entries are recorded in the journals and posted to the ledger. The unadjusted trial balance is a list of general ledger accounts and their account balances, in the following order: assets, liabilities, owners' equity, revenues, expenses, gains, and losses. For accounts with subsidiary ledgers, only the control account balances are entered into the trial balance, after reconciliation with the subsidiary ledger.

The unadjusted trial balance is the starting point for developing adjusting entries and for the worksheet, if used. Exhibit A-5 illustrates an unadjusted trial balance for Sonora Limited, a fictitious retailing company, at the end of the fiscal year. The trial balance reflects Sonora's transaction journal entries recorded during 20X5 and is the basis for the remainder of this accounting cycle illustration.

The unadjusted trial balance is a convenient means for checking that the sum of debit account balances equals the sum of credit account balances. If the sums of debit and credit balances are not equal, the error must be found and corrected. A re-examination of source documents and postings is one way to discover the source of an error. Equality of debits and credits does not, however, imply that the accounts are error-free. A completely unposted journal entry, an incorrectly classified account, and an erroneous journal entry amount are errors that do not cause inequality of total debits and credits.

Sonora uses a **perpetual inventory system**. Under this system, the inventory account balance is updated each time inventory is purchased or sold. Thus, the inventory account balance is up-to-date at the end of the accounting period, and cost of goods sold will reflect all goods sold to date. The inventory balance must be verified by a physical count, and adjusted to the balance determined by the count.

Alternatively, in a **periodic inventory system**, acquisitions during the period are debited to a *purchases* account, not the inventory account. The inventory account balance remains at the 1 January amount all year, and the cost of goods sold is not readily determinable. Merchandise on hand is counted and costed at the end of each accounting period. The resulting inventory amount is used to update the inventory account balance at the report date and to determine cost of goods sold.

As shown in Exhibit A-5, Sonora's retained earnings account reflects the 1 January 20X5 balance, since no transactions directly affected this account during 20X5. Income tax expense is not listed in the unadjusted trial balance because the corporate income tax liability for the current year is not known until pretax income is computed. The loss from discontinued operations also does not yet reflect any tax effect.

EXHIBIT A-5

SONORA LIMITED
Unadjusted Trial Balance

31 December 20X5

Account	Debit	Credit
Cash	$ 67,300	
Accounts receivable	45,000	
Allowance for doubtful accounts		$ 1,000
Notes receivable	8,000	
Inventory	92,000	
Prepaid insurance	600	
Land	8,000	
Building	160,000	
Accumulated depreciation, building		90,000
Equipment	91,000	
Accumulated depreciation, equipment		27,000
Accounts payable		29,000
Bonds payable, 6%		50,000
Common shares, no par, 15,000 shares		170,000
Retained earnings (1 January balance)		41,500
Dividends declared	10,000	
Sales revenue		325,200
Interest revenue		500
Rent revenue		1,800
Cost of goods sold	115,000	
Selling expenses*	104,000	
General and administrative expenses*	23,600	
Interest expense	2,500	
Loss on discontinued operations	9,000	
Totals	$736,000	$736,000

*These broad categories of expenses are used to simplify presentation.

Step 5: Journalize and Post Adjusting Journal Entries

Many changes in a firm's economic resources and obligations occur continuously. For example, interest accrues daily on debts, as does rent expense for an office building. Other resources and obligations, such as employee salaries, originate as service is rendered with payment to follow at specified dates. The end of the accounting period generally does not coincide with the receipt or payment of cash associated with these types of resource changes.

Accrual-basis accounting requires the recording of these changes at the end of the accounting period so that financial statements are faithfully represented. **Adjusting journal entries (AJEs)** are used to record such resource changes to ensure the accuracy of the financial statements. In all cases, AJEs are posted to the general ledger accounts.

Classification of AJEs   AJEs generally record a resource or obligation change and usually involve both permanent and temporary accounts. AJEs are recorded and dated as of the last day of the fiscal period. They are recorded in the general journal and posted to the ledger accounts. Source documents from earlier transactions are the primary information sources for AJEs. AJEs may be classified into three categories: deferral-type, accruals, and other AJEs.

Deferral-type entries are recorded for cash flows that occur *before expense and revenue recognition*. These AJEs are recorded when cash is paid for expenses that apply to more than one accounting period or when cash is received for revenue that applies to a later accounting period, in whole or in part. The portion of the expense or revenue that applies to future periods is deferred as a prepaid expense (asset) or unearned revenue (liability). The chart below clarifies the terminology used:

Deferral Type	Cash Timing	Results in
Deferred revenue	Cash received before revenue recognition is appropriate	Deferred revenue (liability) (perhaps as unearned revenue)
Deferred expense	Cash paid before expense recognition is appropriate	Deferred expense (asset) (perhaps a prepaid)

The exact AJE required for a deferral-type depends on the method used for first recording operational cash payments and receipts. One method, here called the **standard recording method**, records an *asset* upon payment of cash before goods or services are consumed and records a *liability* upon receipt of cash before goods or services are transferred. For example, if a tenant prepays two months' rent on 1 July, the standard method debits prepaid rent for that amount. An adjustment later in the year recognizes rent expense and the reduction of prepaid rent.

A second method, here called the **expedient recording method**, records an *expense* upon payment of cash before goods or services are consumed and records a *revenue* upon receipt of cash before goods or services are transferred. In the case of rent paid in advance, the expedient method debits rent expense for two months' rent. This method is expedient because many cash payments and receipts relate to expenses and revenues that apply only to the year in which the cash flow occurs. No AJE is required in this example because rent expense is correctly stated at year-end. If a portion of the expense or revenue applies to a future accounting period, however, an AJE is required.

Accruals are recorded for cash flows that occur *after expense and revenue recognition*. These AJEs are recorded when cash is to be paid or received in a future accounting period but all or a portion of the future cash flow applies to expenses or revenues of the current period. For example, unpaid wages accrued as wages payable at year-end represent wage costs matched against current year revenues but not to be paid until next year. If the company is a landlord and rents space to tenants, uncollected rent accrued as rent receivable at year-end represents revenue earned in the current year but to be collected next year. In both cases, the expense or revenue is recognized before the cash flow occurs. The chart below clarifies the terminology used:

Accrual Type	Cash Timing	Results in
Accrued revenue	Cash received after revenue recognition is appropriate	Accrued revenue (asset) (perhaps a receivable)
Accrued expense	Cash paid after expense recognition is appropriate	Accrued expense (liability) (perhaps an account payable)

Other types of journal entries are often recorded at the end of the accounting period and are listed here as adjusting journal entries for completeness. These include:

- Reclassifications of permanent accounts;
- Estimation of expenses (e.g., bad debt expense);
- Cost allocations (e.g., depreciation);
- Recognition of cost of goods sold and inventory losses;

• Remeasurements to fair value (e.g., for financial assets or investment properties); and
• Correction of errors discovered at year-end.

Cash generally is not involved in AJEs because of the purpose of AJEs. However, corrections of errors involving the cash account discovered at the end of the accounting period are recorded as AJEs. Also, the entry required to adjust the cash balance upon receipt of the end-of-year bank statement, which lists service charges and other items unknown until receipt, is recorded as an AJE.

In the following discussion, Sonora's 31 December 20X5 unadjusted trial balance (see Exhibit A-5) and additional information are used to illustrate AJEs.

Deferral-Type Examples **Deferred expenses** Some costs are paid in advance and deferred as assets until they are recognized as an expense. For example, on 1 November 20X5, Sonora paid a six-month insurance premium of $600 in advance for the period 1 November to 30 April 20X6. On that date, the $600 payment is recorded as a debit to prepaid insurance and a credit to cash (the standard method). In the unadjusted trial balance, the full $600 payment is reflected in prepaid insurance. One third of this payment ($200) is applicable to 20X5. A $200 expense, indicating the partial expiration of the asset, must be recognized. Sonora records insurance expense and other similar expenses in the general and administrative expense account. AJE (a) adjusts prepaid insurance and recognizes the expense:

a. 31 December 20X5		
General and administrative expenses	200	
Prepaid insurance		200

The credit to prepaid insurance records the reduction in the asset that took place during the last two months of 20X5 as insurance benefits were used up. The remaining $400 of prepaid insurance reflects insurance coverage for the first four months of 20X6.

Deferred revenue Some revenues are received in advance and must be deferred as liabilities until they are recognized in earnings. For example, Sonora leased a small office in its building to a tenant on 1 January 20X5. The lease required an initial payment of $1,800 for 18 months' rent, which is recorded as a debit to cash and a credit to rent revenue (the expedient method). On 31 December 20X5, the unadjusted trial balance reports $1,800 in rent revenue, which is overstated by the $600 (one-third) relating to 20X6. AJE (b) is required to reduce the rent revenue recognized in 20X5 from $1,800 to $1,200 and to create a liability equal to the amount of rent relating to 20X6 ($600).

b. 31 December 20X5		
Rent revenue	600	
Rent collected in advance (liability)		600

The result of this adjustment is a liability equal to the resources received for future services.

Accrual Examples **Accrued expenses** Some expenses must be recognized before they are paid, which results in the recognition of a liability. For example, Sonora has issued, at face value, $50,000 of 6% bonds paying interest annually each 31 October. For the current accounting period, a two-month interest obligation accrues between 31 October 20X5 and 31 December 20X5. Sonora must recognize the liability and the resulting expense. The amount for the two-month period is $500 ($50,000 × 6% × 2/12). Therefore, on 31 December 20X5, both the interest expense and the associated payable are recognized in AJE (c):

c. 31 December 20X5		
Interest expense	500	
Interest payable		500

Accrued revenue Some revenues must be recognized before they are received, which results in the recognition of a receivable. Sonora's unadjusted trial balance lists $8,000 in notes receivable. The interest rate on these notes is 15%, payable each 30 November. As of 31 December 20X5, the payer of the notes is obligated to Sonora for one month's interest of $100 ($8,000 × 15% × 1/12). AJE (d) records the resulting receivable and revenue:

d. 31 December 20X5		
Interest receivable	100	
Interest revenue		100

Other Examples Other common adjusting journal entries are illustrated below.

Depreciation expense Property, plant, and equipment includes many productive assets with a useful life exceeding one year. The cost of these assets is recognized as an expense over their period of use. *Depreciation* or *amortization* is a systematic and rational allocation of asset cost over a number of accounting periods. The amount of depreciation expense recognized depends on a number of factors:

- The original expenditure and subsequent capitalized expenditures;
- The asset's useful life;
- The method chosen for depreciation measurement; and
- The asset's residual value.

Many methods of depreciation are permitted under GAAP. All entail systematic and rational allocation of the cost of a capital asset over its useful life.

AJE (e) illustrates depreciation recorded for Sonora at the end of 20X5 under the straight-line method. Sonora debits two expense accounts because the company uses the building and equipment assets both for selling and for general and administrative functions. Depreciation is commonly allocated to several functions, including manufacturing operations. The adjusting entry for depreciation is as follows:

e. 31 December 20X5		
Selling expense (depreciation)	8,200	
General and administrative expense (depreciation)	10,800	
Accumulated depreciation, building		10,000
Accumulated depreciation, equipment		9,000

The calculations:

Asset	Cost	Residual Value	Useful Life Years	Proportionate Use by Function Selling Function	Proportionate Use by Function G & A* Function
Building	$160,000	$10,000	15	46%	54%
Equipment	91,000	1,000	10	40	60

Computation:

Building:

[($160,000 − $10,000)/15 yrs.] = $10,000 × 0.46 = $4,600; $10,000 × 0.54 =   5,400

Equipment:

[($91,000 − $1,000)/10 yrs.]   =   9,000 × 0.40 =   3,600; $9,000 × 0.60 =   5,400

Totals $19,000 $8,200 $10,800

*General and administrative

AJE (e) reduces the *net book value* of the building and equipment accounts by crediting accumulated depreciation. Accumulated depreciation is a **contra account**, which has the opposite balance of the related asset account. A contra account is always reported on the financial statements along with its main account, producing a net amount for the two accounts taken together. That is, accumulated depreciation is subtracted from the asset value recorded in the building and equipment accounts. The net result is called *net book value*, which is the net undepreciated amount, or cost less accumulated depreciation. Sonora's statement of financial position illustrates this offset.

Bad debt expense Goods and services are often sold on credit. Accounts that are never collected result in bad debt expense, which is a risk of doing business on credit terms. Firms use a bad debt estimate to reduce earnings and net accounts receivable in the period of sale. This practice prevents overstatement of both earnings and assets and is required whenever bad debts are probable and estimable. Recognition of bad debt expense is accomplished with an AJE that debits bad debt expense and credits the allowance for doubtful accounts, a contra account to the accounts receivable account.

Estimates of uncollectible accounts may be based on credit sales for the period or the year-end accounts receivable balance. Assume that Sonora extends credit on $120,000 of sales during 20X5. Prior experience indicates an expected 1% average bad debt rate on credit sales. Sonora treats bad debt expense as a component of selling expenses and records AJE (f):

f. 31 December 20X5		
Selling expense ($120,000 × .01)	1,200	
Allowance for doubtful accounts		1,200

The credit is made to the allowance account, rather than to accounts receivable, because the amount is still an estimate. Write-off of any particular accounting receivable is still premature.

The $1,200 allowance is the portion of 20X5 credit sales not expected to be collected. Net accounts receivable, the difference between the balance in accounts receivable and the allowance account, is an estimate of the cash ultimately expected to be received from sales on account. Bad debt expense appears on the SCI.

Cost of goods sold—perpetual system The methodology used to determine cost of goods sold depends on whether a perpetual or a periodic inventory system is used. Sonora uses a perpetual inventory system. As background, recall that a perpetual inventory system maintains an inventory record for each item stocked. This record contains data on each purchase and issue. The cost of each item purchased is debited to the inventory account when it is bought and removed each time goods are sold to maintain a record of inventory on hand. Suppose an item that sells for $300 is carried in inventory at a cost of $180. The sale of this item requires two entries:

Cash (or accounts receivable)	300	
Sales revenue		300
Cost of goods sold	180	
Inventory		180

In a perpetual inventory system, the balance in the inventory account and the balance in cost of goods sold should reflect all transactions to date. A physical count is done to verify the inventory balance. If the result of the physical count is a different inventory amount than that recorded, an adjusting entry to decrease or increase inventory is recorded, with the other side of the entry changing cost of goods sold. For Sorona, a physical count determines that ending inventory is $90,000. The trial balance shows a balance of $92,000 and must be adjusted to the verified balance.

g. *31 December 20X5*		
Cost of goods sold	2,000	
Inventory		2,000

Periodic system A periodic system does not maintain a current balance in inventory or cost of goods sold. Instead, the physical inventory count at the end of the period is used to determine the balances of these two accounts. The purchases account, rather than the inventory account, is debited for all purchases during the period. In this case, the unadjusted trial balance at the end of an accounting period reflects the beginning inventory, and cost of goods sold does not yet exist as an account. An AJE can be used to set purchases, purchases returns, and other purchase-related accounts to zero (i.e., close these accounts), to replace the beginning inventory amount with the ending inventory amount in the inventory ledger account, and to recognize cost of goods sold for the period.

To illustrate, assume that Sonora had an opening inventory of $75,000, closing inventory of $90,000, and purchases of $132,000. *Opening inventory and purchases* would be listed in the unadjusted trial balance. The cost of goods sold would be recorded only at year-end, as follows:

31 December 20X5		
Inventory (ending)	90,000	
Cost of goods sold ($75,000 + $132,000 − $90,000)	117,000	
Inventory (beginning)		75,000
Purchases		132,000

Alternatively, the accounts related to cost of goods sold may be left in the adjusted trial balance, untouched, and used in detail to create the financial statements. They would then be eliminated in closing entries. Both approaches are widely used in practice and result in the same reported earnings and financial position. It is really a question of which method is preferred by a particular accountant and/or computerized reporting package.

Income tax expense The recognition of income tax expense is often the final AJE. Many firms accrue and pay estimated income taxes monthly, necessitating an AJE at the end of the accounting period only to record any additional taxes due. For simplicity, assume that Sonora pays its income tax once each year after the end of the full accounting period. Sonora's adjusted income before tax must be calculated to determine tax expense.

Assume that Sonora faces an average income tax rate of 40%, depreciation expense equals tax depreciation, and the loss from discontinued operations and all other expenses are fully tax deductible. Calculation of the $50,000 pretax earnings is shown below. AJE (h) recognizes the resulting $20,000 ($50,000 × 40%) income tax expense:

h. 31 December 20X5		
Income tax expense	20,000	
Income tax payable		20,000

Calculation of Pre-tax Earnings
For the Year Ended 31 December 20X5

Revenues:		
Sales revenue	$325,200	
Interest revenue [$500 + $100 (d)]	600	
Rent revenue [$1,800 − $600 (b)]	1,200	$327,000
Expenses and losses:		
Cost of goods sold [$115,000 + $2,000(g)]	117,000	
Selling expenses [$104,000 + $8,200 (e) + $1,200 (f)]	113,400	
General and administrative expenses [$23,600 + $200 (a) + $10,800 (e)]	34,600	
Interest expense [$2,500 + $500 (c)]	3,000	
Discontinued operations (pretax)	9,000	277,000
Pre-tax earnings		$ 50,000
Income tax expense ($50,000 × 0.4)		$ 20,000

For simplicity, the entire income tax expense is recorded in one account. Sonora's statement of comprehensive income (see Exhibit A-7) separates the $3,600 income tax *reduction* associated with the loss from discontinued operations ($9,000 × 40%) from income tax on earnings before the discontinued operation of $23,600. This practice is called *intraperiod tax allocation.*

Step 6: Prepare Adjusted Trial Balance

At this point in the cycle, the transaction journal entries and the AJEs have been journalized and posted, and an adjusted trial balance is prepared. The adjusted trial balance lists all the account balances that will appear in the financial statements, with the exception of retained earnings, which does not reflect the current year's earnings or dividends. The purpose of the adjusted trial balance is to calculate adjusted balances and then confirm debit–credit equality. Exhibit A-6 presents the adjusted trial balance for Sonora.

New accounts emerge from the adjustment process, while other accounts may disappear. For Sonora, the new accounts are interest receivable, interest payable, rent collected in advance, income tax payable, and income tax expense. The financial statements now can be prepared from the adjusted trial balance.

EXHIBIT A-6

SONORA LIMITED
Adjusted Trial Balance

31 December 20X5

Account	Debit	Credit
Cash	$ 67,300	
Accounts receivable	45,000	
Allowance for doubtful accounts		$ 2,200
Notes receivable	8,000	
Interest receivable	100	
Inventory	90,000	
Prepaid insurance	400	
Land	8,000	
Building	160,000	
Accumulated depreciation, building		100,000
Equipment	91,000	
Accumulated depreciation, equipment		36,000
Accounts payable		29,000
Interest payable		500
Rent collected in advance		600
Income tax payable		20,000
Bonds payable, 6%		50,000
Common shares, no par, 15,000 shares		170,000
Retained earnings (1 January balance)		41,500
Dividends declared	10,000	
Sales revenue		325,200
Interest revenue		600
Rent revenue		1,200
Cost of goods sold	117,000	
Selling expenses	113,400	
General and administrative expenses	34,600	
Interest expense	3,000	
Income tax expense	20,000	
Loss on discontinued operations	9,000	
Totals	$776,800	$776,800

Step 7: Prepare Financial Statements

The financial statements are the culmination of the accounting cycle. Financial statements can be produced for a period of any duration. However, monthly, quarterly, and annual statements are the most common.

The SCI, statement of changes in equity, and SCF are prepared directly from the adjusted trial balance. The SCI is prepared first because earnings must be known before the statement of changes in equity and then the SFP can be completed. The temporary account balances are transferred to the SCI (except for dividends), and the permanent account balances (except for equity accounts) are transferred to the statement of financial position. Exhibit A-7 illustrates Sonora's 20X5 SCI and statement of changes in equity.

Total income tax expense ($20,000) is allocated $23,600 to income before discontinued operations and $3,600 tax *savings* to the loss from discontinued operations. Discontinued operations are disclosed separately at the end of the statement.

EXHIBIT A-7

SONORA LIMITED

Statement of Comprehensive Income

For the year ended 31 December 20X5

Revenues:		
Sales	$325,200	
Interest	600	
Rent	1,200	
Total revenues		$327,000
Expenses:		
Cost of goods sold	117,000	
Selling	113,400	
General and administrative	34,600	
Interest	3,000	
Total expenses before income tax		268,000
Earnings before tax and discontinued operations		59,000
Income tax on earnings before discontinued operations ($59,000 × 40%)		23,600
Earnings before discontinued operations		35,400
Loss from discontinued operations	9,000	
Less tax savings ($9,000 × 40%)	3,600	5,400
Net earnings and comprehensive income		$ 30,000

Statement of Changes in Equity

For the year ended 31 December 20X5

	Common shares	Retained earnings
Opening balance, 1 January 20X5	$170,000	$ 41,500
Net earnings and comprehensive income		30,000
		$ 71,500
Less: dividends declared		10,000
Closing balance, 31 December 20X5	$170,000	$ 61,500

The statement of changes in equity includes a column for each equity account. There is no change to the common share account. Retained earnings, however, has increased by earnings and decreased by dividends declared. Dividends are a distribution of capital to shareholders. *They are not an expense and do not belong on the SCI when the corresponding shares are reported as equity.*[1]

EXHIBIT A-8

SONORA LIMITED
Statement of Financial Position

At 31 December 20X5

Assets
Current assets:

Cash		$ 67,300
Accounts receivable	$ 45,000	
Allowance for doubtful accounts	(2,200)	42,800
Notes receivable		8,000
Interest receivable		100
Inventory		90,000
Prepaid insurance		400
Total current assets		208,600

Property, plant and equipment:

Land		8,000	
Building	$160,000		
Accumulated depreciation, building	(100,000)	60,000	
Equipment	91,000		
Accumulated depreciation, equipment	(36,000)	55,000	
Total capital assets			123,000
Total assets			$331,600

Liabilities
Current liabilities:

Accounts payable		$ 29,000
Interest payable		500
Rent collected in advance		600
Income tax payable		20,000
Total current liabilities		50,100

Long-term liabilities:

Bonds payable, 6%		50,000
Total liabilities		100,100

Shareholders' Equity
Contributed capital:

Common shares, no par, 15,000 shares issued and outstanding	$170,000	
Retained earnings	61,500	
Total shareholders' equity		231,500
Total liabilities and shareholders' equity		$331,600

[1] In cases where certain types of preferred shares are recognized as liabilities, the related dividends would be recognized on the SCI.

Exhibit A-8 illustrates the 20X5 SFP. The ending retained earnings balance is taken from the statement of changes in equity rather than from the adjusted trial balance.

Step 8: Journalize and Post-closing Entries

The balances of the revenue, expense, gain, and loss accounts, which are the nominal accounts, are reduced to zero at the end of each accounting period through a transfer to retained earnings. Dividends accounts are also closed. This allows a fresh start for the next fiscal period. Earnings are measured for a specific interval of time, and are not cumulative. Permanent accounts are not closed because they carry over to the next accounting period. Closing entries:

- Reduce to zero (close) the balances of temporary accounts related to earnings measurement and dividends;
- Are recorded in the general journal at the end of the accounting period; and
- Are posted to the ledger accounts.

While some accountants prefer to close temporary accounts directly to retained earnings, it is quite common to use an account called "income summary" to accumulate the balances of temporary accounts in the closing entry process. The income summary is a clearing account—an account used on a short-term basis for a specific purpose. The balances in expenses and losses are reduced to zero and transferred to the income summary by crediting each of those accounts and debiting income summary for the total. Revenues and gains are debited to close them, and the income summary account is credited.

This process leaves a net balance in the income summary account equal to earnings (credit balance if earnings are positive and debit balance if a loss.) The income summary account is then closed by transferring the earnings amount to retained earnings. Sonora makes three closing entries to transfer 20X5 earnings to retained earnings:

31 December 20X5		
1. *To close the revenue and gain accounts to the income summary*		
Sales revenue	325,200	
Interest revenue	600	
Rent revenue	1,200	
Income summary		327,000
2. *To close the expense and loss accounts to the income summary*		
Income summary	297,000	
Cost of goods sold		117,000
Selling expense		113,400
General and administrative expenses		34,600
Interest expense		3,000
Loss from discontinued operations		9,000
Income tax expense		20,000
3. *To close the income summary (i.e., transfer earnings to retained earnings)*		
Income summary	30,000	
Retained earnings		30,000
4. *To close dividends to retained earnings*		
Retained earnings	10,000	
Dividends declared		10,000

After the first two closing entries are recorded and posted, the balance in the income summary equals earnings ($30,000):

Income Summary			
(2)	297,000	(1)	327,000
		Balance	30,000

The temporary accounts now have zero balances and are ready for the next period's accounting cycle. The third entry closes the income summary account and transfers earnings to retained earnings. Finally, dividends declared is closed to retained earnings. The retained earnings account in the ledger now has a balance of $61,500, per the statement of financial position.

Step 9: Prepare Post-closing Trial Balance

A post-closing trial balance lists only the balances of the permanent accounts after the closing process is finished. The temporary accounts have balances of zero. This step is taken to check for debit–credit equality after the closing entries are posted. Firms with a large number of accounts find this a valuable checking procedure because the chance of error increases with the number of accounts and postings. The retained earnings account is now stated at the correct ending balance and is the only permanent account with a balance different from the one shown in the adjusted trial balance. Exhibit A-9 illustrates the post-closing trial balance.

EXHIBIT A-9

SONORA LIMITED
Post-closing Trial Balance

31 December 20X5

Account	Debit	Credit
Cash	$ 67,300	
Accounts receivable	45,000	
Allowance for doubtful accounts		$ 2,200
Notes receivable	8,000	
Interest receivable	100	
Inventory	90,000	
Prepaid insurance	400	
Land	8,000	
Building	160,000	
Accumulated depreciation, building		100,000
Equipment	91,000	
Accumulated depreciation, equipment		36,000
Accounts payable		29,000
Interest payable		500
Rent collected in advance		600
Income tax payable		20,000
Bonds payable, 6%		50,000
Common shares, no par, 15,000 shares		170,000
Retained earnings (31 December balance)		61,500
Totals	$469,800	$469,800

Step 10: Journalize and Post Reversing Journal Entries

Depending on the firm's accounting system and its accounting policies, **reversing journal entries (RJEs)** may be used to simplify certain journal entries in the *next* accounting period. RJEs are optional entries that:

- Are dated the first day of the next accounting period;
- Relate to a specific AJE;
- Use the same accounts and amounts as an AJE but with the debits and credits reversed; and
- Are posted to the ledger.

RJEs are appropriate only for AJEs that defer the recognition of revenue or expense items originally recorded under the expedient method, or entries that accrue revenue or expense items during the current period (e.g., wages expense).

Thus, if a deferral or accrual AJE creates or increases an asset or liability, an RJE is appropriate. RJEs are inappropriate for AJEs that adjust assets and liabilities recorded for cash flows preceding the recognition of revenues and expenses (the standard method) and for some other AJEs, such as reclassifications, error corrections, and estimates.

In the following examples, assume a 31 December year-end.

Deferred item   Assume that on 1 November 20X5, $300 is paid in advance for three months' rent:

1 November 20X5—originating entry		
Rent expense	300	
Cash		300
31 December 20X5—adjusting entry		
Prepaid rent	100	
Rent expense		100

		With Reversing Entry		**Without Reversing Entry**	
1 January 20X6					
Reversing entry:	Rent expense	100			
	Prepaid rent		100		
31 January 20X6					
Subsequent	(No entry			Rent expense	100
entry:	needed)			Prepaid rent		100

With or without the RJE, rent expense recorded in 20X6 is $100. Use of the RJE, however, saves the cost and effort of reviewing the relevant accounts and source documents to determine the subsequent year's entry. The RJE makes the necessary adjustments to the accounts while the information used in making the AJE is available.

Now consider the standard method applied to the same example.

1 November 20X5—originating entry		
Prepaid rent	300	
Cash		300
31 December 20X5—adjusting entry		
Rent expense	200	
Prepaid rent		200

The RJE is not appropriate. No purpose is served by reinstating (debiting) prepaid rent $200 because that amount has expired.

Accrued item Assume that the last payroll for 20X5 is on 28 December. Wages earned through 28 December are included in this payroll. The next payroll period ends 4 January 20X6, at which time $2,800 of wages will be paid. Wages earned for the three-day period ending 31 December 20X5 are $1,500, which will be paid in 20X6. The following AJE is necessary to accrue these wages:

31 December 20X5—adjusting entry		
Wages expense	1,500	
Wages payable		1,500

		With Reversing Entry		**Without Reversing Entry**		
1 January 20X6						
Reversing entry:	Wages payable	1,500				
	Wages expense		1,500			
4 January 20X6						
Subsequent entry:	Wages expense	2,800		Wages expense	1,300	
	Cash		2,800	Wages payable	1,500	
				Cash		2,800

In this example, the RJE simplifies the subsequent payroll entry, which can now be recorded in a manner identical to all other payrolls. With or without reversing entries, total 20X6 wage expense recognized through 4 January 20X6 is $1,300. RJEs often create abnormal short-term account balances. In the above 1 January 20X6 entry, the RJE creates a credit balance in wages expense. The subsequent entry changes the net balance of wages expense to a $1,300 debit.

Some of Sonora's AJEs could be reversed: entry (b) for rent revenue (expedient method—deferred item); entry (c) for interest expense (accrual); entry (d) for interest revenue (accrual); and perhaps entry (h) for income tax expense (accrual).

SUBSIDIARY LEDGERS

Companies typically maintain both *control* and *subsidiary* ledger accounts. **Subsidiary ledgers** are often kept for accounts payable and accounts receivable, and also inventory, although any ledger account can be supported by a subsidiary ledger if size and complexity warrant.

The sum of all account balances in a subsidiary ledger must equal the related control account balance in the general ledger. To ensure that the control account and its subsidiary ledger are equal, frequent reconciliations are made. All posting must be complete, both to the control account and to the subsidiary ledger, before a reconciliation can be accomplished. Postings are made *in total* to the control account and *to individual accounts* in the subsidiary ledger. These postings are described in more depth in the next section.

To illustrate a reconciliation, refer ahead to the accounts receivable subsidiary ledger in Exhibit A-14. A reconciliation for accounts receivable control and the accounts receivable subsidiary ledger based on the information in Exhibit A-14 follows:

RECONCILIATION OF ACCOUNTS RECEIVABLE SUBSIDIARY LEDGER

At 31 January 20X5	**Amount**
Subsidiary ledger balances	
112.13 Adams Co.	$ 980
112.42 Miller, J. B.	196
112.91 XY Manufacturing Co.	1,960
Total	$3,136
General ledger balance	
Accounts receivable control ($5,000 + $9,360 − $11,224)	$3,136

Subsidiary ledgers contain information that help the company operate efficiently—individual account receivable and payable balances are essential information. In smaller companies, subsidiary ledgers can be maintained through a simple filing system. For example, a copy of a sales invoice that is not paid can be kept in a special file until the money is received. At any time, the outstanding receivables are equal to the total of the invoices in the file. The same can be done with accounts payable, if all unpaid bills are kept in an accounts payable file. The point is that formal accounting systems are made necessary by size and complexity, but simple methods in simple situations can be just as effective if efficiently operated.

SPECIAL JOURNALS

Both *general journals* and *special journals* are used in many accounting systems. Even when extensive use is made of special journals, a need exists for a general journal to record the adjusting, closing, reversing, and correcting entries and those transactions that do not apply to any of the special journals. A general journal was illustrated in Exhibit A-3.

A special journal is designed to expedite the recording of similar transactions that occur frequently. Each special journal is constructed specifically to simplify the data-processing tasks involved in journalizing and posting those types of transactions. Special journals can be custom designed to meet the particular needs of the business. Commonly used special journals include:

1. *Sales journal* for recording sales of merchandise *on credit*, and the related cost of goods sold;

2. *Purchases journal* for recording purchases of merchandise inventory *on credit*;

3. *Cash receipts journal* for recording only cash receipts, including cash sales and the related cost of goods sold; and

4. *Cash disbursements journal* for recording only cash payments, including cash purchases of merchandise inventory.

The special journals illustrated in this appendix carry page numbers preceded by letters indicating the journal name. The S in the page number of Exhibit A-10 denotes the sales journal, for example.

Sales Journal This special journal is designed to record sales on account, which otherwise would be recorded as follows in a general journal:

2 January 20X5		
Accounts receivable	980	
Sales revenue		980
Cost of goods sold	410	
Inventory		410
(Credit sale to Adams Company; invoice price, $980; terms n/30. the related inventory sold has a cost of $410)		

The sales journal can accommodate any entry that involves a debit to accounts receivable and a credit to sales, along with its related cost of goods sold. However, this is the *only* situation it can record. If the debit is to cash, or notes receivable, another journal must be used. Exhibit A-10 illustrates a typical sales journal for credit sales. The above entry is shown as the first entry in 20X5. The amount of sale, and the cost of goods sold, are each recorded only once. Each entry in the sales journal records the same information found in the traditional debit–credit format.

The posting of amounts from the sales journal to the general and subsidiary ledgers is simplified. The two phases in posting a sales journal are the following:

1. *Daily posting.* The amount of each credit sale is posted daily to the appropriate individual account in the accounts receivable subsidiary ledger. Each reduction to inventory is

posted daily to the relevant inventory account in the inventory subsidiary ledger. Posting is indicated by entering the account number in the posting reference column. For example, the number 112.13 entered in the posting reference column in Exhibit A-10 is the account number assigned to Adams Company and shows that $980 is posted as a debit to Adams Company in the subsidiary ledger. The number 112 is the general number used for accounts receivable (see Exhibit A-14). The inventory number has a similar logic. The number would be the SKU, or *stock-keeping unit*, assigned to the inventory item.

2. *Monthly posting.* At the end of each month, the numeric columns are totalled. Two journal entries result in the general journal. One is a debit to accounts receivable and a credit to sales for $9,360. The other is a debit to cost of goods sold and a credit to inventory for $3,753. Posting to the subsidiary ledgers would be completed prior to this. The T-accounts shown in Exhibit A-14 illustrate how these postings for sales and accounts receivable are reflected in both the general ledger and the subsidiary ledger. The ledgers reference the journal page (S-23) from which each amount is posted.

Purchases Journal This special journal is designed to accommodate frequent purchases of merchandise inventory on account. Again, there is only one transaction that can go into this journal—a debit to inventory, and a credit to accounts payable. Other entries, including the acquisition of inventory for cash, go elsewhere. Consider the following entry, recorded in general journal format:

3 January 20X5		
Inventory ($1,000 × .99)	990	
Accounts payable (PT Mfg. Co.)		990
(terms 1/20, n/30)		

Terms of 1/20 mean that if the invoice is paid within 20 days, a 1% discount can be applied to the invoice amount. In this case, the invoice is recorded at its net amount, after the 1% discount. Some companies prefer to record purchase invoices gross and record purchase discounts taken when they record payment. Note also that the entry assumes a perpetual inventory system. Under a periodic inventory system, the debit would always be to the purchases account.

This entry is recorded as the first 20X5 entry in the purchases journal illustrated in Exhibit A-11. The accounting simplifications found in the sales journal are present in the

---

EXHIBIT A-10

Page S-23

SALES JOURNAL

Date 20X5	Sales Invoice No.	Accounts Receivable (name)	Terms	Post. Ref.	Receivable and Sale Amount	Post. Ref.	Cost of Goods Sold and Inventory Amount
2 Jan.	93	Adams Co.	n/30	112.13	$ 980	120.899	$ 410
3	94	Sayre Corp.	n/30	112.80	490	120.113	165
11	95	Cope & Day Co.	net	112.27	5,734	120.189	2,450
27	96	XY Mfg. Co.	n/30	112.91	1,960	120.998	671
30	97	Miller, J. B.	n/30	112.42	196	120.003	57
31	—	Total			$9,360		$3,753
31	—	Posting			(112/500)		(120/650)

EXHIBIT A-11

Page P-6   **PURCHASES JOURNAL**

Date 20X5	Purchase Order No.	Accounts Payable (name)	Terms	Posting Ref.	Inventory and Payable Amount
3 Jan.	41	PT Mfg. Co.	1/20, n/30	120.998 210.61	$ 990
7	42	Able Suppliers Ltd.	net	120.431 210.12	150
31	—	Total	—	—	$6,760
31	—	Postings	—	—	(120/210)

purchases journal as well. Each amount is posted daily as a debit to the individual inventory account in the inventory subsidiary ledger. Each amount is also posted each day as a credit to the account of an individual creditor in the accounts payable subsidiary ledger. At the end of the month, the total of the inventory purchases and payable amount column ($6,760 in Exhibit A-11) is posted to the general ledger as a debit to the inventory account (no. 120) and as a credit to the accounts payable control account (no. 210). Posting references refer to both the subledger for inventory and for accounts payable.

Cash Receipts Journal A special cash receipts journal is used to accommodate a large volume of cash receipts transactions. This journal can accommodate any entry that involves a debit to cash. Multiple sources of cash (the credits) are accommodated by designing several credit columns for recurring credits, and a miscellaneous accounts column for infrequent credits, as shown in Exhibit A-12. Space is also provided for the names of particular accounts receivable.

During the month, each amount in the accounts receivable column is posted daily as a credit to an individual customer account in the accounts receivable subsidiary ledger. At the end of the month, the individual amounts in the miscellaneous account column are posted as credits to the appropriate general ledger accounts, and the totals for the cash, accounts receivable, and sales revenue columns are posted to the general ledger as indicated by the posting reference. The total of the miscellaneous accounts column is not posted because it consists of changes in different accounts. However, this column is totalled to ascertain overall debit–credit equality.

Cash Disbursements Journal Most companies use some form of a cash disbursements journal, which is also sometimes called a *cheque register*. This journal can accommodate any entry that involves a credit to cash, and has columns for the common debits and a miscellaneous debits column to make it flexible. Exhibit A-13 illustrates a typical cash disbursements journal. Journalizing and posting follow the same procedures explained for the cash receipts journal.

The General Journal Special journals can be used to record common entries, but there will always be entries that do not fit the format for any special journal and must be recorded in general journal format (Exhibit A-14). Adjusting and reversing entries are prime examples, but unusual operating transactions will also be recorded in this format. The general journal is an essential element of accounting record keeping.

EXHIBIT A-12

Page CR-19

CASH RECEIPTS JOURNAL

Date 20X5	Explanation	Debit Cash	Account Title	Post. Ref.	Accounts Receivable	Sales Revenue	Misc. Accounts	Cost of Goods Sold and Inventory Amount
							Credits	Debit and Credit
4 Jan.	Cash sales	$ 11,200		120.431		$11,200		$ 5,998
7	On acct.	4,490	Sayre Corp.	112.80	$ 4,490			
8	Sale of land	10,000	Land	123			$ 4,000	
			Gain on sale of land	510			6,000	
10	On acct.	1,000	Adams Co.	112.13	1,000			
19	Cash sales	43,600		120.875		43,600		24,320
20	On acct.	5,734	Cope & Day Co.	112.27	5,734			
31	Totals	$116,224		—	$11,224	$71,000	$34,000	$32,116
31	Posting	(101)		—	(112)	(500)	(NP)*	(650/120)

*NP—not posted as one total because the individual amounts are posted as indicated in the posting reference column.

EXHIBIT A-13

Page CD-31

CASH DISBURSEMENTS JOURNAL

Date 20X5	Cheque No.	Explanation	Credit Cash	Account Name	Post. Ref.	Accounts Payable	Inventory	Misc. Accounts
						Debits		
2 Jan.	141	Pur. inv.	$ 3,000		120.899		$ 3,000	
10	142	On acct.	990	PT Mfg. Co.	210.61	$ 990		
15	143	Jan. rent	660	Rent exp.	1300			$ 660
16	144	Pur. inv.	1,810		120.351		1,810	
31	—	Totals	$98,400		—	$5,820	$90,980	$1,600
31	—	Posting	(101)		—	(210)	(120)	(NP)

EXHIBIT A-14

GENERAL LEDGER AND SUBSIDIARY LEDGER GENERAL LEDGER (PARTIAL)

Cash   Acct. 101

20X5			20X5		
1 Jan.	Balance	18,700	31 Jan.	CD-31	98,400
31	CR-19	116,224			

Accounts Receivable Control   Acct. 112

20X5			20X5		
1 Jan.	Balance	5,000	31 Jan.	CR-19	11,224
31	S-23	9,360			

Sales Revenue   Acct. 500

			20X5		
			31 Jan.	S-23	9,360
			31	CR-19	71,000

Subsidiary Ledger for Accounts Receivable (Acct. No. 112)

Date 20X5	Post Ref.	Explanation	Debit	Credit	Balance
Adams Company—Acct. No. 112.13					
1 Jan.		Balance			1,000
2	S-23		980		1,980
10	CR-19			1,000	980
Cope & Day Company—Acct. No. 112.27					
11 Jan.	S-23		5,734		5,734
20	CR-19			5,734	0
Miller, J. B.—Acct. No. 112.42					
30 Jan.	S-23		196		196
Sayre Corporation—Acct. No. 112.80					
1 Jan.		Balance			4,000
3	S-23		490		4,490
7	CR-19			4,490	0
XY Manufacturing Company—Acct. No. 112.91					
27 Jan.	S-23		1,960		1,960

WORKSHEETS

A worksheet is a multicolumn work space that provides an organized format for performing several end-of-period accounting cycle steps and for preparing financial statements before posting AJEs. It also provides evidence, or an audit trail, of an organized and structured accounting process that can be more easily reviewed than other methods of analysis.

Use of a worksheet is always optional. The worksheet is not part of the basic accounting records. Worksheets assist with only a portion of the accounting cycle. Formal AJEs are recorded in the accounts in addition to those entered on the worksheet. Worksheets are also often used in preparing consolidated statements.

Illustration of the Worksheet Approach

Exhibit A-15 illustrates the completed worksheet for Sonora Limited, the company used in this appendix to present the accounting cycle. The worksheet has a debit and a credit column for each of the following: unadjusted trial balance, AJEs, adjusted trial balance, SCI, retained earnings, and SFP. The worksheet is prepared in four steps:

Step 1 *Enter the unadjusted trial balance in the first set of columns of the worksheet by inserting the year-end balances of all ledger accounts.*

- The retained earnings balance is the beginning-of-year balance because no transactions have yet affected this account.

Step 2 *Enter the adjusting entries.*

- The lowercase letters refer to the same AJEs discussed in this appendix for Sonora Limited.
- The worksheet AJEs are facilitating entries only and are not formally recorded in the general journal at this point. If a new account is created by an AJE, it can be inserted in its normal position or at the bottom of the worksheet.
- Determine income tax expense and payable. (Sonora's tax computation was illustrated earlier.) Enter the accounts and the amounts in the AJE columns. Income tax expense (entry [h]) is positioned below the totals of the AJE columns because this reflects its sequence in the adjustment process.

Step 3 *Cross-add.*

- Enter the adjusted trial balance by adding or subtracting across the unadjusted trial balance columns and AJE columns, for each account. For example, the adjusted balance of the allowance for doubtful accounts is the sum of its $1,000 unadjusted balance and the $1,200 increase from AJE (f).
- Confirm the debit–credit equality of all totals.

Step 4 *Extend the adjusted trial balance amounts to the financial statements; complete the worksheet.*

- Each account in the adjusted trial balance is extended to one of the three sets of remaining debit–credit columns. Temporary accounts are sorted to the SCI columns (revenues to the credit column, expenses to the debit column). Permanent accounts are sorted to the SFP columns except for the beginning balance in retained earnings, which is extended to the retained earnings columns. Dividends go in the retained earnings columns in this example.
- Total the SCI columns before income tax expense. Pre-tax income is the difference between the debit and credit column totals. A net credit represents positive earnings; a net debit represents a loss. For Sonora, pretax earnings are $50,000 ($327,000 − $277,000). Next, determine earnings after taxes by extending the income tax expense amount ($20,000) into the debit column and again totalling the columns. Earnings is the difference between the columns, or $30,000 ($327,000 − $297,000).

EXHIBIT A-15

COMPLETED WORKSHEET FOR SONORA LTD.

	Unadjusted Trial Balance		Adjusting Entries		Adjusted Trial Balance		Statement of Comprehensive Income		Retained Earnings		Statement of Financial Position	
	Debit	Credit	Debit	Credit	Debit	Credit	Debit	Credit	Debit	Credit	Debit	Credit
Cash	67,300				67,300						67,300	
Accounts receivable	45,000				45,000						45,000	
Allowance for doubtful accounts		1,000		(f) 1,200		2,200						2,200
Notes receivable	8,000				8,000						8,000	
Interest receivable			(d) 100		100						100	
Inventory	92,000			(g) 2,000	90,000						90,000	
Prepaid insurance	600			(a) 200	400						400	
Land	8,000				8,000						8,000	
Building	160,000				160,000						160,000	
Accumulated depreciation, building		90,000		(e) 10,000		100,000						100,000
Equipment	91,000				91,000						91,000	
Accumulated depreciation, equipment		27,000		(e) 9,000		36,000						36,000
Accounts payable		29,000				29,000						29,000
Interest payable				(c) 500		500						500
Rent collected in advance				(b) 600		600						600
Bonds payable, 6%		50,000				50,000						50,000
Common shares, no par, 15,000 shares		170,000				170,000						170,000
Retained earnings		41,500				41,500				41,500		
Dividends declared	10,000				10,000				10,000			
Sales revenue		325,200				325,200		325,200				
Interest revenue		500		(d) 100		600		600				
Rent revenue		1,800	(b) 600			1,200		1,200				
Cost of goods sold	115,000		(g) 2,000		117,000		117,000					
Selling expenses	104,000		(e) 8,200 (f) 1,200		113,400		113,400					
General and administrative expenses	23,600		(a) 200 (e) 10,800		34,600		34,600					
Interest expense	2,500		(c) 500		3,000		3,000					
Loss on discontinued operations	9,000				9,000		9,000					
	736,000	736,000	23,600	23,600	756,800	756,800	277,000	327,000				
Income tax expense			(h) 20,000		20,000		20,000					
Income tax payable				(h) 20,000		20,000						20,000
			20,000	20,000	776,800	776,800	297,000	327,000				
Earnings to retained earnings							30,000			30,000		
Retained earnings to SFP									61,500			61,500
Totals							327,000	327,000	71,500	71,500	469,800	469,800

- Next, add a line description (earnings to retained earnings) and enter the $30,000 earnings amount as a balancing value in the SCI columns: positive earnings are a debit balancing value; negative earnings are a credit. Then complete this entry by recording $30,000 in the credit column under the retained earnings columns. (Positive earnings are a credit entry, and negative earnings are a debit entry.)

- Total the retained earnings columns and enter a balancing amount (the ending retained earnings balance) in the appropriate column to achieve debit–credit equality. For Sonora, the balancing amount is a $61,500 debit. Add a line description (retained earnings to SFP) and enter the balancing amount in the appropriate SFP column.

- Total the SFP columns and confirm debit–credit equality.

The worksheet is now complete, and the financial statements are prepared directly from the last three sets of worksheet columns. The formal AJEs are then journalized and posted.

Combined Version   To save space, the retained earnings and SFP columns can be combined. If this is done, the opening retained earnings account and dividends are entered in the SFP columns and the earnings figure is included at the bottom of the SFP columns to balance the worksheet.

ACCOUNTING STANDARDS FOR PRIVATE ENTERPRISES

Transaction recording mechanics are the same regardless if the company has adopted ASPE or IFRS. Only the titles and nature of the statements have changed. The basic financial statements are also the same, with ASPE requiring an income statement, balance sheet, and a statement of retained earnings. A retained earnings statement shows the opening retained earnings balance, itemizes each increase and decrease in retained earnings for the year, and then concludes with the closing balance in the account. A statement of changes in equity is not required under ASPE. ASPE also does not have any other comprehensive income items to be reported.

SUMMARY OF KEY POINTS

1. The AIS provides information for daily management information needs and for preparation of financial statements.

2. The SFP discloses the balances of the permanent accounts, which include assets, liabilities, and owners' equity accounts. The SCI includes the preclosing balances of most temporary accounts, which include revenues, gains, expenses, and losses.

3. Transactions are recorded in a double-entry system, where each transaction changes two or more accounts. Debits to assets, expenses, losses, and dividends declared increase those accounts. Credits to liabilities, owners' equity, revenues, and gains increase those accounts.

4. There are 10 steps in the accounting cycle that culminate in the financial statements. Refer to Exhibit A-2.

5. AJEs are required under accrual accounting to complete the measurement and recording of changes in resources and obligations.

6. RJEs are optional entries, dated at the beginning of the accounting period, that reverse certain AJEs from the previous period and are used to facilitate subsequent journal entries.

7. Subsidiary ledgers are used to maintain records on the component elements of ledger control accounts.

8. Special journals are used to record repetitive entries, such as sales, inventory purchases, cash receipts, and cash disbursements. A general journal is used to record entries that do not fit into special journals.

9. A worksheet may be used to organize the adjustment and financial statement preparation phases of the accounting cycle.

KEY TERMS

accounting identity
accounting information system (AIS)
adjusting journal entries (AJEs)
contra account
debit–credit convention
deferral-type entries
double-entry system
expedient recording method
financial statement
general journal
general ledger
journal
journal entry
nominal accounts

nonreciprocal transfer
periodic inventory system
permanent accounts
perpetual inventory system
posting
real accounts
reciprocal transfer
reversing journal entries (RJEs)
special journal
standard recording method
subsidiary ledger
T-account
temporary accounts
transactions

REVIEW PROBLEM

Bucknell Company developed its unadjusted trial balance dated 31 December 20X5, which appears below. Bucknell uses the expedient recording method whenever possible, adjusts its accounts once per year, records all appropriate RJEs, and uses a perpetual inventory system. Ignore income taxes.

BUCKNELL COMPANY
UNADJUSTED TRIAL BALANCE

31 December 20X5	Debit	Credit
Cash	$ 40,000	
Accounts receivable	60,000	
Allowance for doubtful accounts		$ 6,000
Inventory	75,000	
Equipment	780,000	
Accumulated depreciation		100,000
Land	150,000	
Accounts payable		22,000
Notes payable, 8%, due 1 April 20X10		200,000
Common shares, no-par, 60,000 shares		400,000
Retained earnings		50,000
Sales revenue (all on account)		900,000
Subscription revenue		24,000
Cost of goods sold	265,000	
Rent expense	60,000	
Interest expense	12,000	
Selling expense	40,000	
Insurance expense	30,000	
Wages expense	110,000	
General and administrative expense	80,000	
Totals	$1,702,000	$1,702,000

Additional information:

a. Ending inventory by physical count is $70,000.

b. The equipment has a total estimated useful life of 14 years and an estimated residual value of $80,000. Bucknell uses straight-line depreciation and treats depreciation expense as a general and administrative expense.

c. Bad debt expense for 20X5 is estimated to be 1% of sales.

d. The note payable requires interest to be paid semi-annually, every 1 October and 1 April.

e. $5,000 of wages were earned in December but not recorded or paid.

f. The rent expense represents a payment made on 2 January 20X5, for two years' rent (20X5 and 20X6).

g. The insurance expense represents payment made for a one-year policy, paid 30 June 20X5. Coverage began on that date.

h. The subscription revenue represents cash received from several university libraries for an 18-month subscription to a journal published by Bucknell. The subscription period began 1 July 20X5.

Required:

1. Record the required AJEs.
2. Prepare the adjusted trial balance.
3. Prepare an SCI and an SFP for 20X5.
4. Prepare closing entries.
5. Prepare RJEs.

REVIEW PROBLEM—SOLUTION

Requirement 1

a. Cost of goods sold	5,000	
Inventory ($75,000 − $70,000)		5,000
b. General and administrative expense		
($780,000 − $80,000)/14	50,000	
Accumulated depreciation		50,000
c. Bad debt expense (0.01 × $900,000)	9,000	
Allowance for doubtful accounts		9,000
d. Interest expense ($200,000 × 0.08 × 3/12)	4,000	
Interest payable		4,000
e. Wages expense	5,000	
Wages payable		5,000
f. Prepaid rent ($60,000 × 1/2)	30,000	
Rent expense		30,000
g. Prepaid insurance ($30,000 × 6/12)	15,000	
Insurance expense		15,000
h. Subscription revenue ($24,000 × 12/18)	16,000	
Unearned subscriptions		16,000

Requirement 2

BUCKNELL COMPANY
ADJUSTED TRIAL BALANCE

31 December 20X5	Debit	Credit
Cash	$ 40,000	
Accounts receivable	60,000	
Allowance for doubtful accounts (9,000 + 6,000 (c))		$ 15,000
Inventory (75,000 – 5,000 (a))	70,000	
Prepaid rent (30,000 (f))	30,000	
Prepaid insurance (15,000 (g))	15,000	
Equipment	780,000	
Accumulated depreciation (100,000 + 50,000 (b))		150,000
Land	150,000	
Accounts payable		22,000
Interest payable (4,000 (d))		4,000
Wages payable (5,000 (e))		5,000
Unearned subscriptions(16,000 (h))		16,000
Notes payable, 8%, due 1 April 20X10		200,000
Common shares, no-par, 60,000 shares		400,000
Retained earnings		50,000
Sales revenue		900,000
Subscription revenue (24,000 – 16,000 (h))		8,000
Cost of goods sold (265,000 + 5,000 (a))	270,000	
Rent expense (60,000-30,000 (f))	30,000	
Interest expense (12,000 + 4,000 (d))	16,000	
Selling expense	40,000	
Insurance expense (30,000-15,000 (g))	15,000	
Wages expense (110,000 + 5,000 (e))	115,000	
Bad debt expense (9,000 (c))	9,000	
General and administrative expense (80,000 + 50,000 (b))	130,000	
Totals	$1,770,000	$1,770,000

Requirement 3

BUCKNELL COMPANY
STATEMENT OF COMPREHENSIVE INCOME

For the year ended 31 December 20X5

Revenues:		
Sales revenue	$900,000	
Subscription revenue	8,000	
Total revenue		$908,000
Expenses:		
Cost of goods sold	270,000	
Rent expense	30,000	
Interest expense	16,000	
Selling expense	40,000	
Insurance expense	15,000	
Wages expense	115,000	
Bad debt expense	9,000	
General and administrative expense	130,000	
Total expenses		625,000
Net earnings and comprehensive income		$283,000

BUCKNELL COMPANY
STATEMENT OF FINANCIAL POSITION

31 December 20X5

Assets
Current assets
Cash		$ 40,000
Accounts receivable	$ 60,000	
Allowance for doubtful accounts	(15,000)	45,000
Inventory		70,000
Prepaid rent		30,000
Prepaid insurance		15,000

Noncurrent assets $200,000
Equipment	780,000		
Accumulated depreciation	(150,000)	630,000	
Land		150,000	780,000
Total assets			$980,000

Liabilities
Current liabilities
Accounts payable	$ 22,000	
Interest payable	4,000	
Wages payable	5,000	
Unearned subscriptions	16,000	$ 47,000

Noncurrent liabilities
Notes payable, 8%, due 1 April 20X10	200,000
Total liabilities	$247,000

Owners' Equity
Common shares, no-par,
60,000 shares outstanding	400,000	
Retained earnings	333,000*	
Total owners' equity		733,000
Total liabilities and owners' equity		$980,000

*$50,000 + $283,000

Requirement 4

Sales revenue	900,000	
Subscription revenue	8,000	
Income summary		908,000
Income summary	625,000	
Cost of goods sold		270,000
Rent expense		30,000
Interest expense		16,000
Selling expense		40,000
Insurance expense		15,000
Wages expense		115,000
Bad debt expense		9,000
General and administrative expense		130,000
Income summary	283,000	
Retained earnings		283,000

Requirement 5

Interest payable	4,000	
Interest expense		4,000
Wages payable	5,000	
Wages expense		5,000
Rent expense	30,000	
Prepaid rent		30,000
Insurance expense	15,000	
Prepaid insurance		15,000
Unearned subscriptions	16,000	
Subscription revenue		16,000

TECHNICAL REVIEW

connect

TRApp1-1 Deferred Expenses: On 1 November, a payment of $600 was made for six months' insurance.

Required:
Prepare the journal entry using the standard method to record the payment and the year-end adjustment as at 31 December.

connect

TRApp1-2 Accrued Expenses and Reversing Journal Entries: The company has a year-end of 30 April and the last pay period ended 25 April. On 9 May, the payroll was completed, totalling $14,000, and was recorded using the expedient recording method.

Required:
Prepare the journal entries required at the end of April to accrue any wage expense, the reversing journal entry at 1 May and the payment entry on 9 May. Determine the balance in the wage expense amount on 9 May after these entries. (*Note:* There are 14 days in the pay period).

connect

TRApp1-3 Adjusting Journal Entries: A company has machinery that had an original cost of $250,000, a residual value of $5,000, and a useful life of seven years. The machinery is depreciated on a straight-line basis. The balance in the allowance for doubtful accounts is currently $45,000, but the company has estimated that the amount of receivables that are unlikely to be collected totals $56,000, using the percentage of receivables method.

Required:
Prepare the adjusting journal entries required to record depreciation and the bad debts expense for the year.

connect

TRApp1-4 Closing Entries: A company has the following SCI for the year ended 31 October 20X4.

Revenues:		$1,082.000
Expenses:		
Cost of goods sold	$350,000	
Rent expense	50,000	
Selling expense	75,000	
Insurance expense	15,000	
Wages expense	295,000	
General and administrative expense	130,000	
Total expenses		$ 915,000
Net earnings and comprehensive income		$ 167,000

Required:

Prepare the closing entries for this company.

■connect

TRApp1-5 Adjusted Trial Balance: At the year-end, the company had $1,567,000 in marketing expenses and $3,670,000 in sales. The following adjusting journal entries were made by the company:

Prepaid advertising	115,000	
Marketing expenses		115,000

To adjust for costs related to advertising brochures to be received next year.

Marketing expenses	92,000	
Sales		92,000

To correct an error made in posting.

Sales	69,000	
Unearned revenue		69,000

To record a customer deposit paid in advance for work to be completed next year.

Required:

Calculate the adjusted balances for marketing expenses and sales after these entries have been posted.

ASSIGNMENTS

AApp1-1 Journalize Transactions: The Fardy Information Management Inc. follows the expedient recording method. It engaged in transactions during the month of May:

a. Paid $6,000 for May rent.
b. Bought $4,000 of office supplies on account.
c. Payroll for May was $56,000. Employees were paid $43,500, and the remainder was payroll deductions (income tax etc.) All payroll deductions were immediately remitted to the Receiver General.
d. Customers were billed $87,800 for completed assignments.
e. Utilities of $2,600 were paid.
f. Declared a cash dividend of $2 per preferred share and $0.50 per common share, payable 6 June. There are 50,000 preferred shares and 160,000 common shares outstanding.
g. Sold used computer equipment with an original cost of $35,900 accumulated depreciation to date of $23,600, for $15,000.
h. Paid suppliers $3,000 on account for supplies in (b).
i. Collected $65,800 from customers on account in (d).

Required:

1. Journalize each of the above transactions in general journal form.
2. Which entries would be different if the standard recording method were used? Repeat these entries, using the standard reporting method. Explain how the (eventual) adjusting journal entries for these accounts would be different under this approach.
3. Indicate in which journal each transaction would normally be recorded, assuming that the company keeps a journal for purchases (merchandise for resale/inventory purchases), sales, cash receipts, cash disbursements, and also a general journal.

★★ **AApp1-2 Journalize Transactions and Adjustments—Valuation:** Zfind Corporation reports the following in the month of April:

a. Issued 17,000 no-par common shares for cash, $68,000.

b. Issued 15,000 no-par common shares for a piece of used equipment with an appraised value of $52,000. The equipment had an original cost of $76,000 to the seller three years ago. The net book value (cost less accumulated depreciation) on the books of the seller was $42,900 on the date of sale.

c. Bought land with an appraised value of $70,000. An 8%, three-year note payable was issued in the amount of $50,000, and $20,000 was paid in cash.

d. Bought office supplies on account, $1,200. An asset account is debited.

e. Hired three employees at the beginning of the month. All employees are paid on a monthly basis. Monthly salaries for the three will amount to $8,000. (Two will be paid $3,000 per month each, and one will be paid $2,000 per month.)

f. Three months' rent is paid in advance. The lease calls for $1,000 of rent per month. An asset account is debited.

g. Goods for resale in the amount of $120,000 are bought. Twenty percent of the price is paid in cash, and the rest is on account. These goods are priced to sell at $266,000.

h. Received an order from a customer for goods worth $50,000. The goods will be shipped in the next week (see [j]).

i. Miscellaneous operating expenses are paid in the amount of $14,400, cash.

j. Goods are delivered to customers and they are billed, on account, $245,000. The order, in (h) above, is included in this total. The goods delivered to the customers cost $110,000. There are still goods that cost $10,000, with a retail value of $21,000, in inventory.

k. One month has gone by, and monthly rent expense is recorded.

l. Employee salaries for one month are paid.

m. The Board of Directors declares, but does not pay, a dividend in the amount of $13,600.

n. Office supplies on hand at year-end, per physical count, are $400.

o. Goods purchased on account in (g) above are paid for in full.

p. Eighty percent of the accounts receivable from customers, as recorded in (j) above, are received.

Required:

1. Journalize the transactions and events listed above. If no journal entry is needed, write "no entry." Zfind uses a perpetual inventory system. If there is a choice of value to use, justify your choice.

2. Which entries recorded are transactions, and which are adjustments? Explain.

★★ **AApp1-3 Journalize and Post—Unadjusted Trial Balance:** The following selected transactions or events were completed during 20X5 by HUP Inc., a retailer of makeup and skin care products:

a. Issued 25,000 shares of its own no-par common shares for $7 per share and received cash in full.

b. Borrowed $500,000 cash on a 6%, one-year note, interest payable at maturity on 30 April 20X6.

c. Paid $350,000 for leasehold improvements on a shopping mall location that will be the major retail outlet; also paid one year's rent of $100,000 in full.

d. Purchased merchandise inventory for resale at a cash cost of $260,000.

e. Purchased merchandise inventory for resale on credit for $58,800.

f. Sold merchandise that cost $96,000 for $198,000 cash.

g. Paid $87,000 cash for operating expenses.

h. Paid two-thirds of the balance for the merchandise purchased in (e).

i. Paid cash for an insurance premium, $3,600; the premium is for two years' coverage (debit prepaid insurance).

j. Counted inventory and had $219,000 of merchandise on hand.

k. Paid damages to a customer who was injured through use of a company product, $4,000 cash.

Required:

1. Enter transactions in a general journal; use "J1" for the first journal page number. Use the letter of the transaction in place of the date.

2. Set up appropriate T-accounts, and post the journal entries. Use posting reference numbers in your posting. Assign each T-account an appropriate title, and number each account in statement of financial position order followed by the temporary accounts; start with "Cash, No. 101."

3. Prepare an unadjusted trial balance.

★★   **AApp1-4 Adjusting Entries:** Manitoba Mini Homes Corp. has annual earnings of $24,600 in its unadjusted trial balance. The company prepares financial statements annually,

 with adjusting journal entries recorded at year-end. The following items have not yet been addressed for the fiscal period ended 31 December:

a. A 12-month, $1,560 insurance policy that commenced on 1 September was paid on 1 September and debited to prepaid insurance at that time. The prepaid insurance account already had a balance of $960 on 1 September in relation to the prior insurance coverage, which expired on 30 August.

b. The office supplies inventory account had a balance of $1,300 at the beginning of the year. Supplies costing $3,900 were purchased during the year and expensed as bought. There is an inventory of $1,700 physically on hand at the end of the year.

c. Manitoba completed a mini-home sale on the last day of the fiscal year but has not yet recorded the transaction. The mini-home was sold for $56,000, and the proceeds were to be paid in early January. The unit has a cost of $43,100 and was still in inventory on the books as of 31 December.

d. A service charge of $135, a deduction from the cash account per the bank statement for December, has not yet been recorded. Interest on outstanding loans for $560 was also taken out of the bank account in December but is not recorded.

e. A customer paid a $10,000 deposit for repairs in December. This amount was credited to revenue, but the work is not expected to be done until January.

f. A customer paid $5,160 in early November for one year's rent on a mini-home, a rental arrangement effective on 1 November. The cash received was credited to revenue in November.

g. A customer paid $6,000 in early August for one year's rent on a mini-home, a rental arrangement commencing on 1 August. The cash received was credited to unearned revenue in August.

h. A customer who rents a mini-home did not pay her rent in November or December, although the company believes that the amount will be paid in January. Nothing has been recorded for November or December. Monthly rental is $500 on this unit.

Required:

1. Journalize each of the above transactions in general journal form, as needed.

2. Calculate the revised earnings for the period, reflecting the adjustments in requirement 1.

★   **AApp1-5 Adjusting Entries:** Signal Corporation adjusts and closes its accounts each 31 August. The following situations require adjusting entries at the current year-end:

a. Fuel supplies that cost $6,500 were purchased during the year and debited to fuel inventory. At the year-end, the amount of fuel still on hand was $3,100.

b. Signal sold goods for cash to customers on 31 August for $65,200. These sales have not yet been recorded.

c. Equipment is to be depreciated for a half year. It cost $820,000, and the estimated useful life is nine years with an estimated residual value of $10,000. Use straight-line depreciation.

d. The allowance for doubtful accounts currently has a balance of $87,500. Signal has estimated that the amount of uncollectible customer accounts to be $75,600.

e. Signal signed a maintenance contract for office cleaning for 24 months starting for $120,000. The entire amount was set up as prepaid maintenance at the time of payment and no amount for the current year has yet been expensed.

f. Late in August, it was found that a posting error had been made. A deposit of $2,500 from a customer had been recorded as other income and should have been recorded as unearned revenue.

g. On August 15, the company received its statement for vehicle insurance, which is for one year commencing September 9. The amount of $8,700 is due on 2 September.

Required:
Prepare adjusting entries in the general journal for each situation. If no entry is required for an item, explain why.

★★ **AApp1-6 Adjusting Entries:** The following items are independent. Assume that the original transactions have been recorded correctly or as described. Assume a December 31 year-end unless otherwise noted.

a. Prepaid insurance had a debit balance of $18,200 at the beginning of January. This represents the remaining 14 months in an insurance policy that was purchased in a prior year. On 1 April of the current year, a 30-month policy was bought for $50,400, which was debited to prepaid insurance. There were no other entries to the prepaid insurance account during the year. On 1 November, an 18-month policy was bought for $9,360. This policy was debited to insurance expense.

b. Certain invoices had not been recorded at 31 December: a $7,400 bill for power, a $920 phone bill, and a repair bill for $1,350. All these bills are due in January.

c. Salaries payable has a balance of $3,700, unadjusted from the last year-end. There are 14 employees. They were paid up to Friday, 27 December. There were two additional working days prior to the year-end. Three employees earn $600 per (five-day) week each, three earn $500 per week, and eight earn $400 per week.

d. There are two notes payable outstanding. The first is an $890,000, 4% note, issued on 1 September; no interest has been paid to date. The second is a $700,000, 3.5% note issued on 1 April; six months' interest was paid on 1 October. The notes payable themselves were properly recorded on issuance, but interest must be accrued to 31 December, the year-end.

e. There is an unearned revenue account with a balance of $160,000. This includes a $10,000 security deposit from a tenant. This deposit will be returned when the tenant eventually vacates. The remaining $150,000 is six months' rent received, on a lease beginning 1 December, on commercial property.

f. Supplies inventory had a balance of $23,600 at the end of last year. During the year, $69,800 of supplies were purchased, and were debited directly to supplies expense. At year-end, an inventory count was conducted, and the balance was ascertained to be $24,750.

g. Advertising expense of $94,800 includes a $6,300 payment for an advertisement that will run in January of next year.

Required:
1. Prepare adjusting journal entries to reflect the facts above.
2. Prepare reversing entries for adjusting journal entries that must be reversed.

★ **AApp1-7 Adjusting Entries:** Zeonan Inc., an accounting firm, adjusts and closes its accounts each 31 August.

1. On 1 March 20X4, the company collected cash, $21,510, which was for rent collected in advance from a tenant for the next 12 months. Give the adjusting journal entry as at 31 August 20X4 assuming the following at the time of the collection:

Case A $21,510 was credited to rent revenue.

Case B $21,510 was credited to rent collected in advance.

2. On 31 August 20X5, the maintenance supplies inventory account showed a balance on hand amounting to $8,700. During 20X6, purchases of maintenance supplies amounted to $11,000. An inventory of maintenance supplies on hand at 31 August 20X6 reflected unused supplies amounting to $5,600. Give the adjusting journal entry that should be made on 31 August 20X6, under the following conditions:

Case A   Purchases were debited to the maintenance supplies inventory account.

Case B   Purchases were debited to maintenance supplies expense.

3. On 31 August 20X5, the prepaid insurance account showed a debit balance of $7,200, which was for coverage for the three months, September to November. On 1 December 20X5, the company obtained another policy covering a two-year period from that date. The two-year premium, amounting to $62,400, was paid on 1 December. Give the adjusting journal entry that should be made on 31 August 20X6.

Case A $62,400 was debited to prepaid insurance.

Case B $62,400 was debited to insurance expense.

Required:
Provide adjusting journal entries.

★★   **AApp1-8 Adjusting Entries:** Gilby Repairs Limited has transactions that can be used to illustrate terminology and also the recording and adjustment decisions in the accounting cycle. The company prepares complete monthly financial statements and uses reversing entries, where appropriate. Four transactions are described below:

Transaction 1
The company received $15,000 in July from a customer for repairs to be done in the month of August. The repairs were completed in August as scheduled. Assume that the standard recording method is used. Prepare an entry to record the cash receipt in July; an adjusting entry at the end of July, if needed; a reversing entry for the first of August, if needed; and an entry for the work done in August, if needed. Repeat these entries, assuming that the expedient recording method is used.

Transaction 2
The company did work worth $17,000 for a customer in July and then delivered and invoiced the job in July. The customer paid in August. Prepare an entry to record the work done in July, if needed; a reversing entry for the first of August, if needed; and the cash transaction in August.

Transaction 3
Gilby began the month of July with a $4,200 balance in the supplies inventory asset account. Gilby purchased $6,700 of supplies in July for cash, and a physical count revealed $1,200 of supplies on hand at the end of the month. Assume that the standard recording method is used. Prepare an entry to record the cash payment in July, an adjusting entry at the end of July, if needed; and a reversing entry for the first of August, if needed. Repeat these entries, assuming that the expedient recording method is used.

Transaction 4
Gilby used $5,900 of services from the Carleton Consulting Company during the month of July. The bill for this was received and paid in August. Prepare entries needed in July, any reversing entry on the first of August, if needed, and any entry needed in August.

Required:
Prepare journal entries as requested in the transactions above.

★★   **AApp1-9 ASPE—Adjusting Entries:** Eastern Trading Corporation has a preliminary figure for earnings of $250,000, for the year ended 31 December 20X2. The company also has provided the following information in relation to its annual financial information:

a. No income tax has been recorded, but the tax rate is 25%.

b. The company has a bank loan outstanding for $200,000, which has been outstanding for the entire year. The interest has not been paid or recorded for the final quarter. Interest is based on an annual rate of 6%.

c. Property taxes of $19,200 were paid in August and were for the 12-month period starting on 1 September. The amount was expensed in August.

d. Accounts receivable were reviewed for bad debts, and it was determined that $8,000 of the $50,000 owing was unlikely to be collected. At present, there is a balance of $3,000 (credit) in the allowance for doubtful accounts.

e. The merchandise inventory account has a balance of $260,000. The company uses a perpetual inventory system, so cost of goods sold has been recorded as the year has progressed. However, the physical inventory count at the end of the year showed a total of $252,000 of goods on hand. The difference between this and the accounting records was probably due to theft.

f. A customer paid $30,000 on an outstanding account receivable in December. This amount was credited to sales, in error.

g. Depreciation of equipment in the amount of $16,400 has not been recorded.

h. Accounting fees paid, in the amount of $7,600, were debited to dividends instead of an expense account.

i. A customer paid $50,000 as a deposit in June. This was credited to unearned revenue, but the transaction was completed in October, and the goods delivered. Cost of goods sold was correctly recorded at that time, but the unearned revenue was not changed.

j. At the beginning of the year, there was a balance of $2,240 in the prepaid insurance account, for a policy that will expire at the end of February 20X3. During the year, a second policy for different coverage came into effect on June 1. This policy cost $4,770 and covers 18 months. The payment was debited to insurance expense when it was made.

Required:

Journalize each of the above transactions in general journal form.

★★   **AApp1-10 Adjusting Entries:** Triple Y Exports Ltd. uses a perpetual inventory system, recording cost of goods sold each time there is a sale, and updating inventory records for each new purchase of goods. The company has the following transactions and events at 31 December 20X5, the end of the accounting period:

a. On 1 November 20X5, Triple Y invested $75,000 excess cash in an interest-bearing investment for a yield of 4%. Interest will be paid at maturity at the end of April 20X6. The investment has been recorded but the interest for the year has not.

b. Triple Y has a term loan from its bank, of $200,000. Interest at the rate of 6% per annum is paid at the end of each month. Interest for December was not paid until 2 January, in an oversight. A payment of $10,000 principal was also paid on 2 January 20X6.

c. At the beginning of 20X5, office supplies inventory amounted to $600. At the end of 20X5, a count of inventory showed that there was $750 on hand. During 20X5, office supplies amounting to $8,800 were purchased and the inventory account was increased as a result.

d. At the beginning of 20X5, there was a balance of $4,960 in the prepaid insurance account related to a general fire insurance policy that will expire on 1 May 20X6. There was also a prepaid amount of $1,500 relating to vehicle insurance, expiring 28 February 20X5. In 20X5, a six-month vehicle policy costing $4,800 was purchased on March 1, and a further six-month policy costing $5,160 was purchased after the first one expired. The policies purchased in 20X5 were debited to prepaid insurance.

e. A customer returned goods for full credit. The goods have a cost of $1,700 and a retail price of $6,700. The goods had been purchased by the customer on account and correctly recorded on initial sale. When the return was made, inventory was debited and accounts receivable credited for $1,700.

f. The bank statement indicates that the bank, in error, cashed a cheque on the company's bank account in December 20X5 for $4,600. This cheque was written by YYY Exports Limited, not Triple Y Exports. Triple Y has reported the issue to the bank, and the bank has promised to reverse the amount.

g. The accountant has reviewed the invoices that arrived in early January 20X6. The following items are for goods and services purchased or consumed in December: Target Advertising Limited $3,600, BlueWave Cell Communications, $650, Econ Electricity, $1,200, and Forward Oil, $3,200.

h. The accountant reviewed the invoices that were issued to customers in early January and noted the following sales that took place in December: Customer Lui, $54,000 (cost of goods shipped, $34,600), Customer O'Grady, $75,900 (cost of goods shipped, $54,100); and Customer Sami, $23,400 (cost of goods shipped, $12,900). Neither the sale nor the product removed from inventory was recorded in December.

i. There was a payroll of $45,600 paid on 3 January; this covered the period of 30 December to 3 January.

j. A tenant in the administration building pays $1,350 rent per month. The tenant paid one year's rent on 1 March 20X5. The cash received was credited to rental revenue at that time.

Required:

Give the adjusting entry (or entries) that should be made on 31 December 20X5, for each item. If an adjusting entry is not required, explain why. Prepare any reversing entries that might be appropriate.

★★ **AApp1-11 Adjusting Entries:** Set forth below is the adjusted trial balance of the Trough Corporation as of 31 March 20X2:

Account	Debit	Credit
Cash	$ 24,400	
Accounts receivable	71,000	
Merchandise inventory	86,000	
Prepaid rent	8,000	
Equipment	35,200	
Accumulated depreciation		$ 6,500
Accounts payable		40,100
Note payable		40,000
Accrued interest payable		800
Capital stock		10,000
Retained earnings		127,200
	$224,600	$224,600

The following information describes the company's April transactions and provides the data required for month-end adjustments:

- Cash sales were $85,900.
- Sales on account were $78,500.
- Repaid $10,000 of note payable principal on 1 April.
- Operating expenses of $25,000 were paid in cash.
- Collected $41,000 in cash from customers on account.
- Wrote off $2,000 of accounts receivable as uncollectible. No other accounts receivable are in doubt of collection.
- Shareholders invested $20,000 in the business in exchange for 1,000 common shares.
- Bought $82,000 of merchandise on account.
- Ending merchandise inventory was $53,400.
- Paid suppliers $37,000 on account.
- Spent $5,000 for advertising to take place in May 20X2.
- Paid $14,300 in cash for wages, and still owed $2,500 for wages at month-end.
- The rent had previously been paid in advance to 31 July 20X2.
- The equipment has a total useful life of 10 years, and salvage of $4,000. These estimates have not changed since the asset was first acquired.
- The note payable bears an interest rate of 6% per year, and interest is due on 1 May.

Required:

1. Journalize the April transactions and adjusting journal entries.
2. Prepare an SCI and SFP for the month of April.

★★ **AApp1-12 Entries and Financial Statements:** The trial balance for Computer Guru Consulting Ltd., on 31 December 20X2, for the 20X2 fiscal year. No adjustments have been made in 20X2.

connect

Cash	$ 11,300	
Accounts receivable	18,200	
Allowance for doubtful accounts		$ 650
Inventory	94,140	
Equipment	157,500	
Accumulated depreciation, equipment		24,200
Accounts payable		75,200
Unearned revenue		12,000
Note payable		94,000
Common shares		40,000
Retained earnings		96,000
Dividends	18,600	
Sales		850,000
Cost of goods sold	580,000	
Wages	196,000	
Operating expenses	69,800	
Sales salaries	46,510	

Other information:

a. The note payable had an interest rate of 6%. $50,000 was borrowed on 1 February, and the balance was borrowed on 1 June 20X2. No interest was paid in 20X2.

b. An inventory count showed that goods with a cost of $89,200 were on hand at the end of the year.

c. Operating expenses include an insurance policy that was effective on 1 January 20X2 and runs for three years. The policy cost $5,400.

d. An unpaid supplier invoice for heating oil for $3,600 has been recorded for $6,300 in error.

e. A customer paid a $9,000 down payment on a job in December; this amount was credited to unearned revenue. The job is about 50% complete but has not been finished or reviewed with the customer. The remaining $3,000 in unearned revenue is an advance from a customer, for a job that has been cancelled; this amount will be refunded to the customer shortly.

f. Depreciation on equipment has not yet been recorded. The equipment is three years old at the end of 20X2, and estimates of useful life and salvage value have not changed since it was acquired. Depreciation is recorded on a straight-line basis.

g. A review of invoices sent to customers in January 20X3 showed that sales of $41,200 actually took place in December. These sales were connected with goods that cost $13,400. The product had been physically removed from inventory in December, and inventory and cost of sales were properly recorded in December. Sales were not recorded until January.

h. A review of invoices and payments in early January 20X3 showed some expenses that were related to December but not recorded until January: operating expenses, $5,675, and sales salaries, $4,200.

i. A payment for business operating expenses was made by one of the shareholders in 20X2, and he then submitted the $12,500 invoice for payment. When he was reimbursed, the amount was debited to dividends.

j. Accounts receivable were reviewed, and it was determined that $6,500 of accounts receivable are unlikely to be collected, although the company is still making collection attempts. (Percentage of accounts receivable method is used by the company.)

Required:

1. Record adjusting entries, as needed, for the additional information provided above.
2. Calculate the revised earnings for the period, reflecting the adjustments in requirement 1.
3. Record any reversing entries that are appropriate.

★★ **AApp1-13 Adjustments and Financial Statements:** Dan Richards incorporated an appliance repair shop on 1 January 20X2 and has been quite pleased with the results of his first year. His cash receipts and disbursements are:

Inflows:

Repair revenue received	$49,000
Rent revenue received	6,000
Cash refunds from suppliers, for returned parts	1,200
Cash originally invested by Dan	3,000
Bank loan	18,000
	$77,200

Outflows:

Wages paid	18,000
Dividends paid	3,400
Parts and supplies paid for	9,000
Insurance premiums paid	2,000
Rent paid	12,500
Equipment purchased	9,500
Other operating expenses paid	2,000
	$56,400

Other information:

- Equipment has a 10-year life and a $500 salvage value and is to be depreciated using the declining-balance method, using a rate of 20%.
- Parts still on hand amount to $2,760.
- The insurance premium was paid on 1 August for an eight-month policy.
- Rental revenue is from a tenant who rents excess space. She paid 12 months rent on 1 April when she moved in.
- Dan owes his workers another $1,200 in wages, and customers owe him $7,560 for repair work done.
- Dan owes his suppliers $1,490 for parts.
- The bank loan was taken out on 1 March and has an interest rate of 12%.
- Bad debts are likely 4% of repair revenue.
- Rent paid was for the 12-month calendar year of 20X2. Dan must also pay 1% of repair revenue to his landlord but has not done this yet.
- For simplicity, assume that there are no income taxes.

Required:

1. Prepare an SCI for Dan for the year ended 31 December 20X2.
2. Prepare an SFP as of 31 December 20X2.

★★ **AApp1-14 Adjustments and Statement of Financial Position:** On 31 December 20X4, the Hearth & Stove Corp. is preparing financial statements. The following unadjusted trial balance has been prepared:

HEARTH & STOVE CORP.

Trial Balance

	Debit	Credit
Accounts payable		$ 44,300
Accounts receivable	$ 211,090	
Advertising expense	12,800	
Accumulated depreciation—office equipment		39,800
Allowance for doubtful accounts		4,500
Cash	16,800	
Cost of goods sold	660,000	
Common shares		45,000
Dividends declared	10,400	
Insurance expense	1,800	
Interest expense	2,640	
Interest revenue		840
Inventory	50,000	
Land	145,000	
Long-term investments	312,600	
Mortgage payable		297,000
Notes payable—short term		10,800
Office equipment	72,000	
Office expense	13,100	
Prepaid insurance	0	
Retained earnings, opening		45,820
Revenue received in advance		34,800
Sales		1,222,000
Supplies inventory	400	
Supplies expense	4,200	
Miscellaneous expense	15,430	
Rent expense	72,000	
Wages expense	144,600	
	$1,744,860	$1,744,860

The following facts are also available at the end of 20X4:

a. The inventory on hand is $46,700 according to the physical count.
b. The allowance for doubtful accounts should have a balance of $5,600.
c. The office equipment is depreciated at a rate of 8% per year (straight-line).
d. There are supplies of $1,200 on hand.
e. On 31 March of this year, the company bought a $1,800 insurance policy with a 12-month term.
f. Customers have not yet been billed for products delivered on the last day of the year. The products have a retail value of $54,000. The cost of goods sold for this transaction was properly recorded.
g. Income tax is estimated to be 40% of all earnings before income tax. No income tax has been recorded or paid.

Required:

1. Prepare adjusting journal entries to reflect the information in (a) to (g) above.
2. Prepare a statement of changes in equity in good form that reflects the trial balance above and your journal entries. There were no changes to common shares during the year.
3. Prepare a classified SFP in good form that reflects the trial balance above and your journal entries.

★★ **AApp1-15 Adjustments and Financial Statements:** Toronado Ltd. reported the following items in its unadjusted trial balance as of 31 December 20X4 for the 20X4 fiscal year.

This trial balance is listed in alphabetical order. Note that this is a *partial* trial balance and does not include all accounts. Accounts have normal (debit or credit) balances.

Administration expense	$ 235,700
Accounts payable	76,800
Accounts receivable	99,800
Allowance for doubtful accounts (credit)	2,000
Cash dividends declared	31,000
Freight-out (delivery to customers)	26,900
Gain on sale of automobile	1,400
Insurance expense	38,400
Interest expense	27,100
Loans receivable, 8%	75,000
Merchandise inventory, 1 January	89,400
Notes payable, 6%	500,000
Purchases	560,300
Salaries and employee benefits	120,900
Sales returns and allowances	42,100
Sales revenues	1,876,000
Selling expense	34,000
Supplies expense	45,900
Supplies inventory	600
Retained earnings, 1 January	568,300
Unearned revenue	32,000
Utilities expense	65,400

Other information:

- The tax rate is 30%, but no tax has yet been recorded.
- Closing merchandise inventory is $76,500. Closing supplies inventory is $1,300.
- The insurance expense represents a payment made on 1 May for a 24-month fire insurance policy.
- Customers owe $53,000 for goods delivered on 31 December; this amount has not yet been recorded.
- All sales are on account, except those that are prepaid.
- Unearned revenue represents all customer deposits received during the year. Of this amount, 60% is still unearned at the end of the year.
- Bad debt expense is to be recognized as 1% of total sales.
- Interest on the note payable was last paid and recorded on 31 October.
- The company owes $3,200 in utilities.
- Interest on the loan receivable has not been paid or recorded all year.

Required:

1. Prepare journal entries to reflect the required adjustments. Round adjustments to the nearest $100, if necessary.
2. Prepare an SCI based on the adjusted balances.
3. Prepare a statement of changes in equity (for retained earnings only) based on the adjusted balances.

★

AApp1-16 Preparing a Statement of Financial Position: Your assistant has prepared the following *partial* adjusted trial balance data for the Green Solutions Cleaning Products Corporation as of 31 December 20X8. The accounts are arranged in alphabetical order; unfortunately, the debit and credit balances have been listed in the same column. Some revenue, expense, gain or loss accounts may be missing.

Accounts payable	$ 288,000
Accounts receivable	537,600
Accumulated depreciation—buildings	158,400
Accumulated depreciation—equipment	80,000
Advertising expense	38,400

Bonds payable	1,320,000
Buildings	576,000
Capital stock	428,000
Cash	96,000
Depreciation expense—buildings	64,000
Depreciation expense—equipment	12,000
Dividends declared	115,200
Dividends payable	50,000
Equipment	434,240
Expired insurance	11,600
Interest earned	4,590
Interest receivable	2,400
Inventory (merchandise) (closing balance)	484,800
Land	556,800
Long-term investments	436,800
Mortgage payable	384,000
Notes payable—short term	120,000
Office expenses	128,160
Premium on bonds payable	10,000
Prepaid insurance	6,000
Property tax expense	60,960
Retained earnings—31 December 20X7	78,720
Sales	1,968,000
Supplies on hand	6,500
Unearned revenue	12,400

Required:

Prepare the 31 December 20X8 SFP. For the closing retained earnings, use the value that will make the statement balance.

★★ **AApp1-17 ASPE—Preparing Financial Statements:** The following trial balance for Falcon Corporation is in alphabetical order.

31 December 20X7	Debit	Credit
Accounts payable		235,900
Accounts receivable	344,000	
Accumulated amortization, building		200,700
Allowance for doubtful accounts		46,200
Bank loans payable short term		460,000
Building	456,000	
Cash	26,500	
Common shares		170,000
Cost of goods sold	933,100	
Dividends	24,000	
Income tax expense	116,000	
Interest expense	52,100	
Inventory, 31 December 20X7	291,700	
Land	36,000	
Long-term bond payable		120,000
Long-term investments	230,000	
Notes receivable—short term	100,000	
Office supplies	3,600	
Operating expenses	458,000	
Operating expenses payable		48,900
Prepaid insurance	1,500	
Rent revenue		24,700
Retained earnings (1 January 20X7)		44,300
Sales		1,822,200
Selling expenses	107,800	
Unearned revenue		4,000
Wages payable		3,400
	$3,180,300	$3,180,300

Required:

1. Prepare an income statement from the information given.
2. Prepare a balance sheet and a statement of retained earnings.

★★ **AApp1-18 Entries and Worksheet:** Pinehill Ltd. is a retail operation that uses a perpetual inventory system. The unadjusted trial balance for the year ended 31 December 20X8 follows:

PINEHILL LTD.

Unadjusted Trial Balance

Cash	$ 50,000	
Accounts receivable	150,000	
Allowance for doubtful accounts		$ 12,000
Merchandise inventory	305,000	
Store equipment	160,000	
Accumulated depreciation, store equipment		20,000
Accounts payable		200,000
Loan payable—long term		134,000
Common shares		120,000
Retained earnings		66,000
Sales revenue		1,560,000
Sales returns and allowances	35,000	
Cost of goods sold	987,000	
Selling expenses	345,000	
Administrative expenses	80,000	
	$2,112,000	$2,112,000

Additional information:

- The allowance for doubtful accounts should have a balance of $15,000. This is a selling expense.
- The company uses a perpetual inventory system, but the closing inventory is verified by physical count. This count showed that the correct balance for closing inventory is $289,000.
- No depreciation has been recorded for 20X8. The store equipment is being amortized using the straight-line method over an estimated useful life of eight years with no residual value. This is a selling expense.
- The long-term loan was a two-year loan from a local bank. The interest rate is 6%, payable at the end of each 12-month period. The money was borrowed on 1 May 20X8. This is an administrative expense.
- The income tax rate is 40%; no tax has yet been paid or recorded.

Required:

1. Prepare adjusting entries for the year ended 31 December 20X8.
2. Complete the year-end worksheet. Combine the SFP and retained earnings columns.

★★ **AApp1-19 Entries and Worksheet:** The following information pertains to the first year of operations for Carmen Corp.:

CARMEN CORP.
Unadjusted Trial Balance

31 December 20X6	Debit	Credit
Cash	$ 5,100	
Accounts receivable	11,700	
Office equipment	6,900	
Computer equipment	5,400	
Accounts payable		7,550
Loan payable—long term		30,000
Common shares		70
Sales revenue		36,300
Rent expense	12,000	
Supplies inventory	18,100	
Interest expense	2,100	
Insurance expense	1,320	
Miscellaneous expense	11,300	
	$73,920	$73,920

Additional information:

a. On 1 July, the company signed a five-year lease for office space in a new industrial park. The company moved immediately. Rent is $1,500 per month and some rent was paid upfront as a deposit.

b. On 15 June, the company borrowed $30,000 from the bank. Interest at 14% is payable at the middle of every month. Payments have been made to date.

c. Leasehold improvements were made to the rented premises. Total cost for such things as partitions, painting, and wiring was $8,000 and was charged to miscellaneous expense.

d. Used computer equipment was purchased at an auction for $5,400. It was worth $9,000.

e. There was one job completed at year-end but not billed in the amount of $10,000.

f. Bad debts relating to the year-end accounts receivable are expected to be $350.

g. Year-end accounting fees are estimated to be $1,800.

h. On 1 October the company bought a used car for $7,600. Although the vehicle was to be used primarily on company business, the owner/manager used personal funds to pay for it. Consequently no entry was made in the books of the company. The company will repay the owner/manager when there is enough money.

i. The following depreciation and amortization policies are to be used; a full year of depreciation is charged in the first year of ownership. There are no residual values.

> Office and computer equipment: 5 years straight line
> Vehicles: 8 years straight line
> Leasehold improvements: 5 years straight line

j. Supplies inventory was $3,000 at the year-end count.

k. The effective tax rate for the company is 25%.

Required:

1. Prepare the adjusting journal entries required at year-end (31 December 20X6).
2. Complete the year-end worksheet. Combine the retained earnings and SFP columns.

★★★ **AApp1-20 ASPE—The Accounting Cycle:** At 31 December 20X5, the post-closing trial balance of Fox Ltd., a retailer of health food supplements, reflects the following:

Acct. No.	Account	Debit	Credit
101	Cash	$ 81,000	
102	Accounts receivable	63,000	
103	Allowance for doubtful accounts		$ 3,000
104	Inventory (perpetual inventory system)	105,000	
105	Prepaid insurance (20 months remaining at 1 January)	2,700	
200	Equipment (20-year estimated life, no residual value)	150,000	
201	Accumulated amortization, equipment		67,500
300	Accounts payable		22,500
301	Wages payable		—
302	Income taxes payable (for 20X5)		12,000
400	Common shares, no-par, 100,000 shares		240,000
401	Retained earnings		56,700
500	Sales revenue		—
600	Cost of goods sold	—	
601	Operating expenses	—	
602	Income tax expense	—	
700	Income summary	—	
		$401,700	$401,700

The following transactions occurred during 20X6 in the order given (use the letter at the left in place of date):

a. Sales revenue of $90,000, of which $30,000 was on credit; cost of goods sold, provided by perpetual inventory record, $58,500. (*Note:* When the perpetual system is used, make two entries to record a sale: *first*, debit cash or accounts receivable and credit sales revenue; *second*, debit cost of goods sold and credit inventory.)
b. Collected $51,000 on accounts receivable.
c. Paid income taxes payable (20X5), $12,000.
d. Purchased merchandise, $120,000, of which $24,000 was on credit.
e. Paid accounts payable, $18,000.
f. Sales revenue of $216,000 (in cash); cost of goods sold, $140,400.
g. Paid operating expenses, $57,000.
h. Issued 1,000 common shares for $3,000 cash.
i. Purchased merchandise, $300,000, of which $81,000 was on credit.
j. Sales revenue of $294,000, of which $90,000 was on credit; cost of goods sold, $191,100.
k. Collected cash on accounts receivable, $78,000.
l. Paid accounts payable, $84,000.
m. Paid various operating expenses in cash, $54,000.

Required:

1. Journalize each of the transactions listed above for 20X6; use only a general journal.
2. Set up T-accounts in the general ledger for each of the accounts listed in the above trial balance, and enter the account number and 31 December 20X5 balance.
3. Post the journal entries; use posting reference numbers.
4. Prepare an unadjusted trial balance.
5. Journalize the adjusting entries and post them to the ledger. Assume a bad debt rate of 0.5% of credit sales for the period at 31 December 20X6; accrued wages were $900. The average income tax rate was 40%. Record straight-line amortization and insurance expense. Debit expenses to the operating expense account. (Check your work: Income tax expense is $35,352.)
6. Prepare an adjusted trial balance.
7. Prepare the income statement and balance sheet.
8. Journalize and post the closing entries.

9. Prepare a postclosing trial balance.

★★★ **AApp1-21 The Accounting Cycle:** The post-closing trial balance of Gensing Enterprises Limited, a farming operation, at 31 December 20X6, reflects the following:

Acct. No.	Account	Debit	Credit
101	Cash	$ 42,000	
102	Accounts receivable	35,800	
103	Allowance for doubtful accounts		$ 2,000
104	Inventory, 31 December 20X6	46,000	
105	Fertilizer and supplies inventory	6,700	
106	Prepaid insurance (expires at the end of November 20X7)	9,000	
200	Equipment	344,800	
201	Accumulated depreciation, equipment		124,600
202	Land	682,000	
300	Accounts payable		67,500
301	Unearned revenue		32,000
302	Notes payable		75,000
400	Common shares		400,000
401	Retained earnings		465,200
500	Sales revenue		—
600	Cost of goods sold	—	
601	Operating expenses	—	
700	Income summary	—	
		$1,166,300	$1,166,300

Various transactions occurred in 20X7:

a. Sales amounted to $767,000. Cash sales were 25% of the total, and the rest was on account.
b. At the beginning of the year, there was unearned revenue. This revenue was earned in 20X7, in addition to the sales transactions in part (a).
c. Operating expenses of $67,200 were paid in cash.
d. Fertilizer and other supplies were bought for $46,900, on credit.
e. Harvesting costs of $244,200 were paid. Harvesting costs of the crop are debited to inventory.
f. The cost of all goods sold for the period was $281,400. This should be recorded as a journal entry that increases cost of goods sold and reduces the inventory account.
g. The opening accounts receivable were collected in the amount of $31,000. No accounts were written off. Seventy percent of the current year sales on account were also collected.
h. The opening balance of accounts payable was paid in full.
i. Ninety percent of the fertilizer and other supplies, bought on credit, were paid for.
j. Paid dividends of $22,000.
k. A $10,800, 12-month insurance policy was paid on 1 December. The amount was debited to prepaid insurance.
l. A contract was signed with a customer for a certain quantity of next year's crop. The customer paid the full $50,000 price in cash in advance.
m. The note payable was partially repaid at the end of November, in the amount of $50,000. Interest of $5,500 was also paid on the entire note, all pertaining to 20X7. The remaining $25,000 balance of the note payable has an interest rate of 12% per annum. Interest must be accrued for the month of December 20X7 in requirement (5). The $25,000 balance is long term.

Required:

1. Journalize the transactions for 20X7. Use only a general journal. Debit all operating expenses to a general "operating expense" account, for simplicity. Add other accounts if needed. Interest expense is recorded in a separate account.

2. Set up T-accounts in the general ledger for each of the accounts listed in the above trial balance, and enter the account number and the 31 December balance.

3. Post the journal entries; use posting reference numbers. Assign new account numbers as needed.

4. Prepare an unadjusted trial balance.

5. Journalize and post the following adjusting journal entries:
   a. Depreciation for the year, $45,000.
   b. Bad debts are expected to be 2% of credit sales.
   c. Inventory of fertilizer and other supplies was $7,600 at year-end.
   d. Interest expense was accrued for December 20X7.
   e. Prepaid insurance expired.
   f. Wages earned but unpaid at year-end, $5,000.

   Debit expenses other than interest to operating expenses, and payables to accounts payable, for simplicity. There is no income tax.

6. Prepare an adjusted trial balance.

7. Prepare the SCI and SFP.

8. Journalize and post the closing entries.

9. Prepare a post-closing trial balance.

10. For which adjusting journal entries in requirement 5 above would reversing entries be appropriate? Explain.

★★★   **AApp1-22 Worksheet, Adjusting and Closing Entries, Statements:** Darma Corporation is currently completing the end-of-the-period accounting process. At 31 December

 20X5, the following unadjusted trial balance was developed from the general ledger:

Account	Debit	Credit
Cash	$ 120,520	
Accounts receivable	76,000	
Allowance for doubtful accounts		$ 4,000
Interest receivable	0	
Inventory (perpetual inventory system)	210,000	
Sales supplies inventory	1,800	
Long-term note receivable, 14%	24,000	
Equipment	360,000	
Accumulated depreciation, equipment		128,000
Patent (net)	16,800	
Accounts payable		46,000
Interest payable		0
Property tax payable		0
Rent collected in advance		0
Mortgage payable, 12%		120,000
Common shares, no-par, 10,000 shares		230,000
Retained earnings		64,880
Sales revenue		1,400,000
Investment revenue		2,240
Rent revenue		6,000
Cost of goods sold	760,000	
Selling expenses	328,800	
General and administrative expenses	110,000	
Interest expense	13,200	
Discontinued operations gain (pretax)		20,000
	$2,021,120	$2,021,120

Additional data for adjustments and other purposes:

a. Estimated bad debt loss rate is 0.25% of credit sales. Credit sales for the year amounted to $400,000; classify as a selling expense.

b. Interest on the long-term note receivable was last collected and recorded on 31 August 20X5.

c. Estimated useful life of the equipment is 10 years; residual value, $40,000. Allocate 10% of depreciation expense to general and administrative expense and the balance to selling expense to reflect proportionate use. Use straight-line depreciation.

d. Estimated remaining economic life of the patent is 14 years (from 1 January 20X5) with no residual value. Use straight-line depreciation, and classify as selling expense (used in sales promotion).

e. Interest on the mortgage payable was last paid and recorded on 30 November 20X5.

f. On 1 June 20X5, the company rented office space to a tenant for one year and collected $6,000 rent in advance for the year; the entire amount was credited to rent revenue on this date.

g. On 31 December 20X5, the company received a statement for calendar-year 20X5 property taxes amounting to $2,600. The payment is due 15 February 20X6. Classify the adjustment as a selling expense.

h. Sales supplies on hand at 31 December 20X5 amounted to $600; classify as a selling expense.

i. Assume an average 40% corporate income tax rate on all items including the discontinued operations gain. (Check your work: Total income tax expense is $70,264.)

Required:

1. Enter the above unadjusted trial balance on a worksheet.
2. Complete the worksheet.
3. Prepare the SCI and SFP.
4. Journalize the closing entries.

★★★ **AApp1-23 Perform All Accounting Cycle Steps:** Construction Resources Limited (CRL), a calendar-year firm, began operations as a retailer in January 20X5.

Information about transactions and adjustments in 20X5:

1. Investors contributed $500,000 in exchange for 70,000 shares of no-par common shares.

2. CRL obtained a 6%, $500,000 bank loan on 1 February. This loan is evidenced by a signed promissory note calling for interest payments every 1 February. The note is due in full on 31 January 20X9.

3. A rental contract for production and office facilities was signed on 1 February, which required $12,000 immediate payment covering both the first month's rent and a $7,000 deposit refundable in three years or upon termination of the contract, whichever occurs first. Monthly rent is $5,000. As an added incentive to pay rent in advance, CRL accepted an offer to maintain rent at $5,000 per month for the first three years if CRL paid the 2nd through the 13th (March 20X5 through February 20X6) months' rent immediately. In all, CRL paid $72,000 for rent on 1 February. CRL intends to occupy the facilities for at least three years.

4. Equipment costing $350,000 was purchased for cash in early February. It has an estimated residual value of $35,000 and a six-year useful life. CRL uses the straight-line method of depreciation. A full year of depreciation is recorded in the year of acquisition.

5. CRL recognized various cash operating expenses for the year, including the following:

Wages	$310,000
Utilities	47,000
Selling	92,000
General and administrative	198,000

6. Total merchandise inventory purchases for the year, on account, amounted to $4,815,000.

7. All suppliers were paid for except for $90,000 outstanding at year-end.

8. All sales are made on credit and totalled $5,900,000 in 20X5; $4,925,000 was collected on account during the year. CRL estimates that 0.5% of total sales will be uncollectible and has written off $12,000 of accounts. The inventory sold had a cost of $4,447,000.

9. CRL declared a cash dividend of $114,000, payable in January 20X6.

10. Income tax expense is $342,000. All taxes for a fiscal year are payable in April of the following year.

Required:

Perform the 10 accounting cycle steps for CRL for 20X5. Worksheets, special journals, and subsidiary ledgers are not required. Prepare journal entries in summary (for the year) form. Post to T-accounts. CRL uses the expedient recording system and records reversing entries, whenever appropriate. CRL uses a perpetual inventory system.

 AApp1-24 Special Journals: Imported Delights Limited had the following transactions in April 20X5:

April

4   Sold goods to customers on account, $35,600. The cost of these goods was $14,200.

9   Sold goods to customers for cash, $78,200. The cost of these goods was $24,700.

10 Paid electricity bill, $1,900.

14 Received payment from customers for 60% of 4 April sale.

14 Sold goods to customer on account, $100,700. The cost of these goods was $51,900.

15 Repaid note payable of $50,000, borrowed and properly recorded in January, plus $565 interest.

16 Received goods back from customer of 4 April and issued a credit note for $5,200. The cost of these goods was $2,200.

16 Bought merchandise inventory from a supplier on credit, $31,100.

17 Returned merchandise inventory to supplier from order of 16 April and got a credit note of $3,600.

22 Paid wages and salaries, $53,700.

22 Board of Directors declared a $23,000 dividend. The dividend was both recorded and paid on this date.

24 Purchased merchandise inventory from a supplier on credit, $58,200.

25 Purchased merchandise inventory with cash, $7,350.

26 Borrowed $90,000 from the bank, and signed a 120-day, 8% note payable.

28 Bought office supplies on credit, $3,250.

29 Bought machinery, and issued a 120-day, 12% note payable for the full amount of $68,200.

30 Paid net amount due to supplier for goods purchased on 16 April.

31 Recorded depreciation expense on plant machinery of $9,400 for the month of April.

Required:

1. Draft special journals for cash receipts, cash disbursements, sales, and purchases. Also open a general journal.

2. Record the transactions in the appropriate journal. Leave the column blank if details (e.g., name or account number) are not available. There are no discounts offered to or by the company, so all sales and purchases are recorded gross.

 ★ **AApp1-25 Special Journals:** Gagetron Limited uses a perpetual inventory system. The company maintains special journals:

• Purchases (merchandise inventory for resale);

• Sales (sales on account and the related cost of goods sold);

- Cash receipts (all cash receipts, including payment by customers on account, and cash sales and the related cost of goods sold, but also miscellaneous receipts); and
- Cash disbursements (payments to suppliers on account, but also miscellaneous payments).

The company also maintains a general journal.

The company has the following transactions during the year:

a. Collected $99,800 from customers on account.
b. Collected $67,800 from customers for cash sales; these goods had a cost of $40,700.
c. Sold merchandise on account, $84,800; these goods had a cost of $51,000.
d. Bought merchandise inventory on credit, $395,600.
e. Paid $56,000 for dividends to common shareholders.
f. Paid $12,800 for rent.
g. Borrowed $50,000 from the bank.
h. Accepted a return from a customer and cancelled the related $10,700 sale. These goods had a cost of $6,200.
i. Paid for $272,800 of the inventory previously bought on credit.
j. Return merchandise inventory purchased on credit to the supplier, in the amount of $14,600.

Required:

Indicate the journal in which each of the above transactions would be recorded.

★★ **AApp1-26 Special Journals:** Solid Fields Limited had transactions in August 20X5 as follows:

August

3   Sold merchandise on account to Duane Kennerly, Invoice No. 902, $44,300. (Terms of all credit sales are 2/10, n/30 and sales are recorded at the gross amount.) The inventory sold cost $16,100.

3   Issued cheque No. 546 to Downtown Property Management Limited for rent, $2,175.

3   Issued cheque No. 547 to Charles Milbury for travel costs, $511.

3   Received merchandise and an invoice dated 31 July, terms n/15, from Worthy Company, $97,800.

3   Purchased office equipment on account from Dee Limited Company, invoice dated 3 August, terms n/10 EOM, $62,625.

8   Issued cheque No. 548 to *The Chronicle News* for advertising, $975.

10   Issued cheque No. 549 to Worthy Company in payment of its 31 July invoice.

11   Sold unneeded office supplies at cost for cash, $160.

16   Sold merchandise on account to Sally Gunz, invoice No. 903, $10,735. The inventory sold cost $5,400.

18   Received payment from Duane Kennerly for the sale of 3 August.

20   Received merchandise and an invoice dated 18 August, terms n/60, from WayMobile Company, $47,500.

21   Issued a credit memorandum to Sally Gunz for defective merchandise sold on 16 August and returned for credit, $3,835. The merchandise returned was not saleable and was destroyed.

24   Received a $4,700 credit memorandum from WayMobile Company for defective merchandise received on 20 August and returned for credit.

25   Purchased on account from The Office Stop, merchandise inventory, $42,500, invoice dated 25 August, terms n/10 EOM.

26   Received payment from Sally Gunz for the 16 August sale. She paid the net amount due within the discount period and deducted 2% from the amount owing.

28   Issued cheque No. 550 to WayMobile Company in payment of its 20 August invoice, less the purchase return.

30   Cash sales for the month ended 30 August were $61,230. The inventory sold cost $9,600.

Required:

1. Draft special journals for cash receipts, cash disbursements, sales, and purchases. The company also maintains a general journal.

2. Record the transactions in the appropriate journal. Leave columns blank if details (e.g., account numbers) are not available. Sales are recorded at the gross amount.

★★ **AApp1-27 Special Journals:** Calm Seas Limited had the following transactions in September 20X5:

Sept.

1 Purchased inventory for cash, $5,600.

1 Purchased inventory from a supplier on credit, terms 2/10, n/30, $13,400.

2 Purchased $35,000 of automotive equipment for cash.

2 Purchased office equipment by issuing a note payable, $15,700.

5 Purchased inventory of $54,300 on account, terms 1/15, n/30.

10 Sold merchandise for $16,900 to a customer on account, terms 2/10, n/30. The inventory sold cost $7,600. Sales are recorded at the gross amount.

12 Received a credit memo from the supplier re: the inventory acquired on 5 September, $3,200 gross ($3,168 net).

12 Borrowed $70,000 from the bank at an interest rate of 4%.

13 Paid the supplier for the net purchase of 5 September.

22 Received payment from the customer re: sale on 10 September. This cheque was issued within the discount period.

25 Paid salaries of $6,200.

29 Cash sales for the month of September amounted to $97,250. The inventory sold cost $42,160.

Required:

1. Draft special journals for cash receipts, cash disbursements, sales, and purchases. The company also maintains a general journal.

2. Record the transactions in the appropriate journal. Leave columns blank if details (e.g., account numbers) are not available. Inventory and sales are recorded at the net amount.

★★★ **AApp1-28 Transactions and Financial Statements:** Multimedia Incorporated, a producer of graphics and artwork for movie theatres and other media distributors, provided the following information for 20X5:

Selected Accounts from the Statement of Financial Position, as of 1 January 20X5

Accounts receivable	$ 10,000
Prepaid insurance	20,000
Supplies	5,000
Equipment (net)	80,000
Accounts payable (suppliers)	40,000*
Unearned rent	13,000
Wages payable	7,000
Common shares	27,000
Retained earnings	50,000

*The 31 December 20X5 balance is $50,000.

Statement of Comprehensive Income, year ended 31 December 20X5

Sales	$200,000
Insurance expense	(15,000)
Depreciation expense	(10,000)
Supplies expense	(30,000)
Wages expense	(60,000)
Rent revenue	12,000
Net earnings and comprehensive income	$ 97,000

Statement of Cash Flows, year ended 31 December 20X5

Operating activities:

Collections from customers	$ 90,000
Insurance payments	(25,000)
Payments to suppliers	(45,000)
Payments to employees	(52,000)
Rental receipts	19,000
Net operating cash flow	$ (13,000)
Cash balance, 1 January 20X5	22,000
Cash balance, 31 December 20X5*	$ 9,000

*No investing or financing cash flows.

Required:
Prepare the 31 December 20X5 SCF for Multimedia.

★★ **AApp1-29 Transactions and Financial Statements:** During the first week of January 20X8, James Kenna began an energy-efficiency consulting company, Power Smart Limited. He kept no formal accounting records; however, his record of cash receipts and disbursements was accurate. The business got off to a strong start, but James soon needed financing for day-to-day expenses. He approached his bank for a $40,000 loan and was told that he needed accrual-based SCI and SFP before he would be approved. Knowing very little about accounting, he engaged you to prepare statements requested by the bank. He supplies you with the following information:

	Receipts	Disbursements
Investment	$ 30,000	
Computer and office equipment		$ 75,200
Operating expenses		15,700
Supplies		12,700
Rent payments		12,600
Insurance premium		5,400
Advertising—all ads complete		9,800
Wages of assistant		46,200
Telephone		12,940
Payments to James Kenna		87,000
Received from customers	254,500	
Cash balance		6,960
	$284,500	$284,500

Additional information:

- Equipment purchased includes a $2,000 computer purchased for James' son, for school projects.
- The amount received from customers includes a $5,000 deposit on a project to be done in January, but not yet started.
- Rent payments included $900 per month rental and $1,800 deposit.
- The equipment has an estimated five-year life and $1,200 salvage value.
- Supplies on hand 31 December 20X8 were $5,900.
- There were unpaid bills of $250 for cell phone, $540 for electricity, and $380 for travel at December 20X8.
- Insurance premium was for a three-year policy that expires on 31 December 20X10.
- Wages earned in the last week of December 20X8 to be paid in January 20X9 amounted to $900.
- Design revenue earned but not yet collected amounted to $41,400.
- The organization is set up as a company; the $87,000 withdrawn by James is $74,000 salary and $13,000 dividends.

Required:

Prepare the financial statements as requested.

(CGA-Canada, adapted)

★★ **AApp1-30 Transactions and Financial Statements:** Shirt Shack Limited is a retail store operating in a downtown shopping mall. On 1 January 20X8, it reported the following:

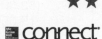

SHIRT SHACK LIMITED

Statement of Financial Position

As of 1 January 20X8

Cash	$ 4,000
Accounts receivable (net of allowance of $2,000)	28,000
Prepaid rent (rental deposit)	1,000
Inventory	36,000
Leasehold improvements (net)	16,000
Total assets	$85,000
Accounts payable	$32,000
Accrued wages payable	3,500
Accrued interest payable	200
Accrued rent payable	0
Notes payable, 10%	14,800
Common shares	10,000
Retained earnings	24,500
Total liabilities plus equity	$85,000

During 20X8, the company reported the following:

a. Cash paid to employees (salaries and commissions), $67,000. Cash paid to suppliers, $90,000.
b. Cash collected from customers, $220,000.
c. On 31 December 20X8, a physical inventory count revealed that inventory was $42,000.
d. At 31 December 20X8, customers owed Shirt Shack $35,000, and the company owed its suppliers $14,000. Of the accounts receivable, aging analysis indicated that $4,000 was expected to be uncollectible. No accounts were written off in 20X8.
e. Cash paid to landlord, $12,000 ($1,000 per month for 12 months). Shirt Shack is required to pay monthly rent and, at year-end, make an additional payment to bring the total rent expense up to 10% of sales. This payment will be made in January 20X9.
f. Cash paid for miscellaneous operating expenses, $6,000.
g. Cash paid in dividends, $14,500; in interest, $1,680. No interest is owing at 31 December 20X8.
h. Shirt Shack owed employees $500 in wages and $1,000 in commissions at year-end.
i. The leasehold improvements were acquired on 1 January 20X7. They had an expected life of 10 years and were installed in leased premises that had a five-year lease on 1 January 20X7.

Required:

1. Prepare journal entries for all transactions and needed adjustments.
2. Prepare an SCI for the year ended 31 December 20X8. Ignore income tax.
3. Show all calculations.

connect LEARNSMART SMARTBOOK

For more information on the resources available from McGraw-Hill Ryerson, go to www.mcgrawhill.ca/he/solutions.

TABLE I-1: Present value of 1: (P/F, i, n)

$$P/F = \frac{1}{(1 + i)^n}$$

n	2%	2.5%	3%	4%	5%	6%	7%	8%	9%	10%	11%	12%	14%	15%
1	0.98039	0.97561	0.97087	0.96154	0.95238	0.94340	0.93458	0.92593	0.91743	0.90909	0.90090	0.89286	0.87719	0.86957
2	0.96117	0.95181	0.94260	0.92456	0.90703	0.89000	0.87344	0.85734	0.84168	0.82645	0.81162	0.79719	0.76947	0.75614
3	0.94232	0.92860	0.91514	0.88900	0.86384	0.83962	0.81630	0.79383	0.77218	0.75131	0.73119	0.71178	0.67497	0.65752
4	0.92385	0.90595	0.88849	0.85480	0.82270	0.79209	0.76290	0.73503	0.70843	0.68301	0.65873	0.63552	0.59208	0.57175
5	0.90573	0.88385	0.86261	0.82193	0.78353	0.74726	0.71299	0.68058	0.64993	0.62092	0.59345	0.56743	0.51937	0.49718
6	0.88797	0.86230	0.83748	0.79031	0.74622	0.70496	0.66634	0.63017	0.59627	0.56447	0.53464	0.50663	0.45559	0.43233
7	0.87056	0.84127	0.81309	0.75992	0.71068	0.66506	0.62275	0.58349	0.54703	0.51316	0.48166	0.45235	0.39964	0.37594
8	0.85349	0.82075	0.78941	0.73069	0.67684	0.62741	0.58201	0.54027	0.50187	0.46651	0.43393	0.40388	0.35056	0.32690
9	0.83676	0.80073	0.76642	0.70259	0.64461	0.59190	0.54393	0.50025	0.46043	0.42410	0.39092	0.36061	0.30751	0.28426
10	0.82035	0.78120	0.74409	0.67556	0.61391	0.55839	0.50835	0.46319	0.42241	0.38554	0.35218	0.32197	0.26974	0.24718
11	0.80426	0.76214	0.72242	0.64958	0.58468	0.52679	0.47509	0.42888	0.38753	0.35049	0.31728	0.28748	0.23662	0.21494
12	0.78849	0.74356	0.70138	0.62460	0.55684	0.49697	0.44401	0.39711	0.35553	0.31863	0.28584	0.25668	0.20756	0.18691
13	0.77303	0.72542	0.68095	0.60057	0.53032	0.46884	0.41496	0.36770	0.32618	0.28966	0.25751	0.22917	0.18207	0.16253
14	0.75788	0.70773	0.66112	0.57748	0.50507	0.44230	0.38782	0.34046	0.29925	0.26333	0.23199	0.20462	0.15971	0.14133
15	0.74301	0.69047	0.64186	0.55526	0.48102	0.41727	0.36245	0.31524	0.27454	0.23939	0.20900	0.18270	0.14010	0.12289
16	0.72845	0.67362	0.62317	0.53391	0.45811	0.39365	0.33873	0.29189	0.25187	0.21763	0.18829	0.16312	0.12289	0.10686
17	0.71416	0.65720	0.60502	0.51337	0.43630	0.37136	0.31657	0.27027	0.23107	0.19784	0.16963	0.14564	0.10780	0.09293
18	0.70016	0.64117	0.58739	0.49363	0.41552	0.35034	0.29586	0.25025	0.21199	0.17986	0.15282	0.13004	0.09456	0.08081
19	0.68643	0.62553	0.57029	0.47464	0.39573	0.33051	0.27651	0.23171	0.19449	0.16351	0.13768	0.11611	0.08295	0.07027
20	0.67297	0.61027	0.55368	0.45639	0.37689	0.31180	0.25842	0.21455	0.17843	0.14864	0.12403	0.10367	0.07276	0.06110
21	0.65978	0.59539	0.53755	0.43883	0.35894	0.29416	0.24151	0.19866	0.16370	0.13513	0.11174	0.09256	0.06383	0.05313
22	0.64684	0.58086	0.52189	0.42196	0.34185	0.27751	0.22571	0.18394	0.15018	0.12285	0.10067	0.08264	0.05599	0.04620
23	0.63416	0.56670	0.50669	0.40573	0.32557	0.26180	0.21095	0.17032	0.13778	0.11168	0.09069	0.07379	0.04911	0.04017
24	0.62172	0.55288	0.49193	0.39012	0.31007	0.24698	0.19715	0.15770	0.12640	0.10153	0.08170	0.06588	0.04308	0.03493
25	0.60953	0.53939	0.47761	0.37512	0.29530	0.23300	0.18425	0.14602	0.11597	0.09230	0.07361	0.05882	0.03779	0.03038
26	0.59758	0.52623	0.46369	0.36069	0.28124	0.21981	0.17220	0.13520	0.10639	0.08391	0.06631	0.05252	0.03315	0.02642
27	0.58586	0.51340	0.45019	0.34682	0.26785	0.20737	0.16093	0.12519	0.09761	0.07628	0.05974	0.04689	0.02908	0.02297
28	0.57437	0.50088	0.43708	0.33348	0.25509	0.19563	0.15040	0.11591	0.08955	0.06934	0.05382	0.04187	0.02551	0.01997
29	0.56311	0.48866	0.42435	0.32065	0.24295	0.18456	0.14056	0.10733	0.08215	0.06304	0.04849	0.03738	0.02237	0.01737
30	0.55207	0.47674	0.41199	0.30832	0.23138	0.17411	0.13137	0.09938	0.07537	0.05731	0.04368	0.03338	0.01963	0.01510
31	0.54125	0.46511	0.39999	0.29646	0.22036	0.16425	0.12277	0.09202	0.06915	0.05210	0.03935	0.02980	0.01722	0.01313
32	0.53063	0.45377	0.38834	0.28506	0.20987	0.15496	0.11474	0.08520	0.06344	0.04736	0.03545	0.02661	0.01510	0.01142
33	0.52023	0.44270	0.37703	0.27409	0.19987	0.14619	0.10723	0.07889	0.05820	0.04306	0.03194	0.02376	0.01325	0.00993
34	0.51003	0.43191	0.36604	0.26355	0.19035	0.13791	0.10022	0.07305	0.05339	0.03914	0.02878	0.02121	0.01162	0.00864
35	0.50003	0.42137	0.35538	0.25342	0.18129	0.13011	0.09366	0.06763	0.04899	0.03558	0.02592	0.01894	0.01019	0.00751
36	0.49022	0.41109	0.34503	0.24367	0.17266	0.12274	0.08754	0.06262	0.04494	0.03235	0.02335	0.01691	0.00894	0.00653
37	0.48061	0.40107	0.33498	0.23430	0.16444	0.11579	0.08181	0.05799	0.04123	0.02941	0.02104	0.01510	0.00784	0.00568
38	0.47119	0.39128	0.32523	0.22529	0.15661	0.10924	0.07646	0.05369	0.03783	0.02673	0.01896	0.01348	0.00688	0.00494
39	0.46195	0.38174	0.31575	0.21662	0.14915	0.10306	0.07146	0.04971	0.03470	0.02430	0.01708	0.01204	0.00604	0.00429
40	0.45289	0.37243	0.30656	0.20829	0.14205	0.09722	0.06678	0.04603	0.03184	0.02209	0.01538	0.01075	0.00529	0.00373
45	0.41020	0.32917	0.26444	0.17120	0.11130	0.07265	0.04761	0.03133	0.02069	0.01372	0.00913	0.00610	0.00275	0.00186
50	0.37153	0.29094	0.22811	0.14071	0.08720	0.05429	0.03395	0.02132	0.01345	0.00852	0.00542	0.00346	0.00143	0.00092

TABLE I-2: Present value of an ordinary annuity of n payments of 1: $(P/A, i, n)$

$$P/A = \frac{1 - \dfrac{1}{(1+i)^n}}{i}$$

n	2%	2.5%	3%	4%	5%	6%	7%	8%	9%	10%	11%	12%	14%	15%
1	0.98039	0.97561	0.97087	0.96154	0.95238	0.94340	0.93458	0.92593	0.91743	0.90909	0.90090	0.89286	0.87719	0.86957
2	1.94156	1.92742	1.91347	1.88609	1.85941	1.83339	1.80802	1.78326	1.75911	1.73554	1.71252	1.69005	1.64666	1.62571
3	2.88388	2.85602	2.82861	2.77509	2.72325	2.67301	2.62432	2.57710	2.53129	2.48685	2.44371	2.40183	2.32163	2.28323
4	3.80773	3.76197	3.71710	3.62990	3.54595	3.46511	3.38721	3.31213	3.23972	3.16987	3.10245	3.03735	2.91371	2.85498
5	4.71346	4.64583	4.57971	4.45182	4.32948	4.21236	4.10020	3.99271	3.88965	3.79079	3.69590	3.60478	3.43308	3.35216
6	5.60143	5.50813	5.41719	5.24214	5.07569	4.91732	4.76654	4.62288	4.48592	4.35526	4.23054	4.11141	3.88867	3.78448
7	6.47199	6.34939	6.23028	6.00205	5.78637	5.58238	5.38929	5.20637	5.03295	4.86842	4.71220	4.56376	4.28830	4.16042
8	7.32548	7.17014	7.01969	6.73274	6.46321	6.20979	5.97130	5.74664	5.53482	5.33493	5.14612	4.96764	4.63886	4.48732
9	8.16224	7.97087	7.78611	7.43533	7.10782	6.80169	6.51523	6.24689	5.99525	5.75902	5.53705	5.32825	4.94637	4.77158
10	8.98259	8.75206	8.53020	8.11090	7.72173	7.36009	7.02358	6.71008	6.41766	6.14457	5.88923	5.65022	5.21612	5.01877
11	9.78685	9.51421	9.25262	8.76048	8.30641	7.88687	7.49867	7.13896	6.80519	6.49506	6.20652	5.93770	5.45273	5.23371
12	10.57534	10.25776	9.95400	9.38507	8.86325	8.38384	7.94269	7.53608	7.16073	6.81369	6.49236	6.19437	5.66029	5.42062
13	11.34837	10.98318	10.63496	9.98565	9.39357	8.85268	8.35765	7.90378	7.48690	7.10336	6.74987	6.42355	5.84236	5.58315
14	12.10625	11.69091	11.29607	10.56312	9.89864	9.29498	8.74547	8.24424	7.78615	7.36669	6.98187	6.62817	6.00207	5.72448
15	12.84926	12.38138	11.93794	11.11839	10.37966	9.71225	9.10791	8.55948	8.06069	7.60608	7.19087	6.81086	6.14217	5.84737
16	13.57771	13.05500	12.56110	11.65230	10.83777	10.10590	9.44665	8.85137	8.31256	7.82371	7.37916	6.97399	6.26506	5.95423
17	14.29187	13.71220	13.16612	12.16567	11.27407	10.47726	9.76322	9.12164	8.54363	8.02155	7.54879	7.11963	6.37286	6.04716
18	14.99203	14.35336	13.75351	12.65930	11.68959	10.82760	10.05909	9.37189	8.75563	8.20141	7.70162	7.24967	6.46742	6.12797
19	15.67846	14.97889	14.32380	13.13394	12.08532	11.15812	10.33560	9.60360	8.95011	8.36492	7.83929	7.36578	6.55037	6.19823
20	16.35143	15.58916	14.87747	13.59033	12.46221	11.46992	10.59401	9.81815	9.12855	8.51356	7.96333	7.46944	6.62313	6.25933
21	17.01121	16.18455	15.41502	14.02916	12.82115	11.76408	10.83553	10.01680	9.29224	8.64869	8.07507	7.56200	6.68696	6.31246
22	17.65805	16.76541	15.93692	14.45112	13.16300	12.04158	11.06124	10.20074	9.44243	8.77154	8.17574	7.64465	6.74294	6.35866
23	18.29220	17.33211	16.44361	14.85684	13.48857	12.30338	11.27219	10.37106	9.58021	8.88322	8.26643	7.71843	6.79206	6.39884
24	18.91393	17.88499	16.93554	15.24696	13.79864	12.55036	11.46933	10.52876	9.70661	8.98474	8.34814	7.78432	6.83514	6.43377
25	19.52346	18.42438	17.41315	15.62208	14.09394	12.78336	11.65358	10.67478	9.82258	9.07704	8.42174	7.84314	6.87293	6.46415
26	20.12104	18.95061	17.87684	15.98277	14.37519	13.00317	11.82578	10.80998	9.92897	9.16095	8.48806	7.89566	6.90608	6.49056
27	20.70690	19.46401	18.32703	16.32959	14.64303	13.21053	11.98671	10.93516	10.02658	9.23722	8.54780	7.94255	6.93515	6.51353
28	21.28127	19.96489	18.76411	16.66306	14.89813	13.40616	12.13711	11.05108	10.11613	9.30657	8.60162	7.98442	6.96066	6.53351
29	21.84438	20.45355	19.18845	16.98371	15.14107	13.59072	12.27767	11.15841	10.19828	9.36961	8.65011	8.02181	6.98304	6.55088
30	22.39646	20.93029	19.60044	17.29203	15.37245	13.76483	12.40904	11.25778	10.27365	9.42691	8.69379	8.05518	7.00266	6.56598
31	22.93770	21.39541	20.00043	17.58849	15.59281	13.92909	12.53181	11.34980	10.34280	9.47901	8.73315	8.08499	7.01988	6.57911
32	23.46833	21.84918	20.38877	17.87355	15.80268	14.08404	12.64656	11.43500	10.40624	9.52638	8.76860	8.11159	7.03498	6.59053
33	23.98856	22.29188	20.76579	18.14765	16.00255	14.23023	12.75379	11.51389	10.46444	9.56943	8.80054	8.13535	7.04823	6.60046
34	24.49859	22.72379	21.13184	18.41120	16.19290	14.36814	12.85401	11.58693	10.51784	9.60857	8.82932	8.15656	7.05985	6.60910
35	24.99862	23.14516	21.48722	18.66461	16.37419	14.49825	12.94767	11.65457	10.56682	9.64416	8.85524	8.17550	7.07005	6.61661
36	25.48884	23.55625	21.83225	18.90828	16.54685	14.62099	13.03521	11.71719	10.61176	9.67651	8.87859	8.19241	7.07899	6.62314
37	25.96945	23.95732	22.16724	19.14258	16.71129	14.73678	13.11702	11.77518	10.65299	9.70592	8.89963	8.20751	7.08683	6.62881
38	26.44064	24.34860	22.49246	19.36786	16.86789	14.84602	13.19347	11.82887	10.69082	9.73265	8.91859	8.22099	7.09371	6.63375
39	26.90259	24.73034	22.80822	19.58448	17.01704	14.94907	13.26493	11.87858	10.72552	9.75696	8.93567	8.23303	7.09975	6.63805
40	27.35548	25.10278	23.11477	19.79277	17.15909	15.04630	13.33171	11.92461	10.75736	9.77905	8.95105	8.24378	7.10504	6.64178
45	29.49016	26.83302	24.51871	20.72004	17.77407	15.45583	13.60552	12.10840	10.88120	9.86281	9.00791	8.28252	7.12322	6.65429
50	31.42361	28.36231	25.72976	21.48218	18.25593	15.76186	13.80075	12.23348	10.96168	9.91481	9.04165	8.30450	7.13266	6.66051

TABLE I-3: Present value of an annuity due of n payments of 1: (P/AD, i, n)

$$P/AD = \left[\frac{1 - \dfrac{1}{(1 + i)^n}}{i} \right] \times (1 + i)$$

n	2%	2.5%	3%	4%	5%	6%	7%	8%	9%	10%	11%	12%	14%	15%
1	1.00000	1.00000	1.00000	1.00000	1.00000	1.00000	1.00000	1.00000	1.00000	1.00000	1.00000	1.00000	1.00000	1.00000
2	1.98039	1.97561	1.97087	1.96154	1.95238	1.94340	1.93458	1.92593	1.91743	1.90909	1.90090	1.89286	1.87719	1.86957
3	2.94156	2.92742	2.91347	2.88609	2.85941	2.83339	2.80802	2.78326	2.75911	2.73554	2.71252	2.69005	2.64666	2.62571
4	3.88388	3.85602	3.82861	3.77509	3.72325	3.67301	3.62432	3.57710	3.53129	3.48685	3.44371	3.40183	3.32163	3.28323
5	4.80773	4.76197	4.71710	4.62990	4.54595	4.46511	4.38721	4.31213	4.23972	4.16987	4.10245	4.03735	3.91371	3.85498
6	5.71346	5.64583	5.57971	5.45182	5.32948	5.21236	5.10020	4.99271	4.88965	4.79079	4.69590	4.60478	4.43308	4.35216
7	6.60143	6.50813	6.41719	6.24214	6.07569	5.91732	5.76654	5.62288	5.48592	5.35526	5.23054	5.11141	4.88867	4.78448
8	7.47199	7.34939	7.23028	7.00205	6.78637	6.58238	6.38929	6.20637	6.03295	5.86842	5.71220	5.56376	5.28830	5.16042
9	8.32548	8.17014	8.01969	7.73274	7.46321	7.20979	6.97130	6.74664	6.53482	6.33493	6.14612	5.96764	5.63886	5.48732
10	9.16224	8.97087	8.78611	8.43533	8.10782	7.80169	7.51523	7.24689	6.99525	6.75902	6.53705	6.32825	5.94637	5.77158
11	9.98259	9.75206	9.53020	9.11090	8.72173	8.36009	8.02358	7.71008	7.41766	7.14457	6.88923	6.65022	6.21612	6.01877
12	10.78685	10.51421	10.25262	9.76048	9.30641	8.88687	8.49867	8.13896	7.80519	7.49506	7.20652	6.93770	6.45273	6.23371
13	11.57534	11.25776	10.95400	10.38507	9.86325	9.38384	8.94269	8.53608	8.16073	7.81369	7.49236	7.19437	6.66029	6.42062
14	12.34837	11.98318	11.63496	10.98565	10.39357	9.85268	9.35765	8.90378	8.48690	8.10336	7.74987	7.42355	6.84236	6.58315
15	13.10625	12.69091	12.29607	11.56312	10.89864	10.29498	9.74547	9.24424	8.78615	8.36669	7.98187	7.62817	7.00207	6.72448
16	13.84926	13.38138	12.93794	12.11839	11.37966	10.71225	10.10791	9.55948	9.06069	8.60608	8.19087	7.81086	7.14217	6.84737
17	14.57771	14.05500	13.56110	12.65230	11.83777	11.10590	10.44665	9.85137	9.31256	8.82371	8.37916	7.97399	7.26506	6.95423
18	15.29187	14.71220	14.16612	13.16567	12.27407	11.47726	10.76322	10.12164	9.54363	9.02155	8.54879	8.11963	7.37286	7.04716
19	15.99203	15.35336	14.75351	13.65930	12.68959	11.82760	11.05909	10.37189	9.75563	9.20141	8.70162	8.24967	7.46742	7.12797
20	16.67846	15.97889	15.32380	14.13394	13.08532	12.15812	11.33560	10.60360	9.95011	9.36492	8.83929	8.36578	7.55037	7.19823
21	17.35143	16.58916	15.87747	14.59033	13.46221	12.46992	11.59401	10.81815	10.12855	9.51356	8.96333	8.46944	7.62313	7.25933
22	18.01121	17.18455	16.41502	15.02916	13.82115	12.76408	11.83553	11.01680	10.29224	9.64869	9.07507	8.56200	7.68696	7.31246
23	18.65805	17.76541	16.93692	15.45112	14.16300	13.04158	12.06124	11.20074	10.44243	9.77154	9.17574	8.64465	7.74294	7.35866
24	19.29220	18.33211	17.44361	15.85684	14.48857	13.30338	12.27219	11.37106	10.58021	9.88322	9.26643	8.71843	7.79206	7.39884
25	19.91393	18.88499	17.93554	16.24696	14.79864	13.55036	12.46933	11.52876	10.70661	9.98474	9.34814	8.78432	7.83514	7.43377
26	20.52346	19.42438	18.41315	16.62208	15.09394	13.78336	12.65358	11.67478	10.82258	10.07704	9.42174	8.84314	7.87293	7.46415
27	21.12104	19.95061	18.87684	16.98277	15.37519	14.00317	12.82578	11.80998	10.92897	10.16095	9.48806	8.89566	7.90608	7.49056
28	21.70690	20.46401	19.32703	17.32959	15.64303	14.21053	12.98671	11.93516	11.02658	10.23722	9.54780	8.94255	7.93515	7.51353
29	22.28127	20.96489	19.76411	17.66306	15.89813	14.40616	13.13711	12.05108	11.11613	10.30657	9.60162	8.98442	7.96066	7.53351
30	22.84438	21.45355	20.18845	17.98371	16.14107	14.59072	13.27767	12.15841	11.19828	10.36961	9.65011	9.02181	7.98304	7.55088
31	23.39646	21.93029	20.60044	18.29203	16.37245	14.76483	13.40904	12.25778	11.27365	10.42691	9.69379	9.05518	8.00266	7.56598
32	23.93770	22.39541	21.00043	18.58849	16.59281	14.92909	13.53181	12.34980	11.34280	10.47901	9.73315	9.08499	8.01988	7.57911
33	24.46833	22.84918	21.38877	18.87355	16.80268	15.08404	13.64656	12.43500	11.40624	10.52638	9.76860	9.11159	8.03498	7.59053
34	24.98856	23.29188	21.76579	19.14765	17.00255	15.23023	13.75379	12.51389	11.46444	10.56943	9.80054	9.13535	8.04823	7.60046
35	25.49859	23.72379	22.13184	19.41120	17.19290	15.36814	13.85401	12.58693	11.51784	10.60857	9.82932	9.15656	8.05985	7.60910
36	25.99862	24.14516	22.48722	19.66461	17.37419	15.49825	13.94767	12.65457	11.56682	10.64416	9.85524	9.17550	8.07005	7.61661
37	26.48884	24.55625	22.83225	19.90828	17.54685	15.62099	14.03521	12.71719	11.61176	10.67651	9.87859	9.19241	8.07899	7.62314
38	26.96945	24.95732	23.16724	20.14258	17.71129	15.73678	14.11702	12.77518	11.65299	10.70592	9.89963	9.20751	8.08683	7.62881
39	27.44064	25.34860	23.49246	20.36786	17.86789	15.84602	14.19347	12.82887	11.69082	10.73265	9.91859	9.22099	8.09371	7.63375
40	27.90259	25.73034	23.80822	20.58448	18.01704	15.94907	14.26493	12.87858	11.72552	10.75696	9.93567	9.23303	8.09975	7.63805
45	30.07996	27.50385	25.25427	21.54884	18.66277	16.38318	14.55791	13.07707	11.86051	10.84909	9.99878	9.27642	8.12047	7.65244
50	32.05208	29.07137	26.50166	22.34147	19.16872	16.70757	14.76680	13.21216	11.94823	10.90630	10.03624	9.30104	8.13123	7.65959

Index